INVESTOR-STATE ARBITRATION

INVESTOR-STATE ARBITRATION

Christopher F. Dugan
Don Wallace, Jr.
Noah Rubins
Borzu Sabahi

OXFORD
UNIVERSITY PRESS

Oxford University Press, Inc., publishes works that further Oxford University's objective of excellence in research, scholarship, and education.

Copyright © 2008 by Oxford University Press, Inc.
Published by Oxford University Press, Inc.
198 Madison Avenue, New York, New York 10016

Oxford is a registered trademark of Oxford University Press
Oxford University Press is a registered trademark of Oxford University Press, Inc.

All rights reserved. No part of this publication may be reproduced, stored in a retrieval system, or transmitted, in any form or by any means, electronic, mechanical, photocopying, recording, or otherwise, without the prior permission of Oxford University Press, Inc.

First printing in paperback, 2011. ISBN 978-0-19-979572-7 (paperback : alk. paper)

The Library of Congress has cataloged the hardcover edition as follows:

Library of Congress Control Number: 2005926262

ISBN 978-0-379-21544-1

Printed in the United States of America on acid-free paper.

Note to Readers:

This publication is designed to provide accurate and authoritative information in regard to the subject matter covered. It is based upon sources believed to be accurate and reliable and is intended to be current as of the time it was written. It is sold with the understanding that the publisher is not engaged in rendering legal, accounting, or other professional services. If legal advice or other expert assistance is required, the services of a competent professional person should be sought. Also, to confirm that the information has not been affected or changed by recent developments, traditional legal research techniques should be used, including checking primary sources where appropriate.

(Based on the Declaration of Principles jointly adopted by a Committee of the American Bar Association and a Committee of Publishers and Associations.)

You may order this or any other Oxford University Press publication by visiting the Oxford University Press website at www.oup.com

Summary of Contents

I. Introduction 1

II. History and Limitations of the Traditional System for Resolving
    Investment Disputes 11

III. The Modern System of Investor-State Arbitration 45

IV. Commonly Used Procedural Rules 77

V. Procedural Law Applicable in Investor-State Arbitration 91

VI. National Court Interference: Anti-Arbitration Injunctions 101

VII. The Course of an Investment Arbitration 117

VIII. Consolidation under Relevant Arbitration Rules or Treaties 185

IX. Governing Law in Investment Disputes 201

X. Consent to Arbitral Jurisdiction 219

XI. The Concept of Investment 247

XII. The Nationality of the Investor 291

XIII. Exhaustion of Local Remedies 347

XIV. Election of Forum: National Courts and Contract Arbitrations 367

XV. Discrimination 397

XVI. Expropriation 429

XVII. "Fair and Equitable Treatment" and "Full Protection and Security" 491

SUMMARY OF CONTENTS

XVIII. Umbrella Clauses 541

XIX. Damages, Compensation, and Non-Pecuniary Remedies 563

XX. Annulment and Set Aside 627

XXI. Enforcement of Awards 675

XXII. The Future of International Investment Arbitration 701

Select Bibliography 715

Index 743

Table of Cases 765

Index of Treaties, Conventions, and International Agreements 785

Table of Contents

Summary of Contents v

Preface xvii

Guidance on Citations and Sources xviii

Abbreviations xix

About the Authors xxiii

I. Introduction 1
   A. The Importance of Investment Flows for Capital Importers
      and Exporters 4
   B. The Purpose of Investment Protection 6

**II. History and Limitations of the Traditional System for Resolving Investment
    Disputes** 11
   A. Harms Suffered by Foreign Investors 11
   B. Barriers to Recovery by Foreign Investors 13
      1. Barriers in Host Country Courts 13
         a. Local Bias 13
         b. State Immunity 14
         c. Inefficient Local Courts 15
         d. Calvo Doctrine 16
      2. Barriers in Foreign Investor's Home Courts 19
         a. Jurisdiction 19
         b. Foreign Sovereign Immunity 20
         c. Act of State Doctrine 20
         d. Choice of Law 23
      3. Political Barriers: The New International Economic Order 23
   C. Traditional Remedies for Foreign Investors 26
      1. Gunboat Diplomacy 26

TABLE OF CONTENTS

    2. Diplomatic Espousal 27
        a. Practice of Espousal 27
        b. The Limitations of Espousal 30
            i. Exhaustion of Local Remedies 30
            ii. Nationality of the Investor 32
  D. Some Early Investment Protection Regimes 34
    1. Jay Treaty (1794) 34
    2. Ad Hoc Arbitration 35
    3. Binational Claims Commissions 36
    4. Friendship, Commerce, and Navigation Treaties 37
    5. Lump Sum Settlement Agreements 38
    6. Investment Guarantee Programs 40
    7. The Algiers Accords 41
  E. Limitations of Historic Dispute
     Settlement Processes 42

III. The Modern System of Investor-State Arbitration 45
  A. Origins 45
  B. ICSID and Its Central Role in the New System of
     Investor-State Arbitration 50
  C. Bilateral Investment Treaties 51
  D. Multilateral Investment Treaties 54
    1. Lomé Conventions 54
    2. North American Free Trade Agreement 56
    3. Energy Charter Treaty 61
    4. Mercado Común del Sur (Mercosur or Mercosul) 64
    5. The Association of South East Asian Nations 67
    6. Free Trade Area of the Americas 68
    7. The Dominican Republic–Central American–United States Free Trade
       Agreement 71
    8. Multilateral Agreement on Investment 74
  E. National Investment Legislation 75

IV. Commonly Used Procedural Rules 77
  A. Introduction 77
  B. ICSID Rules 78
  C. Stockholm Chamber of Commerce Rules 79
  D. International Chamber of Commerce Rules 79

E. UNCITRAL Arbitration Rules 80
F. Comparison of the ICSID and UNCITRAL Rules 81
   1. ICSID Convention Requirements and the ICSID
      Screening Role 82
   2. Place of Arbitration 83
   3. Language of Arbitration 83
   4. Appointment of Tribunal 84
   5. Governing Law 84
   6. Cost and Speed 85
   7. Interim Measures 86
   8. Challenge of Award and Enforcement 87
   9. Multiparty Investment Arbitration—Consolidation 89

V. Procedural Law Applicable in Investor-State Arbitration 91
A. Choice of Procedural Law of Arbitration 92
B. Mandatory Procedural Law of the Forum 93
C. Procedural Law Applicable Under the International Centre for Settlement of
   Investment Disputes Convention 95

VI. National Court Interference: Anti-Arbitration Injunctions 101
A. Introduction 101
B. Anti-Arbitration Injunctions 105
C. Anti-Arbitration Injunctions and the International Centre for Settlement
   of Investment Disputes Convention 110

VII. The Course of an Investment Arbitration 117
A. Introduction 117
B. Waiting Periods 117
C. Local Remedies 119
D. Notice of Claim and Request for Arbitration 120
   1. Notice of Claim 121
   2. Request for Arbitration 122
E. "Registration" or Approval by Arbitral Institution 125
F. Default of a Party 126
G. Composition of Tribunal 128
   1. Appointment of Arbitrators 128
   2. Situs of Arbitration 132
   3. Language of Arbitration 133

TABLE OF CONTENTS

    H. Initial Session of the Tribunal 134
    I. Arbitrator-Ordered Interim Relief 137
        1. The Legal Framework 138
        2. Effect of ICSID Recommendation 140
        3. Review of Investment Arbitration Case Law 140
            a. Obtaining Evidence 141
            b. Securing Financial Guarantees 142
            c. Preserving Confidentiality 142
            d. Enjoining Parallel Domestic Proceedings and Protecting Rights in Dispute 143
        4. Interim Measures in Other Contexts 146
        5. Timing 146
    J. Jurisdictional Phase 147
    K. Merits Phase 153
        1. Briefing 153
        2. Counterclaims 153
        3. Host State Defenses 156
        4. Witness Statements and Other Evidence 158
            a. Witness Statements 159
            b. Document Production from Parties to the Dispute 161
            c. Evidence Collection from Third Parties 163
        5. U.S. Procedures and Third-Party Evidence Taking 163
        6. Third Party Amicus Curiae Submissions 167
    L. Damages Phase 177
    M. Hearings 177
    N. Posthearing Briefs 179
    O. Award 179
    P. Enforcement and Challenge of Award 182

VIII. Consolidation under Relevant Arbitration Rules or Treaties 185

    A. International Centre for Settlement of Investment Disputes 186
    B. United Nations Commission on International Trade Law 189
    C. North American Free Trade Agreement Article 1126 190
    D. Consolidation Provisions in Other Bilateral and Multilateral Investment Treaties 195
    E. International Chamber of Commerce Rules 196

1. Consolidation by Courts 197
  2. Ramifications for Enforcement of Award 198

IX. Governing Law in Investment Disputes 201
A. Introduction 201
B. Rules Chosen by the Parties 202
C. Investment Treaties and Their Interpretation 204
D. Host State Law 209
E. Public International Law 213

X. Consent to Arbitral Jurisdiction 219
A. Introduction 219
B. Fundamental Concepts Relating to Consent 220
  1. Methods of State Consent to Arbitration 220
  2. Methods of Accepting the Government's Offer to Arbitrate ... 221
  3. Irrevocability of Consent 222
  4. Limitations on Consent Clauses 223
C. Arbitration Clauses in Investment Contracts 225
D. National Investment Legislation 230
E. Investment Protection Treaties as Consent to Arbitration 236
F. Investment Arbitration Based on *Compromis* 242

XI. The Concept of Investment 247
A. The Changing Definition of Investment: The Historical Perspective 247
B. Definitions of Investment in Investment Protection Instruments 250
  1. Definitions of Investment in Investment Treaties 250
  2. Definition of Investment in National Investment Laws 254
C. Definition of Investment and Its Implications for the Jurisdiction of
   Arbitral Tribunals Under the Washington Convention 256
  1. Travaux Preparatoire of the Washington Convention Regarding the Notion of
     Investment Under Article 25 256
  2. Dual Jurisdictional Requirements for Submitting a Case Under the Washington
     Convention and an Investment Treaty or Law 259
  3. Survey of Jurisdictional Decisions Under the Washington Convention Based on the
     Type of Investment 260
  4. Characteristics of Investment Under Article 25 of Washington Convention ... 265
    a. Duration of an Activity 266
    b. Regularity of Profit and Return 269

c. Assumption of Risk by Both Parties 269
d. Commitment Should Be Substantial 271
e. Contribution to Economic Development of the Host State 272
D. The Concept of Unity of Investment Under the Washington Convention 276
E. Concept of Investment and Its Implications for the Jurisdiction of Arbitral Tribunals Under Arbitral Rules Other Than the Washington Convention 280
F. Preinvestment Protection 285

XII. The Nationality of the Investor 291
A. Nationality of Natural Persons Under Customary International Law: Effective Nationality Principle 292
B. Qualified Investors Under Investment Treaties and the Washington Convention .. 294
  1. Natural Persons 295
    a. Investment Treaty and Washington Convention Provisions 295
    b. Applicable Law 296
    c. Status of Dual Nationals Under the Washington Convention and Other Arbitral Rules 300
  2. Corporations and other Legal Persons 304
    a. Treaty Provisions 304
    b. Customary Law on Nationality of Corporations and Shareholder Standing 308
    c. Washington Convention 313
  3. Shareholders Standing Under Investment Treaties and the Washington Convention 314
    a. Minority and Noncontrolling Shareholders 315
      i. Standing Under Investment Treaties 315
      ii. Standing Under the Washington Convention 315
      iii. Damages Due Minority Shareholders 318
    b. Indirect Shareholders Controlling an Entity Incorporated in the Host State: Case Studies 319
      i. Amco v. Indonesia 320
      ii. Tokios v. Ukraine 322
      iii. CME Cases 325
      iv. Waste Management v. Mexico 327
      v. Aguas del Tunari v. Bolivia 329
      vi. Aucoven v. Venezuela 331
      vii. Saluka v. Czech Republic 335

      viii. An Unusual Case: When a Tribunal Pierced the Veil but Denied
          Jurisdiction: Loewen v. United States 337

C. Change of National Identity 340

   1. Continuous Nationality Rule Under Customary International Law 340

   2. Change of Nationality and the Jurisdiction of Arbitral Tribunals
      Under Investment Treaties 341

   3. Change of Nationality and Jurisdiction of Arbitral Tribunals Under
      the Washington Convention 343

XIII. Exhaustion of Local Remedies 347

A. Exhaustion of Local Remedies Under Customary International Law 347

B. Exhaustion of Local Remedies in Investment Treaty Arbitration 357

C. Exhaustion of Local Remedies and the Loewen Case 360

XIV. Election of Forum: National Courts and Contract Arbitrations 367

A. National Courts and Treaty Arbitration 367

   1. Fork in the Road and Waiver: Treaty Texts 368

      a. True Fork in the Road Provisions 368

      b. Waiver Provisions 369

   2. The Policy Behind Fork in the Road and Waiver Provisions 370

   3. Choice of Forum with Respect to Disputes 371

   4. Choice of Forum with Respect to Measures 377

B. Investment Treaties and Contractual Forum Selection Clauses 380

XV. Discrimination 397

A. National Treatment 398

   1. Introduction 398

   2. Application of the National Treatment Standard 400

      a. Relevant Class of Comparators: Like Circumstances 400

      b. Relevant Standard of Treatment: No Less Favorably 408

      c. Proof of Discriminatory Intent Based on Nationality 411

B. Most Favored Nation Treatment 413

   1. Introduction 413

   2. Scope and Interpretation of Most Favored Nation Clauses 415

   3. Application of MFN Clauses to Substantive and Procedural Rights 417

      a. Procedural Rights 418

      b. MFN and Substantive Rights 423

C. Discriminatory Impairment 426

XVI. Expropriation 429

A. Historical Overview of Expropriation 430

    1. Introduction 430

    2. Pre–World War II Period 433

    3. Post–World War II Period Until Present 435

B. Investments and Property Protected Against Expropriation 438

C. The Role of Investment Treaties and Investment Insurance Regimes 442

D. The Problem of Indirect or Regulatory Expropriation 450

    1. The Effect of the Government Measures 455

    2. The Intent, Purpose, Nature, or Character of the Governmental Act
       or Measure 461

    3. Legitimate Reliance on Government Representations 465

    4. Duration of Effect of Act or Measure 468

    5. Domestic Remedies Sought 469

    6. Transfer of the Investment to the Government or to Third Parties 469

    7. Other Factors 470

E. Case Study: Metalclad v. Mexico 476

F. The Current U.S. Approach to Indirect or Regulatory Expropriation 482

XVII. "Fair and Equitable Treatment" and "Full Protection and Security" 491

A. The Relationship of "Fair and Equitable Treatment" and "Full Protection and
    Security" to Customary International Law 493

    The NAFTA Free Trade Commission Interpretation of July 2001 500

B. The Meaning of Fair and Equitable Treatment 502

    1. History of the "Fair and Equitable Treatment" Standard 503

    2. The Definition of "Fair and Equitable" Treatment 504

        a. Arbitrary Treatment 507

        b. Legitimate or Reasonable Expectations and Stability 510

        c. Transparency 519

        d. Coercion of Foreign Investors 523

        e. Denial of Justice 525

C. Full Protection and Security 531

    1. Historical Development of the Obligation to Ensure
       Protection and Security 532

    2. Modern Investment Treaties and the Meaning of Protection and Security 534

XVIII. Umbrella Clauses ... 541
A. Introduction ... 541
B. Historical Background and Various Formulations of Umbrella Clauses ... 542
C. Arbitral Decisions Involving Umbrella Clauses ... 544
D. Conclusion ... 558

XIX. Damages, Compensation, and Non-Pecuniary Remedies ... 563
A. Introduction ... 563
B. The Function of Reparation: To Eliminate the Consequences of an Illegal Act ... 567
C. Non-Pecuniary Remedies: Specific Performance and Other Injunctive Relief ... 569
D. Standard of Compensation ... 573
   1. Standard of Compensation for Expropriation ... 573
   2. The Standard of Compensation for Breach of Investment Treaty Obligations Other than Expropriation ... 578
E. Valuation of Assets ... 583
F. Valuation of Enterprises or Projects That Have Not Become Profitable ... 587
G. Awarding Lost Profits for Breach of Contract ... 589
H. Factors Potentially Limiting the Amount of Compensation ... 596
   1. Causation ... 597
   2. Contributory Fault ... 602
   3. Obligation to Mitigate Losses ... 603
I. Role of Equity ... 603
J. Interest ... 605
   1. Overview ... 605
   2. Compound or Simple Interest? ... 609
K. Arbitration Costs and Attorneys' Fees ... 611
   1. Introduction ... 611
   2. Survey of Some Investment Arbitration Awards Rendered under the United Nations Commission on International Trade Law Rules ... 615
   3. Awards Rendered under the International Centre for Settlement of Investment Disputes Rules ... 620
   4. Calculation of Government Legal Fees ... 624

XX. Annulment and Set Aside ... 627
A. International Centre for Settlement of Investment Disputes Annulment ... 629
B. Challenge to Non-ICSID Investment Arbitration Awards ... 635
   1. The Standard of Judicial Review ... 636

TABLE OF CONTENTS

  2. Grounds for Setting Aside Relevant to Investment Arbitration 637
    a. Excess of Authority 637
    b. Nonarbitrability 639
    c. Public Policy 640
    d. Procedural Irregularity 642
    e. "Manifest Disregard of the Law" and Other "Substantive" Grounds 644
 C. Waiver of Objections 647
 D. Agreements to Narrow the Grounds for Annulment 647
 E. The Effect of Annulled Investment Arbitration Awards 649
 F. Case Studies of Non-ICSID Challenge Proceedings 651
  1. Metalclad v. United Mexican States 651
  2. CME v. Czech Republic 660
  3. S.D. Myers v. Canada 664

XXI. Enforcement of Awards 675
 A. Confirmation 677
 B. Enforcement of Awards Under the New York Convention 679
 C. Execution in Investment Arbitrations 684
 D. Sovereign Immunity and the Washington Convention 699
 E. Conclusion 700

XXII. The Future of International Investment Arbitration 701
 A. Trends in the Conclusion and Amendment of Investment Treaties 702
 B. Trends in the Development of Substantive and Procedural Provisions
   of Investment Treaties 705
  1. Confidentiality in Investor-State Arbitration 706
  2. Amicus Curiae Briefs in Investor-State Arbitration 707
 C. Future Jurisprudence of Investment Protection: Possible Problems
   and Solutions 709

Select Bibliography 715

Index 743

Table of Cases 765

Index of Treaties, Conventions, and International Agreements 785

Preface

This book is the product of many years of teaching and practice in the field of investment arbitration. It was originally written as a textbook for the students of a seminar on investor-State arbitration, which we have taught for several years at Georgetown University Law Center. With the proliferation of investment treaties, and the resulting expansion of investment arbitration as a practice area in which we have been actively involved, the focus of the book changed to suit a wider audience. We hope it will be useful for legal practice as well as for academic purposes. In various chapters of the book, we have sometimes cited cases in which we have been involved as counsel or arbitrator, including: *Berschader v. Russian Federation, Biloune v. Ghana Investments Center, Biwater Gauff v. Tanzania, CMS v. Argentina, Champion Trading v. Egypt, Duke Energy v. Peru, Karaha Bodas Company v. Pertamina, Loewen v. United States, Methanex v. United States, Middle East Cement v. Egypt, Parkerings v. Lithuania,* and *Wena Hotels v. Egypt.*

The writing of this book has been a truly collaborative exercise. While we have sought to reach agreement on all of the issues presented here, including the most controversial, each of us came to the project with our own views and experience. As a result, not all of the statements made represent precisely the opinions of all of us. More importantly, the material presented does not necessarily reflect the views of the law firms with which we are affiliated, or the views of the clients of those firms.

We wish to thank the following individuals for their assistance in various stages of writing this book: James Berger, Kristin Cleary, Matt Dunne, Francine Forrester, Suzanne Garner, Sarah Hagans, Bernhard Lauterburg, Robin Lupton, Stephanie K. Rosenthal, and Seung-Hyun Ryu. Our special thanks go to Nicholas J. Birch for his excellent research and editorial assistance.

We would also like to thank Oxford University Press, particularly Peter Rocheleau, Larry Selby, Edward Burchell, and Susan De Maio.

Finally, we would like to thank our families for their constant support and encouragement, without which this work could not have been completed. In particular, we would like to thank our wives, Susan, Daphne, Masha, and Guly for their tolerance and forbearance during this long process.

Guidance on Citations and Sources

This volume contains a combination of monograph text and some extensive extracts, or excerpts, from cases and other materials. Citations follow the Blue Book (a standard citation manual for U.S. legal writing), practitioner's style, with some exceptions.

To identify footnotes that were drawn from (were part of) the original extract, and to distinguish them from the footnotes that we the authors have created: the notation "SN" appears at the beginning of each footnote of the former type (was part of the original text). It is an abbreviation for "Source Note." However, where SN appears: the footnote number appearing as superscript in text (and at the foot of the page) is different from the footnote number appearing in the original text.

To facilitate the use of this book, we have included extensive cross-references to alert the reader to related discussions in other chapters or other sections of the same chapter.

Citations to online sources are provided for many of the cited materials, but are omitted for very common sources to avoid excessive repetition. We have referred to a number of bilateral investment treaties, which are most commonly found at UNCTAD's Investment Instruments Online Web site: *http://www.unctadxi.org/templates/DocSearch_779.aspx*.

Similarly, we have referred to a number of investment treaty arbitration decisions and awards. The vast majority of these decisions can be found at Oxford University Press's site: www.investmentclaims.com. Other important online sources for jurisprudence include: www.naftaclaims.com (for NAFTA awards and related documents, such as written submissions) and *http://ita.law.uvic.ca/*.

We have referred almost universally to the relevant paragraph numbers in the decisions cited. In instances where we have referred to a page or a range of pages within an award or other arbitration-related document, the reference is to the page number in the original document, which may be found at one of the two websites named immediately above, unless otherwise indicated.

Abbreviations

Journals

ABA Sec. Int'l L. & Pract.	American Bar Association Section of International Law and Practice Newsletter
Advocate's Q.	Advocate's Quarterly
Am. J. Econ. and Sociology	American Journal of Economics and Sociology
Am. J. Int'l L. Spec. Supp.	American Journal of International Law Special Supplement
Am. J. Int'l. L.	American Journal of International Law
Am. Rev. Int'l Arb.	American Review of International Arbitration
Am. U. Int'l L. Rev.	American University International Law Review
Am. U. L. Rev.	American University Law Review
Arb. and Disp. Res. L.J.	The Arbitration and Dispute Resolution Law Journal
Arb. Int'l	Arbitration International
Arb. J.	Arbitration Journal
ASIL Insights	American Society of International Law Insights
ASIL Proc.	American Society of International Law Proceedings
Brit. Y.B. Int'l L.	British Yearbook of International Law
Bus. L. Int'	Business Law International
Can.-U.S. L.J.	Canada-United States Law Journal
Can.Y. B. Int'l L.	The Canadian Yearbook of International Law
Cath. U. L. Rev.	Catholic University Law Review
Chi. J. Int'l L.	Chicago Journal of International Law
Colum. J. Transnat'l L.	Columbia Journal of Transnational Law
Comp. L. Y.B. Int'l Bus.	Comparative Law Yearbook of International Business
Cornell Int'l L.J.	Cornell International Law Journal
Delhi L. R.	Delhi Law Review
Duke L.J.	Duke Law Journal
Eur. J. Int'l L	European Journal of International Law
Fordham Int'l L.J.	Fordham International Law Journal
Fordham L. Rev.	Fordham Law Review
German Y.B. Int'l L.	German Yearbook of International Law
Harv. Int'l L.J.	Harvard International Law Journal
Hastings Int'l & Comp. L. Rev.	Hastings International & Comparative Law Review
I.C.J. Reports	International Court of Justice Reports
I.L.M.	International Legal Materials

ABBREVIATIONS

ICC Int'l Ct. Arb. Bull.	International Chamber of Commerce International Court of Arbitration Bulletin
ICSID Rev.-F.I.L.J.	ICSID Review – Foreign Investment Law Journal
Int'l Arb. L. Rev.	International Arbitration Law Review
Int'l Bus. L.J.	International Business Law Journal
Int'l Bus. Law.	International Business Lawyer
Int'l Comp. L. Q.	International and Comparative Law Quarterly
Int'l L. Practicum	International Law Practicum
Int'l Law.	International Lawyer
Int'l L. Prosp.	International Legal Prospectives
Iran-US Cl. Trib. Rep.	Iran-United State Claims Tribunal Reporter
J. Chartered Inst. Arb.	Journal of the Chartered Institute of Arbitrators
J. Comp. Econ.	Journal of Comparative Economics
J. Comp. Legis. & Int'l L	Journal of Comparative Legislation and International Law
J. Econ. L.	Journal of Economic Law
J. Int'l Arb.	Journal of International Arbitration
J. Int'l Econ. L.	Journal of International Economic Law
J. Marshall L. Rev.	John Marshall Law Review
J. Public L.	Journal of Public Law
J. Transnat'l L. & Pol'y	Journal of Transnational Law and Policy
J. World Inv.	Journal of World Investment
J. World Inv. & Trade	Journal of World Investment and Trade
Kan. L. Rev.	Kansas Law Review
L. & Pol'y in Int'l Bus.	Law & Policy in International Business
L. & Pract. of Int'l Ct. & Trib.	The Law and Practice of International Courts and Tribunals
L. Q. Rev.	Law Quarterly Review
L. Rev. (India)	The Law Review (Punjab University, Chandigarh, India)
La. L.R.	Louisiana Law Review
Mealey's Int'l Arb. Rep.	Mealey's International Arbitration Report
Mich. J. Int'l L.	Michigan Journal of International Law
Mich. L. Rev.	Michigan Law Review
Minn. J. Global Trade	Minnesota Journal of Global Trade
N.Y. Int'l L. Rev.	New York International Law Review
N.Y.L.J.	New York Law Journal
N.Y.U. J. Int'l L. & Politics	New York University Journal of International Law and Politics
NAFTA L. & Bus. Rev. Am.	North American Free Trade Agreement Law and Business Review of the Americas
Nat'l L.J.	National Law Journal
Netherlands Int'l L. Rev.	Netherland International Law Review
Nw. J. Int'l L. & Bus.	Northwest Journal of International Law & Business
NW. U.L. Rev.	Northwest University Law Review
Penn. St. Int'l L. Rev.	Penn State International Law Review
Pol'y & Society	Policy and Society
Pol'y Papers Transn'l Econ. L.	Policy Papers on Transnational Economic Law
Rev. de Droit Int'l	Revue de Droit International
Rev. de Droit Int'l	Revue de Droit International
Rev. Int'l Political Econ.	Review of International Political Economy

S. Texas L. R.	South Texas Law Review
Spanish Y.B. Int'l L.	Spanish Yearbook of International Law
Stan. L. Rev.	Stanford Law Review
Stock. Arb. Rep.	Stockholm Arbitration Report
Stock. Int'l Arb. Rev.	Stockholm International Arbitration Review
Swiss Arb. Assn. Bull.	Swiss Arbitration Association Bulletin
Syracuse J. Int'l L. & Com.	Syracuse Journal of International Law and Commerce
T.D.M.	Transnational Dispute Management
Tex. Int'l L.J.	Texas International Law Journal
Touro Int'l L. Rev.	Touro International Law Review
Tul. L. Rev.	Tulane Law Review
Tulsa J. Comp. & Int'l L.	Tulsa Journal of Comparative and International Law
U. Miami Inter-Am. L. Rev.	University of Miami Inter-American Law Review
U. Pa. J. Int'l Econ. L.	University of Pennsylvania Journal of International Economic Law
Va. J. Int'l L.	Virginia Journal of International Law
Vand. J. Int'l L.	Vanderbilt Journal of International Law
Vand. J. Transnat'l L.	Vanderbilt Journal of Transnational Law
Vt. L. Rev.	Vermont Law Review
Willamette J. Int'l L. & Disp. Res.	Willamette Journal of International Law and Dispute Resolution
Wm. Mitchell L. Rev.	William Mitchell Law Review
World Arb. & Med. Rep.	World Arbitration and Mediation Report
Y.B. Comm. Arb.	Yearbook of Commercial Arbitration
Y.B. Int'l L. Comm'n	Yearbook of the International Law Commission
Yale J. Int'l L.	Yale Journal of International Law
Yale L.J.	Yale Law Journal

Treaties

ASEAN	Association of Southeast Asian Nations
DR-CAFTA	Dominican Republic-Central America-United States Free Trade Agreement
ECT	Energy Charter Treaty
FTAA	Free Trade Area of the Americas
ICSID Convention	Convention on the Settlement of Investment Disputes between States and Nationals of Other States
GATT	General Agreement on Tariffs and Trade
MAI	Multilateral Agreement on Investment
Mercosur	Southern Common Market Regional Trade Agreement
NAFTA	North American Free Trade Agreement
New York Convention	1958 Convention on the Recognition and Enforcement of Foreign Arbitral Awards
USSFTA	United States-Singapore Free Trade Agreement
VCLT	Vienna Convention on the Law of Treaties
Washington Convention	Convention on the Settlement of Investment Disputes between States and Nationals of Other States

Other

AAA	American Arbitration Association
ALADI	Latin American Integration Association
ASIL	American Society of International Law
BIT	Bilateral Investment Treaty
CIEL	Center for International Environmental Law
DCF	Discounted Cash Flow
FAA	Federal Arbitration Act
FMV	Fair Market Value
FTA	Free Trade Agreement
IBA	International Bar Association
ICC	International Chamber of Commerce
ICJ	International Court of Justice
ICSID	International Centre for Settlement of Investment Disputes
IISD	International Institute for Sustainable Development
ILC	International Law Commission (United Nations)
IMF	International Monetary Fund
Iran-U.S. Cl. Trib.	Iran-United States Claims Tribunal
LCIA	London Court of International Arbitration
NGO	Non-Governmental Organization
NPV	Net Present Value
OECD	Organisation for Economic Co-operation and Development
OEEC	Organisation for European Economic Co-operation
OGEMID	Oil Gas Energy Mining Infrastructure and Investment Disputes
SCC	Stockholm Chamber of Commerce
U.S. G.P.O.	United States Government Printing Office
UN	United Nations
UNCITRAL	United Nations Commission on International Trade Law
UNCTAD	United Nations Conference on Trade and Development
WTO	World Trade Organization

About the Authors

Christopher Dugan is a partner at Paul, Hastings, Janofsky & Walker in Washington, D.C.; he is the chair of the firm's international dispute practice and its Washington litigation department. He has been an adjunct professor at Georgetown University Law Center since 1994, teaching a course on international aspects of U.S. civil litigation (until 2001), and in 2002 he began teaching a course on investor-state arbitration. He focuses his practice on international arbitrations, international litigation, and FCPA investigations, and was named one of Chambers Leading Lawyers in international arbitration for 2006 and 2007. He has been lead counsel in numerous significant representations, including *Karaha Bodas v. Pertamina,* et al., a global enforcement of a US$261 million arbitration award against the Indonesian national oil company; *The Loewen Group v. United States*, an $800 million NAFTA arbitration claim (the first NAFTA claim filed against the U.S.); and a dispute with the Dominican Republic concerning electricity distribution, which resulted in one of the first DR-CAFTA arbitration filings. He received his B.A. degree from the Johns Hopkins University and his J.D. degree, cum laude, from the Georgetown University Law Center in 1980. From 1980–1981, he was a law clerk to the Hon. John Lewis Smith, Jr., Chief Judge, United States District Court for the District of Columbia, and then practiced with Jones Day for 22 years in Hong Kong and Washington.

Don Wallace Jr. is chairman of the International Law Institute and professor of law at Georgetown University Law Center. He is counsel to the law firm of Morgan, Lewis & Bockius, LLP. Professor Wallace specializes in the fields of international law and foreign affairs. He has taught a number of courses on various aspects of international economic law, including international trade and investment. He currently teaches a seminar on investor-state arbitration and one on foreign affairs and the constitutional law of the United States. Professor Wallace has authored and edited a number of books, book chapters, and articles, including one of the earliest guides on negotiating investments for the developing world. He has been on the roster of World Trade Organization (WTO) panelists. Professor Wallace has served as arbitrator in a number of ICSID, UNCITRAL, and AAA proceedings. He has also acted as counsel in various arbitrations. Professor

Wallace was the Regional Legal Advisor for the Middle East and Deputy Assistant General Counsel to AID in the Department of State from 1962-in 66, a founding board member of the International Development Law Organization in Rome, and has been the head of the International Law Institute since 1970. He chaired the Advisory Committee on World Trade and Technology to the Office of Technology Assessment of the U.S. Congress from 1976–79, and is currently a member of the Secretary of State's Advisory Committee on Private International Law, a U.S. Delegate to UNCITRAL, and a correspondent of UNIDROIT and the vice president of the UNIDROIT Foundation in Rome. He has also been chair of the Section of International Law and Practice of the American Bar Association and a member of the ABA House of Delegates. He received an LL.B. from Harvard (1957 *cum laude*) and a bachelor's degree from Yale (1953 with high honors). He was a Fulbright Fellow in Turkey (1967); a Fellow at St. Antony's College, Oxford (1973–74); and an Eisenhower Exchange Fellow (1976).

Noah Rubins is Counsel in the international arbitration and public international law groups at Freshfields Bruckhaus Deringer in Paris. He has advised and represented clients in arbitrations under the ICSID, ICSID Additional Facility, International Chamber of Commerce, American Arbitration Association, Stockholm Chamber of Commerce, and UNCITRAL rules. He specializes in investment arbitration, particularly under the auspices of bilateral investment treaties, the Energy Charter, and the North American Free Trade Agreement. Before arriving in Paris in 2004, he practiced law in New York, Washington, Houston, and Istanbul, having embarked on a legal career only after serving in the US Embassy in Moscow and working in the NGO sector in Kyrgyzstan. Noah has served as arbitrator in a range of disputes, conducted under the ICC, Stockholm Chamber of Commerce, LCIA and UNCITRAL rules. He received a masters degree in dispute resolution and public international law from the Fletcher School of Law and Diplomacy, a JD from Harvard Law School, and a bachelor's degree in international relations from Brown University. He speaks fluent English, French and Russian, and has a working knowledge of Spanish, Hebrew and Turkish.

Borzu Sabahi is an adjunct professor at Georgetown University Law Center. He specializes in international investment law. He co-teaches a seminar on investor-state arbitration. He has lectured on various aspects of international investment law in a number of countries, and to varied audiences including government officials in charge of negotiation of investment treaties. He has authored book chapters and articles on various aspects of international investment law, particularly on the subject of damages. He is an associate editor of www.investmentclaims.com (Oxford University Press) and an associate editor of Transnational Dispute Management (TDM). He is a member of the New York bar. He has been involved in a number of investment treaty arbitrations under the ICSID, Additional Facility and UNCITRAL Rules. He has been a clerk at the ICC Court of Arbitration in Paris, and is familiar with ICC Rules and working procedures. He is currently pursuing a Doctor of Juridical Science (SJD) degree on damages in investment treaty arbitration at Georgetown University Law Center. He received an LL.M. from Georgetown, and a masters degree (Public International Law), and an LL.B. (Judicial Law) from University of Tehran. He is fluent in English and Persian. He has limited reading proficiency in Arabic and French.

I. Introduction

Cross-border investment is fundamental to twenty-first century commerce, but it is hardly a new phenomenon. Although national and political frontiers have traditionally slowed the migration of both people and capital from one country to another, only in rare instances have such barriers proven insurmountable. And for good reason: Although the emigration of capital necessarily means that the funds do not promote development at home, it is likely that the funds have found a more productive use elsewhere, and some portion of the investment proceeds will find a way back to the investor's home economy.[1]

There are three broad categories of cross-border investment: portfolio investment, direct investment, and indirect investment.[2] Portfolio investments include publicly traded securities, such as stocks and bonds of foreign companies. Foreign direct investment (FDI) typically consists of medium- and long-term infusions of cash, equipment, expertise, or other assets in another country, into either ongoing enterprises or new companies created for the purpose of carrying on some business. The International Monetary Fund (IMF) defines this kind of investment as "investment that is made to acquire a lasting interest in an enterprise operating in an economy other than that of the investor, the investor's purpose being to have an effective voice in the management of the enterprise."[3] As a result of a scarcity of commercial bank loans, improved macroeconomic conditions, and liberalizing regulatory regimes, the flow of direct investment across borders grew

---

[1] Bernardo M. Cremades, *Promoting and Protecting International Investments,* Int'l Arb. L. Rev. 53 (2000) ("Capital tends to flow to places where it can be more productive (i.e., where the return is higher), and from economies where it is abundant, such as developed countries and financial centres, towards countries where capital is scarce and where the capabilities associated with private enterprises are lacking.").

[2] K. V. S. K. Nathan, *The ICSID Convention: The Law of the International Centre for Settlement of Investment Disputes* 111 (Juris Publishing 2000) [hereinafter Law of ICSID].

[3] *IMF Balance of Payments Manual* 136 (4th ed. 1977).

exponentially during the last decades of the twentieth century.[4] Indirect investments, meanwhile, are methods used to move resources across borders in a targeted fashion without actually participating in the resulting program or project.[5] Examples include patent licenses and other intellectual property transfers, technical assistance agreements, and joint marketing arrangements.[6]

Likewise, the concentration of natural resources and labor in developing countries of the metaphorical *south* made cross-border investment an essential part of sustainable development and continued economic growth for the entire world. Because the expertise and initial capital necessary for exploiting resources remained largely in the *north,* less developed countries (LDCs) could not unlock the potential of their natural assets without at least a boost of FDI at the outset of development initiatives.

The increasing importance of international investment has been accompanied by the rapid development of a largely new field of international law, defining the obligations of host states toward foreign investors and creating procedures for resolving disputes in connection with those obligations. Primarily, this new law is codified in a vast network of bilateral and multilateral investment treaties, supported by an ever-evolving body of customary international law. In general under these treaties, foreign entities from a signatory state that have made a qualifying investment in the territory of another signatory state enjoy a range of protections, in particular from discrimination and expropriation without compensation, as well as a requirement of fair and equitable treatment and full protection and security of investments. When an investor feels that its rights under the treaty have been violated, it can bring a complaint for redress before an international arbitration tribunal, normally composed and administered under the auspices of a prominent arbitral institution but occasionally created ad hoc.

In contrast to traditional systems, investor beneficiaries of investment treaties of this sort no longer need to appeal to their own governments to espouse their claim diplomatically. They can proceed directly to arbitration against the host state, thus eliminating the diplomatic and political barriers to direct dispute resolution that exist at customary international law.[7] The subject of investor-state arbitration lies at the cutting edge of international law and dispute resolution, and promises to

---

[4] Ibrahim Shihata, *Legal Treatment of Foreign Investment: The World Bank Guidelines* 2 (Martinus Nijhoff 1993) [hereinafter Treatment of Investment]. Annual FDI flows to the developing world increased from US$500 million in 1965 to US$38 billion in 1992. World Bank, *Global Economic Prospects and Developing Countries* 27 (1993).

[5] World Bank, *The Role of Foreign Direct Investment in Development,* Presentations to the 41st Meeting of the Development Committee 39 (1991).

[6] Nathan, *Law of ICSID, supra* note 2, at 111.

[7] On the right of investors to directly initiate arbitration against a state, *see* Chapter X on consent.

play an increasingly important role in the development of the global economic system. Furthermore, study of this form of arbitration provides insight into the evolving content of customary international law, the inevitable conflict between capital-importing and capital-exporting states, and the status of individuals and corporations in the international legal order.

Chapters I–III of this book cover the history of the treatment of aliens and investments under international law and provide an overview of the most important international treaties that give investors a right to arbitration of claims. This historical analysis is essential for understanding the development of investor-state arbitration and such concepts as state responsibility, denial of justice, exhaustion of local remedies, and espousal. Chapters IV–VIII provide an analysis of the arbitration rules most commonly employed in investor-state dispute resolution. Chapters IX–XIX outline the most important elements of substance and procedure that characterize investor-state arbitration, including applicable law, consent, national and most-favored nations treatment, fair and equitable treatment, minimum standard, full protection and security, expropriation, umbrella clauses, and finally the issue of damages. Chapters XX and XXI deal with challenge and enforcement of the awards, especially annulment proceedings under the *Law of the International Centre for Settlement of Investment Disputes* (ICSID) Convention. Chapter XXII considers the future development of investor-state arbitration. Central themes in this concluding section include the challenges of globalization, the clash of capital-importing and capital-exporting countries, restrictions on state sovereignty, and the evolution of an international investment jurisprudence.

The topic of investor-state dispute resolution differs markedly from other related areas of law. It differs from public international law (and the subtopic of diplomatic protection) in that one of the parties involved is nearly always a private party, not traditionally considered a subject of international law at all.[8] Although investor-state arbitration borrows a great deal of procedure from international commercial arbitration,[9] the standards for liability and compensation in this new category of disputes are derived not from the parties' agreement but largely from the language of treaties and the free-standing body of customary international law.[10]

---

[8] I. Brownlie, *Principle of Public International Law* 57–8 (Oxford University Press 6th ed. 2003) (referring to states and international organizations as "normal types of persons on the international plane"); *see also* 1 *Restatement (Third) of the Foreign Relations Law of the United States*, 70 (American Law Institute 1987).

[9] This is especially so when an investment treaty arbitration is conducted under the United Nations Commission on International Trade Law (UNCITRAL) Arbitration Rules and any other set of rules except the ICSID Convention. For a comparison of the differences between the UNCITRAL and the ICSID rules *see* Chapter IV.

[10] *See* Chapter IX on applicable law. *See also* Chapter XIX on damages.

INTRODUCTION

A. The Importance of Investment Flows for Capital Importers and Exporters

Cross-border investment brings benefits not only to the investors, but also to the recipients in both developed and developing countries. A developed country such as the United States can be both an importer and exporter of capital.[11] Foreign investment has tremendously contributed to the prosperity of the United States.[12]

In developing countries, the positive effects of FDI are more than simply providing scarce financing for needed improvements. Management experience, new technologies, and the establishment of lasting commercial links with other countries that can be used to increase future exports are all felicitous side effects of increased foreign investment.[13]

The effect of FDI on the economy of developing countries is hardly undisputed, however.[14] Some argue that freedom of investment equals a license for multinational corporations to pillage the assets of poorer countries, buying resources for less than their true value, and expatriating them to their home country. At the very least, the influx of capital does not necessarily mean that the profits gained from that investment will remain in the developing host country. Between 1965 and 1986, "net transfers" on FDI, meaning the flow of investment adjusted for the repatriation of profits, was either negative or only slightly positive for developing

---

[11] In fact, at the beginning of the twentieth century, the United States was nicknamed "the greatest debtor nation in history." Mira Wilkins, *The History of Foreign Investment in the United States to 1914*, at 144 (Harvard University Press 1989). After World War I, it gradually emerged as one of the main lenders in international markets and until the 1980s was a net exporter of capital. At that time, however, the tide changed again. Curtis M. Jolly et al., *U.S. Competitive Position and Capital Investment Flows in the Economic Citizen Market: Constraints and Opportunities of the U.S. Investor Program*, 57(2) Am. J. Econ. & Soc. 155, 157 (1998). At the end of 2005, for example, the United States was by far a net importer of foreign capital. *See* Bureau of Econ. Analysis, U.S. Dep't of Commerce, *News Release: U.S. Net International Investment Position at Yearend 2005* (June 29, 2006), http://www.bea.gov/bea/newsrel/intinvnewsrelease.htm.

[12] For statistics regarding the positive effects of FDI on the United States economy *see* U.S. Department of State Fact Sheet, *How Foreign Direct Investment Benefits the United States* (Mar. 13, 2006), http://www.state.gov/r/pa/prs/ps/2006/63041.htm (based on data provided by the Bureau of Economic Analysis of the U.S. Department of Commerce showing that FDI creates jobs, boosts wages, and strengthens U.S. manufacturing).

[13] Shihata, *Treatment of Investment, supra* note 4, at 11.

[14] For an assessment of the effect of FDI on the economic welfare of the host countries, *see, e.g.,* United Nations Conference on Trade & Development (UNCTAD), *World Investment Report 2006: FDI from Developing and Transition Economies: Implications for Development* 183 (United Nations 2006).

countries.[15] Therefore, some argue that an increase in direct investment into a less-developed country may not necessarily provide substantial support for long-term development projects, infrastructure improvements, or other welfare-enhancing activities.[16] Furthermore, the drain of repatriating profits may in fact harm a capital-importing country's balance of payments if FDI flows are inconsistently renewed, and the outward transfer of profits continues.

These concerns were part of the impetus that drove the new international economic order (NIEO) movement among developing countries, one aim of which was to remove the act of nationalization from the protections of international law.[17] The NIEO ultimately had little effect on targeted institutions such as the Bretton Woods system, the General Agreement on Tariffs and Trade (GATT), and the World Trade Organization (WTO). Subsequent attempts to include NIEO principles in U.N. documents elaborating development strategy also failed to achieve any consensus.[18]

In its place a more balanced, pragmatic approach to foreign economic participation gained currency, one that recognized both the humanitarian risks of unregulated capitalism and the simple fact that "less-developed countries compete on a worldwide scale for scarce private investment capital, and that capital will not come unless there is security and a good chance of profit making."[19] Thus, in 2000, the United Nations Conference on Trade & Development (UNCTAD) urged, "Continuing efforts to ensure a pro-investment policy regime through an appropriate mix of macroeconomic and market pressures and incentives will be required to meet target growth rates of 6 percent and above [in developing countries]."[20] Indeed, even non-governmental organizations (NGOs) sympathetic to the developing world now recognize the importance of investment flows.[21]

---

[15] The World Bank, 1 *World Debt Tables* 1992–93, at 20–21 (1992).

[16] Shihata, *Treatment of Investment*, supra note 4, at 9.

[17] *See* Chapter II.

[18] Russel Lawrence Barsh, *A Special Session of the U.N. General Assembly Rethinks the Economic Rights and Duties of States*, 85 Am. J. Int'l L. 192, 192–93 (1991).

[19] Frank Ruddy, *Book Review: Foreign Investment in the Present and a New International Economic Order*, 84 Am. J. Int'l L. 961, 962 (1990).

[20] UNCTAD, *Trade and Development Report, 2002*, U.N. Doc. UNCTAD/TDR/(2002), at XI, *available at* http://www.unctad.org/en/docs/tdr02.en.pdf.

[21] *See, e.g.*, Luke E. Peterson, *Bilateral Investment Treaties and Development Policy-Making* (International Institute for Sustainable Development 2004), *available at* www.iisd.org/pdf/2004/trade_bits.pd; *see also* Center for International Environmental Law (CIEL), Foreign Investment and Sustainable Development (CIEL 2002).

B. The Purpose of Investment Protection[22]

Investors have choices regarding the placement of their resources, but one key to any investment decision is the issue of security. One commentator notes the following:

> Private investors invest to make profits and not for reasons of benevolence. Thus, if they make profits they expect, albeit not unnaturally, to keep them, subject to payment of appropriate taxes to the local authorities; if they acquire property they expect to be entitled to keep it. The feeling of insecurity in these respects is, perhaps, the major deterrent to the flow of direct foreign investment in less-developed countries (LDC[s]).[23]

Thus, one of the principal purposes of the global investment protection regime is to reduce this investor insecurity, increase investment, and reduce poverty, especially in the developing world. Opportunities for investment exist throughout the world, and the market for capital placement is driven by the realistic rate of return investors can expect. The real rate of return, meanwhile, is determined not only by the expected income of a given project, but by the risks—especially political risks—to which a given investment will be subjected. By submitting themselves to the institutions of investment arbitration, states raise the sword of Damocles high over their own heads, constraining their own future action within accepted international limits, and assuring potential investors that an arbitral tribunal will vindicate their risk expectations, even if the state eventually chooses to disregard its own commitments.

> It is at first sight perhaps difficult to understand why governments would voluntarily limit their sovereignty by submitting to such processes of arbitration-enforced discipline. One needs to realise, though, that by accepting such external, politically less malleable discipline, a country gains in reputation, in lowering its political risk reputation and enhancing its ability to participate and benefit fully from the global economy. Governments who don't are seen as higher risk and therefore penalised, usually with good reason, in many ways by investors and the global markets. Submitting to such external disciplines also provides governments with a defense against domestic pressure groups—business lobbies and ideological interest groups—which can often capture the domestic regulatory machinery and manoeuvre it for protectionist policies which in the end damage the country at large and the wealth-creating potential of the global economy.[24]

---

[22] See generally *Economic Development, Foreign Investment and the Law* (Robert Pritchard ed., Kluwer Law International/International Bar Association 1996).

[23] Adeoye Akinsanya, *International Protection of Direct Foreign Investments in the Third World*, 36 Int'l Comp. L. Q. 58 (1987).

[24] Todd Weiler & Thomas W. Wälde, *Investment Arbitration under the Energy Charter Treaty in the Light of New NAFTA Precedents: Towards a Global Code of Conduct for Economic Regulation*, 1(2) Oil, Gas & Energy Law Intelligence 2, http://www.gasandoil.com/ogel/samples/freearticles/article_51.htm.

This axiom, that limits on sovereignty are as beneficial to capital-importing states as they are for the world's wealthy nations, has long been central to the mandate of organizations such as the Organization for Economic Cooperation and Development (OECD) and the World Bank in the field of investment protection.[25] The OECD has been active for several decades in promulgating guidelines for its member states on the management and liberalization of capital flows. For example, the organization's Code of Liberalization of Capital Movements and Code of Current Invisible Operations gradually helped loosen the grip of capital account controls and similar constraints on cross-border transactions in services.[26] According to the International Bank for Reconstruction and Development (IRBD), "creation of an institution designed to facilitate the settlement of disputes between states and foreign investors can be a major step toward promoting an atmosphere of mutual confidence and thus stimulating a larger flow of private international capital into those countries which wish to attract it."[27]

But whether formalized investment protection actually increases investment flows is hotly disputed. One recent article by a distinguished commentator concludes that strong protections do indeed increase flows:

> But it is clear that a U.S. BIT is more correlated with FDI inflows than other BITs . . . The regression results indicate that the presence of a U.S. BIT has large, positive, and significant association with a country's overall FDI inflows.
>
> . . .
>
> If a developing country truly wishes to promote foreign investment, it is better to sign a BIT with high protection standards, like those advocated by the [United States], than one with weaker standards as evidenced by certain other OECD countries. Signing a US BIT may also tend to lead to increased FDI flows from other OECD countries because OECD investors by virtue of the MFN clause . . . gain the protection of the high protective standards in U.S. BITs.[28]

---

[25] *Amco Asia Corp. v. Republic of Indonesia,* ICSID Case No. ARB/81/1 (Award on Jurisdiction, Sept. 25, 1983), *reprinted in* 10 Y.B. Comm. Arb. 61, 66 (1983) (investor-state arbitration "is aimed to protect, to the same extent and with the same vigour the investor and the host-state, not forgetting that to protect investments is to protect the general interest of development and of developing countries").

[26] *See* OECD, *OECD Code of Liberalization of Capital Movements* (2003); *see also* OECD, *Code of Liberalization of Current Invisible Operations* (1997), *available at* http://www.oecd.org/dataoecd/41/21/2030182.pdf; Rainer Geiger, *Towards a Multilateral Agreement on Investment,* 31 Cornell Int'l L. J. 467, 468 (1998).

[27] International Bank for Reconstruction and Development, *Report of the Executive Directors on the Convention on the Settlement of Investment Disputes between States and Nationals of Other States,* 4 I.L.M. 524, 525 (1965).

[28] J. Salacuse & N. Sullivan, *Do BITs Really Work: An Evaluation of Bilateral Investment Treaties and Their Grand Bargain,* 46 Harv. Int'l L. J. 67, 106–7 (2005).

Other commentators have reached similar conclusions, finding that investment treaties exert a significant positive effect on FDI.[29] Conversely, and in contrast to the aforementioned studies, many earlier studies found little correlation between investment protection and increased capital flows, or were "agnostic."[30]

But even assuming that foreign investor protection increases investment flows, some have disputed the assertion that such increases are unquestionably in the interest of the developing world. Developing countries may well be concerned about increased economic domination by foreign interests, loss of public control over vital industrial sectors, undue influence of foreign investors over internal politics, and so on.[31] For example, one commentator takes issue with the World Bank's claim that investor-state arbitration promotes "an atmosphere of mutual confidence" between capital importing countries and foreign investors:

> The whole idea of "confidence" in an economic context is linked inexorably to Western, market-oriented, conceptions of economic organisation. In no sense does the ICSID Convention increase a developing state's "confidence" that a foreign private investor will behave in a manner consistent with public policy or national aspirations. The only real increase in "confidence" that may be experienced by the host state is derived from the fact that, under the ICSID régime, confidentiality is assured, so that disputes can be set-

---

[29] Peter Egger & Michael Pfaffermayr, *The Impact of Bilateral Investment Treaties on Foreign Direct Investment*, 32 J. Comp. Econ. 788 (2004), *available at* http://papers.ssrn.com/s013/papers.cfm?abstract_id=694283; Eric Neumayer & Laura Spess, *Do Bilateral Investment Treaties Increase Foreign Direct Investment to Developing Countries?* (May 2005), http://papers.ssrn.com/s013/papers.cfm?abstract_id=616242.

[30] Bruce A. Blonigen & Ronald B. Davies, *Do Bilateral Tax Treaties Promote Foreign Direct Investment?* (National Bureau of Economic Research, Working Paper No. W8834, Mar. 2002), http://papers.ssrn.com/s013/papers.cfm?abstract_id=303556; Zachary Elkins, Andrew T. Guzman, & Beth Simmons, *Competing for Capital: The Diffusion of Bilateral Investment Treaties, 1960–2000* (UC Berkeley Public Law Research Paper No. 578961, Aug. 2004), http://papers.ssrn.com/s013/papers.cfm?abstract_id=578961; M. Hallward-Driemeier, *Bilateral Investment Treaties: Do They Increase FDI Flows?* (Background paper for Global Economic Prospects 2003: Investing to Unlock Global Opportunities, World Bank, Wash., D.C. 2002). *See also* Jennifer Tobin & Susan Rose-Ackerman, *Foreign Direct Investment and the Business Environment in Developing Countries: The Impact of Bilateral Investment Treaties,* (Yale Law & Economics Research Paper No. 293, May 2, 2005), http://papers.ssrn.com/s013/papers.cfm?abstract_id=557121; Kevin P. Gallagher & Melissa Birch, *Do Investment Agreements Attract Investment? Evidence from Latin America,* 7(6) J. World Inv. & Trade 961 (2006); J. P. Tumman & C. F. Emmert, *The Political Economy of U.S. Foreign Direct Investment in Latin America: A Reappraisal,* 39(3) Latin Am. Res. Rev. 9–29 (2004); Mary Hallward-Driemeier, *Do Bilateral Investment Treaties Attract FDI? Only a Bit . . . And It Might Bite* (World Bank Policy Research Working Paper Series, No. 3121, Wash., D.C. 2003); UNCTAD, *Bilateral Investment Treaties in the Mid-1990s* (United Nations, New York 1998).

[31] Stephen J. Toope, *Mixed International Arbitration: Studies in Arbitration between States and Private Persons* 220, n.7 (Grotius 1990).

tled without negative publicity. Otherwise, the foreign investor is the only party whose level of confidence is enhanced significantly.[32]

This position seems both petulant and untenable. Although capital-importing and capital-exporting states enjoy increased *confidence* of different varieties, it can hardly be said that the only security developing countries enjoy as a result of investment treaties is secrecy for their misdeeds. This position neglects small countries' desire that investment disputes will *not* be resolved by diplomatic and economic pressure from the investor's home government, regardless of the merits of the investor's claim. Developing states may well be more satisfied dealing with a neutral arbitral tribunal than with officials from one of the world's larger economies, whose leverage over smaller states on a range of unrelated issues is likely to be considerable. Indeed, until the United Nations Charter outlawed the unprovoked use of force, powerful states frequently employed the threat of military action, or *gunboat diplomacy,* to prevent harm to investors or to induce a favorable settlement of investment disputes with less developed countries.[33]

Just as importantly, capital-importing states may derive benefits from the mere codification of standards of treatment. By agreeing to a level of investment protection that is clearly defined, governments in the developing world can avoid *overpaying,* implementing too-generous (and politically unpopular) legislation to ensure that foreign investors do not petition their home governments to intervene on their behalf under vague standards of customary law. Finally, investment treaties may give capital-importing states confidence in the continued flow of foreign direct investment—no small assurance when economic reform, infrastructure development, health initiatives, and other improvement programs must be planned, justified, funded, and implemented over long periods of time.

Although there are doubtless other ways for developing states to obtain development financing, most importantly through lending by international organizations (such as the World Bank, the IMF and foreign aid agencies of the industrialized democracies), the potential for mutually beneficial symbiosis

---

[32] *Id.* at 221.

[33] M. Sornarajah, *The International Law on Foreign Investment* 8–9 (Cambridge University Press 1994) [hereinafter *Foreign Investment*]; *see also generally* M. Sornarajah, *Power and Justice in Foreign Investment Arbitration,* 14(3) J. Int'l Arb. 103 (1997); J. Cable, *Gunboat Diplomacy: Political Applications of Limited Naval Force* (Praeger 1981); Matthew B. Cobb, *The Development of Arbitration in Foreign Investment,* 16(4) Mealey's Int'l Arb. Rep., Apr. 2001, at 48, 49.

between developing governments and private foreign investors is prodigious. Even smaller states can establish relatively favorable conditions for foreign participation in the local economy, as long as they are prepared to offer treatment at or above international standards after the investment has been made.[34]

In the end, of course, the central purpose of investment treaties is investment protection, and there is evidence that that goal is being achieved:

> MORALES STATES THAT INTERNATIONAL ARBITRATION IS STOPPING NATIONALIZATION
>
> The Bolivian president, Evo Morales, stated today that the threat of multinationals demanding millions in international arbitration is "stopping" the advancement in "the recuperation of companies and natural resources."
>
> During a visit to a plant expropriated a year ago from the Swiss company Glencore, Morales stated "when we nationalize, multinationals complain . . . to international arbitrations . . . ."[35]

Undoubtedly, the rapidly developing regime of investor protection is one manifestation of *globalization*. And like other manifestations—in particular, world trade—the growth of this regime is unlikely to be reversed or even slowed in coming years.

---

[34] See Ian Brownlie's remarks on the purpose of the Dutch-Czech bilateral investment treaty in *CME Czech Republic B.V. v. Czech Republic*, UNCITRAL Arbitration (Final Award of Mar. 13, 2003), (Concurring Op., ¶ 17), http://www.cetv-net.com/arbitration.asp ("The object and purpose is not the protection of foreign property as such but the encouragement and protection of 'investments.' However, there is more to the terms of the treaty than this. One of the objects is the stimulation of the economic development of the parties, as indicated in the preamble. In this connection, the context includes the end of the Cold War (the treaty was concluded in 1991) and the promotion of a market economy in the region").

[35] Los Tiempos (La Paz, Bolivia) February 7, 2008. Author's translation.

II. History and Limitations of the Traditional System for Resolving Investment Disputes

A. Harms Suffered by Foreign Investors

Investment is by definition a risky enterprise, and foreign investment particularly so. History is replete with government actions that, while viewed as necessary or constructive from the local point of view, brought disaster to economic actors from abroad.

For example, in 1938 Mexico's President Lázaro Cárdenas nationalized the country's petroleum industry, which was then dominated by U.S. and U.K. corporations. Cárdenas' action delivered to the Mexican government a monopoly in the exploration, production, refining, and distribution of oil and natural gas and in the manufacture and sale of basic petrochemicals. Although President Cárdenas offered compensation, U.S. oil companies pressured their government to place an embargo on all imports from Mexico to discourage similar nationalizations in other countries. The boycott was in effect briefly, but the U.S. government soon convinced the oil companies to come to terms with Mexico in furtherance of President Franklin D. Roosevelt's Good Neighbor Policy and U.S. security interests arising from World War II. In 1943 Mexico and the oil companies reached a final settlement, under which the companies received US$24 million (a fraction of the book value of the expropriated facilities) as compensation.[1] The date of the nationalization is still celebrated in Mexico as a national holiday. In Spain the Franco regime's seizure of a Barcelona street car company set in motion one of the longest-running disputes in international law, justifying Dickensian depictions of the futility of legal process.[2] Lacking the political

---

[1] See Mexico, The Economy, Oil, http://countrystudies.us/mexico/78.htm. Daniel Yergin, *The Prize: The Epic Quest for Oil, Money & Power* 271–79 (1992).

[2] *Case Concerning the Barcelona Traction, Light and Power Company* (Belgium v. Spain), 1970 I.C.J. Rep. 1970.

influence of their domestic competitors, foreign investors in such circumstances often find themselves at the mercy of host governments.

Such government actions can have serious long-term consequences. The following newspaper article describes how one country's lack of an impartial legal regime and reliable forum to resolve economic disputes has raised the cost of capital and diverted investment flows to other parts of the world.

[handwritten: Indonesia example]

Beneath the jungles and volcanoes of the Indonesian archipelago are buried some of Asia's richest treasures—vast deposits of gold, copper, coal and other natural resources. But foreign companies have all but stopped investing in new operations to mine them.

Despite huge reserves of oil and natural gas, Indonesia faces the prospect in the next few years of crippling power outages, like those that darkened most of the capital for two days last month. No new power stations are being built on the main Java-Bali electric grid. Foreign investors, whose money is needed for projects of this size, say they are not interested in developing new plants.

In both the mining and power industries, investors say that the poverty of Indonesia's legal system is a major part of why they're staying away. It has contributed to a general lack of confidence that is draining away badly needed capital and undermining the country's struggle to recover from the 1997–98 Asian financial crisis.

Foreign investors complain they are subject to the arbitrary demands of government officials, tax collectors and local partners. They have little meaningful recourse in the courts, where bribery is rampant and favoritism the legal standard.

. . . .

"Investors in Indonesia doubt whether their rights will be preserved and about the sanctity of contracts," said Hikmahanto Juwana, a professor of international economic law at the University of Indonesia. "The main thing is that Indonesia is no longer a good place to invest."

. . . .

The most jarring example, foreign investors say, came this summer. A three-judge panel held that the local unit of Canadian insurer Manulife Financial Corp. was bankrupt, even though the company insisted it was still solvent. The ruling came in response to a claim by Manulife's former Indonesian partner in a joint venture, which had been seeking to win millions of dollars through the bankruptcy process. After the ruling, Manulife claimed it had been the victim of a "public mugging." For a time, it seemed the local Manulife unit, which has 4,000 employees and 400,000 policyholders in the country, would have to close, even though it had assets now worth about $522 million and profits in its insurance business that exceeded $8 million last year, according to Syarifudin Yunus, Manulife's local spokesman.

The Canadian government threatened sanctions. U.S. and other diplomats in Jakarta launched a petition drive on behalf of the company, raising their objections directly with President Megawati Sukarnoputri. A month later, facing intense political pressure, the Supreme Court overturned the decision. The three judges who declared the unit bankrupt were suspended on suspicion of taking bribes. Foreign and Indonesian corporate executives said the Manulife decision was unique only for the extensive political fallout that forced a reversal of the decision. "In almost every way, the law is manipulated. If we are truly interested in restoring our economic development, the most important thing is certainty in the implementation of the law," said Eddie Lembong, who runs Pharos Indonesia Ltd., a big pharmaceutical company.[3]

Foreign investors may be subject to unusual and unpredictable problems, and in attempting to overcome those problems, they face many obstacles.

B. Barriers to Recovery by Foreign Investors

1. Barriers in Host Country Courts

In general, foreign investors usually face serious obstacles to obtaining redress in the host country's courts. Although judicial systems vary widely, even within the developing world, certain systemic barriers are pervasive and tend to affect foreign businesses in a range of less developed countries.

a. Local Bias

One serious barrier to obtaining redress in some host-country courts is local bias. Although judges are not necessarily more sympathetic to their countrymen than to foreigners, the contrary perception is common, in some cases with good reason.[4] Indeed, the possibility of local bias is a phenomenon not unique to developing countries. The U.S. Constitution acknowledges and expressly addresses the problem. To account for "apprehended discrimination in state courts against those not citizens of the state,"[5] the constitution's drafters created what is known as "diversity" jurisdiction in the U.S. federal courts; so in a lawsuit involving citizens of different states, the out-of-state defendant can demand a presumably more neutral federal court. Similar protection against local prejudice is a prominent feature of the international legal system, especially in the investment treaty system.[6]

---

[3] Alan Sipress, *Flawed Legal System Impeding Indonesia; Lacking Confidence, Foreign Investors Flee,* Wash. Post, Oct. 29, 2002, at A17.

[4] *See, e.g.,* the difficulties encountered by Western investors in resolving disputes before courts and arbitral tribunals in Pakistan and Indonesia, Peter Cornell & Arwen Handley, *Himpurna and Hub: International Arbitration in Developing Countries.* Mealey's Int'l Arb. Rep., Sept. 2000, at 39.

[5] *Erie Railroad Co. v. Tompkins,* 304 U.S. 64, 74 (1938). *See also Bank of the U.S. v. Devaux,* 9 U.S. (5 Cranch) 61, 87, 3 L.Ed. 38, 45 (1809) ("However true the fact may be, that the tribunals of the states will administer justice as impartially as those of the nation, . . . it is not less true that the constitution itself either entertains apprehensions on this subject, or views with such indulgence the possible fears and apprehensions of suitors, that it has established national tribunals for the decision of controversies . . . between citizens of different states").

[6] *See generally* John P. Gaffney, *Due Process in the World Trade Organization,* 14 Am. U. Int'l L. Rev. 1173, 1196 (1999) (discussing the 1903 arbitration proceeding between a U.S. citizen and the Venezuelan government, *Rudolf v. Venezuela*).

b. State Immunity

Until the second half of the twentieth century, foreign investors and traders faced a serious and immediate barrier to judicial remedies for uncompensated expropriation and other harm suffered at the hands of host governments. Both the local courts and the judiciary of the investor's home state were unlikely to adjudicate such a dispute, out of deference to sovereign immunity. Such immunity was widely viewed as absolute, even if the foreign investor's claim would have been cognizable against a private party in similar circumstances.

The concept of sovereign immunity can be traced far back into the recesses of international legal development.[7] A state's immunity from the jurisdiction of its own courts is somewhat different in origin and justification from its insulation from suit before foreign judges. The former situation, whereby a government is protected from suit in its own court system absent consent, is the product of the age-old axiom that "the king can do no wrong."[8] Particularly in common-law countries, it was reasoned that the law-making authority, which freely dispenses of rights and obligations within its own territory, should not—or could not—be subordinated to its own power. Thomas Hobbes reasons as follows:

> The sovereign of a Commonwealth, be it an assembly or one man, is not subject to the civil laws. For having power to make and repeal laws, he may, when he pleaseth, free himself from that subjection by repealing those laws that trouble him, and making of new; and consequently he was free before.[9]

The same tradition existed in the civil law:

> [T]he development of the restrictive theory regarding state immunity has its basis in the Napoleonic system, which was created in the first decade of the nineteenth century. At that time, following the absolutist approach, no one could sue the state. However, there was a struggle for more than a century over the means for making the state responsible for its actions and wrongs.
>
> Eventually, the courts differentiated between public acts and private acts. Under that approach, a citizen could sue the domestic sovereign in an ordinary court when it acted in a "private capacity" and before the Conseil d'Etat when it acted in a "public capacity." That way of thinking transferred to the problem of foreign sovereigns, creating the practice known as the "restrictive theory of foreign states." Concerning the domestic sovereign

---

[7] See generally Richard B. Lillich, *The Protection of Foreign Investment* 3–9 (1965).

[8] Edwin Borchard, *Government Liability in Tort*, 34 Yale L. J. 1, 2 (1924).

[9] Thomas Hobbes, *Leviathan* (1660), chapter XXVI, 2. *See also The Western Maid*, 257 U.S. 419, 432 (1922) (Holmes, J.) ("the authority that makes the law is itself superior to it").

immunity (and later, foreign state immunity), the courts examined the nature of the act, i.e., whether the state acted in a private or public capacity.[10]

Two distinct approaches to the public/private divide have coalesced since then, one emphasizing the purpose of the state's act and the other emphasizing the nature of the act. For the most part, civil law systems have adopted the latter approach. Moreover, most civil law countries have a divided legal system, with separate fora for the adjudication of administrative law issues and civil disputes.[11] As discussed in the following text, this *divided* approach to state immunity still appears in various guises, including the extent to which states may be found liable for breach of contract. Regardless of the particular approach to immunity, the consequence for foreign investors is that in cases where the host country government is the cause of the foreign investor's damage, local courts may not be authorized to provide any remedy.

c. Inefficient Local Courts

Efficiency of local courts is another concern of many foreign investors, because developing countries often lack responsive, robust legal systems capable of effectively and quickly adjudicating complex claims. A particularly telling example concerns the 1984 Union Carbide gas plant tragedy in India, in which more than 2,000 deaths and 200,000 injuries resulted from a toxic gas leak at a chemical gas plant owned by Union Carbide India Limited, a company incorporated under Indian law but majority-owned by Union Carbide Corporation of New York.[12] Rather than processing claims in Indian courts, the government of India enacted legislation to vest in the Indian government the exclusive right to represent Indian plaintiffs anywhere in the world.[13] And it then filed claims on behalf of Indian citizens in New York federal courts.[14] In resisting the defendant's efforts to transfer the cases back to India, the Indian government acknowledged the inefficiency

---

[10] Reinhard Von Hennigs, *25th Anniversary of the Foreign Sovereign Immunities Act: European Convention on State Immunity and Other International Aspects of Sovereign Immunity*, 9 Williamette J. Int'l L. & Disp. Res. 185, 190 (2001).

[11] See discussion below at p. 18.

[12] *In re Union Carbide Corp. Gas Plant Disaster at Bhopal, India*, 634 F. Supp. 842 (S.D.N.Y. 1986), aff'd, 809 F.2d 195 (2d Cir.), cert. denied, 484 U.S. 871 (1987).

[13] *Id.*

[14] The unusual posture of this case—a U.S. corporation strenuously trying to escape U.S. jurisdiction, and a foreign government strenuously trying to invoke it—is almost certainly attributable to Union Carbide's justifiable fear of the extremely high awards that U.S. courts are prone to award, especially in personal injury cases.

of its own courts. It argued to the New York court that India's judicial system suffered from "procedural and discovery deficiencies that would thwart the victims' quest for justice."[15] The U.S. court ultimately determined that Indian courts would be a more appropriate forum for the litigants, but the Indian government's characterization of its own judicial system reflects the experience of many foreign investors.

d. Calvo Doctrine

In the past, partially in response to perceived abuses by foreign investors, some host nations tried to restrict a foreign investor's remedies to its local courts and deprive them of the protection of international law, aware that any remedy there would likely be illusory. According to this doctrine, international liability cannot be triggered so long as the host state provides a judicial or administrative adjudicative system that is impartial and comports with generally accepted standards of due process, regardless of the outcome of the investor's local claim.[16] This doctrine, known as the Calvo clause after its chief proponent the Argentinean lawyer and statesman, Carlos Calvo, was especially prevalent in South America:

> The impact of [the] Calvo doctrine on the legal traditions of Latin American States is reflected in the following propositions: (a) international law requires that the host State accord national treatment to aliens; (b) national law governs the rights and privileges of aliens; (c) national courts have exclusive jurisdiction over disputes involving aliens, who may therefore not seek redress by recourse to diplomatic protection; (d) international adjudication is inadmissible for the settlement of disputes with aliens.[17]

The opposite position has been held just as strongly for an equally long time, namely that "the state to which a foreigner belongs may intervene for his protection when he has been *denied* ordinary justice in the foreign country, and also in case of a plain *violation* of the substance of natural justice."[18] Mexico was one of the most prominent proponents of the Calvo Doctrine (and did not effectively abandon it until the advent of the North American Free Trade Agreement), as the following case illustrates.

---

[15] *Id.* at 847.

[16] *See, e.g.*, Alwyn Freeman, *International Responsibility of States for Denial of Justice* 330 (1938); Charles Hyde, *International Law* 731–32 (1945).

[17] Louis Henkin, et al., *International Law* 685 (3d ed. 1993); *see also* Edwin M. Borchard, *Decisions of the Claims Commissions, United States and Mexico*, 20 Am. J. Int'l Law 536, 538 (1926); Sir John H. Percival, *International Arbitral Tribunals and the Mexican Claims Commissions*, 19(3) J. Comp. Legis. & Int'l L. 98, 102 (1937); G. Godfrey Phillips, *The Anglo-Mexican Special Claims Commission*, 49 L. Q. Rev. 226, 234 (1933); Lionel Summers, *La Clause Calvo: Tendences Nouvelles*, 12 Rev. de Droit Int'l 229, 232 (1933).

[18] Letter from U.S. Secretary of State to Mr. McLane, Minister to France from the United States, June 23, 1886, *reprinted in* 6 Moore's Int'l Law Digest 266 (1906).

North American Dredging Company of Texas (U.S.A.) v. United Mexican States

4 R.I.A.A. 26 (1926)

This case is before this Commission on a motion of the Mexican Agent to dismiss. It is put forward by the United States of America on behalf of North American Dredging Company of Texas, an American corporation, for the recovery of the sum of $233,523.30 with interest thereon, the amount of losses and damages alleged to have been suffered by claimant for breaches of a contract for dredging at the port of Salina Cruz, which contract was entered into between the claimant and the Government of Mexico, November 23, 1912. The contract was signed at Mexico City. The Government of Mexico was a party to it. It had for its subject matter services to be rendered by the claimant in Mexico. Payment therefore was to be made in Mexico. Article 18, incorporated by Mexico as an indispensable provision, not separable from the other provisions of the contract, was subscribed to by the claimant for the purpose of securing the award of the contract. Its translation by the Mexican Agent reads as follows:

> "The contractor and all persons who, as employees or in any other capacity, may be engaged in the execution of the work under this contract either directly or indirectly, shall be considered as Mexicans in all matters, within the Republic of Mexico, concerning the execution of such work and the fulfilment of this contract. They shall not claim, nor shall they have, with regard to the interests and the business connected with this contract, any other rights or means to enforce the same than those granted by the laws of the Republic to Mexicans, nor shall they enjoy any other rights than those established in favor of Mexicans. They are consequently deprived of any rights as aliens, and under no conditions shall the intervention of foreign diplomatic agents be permitted, in any matter related to this contract."

1. The jurisdiction of the Commission is challenged in this case on the grounds . . . (second) that a contract containing the so-called Calvo clause deprives the party subscribing said clause of the right to submit any claims connected with his contract to an international commission.

The Calvo clause

3. The Commission is fully sensible of the importance of any judicial decision either sustaining in whole or in part, or rejecting in whole or in part, or construing the so-called "Calvo clause" in contracts between nations and aliens. It appreciates the legitimate desire on the part of nations to deal with persons and property within their respective jurisdictions according to their own laws and to apply remedies provided by their own authorities and tribunals. . . .

4. The Commission does not feel impressed by arguments either in favor of or in opposition to the Calvo clause, in so far as these arguments go to extremes. The Calvo clause is neither upheld by all outstanding international authorities and by the soundest among international awards nor is it universally rejected. . . .

. . . .

Lawfulness of the Calvo clause

8. The contested provision, in this case, is part of a contract and must be upheld unless it be repugnant to a recognized rule of international law. What must be established is not that the Calvo clause is universally accepted or universally recognized, but that there exists a generally accepted rule of international law condemning the Calvo clause and denying to an individual the right to relinquish to any extent, large or small, and under any circumstances or conditions, the protection of the government to which he owes allegiance . . .

9. The commission does not hesitate to declare that there exists no international rule prohibiting the sovereign right of a nation to protect its citizens abroad from being subject to any limitation whatsoever under any circumstances. The right of protection has been limited by treaties between nations in provisions related to the Calvo clause. While it is true that Latin-American countries—which are important members of the family of nations and which have played for many years an important and honorable part in the development of international law—are parties to most of these treaties, still such countries as France, Germany, Great Britain, Sweden, Norway, and Belgium, and in one case at least even the United States of America (Treaty between the United States and Peru dated September 6, 1870, Volume 2, Malloy's United States Treaties, at page 1426; article 37) have been parties to treaties containing such provisions.

10. What Mexico has asked of the North American Dredging Company of Texas as a condition for awarding it the contract which it sought is, "If all of the means of enforcing your rights under this contract afforded by Mexican law, even against the Mexican Government itself, are wide open to you, as they are wide open to our own citizens, will you promise not to ignore them and not to call directly upon your own Government to intervene in your behalf in connexion with any controversy, small or large, but seek redress under the laws of Mexico through the authorities and tribunals furnished by Mexico for your protection?" and the claimant, by subscribing to this contract and seeking the benefits which were to accrue to him thereunder, has answered, "I promise."

11. Under the rules of international law may an alien lawfully make such a promise? The Commission holds that he may, but at the same time holds that he can not deprive the government of his nation of its undoubted right of applying international remedies to violations of international law committed to his damage. . . . But while any attempt to so bind his Government is void, the Commission has not found any generally recognized rule of positive international law which would give to his Government the right to intervene to strike down a lawful contract, in the terms set forth in the preceding paragraph 10, entered into by its citizen.

. . . .

The Calvo clause and the claimant

18. If it were necessary to demonstrate how legitimate are the fears of certain nations with respect to abuses of the right of protection and how seriously the sovereignty of those nations within their own boundaries would be impaired if some extreme conceptions of this right were recognized and enforced, the present case would furnish an illuminating example. The claimant, after having solemnly promised in writing that it would not ignore the local laws, remedies, and authorities, behaved from the very beginning as if article 18 of its contract had no existence in fact. It used the article to procure the contract, but this was the extent of its use. It has never sought any redress by application to the local authorities and remedies which article 18 liberally granted it and which, according to Mexican law, are available to it, even against the Government, without restrictions, both in matter of civil and of public law . . . The record before this Commission strongly suggests that the claimant used article 18 to procure the contract with no intention of ever observing its provisions.

. . . .

20. Under article 18 of the contract declared upon, the present claimant is precluded from presenting to its Government any claim relative to the interpretation or fulfillment of this contract. If it had a claim for denial of justice, for delay of justice or gross injustice, or

for any other violation of international law committed by Mexico to its damage, it might have presented such a claim to its Government, which in turn could have espoused it and presented it here.

Extent of the present interpretation of the Calvo clause

. . . .

23. Even so, each case involving application of a valid clause partaking of the nature of the Calvo clause will be considered and decided on its merits. Where a claim is based on an alleged violation of any rule or principle of international law, the Commission will take jurisdiction notwithstanding the existence of such a clause in a contract subscribed by such claimant. But where a claimant has expressly agreed in writing, attested by his signature, that in all matters pertaining to the execution, fulfilment, and interpretation of the contract he will have resort to local tribunals, remedies, and authorities and then wilfully ignores them by applying in such matters to his Government, he will be held bound by his contract and the Commission will not take jurisdiction of such claim . . . .

The North American Dredging tribunal thus drew a crucial distinction. With respect to breach of contract, a foreign investor or contractor could indeed waive its rights to certain types of international protection by signing on to a Calvo clause. But this was not the case for other state acts constituting violations of international law, such as denial of justice or expropriation. As discussed in the following text, this distinction reappears in other forms in international jurisprudence.

2. Barriers in Foreign Investor's Home Courts

As a result of the potential shortcomings previously described, foreign companies often hesitate to entrust their disputes to the judicial system of the host state. Rather, they frequently look to courts in other countries with a factual connection to the dispute, most often the investor's domicile. But then they face an entirely different, but no less challenging, series of obstacles.

a. Jurisdiction

Absent contractual provisions to the contrary, the courts in the investor's home country are unlikely to exercise in personam jurisdiction over the host state actor. In most investment disputes, the material events have taken place in the host country, and the critical actors are the host country government or corporations operating in the host country. Often in such circumstances there is an insufficient nexus of fact with the investor's country to provide a foundation for jurisdiction.

In the United States, for example, a court may only exercise personal jurisdiction if the foreign entity has sufficient "minimum contacts" with the United States, "such that the maintenance of the suit does not offend 'traditional notions of fair play and substantial justice.'"[19] Other countries have similar restrictions.[20] This initial jurisdictional barrier precludes the resolution of many disputes in the investor's home courts.

b. Foreign Sovereign Immunity

Just as a host government is often immune from suit in its home courts, it is usually also immune in the foreign investor's courts.[21] Judge Higgins of the International Court of Justice explains:

> Under classical international law, states, including governments thereof, were granted immunity from the territorial jurisdiction of other states. Various reasons of policy have been suggested, all interrelated. First, the reason may be found in the doctrine of Sovereign equality . . . which means that no state could be expected to submit to the laws of another. Secondly, it has been said that it would offend the dignity of a state to submit to the jurisdiction of another.[22]

Until the middle of the twentieth century, most commentators agreed—and most states insisted—that the shield of sovereign immunity was absolute. As a result private disputes with government-owned entities were outside the jurisdiction of national courts.[23]

Even now, exceptions to sovereign immunity exist only in limited circumstances. In the United States, for example, the Foreign Sovereign Immunities Act (FSIA) establishes the narrow circumstances in which foreign states can be sued.[24] In general, the FSIA only allows actions that result from a sovereign's *commercial* activity. This may not include sovereign acts such as expropriation or even regulatory acts. Consequently, even if the investor's home courts could exercise jurisdiction, they are unlikely to adjudicate many claims.

c. Act of State Doctrine

In addition to immunity, some courts, especially those in the United States, are reluctant to pass judgment on the actions of foreign states. What is known as the "act of state doctrine" effectively forecloses most legal actions in an investor's domestic courts against foreign governments for harm to the investor's foreign investments

---

[19] See *International Shoe Co. v. Washington*, 326 U.S. 310 (1945).

[20] See, e.g., the limitations set on service of documents on defendants who are located outside of England under the Civil Procedure Rules of the United Kingdom, Section III, Special Provisions on Service Out of Jurisdiction, ¶ 6.17 *et seq.*, available at http://www.dca.gov.uk/civil/procrules_fin/contents/parts/part06.htm#ruleIDAXHUYC.

[21] Troland S. Link, *Foreign Sovereign Immunity, Expropriation, Act of State, and Community*, 703 PLI/Comm. L. & Prac. Handbook Series 183 (1994); Noah Rubins & Stephan Kinsella, *International Investment, Political Risk, and Dispute Resolution* 140–51 (2005).

[22] Rosalyn Higgins, *Problems and Process: International Law and How We Use It* 78–79 (1994).

[23] *Schooner Exchange v. McFadden*, 11 U.S. 116 (1812).

[24] Foreign Sovereign Immunity Act, 28 U.S.C. § 1330 *et seq.* (1976).

through expropriation and other governmental measures.[25] The United States Supreme Court's decision in *Banco Nacional de Cuba v. Sabbatino* is perhaps the most celebrated case where the doctrine was applied:

Banco Nacional de Cuba v. Sabbatino

176 U.S. 398 (1964) [footnotes omitted]

Mr. Justice Harlan delivered the opinion of the Court.

The question [that] brought this case here, and is now found to be the dispositive issue, is whether the so-called act of state doctrine serves to sustain petitioner's [(Banco Nacional's)] claims in this litigation. Such claims are ultimately founded on a decree of the Government of Cuba expropriating certain property, the right to the proceeds of which is here in controversy. The act of state doctrine in its traditional formulation precludes the courts of this country from inquiring into the validity of the public acts a recognized foreign sovereign power committed within its own territory.

In February and July of 1960, respondent Farr, Whitlock & Co., an American commodity broker, contracted to purchase Cuban sugar, free alongside the steamer, from a wholly owned subsidiary of Compania Azucarera Vertientes-Camaguey de Cuba (C.A.V.), a corporation organized under Cuban law whose capital stock was owned principally by United States residents. Farr, Whitlock agreed to pay for the sugar in New York upon presentation of the shipping documents and a sight draft.

On July 6, 1960, the Congress of the United States amended the Sugar Act of 1948 to permit a presidentially directed reduction of the sugar quota for Cuba. On the same day President Eisenhower exercised the granted power. The day of the congressional enactment, the Cuban Council of Ministers adopted "Law No. 851," which characterized this reduction in the Cuban sugar quota as an act of "aggression, for political purposes" on the part of the United States, justifying the taking of countermeasures by Cuba. The law gave the Cuban President and Prime Minister discretionary power to nationalize by forced expropriation property or enterprises in which American nationals had an interest. Although a system of compensation was formally provided, the possibility of payment under it may well be deemed illusory. Our State Department has described the Cuban law as "manifestly in violation of those principles of international law which have long been accepted by the free countries of the West. It is in its essence discriminatory, arbitrary and confiscatory."[26]

Between August 6 and August 9, 1960, the sugar covered by the contract between Farr, Whitlock and C.A.V. was loaded, destined for Morocco, onto the [SS] *Hornfels,* which was standing offshore at the Cuban port of Jucaro (Santa Maria). On the day loading commenced, the Cuban President and Prime Minister, acting pursuant to Law No. 851, issued Executive Power Resolution No. 1. It provided for the compulsory expropriation of all property and enterprises, and of rights and interests arising therefrom, of certain listed

---

[25] *See generally* Richard B. Lillich, *The Protection of Foreign Investment* 45–113 (1965). On the act of state doctrine in England, *see* Jones, *Act of Foreign State in English Law: The Ghost Goes East,* 22 Va. J. Int'l L. 433 (1982); Michael Singer, *The Act of State Doctrine of the United Kingdom: An Analysis, with Comparison to United States Practice,* 75 Am. J. Int'l L. 283 (1981). On application of the doctrine in Hong Kong, *see* Donna Lee, *Discrepancy between Theory and Reality: Hong Kong's Court of Final Appeal and the Acts of State Doctrine,* 35 Colum. J. Transn. L. 175 (1997).

[26] SN: *See* State Dept. Note 397, July 16, 1960 (to Cuban Ministry of Foreign Relations).

companies, including C.A.V., wholly or principally owned by American nationals. The preamble reiterated the alleged injustice of the American reduction of the Cuban sugar quota and emphasized the importance of Cuba's serving as an example for other countries to follow "in their struggle to free themselves from the brutal claws of imperialism."

. . . .

The classic American statement of the act of state doctrine, which appears to have taken root in England as early as 1674, *Blad v. Bamfield*, 3 Swans. 604, 36 Eng. Rep. 992, and began to emerge in the jurisprudence of this country in the late eighteenth and early nineteenth centuries, see, e.g., *Ware v. Hylton*, 3 Dall. 199, 230; *Hudson v. Guestier, 4 Cranch 293, 294; Schooner Exchange v. M'Faddon, 7 Cranch 116, 135,* 136; *L'Invincible, 1 Wheat. 238, 253; The Santissim*a Trinidad, 7 Wheat. 283, 336, is found in *Underhill v. Hernandez*, 168 U.S. 250, where Chief Justice Fuller said for a unanimous Court (p. 252):

> Every sovereign State is bound to respect the independence of every other sovereign State, and the courts of one country will not sit in judgment on the acts of the government of another done within its own territory. Redress of grievances by reason of such acts must be obtained through the means open to be availed of by sovereign powers as between themselves.

Following this precept the Court in that case refused to inquire into acts of Hernandez, a revolutionary Venezuelan military commander whose government had been later recognized by the United States, which were made the basis of a damage action in this country by Underhill, an American citizen, who claimed that he had been unlawfully assaulted, coerced, and detained in Venezuela by Hernandez.

Therefore, rather than laying down or reaffirming an inflexible and all-encompassing rule in this case, we decide only that the Judicial Branch will not examine the validity of a taking of property within its own territory by a foreign sovereign government, extant and recognized by this country at the time of suit, in the absence of a treaty or other unambiguous agreement regarding controlling legal principles, even if the complaint alleges that the taking violates customary international law.

Respondents claim that the economic pressure resulting from the proposed exception to the act of state doctrine will materially add to the protection of United States investors. We are not convinced, even assuming the relevance of this contention. Expropriations take place for a variety of reasons, political and ideological as well as economic. When one considers the variety of means possessed by this country to make secure foreign investment, the persuasive or coercive effect of judicial invalidation of acts of expropriation dwindles in comparison. The newly independent states are in need of continuing foreign investment; the creation of a climate unfavorable to such investment by wholesale confiscations may well work to their long-run economic disadvantage. Foreign aid given to many of these countries provides a powerful lever in the hands of the political branches to ensure fair treatment of United States nationals. Ultimately the sanctions of economic embargo and the freezing of assets in this country may be employed. Any country willing to brave any or all of these consequences is unlikely to be deterred by sporadic judicial decisions directly affecting only property brought to our shores. If the political branches are unwilling to exercise their ample powers to effect compensation, this reflects a judgment of the national interest which the judiciary would be ill-advised to undermine indirectly.

. . . .

However offensive to the public policy of this country and its constituent States an expropriation of this kind may be, we conclude that both the national interest and progress toward the goal of establishing the rule of law among nations are best served by maintaining intact the act of state doctrine in this realm of its application.

Although this specific articulation of the doctrine is applicable only in the United States, it illustrates the reluctance of many courts to condemn the sovereign, political acts of foreign governments. Whether or not this reluctance is codified in legal doctrine, it undoubtedly exists and forms an important barrier to investors seeking recovery of their investment.

d. Choice of Law

Even if a foreign investor is able to surmount the problems of jurisdiction, immunity, and act of state doctrine, the foreign investor's home courts may apply the host country's laws in resolving the dispute. Investment disputes are normally centered around events that took place in the country where the investment was made. Under most law regimes, the controlling law is that of the country where the transaction and dispute are centered.[27] But host country law may well be hostile to foreign investors; indeed, the host country law may have been changed expressly to curtail the rights of the foreign investor. Nonetheless, it is certainly possible, perhaps probable, that the investor's home court, applying normal choice of law principles, would apply that hostile body of law. Because the host state's actions are usually consistent with its own law, this choice of applicable law may well result in dismissal of the investor's claim.[28]

3. Political Barriers: The New International Economic Order

In addition to the formal legal hurdles noted above, foreign investors have at various times faced significant political hostility to their attempts to recover their investments. Although such hostility is perhaps predictable in the host state in the aftermath of an investment dispute, overt anti-investor hostility has surfaced in international institutions, and even in the political attitudes of the investor's home country. Prior to the demise of communism, such sentiment was (and to some degree still is) particularly prevalent in leftist sectors.

One striking example of anti-investor sentiment was the New International Economic Order (NIEO). The governments supporting the NIEO movement—developing countries and communist regimes—sought to counter the development of customary international law standards protecting foreign investments from uncompensated expropriation. In the 1960s and 1970s (the peak of the NIEO movement's strength), these states sponsored a number of United Nations

---

[27] See, e.g., Restatement (First) of Conflicts of Laws, § 311, Place of Contracting (1934).

[28] Sometimes, however, the public policy of the investor's home state may intervene in its favor. In the 1920s and 1930s, after the Soviet government confiscated the property of foreigners, a wave of litigation ensued around the world. In one of the cases brought in New York, the court accepted that by operation of the conflict of law principles, the Soviet law should govern the issue; and accordingly, the confiscation should be enforceable. Yet, it refused to recognize the confiscation, on the ground that it was in conflict with New York's public policy. See Vladikavkazsky Ry. Co. v. N.Y. Trust Co., 263 N.Y. 369, 189 N.E. 456 (1934).

General Assembly (UNGA) resolutions reserving for themselves broad discretion to protect their economic interests, to the detriment of capital exporters.[29] The first of these was UNGA Resolution 1803, which set forth two important principles: Foreign investments remain subject to the domestic law of the host state;[30] and the compensation an investor is due in exchange for its expropriated assets should be "appropriate," rather than the "prompt, adequate and effective" compensation advocated by the developed world.[31] In relevant part Resolution 1803 provided the following:

> 3. In cases where authorization is granted, the capital imported and the earning on that capital shall be governed by the terms thereof, by the national legislation in force, and by international law . . .
>
> 4. Nationalization, expropriation or requisitioning shall be based on grounds or reasons of public utility, security or the national interest which are recognized as overriding purely individual or private interests, both domestic and foreign. In such cases the owner shall be paid appropriate compensation, in accordance with the rules in force in the State taking such measures in the exercise of its sovereignty and in accordance with international law. . . .

Thereafter, a debate ensued as to the norm-creating ability of General Assembly resolutions and the jurisprudential value of the NIEO resolutions.[32] Professor Dupuy considered the issues in the *Texaco Overseas Petroleum Company v. Libyan Arab Republic* arbitration:

> 88. . . . Resolution 1803 (XVII) appears to a large extent as the expression of a real general will[;] this is not[, however,] at all the case with respect to the other Resolutions mentioned above. . . . In particular, as regards the Charter of Economic Rights and Duties

---

[29] Permanent Sovereignty over Natural Resources, G.A. Res. 1803, U.N. GAOR, 17th Sess., Supp. No. 17, at 15, U.N. Doc. A/5217 (1962) [hereinafter Res. 1803]; Declaration on the Establishment of the New International Economic Order, G.A. Res. 3201, U.N. GAOR, 6th Spec. Sess., Supp. No. 1, at 3, U.N. Doc. A/9559 (1974); The Charter of Economic Rights and Duties of States (CERDS), G.A. Res. 3281, U.N. GAOR, 29th Sess., Supp. No. 31, at 51, U.N. Doc. A/9631 (1974).

[30] *See also* pp. 13 *et seq.* above on Calvo doctrine.

[31] For a more detailed discussion of the Hull formula, *see* Chapter XVI on expropriation.

[32] With respect to the normative value of General Assembly resolutions, *see Legality of the Threat or Use of Nuclear Weapons*, ICJ Advisory Opinion (1996), ¶ 70, *available at* http://www.icj-cij.org/icjwww/icases/iunan/iunanframe.htm (last viewed Sept. 8, 2004). ("It is necessary to look at [a General Assembly resolution's] content and the conditions of its adoption; it is also necessary to see whether an *opinio juris* exists as to its normative character. Or a series of resolutions may show the gradual evolution of the *opinio juris* required for the establishment of a new rule").

of States, several factors contribute to denying legal value to those provisions of the document which are of interest in the instant case.[33]

Thus, although the NIEO failed to achieve most of its goals, Resolution 1803 may have had some effect on certain norms of customary international law, and in particular the Hull formula for the standard of compensation for expropriated property.[34]

In 1974, a campaign initiated against the prevailing norms of equal and nondiscriminatory treatment for foreign investors resulted in another UNGA resolution known as the Charter of Economic Rights and Duties of States (CERDS),[35] which envisaged preferential treatment for local capital. Moreover, CERDS set forth a new standard for the treatment of investments, one vehemently opposed by developed countries in the General Assembly: "Every State has and shall freely exercise full permanent sovereignty, including possession, use and disposal, over all its wealth, natural resources and economic activities."[36] Although the general exhortatory provisions of CERDS were approved by a wide margin, the most controversial provision—Article 2, which purported to remove the act of nationalization from the protections of international law—was adopted only over the objections of all the major industrialized and capital-exporting nations, as well as several developing countries.[37]

The CERDS marked the peak of NIEO influence, as well as the start of its decline. Several factors contributed to this process, including the failure of NIEO prescriptions to ameliorate conditions in developing countries; the collapse of Soviet Union, which had supported the NIEO cause[38]; and the conclusion of hundreds of

---

[33] *Texaco Overseas Petroleum Company v. Libyan Arab Republic*, 17 I. L. M. 1, 30 (1978); Professor Brownlie believes that Res. 1803 is the evidence of existing customary law, *see* Ian Brownlie, *Principles of Public International Law* 519 (6th ed., Oxford University Press 2003); *see also* C. F. Amerasinghe, *Issue of Compensation for the Taking of Alien Property in the Light of Recent Cases and Practice*, 41 Int'l & Comp. L. Q. 22, 36 (1992); *cf.* Haliburton Fales, *A Comparison of Compensation for Nationalization of Alien Property with Standards of Compensation under United States Domestic Law*, 5 Nw. J. Int'l & Bus. 871, 881 (1983); Brice M. Clagett, *The Expropriation Issue Before the Iran-United States Claims Tribunal: Is "Just Compensation" Required by International Law or Not?*, 16 L. & Pol'y in Int'l Bus. 813, 818 (1984).

[34] The conclusion of several lump sum agreements settling disputes as to the proper standard of compensation also supports this conclusion. *See* Malcolm N. Shaw, *International Law* 750 (5th ed., Cambridge University Press 2003).

[35] G.A. Res. 3281, 29 U.N. GAOR, 29th Sess., Supp No. 31, at 50, 51–55, U.N. Doc. A/9631 (1974), *reprinted in* 14 I.L.M. 251, 252–60 (1975) [hereinafter CERDS]. *See* Patricia Robin, *The BIT Won't Bite: The American Bilateral Investment Treaty Program*, 33 Am. U. L. Rev. 931, n.93 (1984).

[36] CERDS, *supra* note 35, at 254–55.

[37] Robert von Mehren & P. Nicholas Kourides, *International Arbitration between States and Foreign Private Parties: The Libyan Nationalization Cases*, 75 Am. J. Int'l L. 476, 523 (1981).

[38] Thomas W. Wälde, *A Requiem for the "New International Economic Order"—Rise and Fall of Paradigms in International Economic Law*, in *International Legal Issues Arising under the United Nations Decade of International Law* 1323–26 (Najeeb Al-Nauimi & Richard Meese eds., Martinus Nijhoff Publishers 1995).

bilateral investment treaties that codified high levels of investment protection in accords that trumped the attempted dilution of customary law norms.[39] The central declarations in the NIEO movement have therefore receded largely into irrelevance, but some studies suggest that the Hull formula has not entirely recovered from NIEO attacks.[40]

C. Traditional Remedies for Foreign Investors

Faced with the many legal and political barriers to recovery of property seized or damaged by local government, foreign investors historically had little choice in remedies to seek. Until the Second World War, one possible remedy for expropriation was the use of military force. A more common and less extreme form of redress, and one still occasionally applied today, was diplomatic espousal by the investor's home state.

1. Gunboat Diplomacy

Gunboat diplomacy is not some colorfully exaggerated historic term: It was the literal practice of capital-exporting nations well into the 1890s.

> In the early 1800s, Latin American nations who had recently achieved independence from the colonial powers eagerly sought foreign investment. Shielding their local economies from foreign penetration was a secondary concern. To encourage investment by foreigners, these countries' new constitutions promised foreigners equality of treatment with nationals, which was surprising in light of the lingering political hostility towards many European nations and the United States. The effort by these countries to attract foreign investment was initially a great success.
>
> By 1833, however, every Latin American bond issue was in default, and most of the foreign companies established to conduct business in the area had collapsed. In the following years, foreigners as well as nationals were exposed to economic losses. The inability of Latin American governments and judicial institutions to protect foreigners' property led many foreigners to appeal to their governments for relief either through diplomatic intervention or the use of armed force.[41]

---

[39] S. Schwebel, *Investor-State Disputes and the Development of Customary International Law: The Influence of Bilateral Investment Treaties on Customary International Law*, 98 ASIL Proc. 27, 28 (2004).

[40] *See* World Bank, *Report to the Development Committee and Guidelines on the Treatment of Foreign Direct Investment*, 31 I.L.M. 1363, 1376 (1992) (suggesting that only the "adequate" element of the formula is part of the customary law, and that there is no consistent body of precedent to support "promptness" and "effectiveness" elements).

[41] Christopher K. Dalrymple, *Politics and Foreign Investment: The Multilateral Investment Guarantee and the Calvo Clause*, 29 Cornell Int'l L. 161, 164 (1996).

Thus, in 1900 the U.S. secretary of state approved the dispatch of a naval vessel to Venezuela to prevent the destruction of property belonging to the New York & Bermudez Company, an American corporation. The secretary instructed the secretary of the navy that "the gunboat should also protect all existing rights and maintain the status quo pending an investigation and decision as to an attempt which was alleged then to be in contemplation to deprive the company of its property by executive action."[42]

One of the more notorious examples of the use of armed force to obtain relief in an investment dispute arose out of the *Jecker* claim, which was triggered when the Mexican government defaulted in 1860 on a loan from J. B. Jecker and Company, a Franco-Swiss bank.[43] Mexico had originally arranged for a loan of 75 million francs, but actually borrowed only 3.75 million francs. When it defaulted on that sum, it was deemed to have defaulted on the entire contracted amount.[44] The inability of French investors to secure compensation through Mexican courts and administrative bodies triggered a French invasion in 1861 to 1862,[45] and France maintained a puppet government in Mexico until 1867. The French-installed ruler of Mexico, Emperor Maximilian, was eventually overthrown and executed by firing squad.[46]

Investment disputes today are rarely so dramatic. The CERDS has outlawed the use or threat of force by all states, including by militarily powerful capital-exporting states, except in self-defense.[47] And in any event, gunboat diplomacy rarely produced what foreign investors most frequently sought: full compensation.

2. Diplomatic Espousal

a. Practice of Espousal

Another mode of redress for mistreatment of foreigners and their property under customary international law was diplomatic espousal: intervention by the foreign citizen's home government in the form of diplomatic correspondence. Elements of

---

[42] Letter from Mr. Hay to Sec. of Navy, Dec. 28, 1900, 250 MS. Dom. Let. 8, *reprinted in* 6 Moore's Int'l Law Digest 258 (1906).

[43] Dalrymple, *supra* note 41, at 165.

[44] *Id.*

[45] D. Shea, *The Calvo Clause* 14 (1955); Ibrahim Shihata, *Towards a Greater Depoliticization of Investment Disputes: The Roles of ICSID and MIGA* 1 n.2 (1992).

[46] Dalrymple, *supra* note 41, at 165.

[47] M. Sornarajah, *The International Law on Foreign Investment* 8–9 (1994); *see also generally* M. Sornarajah, *Power and Justice in Foreign Investment Arbitration*, 14 J. Int'l Arb. 103 (1997); J. Cable, *Gunboat Diplomacy: Political Applications of Limited Force* (1981); Matthew B. Cobb, *The Development of Arbitration in Foreign Investment*, Mealey's Int'l Arb. Rep. Apr. 2001.

this long, cumbersome, and generally ineffectual procedure[48] were described in an early guidebook for U.S. diplomatic officials:

> Printed Instructions to Diplomatic Officers of the United States § 170 (1897)
>
> When a diplomatic representative is satisfied that an applicant for protection has a right to his intervention, he should interest himself in his behalf, examining carefully into his grievances. If he finds that the complaints are well founded, he should interpose firmly, but with courtesy and moderation, with the authorities in his behalf and report the case to the Department of State for its further action, if any be required.

Following is a communiqué from the U.S. secretary of state to the American minister to Turkey, instructing him to bring a formal complaint to the Greek government on behalf of Jonas King, a U.S. citizen who had been banished and whose property had been confiscated by Greece after a trial:

> Letter from Mr. Everett, U.S. Secretary of State to Mr. Marsh, Minister to Turkey, Feb. 5, 1853, reprinted in 6 Moore's Int'l Law Digest 264 (1906)
>
> There is a single point only in which, at first view, Dr. King's claim upon his own government to interfere in his behalf may seem premature, and that is his omission to seek redress by bringing an action against the Greek government, as authorized by the code of civil procedure. The rule of public law is settled, that a private citizen in a foreign country is not entitled to the forcible interference of his government to procure him redress of wrongs till justice has been denied him by the local tribunals. This consideration would perhaps prevent the President, at this time, from interfering, had not the conduct of the courts of Greece, in the trial of Dr. King, sufficiently shown that he could not expect justice at their hands. . . . Such being the state of things, the President feels it his duty to interfere to procure redress to Dr. King.
>
> You will therefore, if still in Austria, immediately on the receipt of this letter, repair to Spezzia, which is the rendezvous of the United States squadron in the Mediterranean. Commodore Stringham will be instructed to convey you to Athens, where you will forthwith put yourself in communication with the proper department of the Greek government. You will state, in general terms, the opinion entertained by the President of Dr. King's trial and condemnation as above intimated, and his expectation that a formal remission of the sentence of banishment should be granted by the proper department; and you will state in a general way the reasons why the President forbears in any other respect to make a national question of the treatment of Dr. King on this occasion. You will then represent the affair of Dr. King's land in the light in which it is placed in your report.

---

[48] According to one contemporary lawyer involved in the prosecution of investor-state claims, "If you use a general diplomatic note [to obtain redress for injury to investments], you can all have coffee and talk for years and be seen to be doing something about it." Barry Appleton, *Canadians Docile in Face of Extraterritorial U.S. Laws*, Law Times, Aug. 23–29, 1999.

State strongly and briefly the results of your inquiry, taking care, as far as possible, not to be drawn into a lengthened discussion for the purposes of delay. Avoid the tone or language of menace, but let the government of Greece perceive that the President is quite in earnest . . . .

Having . . . ascertained, as far as practicable, what sum of money would be a reasonable compensation to Dr. King, propose at once to the Greek government to allow it, and urge upon it the expediency of at once putting an end to this long delayed and vexatious affair. If the Greek government is discreet, they will immediately close with this offer, and you will use all your address to induce them to do so. If they decline, you will then make them this proposition, viz: to refer the whole question to the arbitration of a friendly power. . . .

Despite the somewhat hesitant tone of the secretary's instructions, Mr. Marsh's visit to Greece resulted in the reversal of the banishment sentence, but he was unable to obtain compensation for Dr. King's land. Two years later, however, a special envoy was sent to Greece to negotiate an indemnity and succeeded in obtaining US$25,000 in compensation for the seizure,[49] a rare instance of limited espousal success.

The general practice of diplomatic espousal has changed relatively little in the century since then.[50] In particular, states tend to be quite selective about the claims they agree to espouse. Some limitations on diplomatic protection are clear from the Canadian Foreign Ministry's informational bulletin for foreigners abroad.

State Responsibility: Espousal of Claims by the Canadian Government by the Intervention of the Foreign Ministry

1. General Principles

a. The Canadian government cannot, in accordance with generally recognized principles of customary international law, espouse claims related to the loss of human life, to assets, to interest, or to the debts of Canadians, unless such individuals are Canadian citizens at the moment of the loss, confiscation, expropriation, or nationalization. Furthermore, claims must have belonged to Canadian citizens since the events that gave rise to them, and the claimants must be Canadian citizens at the moment of the presentation of claims.

b. Normally, the government of Canada will not espouse any claim of a Canadian against a foreign State unless the claimant has exhausted all legal remedies provided by the internal law of the country in question (that is all available remedies up to an appeal to the court of last resort in the foreign State) without obtaining redress. However, if in exhausting these local judicial remedies, the claimant has been subjected to prejudice or has met with obstructions constituting a denial of justice, the government of Canada may have reason to intervene in his name to obtain the appropriate redress.

. . . .

---

[49] President Franklin Pierce, Annual Address, Dec. 31, 1855.

[50] *See generally* United Nations Commission on Trade and Development, *Dispute Settlement: State-to-State* (2003); Rubins & Kinsella, *supra* note 21, at 405–16.

d. As for claims made by corporations, the Government of Canada cannot, pursuant to customary international law, espouse claims related to assets nationalized or otherwise confiscated abroad, unless the claims originate from a company formed under the law of Canada or a Canadian province, and unless the corporation was formed before the date of the claim.[51]

b. The Limitations of Espousal

Even where an investor's home government is willing to espouse the investor's cause, numerous barriers to compensation remain.

i. Exhaustion of Local Remedies

Under customary international law, diplomatic espousal is normally impermissible unless the foreign investor has exhausted all remedies available within the judicial or administrative system of the country where the investment is located. This doctrine of exhaustion of local remedies has evolved in customary international law from the middle ages to the present day.[52]

The local remedies rule is based on the premise that "the home government of the complaining citizen must give the offending government an opportunity of doing justice to the injured party in its own regular way, and thus avoid, if possible, all occasion for international discussion."[53] The rule is designed at once to protect state sovereignty to the extent possible and reduce the number of international claims initiated.[54]

The application of the exhaustion rule, however, can be quite complex. One particular point of dispute is whether a foreign national must raise all arguments, including allegations of breaches of international law, at the national level before his or her state can pursue an international claim on his behalf. On the one hand, there would seem to be little reason for foreign investors to assert claims based on international law in the context of municipal court or administrative proceedings, so long as they introduce all the relevant issues of fact. On the other hand, some tribunals have required that claimants assert international causes of action as a necessary element of exhausting local remedies, even if such claims are unrecognized by the

---

[51] Government of Canada, *L'Entraide Judiciaire Internationale: Services Juridiques Fournis par le Ministère des Affaires Extérieures Concernant L'Entraide Judiciaire Internationale et Certains Autre Matières* (63) 1987.

[52] C. F. Amerasinghe, *Local Remedies in International Law* 11 (2004); *Interhandel Case (Switzerland v. U.S.)*, 1959 I.C.J. Rep. 5, 27 ("the rule that local remedies must be exhausted before international proceedings may be instituted is a well-established rule of customary international law").

[53] Edwin Borchard, *Diplomatic Protection of Citizens Abroad* 817 (1915); Amerasinghe, *supra* note 52, at 97; William S. Dodge, *Exhaustion of Remedies and Res Judicata under Chapter Eleven of NAFTA*, 23 Hastings Int'l & Comp. L. Rev. 357, 361–62 (2000).

[54] M. N. Shaw, *supra* note 34, at 730; Rubins and Kinsella, *supra* note 21, at 133.

relevant system of domestic law. In the *Finnish Ships Arbitration*,[55] the tribunal held not only that assertions of fact must have been made in prior litigation, but furthermore "propositions of law which are brought forward by the claimant government [before the international tribunal] . . . must have been investigated and adjudicated upon by the municipal Courts."[56] The *Finnish Ships* tribunal was neither the first nor the last to take so broad a view of exhaustion.[57]

From Robert Bruno, ACCESS OF PRIVATE PARTIES TO INTERNATIONAL DISPUTE SETTLEMENT: A COMPARATIVE ANALYSIS (1997), *available at* http://www.jeanmonnetprogram.org/papers/97/97-13.html

[According to the principle of exhaustion,] resort[ing] to dispute settlement on the international level through diplomatic protection is not admissible until the injured person has exhausted the legal remedies (judicial or administrative proceedings) available in the state allegedly responsible for the injury, unless the application of the rule is dispensed with either by an agreement between the claimant and the responding states, or by estoppel on the part of the latter.

. . . .

It has been rightly observed that this rule, which certainly works as a restriction on the applicability of diplomatic protection, is not the necessary consequence of the system of international law as a whole, but rather it is the consequence of political and practical considerations.[58] As to the former, the ICJ [International Court of Justice] held in the *Interhandel* case that "the rule requiring the exhaustion of domestic remedies as a condition of the presentation of an international claim is founded upon the principle that the respondent State must first have an opportunity to redress by its own means within the framework of its own domestic legal system the wrong alleged to have been done to the individual."[59] Furthermore, it may be submitted that another policy ground for the application of the rule is that the alien, by conducting activities within the territory of the host state, both enjoys protection and is correspondingly accountable under the laws and before the courts of that state; thus, it may be fair to hold that she should first seek redress under those laws and before those courts. These two arguments seek not to make the international dispute settlement machinery vexatious to states and to accord a high degree of deference to their sovereignty as expressed by the exercise of their jurisdiction. As to the latter, among various practical considerations put forward from time to time, there are some [that] are worth mentioning, such as: the need to avoid a flood of claims on the international law level, which is undesirable due to the limited resources of international tribunals and to the adverse impact they may have on the delicate relations between states; the fact that domestic courts have often a higher degree of expertise and sophistication than international tribunals; the fact that the determinations made by domestic courts may provide international tribunals

---

[55] *Finish Ships Arbitration* (Finland v. U.K.), 3 U.N.R.I.A.A. 1479 (1934).

[56] *Id.* at 1502.

[57] *Case of Certain Norwegian Loans* (France v. Norway), 1957 I.C.J. Rep. 9, 41–42 (separate opinion of Lauterpacht, J.); *see also* Amerasinghe, *supra* note 52, at 196.

[58] SN: Brownlie, *Principles of Public International Law* 435 (4th ed. 1990).

[59] SN: ICJ Rep. 27 (1959).

with extremely useful if not unique elements for the settlement of the dispute pending before them. . . .

Similarly, it can be observed that some issues arise out of the basic idea that the rule implies seeking redress before a local court. For instance, it may be relevant whether the action is brought for breach of either municipal law or international law or both; moreover, it may be asked whether the local court needs [to] have jurisdiction under either municipal law or international law.

Other important aspects of the rule of exhaustion of local remedies concern the question when such remedies can be deemed available and/or exhausted. On the one hand, reference is to be made to the structure of the relevant proceedings before the local courts. Usually the plaintiff will have to go through all the various (normally no more than three) instances, and rights of actions are afforded even in respect of acts or omissions of the executive power. On the other hand, the international tribunal assessing the admissibility of the claim has to address this question very carefully, because sometimes remedies may prove ineffective even if formally accorded to the injured party. This may be the case when an appeal would be still available, but either because of legislative intervention or because of the *stare decisis* principle, it would not be effective being the outcome of the claim already set forth. This may also be the case when judicial or administrative proceedings are flawed by interference of the executive power. In these as well as in other cases the *de jure* or de facto ineffectiveness of the remedy produces the same result as its exhaustion in more traditional forms, and the claim should be admissible before an international forum. Moreover, in some instances, ineffective remedies may also be regarded as somewhat connected to the concept of denial of justice.

Finally, the most recent developments of the rule by the ICJ's case law are contained in the *ELSI* case.[60] One of the major issues arising out of this case . . . was that the case was brought by the US against Italy under their Treaty of Friendship, Commerce and Navigation of 1948. The Treaty provided that disputes between the two states arising from its implementation be brought before the ICJ, but it did not expressly dispense the parties with complying with the rule of exhaustion of local remedies. While the US interpreted this provision as implicitly dispensing the parties with the application of the rule, the ICJ held that "it finds itself unable to accept that an important principle of customary international law should be held to have been tacitly dispensed with." As Shaw puts it, "in other words, the presumption that local remedies need to be exhausted can only be rebutted by express provision to the contrary."[61] . . . In conclusion, it may be observed that the rule of exhaustion of local remedies is not necessarily bad, in the sense that its underlying rationale can be deemed sound, and it will be seen that it may also work as a useful, if not necessary, device to filter claims in those mechanisms of international dispute settlement where the injured individual can or should be entitled to directly enforce her rights against the host state before an international forum. . . . The main criticism this rule attracts is that it is in its same nature to work against the process of delocalization of international economic disputes.

ii. Nationality of the Investor

The success of diplomatic espousal claims often turns on whether the individual or corporation at the heart of the dispute is internationally recognized as a *national* of the espousing state. Customary international law, from which espousal derives its

---

[60] SN: ICJ Rep., 15, 42 (1989).

[61] SN: Shaw, *International Law* (3d ed., 1991).

force and legitimacy, accords rights to states in relation to the harm suffered by individuals[62] and corporations only if the state can demonstrate a bond of nationality with the harmed entity. Although many international non–investment-related disputes involve relatively straightforward sales or licensing agreements, investment disputes often arise out of large-scale construction or energy-related projects financed by investors from more than one state and can raise complex issues of nationality.

One prominent example of an investor's claim that failed for want of proper nationality is the *Barcelona Traction* case.[63] That case involved a company incorporated in Canada that had developed an electricity generation plant and distribution system in Spain. Most of the Canadian company's shareholders were nationals of Belgium. In 1936 the Spanish government suspended payment on the company's bonds as a result of the Spanish Civil War. Although some restrictions were relaxed during World War II, the company was never again able to pay creditors outside Spain, and it was placed in bankruptcy in 1948. In the 1950s, the Belgian government, on behalf of Belgian shareholders, sought reparations from the Spanish government for its destruction of the shareholders' investment in the Canadian electric company. In 1970 the ICJ ultimately determined that Belgium lacked standing to espouse its nationals' claims, because the Spanish government's actions were aimed at the Canadian company rather than at Belgian investors. The case was dismissed.[64]

Barcelona Traction arose some years before the era of modern investment treaties. If a modern investment agreement had been in force between Spain and Belgium, the Belgian shareholders might well have had standing to recover some or all of their lost investment. One chief purpose of the modern investment protection regime is to allow the substance of capital investments to take precedence over the type of legal formalities that ultimately led to the dismissal in *Barcelona Traction*,[65] which is clarified later in this book.

---

[62] Fransisco Orrego Vicuña, *Changing Approaches to the Nationality of Claims in the Context of Diplomatic Protection and International Dispute Settlement*, in Liber Amicorum Ibrahim Shihata: International Finance & Development Law 503 (Schlemmer-Schulte & Tung eds., 2001); Ian Sinclair, *"Nationality of Claims: British Practice*, 27 Brit. Y. B. Int'l L. 125 (1950); Rubins & Kinsella, *supra* note 21, at 135–40.

[63] *Barcelona Traction, Light & Power Co. Ltd. (Belgium v. Spain)*, Second Phase, 1970 I.C.J. 3.

[64] For an interesting journalistic account of the *Barcelona Traction* case and its fate, see John Brooks, *Annals of Finance, Parts I and II*, New Yorker (1979).

[65] The rule of continuous nationality in international law, which deals with the nationality of claims, may also prevent investors from pursuing their claims. Continuous nationality rule requires that "claims must continuously without interruption have belonged to a person or to a series of person (a) having the nationality of the State by whom it is put forward, and (b) not having the nationality of the State against whom it is put forward. . . ." *See generally* Brownlie, *supra* note 33, at 459–60; for a discussion of the application of this rule and its implications in the modern investment treaty arbitration *see* Maurice Mendelson, *Run Away Train, "Continuous Nationality" Rule from* Panavezys-Saldutiskis *Railway Case to* Loewen, in *International Investment Law and Arbitration: Leading Cases from the ICSID, NAFTA, Bilateral Treaties and Customary International Law* 97 (Weiler ed., Cameron May 2005).

D. Some Early Investment Protection Regimes

Although the current legal structure and formalized practice of investor-state arbitration developed only during the last three decades of the twentieth century, the concerns that led to that innovation are not recent. The desire of both capital exporters and importers to establish a legal regime that would keep capital flowing resulted in occasional attempts to conclude an appropriate framework agreement, or to resolve a particular set of investment-related disputes. The legacy of these attempts is to some degree reflected in the present system of investor-state arbitration.

1. Jay Treaty (1794)

Perhaps the first use of special-purpose tribunals to resolve investment disputes was the 1794 Jay Treaty, concluded between the United States and Great Britain in the aftermath of the American Revolution.[66] The Jay Treaty was intended to ensure a continued flow of capital from Britain, then one of the largest economies in the world, by resolving the British claims of property damage, expropriation, and breach of contract that arose during the conflict. The treaty established a standing international arbitration tribunal to hear all such claims by British investors, where "full compensation for [their] losses and damages [could] not . . . be actually obtained . . . in the ordinary course of justice."[67]

Prominent American political figures such as Alexander Hamilton campaigned hard for ratification of the pact, recognizing that America was in dire need of foreign capital to help its fledgling economy grow. These leaders understood that without investment guarantees and a neutral forum in which to resolve past disputes, the flow of foreign capital could be curtailed.[68] The commissioners who would adjudicate claims were appointed in 1797, and the following year Congress allocated $300,000 to establish a fund for payment of the commission's awards.[69]

---

[66] Treaty of Amity, Commerce, and Navigation, Nov. 19, 1794, U.S.-Grt. Brit., 8 Stat. 116. *See generally* Barton Legum, *Federalism, NAFTA Chapter Eleven and the Jay Treaty of 1794*, News from ICSID (Spring 2001).

[67] Jay Treaty, art. 6; Barton Legum, *The Innovation of Investor-State Arbitration Under NAFTA*, 43 Harv. Int'l L. J. 531, 534 (2002).

[68] Alexander Hamilton & Rufus King, *The Defence No. XIV*, Sept. 9, 1795, *reprinted in* 19 The Papers of Alexander Hamilton 245, 249–50 (Harold C. Syrett ed., 1974).

[69] Legum, *supra* note 66.

> The Jay Treaty of Amity, Commerce, and Navigation
> *Signed at London, November 19, 1794*
>
> 2 Treaties and Other International Acts of the U.S. 245, 249–53 (1931)
>
> ARTICLE 6
>
> Whereas it is alleged by divers British Merchants and others His Majesty's Subjects, that Debts, to a considerable amount, which were bona fide contracted before the Peace, still remain owing to them by Citizens or Inhabitants of the United States, and that by the operation of various lawful Impediments since the Peace, not only the full recovery of the said Debts has been delayed, but also the Value and Security thereof, have been in several instances impaired and lessened, so that by the ordinary course of Judicial proceedings the British Creditors, cannot now obtain and actually have and receive full and adequate Compensation for the losses and damages which they have thereby sustained: It is agreed that in all such Cases where full Compensation for such losses and damages cannot, for whatever reason, be actually obtained had and received by the said Creditors in the ordinary course of Justice, The United States will make full and complete Compensation for the same to the said Creditors.
>
> For the purpose of ascertaining the amount of any such losses and damages, Five Commissioners shall be appointed and authorized to meet and act in manner following— viz—Two of them shall be appointed by His Majesty, Two of them by the President of the United States by and with the advice and consent of the Senate thereof, and fifth, by the unanimous voice of the other Four; and if they should not agree in such Choice, then the Commissioners named by the two parties shall respectively propose one person, and of the two names so proposed, one shall be drawn by Lot in the presence of the Four Original Commissioners.

The commission's activities were permanently discontinued after only a year of work, in July 1799, in part because of personality clashes and disagreement among the commissioners over the local remedies rule,[70] but the structure and operation of the Jay Treaty tribunal lent much to the modern investor-state arbitration system of the late twentieth century.

2. Ad Hoc Arbitration

Many of the disputes concerning mistreatment of foreigners that arose in the nineteenth and early twentieth centuries were resolved by ad hoc tribunals or umpires, who were charged with the case either by treaty provision or by mutual agreement of the two governments involved to submit to neutral dispute resolution. These arbitrators operated without any particular procedural framework, specific scope of jurisdiction, rules of evidence, or other guidelines; and

---

[70] *Id.*

therefore they faced serious challenges in rendering awards efficiently and on a consistent and coherent basis.

The *Gentini*[71] case exemplifies the procedural and substantive ambiguity inherent in ad hoc tribunals. In that case Italy brought a claim against Venezuela in 1903 to seek compensation on behalf of an Italian national whose store was looted by Venezuelan soldiers in 1871. The umpire decided that potentially applicable municipal statutes of limitation could not bar international claims but also held that the concept of a limitation in time is essential to the administration of justice and therefore must apply to international claims in some way. Without expressing an opinion regarding the number of years that would bar such a claim, the umpire dismissed the case on grounds that the claimant "had so long neglected his supposed rights as to justify a belief in their non-existence."[72] Such lack of precision came to characterize the development of customary international law on foreign investment.

3. Binational Claims Commissions

Periods of protracted civil unrest or instability in particular countries in the nineteenth and twentieth centuries often spawned entire sets of disputes. These were sometimes resolved by international claims commissions with jurisdiction over a broad category of disputes.[73]

Longstanding problems between Mexico and the United States resulted in one such international commission. The U.S.-Mexico General Claims Commission was constituted under the terms of the General Claims Convention in 1923.[74] The convention, which took effect in 1924, was intended to improve relations between the countries by forming a quasi-judicial organ to settle claims arising in the previous fifty-five years (after 1868). Its jurisdiction encompassed claims against one government by nationals of the other "for losses or damages suffered by such nationals or their properties" and "for losses or damages originating from acts of officials or others acting for either government and resulting in injustice." Most commission

---

[71] *Gentini (Italy v. Venezuela)*, Mixed Claims Commission, 1903, J. H. Ralston, *Venezuelan Arbitrations of 1903*, 720 (1904).

[72] *Id.*

[73] *See, e.g.*, Report of Fred Nielsen, *American and British Arbitration under the Special Agreement of August 18, 1910* (Wash., D.C., Gov't Printing Off. 1926); B. Hunt, *American and Panamanian General Claims Arbitration, Reports of the Agents for the United States* (1934); Claims Commission between France and Mexico, *La Reparation des Dommages causes aux etrangers par des mouvements revolutionnaires, Jurisprudence de la Commission franco-mexicaine des Reclamations* (1924–1932) (Pedone 1933); Report of B. Hunt, *American-Turkish Claims Settlement under the Agreement of December 17, 1932* (Wash., D.C., Gov't Printing Off. 1934); Jackson Ralston, *Venezuelan Arbitrations of 1903* (1923); Jackson Ralston, *French Venezuelan Mixed Claims Commission of 1902* (1905).

[74] See generally A. H. Feller, *The Mexican Claims Commissions, 1923–1934, A Study in the Law and Procedure of International Tribunals* (Macmillan 1935).

rulings arose from claims for cases of wrongful killing, denial of justice, seizure of property, unlawful arrest and detention, breach of contract, and disputes over taxes. Cases stemming from events related to revolutions or other civil disturbances in Mexico were excluded from the jurisdiction of the General Claims Commission.[75]

The commission was composed of three members—one from the United States, one from Mexico, and one from a neutral country—and it applied principles of international law in resolving disputes. The commission met from 1924 to 1931 in Washington, D.C., and Mexico City. Work resumed in 1934 under a new agreement and format and ended in 1937, but final settlement was not reached until 1941.[76] Although ad hoc in nature, the structure of the commission embodied many of the structural elements now present in the investment treaty regime.

4. Friendship, Commerce, and Navigation Treaties

Beginning in the nineteenth century, developed countries (primarily the colonial powers) entered into commercial agreements with less developed trading partners known as Friendship, Commerce, and Navigation (FCN)[77] treaties. The FCN treaties emerged from the tradition of jurisdictional treaties and treaties of amity, but established a more formally equal status between the parties, and preserved a greater degree of sovereignty for the developing state parties. These agreements were primarily designed to ensure developed states access to expanding markets for the sale of finished goods in the developing world, and therefore focused primarily on rules regarding free trade and transport of goods, although they sometimes also regulated compensation for expropriation and the protection of foreign property.[78] The FCN treaties have largely been superseded by bilateral investment treaties (BITs), free trade agreements (FTAs), and multilateral agreements in the area of investment protection; but they remain important both as historical background to the development of modern investor-state dispute resolution and as a source of law and interpretative guidance still frequently used in modern arbitration.[79]

---

[75] Herbert W. Briggs, *The Settlement of the Mexican Claims Act of 1942*, 37 Am. J. Int'l L. 222, 227 (1943).

[76] The final settlement was memorialized in the Convention Respecting Claims between the United States and Mexico, Nov. 19, 1941, U.S.-Mex., 56 Stat. 1347.

[77] Dieter Blumenwitz, *Treaties of Friendship, Commerce and Navigation*, EPIL IV 953 (2000).

[78] Michael Avramovich, *The Protection of International Investment at the Start of the Twenty-First Century: Will Anachronistic Notions of Business Render Irrelevant the OECD's Multilateral Agreement on Investment?* 31 J. Marshall L. Rev. 1201, 1233–34 (1998).

[79] F. A. Mann, *British Treaties for the Promotion and Protection of Investments*, 52 Brit. Y.B. Int'l L. 241, 249 (1981) ("The importance of the [Friendship, Commerce and Navigation (FCN) treaties] lies in the contribution they make to the development of customary international law, in their being a source of law. . . . [T]hese treaties establish and accept and thus enlarge the force of traditional conceptions."); *see generally Restatement (Third) of Foreign Relations Law*, Introductory Note, at 18 (1987) (treaties are an important source of "international law" because they "have become the principal vehicle for making law for the international system").

5. Lump Sum Settlement Agreements

After World War II, bilateral treaties known as *lump sum agreements* became a prominent means for the settlement of international claims for damage to and expropriation of foreign property by governments.[80] Lump sum agreements relegated large classes of complex individual claims to adjudication by an administrative tribunal within the home state of the injured parties, allowing the states in question to resolve complex outstanding legal issues and improve diplomatic relations more generally. Pursuant to a typical lump sum agreement, the host state transferred a particular amount of money, normally arrived at through a political negotiation process, to the injured individuals' home state. In return, both states agreed to prohibit any further private claims arising out of the same government measures, either in national courts or at international law. The injured parties' state then established an internal administrative process, or employed existing structures, to distribute the lump sum to qualifying citizens.[81] Excerpts from a lump sum settlement agreement are set forth in the following text.

> Agreement Between the Republic of Austria and the German Democratic Republic on the Settlement of Unresolved Questions Relating to Property Rights
>
> August 21, 1987 (entered into force June 1, 1988)
>
> [1988] B.G.B.1 1887
>
> The Republic of Austria and the German Democratic Republic, desiring to contribute to the further development of friendly relations between the Republic of Austria and the German Democratic Republic, in an effort to settle finally the unresolved questions relating to property rights . . . in the interest of both parties, have agreed as follows:
>
> Article 1
>
> The German Democratic Republic shall pay to the Republic of Austria a lump sum of 136,400,000. . . . Austrian schillings in settlement of property claims of the Republic of Austria, Austrian citizens, or Austrian juridical persons because their property has come

---

[80] Burns H. Weston, et al., *International Claims: Their Settlement by Lump Sum Agreements* 7 (1999); M. A. Ruíz Colomé, *Lump Sum Agreements in Spanish Practice*, 6 Spanish Y.B. Int'l L. 1(2002).

[81] In the United States, the Foreign Claims Settlement Commission (FCSC), which is an independent quasi-judicial federal agency, is in charge of determining "the validity and valuation of claims of United States nationals for loss of property in foreign countries, as authorized by Congress or following government-to-government claims settlement agreements." Foreign Claims Settlement Commission of the United States, *1995 FCSC Ann. Rep.*, 1; *see also* the Web site of Foreign Claims Settlement Commission, http://www.usdoj.gov/fcsc/.

exclusively within the control of the German Democratic Republic through a takeover by a public administrator or though other public measures by the German Democratic Republic.

Article 2

This Agreement also shall settle property claims of the German Democratic Republic, as well as of citizens and juridical persons of the German Democratic Republic, against the Republic of Austria, Austrian citizens, or Austrian juridical persons in relation to the property referred to in Article 1.

Article 6

1. The distribution of the lump sum referred to in Article 1 shall be within the exclusive jurisdiction of the Republic of Austria.

Article 7

With the full payment of the sum referred to in Article 1, all property claims referred to in Articles 1 and 2 shall be finally settled. Neither of the parties, after the entry into force of this Agreement, shall raise or in any way support claims settled by the present Agreement vis-à-vis the other party.

Article 8

1. The German Democratic Republic shall fulfill its payment obligation set out in Article 1 as follows:

> The total amount shall be paid from the State Bank of the German Democratic Republic to the Austrian National Bank in successive yearly installments.
>
> The first installment of 31,400,000 . . . Austrian schillings shall be due 6 (six) months after the entry into force of this Agreement.
>
> The amount of further yearly installments shall always equal 0.8% of the proceeds of the trade export of the German Democratic Republic to the Republic of Austria, which shall be based upon the official Austrian statistics for foreign trade for the preceding calendar year. . . .

In the eyes of the ICJ, such lump sum agreements are the product of politics and economics rather than of legal norms; and, therefore, despite their prominence, they have contributed relatively little to the development of investment protection jurisprudence:

> Also distinct are the various arrangements made in respect of compensation for the nationalization of foreign property. Their rationale . . . derived as it is from structural changes in a State's economy, differs from that of any normally applicable provisions. Specific agreements have been reached to meet specific situations, and the terms have varied from case to case. Far from evidencing any norm as to the classes of beneficiaries of compensation, such arrangements are sui generis. . . . It should be clear that the developments in question have to be viewed as distinctive processes, arising out

of circumstances peculiar to the respective situations. To seek to draw from them analogies or conclusions held to be valid in other fields is to ignore their specific character as lex specialis and hence to court error.[82]

Some commentators disagree, however, asserting that the decisions of arbitrators in the context of lump-sum arrangements "must be treated in the same manner as any other international prescription," and in particular as an important source of customary international law.[83]

6. Investment Guarantee Programs

Some developed countries have established investment guarantee programs to provide some level of security for the investment of their citizens abroad, mainly by insuring their nationals' investments against the occurrence of political risk. These guarantees have the advantage of enabling an investor claiming injury to deal with its own governmental agencies. In this way, the "safety of the invested capital [became] . . . independent of the actions of the country of investment."[84] The following excerpt concerning the United States government's investment insurance initiatives is illustrative in this regard.

Kenneth J. Vandevelde, *Reassessing the Hickenlooper Amendment*, 29 Va. J. Int'l L. 115, 123–4 (1988)[85]

The period following World War II saw the initiation of . . . [an] effort to protect U.S. investment overseas. The Economic Cooperation Act of 1948 authorized the sale of insurance to overseas investors against the risk, initially, of nonconvertible currency, and, after 1950, of expropriation. Subsequent legislation broadened the authority and revamped the bureaucratic management of the investment guarantee program, creating in 1969 the Overseas Private Investment Corporation (OPIC) which administers the program today. Under this program, investors purchase insurance from the federal government and are reimbursed for losses due to expropriation within the limits of the policy. Insurance whereby investors, through the pooling of the premiums, actually pay for the loss, however, must be distinguished from a remedy, whereby the wrongdoer is compelled to pay for the loss. Thus, an insurance program is, from one perspective, technically no remedy at all. Moreover, OPIC, like any insurer, only covers specified risks for certain people at a cost to the insured.

---

[82] *Barcelona Traction, Light & Power Co. Ltd.* (*Belgium v. Spain*), 1970 I.C.J. 3 (Second Phase), Judgment of Feb. 5, 1970, at 39–40.

[83] Weston et al., *supra* note 80, at 1; Richard B. Lillich & Burns H. Weston, *Lumps Sum Agreements: Their Continuing Contribution to the Law of International Claims*, 82 Am. J. Int'l L. 69 (1988).

[84] *See* Progress Report by the Secretary-General, E.S.C., 29th Sess., U.N. Doc. E/3325 (1960), ¶ 170 [hereinafter E/3325]. *See also* A. A. Fatouros, *Government Guarantees to Foreign Investors* 101–3 (Columbia University Press 1962); *Oppenheim's International Law* 915, n. 8 (Sir Robert Jennings & Sir Arthur Watts eds., 9th ed. 1992).

[85] Source notes have been deleted.

Nevertheless, the investment guarantee program for the first time provided expropriated investors with a source of recovery which was not dependent upon the agreement of the expropriating country to negotiate or the agreement of the U.S. government to espouse the claim. The U.S. government does become involved to the extent of negotiating agreements with other countries in order to include those nations in the OPIC program. Further, in accordance with the agreements, the U.S. government, through OPIC, has the right to demand arbitration of the insured's claim, to which OPIC becomes subrogated as the insurer. Investors, however, are compensated regardless of OPIC's decision to arbitrate or not to arbitrate.

To the extent that the U.S. government through OPIC does pursue claims and obtain compensation, the investment insurance program may be regarded as an indirect remedy. But precisely to the extent that the program is a remedy, it is dependent upon the involvement of the U.S. government in the dispute.[86]

As early as 1948, the World Bank sponsored multilateral discussions regarding the promotion of international investment through political risk insurance. After much discussion, negotiation, and numerous drafts, these talks led to the creation of Multilateral Investment Guarantee Agency (MIGA) under auspices of the World Bank.[87]

7. The Algiers Accords

In the aftermath of the Iranian revolution of 1979 and the subsequent taking of American hostages by Iranian student protesters, the United States froze all Iran's assets in the United States, pending the resolution of claims put forward by U.S. citizens against Iran. As part of the agreement that led to the hostages' release, the United States was able to negotiate a binding dispute resolution arrangement with Iran, codified in the Algiers Accords of 1981. Pursuant to this treaty, the United States was to unblock restrained assets, and the payment of all claims would be adjudicated by a standing tribunal of international arbitrators drawn from U.S., Iranian and third-country jurists.[88]

---

[86] A related effort, which started earlier, was creation of Export Credit Agencies (ECAs) by the governments of developed and then developing countries. ECAs provided export credit guarantee and insurance to promote export of products from the issuing states abroad. The first such agency was Federal of Switzerland (1906); thereafter other countries followed suit. The United States created its own ECA (Export Import Bank) in 1934. *See generally* Delio E. Gianturco, *Export Credit Agencies—The Unsung Giants of International Trade and Finance* (Quorum Books 2001).

[87] *See generally* Chapter One in Ibrahim F. I. Shihata, *MIGA and Foreign Investment* (Martinus Nijhoff Publishers 1988).

[88] *See generally* George H. Aldrich, *The Jurisprudence of the Iran-United States Claims Tribunal* (1996) (*see, e.g.,* nationality issues (44 *et seq.*), standing and admissibility (124 *et seq.*), expropriations/takings (171 *et seq.*), damages (293 *et seq.*), evidence (332 *et seq.*), and the table of cases (524 *et seq.*); *see also* Charles N. Brower & Jason Brueschke, *The Iran-United States Claims Tribunal* (Martinus Nijhoff 1998).

By July 2005, nearly 4,000 claims had been submitted, with approximately a thousand adjudicated. Approximately US$2.5 billion was paid out to U.S. investors in Iran.[89]

E. Limitations of Historic Dispute Settlement Processes

Some of the limitations characterizing domestic law and customary international law as far as the private investor is concerned have been outlined above. Within the courts of the host country a variety of barriers such as partiality of the forum, immunity of the state, adoption of the Calvo doctrine and the inefficiency of such courts often left no meaningful means of redress for the aggrieved foreign investor. Further, because of the immunity of foreign sovereigns in national courts and the application of the act of state doctrine and similar legal rules, courts of the home country of the investor often did not provide a viable option either.

Meanwhile, customary international law frequently proved inadequate to provide relief to private investors that had suffered harm as a result of host government measures. Procedurally, remedies were normally dependent on espousal by the investor's home state, which could depend on political factors and was not always available to all nationals on an equal basis. Even if an investor managed to persuade its home country to espouse its claim, customary international law requirements of exhaustion of local remedies and continuous nationality had to be satisfied before a tribunal would examine the merits of the case.[90] Substantively, once procedural barriers were overcome, investors could find themselves without a cognizable claim against the host state, because the threshold of state liability at customary international law left a range of inequitable treatment unactionable.[91]

The dilemma that foreign investors faced was summarized in 1968 by Aron Broches, the former General Counsel of the World Bank:

---

[89] Mark Clodfelter, *U.S. State Department Participation in International Economic Dispute Resolution*, 42 S. Texas L.R. 1273, 1274 (2001). For more recent data *see* Iran-U.S. Claims Tribunal, Communiqué No. 05/3 (July 26, 2005), *available at* http://www.iusct.org/communique-english.pdf. Unlike lump sum settlements, here the winning investors receive 100 percent on a dollar.

[90] A good example of jurisdictional hurdles is the claim of *Anglo-Iranian Oil Co. v. Iran*. The United Kingdom espoused the claim of Anglo-Iranian Oil Co. and brought a claim against Iran for nationalization of the assets of Anglo-Iranian before the ICJ. The ICJ, however, held that it lacked jurisdiction, because Iran had not accepted the jurisdiction of the court for disputes that had arisen out of treaties concluded before 1932. Anglo-Iranian Oil Co. Case (*U.K. v. Iran*), Preliminary Objections, 1952 I.C.J. Reports 20 (Judgment of July 22, 1952); a summary of the judgment is available at http://www.icj-cij.org/icjwww/idecisions/isummaries/iukisummary520722.htm.

[91] *See, e.g.*, Oscar Chin Case, (*UK v. Belgium*) (Dec. 12, 1934). 1934 P.C.I.J. Reports, Series A/B, No. 63. For a detailed discussion of this case *see* Todd Weiler, *Saving Oscar Chin: Non-Discrimination in International Investment Law*, in *Arbitrating Foreign Investment Disputes: Procedural and Substantive Aspects* 159 (Horn ed., Kluwer Law Int'l 2004).

Economic Disputes Between Governments and Private Individuals or Corporations

1. The nature of the problem may be briefly described as follows:

> (a) in the absence of an agreement to the contrary between the foreign investor and the host Government, the investment is subject to the laws of that Government (local law) and the redress of grievances which the investor may seek by direct access to that Government is equally determined by local law.
>
> (b) If the investor feels aggrieved by actions of the host Government he may invoke the diplomatic protection of his national State or he may request his national State to espouse his case and bring a claim before an international tribunal. It is to be noted, of course, *first*, that in some countries the foreign investor may, as a condition of entry, be required to waive diplomatic protection and, *second*, that even if the national State is willing to espouse the investor's case, it may find that the host Government is unwilling to submit to the jurisdiction of an international tribunal. However, even in the absence of these obstacles, the present situation may be regarded as unsatisfactory because of the investor's inability to proceed with an international claim *directly* against the host Government. The necessity of espousal of his case by his national Government before an international claim can be lodged, introduces a political element. An investor may well find that his national Government refuses to espouse a meritorious case because it fears that to do so would be regarded as an unfriendly act by the host Government. And this consideration is even more likely to cause the national Government to refrain from acting if the merits of the investor's case are not wholly clear in its view, thus withholding from the investor an opportunity to have his case judged by an impartial tribunal.
>
> (c) In an attempt to overcome these difficulties, some investors, mostly large corporations especially in the field of extractive industry, have been able to negotiate arbitration agreements with host Governments, providing for detailed rules regarding the selection of arbitrators, the arbitral procedure and, in some cases, the law to be applied by the arbitral tribunal. It is quite clear that only a few investors can be in a position to negotiate such agreements. However, the validity of such agreements is sometimes questioned. If the Government refused to proceed with the arbitration, the investor's remedy would once again be either a request to his national State for diplomatic intervention or for an espousal of his case before an international tribunal.
>
> (d) The absence of adequate machinery for international conciliation and arbitration often frustrates attempts to agree on an appropriate mode of settlements of disputes. Tribunals set up by private organizations such as the International Chamber of Commerce are frequently unacceptable to governments and the only public international arbitral tribunal, the Permanent Court of Arbitration, is not open to private claimants. . . .[92]

Out of this dilemma evolved the Washington Convention and the modern system of investment treaties.

---

[92] Note by Aron Broches, General Counsel, transmitted to the Executive Directors: "Settlement of Disputes between Governments and Private Parties," SecM 61–192 *in* 2 *Convention on the Settlement of the Investment Disputes between States and Nationals of Other States, Documents Concerning the Origin and Formulation of the Convention*, 1–2 (1968).

III. The Modern System of Investor-State Arbitration

A. Origins

During the second half of the twentieth century, widespread recognition of the shortcomings of both national and international remedies for government interference with foreign property rights led to the development of depoliticized alternatives. These efforts were naturally supported by developed countries, which sought both greater protection and greater access to markets for their citizens' capital, intellectual property, and assets. The effects were also supported by many developing countries.[1] It had been evident for some time that to achieve their development goals, developing countries would need to supplement the aid flowing from bilateral and multilateral governmental sources with private capital.[2] In the early 1950s, discussions in the U.N. General Assembly led to the adoption of a series of resolutions, as well as to the preparation of reports by the U.N. Secretary General, regarding the "international flow of private capital for the economic development of underdeveloped countries." Resolution 824 introduced several recommendations addressed to both developed and developing countries for the promotion of private capital flows.[3] The General Assembly also requested that the Secretary General prepare annual reports describing the measures taken by governments to facilitate and protect the flow of private capital.[4] According to the reports of the Secretary General, these measures were "designed to provide assurance either directly against the occurrence of non-business risks [mainly expropriation] or toward the indemnification of the investor, should they

---

[1] *See* Progress Report by the Secretary-General, E.S.C., 29th Sess., U.N. Doc. E/3325 (1960), ¶¶ 170–73 [hereinafter E/3325].

[2] *See* 1 *Convention on the Settlement of the Investment Disputes between States and Nationals of Other States, Analysis of Documents Concerning the Origin and Formulation of the Convention*, 2 (1968).

[3] G.A. Res. 824, U.N. GAOR, 9th Sess. (1954).

[4] *Id.* at ¶ 6.

occur."[5] Developed and developing countries also started negotiating bilateral investment treaties (BITs) to address both procedural and substantive limitations of the international legal system.[6]

As a result of the disagreements as to the content of the substantive international legal rules governing the protection of foreign investments, the establishment of arbitral procedures for the settlement of disputes between private investors and government entities acquired particular significance.[7] Beginning in the 1950s, an increasing number of host states began to offer pre-dispute consent to arbitration in contracts signed with foreign investors for high-profile, capital-intensive projects.[8]

In 1961, the U.N. Secretary General prepared a questionnaire and circulated it among member states to gather information about the views of U.N. members on foreign investment. The results of the inquiry were reflected in a report that now offers important insights on the historical development of international investment law:

> 278. In calling for a further report on the promotion of the international flow of private capital, the Economic and Social Council specifically referred to "measures to facilitate the adjustment of disputes related to private investments." In effect, the consultations carried out in the course of the preparation of the present report tend towards the conclusion that apprehension of non-business risks constitutes an impediment to foreign private investment which may be substantially lessened by the assurance of an effective machinery for the

---

[5] E/3325, *supra* note 1, at ¶ 173. Developing states provided such assurances unilaterally through domestic laws, formal policy statements, or individual investment contracts; bilaterally, through bilateral investment treaties; and multilaterally, through instruments prepared by intergovernmental organizations such as the Organization for European Economic Cooperation (OEEC) (which later became the Organization for Economic Cooperation and Development (OECD)) and Council of Europe. *See* Further Report by the Secretary-General, E.S.C., 32d Sess., U.N. Doc. E/3492 (1961), ¶¶ 249–56 [hereinafter UN E/3492].

[6] The first bilateral investment treaty was signed in 1959 between Germany and Pakistan: The Treaty between the Federal Republic of Germany and Pakistan for the Promotion and Protection of Investments, signed on Nov. 25, 1959 [hereinafter Germany-Pakistan BIT]. This treaty, like several dozen others concluded during the 1960s, provided for broad substantive protection of investments from uncompensated expropriation and unfair treatment but relegated dispute resolution to a government-to-government mechanism. Texts of these treaties and other BITs can be found through the search engine maintained by the United Nations Conference on Trade and Development (UNCTAD) *available at* http://www.unctadxi.org/templates/DocSearch_779.aspx. [hereinafter UNCTAD Search Engine].

[7] *Id.* at ¶ 262.

[8] *See, e.g.,* the Libyan nationalization cases, which arose in the 1970s as a result of Libya's expropriation of nine international oil companies. Many of these companies had signed concession agreements in the 1950s with the Libyan government that included arbitration clauses, and the expropriation that followed led to such cases as *TOPCO/CALASIATIC v. Libya* and *LIAMCO v. Libya*. Robert von Mehren & P. Nicholas Kourides, *International Arbitration between States and Foreign Private Parties: The Libyan Nationalization Cases*, 75 Am. J. Int'l L. 476 (1981).

adjustment of investor's claims arising from disputes with the government of the country of investment. In order to be effective, such machinery should be international in character, so as to assure complete independence in interest from both parties to the dispute.

279. Several proposals for such international machinery, in the form of an investment tribunal or arbitral body, have recently been put forward and are under active consideration by various public and private agencies. . . .

281. The principles underlying these various proposals do not differ widely. All contemplate the possibility of direct access by investor to the arbitral body, as a party in interest, thus avoiding the political and practical complications of requiring him to seek espousal of his claim by his home government. This possibility may be considered as providing strong assurance to the investor, while at the same time offering to the governments of investment countries a ready alternative to the intervention of the investor's home government—a contingency rejected by the laws and constitutions of many of these countries. . . .

284. All the . . . proposals contemplate the establishment of new arbitral facilities, rather than reliance on such existing tribunals as the Permanent Court of Arbitration in The Hague or the Court of Arbitration of [the] International Chamber of Commerce. In so far as this preference is expressly discussed, it appears to derive, in the case of the Court of the International Chamber of Commerce, from its identification with commercial arbitration, chiefly between private business men, and its wholly non-governmental character. Nevertheless, it is a fact that its jurisdiction has been accepted in many commercial contracts between parties and government agencies.

285. In the case of [the] Permanent Court of Arbitration, the reverse point has been noted, namely, that it is not specialized in the commercial or investment field, inasmuch as it was established under the Hague Conventions for the Pacific Settlement of International Disputes of 1899 and 1907 for the purpose of "obviating as far as possible recourse to force in the relations between states."

286. In pursuance of the mandate contained in resolution 762 (XXIX), the Secretary-General circulated an inquiry among Member States, specialized agencies and appropriate inter-governmental and non-governmental sources in order to secure their views on the "measures to facilitate the adjustment of disputes related to private investments." The inquiry posed essentially two questions, namely, whether the expansion and institutionalization of the arbitration (or conciliation) of investment disputes were likely to add substantially to the security of foreign investments, and thus to encourage the flow of such investments; and if so, what role might usefully be played by the United Nations in this connexion.

287. Most of the governments replying to the first question expressed interest in the possibilities of international arbitration as a means not only of adjusting investment disputes but also of forestalling their occurrence and thereby improving the international climate for private foreign investments. . . .

293. In reply to the second question, regarding the possible role of the United Nations in this context, several governments stressed the advances which had been achieved more recently under the impulsion of the United Nations in the arbitration of international commercial disputes. Reference was made in this connexion to recent agreements, including the United Nations Convention on the Recognition and Enforcement of Foreign Arbitral Awards of 1958. . . . The governments which expressed interest in the availability of international machinery for the adjustment of investment disputes felt that the United Nations provided an appropriate forum for examining the desirability and appropriate forms of such arbitral machinery. . . .

294. . . . One government, however, felt that the subject was of such technical complexity that it might be more effectively dealt with by an international organization more directly concerned with foreign investments.

> 295. Among specialized agencies and inter-governmental organizations ... [the IBRD] stated that the time was ripe for the discussion and establishment of international arbitration and conciliation machinery to which parties could resort for the adjustment of investment disputes.[9]

The desire to promote the flow of private capital resulted in four important multilateral attempts after the Second World War to increase such flows.[10] The first was the 1948 Havana Charter on Trade and Employment, which was intended to create the International Trade Organization (ITO). The initiative to create the ITO came principally from the United States, which had become the dominant economic power after the Second World War. At the first meeting of the U.N. Economic and Social Council (ECOSOC) in 1946, "the United States introduced a resolution, which was adopted, calling for the convening of a United Nations Conference on Trade and Employment with the purpose of drafting a charter for an international trade organization." The preparatory work on the ITO charter began in the fall of the same year, and was concluded in 1948 at the Havana Conference.[11] However, the governments of developing countries were hostile to certain provisions of the charter, especially those related to the protection of foreign investments. The primary incentive for them to continue negotiations toward a final draft of the charter was to continue to receive development assistance from the United States. Once the United States lost interest in the ITO, developing countries also ceased supporting the project.[12]

The second attempt was a private initiative, the Abs-Shawcross Draft Convention on Investments Abroad (1959). However, this text also failed to gain widespread government support. "The automatic arbitration of investment disputes occupied [a] central place in the Abs-Shawcross Draft Convention and was coupled with far-reaching rights for the unilateral enforcement of awards. These features of the Draft Convention probably contributed as much as any to deter [developing countries]."[13]

The third and most direct approach to investment protection was the Draft Convention on the Protection of Foreign Property, negotiated in the 1960s under the auspices of the Organization for Economic Cooperation and Development

---

[9] UN E/3492, *supra* note 5. This report was prepared pursuant to Resolution 762 of the U.N. Economic and Social Council. E.S.C. Res. 762, 29th Sess. (1960) (citations omitted).

[10] Georg Schwarzenberger, *Foreign Investments and International Law* 136 (Fredrick A. Praeger 1969).

[11] J. Jackson, W. Davey, A. Sykes, *Legal Problems of International Economic Relations* 212–13 (4th ed., West Group 2002).

[12] *Id.* at 137.

[13] *Id.* at 191.

(OECD).[14] The OECD took up the work of the Abs-Shawcross drafters, but moderated a number of provisions included in Abs-Shawcross. Nonetheless, because this convention was perceived as primarily reflecting the interests of developed countries, it failed to obtain the support of the developing world.[15]

Finally, the World Bank at roughly the same time attempted to draft a multilateral convention on investment, observing the mistakes of others and relying on the results of previous U.N. reports.[16] In 1961, World Bank President Eugene R. Black declared in a note to the executive directors his intention to explore and promote the establishment of machinery for arbitration and conciliation of international investment disputes.[17] The World Bank was indeed a more productive forum for conducting the necessary studies on the subject, because (in contrast to the OECD), it included a wide range of member states from both the developed and developing world. At the same time, its economics-oriented and largely apolitical approach, far removed from the (sometimes) charged atmosphere of the U.N. General Assembly, allowed discussion of investment protection without the distraction of ideological debates.[18]

Some of the distinctive features of the World Bank's proposed dispute resolution mechanism, which became the foundation of the Convention on the Settlement of Investment Disputes between States and Nationals of other States,[19] are set forth in the following excerpt from a paper prepared by the General Counsel of the World Bank in 1963:

> 8. The Bank's approach to the problem is more modest than the other two efforts [i.e., OECD effort and the proposals for a multilateral insurance system]. While they aim at improving the investment climate, the proposals submitted to the Executive Directors neither contemplate rules for the treatment of foreign property nor compulsory adjudication of disputes. They would make available to foreign investors and host governments facilities for conciliation or arbitration of disputes between them. Use of these facilities would be entirely voluntary. No government and no investor would ever be under an obligation to go to conciliation or arbitration without having consented thereto. . . . [T]he initiative for conciliation or arbitration proceedings might come from a government as well as from an investor and they are concerned with the protection of the interests of one as well as the other. Furthermore, they proceed on the assumption that if a government has

---

[14] OECD Draft Convention on Protection of Foreign Property, 7 I.L.M. 117 (1967).

[15] Jackson et al., *supra* note 11, at 138.

[16] See p. 46 *supra*.

[17] Excerpt from address by President Eugene R. Black to the Annual Meeting of the Board of Governors, Sept. 19, 1961, 2 *Convention on the Settlement of Investment Disputes between States and Nationals of Other States, Documents Concerning the Origin and Formulation of the Convention,* at 3 (IBRD 1968) [hereinafter History of the ICSID Convention].

[18] Aron Broches, *Development of International Law by the International Bank for Reconstruction and Development,* Proc. Am. Soc. Int'l L. 33, 81 (1965).

[19] Convention on the Settlement of Investment Disputes between States and Nationals of Other States, 575 U.N.T.S. 159 (1966). This multilateral treaty is also known as the "Washington Convention."

consented to arbitrate a dispute with a private investor, the investor should then be deemed to have waived the right to seek the protection of his own government and his government would not be entitled to take up his case. These and other matters will be governed by the provisions of an intergovernmental agreement (the Convention). But, and this cannot be sufficiently stressed, none of these provisions would apply except where a government and a foreign investor had voluntarily agreed to use the facilities for conciliation or arbitration, as the case may be, established by the Convention. And the parties to the Convention would not by the fact of their signature of or adherence to the Convention undertake any obligation to make use of these facilities in any specific area.

9. Finally, the proposals are not to be regarded as an expression of the view that international conciliation or arbitration should be regarded as [the] normal or preferred method of settlement of disputes between governments and foreign investors. Such disputes should normally and preferably be settled through such mechanisms as are provided by local law. . . .[20]

After several years of preparatory work, the text of the Washington Convention was presented to the member governments of the World Bank for signature and ratification in March 1965. The Convention entered into force on September 14, 1966.[21]

B. ICSID and Its Central Role in the New System of Investor-State Arbitration

The International Centre for the Settlement of Investment Disputes (ICSID), created pursuant to Article 1 of the Washington Convention, has come to play a central role in the new system of investor-state arbitration. The cornerstone of ICSID's jurisdiction is the consent of host countries to resolve investment disputes with foreign investors through international arbitration administered by ICSID, an institution under the umbrella of the World Bank. Host states may provide their consent in individual investment contracts, in national domestic investment laws, or through bilateral and multilateral investment treaties.[22] As of November 4, 2007, 155 countries had signed the Convention, of which 143 had deposited their instruments of ratification with the ICSID Secretariat.[23] The following extract from ICSID's Web site describes the organization and its objectives and facilities:

> ICSID is an autonomous international organization. However, it has close links with the World Bank. All of ICSID's members are also members of the Bank. Pursuant to the Washington Convention, ICSID provides facilities for the conciliation and arbitration of

---

[20] Paper prepared by the General Counsel and transmitted to the members of the Committee of the Whole, SID/63-2 (Feb. 18, 1963) in 2 *History of the ICSID Convention, supra* note 17, at 72–73.

[21] Aron Broches, *The Convention of the Settlement of Investment Disputes: Some Observations on Jurisdiction*, 5 Colum. J. Trans. L. 263 (1966).

[22] See Chapter X.

[23] List of Contracting States and other Signatories of the Convention, *available at* http://icsid.worldbank.org, visited on Feb. 25, 2008.

disputes between member countries and investors who qualify as nationals of other member countries. Recourse to ICSID conciliation and arbitration is entirely voluntary. However, once the parties have consented to arbitration under the ICSID Convention, neither can unilaterally withdraw its consent. Moreover, all ICSID Contracting States, whether or not parties to the dispute, are required by the Convention to recognize and enforce ICSID arbitral awards.[24]

Besides providing facilities for conciliation and arbitration under the ICSID Convention, the Centre has since 1978 had a set of Additional Facility Rules authorizing the ICSID Secretariat to administer certain types of proceedings between States and foreign nationals which fall outside the scope of the Convention. These include conciliation and arbitration proceedings where either the State party or the home State of the foreign national is not a member of ICSID. Additional Facility conciliation and arbitration are also available for cases where the dispute is not an investment dispute provided it relates to a transaction which has "features that distinguish it from an ordinary commercial transaction."[25]

Provisions on ICSID arbitration are commonly found in investment contracts between governments of member countries and investors from other member countries. Advance consents by governments to submit investment disputes to ICSID arbitration can also be found in [several investment laws and many bilateral investment treaties].[26] Arbitration under the auspices of ICSID is similarly one of the main mechanisms for the settlement of investment disputes under four recent multilateral trade and investment treaties (the North American Free Trade Agreement, the Energy Charter Treaty, the Cartagena Free Trade Agreement and the Colonia Investment Protocol of Mercosur).[27]

C. Bilateral Investment Treaties[28]

The next significant development in the area of investment protection was the widespread adoption of BITs. Although the first bilateral investment treaty was entered into in 1959,[29] the adoption and use of such treaties was sporadic until the 1980s. Of the over 2,495[30] BITs, more than 1,900 were concluded after 1987. A wider group of countries have concluded BITs in recent years. A number of countries that initially refrained from concluding BITs changed their policies and

---

[24] About ICSID, http://www.worldbank.org/icsid/about/about.htm, visited January 2006.

[25] *Id.*

[26] See Chapter X *infra.*

[27] *Id.*

[28] The first three paragraphs of this section have been taken from the ICSID Web site (http://www.worldbank.org/icsid/treaties/intro.htm, visited December 2005) with some additions, changes, and updates. The footnotes are those of the authors.

[29] Germany-Pakistan BIT, *supra* note 6. The Germany-Pakistan BIT did not include a dispute resolution provision permitting arbitration between the host state and private investors. The first such BIT was signed by France and Tunisia in 1969. For more on the development of the BIT program in the United States, *see generally* Kenneth J. Vandevelde, *United States Investment Treaties: Policy and Practice* (Kluwer 1992).

[30] UNCTAD, *The Entry into Force of Bilateral Investment Treaties (BITs)*, U.N. Doc. UNCTAD/WEB/ITE/IIA/2006/9, *available at* http://www.unctad.org/en/docs/webiteiia20069_en.pdf [hereinafter *BITs Entry into Force*].

began to negotiate and sign such treaties.[31] The rapid growth in the number of investment treaties continued until 2002—when some degree of saturation was achieved—and then the rate of growth started to decline.[32] However, most countries that have an established BIT program still continue to pursue opportunities to enter into new treaties. Moreover, BITs are no longer concluded exclusively between traditional capital-exporting and capital-importing countries: an increasing number of BITs are concluded between developing countries.[33]

Despite some significant variations, modern BITs are broadly similar in their provisions.[34] They typically determine the scope of the application of the treaty, define which investments and investors qualify for protection, provide a number of substantive protections, and create procedures for the settlement of disputes. In this latter respect, most BITs provide for arbitration under the Washington Convention, as well as alternative procedures.

There is considerable debate as to why BITs have proliferated so dramatically in the last twenty years. To some extent, BITs were developed as a response to the perceived erosion of customary international law with respect to foreign investment during the New International Economic Order (NIEO) period.[35] As noted earlier, by the late 1960s and early 1970s, an ideological and political conflict characterized the relationship between developed and certain developing countries

---

[31] Latin American countries, for instance, appeared initially reluctant to enter into BITs. However, at the end of 1980s, many modified their development strategies, and by the end of the 1990s had signed close to three hundred BITs. *Bilateral Investment Treaties 1959–1999*, UNCTAD/ITE/IIA/2 at 15, http://www.unctad.org/en/docs/poiteiiad2.en.pdf. [hereinafter *BITs (1959–1999)*] See also the list of the BITs, http://www.worldbank.org/icsid/treaties/treaties.htm, which shows how the network of BITs has expanded since 1959 in all parts of the world.

[32] *Id.* at 6–7. Despite the decline, seventy BITs were signed in 2005. UNCTAD, *BITs Entry into Force, supra* note 30, at 3.

[33] "By the end of 1999, out of the total 1,857 BITs . . . 476 (26 per cent) BITs were between developing countries (compared with 40—or 10 per cent—at the end of 1989)." *Id.* at 3–4. *See, e.g.,* BITs between Algeria and Jordan, Brazil and Chile, and Cameroon and Guinea. Texts of these treaties are available through the UNCTAD Search Engine, *supra* note 6.

[34] Jennifer Tobin & Susan Rose-Ackerman, *Foreign Direct Investment and the Business Environment in Developing Countries: The Impact of Bilateral Investment Treaties* (Yale Law & Economics Research Paper No. 293, 2004), *available at* http://papers.ssrn.com/s013/papers.cfm?abstract_id=557121.

[35] Eileen Denza & Shelagh Brooks, *Investment Protection Treaties: United Kingdom Experience*, 36 Int'l & Comp. L. Q. 908, 909–10 (1987). Denza and Brooks suggest that BIT programs were initiated by developed countries in response to the NIEO resolutions. *Id.* Tobin and Rose-Ackerman believe that "The treaties are a response to the weaknesses and ambiguities of customary international law as applied to investments by international firms in countries at low levels of development. Customary law mainly developed in response to trade and investment between developed countries and was not adequate to conditions in these more risky and institutionally weak environments." Tobin et al., *supra* note 34. *See also* M. Sornarajah, *International Law of Foreign Investment* 233 (Cambridge University Press 1995).

with respect to expropriation of foreign investment, and for a time the positions of the two camps seemed irreconcilable, especially at the multilateral level. Nevertheless, there also was a growing awareness that continuation of that difference was not in the best interest of either developed countries or developing countries, and that some measures were necessary to restore a climate favorable to the cross-border movement of capital. Because a multilateral solution was not forthcoming, "states had to resort to the second best solution by making bilateral investment treaties to ensure that, as between them at least, there would be definite rules relating to foreign investment."[36]

As a result, a number of developed countries adopted an ambitious policy, concluding reciprocal BITs with developing countries that had demonstrated a willingness to cooperate. Developed countries made negotiation offers to these developing countries individually, often modeling their offers on the provisions in the draft multinational convention for the protection of foreign property prepared by the OECD.[37]

The OECD draft convention on the protection of foreign property[38] became the template for model treaties that many OECD members use in bilateral investment negotiations today.[39] As a consequence, BITs patterned after this model are broadly similar. Definition clauses are normally identical; most OECD treaties permit national control over the admission of foreign investment; and the substantive standards of treatment, such as fair and equitable treatment and full protection and security, are expressed using standard or similar wording.

A number of countries, in particular the United States and the United Kingdom, have produced their own model treaties, which they consider better adapted to their particular relations with developing countries.[40] The U.K. model and the earlier U.S. model treaties were broadly similar to the OECD text. The 2004 U.S. model, however,

---

[36] Sornarajah, *supra* note 35, at 234.

[37] *See* p. 48 *supra*. The drafters of the Abs-Shawcross Convention, which was taken up later by the OECD, relied on some of the provisions of the U.S. Friendship, Commerce, and Navigation (FCN) treaties, which were also incorporated into certain later bilateral treaties, such as that concluded by United Kingdom and Iran. *See The Proposed Convention to Protect Private Foreign Investment*, 9 J. Pub. L. 115, 120 (1960).

[38] "The OECD in turn was helped by the initiative of the ICC in preparing and disseminating a Model Code." *Bilateral Treaties for International Investment* 7–8 (Int'l Chamber Comm. 1977).

[39] The concept of a model treaty had little precedent in international economic law prior to the adoption of model BITs. One instance involved taxation. The League of Nations, when it started exploring the issue of double taxation, originally intended to promote a single multilateral instrument. This proved impossible for both political and technical reasons, and the League instead promulgated model bilateral treaties for the avoidance of double taxation, which member states could use in their dealings with other countries. David M. Hudson & Daniel C. Turner, *International and Interstate Approaches to Taxing Business Income*, 6 Nw. J. Int'l L. & Bus. 562, 563 (1984); H. David Rosenbloom & Stanley I. Langbein, *United States Tax Treaty Policy: An Overview*, 19 Colum. J. Transnat'l L. 359, 366 (1981).

[40] Tobin et al., *supra* note 34, at 8.

no longer follows the OECD model. The 2004 U.S. model, perhaps in reaction to the development of jurisprudence through arbitral awards, especially under the Chapter Eleven of NAFTA, has become significantly more detailed and complex. According to some observers, the new template curtailed some of the protections that were available to the investors under the previous model.[41]

Despite the general uniformity of BITs, there has been significant evolution of provisions over time. The once-prevalent conflicts in negotiating positions between developed countries and developing countries with regard to levels of protection have faded somewhat, although certain differences have emerged among certain developed countries regarding the appropriate scope and nature of treatment standards. There are therefore noticeable differences between model BITs used by many European states and those used by the United States. For example, European models are still generally premised on national control over admission of foreign investment, whereas the U.S. model favors an open-door policy, calling for national treatment in the preinvestment phase.

D. Multilateral Investment Treaties

As already noted, attempts to formulate a single, comprehensive multilateral investment protection treaty have not been successful. The OECD instrument of 1967 was not adopted, and a similar attempt in the 1990s to draft a Multilateral Agreement on Investment (MAI) also failed.[42] Nonetheless, a number of regional multilateral investment treaties have been concluded, although the scope and nature of protection differs markedly from treaty to treaty.

1. Lomé Conventions

The first multilateral instrument to embody investment protection principles is the series of treaties known collectively as the Lomé Conventions.[43] These agreements have evolved since 1975 to govern the economic relations between the European Union and the African, Caribbean, and Pacific (ACP) Group of States.[44] The EU's

---

[41] Noah Rubins, *The Arbitral Innovations of Recent U.S. Free Trade Agreements: Two Steps Forward, One Step Back,* Int'l Bus. L. J. 865 (2003). One commentator has described this curtailment of protections as "a regressive, rather than progressive, development of international law." See Stephen M. Schwebel, *The United States 2004 Model Bilateral Investment Treaty: An Exercise in the Regressive Development of International Law,* in Global Reflections on International Law, Commerce and Dispute Resolution 815–23, Liber Amicorum in honor of Robert Briner (ICC Publishing, Publication 693, Nov. 2005).

[42] See pp. 74–75 *infra.*

[43] Austin Amissah, *The ACP/EEC Conciliation and Arbitration Rules,* 8 Arb. Int'l 167 (1992).

[44] Jan Paulsson, *Arbitration without Privity,* 10 ICSID Rev.-F.I.L.J. 232, 241 (1995). See generally Ramesh F. Ramsaran, *Negotiating the Lomé IV Convention* (1990); Gianluca Brusco, *Eurocentrism and Political Conditionality: The Case of the Lomé Convention,* in Europe, Diplomacy and Development 103 (Carol Cosgrove-Sacks & Carla Santos eds., 2001).

European Development Fund (EDF),[45] which finances infrastructure projects in the ACP countries, and the European governments sought to provide protection for Western contractors involved in these projects. As a result, Lomé III[46] and Lomé IV[47] incorporated arbitration clauses similar to those found in BITs, although more limited in scope and more complex.[48] Lomé III provided:

> Any dispute arising between the authorities of an ACP State and a contractor, supplier or provider of services, candidate or tenderer, on the occasion of the placing or performance of a contract financed by the Fund [(EDF)] shall be settled by arbitration in accordance with procedural rules adopted by the Council of Ministers.[49]

Thus, although the treaty created the real possibility of direct dispute resolution with a large number of host states, the subject matter of the submission to arbitration was limited to transactions financed by the EDF. Nevertheless, the category of potential claimants was relatively broad, including any "candidate" or "tenderer," as well as actual contractors and service providers.[50] The Lomé Council of Ministers never adopted procedural rules, however, and as a "transitional measure" disputes were to be referred to the International Chamber of Commerce (ICC).[51]

In 1989, a fourth Lomé Convention was concluded. Rather than clarifying the arbitration clause of Lomé III or providing a procedural system for the conduct of dispute resolution, Lomé IV replaced the existing clause with an arbitral submission that is difficult to parse.[52] In any event, owing to the limited scope of the Lomé dispute resolution clause and close monitoring by local EDF representatives, few cases have been brought to arbitration pursuant to these conventions. Most disputes have

---

[45] "The European Development Fund (EDF) is the main instrument for Community aid for development cooperation in the ACP countries and the Overseas Countries and Territories (OCT). Articles 131 and 136 of the 1957 Treaty of Rome provided for its creation with a view to granting technical and financial assistance to African countries that were still colonised at that time and with which certain countries had historical links." EUROPA, *European Development Fund,* http://europa.eu.int/scadplus/leg/en/lvb/r12102.htm.

[46] Third ACP-EEC Convention, Signed at Lomé on Dec. 8, 1984 (Lomé III), 24 I.L.M. 574 (1985).

[47] Fourth ACP-EEC Convention, Signed at Lomé on Dec. 15, 1989 (Lomé IV), 29 ILM 783 (1991).

[48] Lomé III deals with issues related to the promotion of private investment under Title IV of Part III—"Investment, capital movements, establishment and services"–which does not contain any arbitration clause. The dispute resolution provision is in Chapter 4 of Title III ("Financial and Technical Cooperation") called "Implementation Procedures."

[49] Lomé III, art. 238(1). According to Article 23(1) of Lomé III, the Council of Ministers consists of "the members of the Council of the European Communities and of members of the Commission of the European Communities and, on the other hand, of the member of the government of each of the ACP States."

[50] Article 253 of the Convention.

[51] Lomé III, art. 238(3).

[52] For a discussion of various submission clauses, *see* Chapter X *infra* on consent.

been settled amicably prior to the arbitration stage, or the relevant contract has contained "an agreement under Article 307(b)(i) that obviate[d] the use of the unsatisfactory mechanism of (b)(ii)."[53]

2. North American Free Trade Agreement[54]

The North American Free Trade Agreement (NAFTA) entered into force on January 1, 1994, between the United States, Canada, and Mexico.[55] It created a free trade area among the parties in order to "a) eliminate barriers to trade in, and facilitate the cross-border movement of, goods and services between the territories of the Parties; b) promote conditions of fair competition in the free trade area; c) increase substantially investment opportunities in the territories of the Parties; . . .e) create effective procedures for the implementation and application of the Agreement [NAFTA] . . .and for the resolution of disputes."[56] NAFTA, therefore, regulates both trade and investment-related activities of the member states within the free trade area. Chapter 11 of NAFTA deals specifically with foreign investment. It provides various protections to the investors and their investments such as national treatment[57] and fair and equitable treatment.[58] In addition, it contemplates the possibility of direct investor-state arbitration between investors of one state party and another state party.[59]

Several institutions facilitate the implementation of NAFTA, including a secretariat that is in charge of the administration of dispute resolution provisions of the agreement.[60] Another important NAFTA institution is the Free Trade Commission (FTC). The FTC is composed of three cabinet-level representatives of the member countries.[61] Its primary duties are to "(a) supervise the implementation of this

---

[53] Id. at 245–46. For an extended analysis of the dispute settlement mechanism of the Lomé Conventions, see id. at 241–46, and Amissah, supra note 43.

[54] For a detailed analysis of the issues related to NAFTA, see NAFTA Investment Law and Arbitration: Past Issues, Current Practice, Future Prospects (Weiler ed., Transnat'l 2004).

[55] North American Free Trade Agreement (NAFTA), Dec. 17, 1992, Can.–Mex.–U.S., 32 I.L.M. 289 (1993), art. 2203.

[56] Article 102, objectives of NAFTA.

[57] NAFTA, art. 1102. See Chapter XV infra for a detailed discussion of this standard. The main substantive protections of NAFTA Chapter 11, which have equivalents in other investment treaties, are contained in Articles 1102 (national treatment), 1103 (most-favored nation treatment), 1105 (fair and equitable treatment and full protection and security), and 1110 (expropriation and compensation). These standards are discussed in Chapters XV–XVII of this book in detail.

[58] NAFTA, art. 1105. See Chapter XVII infra for a detailed discussion of this standard.

[59] See arts. 1116 (Claim by an Investor of a Party on Its Own Behalf), and 1117 (Claim by an Investor of a Party on Behalf of an Enterprise), available at http://www.sice.oas.org/trade/NAFTA/chap-111.asp.

[60] NAFTA, art. 2002. The Web site of the NAFTA Secretariat is http://www.nafta-sec-alena.org/DefaultSite/index_e.aspx.

[61] Id. Article 2001(1).

Agreement [(NAFTA)]; . . . and (c) resolve disputes that may arise regarding its interpretation or application."[62] Article 1131(2) of NAFTA provides that "[a]n interpretation by the Commission [FTC] of a provision of this Agreement shall be binding on a Tribunal established under this Section." The FTC has exercised this power to render several opinions, including a note on the interpretation of the scope of the obligations of the state parties under Article 1105 (minimum standard of treatment) of NAFTA, which provoked extensive debate and criticism.[63]

The following text by Todd Weiler explains the significance and novelty of Chapter 11 of NAFTA as well as its contribution to the development of international economic law. The second excerpt, by Charles N. Brower and Lee Stevens, examines different sections of NAFTA Chapter 11 and their role in achieving the objectives of the NAFTA parties. In so doing, it emphasizes the superior role of the investor-state arbitration mechanism of Chapter 11 in reaching those objectives.

Todd Weiler, *The Significance of NAFTA Chapter 11 for the Development of International Economic Law*, in *NAFTA Arbitration* 3–27

NAFTA Chapter 11 can be granted the "revolutionary" sobriquet because its usage has presaged what may be a paradigmatic shift in the way international economic law is conceived. Before NAFTA Chapter 11, investor-state dispute settlement simply did not exist on the radar screens of trade policy analysts, antitrade activists or most international lawyers. It was the province of a small clique of practitioners specializing in international commercial arbitration, working either for investors or governments of developing countries on disputes arising from relationships that had gone awry. Although it lay dormant for the first few years of its existence, NAFTA Chapter 11 became the catalyst which would change this status quo. A few "entrepreneurial" lawyers . . . realized that the obligations contained within Chapter 11 were as applicable to the conduct of governments in economically developed countries as they were to those from the developing world. In fact, the basic obligations contained within NAFTA Chapter 11—"national treatment," "fair and equitable treatment," "most-favored nation treatment" and the prohibitions against expropriation and the imposition of performance requirements—have enjoyed a long history in international investment law, and share many traits with analogous provisions contained within international trade treaties such as the WTO. As the early cases have borne out, not only was it incorrect to view the obligations contained within NAFTA Chapter 11 as being for the sole protection of investors in less-developed Mexico; it was also incorrect to think in segregationist terms about investment obligations and trade obligations. Both kinds of obligation could be used to "regulate the regulator," in order to ensure fair treatment for individual economic operators as against the state.

---

[62] *Id.* Article 2001(2).

[63] Free Trade Commission, *Notes of Interpretation of Certain Chapter 11 Provisions* (July 31, 2001). For a discussion of the debates surrounding these notes *see* Chapter XVI *infra*. The FTC has also issued a statement regarding the "notice of intent to submit a claim to arbitration," and another one on "non-disputing party participation." These documents are available at www.naftaclaims.com.

Charles N. Brower & Lee A. Steven, NAFTA CHAPTER 11: Who Then Should Judge?—Developing the International Rule of Law under NAFTA Chapter 11, 2 Chi. J. Int'l L. 193 (2001)[64]

Section A of Chapter 11 establishes the substantive investment protections that each NAFTA Party is required to honor, including the better of national treatment or most favored nation treatment, the minimum international standard of treatment, elimination of performance requirements, free transfer of funds, and expropriation protection. The point of these protections is to establish a rule-based investment regime in which foreign direct investment can thrive. Specific barriers to and restrictions on investment are eliminated and positive guarantees are extended. Moreover, all of this is done at the international level so as to place all three NAFTA countries and their investors, so far as possible, on an equal footing.

Section B of Chapter 11 is intended to reinforce that regime and make it work by giving foreign investors standing to bring claims in arbitration against the NAFTA Parties for breach of the substantive investment protections found in Section A. A rule-based system must have an enforcement mechanism if its substantive rules are to have any meaning over the long term. Just as important, however, is the form which that enforcement mechanism takes. After all, giving private individuals standing to sue a State before an international tribunal was not the only means of enforcement open to the NAFTA Parties. Consistent with existing international practice, the Parties could have relied on diplomatic protection, requiring the government of each NAFTA country to espouse the claims of its nationals. Alternatively, the Parties could have required that Chapter 11 claims be litigated in the domestic courts of the three NAFTA countries.[65]

Neither of these alternative options, however, would serve the aims of Chapter 11 as well as does investor-State arbitration. Investor confidence, for example, is not furthered by requiring domestic litigation. . . . Further, domestic courts often do not have the legal expertise and experience to free themselves from the confines of their own domestic regimes so as to give proper attention and respect to international law (which, along with NAFTA itself, expressly governs Chapter 11 disputes).[66] Another factor is that the interests of alien investors are more vulnerable than those of local investors because, as aliens, they are cut off from a direct participation in the host State's political [—both as investors and as claimants—] process and are therefore in greater need of protection at the international level. An international dispute resolution mechanism best serves Chapter 11 precisely because the NAFTA Parties are trying to build an international investment protection and promotion regime, a rule-based system that will be elaborated and enforced uniformly and consistently in each of the three NAFTA countries.

Equally important was the choice of investor-State dispute resolution over State-to-State adjudication. A system that originates in diplomatic protection—a product of expediency, it may be noted, from a time when the international legal order did not recognize the individual as able to invoke international law—places the burden and expense of prosecuting an investment dispute on the investor's government, a process that can be highly inefficient, arbitrary, and politically explosive: inefficient because governments are pressured to prosecute, or at least investigate, a great number of frivolous claims that would not

---

[64] Some of the source notes have been omitted.

[65] SN: Yet another alternative would have been to create a standing NAFTA tribunal to resolve investment disputes. The great advantage of this kind of system is the ability to generate a uniform body of substantive and procedural law, creating greater consistency over time, but the significant cost to the NAFTA parties of maintaining such a body makes its realization improbable.

[66] SN: *See* North American Free Trade Agreement, art. 1131(1), 32 ILM 605, 645 (1993).

otherwise be pressed if the responsibility and cost of prosecution remained with the individual investor; arbitrary because the exigencies of time, money, political priorities, and the whims of individual bureaucrats may cause a government to downgrade, or even ignore, meritorious claims; and politically explosive because diplomatic protection has the distinct disadvantage of pitting two States against one another in an inherently confrontational setting where, once a case is commenced, government officials cannot be seen as acting indifferently to the interests of their nationals. International "incidents," and the longstanding resentment and ill will between nations they generate, simply are not as likely to occur when the private investor itself has the right and the responsibility to prosecute its own claim and hence only one government is actively involved in the litigation.

In the early days of NAFTA, there was only limited public discussion of the potential impact of Chapter 11 on the legal systems of the parties. Once the first arbitration awards under the NAFTA Chapter 11 were released and the potential scope of NAFTA's investment protection regime became apparent, opposition grew. The following excerpt by Patti Ryan provides a contemporary Canadian perspective assessing the benefits of NAFTA Chapter 11. A second text by Don Wallace generally summarizes the controversial aspects of Chapter 11 and the views of different interest groups in this respect.

Patti Ryan, *David vs. Goliath*, 11(7) Nat'l Canadian Bar Assn. J. 30, 35 (Nov. 2002)

Barry Appleton, a Toronto lawyer who has brought all of the four leading cases against the Canadian government, says assigning a "good news" or "bad news" label to Chapter 11 provisions is beside the point. But he concedes that the provisions have created some certainty for both governments and investors.

"It's a positive process that's taking place in the context of a wider process of economic integration," he says. "The fact of the matter is that you need to have institutions and approaches that are rule-based, so you can decide things on the basis of what's right rather than who's bigger—what they call 'trade right, not trade might.'"

For a country like Canada, he says, there are real benefits to having a system that requires U.S. activity to be assessed against a set of agreed-upon rules. "And the price for that," he says, "is that our activity also has to be checked against rules."[67]

Meg Kinnear, general counsel at the Trade Law Bureau of the federal government, is less ambivalent. NAFTA Chapter 11, she says, is absolutely a positive way to resolve disputes.

---

[67] Although NAFTA Chapter 11 has had a positive impact on the process of resolving investment disputes, it has also had "unhappy outcomes," especially for Canadians. In the *Loewen* case, a jury in Mississippi returned a US$500 million verdict against a Canadian investor. The investor started arbitration proceedings under NAFTA Chapter 11 claiming, *inter alia*, denial of justice; the tribunal, however, dismissed the case. For a detailed discussion of this issue *see* Don Wallace, Jr., *Fair and Equitable Treatment and Denial of Justice:* Loewen v. U.S. *and* Chattin v. Mexico, in *International Investment Law & Arbitration: Leading Cases from the ICSID, NAFTA, Bilateral Treaties and Customary International Law* (Weiler ed., Cameron May 2005); Noah Rubins, Loewen v. United States*: The Burial of an Investor-State Claim*, 21(1) Arb. Int'l 1 (2005); and Michael D. Goldhaber, *A "Completely Appalling" Decision*, Am. Law. (Summer 2004), *available at* http://www.americanlawyer.com/focuseurope/appalling04.html.

"In particular, it gives Canadians investing in the United States or Mexico an additional avenue to resolve investment disputes arising from investments in those countries, without having to get their government to advance the claim on their behalf," she points out. "This gives investors additional security and comfort, and hopefully encourages investment among the NAFTA countries."

It also gives foreign investors operating in Canada the same security, which is important. "Investment is vital as an engine of economic growth for Canada," says Kinnear. Chapter 11 is therefore good news for governments, she argues, because there has been a marked increase in investment in the NAFTA countries.

"While it obviously entails some litigation against the NAFTA countries, there has been relatively little litigation when put in the perspective of a huge amount of trade and investment taking place daily among the NAFTA parties."

Appleton points out that considering there are more than 300 million citizens in the three NAFTA countries, and "countless million" corporations, there really haven't been very many claims filed. Whether many more will follow depends at least in part on how well governments follow their obligations, he says.

The fact that governments are such large entities, he adds, will help limit the numbers of frivolous claims being brought. "Nobody lightly brings a case against a government," he says. "Governments are big beasts."

Don Wallace, Jr., *Case Study under NAFTA: Lessons for the Wise*, in *Arbitrating Foreign Investment Disputes* 257 (N. Horn and S. Kröl eds., Kluwer Law International 2004)[68]

The Chapter 11 cases and awards have attracted their share of the species of criticism that has been addressed to WTO dispute settlement, and the more general criticism of international economic arrangements, trade, multinational corporations, and even international commercial arbitration, as well as that animated by the unhappiness of the NAFTA parties themselves.[69] A veritable sea of troubles: the secrecy and confidentiality allowed by party autonomy in commercial arbitration is said to be inappropriate in disputes involving public matters such as policy toward the environment,[70] hearings should be public and NGOs and others allowed to submit amicus briefs and otherwise participate;[71] there should be an appellate body.[72] These matters are being and will have to be further sorted out. . . .

Some detachment is in order, however; the motive of Chapter 11 and comparable arrangements is the belief that investors require a reliable, neutral dispute settlement machinery of

---

[68] Some of the source notes have been omitted.

[69] SN: *See* Ralph Nader, *Introduction*, in *The WTO: Five Years of Reasons to Resist Corporate Globalization* 6 (Lori Wallach & Michelle Sforza eds., Seven Stories 1999) (insisting that WTO and NAFTA represent "an unaccountable system of transnational governance designed to increase corporate profit").

[70] SN: *See* Charles H. Brower, *Structure, Legality, and NAFTA's Investment Chapter*, 36 Vand. J. Trans. L. 37 at 67, at 64–65 & 71–72 (2003); Marcia J. Staff & Christine W. Lewis, *Arbitration under NAFTA Chapter 11: Past, Present and Future*, 25 Hous. J. Int'l L. 301, 327–28; NAFTA Chapter 11 Investor-to-State Cases: Bankrupting Democracy, Public Citizen, *available at* http://www.citizen.org/publications/release.cfm?ID=7076 (last viewed June 5, 2003).

[71] SN: Chris Tollefson, *Games without Frontiers: Investor's Claims and Citizens Submissions under the NAFTA Regime*, 27 Yale J. Int'l L. 141, 163–64 (2002).

[72] SN: *See* Chapter XXII on this issue.

their choice if they are to invest abroad, and that such investment is the great contemporary engine of economic development for the developing countries, whatever the 'anti-globalizers' may think to the contrary.[73] To be sure organized society, a domestic one, or more than one if they agree as by the NAFTA treaty or future treaties, can limit and condition the choices of party autonomy. . . . In other words treaties are enacted and ratified by a population's elected representatives (just as environmental laws may be), and that is the time to oppose or modify such treaties, rather than to question their legitimacy and try to obstruct their implementation after the people's representative have spoken.

Efficient dispute settlement is also a good, and much so called ordinary commercial and other dispute settlement in courts and arbitral tribunals both international and domestic involves and touches on public issues and is nonetheless protected from promiscuous publicity, third party participation and the belief that it is a public forum, circus or legislature. The shibboleth 'environment,' the moralizing righteousness of the NGOs (when allied with protectionists, reminiscent of the 'Baptists and bootleggers' alliance of Prohibition times in the 1920's US) should not be allowed to sweep away institutions and arrangements otherwise serving social purposes of equal and possibly greater value. The defenders of these institutions should strengthen their nerves.

3. Energy Charter Treaty[74]

The Energy Charter Treaty (ECT) is a multilateral investment treaty binding the nations of Europe, including the former Communist bloc, and Australia and Japan.[75] When the ECT was signed in Lisbon in 1994, forty-one countries were parties. Presently, forty-nine countries have ratified the ECT. The Treaty entered into force in 1998, after it was ratified by thirty states.[76]

---

[73] SN: *See, e.g.*, MAI Proposals and Propositions: An Analysis of 1998 text, available at http://www.publiccitizen.org/trade/issues/mai/articles.cfm?ID=7415 (last viewed July 31, 2003); *see also* Jeff Faux, A Global Strategy for Labor, 2002 World Social Forum, Porto Alegre, Brazil (Jan. 30–Feb. 4, 2002), *available at* http://www.gpn.org/faux2002wsf.html (last viewed June 17, 2003); or *see* John J. Sweeney, World Economic Forum Annual Meeting (Jan. 30, 1999), *available at* http://www.aflcio.org/mediacenter/prsptm/sp01301999.cfm (last viewed June 17, 2003); *see generally* positions of Ralph Nader, American Federation of Labor–Congress of Industrial Organizations (AFL-CIO), and Dick Armey, the former house majority leader.

[74] The Energy Charter Treaty, 33 I.L.M. 360 (1995), *available at* www.encharter.org. *See generally The Energy Charter Treaty: An East-West Gateway for Investment and Trade* (Thomas W. Wälde ed., 1996).

[75] Jeswald Salacuse, *The Energy Charter Treaty and Bilateral Investment Treaty Regimes, in The Energy Charter Treaty* (Wälde ed., 1996).

[76] *Energy Charter Treaty Enters into Force* 15(2) *News from ICSID* 1 (Summer 1998), *available at* http://icsid.worldbank.org. As of February 2008 the ECT was ratified by Albania, Armenia, Austria, Azerbaijan, Belgium, Bosnia and Herzegovina, Bulgaria, Croatia, Czech Republic, Cyprus, Denmark, Estonia, European Communities, Finland, France, Georgia, Germany, Greece, Hungary, Ireland, Italy, Japan, Kazakhstan, Kyrgyzstan, Latvia, Liechtenstein, Lithuania, Luxembourg, Malta, Moldova, Mongolia, Netherlands, Poland, Portugal, Romania, Slovakia, Slovenia, Spain, Sweden, Switzerland, Tajikistan, The former Yugoslav Republic of Macedonia, Turkey, Turkmenistan, Ukraine, Uzbekistan, United Kingdom. Australia, Belarus, Iceland, the Russian Federation and Norway have signed the treaty but have yet to ratify it. *See* Energy Charter Treaty, Members and Observers, *available at* http://www.encharter.org.

[The ECT] constitutes the so far most ambitious project to set up an international investment (plus trade) regime. Different from previous attempts . . . it has succeeded in achieving the status of a legally binding multilateral convention. . . . The Energy Charter Treaty followed the non-binding 1991 "European Energy Charter." It was originally meant by the Western countries to be a multilateral version of the by now familiar bilateral investment treaties (BITs), mainly to protect Western foreign investment in the volatile, but very strategic CIS oil & gas industries. The quid pro quo . . . [for] protection of Western investment (BIT-style) . . . [was] access of Eastern energy trade to Western markets (GATT-style). As a consequence of bargaining dynamics, it has now become as well a multilateral treaty affecting West-West (and East/East) investment. In consequence, it is not only influenced by BIT-type obligations and procedures, but also characterised by a diluted version of Western (mainly European, but also NAFTA [style]) economic integration law.[77]

Article 2 of the ECT describes the treaty's purpose as "establish[ing] a legal framework in order to promote long-term cooperation in the energy field, based on complementarities and mutual benefits, in accordance with the objectives and principles of the charter." The investor-state arbitration mechanism, contained in Article 26 of the ECT, constitutes an integral part of this legal framework. "The [ECT']s arbitral system has been shaped very much in response to, and partly in further development of, comparable methods which have evolved over the last 30 years in bilateral and multilateral treaties; NAFTA's Chapter 11 (B) – sections 1115 to 1138 seem to have served as one major precedent."[78]

The ECT provides a range of investment protections similar to those contained in BITs.[79] Once a qualifying investment is in place, it enjoys a range of protections from measures taken by member states, including fair and equitable treatment; constant protection and security; freedom from unreasonable or discriminatory measures; most-favored nation (MFN) treatment, national treatment, and treatment according to international law, whichever is most favorable; limitations on and compensation for expropriation and losses caused by war and civil disturbance; free repatriation of related capital and profits; and good faith consideration of requests for entry and temporary employment of key personnel.

Because the ECT deals exclusively with the energy sector, environmental issues were a primary point of contention during the drafting stage. The ECT embodies the "polluter pays" principle, promoting the objective of market-oriented pricing that fully reflects environmental costs and benefits.[80] A separate protocol on Energy Efficiency and Related Environmental Aspects, which came into full force in 1998, defines policy principles for the promotion of energy efficiency and provides a framework for cooperation. Reflecting the lingering influence of the New International Economic

---

[77] Thomas W. Wälde, *Investment Arbitration under the Energy Charter Treaty—From Dispute Settlement to Treaty Implementation*, 12 Arb. Int'l 429, 429–30 (2004).

[78] *Id.*

[79] *See* Part III of the ECT.

[80] *See* ECT, art. 19.

Order, the ECT recognizes that each signatory has sovereignty over its energy resources and the right to decide the geographical areas that are to be made available for exploration and development. State sovereignty and sovereign rights, however, are to be exercised in accordance with the rules of international law.[81]

Unlike some BITs and NAFTA, the commitments of ECT signatory states concerning the preinvestment phase are limited to the undertaking that "best efforts" will be made to ensure nondiscrimination, national and most-favored treatment, that is, equal market access, for qualifying foreign investors.[82] Moreover, although breach of treatment obligations with regard to established investments are subject to arbitration, violations of the promise of equal market access do not give rise to any direct investor recourse against the host state.[83] Negotiation is currently underway to conclude a supplemental protocol dealing with the establishment of energy-related investments.

The investor-state arbitration provision of Article 26 applies only to disputes arising out of obligations undertaken in Part III of the ECT on investment protection. Other obligations, such as those related to trade, transit, technology transfer, and other aspects of the energy sector, are subject to resolution pursuant to the state-to-state mechanism of Article 27.

One of the main controversies of the ECT is whether investors may have recourse to the investor-state dispute resolution mechanism of the ECT (Article 26) during the provisional application period.

> U. Klaus, *The Gate to Arbitration—The Yukos Case and the Provisional Application of the Energy Charter Treaty in the Russian Federation*. 2(3) Transnat'l Disp. Mgmt. (June 2005).[84]
>
> The quick economic integration of energy markets in the former East and West was considered vital to the restructuring and reform of the former communist economies, and to safeguard the energy supply to energy-dependent western nations. Therefore, in Art. 45 (1), the ECT prescribes its provisional application, including an opt-out clause for those members unwilling to apply the treaty provisionally in Art. 45 (2) ECT.
>
>> "(1) Each signatory agrees to apply this Treaty provisionally pending its entry into force for such signatory (. . .), to the extent that such provisional application is not inconsistent with its constitution, laws or regulations.
>>
>> (2) a) Notwithstanding paragraph (1) any signatory may, when signing, deliver (. . .) a declaration that it is not able to accept provisional application. The obligation contained in paragraph (1) shall not apply to a signatory making such a declaration. (. . .)"

---

[81] ECT, art. 18.
[82] Wälde, *supra* note 77. See also Gillian Turner, *Investment Protection through Arbitration: The Dispute Resolution Provisions of the Energy Charter Treaty*, 1 Int'l Arb. L. Rev. 166, 167 (1998).
[83] Turner, *supra* note 82, at 168.
[84] Source notes have been omitted.

This resulted in provisional application of the treaty by all signatory states between its signature in December 1994 and its entry into force in April 1998 (Art. 44 ECT), unless a member state expressly declared that it was unable to apply the ECT provisionally (Art. 45 2) a) ECT). After April 1998, provisional application was restricted to those signatory states which had signed but not yet ratified the treaty and had not invoked Art. 45 (2) ECT.

The debate about the meaning of Article 45 and "provisional" application continues today. It is worth noting that this concept, at least in the early years of the life of ECT, was considered novel, because it not only provided direct recourse to arbitration against a sovereign (which was new) but also allowed such recourse based on an unratified treaty, which under international law was not a solid source of obligation.[85] Nevertheless, there seems to be nothing in Article 45 or Article 26 that could preclude the provisional application of Article 26.[86] At least one tribunal, *Plama v. Bulgaria*, has made a general statement to the effect that Article 26 may be provisionally applied.[87] Some scholarly writings support this view.[88]

4. Mercado Común del Sur (Mercosur or Mercosul)[89]

Four nations are currently party to the "Southern Cone" free trade zone known as Mercosur: Brazil, Argentina, Paraguay, and Uruguay. Bolivia, Chile, Columbia, Ecuador, Peru, or Venezuela are associate members, which means that they do not have voting rights or full trading privileges.[90] The Mercosur agreement itself deals exclusively with issues of trade and tariffs, and does not touch on questions of

---

[85] On the legal effect of unratified treaties, see W. Michael Reisman, *Unratified Treaties and Other Unperfected Acts in International Law: Constitutional Functions*, 35(3) Vand. J. Int'l L. 729 (2003).

[86] Klaus, *supra* p. 63, text accompanying notes 19–20; *see also* Richard Happ, *Dispute Resolution under Energy Charter Treaty*, 45 German Y.B. Int'l L. 331, 339 (2003).

[87] *Plama v. Bulgaria*, ICSID Case No. ARB/03/24 (Decision on Jurisdiction, 2005, ¶ 140).

[88] *See generally* Happ, *supra* note 86; Wälde, *supra* note 77; and Klaus, *supra* p. 63.

[89] *See generally* Bernardo M. Cremades, *Promoting and Protecting International Investments*, Int'l Arb. L. Rev. 53 (2000); Noah Rubins, *Investment Arbitration in Brazil*, 4 J. World Inv. & Trade 1071 (2003).

[90] Mercosur was created by the Treaty of Asuncion, Mar. 26, 1991, 30 I.L.M. 1041 (1991). For the latest information regarding the membership status in Mercosur, see www.mercosur.org.uy. "Because neither the Treaty of Asuncion nor the [Additional Protocol to the Treaty of Asuncion on the Institutional Structure of Mercosur (Protocol of Ouro Preto)] contemplated the expansion of MERCOSUR's membership, the common market lacks formal procedures for admitting new members. Therefore, instead of incorporating [the current associate members] . . . directly into its existing institutions, which would have required a major overhaul of its foundations, MERCOSUR chose to grant its associates indirect relationships through the mechanisms of the Latin American Integration Association (ALADI)." Samuel A. Arieti, *The Role of Mercosur as a Vehicle for Latin American Integration*, 6 Chi. J. Int'l L. 761, 765 (2006). *See also id.*, for a discussion of the Decision 18/04 of the Council of the Common Market, which grants further

investment protection. In 1994, however, the Mercosur Council[91] adopted[92] two protocols that not only include provisions creating rights for investors from the member countries to initiate arbitration proceedings against other member states, but also provide access to the dispute settlement mechanism to the investors of nonmembers.

The first protocol, known as the Colonia Protocol,[93] extends some BIT-type protections to investors from the Mercosur member states. The Colonia Protocol accords to investments of the nationals of Mercosur countries both national treatment and treatment at least as favorable as that provided to investors from non-Mercosur states.[94] Furthermore, the document establishes obligations of fair and equitable treatment and a prohibition on "unjustified or discriminatory measures,"[95] limits the imposition of performance requirements,[96] and ensures the free transfer of profits and capital out of member countries.[97]

Article 7 is perhaps the most progressive provision:

> When the provisions of the legislation of a Contracting Party or the obligations, present or future, of international law, or an agreement between an investor of one Contracting Party and the Contracting Party in whose territory the investment has been established contain norms that give investments treatment more favorable than that set forth in the present Protocol, these norms shall prevail over the present Protocol to the extent that they are more favorable.[98]

---

[91] Article 3 of the Protocol of Ouro Preto provides that "The Council of the Common Market [(Mercosur Council)] is the highest organ of Mercosur, with responsibility for the political leadership of the integration process and for making the decisions necessary to ensure the achievement of the objectives defined by the Treaty of Asuncion and the final establishment of the common market." 31 I.L.M. 1244 (1995).

[92] Article 38 of the Protocol of Ouro Preto provides that "[t]he States Parties undertake to take all the measures necessary to ensure, in their respective territories, compliance with the decisions adopted by the Mercosur organs." Chapter V of the protocol titled "Legal Sources of Mercosur" clarifies the normative value of the decisions of the Council in Articles 41 and 42. Article 41 of the protocol provides that "[t]he Decisions of the Council . . . adopted since the entry into force of the Treaty of Asuncion" constitute legal sources of Mercosur. Article 42 provides that "[t]he decisions adopted by the Mercosur organs . . . shall be binding and, when necessary, must be incorporated in the domestic legal systems in accordance with the procedures provided for in each country's legislation."

[93] Protocol for the Reciprocal Promotion and Protection of MERCOSUR Investments, approved by Common Market Council Decision No. 11/93 of Jan. 17, 1994. Unofficial English translation of this protocol is available at http://www.cvm.gov.br/ingl/inter/mercosul/coloni-e.asp.

[94] Colonia Protocol, art. 3(2).

[95] Colonia Protocol, art. 3(1).

[96] Colonia Protocol, art. 3(4).

[97] Colonia Protocol, art. 5.

[98] Colonia Protocol, art. 7.

This provision ensures that the standards of treatment guaranteed to Mercosur investors will evolve as international law evolves, and that the Protocol will remain relevant even with the passage of decades. The treaty gives qualified investors the right to bring arbitration claims against the host state under the ICSID or UNCITRAL rules to vindicate these rights, just as would a BIT or NAFTA.[99]

The second protocol, known as the Buenos Aires Protocol,[100] is unique in the annals of investment treaties. It provides much the same substantive protection and access to arbitration as NAFTA or other investment treaties, but bestows such rights on investors from *any non-member country*. In other words, the Buenos Aires Protocol operates as a multilateral investment treaty, with benefits extended simultaneously to *every country in the world, without reciprocity*.[101]

It should be noted, however, that the purpose of the Buenos Aires Protocol is somewhat different from that of BITs; although the underlying purpose of most investment treaties is the promotion of a more efficient international allocation and use of capital, the Protocol's investment provisions are designed to promote other goals as well.[102] Although the Protocol lays down general standards of treatment that are similar to those contained in the Colonia Protocol, the parties enjoy discretion to decide whether or not to accord national treatment and MFN treatment to established investments of investors of third countries. Furthermore,

---

[99] Colonia Protocol, art. 9.

[100] Protocol for the Promotion and Protection of Investments in Mercosur from Non-Member Countries, approved by Common Market Council Decision No. 11/94 of Aug. 5, 1994.

[101] At least one experienced commentator holds the opinion that the Buenos Aires protocol is not a self-executing investment protection agreement at all, but instead only an attempt to harmonize future protections granted to foreign investors. According to this interpretation, the Protocol "only provides a ceiling on the scope of protection to non-Mercosur country investors that may be granted, for example under the discrete investment treaties each Member country may conclude with non-Mercosur countries and does not give rise to any specific rights from non-Mercosur country investors to claim rights directly arising from this Protocol." Horatio Grigera Naòn, *The Settlement of Investment Disputes Between States and Private Parties*, 1 J. World Invest. 59, 63 (2000); Horatio Grigera Naòn, *Foreign Investment Arbitration in Latin America: The New Environment*, A.B.A. Section of Int'l Law & Prac. Newsl. 14–23 (Winter 1995). *But see* Maryse Robert, et al., *Negotiating Investment Rules*, in *An Integrated Approach to the European Union-Mercosur Association* 265, 270–79 (Paolo Giordano ed., 2002) (suggesting that the Buenos Aires and Colonia Protocols provide direct protections to covered investors); U.S. Dept. of State, *Investment Climate Brazil 2000*, available at http://www.mac.doc.gov/ola/brazil/climate.htm (describing Buenos Aires protocol as an "investment protection treaty" like a BIT); *see also* Peter Malanczuk, *State-State and Investor-State Dispute Settlement in the OECD Draft Multilateral Investment Agreement*, 3 J. Econ. L. 417, 423 (2000); Sistema Economico Latinamericano, *International Negotiations on Foreign Investment: Elements for the Latin American and Caribbean Position*, http://lanic.utexas.edu/~sela/AA2K/EN/docs/ 97/spdredi18-97.htm.

[102] OECD Trade Directorate, The Relationship between Regional Trade Agreements and the Multilateral Trading System: Investment, document TD/TC/WP (2002) 18/FINAL, p. 11 (Working Paper, June 13, 2002), *available at* http://www.oecd.org.

the Buenos Aires Protocol contains no provisions on performance requirements, normally an important subsidiary protection of investment treaties.[103]

Whatever their precise limits, the Mercosur investment protocols are for now only a vision of a possible future legal landscape in the Southern Cone. Protocols within the Mercosur rule-making framework are ineffective until thirty days after all four member states have converted the protocol into domestic law. As of March 2005, only Argentina had incorporated the Colonia Protocol into domestic law, and only Argentina and Paraguay had adopted the Buenos Aires Protocol.[104] There is no indication when or if the remaining Mercosur states will ratify these documents, and because the governments themselves did not participate directly in the drafting of the protocols, they may never enter into force.[105] Should Mercosur's investment protocols ever take effect, however, they could well catapult Brazil and its three treaty partners to the forefront of investment protection in Latin America.

5. The Association of South East Asian Nations

Rubins and Kinsella, *International Investment, Political Risk and Dispute Resolution* 199–200 (Oceana Publications 2005)

The Association of South East Asian Nations (ASEAN) concluded the Agreement for the Promotion and Protection of Investments in December 1987.[106] The ASEAN Investment Agreement covers investments made within ASEAN members states by nationals and companies of other ASEAN members.[107] The agreement establishes various host State obligations to create favorable conditions for qualifying investments, including simplification of investment procedures and approval process;[108] to ensure transparency and predictability by providing up-to-date public information on laws and regulations;[109] to accord fair and equitable treatment and full protection and security;[110] compensation for expropriation;[111]

---

[103] *Id.*

[104] Communication with Manueal Olarreaga, Mercosur Secretariat (Sept. 29, 2002). *See* Argentina Law No. 24891 of May 11, 1997 (incorporating Colonia Protocol); Argentina Law No. 24554 of Sept. 13, 1995 (incorporating Buenos Aires Protocol); Paraguay Law No. 593/95 of June 15, 1995 (incorporating Buenos Aires Protocol).

[105] Recently the Common Market Group created the Sub Working Group No. 12 on Investment, which will "analyze the difficulties member states face in the approval and implementation of the Colonia Protocol and the Buenos Aires Protocol and recommend courses of action." Common Market Group Resolution 13/00.

[106] SN: Agreement among the Governments of Brunei Darussalam, the Republic of Indonesia, Malaysia, the Republic of Philippines, the Republic of Singapore, and the Kingdom of Thailand for the Promotion and Protection of investments [hereinafter ASEAN Investment of Agreement] of Dec. 15, 1987, 27 I.L.M. 612 (1988).

[107] SN: *Id.* at preamble and art. II.

[108] SN: Protocol to Amend ASEAN Investment Agreement of Sept. 12, 1996, art. III-A.

[109] SN: *Id.* at Art. III-B.

[110] SN: ASEAN Investment Agreement, *supra* note 106, arts. IV(2) and III(2).

[111] SN: *Id.* at art. IV.

and to observe "any obligation arising from a particular commitment" made with regard to a specific investment of investors of another contracting party.[112] Article IV protects investments against unjustified and discriminatory measures with regard to management, maintenance, use, enjoyment, extension, disposition or liquidation of investments, and MFN treatment has been accorded in respect of a limited range of benefits.[113] The ASEAN Investment Agreement contains no national treatment provision. Further, tax measures are excluded expressly from the agreement's scope of protection.[114] Article IX, as amended by a 2004 protocol, provides for investor-State dispute resolution under a variety of auspices, including the Kuala Lumpur arbitration center.[115] Only one case has been filed under the ASEAN Investment Agreement to date, *Yaung Chi Oo v. Myanmar.* That arbitration was dismissed on jurisdictional grounds . . . .

6. Free Trade Area of the Americas[116]

Free Trade Area of the Americas (FTAA) is an ambitious effort to integrate the economies of American nations into a single free trade area. According to the U.S. Chamber of Commerce, "[t]he proposed FTAA would create the largest trading block in the world, encompassing 34 nations with more than 800 million citizens and a collective GDP that would exceed $13 trillion."[117] Preliminary negotiations for the FTAA started at the 1994 Summit of the Americas, in Miami.[118] At their eighth meeting in Miami on November 20, 2003, ministers of the states participating in the FTAA negotiations reaffirmed their commitment to conclude the FTAA negotiations by January 2005.[119] This target date was not met, however. A complete discussion of the reasons underlying this failure goes beyond the scope of this book. Some of the issues, however, that could arise with respect to the investor-state arbitration mechanism of FTAA have been explained below.

---

[112] SN: *Id.*, art. III(3).

[113] SN: *Id.* art. IV (MFN treatment limited to fair and equitable treatment and restitution, compensation, or other remedies).

[114] SN: *Id.* art. V.

[115] SN: If the disputing parties cannot agree on the applicable procedural rules within three months, then the agreement provides as a default a purely ad hoc three-member tribunal. The chairman in such cases must be a national of third ASEAN State. In such cases, the International Court of Justice acts as the appointing authority. ASEAN Investment Agreement, *supra* note 106, art. X(3)–(4).

[116] For general information regarding the FTAA, the status of the negotiations, and the latest draft text of the FTAA (currently third draft) investment chapter (Chapter XVII), see the official Web site of the FTAA at http://www.ftaa-alca.org/alca_e.asp. See also Christopher M. Bruner, *Hemispheric Integration and the Politics of Regionalism: The Free Trade Area of the Americas (FTAA)*, 33 U. Miami Inter-Am. L. R. 1 (2002); *see also Free trade for the Americas?: The United States' Push for the FTAA Agreement* (Paulo Vizentini & Marianne Wiesebron eds., Zed, Palgrave Macmillan 2004).

[117] *U.S. Chamber of Commerce, Grassroots Newsletter* 3 (July-Aug. 2004), *available at* http://www.traderoots.org/Newsletter/August%2003(for%20web).pdf.

[118] *See Summit of the Americas Action Plan*, *available at* http://www.summit-americas.org/miamiplan.htm.

[119] Ministerial Declaration, Free Trade Area of the Americas, Eighth Ministerial Meeting, ¶ 5 (Nov. 20, 2003), *available at* http://www.ftaa-alca.org/Ministerials/Miami/Miami_e.asp# note1.

Jessica S. Wiltse, *An Investor-State Dispute Mechanism in the Free Trade Area of the Americas: Lessons from NAFTA Chapter Eleven,* 51 Buffalo L. Rev. 1145, 1172–1196 (2003)

The [FTAA] negotiations can be characterized as a bargaining process between the trading blocs led by the U.S., for NAFTA, and Brazil, for . . . MERCOSUR . . . as each attempts to gain the upper hand.

The second draft text of the FTAA, released in November 2002, includes an investment chapter similar to that contained in NAFTA. However, much of the Chapter remains open for negotiation, as almost every provision contained therein is still in brackets. The following discussion provides a general overview of several issues that are important in considering an investor-state dispute mechanism in the FTAA. Besides the practicalities of completing such a large-scale investment agreement, there are several issues that are particular to Latin America, principally the historical dominance of the Calvo Doctrine and the increasing salience of Latin American environmental politics and protection. . . .

A. The Calvo Doctrine in Latin America

Latin America has undergone something of a paradigm shift in recent years . . . to attract more and more foreign direct investment (FDI) . . . to fund economic growth and import new technology. Yet, capital-exporting nations were reluctant to heavily invest in Latin America for a number of reasons, among them the use of so-called Calvo Clauses. . . . [The Calvo Doctrine, however, seems to be in decline in Latin America.]

The abandonment of the Calvo Doctrine in Latin America is evident in several ways. First, arbitration is increasingly common in Latin America . . . Second, the U.S. **Bilateral Investment Treaty** program with Latin America undoubtedly contributed to the demise of the Calvo Doctrine. . . .

In sum, the Calvo Doctrine may have, in the recent past, posed a formidable obstacle to including investor-state arbitration in the FTAA. However, a number of political forces have slowly eroded the necessity of Calvo Clause protections in Latin America. . . .

However, as Brazil is the major player in the FTAA negotiations for Latin America, and Brazil is one of the few countries that is not associated with ICSID or in a BIT with the United States, it is possible that Brazil may be less willing to abandon the Calvo Doctrine [than] . . . some of her neighbors. MERCOSUR currently does not provide for binding investor-state arbitration without the investor first seeking consultations, and its investment provisions are decidedly less comprehensive than those of NAFTA. Until recently, Chile seemed similarly attached to Calvo principles, and with the United States' failure to negotiate Chile's accession to NAFTA and Chile's subsequent association with MERCOSUR, it appeared Chile would remain that way for some time. An encouraging sign emerged very recently, however, with the United States and Chile entering into a bilateral Free Trade Agreement, which provides investment protection and investor-state arbitration similar to NAFTA Chapter 11. Whether the remaining Latin American countries similarly still attached to Calvo principles will eventually follow suit, especially in investment agreements with non-Latin American countries, remains unknown. Yet, it is difficult to envision the United States accepting the FTAA without an investor-state arbitration mechanism. Thus, this issue may present a major stumbling block in the FTAA negotiations as controversy continues to rise over the merits of investor-state arbitration.

B. Environmental Politics in Latin America

The strongest criticism of [NAFTA] Chapter 11 is that foreign investors use it to challenge legitimate national environmental regulations on the grounds that they are "tantamount to expropriation" of their investment. The Metalclad decision exacerbated this fear among environmentalists and other civil society critics when it awarded almost $17 million in damages in connection with the investor's hazardous waste facility in Mexico. Indeed, a significant number of the cases brought under Chapter 11 thus far deal with environmental regulation, public health, or resource management policies. Many environmentalists oppose the inclusion of an investor-state dispute mechanism in the FTAA for fear that it will be used to challenge environmental and public health laws of those governments. Interestingly, it is also for this reason that Canadian trade ministers have demonstrated eroding support for investor-state dispute settlement, saying that they will not ratify the FTAA if it includes a provision similar to NAFTA Chapter 11.

Although Latin America has abundant natural resources, it has traditionally allowed exploitation of those resources as a means to economic development. "As a result of this relentless drive to develop, [the region] acquired not only a reputation as a haven for environmentally negligent industries, but also a host of environmental problems that threaten the region's biodiversity and human health." Yet recently, and in response to two complementary sources of pressure – growing concern from Latin American citizens and environmental NGOs and increasing widespread awareness of the environmental side effects associated with increased international trade – many Latin American countries have adopted much stronger environmental laws. Many international environmental and development organizations see this as a step in the right direction for Latin America, as countries find new ways to develop economically while also taking steps to protect their environment and natural resources. But the fact remains that many of Latin America's national environmental regulations, and especially the enforcement thereof, are still below the standards of the NAFTA Parties.

The lower environmental standards in Latin America raise some important issues. The most significant is how to prevent the lower standards from creating a foreign investment "race to the bottom." Those countries with less strict environmental laws make doing business there less costly, and many Latin American countries have decided to maintain the lower standards in order to attract investment.

This race to the bottom was also an issue when the Canada-U.S. Free Trade Agreement [CUSFTA] was extended to Mexico and NAFTA was created. As a result of political pressure in the United States, the newly elected Clinton Administration negotiated supplementary labor and environment "side agreements" to dispel fears of lenient regulations and enforcement in Mexico. To the United States, the inclusion of the side agreements was a political necessity, "to allay the primary American suspicion of the agreement prior to its adoption: that lax standards south of the border would prompt industry to save money on environmental compliance by relocating to such areas." Such side agreements may again become necessary to the NAFTA Parties in the process of negotiating the FTAA, especially to Mexico, which had to improve its enforcement of environmental laws when NAFTA came into force, and will not want to "lose" foreign investment to those Latin American countries with lower standards and lax enforcement. But whether the Latin American countries will be willing to agree to such provisions is doubtful, as they are likely to view such requirements as an infringement on their national sovereignty and their ability to compete internationally.

In summary, Latin American integration into the FTAA faces at least two significant challenges with regard to environmental issues. First, the use of Chapter 11-like investor-state arbitration should be a source of concern for those who do not wish to see Latin American environmental regulations "chilled" or even clawed back. The newly developing environmental awareness in some Latin American countries is a step in the right direction for these countries, and concern that investor-state arbitration will have a negative impact on new environmental regulation is well-founded. For example, according to author Howard Mann of the International Institute for Sustainable Development, between 1994, when NAFTA came into force, and 2001, the Canadian government enacted only two new environmental regulations, and both have been challenged. Second,

> the goal of attracting foreign investment in Latin America may cause some countries to resist increasing environmental enforcement standards, and thus a mechanism similar to the environmental side agreement of NAFTA may be necessary to both level the playing field and promote sustainable development. The tension between the promotion of free trade and investment on the one hand, and environmental protection on the other, is likely to generate heated controversy as the negotiations for the FTAA conclude and the ratification process commences.

In November 2005, the FTAA-negotiating governments pledged to instruct their officials to resume negotiations in order to examine and overcome the difficulties in the FTAA process.[120] Currently, the third draft of the FTAA is under negotiation, including Chapter 17 on the protection of investments.

7. The Dominican Republic–Central American–United States Free Trade Agreement

The Dominican Republic–Central American–United States Free Trade Agreement (DR-CAFTA) is a free trade agreement that has been entered into between the United States and the Central American countries of Costa Rica, El Salvador, Guatemala, Honduras, and Nicaragua. Dominican Republic is also a member of this agreement, although it joined the negotiations later. With the entry of Dominican Republic, the name of the agreement, which was originally CAFTA, changed to DR-CAFTA and the agreement was signed on August 5, 2004. As of December 2006, DR-CAFTA was in force for all the above signatories except Costa Rica.

The objectives of DR-CAFTA are set forth in Article 1.2 of the agreement:[121]

> 1. The objectives of this Agreement, as elaborated more specifically through its principles and rules, including national treatment, most-favored-nation treatment, and transparency, are to:
>
>   (a) encourage expansion and diversification of trade between the Parties;
>
>   (b) eliminate barriers to trade in, and facilitate the cross-border movement of, goods and services between the territories of the Parties;
>
>   (c) promote conditions of fair competition in the free trade area;
>
>   (d) substantially increase investment opportunities in the territories of the Parties;
>
>   (e) provide adequate and effective protection and enforcement of intellectual property rights in each Party's territory;

---

[120] Fourth Summit of the Americas, *Declaration of Mar Del Plata*, ¶ 19 (Nov. 2005), *available at* http://www.ftaa-alca.org/Summits_e.asp.

[121] Text of DR-CAFTA and other related documents are available at the CAFTA Briefing Book at the United States Trade Representative's Web site, http://www.ustr.gov.

(f) create effective procedures for the implementation and application of this Agreement, for its joint administration, and for the resolution of disputes; and

(g) establish a framework for further bilateral, regional, and multilateral cooperation to expand and enhance the benefits of this Agreement.

2. The Parties shall interpret and apply the provisions of this Agreement in the light of its objectives set out in paragraph 1 and in accordance with applicable rules of international law.

According to some observers, the two agreements together should be considered as steps toward the creation of FTAA.[122] Chapter 10 of DR-CAFTA deals with investments. It is modeled after United States Model BIT of 2004 and provides for direct investor-state arbitration.[123] DR-CAFTA has attracted its own share of criticism.[124] These concerns are briefly explained in the following excerpt.

Lauren A. Hopkins, *Protecting Costa Rica's Osa Peninsula: CAFTA's Citizen Submission Process and Beyond*, 31 Vt. L. Rev. 381, 391–3 (2007)[125]

[CAFTA was approved in the U.S. House of Representatives by a vote of 217 to 215.] In the United States, this close vote reflects the nation's polarization on the CAFTA issue. Those in favor of the agreement believe it will increase trade and employment in all the member countries.[126] Those opposed to the agreement, including a majority of House Democrats and several Republicans from textile and sugar producing states, fear that CAFTA will lead to a loss of jobs and do little to prevent the exploitation of Central American workers.[127]

CAFTA's signatory countries faced strong internal opposition to the agreement as well. In El Salvador, the first country to ratify CAFTA, protestors interfered with congressional debate, delaying the vote on CAFTA for two days. Similarly, in Honduras, thousands protested the legislature's ratification of CAFTA and set up highway blockades that halted cross-country commerce. Protesters invaded the national assembly in Honduras and, after the ratification passed, broke into the building and smashed up windows and chairs. After legislators ratified CAFTA in Guatemala, police sealed the streets surrounding the Guatemalan Congress and clashed with protesters, injuring more than fifty protesters.

---

[122] Lauren A. Hopkins, *Protecting Costa Rica's Osa Peninsula: CAFTA's Citizen Submission Process and Beyond*, 31 Vt. L. Rev. 381, 386 (2007).

[123] DR-CAFTA, art. 10.17.

[124] *See also* the similar debate in the context of NAFTA discussed by Don Wallace at p. 60 *supra*.

[125] Some of the source notes have been omitted.

[126] SN: K. Subramanian, *The Difficult Road to CAFTA*, Hindu Bus. Line (Aug. 13, 2005), *available at* http://thehindubusinessline.com/2005/08/13/stories/2005081300031000.htm. Subramanian, *supra* note 31.

[127] SN: *Id.*

Like NAFTA, much of the public debate over CAFTA centers on the extent to which CAFTA protects the environment. Proponents of CAFTA say the inclusion of an environmental chapter in the text of the agreement "is in itself a victory."[128] The public submissions mechanism, allowing citizens to "raise specific problems associated with enforcement of environmental laws,"[129] is the first free trade agreement of its kind to incorporate environmental and trade provisions simultaneously in one text.[130] In addition, the Environmental Cooperation Agreement (ECA) gives additional "teeth" to CAFTA by providing for benchmarks to measure environmental performance and outside monitoring of progress in meeting the benchmarks.[131]

Opponents, on the other hand, complain that CAFTA's environmental provisions are "pure rhetoric"[132] and have merely "added a bit of green sweetener to a truly toxic stew."[133] Because CAFTA does not require the adoption or maintenance of any uniform set of environmental laws, Central American signatories will simply maintain their existing "'poor' environmental standards."[134] Moreover, the formal dispute settlement procedure is unavailable to individual citizens, and member governments may only invoke it when there has been a "sustained or recurring course of action or inaction."[135] Countries, critics fear, might also attempt to evade enforcement of environmental laws through a CAFTA provision recognizing countries' need to allocate enforcement resources as they see fit.[136] Finally, environmentalists see a potential loophole in CAFTA's exception for laws whose "primary purpose" is natural resource management.[137] These criticisms, though directed at CAFTA for the moment, may reflect environmentalists' underlying dissatisfaction with NAFTA's environmental performance.

Unlike NAFTA, CAFTA contains its key environmental provisions in the main text of the treaty itself; these provisions are modeled on the NAAEC [North American Agreement on Environmental Cooperation]. First, CAFTA requires each country to "ensure that its laws and

---

[128] SN: Diego Cevallos, *The "Green" Promises of CAFTA*, Tierramerica (Feb. 14, 2005), *available at* http://www.tierramerica.net/2005/0212/iacentos.shtml.

[129] SN: Office of the U.S. Trade Representative, *CAFTA Briefing Book, CAFTA Policy Brief: Environmental Firsts in CAFTA* (Feb., 2005), *available at* http://www.ustr.gov/assets/Trade_Agreements/Bilateral/CAFTA/Briefing_Book/asset_upload_file601_7194.pdf [hereinafter *CAFTA Policy Brief*].

[130] SN: Press Release, Office of the U.S. Trade Representative, U.S., CAFTA-DR Countries Sign Two Supplemental Agreements to Facilitate Implementing the FTA's Environmental Provisions (Feb. 18, 2005), *available at* http://www.ustr.gov/Document_Library/Press_Releases/2005/February/US,_CAFTA-DR_Countries_Sign_Two_Supplemental_Agreements_to_Facilitate_Implementing_the_FTAs_ Environmental_Provisions.html [hereinafter USTR Press Release].

[131] SN: *Id.*

[132] SN: Cevallos, *supra* note 128.

[133] Angel Ibarra, *Environment, in Why We Say No to CAFTA. Analysis of the Official Text* 27 (Raul Moreno ed., Karen Hansen-Kuhn trans., ed., 2004), *available at* http://www.ssc.org/resources/pdf/WhyWeSayNOtoCAFTA.pdf.

[134] SN: Cevallos, *supra* note 128.

[135] SN: Sierra Club & Friends of the Earth, CAFTA's Environmental Provisions: Weak, Unenforceable, and Full of Loopholes (2005) (quoting Article 17.2:1(a) of CAFTA), *available at* http://www.sierraclub.org/trade/cafta/weak_ provisions.pdf.

[136] SN: *Id.*; *see also* CAFTA, art. 17.2 ("[E]ach Party retains the right to exercise discretion with respect to investigatory, prosecutorial, regulatory, and compliance matters and to make decisions regarding the allocation of resources to enforcement with respect to other environmental matters determined to have higher priorities.").

[137] SN: Sierra Club & Friends of the Earth, *supra* note 135 (quoting art. 17.2:13 of CAFTA).

policies provide for and encourage high levels of environmental protection," and demands that each country "strive to continue to improve those laws and policies."[138] CAFTA also establishes an Environmental Affairs Council (EAC) made up of "cabinet-level or equivalent" representatives of each country.[139] CAFTA is similar to the NAAEC in that it offers both a citizen submission and consultation mechanism.[140]

Concerns and criticisms related to environmental and labor standards of DR-CAFTA mirror the grassroots opposition to NAFTA in both the United States and Canada. Nevertheless, DR-CAFTA is now fully in force, and may already be influencing the conduct of both investors and governments in Central America.[141]

8. Multilateral Agreement on Investment[142]

Jessica S. Wiltse, *An Investor-State Dispute Mechanism in the Free Trade Area of the Americas: Lessons from NAFTA Chapter Eleven*, 51 Buffalo L. Rev. 1145, 1172–1196 (2003).

No discussion of investment treaties and investor protections would be complete without at least a brief consideration of the difficulty of negotiating a multilateral treaty that includes investment provisions. A comprehensive multilateral treaty on foreign investment currently does not exist. NAFTA contains a comprehensive investment chapter, but it only covers three countries, while the Trade Related Aspects of Investment Measures (TRIMs) Agreement applies to every member state of the WTO, but it creates only minimal obligations. "One major reason for the difficulty in establishing an international treaty on investments has been the great difficulty in striking a compromise between industrialized nations' [sic] desire for security of their investments and developing nations' desire for flexibility."

In 1995, the Organization for Economic Cooperation and Development began negotiating the Multilateral Agreement in Investment, which would be a comprehensive investment treaty containing an investor-state dispute mechanism among the twenty-nine members, most of which are developed countries. The MAI [Multilateral Agreement on Investment] Negotiating Text revealed that its provisions were essentially identical to NAFTA Chapter 11. Thus, it was susceptible to many of the same criticisms levied at Chapter 11, especially with respect to environmental protection and sovereignty. Yet the MAI was even broader

---

[138] SN: CAFTA, art. 17.1.

[139] SN: CAFTA, art. 17.5.

[140] SN: Compare CAFTA arts. 17.7, 17.10, with NAAEC arts. 14, 22.

[141] In 2007 alone, two claims were filed under the DR-CAFTA, against Guatemala and the Dominican Republic. See *Two Investors Bring CAFTA Claims*, Global Arbitration Review (Mar. 23, 2007), http://www.globalarbitrationreview.com/news/news_item.cfm?item_id=3747; *see also Second DR-CAFTA Arbitration Launched*, Global Arbitration Review (Mar. 30, 2007), *available at* http://www.globalarbitrationreview.com/news/news_item.cfm?item_id=3754.

[142] *See also* G. Kelley, *Multilateral Investment Treaties: A Balanced Approach to Multinational Corporations*, 39 Colum. J. Transnat'l L. 483 (2001) (prize-winning student note, discussing the reasons for the MAI's failure); Rainer Geiger, *Towards a Multilateral Agreement on Investment*, 31 Cornell Int'l L. J. 467 (1998); Wesley Sholz, *International Regulation of Foreign Direct Investment*, 31 Cornell Int'l L. J. 485, 486 (1998).

than Chapter 11. Specifically, it potentially applied to both portfolio investments and foreign direct investment. This would effectively have extended the benefits of the MAI and its investor-state dispute mechanism to investors from non-OECD countries, because non-OECD investors would be able to establish shell corporations in MAI member countries to take advantage of MAI benefits. Essentially, almost any corporation in the world would have legal standing under the MAI, regardless of whether their home country is an MAI Party.

Another significant problem with the MAI had to do with the nature of the negotiating parties. The OECD is dominated by the wealthiest of nations, meaning the MAI focused mostly on the concerns of multinational corporations, rather than the concerns of the developing nations that host investment. Two major problems arose during the MAI negotiations: (1) disputes among the negotiating states, particularly the United States, Canada and the European Union, over exemptions from MAI provisions for cultural industries and preferential trade agreements, and (2) an aggressive campaign against the MAI by an international coalition of NGOs, opposed to the MAI on similar grounds to those given for opposing NAFTA Chapter 11, specifically the environmental and other negative consequences of economic globalization. Ultimately these troubles overwhelmed the negotiations: the MAI was a failure, and in October 1998, the negotiations were abandoned as a result of concerns that the agreement would negatively affect national sovereignty, labor rights and the environment.

E. National Investment Legislation

National investment laws also play a part in the modern system of investment protection. This role was contemplated as early as the 1960s, when the initiators of the ICSID Convention indicated that national investment laws could be one of the sources of consent of state parties to submit their future disputes with foreign investors to arbitration.[143] Indeed, several of the earliest ICSID investment arbitration cases were initiated based on national investment legislation.[144]

Some of these laws contain substantive protections similar to those in bilateral investment treaties and provide for national treatment, or prohibit expropriation without compensation.[145] A number of them contain dispute resolution clauses that allow direct investor-state arbitration similar to the clauses in BITs.[146] Their importance in this sense, however, has diminished as they have been substantially outnumbered by BITs. More information on the dispute resolution provisions of national investment protection laws is provided in Chapter X.

---

[143] *Report of the Executive Directors on the Convention on the Settlement of Investment Disputes between States and Nationals of other States* ¶ 24 (Mar. 18, 1965), *available at* http://www.worldbank.org/icsid/basicdoc/partB-section05.htm#02.

[144] *Southern Pacific Properties v. Arab Republic of Egypt*, ICSID Case No. ARB/84/03 (1992). For a more detailed discussion of this case, *see* Chapter X *infra*.

[145] *See, e.g.*, Article 2 (national treatment) and Article 4 (expropriation) of Albanian Law on Foreign Investment (1993), http://pbosnia.kentlaw.edu/resources/legal/albania/forinv.htm.

[146] *See* Chapter X *infra*.

IV. Commonly Used Procedural Rules

A. Introduction

Although the confidentiality of arbitration outside the International Centre for Settlement of Investment Disputes (ICSID) system makes it difficult to determine the exact distribution of investment arbitration cases among different arbitration institutions and ad hoc proceedings, anecdotal evidence indicates that the ICSID and the United Nations Commission on International Trade Law (UNCITRAL) arbitration rules govern the vast majority of investment arbitration cases.[1]

Some investment treaties, national foreign investment laws, and other forms of written submission to arbitration allow claimants to opt for other arbitration systems.[2] Most international arbitrations today, whether between private commercial parties or between investors and host states, are conducted under the auspices of one of several arbitration "institutions" around the world. These institutions are not arbitration "courts," in the sense that they do not decide the outcome of disputes. Rather, they "administer arbitrations including receiving and distributing pleadings, and perhaps appointing arbiters or reviewing an

---

[1] The 2006 statistics from the United Nations Conference on Trade and Development (UNCTAD) indicate that as of November 2006, the number of known treaty-based cases reached 255. Of this number, 156 cases were filed with ICSID (or the ICSID Additional Facility), 65 under the UNCITRAL rules, 18 with the Stockholm Chamber of Commerce, 4 with the International Chamber of Commerce, and 4 others as ad hoc arbitrations. One case was filed in the Cairo Regional Centre for International Commercial Arbitration, and for seven cases the exact venue was declared unknown at the time of the release of the UNCTAD report. *Latest Developments in Investor-State Dispute Settlement,* IIA Monitor No. 4 (2006), U.N. Doc. UNCTAD/WEB/ITE/IIA/2006/11, at 2, *available at* http://www.unctad.org/.

[2] The U.S.-Haiti bilateral investment treaty (BIT), for instance, provides for International Chamber of Commerce (ICC) arbitration as an option. *See* Treaty Between the United States of America and Republic of Haiti Concerning Reciprocal Protection and Encouragement of Investment, art. VII(3)(a). The Energy Charter Treaty (ECT), as described in Chapter III, allows investors to choose the Stockholm Chamber of Commerce arbitration rules, in deference to the long-standing preference of enterprises from the former Soviet bloc. *See* ECT, art. 26(4)(c).

award for technical accuracy usually in connection with a decision by the parties to use the arbitration rules of the institution."[3] The major institutional arbitration systems are broadly similar in procedural approach, as a result of the process of harmonization that has taken place in recent years through revisions in the rules of the International Chamber of Commerce (ICC), American Arbitration Association (AAA), and China International Economic and Trade Arbitration Commission (CIETAC), among others.[4]

B. ICSID Rules[5]

The ICSID Rules of Procedure for Arbitration Proceedings (Arbitration Rules) set forth procedures for the conduct of an arbitration proceeding under the ICSID Convention, including the constitution of the arbitral tribunal, the presentation by the parties of their case, and the preparation of the arbitral award.[6] The ICSID Arbitration Rules were first adopted by the Administrative Council of ICSID in 1967. "They were amended by [a] decision of the Administrative Council adopted in 1984. The amendments . . . mainly intended to simplify certain provisions and to update others in the light of experience."[7] In 2002 and 2006, for the second and third times, the Arbitration Rules were amended.[8]

The Rules of Procedure for Arbitration Proceedings may be reviewed at http://icsid.worldbank.org.

---

[3] Clifford Larsen, *International Commercial Arbitration*, 2 ASIL Insights (Apr. 1997), *available at* www.asil.org/insights/insight97041.pdf.

[4] *See, e.g.*, Eugene Lenehan, *A Comparison Between ICC Arbitration Rules and UNCITRAL Arbitration Rules* (2005), *available at* http://www.alway-associates.co.uk/legal-update/article.asp?id=72 ("The similarities between the ICC Rules and the UNCITRAL Rules are many and it is suggested that they outweigh the differences.").

[5] *See* Chapter III *supra* for the discussion of the origins of ICSID.

[6] News Release, ICSID, New Amendments of the ICSID Regulations and Rules and Additional Facility Rules, ICSID (Sept. 30, 2002), *available at* http://icsid.worldbank.org/. ICSID also has another set of arbitration rules, called Additional Facility. ICSID Additional Facility Rules authorize the Secretariat of ICSID to administer certain categories of proceedings between States and nationals of other States that fall outside the scope of the ICSID Convention. These are (i) fact-finding proceedings; (ii) conciliation or arbitration proceedings for the settlement of investment disputes between parties one of which is not a Contracting State or a national of a Contracting State; and (iii) conciliation and arbitration proceedings between parties at least one of which is a Contracting State or a national of a Contracting State for the settlement of disputes that do not arise directly out of an investment, provided that the underlying transaction is not an ordinary commercial transaction. Introduction, Additional Facility Rules, *available at* http://www.worldbank.org/icsid/facility/facility.htm.

[7] *Id.*

[8] *Id. See also* Amendment to the ICSID Rules, 23(1) *News from ICSID* 1 (2006).

C. Stockholm Chamber of Commerce Rules

The Arbitration Institute of the Stockholm Chamber of Commerce (SCC) was established in 1917 as a separate entity within the Chamber.[9] During the 1970s, the SCC came to be used frequently in disputes between the Soviets and Western companies and was viewed by Eastern Bloc entities as neutral ground for the resolution of commercial disputes.[10] Following the collapse of the Soviet Union, and by November 2006, more than a dozen investment arbitration cases had been filed at the SCC, all involving respondent states of the Commonwealth of Independent States or the Baltic region.[11] With the increase of arbitration under the Energy Charter Treaty,[12] which provides for SCC arbitration as a dispute resolution option, investment arbitration may become an even larger portion of the SCC docket.

The SCC Rules may be reviewed at http://www.chamber.se/arbitration/english/.[13]

D. International Chamber of Commerce Rules[14]

The International Chamber of Commerce (ICC) International Court of Arbitration, created in 1923, is one of the central activities of the ICC, which was established in 1919. The ICC also acts as an advocate for transnational business interests and initiatives before national governments and international organizations, including the World Trade Organization. The ICC Arbitration Rules were first promulgated in 1923 and have been revised on several occasions since. The most recent amendments, enacted in 1998, were widely hailed as a major improvement in an already often-used and efficient dispute resolution system. The ICC Rules are only infrequently employed in investment disputes, as a small fraction of bilateral investment treaties (BITs) and national investment

---

[9] *See generally* Edwin R. Alley, *International Arbitration: The Alternative of the Stockholm Chamber of Commerce*, 22 Int'l L. 837 (1988).

[10] More information is available at http://www.chamber.se/arbitration/english.

[11] *See* UNCTAD IIA Monitor No. 4 (2006), *supra* note 1.

[12] The first investor-state arbitration award under the ECT was issued under the auspices of SCC on December 16, 2003. *See generally* Jonas Wetterfors, *The First Investor-State Arbitration Award under the 1994 Energy Charter Treaty, Nykomb Synergetics Technology Holding AB, Sweden (Nykomb) v. The Republic of Latvia: A Case Comment*, 2(1) TDM (Jan. 2005).

[13] Other well-known international arbitration institutions such as the London Court of International Arbitration (LCIA) and the AAA have not been discussed, mainly because they have yet to be used in investor-state arbitration.

[14] *See generally* W. L. Craig, W. W. Park, & J. Paulsson, *International Chamber of Commerce Arbitration* (3d ed. 2000); Horatio Grigera Naón, *The Administration of Cases under the 1998 Rules of Arbitration of the International Chamber of Commerce*, Presentation on Oct. 24, 1997 at Biennial IFCAI Conference, *available at* http://arbiter.wipo.int/events/conferences/1997/october/grigeranaon.html.

laws provide an ICC dispute resolution option,[15] and none of the important regional treaties do so.

The ICC Rules may be reviewed at http://www.iccwbo.org/court/english/arbitration/rules.asp.

E. UNCITRAL Arbitration Rules

UNCITRAL is the central legal entity within the United Nations system responsible for activities in the field of international commercial law, particularly the progressive harmonization and unification of the law of international trade.[16] The UNCITRAL Arbitration Rules (UNCITRAL Rules), adopted by the United Nations General Assembly in 1976, are among the most widely used arbitration rules. Arbitration by these Rules is by far the most commonly selected ad hoc arbitral system,[17] whereby arbitration procedures are conducted without supervision by any administrative institution.[18]

The UNCITRAL Rules may be reviewed at http://www.jus.uio.no/lm/un.arbitration.rules.1976/index.html.

The absence of an administering institution may offer some advantage in terms of cost, as the parties incur no direct administrative expenses. However, the fees charged by the arbitrators are rather difficult to predict in UNCITRAL arbitrations, as they

---

[15] *See, e.g.*, Agreement Between Republic of Turkey and the Arab Republic of Egypt Concerning the Reciprocal Promotion and Protection of Investment (1996), art. VII(2)(c); Agreement between the Government of the United Kingdom of Great Britain and Northern Ireland and the Government of Republic of Bolivia (1988), art. 8(2)(a); and U.S.-Haiti BIT (1983), art. VII(3)(a), *supra* note 2.

[16] U.N. G.A. Res. 2205 (XXI), *available at* http://www.uncitral.org/en-index.htm.

[17] For instance, the Iran-U.S. Claims Tribunal adopted UNCITRAL Rules as its rules of procedure. *See* J. J. Van Hof, *Commentary on the UNCITRAL Arbitration Rules: The Application by the Iran-U.S. Claims Tribunal* (Deventer, Kluwer Law & Taxation 1991). UNCITRAL Rules are also frequently used in disputes brought under Chapter 11 of the North American Free Trade Agreement (NAFTA). This is mainly because of the failure of Canada and Mexico to ratify the Washington Convention, which effectively excluded ICSID as a dispute resolution option. In 2006, however, Canada ratified the ICSID Convention. It remains to be seen whether this fact will reduce resort to the UNCITRAL Rules in favor of the ICSID Rules within the NAFTA system. For some of the practical consequences of investment treaty arbitration under the UNCITRAL Rules, *see* R. Doak Bishop & William Russell, *Survey of Arbitration Awards under Chapter 11 of the North American Free Trade Agreement*, 19 J. Int'l Arb. 505–506, 511, 522–24 (2002). Working Group II of UNCITRAL is at work on the revision of rules, including a revision of the rules related to investment disputes. *See* www.uncitral.org.

[18] Ample guidance on the application of the UNCITRAL Rules is nevertheless available. *See, e.g.*, David D. Caron, Lee M. Caplan, & Matti Pellonpää, *The UNCITRAL Arbitration Rules: A Commentary* (Oxford University Press 2006).

must be negotiated directly between the parties and the tribunal—a negotiation in which the parties have relatively little bargaining leverage or incentive to use it.[19]

F. Comparison of the ICSID and UNCITRAL Rules

Given that the overwhelming majority of investment arbitration cases are conducted under either the ICSID or UNCITRAL Rules,[20] a comparison of these two systems follows.[21]

The UNCITRAL Rules were designed to accommodate the widest possible range of disputes. They provide the parties with a great deal of flexibility in crafting a procedure that suits their needs.[22] In the absence of an agreement, arbitrators under the UNCITRAL system are given broad discretion to fashion appropriate procedures.[23] Although such flexibility can be a great boon in the commercial context, where parties incorporate and supplement the Rules in their predispute arbitration agreement, there is arguably less to be gained in the investment arbitration situation, where there is no arbitration agreement, in the traditional sense, and the arbitration is based on the consent of the host government provided in a bilateral or multilateral investment treaty or a law.

A considerable jurisprudence has evolved interpreting and applying the UNCITRAL Rules. This clarifying case authority, relatively uncommon in the usually confidential world of arbitration, is caused both by the broad usage of UNCITRAL procedures in commercial disputes and by their successful adaptation

---

[19] Alan Redfern, Martin Hunter, Nigel Blackaby, & Constantine Partasides, *The Law and Practice of International Commercial Arbitration* 230 (4th ed. 2004); *see also* the discussion at p. 85 *infra*; Pierre Karrer, *Arbitration Saves! Costs: Poker and Hide-and-Seek*, 3(1) J. Int'l Arb. 35, 39 (1986).

[20] *See* note 1 *supra*.

[21] Comparison can also be found in Cedric Chao & James Schurz, *International Arbitration: Selecting the Proper Forum*, 17(2) Mealey's Int'l Arb. Rep. 41 (2002).

[22] UNCITRAL Arbitration Rules, art. 1(1) provides that "[w]here the parties to a contract have agreed in writing that disputes in relation to that contract shall be referred to arbitration under the UNCITRAL Arbitration Rules, then such disputes shall be settled in accordance with these Rules *subject to such modifications as the parties may agree in writing*" [emphasis added].

[23] UNCITRAL Arbitration Rules, art. 15(1) provides that "[s]ubject to these Rules, the arbitral tribunal may conduct the arbitration in such manner as it considers appropriate, provided that the parties are treated with equality and that at any stage of the proceedings each part is given a full opportunity of presenting its case." *See also* UNCITRAL Notes on Organizing Arbitral Proceedings ¶¶ 4 & 16 (1996), *available at* http://www.uncitral.org/english/texts/arbitration/arb-notes.htm.

at the Iran-U.S. Claims Tribunal,[24] which has adjudicated more than a thousand cases since 1981.

However, some practitioners contend that ICSID's procedural provisions are better suited to the particular demands of investor-state disputes. Although in some ways similar to the UNCITRAL Rules, the ICSID rules are specially tailored for arbitration with the participation of a government party. Furthermore, the oversight of the ICSID Secretariat and the availability of the institution's resources and experienced personnel to facilitate the conduct of arbitration is widely viewed as a major asset in investment disputes, which tend to be complex and often involve voluminous submissions and documentation.

Ultimately, the choice of UNCITRAL, ICSID, or some other arbitration system will depend on the specific characteristics of the particular dispute. The following is a review of a number of the significant differences between the rules that may influence the claimant's choice.

1. ICSID Convention Requirements and the ICSID Screening Role

An important factor to consider in making a choice between the ICSID Convention and the UNCITRAL Rules concerns the jurisdictional requirements of the ICSID Convention and the ICSID's screening role. Filing a case under the ICSID Convention entails both satisfying the jurisdictional requirements of the ICSID Convention, such as the requirement that there must be an "investment dispute" (*ratione materiae*),[25] as well as jurisdictional requirements of the relevant investment treaty pursuant to which a claim is filed. Therefore, filing a claim under the ICSID Convention practically requires passing through two layers of jurisdictional requirements. In addition, although the ICSID Secretariat may not thoroughly examine whether the jurisdictional requirements of the respective investment treaty have been complied with, it must determine whether the claim as submitted is not manifestly outside[26] of the jurisdiction of the ICSID. Admittedly, this standard is not difficult to meet, but it still requires some legal work and adds to the aggregate time, complexity, and costs of the proceeding.

Bringing a claim under the UNCITRAL Rules, however, does not require going through such an initial screening process by the arbitral institution that administers the case.

---

[24] *See* Article 3(2) of Declaration of the Government of the Democratic and Popular Republic of Algeria Concerning the Settlement of Claims by the Government of the United States of America and the Government of the Islamic Republic of Iran, 20 I.L.M. 223 (1981).

[25] Washington Convention, art. 25(1).

[26] ICSID Institutional Rules, art. 6(1)(b).

2. Place of Arbitration

Under both the ICSID and UNCITRAL Rules, the parties are free to agree on any arbitral situs. However, the ICSID Rules and Washington Convention provide that where there is no contrary agreement of the parties, arbitration will be held at the World Bank in Washington, D.C.[27] The UNCITRAL Rules, meanwhile, require the arbitral tribunal to determine the place of arbitration if the parties cannot agree.[28]

In addition, when arbitrating under UNCITRAL Rules, the choice of the situs has significant legal consequences.[29] In particular, the law of the place of arbitration will normally form the *lex arbitri* for the proceeding, and the courts at the place of arbitration have supervisory jurisdiction to provide interim relief. Under the ICSID Rules, choice of "situs" does not have as important an effect, as the arbitration is conducted largely in isolation from domestic law. In particular, the courts at the place of arbitration have little role to play, as court-ordered interim measures are prohibited, and challenge of awards is limited to the ICSID annulment structure.[30] As a result, the primary considerations in selecting an arbitral situs are convenience and comparative cost.[31]

3. Language of Arbitration

Under both ICSID and the UNCITRAL rules, the parties are free to jointly designate one or more languages in which the proceedings will be conducted. UNCITRAL provides no default procedural language, leaving full discretion in this matter to the arbitral tribunal in the absence of party agreement.[32] The Tribunal may designate more than one language to be employed in the arbitration. The ICSID Rules, meanwhile, specify that French, English, and Spanish are the official languages and that another language can be selected by the parties only with the approval of the Tribunal.[33] Under the ICSID Arbitration Rules, two languages can be selected, and if no agreement can be reached by the parties, each side may select one of the three official languages, and both languages will be used in the proceeding.[34]

---

[27] *See* ICSID Arbitration Rule 13(3); and Washington Convention, art. 62.

[28] *See* UNCITRAL Rules, art. 16; *see also Ethyl Corp. v. Gov't of Canada* (UNCITRAL Arbitration under Chapter 11 of NAFTA, Award on Place of Arbitration, Nov. 1997), *available at* www.naftaclaims.com.

[29] Noah Rubins, *The Arbitral Seat Is No Fiction*, Mealey's Int'l Arb. Rep., Jan. 2001, at 23; William Park, *The Lex Loci Arbitri and International Commercial Arbitration*, 32 Int'l Comp. L. Q. 21 (1983).

[30] Washington Convention, arts. 26 & 52.

[31] Abbey Cohen Smutny, *Arbitration before International Center for the Settlement of Investment Disputes*, 1(2) Oil, Gas, and Energy Law Intelligence (Mar. 2003), *available at* http://www.gasandoil.com/ogel.

[32] UNCITRAL Rules, art. 17(1).

[33] Arbitration Rule 22(1).

[34] Arbitration Rule 22(2).

4. Appointment of Tribunal

Various techniques have emerged over the decades to select the individuals who will form the arbitral tribunal. Most international arbitration tribunals in disputes of significant size are appointed in the same way: each party names one arbitrator, and the two party-appointed members together agree on a third arbitrator, who serves as the tribunal chairman. Absent contrary agreement of the parties, this is the procedure envisaged by the UNCITRAL Rules.[35] The ICSID Rules and Washington Convention provide that absent contrary agreement, the *parties*, and not the party-appointed arbitrators, are to jointly select the chairman of the tribunal.[36] To do this, one party suggests two names to the other party, who then either accepts one of the candidates or counters with two proposals of its own.[37] If no agreement is reached within 90 days, the ICSID Secretariat will appoint the tribunal chairman.

5. Governing Law

Many investment protection treaties include a provision specifying the substantive legal rules that must be applied by arbitral tribunals constituted pursuant to the treaty. The France-Argentina bilateral investment treaty (BIT), for example, provides:

> The arbitration body shall rule, pursuant to the provisions of this Agreement, according to the law of the contracting Party that is a party to the dispute, including the rules governing conflicts of law, according to the terms of specific agreements, if any, that may have been entered into with regard to the investment, and according to applicable principles of international law.[38]

Although this designation of governing law is likely to be controlling, differences between the UNCITRAL and ICSID arbitration rules in their treatment of the applicable substantive law of the proceeding may influence the arbitral tribunal's decision in this respect.

The ICSID Rules and Washington Convention explicitly define the law applicable to the merits of disputes, using language almost identical to that found in the France-Argentina BIT, reproduced above. In the absence of agreement between the parties, ICSID arbitrators must adjudicate disputes in accordance with the law

---

[35] If the parties fail to appoint arbitrators, or if the party-appointed arbitrators cannot agree on a tribunal chairman, this task falls to the "Appointing Authority," which under the default provisions of the UNCITRAL Rules is an institution chosen by the Permanent Court of Arbitration (PCA) at the Hague (which would not normally itself serve as Appointing Authority). In investment disputes, the PCA frequently designates the ICSID Secretariat as the Appointing Authority. This two-step process, however, can create some delay in the constitution of the arbitral tribunal.

[36] Washington Convention, art. 37(2)(b).

[37] Arbitration Rule 3(1).

[38] Accord Entre le Gouvernement de la Republique Francaise et le Gouvernement de la Republique Argentine sur l'encouragement et la Protection Reciproques des Investissements, art. 8(4) (1993).

of the state party to the dispute (including its rules on conflict of laws) and such rules of international law as may be applicable.[39] Thus, selecting the ICSID Rules increases the likelihood that both the host state's law and international law will play a major part in the arbitrators' deliberations.[40]

Because the UNCITRAL system was designed to resolve commercial disputes, which are normally governed by private contracts containing governing law clauses, it does not provide a great deal of guidance to arbitrators in selecting the applicable law. If the parties have not agreed on the governing law, the Arbitral Tribunal is instructed to "determine the applicable law in applying the conflict of laws rules it deems applicable."[41]

6. Cost and Speed[42]

It is generally accepted that ad hoc arbitration is less expensive than institutional or administered arbitration. Higher administrative costs are a natural consequence of the services provided by the arbitral institution, including facilitation of correspondence, filing and other ministerial work, and the hosting and conduct of oral hearings. Where the amount in dispute is large, however, and where disputes are complex, the difference in administrative cost relative to legal costs and arbitrator fees, although potentially substantial, is not normally a decisive factor.

Furthermore, a number of factors may in effect increase the cost of ad hoc arbitration relative to institutional proceedings. First, ad hoc rules such as the UNCITRAL regime do not provide a schedule of arbitrator's fees.[43] This leaves the parties in the unenviable position of negotiating over payment with arbitrators on whom they will depend for a favorable result. Neither party will likely be anxious to oppose an arbitrator's suggestion as to compensation, or request that those fees be lowered. Second, the lack of a supervisory body such as the ICSID Secretariat may allow recalcitrant parties (particularly sovereign parties) to delay the proceedings at various stages. This is of particular concern in investment arbitration, where there is no specific agreement to arbitrate and where so many details of arbitral procedure will have to be negotiated as issues arise. Such delays will invariably increase the cost of arbitration. Furthermore, ICSID, as a subdivision of the World Bank, may

---

[39] Washington Convention, art. 42.

[40] *See generally* Emmanuel Gaillard & Yas Banifatemi, *The Meaning of "and" in Article 42(1), Second Sentence, of the Washington Convention: The Role of International Law in the ICSID Choice of Law Process*, 18 ICSID Rev.-F.I.L.J. 375, 389–93 (2003).

[41] UNCITRAL Rules, art. 33(1).

[42] *See generally* John Y. Gotanda, *Awarding Costs and Attorney's Fees in International Commercial Arbitrations*, 21 Mich. J. Int'l L. 1 (1999).

[43] Craig et al., *supra* note 14, at 31 ("As for ad hoc proceedings arranged outside an institutional framework, they often turn out to be frighteningly expensive.").

be able to use the World Bank's stature to prevent a recalcitrant country that has received substantial funds through the lending system of the Bank from obstructing the arbitration process.[44]

One additional distinction between the ICSID and UNCITRAL Rules relates to the allocation of costs between the parties after an award is rendered. The ICSID Rules allow arbitrators full discretion to decide whether each side will bear its own costs or if some portion of those costs should be borne by the losing side in the arbitration.[45] The UNCITRAL Rules, meanwhile, assume that the loser in arbitration will normally cover both sides' administrative costs, although not necessarily legal fees.[46] Although the arbitrators have the power to allocate costs as they see fit in the circumstances, allocation of all arbitration costs to the losing party is not uncommon in UNCITRAL arbitration.

7. Interim Measures

A seeming difference between the UNCITRAL Rules and ICSID is the availability of binding interim measures of protection. Although ICSID arbitrators are only authorized to "recommend" preliminary relief,[47] the UNCITRAL Rules provide that a tribunal may "take any interim measures it deems necessary."[48] However, in practice the distinction between *recommendations* and *orders* should not be overstated. In most instances, the provisional orders of ICSID tribunals have been respected by the subject party.[49] Indeed, several decisions suggest that despite the

---

[44] Although the existence of a schedule of fees for arbitrators as well as other factors in institutional arbitration gives it a relative advantage over ad hoc arbitration in determining the costs and providing a speedier process, there have been exceptional cases in which the arbitration process was delayed because the arbitrators were unable to reach an agreement with the parties on a schedule of fees higher than what was provided by the institution, and they subsequently resigned. See *MTD Equity Sdn. Bhd. & MTD Chile S.A. v. Chile*, ICSID Case No. ARB/01/7 (Award of May 25, 2004), ¶¶ 6–12. In this case it took 103 days to constitute a new tribunal. *Id.* ¶ 27.

[45] ICSID Rules, art. 28. In the *SPP* case, for instance, the tribunal held that US$5,093,000 in legal, audit, and arbitration costs be entirely borne by Egypt (the respondent). *SPP v. Egypt*, ICSID Case No. ARB/84/3 (Award of May 20, 1992) 3 ICSID Rep. 189, 248 (1995), also known as the Pyramids Case. But in *Middle East Cement*, the tribunal held that each party was to bear its own legal costs, and to share administrative and arbitrators' fees equally. *Middle East Cement Shipping & Handling Co. v. Arab Republic of Egypt*, ICSID Case No. ARB/99/6 (Award of Apr. 12, 2002), ¶ 176. On cost shifting in investor-state arbitration, *see generally* Noah Rubins, *The Allocation of Costs and Attorney's Fees in Investor-State Arbitration*, 18 ICSID Rev.-F.I.L.J. 109 (2003).

[46] UNCITRAL Rules, art. 40(1)-(2). *See also* Isaak Dore, *The UNCITRAL Framework for Arbitration in Contemporary Perspective* 44 (Graham & Trotman/Martinus Nijhoff 1993).

[47] Washington Convention, art. 47; ICSID Rules, art. 39.

[48] UNCITRAL Rules, art. 26.

[49] *See, e.g., Maritime Int'l Nominees Establishment (MINE) v. Republic of Guinea*, ICSID Case No. ARB/84/4 (Award of Jan. 6, 1988), 4 ICSID Rep. 54 (1997).

difference in wording, ICSID interim recommendations carry full binding force. The tribunal in *Maffezini* reasoned:

> While there is a semantic difference between the word "recommend" as used in Rule 39 and the word "order" as used elsewhere in the Rules to describe the Tribunal's ability to require a party to take a certain action, that difference is more apparent than real. It should be noted that the Spanish text of that Rule uses also the word "dictación." The Tribunal does not believe that the parties to the Convention meant to create a substantial difference in the effect of these two words. *The Tribunal's authority to rule on provisional measures is no less binding than that of a final award.* Accordingly, for the purposes of this Order, the Tribunal deems the word "recommend" to be of equivalent value as the word "order."[50]

Perhaps more important is the potential involvement of national courts themselves granting interim measures. In arbitration conducted pursuant to the UNCITRAL Rules, the parties are free to seek urgent measures of protection from local courts, without affecting their agreement to submit the merits of the dispute to arbitration.[51] Court-ordered interim relief can be extremely important in certain circumstances, as the arbitral tribunal may not yet be constituted and in a position to take a decision on the matter. Moreover, in some jurisdictions mandatory norms of local law can prohibit arbitrators from granting interim measures of protection.[52] Therefore, the exclusion of local court jurisdiction contained in the Washington Convention can prove problematic in cases where urgent interim measures are required at the outset of a proceeding.

8. Challenge of Award and Enforcement

Perhaps the most important procedural distinction between the ICSID and UNCITRAL arbitration rules comes into play after the award has been rendered. UNCITRAL awards are treated as standard international commercial awards for purposes of enforcement under the New York Convention on the Recognition and Enforcement of Foreign Arbitral Awards (the New York Convention).[53] Therefore, an UNCITRAL award is subject to confirmation and

---

[50] *Emilio Augustín Maffezini v. Kingdom of Spain*, ICSID Case No. ARB/97/7 (Proc. Ord. No. 2 of Oct. 28, 1999), 27 Y.B. Comm. Arb. 13, at ¶ 6 (2002). *See also Victor Pey Casado v. Chile*, ICSID Case No. ARB/98/2 (Decision on Interim Measures of Sept. 25, 2001), at ¶ 17 (the question whether orders under Rule 39 can be binding "can be considered closed").

[51] UNCITRAL Rules, art. 26(3) ("A request for interim measures addressed by any party to a judicial authority shall not be deemed incompatible with the agreement to arbitrate, or as a waiver of that agreement"). *See generally* Caron et al., *supra* note 18, at 532–39.

[52] *See id.* at 543–45.

[53] 330 U.N.T.S. 3 (1959). As of March 2008, New York Convention had 142 members. *See* Status, 1958—United Nations Convention on Recognition and Enforcement of Foreign Arbitral Awards, *available at* www.uncitral.org/.

enforcement by local court judgment in more than 140 New York Convention member countries. The New York Convention ensures that national courts will recognize such awards, unless the losing party can demonstrate that the award is tainted by one of seven procedural defects listed in Article V of the New York Convention.

Recourse against an award in relation to the merits of the dispute can be had only at the seat of arbitration, and the law of most developed countries tightly restricts grounds for such challenge. In the United States, for example, an arbitral award can only be vacated on the merits if the challenging party can demonstrate "manifest disregard of law."[54]

The ICSID Rules and Washington Convention establish an arbitration system almost completely divorced from national courts at the enforcement stage. Enforcement is meant to be semiautomatic, as member states are required to recognize and enforce the pecuniary obligations of ICSID awards as if they were local court judgments.[55] This means that execution can be had immediately in any member state's courts without the loser having any opportunity to challenge the merits of the award[56] subject to the immunities that a state may enjoy under the laws of the Contracting Party where the enforcement is sought.[57] Nor can awards be independently appealed or vacated through national courts.[58]

Instead, a party seeking to challenge an ICSID award may institute an "annulment proceeding," which entails the composition of an entirely new, three-member annulment committee. The ICSID grounds for annulment are roughly equivalent to the narrow grounds for nonrecognition provided in the New York Convention.[59] Despite the apparent restriction of grounds for annulment to procedural matters, the first three ICSID awards that were referred to annulment panels were in fact set aside.[60] This raised some concerns in the arbitration community as to the

---

[54] *Wilko v. Swan*, 346 U.S. 427, 436–37 (1953); Noah Rubins, *"Manifest Disregard of the Law" and Vacatur of Arbitral Awards in the United States*, 12 Am. Rev. Int'l Arb. 363 (2001). *See also* Gary B. Born, *International Commercial Arbitration—Commentary and Materials* 797–99 (2d ed. Transnat'l & Kluwer Law Int'l 2001).

[55] Washington Convention, art. 54(1). *See generally Annulment of ICSID Awards* (Gaillard & Banifatemi, eds., Juris 2004). It is, however, unclear to what extent some states feel obliged to enforce ICSID awards. In fact, as of April 2007, the Argentine Republic had refused to enforce three ICSID awards that were rendered against it.

[56] Washington Convention, art. 54(3).

[57] Washington Convention, art. 55.

[58] Washington Convention, art. 53(1).

[59] Washington Convention, art. 52.

[60] *See Holiday Inns S.A. v. Morocco*, ICSID Case No. ARB/72/1; *Klockner v. Cameroon*, ICSID Case No. ARB/81/2; and *Amco v. Indonesia*, ICSID Case No. ARB/81/1.

finality and legitimacy of ICSID awards.[61] A more recent case demonstrates that annulment panels may be becoming more circumspect about award challenges.[62]

9. Multiparty Investment Arbitration—Consolidation[63]

The question of consolidation of investment arbitration has become increasingly important in recent years. As more foreign investors become aware of the rights they may enjoy under the provisions of investment protection treaties and investment laws, certain government measures may inspire large groups of claimant investors to initiate arbitration against a single state, rather than just one or two as was previously common. The case of Argentina is a clear demonstration of this phenomenon. By mid-2006, more than thirty companies had initiated investment treaty arbitration against Argentina.

Within the commercial arbitration context, the issue of multiparty consolidation of related disputes is a hotly disputed issue.[64] The difficulties of multilateral arbitration arise out of the contractual basis of arbitration. Under normal circumstances, only the common will of the contracting parties can give an arbitral tribunal jurisdiction over them and oblige parties to appear before it. Therefore, commentators tend to agree that "[t]he greater the number of such persons, the greater the degree of care which should be taken to ensure that none of them is joined in the proceeding against its will."[65]

Neither the ICSID Rules nor the UNCITRAL Rules explicitly provide for consolidation of related claims brought against a single state by several investors. For the time being the only solution seems to be reappointment of the same tribunal to hear the related cases. This practical solution has been adopted in the past in several cases

---

[61] *See, e.g.*, M. Reisman, *The Breakdown of the Control Mechanism in ICSID Arbitration*, 4 Duke L. J. 739 (1989); Mark Feldman, *The Annulment Proceedings and the Finality of ICSID Arbitral Awards*, 2 ICSID Rev.-F.I.L.J. 85 (1987).

[62] *Wena Hotels Ltd. v. Republic of Egypt*, ICSID Case No. ARB/98/4 (2000). For a more in-depth discussion of this issue *see* Chapter XX *infra*.

[63] For a more detailed discussion of the issues related to consolidation *see* Chapter VIII *infra*.

[64] Emmanuel Gaillard, *L'affaire Sofidif ou les difficultés de l'arbitrage multipartite*, 3 Revue de l'Arbitrage 275 (1987); Dominique T. Hascher, *Consolidation of Arbitration by American Courts: Fostering or Hampering International Commercial Arbitration*, 1(2) J. Int'l Arb. 127 (1984); William M. Barron, *Court-Ordered Consolidation of Arbitration Proceedings in the United States*, 4(1) J. Int'l Arb. 81 (1987); Julie Chiu, *Consolidation of Arbitral Proceeding and International Arbitration*, 7(2) J. Int'l Arb. 53 (1990); Jan van den Berg, *Consolidated Arbitrations and the 1958 New York Arbitration Convention*, 2(4) Arb. Int'l 367 (1986); V. V. Veeder, *Multi-Party Disputes: Consolidation under English Law*, 2(4) Arb. Int'l 310 (1986); V. V. Veeder, *Consolidation: More News from the Front Line*, 3(3) Arb. Int'l 262 (1987); Jacomijn von Haersolte-van Hof, *Consolidation under the English Arbitration Act 1996*, 13(4) Arb. Int'l 427 (1997).

[65] M. Jean-Louis Delvolvé, *Final Report on Multi-Party Arbitrations*, Commission on International Arbitration, Paris, June 1994, ¶ 5.

that were filed against Argentina in the aftermath of the Argentine financial crisis. In March 2004, for instance, the parties to *Sempra Energy International v. Argentina* and *Camuzzi International A.A. v. Argentina* agreed that a single tribunal hears both cases.[66]

NAFTA Chapter 11, however, allows consolidation.[67] So does the U.S. Model BIT of 2004.[68]

---

[66] *See Sempra Energy Int'l v. Argentina*, ICSID case No ARB/02/16 (Decision on Objections to Jurisdiction, May 11, 2005), ¶ 4. *Camuzzi Int'l A.A. v. Argentina*, ICSID Case No ARB/03/2 (Decision on Objection to Jurisdiction, May 11, 2005), ¶ 5. For a discussion of the recent jurisprudence in this respect *see also* OECD, *Improving the System of Investor-State Dispute Settlement: An Overview* 21–26 (Working Papers on International Investment, 2006/1), available at http://www.oecd.org/dataoecd/3/59/36052284.pdf.

[67] *See* NAFTA Chapter 11, art. 1126, ¶ 1: "[a] Tribunal established under this Article shall be established under the UNCITRAL Arbitration Rules and shall conduct its proceedings in accordance with those Rules, except as modified by this Section."

[68] *See* U.S. Model BIT of 2004, art. 33, *available at* http://www.ustr.gov/assets/Trade_Sectors/Investment/Model_BIT/asset_upload_file847_6897.pdf. *See also* U.S.-Chile Free Trade Agreement, art. 10.24 and U.S.-Morocco Free Trade Agreement, art. 10.24, *available at* http://www.ustr.gov/Trade_Agreements/Bilateral/Section_Index.html.

V. Procedural Law Applicable in Investor-State Arbitration

Although the arbitration rules selected by the investor normally provide answers to the most common questions that arise with respect to the proper method of conducting the arbitral proceeding, nevertheless, issues inevitably arise that are not addressed in the applicable arbitration rules. Therefore, an important and often overlooked issue in investment treaty arbitration concerns the determination of the system of law governing procedural aspects of the arbitration. The nationality of the law governing arbitral procedure may well differ from that applicable to the merits of the dispute, which is most often subject to some combination of international law and the law of the host state.[1]

In arbitration pursuant to commercial arbitration rules, the law governing procedure—known as the *lex arbitri*—is normally the law of the legal place of the arbitration, unless the parties agree otherwise. This is not the case in International Centre for Settlement of Investment Disputes (ICSID) arbitration; the ICSID Convention establishes a *self-contained* procedural system, which is normally considered *a-national,* independent of any particular legal situs.

Sections A and B in the following text discuss the different issues of applicable procedural law that may arise in non-ICSID arbitration proceedings. Section C examines the same questions in the context of the ICSID Convention.

---

[1] On the choice of governing substantive law, *see* Chapter IX *infra*.

A. Choice of Procedural Law of Arbitration[2]

Pippa Read, *Delocalization of International Commercial Arbitration: Its Relevance in the New Millennium*, 10 Am. Rev. Int'l Arb. 177, 178–80 (1999)

The procedural law governs the arbitral process. This usually includes such matters as the appointment and dismissal of arbitrators, the composition of the tribunal (the number and qualifications of arbitrators), the conduct of the proceedings (the type of hearing, the rules of evidence, and the level of local court involvement) and ultimately the law governing the validity of awards (the required form of the award, and the grounds for setting aside awards[3]).

It has long been established that the law of procedure in an arbitration need not necessarily be of the same nationality as the substantive "proper law" governing the merits of the dispute. In the English case of *James Miller Ltd. v. Whitworth Street Estates*,[4] the House of Lords found that a Scottish arbitration, which applied English law as the substantive law of the contract, was not bound by English procedural law. In that case, the court upheld the Scottish arbitrator's refusal to submit his award in the form of a "case stated" to the English High Court, which was, at that time, a remedy available to parties under English procedural law. The court found that the arbitration was governed instead by Scottish procedural law, as Scotland was the place of arbitration.

It is also clear that the law of procedure applied to an arbitration need not be that of the place of arbitration. Whilst parties (or arbitrators) may choose to adopt the procedural law of the place of arbitration for the sake of convenience, there is no mandatory requirement to do so. In fact, parties to an arbitration are expressly permitted to choose their own procedural law, [which may] be the procedural law of the situs, or [of] another country, or even a-national rules of procedure which are selected by the parties. This is acknowledged in Article V (1)(d) of the United Nations Convention on the Recognition and Enforcement of Foreign Arbitral Awards ("New York Convention"), which states that recognition and enforcement may be refused where ". . . the arbitral procedure was not in accordance with the agreement of the parties, or, failing such agreement, was not in accordance with the law of the country where the arbitration took place." This ground of refusal indicates that parties are entitled to choose a procedural law other than the law of the situs, and that the law of the place of arbitration is only applied if the parties fail to agree upon an alternative. Such an alternative may be the procedural law of a specified country, or parties may even attempt to exhaustively outline the rules of procedure in their initial agreement or when a dispute arises. To avoid such a labor-intensive exercise,

---

[2] *See also* in this regard Gary Born, *International Commercial Arbitration: Commentary and Materials* 411–16 (2d ed., Transnational & Kluwer Law Int'l 2001).

[3] SN: Note, however, that in some jurisdictions, the view is taken that the law governing the validity of the award is not the procedural law; rather it is [part of] the [substantive] law governing the arbitration agreement. *See, e.g.,* the approach of the Supreme Court of Pakistan taken in *Hitachi Ltd. v Rupali Polyester,* 1998 S.C.M.R. 1618 (June 10, 1998) reported in *Pakistan's Highest Court Rules on Jurisdiction in International Arbitration,* 10(6) World Arb. & Med. Rep. 155 (1999).

[4] SN: *James Miller Ltd. v. Whitworth Street Estates,* [1970] *1 All E.R.* 796 (H.L.).

it is more common for parties to nominate a set of procedural rules for arbitration which have been established by international institutions or arbitration bodies, such as the UNCITRAL [United Nations Commission on International Trade Law] Arbitration Rules or the International Chamber of Commerce ("ICC") Rules of Arbitration. These Rules contain the procedure necessary for an international arbitration, but are not exhaustive. For example, the UNCITRAL Rules include provisions relating to the appointment and replacement of arbitrators, the place and language of the arbitration, the statements to be provided by parties, the making of awards and the distribution of costs. In addition, the UNCITRAL Rules specify in Article 15(1) that in relation to the actual arbitral proceedings, the "arbitral tribunal may conduct the arbitration in such manner as it considers appropriate" subject to the requirement that parties are treated equally and are given full opportunity to present their case. This gives the tribunal the power to determine such issues as the type of hearing and the rules of evidence to be applied. The ICC Rules convey a similar power in Article 15, by allowing the parties, or failing them, the arbitral tribunal, to determine the rules of procedure applicable to the arbitration for matters in which the Rules are silent.

B. Mandatory Procedural Law of the Forum

National laws include mandatory norms, subjecting locally conducted arbitrations, including *international* arbitration, to the procedural and arbitration laws of the forum.[5] In both cases, the applicability of a foreign law to the arbitral proceedings is limited by the mandatory rules of public policy or other statutory restrictions of the forum.[6] The following excerpt explains some of the issues relating to the selection of the law governing the procedure.

> Pippa Read, *Delocalization of International Commercial Arbitration: Its Relevance in the New Millennium*, 10 Am. Rev. Int'l Arb. 177, 180
>
> Whilst parties are free to select an arbitral law of procedure other than the lex loci arbitri, there is some doubt as to whether they may exclude the mandatory procedural law of the forum. Article 1(2) of the UNCITRAL Rules states:
>
>> "These Rules shall govern the arbitration except that where any of these Rules is in conflict with a provision of the law applicable to the arbitration from which the parties cannot derogate, that provision shall prevail."

---

[5] *See, e.g.,* Article 223 of the Organic Law of the Judiciary (Chile), Law 7421 of June 15, 1953 (". . . A de jure arbitrator shall decide in accordance with the law and shall follow the rules established for ordinary judges as to the conduct of the proceedings"). Born, *supra* note 2, at 418 *et seq.* For more examples *see id.* at 417 *et seq.*

[6] *Id.* at 415.

This indicates that the Rules are subject to the mandatory law applicable to the parties, which may include any mandatory procedural law of the forum. It has been argued that this section does not conclusively support the view that lex loci arbitri is binding upon international arbitrations. According to Shindler, there is nothing in the UNCITRAL Rules which indicates how the "applicable law" is to be determined.[7] Arguably, the Rules could have specified that the "law of the place of arbitration from which the parties cannot derogate" would prevail, if that were the result intended. The status of mandatory lex loci arbitri is therefore ambiguous under the UNCITRAL Rules.

. . . .

The specific mandatory provisions of procedural law will obviously differ amongst jurisdictions but the most prevalent mandatory laws of procedure relate to matters of public policy and procedural fairness. It may be against the public policy of the forum to permit specific types of disputes to be arbitrated,[8] or to permit the rendering of awards which breach certain norms, for example an award enforcing a contract which breached national boycott laws.[9] Fundamental standards of procedural fairness, such as arbitrator impartiality and the requirement that both parties have an equal opportunity to present their case, will also be mandatory in most jurisdictions.

Some jurisdictions, however, will have mandatory procedural laws that differ from the universally accepted grounds stated above. In these jurisdictions, parties to an international arbitration can often be caught unaware and risk jeopardizing the enforceability of their award if they fail to comply with these mandatory laws. This was illustrated in the famous arbitral award in *Société Européenne d'Etudes et d'Entreprise v. People's Federal Republic of Yugoslavia* (SEEE).[10] This award was rendered in Switzerland, according to Swiss procedure, but involved an agreement between a French company and the Republic of Yugoslavia. In accordance with the contractual agreement to arbitrate, only two arbitrators were appointed. This was unfortunately contrary to the procedural law of Vaud (the Swiss canton that was the site of the arbitration), which required arbitral tribunals to be composed of an odd number of arbitrators. Accordingly, the Vaud Cantonal Tribunal refused to enforce the award, as it did not comply with the applicable procedural law. This award led to a plethora of litigation in multiple jurisdictions . . . yet it provides a simple example of where parties to an international arbitration were prevented from obtaining an enforceable award by virtue of unforeseen, mandatory procedural law of the forum.

---

[7] SN: A. Shindler, *Arbitration Still Bound*, 102 L. Q. Rev. 500, 502 (1986).

[8] SN: *See, e.g.,* William W. Park, *The Lex Loci Arbitri and International Commercial Arbitration*, 32 I.C.L.Q. 21, 23 (1983), who gives the examples of disputes involving sensitive public interests such as securities [regulations] or contracts with state agencies. Alternatively, it may be argued that these matters are issues going to the validity of the arbitration agreement itself and would therefore not be dealt with by the procedural law of the arbitration.

[9] SN: This was a ground of challenge raised in the French decision concerning the award [in] . . . *Gotaverken Arendal AB [v.] . . . the Libyan General National Maritime Transport Co.*. In that case, a French award rendered against the Libyan Maritime Transport Company in favor of a Swedish shipyard (Gotaverken) was challenged on the ground that it breached French boycott laws against Libya. This challenge was unsuccessful in the French Court of Appeals. *See* Jan Paulsson, *Arbitration Unbound: An Award Detached from the Law of the Country of Origin*, 30 I.C.L.Q. 358 (1981), and further discussion in the following text.

[10] SN: *24 I.L.R. 761, 767 (1957)* (Trib. Canton. Vaud. Feb. 12, 1957) *reprinted in* 1958 R.C.D.I.P. 358 (French Text) *as discussed in* Jan Paulsson, *The Extent of Independence of International Arbitration from the Law of the Situs*, in *Contemporary Problems in International Arbitration* 141 (Julien D. M. Lew ed., 1987).

While lex arbitri is in most cases a background issue, in many proceedings the lex arbitri can resolve decisive procedural issues, such as consolidation, discovery, or interim relief. As with so many aspects of investment arbitration law, the precise contours of the importance of lex arbitri are still evolving.

C. Procedural Law Applicable Under the International Centre for Settlement of Investment Disputes Convention

As noted earlier, the ICSID Convention imposes a self-contained system of procedural rules for conducting arbitration proceedings. Some rules are contained in the ICSID Convention itself.[11] Most of them are found in the ICSID Arbitration Rules.[12] The ICSID Institution Rules also contain some rules of procedure.[13]

Article 44

Any arbitration proceeding shall be conducted in accordance with the provisions of this Section and, except as the parties otherwise agree, in accordance with the Arbitration Rules in effect on the date on which the parties consented to arbitration. If any question of procedure arises which is not covered by this Section or the Arbitration Rules or any rules agreed by the parties, the Tribunal shall decide the question.

C. H. Schreuer, *The ICSID Convention: A Commentary* 666–7 (Cambridge University Press 2001) [Commentary on Article 44]

1. The Convention itself contains a number of provisions of procedure. Art. 44 is a residual rule directing a tribunal and the Convention. The parties are free to exclude or adapt these Rules subject to certain limits . . . The tribunal is authorized to fill any remaining gaps.

2. In the Convention's drafting, the text of what eventually became Art. 44 underwent only few changes and was largely uncontested (History Vol. I, pp. 198–200) . . . The only major point of debate was to what extent procedural questions should be regulated in the Convention itself rather in the Arbitration Rules. . . .

3. Art. 44 is the procedural counterpart to the choice of law provisions of Art. 42(1). Art. 42(1) only applies to substantive questions but not to the procedure before an ICSID tribunal (see Art. 42, para. 3). Whereas Art. 42(1) contains reference to the law of the State party to the dispute, Art. 44 creates a comprehensive and self-contained system that is insulated from national rules of procedure. In particular, the place of proceedings has no

---

[11] *See, e.g.,* ICSID Convention, articles 44, 48–51, 57, 60–63.

[12] Rules of Procedure for Arbitration Proceedings, *available at* http://icsid.worldbank.org/.

[13] Rules of Procedure for the Institution of Arbitration and Conciliation Proceedings, *available at* http://icsid.worldbank.org/.

influence on procedure before an ICSID tribunal[14] . . . if the place is in a Contracting State to the ICSID Convention (see Art. 62 . . .). But points of contact with the procedure under national law arise in the context of provisional measures by domestic courts[15] under Arbitration Rule 39(5) (see Art. 26 . . .) and in the context of recognition and enforcement under Art. 54.[16]

4. A violation of the procedural provisions of the Convention and of the Arbitration Rules may expose an award to annulment. Art. 52(1)(d) states that annulment may be requested on the ground that there has been a serious departure from a fundamental rule of procedure. But not every violation of a rule of procedure would automatically lead to nullity. The violation must be serious and the rule thus violated must be fundamental. In the course of the Convention's drafting, Mr. *Broches* pointed out that fundamental rules of procedure might have a wider connotation than the concrete rules adopted by ICSID's Administrative Council. They could comprise principles of natural justice, e.g., that both parties must be heard and that there must be adequate opportunity for rebuttal (History, Vol. II, p. 480) (see also paras. 21, 22 *infra*).

Article 44, therefore, gives the parties the necessary latitude to choose the procedural rules of their choice to govern the arbitration proceedings.[17] In the event that the parties do not specify their choice, an ICSID tribunal may use the discretion granted to it in Article 44 to conduct the proceedings as it sees fit.[18]

---

[14] SN: E. Lauterpacht, *The World Bank Convention on the Settlement of International Investment Disputes*, in Recueil de droit international en hommage a Paul Guggenheim 642, 650/1 (1968); G. R. Delaume, *Le Centre International pour le règlement des Différends relatifs aux Investissements* (CIRDI), 109 J. du Droit Int'l 775, 809/10 (1982); S. J. Toope, *Mixed International Arbitration: Studies in Arbitration Between States and Private Persons* 234/5 (1990). For a comparison of non-ICSID arbitration *see* K. Lipstein, *International Arbitration between Individuals and Governments and the Conflict of Laws*, in Contemporary Problems of International Law: Essays in Honour of Georg Schwarzenberger 177, 189–93 (1988).

[15] *See* Chapter VII *infra* for a discussion of provisional measures.

[16] *See* Chapter XXI *infra* for a discussion of recognition and enforcement of awards.

[17] In *Gruslin v. Malaysia*, ICSID Case No. ARB/99/3 (Award of Nov. 27, 2000), 5 ICSID Rep. 483, 486, for instance, the parties agreed that proceedings should be conducted in accordance with the Arbitration Rules in effect from Sept. 26, 1984. "They also agreed that within the ambit of the Arbitration Rules the Tribunal could make directions appropriate to ensure efficiency, economy and fairness to the parties, including directions to ensure that the case proceeded as quickly as possible to a final result." *Id.*

[18] In *Santa Elena v. Costa Rica*, the tribunal stated: "In the absence of any agreed request by the parties to the Tribunal to vary the rules of procedure laid down in the Convention and the ICSID Rules of Procedure for Arbitration Proceedings, in effect from 26 September 1984 (hereinafter, the "Arbitration Rules"), the Tribunal has followed the discretion given in Article 44 of the Convention to the effect that the proceedings shall be conducted in accordance with Section 3 of Chapter IV of the ICSID Convention and the Arbitration Rules." *Compañia del Desarrollo de Santa Elena S.A. v. Republic of Costa Rica*, ICSID Case No. ARB/96/1 (Award of Feb. 17, 2000), 5 ICSID Rep. 153, 158. *See also Aguas Argentinas, S.A., Suez, Sociedad General de Aguas de Barcelona, S.A. & Vivendi Universal, S.A. v. Argentina*, ICSID Case No. ARB/03/19 (Order on *Amicus Curiae* Petition, May 19, 2005), at 10 (applying Article 44 to establish the Tribunal's power to entertain *amicus curiae* petitions).

> C. H. Schreuer, *The ICSID Convention: A Commentary* 678 (Cambridge University Press 2001) [Commentary on Article 44]
>
> 34. The Arbitration Rules give detailed guidance to the tribunal and the parties leaving few gaps to be filled by the tribunal in accordance with the last sentence of Art. 44. They address the various stages of the proceedings such as the establishment of the tribunal, the written and oral procedure, the award as well as the post-award remedies of interpretation, revision and annulment. Particular procedures such as provisional measures, ancillary claims, jurisdictional objections, default as well as settlement and discontinuance are addressed separately. In addition, the Rules provide general guidance on the working of the tribunal and regulate such matters as languages, documentation, time limits and costs.
>
> 35. The Arbitration Rules are designed to reflect the best features of common law and civil law approaches. This is evident, in particular, in the balance between the written and oral parts of the proceedings and in the rules on the taking of evidence.

This contemplates that the parties will rely on the text of the Convention and the Arbitration Rules to conduct their arbitration proceedings. Yet, it leaves some room for the parties' autonomy to tailor the arbitration proceedings according to their needs. This possibility was referred to in the Report of the Executive Directors of the World Bank on the ICSID Convention:[19]

> In keeping with the consensual character of proceedings under the Convention, the parties to conciliation or arbitration proceedings may agree on the rules of procedure which will apply in those proceedings. However, if or to the extent that they have not so agreed the Conciliation Rules and Arbitration Rules adopted by the Administrative Council will apply (Articles 33 and 44).

It should be noted that although the ICSID Arbitration Rules may be modified by the parties, the Institution Rules and the Center's Administrative and Financial Regulations are not generally subject to modification unless the relevant rules themselves provide for such a possibility.[20] The parties' choice is further limited by "fundamental rules of procedure," the violation of which may be ground for annulment according to Article 52(1)(d) of the ICSID Convention. It is not clear which rules fall within this category. The annulment committee in *MINE v. Guinea* gave the following example:

> The Committee considers that a clear example of such a fundamental rule is to be found in Article 18 of the UNCITRAL Model Law on International Commercial Arbitration which provides: "The parties shall be treated with equality and each party shall be given full opportunity of presenting his case."

---

[19] International Bank for Reconstruction and Development, *Report of the Executive Directors on the Convention on Settlement of Disputes among States and Nationals of other States* (Mar. 18, 1965), *available at* http://icsid.worldbank.org/.

[20] Schreuer, *supra* p. 95, at 669–70.

> The term "fundamental rule of procedure" is not to be understood as necessarily including all of the Arbitration Rules adopted by the Centre.[21]

Apart from certain established principles referred to in *MINE v. Guinea*, it is difficult to identify fundamental procedural rules and distinguish them from those rules that are not fundamental. Some ICSID tribunals, however, have taken a more lenient approach toward certain procedural issues. In *Bayindir v. Pakistan*, for example, the tribuanl refused to dismiss the case on the grounds that the claimant had failed to give a formal notice of dispute under the applicable BIT.[22]

There is also a similar tendency in the practice of other international tribunals to avoid taking an overly formalistic approach toward procedural requirements. The International Court of Justice, for example, has not allowed a mere procedural defect to hamper its proceedings when the alleged deficiency could have been cured by the party.[23]

Similarly, the tribunal in *Lauder v. Czech Republic* stated with respect to the respondent's allegation that the claimant had not observed the required waiting periods under the bilateral investment treaty between the United States and the Czech Republic:

> To insist that the arbitration proceedings cannot be commenced until 6 months after the 19 August 1999 Notice of Arbitration would, in the circumstances of this case, amount to an unnecessary, overly formalistic approach which would not serve to protect any legitimate interests of the parties.[24]

---

[21] *MINE v. Guinea*, ICSID Case No. ARB/84/4 (Decision on Annulment of 1984), 4 ICSID Reports 87 *cited in* Schreuer, *supra* p. 95, at 673.

[22] *Bayindir Insaat Turizm Tecaret ve Sanayi v. Pakistan*, ICSID Case No. ARB/03/29 (Decision on Jurisdiction of 2005), ¶¶ 98–99 and 103. *See also Salini v. Morocco*, ICSID Case No. ARB/00/4 (Decision on Jurisdiction of 2001), ¶ 20.

[23] *See, e.g., Military and Paramilitary Activities in and Against Nicaragua (Nicaragua v. U.S.)* (Judgment on Jurisdiction and Admissibility), 1984 ICJ Rep. 428–29 (in response to the contention that Nicaragua had not expressly invoked the treaty in dispute, the International Court of Justice (ICJ) concluded: "In the view of the Court, it does not necessarily follow that, because a State has not expressly referred in negotiations with another State to a particular treaty as having been violated by conduct of that other State, it is debarred from invoking a compromissory clause in that treaty. The United States was well aware that Nicaragua alleged that its conduct was a breach of international obligations before the present case was instituted; and it is now aware that specific articles of the 1956 Treaty are alleged to have been violated. It would make no sense to require Nicaragua now to institute fresh proceedings based on the Treaty, which it would be fully entitled to do." *Id.* at 428–29.

[24] *Ronald Lauder v. Czech Republic* (UNCITRAL Arbitration, Final Award, Sept. 3, 2001), ¶ 190. *See also Consorzio Groupement L.E.S.I-DIPENTA v. Algeria*, ICSID Case No. ARB/03/8 (Award of Jan. 10, 2005), ¶ 32 ("La règle doit être interprétée dans ce contexte, ce qui exclut qu'on en fasse une lecture exagérément formaliste.").

In the same vein, the NAFTA tribunal in *Ethyl v. Canada,* with respect to the prearbitral negotiation requirements of Article 1118 of NAFTA said that "no purpose would be served by any further suspension of Claimant's right to proceed."[25]

It follows that although some rules of procedure such as those related to equality of the parties may not be ignored, others may under certain circumstances be dispensed with. The main criteria in this context seem to be that the other party to the dispute would not suffer any prejudice and that the observance of the rule would not materially affect the outcome of the case.

---

[25] *Ethyl Corp. v. Canada* (Decision on Jurisdiction, June 24, 1998), 38 I.L.M. 708, ¶ 84 (1999). See also *CMS v. Argentina,* ICSID Case No. ARB/01/8 (Decision on Jurisdiction, July 17, 2003), 42 I.L.M. 788, 806–7 (2003); *Wena v. Egypt,* ICSID Case No. ARB/98/4 (Decision on Jurisdiction, May 25, 1999), 41 I.L.M. 881, 891 (2002).

VI. National Court Interference: Anti-Arbitration Injunctions

A. Introduction

Historically, the relationship between arbitration and national courts has been complex and at times conflictual. On the one hand, parties normally select arbitration—and in particular international arbitration—for the resolution of their disputes precisely to reduce or eliminate the role of national courts. On the international level, this is largely because of the mistrust that each side feels toward the municipal law and judges of the other side as well as to avoid giving the other side a *home court advantage* in the dispute resolution process. On the other hand, governments for many years expressed a certain deep-seated mistrust of the adjudication of disputes on a purely private footing, because dispute resolution was traditionally viewed as the proper bailiwick of the state, and not for private parties to resolve as they will.

At the end of the day, national courts are an essential component of successful international arbitration. Arbitrators, as private persons, lack the coercive police power of the state, which is reserved to government. At various stages[1] in the arbitration process, effective adjudication may therefore become difficult to achieve without implementation or the threat of implementation by a national court. International conventions are of some assistance in this regard, as the New York Convention and Washington Convention attempt to ensure court enforcement of arbitration agreements and final awards in most countries around the world.[2]

Increasingly over the last half century, most parts of the world have realized that excessive intervention by state courts can deprive arbitration of its usefulness. Court interference slows the process, makes it more expensive, and can tilt the playing field if a party turns to its own national courts for support in an arbitrable dispute.

---

[1] *See* Chapter VII for an overview of the different stages of an arbitration proceeding.

[2] New York Convention, art. V; Washington Convention, art. 53–55.

This problem is more acute in investor-state arbitration, where the respondent-state may be able to influence or control its judicial system.

Perhaps the most notorious example of excessive state interference in the arbitral process occurred in 1999 in the *Himpurna*[3] case, a contractual arbitration conducted under the United Nations Commission on International Trade Law (UNCITRAL) Rules, in which Indonesia appeared as a respondent. In *Himpurna,* the contract called for arbitration in Jakarta, with Indonesian law applicable to both substance and procedure. Shortly after the case began, Indonesia sought and obtained an injunction from the Jakarta District Court against all participants in the arbitration, including the arbitrators, ordering them to cease all arbitration-related activities. Failure to comply would result in a fine of US$1 million per day. The tribunal, composed of French national Jan Paulsson, Australian Antonio Albert de Fina, and Indonesian Professor Priyatna Abdurrasyid, decided to move the hearings to The Hague, in the Netherlands.[4] But Indonesia's campaign to prevent the rendering of an award against it was not yet over, as the arbitrators learned on arriving for deliberations in The Hague. Well-known arbitration practitioner Albert Jan van den Berg was a witness to what happened next and provided a detailed account:

> I became involved in this case when, on Friday afternoon, 18 September 1999, my partner Jan Paulsson in the Paris office called me in his capacity of President of the Arbitral Tribunal . . . . He asked me to be present in summary court proceedings [in the Netherlands] that had been instituted earlier that day by the Republic of Indonesia against the claimants and all three arbitrators in that case with the purpose of enjoining the holding of a hearing determined by the arbitral tribunal to take place in the Peace Palace . . . . Mr. Paulsson informed me that he could not reach the two other arbitrators as they were travelling to The Hague.
>
> . . . .
>
> After the court hearing was over, on Monday evening, 20 September 1999, Mr. Paulsson told me by telephone he had been able to reach Mr. de Fina but that the Carlton Ambassador Hotel at The Hague had advised that the reservation for Professor Priyatna had been cancelled. On Tuesday morning, 21 September 1999, I received a telephone call at about 09.10 a.m. from The Hague District Court, informing me that all injunctions sought by the Republic of Indonesia had been rejected. I relayed this information to Mr. Paulsson in Paris. He then asked me to pick up Mr. de Fina at Schiphol Airport in order to apprise him of the outcome of the Dutch Court proceedings.
>
> Accompanied by my driver, . . . I picked Mr. de Fina up [sic] at the airport at approximately 14.00 hours. We brought Mr. de Fina to The Hague. During the trip, I informed Mr. de Fina of the court proceedings.

---

[3] *Himpurna California Energy Ltd. (Bermuda) v. Republic of Indonesia* (UNCITRAL Interim Award of Sept. 26, 1999, and Final Award of Oct. 16, 1999), 25 Y.B.. Comm. Arb. 11, 157 (2000) [hereinafter Himpurna Interim Award].

[4] The legal seat of the arbitration was not altered and remained Jakarta, Indonesia in accordance with the parties' agreement.

During the same trip, Mr. de Fina told me that he had tried to contact Professor Priyatna at the Carlton Ambassador Hotel at The Hague on Monday, 20 September 1999, but was advised by the hotel that another gentleman had cancelled the reservation of Professor Priyatna and that a message was left for him at the hotel in which it was said that Professor Priyatna would not come.

We arrived at the Carlton Ambassador Hotel at approximately 15.15 hours. Mr. de Fina wanted to know what had actually happened with the cancellation of Professor Priyatna's reservation and wanted also to have more information about the messages. Both of us then spoke with . . . the front office manager, and thereafter with . . . a trainee who had both received the telephone calls and messages. [They] told us two telephone calls had been received with respect to Professor Priyatna, one in the morning between 11.45 and 12.15 hours, which she had taken, and one in the afternoon at around 14.30 hours. . . . [T]he person who had called . . . was Mr. R[ossidi] M. "Hosen" (her phonetic spelling for "Husein") from the Embassy of the Republic of Indonesia. . . . Mr. Husein said . . . that he wanted to leave a message for Mr. de Fina and Mr. Paulsson that "Mr. Priyatna cannot come to the hotel to meet you" and that he cancelled the reservation . . . . Mr. Husein called at 14.30 hours [to say] that "Mr. Abdurrasyid" would not come to the hotel and that his reservation could be cancelled . . . . Mr. Husein asked [the clerk] to give a message to Mr. de Fina and Mr. Paulsson that "Mr. Abdurrasyid does not come. . . ."

Thereupon, Mr. de Fina and I went to the Embassy of the Republic of Indonesia . . . at The Hague. . . . I asked the guard to see Mr. Husein. The guard answered that he had gone to Schiphol Airport. I then asked whether he knew where Professor Priyatna was. The guard answered that he did not know of Professor Priyatna. I said that I had an urgent message for Mr. Husein and would like to have his mobile telephone number. The guard wrote down for me the mobile telephone number of Mr. Husein. . . .

Back in the car, I tried to call Mr. Husein on my mobile but there was no answer. Two minutes later I received a call from Mr. Husein who wanted to know who had called and why. . . . I asked Mr. Husein whether Professor Priyatna was with him since I wanted to give him documents. Mr. Husein answered that Professor Priyatna was not with him. I asked him then whether he knew where he was. Mr. Husein answered that he did not know but that he would call me if he knew where he was. I then asked him whether he was in the airport. He answered that he was bringing other people to the airport. . . . I asked Mr. Husein whether he knew where Professor Priyatna had gone. Mr. Husein answered that he did not know. Mr. Husein repeatedly said to me that when he would know where Professor Priyatna was, he could call me back[;] and, upon his request, I gave him my mobile number. After this telephone conversation, I obtained information by phone through the airlines booking system that Professor Priyatna was booked on a flight from Amsterdam to Jakarta the same evening. . . . Mr. de Fina and I then proceeded to Schiphol Airport, where we arrived at 17.15 hours. Together with my driver . . . , we waited at the KLM check in counter in the departure hall. At around 17.50 hours we noticed two people of possible Indonesian nationality, but not Professor Priyatna. We followed them from the check in counter and saw them going to a group of approximately 8 Indonesian looking persons, one of whom was Professor Priyatna. Professor Priyatna immediately shook hands with Mr. de Fina and myself and both went some 10 meters aside for a conversation. In the meantime, I shook hands with the Indonesian looking persons, one of whom introduced himself as Mr. Husein with whom I had the aforementioned telephone conversation. A number [of] persons of the group thereafter spread out through the departure hall, watching us closely. My driver took position in the middle.

After having been with what was left of the group of Indonesian looking persons, I walked over to Professor Priyatna and Mr. de Fina. . . . I informed Professor Priyatna that the injunctions sought by the Republic of Indonesia had been rejected by the District Court.

When I told him that these injunctions meant that the Dutch Court does not prevent him from attending the hearing on 22 September in the Peace Palace, Professor Priyatna said that a person had travelled from Jakarta to Washington to read him a letter that the person said was from a [m]inister, asking him not to take part in the arbitration, and that he felt obliged to return to Jakarta. . . . Professor Priyatna also said that he considered Mr. de Fina and Mr. Paulsson as his friends and did not want to lose friendship but that he could not continue the case. . . . During the conversation, which lasted approximately 10 minutes, Professor Priyatna appeared to be quite shaken and at certain moments I noticed that he was on the verge of crying.

After this conversation, Professor Priyatna rejoined the group of Indonesian looking persons[;] and when my driver left his position to follow us, the other persons of apparent Indonesian origin also rejoined the group.[5]

Although the apparent kidnapping of Professor Priyatna is shocking and extreme, the intervention of the Indonesian courts in the *Himpurna* case was hardly unprecedented or even unexpected. As one commentator explains, the extent of national court intervention in international commercial arbitration is to a large degree a function of the law on arbitration at the arbitral seat.

Pippa Read, *Delocalization of International Commercial Arbitration: Its Relevance in the New Millennium,* 10 Am. Rev. Int'l Arb. 177, 179–84 (1999)

One of the more controversial aspects of mandatory procedural law concerns the extent to which the local court system is permitted to intervene . . . in the arbitration. Court assistance is unquestionably a necessary element of the arbitration system, yet national procedural laws, which permit local courts to unduly intervene in the arbitral process often provide unwilling (or losing) parties with the power to frustrate the arbitration, or delay the enforcement of the award.

Court intervention can occur in a number of different ways at various stages throughout the arbitration.[6] The court can exercise its power to enforce the contractual promises in the arbitration agreement firstly by staying any local court proceedings in favor of the arbitration, and secondly, by enforcing awards. In addition, many jurisdictions permit a local court to constitute or reconstitute the arbitral tribunal in certain circumstances (e.g., the death of an arbitrator), to prevent the reference from becoming abortive.[7] The court can also assist by providing remedies that are outside the scope of the arbitrator's jurisdiction. Whilst arbitrators have extensive powers over parties to an arbitration, they do not have jurisdiction over third parties. Therefore, local court assistance is necessary when, for instance, property in the hands of third parties needs to be preserved, or

---

[5] Himpurna Interim Award, *supra* note 3, and Final Award of Oct. 16, 1999, 25 Y.B.. Comm. Arb. 11, 157 (2000). On the *Himpurna* and *Patuha* arbitrations against Indonesia, *see generally* Peter Cornell & Arwen Handley, *Himpurna and Hub: International Arbitration in Developing Countries,* 15 Mealey's Int'l Arb. Rep., Sept. 2000 at 39.

[6] SN: *See* S. C. Boyd, *The Role of National Law and the National Courts in England,* in *Contemporary Problems in International Arbitration* 149 (Julian D. M. Lew ed., 1987).

[7] SN: *Id.* at 150.

witnesses and ... evidence held by third parties need to be examined. These procedures actively assist the arbitration process but many jurisdictions also permit the court to implement a variety of "corrective" or "supervisory" remedies[8] whereby the court can supervise the arbitral process and "correct" any procedural abuses. This includes the broad power to set aside the final award as well as the power to remove an arbitrator, to correct substantive errors of law in the award itself or even to bring the arbitration to an end by injunction. In jurisdictions where these powers exist, a party could theoretically appeal to the court ... and thereby delay the arbitration or frustrate it entirely, in substance reducing the arbitral process to simply a preliminary level in the ... court system. ...

Unforeseen mandatory procedural laws peculiar to the place of arbitration and procedural laws which permit a high level of local court involvement both pose difficulties for parties to an international arbitration. Such difficulties have raised the theoretical question, "Should international arbitration be subject to the mandatory procedural law of the forum?" Those commentators in favor of removing the harness of the mandatory lex loci arbitri have argued strongly for the "delocalization" of arbitration.[9] Other commentators, who support the territorial theory of arbitration, contend that this theory is impractical and contrary to the fundamental principles of the legal system as we know it.[10]

B. Anti-Arbitration Injunctions[11]

The most extreme form of national court intervention in arbitral proceedings is an anti-arbitration injunction, such as the one issued by the Jakarta court in *Himpurna*. In principle, the New York Convention requires courts in member states to refrain from adjudicating the merits of disputes subject to a valid agreement to arbitrate.[12] In practice, however, courts in certain countries have sought to enjoin arbitral proceedings despite the restrictions of the New York Convention, relying on exceptions to the general rule such as public policy or the invalidity of the underlying agreement between the parties. In recent years courts in developed countries have been reluctant to order the stay of arbitration where there is evidence of a valid arbitration agreement covering the

---

[8] SN: *Id.*

[9] SN. *See, e.g.*, Jan Paulsson, *Arbitration Unbound: Award Detached from the Law of its Country of Origin*, 30 Int'l Comp. L. Q. 358 (1981).

[10] *See, e.g.*, William W. Park, *The Lex Loci Arbitri and International Commercial Arbitration*, 32 Int'l & Comp. L.Q. 21 (1983) (Park, however, concludes that the lex loci arbitri "should be limited to ensuring respect for traditional standards of fairness, the limits of the arbitral mission and the rights of third parties").

[11] *See generally Anti-Suit Injunctions in International Arbitration* (Gaillard ed., Juris Publishing & Staempfli Publishers 2005).

[12] New York Convention, art. II(3); Julian D. M. Lew, *Anti-Suit Injunctions Issued by National Courts to Prevent Arbitration Proceedings*, in *Anti-Suit Injunctions in International Arbitration* 25, 31–32 (Gaillard ed., 2005).

dispute.[13] Indeed, in some countries the public policy favoring arbitration routinely leads local courts to stay judicial proceedings in favor of arbitration.[14] However, particularly in politically charged cases such as those involving the participation of the government or state-owned entities of the country where the reviewing court is located, arguments that objections to arbitrability and

---

[13] *See, e.g., Compania Minera Condesa SA and Compania de Minas Buenaventura SA v. BRGM-Pérou S.A.S.*, Bundesgericht [BGer][Fed. Ct.] Dec. 19, 1997, 124, Entscheidungen des Schweizerischen Bundesgerichts [BGE] III 84 (Switz.), where the Federal Court held that arbitral proceedings in Switzerland must be stayed when court proceedings in the same matter have been commenced before a foreign court prior to the commencement of arbitration proceedings. However, arbitration may proceed when the judgment of a foreign court is not legally enforceable. A foreign judgment that ignores an arbitration agreement that is valid under the New York Convention falls within this category and is not enforceable in Switzerland. In *Fomento v. CCT.*, Bundesgericht [BGer][Fed. Ct.] May 14, 2001, 127, Entscheidungen des Schweizerischen Bundesgerichts [BGE] III 279 (Switz.), however, the Swiss Federal Court granted an injunction ordering the stay of arbitration, because it appeared that the parties had altered the original arbitration agreement and instead agreed on court proceedings in Panama. After Fomento initiated court proceedings in Panama, CCT filed for arbitration in Switzerland, and Fomento objected successfully, because it could demonstrate that the judgment being rendered by the Panamanian court could be enforced in Switzerland.

The fundamental and general rule deriving from these judgments, that anti-arbitration injunctions are incompatible with Swiss law, was recently affirmed in *Air (PTY) Ltd. v. Int'l Air Transport Assoc. (IATA) & CSA in liquidation,* Case No. C/1043/2005–15SP (Republic and Canton of Geneva Judiciary, Court of First Instance, May 2, 2005). *See also* Julian D. M. Lew, *Control of Jurisdiction by Injunctions Issued by National Courts,* Report presented at ICCA Montreal 2006–International Arbitration 2006: Back to Basics?, June 1, 2006, http://www.iccamontrea l2006.org/english/pdf/program/presentations/JulianDMLew.pdf; Matthias Scherer & Teresa Giovannini, *Anti-Arbitration and Anti-Suit Injunctions in International Arbitration: Some Remarks Following a Recent Judgment of The Geneva Court,* 3 Stockholm Int'l Arb. Rev. 201 (2005).

[14] In the United States, for example, Section 206 of Federal Arbitration Act (FAA), which implements Article II of New York Convention of 1958 on Recognition and Enforcement of Foreign Arbitral Awards, provides a basis for the courts to direct the parties to a valid arbitration agreement to submit their case for resolution through international arbitration. Section 206 provides that "A court having jurisdiction under this chapter may direct that arbitration be held in accordance with the agreement at any place therein provided for, whether that place is within or without the United States. Such court may also appoint arbitrators in accordance with the provisions of the agreement." 9 U.S.C. § 206. Several U.S. courts have found that under FAA § 206, they are compelled to order the parties to go to arbitration. *See, e.g., Francisco v. M/T Stolt Achievement,* 293 F.3d 273 (2001); *Sedco, Inc. v. Petroleos Mexicanos Mexican Nat. Oil Co. (Pemex),* 767 F.2d 1140, 1145 (1985). *See also* Section 9 of the 1996 Arbitration Act of the United Kingdom, which provides in the relevant part that "(1) A party to an arbitration agreement against whom legal proceedings are brought . . . in respect of a matter which under the agreement is to be referred to arbitration may . . . apply to the court in which the proceedings have been brought to stay the proceedings so far as they concern that matter." The Queens Bench Division in *Cable & Wireless Plc v. IBM U.K. Ltd.,* [2002] EWHC 2059, applying this provision, stayed a court proceedings for interim relief, until the parties resolve all their outstanding disputes through ADR as contemplated in their contract. Swiss courts have taken a similar approach; *see SGS Société Générale de Surveillance S.A. v. Islamic Republic of Pakistan,* ICSID Case No. ARB/01/13 (Decision of the Tribunal on Objections to Jurisdiction, Aug. 6, 2003), 42 I.L.M. 1290 (2003), ¶ 23.

validity of the agreement are properly aired before the arbitral tribunal, and not the court, have met with mixed success.[15]

A prime example of the persistent risk of anti-arbitration injunctions is the *Hubco v. WAPDA*.[16] The dispute concerned a power purchase agreement between Hub Power Co. Ltd. (Hubco) and the Water and Power Development Authority of Pakistan (WAPDA). Pursuant to the terms of the agreement, Hubco was to develop a power plant and to sell the electricity produced to WAPDA, which would pay the tariff in U.S. dollars. The agreement was amended three times, under different Pakistani administrations.[17] Subsequently, as a result of a change of administration, as well as other political and economic developments, independent power producers, particularly Hubco, came under intense scrutiny.[18] In 1998 the government of Pakistan started formal proceedings to investigate possible irregularities in the Hubco deal. Concurrently, a consumer commenced litigation against Hubco, WAPDA, and the government of Pakistan "claiming that his power bill was too high because of corruption in negotiations of [the] Hubco power purchase agreement."[19] Pakistani courts, including the supreme court, ruled that the tariff should be reduced and adjusted it accordingly. Hubco then filed for International Chamber of Commerce (ICC) arbitration in London based on the arbitration clause of the power purchase agreement. Soon thereafter, WAPDA sent a letter to Hubco informing it that the amendments to the agreement were obtained through corruption and other irregularities, hence, they were void ab initio; it unilaterally further reduced the tariff. In addition, it sought repayment of Rupee 16 billion plus 18 percent interest. Hubco immediately sought an injunction from the local Pakistani court seeking to enjoin WAPDA from pursuing its allegations in any forum other than the ICC arbitration. WAPDA in turn sought an anti-arbitration injunction.[20] After a series of restraining orders, the Supreme Court of Pakistan had to decide whether the dispute was arbitrable. In a 3-to-2 decision the court ruled that the dispute was not arbitrable, because it involved, among other issues, criminal behavior. The following is an excerpt of the supreme court's judgment in this case.

---

[15] Walid Ben Hamida, *L'Arbitrage Transnational Face à un Desordre Procedural: La Concurrence des Procedures et les Conflits de Juridictions,* Conference Presentation, Tunis, Mar. 3 4, 2006, at 34 36.

[16] Louise Barrington, *Hubco v. WAPDA: Pakistan Top Court Rejects Modern Arbitration,* 11 Am. Rev. Int'l Arb. 385 (2000). Nudrat Majeed, *Commentary on the Hubco Judgment,* 16 Arb. Int'l 431 (2000). For a detailed discussion of the facts surrounding this case *see* Mark Kantor, *International Project Finance and Arbitration with Public Sector Entities: When Arbitrability Is a Fiction?* 24 Fordham Int'l L. J. 1122 (2000–1).

[17] Rumu Sarkar, *Transnational Business Law, A Development Perspective* 364 (Kluwer Law Int'l 2003).

[18] *Id.* at 1150.

[19] *Id.* at 1152.

[20] *Id.* at 1153–54.

Hub Power Co. Ltd v. Pakistan WAPDA

Supreme Court of Pakistan, Judgement of June 20, 2000, 16(4) Arb. Int'l 439 (2000)

SH. RIAZ AHMAD, J:

... The only question which this Court is required to answer by agreement of both the parties is noted down in the leave granting order which is to the following effect:

> Whether the nature of the dispute and the question of mala fide, fraud, illegalities and the legal incompetence raised preclude resolution of the matter through arbitration as a matter of public policy and as such the dispute between the parties is not arbitrable and cannot legitimately be subject matter of ICC arbitration? What is the effect of joining a stranger to the agreement in making reference to the arbitration.

Case of the WAPDA at the very outset was that supplemental deed 16.11.1993, the first amendment dated 24.2.1994 and the second amendment dated 17.10.1994 were obtained by HUBCO in collusion with the concerned authorities of WAPDA and the high officials of the Federal Government who were in a position to exert influence on the WAPDA "456" authorities through the payment of bribe and kick backs as such it was void under section 23 of the Contract Act and not voidable simplicitor. The main question falling for determination according to our view, was that if an agreement prima facie had been obtained through fraud or bribe would it not then be sufficient to take it out of the pale of the arbitrability as distinguished from a commercial dispute raised under a valid agreement, therefore, we have heard learned counsel for the parties as to whether there was prima facie material and circumstances brought on the record in support of these allegations, as mere allegations were not sufficient in order to come to the conclusion, whether the dispute between the parties is arbitrable or not.

Since these circumstances have been dealt with by our learned brother Muhammad Bashir Jehangiri, J. in his proposed judgment, we need not repeat the same but the following salient features and circumstances noted by us have persuaded us to hold that these prima facie furnish evidence in support of the allegations made in respect of the disputed documents that the dispute is not arbitrable as such [and] should be decided by a Court of law as a matter of public policy:

(a) In the original agreement cost of plant was 1275 Million Dollar which HUBCO wanted to raise and was in fact subsequently raised. The documents produced on the record by both the parties show that WAPDA had throughout been contesting the case of HUBCO to raise the said cost of construction but the same was raised to more than 1500 Million Dollars which prima facie gave one sided benefit to HUBCO as CPP [Capacity Purchase Price, the fixed component of Hubco's tariff] was also raised, as a consequence thereof it was payable on the amount of cost of construction on the plant.

(b) The debt and equity ratio as fixed in the original agreement was 80% and 20% respectively which was changed and was converted to 75% and 25% respectively which allegedly burdened the WAPDA and gave undue advantage to HUBCO, for, on the amount of equity the rate of interest to be paid by WAPDA is 17% called IRP [Interest Rate Parity], whereas on the part of debt it is for less maybe about 6%.

(c) According to the original agreement and its schedule 6, such matters were to be referred to Experts, in case of difference of opinion, whose decision was to be final and such matters were kept out of the pale of the arbitration clause and through impugned amendments the provisions contained in Schedule 6 for reference of these matters to expert was done away with, as a consequence of which HUBCO allegedly had free hand to get tariff and CPP amount arbitrarily raised, as a consequence of which the WAPDA allegedly would have to pay an amount of 30 Billion Dollars in excess in the entire period of the contract, which prima facie seems to be unconscionable and without consideration.

(d) From the documents placed on the record by both the parties and particularly the learned counsel for the appellant/HUBCO it is manifest that there was a prolonged negotiation between HUBCO and WAPDA on these matters and WAPDA had throughout been resisting and opposing the demands of HUBCO about the raise of tariff, CPP etc., but after the installation of new Government after Elections in October 1993 the disputed documents were executed and it is not clear from the record as to how these hotly contested matters, for such a long time, were brought to an end suddenly and further for what considerations supplementary deed first amendment and second amendment were abruptly executed and so on whose behest and for what consideration. It is pertinent to note that the allegations of corruption as are disclosed in the FIRs [First Information Reports; a First Information Report is a written document prepared by Pakistani police when they receive information about a cognizable offense] lodged by WAPDA are against specified persons with particularity of the newly installed high officials in the Ministry. These circumstances prima facie do establish the case of misuse of power by public functionary for extraneous considerations requiring detailed examination and decision by a Court of law after full-fledged trial.

In arriving this conclusion we have taken note of the following circumstances:

(a) Though in supplemental deed reference has been made to newly Schedule 6 but surprising the same was not annexed with the said deed as its part. The said new schedule 6 was not got signed [sic] by HUBCO from the Chairman WAPDA, whereas the same was signed by one Muhammad Ashraf, who later on expressly declared that he was not authorized to sign the said document, but no steps were taken to get this Schedule 6 regularized by HUBCO by insisting that the same should be got signed [sic] by some authorized person.

(b) Likewise Schedule 1(A), 1(B) and 1(C) which were placed in place of the previous Schedule containing rates of tariff etc., were not signed by WAPDA but by Chief Economist of WAPDA.

(c) We have also taken note that officers of WAPDA left the service of WAPDA conveniently, one of whom was paid the huge amount of security which he provided at the time of joining service and joined the service of HUBCO at an exuberant salary, which fact during arguments was not denied by the learned counsel for HUBCO.

(d) The payment of IRP on the equity amount was allowed retrospectively w.e.f. from 17.11.1993 by providing that the actual amount shall be deemed to have been injected on the said date though the same was allegedly injected later on burdening the WAPDA with huge amount to be paid to HUBCO.

(e) According to the original arrangement between the parties, at the expiry of the contract period, the ownership of the plant was to vest in the WAPDA whereas subsequently it was decided that the same would vest in HUBCO, prima facie without any consideration or benefit to WAPDA, the amount of CPP and rates of tariff had been allegedly unreasonably raised without any plausible reasons.

The allegations of corruption in support of which the above-mentioned circumstances do provide prima facie basis for further probe into matter judicially and, if proved, would render these documents as void, therefore, we are of the considered view that according to the public policy such matters, which require finding about alleged criminality, are not referable to Arbitration. The disputes between the parties are not commercial dispute arising from an undisputed legally valid contract, or relatable to such a contract, for, according to the case of WAPDA on account of these criminal acts disputed documents did not bring into existence any legally binding contract between the parties, therefore, the dispute primarily relates to very existence of a valid contract and not a dispute under such a contract.

Additionally we have also noted from the documents on record that WAPDA has throughout been asking HUBCO to furnish documents to ascertain the correctness of their stand in the matter of cost of construction and tariff but a deaf ear was turned. Parties to bear their own costs.

Order of the Court

We hold by majority of (3 to 2) that Civil Appeal No. 1399/99 filed by WAPDA against HUBCO is allowed, and the respondent HUBCO is restrained from invoking the arbitration clause of the agreement and Civil Appeal No. 1398 HUBCO v. WAPDA stands dismissed.

The judgment of the Supreme Court of Pakistan disregards the separability of the arbitration agreement and the underlying agreement, which is an established principle and "part of the fabric of international arbitration."[21] According to this doctrine, the arbitration clause is viewed as a separate agreement so that the invalidity of the underlying agreement—here the power purchase agreement—does not affect the validity of the arbitration clause. The invalidity of any amendments to the underlying agreement, where the underlying agreement is not tainted, a fortiori should not affect the arbitration clause.

C. Anti-Arbitration Injunctions and the International Centre for Settlement of Investment Disputes Convention

The Washington Convention, which governs proceedings under the auspices of the International Centre for Settlement of Investment Disputes (ICSID), contains specific additional protection from anti-arbitration injunctions and other types of interference by national courts. Article 26 of the Washington Convention provides the following:

> Consent of the parties to arbitration under this Convention shall, unless otherwise stated, be deemed consent to such arbitration to the exclusion of any other remedy.[22]

Christoph H. Schreuer, *The ICSID Convention, A Commentary* 347 (2001) Commentary on Art. 26

2. The first sentence of Art. 26 has two main features. The first is that, once consent to ICSID arbitration has been given, the parties have lost their right to seek relief in another forum, national or international, and are restricted to pursuing their claim through ICSID. This principle operates from the moment of valid consent. This exclusive remedy rule

---

[21] Lew, *supra* note 12, at 38.
[22] Washington Convention, art. 26.

of Art. 26 is subject to modification by the parties. The words "unless otherwise stated" in the first sentence give the parties the option to deviate from it by agreement.

3. The second feature of Art. 26, first sentence, is that of non-interference with the ICSID arbitration process, once it has been instituted. The principle of noninterference is a consequence of the self-contained nature of proceedings under the Convention. The Convention provides for an elaborate process designed to make arbitration independent of domestic courts. Even in the face of an uncooperative party, ICSID arbitration designed to proceed independently without the support of domestic courts. This is evidenced by the provisions on the constitution of the tribunal (Arts. 37–40), on proceedings in the absence of a party (Art. 45(2)), on autonomous arbitration rules (Art. 44), on applicable law (Art. 42(1)), and on provisional measures (Art. 47). It is only in the context of enforcement that domestic courts may enter the picture (Arts. 54–5). In addition, the arbitration process is also insulated from inter-State claims, by the exclusion of diplomatic protection (Art. 27).

4. The underlying idea of the exclusive remedy rule and of the principle of noninterference is to provide an effective forum and to dispense with other proceedings which for a variety of reasons appear unattractive to the parties. Investors often do not perceive litigation in the courts of host States as a reliable way of protecting their interests. In turn, host States dislike getting involved in litigation abroad. This applies not only to proceedings on the merits but also to those ancillary to arbitration. In addition, State immunity tends to have a distorting effect on litigation between States and non-State parties before domestic courts. The principle of autonomy for ICSID arbitration, as expressed in Art. 26, therefore, meets a number of needs of the host States and of the foreign investors.

In *MINE v. Guinea*, a Swiss court applied ICSID's rule of abstention under Article 26 and determined that a party to an ICSID case may not bring the same issue before a national court while the ICSID case is pending.[23] The dispute between Maritime International Nominees Establishment (MINE), a Liechtenstein corporation, and the Republic of Guinea concerned a 1971 contract for shipping services in which MINE was to transport Guinean bauxite to foreign markets.[24] Article XVIII of that contract provided that any conflict should be resolved by a panel of three arbitrators "selected by the President of ICSID at the joint request of the parties or, failing this, at the request of the most diligent party."[25] After a rift between the parties, MINE filed a motion with the U.S. District Court for the District of Columbia to compel arbitration. Acting on MINE's request, in 1978 the District Court designated the American Arbitration Association (AAA) to resolve the dispute; and in Guinea's absence, on June 9, 1980, an AAA panel

---

[23] Geneva Surveillance Authority (Office of Pursuits for Debts and Bankruptcy), *Guinea v. Maritime Int'l Nominees Establishment* (Decision of Oct. 7, 1986), 26 I.L.M. 382, 383 (1987) [hereinafter Geneva Magistrate's Decision].

[24] *In the Matter of the Arbitration between Maritime Int'l Nominees Establishment v. Republic of Guinea*, 693 F.2d 1094, 1095 (D.C. Cir. 1982) [hereinafter 1982 DC Cir.].

[25] Geneva Magistrate's Decision, *supra* note 23, at 383.

declared that the Republic of Guinea was to pay MINE more than $25 million for breach of contract damages.[26] The District Court confirmed the award of the AAA, but the U.S. Court of Appeals for the District of Columbia reversed the confirmation on grounds that Guinea was immune from the suit under the Foreign Sovereign Immunities Act.[27]

Without a judgment entered on the AAA arbitration award, on May 7, 1984, MINE submitted to ICSID the same dispute it had submitted to AAA five years earlier. While that ICSID case was pending, on May 28, 1985, MINE requested attachment of Republic of Guinea assets in Switzerland based on the award rendered by the AAA. On May 30, a Swiss magistrate authorized the attachment of a deposit of Guinea in a Swiss bank.[28] On appeal, Guinea argued that the magistrate violated Article 26 of the ICSID Convention by entertaining MINE's request for attachment after the parties agreed to submit the dispute to ICSID. The appellate panel accepted Guinea's argument and lifted the attachment, concluding that consent to arbitration under the ICSID Convention is "a waiver of all other recourse." Because Switzerland had ratified the ICSID convention, it would be a violation of Swiss law for Swiss courts to permit attachment proceedings for an issue pending before ICSID.[29]

National courts have not always been equally respectful of ICSID arbitration and Article 26 of the Washington Convention. In *SGS v. Pakistan*,[30] the claimant's contract to provide customs security services was cancelled by Pakistan after a change in government. The contract provided for domestic arbitration in Islamabad, but SGS sought to litigate the contract cancellation in Swiss courts, arguing that it would not obtain a fair hearing in Pakistan. The Swiss courts dismissed this petition, and Pakistan ultimately initiated domestic arbitration against SGS pursuant to the contractual arbitration agreement.[31] SGS contested jurisdiction and soon initiated ICSID arbitration against Pakistan pursuant to the Pakistan–Switzerland bilateral investment treaty (BIT), seeking interim relief in the Islamabad district court to suspend the local arbitration pending a decision of the ICSID tribunal. Pakistan, meanwhile, sought an order from the same court enjoining SGS from pursuing the ICSID arbitration.[32] The case rose eventually to Pakistan Supreme

---

[26] 1982 DC Cir., *supra* note 24, at 1095.

[27] *Id.* at 1111.

[28] Geneva Magistrate's Decision, *supra* note 23, at 385.

[29] *Id.* at 388.

[30] *SGS v. Pakistan, supra* note 14.

[31] Martin Lau, *Note on Société Générale de Surveillance SA v. Pakistan,* 19 Arb. Int'l 179 (2003).

[32] Walid Ben Hamida, *L'Arbitrage Transnational Face à un Desordre Procedural: La Concurrence des Procedures et les Conflits de Juridictions,* Conference Presentation, Tunis, Mar. 3–4, 2006, at 35.

Court. That court held that SGS could not proceed with the ICSID arbitration, on two grounds. First, it stated that the Pakistan–Switzerland BIT was improperly incorporated into Pakistani law through implementing legislation; hence, no Pakistani court had jurisdiction or power to enforce the rights arising under the treaty. Then, notwithstanding this finding, it went on to examine whether the business under the parties' contract could be considered an investment within the meaning of Article 2(1) of the BIT. It held that it could not. Excerpts of the relevant parts of the court's decision are reproduced in the following text:[33]

> *SGS Société Générale de Surveillance S.A. v. Pakistan*
>
> *Supreme Court of Pakistan (Appellate Jurisdiction), Judgment of July 3, 2002, 19 Arb. Int'l 181 (2003)*
>
> 22. Learned Attorney General has also referred to Article VI of the United States Constitution to demonstrate that wherever it was intended to give effect to a treaty by a State as Municipal Law of the country for enforcement of rights thereunder as such through courts, law was made through statutes to incorporate the provisions of the treaty in the Municipal Law of the country. Article VI of the said Constitution reads as follows:
>
>> *(2) This Constitution, and the Laws of the United States which shall be made in pursuance thereof; and all treaties made, or which shall be made, under the Authority of the United States, shall be the supreme Law of the Land; and the Judges in every State shall be bound thereby, anything in the Constitution or Laws of any State to the contrary notwithstanding.*
>
> 23. The argument raised by the learned Attorney General has considerable force. Admittedly, in Pakistan, the provisions of the Treaty were not incorporated through legislation into the laws of the country, therefore, the same did not have the effect of altering the existing laws, as such, rights arising therefrom called treaty rights cannot be enforced through courts as in such a situation, the court is not vested with the power to do so. It may be significantly mentioned here that according to Article 175(2) of the Constitution of Islamic Republic of Pakistan, no court has any jurisdiction unless conferred by or under any law or the Constitution, therefore, unless the treaty was incorporated into the law so that it become part of the Municipal Law of the country, no court shall have jurisdiction to enforce any right arising therefrom.
>
> 24. Faced with this difficulty, Mr. K. M. A. Sarndani, learned counsel for the appellant, attempted to overcome it by arguing that by reason of the unilateral act of the Federation of Pakistan itself of omission or inaction to incorporate into the laws of the country the provisions of the Treaty by legislation it should not be allowed to raise such a plea to avoid the enforcement of the provisions of the Treaty. He further argued that according to Article 97 of the Constitution of the Islamic Republic of Pakistan, 1973, the executive authority of the Federation "188" extends to the matters enumerated in Part I of the Fourth Schedule regarding which the Parliament could legislate,

---

[33] In the meantime the ICSID arbitration continued on the basis that the Washington Convention was signed and ratified by Pakistan (Agreement between the Swiss Confederation and the Islamic Republic of Pakistan on the Promotion and Reciprocal Protection of Investments, Systematische Sammlung des Bundesrechts [SR] 0.975.262.3, *available at* http://www.admin.ch/ch/f/rs/c0_975_262_3.html [French original]), and that the BIT became effective by virtue of an exchange of letters between Switzerland and Pakistan on May 6, 1996.

therefore its acts of ratification of the Bilateral Investment Treaty amounted to give it the status of law.

25. Article 97 of the Constitution only provides that, subject to the Constitution, the executive authority of the Federation shall extend only to those matters with respect to which Majlis-e-Shoora (Parliament) has the power to make laws, including exercise of rights, authority and jurisdiction in, and in relation to, areas outside Pakistan: the Fourth Schedule embodies the list of those matters with respect to which Majlis-e-Shoora has the power to make laws, Item 3 of which is very relevant which reads as follows:

> 6. *External affairs: the implementing of treaties and agreements, including educational and cultural pacts and agreements, with other countries; extradition, including the surrender of criminals and accused person to Governments outside Pakistan.*

Since Majlis-e-Shoora has the power to make laws in respect of those matters, therefore, by virtue of Article 97 of the Constitution, the Federal Government of Pakistan has the power to exercise executive authority in respect thereof which was exercised to ratify the Treaty, but it has not conferred power on the executive authority to legislate for a statute.

. . . .

27. As regards resolution of dispute arising from investment as per terms of the Bilateral Investment Treaty in this case, no law has been made in Pakistan of the nature as was made by the Zambia Government or other States, therefore, the same could not be enforced as law in order to claim that the alleged choice given to the appellant under the said Treaty to approach ICSID for arbitration had preference over the existing lawful contract between the parties inclusive of the arbitration clause which is binding on the parties.

28. It is demonstrably clear to which no exception can be taken that the act of the appellant to approach the court of general jurisdiction in Switzerland seeking recovery of specific amounts under the agreement, alleging that Arbitration Clause 11.1 embodied therein could not be invoked for the reason of termination of contract and that fair trial in the courts of Pakistan was not possible and not on account of ICSID arbitration under the Treaty, amounted to admission that otherwise the said clause was valid, legally operative and binding on the parties.

29. The next question which falls for consideration is whether the agreement between the parties is relatable to any investment to attract the provisions of the Bilateral Investment Treaty because the said Treaty governs the dispute about investment of a party of the country signatory to the said Treaty as is the case here, so as to raise a plea that the arbitration clause of the agreement in dispute no longer remained binding between the parties and the choice of the appellant had to be preferred as to the forum of ICSID arbitration. Answer to this question revolves around the answer as to what is meant by the word or expression 'investment.' The word 'investment' has been defined in Article 1(2) of the Bilateral Investment Treaty as follows:

> *(2) The term 'investments' shall include every kind of assets and particularly: (a) movable and immovable property as well as any other rights in rem, such as servitudes, mortgages, liens, pledges; (b) shares, parts or any other kinds of participation in companies; (c) claims to money or to any performance having an economic value; (d) copyrights, industrial property rights (such as patents, utility models, industrial designs or models, trade or service marks, trade names, indications of origin) know-how and good will; (e) concessions under public law, including concessions to search for, extract or exploit natural resources as well as all other rights given by law, by contract or by decision of the authority in accordance with the law.*

. . . .

31. The agreement between the parties the subject matter of these appeals is to be tested on the touchstone of true meaning of the word 'investment.' In order to decide this question, it would be necessary to examine the agreement itself to arrive at a decision as to its scope and nature. It has to be construed strictly, carefully keeping in view the purpose for which the same was executed.

[The Court proceeded to examine the subject matter of the parties' contract.]

. . . .

33. From a bare reading of these clauses of the agreement in particular and the agreement as a whole, it is manifest that it was an agreement through which the services of the appellant were hired for carrying out pre-shipment inspection of the goods to determine their value for the purposes of charging custom duty on their import in Pakistan according to the rates prescribed under the relevant laws of Pakistan and the major portion of the exercise was to be undertaken out of Pakistan at the stage of shipment of the goods from the foreign countries from where they were to be imported, and in case re-inspection in warehouse in Pakistan was necessary, the appellant was given authority to carry out the same through SGS Pakistan and nothing else.

34. Considering the nature of these functions for which the services of the appellant were hired in juxtaposition with the meaning of the word 'investment,' it can safely be held for reasons to follow, that it is not agreement of the kind and nature relating to any investment, as such, is not covered by the said Bilateral Investment Treaty or the Washington Convention. It was an agreement between the two parties for hiring services simpliciter involving no investment, therefore, Arbitration Clause 11.1 embodied therein would not in any manner be adversely affected as to its enforcement through a court of law by any of the clauses of Bilateral Investment Treaty, inclusive of ICSID arbitration, being not a dispute related to investment.

35. As is evidenced by the definition of 'investment' given in the Bilateral Investment Treaty, the definition is not exhaustive as it is controlled by the expression 'includes.' Learned counsel for the appellant, when questioned as to how it could be claimed in view of the terms of the agreement in question, being an agreement for hiring services simpliciter, that the same involves any 'investment' such as is referred to in Clause C in the Treaty, argued that any claim to money simpliciter or any performance having an economic value is also 'investment,' therefore, the claim of the appellant for the recovery of the amounts in question for the services rendered by it would be covered by this clause. We are afraid, however, that the argument in our view is not only devoid of any force but also plainly unsound. By raising this argument, learned counsel for the appellant has overlooked that all claims to money, or any performance having an economic value, must relate to investment. Clause C on which reliance has been placed by the learned counsel for the appellant as a matter of fact is of the species of assets earnable by an investor from his investment and not the investment itself. The expression 'investment' has a legal connotation and meaning has to be assigned to determine whether the dispute between the parties relate to or has any nexus with investment.

. . . .

37. It is sufficiently clear from this that laying out of money in the acquisition of some species of property was a necessary ingredient to determine whether an "200" entry or transaction was relatable to investment or not. Keeping in view this meaning and interpretation of the expression 'investment' and examining the terms of the agreement in question in the light thereof, it can safely be concluded that the same does not fall within the scope and ambit of investment, for as observed above, it is simpliciter an agreement through which mere services had been acquired for a valuation of the goods, mostly in foreign countries, and there is no element of laying out of money by the appellant for acquisition of any species of property, as such, it is not a case of investment which is

covered by the Treaty, and no right in the appellant has been created to invoke its provisions for ICSID arbitration.

. . . .

39. From what has been discussed above, we are of the view that the arbitration agreement between the parties dated 29.9.1994 was binding and continued to be binding upon them notwithstanding the ratification of the Bilateral Investment Treaty which provided another parallel forum for arbitration before ICSID in that the appellant was not an investor within the meaning of the word used in the said Treaty and for the reasons discussed above, the findings of the High Court do not suffer from any legal infirmity.

. . . .

77. Civil Appeal No. 460 of 2002 filed by the Federation of Pakistan is accepted and SGS (appellant in CA 459 of 2002) is hereby restrained from taking any step, action or measure to pursue or participate or to continue to pursue or participate in the ICSID arbitration.

In particular, the Pakistani court's consideration of the investment issue seems a clear invasion of the ICSID tribunal's jurisdiction. In any case, the decision illustrates well the inherent tensions between local courts and international arbitral tribunals concerning the appropriate forum as well as under what circumstances a local court will attempt to interfere with an arbitration.

VII. The Course of an Investment Arbitration

A. Introduction

Investment arbitrations resemble commercial arbitrations in many ways but are dramatically different in others. Above all, the presence of a sovereign state in every such dispute can transform the tone and nature of an investment dispute. Tribunals are sometimes more solicitous of the position of a sovereign than they would be of a private party, if only because of the public policy and other noncommercial issues that often arise in investment disputes. The following description of the course of an investment arbitration attempts to identify some of these similarities and differences.

B. Waiting Periods

Many bilateral investment treaties (BITs) provide for a consultation or amicable negotiation period before disputes are submitted to arbitration.[1] Other BITs establish a "cooling off" period, most commonly six months, that must elapse between the government act that triggers the dispute and the commencement of the arbitration.[2] The waiting period time is normally to be spent seeking amicable settlement or pursuing remedies in local courts or administrative tribunals.[3] In most instances, the time period is short enough that the investor need not be overly concerned

---

[1] France-Chile BIT, art. 8(1)-(2) (requiring amicable negotiation, but "[i]f the dispute has not been resolved within six months of the date it arose, it shall be submitted, at the investor's request," to arbitration).

[2] U.S.-Argentina BIT, art. VII(3)(a) ("Provided that . . . six months have elapsed from the date on which the dispute arose, the national or company concerned may choose to consent in writing to the submission of the dispute for settlement by binding arbitration"); *cf.* U.S.-Azerbaijan BIT, art. IX(3)(a) (three-month waiting period from time dispute arises).

[3] In some Indian BITs, the investor must not only seek amicable settlement through negotiation for six months, but is also compelled to initiate conciliation proceedings before arbitration can begin. *See, e.g.,* Sweden-India BIT, art. 9; Australia-India BIT, art. 12; and Croatia-India BIT, art. 9.

about the effect of such provisions: Often the preparation of a request for arbitration will take several months in any event, particularly if the request is to be detailed and bolstered by supporting evidential materials. Furthermore, the expense and risk of the arbitral process means that a settlement is normally a desirable option for the claimant, who therefore may welcome the opportunity to engage in last-minute negotiations with the host state to avert an adversarial process. In this sense, the existence of a definite waiting period may add gravity to the investor's demands, as the government is made aware that negotiation can only be drawn out so long, after which arbitration will begin. Despite these considerations, claimants may seek to bypass the strictures of the waiting period provision and initiate arbitration as soon as possible. In such cases, a number of different issues can arise.

First, a tribunal may be faced with the question of whether the claimant's behavior since the claim arose satisfies the amicable settlement provision of the submission to arbitration. Practitioners have noted that where disputes are serious, negotiation may be futile by the time the decision is made to arbitrate. This is one reason why many refer to the cooling-off requirement as a "waiting period," rather than as a negotiation period. But, what would a tribunal think of a claimant who simply waited for the period to elapse, without making any attempt to communicate with the respondent government? Technically speaking, in such a case the period may be held not to have begun at all, depending on the wording of the clause.

A. Biloune and Marine Drive Complex Ltd. v. Ghana Inves. Center, Ad Hoc UNCITRAL Arbitration, Awards of Oct. 27, 1989 and June 30, 1990, XIX Y.B. Comm. Arb. 11 (1994)

[2] "The respondents' initial communication to the Tribunal raised the preliminary objection that the arbitral proceedings were instituted before opportunity for reconciliation or consultation. This assertedly is in violation of the arbitration clause at Art. 15 of the GIC [Ghana Investment Centre] Agreement, which requires that before arbitration is commenced, 'all efforts shall be made through mutual discussions to reach an amicable settlement.' The Tribunal previously deferred this issue to the merits phase of the proceedings, and it is now addressed . . . .

[3] "The Tribunal believes that the claimants have made a clear showing of their efforts to reach an amicable settlement. On more than one occasion the claimants invited negotiations with the respondents on this matter. GIC failed to make any response to those invitations. GIC and the Government were fully informed by the claimants, by the Designating Authority under the UNCITRAL Rules, Mr. Varekamp, by the Appointing Authority, Dr. Shihata, and by this Tribunal of the establishment and composition of the Tribunal. The respondents had ample opportunity to negotiate an amicable settlement. GIC did not respond to the claimants' request for an inquiry into the situation. Nor did the respondents object to the establishment of the Tribunal until well after proceedings had begun and the claimants had already prepared and served their Statement of Claim and their evidence concerning the Claim to the respondents. Although the minutes of GIC board meetings submitted in evidence show that extensive consideration was given to the MDCL problem, including requests for its settlement or arbitration, the fact and content of those deliberations were not communicated to the claimants until the pleadings were filed in these proceedings.

[4] "In light of these findings, the Tribunal holds that the legal and contractual prerequisite to arbitration – failure of attempts at amicable settlement – was satisfied by the claimants' efforts and the respondents' inaction."

It should be observed that arbitral tribunals tend to take a less formalistic approach to such matters.[4] In fact, they normally do not dismiss a case for failure to abide by these requirements. Yet, there are tribunals such as *Ethyl v. Canada* that have sanctioned a claimant for not complying with a waiting requirement, by ordering it to bear the costs associated with litigating the issues arising out of the premature filing of a case.

An additional question arises with regard to the effect of an applicable most favored nation (MFN) clause on waiting, settlement, or litigation periods to which consent to arbitration is subject. It is in such situations that an MFN clause could possibly have a positive impact for a claimant; where the basic treaty contains a restriction such as a waiting, settlement, or litigation period and another investment treaty to which the respondent state is a party does not contain such limitations, the claimant arguably could enjoy the benefit of the latter treaty without risking sanctions for a premature filing. The question of the applicability of MFN clauses in this context has not arisen so far. These matters, however, as procedural preconditions to arbitration, may be compared to the requirement of exhaustion of local remedies. In the latter context, a line of cases following *Maffezini v. Spain*[5] has held that investors through the application of MFN may enjoy the benefits of the BIT that does not contain the exhaustion requirement.[6] The exhaustion of local remedies and the *Maffezini* line of cases is briefly discussed in the section that follows.

C. Local Remedies[7]

Under customary international law, the home state of a foreign investor cannot espouse the latter's claim against the host state until the investor has exhausted the available local remedies. The foreign investor is excused from exhausting local remedies if it can prove that the remedies are futile.[8]

---

[4] *See* Chapter V *supra*.

[5] *Maffezini v. Kingdom of Spain*, ICSID Case No. ARB/97/7 (Decision on Objections to Jurisdiction, Jan. 25, 2000). *See also* cases cited in note 11 *infra*.

[6] The tribunal's reasoning in *Maffezini* was criticized in *Plama Consortium Ltd. v. Republic of Bulgaria*, ICSID Case No. ARB/03/24 (Decision on Jurisdiction, Feb. 8, 2005).

[7] On exhaustion of local remedies, *see generally* Chapter XIII *infra*. *See also* C. F. Amerasinghe, *Local Remedies in International Law* (Cambridge University Press 2004); S. Schwebel & G. Wetter, *Arbitration and the Exhaustion of Local Remedies*, in *Justice in International Law* 171 (Schwebel ed., 1994).

[8] *Finish Shipowners Arbitration (Finland v. U.K.)*, Award of May 9, 1934, 3 U.N.R.I.A.A. 1479 (1934).

Modern investment treaties have generally done away with the exhaustion requirement.[9] A few BITs, however, still contain an "exhaustion" requirement,[10] requiring an aggrieved investor to first file local court proceedings in the host state before it may bring a claim to international arbitration.

Where a BIT contains such an exhaustion provision, and another BIT signed by the same host country includes a shorter period or has no waiting period at all, it is possible that the shorter period would apply under the MFN provisions of the BIT in question. This was the holding of the arbitral tribunal in *Maffezini v. Spain*,[11] where the MFN provision of the Argentina-Spain BIT entitled an Argentine investor to the more relaxed procedural requirements of the Chile-Spain BIT and allowed it to immediately commence arbitration against Spain; whereas under the Argentina-Spain BIT, the investor was required to pursue its claims in the courts of the host state for 18 months before it would be allowed to initiate arbitration against the host state.

D. Notice of Claim and Request for Arbitration

Modern investment arbitration normally commences with a two-stage process. The investor first sends the host state a Notice of Claim or Letter of Intent, informing the respondent state that a dispute exists, and describing the basis of the claim in general terms. Thereafter, the investor submits a more detailed Request for Arbitration, in which the investor lodges its complaint formally with the arbitration institution (if any) and initiates the arbitrator selection process.[12]

---

[9] N. Rubins & S. Kinsella, *International Investment, Political Risk and Dispute Resolution* 272 (Oceana Publications 2005).

[10] *See, e.g.,* Malaysia-Netherlands BIT, art. 12 ("In the event of any dispute arising between a national or a company of one Contracting Party and the other Contracting Party in connection with an investment in the territory of the other Contracting Party, the other Contracting Party shall, after the exhaustion of all local administrative and judicial remedies, agree to such dispute being submitted for conciliation or arbitration . . ."); and Ghana-Romania BIT, art. 4(3).

[11] *Maffezini v. Spain* (Decision on Objections to Jurisdiction), *supra* note 5, ¶ 56; *see also Siemens A.G. v. Argentine Republic*, ICSID Case No. ARB/02/8 (Decision on Jurisdiction Aug. 3, 2004), ¶¶ 102–103; and *Gas Natural SDG, S.A. v. Argentine Republic*, ICSID Case No. ARB/03/10 (Decision of the Tribunal on Preliminary Questions on Jurisdiction, June 17, 2005), ¶ 49; *cf. Salini Costruttori S.p.A. & Italstrade S.p.A. v. Hashemite Kingdom of Jordan*, ICSID Case No. ARB/02/13 (Decision on Jurisdiction, Nov. 29, 2004); and *Plama Consortium Ltd. v. Republic of Bulgaria*, ICSID Case No. ARB/03/24 (Decision on Jurisdiction, Feb. 8, 2005). Although the first group of cases support the application of MFN clauses to procedural matters, the latter group, which includes *Salini v. Jordan* and especially *Plama v. Bulgaria*, reject and deny the applicability of MFN clauses to procedural matters. *See also Telenor v. Hungary*, ICSID Case No. ARB/04/15 (Award, Sept. 6, 2006), ¶¶ 90–95 & 99–100.

[12] *See, e.g.,* UNCITRAL Arbitration Rules, art. 3 ("Notice of Arbitration"); ICSID Arbitration Rules, art. 36 ("Request for Arbitration").

1. Notice of Claim

The notice of claim is normally a very simple document that can be filed relatively quickly. Although filing a notice may not be required under the relevant contract or investment treaty, such a step can offer significant advantages to foreign investors interested in achieving improved treatment from the host state during a crisis period. The notice makes the government aware that its conduct could give rise to international liability. In addition, it may serve as the starting date for the calculation of waiting periods, or other periods where lapse of a certain period of time is a prerequisite to commencing arbitration. Most arbitration rules do not require prospective claimants to file a notice of claim. However, many investment treaties do so require. Article 1119 of North American Free Trade Agreement (NAFTA), for instance, provides that:

> "[t]he disputing investor shall deliver to the disputing Party written notice of its intention to submit a claim to arbitration at least 90 days before the claim is submitted, which notice shall specify: (a) the name and address of the disputing investor and, where a claim is made under Article 1117, the name and address of the enterprise; (b) the provisions of this Agreement alleged to have been breached and any other relevant provisions; (c) the issues and the factual basis for the claim; and (d) the relief sought and the approximate amount of damages claimed."[13]

Under normal circumstances, a notice of claim in investor-state arbitration is not served on the respondent government through diplomatic channels or pursuant to treaties dealing with the service of process.[14] Instead, depending on the arbitration rules chosen, the claimant in such a case may deliver a copy of the notice of claim to the head of state or the responsible ministry of the host state. Article 2 of the UNCITRAL Arbitration Rules, for example, contains a general provision that sets the procedure for filing various notices by the parties.[15] Sometimes investment instruments specify the procedure for the service of documents. NAFTA Annex 1137.2, for example, required NAFTA Parties to designate a place for delivery of the documents. The Free Trade Commission of NAFTA in 2004 issued a statement on notices of intent in which it specified the appropriate recipient authority within each NAFTA government.[16]

---

[13] NAFTA, art. 1119. *See also* U.S.-Chile Free Trade Agreement (FTA), art. 10.15(4); U.S. Model BIT of 2004, art. 24 (2).

[14] "Service of Process" refers to formal delivery of a writ, summons, or other legal process. *See* Service, *Black's Law Dictionary* (8th ed. 2004). The most important multilateral convention on service of process is Convention on Service Abroad of Judicial and Extra Judicial in Civil or Commercial Matters (entered into force in Feb. 1969), *available at* http://www.hcch.net/index_en.php?act=conventions.text&cid=17.

[15] *See* Article 2(1) of UNCITRAL Arbitration Rules at p. 122 *infra*. ICSID Rules, although they contain detailed provisions regarding serving the request for arbitration (see subsection 2 below), do not have a corresponding provision regarding service of a notice of claim.

[16] Statement of the Free Trade Commission on notices of intent to submit a claim to arbitration (October 7, 2004), *available at* www.naftaclaims.com. In contract arbitration, the notice is to be delivered to the contractually agreed-upon recipient. Rubins et al. *supra* note 9, at 331.

2. Request for Arbitration

Once the necessary periods of time or other prearbitration conditions have been satisfied, the claimant may commence the arbitration proceedings by filing a document widely referred to as a "Request for Arbitration."[17] Various arbitral rules contain detailed instructions prescribing the information that must be included in a request for arbitration.[18]

The International Centre for the Settlement of Investment Disputes (ICSID) provides explicitly for the procedure to be followed to effect service of process on the host state in its Rules of Procedure for the Institution of Conciliation and Arbitration Proceedings (Institution Rules). These rules require the claimant to send the Request in writing to the Secretary-General of ICSID, containing basic information.[19] After receiving the required fee from the claimant, the Secretary-General sends a copy of the Request to the respondent.[20] The Secretary-General will then review the Request to determine if it is manifestly outside the scope of ICSID jurisdiction, and if it is not, he or she will register the arbitration Request at the Center. Once the Request is registered, the arbitration is deemed commenced.[21] After arbitration is commenced in this manner, the respondent state cannot avoid the proceedings by refusing to respond to the Request for Arbitration; the ICSID Rules mandate that the proceeding will continue even if the respondent fails to participate.[22]

The UNCITRAL Rules provide for a simplified method of service of process. These Rules provide that "any notice, including a notification, communication or proposal, is deemed to have been received if it is physically delivered to the addressee or if it is delivered at his habitual residence, place of business or mailing address...."[23] The UNCITRAL Rules also specify that "Notice shall be

---

[17] See, e.g., ICSID Convention, art. 36; International Chamber of Commerce (ICC) Arbitration Rules, art. 4; London Court of International Arbitration (LCIA) Rules, article 1; Stockholm Chamber of Commerce (SCC) Rules, art. 5. Article 3 of the UNCITRAL Rules calls this document "Notice of Arbitration."

[18] ICSID Institution Rules, art. 2; SCC Rules, art. 5; ICC Rules, art. 4; UNCITRAL Rules, art. 3; *see also* Arbitration (Additional Facility) Rules, art. 3.

[19] Institution Rules, art. 1–2.

[20] Institution Rules, art. 5. *See, e.g., Vacuum Salt Prod. Ltd. v. Ghana,* ICSID No. ARB/92/1 (Award of Feb. 16, 1994) ("On 28 May 1992, ICSID received the Request for Arbitration in this case submitted by [claimant].... Pursuant to Rule 5 of the Rules of Procedure for the Institution of Conciliation Arbitration Proceedings, the Secretary-General of ICSID by letters dated 29 May 1992 ... transmitted a copy of the Request and of the accompanying documentation to Ghana").

[21] Institution Rules, art. 6.

[22] *See, e.g., Tradex Hellas, S.A. (Greece) v. Albania,* ICSID No. ARB/94/2 (Award on Jurisdiction, Dec. 24, 1996) (Albania's failure to respond to Request led to Secretary-General's appointment of its arbitrator).

[23] UNCITRAL Rules, art. 2(1).

deemed to have been received on the day it is so delivered,"[24] and "Arbitral proceedings shall be deemed to commence on the date on which the notice of arbitration is received by the respondent."[25]

ICSID Arbitration Rules

Rule 1. The Request

(1) Any Contracting State or any national of a Contracting State wishing to institute conciliation or arbitration proceedings under the Convention shall address a request to that effect in writing to the Secretary-General at the seat of the Centre. The request shall indicate whether it relates to a conciliation or an arbitration proceeding. It shall be drawn up in an official language of the Centre, shall be dated, and shall be signed by the requesting party.

(2) The request may be made jointly by the parties to the dispute.

Rule 2. Contents of the Request

(1) The request shall

    (a) designate precisely each party to the dispute and state the address of each;

    (b) state, if one of the parties is a constituent subdivision or agency of a Contracting State, that it has been designated to the Centre by that State pursuant to Article 25(1) of the Convention;

    (c) indicate the date of consent and the instruments in which it is recorded, including, if one party is a constituent subdivision or agency of a Contracting State, similar data on the approval of such consent by that State unless it had notified the Centre that no such approval is required;

    (d) indicate with respect to the party that is a national of a Contracting State:

        (i) its nationality on the date of consent; and

        (ii) if the party is a natural person:

            (A) his nationality on the date of the request; and

            (B) that he did not have the nationality of the Contracting State party to the dispute either on the date of consent or on the date of the request; or

        (iii) if the party is a juridical person which on the date of consent had the nationality of the Contracting State party to the dispute, the agreement of the parties that it should be treated as a national of another Contracting State for the purposes of the Convention; and

---

[24] *Id.*

[25] UNCITRAL Rules, art. 3(2). *See also Lauder v. Czech Republic* (UNCITRAL Arbitration, Award of Sep. 1, 2001) ("On 19 August, 1999, Ronald S. Lauder initiated these arbitration proceedings by giving notice of arbitration to the Czech Republic"); *Adams v. Mexico* (NAFTA), Notice of Claim, Feb. 16, 2001 (UNCITRAL claim served directly upon the Secretary of Economy at the Foreign Investment Directorate of Mexico).

(e) contain information concerning the issues in dispute indicating that there is, between the parties, a legal dispute arising directly out of an investment.

(2) The information required by subparagraphs (1)(c) and (1)(d)(iii) shall be supported by documentation.

(3) "Date of consent" means the date on which the parties to the dispute consented in writing to submit it to the Centre; if both parties did not act on the same day, it means the date on which the second party acted.

Neither the ICSID nor the UNCITRAL arbitration rules require that a Request for Arbitration set forth the legal or factual basis of a claim in detail. However, some claimants have used the Request for Arbitration to provide a full analysis of both facts and law, occasionally in a lengthy document.[26] Although such a substantial document entails greater expense and longer preparation time than a summary notice of claim, the more detailed approach can provide some important advantages to claimants.

First, the Request for Arbitration may be the only substantive document the arbitral tribunal reviews in the first instance, and for a significant period of time it will not be subject to rebuttal by the respondent. By presenting its position persuasively and comprehensively at the outset, a claimant may be able to establish a lasting, favorable impression of the case in the arbitrators' minds. A strongly formulated Request for Arbitration may be particularly advantageous during preliminary jurisdictional challenges. If the arbitrators are familiar with the details of the claim first from the claimant's perspective, and are convinced that it has a legitimate basis, the tribunal may be less persuaded by technical defenses that might otherwise block recovery.

Second, a thorough and convincing Request for Arbitration can strengthen a private claimant's position in negotiations with the host state, regardless of whether the arbitration continues to conclusion. By taking the opportunity in the Request for Arbitration to describe the factual and legal basis for the claim and provide comprehensive analysis in support of its assessment of damages, claimants may be able to gain bargaining leverage, having demonstrated a reasonable probability of success and an approximate value of the arbitration claim.

This kind of detailed Request for Arbitration normally includes, in addition to the information required by the applicable rules:

(1) a thorough presentation of the factual background;
(2) an explanation of the basis for jurisdiction, including the consent to arbitration and preemptive responses to expected jurisdictional challenges;

---

[26] The Notice of Claim in *Loewen Group. v. U.S.*, which served as the Request for Arbitration, was 67 pages long and had nearly 120 pages of supporting affidavits and other materials.

(3) a description of the substantive legal regime established by relevant treaties and international law, applicable domestic laws, as well as the application of the law to the case at hand; and

(4) a preliminary assessment of the claimant's damages and requests for other relief.

Some practitioners, however, insist that a relatively short request for arbitration is preferable in most cases.[27] According to this approach, presenting the full panoply of legal arguments at the earliest stage of the arbitration simply provides the respondent additional time in which to prepare a response. Instead, the claimant may include a relatively full description of the background facts of the case, but withhold the details of legal argument for its full memorial, to be filed after the tribunal is formed.

E. "Registration" or Approval by Arbitral Institution

Under the ICSID Rules and Washington Convention and some other arbitration systems,[28] the arbitral institution is charged with screening requests for arbitration. Under the ICSID regime, the ICSID Secretary-General reviews all requests for arbitration to establish that the claimant has presented a case that prima facie falls within the jurisdiction of the Centre.[29] The ICSID Secretary-General is not authorized to engage in an in-depth analysis of jurisdictional issues. Instead, the goal is to eliminate jurisdictionally frivolous claims that are clearly outside the scope of any valid submission to arbitration, before either side invests substantial assets in the prosecution of the arbitration.[30] This basic oversight protects states from abusive litigation tactics aimed at applying unreasonable pressure during negotiations.[31] As noted above, the decision to register or reject an ICSID claim is based solely on the materials submitted by the claimant in its request; the respondent has no opportunity actively to oppose registration.[32]

---

[27] *E.g.,* Lucy Reed & John Beechey, panel discussion at International Dispute Resolution by the Rules Conference sponsored by the A.B.A., Sept. 12, 2003, Washington, DC

[28] *See, e.g.,* Stockholm Chamber of Commerce Rules, art. 7 ("If it is clear that the SCC Institute lacks jurisdiction over the dispute or if the Registration Fee has not been paid in due time, the Claimant's Request for Arbitration shall be dismissed"); and ICC Rules, art. 6(2).

[29] ICSID Convention, art. 36(3).

[30] Antonio Parra, *The Screening Power of the ICSID Secretary,* 2(1) ICSID News 10 (1985).

[31] *Id.,* at 10; Moshe Hirch, *The Arbitration Mechanism of the International Centre for the Settlement of Investment Disputes* 43 (1993).

[32] Parra, *supra* note 30, at 12. In practice, where there is doubt as to whether a Request for Arbitration should be registered, ICSID often requests that the claimant provide additional information.

> Washington Convention, art. 36
>
> . . . .
>
> (3) The Secretary-General shall register the request unless he finds, on the basis of the information contained in the request, that the dispute is manifestly outside the jurisdiction of the Centre. He shall forthwith notify the parties of registration or refusal to register.

If the Secretary-General refuses to register a Request for Arbitration, the claimant has no recourse to appeal or other review of the decision.[33] Conversely, registration of Request does not mean that ICSID jurisdiction has been established definitively. Once the tribunal has been composed, the respondent is free to challenge the competence of the arbitral tribunal on any grounds.[34]

This is different from the International Chamber of Commerce (ICC) procedure, which calls for prima facie review by the Court of Arbitration only where the responding party has submitted initial objections to the validity of the arbitration agreement (or has failed to appear).[35]

The UNCITRAL Rules, like many institutional commercial arbitration rules, do not provide for any prima facie initial review of requests for arbitration. Instead, the respondent must raise all jurisdictional arguments before the arbitral tribunal after it is formed.

F. Default of a Party

It is not uncommon that the host state will refuse to participate in arbitration proceedings. A party may refuse to participate at all, or may stop responding or appearing at a particular stage in the proceedings. However, a submission to arbitrate is normally binding on both parties, and irrevocable. Indeed, it is considered central to the efficient working of any private dispute resolution system that the noncooperation of a party cannot be permitted to frustrate the process and prevent the claimant from obtaining relief.[36] Despite the obvious tension between this

---

[33] The claimant, however, may file a new request for arbitration involving the same issues. The rejection of the initial request by the ICSID Secretariat does not necessarily mean that the second request will automatically be dismissed.

[34] Washington Convention, art. 41(1) ("The Tribunal shall be the judge of its own competence"); Washington Convention, art. 41(2) (directing the tribunal to consider "any objection by a party to the dispute that that dispute is not within the jurisdiction of the Centre, or for other reasons is not within the competence of the Tribunal").

[35] ICC Rules (1998), art. 6(2).

[36] *See* C. Schreuer, *The ICSID Convention: A Commentary* 694 (2001); ICC Rules (1998), art. 21(2); UNCITRAL Rules, art. 28.

principle and the fundamental goal of due process for all parties, default judgments are well founded in international law, including explicit incorporation into the procedures of the International Court of Justice.[37] Therefore, under normal circumstances, the arbitration will proceed to a "default" ruling, despite the fact that only one side has presented its case.[38]

The Washington Convention is no exception, providing in considerable detail the procedure to be followed in case of default:

> Article 45
>
> (1) Failure of a party to appear or to present his case shall not be deemed an admission of the other party's assertions.
>
> (2) If a party fails to appear or to present his case at any stage of the proceedings the other party may request the Tribunal to deal with the questions submitted to it and to render an award. Before rendering an award, the Tribunal shall notify, and grant a period of grace to, the party failing to appear or to present its case, unless it is satisfied that that party does not intend to do so.

Other rules deal with default in other ways. The ICC Rules, for instance, allow the Court of Arbitration (rather than the tribunal) to decide whether an arbitration should proceed to default:

> Article 6
>
> Effect of the Arbitration Agreement
>
> 1. Where the parties have agreed to submit to arbitration under the Rules, they shall be deemed to have submitted ipso facto to the Rules in effect on the date of commencement of the arbitration proceedings, unless they have agreed to submit to the Rules in effect on the date of their arbitration agreement.

---

[37] Statute of the International Court of Justice, art. 53, *available at* http://www.icj-cij.org/icjwww/ibasicdocuments/ibasictext/ibasicstatute.htm. "1. Whenever one of the parties does not appear before the Court, or fails to defend its case, the other party may call upon the Court to decide in favour of its claim. 2. The Court must, before doing so, satisfy itself, not only that it has jurisdiction in accordance with Articles 36 and 37, but also that the claim is well founded in fact and law." *See also* Stanimir Alexandrov, *Non-Appearance before the International Court of Justice*, 33 Colum. J. Transnat'l L. 41 (1995); K. Highet, *Nonappearance and Disappearance before the ICJ*, 81 Am. J. Int'l L. 237 (1987); Noah Rubins, *Swembalt v. Latvia: Introduction and the Dilemma of Default*, 2 Stock. Int'l Arb. Rep. 119 (2004).

[38] *See generally* Aron Broches, *The Convention on the Settlement of Investment Disputes between States and Nationals of Other States: Applicable Law and Default Procedure*, in *International Arbitration Liber Amicorum for Martin Domke* 12 (1967); A. Masood, *Default Procedure in Arbitration under the World Bank Convention*, 22 L. Rev. 1 (1970); William Northcote, *Default, Ex parte and Want of Prosecution Proceedings in International Commercial Arbitration*, 14 Advoc. Q. 319 (1992); G. Fitzmaurice, *The Problem of the "Non-Appearing" Defendant Government*, 51 Brit. Y. Int'l L. 89 (1980); Rubins, *supra* note 37.

2. If the Respondent does not file an Answer, as provided by Article 5, or if any party raises one or more pleas concerning the existence, validity or scope of the arbitration agreement, the Court may decide, without prejudice to the admissibility or merits of the plea or pleas, that the arbitration shall proceed if it is prima facie satisfied that an arbitration agreement under the Rules may exist. In such a case, any decision as to the jurisdiction of the Arbitral Tribunal shall be taken by the Arbitral Tribunal itself. If the Court is not so satisfied, the parties shall be notified that the arbitration cannot proceed. In such a case, any party retains the right to ask any court having jurisdiction whether or not there is a binding arbitration agreement.

3. If any of the parties refuses or fails to take part in the arbitration or any stage thereof, the arbitration shall proceed notwithstanding such refusal or failure.

G. Composition of Tribunal

1. Appointment of Arbitrators[39]

Outside the ICSID system, the majority of international arbitration tribunals in disputes of significant size are appointed in a similar way: each party names one arbitrator, and the two party-appointed tribunal members together agree on a third arbitrator, who serves as the tribunal chairman. The increased expertise, breadth of knowledge, and consultation that results from a three-member tribunal arguably makes such a panel less likely to err than would a single arbitrator, and therefore the additional cost and time when compared to a sole arbitrator is normally considered to be justified.[40] Absent contrary agreement of the parties, this is the procedure envisaged by the UNCITRAL Rules.[41] Absent contrary agreement, the ICSID Rules and Washington Convention provide that the *parties*, and not the party-appointed arbitrators, are jointly to select the chairman of the tribunal.[42] To do this, one party suggests two names to the other party as

---

[39] *See generally* Gavan Griffith, *Constitution of Arbitral Tribunals: The Duty of Impartiality in Tribunals or Choose Your Arbitrator Wisely*, 16 Arbitrator: J Inst. Arb. Austl. 229 (1998); Wendy Miles, *Practical Issues for Appointment of Arbitrators*, 20 J. Int'l Arb. 219 (2003); Douglas E. McLaren, *Party-Appointed vs. List-Appointed Arbitrators*, 20 J. Int'l Arb. 233 (2003).

[40] Nevertheless, a number of investment disputes have been presided over by sole arbitrators. *See, e.g., Misima Mines Pty., Ltd. v. Papua New Guinea*, ICSID Case No. ARB/96/2; *Gruslin v. Malaysia*, ICSID Case No. ARB/94/1.

[41] If the parties fail to appoint arbitrators, or if the party-appointed arbitrators cannot agree on a tribunal chairman, this task falls to the "Appointing Authority," which in investment arbitration cases (where there is no party agreement on the appointing authority) is designated by the Permanent Court of Arbitration (PCA) at the Hague. UNCITRAL Rules, art. 2(b). It has become common that the PCA chooses the ICSID Secretariat as the appointing authority in investment treaty arbitration.

[42] Washington Convention, art. 37(2)(b).

potential tribunal chairmen. The other party then either accepts one of the candidates or counters with two proposals of its own.[43] If no agreement is reached within 90 days, then on the request of any of the parties, the ICSID Secretariat will appoint the tribunal chairman.[44] In practice, it is relatively rare for either of the parties to accept the nomination put forward by the other side, and therefore the ICSID Secretariat normally is often left with the task of appointing the President of the tribunal.[45]

One requirement in all the major arbitration rules and most national laws is that arbitrators be unbiased and independent.[46] Under the UNCITRAL arbitration rules, for example, an arbitrator can be disqualified for any fact that could be seen as giving rise to justifiable doubts as to the arbitrator's impartiality and independence.[47] The basic rule is now very developed in greater detail and is actually applied in the investment arbitration context.[48]

---

[43] ICSID Rules, art. 3(1).

[44] ICSID Rules, art. 4(2). *See also* A. A. de Fina, *Different Strokes for Different Folks: Institutional Appointment of Arbitrators*, Arb. & Disp. Res. L. J. 31–35 (Mar. 2000).

[45] On the institutional process of selecting arbitrators, *see* Eva Muller, *How Do International Institutions Select Arbitrators?*, 17 J. Int'l Arb. 157 (2000). Another common method of forming the arbitration tribunal is known as the "list method," whereby the appointing institution provides list from which each party strikes names. The parties then rank remaining candidates, and the appointing institution appoints the highest-ranked arbitrators as a panel.

[46] On independence and impartiality of arbitrators *see generally* Dominique Hascher, *ICC Practice in Relation to the Appointment, Confirmation, Challenge and Replacement of Arbitrators*, 6(2) ICC Int'l Ct. Arb. Bull. 4, 6 (Nov. 1995); D. Bishop & L. Reed, *Practical Guidelines for Interviewing, Selecting, and Challenging Party-Appointed Arbitrators in International Commercial Arbitration*, 14 Arb. Int'l 395, 408–409 (1998); W. Michael Tupman, *Challenge and Disqualification of Arbitrators in International Commercial Arbitration*, 38 Int'l & Comp. L. Q. 26, 50 (1989); W. L. Craig, W. W. Park, J. Paulsson, *International Chamber of Commerce Arbitration*, at 203–206 (2000); M. Hunter & J. Paulsson, *A Code of Ethics for Arbitrators in International Commercial Arbitration*, 13 Int'l Bus. L. 153, 155 (1985); and H.-L. Yu & L. Shore, *Independence, Impartiality and Immunity of Arbitrators—US and English Perspectives*, 52 Int'l & Comp. L. Q. 935, 963 (2003).

[47] UNCITRAL Rules, art. 10(1); *see also* ICC Arbitration Rules, art. 7(1); LCIA Rules, art. 5(2).

[48] Most arbitral rules lack guidelines to assist parties, arbitrators, and arbitral institutions in determining whether a particular relationship should raise doubts as to the impartiality of a challenged arbitrator. The International Bar Association (IBA), however, has promulgated Guidelines on Conflicts of Interest in International Arbitration, which are now widely cited. *See* International Bar Association Guidelines on Conflicts of Interest in International Arbitration, Approved on May 22, 2004 by the IBA Council, *available at* http://www.ibanet.org/legalpractice/Arbitration.cfm#Guides. *See also* Nathalie Voser & Neomi Rao, *Background Information on the IBA Guidelines on Conflicts of Interest in International Arbitration*, 5 Bus. L. Int'l 433, 442 (2004). The American Bar Association (ABA) Dispute Resolution Section has prepared a set of "best practices" guidelines for arbitrator disclosure. *See* The Arbitrator's Disclosure Conundrum Draft Guidelines 1-10-08, *available at* www.abanet.org.

Much has been written about the complex task of choosing the optimal candidate for party-appointed arbitrator.[49] Basic qualifications include a nationality other than that of the opposing party, a command of the language of the dispute (and, preferably, the primary language of the disputing parties), technical and legal knowledge appropriate to the dispute, organizational skills, and availability.[50] However, other less tangible attributes may be equally important in the selection of an arbitrator, making the appointment process more of an art than a science. Some of these characteristics include decisiveness, procedural competence, sound judgment, and perhaps most importantly, persuasiveness. The ability to persuade is essential, because although all three arbitrators must be unbiased and independent of the parties, in practice each party-appointed arbitrator may find himself or herself in the position of presenting to the President the positions of the party that appointed him or her.

To determine the proper qualifications, counsel to the arbitrating parties often conduct an interview of arbitrator candidates. This initial conversation must be carefully limited to avoid tainting the candidate with bias in any way.

A. A. de Fina, *The Party Appointed Arbitrator in Int'l Arbitrations: Role and Selection*, 15 Arb. Int'l 381, 392 (1999)

Although a possibly costly exercise, but one which might be both appropriate and justified in the context of a particular international arbitration, is an interview of prospective arbitrators. The circumstances of such an interview must be carefully orchestrated and controlled, particularly in the case of a prospective party appointed arbitrator.

Whilst interview for a sole arbitrator may properly be conducted by both parties to an arbitration, the nature of a party appointment will mean in most instances that only the appointing party through their lawyers will conduct the interview. Nothing can be done or said at such an interview which may prejudice the prospective appointee if ultimately appointed, or which might give rise to challenge and disqualification. An interview must therefore be limited to such matters as availability, conflict, experience, training, qualification, specialist expertise and the like. Under no circumstances can aspects going to the nature of the dispute or its merits be raised or canvassed even indirectly. In any event, the interview should be carried out only by counsel for a party and in the absence of that party. Whether or not to conduct an interview is a very delicate and possibly controversial issue, particularly as it would ordinarily be appropriate to compensate for out of pocket expenses and to pay some fee for attendance. However, this is now a relatively common practice, particularly in very large and complex arbitrations, and appears to work to [the] benefit of and without compromising the arbitral process.

---

[49] See, e.g., Andreas Lowenfeld, *The Party-Appointed Arbitrator in International Controversies*, 30 Tex. Int'l L. J. 59 (1995).

[50] David Hacking, comments at the meeting of the Chicago International Dispute Resolution Association, Chicago, Ill., Oct. 15, 1999.

In practice, other considerations sometimes take precedence in arbitrator selection. Counsel routinely scour the candidate's published writings and other professional activities, seeking to ascertain whether the individual would be naturally disposed to the appointing party's positions. A claimant in investment arbitration, for example, may look for an arbitrator who has represented clients against governments or state-owned enterprises, or who has opined positively about expanded protection standards for investors. As one practitioner has noted:

> The point here is, strictly *neutral* panels are not what the disputants seek; rather, rational disputants with so much at stake want to retain some measure of control over who decides the dispute. They want to choose their own arbitrator and to constitute a panel of arbitrators who can truly appreciate, from personal experience or involvement, the points each makes and *particularly* the point of view of the selecting party.
>
> Thus, a rational party will start with a field including only disinterested candidates, whose integrity is unimpeachable, ... but he will then choose those who will give him the greatest confidence that he will prevail.[51]
>
> Therefore, additional criteria often play a role in arbitrator selection. For example, an established reputation within the industry in which the dispute arose or with regard to the legal issues in dispute ensures the candidate's "gravitas" among his colleagues on the panel, and may give him disproportionate influence in the final result. Likewise, a forceful personality (assuming that the arbitrator agrees with the appointing party's position) will allow the candidate to make his voice heard over that of the other party-appointed arbitrator.[52]

The participation of state parties has an important effect on the appointment of arbitrators. Most significantly, inexperienced arbitrators may be unacceptable to the claimant, since it is widely perceived that only well-established jurists have the self-confidence to render large awards against states, which may have serious economic consequences for the country involved. From the opposite perspective, at least one practitioner has noted that developing governments often select their investment arbitrators from a very short list of names, such that some of their appointees will derive a majority of their income from such appointments. In one case, according to the attorney, it was discovered that an arbitral appointee had served fifteen times in different proceedings on tribunals as the government-appointed adjudicator.[53] Seen from the most charitable point of view, host states may want to be sure that their party-appointed arbitrator is familiar with conditions in their country, including humanitarian and development concerns they may feel justify the measures they have implemented.

---

[51] James D. Wangelin, *Effective Selection of Arbitrators in International Arbitration*, available at http://www.sdma.com/sedgwick.updates/articles/litigation-trial/?internationalarbitration.html.

[52] For more on suggested criteria for choosing arbitrators, *see* Claudia T. Salomon, *Selecting an International Arbitrator: Five Factors to Consider,* Mealey's Int'l Arb. Rep., Oct. 2002, at 25.

[53] Mark Baker, Fulbright & Jaworski Conference on Arbitration, Washington, D.C., Sept. 26, 2002.

2. Situs of Arbitration

Under both ICSID and UNCITRAL Rules, the parties are free to agree on any arbitral situs, and to jointly designate one or more languages in which the proceedings will be conducted. However, the Washington Convention and ICSID Rules provide that where there is no contrary agreement of the parties, the seat of the arbitration will be at the World Bank in Washington, D.C.[54] The UNCITRAL Rules meanwhile, require the arbitral tribunal to determine the place of arbitration if the parties cannot agree.[55] Under other arbitration regimes as well, the arbitrators (or the arbitral institution, as in the case of the ICC[56]) retain wide discretion in choosing the arbitral situs that best suits the needs of the parties to the dispute.

UNCITRAL, *Notes on Organizing Arbitral Proceedings*, U.N. Doc. A/CN.9/410, n.21–23

3. Place of arbitration

(a) Determination of the place of arbitration, if not already agreed upon by the parties

21. Arbitration rules usually allow the parties to agree on the place of arbitration, subject to the requirement of some arbitral institutions that arbitrations under their rules be conducted at a particular place, usually the location of the institution. If the place has not been so agreed upon, the rules governing the arbitration typically provide that it is in the power of the arbitral tribunal or the institution administering the arbitration to determine the place. If the arbitral tribunal is to make that determination, it may wish to hear the views of the parties before doing so.

22. Various factual and legal factors influence the choice of the place of arbitration, and their relative importance varies from case to case. Among the more prominent factors are: (a) suitability of the law on arbitral procedure of the place of arbitration; (b) whether there is a multilateral or bilateral treaty on enforcement of arbitral awards between the State where the arbitration takes place and the State or States where the award may have to be enforced; (c) convenience of the parties and the arbitrators, including the travel distances; (d) availability and cost of support services needed; and (e) location of the subject-matter in dispute and proximity of evidence.

(b) Possibility of meetings outside the place of arbitration

23. Many sets of arbitration rules and laws on arbitral procedure expressly allow the arbitral tribunal to hold meetings elsewhere than at the place of arbitration. For example, under the UNCITRAL Model Law on International Commercial Arbitration "the arbitral tribunal may, unless otherwise agreed by the parties, meet at any place it considers appropriate for consultation among its members, for hearing witnesses, experts or the parties, or for inspection of goods, other property or documents"

---

[54] ICSID Rules, art. 13(1); Washington Convention, art. 63. Unlike the ICSID Rules, ICSID Additional Facility Rules do not designate a default seat.

[55] UNCITRAL Rules, art. 16.

[56] Herman Verbist, *The Practice of the ICC International Court of Arbitration with Regard to the Fixing of the Place of Arbitration*, 12 Arb. Int'l 347 (1996).

(article 20(2)). The purpose of this discretion is to permit arbitral proceedings to be carried out in a manner that is most efficient and economical.

The choice of arbitral situs has more significance than simply efficiency and economy. The decision to designate a particular country as the place of arbitration may bring with it a choice of *lex arbitri*, importing to a large degree the mandatory (nonderogable) rules of the forum with regard to the conduct of arbitration, ethical standards for counsel and arbitrators, and other important legal standards.[57] Perhaps most important, unless the investment arbitration in question is conducted within the ICSID system, the arbitral situs will be the proper place to challenge any eventual award in national courts.[58]

3. Language of Arbitration

The UNCITRAL Rules provide no default language, leaving full discretion in this matter to the arbitral tribunal in the absence of party agreement.[59] The tribunal may designate more than one language to be employed in the arbitration. ICSID, meanwhile, specifies that French, English, and Spanish are the official languages, and that another language can be selected by the parties only with the approval of the tribunal.[60] Under the ICSID rules, one or two languages can be designated as working languages by the parties, and if no agreement can be reached by the parties, each side may select one of the three official languages, and both languages will be used in the proceeding.[61]

UNCITRAL, *Notes on Organizing Arbitral Proceedings*, U.N. Doc. A/CN.9/410, n.17–20

2. Language of proceedings

17. Many rules and laws on arbitral procedure empower the arbitral tribunal to determine the language or languages to be used in the proceedings, if the parties have not reached an agreement thereon.

(a) Possible need for translation of documents, in full or in part

18. Some documents annexed to the statements of claim and defence or submitted later may not be in the language of the proceedings. Bearing in mind the needs of the proceedings and economy, it may be considered whether the arbitral tribunal should order that

---

[57] *See, e.g.,* Noah Rubins, *The Arbitral Seat is No Fiction*, Mealey's Int'l Arb. Rep., Jan. 2001, at 23.
[58] New York Convention, art. V(1)(e).
[59] UNCITRAL Rules, art. 17(1).
[60] ICSID Rules, art. 22(1).
[61] *Id.*

any of those documents or parts thereof should be accompanied by a translation into the language of the proceedings.

(b) Possible need for interpretation of oral presentations

19. If interpretation will be necessary during oral hearings, it is advisable to consider whether the interpretation will be simultaneous or consecutive and whether the arrangements should be the responsibility of a party or the arbitral tribunal. In an arbitration administered by an institution, interpretation as well as translation services are often arranged by the arbitral institution.

(c) Cost of translation and interpretation

20. In taking decisions about translation or interpretation, it is advisable to decide whether any or all of the costs are to be paid directly by a party or whether they will be paid out of the deposits and apportioned between the parties along with the other arbitration costs.

H. Initial Session of the Tribunal

Once the tribunal has been formed, it will almost invariably call the parties to attend, either in person and/or telephonically, an initial conference or hearing to discuss preliminary matters and to confirm the agreement of the parties or decision of the tribunal on issues of situs, language, arbitral rules and modifications thereto, and the like. Under the ICSID Rules, for example, the tribunal "shall hold its first session within 60 days after its constitution or such other period as the parties may agree."[62] Most frequently, the initial session will also be used to establish the initial briefing schedule, which often begins with a Statement of Claim and Statement of Defense from the claimant and respondent, respectively. Under the ICC Rules, the Terms of Reference are often negotiated, drafted, and/or signed during the initial session.

ADF Group, Inc. v. U.S., ICSID Case No. ARB(AF)/00/1 ((NAFTA) Minutes of the First Session of the Tribunal Feb. 3, 2001), *available at* www.naftaclaims.com

As agreed with the parties, the first session of the Arbitral Tribunal was held by videoconference on February 3, 2001 from 10:00 a.m. to 11:00 a.m., from the offices of the World Trade Organization in Geneva (Switzerland), the offices of Fasken Martineau Du Moulin LLP in Montreal (Canada), and the offices of the World Bank in Washington, DC (United States).

Participating in the session, with an indication of their location, were:

Members of the Tribunal
Judge Florentino P. Feliciano, President (Geneva)

---

[62] ICSID Rules, art. 13.

Professor Armand de Mestral, Arbitrator (Montreal)
Ms. Carolyn B. Lamm, Arbitrator (Washington, DC)

ICSID Secretariat
Mr. Alejandro A. Escobar, Secretary of the Tribunal (Washington, D.C.)

Representing ADF Group Inc. (Claimant)
Mtre. Peter E. Kirby (Montreal) Fasken Martineau Du Moulin LLP
Mtre. René Cadieux (Montreal) Fasken Martineau Du Moulin LLP
Mtre. Diane Bertrand (Montreal) Fasken Martineau Du Moulin LLP
Mtre. Pierre Labelle (Montreal) Fasken Martineau Du Moulin LLP

Representing the United States of America (Respondent)
Mr. Mark A. Clodfelter (Washington, D.C.) Assistant Legal Adviser for
International Claims & Investment Disputes
United States Department of State
Mr. Barton Legum (Washington, D.C.) Chief,
NAFTA Arbitration Division
Office of International Claims & Investment
Disputes, United States Department of State

. . . .

The session considered matters listed on the Provisional Agenda, circulated by the Secretary and attached to these Minutes as Attachment 1.

The President noted that, by a joint letter of February 2, 2001, the parties had informed the Tribunal of the agreements the parties had reached on a number of the matters listed in the Provisional Agenda.

I Procedural Matters

1. Constitution of the Tribunal and the Tribunal Members' Declarations

The Tribunal had been constituted on January 11, 2001. The President noted the parties' agreement that it had been duly constituted in accordance with the Additional Facility Arbitration Rules, and that the Claimant had supplied correspondence on behalf of itself and of ADF International Inc. agreeing to the appointment of each individual member of the Tribunal under NAFTA Article 1125. It was noted that the parties had received from the Secretariat copies of the declarations, and of their respective attached statements, signed by each arbitrator pursuant to Additional Facility Arbitration Rule 14.

. . . .

3. Arbitration Rules

The President noted the parties' agreement that the ICSID Additional Facility Arbitration Rules govern the proceeding, which was instituted under the provisions of Chapter Eleven of NAFTA. The President noted that the parties are attempting to reach agreement regarding any additional rules to address document production, the testimony of witnesses and experts, the submission of evidence and treatment of claimed confidential business information. If necessary, the parties were to make submissions with their proposals on such matters within the time periods set forth in section 14 below.

4. Fees and Expenses of Tribunal Members

It was noted that, in addition to receiving reimbursement for any direct expenses reasonably incurred, each member of the Tribunal would receive:

a fee of US$1,500, or such other fee as may be set forth from time to time in the Centre's Schedule of Fees, for each day of meetings or other work performed in connection with the proceeding, without prejudice to any suggestions in respect of arbitrators' fees which the Tribunal might, at an appropriate time, make for the consideration of the parties; and subsistence allowances and reimbursement of travel and other expenses within limits set forth in Additional Facility Administrative and Financial Rule 6.

. . . .

6. Apportionment of Costs

The President noted the parties' agreement that, in accordance with Article 59 of the Additional Facility Arbitration Rules, the parties would defray the expenses of the proceeding in equal parts, without prejudice to the final decision of the Tribunal as to costs.

7. Records of Hearings

The President noted the parties' agreement that an audio or video recording shall be made of procedural hearings, and that a verbatim transcript of substantive hearings shall be made. In addition, the parties agreed that either party may decide in its sole discretion whether a hearing is substantive for this purpose. The Secretary is to keep minutes in summary form under Article 44 of the Additional Facility Arbitration Rules.

8. Means of Communication

It was noted that all communications by a party to the Tribunal or any of its members shall be made through ICSID. The Tribunal took note of the parties' agreement that delivery of pleadings to ICSID shall be made by overnight courier service to arrive on or before the date that the submission is due. For submissions other than pleadings, the parties agreed that delivery may be made by facsimile on or before the date the submission is due, followed by hard copy sent by mail or courier service.

9. Copies of Instruments

It was agreed that all written submissions would be introduced by a party into the proceeding by sending the original and five copies to the Centre, which would arrange for the appropriate distribution of copies. In addition, each party agreed to serve two copies of all submissions directly on the other party.

10. Quorum

The President noted the parties' agreement that the quorum for all sittings of the Tribunal would be constituted by all three of its members, unless the parties otherwise agreed.

11. Procedural Languages

The President noted the parties' agreement that the language of the proceeding would be English. In addition, the parties agreed that the foregoing is without prejudice to either party's ability to rely upon, and to provide the Tribunal with copies of, legal authorities rendered in other languages. A party relying on legal authority in a language other than English, French or Spanish shall, within a reasonable time after the date it submits such legal authority, provide to the Tribunal and the other party a translation of the portion or portions of the legal authority upon which the party relies.

12. Place of Arbitration

The parties agreed that they would make further submissions on the question of the place of arbitration, as indicated in their joint letter of February 2, 2001.

The President noted the parties' agreement on the following schedule: The Claimant's submission on place of arbitration shall be filed by February 26, 2001, and the Respondent's submission on place of arbitration shall be filed by March 19, 2001. If the Claimant deems it necessary, it may file a response to the Respondent's submission by April 2, 2001, and the Respondent may file observations on the Claimant's response by April 16, 2001.

The parties agreed that it will not be necessary to hold a hearing on this issue and requested, if necessary, that the Tribunal render its decision based on the written argument.

13. Written and Oral Proceedings

The President noted the parties' agreement that, notwithstanding paragraphs 2 and 4 of Article 46 of the Additional Facility Arbitration Rules, there shall be a single written proceeding that addresses both the question of liability and any defenses that might be characterized as objections to the competence of the Tribunal. After completion of the written procedure, the parties agree that there shall be a hearing to address both legal and factual issues pertaining to competence and liability. The parties agree to bifurcate the issue of liability from that of damages.

14. Pleadings: Number, Sequence, Time Limits

The President noted the parties' agreement that the written procedure for the phase of the proceeding concerning competence and liability shall consist of the Claimant's memorial, the Respondent's counter-memorial, the Claimant's reply and the Respondent's rejoinder. The parties recognize that the Governments of Canada and Mexico have the right to make written and oral submissions pursuant to NAFTA Article 1128.

The parties agreed to make written submissions to the Tribunal on the matter of the schedule for their respective pleadings, setting forth their respective positions within the following timeframe: the Claimant shall make its submission regarding the schedule on or before February 12, 2001, and the Respondent shall make its submission regarding the schedule on or before February 20, 2001.

15. Subsequent Sessions

The parties stated that they were attempting to reach agreement on a proposal to the Tribunal regarding subsequent sessions. The President noted that the parties could submit their respective positions on this matter, if necessary, simultaneously with their submissions regarding the schedule of the proceeding, mentioned at section 14 above. It was noted that Ms. Lamm and Professor de Mestral would provide the Secretary with the dates on which they were currently unavailable for holding subsequent sessions, and that the Secretary would transmit those dates to the parties for their information. This was subsequently done by the Secretary's letter to the parties of February 13, 2001.

I. Arbitrator-Ordered Interim Relief

The ICSID Arbitration Rules allow arbitral tribunals to recommend interim assistance to parties in the context of ongoing arbitration proceedings. However, owing to the realities of arbitration against sovereign states and the wording of the ICSID rules, enforcement of such remedies may sometimes be difficult. Nevertheless, parties to investment arbitration frequently request recommendations of provisional measures, and in some cases arbitrators have ordered the requested interim relief such as the suspension of related proceedings in national courts.

The UNCITRAL Rules, rooted as they are in the less politically complicated circumstances of international commercial arbitration, provide more explicit support for binding interim relief. On the other hand, the lack of treaty support means that arbitrators' interim orders may be impossible to enforce when the order is directed against a national government. In particular, the exclusivity provision contained in Article 26 of the Washington Convention might make orders barring a government respondent from pursuing remedies in its own courts more easily obtainable and enforceable in ICSID than in UNCITRAL proceedings.

1. The Legal Framework

The Washington Convention establishes the basis for ICSID tribunals' power to provide interim relief:

> Except as the parties otherwise agree, the Tribunal may, if it considers that the circumstances so require, *recommend any provisional measures* which should be taken to preserve the respective rights of either party.[63]

This language was the result of a compromise during treaty-drafting sessions between those states that wanted to provide for binding measures and the power to impose sanctions for noncompliance and those that sought to exclude provisional measures altogether.[64] The ICSID Arbitration Rules follow the basic model for interim relief found in the Washington Convention, and set up the applicable procedural framework:

> (1) At any time during the proceeding a party may request that provisional measures for the preservation of its rights be recommended by the Tribunal. The request shall specify the rights to be preserved, the measures the recommendation of which is requested, and the circumstances that require such measures.
>
> (2) The Tribunal shall give priority to the consideration of a request made pursuant to paragraph (1).
>
> (3) The Tribunal may also recommend provisional measures on its own initiative or recommend measures other than those specified in a request. It may at any time modify or revoke its recommendations.

---

[63] Washington Convention, art. 47 (emphasis added).
[64] Schreuer, *supra* note 36, at 746.

(4) The Tribunal shall only recommend provisional measures, or modify or revoke its recommendations, after giving each party an opportunity of presenting its observations.[65]

. . . .

Although the ICSID Rules, like the Washington Convention, empower arbitrators only to "recommend" provisional measures, the Additional Facility Rules—used when one of the countries involved in the dispute is not a party to the Washington Convention—allow parties to request that the tribunal *order* interim relief.[66]

The UNCITRAL Arbitration Rules also provide for binding provisional measures of protection:

> At the request of either party, the arbitral tribunal may take any interim measures it deems necessary in respect of the subject-matter of the dispute . . . . Such interim measures may be established in the form of an interim award. The arbitral tribunal shall be entitled to require security for the costs of such measures.[67]

Although UNCITRAL provisional measures therefore appear at first glance to be more enforceable than recommendations under ICSID, the difference may be minimal in the investment arbitration context. Although a state party is clearly bound by the UNCITRAL Rules to implement interim measures, there is probably no practical means of enforcing this obligation through the host state's courts. And although monetary awards rendered under the UNCITRAL Rules can be enforced by execution on assets through the New York Convention, foreign courts will normally lack jurisdiction to compel compliance with an arbitral tribunal's injunctive order against a host state. Further, it is an open question whether interim orders are enforceable at all in national courts as "foreign awards" under the New York Convention.[68] As a result, the practical

---

[65] ICSID Rules, art. 39.

[66] ICSID Additional Facility Rules, art. 47.

[67] UNCITRAL Arbitration Rules, art. 26. *See also* Chapter IV bis of the UNCITRAL Model Law on International Commercial Arbitration. On July 7, 2006, UNCITRAL adopted several amendments to the law including Chapter IV bis, which replaced the former Article 17 on interim measures. This new chapter substantially expands the treatment of the subject in the model law. It has 5 sections and 11 articles, which cover a wide spectrum of issues relating to interim measures, ranging from the power of arbitral tribunals to order such measures to court-ordered interim relief. See UNCITRAL: Model Law on International Commercial Arbitration 1985 with Amendments as adopted in 2006 (United Nations 2008), *available at* www.uncitral.org.

[68] Marc J. Goldstein, *Interpreting the New York Convention: When Should an Interlocutory Arbitral "Order" be Treated as an "Award"?* Swiss Arb. Assn. Bull. 830–837 (2000); Publicis Communication v. True North Communications: *Recognition and Enforcement of an Arbitral Tribunal's "Order,"* 4 Int'l Arb. L. R., N45–N46 (2000).

legal effect of an UNCITRAL interim order will likely be the same as an ICSID recommendation.[69] This effect is explained below.

2. Effect of ICSID Recommendation

The drafting history of the Washington Convention demonstrates that delegates made a conscious decision not to grant ICSID tribunals the power to order binding provisional measures. Nevertheless, Article 47 recommendations have legal significance. First, the parties are under a general obligation not to frustrate the object of the proceedings. Second, there is some authority indicating that a recommendation has effectively the same legal force as an "order," and that state parties to the Washington Convention are therefore legally obligated to fully implement ICSID interim measures.[70] Third, the tribunal can (and probably will) take the parties' conduct into account when making its award, and therefore a government respondent may be reluctant to ignore even nonbinding provisional measures. Both the drafting history and commentators agree that it is likely and desirable that arbitrators consider noncompliance with provisional measures when rendering an award.[71] At least one tribunal ordered a party that did not swiftly obey its recommendation to pay part of the other side's legal fees and administrative costs.[72]

3. Review of Investment Arbitration Case Law

Despite the enforcement problems described above, requests for interim relief are not uncommon in investment arbitration: as of 2006, parties have requested recommendations of interim relief in at least ten reported ICSID cases.[73] Because very

---

[69] On interim measures in other arbitration systems, *see* Grégoire Marchac, *Interim Measures in International Commercial Arbitration under the ICC, AAA, LCIA and UNCITRAL Rules*, 10 Am. Rev. Int'l Arb. 123–138 (1999).

[70] *Casado & Allende Foundation v. Chile*, ICSID Case No. ARB/98/2 (Decision on Conservatory Measures of Sept. 25, 2001), at ¶¶ 18–26, *reprinted in* 16 ICSID Rev.-F.I.L.J. 567, 573 (2001).

[71] Schreuer, *supra* note 36, at 761; P. Friedland, *Provisional Measures and ICSID Arbitration*, 2 Arb. Int'l 335, 337 (1986); A. Masood, *Provisional Measures of Protection in Arbitration under the World Bank Convention*, 1 Delhi L. R. 138, 146 (1972); Antonio Parra, *The Practices and Experience of ICSID*, in Conservatory and Provisional Measures in International Arbitration (International Chamber of Commerce ed., 1993).

[72] *MINE v. Guinea*, ICSID Case No. ARB/84/4 (Award of Jan. 6, 1988), *reprinted in* 4 ICSID Rep.-F.I.L.J. 77.

[73] *AGIP S.p.A. v. People's Republic of the Congo*, ICSID Case No. ARB/77/1; *Holiday Inns v. Morocco*, ICSID Case No. ARB/72/1; *Vacuum Salt v. Ghana*, ICSID Case No. ARB/92/1; *CSOB v. Slovakia*, ICSID Case No. ARB/92/1; *Amco Asia Corp. v. Republic of Indonesia*, Case No. ARB/81/1; *MINE v. Guinea*, ICSID Case No. ARB/84/4; *Atlantic Triton v. Guinea*, ICSID Case No. ARB/84/1; *SGS Société Générale de Surveillance S.A. v. Islamic Republic of Pakistan*, ICSID Case No. ARB/01/13; *Maffezini v. Kingdom of Spain*, ICSID Case No. ARB/97/7; *Plama v. the Republic of Bulgaria*, ICSID Case No. ARB/03/24; *Biwater Gauff Ltd. v. United Republic of Tanzania*, ICSID Case No. ARB/05/22. In addition, there have been such requests in the following ICSID Additional Facility cases: *Metalclad v. Mexico*, ICSID Case No. ARB(AF)/97/1; and *Loewen v. U.S.*, ICSID Case No. ARB (AF)/98/3.

few UNCITRAL arbitration decisions are published, no recent requests for interim relief under Article 26 were found.[74] However, tribunals in an investment arbitration will probably consider similar factors when reviewing requests for interim measures of protection, regardless of whether the ICSID or UNCITRAL rules apply.

It is clear that tribunals enjoy wide discretion when considering requests for recommendations of interim measures of protection. A survey of reported cases reveals that in three of those cases interim relief was granted, more or less as requested. In one case, the tribunal granted relief but departed significantly from the request. In three instances, requests for interim measures were denied. The legislative history of the Washington Convention indicates that interim measures are to be recommended only in situations of absolute necessity, and that tribunals should exercise self-restraint in their use.[75] The most common situations that the drafters envisioned where interim relief would be appropriate include:

- To compel parties to cooperate in the proceedings and to furnish all relevant evidence;

- To secure compliance with an eventual award;

- To stop the parties from resorting to self-help, or seeking relief through remedies other than the arbitration process; and

- To prevent a general aggravation of the situation through unilateral action.

The requests for provisional measures made thus far in ICSID proceedings fall into four general categories: obtaining evidence, securing financial guarantees, preventing excessive disclosure of information, and enjoining parallel domestic proceedings.

a. Obtaining Evidence

In at least two cases, claimants have sought to use Article 39 of the ICSID Rules to preserve and gain access to potentially important documentary evidence held by the host state. In *AGIP v. Congo*, the tribunal granted the claimant's request for a recommendation that the Congolese government provide a complete list of relevant documents and to make them available for presentation to the tribunal. Congo did not comply with the recommendation.[76] In *Vacuum Salt v. Ghana*, the claimant submitted a request for provisional measures seeking the preservation of

---

[74] In *Biloune v. Ghana*, p. 118 *supra*, the arbitrators issued an interim order to Ghana to produce certain documents. Ghana complied. *See also* the jurisprudence of Iran-U.S. Claims Tribunal as summarized in D. Caron, L. Caplan, M. Pelonpää, *The UNCITRAL Arbitration Rules: A Commentary* 546 *et seq.* (Oxford University Press 2006).

[75] Schreuer, *supra* note 36, at 751.

[76] *AGIP S.p.A. v. People's Republic of the Congo*, ICSID Case No. ARB/77/1 (Award of Nov. 30, 1979), *reprinted in* 1 ICSID Rep. 311.

its corporate records, which had been expropriated along with the rest of the enterprise. The tribunal noted in its decision that Ghana had voluntarily agreed to give the claimant free access to its records.[77]

b. Securing Financial Guarantees

In one ICSID arbitration, the claimant sought a recommendation that the respondent state post a guarantee securing the amount of the claim, asserting that the state might be unable or unwilling to pay an eventual award. The respondent state also requested security, in this case to cover expenses incurred as a result of attachments the claimant had obtained on its property. The tribunal considered these two requests and rejected both, finding that neither party had established the requisite circumstances for interim relief under Article 47 of the Washington Convention.[78] In *Maffezini v. Kingdom of Spain*, the tribunal similarly rejected Spain's request for a recommendation of security for costs, primarily because it found that such a measure would not secure any present right, but only a "purely hypothetical" right to receive a costs award at some time in the future.[79]

In the commercial arbitration context, arbitrators sometimes, although not frequently, order claimants to provide security to cover the costs of arbitration. When disputes are contract-based and between private parties and where cost-shifting is a real possibility, it is thought that "arbitration can become a means for a small firm to extract economic concessions from a larger company, rather than purely a conflict-resolution tool."[80] When arbitration is against a foreign government on the basis of an investment treaty, the policy concerns are somewhat different and the rationale for security is weaker.[81]

c. Preserving Confidentiality

In one ICSID case, *Amco v. Indonesia*, the host state requested provisional measures against the private claimant. The request grew out of a news report published in a Hong Kong newspaper presenting the claimant's version of the facts underlying the dispute, allegedly designed to bring pressure on Indonesia by criticizing the investment climate in the country. Indonesia asked the tribunal to enjoin the claimant from

---

[77] *Vacuum Salt v. Ghana*, ICSID Case No. ARB/92/1 (Award of Feb. 16, 1994), *reprinted in* 4 ICSID Rep. 331.

[78] Unpublished award, described in Paul Friedland, *Provisional Measures and ICSID Arbitration*, 2 Arb. Int'l 335, 348 (1986).

[79] *Maffizini v. Kingdom of Spain*, ICSID Case No. ARB/97/7 (Decision on Request for Provisional Measures of Oct. 28, 1999), *reprinted in* 16 ICSID Rev.-F.I.L.J. (2001).

[80] Noah D. Rubins, *In God We Trust, All Others Pay Cash: Security for Costs in International Commercial Arbitration*, 11 Am. Rev. Int'l Arb. 307, 361 (2000).

[81] On allocation of costs *see* Chapter XIX.

engaging in propaganda that "might aggravate or extend the dispute." The tribunal rejected Indonesia's request,[82] finding that the article "could not have done any actual harm to Indonesia, nor aggravate or exacerbate the legal dispute."[83]

In *Biwater v. Tanzania*,[84] another ICSID case, the request for provisional measures on confidentiality was filed by claimant-investor. The claimant argued that Tanzania had unilaterally disclosed Procedural Order No. 2 and the minutes of the first session of the tribunal to a third party, and the latter had published them on an Internet Web site (http://ita.law.uvic.ca/). Consequently, the claimant requested that the tribunal recommend that "the parties refrain from taking any steps which might undermine the procedural integrity, or the orderly working, of the arbitral process and/or which might aggravate or exacerbate the dispute . . . ."[85] Tanzania replied that these proceedings were conducted under public international law and that the claimant's request would limit the transparency of the proceedings, which is an established principle in ICSID arbitrations. The tribunal examined the parties' arguments in great length. In the end, it agreed that there was a trend toward greater transparency,[86] but it also found that in the context of this dispute, considerations of procedural integrity and "non-aggravation/non-exacerbation" of the dispute tipped the balance in favor of confidentiality of some of the arbitration proceedings, including the minutes or record of the hearings.[87]

d. Enjoining Parallel Domestic Proceedings and Protecting Rights in Dispute

The most common provisional relief requested in ICSID arbitration is the stay of parallel lawsuits or administrative proceedings initiated before national courts or other bodies.[88] At least five tribunals have considered this kind of request, aimed at both preserving the exclusivity of ICSID jurisdiction and safeguarding the parties' disputed rights pending arbitral adjudication.

In *Holiday Inns v. Morocco*, for example, the Moroccan government turned to its own courts to force the resumption of the construction project (at the claimant's expense)

---

[82] *Amco Asia Corp. v. Republic of Indonesia*, Case No. ARB/81/1 (Decision on Request for Provisional Measures, Dec. 9, 1983), 1 ICSID Rep. 410 (1986).

[83] Procedural Order of Dec. 9, 1983, *unpublished, described in id.*

[84] *Biwater Gauff Ltd. v. United Republic of Tanzania*, ICSID Case No. ARB/05/22 (Procedural Order No. 3, Sept. 29, 2006), ¶ 5.

[85] *Id.* ¶ 12.

[86] *Id.* ¶ 133.

[87] *Id.* ¶¶ 145–47. For a summary of the tribunal's recommendations *see id.* ¶ 162.

[88] *See generally* Charles N. Brower & Ronald E. M. Goodman, *Provisional Measures and the Protection of ICSID Jurisdictional Exclusivity Against Municipal Proceedings*, 6 ICSID Rev.-F.I.L.J. 431 (1991).

that had given rise to the ICSID claim. This domestic action was commenced after the arbitration had already begun. The claimant sought a provisional recommendation instructing Morocco to terminate its domestic court action. Rather than grant the request, the tribunal issued a recommendation that the parties abstain from measures incompatible with their contractual obligations and that they cooperate fully to resolve their dispute. In dicta, however, the tribunal stated that Moroccan courts should defer to arbitration tribunals, even in matters not directly related to the dispute, and "should refrain from making decisions until the Arbitration Tribunal has decided [jurisdictional] questions, or if the Tribunal has already decided them, the Moroccan tribunals should follow its opinion."[89]

The tribunal in *MINE v. Guinea* granted the host state's request for relief from the private claimant's ongoing attempts to enforce a commercial arbitration award (rendered under the American Arbitration Association [AAA] Rules) in the domestic courts of Switzerland. The tribunal's strongly worded ruling could serve as a useful model for the sort of recommendation parties in ICSID arbitration might seek:

> The Tribunal recommends that MINE immediately withdraw and permanently discontinue all pending litigation in national courts, and commence no new action, arising out of the dispute.... The Tribunal further recommends that MINE dissolve every existing provisional measure in litigation in national courts ... and seek no new provisional remedy in national courts.[90]

Because the claimant did not comply promptly with the tribunal's "recommendation," Guinea eventually received an award of damages for costs and legal fees relating to the parallel proceedings in domestic court.[91]

The arbitral tribunal in *CSOB v. Slovakia* also recommended the suspension of domestic proceedings, in this case at the claimant's request. There, an agreement between the parties assigned the claimant bank's nonperforming receivables to a collection company, which was to pay the bank in exchange through a loan arrangement, guaranteed by the Slovak government. The collection company defaulted, and CSOB initiated arbitration to collect on the guarantee. Meanwhile, Slovak bankruptcy proceedings began against the collection company, and the bankruptcy court was to determine whether CSOB

---

[89] Pierre Lalive, *The First "World Bank" Arbitration (Holiday Inns v. Morocco)—Some Legal Problems,* 1980 Brit. Y.B. Int'l L. 123, 160. *See also Atlantic Triton v. Guinea, described in* Friedland, *supra* note 71, at 343 (state respondent attempted to enjoin parallel domestic court proceedings where the claimant had attached three of Guinea's vessels through court actions in France. Because the French courts lifted the attachment before the tribunal rendered its decision, the issue was declared moot).

[90] *MINE v. Guinea,* ICSID Case No. ARB/84/4 (unpublished decision), *described in* 4 ICSID Rep. 41.

[91] *MINE v. Guinea,* ICSID Case No. ARB/84/4 (Award of Jan. 6, 1988), *reprinted in* 4 ICSID Rep. 77.

had a right to receive funds from the Slovak government under the guarantee contract between them. The tribunal agreed with the claimant that the bankruptcy action would probably determine some issues that were also before the tribunal, and recommended that Slovakia discontinue the court proceedings.[92] Slovakia, however, ignored the recommendation, even after it was repeated in a second interim decision.[93]

Of particular interest is the decision on interim relief rendered in the *Casado and Allende Foundation v. Chile* case. There, the claimants brought an ICSID arbitration against Chile for the expropriation of corporate shares during its military dictatorship. A central issue in the case was whether the claimants had actually been shareholders in the disputed companies. The claimants requested that the tribunal recommend suspension of a Chilean ministerial decision that allowed certain private parties to claim title to and compensation for assets belonging to the disputed companies. The claimant argued that the ministerial decree dealt directly with the question of company ownership, and would also affect the amount of its recovery, if any, and therefore should be suspended until the conclusion of arbitration. The tribunal stated that such relief was available in principle, and that it could be granted "if it were shown that the question 'of the ownership of shares in [the disputed companies]' ... was truly an object, at least the primary or essential object, of both Decision No. 43 ... and the proceeding submitted to ICSID."[94] The tribunal refused the request, however, finding that the decree, "in its operative part, does not touch upon the same dispute as that which the Claimants seeks to submit to the jurisdiction of the ICSID Tribunal, although it appears that certain of its themes could affect, at least indirectly, the interests that the Claimants have emphasized."[95]

In *Plama v. Bulgaria*,[96] the claimant requested similar interim relief.[97] Plama sought an order compelling the Republic of Bulgaria to discontinue or cause to be discontinued all proceedings before the Bulgarian courts relating to the bankruptcy of a related company on the basis that these proceedings aggravated the dispute before the tribunal. The tribunal noted that Plama, in its request for relief, had only sought damages, rather than nonpecuniary relief such as restitution. Therefore, the tribunal reasoned, insolvency proceedings could not

---

[92] *CSOB v. Slovakia*, ICSID Case No. ARB/97/4 (Decision on Jurisdiction of May 24, 1999), *reprinted in* 14 ICSID Rev.-F.I.L.J. 251, 255 (1999).

[93] *See* Schreuer, *supra* note 36, at 757.

[94] *Casado and Allende Foundation v. Chile*, ICSID Case No. ARB/98/2 (Decision on Conservatory Measures of Sept. 25, 2001), *reprinted in* 16 ICSID Rev.-F.I.L.J. 567, 573 (2001).

[95] *Id.* ¶ 59.

[96] *Plama v. the Republic of Bulgaria*, ICSID Case No. ARB/03/24.

[97] *Plama v. Bulgaria*, ICSID Case No. ARB/03/24 (Order of Sept. 6, 2005), *available at* http://icsid.worldbank.org.

prevent the claimant from obtaining the relief it sought.[98] It further noted that the bankruptcy proceedings had been brought by private entities that were not parties to the arbitration. Consequently, the tribunal was reluctant to recommend that Bulgaria order its courts to deny third parties the right to pursue judicial remedies available to them under local law.[99]

4. Interim Measures in Other Contexts

There is some precedent in international law outside the investment arbitration context that supports the application of interim measures against states. In a 1951 case between Iran and the United Kingdom, for instance, the International Court of Justice issued an interim order in response to damage to nationalized oil facilities allegedly caused by the Iranian government. The ICJ stated that the parties "should each ensure that no action of any kind is taken which might aggravate or extend the dispute submitted to the court."[100] In a more recent case, when the United States requested that the ICJ issue provisional measures to safeguard hostages held in the American Embassy in Teheran, the Court issued a very similar statement, that the parties "should not take any action and should ensure that no action is taken which may aggravate the tension between the two countries or render the existing dispute more difficult of solution."[101]

5. Timing

Under the ICSID Rules, until fairly recently the parties could only request a recommendation of provisional measures *after* the arbitral tribunal was constituted. The tribunal in *Casado v. Chile* specifically underlined the preemptive nature of provisional measures:

> These measures must therefore be able to be taken, recommended, stipulated or ordered ... at any stage of the proceedings, and this could be *before* the Arbitral Tribunal has been able to rule upon eventual objections to its jurisdiction or the validity of the merits of the claim.[102]

On April 10, 2006, amendments to ICSID Arbitration Rules entered into force, including a new paragraph added to Article 39 on provisional measures. This paragraph provides that:

---

[98] *Id.* ¶ 42.

[99] *Id.* ¶ 43.

[100] *Anglo-Iranian Oil Co. Case*, 1951 I.C.J. Rep. 89, 93–94.

[101] *Case Concerning U.S. Diplomatic and Consular Staff in Teheran*, 1979 I.C.J. Rep. 7, 19 I.L.M. 139 (1980).

[102] *Casado & Allende Foundation v. Chile*, ICSID Case No. ARB/98/2 (Decision on Conservatory Measures of Sept. 25, 2001), *reprinted in* 16 ICSID Rev.-F.I.L.J. 567, 573 (2001). *See also* Schreuer, *supra* note 36, at 229 ("the urgency of the matter may make it impossible to defer provisional measures until the Tribunal's jurisdiction has been fully argued and decided").

> (6) Nothing in this Rule shall prevent the parties, provided that they have so stipulated in the agreement recording their consent, from requesting any judicial or other authority to order provisional measures, prior to or after the institution of the proceeding, for the preservation of their respective rights and interests.

This provision, which creates an expedited procedure for examining requests for interim relief, allows the parties to seek interim relief even *before* a tribunal is constituted. Once the arbitral tribunal is formed, it will consider the request prior to examining other issues.

J. Jurisdictional Phase

After the arbitration has commenced, the tribunal may divide the arbitral procedure into two parts—jurisdiction and merits—or even three parts—jurisdiction, liability, and damages. Frequently, bifurcation or trifurcation is at the request of one of the parties, but this is not universally so. Some arbitration rules, including the ICSID Additional Facility Rules, explicitly provide for separating jurisdiction (competence) and the merits into separate phases.[103] Such a division of the proceedings is designed to reduce the cost incurred by the parties in connection with claims that the tribunal will ultimately find are outside the scope of its competence. Bifurcation also permits the parties and the arbitrators to focus discussions and deliberation on a limited universe of issues, and more clearly analyze the questions posed during each phase. The issuance of a series of awards on different aspects of a dispute may also offer the parties an opportunity to negotiate a solution to the dispute after the *bona fides* of the case are established, or after the issues separating the parties have been narrowed.

The line between objections to jurisdiction and the merits of a claim is often less than clear. Nevertheless, as noted above, it is common practice for arbitral tribunals, particularly in investment arbitration, to separate the proceedings into two phases, such that a claimant must first overcome jurisdictional objections before presenting the heart of its case.[104] In many cases, separating out issues in this way can be an effective means of reducing arbitration costs, clarifying complex legal questions, and discouraging frivolous claims.

---

[103] Additional Facility Rules, art. 46(2), 46(4); *ADF Inc. v. U.S.,* ICSID Case No. ARB(AF)/00/1, (Minutes of First Session of Tribunal, Feb. 3, 2001).

[104] Under the ICSID Convention system "Upon the formal raising of an objection [to jurisdiction] . . . the Tribunal may decide to suspend the proceeding on the merits. The President of the Tribunal, after consultation with its other members, shall fix a time limit within which the parties may file observations on the objection." ICSID Convention, art. 41(3).

United Parcel Service of America, Inc. v. Canada ((NAFTA/UNCITRAL), Award on Jurisdiction, Nov. 22, 2002), ¶¶ 30–37, *available at* www.naftaclaims.com

Basis for determining jurisdictional disputes

30. International judicial practice has long recognized that challenges to jurisdiction may be able to be determined in advance of the hearing of the merits of the claim. So article 21(4) of the UNCITRAL Arbitration Rules provides:

> In general, the arbitral tribunal should rule on a plea concerning its jurisdiction as a preliminary question. However, the arbitral tribunal may proceed with the arbitration and rule on such a plea in their final award.

31. This power both supports the efficient and effective administration of the arbitral process and reflects the fact that parties, notably State parties, to arbitration processes are subject to jurisdiction only to the extent they have consented.

32. What is the test to be applied to resolving disputes about jurisdiction? The parties were agreed from the outset of the written submissions on one matter. For the purpose of Canada's challenge to jurisdiction, the facts alleged in the [Amended Statement of Claim] . . . are to be accepted as correct. While Canada accepts that proposition, it does not contend, however, that the legal inferences to be drawn from the facts are [not] another matter: the Tribunal must be free to decide questions of law which are relevant to its jurisdiction.

33. In the course of their written argument, the parties formulated the test the Tribunal is to apply in determining jurisdictional disputes in various ways. They made extensive references to decisions of the International Court of Justice and of NAFTA tribunals, as well as other tribunals. The differences between their positions appeared to narrow through that written process and, at the oral hearing, counsel for UPS accepted the test stated by Canada in its reply Memorial:

> [The Tribunals] must conduct a prima facie analysis of the NAFTA obligations, which UPS seeks to invoke, and determine whether the facts alleged are capable of constituting a violation of these obligations.

34. That formulation rightly makes plain that a claimant party's mere assertion that a dispute is within the Tribunal's jurisdiction is not conclusive. It is the Tribunal that must decide. The formulation also importantly recognizes that the Tribunal must address itself to the particular jurisdictional provisions invoked. There is a contrast, for instance, between a relatively general grant of jurisdictional over "investment disputes" and the more particularized grant in article 1116 which is to be read with the provisions to which it refers and which are invoked by UPS. Those provisions impose "obligations," as the test proposed by Canada and accepted by UPS indicates.

35. The International Court of Justice in the Case Concerning Oil Platforms (Islamic Republic of Iran v. United States of America) 1966 ICJ Reports 803, para 16 puts the test in this way:

> [The Court] must ascertain whether the violations of the Treaty . . . pleaded by Iran do or do not fall within the provisions of the Treaty and whether, as a consequence, the dispute is one which the Court has jurisdiction ratione materiae to entertain, pursuant to Article XXI, paragraph 2.

That paragraph gave the Court jurisdiction over any dispute between the Parties about "the interpretation or application" of the Treaty.

36. The reference to the facts alleged being "capable" of constituting a violation of the invoked obligations, as opposed to their "falling within" the provisions, may be of little or no consequence. The test is of course provisional in the sense that the facts alleged have still to be established at the merits stage. But any ruling about the legal meaning of the jurisdictional provision, for instance about its outer limits, is binding on the parties.

37. Accordingly, the Tribunal's task is to discover the meaning and particularly the scope of the provisions which UPS invokes as conferring jurisdiction. Do the facts alleged by UPS fall within those provisions; are the facts capable, once proved, of constituting breaches of the obligations they state? It may be that those formulations would differ in their effect in some circumstances but in the present case that appears not to be so.

Tribunals have not always been successful in untangling issues of jurisdiction and liability. Indeed, despite its clear framing of the difference between jurisdiction and the merits, the *UPS* tribunal, later in the award reproduced above, appeared to determine the admissibility of the claim presented, in part based on the strength of the claimant's factual allegations of unfair and inequitable treatment.[105]

Similarly, the tribunal in *Methanex v. United States* appeared to struggle with the division between preliminary and merits issues. In that case, the tribunal found that NAFTA Article 1101 imposed a requirement that as a preliminary matter, the claimant establish a "legally significant connection" between the disputed government measures and the harm caused to the investment or investor. Because the claimant's case in chief included allegations that the Governor of California implemented the measures to benefit an American company and to the detriment of the Canadian competitor, the tribunal ultimately required Methanex to present evidence on the merits during the jurisdictional phase.

Methanex Corp. v. U.S. ((NAFTA/UNCITRAL), Preliminary Award on Jurisdiction and Admissibility, Aug. 7, 2002), ¶¶ 110–61 (source notes selectively omitted)

110. The Tribunal faces an obvious practical problem in addressing the USA's various challenges. The parties' respective cases raise a large number of disputed issues of fact and law. Apart from any jurisdictional challenge, such issues would be decided by the Tribunal after a full hearing on the merits and a complete investigation of the relevant factual evidence and the legal principles to be applied specifically to such evidence. This arbitration, however, has only reached the jurisdictional phase. The Disputing Parties have not adduced any factual evidence on disputed issues (nor have they been entitled to do so); and the Tribunal cannot pre-judge any eventual decision on the merits, still less pre-determine any issue of disputed fact.

---

[105] *UPS v. Canada* (Award on Jurisdiction, Nov. 22, 2002), ¶ 36.

111. There is therefore a preliminary question as to the standard to which Methanex is required, in the face of the USA's several challenges, to establish the two essential components of its claim: (i) its allegations of fact and (ii) its allegations as to the legal meaning of the provisions of NAFTA Chapter 11 on which its case depends.

112. (i) Fact: It was common ground between the Disputing Parties that, for the purpose of this jurisdictional phase, Methanex was not obliged to prove its allegations of fact and that it was sufficient that Methanex should credibly allege the factual elements of its claim (Counter Memorial on Jurisdiction, page 2; Reply of 12th April 2001, page 5). According to Methanex, this means that its allegations suffice unless the Tribunal determined that these allegations were incredible, frivolous or vexatious. If there was a material difference in these submissions from the submissions made by the USA, albeit in different terms, it was not perceptible to the Tribunal; and in any event, the Tribunal accepts Methanex's submissions. It follows that the correct approach is to assume that Methanex's factual contentions are correct (insofar as they are not incredible, frivolous or vexatious) and to apply, under whatever appropriate test, the relevant legal principles to those assumed facts.

113. (ii) Law: This test proved highly contentious between the Disputing Parties; and it raised two successive questions. First, in applying the relevant legal principles to the assumed facts, does the Tribunal have definitively to decide the legal meaning of the relevant provisions of Chapter 11? Or is it sufficient for the Tribunal to establish that Methanex's interpretation is "arguable" or (since such interpretations were indeed argued by Methanex) "well arguable" or argued to some higher standard? There is then a second question: is the same test to be applied to the provisions of Chapter 11 creating jurisdiction, i.e. Articles 1101, 1116, 1117 NAFTA as to those creating substantive obligations, i.e. Articles 1102, 1105 and 1110 NAFTA?

114. There are significant differences between the Disputing Parties on these two questions. For Methanex, relying on the separate opinion of Judge Shahabuddeen in *Case Concerning Oil Platforms*,[106] it is sufficient that its interpretations of the relevant provisions of Chapter 11 should be "arguable." It may also be that Methanex adopted the conclusion of Judge Shahabuddeen in the *Oil Platforms* case to the effect that the International Court of Justice there had to decide definitively (and not provisionally) that the particular dispute was within the category of disputes for which the respondent had accepted the jurisdiction of the Court.[107] In other words, whilst an "arguable" interpretation would suffice in relation to provisions creating substantive obligations, it might not suffice in respect of procedural provisions creating jurisdiction: the interpretation would there have to be conclusively correct.

115. According to the USA, the correct approach was to ascertain whether on the basis of the assumed facts there could be a violation of the relevant provisions; and this exercise required the Tribunal to make a definitive interpretation of all relevant NAFTA provisions. The USA rejected the reasoning of Judge Shahabuddeen; and the USA maintained that even on the basis of such reasoning, it would remain necessary for the Tribunal definitively to determine the meaning of the relevant jurisdictional clauses: e.g. Article 1101(1) NAFTA.

. . . .

---

[106] SN: *Case Concerning Oil Platforms (Islamic Republic of Iran v. U.S.)*, ICJ Rep. 803 (1996) and *Ambatielos, Preliminary Objections*, ICJ Rep. 28 (1952). (The *Oil Platforms* case is to be found on the Web at http://www.icj-cij.org/icjwww/ido . . . /iop_ijudgment_19961212_Preliminary%20Objection.htm.)

[107] SN: ICJ Rep. 831 (1996).

127. The Scope and Coverage of Chapter 11 NAFTA is limited expressly by Article 1101(1) NAFTA. It provides that Chapter 11

"... applies to measures adopted or maintained by a Party relating to: (a) investors of another Party [or] (b) investments of investors of another Party in the territory of a Party."

....

128. The issue that divides the Disputing Parties is whether these US measures, on the assumed facts, *"relate to"* Methanex because, as recited above, neither measure was expressly directed at methanol, methanol producers or Methanex. Applying the approach described in the previous chapter, it is necessary first to interpret definitively this phrase; and second to determine on the basis of the assumed facts, whether or not any of these measures relate to Methanex and its investments.

....

147. Conclusion: We decide that the phrase "relating to" in Article 1101(1) NAFTA signifies something more than the mere effect of a measure on an investor or an investment and that it requires a legally significant connection between them, as the USA contends. Pursuant to the rules of interpretation contained in Article 31(1) of the Vienna Convention, we base that decision upon the ordinary meaning of this phrase within its particular context and in the light of the particular object and purpose in NAFTA's Chapter 11.

....

153. The relevant assumed facts, summarised in Chapter E above, can be recalled briefly: ADM drives the US ethanol industry's political and lobbying machine; ADM has launched a systematic attack on MTBE; ADM has characterised MTBE as a "foreign" product; ADM had a secret meeting with Governor Davis during his election campaign; this meeting concerned ethanol; ADM made substantial campaign contributions to Governor Davis; and after being elected, Governor Davis made the California Executive Order (leading to the California Regulations) banning MTBE, notwithstanding that MTBE is a safe product and other rational solutions exist for addressing California's drinking water problems. From these alleged facts, Methanex also invites the Tribunal to make a series of inferences:

(i) That, at the secret meeting, ADM stated that MTBE was a "foreign" product and that banning MTBE would be a patriotic step to reduce US dependence on fuels;

(ii) That in bringing about the US measures Governor Davis acted on what he was told by ADM;

(iii) That in bringing about the measures Governor Davis acted to favour ADM and the US ethanol industry; and

(iv) That Governor Davis also acted to disadvantage, relative to ADM and the US ethanol industry, the "foreign" producers of MTBE.

154. On the sole basis of these assumed facts and inferences, it is doubtful that the essential requirement of Article 1101(1) is met. It could be said with force that the intent behind the measures would be, at its highest, to harm foreign MTBE producers with no specific intent to harm suppliers of goods and services to such MTBE producers. If so, the measures would not relate to methanol suppliers such as Methanex; and accordingly, even with such intent as alleged by Methanex, we would have no jurisdiction to decide Methanex's amended claim. However, Methanex's case does not stop here. It is further alleged that Governor Davis had a broader objective: to favour ADM and the US ethanol industry, to penalise "foreign" MTBE producers and "foreign" methanol producers, such as Methanex.

155. The USA responds that this cannot be a credible allegation, for several reasons. First, on the assumed facts, there is no reason why ADM should be concerned with disadvantaging methanol suppliers because ADM's commercial objective is already

achieved by the ban on MTBE. Second, on the assumed facts, Governor Davis fulfils his own objectives by penalising MTBE producers; and there is no reason why he should also be concerned with the suppliers to these producers or their products, such as methanol and Methanex. Third, the USA contends that there are strong grounds for inferring that Governor Davis could not have intended to penalise "foreign" methanol producers because there is a substantial US methanol industry equally subject to such intentional harm.

156. In addition, the USA contends that there is no sufficient reason for attributing ADM's motives to Governor Davis; it cannot be inferred that the meeting had any significant influence on Governor Davis when it is not alleged that ADM representatives said anything beyond ADM's usual public statements; it is significant that no bribery or corruption is alleged by Methanex; the California Bill significantly pre-dates the meeting; and as provided by the California Bill, a study was carried out by the University of California on the human health and environmental risks and benefits associated with the use of MTBE; this study was subjected to public scrutiny in February-March 1999 and only thereafter was the California Executive Order made; and on the face of this Order, Governor Davis acted on the basis that there was a significant risk to the environment and public health from using MTBE in gasoline in California, as reported by the University of California, public testimony and regulatory agencies.

157. These are powerful points; and if it were possible for us safely to conclude at this stage that there was nothing more to Methanex's case, we would be minded to decide that the requirements of Article 1101(1) were still not met with a sufficiently credible allegation of intent. However, Methanex also alleges that it supplies the majority of methanol in California; that California had no methanol industry of its own; and that as regards MTBE in California, it is essentially Methanex's methanol which provides the relevant "foreign" characteristic which allowed ADM to promote ethanol to Governor Davis to the disadvantage of MTBE. Whatever the position elsewhere in the USA, methanol and Methanex were "foreign" in California; and this, it is suggested, explains why anti-foreigner action could be taken against methanol in California which on its face would appear to hurt US producers of methanol. In short, it is contended, as regards Governor Davis, that his constituency was the State of California; a "foreign" product was a product foreign to California, which to him, as influenced by ADM, signified methanol produced by Methanex, a "foreign" product produced by "foreigners"; and his intent was to harm Methanex.

158. In these circumstances, we do not consider the case clear enough to determine whether or not Methanex's allegations based on "intent" are sufficiently credible. Accordingly, it is not possible for us to decide, at this stage, that any measure does or does not relate to Methanex or its investments. In particular, decrees and regulations may be the product of compromises and the balancing of competing interests by a variety of political actors. As a result, it may be difficult to identify a single or predominant purpose underlying a particular measure. Where a single governmental actor is motivated by an improper purpose, it does not necessarily follow that the motive can be attributed to the entire government. Much if not all will depend on the evidential materials adduced in the particular case.

159. Accordingly, given the procedural solution on which we have decided below, it would be inappropriate here to develop any further analysis of Methanex's factual case. As we have said already, we do not wish to pre-judge the evidence on disputed issues or indeed further submissions on that evidence; and so far we have heard neither.

(5) Article 21(4) of the UNCITRAL Arbitration Rules

160. Article 21(4) of the UNCITRAL Arbitration Rules requires the arbitration tribunal, in general, to rule on a jurisdictional plea as a preliminary question; and indeed this is the procedure which has so far been followed in these arbitration proceedings. If the Tribunal had no jurisdiction, a decision to that effect could save the Disputing

Parties much time and cost. However, as Article 21(4) also provides, the tribunal "may proceed with the arbitration and rule on such a plea in their final award." The discretion whether to choose the general or the exceptional procedure lies with the arbitration tribunal; and the exercise of that discretion is not confined to economic factors: e.g. where jurisdictional issues are intertwined with the merits, it may be impossible or impractical to decide the former without also hearing argument and evidence on the latter. In these proceedings, two factors have influenced us in selecting the exceptional procedure.

161. Fresh Pleading: First, the effect of the Tribunal's decision on Article 1101(1) NAFTA in this Award will require Methanex to re-plead its case in a fresh Statement of Claim. Its Original Statement of Claim fails the jurisdictional test under Article 1101; and potentially only a part of its Amended Statement of Claim can survive that test. It is inappropriate for Methanex to re-amend its Amended Statement of Claim. In our view, a fresh pleading is required both for the Tribunal and as a matter of procedural fairness to the USA, which is entitled to know precisely the case advanced against it.

K. Merits Phase

1. Briefing

As with the jurisdictional phase, the merits of an investment arbitration are normally conducted first through the parties' exchange of written memorials, which serve as the primary basis of decision for the arbitral tribunal. Most commonly, the claimant submits a memorial on the merits, followed by the respondent's countermemorial, the claimant's reply, and the respondent's sur-reply or rejoinder.[108] After these rounds of briefings, a hearing takes place, and at the end there may be one or two rounds of posthearing briefs.

2. Counterclaims

All arbitral rules contemplate the possibility of asserting counterclaims,[109] provided that these counterclaims are within the scope of the parties' arbitration agreement. Under the ICSID Arbitration Rules, any ancillary claim, including a counterclaim or additional claim, could be asserted, provided that it is within the scope of the parties' consent to arbitration.[110] The great majority of arbitral rules provide that counterclaims may be filed in the response to a request for arbitration or statement of defense.[111]

---

[108] *See, e.g.,* ICSID Arbitration Rules, art. 31; and UNCITRAL Rules, arts. 18 & 19.

[109] *See, e.g.,* AAA International, art. 3(2); ICC, art. 5(5); ICSID Arbitration Rules, art. 40; ICSID Convention, art. 46; SCC Rules, art. 10(3); UNCITRAL Rules, art. 19.

[110] ICSID Arbitration Rules, art. 40.

[111] *See* note 109 *supra.*

Notwithstanding this rule, counterclaims by the host state are rare in investor-state disputes.[112] Jurisdiction over counterclaims in such cases depends on whether the counterclaim arises out of a contract or a treaty, and on the text of the arbitration rules that govern the proceedings. Under the Washington Convention, for example, the *Amco* tribunal in the resubmitted case found that Indonesia's allegation of tax fraud did not fall within Article 25(1) of the ICSID Convention.[113] The tribunal stated:

> In answering this question the Tribunal believes that it is correct to distinguish between rights and obligations that are applicable to legal or natural persons who are within the reach of a host State's jurisdiction, as a matter of general law; and rights and obligations that are applicable to an investor as a consequence of an investment agreement entered into with that host state. Legal disputes relating to the latter will fall under Article 25(1) of the Convention. Legal disputes concerning the former in principle fall to be decided by the appropriate procedures in the relevant jurisdiction unless the general law generates an investment dispute under the Convention.
>
> The obligation not to engage in tax fraud is clearly a general obligation of law in Indonesia. It was not specially contracted for in the investment agreement and does not arise directly out of the investment.[114]

In *Saluka v. Czech Republic*, Saluka Investments B.V., a Dutch company, brought a case against the Czech Republic under the 1991 Czech Republic-Netherlands BIT for the forced administration of the Investicní a poštovní banka a.s. (now known as IP banka a.s. [IPB]), a Czech Bank partly owned by Saluka. IPB was one of the four large state-owned commercial banks in the Czech Republic, which was privatized in the 1990s. Saluka obtained its shareholding through its U.K. parent company, Nomura. In 1998, Nomura purchased the IPB's shares from the Czech National Property Fund (NPF), a state-owned entity, by signing a Share Purchase Agreement (SPA) and later transferred them to Saluka. Subsequent events led to the forced administration of IPB by the Czech government and transfer of its shares to CSOB, another Czech bank.

During the arbitral proceedings, the Czech Republic raised several counterclaims against Saluka. The counterclaims alleged violations of the Czech banking, competition, and tax laws, as well as the SPA.[115] Article 8 of the Czech

---

[112] *See, e.g., Am.n Bell Int'l v. Gov't of the Islamic Republic of Iran* (Award of June 11, 1984), 6 Iran-US Cl. Trib. Rep. 74, 83–84. *Owens-Corning Fiberglass Corp. v. Gov't of Iran* (Award of May 13, 1983), 2 Iran-US Cl. Trib. Rep. 322, 324.

[113] *See also Amco v. Indonesia*, ICSID Case No. ARB/81/1 (Resubmitted Case, Decision on Jurisdiction, May 10, 1988), 1 ICSID Rep. 543, 565.

[114] *Saluka Inves. B.V. v. Czech Republic* (UNCITRAL Arbitration, Decision on Jurisdiction over the Czech Republic's Counterclaim, May 7, 2004).

[115] It should be noted that one of the central issues at this case was whether Saluka and Nomura were one and the same. The tribunal, just for the purpose of determining its jurisdiction, assumed that they were. In its decision on liability, however, it found that they were separate entities. *Saluka v. Czech Republic* (UNCITRAL Arbitration, Decision on Liability, Mar. 17, 2006), ¶ 230. *See also* Chapter XII *infra* for a discussion of this issue.

Republic-Netherlands BIT[116] gave the tribunal jurisdiction over "all disputes," and the Czech Republic argued that that text encompasses both claims and counterclaims. Saluka denied that the tribunal had jurisdiction *ratione materiae* over the counterclaims, because under Article 19.3 of the UNCITRAL Rules[117] only counterclaims arising out of the same legal instrument containing the reference to arbitration, that is, the BIT, were permitted, whereas Czech Republic's counterclaims did not arise out of the BIT. Saluka also asserted that Czech Republic failed to establish the necessary connection between its counterclaim and the primary investment dispute before the tribunal.[118]

The *Saluka* tribunal noted that the issue was one of first impression, as no tribunal had dealt with the admissibility of counterclaims in the context of a BIT arbitration under the UNCITRAL Rules before. It then engaged in a systematic survey of the case law of the Iran-U.S. Claims Tribunal and ICSID tribunals, holding that if a counterclaim has a "close connexion" with the original claim, it is within the jurisdiction of the tribunal. The tribunal summarized its findings as follows:

> 76. The Tribunal acknowledges that the several decisions referred to were based on the terms of instruments which differ from those of Article 8 of the Treaty in issue in the present arbitration and of the UNCITRAL Rules, or (particularly in relation to the decisions of the Iran-US Claims Tribunal) turned on the particular relationship between a counterclaim and a contract-based original claim. Nevertheless, Article 19.3 of the UNCITRAL Rules, Articles 25(1) and 46 of the ICSID Convention and Article II(1) of the Iran-US Claims Settlement Declaration, all reflect essentially the same requirement: the counterclaim must arise out of the "same contract" (UNCITRAL Rules, Article 19.3), or must arise "directly out of an investment" and "directly out of the subject-matter of the dispute" (ICSID, Articles 25(1) and 46), or must arise "out of the same contract, transaction or occurrence that constitutes the subject matter of [the primary] claims" (Article II(1) of the Claims Settlement Declaration). The Tribunal is satisfied that those provisions, as interpreted and applied by the decisions which have been referred to, reflect a general legal principle as to the nature of the close connexion which a counterclaim must have with the primary claim if a tribunal with jurisdiction over the primary claim is to have jurisdiction also over the counterclaim. The Tribunal notes that the parties, in their written and oral submissions on the question of counterclaims, have said nothing to suggest that Czech law does not accord with that general legal principle.[119]

---

[116] Article 8 of the Czech Republic-Netherlands BIT provides in the relevant part that "1. All disputes between one Contracting Party and an investor of the other Contracting Party concerning an investment of the latter shall, if possible, be settled amicably. 2. Each Contracting Party consents to submit a dispute referred to in paragraph (1) of this Article, to an arbitral tribunal, if the dispute has not been settled amicably within [a stated] period . . ."

[117] Article 19(3) of UNCITRAL Rules provides that "3. In his statement of defence, or at a later stage in the arbitral proceedings if the arbitral tribunal decides that the delay was justified under the circumstances, the respondent may make a counter-claim arising out of the same contract or rely on a claim arising out of the same contract for the purpose of a set-off."

[118] *Saluka* (Decision on Objections to Jurisdiction), ¶¶ 25–27.

[119] *Id.* ¶ 76.

> 77. The Tribunal considers that Article 8 of the Treaty has to be understood and applied in the light of that general legal principle.[120]

On the basis of this analysis and taking into account other criteria, the *Saluka* tribunal dismissed the counterclaims of the Czech Republic that were based on violations of the Czech domestic laws.[121]

3. Host State Defenses

Respondent states may assert a variety of defenses to justify their failure to abide by international law obligations. The Draft Articles on State Responsibility of the International Law Commission (the ILC Articles) refer to a group of such defenses as "circumstances precluding wrongfulness."[122] These circumstances include absence of consent (Article 20), self-defense (Article 21), countermeasures (Article 22), *force majeure* (Article 23), distress (Article 24), and necessity (Article 25). It should be noted that these grounds "do not annul or terminate the [international] obligation; rather they provide a justification or excuse for non-performance while the circumstances in question subsists."[123] Once the relevant circumstances no longer exist, the state is required to again comply with its international obligation and the obligation regains its full force.[124] The invocation of one of the circumstances precluding wrongfulness is without prejudice to the question of any material loss caused by the act in question. The state invoking necessity will be still liable to compensate the injured party for its losses. The measure of compensation, however, in the ILC's parlance is "narrower" than that applicable in cases involving wrongful acts, which presumably is governed by the *Chorzów Factory* dictum.[125]

---

[120] *Id.* ¶ 77.

[121] *Id.* ¶¶ 76–79. The tribunal also dismissed the counterclaims that were based on the SPA; because, among other things, Article 21 of the SPA referred any dispute arising out of that agreement to arbitration in Zurich. As the *Vivendi Annulment Committee* held "[i]n a case where the essential basis of a claim brought before an international tribunal is a breach of contract, the tribunal will give effect to any valid choice of forum clause in the contract." Furthermore, the SPA's arbitration clause was a "special agreement relating to the investment" within the meaning of Article 8(6) of the BIT, which the tribunal was required to take into account. *Id.* ¶¶ 53–56. For excerpts from the Vivendi Annulment Decision, *see* Chapter XIV *infra*.

[122] *Draft Articles on Responsibility of States for Internationally Wrongful Acts*, in Report of the International Law Commission on the Work of Its Fifty-third Session, U.N. GAOR, 56th Sess., Supp. (No. 10), at 43, UN Doc. A/56/10 (2001), [hereinafter ILC Articles], Chapter V, *available at* http://www.un.org/law/ilc.

[123] J. Crawford, *The International Law Commission's Articles on State Responsibility: Introduction, Text, and Commentaries* 160 (Cambridge University Press 2002). *See also* Case Concerning Gabcikovo-Nagymaros Project (Hungary/Slovakia), 1997 ICJ Rep. 7, ¶ 39.

[124] ILC Articles, art. 27(a) [hereinafter ILC Articles]. Crawford, *supra* note 123, at 189.

[125] ILC Articles, art. 27(b). *See also* Crawford, *supra* note 123, at 190. For a discussion of the *Chorzów Factory* dictum, *see generally* Chapter XIX *infra*.

In modern investment treaty practice, as of May 2007, "necessity" has been the centerpiece of three ICSID cases involving Argentina: *CMS v. Argentina*,[126] *LG&E v. Argentina*,[127] and *Enron v. Argentina*.[128] Article 25 of the International Law Commission Articles on Responsibility of States for Internationally Wrongful Acts describes the necessity defense:

> Article 25
>
> Necessity
>
> 1. Necessity may not be invoked by a State as a ground for precluding the wrongfulness of an act not in conformity with an international obligation of that State unless the act:
>
> (a) Is the only way for the State to safeguard an essential interest against a grave and imminent peril; and
>
> (b) Does not seriously impair an essential interest of the State or States towards which the obligation exists, or of the international community as a whole.
>
> 2. In any case, necessity may not be invoked by a State as a ground for precluding wrongfulness if:
>
> (a) The international obligation in question excludes the possibility of invoking necessity; or
>
> (b) The State has contributed to the situation of necessity.

Article 25, which embodies customary international law on the subject, has several elements (e.g., grave and imminent peril to the state, no contribution by the state to the situation) that must be "cumulatively satisfied."[129] Another important question is whether a state can "self-judge" the necessity defense, or in other words, whether the crisis-stricken state's own determination of necessity is determinative. The commentary on the ILC Articles answers this question in the negative.[130]

The Argentina cases were commenced in the wake of the late 1990s and early 2000 Argentine financial crisis. The cases were brought by American companies alleging that Argentina through an Emergency Law and other measures adopted to combat the financial crisis had violated its obligations toward them under the United States-Argentina BIT by substantially diminishing the value of their

---

[126] *CMS Gas Transmission Co. v. Argentine Republic*, ICSID Case No. ARB/01/8 (Final Award, May 12, 2005).

[127] *LG&E v. Argentina*, ICSID Case No. ARB/02/1 (Decision on Liability, Oct. 3, 2006).

[128] *Enron Corp. & Ponderosa Asset v. Argentina*, ICSID Case No. ARB/01/3 (Award, May 22, 2007).

[129] *Gabčíkovo-Nagymoros*, 1997 I.C.J. 40.

[130] Crawford, *supra* note 123, at 184. *See also LG&E v. Argentina*, *supra* note 127, ¶ 212, (holding that Article XI of the U.S.-Argentina BIT, which the tribunal interpreted in light of the ILC Articles articulation on the state of necessity, is not self-judging).

investments. One of Argentina's defenses was that the financial crisis constituted a state of necessity under international law, and consequently that both Article 25 of the ILC Articles and the analogous emergency clause of the United States-Argentina BIT[131] relieved it from any responsibility.

The *CMS* and *Enron* tribunals rejected Argentina's plea of necessity on these bases and awarded damages. The *LG&E* tribunal, however, accepted the necessity defense for the duration of the state of necessity, which it held was the period during which the Argentine Emergency Law was in force (December 2001–October 2003). Argentina was thus exempted from paying compensation during the period of emergency. The *LG&E*'s finding, however, was mainly based on the BIT emergency provisions, Article XI, rather than the Article 25 of the ILC Articles.[132] The *LG&E* tribunal found that the BIT provisions set a lower threshold than ILC Article 25 for invoking the state of necessity. A rigorous approach to this issue would determine whether Article XI was clear, in which case it would control. If ambiguous however, it is possible that Article 25 controls to remedy the ambiguity.

It is not comforting (and indicative of a fundamental structural problem in the investment treaty system) that tribunals evaluating the same nucleus of facts and the same legal standards reached different conclusions as to the necessity defense. On the other hand, there is very little precedent on this issue and it remains to be seen how future arbitral tribunals involved in the Argentine cases deal with Argentina's state of necessity defense.

4. Witness Statements and Other Evidence[133]

The marshalling of evidence in investment arbitration is generally similar to the process in commercial arbitrations. As in commercial arbitration and litigation, the presentation of written evidence is to a degree idiosyncratic, depending on the rules chosen, the procedural law applicable to the arbitration, the particular experience of the arbitrators, and the location of the relevant evidence. Participation of lawyers from both common and civil law traditions in international arbitration has led

---

[131] Article XI of the U.S.-Argentina BIT provides: "This Treaty shall not preclude the application by either Party of measures necessary for the maintenance of public order, the fulfillment of its obligations with respect to the maintenance or restoration of international peace or security, or the protection of its own essential security interests."

[132] See *LG&E*, supra note 127, ¶¶ 229–30.

[133] See generally Robert Pietrowski, *Evidence in International Arbitration*, 22(3) Arb. Int'l 373–410 (2006); C. F. Amerasinghe, *Evidence in International Litigation* (Martinus Nijhoff 2005); Alan Redfern, *The Standards and Burden of Proof in International Arbitration*, 10(3) Arb. Int'l 317–64 (1994); M. Kazazi, *Burden of Proof and Related Issues* (Kluwer Law International 1996); Durward Sandifer, *Evidence Before International Tribunals* (University Press of Virginia 1975).

to the emergence of a hybrid system of evidence taking,[134] which is reflected to some degree in the International Bar Association's (IBA) Rules on the Taking of Evidence in International Commercial Arbitration (the IBA Rules).[135] The IBA Rules are not binding on the parties unless agreed or ordered by the tribunal and are "designed to be used in conjunction with, and adopted together with, institutional or ad hoc rules or procedures governing international commercial arbitrations."[136] Many parties to arbitration proceedings voluntarily adopt the IBA Rules to ensure predictability with respect to a range of issues relating to documents and witnesses.[137]

> Whenever the Parties have agreed or the Arbitral Tribunal has determined to apply the IBA Rules of Evidence, the Rules *shall* govern the taking of evidence, except to the extent that any specific provision of them may be found to be in conflict with any mandatory provision of law determined to be applicable to the case by the Parties or by the Arbitral Tribunal.[138] . . . The Rules [, however,] are not intended to limit the flexibility that is inherent in, and an advantage of, international arbitration, and Parties and Arbitral Tribunals are free to adapt them to the particular circumstances of each arbitration.[139]

a. Witness Statements

Arbitration procedure differs from court practice in many countries in that most witness evidence, of both fact and expert witnesses, is submitted in the form of written statements rather than oral testimony. Witness statements therefore often comprise a substantial portion of the parties' submissions in investment arbitration.[140]

International Bar Association, *Rules on the Taking of Evidence in International Commercial Arbitration*, available at http://www.ibanet.org/legalpractice/Arbitration.cfm#Guides

Article 4

Witnesses of Fact

1. Within the time ordered by the Arbitral Tribunal, each Party shall identify the witnesses on whose testimony it relies and the subject matter of that testimony.

---

[134] S. Elsing & J. Townsend, *Bridging the Common Law-Civil Law Divide in International Arbitration*, 18(1) Arb. Int'l 59, 61 (2002).

[135] International Bar Association (IBA) Rules on the Taking of Evidence in International Commercial Arbitration, *available at* http://www.ibanet.org/legalpractice/Arbitration.cfm #Guides.

[136] *Id.* Foreword; *see also* Preamble, ¶ 1.

[137] *See, e.g., Lauder v. Czech Republic* (Final Award, Sept. 3, 2001), ¶ 16, 9 ICSID Rep. 68 (2006).

[138] IBA Rules, *supra* note 135, art. 2(1) (emphasis added).

[139] *Id.*, Preamble, ¶ 2. *See, e.g., CME v. Czech Republic* (Partial Award on Liability, Sept. 13, 2001), ¶ 45 (the parties adopted IBA Rules with some modifications).

[140] George M. von Mehren, *Submitting Evidence in International Arbitration: A Common Lawyer's Guide*, 20 J. Int'l Arb. 285 (2003); Thomas J. Tallerico, *Bifurcation and Direct Testimony Witness Statements in International Commercial Arbitration*, 20 J. Int'l Arb. 295 (2003).

2. Any person may present evidence as a witness, including a Party or a Party's officer, employee or other representative.

3. It shall not be improper for a Party, its officers, employees, legal advisors or other representatives to interview its witnesses or potential witnesses.

4. The Arbitral Tribunal may order each Party to submit within a specified time to the Arbitral Tribunal and to the other Parties a written statement by each witness on whose testimony it relies, except for those witnesses whose testimony is sought pursuant to Article 4.10 (the "Witness Statement"). If Evidentiary Hearings are organized on separate issues (such as liability and damages), the Arbitral Tribunal or the Parties by agreement may schedule the submission of Witness Statements separately for each Evidentiary Hearing.

5. Each Witness Statement shall contain: (a) the full name and address of the witness, his or her present and past relationship (if any) with any of the Parties, and a description of his or her background, qualifications, training and experience, if such a description may be relevant and material to the dispute or to the contents of the statement; (b) a full and detailed description of the facts, and the source of the witness's information as to those facts, sufficient to serve as that witness's evidence in the matter in dispute; (c) an affirmation of the truth of the statement; and (d) the signature of the witness and its date and place.

6. If Witness Statements are submitted, any Party may, within the time ordered by the Arbitral Tribunal, submit to the Arbitral Tribunal and to the other Parties revised or additional Witness Statements, including statements from persons not previously named as witnesses, so long as any such revisions or additions only respond to matters contained in another Party's Witness Statement or Expert Report and such matters have not been previously presented in the arbitration.

7. Each witness who has submitted a Witness Statement shall appear for testimony at an Evidentiary Hearing, unless the Parties agree otherwise.

8. If a witness who has submitted a Witness Statement does not appear without a valid reason for testimony at an Evidentiary Hearing, except by agreement of the Parties, the Arbitral Tribunal shall disregard that Witness Statement unless, in exceptional circumstances, the Arbitral Tribunal determines otherwise.

9. If the Parties agree that a witness who has submitted a Witness Statement does not need to appear for testimony at an Evidentiary Hearing, such an agreement shall not be considered to reflect an agreement as to the correctness of the content of the Witness Statement.

10. If a Party wishes to present evidence from a person who will not appear voluntarily at its request, the Party may, within the time ordered by the Arbitral Tribunal, ask it to take whatever steps are legally available to obtain the testimony of that person. The Party shall identify the intended witness, shall describe the subjects on which the witness's testimony is sought and shall state why such subjects are relevant and material to the outcome of the case. The Arbitral Tribunal shall decide on this request and shall take the necessary steps if in its discretion it determines that the testimony of that witness would be relevant and material.

11. The Arbitral Tribunal may, at any time before the arbitration is concluded, order any Party to provide, or to use its best efforts to provide, the appearance for testimony at an Evidentiary Hearing of any person, including one whose testimony has not yet been offered.

b. Document Production from Parties to the Dispute

Production of evidentiary documents is one of the most important aspects of any international arbitration. In investment treaty arbitration, document collection becomes especially significant insofar as it assists the attorneys to develop a detailed factual background to make up for the uncertainties associated with applying some of the flexible standards of protection under various investment treaties. In these disputes, document production can be equally important for developing legal arguments, as the investor may, for example, need to find evidence of government's intent in the *travaux preparatoire* to support a particular interpretation of an investment treaty.[141]

All arbitral rules contain provisions dealing with production and evaluation of evidence.[142] The ICSID Rules, for instance, require the parties to inform the ICSID Secretary-General about the evidence that they intend to produce and also the evidence that they intend to request the tribunal to call for.[143] They also permit the arbitrators, on their own initiative, to request the parties to produce certain documents.[144] The ICSID Rules, additionally, provide that "[t]he Tribunal shall be the judge of the admissibility of any evidence adduced and of its probative value."[145] Articles 24(2),[146] 24(3),[147] and 25(6)[148] of the UNCITRAL Arbitration Rules contemplate similar procedures for document collection.

The following excerpt from IBA Rules on the Taking of Evidence outlines some of the procedures that the parties and the arbitral tribunals use with respect to documents.

---

[141] This was the case in the NAFTA Chapter 11 case of *Methanex v. U.S.* where the investor asked the tribunal to order the U.S. government to produce the preparatory works of NAFTA.

[142] *See, e.g.,* ICSID Arbitration Rules, arts. 33 and 34; SCC Rules, art. 26; UNCITRAL Rules, art. 24.

[143] ICSID Arbitration Rules, art. 33.

[144] *Id.* art. 34. *See also* the discussion of interim measures at p. 137 *supra*.

[145] *Id.* art. 34(1).

[146] Art. 24(2) of the UNCITRAL Rules provides that "The arbitral tribunal may, if it considers it appropriate, require a party to deliver to the tribunal and to the other party, within such a period of time as the arbitral tribunal shall decide, a summary of the documents and other evidence which that party intends to present in support of the facts in issue set out in his statement of claim or statement of defence."

[147] Article 24(3) of the UNCITRAL Rules provide that "At any time during the arbitral proceedings the arbitral tribunal may require the parties to produce documents, exhibits or other evidence within such a period of time as the tribunal shall determine."

[148] Article 25(6) of the UNCITRAL Rules provides that "The arbitral tribunal shall determine the admissibility, relevance, materiality and weight of the evidence offered."

International Bar Association, *Rules on the Taking of Evidence in International Commercial Arbitration* (Adopted on June 1, 1999), *available at* http://www.ibanet.org/legalpractice/Arbitration.cfm#Guides

Article 3 Documents

1. Within the time ordered by the Arbitral Tribunal, each Party shall submit to the Arbitral Tribunal and to the other Parties all documents available to it on which it relies, including public documents and those in the public domain, except for any documents that have already been submitted by another Party.

2. Within the time ordered by the Arbitral Tribunal, any Party may submit to the Arbitral Tribunal a Request to Produce.

3. A Request to Produce shall contain:

>(a) (i) a description of a requested document sufficient to identify it, or (ii) a description in sufficient detail (including subject matter) of a narrow and specific requested category of documents that are reasonably believed to exist;

>(b) a description of how the documents requested are relevant and material to the outcome of the case; and

>(c) a statement that the documents requested are not in the possession, custody or control of the requesting Party, and of the reason why that Party assumes the documents requested to be in the possession, custody or control of the other Party.

4. Within the time ordered by the Arbitral Tribunal, the Party to whom the Request to Produce is addressed shall produce to the Arbitral Tribunal and to the other Parties all the documents requested in its possession, custody or control as to which no objection is made.

5. If the Party to whom the Request to Produce is addressed has objections to some or all of the documents requested, it shall state them in writing to the Arbitral Tribunal within the time ordered by the Arbitral Tribunal. The reasons for such objections shall be any of those set forth in Article 9.2. [They include: irrelevance or immateriality; privilege under the applicable legal or ethical rules; unreasonable burden; loss of documents; commercial or technical confidentiality; special political or institutional sensitivity; and considerations of fairness.]

6. The Arbitral Tribunal shall, in consultation with the Parties and in timely fashion, consider the Request to Produce and the objections. The Arbitral Tribunal may order the Party to whom such Request is addressed to produce to the Arbitral Tribunal and to the other Parties those requested documents in its possession, custody or control as to which the Arbitral Tribunal determines that (i) the issues that the requesting Party wishes to prove are relevant and material to the outcome of the case, and (ii) none of the reasons for objection set forth in Article 9.2 apply.

7. [contemplates the possibility that an independent expert reports to the tribunal about objections to production]

. . . .

9. The Arbitral Tribunal, at any time before the arbitration is concluded, may request a Party to produce to the Arbitral Tribunal and to the other Parties any documents that it believes to be relevant and material to the outcome of the case. A Party may object to such a request based on any of the reasons set forth in Article 9.2. If a Party raises such an objection, the Arbitral Tribunal shall decide whether to order the production

of such documents based upon the considerations set forth in Article 3.6 and, if the Arbitral Tribunal considers it appropriate, through the use of the procedures set forth in Article 3.7.

c. Evidence Collection from Third Parties

Because arbitration is the product of contractual consent, there are built-in barriers with regard to obtaining evidence from nonparties. The ability to obtain such evidence varies depending on the governing rules, as well as the laws of both the situs of the arbitration and the location of the evidence. Once again, the IBA rules provide a kind of template for arbitral tribunals considering evidence in the possession of third parties:

> IBA Rules, art. 3.8
>
> If a Party wishes to obtain the production of documents from a person or organization who is not a Party to the arbitration and from whom the Party cannot obtain the documents on its own, the Party may, within the time ordered by the Arbitral Tribunal, ask it to take whatever steps are legally available to obtain the requested documents. The Party shall identify the documents in sufficient detail and state why such documents are relevant and material to the outcome of the case. The Arbitral Tribunal shall decide on this request and shall take the necessary steps if in its discretion it determines that the documents would be relevant and material.

5. U.S. Procedures and Third-Party EvidenceTaking

The processes available in the United States for obtaining evidence from third parties for use in investment arbitrations are important for two reasons. First, the U.S. is likely to be the venue of many investment arbitrations because of the presence of ICSID in Washington, D.C.[149] Second, the U.S. has comparatively well-developed procedures for obtaining evidence from third parties for use in international arbitration. Thus, a brief survey of such rules is instructive.

In the United States, parties to arbitration can obtain evidence from third parties[150] by resorting to two statutes. First, the Federal Arbitration Act (FAA) allows tribunals, but not parties independently, to obtain evidence from persons

---

[149] The ICSID Convention designates Washington, D.C., as the default seat for ICSID arbitrations subject to the parties' autonomy to choose other possible venues. ICSID Convention, art. 62.

[150] Discovery in the United States is a method of "[c]ompulsory disclosure, at a party's request, of information that relates to the litigation . . . " *See* Fed. R. Civ. P. 26–37; Fed. R. Crim. P. 16. "The primary discovery devices are interrogatories, depositions, requests for admissions, and requests for production. Although discovery typically comes from parties, courts also allow limited discovery from nonparties." *Black's Law Dictionary* (8th ed. 2004).

not party to the dispute.[151] Second, a federal procedural statute, 28 U.S.C. § 1782,[152] permits broader evidence production than the FAA and allows any interested party, and not only the tribunal, to request a disclosure order from an appropriate U.S. federal district court.[153]

The FAA establishes the arbitrators' authority to invoke the powers of federal district courts to assist an arbitration in obtaining evidence:

> The arbitrators selected either as prescribed in this title or otherwise, or a majority of them, may summon in writing any person to attend before them or any of them as a witness and in a proper case to bring with him or them any book, record, document, or paper which may be deemed material as evidence in the case .... Said summons shall issue in the name of the arbitrator or arbitrators, or a majority of them, and shall be signed by the arbitrators, or a majority of them, and shall be directed to the said person and shall be served in the same manner as subpoenas to appear and testify before the court; if any person or persons so summoned to testify shall refuse or neglect to obey said summons, upon petition the United States district court for the district in which such arbitrators, or a majority of them, are sitting may compel the attendance of such person or persons before said arbitrator or arbitrators, or punish said person or persons for contempt in the same manner provided by law for securing the attendance of witnesses or their punishment for neglect or refusal to attend in the courts of the United States.[154]

This provision explicitly confers authority only on the arbitrators themselves to order the production of evidence.[155] As the *Burton* court stated, "While an arbitration panel may subpoena documents or witnesses, the litigating parties have no comparable privilege."[156] Furthermore, under the FAA, federal district courts' authority to enforce arbitrators' orders is extremely limited geographically, usually operating only within the district in which a majority of the arbitrators sit.[157] However, if witnesses fail to comply with the arbitrators' order to appear, the federal district court where the majority of the arbitrators are sitting may compel compliance.[158]

---

[151] 9 U.S.C. § 7.

[152] The pertinent parts of 28 U.S.C. § 1782 has been reproduced at pp. 165–66.

[153] Several courts have noted a potential conflict between 28 U.S.C. § 1782 and Federal Arbitration Act § 7. Because investment arbitration cases could be viewed by U.S. courts as akin to private commercial arbitration, any district court receiving a discovery request from a party to such proceedings may have to decide which of the two statutes applies. *NBC*, 165 F.3d at 188 (noting that "[i]f the broader evidence-gathering mechanisms provided for in § 1782 were applicable to proceedings before non-governmental tribunals such as private arbitral panels, we would need to decide whether [§ 7] is exclusive, in which case the two statutes would conflict.").

[154] *Id.*

[155] *Burton v. Bush*, 614 F.2d 389, 390 (4th Cir. 1980), *cited with approval in St. Mary's Med. Ctr. of Evansville, Inc. v. Disco Aluminum Prods. Co.*, 969 F.2d 585, 591 (7th Cir. 1992).

[156] *Burton*, 614 F.2d at 390 (citations omitted).

[157] 9 U.S.C. § 7.

[158] *NBC v. Bear Stearns*, 165 F.3d 184, 187 (2d Cir. 1999).

Finally, the FAA refers exclusively to testimony "before [the] arbitrator or arbitrators" and to the physical evidence such witnesses may bring with them.[159] It is unclear, therefore, whether this language can also be invoked to require prehearing depositions and document discovery,[160] as is customary in U.S. litigation. Most courts appear to agree that the FAA does empower an arbitrator to compel the production of documents prior to a hearing.[161] There is, however, considerable disagreement regarding whether prehearing depositions are available under the FAA. Some courts have refused to allow arbitrators to use the statute to require nonparties to appear for deposition prior to hearing.[162] Other courts, meanwhile, have held that to realize the purposes of the FAA, arbitrators should be allowed to order such depositions.[163]

28 U.S.C. § 1782 is a more controversial U.S. statute, potentially providing for the compulsory production of evidence in investment arbitration cases. Section 1782 expressly permits an "interested" person to obtain an order from a federal district court compelling testimony or the production of documents from persons residing or found in that district for use in a "foreign or international tribunal."[164] Section 1782 provides, in pertinent part:

> The district court of the district in which a person resides or is found may order him to give his testimony or statement or to produce a document or other thing for use in a proceeding in a foreign or international tribunal . . . . The order may be made pursuant

---

[159] 9 U.S.C. § 7.

[160] *See NBC,* 165 F.3d at 188 (noting split in authority); *Integrity Ins. Co. v. Am. Centennial Ins. Co.,* 885 F. Supp. 69, 72–73 (S.D.N.Y. 1995) (arbitrator may not rely on § 7 to obtain pre-hearing depositions from non-parties); *Meadows Indem. Co. v. Nutmeg Ins. Co.,* 157 F.R.D. 42, 45 (M.D. Tenn. 1994) (§ 7 power to compel document production from third parties at hearing encompasses lesser power to compel production prior to hearing); *accord Stanton v. Paine Webber Jackson & Curtis, Inc.,* 685 F. Supp. 1241, 1242–43 (S.D. Fla. 1988) (§ 7 power to compel document production from third parties at hearing encompasses lesser power to compel production prior to hearing).

[161] *See Arb. Between Security Life Insurance Co. of Am. & Duncanson & Holt, Inc.,* 228 F.3d 865, 870–71 (8th Cir. 2000) (noting belief that "interest in efficiency [in arbitrations] is furthered by permitting a party to review and digest relevant documentary evidence prior to the arbitration hearing); *Amgen, Inc. v. Kidney Ctr. Del. County, Ltd.,* 879 F. Supp. 878, 880 (N. D. Ill. 1995) (noting that courts have held "that implicit in the power to compel testimony and documents for purpose of a hearing is the lesser power to compel such testimony and documents for purposes prior to hearing.").

[162] *See, e.g., Integrity Ins. Co., in Liquidation v. Am. Centennial Ins. Co.,* 885 F. Supp. 69, 72–73 (holding that "an arbitrator may not compel attendance of a nonparty at a pre-hearing deposition").

[163] *See Stanton.,* 685 F. Supp. at 1242–43 (holding that "Plaintiff's contention that § 7 . . . only permits the arbitrators to compel witnesses at the hearing, and prohibits pre-hearing appearances, is unfounded"); *Amgen,* 879 F. Supp. at 880 (power to compel testimony during hearing necessarily encompasses power to do so for pre-hearing depositions).

[164] *See generally* Johnson Schwartz, *Court-Assisted Discovery in Aid of International Commercial Arbitrations: Two Recent U.S. Cases Regarding the Applicability of 28 U.S.C. § 1782,* 15(9) J. Int'l Arb. 53 (1998); B. Bomstein & J. Levitt, *Much Ado About 1782: A Look at the Recent Problems with Discovery in the United States for Use in Foreign Litigation under Section 1782,* 20 U. Miami Inter-Am. L. Rev. 429 (1989).

to a letter rogatory issued, or request made, by a foreign or international tribunal or upon the application of any interested person and may direct that testimony or statement be given, or the document or other thing be produced, before a person appointed by the court.[165]

There is uncertainty whether parties to investment arbitration can take advantage of § 1782 to obtain documentary and witness evidence from parties and nonparties in the United States. Prevailing opinion in U.S. courts until recently was that international commercial arbitration tribunals do not qualify as "tribunals" within the meaning of § 1782, and therefore parties to such proceedings cannot obtain discovery by way of the statute. The U.S. Courts of Appeal for the Second and Fifth Circuits held that the word *tribunal* as used in § 1782 was intended to cover only "governmental or intergovernmental arbitral tribunals and conventional courts and other state-sponsored adjudicatory bodies."[166] The Second Circuit in *NBC* reasoned that the term *foreign or international tribunal* was sufficiently ambiguous to require the court to examine the legislative history and purpose of § 1782 to determine the meaning of the term.[167] The court found especially telling the legislative history's silence regarding § 1782's application to private tribunals, and concluded that the statute was intended more to assist tribunals created by intergovernmental agreement.[168] Many commentators, however, have criticized these holdings. Professor Hans Smit, who played an important role in the drafting of the statute, has led this critique, and many scholars have joined him in opining that judicial assistance under §1782 should be available in all arbitration proceedings.[169]

In June 2004, the U.S. Supreme Court issued an important ruling on § 1782 in *Intel Corp. v. Advanced Micro Devices, Inc.*[170] The *Intel* case did not squarely

---

[165] 28 U.S.C. § 1782.

[166] *NBC v. Bear Stearns*, 165 F.3d 184, 190 (2nd Cir. 1999); *accord, Republic of Kaz. v. Biedermann Int'l*, 168 F.3d 880, 881 (5th Cir. 1999).

[167] *NBC*, 165 F.3d at 188.

[168] *Id.* at 190; *see also Biedermann*, 168 F.3d at 882 (same).

[169] *See Biedermann*, 168 F.3d at 882 n.5 (noting that "majority view of commentators [is] that private commercial arbitrations are within § 1782"); Hans Smit, *American Assistance to Litigation in Foreign and International Tribunals: Section 1782 of Title 28 of the U.S.C. Revisited*, 25 Syracuse J. Int'l L. & Com. 1, 5–8 (1998) (noting that "the broad term 'international tribunal' was intended to cover all international arbitral tribunals"); J. C. Green, *Are International Institutions Doing Their Job?*, 90 Am. Soc'y Int'l L. Proc. 62, 70 (1996) (noting that it is difficult to imagine an international tribunal as anything besides an international court or arbitration panel); P. Schlosser, *Coordinated Transnational Interaction in Civil Litigation and Arbitration*, 12 Mich. J. Int'l L. 150, 170 n.84 (1990) (stating that scope of "tribunal" should include international arbitrations). Even more convincingly, Professor Smit, in a 1965 article definitively stated that, "[t]he term 'tribunal' embraces all bodies exercising adjudicatory power, and includes investigating magistrates, administrative and arbitral tribunals and quasi-judicial agencies . . . ." Hans Smit, *International Litigation Under the United States Code*, 65 Colum. L. Rev. 1015, 1026 n.71 (1965).

[170] 542 U.S. 241 (2004).

address whether the statutory term *tribunal* encompasses international arbitration tribunals, either commercial or treaty-based, but its expansive interpretation of § 1782 seriously undermines the prior holdings in *NBC* and *Biedermann*. The Supreme Court cited in particular Congress's intent to provide discovery assistance to "foreign courts and quasi-judicial agencies," and held that the term *tribunal* was broad enough to include a "first-instance decisionmaker."[171]

In the wake of *Intel,* two recent decisions by U.S. courts, *Oxus*[172] and *Roz Trading,*[173] have extended the scope of § 1782 to include both investment treaty and commercial arbitrations. In *Oxus,* the applicant was Oxus Gold, which was the claimant in an investment treaty arbitration under the United Kingdom-Kyrgyz BIT, and which was seeking to obtain discovery from a U.S. citizen.[174] Relying on *Intel,* the court held that:

> In the case at bar, Article 8 of the BIT Agreement between the United Kingdom and Kyrgyzstan specifically mandates that disputes between nationals of the two countries would be resolved by arbitration governed by international law. The Arbitration at issue in this case, between admittedly private litigants, is thus being conducted within a framework defined by two nations and is governed by the Arbitration Rules of the United Nations Commission on International Trade Law (the "UNCITRAL rules"). In light of these facts, this Court concludes that the Magistrate Judge's holding that the arbitration panel in the case at bar constituted a "foreign tribunal" for purposes of a 28 U.S.C. Section 1782 analysis was not clearly erroneous or contrary to law.

The court in *Roz Trading* allowed the use of § 1782 in international commercial arbitration, holding that the term *tribunal* encompassed a commercial arbitral tribunal at the International Arbitral Centre of the Austrian Federal Economic Chamber.[175] Also relying on *Intel,* the court expressly declined to follow the previous contrary rulings in *NBC* and *Biedermann*.[176] Although the matter is not yet settled, it is entirely possible that future investment treaty arbitration tribunals sitting in the U.S., including ICSID panels, will be able to turn to U.S. courts to assist them in obtaining evidence from nonparties in the United States and possibly elsewhere.

6. Third Party Amicus Curiae Submissions

The possibility of submissions by nonparty public interest groups or nongovernmental organizations (NGOs) has become a controversial and recurring issue in investment arbitrations.[177] Because arbitration against states frequently raises

---

[171] *Id.* at 258.

[172] *In the Matter of the Application of Oxus Gold plc for Assistance Before a Foreign Tribunal,* 2007 U.S. Dist. LEXIS 24061 (D.N.J. 2007).

[173] *In re Roz Trading, Ltd.,* 469 F. Supp. 2d 1221 (N.D. Ga. Dec. 19, 2006).

[174] *In the Matter of Application of Oxus Gold,* 2007 U.S. Dist. LEXIS at 24064.

[175] *Roz Trading,* 469 F. Supp. 2d at 1228.

[176] *Id.*

[177] *See* Chapter XXII.

concerns of the public good, interested third parties, especially in common law jurisdictions, believe they should have access to the decision-making process.[178]

One of the first investment treaty disputes in which this issue arose was the NAFTA arbitration *Methanex Corp. v. United States*.[179] After weighing the opinions of Mexico, Canada, and the disputing parties, the tribunal ruled that it had the authority to accept *amicus* written submissions from the International Institute for Sustainable Development (IISD). The Institute voiced concern that a recent award rendered in *Metalclad Corp. v. United Mexican States* had failed to consider the environmental and sustainable development goals of NAFTA, and it argued that there is no overriding principle of confidentiality in NAFTA proceedings that would operate to exclude amici.[180] Moreover, the Institute maintained that the absence of an appeal from the tribunal's award supported the tribunal's acceptance of briefs from amici, and that such submissions would be necessary for the tribunal to render an informed decision.[181]

Mexico (which was not a party to the arbitration) objected to the Institute's petition to intervene, asserting that Chapter 11 of NAFTA does not provide for the intervention of third parties, other than the right of nonparty NAFTA governments to provide limited comments pursuant to Article 1128. Mexico further noted that the right of intervention sought by the Institute would confer greater rights on

---

[178] *See, e.g.*, the submission of the Canadian based International Institute for Sustainable Development (IISD) in *Methanex v. U.S* (Petition to Arbitration Arbitral, Aug. 25, 2000), *available at* www.naftaclaims.com. In the ICSID Convention context, a Petition for Transparency and Participation as Amicus Curiae was submitted by five non-governmental organizations (NGOs): Association Civil por la Igualdad y la Justicia (ACIJ), Centro de Estudios Legales y Sociales (CELS), Center for International Environmental Law (CIEL), Consumidores Libres Cooperativa Ltda. de Provisión de Servicios de Acción Comunitaria, and Unión de Usuarios y Consumidores. This petition was submitted in *Aguas Argentinas, S.A., Suez, Sociedad General de Aguas de Barcelona, S.A. & Vivendi Universal, S.A. v. Argentina*, ICSID Case No. ARB/03/19 (Jan. 23, 2005). The text of the petition is *available at* http://www.ciel. org/Tae/ Suez_ICSID_8Feb05.html. *See also* Petition of La Coordinadora para la Defensa del Agua y Vida, La Federación Departamental Cochabambina de Organizaciones Regantes, SEMAPA Sur, Friends of the Earth-Netherlands, Oscar Olivera, Omar Fernandez, Father Luis Sánchez, and Congressman Jorge Alvarado, in *Aguas del Tunari S.A. v. Republic of Bol.*, ICSID Case No. ARB/02/3 (Aug. 29,2002); Jeffery Atik, *Legitimacy, Transparency and NGO Participation in the NAFTA Chapter 11 Process*, in *NAFTA Investment Law and Arbitration: Past Issues, Current Practice, Future Prospects* (Weiler ed., Transnational Publishers 2004); Meg Kinear, *Transparency and Third Party Participation in Investor-State Dispute Settlement*, Paper presented in Symposium Organized by ICSID, UNCITRAL, and UNCTAD: Making the Most of International Investment Agreements: A Common Agenda (OECD, ICSID, UNCTAD Dec. 2005); Loukas Mistelis, *Confidentiality and Third Party Participation*, Int'l L. & Pol'y 170 (2005); Ruth Mackenzie, *The Amicus Curiae in International Courts: Towards Common Procedural Approaches?* in *Civil Society, International Courts and Compliance Bodies* 295, 298 (Treves et al., eds., 2005).

[179] *Methanex Corp. v. U.S.* (Decision of the Tribunal on Petitions from Third Persons to Intervene as Amici Curiae, Jan. 15, 2001), *available at* www.naftaclaims.com.

[180] *Id.* ¶ 6.

[181] *Id.*

amicus curiae than NAFTA governments enjoy, given the limited scope of Article 1128 submissions.[182] By contrast, Canada (also not a party) wrote to the tribunal, supporting greater general transparency in NAFTA proceedings and the acceptance of amicus curiae submissions. At the same time, Canada reminded the arbitrators that only NAFTA Parties have the right to make submissions with respect to the interpretation of NAFTA provisions.[183]

The claimant first sought dismissal of the Institute's petition to intervene on grounds that Article 25(4) of the governing UNCITRAL Arbitration Rules requires that hearings be held in camera, and that by implication this provision must also require that documents prepared for the arbitration be confidential.[184] Second, the claimant argued that granting the Institute the status of amicus curiae would be equivalent to adding a party to the proceedings, and that the UNCITRAL Rules prevent the tribunal from adding parties without the agreement of all parties.[185] Third, the claimant argued that the protection of the public interest was already ensured by Article 1128 of NAFTA, which allows public interest groups to convey information to NAFTA Parties that can intervene on questions of interpretation.[186]

The United States argued that the rules governing arbitration do permit the acceptance of amicus curiae submissions, and that a tribunal should accept such submissions if the material is likely to be useful to the tribunal in deciding the case at hand. The United States argued that Article 15(1) of the UNCITRAL Arbitration Rules empowers an arbitral tribunal to "conduct the proceedings as it deem[s] appropriate subject to the proviso that the parties be treated equally and given a full opportunity of presenting their cases."[187] Furthermore, the United States opined that nothing in Article 25(4) of the UNCITRAL Arbitration Rules nor in Chapter 11 of NAFTA prevents an arbitral tribunal from accepting amicus submissions.[188]

In reaching its decision, the tribunal recognized that because nothing in the UNCITRAL Arbitration Rules or Chapter 11 of NAFTA expressly addresses the issue, the power to accept amicus curiae submissions must be inferred. The tribunal considered Article 15(1) of the UNCITRAL Arbitration Rules.[189] Stressing the importance of Article 15(1), the tribunal hailed it as a "hallmark" of arbitral procedure, the

---

[182] *Id.* ¶ 9.
[183] *Id.* ¶ 10.
[184] *Id.* ¶ 12.
[185] *Id.* ¶ 13.
[186] *Id.* ¶ 14.
[187] *Id.* ¶ 18.
[188] *Id.* ¶¶ 19–20.
[189] *Id.* ¶ 26.

"heart" of UNCITRAL Arbitration Rules, and the "Magna Carta" of international commercial arbitration.[190]

Evaluating the issue in the context of Article 15(1), the tribunal first decided that allowing a third party to participate in UNCITRAL proceedings as an amicus curiae submission remains within the general authority accorded to the arbitral tribunal by Article 15(1), because such a submission does not affect the legal rights of the disputing parties.[191] The tribunal also reasoned that acceptance of amicus submissions would not create an immediate risk of unfair or unequal treatment, because both disputing parties must bear an equal burden in responding to the information and argument provided in such interventions.[192] The tribunal added that no other provision of the UNCITRAL Rules or NAFTA modifies the effect of Article 15(1) in the case at hand.[193]

In conclusion, the *Methanex* tribunal found that it had the power to accept amicus curiae submissions under Article 15(1), and that given public interest in the proceeding and the minimal expense that the amicus submission would add to the overall cost of the arbitration, it was appropriate to allow the Institute to intervene.[194] The *Methanex* tribunal's conclusion illustrates one line of reasoning tribunals may follow in the future, especially in light of the increasing public interest in investment arbitrations.

Nine months after this decision of the *Methanex* tribunal, another NAFTA tribunal, in *United Parcel Service (UPS) v. Canada*,[195] based upon the same UNCITRAL provisions and relying largely on the above decision of the *Methanex* tribunal, allowed the interested parties, in that case the Canadian Union of Postal workers and the Council of Canadians, to make amicus curiae submissions; it however denied their request to participate as a party.[196]

In 2003, the Free Trade Commission of NAFTA published a statement in which it set forth certain procedures for filing amicus curiae submissions in the context of NAFTA arbitrations.[197] This move was partly in response to the multiple requests

---

[190] *Id.*

[191] *Id.* ¶ 30.

[192] *Id.* ¶¶ 35–37.

[193] *Id.* ¶¶ 38–46.

[194] *Id.* ¶¶ 47–52.

[195] *United Parcel Service of Am., Inc. (UPS) v. Canada* (NAFTA/UNCITRAL Tribunal, Decision on Jurisdiction, Nov. 22, 2003).

[196] *UPS v. Canada* (Decision of the Tribunal on Petition for Intervention and Participation as Amici Curiae, Oct. 17, 2001), ¶¶ 35–43.

[197] Statement of the Free Trade Commission on Non-Disputing Party Participation (Oct. 7, 2003), *available at* http://www.dfait-maeci.gc.ca/nafta-alena/Nondisputing-en.pdf [hereinafter FTC Statement on Amici Participation].

by civil society groups during the *Methanex* and *UPS* cases to participate or submit amicus briefs in the arbitral proceedings. The procedures provide that any nondisputing party who wishes to file a written submission with a NAFTA tribunal shall apply for a leave from the tribunal to submit such an application document.[198] It also lays out in detail the required content of such an application, method of serving it on the parties, and other procedural issues.[199] Finally, it sets out the criteria that a tribunal should consider before granting a leave:

> 6. In determining whether to grant leave to file a non-disputing party submission, the Tribunal will consider, among other things, the extent to which:
>
> (a) the non-disputing party submission would assist the Tribunal in the determination of a factual or legal issue related to the arbitration by bringing a perspective, particular knowledge or insight that is different from that of the disputing parties;
>
> (b) the non-disputing party submission would address matters within the scope of the dispute;
>
> (c) the non-disputing party has a significant interest in the arbitration; and
>
> (d) there is a public interest in the subject-matter of the arbitration.
>
> 7. The Tribunal will ensure that:
>
> (a) any non-disputing party submission avoids disrupting the proceedings; and
>
> (b) neither disputing party is unduly burdened or unfairly prejudiced by such submissions.
>
> . . . .
>
> 9. The granting of leave to file a non-disputing party submission does not require the Tribunal to address that submission at any point in the arbitration. The granting of leave to file a non-disputing party submission does not entitle the non-disputing party that filed the submission to make further submissions in the arbitration.[200]

In addition to the NAFTA parties' initiatives, the UNCITRAL Working Group is also currently considering to revise the UNCITRAL Rules to allow further access to the proceedings in investment treaty arbitrations.[201]

In the context of the ICSID Convention, several tribunals have received petitions from interested civil society groups for participation in arbitral proceedings as a party or as an amicus curiae.[202] Such ICSID tribunals, noting that the ICSID Convention and the

---

[198] *Id.* ¶ B(1).

[199] *Id.* ¶ B(2)–(5).

[200] *Id.* ¶ B(6)–(9).

[201] *See* U.N. Doc. No. A/CN.9/WG.II/WP.143 (2006), *available at* www.uncitral.org.

[202] *See, e.g., Suez, Sociedad General de Aguas de Barcelona, S.A. & Vivendi Universal, S.A. v. Argentine Republic,* ICSID Case No. ARB/03/19; and *Biwater Gauff Ltd. v. United Republic of Tanzania,* ICSID Case No. ARB/05/22.

Rules then in effect did not deal with this issue, accepted amicus submissions, basing their decision on the broad authority granted by Article 44 of the ICSID Convention.[203] In 2006, however, the new ICSID Arbitration Rules came into force,[204] and they changed the framework for considering amicus curiae submissions. The new Rule 37(2) provides that:

> 2) After consulting both parties, the Tribunal may allow a person or entity that is not a party to the dispute (in this Rule called the "non-disputing party") to file a written submission with the Tribunal regarding a matter within the scope of the dispute. In determining whether to allow such a filing, the Tribunal shall consider, among other things, the extent to which:
>
> (a) the non-disputing party submission would assist the Tribunal in the determination of a factual or legal issue related to the proceeding by bringing a perspective, particular knowledge or insight that is different from that of the disputing parties;
>
> (b) the non-disputing party submission would address a matter within the scope of the dispute;
>
> (c) the non-disputing party has a significant interest in the proceeding.
>
> The Tribunal shall ensure that the non-disputing party submission does not disrupt the proceeding or unduly burden or unfairly prejudice either party, and that both parties are given an opportunity to present their observations on the non-disputing party submission.

These ICSID criteria mirror those in the NAFTA Free Trade Commission (FTC) statement discussed above. They are not exhaustive, however, as the terms *among other things* suggest. Arbitral tribunals on several occasions have considered additional criteria for this purpose such as the extra burden that amicus briefs may place on the parties.[205]

---

[203] Article 44 of the ICSID Convention provides that "Any arbitration proceeding shall be conducted in accordance with the provisions of this Section and, except as the parties otherwise agree, in accordance with the Arbitration Rules in effect on the date on which the parties consented to arbitration. If any question of procedure arises which is not covered by this Section or the Arbitration Rules or any rules agreed by the parties, the Tribunal shall decide the question." See *Aguas Argentinas, S.A., Suez, Sociedad General de Aguas de Barcelona, S.A. & Vivendi Universal, S.A. v. Argentina*, ICSID Case No. ARB/03/19 (Order in Response to Petition for Transparency and Participation as Amicus Curiae, May 19, 2005), ¶¶ 19–20 (accepting submissions) (source notes omitted)).

[204] *See* News Release, ICSID, Amendment to the ICSID Rules and Regulations (Apr. 5, 2006), *available at* http://icsid.worldbank.com.

[205] *See Aguas Argentinas v. Argentina* (Order in Response to a Petition for Transparency and Participation as Amicus Curiae), ICSID Case No. ARB/03/19 (May 19, 2005); *Aguas Provinciales de Santa Fe v. Argentina* (Order in Response to a Petition for Participation as Amicus Curiae), ICSID Case No. ARB/03/17 (March 17, 2006). In these cases, the tribunal listed several additional factors to consider: ". . . all the information in the petition, the view of the Claimants and Respondents; the extra burden which the acceptance of amicus curiae briefs may place on the parties, the Tribunal and the proceedings; and the degree to which the proposed amicus curiae brief is likely to assist the Tribunal in arriving at its decision."

Below are two excerpts from procedural orders deciding requests for participation as amicus curiae. The first order was rendered in the context of *Aguas Provinciales de Santa Fe S.A., et al. v. Argentina*. The investment dispute in this case centered around the water distribution and sewerage systems in the province of Santa Fe, Argentina. Five NGOs submitted a petition to participate. The tribunal, which issued its decision prior to the entry into force of the amended ICSID Rules, rejected the NGOs' petition. The tribunal, noting that the ICSID Rules were silent on the issue of participation of amici, relied on Article 44 of the ICSID Convention as a source of authority to accept them. The second order was rendered in *Biwater Gauff v. Tanzania*, and also involved issues relating to distribution of water. In the *Biwater* decision, which was issued after the entry into force of the new ICSID rules, the tribunal based its authority on the new Rule 37(2) and partly granted the petitioners' request.

The new Rule 37(2), however, directly applies only to cases filed after April 10, 2006, the date of the entry into force of the amendments to the ICSID Rules. Prior cases will, in accordance with Article 44, still be subject to the old rules. This technical difference may not have a practical significance though, as Rule 37(2) contains the same factors that were taken into account by arbitral tribunals in issuing procedural orders prior to the entry into force of that rule.[206]

Aguas Provinciales de Santa Fe S.A., Suez, Sociedad General de Aguas de Barcelona S.A. & Inter Aguas Servicios Integrales del Agua S.A. v. Argentina, ICSID Case No. ARB/03/17 (Order in Response to a Petition for Participation as an *Amicus Curiae*, Mar. 17, 2006)

10. Neither the ICSID Convention nor the Arbitration Rules specifically authorize or specifically prohibit the submission by nonparties of amicus curiae briefs or other documents. Moreover, to the knowledge of the Tribunal, prior to its Order of May 19, 2005, no previous tribunal functioning under ICSID Rules had granted a nonparty to a dispute the status of amicus curiae and accepted amicus curiae submissions. This lack of specificity in the ICSID Convention and Rules requires the Tribunal in this case, as it did in ICSID Case ARB/03/19, to address two basic questions: 1) Does the Tribunal have the power to accept and consider amicus curiae submissions by nonparties to the case? and 2) If it has that power, what are the conditions under which it should exercise it?

11. The Powers of the Tribunal to Accept Amicus Submissions. Article 44 of the ICSID Convention states: "Any arbitration proceeding shall be conducted in accordance with the provisions of this Section and, except as the parties otherwise agree, in accordance

---

[206] *Suez, Sociedad General de Aguas de Barcelona, S.A., & Vivendi Universal S.A. v. Argentina*, ICSID Case No. ARB/03/19 (Order in Response to a Petition by Five Non-governmental Organizations for Permission to Make an Amicus Curiae Submission, Feb. 12, 2007), ¶¶ 14–15.

with the Arbitration Rules in effect on the date on which the parties consented to arbitration. If any question of procedure arises which is not covered by this Section or the Arbitration Rules or any rules agreed by the parties, the Tribunal shall decide the question." The last sentence of Article 44 is a grant of residual power to the Tribunal to decide procedural questions not treated in the Convention itself or in the rules applicable to a given dispute.

12. In applying this provision to the present case, the Tribunal faces an initial question as to whether permitting an amicus curiae submission by a non disputing party is a "procedural question." At a basic level of interpretation, a procedural question is one which relates to the manner of proceeding or which deals with the way to accomplish a stated end. The admission of an amicus curiae submission would fall within this definition of procedural question since it can be viewed as a step in assisting the Tribunal to achieve its fundamental task of arriving at a correct decision in this case.

13. An amicus curiae is, as the Latin words indicate, a "friend of the court," and is not a party to the proceeding. Its role in other fora and systems has traditionally been that of a nonparty, and the Tribunal believes that an amicus curiae in an ICSID proceeding would also be that of a nonparty. The traditional role of an amicus curiae in an adversary proceeding is to help the decision maker arrive at its decision by providing the decision maker with arguments, perspectives, and expertise that the litigating parties may not provide. In short, a request to act as amicus curiae is an offer of assistance—an offer that the decision maker is free to accept or reject. An amicus curiae is a volunteer, a friend of the court, not a party.

14. [The tribunal then relied on the Methanex tribunal's interpretation of Article 15(1) of UNCITRAL Rules. It noted that the latter provision was "substantially similar to Article 44 of the ICSID Convention." Accordingly, similar to the Methanex tribunal, it had the power to accept amicus briefs. It also added, acceptance of amicus submissions is not equivalent to making a person a party to arbitration.]

15. Although it could be argued that amicus submissions would place an increased burden on the parties and the Tribunal, that result is not inevitable. The Tribunal believes that it can exercise its powers under Article 44 in such a way as to minimize the additional burden on both the parties and the Tribunal, while giving the Tribunal the benefit of the views of suitable amici curiae in appropriate circumstances. The Tribunal in the present case finds further support for the admission of amicus submissions in international arbitral proceedings in the practices of NAFTA, the Iran-United States Claims Tribunal, and the World Trade Organization.

16. The Tribunal concludes that Article 44 of the ICSID Convention grants it the power to admit amicus curiae submissions from suitable nonparties in appropriate cases. We turn now to consider the conditions under which the Tribunal may exercise that power.

17. The Conditions for the Admission of Amicus Curiae Briefs. Based on a review of amicus practices in other jurisdictions and fora, the Tribunal has concluded that the exercise of the power conferred on the Tribunal by Article 44 to accept amicus submissions should depend on three basic criteria: a) the appropriateness of the subject matter of the case; b) the suitability of a given nonparty to act as amicus curiae in that case, and c) the procedure by which the amicus submission is made and considered. The Tribunal believes that the judicious application of these criteria will enable it to balance the interests of concerned non disputant parties to be heard and at the same time protect the substantive and procedural rights of the disputants to a fair, orderly, and expeditious arbitral process.

18. The Appropriateness of the Subject Matter of the Case for Amicus Curiae Submissions . . . . The factor that gives this case particular public interest is that the investment dispute

centers around the water distribution and sewage systems of urban areas in the province of Santa Fe. Those systems provide basic public services to hundreds of thousands of people and as a result may raise a variety of complex public and international law questions, including human rights considerations . . . .

20. Given the public interest in the subject matter of this case, it is possible that appropriate nonparties may be able to afford the Tribunal perspectives, arguments, and expertise that will help it arrive at a correct decision . . . .

21. The acceptance of amicus submissions would have the additional desirable consequence of increasing the transparency of investor-state arbitration. Public acceptance of the legitimacy of international arbitral processes, particularly when they involve states and matters of public interest, is strengthened by increased openness and increased knowledge as to how these processes function. It is this imperative that has led to increased transparency in the arbitral processes of the World Trade Organization and the North American Free Trade Agreement. Through the participation of appropriate representatives of civil society in appropriate cases, the public will gain increased understanding of ICSID processes.

22. For the foregoing reasons, the Tribunal concludes that the present case is an appropriate one in which suitable nonparties may usefully make amicus curiae submissions.

23 and 24. The Suitability of Specific Nonparties to Act as Amici Curiae. [The tribunal relied on the NAFTA FTC statement to set out the procedure]

IV. Whether Petitioners Qualify as Appropriate Amici Curiae in This Case

29. Tribunal considers that a nonparty must demonstrate three important attributes to qualify as an amicus curiae: relevant expertise, experience, and independence. To enable the Tribunal to judge whether a nonparty possesses these three vital attributes, the Tribunal asks that it be provided with information on 4 issues: (i) the identity and background of the petitioner; (ii) the interests of the petitioner in the case; (iii) the petitioners' financial or other relationships with the parties; and (iv) the reasons why the Tribunal should accept the petitioners' amicus curiae brief . . . .

34. Conclusion. The Tribunal has decided that the four Petitioners have not provided it with sufficient specific information and reasons to conclude that they qualify as amici curiae in this case. Consequently, the Tribunal declines to grant them permission to make amicus submissions at this time. In the event that the Petitioners were to present a new application for leave to submit amicus curiae submissions, with appropriate and sufficient information and reasons as specified above, the Tribunal would be prepared to consider whether Petitioners qualify as amici curiae and to grant them leave to make amicus submissions in accordance with the conditions stated above.

Biwater Gauff Ltd. v. United Republic of Tanzania, ICSID Case No. ARB/05/22 (Procedural Order No. 5, Feb. 2, 2007)

46. Nature of the Petition: The application before the Arbitral Tribunal is headed: "Petition for *Amicus Curiae* Status." It might be noted at the outset that the ICSID

Rules do not, in terms, provide for an amicus curiae "status," in so far as this might be taken to denote a standing in the overall arbitration akin to that of a party, with the full range of procedural privileges that that might entail. Rather, the ICSID Arbitration Rules expressly regulate two specific—and carefully delimited—types of participation by non-parties, namely: (a) the filing of a written submission (Rule 37(2)) and (b) the attendance at hearings (Rule 32(2)). Each of these types of participation is to be addressed by a tribunal on an ad hoc basis, rather than by the granting of an overall "*amicus curiae* status" for all purposes. Indeed, Rule 37(2) is specifically drafted in terms of the discretion of a tribunal to accept "a" written submission, rather than all submissions from a particular entity. It follows that there may be some written submissions from any given non-disputing party that are accepted as qualifying under the terms of Rule 37(2), and some that are not. It also follows that a "non-disputing party" does not become a party to the arbitration by virtue of a tribunal's decision under Rule 37, but is instead afforded a specific and defined opportunity to make a particular submission.

47. The Arbitral Tribunal considers this an important starting point in terms of safeguarding the expectations of all concerned, as well as the integrity of the arbitral process, lest it be misunderstood that once any type of permission to participate is given to a non-disputing party, the latter may then be entitled as of right to all other procedural rights and privileges.

48. Having said this, the Arbitral Tribunal also recognises that to allow effective access to an *amicus curiae*, there may be certain other procedural mechanisms that need to be put in place.

49. Rule 37(2): The test which the Arbitral Tribunal must apply in deciding whether or not to allow any particular Petitioner to file a written submission in these proceedings is set out in Rule 37(2) . . . .

50. The Arbitral Tribunal has carefully considered each of the conditions in Rule 37(2)(a), (b) and (c). On the basis of the information provided in the Petition, the nature and expertise of each Petitioner, and the submissions summarised above, the Arbitral Tribunal is of the view that it may benefit from a written submission by the Petitioner, and that allowing for the making of such submission by these entities in these proceedings is an important element in the overal discharge of the Arbitral Tribunal's mandate, and in securing wider confidence in the arbitral process itself. In particular the Arbitral Tribunal:

> (a) considers that a written submission by the Petitioners appears to have the reasonable potential to assist the Arbitral Tribunal by bringing a perspective, particular knowledge or insight that is different from that of the disputing parties (Rule 37(2)(a));
>
> (b) accepts the Petitioners' indication that their submissions would address matters within the scope of the dispute, and obviously reserves the right to disregard any submission that does not do so (Rule 37(2)(b));
>
> (c) accepts that each of the Petitioners has a sufficient interest in this proceeding (Rule 37(d)(c)).
>
> . . . .

55. For the above reasons, and subject to the further discretion below, the Arbitral Tribunal grants the Petitioners the opportunity to file a written submission in these arbitral proceedings, pursuant to Rule 37(2).

This trend of increased public participation in the arbitral process is likely to continue.[207]

L. Damages Phase[208]

In most investment treaty arbitrations, the damages are determined along with the merits, with no separate "damages phase." Nonetheless, it is not unusual to see bifurcated or trifurcated arbitral proceedings where the issue of damages is briefed and decided in a separate hearing and award.[209] The nature and calculation of damages often raise important legal issues, which are discussed in detail in Chapter XIX.

M. Hearings

Extensive hearings are a feature of many investment arbitrations. Hearings include both legal argument and the presentation of oral witness evidence, and in particular cross-examination, as most witness testimony will already have been submitted in the form of written witness statements. The organization of hearings is normally left to the discretion of the tribunal, with some participation from the parties. The following notes from the UNCITRAL outline the most important issues with respect to hearings.

UNCITRAL, *Notes on Organizing Arbitral Proceedings*, available at http://www.uncitral.org/english/texts/arbitration/arb-notes.htm

17. HEARINGS

(a) Decision whether to hold hearings

74. Laws on arbitral procedure and arbitration rules often have provisions as to the cases in which oral hearings must be held and as to when the arbitral tribunal has discretion to decide whether to hold hearings.

---

[207] See D. P. Stoger, *Amicus Curiae. Participant or Friend?*, in *European Integration and International Co-Ordination: Studies in Transnational Economic Law in Honour of Claus-Dieter Ehlermann* 419–50 (A. von Bogdandy, P. C. Mavroidis, & Y. Meny eds., 2002); T. Weiler, *Restrictions on Submissions of Amicus Briefs to NAFTA investment Arbitral Tribunals*, 1(2) Ogel (2003).

[208] See generally Chapter XIX.

[209] *CME Czech Republic B.V. v. Czech Republic* (UNCITRAL Arbitration, Partial Award (2001) and Final Award (2003)); *LG&E Capital Corp. and LG&E Int'l Inc. v. Argentine Republic*, ICSID Case No. ARB/02/1; *S.D. Myers, Inc. v. Canada* (UNCITRAL Arbitration under Chapter 11 of NAFTA (2002)); *Pope & Talbot Inc. v. Canada* (UNCITRAL Arbitration under Chapter 11 of NAFTA); *Saluka Inves. v. Czech Republic* (UNCITRAL Arbitration).

75. If it is up to the arbitral tribunal to decide whether to hold hearings, the decision is likely to be influenced by factors such as, on the one hand, that it is usually quicker and easier to clarify points at issue pursuant to a direct confrontation of arguments than on the basis of correspondence and, on the other hand, the travel and other cost of holding hearings, and that the need of finding acceptable dates for the hearings might delay the proceedings. The arbitral tribunal may wish to consult the parties on this matter.

(b) Whether one period of hearings should be held or separate periods of hearings

76. Attitudes vary as to whether hearings should be held in a single period of hearings or in separate periods, especially when more than a few days are needed to complete the hearings. According to some arbitrators, the entire hearings should normally be held in a single period, even if the hearings are to last for more than a week. Other arbitrators in such cases tend to schedule separate periods of hearings. In some cases issues to be decided are separated, and separate hearings set for those issues, with the aim that oral presentation on those issues will be completed within the allotted time. Among the advantages of one period of hearings are that it involves less travel costs, memory will not fade, and it is unlikely that people representing a party will change. On the other hand, the longer the hearings, the more difficult it may be to find early dates acceptable to all participants. Furthermore, separate periods of hearings may be easier to schedule, the subsequent hearings may be tailored to the development of the case, and the period between the hearings leaves time for analysing the records and negotiations between the parties aimed at narrowing the points at issue by agreement.

(c) Setting dates for hearings

77. Typically, firm dates will be fixed for hearings. Exceptionally, the arbitral tribunal may initially wish to set only "target dates" as opposed to definitive dates. This may be done at a stage of the proceedings when not all information necessary to schedule hearings is yet available, with the understanding that the target dates will either be confirmed or rescheduled within a reasonably short period. Such provisional planning can be useful to participants who are generally not available on short notice.

(d) Whether there should be a limit on the aggregate amount of time each party will have for oral arguments and questioning witnesses

78. Some arbitrators consider it useful to limit the aggregate amount of time each party has for any of the following: (a) making oral statements; (b) questioning its witnesses; and (c) questioning the witnesses of the other party or parties. In general, the same aggregate amount of time is considered appropriate for each party, unless the arbitral tribunal considers that a different allocation is justified. Before deciding, the arbitral tribunal may wish to consult the parties as to how much time they think they will need.

79. Such planning of time, provided it is realistic, fair and subject to judiciously firm control by the arbitral tribunal, will make it easier for the parties to plan the presentation of the various items of evidence and arguments, reduce the likelihood of running out of time towards the end of the hearings and avoid that one party would unfairly use up a disproportionate amount of time.

(e) The order in which the parties will present their arguments and evidence

80. Arbitration rules typically give broad latitude to the arbitral tribunal to determine the order of presentations at the hearings. Within that latitude, practices differ, for example, as to whether opening or closing statements are heard and their level of detail; the sequence in which the claimant and the respondent present their opening

statements, arguments, witnesses and other evidence; and whether the respondent or the claimant has the last word. In view of such differences, or when no arbitration rules apply, it may foster efficiency of the proceedings if the arbitral tribunal clarifies to the parties, in advance of the hearings, the manner in which it will conduct the hearings, at least in broad lines.

(f) Length of hearings

81. The length of a hearing primarily depends on the complexity of the issues to be argued and the amount of witness evidence to be presented. The length also depends on the procedural style used in the arbitration. Some practitioners prefer to have written evidence and written arguments presented before the hearings, which thus can focus on the issues that have not been sufficiently clarified. Those practitioners generally tend to plan shorter hearings than those practitioners who prefer that most if not all evidence and arguments are presented to the arbitral tribunal orally and in full detail. In order to facilitate the parties' preparations and avoid misunderstandings, the arbitral tribunal may wish to clarify to the parties, in advance of the hearings, the intended use of time and style of work at the hearings.

N. Posthearing Briefs

The parties to a dispute may agree, or the tribunal may require, one or two rounds of posthearing briefs. Posthearing briefs typically address questions that may have arisen during the hearing, whether raised by the tribunal, by a party, or through the dynamics of litigation. Depending on the arrangement of the parties and instructions of the arbitral tribunal, some parties may choose to provide a summary of their case in posthearing briefs, but more often posthearing briefs focus on the issues that the arbitral tribunal asks the parties to address. Indeed, it is not uncommon to see posthearing briefs that have been prepared in a very concise way and in a question-and-answer format.

O. Award

Once the proceedings are closed, the tribunal deliberates and issues an award. It is difficult to generalize about the amount of time that normally elapses between the parties' final submissions and the release of the arbitrators' decision. Even when arbitration rules establish a time limit for the issue of an award,[210] tribunals often ask for additional time from the parties or the arbitral institution, and such an extension is unlikely to be refused. Naturally, the amount of time required varies

---

[210] ICC Arbitration Rules, art. 24(1) (setting six-month time limit for issue of award after signing of Terms of Reference); SCC Rules of Arbitration, art. 37 (the final award shall be made not later than six months from the date on which the arbitration was referred to the Arbitral Tribunal).

widely according to the complexity of the case and the schedule of the arbitrators. The most common period between the end of hearings and the release of an investment arbitration award is six to nine months.

The drafting of the award normally begins with a meeting of the arbitrators, without the presence of the parties. Although this deliberation session sometimes takes place immediately after the close of oral hearings, it may take more time for the arbitrators to gather, particularly if the schedule calls for an additional round of posthearing briefs. During the closed discussion session, the arbitrators will discuss the merits of each side's presentation, attempting to come to a consensus on the proper outcome of the case. After deliberations are complete, the chairman is normally charged with writing the first draft of the award, attempting to incorporate the concerns and comments of his coarbitrators to achieve a unanimous decision, if possible. The chairman then circulates the draft to the other members of the tribunal for comment. The process of comments and redrafting may be repeated several times before a final version of the award is ready. An arbitrator who does not agree with the conclusions of the majority may file a separate or dissenting opinion, which will be delivered to the parties along with the award. A separate or dissenting opinion has no legal force, although it may have persuasive force in subsequent cases.[211]

The deliberation and drafting that lead to the release of an international arbitration award is one of the least understood aspects of the arbitration process. Although parties could learn a great deal about case management strategy from a detailed analysis of the dynamics of this process, only those who have served as arbitrators know precisely how the interaction of three disparate personalities finally give rise to a single, coherent award. The case of *CME Czech Republic B.V. v. Czech Republic* has provided practitioners with some useful anecdotal information in this area, however. After losing in the liability phase of the arbitration brought against it by a Dutch claimant company, the Czech Republic sought to set aside the tribunal's decision before a national court in Stockholm, the place of the arbitration. Among many challenges to the award, the Czech Republic insisted that the arbitrator it had appointed was excluded from deliberations between the other two tribunal members, in violation of the UNCITRAL Rules and Swedish law. In considering this attack, the Swedish courts took evidence from the arbitrators themselves, and in their decision provided a detailed description of deliberation in investment arbitration.

---

[211] On dissenting opinions *see generally* Fouchard, Gaillard, Goldman on *International Commercial Arbitration* ¶¶ 1396–1405 (Kluwer Law International, 1999); A. Redfern, M. Hunter, N. Blackaby & C. Partasides, *Law and Practice of International Arbitration* § 8–77 *et seq* (Kluwer Law International 2004); A. Redfern, *The 2003 Freshfields—Lecture Dissenting Opinions in International Commercial Arbitration: The Good, the Bad and the Ugly,* 20(3) Arb. Int'l 223 (2004); A. Redfern, *Dangerous Dissents,* 71(3) J. Chartered Inst. Arb. 200 (2005).

AWARD

Czech Republic v. CME Czech Republic, B.V. (Svea Court of Appeal Judgement, Case No. T 8735–01, Decision of May 15, 2003)

After the hearing was concluded on May 2, 2001, [Tribunal Chairman] Kühn drafted a list of questions. The various issues were set out in this list of questions and testimony has been given in the case that Kühn had thereby carried out very serious and ambitious work. In addition, in a cover letter, Kühn also invited both of the other arbitrators to make their own supplements to the list of questions. The list of questions was answered in detail by [Claimant-appointed arbitrator] Schwebel and [Respondent-appointed arbitrator] Hándl. Kühn thereafter processed the list of questions so that it could serve as a basis for the oral deliberations in Düsseldorf which, from what appears to have been proven, were held during the whole of June 1 and for a couple of hours in the morning of June 2.

It has been testified that essentially all significant issues were discussed at the meeting. Both Schwebel and Kühn have stated that Hándl was the one who spoke most. The focal point of the deliberations must be deemed to have been the list of questions, the answers thereto, and the discussions between the arbitrators in Düsseldorf . . . .

Prior to the meeting in Düsseldorf, both Schwebel's and Hándl's positions in the dispute were probably clear to the others, while Kühn had not yet reached a decision. Following the meeting, it was clear what the outcome would be since Kühn had then decided to side with Schwebel's opinion that the Republic had breached the Treaty, while Hándl was of the opposite opinion.

Schwebel has stated that he believed that Hándl, directly after the meeting, would begin writing a dissenting opinion. Kühn has stated that he proposed that Hándl write the introduction to the award—"to keep him in the team"—since he would not be able to participate in the drafting of the reasons for the award. Schwebel has also stated that Hándl made it entirely clear that he did not wish to participate in the production of the draft award . . . .

On July 30, Kühn had prepared a complete draft award, which he distributed to Schwebel and Hándl. Hándl commented on the award in detail in a letter dated August 16, which Kühn responded to two weeks later. Both Kühn and Schwebel have stated that they regarded Hándl's comments as largely constituting a repetition of his reply to the list of questions and what he stated at the deliberations in Düsseldorf . . . .

[T]hrough the testimony of Kühn and Schwebel it must be deemed proven that it was entirely clear to the arbitrators—without any formal voting having taken place—that Hándl had a dissenting opinion at the Düsseldorf meeting. The Republic argues that from the commencement of the drafting of the award, Hándl no longer participated on the same terms as the two other arbitrators; the two other arbitrators held discussions without him, he was not awarded sufficient time to rebut the various draft awards, and he was thereby deprived of the possibility to express his opinion on certain essential questions . . . .

Hándl has received all essential communications between the arbitrators. The evidence in the case does not support the Republic's allegations that the two other arbitrators deliberated without Hándl and that Hándl did not have an opportunity to participate on equal terms, that they worked against him, and that the two other arbitrators ignored his opinions. On the contrary, Kühn appears the whole time to have treated Hándl correctly and Hándl appears to have been afforded an opportunity to submit his comments to the extent which reasonably may be dictated by considerations of courtesy between colleagues. Hándl's feeling of having been excluded is probably, in all essential regards, connected to the fact that he did not meet with

> support for his opinion in the case . . . . [A]s the arbitrator in the minority, Hándl no longer played any necessary role with respect to [the] reasons for the majority's award . . . . Accordingly, the Court of Appeal finds that Hándl received due time to submit comments to the draft award.

Finally, it is becoming increasingly common for arbitrators to draft separate or dissenting opinions. When one of the arbitrators disagrees with the others regarding certain issues of law or fact, he or she may choose to write such opinions explaining his or her own views with respect to those issues. In *CME v. Czech Republic*, for instance, Mr. Hándl wrote a dissenting opinion.[212]

P. Enforcement and Challenge of Award

One of the primary attractions of the international arbitral system is the possibility of voluntary compliance, either with the respondent's payment of amounts ordered by the tribunal or with the abandonment of the dispute (should the claimant be defeated).[213] This widespread compliance with arbitration awards is due in large part to the effectiveness of the New York and ICSID Conventions enforcement provisions, which ensure that in most circumstances a losing respondent will be unable to avoid execution on assets in scores of national court jurisdictions around the world.[214]

Nevertheless, a losing party sometimes seeks to alter or overturn arbitration awards, in particular when it is dissatisfied with the result or perceives defects in the process that led to the award. Challenge of investment arbitration awards appears to be somewhat more prevalent in investment arbitration cases than in commercial disputes. This may be the result of political pressure on governments, or simply a function of the very large stakes in many treaty cases. Losing parties have several avenues to follow; the first instance of redress for a losing party may well be the tribunal itself. The losing party may file a request for the interpretation or alteration of award to the same tribunal, although under most arbitration rules

---

[212] *CME v. Czech Republic* (Dissenting Opinion of Dr. Hándl on Partial Award of Sept. 13, 2001). Even the Chairman of an arbitral tribunal may dissent from the majority, although this is exceedingly rare. *See Tokios Tokeles v.Ukraine,* ICSID Case No. ARB/02/18 (Dissenting Opinion of Prof. Weil, Apr. 29, 2004).

[213] Redfern et al., *supra* note 211, § 10–01; *see also* D. Wang, *Binding Force and Enforcement: International Center for the Settlement of Investment Disputes,* UNCTAD Course on Dispute Settlement, International Centre for the Settlement of Investment Disputes, Module 2.9, UNCTAD/EDM/Misc.232/Add. 8, at 1.

[214] The enforcement provisions of the ICSID Convention are even stronger than the New York Convention, in so far as they require the member states consider the ICSID awards as a final judgment of their courts. ICSID Convention, art. 54(1).

such modification is limited to the correction of clerical and mathematical errors. Alternatively, it may challenge the award in national courts of the place where the award was rendered or the place of enforcement;[215] finally, when the award is rendered under the ICSID Convention regime, the losing party will have the opportunity to seek to annul the award.[216] These issues have been explored in great detail in Chapters XX and XXI.

---

[215] For example, New York Convention, art. V, and UNCITRAL Model Law, art. 34(2), each contemplate several grounds for setting aside an award.

[216] *See* ICSID Convention, art. 54.

VIII. Consolidation under Relevant Arbitration Rules or Treaties

Consolidation of related claims in international commercial arbitration is not uncommon.[1] In the context of investment treaty arbitration, however, only a limited number of cases have arisen so far where arbitral tribunals had to decide on the consolidation of different arbitrations with related factual and legal issues.[2]

Consolidation in the context of investment treaty arbitration is a challenging task. Apart from the complexity of legal and factual issues involved, which makes it difficult to assess whether separate arbitrations are similar enough to allow a tribunal to consolidate them, the institutional and ad hoc rules governing investment treaty arbitrations usually do not have any rules governing this matter. In fact, the International Centre for Settlement of Investment Disputes (ICSID), Additional Facility, and United Nations Commission on International Trade Law (UNCITRAL) Rules, which are used in the majority of investment treaty arbitrations, do not contain provisions regarding consolidation of claims.

Some investment treaties, however, contain provisions governing consolidation of related disputes, which would fill this gap in the arbitration rules. Article 1126 of the North American Free Trade Agreement (NAFTA) is an example of such a provision in a multilateral investment treaty. In addition, the U.S. Model bilateral investment treaty (BIT) of 2004 and some more recent investment

---

[1] Emanuel Gaillard, *Consolidation of Arbitral Proceedings and Court Proceedings*, in *Complex Arbitrations: Perspectives on Their Procedural Implications*, Special Supplement, ICC Int'l Cr. Arb. Bull. (Dec. 2003). *See generally* B. Hanotiau, *Complex Arbitrations: Multiparty, Multicontract, Multi-Issue and Class Actions* (Kluwer Law Int'l 2006).

[2] Two of the earlier cases were *CME v. Czech Republic* and *Lauder v. Czech Republic*, both of which were brought against the Czech Republic based on the same facts but different BITs with similar protections. These cases were not consolidated, because the Czech Republic did not consent to their consolidation. The two tribunals ultimately rendered awards that are widely viewed as contradictory. For a more detailed examination of these cases *see* Chapter XII *infra*.

treaties and free trade agreements contemplate the possibility of consolidation of related claims.[3]

Where applicable arbitral rules or investment treaties contain no provision dealing with consolidation, considerations of efficiency and avoidance of inconsistency in the jurisprudence[4] have led some arbitral tribunals and parties to the disputes to look for practical solutions.[5] For example, parties to disputes pending before ICSID tribunals on several occasions have dealt with this issue by appointing the same arbitrators to hear related cases. In the following pages, consolidation of claims will be examined under the ICSID, UNCITRAL, NAFTA, and International Chamber of Commerce (ICC) rules, as well as the potential ramifications for enforcement of awards under the New York Convention.

A. International Centre for Settlement of Investment Disputes

The ICSID Convention and Arbitration Rules, as indicated earlier, do not expressly provide for consolidation of related claims. It is not impossible, however, to consolidate claims and present them before a single tribunal. According to some observers, a tribunal could exercise its discretion under Article 44 of the ICSID Convention to order consolidation. The second sentence of Article 44 of the ICSID Convention provides that "[i]f any question of procedure arises which is not covered by this Section or the Arbitration Rules or any rules agreed by the parties, the Tribunal shall decide the question."[6] In his commentary on the ICSID Convention, Professor Schreuer explains his view of the history and implications of this sentence:

> C. H. Schreuer, *The ICSID Convention: A Commentary* 678 (Cambridge University Press 2001) (commentary on art. 44)
>
> 50. All drafts leading up to the Convention provided for the residual power of the tribunal to decide on procedural matters not covered by the Arbitration Rules. The relevant

---

[3] See pp. 195–96 *infra*.

[4] For a discussion of advantages of consolidation in investment treaty arbitration *see Canfor Corp., Tembec Inc., Tembec Inves. Inc., Tembec Indus. Inc., Terminal Forests Prod. Ltd. v. U.S.* (Submission on Consolidation of the Resp't, June 3, 2005), pp. 15–21, *available at* www.naftaclaims.com. Some commentators have opined that consolidation undermines the principle of consent, the foundation of any submission to arbitration. H. Alvarez, *Arbitration under North American Free Trade Agreement*, 16(4) Arb. Int'l 393, 412 (2000); *see also Corn Prod. Int'l Inc. v. United Mexican States* and *Archer Daniels Midland Co. and Tate & Lyle Ingredients Americas, Inc. v. United Mexican States* (Decision of the Consolidation Tribunal, May 20, 2005), ¶ 8.

[5] See p. 187 *infra*.

[6] See also Chapter V *supra*.

> parts of the Convention and rules agreed by the parties were added in the course of the drafting to complete the framework within which the tribunal would have to operate (History, Vol. I, pp. 198, 200).
>
> 51. An ICSID tribunal's power to close gaps in the rules of procedure is declaratory of the inherent power of any tribunal to resolve procedural questions in the event of *lacunae*. In exercising this power, the tribunal may not go beyond the framework of the Convention, the Arbitration Rules and the parties' procedural agreements but must, first of all, attempt to close any apparent gaps through the established methods of interpretation for treaties and other legal documents. But the tribunal is free of the constraints of procedural law in any national legal system of law, including that of the tribunal's seat.

According to this view, the fact that consolidation is not expressly authorized by the ICSID Convention does not necessarily preclude such a measure, but the parties seeking consolidation would likely need to convince the tribunal that it is appropriate under the Convention and international law.[7]

Three of the earliest ICSID cases were effectively "consolidated," as all three claimants pursued arbitration against Jamaica before the same panel. When the Government of Jamaica in 1974 introduced legislation for a production levy on bauxite producers, three affected U.S. companies, Alcoa Minerals of Jamaica, Inc., Kaiser Bauxite Co., and Reynolds Jamaica Mines Ltd., requested arbitration under their respective investment contracts, and all appointed the same arbitrator. As the Jamaican Government did not participate in the appointment process, the Secretary-General of ICSID, in accordance with Article 38 of the ICSID Rules, appointed an arbitrator on behalf of Jamaica, as well as the Chairman. All three arbitrators were identical for all three cases, and the disputes were heard jointly. However, the tribunal issued three preliminary awards, one for each claimant. These awards were identical in all material respects, but drafted as if the particular claimant were the only claimant in the case. Despite Jamaica's failure to appeal, the tribunal took up several procedural issues *sua sponte*. It did not raise the issue of multiple claimants. The three cases were withdrawn prior to the issuance of a final award pursuant to a settlement.[8]

The ICSID Secretariat may also take the initiative to recommend consolidation of related claims. Such an initiative was undertaken with respect to the cases of *Salini v.*

---

[7] It is doubtful that the tribunal would agree to such consolidation unless all the parties to both (or more) proceedings gave their consent.

[8] See *Alcoa Minerals of Jamaica, Inc. v. Jamaica*, ICSID Case No. ARB/74/2, *reprinted in* 4 Y.B. Comm. Arb. 206 (1979); *Kaiser Bauxite Co. v. Jamaica*, ICSID Case No. ARB/74/3, *reprinted in* 1 ICSID Rep. 296 (1993); *Reynolds Jamaica Mines Ltd. v. Jamaica*, ICSID Case No. ARB/74/4 (order taking note of the discontinuation of the proceedings 1977). *See also* Joachim G. Frick, *Arbitration and Complex International Contracts* 239 (2001).

Morocco,[9] and *Consortium R.F.C.C. v. Morocco*.[10] Both of these cases were based on the Italy-Morocco BIT and exhibited similar factual and legal backgrounds. In the event, the cases were not consolidated. But the same arbitrators were chosen to decide both cases, which effectively ensured the consistency of the awards as if a single consolidated tribunal had decided them.[11]

The question of consolidation under the ICSID Rules became particularly relevant after Argentina's implementation of emergency measures in response to an economic crisis that began in 2000. These measures included the mandatory and automatic "pesification" of dollar-denominated bank accounts and contracts. Argentina's actions caused significant losses to foreign investors across a broad spectrum of industries, perhaps most of all within the energy sector. As a result, Argentina became the target of an unprecedented wave of investment arbitration claims, with as many as forty foreign companies filing or preparing to file with ICSID by 2005.[12] The fact that many of these cases dealt with the same government measures, albeit in a variety of business and economic sectors, raised the specter of contradictory awards that had so inflamed many critics of the investment arbitration system after the *CME* and *Lauder* cases.[13] By mid-2003, it appeared that both the Argentine government and some private investors had realized that a mutually agreed consolidation would be advantageous. By this time, the government already faced an overwhelming financial burden of more than ten simultaneously prosecuted arbitration proceedings. Some claimants, however, realized the problems of legitimacy and enforcement that could result if some tribunals recognized a violation of applicable investment protection standards, while others did not. As a result, in March 2003, the parties to two ICSID cases, *Sempra Energy v. Argentina* and *Camuzzi v. Argentina,* selected the same three arbitrators,[14] indicating that they would like the cases to proceed together, as had the Jamaica arbitrations thirty years

---

[9] *Salini Costruttori S.p.A. & Italstrade S.p.A. v. Kingdom of Morocco,* ICSID Case No. ARB/00/4, 6 ICSID Rep. 400 (2004).

[10] *Consortium R.F.C.C. v. Kingdom of Morocco,* ICSID Case No. ARB/00/6 (2003).

[11] Antonio Crivellaro, *Consolidation of Arbitral and Court Proceedings in Investment Disputes,* 4(3) L. & Pract. of Int'l Ct. & Trib. 371 (2005).

[12] ICSID, 22(1) *News from ICSID* (Summer 2005), *available at* http://icsid.worldbank.org/. *See also* Paolo de Rosa, *The Recent Wave of Arbitration Against Argentina Under Bilateral Investment Treaties: Background and Principal Legal Issues,* 36 U. Miami Inter-Am. L. Rev. 41 (2004).

[13] *See, e.g.,* Charles N. Brower, *The Coming Crisis in the Global Adjudication System,* 13 World Arb. & Med. Rep. 270 (2002); *see also* Charles N. Brower, *A Crisis of Legitimacy,* Nat'l L. J. (Oct. 7, 2002).

[14] *Sempra Energy Int'l v. Argentine Republic,* ICSID Case No. ARB/02/16 and *Camuzzi Int'l S.A. v. Argentine Republic,* ICSID Case No. ARB/03/2. The three arbitrators selected in the cases were Francisco Orrega Vicuña (chairman), Marc Lalonde, and Sandra Morelli Rico.

earlier. Afterward, several other parties to cases against Argentina followed suit by choosing to submit their disputes to the same group of arbitrators.[15]

B. United Nations Commission on International Trade Law

The UNCITRAL Rules do not explicitly provide for consolidation of related claims, but do not appear entirely incompatible with such a procedure. In the Swiss-based UNCITRAL arbitration of *Karaha Bodas Company, LLC v. Pertamina et al.*,[16] the tribunal consolidated claims KBC had brought against Pertamina and PLN, two Indonesian state-owned entities, under closely related project agreements. The tribunal stated that consolidation absent express agreement is suitable only where there is (1) "connexity" of claims and (2) appropriateness. The tribunal defined the first term as the integration of the underlying agreements to arbitrate. Appropriateness, meanwhile, was held to exist where "the initiation of two separate arbitrations would be artificial and would generate the risk of contradictory decisions," as well as unnecessary costs. The tribunal justified consolidation in the matter at hand in that "the parties did not contemplate the performance of two independent contracts but the performance of a single project consisting of two closely related parties" (internal cites and emphasis omitted).[17] Later, when KBC sought to confirm the award in a U.S. federal district court, the court rejected Pertamina's argument that the arbitral proceeding had been carried out improperly. The court stated:

> The Tribunal based its integration finding on the facts that the contracts were signed on the same day; that the [Joint Operating Contract] [(JOC)] expressly provided that the [(Energy Sales Contract)] [(ESC)] "shall be an integral part of this contract, and to the extent the provisions of the Energy Sales Contract obligate the Parties hereto, shall be deemed incorporated into this contract for all purposes"; and that the ESC provided

---

[15] The parties to *Electricidad Argentina S.A. & EDF Int'l S.A. v. Argentine Republic*, ICSID Case No. ARB/03/22 and *EDF Int'l S.A., SAUR Int'l S.A. and Léon Participaciones Argentinas S.A. v. Argentine Republic*, ICSID Case No. ARB/03/23, on June 2, 2004, simultaneously chose William W. Park (chairman), Gabrielle Kaufmann-Kohler, and Fernando de Trazegnies Granda to hear their cases. Similarly, the parties in three water concession cases of *Aguas Provinciales de Santa Fe, S.A., Suez, Sociedad General de Aguas de Barcelona, S.A. & Interagua Servicios Integrales de Agua, S.A. v. Argentine Republic*, ICSID Case No. ARB/03/19, *Aguas Cordobesas, S.A., Suez, and Sociedad General de Aguas de Barcelona, S.A. v. Argentine Republic*, ICSID Case No. ARB/03/18, and *Aguas Argentinas, S.A., Suez, Sociedad General de Aguas de Barcelona, S.A. & Vivendi Universal, S.A. v. Argentine Republic*, ICSID Case No. ARB/03/17, submitted their disputes to a tribunal consisting of Jeswald W. Salacuse (chairman), Gabrielle Kaufmann-Kohler, and Pedro Nikken.

[16] *Karaha Bodas Co. LLC v. Perusahan Pertambangan Minyak Dan Gas Numi Negara (Indonesia)*, UNCITRAL Arbitration (1999), 16(3) Mealey's Int'l Arb. Rep., 3/01, Doc. C (2001).

[17] The tribunal relied on this conclusion in the decision of the Swiss Federal Tribunal in *Westland*, 1989 Rev. Arb. 514.

that it and the JOC together constitute the entire agreement between the parties. In essence, the Tribunal concluded that the nature of the contracts at issue is such that the parties contemplated arbitration in a single proceeding. This Court strongly concurs. In addition, it is obvious that separate arbitrations of the matters in dispute among the parties under the JOC and ESC would have required substantial duplication of evidence on liability, damages and defensive issues. Pertamina . . . is a party to both the JOC and the ESC. The two Respondents in the arbitration, Pertamina and PLN, were represented by the same counsel at all times during the arbitration. Further, Pertamina has not cited any case in which consolidation was deemed to be in error under similar circumstances.[18]

The experience of the Iran-U.S. Claims Tribunal, employing the UNCITRAL Rules, indicates the difficulties that may be encountered in seeking to consolidate claims despite a party's objection. In *Iran-U.S. Case Nos. 44, 46, and 47*, the tribunal refused to consolidate three related proceedings at the respondent's request after the claimant objected. A comparable conclusion was reached in *Iran-U.S. Case No. B-58* and in *Iran-U.S. Case No. 266*, where tribunals noted in each case that there was insufficient interconnection between the cases claimants sought to consolidate. In *Iran-U.S. Cases A15 and A24*, the tribunal granted Iran's request to consolidate, but it is unclear from the record whether the claimants agreed to the procedure.

C. North American Free Trade Agreement Article 1126

A NAFTA tribunal has noted that consolidation is disfavored by the common law, which requires that neither arbitration tribunals nor the courts compel a party to arbitrate with a nonconsenting party.[19] NAFTA, however, provides that where more than one claim has been submitted and they raise common questions of law and fact, a NAFTA tribunal may decide to hear and determine them together in the interests of fair and efficient resolution of the claims. NAFTA therefore explicitly preempts the widespread presumption against consolidation in Article 1126 but establishes a number of strict procedural requirements to safeguard the rights of the parties in a consolidated case.

Article 1126: Consolidation

1. A Tribunal established under this Article shall be established under the UNCITRAL Arbitration Rules and shall conduct its proceedings in accordance with those Rules, except as modified by this Section.

---

[18] *Karaha Bodas Co., LLP v. Perusahaan Pertambangan Minyak Dan Bumi Negara*, 190 F. Supp. 2d 936, 946 (S.D. Tex. 2001) (citations omitted).

[19] *United Parcel Service of Am., Inc. v. Canada* (Decision of the Tribunal on Amicus Curiae, Oct. 17, 2001), ¶ 31.

2. Where a Tribunal established under this Article is satisfied that claims have been submitted to arbitration under Article 1120 that have a question of law or fact in common, the Tribunal may, in the interests of fair and efficient resolution of the claims, and after hearing the disputing parties, by order:

(a) assume jurisdiction over, and hear and determine together, all or part of the claims; or

(b) assume jurisdiction over, and hear and determine one or more of the claims, the determination of which it believes would assist in the resolution of the others.

3. A disputing party that seeks an order under paragraph 2 shall request the Secretary-General to establish a Tribunal and shall specify in the request:

(a) the name of the disputing Party or disputing investors against which the order is sought;

(b) the nature of the order sought; and

(c) the grounds on which the order is sought.

4. The disputing party shall deliver to the disputing Party or disputing investors against which the order is sought a copy of the request.

5. Within 60 days of receipt of the request, the Secretary-General shall establish a Tribunal comprising three arbitrators. The Secretary-General shall appoint the presiding arbitrator from the roster referred to in Article 1124(4). In the event that no such presiding arbitrator is available to serve, the Secretary-General shall appoint, from the ICSID Panel of Arbitrators, a presiding arbitrator who is not a national of any of the Parties. The Secretary-General shall appoint the two other members from the roster referred to in Article 1124(4), and to the extent not available from that roster, from the ICSID Panel of Arbitrators, and to the extent not available from that Panel, in the discretion of the Secretary-General. One member shall be a national of the disputing Party and one member shall be a national of a Party of the disputing investors.

6. Where a Tribunal has been established under this Article, a disputing investor that has submitted a claim to arbitration under Article 1116 or 1117 and that has not been named in a request made under paragraph 3 may make a written request to the Tribunal that it be included in an order made under paragraph 2, and shall specify in the request:

(a) the name and address of the disputing investor;

(b) the nature of the order sought; and

(c) the grounds on which the order is sought.

7. A disputing investor referred to in paragraph 6 shall deliver a copy of its request to the disputing parties named in a request made under paragraph 3.

8. A Tribunal established under Article 1120 shall not have jurisdiction to decide a claim, or a part of a claim, over which a Tribunal established under this Article has assumed jurisdiction.

9. On application of a disputing party, a Tribunal established under this Article, pending its decision under paragraph 2, may order that the proceedings of a Tribunal established under Article 1120 be stayed, unless the latter Tribunal has already adjourned its proceedings.

10. A disputing Party shall deliver to the Secretariat, within 15 days of receipt by the disputing Party, a copy of:

(a) a request for arbitration made under paragraph (1) of Article 36 of the ICSID Convention;

(b) a notice of arbitration made under Article 2 of Schedule C of the ICSID Additional Facility Rules; or

(c) a notice of arbitration given under the UNCITRAL Arbitration Rules.

11. A disputing Party shall deliver to the Secretariat a copy of a request made under paragraph 3:

(a) within 15 days of receipt of the request, in the case of a request made by a disputing investor;

(b) within 15 days of making the request, in the case of a request made by the disputing Party.

12. A disputing Party shall deliver to the Secretariat a copy of a request made under paragraph 6 within 15 days of receipt of the request.

13. The Secretariat shall maintain a public register of the documents referred to in paragraphs 10, 11 and 12.

Article 1126 was the first provision incorporated into an investment treaty to provide for consolidation. It offers answers to certain questions that would otherwise have caused difficulty. One such question is whether the arbitrators that are hearing related cases should stop hearing the cases by the order of a consolidation tribunal. Article 1126 expressly provides for creation of a new consolidation tribunal, which has the power to enjoin already existing tribunals constituted under Article 1120 of NAFTA from further examination of the cases.

But many other issues of first impression may arise in each particular consolidation scenario that require a case-specific approach. For example, the first two consolidation tribunals constituted under Article 1126 reached opposing conclusions, in light of the circumstances, regarding the argument that consolidation may compromise the confidentiality of investors' trade secrets.

The first request for consolidation under Article 1126 was submitted to the ICSID Secretary-General by Mexico to consolidate two separate Chapter 11 cases, which had been brought against Mexico by American producers of high-fructose corn syrup (HFCS).[20] The dispute arose out of Mexico's imposition of a tax on soft drinks containing HFCS and its failure to impose the same tax on soft drinks containing sugar. In 2003, Corn Products International (CPI), an American investor, started arbitration against Mexico at ICSID,[21] alleging that the tax measure was designed to protect Mexican producers of sugar against competition from HFCS producers in the Mexican

---

[20] *Corn Prod. Int'l, Inc. v. United Mexican States & Archer Daniels Midland Co.* and *Tate & Lyle Ingredients Americas, Inc. v. United Mexican States* (Mexico's Request for Establishment of a Consolidation Tribunal, Sept. 8, 2004), *available at* www.naftaclaims.com.

[21] *Corn Prod. Int'l, Inc. v. Mexico,* ICSID Case No. ARB (AF)/04/01 (Oct. 21, 2003).

soft drink sweetener market. In 2004, Archer Daniels Midland Company and Tate & Lyle Ingredients Americas, Inc., two American producers of HFCS in Mexico, jointly initiated arbitration against Mexico,[22] contesting the same tax measure.

In September 2004, Mexico filed its request for consolidation. With the agreement of all the parties to the dispute, a consolidation tribunal was constituted to examine whether the cases should be consolidated. The American investors strongly opposed the consolidation, and at the end the tribunal ultimately rejected Mexico's request.

The panel first acknowledged that the cases implicated several questions of fact and law in common.[23] Nevertheless, it concluded that other considerations militated against the consolidation. In reaching this conclusion, it took into account the investors' concerns that the confidentiality of their business practices would be compromised in a consolidated proceedings and held that "the direct and major competition between the claimants, and the consequent need for complex confidentiality measures throughout the arbitration process, would render consolidation in this case, in whole or in part, extremely difficult."[24] Consolidation in this situation would run counter to another purpose of Article 1126, which is meant to facilitate the "fair and efficient resolution of the claims."[25] It also noted that three of the four parties involved did not wish to consolidate the cases.[26] In addition, it found that the cases would raise numerous issues of state responsibility and quantum of damages that are better handled in separate proceedings.[27]

The tribunal rejected Mexico's argument that absent consolidation there would be a significant risk of inconsistent awards on similar factual and legal issues. It held that there was no risk of inconsistent decisions, since "different awards with respect to the issues of liability and damages" are not necessarily inconsistent. The Mexican measure could constitute expropriation with respect to one party but not so with respect to another, for example. Also, as the impact of the tax on the various claimants may differ, an application of other protections under NAFTA could be triggered in one of the cases, but not necessarily in the others.[28] In conclusion,

---

[22] *Archer Daniels Midland Co. & Tate & Lyle Ingredients Americas, Inc. v. Mexico*, ICSID Case No. ARB (AF)/04/05 (Aug. 4, 2004).

[23] *Corn Prod. Int'l, Inc. v. Mexico*, ICSID Case No. ARB (AF)/04/01, and *Archer Daniels Midland Co. & Tate & Lyle Ingredients Americas, Inc. v. Mexico* (Order of the Consolidation Tribunal, ICSID Case No. ARB(AF)/04/05, May 20, 2005), ¶ 6, *available at* http://www.economiasnci.gob.mx/sphp_pages/importa/sol_contro/consultoria/Casos_Mexico/Consolidacion/acuerdos/050520_Orden_de_Tribunal_de_Acumulacion.pdf [hereinafter Order of the Consolidation Tribunal].

[24] *Id.* ¶ 8.

[25] *Id.* ¶ 9.

[26] *Id.* ¶ 12.

[27] *Id.* ¶ 14.

[28] *Id.* ¶ 16.

the tribunal was satisfied that "the risk of unfairness to Mexico from inconsistent awards resulting from separate proceedings cannot outweigh the unfairness to the claimants of the procedural inefficiencies that would arise in consolidated proceedings."[29]

The second request for consolidation was filed by the United States with ICSID to consolidate three separate cases involving softwood lumber filed by Canadian investors Canfor Corporation, Terminal Forest Products Limited, and Tembec Inc.[30] The investors had alleged that as a result of certain U.S. antidumping and countervailing duty measures on imports of Canadian softwood lumber, they had suffered losses in violation of the provisions of NAFTA Chapter 11. They also argued that they had suffered injury as a result of the implementation of the United States' Byrd Amendment.[31]

On May 5, 2005, the consolidation tribunal was constituted and on September 7, 2005, after extensive examination of the legislative history of Article 1126 and the arguments of the parties, ordered the three cases to be consolidated.[32] The following excerpt from the tribunal's order summarizes different aspects of the case as well as its points of disagreement with the Corn Products tribunal.

Order of the Consolidation Tribunal in *Canfor Corp. v. U.S.*, *Tembec v. U.S.*, and *Terminal Forest Prod. Ltd. v. U.S.* (Sept. 7, 2005), available at www.naftaclaims.com

> 221. The Consolidation Tribunal concludes that all four conditions of Article 1126(2) of the NAFTA are met in the present proceedings. First, it is common ground that the claims in question have been submitted to arbitration under Article 1120. Second, the Tribunal has found that many questions of law and fact are common in the three Article 1120 arbitrations. Third, the Tribunal has also found that the interests of fair and efficient resolution of the claims merit the assumption of jurisdiction over all of the claims. And fourth, the parties to the present proceedings have been heard.
>
> 222. The result in the present case differs from the one in the *Corn Products* case. There are several reasons for the different outcome, which include the following.

---

[29] *Id.* ¶ 17.

[30] See U.S. Request for the Establishment of a Consolidation Tribunal (Mar. 7, 2005), *available at* www.naftaclaims.com.

[31] The Continued Dumping and Subsidy Offset Act of 2000 (CDSOA), commonly referred to as the "Byrd Amendment," provides for the annual distribution of antidumping (AD) and countervailing duties (CVD) assessed on or after October 1, 2000, pursuant to AD and CVD orders in effect on or after January 1, 1999. The distribution is available to "affected domestic producers for qualifying expenditures." Byrd Amendment, *available at* http://www.usitc.gov/trade_remedy/731_ad_701_cvd/byrd.htm.

[32] Order of the Consolidation Tribunal in *Canfor Corp. v. U.S.*, *Tembec v. U.S.*, and *Terminal Forest Prod. Ltd. v. U.S.* (Sept. 7, 2005).

First, the Order on Consolidation in *Corn Products* is silent about what Article 1126(2) requires for satisfying the term "a question of law or fact in common." The Tribunal there wrote, without any further inquiry expressed in the Order, in ¶ 6: "The Consolidation Tribunal accepts that the claims submitted to arbitration do have certain questions of law or fact in common for purposes of Article 1126(2)," and at ¶ 15: "The Tribunal is persuaded that notwithstanding certain common questions of law and fact, the numerous distinct issues of state responsibility and quantum further confirm the need of separate proceedings." Second, as a general proposition, the present Tribunal disagrees with the statements found in ¶ 9 of the *Corn Products* Order: "Two tribunals can handle two separate cases more fairly and efficiently than one tribunal where the two claimants are direct and major competitors, and the claims raise issues of competitive and commercial sensitivity," and in ¶ 10: "However, confidential information among competitors is much more easily protected in separate proceedings, which in turn also permit a far more efficient arbitration process under such circumstances." Third, in ¶ 14, the *Corn Products* Tribunal notes: "Yet, as CPI pointed out in its written submission, Mexico did not indicate, apart from jurisdiction, common defenses it intends to raise to the claims." While the present case involves also common questions of law and fact relating to jurisdiction, the same applies to liability as well, in respect of which the United States has raised, and intends to raise, common questions of law and fact. Moreover, in the judgment of the present Tribunal, anticipated questions may also be taken into account if there is a degree of certainty that they will be raised. Fourth, while acknowledging the risk of inconsistent awards, in ¶ 16 of the *Corn Products* Order, it is stated that: "This Tribunal does not have before it a large number of identically or very similarly situated claimants . . . . The tax could, for example, constitute an expropriation as to one claimant, but not another." This fact pattern does not apply to the present case. Lastly, in ¶ 19, the *Corn Products* Order emphasizes that the cases there "are not close to procedural alignment," which is not applicable in the present case either.

223. The consequence of the decision of the present Consolidated Tribunal is that the Article 1120 Tribunals cease to function.

224. The next step in the proceedings will be for the Tribunal to consult with the parties about the conduct and sequence of the proceedings. . . .

In June 2006, the consolidated tribunal held that it lacked jurisdiction over the claims of Canfor and Terminal, except to the extent that they concerned the Byrd Amendment.[33]

D. Consolidation Provisions in Other Bilateral and Multilateral Investment Treaties

As indicated above, investment treaties may contain provisions on consolidation that effectively fill the gaps of the arbitral rules in this respect, as does NAFTA Article 1126. The ill-fated Multilateral Agreement on Investment

---

[33] *Canfor, Tembec, & Termina v. U.S.*, Decision on Jurisdiction in the Consolidated Arbitration (June 6, 2006), *available at* www.naftaclaims.com.

(MAI), negotiated in the 1990s among OECD Members, contained express provisions for consolidation of related arbitrations similar to those in NAFTA Article 1126.[34]

The current versions of the U.S. Model BIT[35] and the Canadian Model BIT of 2004[36] also contain provisions on consolidation.

There are several other recent trade and investment agreements that contain consolidation provisions. For example, the Central America-Dominican Republic-United States Free Trade Agreement (DR-CAFTA),[37] the Canada-Chile Free Trade Agreement (CCFTA),[38] the United States-Chile Free Trade Agreement,[39] and the Free Trade Agreement between Mexico and Bolivia all track the provisions of the U.S. and Canada models cited above.[40]

E. International Chamber of Commerce Rules

Although the ICC Rules are rarely used in investor-state arbitration, it is worth mentioning that ICC practice is not significantly different from the UNCITRAL experience. There is no express language in the ICC Rules dealing with multiple parties or consolidation, and the limited precedent available indicates that consolidation is possible but exceedingly rare. In ICC Case No. 7385 (1992), the tribunal consolidated two cases, in part because it found that the respondent in the

---

[34] Under the MAI regime, investors could choose different arbitration rules to govern their disputes. The draft MAI provided that "if the investor parties have not agreed upon a means of arbitration . . . within 30 days after the date of receipt of the request for consolidated consideration . . . , the request shall be submitted to arbitration . . . under the UNCITRAL rules." Under the MAI rules, in such cases, a tribunal would have been allowed to consolidate proceedings against the parties' will: "[t]he arbitral tribunal shall assume jurisdiction over all or part of the disputes . . . , if, after considering the views of the parties, it decides that to do so would best serve the interest of fair and efficient resolution of the dispute." In this regard, priority is given to efficiency, rather than the parties' will. Yoshi Kodama, *Dispute Settlement Under the Multilateral Agreement on Investment: The Quest for an Effective Investment Dispute Settlement Mechanism and Its Failure*, 16(3) J. Int'l Arb. 45, 73 (1999).

[35] U.S. Model Bilateral Investment Treaty 2004, art. 33, *available at* http://ustr.gov/Trade_Sectors/Investment/Model_BIT/Section_Index.html.

[36] *See* Canada's Model Agreement for Promotion and Protection of Investment, art. 32, *available at* www.naftaclaims.com.

[37] *See* DR-CAFTA, art. 10.25, *available at* http://www.ustr.gov/Trade_Agreements/Bilateral/CAFTA/CAFTA-DR_Final_Texts/Section_Index.html.

[38] *See* CCFTA, art. G-27, *available at* www.dfait-maeci.gc.ca/tna-nac/cda-chile/chap-g26-en.asp#II.

[39] *See* U.S.-Chile Free Trade Agreement, art. 10.24, *available at* http://www.ustr.gov/Trade_Agreements/Bilateral/Chile_FTA/Final_Texts/Section_Index.html.

[40] *See* Tratado de Libre Comercio México–Bolivia (Mexico-Bolivia FTA), art. 15(27) (Acumulación de procedimientos), *available at* http://2005.sice.oas.org/Trade/mexbo_s/mbind.asp.

second case could have been impleaded in the first, had the proceedings taken place before a national court. In that case, however, the tribunal first had to convince the parties to agree to consolidation, although they had initially refused to do so, and it was made clear that consolidation would not be possible under the ICC Rules without consent.

1. Consolidation by Courts

Instead of seeking consolidation from the arbitral tribunal or institution at the outset, it may be possible to request a court at the situs of arbitration to order consolidation, in the interest of efficiency and equity.[41]

Most cases involving consolidation of international arbitration have taken place in national courts, where either claimants or (more frequently) respondents have requested that a court exercise its supervisory jurisdiction to consolidate related arbitral proceedings. In *Abu Dhabi Gas Liquefaction v. Eastern Bechtel*,[42] an entity that was the respondent in one arbitration and the claimant in another requested the English High Court to appoint the same arbitrator in both proceedings to avoid the possibility of inconsistent findings of fact. The High Court judge held that because he lacked authority to order consolidation of the proceedings or to appoint an arbitrator subject to conditions (i.e., that the arbitrator order consolidated proceedings), two different arbitrators should be appointed. The Court of Appeal agreed that courts have no power to order consolidation or to impose conditions on an appointed arbitrator,[43] but held that it did have the power under the English Arbitration Act (1950) to appoint the same arbitrator in separate arbitrations. The Court stated that this kind of "consolidation" was appropriate: "It is most undesirable that there should be inconsistent findings by two separate arbitrators on virtually the self-same question, such as causation. It is very desirable that everything should be done to avoid such a circumstance."[44]

Most national courts oppose consolidation, and have ruled that judicial consolidation of arbitration may violate the agreement to arbitrate.[45] For example, the French Court of Cassation has ruled that the judicial consolidation of

---

[41] See generally Dominique T. Hascher, *Consolidation of Arbitration by American Courts: Fostering or Hampering International Commercial Arbitration,* 2 J. Int'l Arb. 127 (1984).

[42] *Abu Dhabi Gas Liquefaction Co. v. Eastern Bechtel Corp.* (London Ct. Appeal, June 23, 1982), 2(5) Lloyds Law Rep. 425 (1982).

[43] See also *Oxford Shipping Co. Ltd. v. Nippon Yusen Kaisha,* [1984] 2 Lloyds Law Rep., 374, where an English court held that not only do courts lack the power to consolidate arbitrations, but the arbitrators themselves may not do so, without the consent of the parties involved.

[44] See also *Taunton-Collins v. Cromie & Others,* [1964] 1 WLR 633.

[45] Many commentators appear to agree that consolidation can amount to a rewriting of the arbitration agreement, as the parties agreed to arbitrate disputes between themselves, not those between themselves and several other parties. See, e.g., T. Carbonneau, *Cases and Materials on the Law and Practice of Arbitration* 27 (2000).

related arbitrations into multiparty proceedings is inimical to the interests of the arbitral process and unlawful under French law.[46]

A few jurisdictions, such as Hong Kong and the Netherlands, nevertheless permit one party to petition a local court for consolidation, even without the consent of the other side.[47] U.S. courts are divided as to whether arbitrations can be consolidated.[48]

2. Ramifications for Enforcement of Award

It should be recalled that forced consolidation of arbitration, whether by an arbitral institution, by a tribunal, or by the supervising national court, could expose any resulting award to challenge pursuant to the New York Convention.[49] Article V(1)(d) of the Convention allows courts to refuse recognition or enforcement of awards if "the composition of the arbitral authority or the arbitral procedure was not in accordance with the agreement of the parties."[50]

In the *Karaha Bodas* case, however, the U.S. district court, which was asked to refuse enforcement of the award under Article V(1)(d) of the New York Convention, looked upon the request with great skepticism, and ultimately enforced the award.[51] Just as tribunals will employ consolidation to avoid breakdown of the arbitral process, reviewing courts tend to view the practice in pragmatic terms when asked to recognize or enforce an award rendered in consolidated proceedings. Nevertheless, where multiple parties are involved, some concerns of due process may arise where consolidation forces entities with incompatible interests to "share"

---

[46] *Dutco* (Court of Cassation, Decision of Jan. 7, 1992), *reported in* 7 Mealey's Int'l Arb. Rep., Feb. 1992, at 20.

[47] Netherlands Arbitration Act 1986, art. 1046(1); 1982 Hong Kong Arbitration Ordinance, Chapter 341, § 6B. *See also In re Sui On Construction Co. Ltd. & Moon Yik Co. Ltd.*, Hong Kong High Court, Decision of Sept. 12, 1986 (consolidation ordered by Hong Kong court under § 6B of arbitration ordinance).

[48] *See, e.g., Compania Espanola de Petroleos, S.A. v. Nereus Shipping, S.A.*, 527 F.2d 966, 968–70 (2d Cir. 1975) (ordering consolidation of ad hoc international arbitration to result in tribunal of five arbitrators); *Maxum Foundations, Inc. v. Salus Corp.*, 817 F.2d 1086, 1087–88 (4th Cir. 1987) (ordering consolidation of related arbitrations); *Weyerhauser Co. v. Western Seas Shipping Co.*, 743 F.2dd 635 (9th Cir. 1984) (refusing to consolidate related arbitrations); *U.K. v. Boeing Co.*, 998 F.2d 68 (2d Cir. 1993) (refusing to consolidate related arbitrations where none of the claimants had jointly signed any underlying agreements).

[49] *See generally* Hascher, *supra* note 41, at 137–38; Sigvard Jarvin, *Consolidated Arbitrations, the New York Convention, and the Dutch Arbitration Act 1986,* 3 Arb. Int'l 254 (1987).

[50] Thus, an award rendered by a tribunal consolidated by court order may be unenforceable in countries not allowing such judicial intervention. *See, e.g.,* Judgment of Apr. 13, 1978, Corte di Appello de Firenze, *reprinted in* 4 Y.B. Comm. Arb. 294 (1979) (award denied enforcement where English Arbitration Act superseded contractual agreement of parties regarding composition of tribunal).

[51] *Karaha Bodas, supra* note 18, at 939.

arbitrators. When the possibility of multiple parties can be foreseen, the solution may be an expanded tribunal of five or more arbitrators; such an arrangement may be unavailable in the case of postdispute consolidation.

Consolidation without party authorization could also lead to an annulment proceeding in arbitrations governed by the ICSID Convention. Article 52 of the ICSID Convention contains language mirroring New York Convention Article V(1)(d), authorizing an ad hoc panel to annul an arbitration award if it finds that the tribunal was improperly constituted.

IX. Governing Law in Investment Disputes

A. Introduction

There are four primary sources of substantive law pertinent to investment disputes: rules or contractual terms agreed to by the parties, if any; the investment treaties themselves; the law of the host state and other relevant rules of national law; and public international law. As the investment treaty regime has developed over the last few decades, tribunals have turned ever more frequently to investment treaty texts and evolving norms of international law. Meanwhile, in many cases national law norms have come to occupy a subsidiary position in the hierarchy of legal sources. This tendency is not without controversy, however.

The aforementioned sources may combine or interact in a variety of ways to provide the rules of law that should govern the substantive aspects of an investment dispute. In this respect, the role of arbitral rules under which the arbitration proceedings are conducted cannot be overlooked. All arbitral rules recognize the parties' autonomy to choose the law applicable to the substance of their dispute.[1] Some also contain choice of law provisions, which in the absence of the parties' agreed preference may supply the applicable substantive rules of law[2] or provide guidance as to how the applicable rules should be chosen.[3] In modern practice, most investment arbitration cases are based on the following combinations: (1) arbitration under the International Centre for Settlement of Investment Disputes (ICSID) Convention pursuant to the consent of the government in an investment treaty or a law; and (2) arbitration under the United Nations Commission on International Trade Law (UNCITRAL) Rules pursuant to the consent of the government in an investment treaty or a law.

---

[1] *See, e.g.,* art. 42(1) of the ICSID Convention, first sentence.
[2] *See* ICSID Convention, art. 42.
[3] *See* United Nations Commission on International Trade Law (UNCITRAL) Rules, art. 33.

The following sections examine different sources of substantive law that may be applicable to the merits of an investment arbitration, as outlined at the beginning of this chapter.

B. Rules Chosen by the Parties

Various arbitral rules anticipate an important role for the parties' agreement over substantive law. Article 42(1) of the Washington Convention, for example, recognizes the principle of party autonomy, mandating that a tribunal apply any "rules of law" that the parties have selected.[4] This provision refers primarily to the situation (common in ICSID's early years but more infrequent today) where ICSID jurisdiction is based on an arbitration clause in an investment contract binding the host state and the private party. Such an arrangement gives the investor and state the opportunity to jointly select the governing law before a dispute arises.

Where arbitral jurisdiction is based on the standing consent of the government in a treaty or in a law,[5] there is no clear opportunity for the "parties to the dispute" to agree on the governing law before a dispute arises. And after the conflict has materialized, agreement is unlikely. The parties to such a dispute are normally bound by the choice-of-law provisions in the treaty or the law, if any.

Only a minority of investment treaties addresses the question of applicable law.[6] Some treaties, such as the North American Free Trade Agreement (NAFTA), exclude most aspects of national law, instead directing arbitrators to determine the rights and obligations of the parties on the basis of the terms of the treaty and applicable international law norms.

---

[4] Article 42(1) of the ICSID Convention provides that "(1) The Tribunal shall decide a dispute in accordance with such rules of law as may be agreed by the parties. In the absence of such agreement, the Tribunal shall apply the law of the Contracting State party to the dispute (including its rules on the conflict of laws) and such rules of international law as may be applicable."

[5] *See* Chapter X *infra*.

[6] *See, e.g.*, Treaty Between the Republic of Canada and the Republic of Panama for Promotion and Encouragement of Investment (1996). *See also* Agreement between the Kingdom of Netherlands and Republic Poland on Encouragement and Reciprocal Protection of Investments (1992), art. 12(6). Most BITs entered into by France, Germany, the United Kingdom, and the United States do not contain specific choice-of-law clauses. *See* E. Gaillard & Y. Banifatemi, *The Meaning of "and" in Article 42(1), Second Sentence of the Washington Convention: The Role of International Law in the ICSID Choice of Law Process*, (hereinafter Gaillard & Banifatemi) at note 16.

NAFTA art. 1131: Governing Law

1. A Tribunal established under this Section shall decide the issues in dispute in accordance with this Agreement and applicable rules of international law.[7]

Some treaties expressly designate national law as a governing source, usually in conjunction with applicable rules of international law. For example, Article 10(7) of the Netherlands-Argentina bilateral investment treaty (BIT) provides the following:

> The arbitration tribunal . . .shall decide on the basis of the law of the Contracting Party which is a party to the dispute (including its rules on the conflict of law), the provisions of the present Agreement, special Agreements concluded in relation to the investment concerned as well as such rules of international law as may be applicable.[8]

When the parties to an investment agreement do not choose the governing law, or the treaty that is the basis of jurisdiction does not contain any governing law clause, the relevant provisions of the arbitration rules that govern the conduct of the arbitral proceedings may provide guidance. Article 42(1) of the ICSID Convention, for example, provides that "[i]n the absence of . . . agreement [regarding the governing law], the Tribunal shall apply the law of the Contracting State party to the dispute (including its rules on the conflict of laws) and such rules of international law as may be applicable."[9]

This provision suggests that in ICSID arbitration, the tribunal will first examine the conflict of law rules of the host state; if these rules do not direct the tribunal to the application of the laws of another country, it may apply the substantive laws of the host country. In practice, conflict of law rules will often direct the tribunal to apply the substantive laws of the host country, because these are the laws that normally are most closely connected to the investment.[10]

---

[7] NAFTA, art. 1131. *See also* Agreement between the Government of Canada and the Government of Republic of Ecuador for the Promotion and Reciprocal Protection of Investments (1996), art. XIII(7); BITs entered into by Argentina, Australia, Belgium, and Luxembourg. *See* Gaillard & Banifatemi, *supra* note 6, at note 7.

[8] Agreement on Encouragement and Reciprocal Protection of Investments between the Kingdom of the Netherlands and the Argentine Republic, art 10(7)

[9] *See also* UNCITRAL Rules, art. 33 ("[t]he arbitral tribunal shall apply the law designated by the parties as applicable to the substance of the dispute. Failing such designation by the parties, the arbitral tribunal shall apply the law determined by the conflict of laws rules which it considers applicable").

[10] M. Sornarajah, *The Settlement of Foreign Investment Disputes* 237 (Cambridge University Press 2000). It has been suggested that even in the absence of the Article 42(1) the choice of the host country's substantive laws may follow by virtue of the application of the ordinary principles of conflict of laws. *See SPP v. Egypt*, ICC Arbitration No. YD/AS No. 3494, 3 ICSID Rep. 45, 64 (1995). However, it is not impossible to imagine a situation where the conflict of law rules of the host country refer the tribunal to the laws of the investor's home country, or of a third state. C. Schreuer, *The ICSID Convention: A Commentary* 605–08 (Cambridge University Press 2001).

In addition, Article 42(1) authorizes ICSID tribunals to apply relevant rules of international law, which include the investment treaty itself.[11] As noted, many treaties select no governing law at all. Whether or not an investment treaty explicitly selects a body of governing law, the treaty itself usually contains substantive international law protections. These typically include protection against discrimination,[12] unfair and inequitable treatment,[13] and improper expropriation,[14] as well as a duty to provide appropriate protection and security.[15] Where the relevant treaty contains these types of international law protections, they usually function as the principal source of governing law.

Outside the ICSID Convention, determination of the applicable rules of law may turn on the interpretation of the choice-of-law clause of the treaty, when the arbitration proceedings have commenced based on the consent of the state party in a BIT. In *CME v. Czech Republic*,[16] which was an arbitration conducted under the UNCITRAL Rules, the parties disagreed about the proper interpretation of the choice-of-law clause of the Netherlands-Czech Republic BIT. Article 8(6) provided that "the arbitral tribunal shall decide on the basis of the law, taking into account in particular but not exclusively, the law in force of the Contracting Party concerned, the provisions of this Agreement, and any other Agreement between the Contracting Parties, the general principles of international law." The respondent argued that under this formulation, the tribunal had first to apply Czech law to assess the propriety of the acts that occurred in the Czech Republic, and only then, if there was a "genuine gap" in Czech law, to apply international law. The tribunal rejected this interpretation, and held that the language of Article 8(6) established no hierarchy among the four enumerated sources.[17]

C. Investment Treaties and Their Interpretation

Regardless of the wording of a choice-of-law clause, investment treaties by definition require that disputes be resolved in accordance with the terms of the treaty itself.[18] The initial task facing any tribunal is to determine what the treaty states and how it is to be interpreted. International law has developed an extensive canon of rules for such interpretation. The following excerpt from the award in

---

[11] See p. 213 *infra* on the application of rules of international law.
[12] See generally Chapter XV *infra*.
[13] See generally Chapter XVII *infra*.
[14] See generally Chapter XVI *infra*.
[15] See pp. 529–537 *infra*.
[16] See *CME Czech Republic BV v. Czech Republic* (UNCITRAL Arbitration, Final Award, Mar. 14, 2003), ¶¶ 396–413.
[17] See *id.*
[18] Vienna Convention on The Law of Treaties, art. 31.

Asian Agricultural Products v. Sri Lanka explains some of the rules and principles that may be used in interpreting a BIT[19]:

> *Asian Agricultural Products Ltd. v. Sri Lanka*
>
> ICSID Case No. ARB/87/3, *reprinted at* 30 I.L.M. 577, 594–97 (1991)
>
> [T]he first task of the Tribunal is to rule on the controversies existing in this respect by indicating what constitutes the true construction of the Treaty's relevant provisions in conformity with the sound universally accepted rules of treaty interpretation as established in practice, adequately formulated by l'Institut de Droit International in its General Session in 1956, and as codified in Article 31 of the Vienna Convention on the Law of Treaties.
>
> 39. The basic rule to be followed by the Tribunal in undertaking its task with regard to the pending controversial interpretation issue has been formulated since 1888 in the Award rendered in the Van Bokkelen case (Haiti/USA), where it was stated that:
>
>> "for the interpretation of treaty language and intention, whenever controversy arises, reference must be made to the law of nations and to international jurisprudence (Repertory of International Arbitral Jurisprudence, Volume I: 1794–1918, Edited by; Vincent COUSSIRAT-COUSTERE and Pierre Michel EISEMANN, Nijhoff, Dordrecht/Boston/London, 1989, § 1015, p.13)."
>
> In essence, the requirement that treaty provisions "must be interpreted according to the Law of Nations, and not according to any municipal code," emerges from the basic premise expressed by Mr. WEBSTER in the following terms:
>
>> "When two nations speak to each other, they use the language of nations" (Quoted by the Germany/Venezuela Mixed Claims Commission in the Christern Case, as reproduced in the Repertory referred to herein-above, § 1017, p. 27).
>
> 40. The other rules that should guide the Tribunal in adjudicating the interpretation issues raised in the present arbitration case may be formulated as follows:
>
>> Rule (A)—"The first general maxim of interpretation is that it is not allowed to interpret what has no need of interpretation. When a deed is worded in clear and precise terms, when its meaning is evident and leads to no absurd conclusion, there can be no reason for refusing to admit the meaning which such deed naturally presents" (passage from VATTEL'S Chapter on Interpretation of Treaties—Book 2, chapter 17,) . . . , and the Mixed Commission did not hesitate in declaring: "to attempt interpretation of plain words . . . would be violative of Vattel's first rule" (Ibid., p. 26); and I. M. SINCLAIR, "The Principles of Treaty Interpretation and Their Application By the English Courts," International and Comparative Law Quarterly, vol. 12, (1963), p. 536—referring to the decisions pronouncing that if the meaning intended to be expressed is clear the Courts are "not at liberty to go further").
>
>> Rule (B)—"In the interpretation of treaties . . . we ought not to deviate from the common use of the language unless we have very strong reasons for it (. . .) words

---

[19] See also C. Schreuer, *Diversity and Harmonization of Treaty Interpretation in Investment Arbitration,* 3(2) TDM (Apr. 2006).

are only designed to express the thoughts: thus the true signification of an expression in common use is the idea which custom has affixed to that expression" (another passage from VATTEL relied upon by the U.S.A./Venezuela Mixed Commission in the Howland case, op.cit., p. 16—cf. Award of the Mexico/U.S.A. Mixed Commission of 1871 in the William Barron case, Ibid., § 1023, p. 30, emphasizing that: "interpretation means finding in good faith that meaning of certain words, if they are doubtful, which those who used the words must have desired to convey, according to the usage of speech (usus loquendi)"; ALEXANDER's award of 1899 in the Treaty of Limits case between Costa Rica and Nicaragua Ibid., § 1025, p. 31, declaring that: "words are to be taken as far as possible in their first and simplest meanings," "in their natural and obvious sense, according to the general use of the same words," "in the usual sense, and not in any extraordinary or unused acceptation"; S. BASTID, op.cit., p. 129, reproducing the Resolution adopted in 1956 by l'Institut de Droit International according to which: "L'accord des parties s'etant realise sur le texte, il y a lieu de prendre le sens naturel et ordinaire de ce texte comme base d'interpretation"; and I. M. SINCLAIR, op.cit., p. 537, reporting that: "the Court . . . is bound to construe them (the words) according to their natural and fair meaning").

Rule (C)—In cases where the linguistic interpretation of a given text seems inadequate or the wording thereof is ambiguous, there should be recourse to the integral context of the Treaty in order to provide an interpretation that takes into consideration what is normally called: "le sens general, l'espirit du Traite," or "son economie generale" (Award rendered in 1914 by the Permanent Court of Arbitration in the Timor Island case between the Netherlands and Portugal, Repertory, op.cit., § 1019, p. 28; decision of the Bulgarian/Greek Mixed Arbitration Tribunal rendered in 1927 in the Sarrapoulos case, Repertory, vol. II: 1919–1945, § 2020, p. 21–22; The 1926 Paula Mendel case where the Germany/U.S.A. Mixed Claims Commission disregarded "a literal construction of the language" since it "finds no support in the other provisions of the Treaty as a whole." Hence, "it cannot stand alone and must fall" Repertory vol. II, § 2025, p. 25; and the Decision of the Germany/Venezuela Mixed Claims Commission of 1903 in the Kummerow case which stated that: "it is a uniform rule of construction that effect should be given to every clause and sentence of an agreement," Repertory, op.cit., vol. I, § 1031, p. 38).

Rule (D) In addition to the "integral context," "object and intent," "spirit," "objectives," "comprehensive construction of the treaty as a whole," recourse to the rules and principles of international law has to be considered a necessary factor providing guidance within the process of treaty interpretation. (Resolution of l'Institut de Droit International, op.cit., Article 1.(2) which stipulates: "les termes des dispositions dutraite doivent etre interpretes dans le contexte entier, selon la bonne foi et a la lumiere des principes du droit international"; Paragraph 3.(c), of Article 31 of Vienna convention on the Law of Treaties containing reference to: "all relevant rule of international law applicable in the relations between the parties," and the Award rendered in 1928 by the France/Mexico Claims Commission in the Georges Pinson case, which stated among "les principes generaux d'interpretation": "Toute convention internationale doit etre reputee s'en referer tacitement au droit international commun, pour toutes les questions qu'elle ne resout pas elle-meme en termes expres et d'une facon differente" Repertory, op.cit., vol. II, § 2023, p. 24).

Rule (E)—"Nothing is better settled, as a canon of interpretation in all systems of law, than that a clause must be so interpreted as to give it a meaning rather than so as to deprive it of meaning (Award of the UK/USA Arbitral Tribunal of 1926 in the Cayuga Indians case, Repertory, vol. II, § 2036, p. 35–36). This is simply an application of the more wider legal principle of "effectiveness" which requires favouring the interpretation that gives to each treaty provision "effet utile."

Rule (F)—"When there is need of interpretation of a treaty it is proper to consider stipulations of earlier or later treaties in relation to subjects similar to those treated in the treaty under consideration" (Award of the Mexico/USA General Claims Commission of 1929 rendered in the Elton case, Repertory, vol. II, § 2033, p. 35). Thus, establishing the practice followed through comparative law survey of all relevant precedents becomes an extremely useful tool to provide an authoritative interpretation.

41. In the light of the above-mentioned canons of interpretation, the relevant provisions of the Sri Lanka/U.K. Bilateral Investment Treaty have to be identified, each provision construed separately, examined within the global context of the Treaty, in order to determine the proper interpretation of each text. . . .

The terms of an applicable treaty can create both procedural and substantive rules. For example, treaty provisions may control which entities have standing to bring a treaty claim[20] or whether there is a pertinent statute of limitations.[21] As noted, the treaty may or may not choose a particular body of governing substantive law.

Because the specific language of a treaty may be decisive to the outcome of a particular dispute, it is important to parse the treaty language carefully. Different states may articulate a particular legal concept—such as expropriation and the limits on its exercise—in different ways, or a state may over time seek to change the formulation and content of a particular principle as its preferences and bargaining position shifts. For example, over time the United States has altered the wording used to articulate the minimum standard of treatment.[22] A number of U.S. BITs concluded in the 1980s and 1990s include the following language: "2. a) Investment shall at all times be accorded fair and equitable treatment, shall enjoy full protection and security and shall in no case be accorded treatment less than that required by international law."[23]

---

[20] Art. 1(2) of the Ukraine-Lithuania BIT, for example, defines an "investor" as any entity properly incorporated in one state that makes an investment in another state. The meaning of this clause was the main contentious issue in *Tokios Tokeles v. Ukraine*. The president of the tribunal, Professor Weil, disagreed with his co-arbitrators regarding the interpretation of this article, wrote a dissenting opinion to the jurisdictional award, and later resigned. See *Tokios Tokeles v. Ukraine*, ICSID Case No. ARB/02/18 (Award on Jurisdiction, Apr. 29, 2004).

[21] *E.g.*, NAFTA Articles 1116 provides that "[a]n investor may not make a claim if more than three years have elapsed from the date on which the investor first acquired, or should have first acquired, knowledge of the alleged breach and knowledge that the investor has incurred loss or damage." *See also* NAFTA art. 1117.

[22] For more detail on the textual alterations in U.S. investment protection treaties that were implemented in the early 2000s, *see* Noah Rubins, *The Arbitral Innovations of Recent U.S. Free Trade Agreements: Two Steps Forward, One Step Back*, Int'l Bus. L. J. 865 (2003).

[23] Treaty between the United States of America and the Argentine Republic Concerning Reciprocal Encouragement and Protection of Investments (1991), art. 2. *See also* BITs that the United States entered into with Ecuador and Kazakhstan during the 1990s; and BITs that the United States entered into with Cameroon, Bangladesh, and Turkey during the 1980s.

In Article 10.5[24] of the recent Central American–Dominican Republic–United States Free Trade Agreement,[25] the language used is very different:

> 1. Each Party shall accord to covered investments treatment in accordance with customary international law, including fair and equitable treatment and full protection and security.
>
> 2. For greater certainty, paragraph 1 prescribes the customary international law minimum standard of treatment of aliens as the minimum standard of treatment to be afforded to covered investments. The concepts of "fair and equitable treatment" and "full protection and security" do not require treatment in addition to or beyond that which is required by that standard, and do not create additional substantive rights. The obligation in paragraph 1 to provide:
>
> (a) "fair and equitable treatment" includes the obligation not to deny justice in criminal, civil, or administrative adjudicatory proceedings in accordance with the principle of due process embodied in the principal legal systems of the world; and
>
> (b) "full protection and security" requires each Party to provide the level of police protection required under customary international law.
>
> 3. A determination that there has been a breach of another provision of this Agreement, or of a separate international agreement, does not establish that there has been a breach of this Article.

At some point, a tribunal may have to compare these articulations carefully, and determine whether the United States has altered the scope of investor protections in its more recent treaties.

Finally, questions concerning the consent of the parties to jurisdiction,[26] in the context of a BIT arbitration, are generally governed by international law.[27] In this context, to determine whether it has jurisdiction, a tribunal must interpret Article 25

---

[24] This Article must be interpreted in light of Annex 10.B of the Agreement, which specifies that customary international law "results from a general and consistent practice of States that they follow from a sense of legal obligation. With regard to Article 10.5, the customary international law minimum standard of treatment of aliens refers to all customary international law principles that protect the economic rights and interests of aliens."

[25] Dominican Republic–Central American–United States Free Trade Agreement (DR-CAFTA) (the parties to this agreement include Costa Rica, Dominican Republic, El Salvador, Guatemala, Honduras, Nicaragua, the United States of America. As of May 2006, the agreement had been approved by the legislature of all the parties except Costa Rica. The text of the agreement is available at www.ustr.gov/Trade_Agreements/Bilateral/CAFTA/CAFTA-DR_Final_Texts/Section_Index.html.).

[26] See Chapter X, infra.

[27] See CSOB v. Slovak Republic, ICSID Case No. ARB/97/4 (Decision on Jurisdiction 1999), ¶ 35; Siemens v. Argentina ICSID Case No. ARB/02/8 (Decision on Jurisdiction 2004), ¶ 31; Enron Corp. & Ponderosa Assets LP v. Argentina, ICSID Case No. ARB/01/3 (Decision on Jurisdiction 2004), ¶ 38; Azurix Corp. v. Argentina, ICSID Case No. ARB/01/12 (Decision on Jurisdiction 2003), ¶¶ 48–50.

of the ICSID Convention (if the case has been commenced under auspices of ICSID) as well as the relevant provisions of the BIT, international treaties subject by their nature to international law. However, the tribunal in *CMS v. Argentina* offered a somewhat more ambiguous view of the choice of law issue in this regard:

> The very option the investor has under the Treaty to submit a dispute to local jurisdictional [sic] also involves to an extent a choice of law provision, as local courts will apply mainly domestic law. In such a case, domestic law might apply together with the Treaty and [ICSID] Convention or separately.[28]

D. Host State Law[29]

The role of host state law in investment disputes—and in particular its relationship with international law—remains controversial. As noted, national law can become relevant where the parties to a dispute have selected it as the law governing their contractual relations, or where the relevant investment treaty mandates a role for it.[30] Further, if an applicable treaty does not expressly designate a governing law, as is often the case, and if the arbitration proceeds under the auspices of ICSID, Article 42(1) of the Washington Convention calls for the application of the host state's national law:

> The Tribunal shall decide a dispute in accordance with such rules of law as may be agreed by the parties. In the absence of such agreement, the Tribunal shall apply the law of the Contracting State party to the dispute (including its rules on the conflict of laws) and such rules of international law as may be applicable.[31]

Three schools of thought have developed in relation to the proper interpretation of this provision, and, more generally, the appropriate role of host state law in the application of investment treaties. The first approach, advocated by Prof. Reisman, posits that international law should be used in only limited circumstances to supplement and occasionally correct host state law:

> International law plays an important role under Article 42(1), but if it is wielded incautiously, it can defeat other parts of this provision. Where there is a genuine *lacuna*, i.e., one for which host State law does not provide a method for filling [it], the Tribunal may turn to international law. In addition, international law may perform

---

[28] *CMS Gas Transmission Co. v. Argentina*, ICSID Case No. ARB/01/8 (Decision on Objections to Jurisdiction 2003), ¶ 88.

[29] *See also* the discussion of consent to arbitration through host state law in Chapter X *infra*.

[30] *See* p. 203 *supra*.

[31] Tribunals occasionally apply a system of law other than that of the host state. By applying the conflicts rules of the host state, or treaty provisions themselves, the tribunal might turn to another state's laws. An example would be when a tribunal is required to determine whether a claimant has standing to maintain a claim, which in turn could require the tribunal to decide if the investor is properly incorporated under the laws of its home state.

a corrective function, but the contingency for correction must be more than a mere difference between international and host State law. *What is required is a veritable collision*. . . . The test, then, is not inconsistency, but whether applying the Contracting State's law would constitute a violation of something fundamental to international law.[32]

The second view of Article 42(1) of the Washington Convention envisions a greater role for international law in the resolution of investment disputes, but with host state law remaining the primary source. This interpretation was adopted in some early ICSID cases, which involved contractual disputes. The ad hoc committee in *Klöckner v. Cameroon* was one of the first tribunals to support this view. The dispute arose out of several contracts between the German company Klöckner and the government of Cameroon for the construction of a fertilizer factory, which Klöckner was then to manage through a Cameroonian joint venture, SOCAME. Klöckner built the factory and started its management operations, but the factory turned out to be unprofitable. It was eventually shut down by the Cameroonian government. In 1981 Klöckner started arbitration proceedings before ICSID. The tribunal concluded that Klöckner was not entitled to recover anything more than what it had already received from Cameroon as part of the price for the factory. Klöckner then sought annulment of the award. In this proceeding, it argued that the arbitral tribunal had manifestly exceeded its powers by failing to apply Cameroonian law, violating Article 42(1) of the ICSID Convention. The tribunal concluded:

> Article 42 of the Washington Convention certainly provides that "in the absence of agreement between the parties, the Tribunal shall apply the law of the Contracting State party to the dispute . . . and *such principles of international law as may be applicable.*" This gives these principles (perhaps omitting cases in which it should be ascertained whether the domestic law conforms to international law) a dual role, that is *complementary* (in the case of a "lacuna" in the law of the State), or *corrective,* should the State's law not conform on all points to the principles of international law. *In both cases,* the arbitrators may have recourse to the 'principles of international law' only *after* having inquired into and established the content of the law of the State party to the dispute (which cannot be reduced to *one* principle, even a basic one) and *after* having applied the relevant rule of the State's law.
>
> Article 42(1) therefore clearly does not allow the arbitrator to base his decision *solely* on the "rules" or "principles of international law."[33]

---

[32] W. M. Reisman, *The Regime for Lacunae in the ICSID Choice of Law Provision and the Question of its Threshold,* 15 ICSID Rev.-F.I.L.J. 362, 374–75 (2000) (emphasis added).

[33] *Klöckner v. Cameroon* (Ad Hoc Committee Decision, May 3, 1985), 2 ICS ID Rep. 95, 122 *et seq.* (1994) (emphasis in original) [hereinafter *Klöckner* First Ad Hoc Committee Decision]. See also A. Broches, *Observations on the Finality of ICSID Awards,* 6 ICSID Rev.-F.I.L.J. 321, 339–41 (1991).

One year later, the tribunal in *Amco Asia v. Indonesia* reached a similar conclusion with respect to applicable law:

> 20. It seems to the *ad hoc* Committee worth noting that Article 42(1) of the Convention authorizes an ICSID tribunal to apply rules of international law *only to fill up lacunae in the applicable domestic law and to ensure precedence to international law norms where the rules of the applicable domestic law are in collision with such norms.*
>
> 21. The above view of the role or relationship of international law norms vis-à-vis the law of the host State, in the context of Article 42(1) of the Convention, is suggested by an overall evaluation of the system established by the Convention. The law of the host State is, in principle, the law to be applied in resolving the dispute. At the same time, applicable norms of international law must be complied with since every ICSID award has to be recognized, and pecuniary obligations imposed by such award enforced, by every Contracting State of the Convention (Art. 54(1), Convention). Moreover, the national State of the investor is precluded from exercising its normal right of diplomatic protection during the pendency of the ICSID proceedings and even after such proceedings, in respect of a Contracting State which complies with the ICSID award (Art. 27, Convention). The thrust of Article 54(1) and of Article 27 of the Convention makes sense only under the supposition that the award involved is not violative of applicable principles and rules of international law.
>
> 22. The above view on the *supplemental and corrective role of international law* in relation to the law of the host State as substantive applicable law, is shared in ICSID case law (Decision of May 3, 1985, of an ICSID *ad hoc* Committee [*Klöckner v. Cameroon*] and in literature (e.g., Broches, 'The Convention for the Settlement of Investment Disputes between States and Nationals of Other States,' *Recueil des Cours* vol. 136 (1972, II) p. 392), and finds support as well in the drafting history of the Convention (see *ICSID Convention, Analysis of Documents Concerning the Origin and the Formulation of the Convention* vol. II/1, p. 804 (Washington, D.C. 1970).[34]

The *corrective* approach to Article 42(1) adopted in both *Klöckner* and *Amco Asia* follows the interpretation favored by Aron Broches, the principal architect of the Washington Convention. Writing at a time before any ICSID tribunal had rendered an award, he explained that the second sentence of Article 42(1) should be understood in the following manner:

> The Tribunal will first look at the law of the host State and that law will in the first instance be applied to the merits of the dispute. *Then the result will be tested against international law.* That process will not involve the confirmation or denial of the validity of the host State's law, but may result in not applying it where that law, or action taken under that law, violates international law. In that sense, as I suggested earlier, international law is hierarchically superior to national law under Article 42(1).[35]

---

[34] *Amco Asia Corp. v. Republic of Indonesia*, ICSID Case No. ARB/81/1 (Decision on the Application for Annulment, May 16, 1986) (hereinafter *Amco* First Ad Hoc Committee Decision), 1 ICSID Rep. 509, 515 (1993).

[35] *See* Aron Broches, *The Convention on the Settlement of Investment Disputes between States and Nationals of Other States*, 136 Recueil Des Cours de L'Academie de Droit Int'l 331, 392 (1972) (emphasis added).

Thus, according to Broches, although international law maintains a role that is theoretically subsidiary, international law nevertheless applies whenever host state law or action violates or is inconsistent with international law. The first two interpretations, therefore, appear to differ primarily as to the degree of *collision* between host state and international law that is necessary to trigger the application of international law.

The third approach to Washington Convention Article 42(1) attributes equal importance to international law and host state law. This interpretation was articulated and adopted by the ad hoc committee in *Wena Hotels v. Egypt*. In that case, debate was centered around the proper method that the tribunal should use to calculate interest as part of the award of damages. Egyptian law provided for simple interest, whereas the claimant contended that international law required compound interest. As outlined in the following excerpt, the ICSID tribunal ruled that compound interest was appropriate to restore the investor's position had Egypt not breached the treaty.[36] Egypt later sought to annul the tribunal's award, in part on grounds that the arbitrators had exceeded their mandate by applying only international law to the issue of interest. In considering the decision on interest, the ad hoc committee first explored the relationship between municipal and international law:

> 38. This discussion brings into light the various views expressed as to the role of international law in the context of Article 42(1). Scholarly opinion, authoritative writings and some ICSID decisions have dealt with this matter. Some views have argued for a broad role of international law, including not only the rules embodied in treaties but also the rather large definition of sources contained in Article 38(1) of the Statute of the International Court of Justice. Other views have expressed that international law is called in to supplement the applicable domestic law in case of the existence of *lacunae*. In *Klöckner I* an *ad hoc* Committee introduced the concept of international law as *complementary* to the applicable law in case of *lacunae* and as *corrective* in case that the applicable domestic law would not conform on all points to the principles of international law. There is also the view that international law has a controlling function of domestic applicable law to the extent that there is a collision between such law and fundamental norms of international law embodied in the concept of *jus cogens*.
>
> 39. Some of these views have in common the fact that they are aimed at restricting the role of international law and highlighting that of the law of the host State. Conversely, the view that calls for a broad application of international law aims at restricting the role of the law of the host State. There seems not to be a single answer as to which of these approaches is the correct one. The circumstances of each case may justify one or another solution. However, this Committee's task is not to elaborate precise conclusions on this matter, but only to decide whether the Tribunal manifestly exceeded its powers with respect to Article 42(1) of the ICSID Convention. Further, the use of the word 'may' in the second sentence of this provision indicates that the Convention does not draw a sharp line for the distinction of the respective scope of international and of domestic law and, correspondingly, that this has the effect to confer on to the Tribunal a certain margin and power for interpretation.

---

[36] *Wena Hotels Ltd. v. Arab Republic of Egypt* (Award, Dec. 8, 2000) 41 ILM 896, 910–11 (2002) (hereinafter *Wena* Award).

40. What is clear is that the sense and meaning of the negotiations leading to the second sentence of Article 42(1) allowed for *both legal orders to have a role.* The law of the host State can indeed be applied *in conjunction with international law* if this is justified. *So too international law can be applied by itself* if the appropriate rule is found in this other ambit.[37]

Although these approaches to applicable law under the Washington Convention appear to differ in theory and methodology, the outcome in terms of the specific rules of law to be applied may be the same, regardless of the analysis used. Consider, for example, the issue before the *Wena* tribunal, in respect of the proper rule for calculating interest. The tribunal could have adopted the international legal principle of *prompt, adequate, and effective* compensation, and then tested Egyptian law against that standard. It could then have found that the Egyptian limitation of simple interest, even if it was not a *veritable collision* with a fundamental principle of international law, nonetheless contradicted the international rule. Because of the inconsistency, the simple interest limitation in host state law could reasonably have been found to give way.

E. Public International Law

As previously described, the past decade has witnessed the growing importance of customary international law in the resolution of investment disputes. As investment treaty decisions multiply, it seems likely that most tribunals will routinely test host state laws and actions taken pursuant to them against the standards of international law. The stricter *veritable collision* theory has found relatively little favor, and tribunals tend to either apply the international law principles expressly contained in the applicable treaty or to use ICSID Article 42 as a vehicle for applying hierarchically superior international law rules. In short, international law is increasingly applied as the governing law for most issues in most investment disputes.

The prospect of applying international law raises the question as to what precisely constitutes international law. One of the most widely accepted guides to the content of international law can be found in Article 38(1) of the Statute of the International Court of Justice (ICJ):

> The Court, whose function is to decide in accordance with international law such disputes as are submitted to it, shall apply:
>
> (a) international conventions, whether general or particular, establishing rules expressly recognized by the contesting states;

---

[37] *Wena Hotels Ltd. v. Arab Republic of Egypt,* ICSID Case No. ARB/98/4 (Decision on Application for Annulment, Feb. 5, 2002) (hereinafter *Wena* Annulment Decision), 41 ILM 933, ¶¶ 38–40 (2002) (emphasis added).

(b) international custom, as evidence of a general practice accepted as law;

(c) the general principles of law recognized by civilized nations;

(d) . . . judicial decisions and the teachings of the most highly qualified publicists of the various nations, as subsidiary means for the determination of rules of law.[38]

All four elements of this definition are potentially relevant to investment disputes. Perhaps most important and controversial is the role of *custom,* normally deemed equivalent to customary international law. Many future disputes will likely require consideration of the legal principles that have become part of that body of law. One frequently encountered issue in this regard, as discussed in Chapter XVII below,[39] is whether the requirement that host states provide fair and equitable treatment has been so widely accepted by governments in the context of investment treaties that it has become a principle of customary international law. Similarly, several tribunals have examined the question of whether the term *fair and equitable treatment* as found in most investment treaties should be informed, interpreted, and applied in accordance with customary international law on the protection of aliens, or independently as an express derogation from the less stringent protections of customary law.[40]

Another contentious issue related to the application of Article 38(1) of the ICJ Statute is the extent to which international investment law can be said to include any "general principles of law."[41] In the *Erdemovic* case, the International Tribunal for the Former Yugoslavia addressed the problem of incorporating general principles of law into international law decisions, in connection with the principle of duress. The separate opinion of Judges MacDonald and Vohrah illustrates one approach to identifying general principles of law as a source of international law.

Prosecutor v. Erdemovic

Int'l Criminal Tribunal for the Former Yugoslavia, Appeals Chamber, Joint Separate Opinion of Judge MacDonald & Judge Vohrah, Oct. 7, 1997

56. It is appropriate now to inquire whether the "general principles of law recognised by civilised nations," established as a source of international law in Article 38(1)(c) of the ICJ Statute, may shed some light upon this intricate issue of duress. Paragraph 58 of the

---

[38] Statute of the International Court of Justice, art. 38, *available at* http://www.icj-cij.org/.
[39] *See* pp. 493–502.
[40] *Mondev Int'l Ltd. v. U.S.,* ICSID Case No. ARB(AF)/99/2 (Award of Oct. 11, 2002), 42 I.L.M. 85 ¶¶ 116 & 123 (2003).
[41] On general principles of law, *see generally* Bin Cheng, *General Principles of Law: As Applied by International Courts and Tribunals* 1–6 (Grotius Publications 1987) (1953).

Report of the Secretary-General of the United Nations presented on 3 May 1993 expressly directs the International Tribunal to this source of law:

> The International Tribunal itself will have to decide on various personal defences which may relieve a person of individual criminal responsibility, such as minimum age or mental incapacity, drawing upon general principles of law recognised by all nations.[42]

Further, Article 14 of the International Law Commission's Draft Code of Crimes Against the Peace and Security of Mankind provides:

> The competent court shall determine the admissibility of defences in accordance with the general principles of law, in the light of the character of each crime.[43]

57. A number of considerations bear upon our analysis of the application of "general principles of law recognised by civilised nations" as a source of international law. First, although general principles of law are to be derived from existing legal systems, in particular, national systems of law,[44] it is generally accepted that the distillation of a "general principle of law recognised by civilised nations" does not require the comprehensive survey of all legal systems of the world as this would involve a practical impossibility and has never been the practice of the International Court of Justice or other international tribunals which have had recourse to Article 38(1)(c) of the ICJ Statute. Second, it is the view of eminent jurists, including Baron Descamps, the President of the Advisory Committee of Jurists on Article 38(1)(c), that one purpose of this article is to avoid a situation of non-liquet, that is, where an international tribunal is stranded by an absence of applicable legal rules.[45] Third, a "general principle" must not be confused with concrete manifestations of that principle in specific rules. As stated by the Italian-Venezuelan Mixed Claims Commission in the Gentini case:

> A rule . . . is essentially practical and, moreover, binding; there are rules of art as there are rules of government, while a principle expresses a general truth, which guides our action, serves as a theoretical basis for the various acts of our life, and the application of which to reality produces a given consequence.[46]

In light of these considerations, our approach will necessarily not involve a direct comparison of the specific rules of each of the world's legal systems, but will instead involve a survey of those jurisdictions whose jurisprudence is, as a practical matter, accessible to us in an effort to discern a general trend, policy or principle underlying the concrete rules of that jurisdiction which comports with the object and purpose of the establishment of the International Tribunal.

58. In order to arrive at a general principle relating to duress, we have undertaken a limited survey of the treatment of duress in the world's legal systems. This survey is necessarily modest in its undertaking and is not a thorough comparative analysis. Its purpose

---

[42] SN: Report of the Secretary-General pursuant to ¶ 2 of Security Council resolution 808 (1993), U.N. Doc. S/25704.

[43] SN: Report of the International Law Commission on the Work of its 48th Session, May 6–July 26, 1996, G.A.O.R., 51st Sess., Supp. No.10, U.N. Doc. A/51/10, at 73.

[44] SN: *See* Permanent Court of International Justice, Advisory Committee of Jurists, *Procés verbaux of the Proceedings of the Committee* (June 16–July 24, 1920) L.N. Publication 335 (1920) (per Lord Phillimore & de La Pradelle).

[45] SN: *Id.* at 336.

[46] SN: *Gentini* case, 10 Rep. Int'l Arbitral Awards, at 551.

is to derive, to the extent possible, a "general principle of law" as a source of international law.

In a similar vein, McNair pointed out in his Separate Opinion in the *South-West Africa Case* that:

> it is never a question of importing into international law private law institutions "lock, stock and barrel," ready made and fully equipped with a set of rules. It is rather a question of finding in the private law institutions indications of legal policy and principles appropriate to the solution of the international problem at hand. It is not the concrete manifestation of a principle in different national systems—which are anyhow likely to vary—but the general concept of law underlying them that the international judge is entitled to apply under paragraph (c).[47]

Through reliance on general principles, international tribunals have recognized the existence of a number of international law rules relevant to investment disputes. For example, in the *North Sea Continental Shelf Case* the ICJ looked to "equitable principles" in its formulation of a rule to delimit international maritime boundaries. In the *Diversion of Water from the Meuse Case (Netherlands v. Belgium)* before the Permanent Court of International Justice, Judge Hudson accepted that equity is a "general principle of law recognised by civilised nations," and stated:

> It would seem to be an important principle of equity that where two parties have assumed an identical or a reciprocal obligation, one party which is engaged in a continuing non-performance of that obligation should not be permitted to take advantage of a similar non-performance of that obligation by the other party.[48]

In the *Chorzów Factory Case,* the Permanent Court of International Justice observed that "it is a principle of international law, and even a general conception of law, that any breach of an engagement involves an obligation to make reparation."[49]

General principles of law may also find application to procedure in investment disputes. In the *Corfu Channel Case (Merits)*, the ICJ drew on the experience of municipal legal systems to conclude that circumstantial evidence is admissible in international law proceedings:

> [T]he other State, the victim of a breach of international law, is often unable to furnish direct proof of facts giving rise to responsibility. Such a State should be allowed a more liberal recourse to inferences of fact and circumstantial evidence. This indirect evidence is admitted in all systems of law, and its use is recognized by international decisions.[50]

---

[47] *South-West Africa Case*, 1950 I.C.J. Rep., at 148.

[48] *Diversion of Water from the Meuse Case (Netherlands v. Belgium)*, 1937 P.C.I.J. Rep., Series A/B, No. 70, at 76–77.

[49] *Chorzow Factory Case (Germany v. Poland)* (Merits) 1928 P.C.I.J. Rep., Series A, No. 17, at 29.

[50] *Corfu Channel Case (U.K. v. Albania)* (Merits) 1949 I.C.J. Rep., at 18.

Another central issue in relation to the content of international law is the extent to which investment tribunal decisions are themselves a source of applicable law that can be persuasive but nonbinding.[51] It is a fundamental precept of arbitration that the decisions of tribunals do not normally carry the weight of precedent as called for by the stare decisis rule. As a product of the parties' will, an arbitration tribunal is only empowered to decide the case presented to it, in accordance with the applicable law.[52] Further, to the extent that tribunals seek to apply international law, the decisions of other arbitrators can have only "subsidiary" importance, falling within the catch-all category of "judicial decisions and the teachings of the most highly qualified publicists of the various nations" in the ICJ Statute's list of legal sources.[53] Nevertheless, investment arbitration tribunals have consistently looked to their brethren for guidance in resolving contentious questions of international law.[54] Moreover, some tribunals have taken the view that arbitral awards rendered pursuant to investment protection treaties actually reflect the current state of public international law in the area of investment protection.[55]

---

[51] See McKesson Corp. v. Islamic Rep. of Iran, 116 F. Supp. 2d 13, 44–45. ("[The] Santa Elena decision thus presents relevant evidence of international law but must still be considered in light of the other evidence available. It thus cannot be authoritative in the sense that a controlling decision of law would be"). See also Paquete Habana, 175 U.S. 677, 700 (1900).

[52] Indeed, this principle is codified in a range of international instruments, including the Washington Convention and the ICJ Statute. See Article 53(1) of the ICSID Convention ("The award shall be binding on the parties . . . ."); see also Article 59 of the ICJ Statute ("The decisions of the Court have no binding force except between the parties in relation to that particular case").

[53] ICJ Statute, art. 38(1)(d).

[54] ICSID tribunals have taken a cautious approach to the issue of precedential value of previous decisions. Yet, they have frequently relied on the decisions of previous tribunals. In so doing, however, they often mention that the decisions of previous tribunals do not bind them, but they find their reasoning instructive in reconfirming their own independent findings. See, e.g., Amco v. Indonesia, ICSID Case No. ARB/81/1 (First Annulment Decision), 1 ICSID Rep. 521, ¶ 44 (1993); see also LETCO v. Liberia (Award Mar. 31, 1986), 2 ICSID Rep. 352; Gas Natural v. Argentina, ICSID Case No. ARB/03/10 (Decision on Jurisdiction, 2005), ¶¶ 36–38; Enron Corp. & Ponderosa Assets L.P. v. Argentina, ICSID Case No. ARB/01/3, ¶ 25 (2004).

[55] See Mondev International Ltd. v. U.S., ICSID Case No. ARB(AF)/99/2 (Final Award of Oct. 11, 2002).

X. Consent to Arbitral Jurisdiction

A. Introduction

The consent of the parties is the basis of the jurisdiction of all international arbitration tribunals.[1] The requirement of consent to arbitral jurisdiction in the context of investor-state arbitration is also a corollary of the principle that "there is no power superior to the states which can force a judge upon them."[2] There is nothing to preclude states from voluntarily submitting a dispute to a court or tribunal, however, and nothing can prevent them from making that submission irrevocable. A fundamental element of state sovereignty is the state's ability voluntarily to limit its own sovereignty.[3] Indeed, without such power, the state would be unable to obtain the economic benefits that can be procured through commercial

---

[1] C. F. Amerasinghe, *Jurisdiction of International Tribunals* 70 (Kluwer 2003).

[2] Report by Baron Descamps: J. B. Scott, Reports to the Hague Conferences of 1899 and 1907 (1917) p. 55 quoted in *id.* at 71 (The rationale for requiring consent in cases of settlement of disputes through arbitration was explained at the First Hague Peace Conference of 1899 as follows: "[Arbitration, as a] voluntary system of jurisprudence in origin as well as in jurisdiction, it agrees with the just demands of sovereignty, of which it is only an enlightened exercise. For, if there is no power superior to the States which can force a judge upon them, there is nothing to oppose their selection of an arbitrator by common agreement to settle their disputes, thus preferring a less imperfect means of securing justice to a method more problematical and more burdensome."). This principle has been characterized as an application of the sovereign equality of states. Hans Kelsen, *The Principle of Sovereign Equality of State as a Basis for International Organization*, 53(2) Yale L. J. 207, 209 (1944).

[3] *Texaco Overseas Petroleum Co. & California Asiatic Oil Co. (TOPCO) v. Gov't of the Libyan Arab Republic*, 17 I.L.M. 1 ("Nothing can prevent a State, in the exercise of its sovereignty, from binding itself irrevocably by the provisions of a concession and from granting to the concessionaire irretractable rights. . . . [I]n entering into concession contracts with the plaintiffs, the Libyan State did not *alienate* but *exercised* its sovereignty"); ICC Case No. 2321, Preliminary Award (1974), Collection of ICC Arbitral Awards 1974–1985, at 8–9 (Jarvin & Derains eds., 1990) ("A sovereign State must be sovereign enough to make a binding promise both under international law and municipal law").

agreements.[4] In the context of investor-state arbitration and the ICSID Convention, the Executive Directors of the World Bank explained, "Consent of the parties is the cornerstone of the jurisdiction of the Centre. Consent to jurisdiction must be in writing and once given cannot be withdrawn unilaterally (Article 25(1))."[5]

B. Fundamental Concepts Relating to Consent

1. Methods of State Consent to Arbitration

States and private entities or individuals may express their consent to binding dispute resolution in a variety of ways. One method is through a direct agreement (*compromis*) referring an existing dispute to ad hoc or institutional arbitration. A second is through an arbitration clause in an investment contract, covering disputes that have not yet arisen. These two methods have been used extensively in commercial disputes as well as inter-state and investor-state arbitrations but are now less frequently encountered in investment disputes between private parties and state entities.

Today, states typically provide their consent to submit future investment disputes to arbitration through bilateral investment treaties (BITs),[6] multilateral treaties, or the state's own domestic legislation.[7] Expression of consent by a state, however, is

---

[4] *Revere Copper & Brass Inc. v. Overseas Private Investment Corp.*, American Arbitration Association Case No. 16 10 0137 76, 17 I.L.M. 1321, 1342–43 (1978) ("If the sovereign power of the State cannot be fettered in this [voluntary] manner by entering into binding contracts, the State would be deprived of the power by contracts to meet essential needs").

[5] Report of the Executive Directors of the World Bank on the ICSID Convention, ¶ 23, *available at* http://icsid.worldbank.org.

[6] Jan Paulsson has called arbitration based on the consent provided in a legislation or treaty, "arbitration without privity," Paulsson, *Arbitration Without Privity*, 10 ICSID Rev.-F.I.L.J. 232 (1995), because this type of arbitration does not necessarily involve any direct contractual relationship between the parties. *Id.* at 232. This expression has gained some currency but has also been criticized. *See, e.g.,* M. Sornarajah, *Settlement of International Investment Disputes* 168 (Kluwer Publications 2000). This type of arbitration also has been referred to as "arbitrage transnational unilateral." *See* Walid Ben Hamida, *L'Arbitrage Etat-Investisseur Etrange: Regards sur les Traités et Projets Récents*, 131 J. du Droit Int'l 419, 420–21 (2004). For a recent commentary, *see* G. Blanke and Borzu Sabahi, *The New World of Unilateral Offers to Arbitrate: Investment Arbitration and EC Merger Control*, 74 Arbitration (2008).

[7] Christoph Schreuer, *The ICSID Convention: A Commentary* 191–224 (Cambridge University Press 2001) [hereinafter "Commentary"]. Report of the Executive Directors of the World Bank, ¶ 24 describes these methods as follows: "24. Consent of the parties must exist when the Centre is seized (Articles 28(3) and 36(3)) but the Convention does not otherwise specify the time at which consent should be given. Consent may be given, for example, in a clause included in an investment agreement, providing for the submission to the Centre of future disputes arising out of that agreement, or in a *compromis* regarding a dispute which has already arisen. Nor does the Convention require that the consent of both parties be expressed in a single instrument. Thus, a host State might in its investment promotion legislation offer to submit disputes arising out of certain classes of investments to the jurisdiction of the Centre, and the investor might give his consent by accepting the offer in writing."

insufficient to bestow jurisdiction on a tribunal; "the investor must perform some reciprocal act to perfect the consent."[8] Consent of a government in a law or a treaty is merely an *offer* to agree to arbitration, rather than a full contractual *compromis* as one would find in an investment contract.[9] The government's unilateral offer is consummated as a binding obligation to arbitrate only with the investor's acceptance of that offer.[10]

2. Methods of Accepting the Government's Offer to Arbitrate

The form of the parties' consent is often controversial, even when arbitration has commenced based on a *compromis* or a contractual arbitration clause.[11] The issue may become even more contentious where the investment law or treaty that constitutes the state's consent to arbitral jurisdiction, or the institutional rules that govern the conduct of the arbitration proceedings, require that consent be expressed in a particular form. Article VII(3)(a) of the United States-Argentina BIT, for example, requires that the investor provide its consent in writing. Among the institutional rules that are used in investment arbitration, the ICSID Convention also requires consent in writing.[12]

The investor's reciprocal consent is normally given through the filing of a request for arbitration or other document initiating the dispute resolution process.[13]

---

[8] Schreuer, "Commentary," *supra* note 7, art. 25, ¶ 276.

[9] Georges Delaume, *Consent to ICSID Arbitration*, in *The Changing World of International Law in the Twenty-First Century* 155, 164 (Kluwer 1998).

[10] *See Tradex Hellax S.A. v. Republic of Albania*, ICSID Case No. ARB/94/2 (Decision on Jurisdiction), 14 ICSID Rev.-Foreign Inv. L. J. 161 (1999) (submission under investment law providing for ICSID arbitration) [hereinafter *Tradex*].

[11] For example, Article II of the New York Convention on Recognition and Enforcement of Foreign Arbitral Award (1958) provides that arbitration agreements shall be in writing. There is, however, a great amount of debate regarding what constitutes "an agreement in writing" under this article. *See generally* F. A. Mann, *An Agreement "In Writing" to Arbitrate*, 3(2) Arb. Int'l 171 (1987); Paul Friedland, *U.S. Courts' Misapplication of the "Agreement in Writing" Requirement for Enforcement of an Arbitration Award Agreement Under the N.Y. Convention*, Mealey's Int'l Arb. Rep., May 1998, at 21; Richard Hill, *The Writing Requirement of the New York Convention Revisited: Are There Black Holes in International Arbitration?*, Mealey's Int'l Arb. Rep., Nov. 1998, at 17. *See also* Noah Rubins, Group of Companies Doctrine and the New York Convention, in *The New York Convention in Practice* (E. Gaillard & D. DiPietro, eds., Sweet and Maxwell 2008) for an analysis of the status of non-signatories as parties to an arbitration agreement under Article II(2) of the New York Convention.

[12] Article 25(1) of the ICSID Convention provides in the relevant part that "(1) The jurisdiction of the Centre shall extend to any legal dispute arising directly out of an investment, between a Contracting State (or any constituent subdivision or agency of a Contracting State designated to the Centre by that State) and a national of another Contracting State, which the parties to the dispute consent in writing to submit to the Centre. When the parties have given their consent, no party may withdraw its consent unilaterally . . . (3) Consent by a constituent subdivision or agency of a Contracting State shall require the approval of that State unless that State notifies the Centre that no such approval is required." *See also* Article 26(2)(a) of the U.S. Model BIT of 2004.

[13] Schreuer, "Commentary," *supra* note 7, art. 25, ¶ 277.

In *Tradex,* for instance, the investor relied, inter alia, on the Albanian law of 1993 to establish Albania's consent to ICSID jurisdiction. The tribunal stated that "the consent [becomes] effective at the latest if and when the foreign investor files its claim with ICSID making use of the respective national law."[14] However, consent is not limited to the filing of a formal arbitration claim. Other ways of accepting the offer provided in a national law or an investment treaty include a simple communication to the host state that consents to jurisdiction in accordance with the relevant instrument[15]; or a statement contained in an application for an investment license; or a mere application, if under the relevant law the successful applicant automatically gets specified benefits, including access to an arbitral institution.[16]

3. Irrevocability of Consent

It is generally accepted that once a state has given its consent to arbitrate investment disputes and this consent has been perfected, it cannot be revoked unilaterally.[17] When an investor accepts the state's open offer to arbitrate, a valid and binding contract is created between the parties. This is "a manifestation of the maxim *'pacta sunt servanda'* and applies to undertakings to arbitrate in general."[18] Thus, Article 25(1) of the ICSID Convention provides specifically that "[w]hen the parties have given their consent, no party may withdraw its consent unilaterally."

---

[14] *Tradex, supra* note 10, at 187. In a non-ICSID context *see CCL v. Kazakhstan,* SCC Case No. 122/2001, at 143 ("the fact of [claimant-investor]'s initiating this arbitration is ample proof of [claimant-investor]'s consent to this procedure for settlement of the dispute between the parties"); *EnCana v. Ecuador,* LCIA Case UN3481 (UNCITRAL Arbitration, Jurisdictional Award of Feb. 2004), ¶ 13 ("consent to arbitration under Article XIII of the BIT is given vis-à-vis the Tribunal itself, by an instrument which . . . is by definition opposable to the Claimant for the purposes of the proceedings . . ."). *See also generally Generation Ukraine v. Ukraine,* ICSID Case No. ARB/00/9 (Award, Sept. 16, 2003), ¶¶ 12.2, 12.3; *SGS v. Philippines* (Decision on Jurisdiction, Jan. 29, 2004), 8 ICSID Rep. 518, ¶¶ 30–31; *Generation Ukraine v. Ukraine* (Award, Sept. 16, 2003), ¶¶ 12.1–12.8; *Impregilo v. Pakistan* (Decision on Jurisdiction, Apr. 22, 2005), ¶¶ 108.

[15] In the *Pyramids Case,* for example, the claimant sent a letter to accept submission of the dispute to ICSID. *SPP v. Egypt,* ICSID Case No. ARB/83/3 (Decision on Jurisdiction, Nov. 27, 1985), 3 ICSID Rep. 112, 119 (1995). *See also El Paso Energy Int'l Co. v. Argentine Republic,* ICSID Case No. ARB/03/15 (Decision on Jurisdiction, Apr. 27, 2006), ¶ 36 (claimant delivered a letter to Argentina accepting the consent and informing it of the potential ensuing arbitration proceedings should the parties fail to resolve the issue through negotiation and consultation).

[16] C. Schreuer, Consent to Arbitration, [United Nations Conference on Trade and Development] UNCTAD Course on Dispute Settlement, International Center for the Settlement of Investment Disputes, Module 2.3, UNCTAD/EDM/Misc.232/Add.2, at 15 [hereinafter UNCTAD Course § 2.3].

[17] Washington Convention, art. 25(1). *See also* Schreuer, "Commentary," *supra* note 7, art. 25, ¶¶ 386–95.

[18] UNCTAD Course, § 2.3, *supra* note 16, at 37.

4. Limitations on Consent Clauses

Some investment laws and investment protection treaties contain language expressly submitting disputes to mandatory arbitration, which permits a qualifying investor to initiate arbitration proceedings.[19] However, other laws and treaties do not contain such conclusive and unambiguous language, which means that further action on the part of both parties is required to bestow jurisdiction on a tribunal. For example, the applicable law or treaty may list various dispute resolution options to which the parties to the dispute may resort.[20]

Limitations are not necessarily found in the consent clause but may instead be set forth in other provisions of the BIT. In *Inceysa Vallisoletana S.L. v. Republic of El Salvador*, for example, such a limitation on the scope of consent was found in the requirement that the investments be made in accordance with the laws of the host state to enjoy the protections of the Spain-El Salvador BIT.[21] This requirement was included in Articles 2 and Article 3 of the BIT, as opposed to Article 11(2), which contained the consent of the state to the BIT. The claimant argued that El Salvador had consented to arbitration without limitation when it signed and ratified the BIT, but El Salvador replied that it had not consented to submit the given dispute to ICSID arbitration because the investment at issue was made in violation of El Salvadoran laws as a result of fraud and misrepresentation. The tribunal accepted El Salvador's argument and ultimately dismissed the case for lack of jurisdiction.

Inceysa Vallisoletana S.L. v. Republic of El Salvador

ICSID Case No. ARB/03/26 (Award, Aug. 2, 2006)

185. States use multiple mechanisms to limit the scope of application of the agreements for the reciprocal protection of investments signed by them. One of the most commonly used refers to the so-called "accordance with the laws of the host State clause." Various tribunals of the [ICSID] have referred to this limitation. This is the case of the tribunal in the *Tokios Tokeles v. Ukraine* case, in which it was decided as follows:

> "The requirement in Article 1(1) of the Ukraine-Lithuania BIT that investments be made in compliance with the laws and regulations of the host state is a common requirement in modern BITs."[22]

---

[19] Investment treaties, for instance, may provide that the state "hereby consents" to arbitration or it "shall submit" the dispute to arbitration. C. H. Schreuer, *Consent to Arbitration*, 2(5) TDM 7 (2005).

[20] *See* Schreuer, "Commentary," *supra* note 7, art. 25, ¶¶ 271–75.

[21] Agreement for Reciprocal Promotion and Protection of Investments between the Kingdom of Spain the Republic of El Salvador ("Spain-El Salvador BIT"), art. 2(1).

[22] SN: *Tokios Tokeles v. Ukraine*, ICSID Case No. ARB/02/18 (Decision on Jurisdiction of Apr. 29, 2004), ¶ 84.

186. There are various forms by which States establish "accordance with the laws of the host State clause." Among the mechanisms used to include this limitation is to add it into the definition of investment itself, making it clear that for the purposes of that reciprocal protection agreement only those made in accordance with the laws of the host State will be deemed *investments*.

187. Furthermore, the signatory States may validly exclude from the protection of a BIT investments made illegally, precisely in the articles that indicate the scope of protection of the BIT in question. In this context, particularly relevant are the indications of the tribunal in *Salini Construttori S.P.A. and Italstrade S.P.A. v. the Kingdom of Morocco* case in which it was decided that:

> "[. . .] In envisaging "the categories of invested assets [. . .] in accordance with the laws and regulations of the said party," the provision in question refers to the legality of the investment and not to its definition. It aims in particular to ensure that the bilateral Agreement does not protect investments which it should not, generally because they are illegal."[23]

188. Consequently, the limitation of consent based on the "accordance with law clause" may be contained not only in the definition of investment, but also in the precepts related to "Protection" or even in the chapter related to "Promotion and Admission."

The parties to investment contracts may also subject their consent to arbitrate to a limited range of circumstances. This was the situation in *Aucoven v. Venezuela*.[24] There, the parties signed a concession contract that included an ICSID arbitration clause and expressly conditioned the parties' consent to ICSID arbitration upon the transfer of Aucoven's majority shares to a national of a state that was a party to the ICSID Convention. The tribunal concluded that this condition was fulfilled when the initial investor, a Mexican company (a national of a non-ICSID member), transferred 75 percent of its shares to a U.S. company (a national of an ICSID member).[25]

Consequently, whether dealing with a consent clause in an investment contract or a unilateral submission to arbitral jurisdiction contained in a treaty or national legislation, it is essential to examine and interpret carefully[26] the text of the relevant consent document to determine whether it includes the unequivocal consent of the

---

[23] SN: *Salini Construttori S.P.A. & Italstrade S.P.A. v. Kingdom of Morocco*, ICSID Case No. ARB/00/4 (Decision on Jurisdiction of July 23, 2001), ¶ 46.

[24] *Autopista Concesionada de Venezuela, C.A. v. Bolivarian Republic of Venezuela*, ICSID Case No. ARB/00/5 (Decision on Jurisdiction, Sept. 27, 2001), 6 ICSID Rep. 417 [hereinafter *Aucoven*].

[25] *Id.* at 438–39 & 446. It is possible to imagine a variety of conditions precedent to consent. Article 26 of the ICSID Convention, for instance, contemplates that a state may subject its consent to the exhaustion of local remedies. Some BITs require written approval of an investment to trigger consent to arbitrate related disputes. *Philippe Gruslin v. Malaysia*, ICSID Case No. ARB/94/1 (Award of Nov. 27, 2000), 5 ICSID Rep. 483, ¶¶ 22.1–25.7.

[26] For a review of the general principles governing the interpretation of investment treaties, *see* Chapter IX.

state or of the parties to arbitrate and, if not, to ascertain the additional steps required to permit the investor to initiate arbitration proceedings. The following sections examine in more detail various methods and forms of expressing consent to arbitrate.

C. Arbitration Clauses in Investment Contracts

As previously noted, investor-state arbitration on the basis of a postdispute contractual submission[27] or through an arbitration clause included in a concession agreement was dominant during the era of the customary law (state-to-state) diplomatic espousal system. This form of submission to arbitration still occurs,[28] but was of greater currency when it was the only means to obtain direct access to binding dispute resolution against the host state, notably before the advent of modern investment protection treaties.

This form of consent to arbitration provides governments a means to induce specific foreign companies to enter the local economy and develop particular areas of activity in need of additional capital or know-how, without extending potentially costly legal protections to existing investors or foreigners already set on investing without such encouragement. The arbitration clause in the well-known Texaco/Libya concession is illustrative.

Texaco Overseas Petr. Co./Cal. Asiatic Oil Co. v. Libyan Arab Republic

(Preliminary Award of Nov. 27, 1975), 53 I.L.R. 389, 402–04 (1979)

> 1. If at any time during or after the currency of this Concession any difference or dispute shall arise between the Government and the Company concerning the interpretation or performance hereof, or anything herein contained or in connection herewith, or the rights and liabilities of either of such parties hereunder and if such parties should fail to settle such difference or dispute by agreement, the same shall, failing any agreement to settle it any other way, be referred to two Arbitrators, one of whom shall be appointed by each such party, and an Umpire who shall be appointed by the Arbitrators immediately after they are themselves appointed.
>
> In the event of the Arbitrators failing to agree upon an Umpire within 60 days from the date of the appointment of the second Arbitrator, either of such parties may request the President or, if the President is a national of Libya or of the Country where the Company was incorporated, the Vice-President, of the International Court of Justice to appoint the Umpire.

---

[27] *See* Subsection F *infra* on *compromis*, at 242.

[28] *See, e.g., Aucoven, supra* note 24; *see also BP Exploration Co. (Libya) Ltd. v. Gov't Libyan Arab Republic*, 53 I.L.R. 297 (1973); *TOPCO, supra* note 3.

2. The institution of Arbitration proceedings shall take place upon the receipt by one of such parties of a written request of Arbitration from the other which request shall specify the matter in respect of which Arbitration is required and name the Arbitrator appointed by the party requiring Arbitration.

3. The party receiving the request shall within 90 days of such receipt appoint its Arbitrator and notify this appointment to the other of such parties failing which such other party may request the President, or in the case referred to in paragraph 1 above, the Vice-President, of the International Court of Justice to appoint a Sole Arbitrator and the decision of a Sole Arbitrator so appointed shall be binding upon both such parties.

. . . .

7. This Concession shall be governed by and interpreted in accordance with the principles of law of Libya common to the principles of international law and in the absence of such common principles then by and in accordance with the general principles of law, including such of those principles as may have been applied by international tribunals.[29]

When investors rely on contractual arbitration agreements with host states to initiate dispute resolution proceedings against the government, the arbitral tribunal, once formed, almost invariably faces questions of jurisdiction and scope similar to those encountered in the commercial arbitration context, such as the validity and effect of the arbitration clause, the severability doctrine, and so forth.[30] Because submission to arbitration is based on a specific contractual provision, there is normally no history of disputes that can be used to inform the decision as to the breadth of the parties' intent to be bound to arbitrate. Instead, the tribunal must determine, based on the national law designated as governing the contract, if there is one, or generally accepted rules of contractual interpretation, whether the particular parties and the particular dispute by its nature are subject to the agreement to arbitrate.[31] Furthermore, tribunals in contract-based investor-state arbitration are frequently faced with the issue of the validity of the underlying

---

[29] *See also* the arbitration clause in Exploration and Production Sharing Agreement Between Government of Qatar and Wintershall Aktiengesellschaft and Others, 3 *Collection of International Concessions and Related Instruments, Contemporary Series* 399 (P. Fischer & T. Wälde eds., 1976) ("The parties by this clause refer their dispute to a tribunal consisting of two arbitrators one of whom shall be chosen by each party and a referee who shall be chosen by the two arbitrators."). *See also* Agreement between the Government of Panama and Foreign Investors for the Development of the Cerro Colorado Copper Deposits. *Id.* at 71. Here also the parties referred "all disputes arising in connection with this Agreement and which are not resolved in [a friendly spirit] shall be finally settled by arbitration under the Rules of Procedure of the Inter-American Commercial Arbitration Commission." *Id.*

[30] *See generally* G. Born, *International Commercial Arbitration in the United States: Commentary and Materials* (Kluwer 2003); A. Redfern & M. Hunter, *Law and Practice of International Commercial Arbitration* (Sweet & Maxwell 4th ed. 2004).

[31] *Id.*

contract and the arbitration clause, a question that does not arise where the consent to arbitration is contained in a long-standing law or treaty of general application. The principle of separability of arbitration clauses normally prevents respondents from escaping the obligation to arbitrate by attacking the validity of the contract as a whole.[32]

The *Biloune* case arose out of a form contract issued to approved investors by an arm of the government of Ghana. The claimant asserted that early in the life of his investment, the government nationalized his property in contravention of that contract. The case, conducted under the United Nations Commission on International Trade Law (UNCITRAL) arbitration rules, included questions of both the scope of the state's submission to arbitration and the validity of the underlying contract.

Biloune (Syria) & Marine Drive Complex Ltd. v. Ghana Investments Center (GIC)

Award of Oct. 27, 1989, 95 I.L.R. 183 (1993)

Jurisdiction over the Dispute

[5] The arbitration clause contained at Art. 15 of the GIC Agreement is broad, providing for arbitration of "[a]ny dispute between the foreign investor and the Government in respect of an approved enterprise." The Agreement contains an explicit guarantee against expropriation by the Government. There can be no question that a claim that the Government has interfered with and expropriated the claimants' interest in the venture with Ghana Tourist Development Company (GTDC) gives rise to a dispute "in respect of an approved enterprise" under the Agreement.

[6] The same cannot be concluded as to the other causes of action alleged, that is, the claim for denial of justice and the claim for violation of Mr. Biloune's human rights. As to the first, the claimants based their claim on the initial failure of the respondents to submit to arbitration under Art. 15 of the Agreement. The Tribunal need not decide whether such a claim could form the basis of a separate claim under the arbitration clause, because that claim is moot. While the respondents did not participate in the constitution of the Tribunal, and for some time left unclear the question of their participation in the arbitration, they eventually did obtain counsel and took part fully in the proceedings, filing briefs and documentary evidence, appearing at the Hearing, and providing their share of the expenses of the Tribunal. Thus no continuing "dispute" between the parties, over which the Tribunal could exercise its

---

[32] *See generally* Born, *supra* note 30; *see also CCL v. Kazakhstan, supra* note 14, at 136 (Kazakhstan argued that there was a distinction between invalidation and termination of a contract and that the principle of severability only applied in the former scenario. It argued that because Kazakh courts had already terminated the contract, the arbitration clause of the contract had also been terminated. The tribunal rejected this argument, holding that the decisions of the Kazakh courts under the applicable law to the arbitration, the Swedish law, did not bind the tribunal.) *World Duty Free Co. Ltd. v. Kenya,* ICSID Case No. Arb/00/7 (Oct., 4, 2003) (jurisdictional issue conceded, contract invalidated on the merits.)

jurisdiction, exists as to the alleged denial of justice for failure of the respondents to participate in the arbitration.

[7] In the final cause of action asserted, the claimants seek recovery for alleged violation by the Government of Ghana of Mr. Biloune's human rights. The claimants assert that the Government's allegedly arbitrary detention and expulsion of Mr. Biloune and violation of his property and contractual rights constitute an actionable human rights violation for which compensation may be required in a commercial arbitration pursuant to the GIC Agreement. They assert that the Tribunal should consider this portion of the claim because this is the only forum in which redress for these alleged injuries may be sought.

[8] Long-established customary international law requires that a State accord foreign nationals within its territory a standard of treatment no less than that prescribed by international law. Moreover, contemporary international law recognizes that all individuals, regardless of nationality, are entitled to fundamental human rights (which, in the view of the Tribunal, include property as well as personal rights), which no government may violate. Nevertheless, it does not follow that this Tribunal is competent to pass upon every type of departure from the minimum standard to which nationals are entitled, or that this Tribunal is authorized to deal with allegations of violations of fundamental human rights.

[9] This Tribunal's competence is limited to commercial disputes arising under a contract entered into the context of Ghana's Investment Code. As noted, the Government agreed to arbitrate only disputes "in respect of" the foreign investment. Thus, other matters—however compelling the claim or wrongful the alleged act—are outside this Tribunal's jurisdiction. Under the facts of this case it must be concluded that, while the acts alleged to violate the international human rights of Mr. Biloune may be relevant in considering the investment dispute under arbitration, this Tribunal lacks jurisdiction to address, as an independent cause of action, a claim of violation of human rights. . . .

Jurisdiction over the Parties

[10] The Tribunal must also establish that each claimant before it has a right, under the arbitration clause, to assert a claim and, likewise, that each respondent against which a claim is asserted is a person bound by and subject to the arbitration clause.

[11] Marine Drive Complex Ltd. (MDCL) was the foreign investor that entered the Agreement with Ghana Investments Centre seeking investment concessions from GIC. Mr. Biloune was and is the majority shareholder and Chairman of MDCL. The respondents have not disputed the right of either MDCL or Mr. Biloune to appear as claimants. The Tribunal finds that MDCL is entitled to invoke arbitration under the GIC Agreement and that Mr. Biloune, as MDCL's Chairman and principal shareholder, may assert MDCL's claims. The Tribunal also finds that, in the circumstances of this case, and particularly having regard to GIC's knowledge of Mr. Biloune's role of financing and directing the project, Mr. Biloune, though not a party to the GIC Agreement, may assert his own claims arising out of his investment in MDCL. The respondents have not disputed this conclusion, which finds support in Art. 22 of the GIC Agreement. The first paragraph of that Article prohibits expropriation of an approved enterprise, and the second expressly protects a "person who owns, whether wholly or in part, the capital" of such an enterprise.

[12] GIC is the entity originally named as the respondent in this arbitration. As signatory to the GIC Agreement, GIC is clearly bound by it and its arbitration clause.

. . . .

[15] Of course, in order to be subject to the Tribunal's jurisdiction, the Government must have consented to the arbitration, either now or previously. We need not consider the possibility that the Government's participation in the proceedings might constitute consent, despite counsel's later objection to the Government's inclusion as a party. This is because the Agreement with GIC, an agency of the Government of Ghana, clearly binds the Government; indeed, the Agreement speaks explicitly of disputes between the investor "and the Government," and the expropriation clause expressly prohibits expropriation "by the Government." Thus the relevant clauses both engage the Government of Ghana, and contemplate claims against it.

. . . .

Validity of the GIC Agreement

[17] The final jurisdictional issue is whether the GIC Agreement, which contains the operative arbitration clause, remains in effect and is binding on the parties. The respondents have asserted that the GIC Agreement should be held inapplicable because MDCL and Mr. Biloune do not qualify as foreign investors as required by the GIC Agreement. They allege that GIC approved the Marine Drive venture for investment concessions on the basis of a 60%–40% shareholding between Mr. Biloune and Mr. Michigan in MDCL. According to the respondents, the fact that over 99% of the financing for the venture was in fact provided by Mr. Biloune constituted a misrepresentation which, under Art. 20 of the GIC Agreement, permits GIC to cancel its approval.

[18] The respondents argue in addition that because MDCL obtained GIC approval as a foreign/Ghanaian joint venture, it was required to make a minimum $60,000 foreign currency investment in MDCL, in cash or in capital goods. They point out further that if MDCL had sought approval as a venture wholly owned by Mr. Biloune, as a foreign national he would have been required to invest $100,000. The respondents assert that the foreign currency investment advanced by the claimants as satisfying this requirement—largely a shipment of building materials needed for the construction work worth £47,000—was too little to satisfy the minimum required for an enterprise wholly owned by a foreign investor. The respondents argue in the alternative that the investment was not registered with the appropriate governmental office, as allegedly required to prove foreign investment in any amount.

[19] The Tribunal does not find these objections sufficient to deprive the GIC Agreement of validity. As to the alleged misrepresentation in describing the capital basis of MDCL, the Tribunal notes that the application submitted to GIC clearly states both that the shares would be split 60%–40% between Mr. Biloune and Mr. Michigan and that Mr. Biloune would provide 24.7 million cedis of MDCL's capital compared to only 150,000 cedis for Mr Michigan. This disclosure of the proposed capital arrangements eliminates any basis for the defense of misrepresentation as now alleged. Thus, if in fact such an arrangement is not normally contemplated by GIC, GIC's approval of the application must be considered a waiver of this defense and an acceptance of a modification of the norm. Moreover, it may also be relevant to note that the project at issue was carried forward by what Lt. Col. Yaache described as a partnership between GTDC (whose shares are wholly owned by the Ghanaian Government) and MDCL.

[20] Much the same can be said about the allegation of insufficient foreign currency investment. The respondents' defense is deficient in two respects. First, it does not appear that any time limit was imposed within which full foreign currency

contributions must be in place. Second, there is no indication in the record that GIC was concerned at the time that MDCL's foreign currency requirement was being implemented too slowly, or, if it was, that the Agreement was voided as a result. On the contrary, the parties consistently acted in accordance with the terms of the GIC Agreement, treating it as in force. During the difficulties experienced by Mr. Biloune at the end of 1987, it was never suggested that the Agreement was invalid. Accordingly, the Tribunal determines that the respondents have failed to establish their contention that the GIC Agreement should be considered invalid. This does not mean that issues as to the amounts actually invested in, and paid out by, the enterprise, may not be relevant to the ultimate determinations of this Tribunal.

[21] Given the Tribunal's determination of the validity of the GIC Agreement, it need not decide whether, if the Agreement were adjudged invalid, the arbitration clause would nevertheless be separable and provide sufficient basis for this Tribunal's jurisdiction. Nor need it decide whether there is an independent basis for arbitration under Art. 20 of the Ghana Investment Code of 1985.

. . . .

[23] For all the above reasons, the Tribunal holds that it has jurisdiction to decide the claim of expropriation as here presented.

D. National Investment Legislation

Some of the earliest ICSID cases were initiated on the basis of a unilateral submission or consent to arbitration by the host state, codified in its own domestic laws governing foreign investment. Before the proliferation of BITs in the 1980s and 1990s, several developing countries opted to encourage foreign direct investment by incorporating substantive investment protection and recourse to arbitration for violations of those standards directly into their municipal laws. With the expansion of investment protection treaties, however, many national laws have been superseded, and in any case offer less favorable conditions than BITs. As a result few cases have been brought under such laws in recent decades.[33]

Consent to arbitration in national legislation may appear in a variety of forms. Some national investment laws provide unambiguously for the settlement of disputes through investor-state arbitration under the auspices of a recognized arbitral institution. Article 8(2) of Albania's 1993 Law on Foreign Investment provides that "a foreign investor may submit the dispute for resolution and the Republic of

---

[33] *But see Petrobart,* which refers to a prior case brought under the Kyrgyz foreign investment law, *Petrobart v. Kyrgyz Republic,* Stockholm Chamber Case No. 126/2003 (Mar. 29, 2005).

Albania hereby consents to the submission thereof, to the International Center for Settlement of Investment Disputes."[34]

Investment laws may also provide access to investor-state dispute settlement institutions like ICSID as one of several dispute settlement options available to an investor.[35] Sometimes these laws explicitly provide that the reference to a particular mode of arbitration constitutes the consent of the government to the ICSID jurisdiction. Such reference is especially common in investment laws of some African countries.[36] Article 7 of Mauritania's Ordinance No. 89.013/CMSN Concerning the Investment Code, for instance, provides the following:

> 7.2 [A]ny dispute between a foreign natural or juridical person and the Islamic Republic of Mauritania related to the application or the interpretation of this code shall be settled according to an arbitration and conciliation procedure as the following:
>
> a) either by agreements and treaties concerning the protection of investments concluded between the Islamic Republic of Mauritania and the State the natural or juridical person is a national thereof,
>
> b) or by an arbitration and conciliation procedure to which both parties have agreed,
>
> c) or according to the Convention of March 18, 1965 for the Settlement of Investment Disputes between States and Nationals of Other States, established under the auspices of the IBRD, ratified by the Islamic Republic of Mauritania by Law No. 65.136 on July 30, 1965,
>
> d) ... this article constitutes consent of the Islamic Republic of Mauritania to the jurisdiction of ICSID. ... .[37]

---

[34] Albanian Law on Foreign Investment, Law No. 7764, 1993, Albania, 1 *Investment Laws of the World*, Looseleaf (Oceana 2003) [hereinafter *Investment Laws of the World*]; *see also* Investment Law of Mali, Law No. 91–048/AN-RM, 1991, art. 21, Mali, 5 *Investment Laws of the World*. In the *Tradex* arbitration, the Tribunal stated that "although consent by written agreement is the usual method of submission to ICSID Jurisdiction, it can now be considered as established and not requiring further reasoning that such consent can also be effected unilaterally by a Contracting State in its national laws, the consent becoming effective at the latest if and when the foreign investor files its claim with ICSID making use of the representative national law. Therefore [Article 8(2) of the Albanian] 1993 Law together with Tradex's Request for Arbitration must be considered as sufficient consent. ... ." *Tradex, supra* note 10, at 186–87.

[35] UNCTAD Course § 2.3, *supra* note 16, at 11; *see also* Tanzanian Investment Act, art. 23 Tanzania, 9 *Investment Laws of the World*; Foreign Investment Law of Somalia, Law No. 19, 1987, art. 19, Somalia, 8 *Investment Laws of the World*,; Tunisia's Law No. 69–35 (June 26, 1969, concerning the Investment Code, art. 19), Tunisia, 9 *Investment Laws of the World*.

[36] Antonio R. Parra, *Principles Governing Foreign Investment, as Reflected in National Investment Codes*, 7 ICSID Rev.-F.I.L.J. 428, 444–45 (1992).

[37] Ordinance No. 89.013/CMSN 23 of Jan. 1989 in regard to Investments Code, art. 7 Mauritania, 5 *Investment Laws of the World*. *See also* Investment Law of El Salvador, art. 15.

Many investment laws, however, do not contain such express consent.[38] Article 19 of Somalia's Investment Act, for example, provides in relevant part the following:

> 1. Disputes in respect of the implementation of this law shall be settled:
>
>   a) In a manner to be agreed upon with the investor, or in the absence of such agreement;
>
>   b) Within the framework of the agreements in force between the Somali Democratic Republic and the investor's home country, or in the absence of (a) and (b);
>
>   c) Within the framework of the ICSID Convention, to which Somali has adhered by virtue of Law No. 11 of 1967, when such convention applies. . . .[39]

Where the investor and the Somali government have not come to some alternative dispute resolution arrangement, and where there is no bilateral investment treaty in force between the investor's home state and Somalia, it is likely that a tribunal would still interpret the mandatory phrasing of the clause (disputes *"shall* be settled") to constitute the Somali government's prior consent to submit the relevant category of disputes to ICSID arbitration.[40]

Not all foreign investment legislation is clear with respect to available dispute resolution methods. Thus, there is debate as to whether Article 22 of the 1999 Venezuelan Investment Law provides for state consent to ICSID jurisdiction.[41] Article 22 provides:

> [D]isputes arising between an international investor whose country of origin has a treaty or agreement for the promotion and protection of investments in force with Venezuela, or the disputes *to which the provisions of the [MIGA] Convention or the [ICSID] Convention are applicable,* shall be submitted to international arbitration under the terms provided for in the respective treaty or agreement, *if it so provides,* without prejudice to the possibility to use, whenever it is possible, the judicial remedies provided for in the Venezuelan laws in force.[42] (emphasis added)

---

[38] UNCTAD Course § 2.3, *supra* note 16, at 11.

[39] The Foreign Investment Law, Law No. 19 of May 9, 1987, art. 19, Somalia, 8 *Investment Laws of the World.*

[40] *See also CCL v. Kazakhstan, supra* note 14, at 141–3 (finding jurisdiction pursuant to Kazakhstan Law on Foreign Investment, Dec. 27, 1994, art. 27, which provides: "(1) Investment disputes shall be settled, whenever possible, by means of negotiations. (2) If such dispute can not be settled by means of negotiations . . . then the dispute at the choice of any of the parties thereof may be transferred for settlement when there exists the written consent of the foreign investor . . .").

[41] Guillaume Lemenez de Kerdelleau, *State Consent to ICSID Arbitration: Article 22 of the Venezuelan Investment Law,* 4(3) TDM (June 2007) ("[Article 22] may lead to two different interpretations.").

[42] *Id.* For original Spanish text, *see* Decree No. 356 of Oct. 3, 1999 on Promotion and Protection of Investments, art. 22, Venezuela, 10 *Investment Laws of the World.*

Some commentators argue that Article 22 only authorizes ICSID arbitration if the Washington Convention is "applicable" and "so provides," which would be the case where all the conditions of Article 25 of the Washington Convention, including state consent, are satisfied.[43] Other commentators disagree, arguing that Article 22 establishes the state's consent to ICSID jurisdiction.[44]

One of the first investor-state cases, which drew a great deal of interest from scholars and practitioners at the time, raised questions about the interpretation of national legislation on foreign investment. In what has come to be known as the *Pyramids Case*,[45] a foreign company involved in developing a tourism project in Egypt initiated arbitration against the Egyptian government pursuant to Article 8 of Law No. 43 of 1974 Concerning the Investment of Arab and Foreign Funds and the Free Zone, which contained a rather ambiguous dispute resolution clause:

> Investment disputes in respect of the implementation of the provisions in this Law shall be settled in a manner to be agreed upon with the investor, or within the framework of the agreements enforced between the Arab Republic of Egypt and the investor's home country, or within the framework of the Convention for the Settlement of Disputes between the State and the nationals of other countries to which Egypt has adhered by virtue of Law No. 90 of 1971, where such Convention applies.[46]

Egypt argued that the clause referring disputes to ICSID arbitration could have no effect absent a separate implementing agreement, expressing consent to arbitrate a specific dispute with the particular investor in question. The arbitral tribunal disagreed with Egypt's defense and found that the foreign investment law established a hierarchical sequence of mandatory dispute settlement procedures. According to the tribunal's decision, this clause constituted an independent and express "consent in writing" to ICSID jurisdiction within the meaning of Article

---

[43] Kerdelleau, *supra* note 41. Arif Ali argues that "if it so provides" ("the *si así éste lo establece*) clause makes it clear that Article 22 cannot serve as an investment law-based consent for the purposes of Article 25 of the ICSID Convention." Similarly, Omar E. Garcia-Bolivar contends that Venezuela is not consenting to ICSID arbitration, and the wording of Article 22 merely indicates that the ICSID arbitration is "an option subject to a subsequent condition." Bolivar also argues that the terms "*to which are applicable the provisions of the Convention*" and "*if so provides*" are not redundant as other commentators suggest. For more discussion, *see* archives of Oil-Gas-Energy-Mining-Infrastructure and Investment Disputes (OGEMID) in TDM, Discussion Thread Entitled "*Venezuela's Consent to ICSID Jurisdiction*," starting on Nov. 6, 2006.

[44] Oscar M. Garibaldi suggests that Article 22 establishes the state's consent to ICSID jurisdiction, relying in part on the *SPP v. Egypt* where the tribunal addressed a similar question of interpretation. *Id.* Kerdelleau also concludes that the wording of Article 22 clearly points to ICSID arbitration, which is also supported by the purpose of the Venezuelan investment law. Kerdelleau further argued that Article 22 should be interpreted in favor of foreign investors and that the principle of good faith should prevent the Government from using the ambiguity to refuse to arbitrate. For more discussion, see Kerdelleau *supra* note 41.

[45] *Southern Pacific Properties (Middle East) Ltd. v. Arab Republic of Egypt,* ICSID Case No. ARB/84/3, 32 I.L.M. 933 (1993).

[46] Egypt: Foreign Investment Law, 1977, art. 8 (16 I.L.M. 1476, 1479 (1977)).

25 of the Convention, where no other method of dispute settlement had been agreed between the parties, and where no bilateral investment treaty applied.

Given the wide variety of legislative texts, in each case it is important to carefully consider whether a reference in national law to international arbitration of disputes is intended as simply an acknowledgment of the possibility of dispute resolution in that forum, or whether it amounts to the binding consent of the host state to arbitral jurisdiction. In some cases the government's *offer* as contained in foreign investment legislation is limited and contingent, requiring further action by the state or the investor before it becomes binding and irrevocable.[47] Naturally, after a dispute arises, the state is unlikely to take the necessary additional steps to submit to arbitration.[48]

The new Egyptian Investment Law of 1989, which appears to have been enacted in light of the decision in the *Pyramids Case* based on the prior law, contains just such an express limitation:

> The parties concerned may also agree to settle such disputes within the framework of the agreements in force between the Arab Republic of Egypt and the investor's home country or within the framework of the ICSID Convention . . . subject to the terms and conditions, and in the instances where such agreements do apply.[49]

With the expansion of the network of BITs around the world, there has been less recourse to international dispute resolution pursuant to domestic investment protection legislation.[50] In particular, this is because of the limited substantive protections and scope of submission to arbitration in many such laws, which is sometimes restricted to compensation for expropriation and denial of national treatment. The following excerpt from the decision in *Tradex v. Albania* is illustrative:

> 67. Before the Tribunal can enter into evaluating the facts and contentions of the Parties in this case for its decision on the merits, it seems appropriate to identify the legal framework in which the relevance of the factual aspects can and must be considered.

---

[47] Delaume, *supra* note 9, at 157. Thus, Article 30 (2) of the Ugandan Investment Code provides in relevant part that "A dispute between a foreign investor and the Authority of the Government in respect of a licensed business enterprise which is not settled through negotiations may be submitted to arbitration in accordance with the following methods as may be . . . agreed by the parties—(a) in accordance with the rules of procedure for arbitration of the International Center for the Settlement of Investment Disputes. . . ." Investment Code of Uganda, 1991 art. 30(2), Uganda, 10 *Investment Laws of the World*.

[48] UNCTAD Course § 2.3, *supra* note 16, at 13.

[49] *Id.*

[50] In 2006, out of twenty-two cases that were registered with ICSID, only two were based on domestic investment legislation. In these two cases, the laws were not asserted as the sole basis of jurisdiction but were asserted along with treaty provisions as alternatives. 23(2) News from ICSID 2 (2006); 23(1) News from ICSID 2 (2006).

> 68. An important limitation of this framework is that, in its Decision on Jurisdiction of 24 December 1996, the Tribunal found that it only had jurisdiction on the basis of the Albanian Law No. 7764 of 2 November 1993 on Foreign Investments (the 1993 Law).
>
> 69. Therefore, in its consideration of the merits, the Tribunal is prevented from examining the claim on any other possible legal basis such as any other of the various investment laws issued in Albania, the Bilateral Investment Treaty between Albania and Greece, as well as other sources of international law. . . .
>
> 70. A further limitation comes from the 1993 Law itself. Art. 8 paragraph 2 of the Law which the Tribunal accepted as the basis of its jurisdiction provides for submission to ICSID only "if the dispute arises out of or relates to expropriation, compensation for expropriation, or discrimination and also for the transfers in accordance of Article 7, . . ."
>
> 71. . . . [I]n view of the above mentioned limitation, for the Tribunal's examination on the merits only the following Articles of the 1993 Law [on Entry and Treatment, Expropriation and Nationalization, and Compensation for Expropriation and Nationalization] must be considered as possible sources of the claim insofar as they may become relevant for an expropriation and a compensation for expropriation.
>
> . . . .
>
> 204. At the end of its examination in this Section 5 of the Award, therefore, the Tribunal concludes that Tradex has not been able to prove that an expropriation occurred regarding its foreign investment in the Joint Venture . . .
>
> 205. In view of this conclusion, if no expropriation occurred there is no jurisdiction according to Art. 8 of the 1993 Law. . . .[51]

An important distinction between national legislation and investment protection treaties is that local laws are subject to amendment or revocation without any need to consult with other states, as would be required to change or abrogate an international agreement. The question arises: Can a host state prevent an investment dispute from proceeding to arbitration by altering its investment laws after the dispute arises? Although no arbitral tribunals have yet addressed this issue directly, there appears to be some consensus among commentators that, at least as far as the Washington Convention is concerned, state consent becomes irrevocable once the investor-claimant has accepted the offer to arbitrate.[52] Under this view, any alteration of the investment legislation after the investor has accepted the unilateral offer available in the legislation (normally by submitting a Request for Arbitration to ICSID) has no effect on the jurisdiction of the arbitral tribunal.[53] For at least two reasons, this approach seems sound. First, the Washington Convention expressly states, "When the parties have given their consent, no party may withdraw its

---

[51] *Tradex, supra* note 10, Award, 14 ICSID Rev.-F.I.L.J. 197 (1999).

[52] Schreuer, "Commentary," *supra* note 7, at 259; Moshe Hirsch, *The Arbitration Mechanism of the International Centre for the Settlement of Investment Disputes* 52–53 (1993).

[53] UNCTAD Course § 2.3, *supra* note 16, at 38.

consent unilaterally."⁵⁴ Because in the case of investment laws the consent of both parties has been given once the investor submits a request for arbitration, it would seem contrary to the Convention if the host state sought to avoid arbitration on the basis of a modification of its own consent by legislative amendment after the investor's submission. One would expect such a modification to be ineffective as a matter of international law for purposes of ICSID registration,⁵⁵ and that the ICSID proceedings could proceed to a judgment, even absent the respondent state's participation. The issue is, however, less clear with respect to arbitration outside the framework of the Washington Convention.

E. Investment Protection Treaties as Consent to Arbitration

In most modern investment protection treaties, contracting states expressly consent to the mandatory submission of certain investment disputes to arbitration, thus satisfying the written consent requirement of Article 25(1) of the Washington Convention. Article IX (4) of United States-Azerbaijan BIT⁵⁶ provides a typical example of this type of consent: "[E]ach party hereby consents to the submission of any investment dispute for settlement by binding arbitration."⁵⁷ Many investment treaties include consent to arbitration outside the ICSID system. For example, Article 8(2) of the Netherlands-Czech Republic BIT contemplates mandatory submission of investment disputes to ad hoc arbitration pursuant to the UNCITRAL arbitration rules:

> 1. All disputes between one Contracting Party and an investor of the other Contracting Party concerning an investment of the latter shall if possible, be settled amicably.
>
> 2. Each Contracting Party hereby consents to submit a dispute referred to in paragraph (1) of this Article, to an arbitral tribunal, if the dispute has not been settled

---

⁵⁴ Washington Convention, art. 25(1).

⁵⁵ Rule 6(2) of ICSID Rules of Procedure of the Institution of Conciliation and Arbitration Proceedings (Institution Rules) provides that "A proceeding under the Convention shall be deemed to have been instituted on the date of the registration of the request." Rule 8 of the Institution Rules, which deals with the withdrawal of the request, provides in the relevant part that "The requesting party may, by written notice to the Secretary-General, withdraw the request *before it has been registered*. . . ." (emphasis added)

⁵⁶ Treaty between the Government of the United States of America and the Government of the Republic of Azerbaijan Concerning the Encouragement and Reciprocal Protection of Investment (1997), art. IX(4).

⁵⁷ *See also* Agreement between the Government of the United Kingdom of Great Britain and Northern Island and the Government of Republic of Albania for Promotion and Protection of Investments, art. 8 ("each Contracting Party hereby consents to submit to [the ICSID] . . . for settlement by arbitration. . . any legal dispute. . . concerning an investment"); Agreement between the Government of the Republic of France and the Government of the Republic of Albania Concerning Reciprocal Encouragement and Protection of Investment, art. 9 (". . . the Contracting Party, which is a party to a dispute, consents to submit the dispute to [ICSID] . . . at the request of the individual or corporate investor").

amicably within a period of six months from the date either party to the dispute requested amicable settlement.[58]

...

5) The arbitration tribunal shall determine its own procedure applying the arbitration rules of the United Nations Commission for International Trade Law (UNCITRAL).[59]

Dispute settlement mechanisms in investment protection treaties do not always contain the host state's complete consent to arbitrate, however. In certain Swedish BITs, for example, the dispute resolution provision appears to constitute a mere agreement to agree: Disputes "shall **upon the agreement by both parties** be submitted for arbitration to [ICSID]."[60] As former ICSID Secretary-General Aron Broches points out, "[s]uch a provision does not, of course, constitute consent to arbitration by the States concerned. . . . Nor does it impose a legal obligation on these States to give such consent."[61] Instead, this language merely establishes ICSID arbitration as the preferred means for the resolution of investment disputes, and provides notice to foreign investors that the host state may be prepared to consider such an avenue. In practice, without significant pressure from the investor's home state, the host state party to an investment dispute normally has little incentive to voluntarily submit to arbitration after the dispute has arisen.[62] According to some observers, however, even these "agreements to agree" in certain BITs have

---

[58] Agreement on Encouragement and Reciprocal Protection of Investments Between the Kingdom of the Netherlands and the Czech and Slovak Federal Republic (1991).

[59] *See also CME Czech Republic B.V. v. Czech Republic* (UNCITRAL Arbitration, Partial Award of Sept. 13, 2001) (the tribunal stated that this clause contained the contracting parties' consent to arbitration). Another major arbitration was recently initiated based on this treaty. *See Saluka Investments B.V. v. Czech Republic* (Ad hoc UNCITRAL Arbitration, Partial Award, 2006). *See also* Agreement between the Portuguese Republic and the United Mexican States on the Reciprocal Promotion and Protection of Investments (1999), art. 10 ("Each Contracting Party hereby gives its unconditional consent to the submission of a dispute to international arbitration in accordance with this Part"). Article 9 of the same BIT gives an investor an option to submit its claim to ICSID, an UNCITRAL tribunal, or other forums. Drafting styles may vary; note also Article XIII(5) of the Canada-Ecuador BIT, in which the contracting parties to the BIT provide their "unconditional consent" to submit a dispute to international arbitration in accordance with that article. This particular provision was invoked in *EnCana v. Ecuador* to grant jurisdiction to an UNCITRAL tribunal administered by LCIA. *EnCana v. Ecuador,* LCIA Case UN3481 (Jurisdictional Award of Feb. 27, 2004).

[60] Agreement between the Government of Sweden and the Government of Malaysia Concerning the Mutual Protection of Investments (1979), art. 6 (emphasis added); Agreement between the Government of Australia and the Government of the People's Republic of China on the Reciprocal Encouragement and Protection of Investments (1988), art. XII(2)(b).

[61] Aron Broches, *Bilateral Investment Protection Treaties and Arbitration of Investment Disputes,* in *The Art of Arbitration* 63, 65 (1982).

[62] *But see Compañía del Desarrollo de Santa Elena S.A. v. Costa Rica,* ICSID Case No. ARB/96/1 (Award, Feb. 17, 2000), described at pp. 245–46 *infra.*

some moral force, placing pressure in and of themselves upon host states to provide consent to arbitrate.[63]

A third category of treaty consent clauses may be found in some Australian BITs. Article 11 of the Australia-Czech Republic BIT, for example, provides in relevant part that:

> (3) Either party to a dispute may ... (a) ... refer the dispute to the [ICSID] ... Where this action is taken by an investor of one Contracting Party the other Contracting Party *shall consent* in writing to the submission of the dispute to the Centre within thirty days of receiving such a request from the investor ... .[64] (emphasis added)

This provision suggests that the investment treaty itself does not contain the consent of the state party to submit to arbitration. Rather, the treaty requires it to provide its consent to arbitrate a given category of disputes after they arise. When compared with the Swedish treaty text noted above, this formulation appears to offer more enforcement options. It could be argued that the state party's refusal to consent to the arbitration of investment disputes constitutes a breach of the state's treaty obligations toward the other contracting party to the BIT. Although the investor may be unable to mount a claim directly against the host state, it may have access to diplomatic espousal by its home state and the state-state arbitration provision of the relevant treaty.

In section B(4) the issue of irrevocability of consent was briefly discussed. The following excerpt from Schreuer provides more detail with respect to that issue in the context of the BITs. In addition, it touches upon other important issues, such as the proper scope of consent to arbitration in the context of investment treaty arbitration.

C. H. Schreuer, Consent to Arbitration, 2 TDM 5 (2005), 1–36, reprinted in *The Oxford Handbook of International Investment Law* (P. Muchlinski, F. Ortino & C. H. Schreuer, eds., Oxford University Press 2008)

A possible withdrawal of an offer of consent before its acceptance is less of a problem in the case of arbitration clauses contained in treaties than in the case of national legislation. An offer of arbitration in a treaty remains valid notwithstanding an attempt to terminate it, unless there is a basis for the termination under the law of treaties. Nevertheless, in order to avoid complications early acceptance is advisable also in the case of offers of consent contained in BITs. Once the arbitration agreement is perfected through the acceptance of the offer contained in the treaty it remains in existence even if the States parties to the BIT agree to amend or terminate the treaty.

. . . .

---

[63] Rudolf Dolzer & Margrete Stevens, *Bilateral Investment Treaties* 132 (Martinus Nijhoff Publishers 1995).

[64] *See also* Agreement between Japan and the Islamic Republic of Pakistan Concerning the Promotion and Protection of Investment (1998), art. 10(2).

3. Scope of Consent[65]

a) All Disputes Concerning Investments

The scope of consent to arbitration offered in BITs varies. Many BITs in their consent clauses contain phrases such as "all disputes concerning investments" or "any legal dispute concerning an investment." These provisions do not restrict a tribunal's jurisdiction to claims arising from the BITs' substantive standards. By their own terms, these consent clauses encompass disputes that go beyond the interpretation and application of the BIT itself and would include disputes that arise from a contract in connexion with the investment.

In *Salini* v. *Morocco*[66] Article 8 of the applicable BIT defined ICSID's jurisdiction in terms of "[t]ous les différends ou divergences . . . concernant un investissement."[67] The Tribunal noted that the terms of this provision were very general and included not only a claim for violation of the BIT but also a claim based on contract:

> . . . Article 8 obliges the State to respect the jurisdictional choice arising by reason of breaches of the bilateral Agreement and of any breach of a contract which binds it directly.[68]

In *Compañía de Aguas del Aconquija, S.A. & Vivendi Universal*[69] Article 8 of the BIT between France and Argentina, applicable in that case, offered consent for "[a]ny dispute relating to investments." In its discussion of the BIT's fork in the road clause, the *ad hoc* Committee said:

> . . . Article 8 deals generally with disputes "relating to investments made under this Agreement between one Contracting Party and an investor of the other Contracting Party." It is those disputes which may be submitted, at the investor's option, either to national or international adjudication. Article 8 does not use a narrower formulation, requiring that the investor's claim allege a breach of the BIT itself. Read literally, the requirements for arbitral jurisdiction in Article 8 do not necessitate that the Claimant allege a breach of the BIT itself: it is sufficient that the dispute relate to an investment made under the BIT. This may be contrasted, for example, with Article 11 of the BIT

---

[65] In the context of the ICSID Convention the most comprehensive commentary on the Washington Convention explains in relation to Article 25(1) that: "The scope of such consent is within the discretion of the parties. In this connection, it should be noted that ratification of the Washington Convention is, on the part of a Contracting State, only an expression of its willingness to make use of the ICSID machinery. As such, ratification does not constitute an obligation to use that machinery. That obligation can arise only after the State concerned has specifically agreed to submit to ICSID arbitration a particular dispute or classes of disputes. In other words, the decision of a State to consent to ICSID arbitration is a matter of pure policy and it is within the sole discretion of each Contracting State to determine the type of investment disputes that it considers arbitrable in the context of ICSID." Christoph Schreuer, *Commentary on the Washington Convention, Article 25*, 11 ICSID Rev.–F.I.L.J. 318, ¶ 243 (1996).

[66] SN: *Salini Construtorri S.p.A. & Italstrade S.p.A. v. Morocco*, ICSID Case No. ARB/00/4 (Decision on Jurisdiction, July 23, 2001), J. de Droit Int'l 196 (2002), 6 ICSID Rep. 400.

[67] SN: Italy/Morocco BIT Art. 8.

[68] SN: *Id.* ¶ 61.

[69] SN: *Compañía de Aguas del Aconquija, S. A. & Vivendi Universal (formerly Compagnie Générale des Eaux) v. Argentine Republic* (Decision on Annulment, July 3, 2002), 6 ICSID Rep. 340.

[dealing with state/state dispute settlement], which refers to disputes "concerning the interpretation or application of this Agreement," or with Article 1116 of the [North American Free Trade Agreement] NAFTA, which provides that an investor may submit to arbitration under Chapter 11 "a claim that another Party has breached an obligation under" specified provisions of that Chapter.[70]

The Tribunal in *SGS v. Pakistan*[71] reached a different conclusion. Article 9 of the applicable BIT between Switzerland and Pakistan referred to "disputes with respect to investments." The Tribunal found that the phrase was merely descriptive of the factual subject matter of the disputes and did not relate to the legal basis of the claims or cause of action asserted in the claims. The Tribunal said:

> ... from that description alone, without more, we believe that no implication necessarily arises that both BIT and purely contract claims are intended to be covered by the Contracting Parties in Article 9.[72]

Therefore, the Tribunal held that it had no jurisdiction with respect to contract claims which did not also constitute breaches of the substantive standards of the BIT.[73]

That decision has attracted some criticism.[74] In *SGS v. Philippines*[75] Article VIII(2) of the Switzerland/Philippines BIT offered consent to arbitration for "disputes with respect to investments." The Tribunal found that the clause in question was entirely general allowing for the submission of all investment disputes. Therefore, the Tribunal found that the term included a dispute arising from an investment contract.[76]

. . . .

c) Limited Expression of Consent

Other BIT clauses offering consent to arbitration circumscribe the scope of consent to arbitration in narrower terms. A provision that is typical for United States BITs is contained in Article VII of the Argentina-U.S. BIT of 1991. It offers consent for investment disputes which are defined as follows:

> a dispute between a Party and a national or company of the other Party arising out of or relating to (a) an investment agreement between that Party and such national or company; (b) an investment authorization granted by that Party's foreign investment authority (if any such authorization exists) to such national or company; or (c) an alleged breach of any right conferred or created by this Treaty with respect to an investment.

Other BITs require that the investment to which the dispute relates must have been specifically approved in writing as a condition for consent. The scope for the jurisdiction of tribunals is even narrower where consent is limited to the amount of

---

[70] SN: *Id.* ¶ 55.

[71] SN: *SGS v. Pakistan* (Decision on Jurisdiction, Aug. 6, 2003), 8 ICSID Rep. 406.

[72] SN: *Id.* ¶ 161.

[73] SN: Loc. cit.

[74] SN: *See also Tokios Tokeles v. Ukraine, supra* note 22, ¶ 52.

[75] SN: *SGS v. Philippines*, ICSID Case No. ARB/02/6 (Decision on Jurisdiction, Jan. 29, 2004), available at www.investmentclaims.com.

[76] SN: *Id.* ¶¶ 131–35. (*See also* Scheuer, *Consent to Arbitration*, at 11–21 for the impact of umbrella clause and "fork in the road" provisions on the scope of consent. Because these issues have been discussed in Chapters XVII and XIII of this book, they have not been reproduced here.)

compensation for expropriation.[77] For instance, the China-Hungary BIT of 1991 provides in Article 10(1):

> Any dispute between either Contracting State and the investor of the other Contracting State concerning the amount of compensation for expropriation may be submitted to an arbitral tribunal.

As with bilateral investment treaties, multilateral investment treaties may also supply the requisite state consent to arbitration. Several multilateral treaties have clauses expressing the consent of the contracting parties to arbitrate disputes involving foreign investments and/or investors. These include the Lomé Conventions, NAFTA,[78] Energy Charter Treaty (ECT),[79] Association of South East Asian Nations (ASEAN),[80] Dominican Republic–Central American–United States Free Trade Agreement (DR-CAFTA),[81] and Mercosur.[82] Multilateral investment treaties often regulate international activities in both the trade and investment spheres. Some, like the ECT, may regulate a specific sector of the economy. These treaties, despite their differences, share one thing in common: They contain the *consent* of the contracting parties to submit disputes involving foreign investment to direct investor-state arbitration.[83]

The U.S. government has initiated a program of concluding Free Trade Agreements (FTAs).[84] Some of these treaties are bilateral, such as the United States-Morocco

---

[77] *See, e.g.,* 1989 Russian Federation–Germany BIT, art. 10 (" (2) If a dispute relating to the amount of compensation or the method of its payment, in accordance with article 4 of this Agreement, or to freedom of transfer, in accordance with article 5 of this Agreement, is not settled within six months from the time when a claim is made by one of the parties to the dispute, either party to the dispute shall be entitled to refer the matter to an international arbitral tribunal. . . ."). This article was invoked in *Sedelmayer v. Russian Federation* (SCC Arbitration, Final Award, July 7, 2001).

[78] *See* NAFTA, art. 1122 ("1. Each Party consents to the submission of a claim to arbitration in accordance with the procedures set out in this Agreement.").

[79] *See* ECT, art. 26 ("(3) (a) Subject only to subparagraphs (b) and (c), each Contracting Party hereby gives its unconditional consent to the submission of a dispute to international arbitration or conciliation in accordance with the provisions of this Article"). But note the exceptions to consent in Article 26(3)(b) and (c), *available at* www.encharter.org.

[80] ASEAN Investment Treaty, art. X(2) ("If such a dispute cannot thus be settled within six months of its being raised, then either party can elect to submit the dispute for conciliation or arbitration and such election shall be binding on the other party . . .").

[81] DR-CAFTA, art. 10.17.

[82] Noah Rubins, *Investment Arbitration in Brazil*, 4(6) J. World Inv. & Trade, 1071, 1088–89 (December 2003) (arguing that Mercosur includes consent to arbitrate); *cf.* Horacio Grigera-Naon, *The Settlement of Investment Disputes between States and Private Parties: An Overview from the Perspective of the ICC*, 1 J. World Inv. & Trade, 59, 62–63 (July 2000) (disagreeing with Rubins).

[83] *See, e.g.,* Lomé IV, art. 307; NAFTA, art. 1122; Energy Charter Treaty, art. 26; and Colonia Protocol in regard to Mercosur, art. 9.

[84] *See generally* the Web site of United States Trade Representative (USTR) at the following link: http://www.ustr.gov/Trade_Agreements/Section_Index.html.

FTA[85]; others are multilateral and regional, such as DR-CAFTA and the Free Trade Area of the Americas (FTAA).[86] Similar to the other multilateral treaties noted above, these treaties regulate both trade and investment activities. Their provisions on regulation of investment activities, especially those related to resolution of disputes between governments and investors, are generally similar to those of the U.S. Model BIT of 2004.[87]

F. Investment Arbitration Based on *Compromis*

The various forms of arbitral consent previously discussed in this chapter are all predispute submissions to arbitration, whereby the host state presents an open offer to arbitrate (either by agreement with the investor's home state, or with the investor in a concession or investment contract, or to all potential investors through investment legislation) before conflict has arisen, and in many cases before the relevant investment has even been made. However, the investment arbitration system can just as easily accommodate a state's consent to arbitrate made *after* a dispute has crystallized. Normally in the form of a separate agreement between both parties to the dispute, such a submission is sometimes referred to as a *compromis*.[88]

In some ways, a *compromis* implies less constraint of state sovereignty than would an investment protection treaty or other predispute consent instrument.[89] For decades it was widely accepted in some developing countries that even private parties should not be permitted to consent irrevocably to binding arbitration before a dispute arises, because the parties cannot know the nature of the disputes they are

---

[85] For the text of the U.S.-Morocco FTA, *see id.*

[86] *See id* for references.

[87] *See, e.g.*, U.S.-Chile FTA, art. 10; *cf.* U.S. Model BIT of 2004, art. 10.

[88] *See, e.g.*, Explanatory Note by the UNCITRAL Secretariat on UNCITRAL Model Law on International Commercial Arbitration, *available at* http://www.sice.oas.org/DISPUTE/comarb/uncitral/icomarbe3.asp. Likewise in investment arbitration *compromis* refers to an agreement to refer an existing dispute to arbitration, *see* Antonio Parra, *Role of ICSID in Settlement of Investment Disputes*, 16(1) ICSID News (Winter 1999), *available at* http://icsid.worldbank.org/. It should be noted, however, that in public international law *compromis* refers to an agreement referring disputes that have arisen or may arise to arbitration. For the definition of *compromis* in public international law *see Encyclopedia of Public International Law* (Berhnhardt ed., 1997).

[89] In the past some jurisdictions did not deem predispute submissions to arbitration valid. *See, e.g.*, Horatio A. Grigera Naón, *Arbitration in Latin America*, 5 Int'l Arb. 137 (1989); Samir Saleh, *Commercial Arbitration in the Arab Middle East* 49–50 (1984). This trend is changing, however; *see, e.g.*, Amazu A. Asouzu, *International Commercial Arbitration and African States: Practice, Participation and International Development* 142 (Cambridge University Press 2001). Nevertheless, several U.S. states still do not recognize predispute arbitration agreements, although this is overridden by the Federal Arbitration Act. Born, *supra* note 30, at 152.

excluding from court jurisdiction. Instead, a predispute agreement to arbitration would be construed as a mere agreement to agree, with constitutional mandates guaranteeing access to court justice often prohibiting enforcement of such submissions. Where the rights to be adjudicated are not only unknown but likely to implicate the public interest, as in investor-state disputes, concerns about predispute submission are only amplified.

But from the investor's perspective, the prospect of a possible postdispute submission to arbitration usually offers small comfort. Once a dispute has arisen, states are unlikely to voluntarily relinquish their sovereignty by submitting disputes to neutral, binding arbitration, preferring instead to resolve them in their own courts. In the absence of a contract or treaty, there is normally little for the state to gain from such a submission. Furthermore, the acrimony that frequently characterizes the parties' relations after the dispute arises can make agreement on even minor points practically impossible, let alone agreement on the possibility and parameters of a complex international arbitration process.

The United States has responded to the difficulty of obtaining consent from developing nations in a particularly direct way. In 1962 the Governor of the Brazilian State of Rio Grande do Sul canceled the operating license of a local subsidiary of International Telephone and Telegraph Company of New York and confiscated the subsidiary's property within the state.[90] Rio Grande do Sul compensated IT&T US$400,000 for property the company had valued at US$8 million.[91] In reaction to the Brazilian expropriation, as well as to similar actions taken by the government of Cuba, the U.S. Congress adopted a law that became known as the Hickenlooper Amendment.[92] This law, which was an amendment to the Foreign Assistance Act of 1961,[93] directly tied the provision of U.S. foreign aid funds to the issue of outstanding uncompensated expropriation. Opposed by President Kennedy and the Department of State,[94] the bill nevertheless was enacted into law. Under the Hickenlooper Amendment, the president was required to deny foreign aid to expropriating governments until they took positive steps to

---

[90] N.Y. Times, Feb. 17, 1962, at 1.

[91] *Id.*

[92] A detailed history of the first Hickenlooper Amendment can be found *in* Richard B. Lillich, *Protection of Foreign Investment* 117–46 (1965). *See also* Vandevelde, *Reassessing the Hickenlooper Amendment*, 29 Va. J. Int'l L. 115, 127 (1988).

[93] Foreign Assistance Act of 1961, Pub. L. No. 87–195, 75 Stat. 424.

[94] Kennedy stated that "Nobody has ever questioned the right of any government to seize property, providing the compensation is fair. . . . We don't want to make those who dislike us work easy [sic] by reacting to things which happen in a way that strengthens them and weakens the influence of the United States." N.Y. Times, Mar. 8, 1962, at 14. The State Department also expressed concern that bypassing traditional diplomatic channels would jeopardize ongoing settlement negotiations. Hearings on 5.2996 Before the Senate on Foreign Relations, 87th Congress, 2d Session at 557–68 (1962).

provide "speedy compensation" for property taken, equivalent to the "full value" of those assets.[95]

The Hickenlooper Amendment was intended to compel expropriating governments either to submit to arbitration or to compensate U.S. investors in appropriate fashion. In the early years after the enactment of the Hickenlooper Amendment, however, neither instance in which it was relevant led to arbitration. The law was applied at least in two instances, to Ceylon and Ethiopia, and resulted in the suspension of foreign aid after these governments expropriated the assets of U.S. companies and declined to compensate the owners in the manner prescribed by the Hickenlooper Amendment.[96] In 1994 Congress passed the Helms Amendment,[97] which superseded the Hickenlooper Amendment.[98] Under the Helms Amendment, the president is no longer required to suspend foreign aid, but rather has the discretion to do so.[99]

The current version of Helms Amendment, 22 USCS § 2370a, provides the following:

> § 2370a. Expropriation of United States Property
>
> (a) Prohibition. None of the funds made available to carry out this Act, the Foreign Assistance Act of 1961, or the Arms Export Control Act may be provided to a government or any agency or instrumentality thereof, if the government of such country (other than a country described if [in] subsection (d))—
>
> > (1) has on or after January 1, 1956—
> >
> > > (A) nationalized or expropriated the property of any United States person,
> > >
> > > (B) repudiated or nullified any contract with any United States person, or
> > >
> > > (C) taken any other action (such as the imposition of discriminatory taxes or other exactions) which has the effect of seizing ownership or control of the property of any United States person, and
> >
> > (2) has not, within the period specified in subsection (c), either—

---

[95] 22 U.S.C. 620(e), as originally passed. This law was known as First Hickenlooper; thereafter, in the wake of the famous *Sabbatino* case, *Banco Nacional de Cuba v. Sabbatino*, 376 U.S. 398 (1964), Congress passed another amendment, known as Second Hickenlooper, which is irrelevant to this discussion. For a clear description of the two see Barry E. Carter, Philip R. Trimble, & Curtis A. Bradley, *International Law* (Aspen 4th ed. 2003).

[96] See cases of Ceylon (1963) and Ethiopia (1979) *in* Vandevelde, *supra* note 92, at 145–48.

[97] Section 527 of 1994–1995 Foreign Relations Authorization Act, PL 103–236, 1994 HR 2333; currently 22 USCS § 2370a.

[98] See *Talenti v. Clinton*, 102 F.3d 573, 578 (D.C. Cir. 1996); *Betteroads Asphalt Corp. v. U.S.*, 106 F. Supp. 2d 262, 267–69 (D.P.R. 2000). See also María L. Pagán, *U.S. Legal Requirements Affecting Trade with Cuba*, 7 Pace Int'l L. Rev. 485, 512 (1996).

[99] *Betteroads Asphalt Corp. v. U.S.*, 106 F. Supp. 2d 262, 264 (D.P.R. 2000).

(A) returned the property,

(B) provided adequate and effective compensation for such property in convertible foreign exchange or other mutually acceptable compensation equivalent to the full value thereof, as required by international law,

(C) offered a domestic procedure providing prompt, adequate and effective compensation in accordance with international law, or

(D) submitted the dispute to arbitration under the rules of the Convention for the Settlement of Investment Disputes or other mutually agreeable binding international arbitration procedure.

(b) Other actions. The President shall instruct the United States Executive Directors of each multilateral development bank and international financial institution to vote against any loan or other utilization of the funds of such bank or institution for the benefit of any country to which assistance is prohibited under subsection (a), unless such assistance is directed specifically to programs which serve the basic human needs of the citizens of that country.

(c) Period for settlement of claims. The period of time described in subsection (a)(2) is the latest of the following—

(1) 3 years after the date on which a claim was filed,

(2) in the case of a country that has a totalitarian or authoritarian government at the time of the action described in subsection (a)(1), 3 years after the date of installation of a democratically elected government, or

(3) 90 days after the date of enactment of this Act [enacted April 30, 1994].

(d) Excepted countries and territories. This section shall not apply to any country established by international mandate through the United Nations or to any territory recognized by the United States Government to be in dispute . . .

(e) Resumption of assistance. A prohibition or termination of assistance under subsection (a) and an instruction to vote against loans under subsection (b) shall cease to be effective when the President certifies in writing to the Speaker of the House of Representatives and to the Committee on Foreign Relations of the Senate that such government has taken one of the steps described in subsection (a)(2). . . .

. . . .

(g) Waiver. The President may waive the prohibitions in subsections (a) and (b) for a country, on an annual basis, if the President determines and so notifies Congress that it is in the national interest to do so.

(h) "United States person" defined. For the purpose of this section, the term "United States person" means a United States citizen or corporation, partnership, or association at least 50 percent beneficially owned by United States citizens.

Although the Helms Amendment has rarely been invoked, at least one investor managed to employ it to force a government to provide consent to investor-state arbitration. In *Santa Elena v. Costa Rica*,[100] Costa Rica had, by a 1978 decree,

---

[100] *Santa Elena, supra* note 62, *reprinted in* 15 ICSID Rev.-F.I.L.J. 169 (2000).

expropriated land for a new national park. The land was owned by Compañía del Desarrollo de Santa Elena, S.A. (CDSE), a development company whose shareholders were mostly American. CDSE had spent approximately US$395,000 for the property and had begun development of a luxury resort there. Costa Rica offered CDSE approximately US$1.9 million as compensation for the property, but CDSE refused, claiming instead that based on its own appraisal, the land was worth US$6.4 million. The parties litigated the issue of compensation before Costa Rican courts for nearly twenty years, without coming to a mutually satisfactory result. At some point in 1994 or 1995, CDSE invoked the Helms Amendment, asking the United States government to vote against a pending US$175 million loan from the Inter-American Development Bank. The United States complied, and the loan disbursement was delayed until Costa Rica consented to submit the case to international arbitration.[101] The resulting tribunal eventually held that US$4.15 million constituted a fair value for the confiscated property and, including compound interest, awarded CDSE US$16 million.[102]

---

[101] *Id.* ¶¶ 24–26.

[102] The tribunal was particularly eminent: The party-appointed arbitrators were Elihu Lauterpacht and Prosper Weil, and the Chairman was Yves Fortier.

XI. The Concept of *Investment*

The notion of investment and its definitions are inherently vague, and the meanings of the term *investment* in economics and investment protection instruments do not necessarily coincide. However, this chapter is only concerned with the definition of the term in investment protection instruments such as international treaties and national investment laws. These instruments set forth definitions of investment that are quite broad and unhelpful; the listed categories of things that constitute investment under these instruments illustrate assets that tribunals would normally find within the scope of protection even without the help of explicit language.[1]

Determining whether a particular economic activity constitutes investment under the definitions of investment protection instruments is one of the prerequisites for jurisdiction of an arbitral tribunal. This chapter examines the definition of the term *investment* under investment treaties, national investment legislations, and the Washington Convention, in light of the relevant case law.

A. The Changing Definition of *Investment*: The Historical Perspective

Investment in the international dispute resolution field has a wide range of both long and short definitions, not all of which are fully consistent with one another. Indeed, there is not even full agreement whether *investment* is a thing or an activity. Although investment treaties tend to view investment as a subset of assets,[2]

---

[1] The two exceptions are: (1) expansions of the concept of investment, such as explicit coverage of initial, preinvestment activity or of purely commercial contractual rights, or (2) particularly narrowed definitions, for example, requiring that a project be government-approved before it can qualify as an investment.

[2] *See, e.g.*, U.S.-Democratic Republic of the Congo bilateral investment treaty (BIT) (1994), art. 1 (1)(b) (" 'investment' means every kind of investment . . . owned or controlled directly or indirectly by [an investor]. . . ."); Canada-Czech BIT (1992), art. 1(a) ("the term 'investment' means any kind of asset held or invested either directly, or indirectly by an investor. . . ."); U.K.-Chile BIT (1996), art. 1(1)(a) (" 'investment' means every kind of asset. . . ."); Viet Nam-Finland BIT (1993), art. 1(1) ("The term "Investment" means any kind of asset, invested by an investor. . . .").

economists and legal commentators more often describe it as a phenomenon, process, or action.[3] This semantic diversity, and at times confusion, has inevitably infused nearly all recent analyses of the notion of investment in the arbitration context.

As noted in Chapter I,[4] cross-border investment in the economic sense falls into three categories: foreign direct investment (FDI), portfolio investment, and indirect investment. Historically, prior to the advent of modern investment treaties, *foreign investment* under customary international law referred to the first category,[5] which among other things required total control and participation in management of the respective enterprise—in contrast to portfolio and indirect investment, which did not require them.[6]

Modern investment protection instruments,[7] however, have expanded the legal definition of *investment* by including the latter two categories within the definition of investment.[8] Participation in management, for example, does not appear among the typical characteristics of investment under the Washington Convention proposed by Schreuer.[9] Similarly, where the respondent government's consent is silent on this point, investment arbitration tribunals seem generally unconcerned with the question of whether the foreign claimant has direct control or participation in the day-to-day business decisions of a venture. This marks the abandonment of the once-important distinction between foreign direct investment and portfolio investment,[10] where the former

---

[3] M. Sornarajah, *The International Law on Foreign Investment* 7 (Cambridge University Press 2004) ("Foreign investment involves the transfer of tangible or intangible assets from one country into another for the purpose of use in that country to generate wealth under the total or partial control of the owner of the assets"); *cf.* Stefan A. Riesenfeld, *Foreign Investments*, in 8 *Encyclopedia of Public International Law* 246 (Rudolf Bernhardt ed., Elsevier Science 1990) (foreign investment is "the transfer of funds or materials from one country . . . to another country . . . to be used in the conduct of an enterprise in that country in return for a direct or indirect participation in the earnings of the enterprise").

[4] *See* pp. 1–2 *supra*.

[5] Sornarajah, *supra* note 3, at 7–8.

[6] *Id.* One characteristic of FDI, thus, was a more lasting interest of the investor in the investment, as compared with portfolio investment, where investors often did not have a long-term interest.

[7] Mainly investment treaties and domestic legislations for protection of foreign investment.

[8] *See, e.g.*, Argentina-U.S. BIT (1991), art. 1.

[9] *See* p. 260 *infra*.

[10] K. V. S. K. Nathan, *The ICSID Convention: The Law of the International Centre for Settlement of Investment Disputes* (2000).

was the true subject of investment protection treaties and the latter beyond the pale of host states' obligations and investor states' right to protect their nationals.[11] Now largely rendered defunct by the definitions contained in most investment treaties, the previous distinction[12] was based in part on the conviction that only participation in management could signal the foreign entity's stable—and therefore constructive—involvement in the host state's economic affairs and its *economic development*. Furthermore, portfolio investment does not lead to technology transfer, training of local cadres, and other beneficial side effects of direct investment—all indicia of contributions to "economic development."[13]

In the language of today's international investment arbitration decisions, however, and therefore in the criteria that give shape to the modern notion of protectable investment, the relevance of management participation and the need to distinguish the subspecies of "portfolio investment" have clearly declined.[14]

---

[11] A statement by the Canadian High Commission regarding the scope of investment guarantees through the Export Development Corporation emphasized that "mainly joint ventures" could be so insured, whereas "portfolio investments . . . are excluded from coverage." Cited in Adeoye Akinsanya, *International Protection of Direct Foreign Investments in the Third World*, 36 Int'l & Comp. L. Q. 58, 69 (1987).

[12] Sornarajah, *supra* note 3, at 7 ("in portfolio investment, there is a divorce between management and control of the company and the share ownership in it"); Edward Graham & Paul Krugman, *Foreign Direct Investment in the United States* 7 (1991) ("foreign direct investment is formally defined as ownership of assets by foreign residents for purposes of controlling the use of those assets"); United Nations Conference on Trade and Development (UNCTAD), *Trends in International Investment Agreements*, at 56, U.N. Doc UNCTAD/ITE/IIT/13-E.99.II.D.23, (1999) ("instruments that concern the cross-border movement of capital and resources usually define investment in narrow terms, distinguishing FDI from other types of investment (e.g. portfolio investment). . . . [while] [i]nstruments mainly directed at the protection of FDI usually define investment in a broad and comprehensive manner").

[13] UNCTAD, *International Investment Agreements: Flexibility for Development* 72, U.N. Doc UNCTAD/ITE/IIT/18-E.00.II.D.6 (2000). The International Monetary Fund's definition of "direct investment" reflects this linkage, to wit: "investment that is made to acquire a lasting interest in an enterprise operating in an economy other than that of the investor, the investor's purpose being to have an effective voice in the management of the enterprise." *IMF Balance of Payments Manual* 136 (4th ed. 1977).

[14] See *American Mfg. & Trading v. Zaire*, ICSID Case No. ARB/93/1 (Award of Feb. 21, 1997) (American company's "investment" was its shares in a Zairian company); *Genin v. Estonia*, ICSID Case No. ARB/99/2 (Award of June 25, 2001), ¶ 324 (U.S. citizen's equity in Estonian company qualified as "investment"). As early as 1967, the OECD Draft Convention on the Protection of Foreign Property, 7 I.L.M. 118 (1968) [hereinafter Draft Convention], adopted a definition that appears to include portfolio investment. Article 1 provides for protection for all foreign "property," which is defined as "all property, rights and interests, whether held directly or indirectly, including the interest which a member of a company is deemed to have in the property of the company. . . ." Draft Convention, art. 9(c).

B. Definitions of *Investment* in Investment Protection Instruments

1. Definitions of *Investment* in Investment Treaties

Most recent bilateral investment treaties, including those based on U.S. and Organization for Economic Cooperation and Development (OECD) models, have adopted broad and descriptive definitions of covered investments.[15] Possibly the broadest such definition is contained in certain bilateral investment treaties (BITs), such as the Ecuador-United Kingdom BIT, describing investment as "every kind of asset."[16] Article 1 of the Ecuador-United Kingdom BIT (1994) provides that:

> (a) "investment" means every kind of asset and in particular, though not exclusively, includes:
>
> (i) movable and immovable property and any other property rights such as mortgages, liens and pledges;
>
> (ii) shares, stock and debentures of companies or interests in the property of such companies;
>
> (iii) claims to money or to any performance under contract having a financial value;
>
> (iv) intellectual property rights and goodwill;
>
> (v) business concessions conferred by law or under contract, including concessions to search for, cultivate, or exploit natural resources.

As noted earlier such definitions do not provide much guidance when a case involves an activity that does not neatly fit within one of the enumerated categories. They are distinct from, and marginally more useful than, the circular approach of the pre-2004 U.S. BITs, which state that investment is "every kind of investment owned or controlled directly or indirectly."[17] Treaties of this latter sort normally illustrate the subject-matter scope of their application by providing a

---

[15] UNCTAD, *Bilateral Investment Treaties 1995–2005: Trends in Investment Rulemaking* 17 (UNCTAD Draft of Apr. 2006) [hereinafter UNCTAD 2006 Report]; UNCTAD, *supra* note 13, at 70; UNCTAD, *supra* note 12, at 45 (in most BITs "[t]he definition of investment is broad and open-ended so that it can accommodate new forms of foreign investment"). Rudolph Dolzer & Margrete Stevens, *Bilateral Investment Treaties* 25–31 (1995).

[16] Agreement among the Government of Brunei Darussalam, Republic of Indonesia, Malaysia, Republic of the Philippines, Republic of Singapore, and the Kingdom of Thailand for the Promotion and Protection of Investments, signed Dec. 15, 1987 (*ASEAN Investment Agreement*), art. I(3). The UNCTAD 2006 Report refers to these definitions as "asset-based" definitions. UNCTAD 2006 Report, *supra* note 15, at 8.

[17] Treaty between the Government of the United States of America and the Government of the Republic of Trinidad and Tobago Concerning the Encouragement and Reciprocal Protection of Investment (1994), art. I(d). The U.S. Model BIT of 2004 abandoned that formula in favor of a new more precise, but still broad and nonexhaustive definition of investment, which defines investment as "every kind of asset . . ." and then goes on to explain the characteristics of investment and finally enumerates various forms that investment may take. *See* 2004 U.S. Model BIT, art. 1, *available at* www.ustr.gov.

nonexhaustive list of asset categories that fall within the definition of *investment*.[18] Typical categories found in most investment treaties include real estate and other direct property rights, shareholdings and other forms of participation in local companies, claims to payment or performance, intellectual property and other intangibles, and concession agreements.[19]

In contrast to the nonexhaustive lists of the above treaties, some treaties such as the North American Free Trade Agreement (NAFTA) set forth a broad but *exhaustive* list of covered assets.[20] NAFTA Article 1139 uses the words "investment means" rather than "investment includes." Investments under NAFTA, for example, extend to both foreign direct investment (an enterprise),[21] portfolio investment (equity securities), partnership and other interests that give the owner a right to share in profits or liquidated assets,[22] and tangible and intangible property "acquired in the expectation . . . of economic benefit."[23] Loan financing, meanwhile, is only protected where funds flow within a business group, or where debt is issued on a relatively long-term basis.[24] Contract rights or claims to money that do not fall under other categories of investment are covered only if they involve a "commitment of capital or other resources in the territory of a Party . . . to economic activity in such territory."[25] NAFTA complements its exhaustive list

---

[18] Such a list would seem somewhat redundant where the treaty definition is "every kind of asset," but disputes could theoretically arise as to the meaning of "asset."

[19] Christoph Schreuer, *The ICSID Convention: A Commentary 129* (Cambridge University Press, 2001). Article 1 of U.S.-Argentine BIT, for example, provides that *investment* includes the following: "[T]angible and intangible property, including rights, such as mortgages, liens and pledges; a company or shares of stock or other interests in a company or interests in the assets thereof; claim to money or a claim to performance having economic value and directly related to an investment; intellectual property which includes, inter alia, rights relating to: literary and artistic works, including sound recordings, inventions in all fields of human endeavor, industrial designs, semiconductor mask works, trade secrets, know-how, and confidential business information, and trademarks, service marks, and trade names; and any right conferred by law or contract, and any licenses and permits pursuant to law. . . ."

[20] *See also* Canada Model Foreign Investment Protection Agreement (2004), *available at* http://www.international.gc.ca/.

[21] North American Free Trade Agreement (NAFTA), art. 1139(a), *reprinted in* 32 I.L.M. 289 (1993).

[22] *Id.* art. 1139(e–f).

[23] *Id.* art. 1139(g).

[24] *Id.* art. 1139(d); Jürgen Kurtz, *A General Investment Agreement in the WTO? Lessons from Chapter 11 of NAFTA and the OECD Multilateral Agreement on Investment*, 23 U. Pa. J. Int'l Econ. L. 713, 734 (2002).

[25] NAFTA, art. 1139(h) (such contracts include those "involving the presence of an investor's property in the territory of the Party, including turnkey or construction contracts, or concessions," and "contracts where remuneration depends substantially on the production, revenues or profits of an enterprise").

of investment categories with a negative definition, establishing certain kinds of property that are *not* to be considered investments under the treaty:

> [I]nvestment does not mean,
>
> (i) claims to money that arise solely from
>
> > (i) commercial contracts for the sale of goods or services by a national or enterprise in the territory of a Party to an enterprise in the territory of another Party, or
> >
> > (ii) the extension of credit in connection with a commercial transaction, such as trade financing, other than a loan covered by subparagraph (d); or
>
> (j) any other claims to money that do not involve the kinds of interests set out in subparagraphs (a) through (h) . . .[26]

Certain post-NAFTA accords have followed the NAFTA exhaustive-list model for defining *investment*, including the Canada-Chile Free Trade Agreement.[27]

A more useful recent approach to definition of investment can be found in the investment chapter of the U.S.-Singapore Free Trade Agreement (USSFTA), which was signed in May 2003 and U.S. Model BIT of 2004.[28] Like the 2004 U.S. Model BIT, the USSFTA defines investment broadly, as "every asset owned or controlled, directly or indirectly, by an investor, that has the characteristics of an investment,"[29] and includes a nonexhaustive list of forms such investment may take. Besides the typical *core* investment types, such as enterprises, shares, intellectual property rights, and movable or immovable property,[30] these forms also cover various debt instruments,[31] "futures, options, and other derivatives,"[32] and "turnkey, construction, management, production, concession, revenue-sharing, and other similar contracts."[33] The USSFTA is further innovative in that it includes explanatory notes, designed to clarify and narrow the seemingly boundless definition. For example, the drafters point out that not only is the list of investment types not exhaustive, but certain activities or assets listed may not qualify as investment, depending on their economic nature: "Where an asset lacks the characteristics of an investment, that asset is not an investment regardless of the form it may take. The characteristics of an investment include the commitment of capital, the expectation of gain or profit, or

---

[26] *Id.*

[27] Canada-Chile Free Trade Agreement (1997), art. G-40, *reprinted at* 36 I.L.M. 1067 (1997).

[28] Alexa Olesen, *Singapore to Ink Landmark Free Trade Pact with the United States*, Associated Press, May 4, 2003.

[29] U.S.-Singapore Free Trade Agreement (USSFTA) (2003), art. 15.1(13). *See also* U.S. Model BIT of 2004, art. 1. *See also* U.S.-Uruguay BIT (2005), art. 1.

[30] USSFTA, *supra* note 29, art. 15.1(13)(a),(b),(f),(h).

[31] *Id.* art. 15.1(13)(c).

[32] *Id.* art. 15.1(13)(d).

[33] *Id.* art. 15.1(13)(e).

the assumption of risk."[34] Similarly, the notes specify the following with regard to debt instruments:

> Some forms of debt, such as bonds, debentures, and long-term notes, are more likely to have the characteristics of an investment, while other forms of debt, such as claims to payment that are immediately due and result from the sale of goods or services, are less likely to have such characteristics.[35]

Thus, the USSFTA's approach is more helpful than both the illustrative list language of the most recent bilateral investment treaties and the exhaustive list approach of NAFTA Article 1139; although conserving a good deal of flexibility and specifically naming certain very modern forms of economic activity as investment, the treaty provides guidance to arbitrators in their case-by-case analysis, directing them to look past the *form* to the economic essence of each project or operation.[36]

By adding *characteristics* as part of the definition of an investment, as well as by providing other explanatory footnotes regarding what certain terms mean, and do not mean, the drafters of USSFTA and 2004 U.S. Model have provided guidance to arbitral tribunals.

Finally, some more recent investment treaties limit the scope of covered investments to those that have been made in accordance with the laws of the host state.[37] There are also other recent investment instruments that exclude certain categories of investment such as portfolio investment from the coverage of the respective treaty.[38]

---

[34] *Id.* at note 15–1. U.S. Model BIT of 2004 has made these characteristics part of the definition in the main body text of the article. 2004 U.S. Model BIT, art. 1.

[35] USSFTA, *supra* note 29, at note 15–2.

[36] Although, as noted earlier, the Canada-Chile FTA follows the NAFTA exhaustive-list model, the U.S.-Chile FTA tracks the USSFTA language essentially verbatim. U.S.-Chile FTA (2006), art. 10.27.

[37] *See* Chile-New Zealand BIT (1999), art. 1 (" 'investment' means any kind of asset or rights related to it provided that the investment has been made in accordance with the laws and regulations of the Contracting Party receiving it"); El Salvador-Spain BIT (1995), art. II (*see also Inceysa Vallisoletana S.L. v. El Salvador*, ICSID Case No. ARB/03/26 (Award of Aug. 2, 2006), ¶¶ 184–207 (discussing the El Salvador-Spain BIT requirement that the investment be made in accordance with the laws of the host state)); Italy-Philippines BIT (1988), art. II(1) (" 'investment' means accepted in accordance with the respective laws and regulations. . . ."); U.K.-Oman BIT (1995), art. 1(a) (" 'Investment' means every kind of asset admitted into the territory of each Contracting party in accordance with its laws and regulations. . . ."); Belgium & Luxemburg-Rwanda BIT (1983), art. 1(3)(a) ("The term 'investments' shall mean any . . . contribution . . . made under the laws of the State. . . ."). These provisions, effectively, establish a screening right for the host state to exclude non-conforming investments.

[38] *See, e.g.*, Association of South East Asian Nations (ASEAN) Agreement, *supra* note 16, art. 2. Other investment treaties may not explicitly exclude portfolio investment but they define investment in such a way that it likely does not include portfolio investment. *See, e.g.*, Denmark–Lithuania BIT (1992), art. 1 (investments must be "acquired for the purpose of establishing lasting economic relations between an investor and an enterprise.").

2. Definition of *Investment* in National Investment Laws[39]

Investment laws define *investment* in a variety of ways. Similar to investment treaties, some national investment laws contain an exhaustive list of activities that may be considered an investment. For example, the Foreign Investment Statute of Chile provides that foreign investment consists of the following:

> a) Freely-convertible foreign currency . . . b) Tangible assets of any description or condition . . . c) Technology in its various forms when eligible for capitalization . . . d) Credits associated with a foreign investment . . . e) Capitalization of external credits and debts in freely convertible currencies when incurred with due authorization . . . and f) Capitalization of profits eligible for transfer abroad.[40]

Other investment laws contain nonexhaustive lists. For example, Armenia's foreign investment law provides in the relevant part that "foreign investment" means "*any type of property, including* financial resources and intellectual values, which are directly invested by a foreign investor in commercial and other activities implemented in the territory of the Republic of Armenia for gaining of profit (revenue) or for achievement of any other beneficial result."[41]

Although these definitions mainly associate foreign investment activity with the purpose of gaining profit, some definitions are broader and encompass nonprofit activities. For example, Ukraine's foreign investment legislation defines foreign investments as "values invested by foreign investors in objects of investment activity according to the legislation of Ukraine to produce revenues or *to achieve a social effect*."[42]

---

[39] See generally Antonio Parra, *Principles Governing Foreign Investment, as Reflected in National Investment Codes*, 7 ICSID Rev.-F.I.L.J. 428 (1992). Domestic laws of a number of countries have traditionally restricted entry of foreign direct investment through a variety of screening mechanisms such as the requirement of obtaining government approvals. General screening is rare today. More limited screening, particularly in regard to important economic sectors, may still exist. *See generally* Thomas Pollan, *Legal Framework for the Admission of FDI* 57 *et seq.* (Eleven 2006).

[40] Chile: Foreign Investment Statute, art. 1. Decree Law 600, *reprinted in* Chile, 1 *Investment Laws of the World* (Oceana 2003) [hereinafter *Investment Laws of the World*]; *see also* Indonesia: Law Number 1 of 1967 Concerning Foreign Investment, art. 2, *reprinted in* Indonesia, 4 *Investment Laws of the World*.

[41] Armenia: The Law of the Republic of Armenia on Foreign Investments, § 1, art. 1, *reprinted in* 1 *Investment Laws of the World, supra* note 40 (Armenia 1995, emphasis added). *See also* Law of the Republic of Moldova on Foreign Investment, No. 998-XII of Apr. 1, 1992, art. 3(1), *reprinted in* 5 *Investment Laws of the World, supra* note 40 (Moldova 2002).

[42] Ukraine: Law on Ukraine on the Status of Foreign Investment (Implemented by the Resolution of Verchova Rada N94/96-BP on Mar. 19, 199), *reprinted in* 10 *Investment Laws of the World, supra* note 40 (Ukraine 1995, emphasis added).

Investment laws may restrict the economic sectors in which foreign investment is permitted, mainly but not exclusively to protect national security.[43] Some investment laws set a threshold amount below which the investment law does not apply. The Republic of Korea's Foreign Investment Promotion Act specifically limits the meaning of foreign investment to "an investment which amounts . . . to 50 million won. . . ."[44] The act does not clarify the status of foreign investments that do not reach the threshold, but there is no ban against their entry. Presumably, such investments are treated in the same manner as investments of nationals.

Not all investment laws provide for arbitration of investment disputes.[45] Investment laws that consent to international arbitration often define investment (and scope of consent) more narrowly than investment treaties.[46] Common limitations within this category of investment laws include the requirement of state approval of the underlying project and a focus on capital contributions.[47] For example, the 1997 foreign investment law of Tanzania defines investment as "the creation or acquisition of new business assets, and includes the expansion, restructuring, or rehabilitation of an existing business enterprise."[48] However, some more recent investment legislation in capital-importing countries tracks broad BIT language on the definition of

---

[43] Laos' investment law, for example, specifically excludes foreign investors from investing in or operating "enterprises which are detrimental to national security, the national environment, public health or the national culture, or which violate the laws and regulation[s] of the Lao PDR." Laos: Law on the Promotion and Management of Foreign Investment in the Lao People's Democratic Republic, § 1 art. 2 (1994), *reprinted in* 4 *Investment Laws of the World, supra* note 40 (Laos 1995). *See also* Tonga: Foreign Investment Act No. 22 of 2002, Schedule 1 (Regulation 3), *reprinted in* 9 *Investment Laws of the World, supra* note 40 (Tonga 2007) (reserving for only Tongan investment such sectors as taxis, used motor vehicle dealers, grocery retail, "[b]aking of white loaf bread," cultural activities, raising chickens for eggs, security, and some types of farming and fishing); Indonesian Decree No. 31 of 1995 Concerning the List of Sectors That Are Closed for Investment, *reprinted in* 4 *Investment Laws of the World* 21, *supra* note 40 (Indonesia 1997) (closes some sectors to investors that are entirely foreign owned, such as seaport construction, electric power, telecom, shipping, airfreight, and potable water; and other sectors to investors with any foreign ownership, such as taxis, local shipping, retail trade, television and radio, and operation of cinema[s]).

[44] Korea: Decree of the Foreign Investment Promotion Act (Mar. 8, 2005), art. 2, *reprinted in* 4 *Investment Laws of the World* 38, *supra* note 40 (Korea 2007). As of Aug. 8, 2007, this amount was approximately US$54,056.

[45] *See generally* Chapter X for the discussion of various ways in which legislation provides for arbitration.

[46] N. V. S. K. Nathan, *Submissions to the International Centre for Settlement of Investment Disputes in Breach of the Convention*, 12 J. Int'l Arb. 27, 29 (1995). *See also, e.g.,* Egypt Investment Law (1977), art. 2.

[47] Angolan investment law, for example, requires an authorization from the Angolan National Private Investment Agency for foreign investments exceeding US$100,000. Private Investment Law (Law No. 11/03 of May 13, 2003), art. 9.3, *reprinted in* 1 *Investment Laws of the World, supra* note 40 (Angola 2003).

[48] Tanzania Investment Act (1997), art. 3, *reprinted in* 9 *Investment Laws of the World, supra* note 40 (Tanzania 1999).

investment.[49] In any case BITs have become the primary source of state consent to investment arbitration, reducing the significance of the *investment* definition contained in national legislation.[50]

C. Definition of *Investment* and Its Implications for the Jurisdiction of Arbitral Tribunals Under the Washington Convention

1. *Travaux Preparatoire* of the Washington Convention Regarding the Notion of Investment Under Article 25

Article 25 of the Washington Convention limits the jurisdiction *ratione materiae*, or subject matter jurisdiction, of the International Centre for Settlement of Investment Disputes (ICSID) to "any legal dispute arising directly out of an *investment*."[51] It gives no definition of *investment*, however. The lack of definition is not for want of trying; during the drafting of the convention, various proposals were made by delegates who sought to provide more explicit guidance as to the scope of the ICSID's jurisdiction. The convention's First Draft set forth a general definition: "any contribution of money or other assets of economic value for an indefinite period, or . . . not less than five years."[52] Problems with this definition soon become clear: the emphasis on time appeared too narrow to some, whereas others argued that the lack of criteria such as *risk* or *profit* would allow adjudication of transactions that contributed little to sustained economic development. Any more specific definition, meanwhile, risked excluding from coverage new and innovative forms of economic activity with development benefits similar to traditional foreign

---

[49] See Law of the Republic of Kazakhstan "On Investments" (2003), art. 1, *reprinted in* 4 *Investment Laws of the World*, *supra* note 40 (Kazakhstan 2004); Madagascar Investment Code (Law No. 89–026 of Dec. 29, 1989), art. 3, *reprinted in* 5 *Investment Laws of the World*, *supra* note 40 (Madagascar 1995); Law of the Kyrgyz Republic on Investments in the Kyrgyz Republic (2003), art. 1, *reprinted in* 4 *Investment Laws of the World*, *supra* note 40 (Kyrgyz Republic 2005). At least one national investment code appears to have taken the exhaustive approach of NAFTA Chapter 11. *See* Albania: Law on Foreign Investments (1993), art. 1(3), *reprinted in* 1 *Investment Laws of the World*, *supra* note 40 (Albania 1995). Some examination of the definition of investment contained in the Albanian investment code was undertaken by the tribunal in *Tradex Hellas, S.A. v. Republic of Albania*, ICSID Case No. ARB/94/2 (Decision on Jurisdiction of Dec. 24, 1996), *reprinted in* 5 ICSID Rep. 47 (2002).

[50] For a general overview of the protections provided in national investment legislation, see Antonio Parra, *The Scope of New Investment Laws and International Instruments*, in 4 *Economic Development, Foreign Investment and the Law* 27 (Pritchard, ed. 1996).

[51] Convention on the Settlement of Investment Disputes between States and Nationals of Other States (1966), art. 25(1) [hereinafter Washington Convention].

[52] *Id.* First Draft, art. 30, *found in* 1 *Analysis of Documents Concerning the Origin and Formulation of the Convention* 116 (1970).

direct investment (technology transfer and contribution of intellectual property, for example).[53]

Ultimately, the definitionless version of the convention prevailed.[54] As Delaume explained shortly after the convention was adopted,

> The term "investment" is not defined in the Convention. This omission is intentional. To give a comprehensive definition . . . would have been of limited interest since any such definition would have been too broad to serve a useful purpose [or] might have arbitrarily limited the scope of the Convention by making it impossible for the parties to refer to the Centre a dispute which would be considered by the parties as a genuine "investment" dispute though such dispute would not be one of those included in the definition in the Convention.[55]

In part delegates felt comfortable omitting a definition because it was realized that the state party to the dispute must specifically consent to arbitration in any case, and it was expected that the terms of that consent in most cases would include a definition (implied or explicit) of *investment*. The approach of the Washington Convention's drafters, therefore, was to provide the parties to a dispute maximum discretion to designate their transactions as investment subject to investor-state arbitration under ICSID auspices. Indeed, the "father" of the convention, Aron Broches, opined that "the requirement that the dispute must have arisen out of an 'investment' may be merged into the requirement of consent to jurisdiction. Presumably, the parties' agreement that a dispute is an investment dispute will be given great weight in any determination of the [ICSID]'s jurisdiction. . . ."[56] A similar position was included in the Directors' Report on the Washington Convention.[57]

---

[53] D. H. Bliesener, *La Compétence du CIRDI dans la Pratique Arbitrale*, 68 Revue de droit international et comparé 95 (1991). For a list of activities considered examples of "investment" at the time of the drafting of the Washington Convention, see Michael M. Moore, *International Arbitration Between States and Foreign Investors—the World Bank Organization*, 18 Stan. L. Rev. 1369, 1362 (1966).

[54] W. M. Tupman, *Case Studies in the Jurisdiction of the International Centre for Investment Disputes*, 35 Int'l & Comp. L. Q. 813, 816 (1986).

[55] G. R. Delaume, *Convention on the Settlement of Investment Disputes Between States and Nationals of Other States*, 1 Int. Law. 64, 70 (1966).

[56] Aron Broches, *The Convention on the Settlement of Investment Disputes: Some Observations on Jurisdiction*, 5 Colum. J. Transnat'l L. 263, 268 (1966). *See also* Tupman, *supra* note 54, at 816 ("In agreeing to [International Centre for Settlement of Investment Disputes] ICSID arbitration . . .the parties would seem to have considerable latitude in determining that theirs is a legal relationship between a host State and a foreign investor").

[57] *Report of the Executive Directors of the World Bank on the Convention on the Settlement of Investment Disputes Between States and Nationals of Other States*, reprinted in 4 I.L.M. 524 (1965) ("No attempt was made to define the term 'investment' given the essential requirement of consent by the parties"). The Directors' Report has been described as the clearest source of the ICSID drafters' "legislative intent." Josef P. Sirefman, *The World Bank Plan for Investment Dispute Arbitration*, 20 Arb. J. 168 (1965). *See also* Nathan, *supra* note 46, at 30 ("it has been suggested by some writers that where the parties have agreed that a dispute involves an investment, the ICSID tribunal is not required to check if the alleged investment is also an investment under the ICSID Convention").

In the end, however, a textual analysis of the convention and institution rules reveals,[58] and commentators now agree,[59] that there is an objective boundary to the definition of *investment* for purposes of ICSID jurisdiction, which is no different from other jurisdictional issues. The parties to an investment dispute

> have considerable freedom to determine for themselves whether, for the purposes of the ICSID Convention, their dispute arises out of an investment. That freedom is not, however, unlimited; it is not so extensive as to permit parties to submit to arbitration under the ICSID Convention disputes that clearly do not relate to investments.[60]

This objective limitation on the parties' discretion to define investment in the context of the Washington Convention has other implications in modern investment arbitration practice. During the era when the Washington Convention was drafted,[61] the main vehicles for submitting an investment dispute to arbitration were arbitration clauses in investment contracts or a *compromis*. The current legal framework governing foreign investment mainly consists of investment treaties and laws, however, which by definition have been drafted prior to the emergence of a dispute, without reference to a particular investment, and hence do not leave any opportunity for the parties to the investment dispute to expressly or specifically agree whether a particular activity constitutes an investment for the purposes of Washington Convention. This limits the application of Aaron Broches' suggestion, to the extent that it envisions and accords a greater weight to the agreement

---

[58] *See* Washington Convention, art. 25(1); ICSID, *Rules of Procedure for the Institution of Conciliation and Arbitration Proceedings (Institution Rules)*, art. 2(1) (requiring potential claimants to submit to the Secretariat not only details concerning the parties' consent, but also evidence that the dispute arises directly out of an investment), *available at* http://www.worldbank.org/icsid/basicdoc/partD.htm.

[59] Schreuer, *supra* note 19, at 125; Moshe Hirsch, *The Arbitration Mechanism of the International Centre for the Settlement of Investment Disputes* 59 (1993); Aron Broches also recognized that "[a]n investment protection treaty could not effectively establish jurisdiction of the Centre beyond [the Article 25(1)] limitation *ratione materiae*. . . ." Aron Broches, *Bilateral Investment Protection Treaties and Arbitration of Investment Disputes, in Selected Essays: World Bank, ICSID, and Other Subjects of Public and Private International Law* 447, 455 (Martinus Nijhoff 1995).

[60] Ibrahim F. I. Shihata & Antonio R. Parra, *The Experience of the International Centre for Settlement of Investment Disputes*, 14 ICSID Rev.-F.I.L.J. 299, 307–08 (1999). The drafters of the convention consciously established the objective limitations of ICSID jurisdiction as distinct from the issue of consent, in part to prevent investors from using overweening bargaining power to compel small host states to submit all disputes to ICSID arbitration. Carolyn Lamm, *The Jurisdiction of the International Centre for Settlement of Investment Disputes*, 6 ICSID Rev.-F.I.L.J. 462, 474 (1991); 2 *Analysis of Documents Concerning the Origin and Formulation of the Convention* (1970), at 203–04.

[61] *See generally* Chapter III.

of the parties, to the small number of cases that are submitted to ICSID based on a *compromis* or contractual arbitration clause.[62]

2. Dual Jurisdictional Requirements for Submitting a Case Under the Washington Convention and an Investment Treaty or Law

As early as the 1975 award in *Alcoa v. Jamaica*, tribunals generally recognized that "the parties' consent to ICSID arbitration [cannot] be dispositive on all points of jurisdiction," including whether there is an investment, and that consent is merely a factor to be given "great weight" in the overall consideration of the issue.[63] In most cases the result of the jurisdictional analysis leads to an identical result for purposes of consent or definition of investment in an investment instrument, on the one hand, and Article 25(1), on the other. It is conceivable that the host state's consent or definition of investment under the respective investment instrument permits adjudication of disputes that are nonarbitrable within the ICSID system, however, and therefore subject to arbitration only under some other agreed-on dispute resolution system, such as the United Nations Commission on International Trade Law (UNCITRAL) Rules or the International Chamber of Commerce (ICC) Rules.[64]

In *Salini v. Morocco*[65] the tribunal clarified the distinct roles of these dual requirements for the purposes of obtaining ICSID jurisdiction. First, the claimant must establish that the transaction underlying the parties' dispute falls within the scope of the consent to arbitration, whether contained in a contract, national investment law, or international investment treaty.[66] Then the claimant must also establish that the transaction falls under Article 25 of Washington Convention.[67] As noted earlier there is no definition of *investment* under the Washington Convention. Thus the claimant must look into other criteria to prove that its activity is an investment within the meaning of the convention. These criteria are explained in sections (3) and (4) below.

---

[62] See, e.g., *Duke Energy Int'l Peru Invs. No. 1, Ltd. v. Peru*, ICSID Case No. ARB/03/28 (Decision on Jurisdiction, Feb. 1, 2006).

[63] *Alcoa Minerals of Jamaica, Inc. v. Gov't of Jamaica*, ICSID Case No. ARB/74/2 (Decision on Jurisdiction and Competence of July 6, 1975) at 9, *described in* John T. Schmidt, *Arbitration under the Auspices of the International Centre for Settlement of Investment Disputes: Implications of the Decision on Jurisdiction in* Alcoa Minerals of Jamaica, Inc. v. Gov't Jamaica, 17 Harv. Int'l L. J. 90, 99 (1976).

[64] Most prominently, this situation could occur with regard to the entry of an investment or certain contractual rights.

[65] *Salini Costruttori S.p.A. v. Kingdom of Morocco*, ICSID Case No. ARB/00/4 (Decision on Jurisdiction of July 23, 2001), ¶ 44, *reprinted in* 129 J. de Droit Int'l 196 (2002). *See also Fedax N.V. v. Venezuela*, ICSID Case No. ARB/96/3 (Award of July 11, 1997).

[66] *Id.* ¶¶ 43–9.

[67] *Id.* ¶¶ 50 *et seq. See also* pp. 122 and 125–26 *supra* in regard to the ICSID's gatekeeping function.

3. Survey of Jurisdictional Decisions Under the Washington Convention Based on the Type of Investment

Schreuer provides five criteria that he suggests can be used as a guide in establishing whether a particular dispute may be considered an "investment dispute" within the meaning of Article 25(1) of Washington Convention.[68] According to Professor Schreuer, investment entails the following: (a) a certain duration; (b) generation of regular profits and returns; (c) participation of both parties in risk; (d) substantial commitment of capital; and (e) contribution to the economic development of the host state.[69] ICSID tribunals that have considered Schreuer's criteria—also partly reflected in the *Salini* case and otherwise known as the *Salini* test—have had no difficulty accepting the purchase of real property,[70] shares in companies,[71] or ownership of companies[72] as investment. In addition, they have held that construction contracts are acceptable as investments under the Washington Convention,[73] as are other major contracts for projects.[74] However, tribunals have refused to accept a law firm,[75] contracts for salvage operations[76] or for sale of equipment,[77] or contingent liabilities[78] as investments. The types of projects that have failed the *Salini* test have generally been short-term projects that do not leave a clear, lasting contribution to the host economy. The following table lists various types of economic activities that claimants have characterized, before ICSID and other arbitral tribunals, as an *investment*. The table also shows the language in the applicable investment treaty on

---

[68] Schreuer, *supra* note 19, at 140.

[69] *Id. compare with* the characteristics of investment in the U.S. Model BIT of 2004, art. 1 ("the commitment of capital or other resources, the expectation of gain or profit, or the assumption of risk. . . .").

[70] *See, e.g., MTD Equity Sdn. Bhd. & MTD Chile S.A. v. Chile*, ICSID Case No. ARB/01/7 (Award of May 25, 2004).

[71] *See, e.g., Siag & Vecchi v. Egypt*, ICSID Case No. ARB/05/15 (Decision on Jurisdiction and Partial Dissenting Opinion of April 11, 2007).

[72] *See, e.g., Kardassopoulos v. Georgia*, ICSID Case No. ARB/05/18 (Decision on Jurisdiction of July 6, 2007).

[73] *See Salini, supra* note 65; *Bayindir Insaat Turizm Ticaret Ve Sanayi A. (Scedil) v. Pakistan*, ICSID Case No. ARB/03/29 (Decision on Jurisdiction of Nov. 14, 2005). In the past, construction contracts were not considered investment. *See* Rubins & Kinsella, *International Investment, Political Risk, and Dispute Resolution* 302–03 (Oceana 2005).

[74] *See Jan de Nul N.V. & Dredging Int'l N.V. v. Egypt*, ICSID Case No. ARB/04/13 (Decision on Jurisdiction, June 16, 2006).

[75] *Patrick Mitchell v. Democratic Republic of the Congo*, ICSID Case No. ARB/99/7 (Annulment Decision of Nov. 1, 2006).

[76] *Malaysian Historical Salvors Sdn. Bhd v. Malaysia* (MHS), ICSID Case No. ARB/05/10 (Award of May 28, 2007).

[77] *Joy Mining Machinery v. Egypt*, ICSID Case No. ARB/03/11 (Award on Jurisdiction of Aug. 6, 2004).

[78] *Id.* ¶ 47.

which the tribunal relied, what arbitral rules were applied, and the decision of the tribunals on the definition of the *investment*. This table does not include all the awards that have considered the definition of investment, nor does it include all the cases that are discussed in this chapter. Its main goal is to list as many categories of investment as possible.

Investment Categories	Cases	Investment Treaty	Arbitral Rules	Jurisdictional Decision
Access to a market[79]	1. *Pope & Talbot Inc. v. Canada*, UNCITRAL/NAFTA Arbitration (2000)	1. NAFTA, art. 1139(g) ("property, tangible or intangible, acquired in the expectation or used for the purpose of economic benefit or other business purposes")	1. UNCITRAL	1. Approved under NAFTA.
Concession contract	1. *Telenor Mobile Communications A.S. v. Hungary*, ICSID Case No. ARB/04/15 (2006)	1. Norway-Hungary BIT (1991), art. 1(III) ("business concessions conferred by law or under contract")	1. ICSID	1. Approved both under the ICSID Convention and under the BIT.
	2. *Suez, Sociedad General de Aguas de Barcelona S.A. & Vivendi Universal S.A. v. Argentina*, ICSID Case No. ARB/03/19 (2006)	2. Argentina-France BIT (1991), Argentina-Spain BIT (1991), and Argentina-United Kingdom BIT (1990) ("business concessions conferred by law or under contract")	2. ICSID	2. Approved both under the ICSID Convention and under the BITs.
Construction contract	1. *Bayindir Insaat Turizm Ticaret Ve Sanayi A.Ş. v. Pakistan*, ICSID Case No. ARB/03/29 (2005)	1. Turkey-Pakistan BIT (1995), art. 1(2) ("The term 'investment,' in conformity with the hosting Party's laws and regulations, shall include every kind of asset")	1. ICSID	1. Approved both under the ICSID Convention and under the BIT.

Continued

---

[79] On market access and relationship between trade and investment see Noah Rubins, *The Notion of "Investment" in International Investment Arbitration*, in *Arbitrating Foreign Investment Disputes: Procedural and Substantive Aspects* 283 (Horn ed., Kluwer 2004).

Investment Categories	Cases	Investment Treaty	Arbitral Rules	Jurisdictional Decision
	2. *Autopista Concesionada de Venezuela, C.A. v. Venezuela*, ICSID Case No. ARB/00/5 (2003)	2. Brought under an arbitration clause in the contract for construction	2. ICSID	2. Approved under both the ICSID Convention and the contract.
	3. *Salini Construtorri S.p.A. & Italstrade S.p.A. v. Morocco*, ICSID Case No. ARB/00/4 (2001)	3. Italy-Morocco BIT (1990), art. 1(1)(e) ("any right of an economic nature conferred by law or by contract")	3. ICSID	3. Approved both under the ICSID Convention and under the BIT.
Governance rights in local companies	1. *Eureko B.V. v. Poland*, Ad Hoc Investment Treaty Case (2006)	1. Netherlands-Poland BIT (1992), art. 1(a)(ii) ("rights derived from shares, bonds and other kinds of interests in companies and joint ventures")	1. Ad hoc UNCITRAL tribunal	1. Approved under the BIT.
Hotel management and operation contract	1. *Helnan Int'l Hotels A/S v. Egypt*, ICSID Case No. ARB/05/19 (2006)	1. Egypt-Denmark BIT (1999), art. 1(v) ("concessions or other rights conferred by law or under contract")	1. ICSID	1. Approved both under the ICSID Convention and under the BIT.
	2. *Wena Hotels Ltd. v. Egypt*, ICSID Case No. ARB/98/4 (2005)	2. U.K.-Egypt IPPA (1976), art. 1(a) (" 'investment' means every kind of asset")	2. ICSID	2. Approved both under the ICSID Convention and under the BIT.
Issuance of public debt	1. *Fireman's Fund Ins. Co. v. Mexico*, ICSID Case No. ARB(AF)/05/1 (2003)	1. NAFTA, art. 1416, ¶ 7 ("investment means . . . a loan to or debt security issued by a financial institution . . . where it is treated as regulatory capitol by the Party in	1. ICSID Additional Facility	1. Approved under NAFTA.

Continued

DEFINITION OF *INVESTMENT* UNDER THE WASHINGTON CONVENTION

Investment Categories	Cases	Investment Treaty	Arbitral Rules	Jurisdictional Decision
		whose territory the financial institution is located")		
Law firm	1. *Patrick Mitchell v. Democratic Republic Congo*, ICSID Case No. ARB/99/7 (2006) (involving a law firm)	1. U.S.-Democratic Republic of Congo BIT (1984), art. I(c) ("tangible and intangible property, including all properly rights," "know how, and goodwill," "any right conferred by law or contract")	1. ICSID	1. Disapproved under the ICSID Convention, approved under the BIT.
Leases	1. *Middle East Cement Shipping & Handling Co. S.A. v. Egypt*, ICSID Case No. ARB/99/6 (2002)	1. Greece-Egypt BIT (1993), art. 1(1)(e) ("goods that under a leasing agreement are placed at the disposal of a lessee in the territory of a Contracting Party")	1. ICSID	1. Approved both under the ICSID Convention and under the BIT.
Licenses	1. *LG&E v. Argentina*, ICSID Case No. ARB/02/1 (2004)	1. Argentina-U.S. BIT (1991), art. I(1)(a)(ii) (" 'investment' means every kind of investment . . . such as equity, debt, and service and investment contracts")	1. ICSID	1. Approved both under the ICSID Convention and under the BIT.
Loans	1. *Ceskoslovenska Obchodni Banka v. Slovakia*, ICSID Case No. ARB/97/4 (1999)	1. Slovakia-Czech Republic BIT (1992), art. 1(1) ("monetary receivables or claims")	1. ICSID	1. Approved both under the ICSID Convention and under the BIT.
Ownership of local companies	1. *Kardassopoulos v. Georgia*, ICSID Case No. ARB/05/18 (2007)	1. Greece-Georgia BIT (1996), art. 1(b) ("shares in and stock and debentures of a company and any other form of participation in a company"	1. ICSID	1. Approved under the ICSID Convention, and under the BIT, and under the Energy Charter Treaty.

Continued

Investment Categories	Cases	Investment Treaty	Arbitral Rules	Jurisdictional Decision
	2. *Int'l Thunderbird Gaming v. Mexico*, UNCITRAL/ NAFTA Award (2006)	2. NAFTA, art. 1117 ("an enterprise ... that the investor owns or controls directly or indirectly")	2. UNCITRAL	2. Approved under NAFTA.
Promissory notes	1. *Fedax N.V. v. Venezuela*, ICSID Case No. ARB/96/3 (1997)	1. The Netherlands-Venezuela BIT (1991), art. 1(a) ("titles to money, or any other assets or performance having monetary value")	1. ICSID	1. Approved both under the ICSID Convention and under the BIT.
Purchase of real property	1. *MTD Equity Sdn. Bhd. & MTD Chile S.A. v. Chile*, ICSID Case No. ARB/01/7 (2004)	1. Malaysia-Chile BIT (1992), art. 1(b) ("all investments approved by the appropriate Ministries or authorities of the Contracting Parties in accordance with its legislation and national policies")	1. ICSID	1. Approved both under the ICSID Convention and under the BIT.
Sales contracts[80]	1. *Joy Mining Machinery v. Egypt*, ICSID Case No. ARB/03/11 (2004)	1. U.K.-Egypt BIT (1976), art. 1(a)(iii) ("claims to money or to any performance under contract having a financial value")	1. ICSID	1. Disapproved under both the Convention and under the BIT.
Salvage contract with the government	1. *Malaysian Historical Salvors Sdn, Bhd v. Malaysia*, ICSID Case No. ARB/05/10 (2007) (involving a maritime salvage operation)	1. U.K.-Malaysia BIT (1981), art. 1(1)(a)(v) ("business concessions conferred under contract")	1. ICSID	1. Disapproved under the ICSID Convention. The tribunal did not examine its jurisdiction under the BIT.

Continued

---

[80] See also Shihata & Parra, *supra* note 60, at 308, note 27 (discussing the refusal of the Secretary-General of ICSID in 1999 to register a request for arbitration arising from a sales contract on the grounds that such a transaction is manifestly not an investment). On standard of review applied by ICSID Secretariat for registration of cases, see p.126 *supra*.

Investment Categories	Cases	Investment Treaty	Arbitral Rules	Jurisdictional Decision
		goodwill," "any right conferred by law or contract")		
Shares in companies	1. *Siag & Vecchi v. Egypt*, ICSID Case No. ARB/05/15 (2007)	1. Italy-Egypt BIT (1989), art. 1(1)(c) ("shares, stocks and debentures of companies, or other rights or interests in such companies")	1. ICSID	1. Approved both under the ICSID Convention and under the BIT.
	2. *Saluka Investments BV v. Czech Republic*, UNCITRAL/BIT Award (2006)	2. Netherlands-Czech and Slovak Federal Republic BIT (1991), art. 1(a)(ii) ("shares, bonds and other kinds of interests in companies and joint ventures, as well as rights derived therefrom")	2. UNCITRAL	2. Approved under the BIT.

4. Characteristics of Investment Under Article 25 of Washington Convention

Schreuer points out that the aforementioned five criteria are not requirements but characteristics that most investments share. Some arbitral tribunals appear to have adopted certain of these factors in reviewing the nature of transactions for jurisdictional purposes.[81] The tribunals have noted that these factors are interdependent and

---

[81] The tribunal in *Salini v. Morocco* adopted a four-prong test mirroring Schreuer's first (duration), third (assumption of risk), fourth (substantial commitment of capital), and fifth (contribution to development) factors. *Salini, supra* note 65, ¶ 52 (referring to Emmanuel Gaillard, *Chronique des sentences arbitrales*, 126 J.D.I. 273, 292 (1999)). Other arbitral tribunals that have applied the combination of these four factors include *MHS, supra* note 76; *Saipem S.p.A. v. Bangladesh*, ICSID Case No. ARB/05/07 (Decision on Jurisdiction and Recommendation on Provisional Measures of Mar. 21, 2007); *Patrick Mitchell supra* note 75; *Bayindir, supra* note 73; *Joy Mining, supra* note 77; *Consortium R.F.C.C. v. Morocco*, ICSID Case No. ARB/00/6 (Decision on Jurisdiction of July 16, 2001). The tribunal in *L.E.S.I. Dipenta v. Algeria*, however, stated that the criterion of contribution to development is implicit in the other three tests suggested by *Salini*. *L.E.S.I. Dipenta v. Algeria*, ICSID Case No. ARB/03/08 (Award of Jan. 10, 2005), ¶ 13; *see also L.E.S.I., S.p.A. & Astaldi, S.p.A. v. Algeria*, ICSID Case No. ARB/05/3 (Decision of July 12, 2006), ¶ 72; *cf. Patrick Mitchell, supra* note 75, ¶ 73 (stating that contribution to development is a requirement). These cases are discussed in more detail below.

should be assessed collectively, even if they are considered individually.[82] In contrast to Schreuer's suggestion that the factors are only guidelines ("characteristics" or "features"), some tribunals seem to have considered and applied them virtually as mandatory requirements;[83] this is especially so with respect to the fifth factor, contribution to development, which so far has been the focal point and the basis for dismissal of at least two cases.[84]

Some arbitral tribunals have not applied Schreuer's criteria in a systematic way, however. Instead, they have determined, without going into detail, that the respective economic activity or transaction constitutes an investment within the meaning of Article 25 of Washington Convention. Such cases seem to involve projects that are "readily recognizable"[85] investments in the sense that no one would doubt the fact that they are investment under the convention. Examples of such projects include the purchase of property[86] or shares in local companies,[87] and the development of a large farming operation.[88] Each of Schreuer's criteria is discussed in the following text in light of the cases.

a. Duration of an Activity

Investment projects tend to have an extended duration. Thus, one-time sales or purchases of goods or short-term commercial credits would normally not be investments.[89] Presumably, this criterion refers to the host state's desire to encourage commitments of capital from abroad on which it can rely for economic development. Capital infusions of limited duration, in the host-state's view, are unpredictable and prone to withdrawal or nonrenewal when conditions deteriorate, worsening financial volatility in the country rather than mitigating it.

---

[82] *Salini, supra* note 65, ¶ 52; *see also Patrick Mitchell, supra* note 75, ¶ 27 ("There are four characteristics of investment identified by ICSID case law and commented on by legal doctrine, but in reality they are interdependent and are consequently examined comprehensively.")

[83] *See, e.g., Joy Mining, supra* note 77, ¶ 53 (referring to these as "elements that an activity *must have* in order to qualify as an investment," (emphasis added)). *See also MHS, supra* note 76, ¶ 69–72, 105 (discussing the two approaches, whether characteristics or mandatory, and concluding that in practice the two are the same.)

[84] *See Patrick Mitchell, supra* note 75, ¶ 48; *MHS, supra* note 76, ¶ 130.

[85] Aron Broches, cited in Schreuer, *supra* note 19, at 124 (". . . while it might be difficult to define the term [investment], an investment was in fact readily recognizable.").

[86] *See, e.g., Siag, supra* note 71; *MTD, supra* note 70.

[87] *See, e.g., Suez, Sociedad General de Aguas de Barcelona S.A. & Vivendi Universal S.A. v. Argentina,* ICSID Case No. ARB/03/19; *CMS Gas Transmission Co. v. Argentina,* ICSID Case No. ARB/01/08; *Azurix Corp. v. Argentina,* ICSID Case No. ARB/01/12.

[88] *See Tradex Hellas, supra* note 49.

[89] As noted, ICSID has refused to register a case involving sale of goods, as it manifestly did not involve an investment. Shihata & Parra, *supra* note 60, at 308.

At the same time, "[i]t is entirely clear from [the] negotiating history that the term 'investment' in article 25(1) of the [Washington] [C]onvention does not exclude from its scope an investment simply because it is a short-term investment."[90]

The required duration seems to vary according to the nature of the activity involved, making it hard to devise a general formula for all types of investments. In *Salini v. Morocco*,[91] which involved a construction project for building a highway, the tribunal opined that the minimum length of time for an investment "according to doctrine" is two to five years.[92] No explanation of this period was given. However, because the governing contract in the case was to be implemented over a period of thirty-six months, the tribunal found the duration test satisfied.

Another case also involving highway construction, *Consortium R.F.C.C. v. Morocco*, had a contract period of twenty months, which would not meet this two-year minimum.[93] However, because the contract had been extended by agreement of the parties an additional six months, the tribunal found the investment "satisfies the minimal duration observed by the doctrine which are 2 to 5 years."[94] In a third highway construction case, *Bayindir v. Pakistan*, the tribunal stated that "duration is the paramount factor which distinguishes investments within the scope of the ICSID Convention and ordinary commercial transactions."[95] Here, the contract was for three years and extended for one more, which the tribunal deemed sufficient.[96] The tribunal did not give a precise minimum duration that must be met, but did state, "one cannot place the bar very high. . . ."[97] Additionally, the tribunal concluded the duration of the contractor's (Bayindir) guarantee on the work should also be taken into account as part of the relevant duration.[98] The tribunal in *Saipem v. Bangladesh* followed a similar line of reasoning. There, the contract for construction of an oil pipeline was originally to be completed in fourteen months, but was extended another twelve months because of delays.[99] Bangladesh argued that the appropriate time period for

---

[90] U.S. Senate, 89th Congress, 2d Session, Exec. Rep. No. 2, at 15. *But see* Gaillard, *supra* note 81, at 292 (naming extended duration as one of three elements of investment).

[91] *Salini*, *supra* note 65.

[92] *Id.*, Decision on Jurisdiction, ¶ 54 (citing D. Carreau et al., *Droit International Economique* 558–78 (3d ed. 1990)); Christoph Schreuer, *Commentary on the ICSID Convention*, 11 ICSID Rev.-F.I.L.J. 318 *et seq.* (1996).

[93] *Consortium R.F.C.C.*, *supra* note 81, ¶ 62.

[94] *Id.*

[95] *Bayindir*, *supra* note 73, ¶ 132.

[96] *Id.*

[97] *Id.* ¶ 133.

[98] *Id.*

[99] *Saipem*, *supra* note 81, ¶¶ 7 & 11.

consideration was the time in which work had actually been performed, amounting to only twelve months, which did not meet the two-year minimum it claimed was necessary to meet the *Salini* test.[100] The tribunal held the proper duration was for the "entire or overall operation," however, including the contract period, actual construction, and the warranty period on the work.[101] The tribunal's reason for using this extended period was to match the relevant duration to the time that the risks of the project existed.[102]

In *Joy Mining*, the tribunal rejected a claim that a contract for the sale of mining equipment qualified as an investment.[103] To determine the relevant duration, the tribunal looked at when payment on the contract was made. Because this occurred early in the contract, the tribunal stated the "duration of the commitment is not particularly significant,"[104] because most risks of the sale ended when payment was made.

However, in *MHS v. Malaysia*, the arbitrator did not limit the duration of the investment to match the risks but to match the period of the fifth criterion: contribution to the economic development of the host state.[105] The dispute in *MHS* was over a contract to salvage a shipwreck, originally lasting eighteen months and then extended by agreement.[106] The arbitrator noted that with the extension, the contract would meet the "minimum length of time of two to five years, as discussed in *Salini*."[107] However, the arbitrator went on to state that "owing to the nature of the Contract, the Claimant only managed to satisfy this factor in a *quantitative* sense."[108] By this the arbitrator evidently meant that the agreement as extended did not have the other characteristics, especially the fifth, to qualify as an investment.[109] Because the period of time involved did meet the other investment criteria, the arbitrator held that "the criterion of duration is not satisfied in the qualitative sense envisaged by ICSID jurisprudence."[110]

---

[100] *Id.* ¶ 101.
[101] *Id.* ¶ 110.
[102] *Id.* ¶ 102.
[103] *Joy Mining, supra* note 77.
[104] *Id.* ¶ 57.
[105] *MHS, supra* note 76, ¶ 111.
[106] *Id.* ¶ 110.
[107] *Id.*
[108] *Id.* (emphasis added). The tribunal also noted the duration of the extension "was dependent, in part, on the element of fortuity," and not caused by the nature of the project itself. *Id.* ¶ 111(a).
[109] *Id.* ¶ 111. *See also L.E.S.I., supra* note 81 (allowing an extended duration because the extension period *did* contribute to the host's economy and development).
[110] *MHS, supra* note 76, ¶ 111(b).

The preceding review of the cases suggests that where the duration of the investment is unclear, the tribunals have often stressed the interdependence of the criteria in considering the duration. The frequently cited minimum duration is two to five years. This might be shortened, however, if the interplay of all the criteria made it appropriate.

b. Regularity of Profit and Return

Investments normally display a certain regularity of profit and return, and even where no profits are eventually realized, the expectation of return is a typical aspect of any investment. In his concurring opinion in *CME*, Brownlie suggested that this was an indispensable aspect of any true investment—"as a form of expenditure or transfer of funds for the precise purpose of obtaining a return."[111] Under this analysis, infusions of capital made without any reasonable, substantiated belief that profit would result could be excluded from the definition of *investment*.[112] In *Joy Mining* the tribunal took this position further and cited the lack of *regularity* in returns as a reason why the sales contract failed to rise to the level of investment, because there was only one payment made instead of regular returns.[113]

However, the *MHS* arbitrator stated "this criterion is not always critical," nor "determinative of the question of 'investment.'"[114] The arbitrator noted that there was no regularity of profit in the salvage contract, because there was only one payment. However, he did note that the regular recovery of salvaged items might be considered regular profit because payment was based on the number of items recovered.[115] Ultimately though, he held the "absence of this hallmark is immaterial."[116]

c. Assumption of Risk by Both Parties

In part because of extended duration and the expectation of profit, investment normally entails the assumption of some form of risk by both parties. Thus, transactions where the risk is primarily or entirely placed on the host state by contract—in particular the prepaid sale of goods and other service agreements where payment is made substantially before completion of the foreigner's

---

[111] *CME Czech Republic, S.A. v. Czech Republic* (UNCITRAL arbitration, Final Award of Mar. 13, 2003, Separate Opinion of Ian Brownlie), ¶ 34.

[112] *Id.* ¶ 20; *see also Metalclad Corp. v. United Mexican States*, ICSID Case No. ARB(AF)/97/1 (Award of Sept. 2, 2000), ¶ 122, *reprinted in* 119 I.L.R. 616, 642 (2000).

[113] *Joy Mining, supra* note 77, ¶ 57.

[114] *MHS, supra* note 76, ¶ 108.

[115] *Id.*

[116] *Id.*

obligations—tend to fall outside the realm of protected investments.[117] The reason for this distinction seems relatively clear: It is precisely the possibility of contractual failure that necessitates international legal protection, to induce entrance into such transactions. However, the element of risk is more complex than it first appears. Even absent the obvious risk of a failed or unprofitable enterprise connected with a long-term infrastructure or resource exploitation project, some tribunals have suggested that the credit risk involved in bond purchases[118] and the risk of default that attaches to any contractual arrangement[119] can also support the conclusion that an investment exists. Although it is the former type of risk, "and not that of contractual breach, which classical doctrine has in mind when it defines investment,"[120] separating these different hazards is difficult in many cases.[121]

Other tribunals have considered the risk of changes in production costs,[122] of a warranty period,[123] of a work stoppage,[124] and in posting guarantee money[125] to be the types of risk that distinguish an investment. The arbitrator in *MHS* stated that the risk criterion must be met in a qualitative sense, not just quantitative. By this he meant the risks must be "other than normal commercial risks."[126] Under the salvage contract, the "no-finds-no-pay" risk was only an ordinary commercial risk, meaning the risk was inherent in the transaction, not a special feature of the project that would affect the investor's decision to invest.[127] Just because there is some risk in the project does not mean there is the type of risk inherent in investment; there must be more than just a "superficial satisfaction" of this condition.[128]

---

[117] *Joy Mining, supra* note 77, ¶ 57 ("Risk there might be indeed, but it is not different from that involved in any commercial contract. . . ."). In the past, construction contracts (civil works) were not deemed investment for similar reasons. The practice of arbitral tribunals, however, seems to indicate a departure from that position. *See* Rubins et al., *supra* note 73, at 302. *See also* p. 266 *supra*.

[118] *Fedax, supra* note 65 (Decision on Objects to Jurisdiction of July 11, 1997), ¶ 40, *reprinted at* 37 I.L.M. 1378 (1998).

[119] *Salini, supra* note 65, ¶¶ 55–56 (also noting that the fact that such risks are freely taken is irrelevant).

[120] Gaillard, *supra* note 81, at 292.

[121] In a complex construction project, for example, a variety of risks may be involved such as cost-overruns, delay, force majeure, contingencies, and so forth. Arbitral tribunals so far have not attempted to identify all of these potential risks in an exhaustive manner. This may partly be caused by the parties' failure to brief them.

[122] *Consortium R.F.C.C., supra* note 81, ¶ 63.

[123] *Bayindir, supra* note 73, ¶ 136.

[124] *Saipem, supra* note 81, ¶ 109.

[125] *Id.*

[126] *MHS, supra* note 76, ¶ 112.

[127] *Id.*

[128] *Id.*

d. Commitment Should Be Substantial

Because the drafters of the Washington Convention considered and rejected a minimum amount in dispute as a jurisdictional requirement for ICSID, amount of the investment should not play a role in defining investment under the convention.[129] Indeed, it would be somewhat arbitrary to read such a threshold into the definition of *investment*. Nevertheless, tribunals frequently examine the magnitude of the claimant's total expenditures in determining whether there is an investment.[130] They may also look beyond the monetary contribution in determining the *magnitude*. The tribunal in *Bayindir*, for example, considered Bayindir's contributions in know-how, equipment, personnel, and finances to be elements showing substantial commitment.[131] In *Joy Mining* the tribunal noted that although the price for the contract and the money the seller put up as guarantees was substantial, it was only a small fraction of the entire project and therefore not substantial enough to be considered an investment.[132] The arbitrator in *MHS* adopted this line of reasoning, stating that the contributions under the salvage contract (of at least US$3.8 million)[133] were "largely similar to those which might have been made under a commercial . . . contract,"[134] and not of the type typical for an investment.

---

[129] 2 *Analysis of Documents Concerning the Origin and the Formulation of the ICSID Convention, supra* note 52, at 34, 257–58, 260, 497–99. *See also* the decision of the annulment committee in *Patrick Mitchell, supra* note 75, ¶ 33 (stating that although investment under the Washington Convention should contribute to development, it does not have to be substantial or successful). The definition of *investment* in certain instruments does include a minimum amount. *See, e.g.*, Community Investment Code of the Economic Community of the Great Lakes Countries, art. 15 (1987) (setting US$1 million minimum "investment"); ASEAN Investment Agreement, *supra* note 16, art. 1 (defining "investor" to exclude owners of *de minimis* stakes); Tanzania Investment Act, *supra* note 48, art. 2(2)(a) (setting minimum capital contribution for protected foreign investment at $300,000).

[130] *Liberian Eastern Timber Corp. v. Republic of Liberia*, ICSID Case No. ARB/83/2 (Decision on Jurisdiction of Oct. 24, 1984), *reprinted at* 2 ICSID Rep. 346, 350 (1994) (in determining that claimant had made an investment, particular emphasis placed on size of expenditure). *But cf. Mihaly Int'l Corp. v. Socialist Democratic Republic of Sri Lanka*, ICSID Case No. ARB/00/2 (Award of Mar. 15, 2002), *reprinted in* 16 ICSID Rev.-F.I.L.J. 142, 151–56 (2001) ("the question whether an expenditure constitutes an investment is hardly to be governed by whether or not the expenditure is large or small"). Moreover, the term *substantial* must depend to a great deal on the position of the parties. A commitment of US$100,000, for example, may be a major dedication of resources for a startup company, but a mere rounding error for Exxon or IBM. Likewise, an amount that would seem insignificant for the United States as a host state could be substantial for Armenia or Guatemala. As a practical matter, it is unlikely that claims worth less than US$100,000 would ever be submitted to investor-state arbitration, because of the expense of prosecuting claims.

[131] *Bayindir, supra* note 73, ¶ 131.

[132] *Joy Mining, supra* note 77, ¶ 57.

[133] *MHS, supra* note 76, ¶ 134.

[134] *Id.* ¶ 109.

e. Contribution to Economic Development of the Host State

Schreuer's final factor is "the operation's significance for the host state's *development*."[135] The role of the foreign-initiated operation in the host state's economy differs from the other four elements in this perspective. Although duration, risk, expectation of profit, and commitment of resources are primarily characteristics of the *investor's* participation, this factor looks at the state's motivation to accept and protect the operation in question. Delaume has suggested that the state's viewpoint should in fact be the dominating one for purposes of defining investment in many cases, and there is some possible merit in this position.[136] Particularly where consent is achieved by way of a state offer to arbitrate contained in a domestic law or international investment treaty, the intended scope of that offer should logically derive primarily from the host state's *ex ante* preferences, not the behavior of the investor.[137] It stands to reason, therefore, that states would only view as *investments* (i.e., economic activity subject to international legal protection) projects that contribute to their development, including some that are largely *commercial, contractual,* or *trade-related* in nature.

Several arbitral tribunals have taken this factor into account.[138] The necessity of this factor has been inferred from the Preamble of the Washington Convention, which describes "economic development" of the host states through private investment as one of the goals of the convention.[139] Although most arbitral tribunals[140] have in principle considered this factor, they have not agreed on the extent to

---

[135] Schreuer, *supra* note 19, at 140. *See also* Convention Establishing the Multilateral Investment Guarantee Agency, art. 12(d)(i), Oct. 11, 1985, *available at* http://www.miga.org/; Walid Ben Hamida, *Two Nebulous ICSID Features: The Notion of Investment and the Scope of Annulment Control: Ad Hoc Committee's Decision in* Patrick Mitchell v. Democratic Republic of Congo, 24 J. Int'l Arb. 287, 296 (2007); *cf.* Martin Endicott, *The Definition of Investment in ICSID Arbitration: Development Lessons for the WTO?*, in Sustainable Development in World Trade Law 375 and 390–91 (Markus Gehring & Marie-Claire Cordonier Segger, eds., 2005).

[136] Delaume, *supra* note 55, at 70.

[137] A range of capital exporting states that provide political risk insurance to their investors through agencies analogous to the U.S. Overseas Private Insurance Corporation require that the project to be insured contribute to the socioeconomic development of the host state to receive coverage. This is the case in Australia, Denmark, Netherlands, Canada, and other countries. *See* Akinsanya, *supra* note 11, at 69.

[138] *See, e.g., Joy Mining, supra* note 77, ¶ 57; *Consortium R.F.C.C., supra* note 81, ¶ 65.

[139] *See, e.g., Salini supra* note 65, ¶ 52; *see also Patrick Mitchell, supra* note 75; Endicott, *supra* note 135, at 383 ("[The Preamble] confirms the purpose of the Convention is to promote private international investment that contributes to economic development").

[140] *But see L.E.S.I. Dipenta, supra* note 81, ¶ 14 (stating that the investor only has to make an expenditure in pursuit of an economic goal, not considering if the expenditure contributes to the host economy).

which an investment should contribute to economic development of the host state. Some tribunals have stated that the contribution must be significant;[141] others have not required such significant contribution.[142]

Among the cases that have taken into account the "contribution to economic development" criterion are the decision of the Annulment Committee in *Patrick Mitchell* and the tribunal decision in *MHS v. Malaysia*, both of which dismissed the claims for, among other things, the failure of the investment to contribute to host state's development.

Patrick Mitchell[143] involved an issue of first impression turning on the question of whether a law firm could constitute an investment within the meaning of the Washington Convention and the relevant investment treaty. Patrick Mitchell was an American who established a law office in the Democratic Republic of Congo (DRC). In 1999, pursuant to an order by the Military Court of the DRC,

> the premises housing Mr. Mitchell's firm were put under seals, documents qualified as compromising and other items were seized, the employees of the firm were forced to leave the premises, and two lawyers, Mr. Risasi and Mr. Djunga, were put into prison. These individuals remained incarcerated until the day of their release by a decision of the Military Court on November 12, 1999, which also ordered the removal of the seals placed on the premises of Mr. Mitchell's firm.[144]

Mr. Mitchell filed a case before ICSID under the U.S.-D.R.C. BIT[145] and in February 2004 was awarded US$750,000 plus arbitration costs and interest for expropriation of his property. In June 2004 the DRC filed an annulment request with ICSID. In November 2006 the Annulment Committee rendered its decision annulling the award based on several grounds, including the fact that Mr. Mitchell's law firm and its related legal services did not constitute an investment within the meaning of Article 25 of the ICSID Convention, because, among other things, they failed to contribute to the economic development of the DRC.[146] In reaching this conclusion, the tribunal did not deny that a law firm's provision of legal services could constitute *investment*; but it set the standard very high. In analyzing the issue, the tribunal drew a line between the

---

[141] *See, e.g., Ceskoslovenska Obchodni Banka v. Slovakia*, ICSID Case No. ARB/97/4 (Decision on Objection to Jurisdiction of May 24, 1999), ¶ 88 [hereinafter *CSOB*]; *MHS, supra* note 76, ¶ 123; *Bayindir, supra* note 75, ¶ 137; *Joy Mining, supra* note 77, ¶ 57.

[142] *See, e.g., Patrick Mitchell, supra* note 73, ¶ 33; *Consortium R.F.C.C, supra* note 81, ¶ 65.

[143] *See also* Reza Mohtashami, *Patrick Mitchell Annulment Decision (Observations)*, 2006(3) Stockholm Int'l Arb. Rev. 203.

[144] *Patrick Mitchell, supra* note 75, ¶ 1.

[145] U.S.-D.R.C. BIT, *supra* note 2.

[146] *Patrick Mitchell, supra* note 75, ¶ 49.

economic operation or service—in this case provision of services by the law firm—on the one hand and the assets and rights that are part of the operation on the other. According to the tribunal, only the former category constitutes an investment for the purposes of the Washington Convention. The latter, in this case presumably the assets of the law firm, does not meet the requirements of the Convention, although perhaps is covered by the BIT.[147] It went on to state the following:

> As a legal consulting firm is a somewhat uncommon operation from the standpoint of the concept of investment . . . it is necessary for the contribution to the economic development or at least the interests of the State, in this case the DRC, to be somehow present in the operation.[148]

Accordingly, it concluded that the "[a]ward is incomplete and obscure as regards what it considers an investment: it refers to various fragments of the operation . . . without providing the slightest explanation as to the relationship between the 'Mitchell & Associates' firm and the DRC."[149]

The Annulment Committee's application of the *contribution to development* criterion is extreme, inasmuch as it requires a relationship between the law firm and the government as an indication of contribution to development. Such a relationship could, at most, serve as one piece of circumstantial evidence, among many others, to support the argument that the respective activity in fact contributes to the economic development of the country. However, the tribunal seems to have elevated it to the level of a mandatory requirement. This interpretation can potentially exclude a class of cases where the government is not involved in the underlying transactions or investments.[150] Similarly, the tribunal's distinction between economic operation and assets narrows the scope of protected investments under the Washington Convention.[151]

MHS v. Malaysia, another case of first impression, involved a contract with the government to salvage the cargo of the *Diana*, a British ship that had sunk off the Malay coast in 1817. MHS was required to find the wreck; recover,

---

[147] *Id.* ¶ 38.

[148] *Id.* ¶ 39.

[149] *Id.* ¶ 40.

[150] *See, e.g., Loewen Group, Inc. & Raymond L. Loewen v. U.S.*, ICSID Case No. ARB (AF)/98/3 (the underlying dispute involved two private parties, from the United States and Canada, which was tried in a Mississippi court in an unfair manner in favor of the U.S. citizen. The Canadian investor filed a case under NAFTA Chapter 11 alleging inter alia expropriation and denial of justice in the U.S. court. *See generally* Chapter XVII *infra*).

[151] *See also* Ben Hamida, *supra* note 135, at 297–98.

restore, store, and insure the cargo; and arrange for the sale of the recovered items. MHS was to be paid a percentage of the profit from the arranged sale and a share of the best attainable value for any items the government decided to withhold from sale.[152] The salvage operation recovered 24,000 pieces; a sale at auction yielded US$2.98 million.[153] However, MHS claimed that the Malaysian government neither paid the full agreed percentage of the sale proceeds nor paid for items withheld from auction.[154] MHS first brought this claim to arbitration in Malaysia, where the claim was dismissed, as was subsequent challenge by MHS in Malaysian court.[155] MHS then brought the case to ICSID arbitration under the Malaysia-U.K. BIT.[156] Applying all five of the *Salini* factors to the salvage contract, the ICSID arbitrator stated that the final factor, contribution to the economy of the host state, was "of considerable, even decisive, importance."[157] The arbitrator held this was especially true in this case, because "other features of 'investment,' such as risk and duration of contract, only appear to be superficially satisfied on the facts of this case, and not in the qualitative sense envisaged under ICSID practice and jurisprudence,"[158] and further because this was not "a 'readily recognizable' 'investment'" but a case of first impression.[159] Recognizing that "[a]ny contract would have made some economic contribution to the place where it is performed," the arbitrator stated that the contribution must also have a positive effect on the economic *development* of the host state.[160] MHS argued that the contract did develop the local economy, because it employed more than forty local people in the salvage operation, imparted know-how on salvage recoveries to Malaysian museums, raised Malaysia's international profile, and contributed more than US$1 million to the Malaysian treasury.[161] The arbitrator rejected these arguments, replying that "this benefit is not of the same quality or quantity envisaged in previous ICSID jurisprudence."[162] Further, the arbitrator stated he could consider only the economic, not

---

[152] *MHS, supra* note 76, ¶¶ 7–11.
[153] *Id.* ¶ 13.
[154] *Id.* ¶ 14.
[155] *Id.* ¶ 16.
[156] Malaysia-U.K. BIT (1988).
[157] *MHS, supra* note 76, ¶ 123, *see also id.* ¶ 130.
[158] *Id.* ¶ 72.
[159] *Id.* ¶ 129. See also p. 266 *supra*.
[160] *Id.* ¶ 125.
[161] *Id.* ¶¶ 132–33.
[162] *Id.* ¶ 132.

cultural or political benefits of the contract in assessing its effect.[163] Instead, the benefits of the salvage contract were "no different from the benefits flowing to the place of the performance of any normal service contract."[164] By this, the arbitrator meant the benefits from the contract did not create a continuing benefit to the economy, but only lasted so long as the contract itself.[165] Because the benefits from the salvage operation were not shown to have a lasting, significant effect, the arbitrator concluded it was not an *investment* under the Washington Convention.[166]

D. The Concept of Unity of Investment Under the Washington Convention

In general ICSID tribunals have been willing to include straightforward construction, management, and other contracts among investments where they are part of an overall, larger-scale, complex project that meets the basic criteria of investment, even if the respective contracts and investors are legally distinct. This concept has been referred to as "unity of investment."[167] In *Duke Energy v. Peru*, for example, an American energy company, Duke Energy International (DEI or Duke), through a complex series of transactions, acquired the majority of shares of Egenor, a privatized Peruvian state-owned electricity company. Duke's ownership interests in Egenor were maintained through a multilayer structure. The main investor was Duke's Bermudan subsidiary, DEI Bermuda, which made the necessary capital contribution for acquisition purposes to its Peruvian holding company, called DEI Peru Holdings, and the latter used the contributed funds to acquire Duke's interest in Egenor (later called DEI Egenor). DEI Bermuda, DEI Peru Holdings, DEI Egenor, and the Peruvian government entered into four legal stability agreements (LSAs) which provided various guarantees to these entities. DEI Bermuda's LSA contained an ICSID clause. In 2001 the Peruvian Tax Authority, Superintendencia Nacional de Administración Tributaria (SUNAT), made two tax assessments against DEI Egenor for its tax underpayments during the previous years. Duke unsuccessfully challenged these assessments before Peruvian authorities and finally filed a request for arbitration with ICSID in 2003.

At the jurisdictional phase, Peru argued that Duke's investment, for the purposes of Article 25 of Washington Convention, was limited to its capital

---

[163] *Id.* ¶ 138.
[164] *Id.* ¶ 144.
[165] *See id.*
[166] *Id.* ¶ 146.
[167] *Duke, supra* note 62, ¶ 21.

contribution to DEI Peru Holdings and did not include its indirect interest in DEI Egenor. The tribunal rejected this argument based on the concept of unity of investment and summarized the relevant ICSID case law in this respect as follows:

Duke Energy Int'l Peru Invs. No. 1, Ltd. v. Peru

ICSID Case No. ARB/03/28 (Decision on Jurisdiction of Feb. 1, 2006)

119. Finally, in deciding on the nature of the investment, the Tribunal agrees with the position adopted by other ICSID tribunals involving situations in which the parties' consent to ICSID arbitration was included in one of several successive agreements connected to an investment. This is the case in the present arbitration.

120. Respondent has raised the concern that the Tribunal might import into this proceeding, inappropriately, a broad definition of investment of the kind typically found in Bilateral Investment Treaties ("BITs") on this subject. Respondent states:

> Instead of calling on the Tribunal to interpret the Agreement, normally and naturally, as a contract between specified parties, and establishing specified rights and obligations, Claimant would have the Tribunal mistakenly import into this proceeding the general definition of "investment" from bilateral investment treaties ("BITs"), together with inapposite BIT jurisprudence. Because the instrument of consent before this Tribunal contains a narrowly focused definition of investment, and not the broad definition found in BITs, Claimant's arguments are wholly misdirected, and should be ignored. In the case at hand, the relevant investment is precisely delineated in the DEI Bermuda Legal Stability Agreement, and it is not that investment on which Claimant predicates its claims.[168]

121. The Tribunal is not importing into this proceeding a general definition of "investment" from BITs together with inapposite BIT jurisprudence. In the relevant cases, which are discussed below, ICSID tribunals have applied the principle of the "unity of the investment" in situations where consent to ICSID arbitration is found in individual investment agreements or contracts, not in an umbrella instrument such as a BIT. The Tribunal is of the view that the principles derived from those cases are directly applicable to its determination of the investment in relation to which the parties consented to ICSID arbitration in Clause Nine of the DEI Bermuda LSA.

122. In *Holiday Inns v. Morocco*, an ICSID arbitration agreement was included in a "Basic Agreement" for the establishment and operation of hotels. Government financing for the hotels was secured by means of separate loan agreements involving parties affiliated with (but different from) those who signed the Basic Agreement. The loan agreements contained choice of forum clauses in favor of the Moroccan courts.[169] Claimants sought to bring a financing dispute within the jurisdiction of the ICSID tribunal constituted under the dispute-resolution provision of the Basic Agreement.

---

[168] SN: *See* Respondent's Reply, ¶ 3.
[169] SN: *Lalive*, First "World Bank" Arbitration, at 156.

123. Morocco objected to the jurisdiction of the ICSID tribunal, arguing that the dispute related to separate transactions, between separate parties, for which other dispute-settlement procedures had been agreed.[170] The tribunal rejected these contentions and asserted its jurisdiction over the loan agreements. In doing so, it emphasized "the general unity of an investment operation." The tribunal held:

> It is well known, and it is being particularly shown in the present case, that investment is accomplished by a number of juridical acts of all sorts. It would not be consonant either with economic reality or with the intention of the parties to consider each of these acts in complete isolation from the others. It is particularly important to ascertain which is the act which is the basis of the investment and which entails as measures of execution the other acts which have been concluded in order to carry it out.[171]

124. In *CSOB v. Slovakia*, a Consolidation Agreement between the claimant, a former state-owned bank, and the Ministries of Finance of the Czech and Slovak Republics provided for the assignment by CSOB of certain non-performing receivables to two "Collection Companies," one in each Republic, created for this purpose. Each Collection Company was to pay CSOB for the assigned receivables. To enable them to do so, each Collection Company was to receive loans from CSOB, which were to be repaid according to an agreed repayment schedule. The Consolidation Agreement included a clause stating that it was to be governed by the laws of the Czech Republic and the BIT between the Czech and Slovak Republics.

125. After the Slovak Collection Company (SCC) was established, it concluded Loan Agreements with CSOB. Under the terms of both the Consolidation Agreement and the Loan Agreements, the loan was secured by a guarantee of the Slovak Ministry of Finance. When SCC defaulted in its payment, CSOB instituted ICSID proceedings. Slovakia argued that the claims against it did not arise directly out of the loan and were, therefore, outside of the tribunal's jurisdiction, which was based on the arbitration agreement contained in the separate Consolidation Agreement.[172] The tribunal rejected this argument. It held that

> [a]n investment is frequently a rather complex operation, composed of various interrelated transactions, each element of which, standing alone, might not in all cases qualify as an investment. Hence, a dispute that is brought before the Centre must be deemed to arise directly out of an investment even when it is based on a transaction which, standing alone, would not qualify as an investment under the Convention, provided that the particular transaction forms an integral part of an overall operation that qualifies as an investment.
>
> . . . .
>
> The foregoing analysis indicates that the term "directly," as used in Article 25(1) of the Convention, should not be interpreted restrictively to compel the conclusion that CSOB's claim is outside the Centre's jurisdiction and the Tribunals' competence merely because it is based on an obligation of the Slovak Republic which, standing alone, does not qualify as an investment.

---

[170] SN: *Lalive*, First "World Bank" Arbitration, at 156.

[171] SN: Decision on Jurisdiction, May 12, 1974, *Lalive*, First "World Bank" Arbitration, at 159.

[172] SN: As such, the BIT here played only an indirect role, in that it contained the ICSID arbitration agreement that was incorporated by reference in the Consolidation Agreement. The claim itself was not brought under the BIT.

> Hence, in deciding whether the obligation referred to in CSOB's requested relief forms part of an investment, *the Tribunal has to determine whether the purported obligation of the Slovak Republic forms an integral part of a transaction which qualifies as an investment.*
>
> . . . .
>
> The contractual scheme embodied in the Consolidation Agreement shows, however, that the CSOB loan to the SCC is closely related to and *cannot be disassociated from all other transactions involving the restructuring of CSOB*. . . .
>
> . . . .
>
> The Slovak Republic's undertaking and the loan form an integrated whole in the process defined in the Consolidation Agreement. Hence, individual transactions comprising it may still meet the requirements of an investment under the Convention, provided the overall operation for the consolidation of CSOB, to which it is closely connected, qualifies as an investment.[173]

126. The *CSOB* case is particularly instructive for the issue facing this Tribunal. In *CSOB*, as is the case here, it was necessary to consider contracts and transactions outside the scope of the single agreement that contained the ICSID arbitration agreement in order to find, as the tribunal did in that case, that the dispute before it arose directly out of an investment.

127. At the same time, the tribunal confirmed, in a supplementary decision on jurisdiction, that the application of the concept of the unity of the investment (the "overall operation") did not mean that the Tribunal "automatically acquires jurisdiction with regard to each agreement concluded to implement the wider investment operation."[174] As such, the *CSOB* decision was more restrictive than the decision reached by another ICSID tribunal in *Société Ouest-Africaine des Bétons Industriels (SOABI) v. The Republic of Senegal*, a case also involving an ICSID arbitration agreement contained in one of several successive agreements.

128. In *SOABI*,[175] three successive agreements were entered into by the parties in connection with the construction of low-cost dwellings in Senegal. Only the last agreement to be signed (the "Establishment Agreement"), which related to the establishment of a plant for the pre-fabrication of reinforced concrete for the planned dwellings, contained an ICSID arbitration agreement, which by its express terms was limited to disputes between the parties relating to the Establishment Agreement.

129. The majority of the tribunal held that "the agreements between the parties other than the Establishment Agreement, with respect to the construction of the plant as well as the construction of the 15,000 dwelling units, are implicitly encompassed by the Establishment Agreement."[176] The majority reasoned that "one could not dissociate the

---

[173] SN: *Ceskoslovenska Obchodni Banka A.S. v. Slovak Republic*, ICSID Case No. ARB/97/4 (Decision of the Tribunal on Objections to Jurisdiction of May 24, 1999), ¶¶ 72, 74–75, 80, & 82 (emphasis added).

[174] SN: Supplementary Decision of Dec. 1, 2000, ¶ 28.

[175] SN: *Société Ouest-Africaine des Bétons Industriels (SOABI) v. the Republic of Senegal*, ICSID Case No. ARB/82/1 (Award of Feb. 25, 1988), 17 Y.B. Com. Arb. 42–72, ¶ 4.10 (1992).

[176] SN: *Id.* ¶ 4.13.

two parts of the operation,"[177] and accused the dissent of "hid[ing] behind hypotheses that are refuted by . . . reality . . ."[178]

130. Professor Schreuer summarizes these and other cases as follows:

> These cases suggest that ICSID tribunals are inclined to take a broad view of consent clauses where the agreement between the parties is reflected in several successive instruments. Expressions of consent are not applied narrowly to the specific document in which they appear but are read in the context of the parties' overall relationship. Therefore, a series of interrelated contracts may be regarded, in functional terms, as representing the legal framework for one investment operation. ICSID clauses contained in some, though not all, of the different contracts may be interpreted to apply to the entire operation.[179]

131. The Tribunal has no hesitation in applying the unity-of-the-investment principle[180] to refute Respondent's argument that the narrow description of the transaction in Clause Two of the DEI Bermuda LSA necessarily determines the scope of the "investment" for purposes of the DEI Bermuda LSA. The reality of the overall investment, which is clear from the record, overcomes Respondent's objection that it could never have consented to arbitration of a dispute related to the broader investment by Duke Energy in DEI Egenor.

E. Concept of Investment and Its Implications for the Jurisdiction of Arbitral Tribunals Under Arbitral Rules Other Than the Washington Convention

Under arbitral rules other than the ICSID—such as those of the ICSID Additional Facility, ICC, or UNCITRAL—once it has been established that the claimant's activity constitutes an investment within the meaning of the applicable investment instrument, the jurisdictional analysis in that respect is complete; and assuming that the other jurisdictional requirements under the instrument have been met, the claimant has access to arbitration against the host state. Thus, in contrast to the ICSID system, which requires two levels of jurisdictional determination (i.e., under the respective investment instrument and under the Washington Convention)[181] here there is only one level of jurisdictional

---

[177] SN: *Id.* ¶ 4.17.

[178] SN: *Id.*

[179] SN: C. Schreuer, *The ICSID Convention: A Commentary*, 245 (2001).

[180] SN: We are guided here principally by the reasoning adopted by the *CSOB* tribunal in reaching its balanced decision.

[181] See Section C(2) at p. 259 *supra* on dual-jurisdictional requirements of the Washington Convention.

determination,[182] which mainly turns on interpretation of the term *investment* within the applicable investment instrument.[183] It is thus essential to examine the text of the respective treaty, including the exceptions to the definition of investment or other carve-outs carefully. The following cases provide examples of non-ICSID claims filed under various investment treaties. These cases involve a variety of investments such as shares owned in a bank, shareholding in an insurance company in conjunction with corporate control rights derived from the share purchase agreement, a broadcasting license, and so forth. This variety, as well as the differences in treaty language, entails a case-by-case analysis. Thus, any generalization regarding the scope of the term *investment* within a treaty should be approached with utmost care.

In *Saluka v. Czech Republic*,[184] which was commenced pursuant to Czech Republic-Dutch BIT[185] and under the UNCITRAL Arbitration Rules, the government of the Czech Republic alleged among other things that Saluka's holding of the shares of the Czech bank, Investiční a Poštovní banka a.s. (later known as IP banka a.s., or IPB), which was purchased by its parent company Nomura, did not constitute an investment within the meaning of Article 2 of the BIT.[186] The tribunal rejected this argument, relying mainly on the definition of investment in Article 2 of the BIT:

> Saluka Investments v. Czech Republic
>
> UNCITRAL Arbitration, Partial Award of Mar. 17, 2006
>
> 210. The second consideration which is said by the Respondent to undermine any determination that the purchase of IPB's shares was an "investment" appears to be that Saluka itself invested nothing in IPB but was merely a conduit for the investment made by Nomura, which retained the voting rights associated with the IPB shares, participated in the management of IPB, and conducted all the dealings with the Czech authorities. Saluka was a mere surrogate for Nomura, being no more than an agent for Nomura and not itself a true investor.

---

[182] Despite the clear authority supporting a separation of *investment* for purposes of consent and for purposes of ICSID jurisdiction, some ICSID tribunals continue to examine only the definition of investment contained in the consent to arbitration. In *Middle East Cement*, for example, an expropriated ship that was allegedly owned by the claimant's parent company and leased to the claimant was deemed an investment, primarily because the applicable Greece-Egypt BIT included leased property in its definition. No consideration was given to whether this arrangement would satisfy the *investment* requirement of Washington Convention art. 25(1). *Middle East Cement*, *supra* note 67, ¶136.

[183] This issue has been discussed in more detail in Section B at pp. 250–52 *supra*.

[184] *Saluka Inv. v. Czech Republic* (UNCITRAL Arbitration, Partial Award, Mar. 17, 2006).

[185] Czech Republic-Netherlands BIT (1991).

[186] *Id.* art. 2 ("Each Contracting Party shall in its territory promote investments by investors of the other Contracting Party and shall admit such investments in accordance with its provisions of law").

211. To a considerable extent, this argument seeks to replace the definition of an "investment" in Article 2 of the Treaty with a definition which looks more to the economic processes involved in the making of investments. However, the Tribunal's jurisdiction is governed by Article 1 of the Treaty, and nothing in that Article has the effect of importing into the definition of "investment" the meaning which that term might bear as an economic process, in the sense of making a substantial contribution to the local economy or to the wellbeing of a company operating within it. Although the *chapeau* of Article 2 refers to "every kind of asset *invested*," the use of that term in that place does not require, in addition to the very broad terms in which "investments" are defined in the Article, the satisfaction of a requirement based on the meaning of "investing" as an economic process: the chapeau needs to contain a verb which is apt for the various specific kinds of investments which are listed, and since all of them are being defined as various kinds of investment it is in the context appropriate to use the verb "invested" without thereby adding further substantive conditions.

The *Saluka* tribunal's approach, to the extent that it does not consider the contribution of investment to the local economy as a relevant criterion, may be contrasted with Schreuer's fifth criterion, explained earlier, which considers contribution to the local economy as one of the features of an investment under the ICSID Convention. There is no conflict between the two, however, insofar as they relate to different instruments.

In *Eureko B.V. v. Poland*,[187] an arbitration under the Dutch-Polish BIT, the ad hoc tribunal considered whether the strategic corporate control rights acquired along with the stocks in a company through a stock purchase agreement (SPA) qualified as an investment under the treaty. The investors had purchased 30 percent ownership in the state-owned insurance company, Powszechny Zaklad Ubezpieczen S.A. (PZU), as part of a privatization initiative and later entered into an addendum to the SPA with the Polish government to purchase a further 21 percent ownership.[188] Because of the political climate in Poland, the government did not take the necessary steps to sell the additional shares to Eureko and took other measures to limit the investors' interests in the company. The investors filed for arbitration claiming violations of various provisions of the BIT.[189] The treaty stated that investments included "rights derived from shares, bonds, interests, and other kinds of interests in companies and joint ventures."[190] At first the tribunal was reluctant to find the investors' corporate governance rights under the SPA as an investment, because the 30 percent

---

[187] *Eureko B.V. v. Poland* (Ad Hoc Investment Treaty Case, Partial Award on Liability, Aug. 19, 2005).
[188] *Id.* ¶¶ 36–41, 57.
[189] Netherlands-Poland BIT (1992), art. 3.5.
[190] *Id.* art. 1(a)(ii).

ownership only entitled the investors to "exercise substantial influence"[191] and not full control. But because these rights were "a key element of the investment, without which it appears that there would have been no investment at all," and they conferred on the investor more influence than that implied by its 30 percent shareholding, the tribunal concluded the rights had economic value and were therefore protected investments under the BIT.[192] The tribunal also held that the investors' rights under the contract for the purchase of further shares amounted to an investment.[193]

A Stockholm Chamber of Commerce tribunal used similar reasoning in *Nagel v. Czech Republic*,[194] an arbitration brought under the U.K.-Czech Republic BIT.[195] The investor had entered into a co-operation agreement with a state-owned enterprise to obtain a broadcasting license. Later, the government sold that license to another party.[196] The investor claimed his rights under the co-operation agreement qualified as an investment under the BIT.[197] The tribunal disagreed, stating that *financial value* was an underlying concept of *investment* in the BIT,[198] and that the co-operation agreement only set up a framework for future agreement, had no financial value, and hence was not an investment under the BIT.[199]

In *Sedelmayer v. Russian Federation,* another SCC case involving an expropriation claim, the tribunal allowed claims for improvement to real property as an investment under the Germany-Russia BIT.[200] However, the tribunal held that items meant for import that were stopped by the expropriation of the property and personal goods owned by the investor that were seized along with the property were not considered investments under the treaty.[201]

---

[191] *Eureko, supra* note 187, ¶ 140.

[192] *Id.* ¶¶ 139 & 145.

[193] *Id.* ¶¶ 157–58.

[194] *Nagel v. Czech Republic*, SCC Case 49/2002 (Award of Sept. 9, 2003), *reprinted in* 1 Stockholm Arb. Rep. 141 (2004).

[195] U.K.-Czech Republic BIT (1990).

[196] Final Arbitral Award Rendered in 2003 in SCC Case 49/2002, 1 Stockholm Arb. Rep. 141, 142–43 (2004).

[197] *Id.* at 148–49.

[198] *Id.* at 157–58. The treaty presented a nonexhaustive list of included investments, all of which, the tribunal stated, had the common characteristic of financial value. Further, the tribunal found support for this theory in the BIT's requirements for compensation to be paid in event of expropriation and in the "unanimity among writers" on the subject. *Id.*

[199] *Id.* at 64–65.

[200] Federal Republic of Germany-U.S.S.R. Agreement Concerning the Promotion and Reciprocal Protection of Investments (1989).

[201] *Sedelmayer v. Russian Federation* (Final Award, 1998), 2 Stockholm Arb. Rep. 39 (2005).

Tribunals interpreting the definition of *investment* under NAFTA have similarly found ownership of local companies to be straightforward investment. In *United Parcel Service v. Canada*, for example, the tribunal accepted United Parcel Service's ownership of a Canadian subsidy, United Parcel Service Canada Limited, as an investment without any dispute.[202]

Other NAFTA tribunals have found much less straightforward investments, despite the apparently exhaustive definition in NAFTA.[203] In *Pope & Talbot Inc. v. Canada* the tribunal held that the claimant's access to the U.S. market met the definition of *investment* in NAFTA Article 1139(g) as "other property, tangible or intangible, acquired in the expectation or used for the purpose of economic benefit or other business purposes." The tribunal reasoned that the market access was "an abstraction" but was necessary for the claimant to derive any value from its investment, and therefore fit the definition.[204] Other NAFTA tribunals have echoed this holding in *S.D. Myers, Inc. v. Canada*[205] and *Methanex v. United States of America*.[206]

In NAFTA and other free trade agreements, which have several chapters, determining whether an activity constitutes investment sometimes is more difficult. It may require examining chapters other than the investment chapter as well as various annexes of the agreement to decide whether the particular activity falls under carve-outs to the agreement. In *Fireman's Fund Insurance Company v. Mexico*, the claimant purchased US$50 million in debentures to inject capital into a Mexican bank. When the bank failed, the claimant filed a NAFTA claim pursuant to the ICSID Additional Facility Rules and claimed certain actions by the Mexican government prevented it from recovering its investment.[207] Mexico argued that article 1416 of NAFTA, the basis of the claim, had an additional exception to the general definition of investment in Article 1139[208]:

---

[202] *United Parcel Service v. Canada* (UNCITRAL Arbitration, Final Award of June 19, 2007).

[203] See pp. 251–52 *supra*.

[204] *Pope & Talbot Inc. v. Canada* (UNCITRAL Arbitration, Interim Award of June 26, 2000), ¶¶ 97–98.

[205] *S.D. Myers, Inc. v. Canada* (UNCITRAL Arbitration, First Partial Award of Nov. 13, 2000), ¶ 232.

[206] *Methanex v. U.S.* (UNCITRAL Arbitration, Award of Aug. 3, 2005), ¶ 17.

[207] *Fireman's Fund Ins. Co. v. Mexico*, ICSID Case No. ARB (AF)/02/1 (brought under the ICSID Additional Faculty Rules, as Mexico is not a party to the ICSID convention, so the Washington Convention did not apply).

[208] NAFTA, art. 1139 ("investment means: . . . (c) a debt security of an enterprise . . . (d) a loan to an enterprise").

investment means "investment" as defined in Article 1139 (Investment Definitions), except that, with respect to "loans" and "debt securities" referred to in that Article:

(a) a loan to or debt security issued by a financial institution is an investment only where it is treated as regulatory capital by the Party in whose territory the financial institution is located;[209]

Mexico claimed that these particular debentures were not treated as regulatory capital under Mexican law. The tribunal held that they were treated as regulatory capital in the financial statements issued by the bank, however, and these were in accordance with Mexican law.[210] Hence, the tribunal held, the debentures did satisfy the additional requirements of Article 1416 and were an investment.

F. Preinvestment Protection

Most investment treaties, including bilateral agreements based on the OECD model, extend protection only to investments (however defined) once established, leaving host states free to promulgate whatever rules they deem appropriate with regard to admission or entry or establishment of foreign capital.[211] *Preinvestment*, or *investment-making* activity, is most commonly protected only by a loose best-efforts obligation (e.g., Energy Charter Treaty), or a requirement of nondiscriminatory access (guaranteed through a national or most-favored national treatment provision), often with sectoral limitations.[212] Under most arbitral consent documents, therefore, a mere intention to invest, no matter how clearly stated, does not normally entitle a foreign national to the full panoply of legal protection or access to arbitration. Furthermore, according to certain commentators, the ICSID Convention's jurisdiction likewise will not extend to the establishment phase, even

---

[209] *Id.* art. 1416.

[210] *Fireman's Fund, supra* note 207, Decision on the Preliminary Question of Jurisdiction, July 17, 2003, ¶¶ 97–98.

[211] Some treaties are explicit in reserving the host state's right to screen investments. *See, e.g.*, ASEAN Investment Agreement, *supra* note 16, art. II(1) ("This Agreement shall apply only to investments brought into, derived from or directly connected with investments brought into the territory of any Contracting Party by nationals or companies of any other Contracting Party and which are specifically approved in writing and registered by the host country and upon such conditions as it deems fit for the purposes of this Agreement"); China Model BIT, art. 1(1) ("The term 'investment' means every kind of asset invested by investors of one Contracting Party in accordance with the laws and regulations of the other Contracting Party in the territory of the latter"), *quoted in* UNCTAD, *supra* note 13, at 78. There are some important exceptions to this tendency, most notably the U.S. BITs, NAFTA, and more recently some Canadian BITs, such as the Canada-Costa Rica BIT (1998).

[212] Patricia McKinstry Robin, *The BIT Won't Bite: The American Bilateral Investment Treaty Program*, 33 Am. U.L. Rev. 931, 947–48 (1984).

if a particular consent document extends to entry of investments.[213] The question of when a commitment of capital to a project becomes an *investment* for jurisdictional purposes recently led to the dismissal on jurisdictional grounds of the claimant's case in *Mihaly v. Sri Lanka*.

In *Mihaly*,[214] the American claimant corporation, after a formal bidding process, signed a *letter of intent* with the government of Sri Lanka, outlining the framework for negotiations that were to lead to the BOT construction of a 300-megawatt power plant in Sri Lanka.[215] Mihaly had been selected by the government out of twenty-five candidates. It held the exclusive right to enter into the letter of intent, which established benchmarks the company had to meet to obtain final approval to begin work on the plant.[216] On the basis of the letter, Mihaly spent several million dollars obtaining financing, negotiating project documents, and engaging consultants for feasibility analyses. After these expenditures had been made, the Sri Lankan government refused to sign the project agreement, and Mihaly filed its claim with ICSID. The tribunal held that business development expenditures did not rise to the level of *investment* under the U.S.-Sri Lanka BIT and the Washington Convention, even though those costs constituted two to four percent of the total projected investment. The tribunal relied largely on the fact that the letter of intent created no binding obligation for Sri Lanka to conclude a project contract with Mihaly.

Mihaly Int'l Corp. v. Socialist Democratic Republic of Sri Lanka

ICSID Case No. ARB/00/2 (Award of March 15, 2002) 16 ICSID Rev.-F.I.L.J. 142, 151–56 (2001)

32. The most crucial and controversial contentions of the Parties were concentrated upon the existence *vel non* of an "*investment*" for the purpose of Article 25(1) to

---

[213] Schreuer, *supra* note 19, at 130 ("clauses in BITs that cover disputes concerning the admission or establishment of investments cannot create a basis for ICSID's jurisdiction since there is no investment"); Antonio Parra, *Provisions on the Settlement of Investment Disputes in Modern Investment Laws, BITs, and Multilateral Instruments on Investment*, 12 ICSID Rev.-F.I.L.J. 287, 325 (1997) ("where the dispute is over the denial of admission, it might be argued that, since there is in fact no investment, the dispute could not be said to arise out of one, and hence would fall outside the scope of the ICSID Convention").

[214] *Mihaly, supra* note 130. *See also* Walid Ben Hamida, *The* Mihaly v. Sri Lanka *Case: Some Thoughts Relating to the Status of Pre-Investment Expenditures*, in *International Investment Law and Arbitration: Leading Cases from ICSID, NAFTA, Bilateral Treaties and Customary International Law* 47 (Weiler ed., Cameron 2005).

[215] Robert Hornick, *The Mihaly Arbitration: Pre-Investment Expenditure as a Basis for ICSID Jurisdiction*, 20 J. Int'l Arb. 189, 189–90 (2003).

[216] *Mihaly, supra* note 130, ¶ 40.

found the jurisdiction of ICSID Centre and the Tribunal. A *fortiorissime*, without proof of an "*investment*" under Article 25(1), neither Party need to argue further, for without such an "*investment*," there can be no dispute, legal or otherwise, arising directly or indirectly out of it, which could be submitted to the jurisdiction of the Centre and the Tribunal.

33. Neither Party asserted that the ICSID Convention contains any precise *a priori* definition of "*investment*." Rather the definition was left to be worked out in the subsequent practice of States, thereby preserving its integrity and flexibility and allowing for future progressive development of international law on the topic of investment.

. . . .

48. [T]he Tribunal has been asked to consider whether or not the undoubted expenditure of money, following upon the execution of the Letter of Intent, in pursuit of the ultimately failed enterprise to obtain a contract, constituted "investment" for the purpose of the Convention. The Tribunal has not been asked to and cannot consider in a vacuum whether or not in other circumstances expenditure of moneys might constitute an "investment." A crucial and essential feature of what occurred between the Claimant and the Respondent in this case was that first, the Respondent took great care in the documentation relied upon by the Claimant to point out that none of the documents, in conferring exclusivity upon the Claimant, created a contractual obligation for the building, ownership and operation of the power station. Second, the grant of exclusivity never matured into a contract. To put it rhetorically, what else could the Respondent have said to exclude any obligations which might otherwise have attached to interpret the expenditure of the moneys as an admitted investment? The operation of SAEC[217] was contingent upon the final conclusion of the contract with Sri Lanka, thus the expenditures for its creation would not be regarded as an investment until admitted by Sri Lanka.

49. The Tribunal is not unmindful of the need to adapt the Convention to changes in the form of cooperation between investors and host States. However, these changes have to be considered in the context of the specific obligations which the parties respectively assume in the particular case. The Tribunal repeats that, in other circumstances, similar expenditure may perhaps be described as an investment.

50. Again, if the negotiations during the period of exclusivity, or for that matter, without exclusivity, had come to fruition, it may well have been the case that the moneys expended during the period of negotiations might have been capitalised as part of the cost of the project and thereby become part of the investment. By capitalising expenses incurred during the negotiation phase, the parties in a sense may retrospectively sweep those costs within the umbrella of an investment.

51. It is an undoubted feature of modern day commercial activity that huge sums of money may need to be expended in the process of preparing the stage for a final contract. However, the question whether an expenditure constitutes an investment or not is hardly to be governed by whether or not the expenditure is large or small. Ultimately, it is always a matter for the parties to determine at what point in their negotiations they wish to engage the provisions of the Convention by entering into an investment. Specifically, the Parties could have agreed that the formation of a South Asia Electricity Company was to be treated as the starting point of the admitted investment, engaging the responsibility of the Respondent for the Claimant's failure to complete other arrangements to achieve the milestones by the

---

[217] "South Asia Electricity Company, a company formed in Sri Lanka to negotiate and manage the distribution of the supplies of electricity." *Id.* ¶ 45.

due date mentioned in the Letter of Extension. The facts of the case point to the opposite conclusion. The Respondent clearly signalled, in the various documents which are relied upon by the Claimant, that it was not until the execution of a contract that it was willing to accept that contractual relations had been entered into and that an investment had been made. It may be and the Tribunal does not have to express an opinion on this, that during periods of lengthy negotiations even absent any contractual relationships obligations may arise such as the obligation to conduct the negotiations in good faith. These obligations if breached may entitle the innocent party to damages, or some other remedy. However, these remedies do not arise because an investment had been made, but rather because the requirements of proper conduct in relation to negotiation for an investment may have been breached. That type of claim is not one to which the Convention has anything to say. They are not arbitrable as a consequence of the Convention.

In a concurring opinion in *Mihaly*, arbitrator David Suratgar took issue with the majority's reliance on the particular wording of the letter of intent and argued that the line between preinvestment expenditures and investment itself is far finer than the *Mihaly* award suggests.[218] Suratgar noted that the absence of a binding agreement between the parties may have freed Sri Lanka from any *contractual* liability but that liability under Sri Lankan or international law still could "arise from its conduct after the award of the Letter of Intent—including [breach of] a duty to negotiate in good faith."[219] Suratgar nevertheless reluctantly agreed that, based on the evidence presented, there had been no *investment*; but he added an important caveat. He suggested that, had Mihaly's expenditures been made through its local Sri Lankan subsidiary, its shareholdings in the operating company would certainly have constituted an investment, both for purposes of the U.S.-Sri Lanka BIT and the Washington Convention. Although this position seems at first formalistic, it is convincing from an economic standpoint. It is difficult to deny the economic value of the exclusive right to negotiate a contract with the government, and the improved chance of achieving such an agreement that would result from research, feasibility, design, and other expenditures. Certainly, had the Mihaly's local operating company made these expenditures, the resulting value would have been reflected to a large degree in the market value of its shares. As it was, Mihaly's direct expenditures had no vehicle, no presence, within Sri Lankan territory, and therefore fell outside the notion of *investment*. Nevertheless, Suratgar concluded:

> Expenditure incurred by successful bidders do indeed produce "economic value" as specified by Article 1 of the US-Sri Lanka BIT and the protection mechanism developed under the aegis of the World Bank in the form of the ICSID Convention should be available to those who are encouraged to embark on such expensive exercises.[220]

---

[218] *Mihaly, supra* note 130, Individual Concurring Opinion of David Suratgar, *reprinted in* 16 ICSID Rev.-F.I.L.J. 161 (2001).

[219] *Id.* at 163.

[220] *Id.* at 164–65.

The outcome in *Mihaly* seems to correspond to the understanding of the drafters of the Washington Convention, who apparently did not conceive of precontractual expenses as part of the notion of investment.[221] But to some degree, the case conflicts with the thrust of modern investment treaties, which often include in their extensive lists of *investment* activities, including contractual rights, loans, permits, and intellectual property, items which arise long before formal incorporation or the signing of project documents. However, it is still unclear where the line can be drawn between investment and mere preparation to invest. Subsequent tribunals have also been reluctant to find preinvestment expenditures to constitute *investment*, particularly where not expressly included in the scope of the applicable investment protection instrument.[222]

---

[221] This is the assertion of Professor Schreuer, reported in Hornick, *supra* note 215, at 189 note 5 and accompanying text

[222] See, e.g., the discussion of *Nagel* at p. 283 *supra*.

XII. The Nationality of the *Investor*

Investment treaties and laws provide protection to juridical or natural persons who qualify as an *investor* of appropriate nationality, within the definitions of these instruments.[1] Determining whether a foreign investor satisfies the nationality requirements of an investment protection instrument or the Washington Convention can be a complex exercise, given the myriad investment structures by which assets may be held. In some cases a company formed in the home state of the investor with an applicable treaty may have made an investment directly in the host state, giving rise to little debate as to the foreign entity's standing to bring a claim against the host state.[2] In many other cases, however, the factual circumstances are more intricate. The ultimate contributor of capital may have made its investment through several layers of companies, incorporated in different jurisdictions. Some intervening corporate vehicles may benefit from investment treaties with the host country, whereas others may not. Further complications may arise as a result of changes to the ownership structure of an investment between the time the investment was made and the time the dispute arose or later. Factual subtleties such as these can present significant problems in identifying the nationality of the investor for purposes of establishing the jurisdiction of an arbitral tribunal.

In this chapter a range of legal issues are examined, which relate to the qualification of a natural or legal person as an *investor* under customary international law,

---

[1] *Mihaly v. Sri Lanka*, ICSID Case No. ARB/00/2 (Award of Mar. 15, 2002), *reprinted in* 16 ICSID Rev.-F.I.L.J. 142, 151–56 (2001), ¶¶ 20–27. On citizenship and investment arbitration *see generally* Francisco Orrego Vicuña, *Changing Approaches to the Nationality of Claims in the Context of Diplomatic Protection and International Dispute Settlement*, in *Liber Amicorum Ibrahim F. I. Shihata* 503 (S. Schlemmer-Schulte & K.-Y. Tung eds., 2001); Robert Wisner & Nick Gallus, *Nationality Requirements in Investor-State Arbitration*, 5 J. World Inv. & Trade 927 (2004); Pia Acconci, *Determining the Internationally Relevant Link between a State and a Corporate Investor*, 5 J. World Inv. & Trade 139 (2004).

[2] *See, e.g, MTD Equity Sdn. Bhd. & MTD Chile S.A. v. Chile*, ICSID Case No. ARB/01/7 (Award of May 25, 2004) (a national of Malaysia who had made an investment in Chile satisfied the *ratione personae* requirements of both the Chile-Malaysia bilateral investment treaty (BIT) and the Washington Convention).

investment protection treaties and legislation, and the Washington Convention. In particular, the status of minority, noncontrolling, and indirect shareholders are examined. Finally, issues arising out of change of nationality of investors and their implications for jurisdiction of arbitral tribunals under investment treaties and the Washington Convention are examined.

A. Nationality of Natural Persons Under Customary International Law: Effective Nationality Principle

The customary international law rules for determining the nationality of natural persons were developed in the context of diplomatic protection,[3] which a state can only provide to individuals who qualify legally as its nationals. "[N]ationality is a legal bond having as its basis a social fact of attachment, a genuine connection of existence, interests and sentiments, together with the existence of reciprocal rights and duties."[4] However, an individual may be recognized by more than one state as a *national* for internal purposes.[5] Normally, for purposes of diplomatic protection, the nationality of such individuals under customary international law has been determined by the application of the effective nationality rule.[6] The International Court of Justice articulated this principle in the classic *Nottebohm* case.

In *Nottebohm*, Liechtenstein espoused the claims of Nottebohm against Guatemala before the International Court of Justice (ICJ) in relation to his arrest, detention, and expulsion from Guatemala as well as the seizure of his property. Guatemala argued that the claim was inadmissible on a number of grounds, including that Liechtenstein had failed to prove that Nottebohm had properly acquired its nationality in accordance with Liechtenstein laws; "even if such proof were provided, the legal provisions which would have been applied cannot be regarded as in conforming with international law; and because M. Nottebohm appears in any event not to have lost, or not validly to have lost, his German nationality."[7]

Nottebohm was born a German citizen, and acquired Liechtenstein citizenship through naturalization after the outbreak of World War II. He had spent a number of years in Guatemala and had made it the center of his business activities. The ICJ accepted Guatemala's plea of inadmissibility, because Liechtenstein failed to show

---

[3] On diplomatic protection *see* Chapter II at pp. 27 *et seq. supra*.
[4] *Nottebohm (Liecht. v. Guat.)* 1955 I.C.J. 4, 23.
[5] Marjorie M. Whiteman, 8 *Digest of International Law*, 65 (U.S. Dept. of State 1967).
[6] *Nottebohm, supra* note 4, at 22. *See also* Paul Weis, *Nationality and Statelessness*, in *International Law* 173–99 (1979); Ian Brownlie, *Principles of Public International Law* 396 *et seq.* (6th ed. Oxford University Press 2003); Charles N. Brower & Jason D. Brueschke, *The Iran-United States Claims Tribunal* 293–96 (Martinus Nijhoff 1998).
[7] *Nottebohm, supra* note 4, at 6.

that Nottebohm had any effective links to it. The ICJ described the factors that should be taken into account in determining the real and effective nationality:

> International arbitrators have ... given their preference to the real and effective nationality, that which accorded with the facts, that based on stronger factual ties between the person concerned and one of the States whose nationality is involved. Different factors are taken into consideration, and their importance will vary from one case to the next: the habitual residence of the individual concerned is an important factor, but there are other factors such as the center of his interests, his family ties, his participation in public life, attachment shown by him for a given country and inculcated in his children etc.[8]

Guided by these factors, the Court carefully reviewed Nottebohm's connection to various countries:

> *Nottebohm Case*, 25–26 ICJ Rep. (1955)
>
> At the date when he applied for naturalization Nottebohm had been a German national from the time of his birth. He had always retained his connections with members of his family who had remained in Germany and he had always had business connections with that country. His country had been at war for more than a month, and there is nothing to indicate that the application for naturalization then made by Nottebohm was motivated by any desire to dissociate himself from the Government of his country.
>
> He had been settled in Guatemala for 34 years. He had carried on his activities there. It was the main seat of his interests. He returned there shortly after his naturalization, and it remained the centre of his interests and of his business activities. He stayed there until his removal as a result of war measures in 1943. He subsequently attempted to return there, and he now complains of Guatemala's refusal to admit him. There, too, were several members of his family who sought to safeguard his interests.
>
> In contrast, his actual connections with Liechtenstein were extremely tenuous. No settled abode, no prolonged residence in that country at the time of his application for naturalization: the application indicates that he was paying a visit there and confirms the transient character of this visit by its request that the naturalization proceedings should be initiated and concluded without delay. No intention of settling there was shown . . . If Nottebohm went to Liechtenstein in 1946, this was because of the refusal of Guatemala to admit him . . . There is no allegation of any economic interests or of any activities exercised or to be exercised in Liechtenstein, and no manifestation of any intention whatsoever to transfer all or some of his interests and his business activities to Liechtenstein. . . .
>
> These facts clearly establish, on the one hand, the absence of any bond of attachment between Nottebohm and Liechtenstein and, on the other hand, the existence of a long-standing and close connection between him and Guatemala, a link which his naturalization in no way weakened. That naturalization was not based on any real prior connection with Liechtenstein, nor did it in any way alter the manner of life of the person upon whom it was conferred in exceptional circumstances of speed and accommodation. In both respects, it was lacking in the genuineness requisite to an act of such importance, if it is to be entitled to be respected by a State in the position of Guatemala. It was granted without regard to the concept of nationality adopted in international relations.
>
> Naturalization was asked for not so much for the purpose of obtaining a legal recognition of Nottebohm's membership in fact in the population of Liechtenstein, as it was to

---

[8] *Id.* at 22.

> enable him to substitute for his status as a national of a belligerent State that of a national of a neutral State, with the sole aim of thus coming within the protection of Liechtenstein but not of becoming wedded to its traditions, its interests, its way of life or of assuming the obligations—other than fiscal obligations—and exercising the rights pertaining to the status thus acquired. Guatemala is under no obligation to recognize a nationality granted in such circumstances. Liechtenstein consequently is not entitled to extend its protection to Nottebohm vis-à-vis Guatemala and its claim must, for this reason, be held to be inadmissible.

Other international adjudicating bodies, including the Iran-U.S. Claims Tribunal[9] and the United Nations Compensation Commission,[10] have adopted and applied the principle of effective nationality in order to assess the standing of claimants to obtain relief.

B. Qualified *Investors* Under Investment Treaties and the Washington Convention

Investment treaties normally use terms such as *investors*[11] or *nationals*[12] of a country, or sometimes both terms together,[13] to describe individuals or entities that qualify to enjoy the substantive protections of the treaty. These terms are typically phrased with sufficient breadth to encompass both natural persons and legal entities such as corporations.[14] In practice, however, the legal issues that arise in connection with individuals and corporations are rather distinct and are therefore addressed separately.

---

[9] *Iran v. U.S.*, Case No. A/18, Decision No. DEC 32-A18-FT (Apr. 6, 1984), *reprinted in* 5 Iran-U.S. C.T.R. 251. *See generally* Brower & Brueschke, *supra* note 6, at 289–96.

[10] *See* United Nations Compensation Commission Governing Council, *Report and Recommendations Made by the Panel of Commissioners Concerning the Sixth Installment of Claims for Departure from Iraq or Kuwait (Category "A" Claims)*, ¶¶ 27–33, U.N. Doc. S/AC.26/1996/3 (Oct. 16, 1996). (discussing the need for effective nationality other than Iraqi for compensation for losses resulting from Iraq's 1990 invasion of Kuwait).

[11] *See, e.g.*, Canada-South Africa BIT (1995), art. 1(g); South Korea-Egypt BIT (1996), art. 1(1).

[12] *See, e.g.*, U.K.-Tonga BIT (1997), art. 2(2); Germany-Somalia BIT (1981), art. 1(3).

[13] *See, e.g.*, U.K.-U.A.E. BIT (1992), art. 1(c),(e).

[14] *See, e.g.*, Philippines-Sweden BIT (1999), art. 1(2) ("The term 'investor' shall mean natural persons . . . [and] legal entities including companies. . . ."); Tunisia-U.K. BIT (1989), art. 1(c) (" 'nationals' means . . . physical persons . . . and legal persons . . ."). Some investment treaties, such as the Association of South East Asian Nations (ASEAN) investment protection agreement, define physical persons separately as *nationals*, defining legal entities separately as *corporations*. *See, e.g.*, Agreement among the Government of Brunei Darussalam, Republic of Indonesia, Malaysia, Republic of the Philippines, Republic of Singapore, and the Kingdom of Thailand for the Promotion and Protection of Investments art. 1, Dec. 15, 1987; Singapore-Vietnam BIT (1992), art. 1(3)-(4).

1. Natural Persons

a. Investment Treaty and Washington Convention Provisions

As explained in Chapter XI, the definitions of *investment* contained in investment treaties and the Washington Convention are not the same, and International Centre for Settlement of Investment Disputes (ICSID) arbitral tribunals therefore often engage in a two-step analysis to determine whether they have subject-matter jurisdiction under the Washington Convention and the applicable treaty. One might expect the same approach to apply with respect to whether a claimant qualifies as an *investor*. However, the Washington Convention has been interpreted to impose less stringent limitations upon the definition of *investor* than is the case with the concept of *investment*. As a result, with respect to jurisdiction *ratione personae*, the difference between an investment arbitration initiated under the ICSID Rules and the United Nations Commission on International Trade Law (UNCITRAL) Rules may not be substantial.[15] The most important issues would arise in the context of both ICSID and non-ICSID arbitration, such as the law applicable to the determination of nationality, and the status of natural persons (individuals) with more than one nationality. These problems are discussed in the following text.

Investment treaties refer to *nationals, natural persons*,[16] or *physical persons*.[17] The Washington Convention uses the term *natural person*.[18] These terms denote what in some immigration laws is referred to as a *citizen*. However, the personal jurisdiction established by some investment treaties extends beyond citizens, offering coverage to permanent residents as well. Article 1(7) of the Energy Charter Treaty, for example, provides that " 'investor' means . . . a natural person having the citizenship or nationality of or who is permanently residing in that Contracting Party in accordance with its applicable law."[19] Article 1(1)(c) of the Russian Federation-Germany BIT provides that "the term 'investor' means a

---

[15] The Washington Convention does impose certain additional conditions with respect to the time at which the investor's nationality is to be determined for purposes of jurisdiction *ratione personae*. *See* pp. 301 *et seq.* and p. 343 *infra*.

[16] *See, e.g.*, North American Free Trade Agreement (1992), art. 201(1) [hereinafter NAFTA] ("national means a natural person who is a citizen or permanent resident of a Party and. . . ."); *see also* U.K.-Slovenia BIT (1996), art. 1(c) (" 'nationals' means . . . natural persons with citizenship of the [Party] . . ."). *See, also,* U.S.-Ecuador BIT (1993), art. 1(c) (" 'national' of a Party means a natural person who is a national of a Party. . . .").

[17] *See, e.g.*, U.K.-Yemen BIT (1982), art. 1(c) (" 'nationals' means . . . physical persons deriving their status . . . from the law in force. . . .").

[18] Convention on the Settlement of Investment Disputes between States and Nationals of Other States (1966) art. 25 [hereinafter Washington Convention or ICSID Convention].

[19] The Energy Charter Treaty, Annex 1 to the Final Act of the European Energy Charter Conference, at art. 1(7), Dec. 16–17, 1994, Lisbon, Portugal, *available at* http://www.encharter.org/; *see also* NAFTA, art. 201(1) ("national means a natural person who is a citizen or permanent resident of a Party. . . .").

natural person that has the permanent residence, or a legal entity that has its seat, in the respective territories to which this Treaty applies, and that has the right to make investments."[20]

The Washington Convention grants standing for jurisdictional purposes to nationals of other Contracting States. "National of another Contracting State" is defined as:

> (a) any natural person who had the nationality of a Contracting State other than the State party to the dispute on the date on which the parties consented to submit such dispute to conciliation or arbitration as well as on the date on which the request was registered pursuant to paragraph (3) of Article 28 or paragraph (3) of Article 36, but does not include any person who on either date also had the nationality of the Contracting State party to the dispute. . . .[21]

The Washington Convention offers no guidance as to how long an individual must remain a national to be considered a *national* of a Contracting State. Therefore the answer to this question must be sought in external sources of law: national or international. This issue is also discussed in Section C(3) below.

The primary additional condition imposed on individual investors to qualify for protection is that such an investor must have made an *investment*.[22] As a result of the interdependence of the terms *investor* and *investment*, treaties that include a relatively broad definition of *investment* also protect a wider range of putative investors.

b. Applicable Law

As noted earlier the central criterion established in investment treaties for determining whether a natural person qualifies for protection as an *investor* is that the individual is endowed with the nationality of a signatory state other than the state where the individual's investment was made. It is not immediately evident how an arbitral tribunal is to assess an individual claimant's nationality. Helpfully, many investment treaties do provide that the nationality of a person shall be determined in accordance with the national law of the investor's purported home state. For example, the United States-Ecuador BIT provides that *national* of a Party means a natural person who is a national of a Party "under its applicable law."[23] Therefore, the question of nationality should be answered by reference to the domestic laws of the states party to the treaty. Domestic laws of the world generally adopt one or both of two fundamentally different rules on nationality: jus sanguinis and

---

[20] Russian Federation-Germany BIT (1989), art. 1(1)(c).
[21] Washington Convention, art. 25(2)(a).
[22] *See* Chapter XI on definition of investment.
[23] U.S.-Ecuador BIT, art. 1 (emphasis added); *see also* U.K.-U.A.E. BIT, art. 1(c): ("[N]ationals means: (i) in respect of the United Kingdom: physical persons deriving their status as United Kingdom nationals from the law in force in the United Kingdom. (ii) in respect of the United Arab Emirates: natural and physical persons deriving their status as United Arab Emirates nationals from the law in force in the United Arab Emirates").

jus soli.[24] Jus sanguinis refers to the acquisition of citizenship by birth to parents of a particular nationality; and jus soli refers to the acquisition of citizenship by birth in the territory of a state.[25] Domestic laws normally envisage additional methods of acquiring citizenship, such as through marriage or subsequent to an extended period of residency.

Some investment treaties provide more guidance in this respect by specifying the particular laws of the contracting parties that should be consulted for the purpose of determining nationality. For example, Annex 201.1 to North American Free Trade Agreement (NAFTA) Article 201 identifies the Mexican Constitution and the United States Immigration and Nationality Act as the proper reference points for determining who may be considered a national of these countries.[26] Various other drafting variations among investment treaties may narrow or broaden the scope of the persons who would fall under a treaty.[27] These issues naturally must be examined on a case-by-case basis.

Some investment protection treaties, as well as the Washington Convention,[28] do not specify the law that should be applied to determine the nationality of potential claimants who are natural persons. The Austria-Croatia BIT, typical of such treaties, provides that "the term 'investor' means in respect of either Contracting Party . . . nationals of a Contracting Party who make an investment in the other Contracting Party's territory."[29] Most commentators agree that where the relevant treaty provides no guidance, tribunals should normally give substantial deference to the law of the home state of the claimant.[30] The applicable rules of public international law for this purpose, which were developed in the context of diplomatic protection,[31] recognize the rights of states to set the rules for granting nationality

---

[24] Brownlie, *supra* note 6, at 378–79; Albrecht Randelzhofer, *Nationality, in* 3 *Encyclopedia of Public International Law* 501, 503 (R. Bernhardt ed., 1997).

[25] Brownlie, *supra* note 6, at 378–79. In addition to these general rules, various domestic laws may address additional methods of acquiring citizenship, through, for instance, residence in the territory of a country. *See id.* at 379 *et seq. See also* Alfred M. Boll, *Multiple Nationality and International Law* (Martinus Nijhoff 2007).

[26] NAFTA, Annex 201.1.

[27] *See generally* Rudolf Dolzer & Margrete Stevens, *Bilateral Investment Treaties* 32 (Kluwer Academic Publishers 1995).

[28] With respect to Washington Convention, "[q]uestions of nationality are not ruled by the law applicable to the dispute in accordance with art. 42 unless, of course, that law happens to be also the law of the State whose nationality is at issue." Christoph Schreuer, *The ICSID Convention: A Commentary* 267 (Cambridge University Press 2001).

[29] Austria-Croatia BIT (1997), art. 1(2)(a).

[30] *Cf.* Schreuer, *supra* note 28, at 267 ("Whether a person is a nation of a particular State is determined, in the first place, by the law of the State whose nationality is claimed. . . .").

[31] Brownlie, *supra* note 6, at 375; *see also* Schreuer, *supra* note 28, at 268 (adhering to the same view); Chittharanjan F. Amerasinghe, *Jurisdiction of International Tribunals* 258–59 (Kluwer Law International 2003).

to a person in their domestic laws and to apply such rules.[32] However, the international law of diplomatic protection limits the weight that tribunals should accord to the decisions of national institutions to their domestic laws; as the ICJ explained in the *Nottebohm* case,[33] when a state espouses a claim of one of its nationals and initiates proceedings on such person's behalf before an international tribunal, "it place[s] itself on the plane of international law. It is international law which determines whether [it] is entitled to exercise protection. . . ."[34] Therefore, neither a state's grant of nationality to a person under its own laws nor its espousal of a resulting claim is determinative at the international level, and an international tribunal retains its right to independently examine the issue of nationality. In investment treaty arbitration, although investors have a direct right of action, the same rationale should apply. This explains why arbitral tribunals, which generally turn to the laws of the investor's home state in determining the nationality of natural persons, have not completely deferred to that state's interpretation or application of its laws on nationality. Documents of nationality issued by a state in this respect, such as a certificate of nationality, have been considered only as prima facie evidence of nationality.[35] In *Soufraki v. United Arab Emirates* (U.A.E.),[36] for example, the claimant brought a case against U.A.E. under the Italy-U.A.E. BIT. The respondent state contested the jurisdiction of the tribunal on the ground that the claimant was not an Italian national. The claimant provided various documents, including a certificate of nationality from Italian authorities, to prove his Italian nationality. Although the tribunal gave some weight to the documents issued by the Italian authorities, in the end it conducted its own independent

---

[32] Article 1 of the Convention on Certain Questions Relating to the Conflict of Nationality Laws, which was signed in the Hague in 1930 provides that "[i]t is for each State to determine under its own law who are its nationals. This law shall be recognised by other States in so far as it is consistent with international conventions, international custom, and the principles of law generally recognised with regard to nationality." 179 L.N.T.S. 89 (1937). A number of commentators believe that this article reflects a rule of general customary international law. *See* Randelzhofer, *supra* note 24, at 502; *see also* Brownlie, *supra* note 6, at 375; Edwin M. Borchard, *The Protection of Citizens Abroad*, 43 Yale L.J. 359, 374 (1934); *Oppenheim's International Law* 852–52 (Robert Jennings & Arthur Watts eds., 9th ed. 1992) (1905); *Siag v. Egypt*, ICSID Case No. ARB/05/15 (Decision on Jurisdiction, May 28, 2007), ¶ 143. *See also* Schreuer, *supra* note 28, at 267: "But an international tribunal is not bound by the national law in question under all circumstances. Situations where nationality provisions of national law may be disregarded include cases of ineffective nationality lacking a genuine link between the State and the individual. Other instances where national rules need not be followed are certain situations of involuntary acquisition of nationality in violation of international law or cases of withdrawal of nationality that are contrary to international law."

[33] *Nottebohm, supra* note 4.

[34] *Id.* at 20–21.

[35] *Siag, supra* note 32, ¶ 153; *Soufraki v. United Arab Emirates*, ICSID Case No. ARB/02/07 (Award of July 7, 2004), ¶ 55.

[36] *Id.*

analysis of the claimant's nationality under Italian law and concluded that he lacked the requisite nationality.[37]

Soufraki v. U.A.E.

ICSID Case No. ARB/02/07 (Award of July 7, 2007)

53. The first contentious question to be decided is whether, as Claimant maintains, the Certificates of Nationality issued by Italian authorities characterizing Mr. Soufraki as an Italian national, and his Italian passports, identity cards and the letter of the Italian Ministry of Foreign Affairs so stating, constitute conclusive proof that Mr. Soufraki reacquired his Italian nationality after 1992 and that he was an Italian national on the date on which the parties to this dispute consented to submit it to arbitration as well as on the date on which the request to ICSID was registered by it.

54. Claimant contends that it is for the Italian authorities to interpret Italian nationality law, and that this Tribunal should apply their conclusions. He emphasizes that Article 1(3) of the BIT [Italy-U.A.E. BIT (1995)] specifies that the nationality of a natural person shall be determined according to the law of the Contracting State in question.

55. It is accepted in international law that nationality is within the domestic jurisdiction of the State, which settles, by its own legislation, the rules relating to the acquisition (and loss) of its nationality. Article 1(3) of the BIT reflects this rule. But it is no less accepted that when, in international arbitral or judicial proceedings, the nationality of a person is challenged, the international tribunal is competent to pass upon that challenge. It will accord great weight to the nationality law of the State in question and to the interpretation and application of that law by its authorities. But it will in the end decide for itself whether, on the facts and law before it, the person whose nationality is at issue was or was not a national of the State in question and when, and what follows from that finding. Where, as in the instant case, the jurisdiction of an international tribunal turns on an issue of nationality, the international tribunal is empowered, indeed bound, to decide that issue.

---

[37] Similarly, in *Siag & Vecchi v. Egypt*, a case filed under the Egypt-Italy BIT, the tribunal was presented with various documents and legal argument as to the nationality of the claimants. In the end, relying largely on *Soufraki v. U.A.E.*, the tribunal conducted its own examination of the nationality of the claimants and found that they did not have Egyptian nationality and hence were entitled to file a claim against Egypt without being subject to the limitations on dual nationality imposed by the Washington Convention. *Siag*, *supra* note 32, ¶¶ 48, 142–201. The issue of dual nationality is treated in section (c) of the text that follows. *See also Champion Trading Co. v. Egypt*, ICSID Case No. ARB/02/9, 11C 56 (Decision on Jurisdiction of Oct. 21, 2003), at 4–8 (the tribunal conducted its own independent analysis of individual claimants and denied jurisdiction with respect to them, as they were Egyptian nationals and under the Washington Convention they could not file a case against Egypt). *See also* Richard Happ & Noah Rubins, *Awards and Decisions of ICSID Tribunals in 2004*, 47 Germ. Y.B. Int'l L. 878, 904–905 (2004); Wisner & Gallus, *supra* note 1, at 930; Farouk Yala, Soufraki v. United Arab Emirates (*Observations*), Les Cahiers de l'Arbitrage/Gazette du Palais 22 (2004); Anthony Sinclair, *Nationality of Individual Investors in ICSID Arbitration*: Hussein Nuaman Soufraki v. United Arab Emirates, Int'l Arb. L. Rev. 191 (2004).

56. While the Claimant does not dispute the foregoing authority of this Tribunal, it submits that it should exercise it so as to override official Italian affirmations of the Italian nationality of Mr. Soufraki only in response to allegations and proof of fraud.

57. While the Respondent did not in terms maintain that evidence in support of Mr. Soufraki's acquisition or reacquisition of Italian nationality was fraudulent, counsel of the Respondent when cross-examining Mr. Soufraki did characterize the evidence that he submitted in support of his claim that he was resident in Italy for more than a year 1993–94 as "bogus." Nevertheless, the Tribunal wishes to make clear that, in its view, issues of alleged fraud need not be addressed.

58. The question rather comes to this. Mr. Soufraki asserts as a fact that he was resident in Italy for business purposes for more than one year in 1993–94. In accordance with accepted international (and general national) practice, a party bears the burden of proof in establishing the facts that he asserts. Claimant accordingly bears the burden of proving to the satisfaction of the Tribunal that he was resident in Italy for more than one year in 1993–94 and accordingly that he was an Italian national on the relevant dates and that, as a result, he belongs to the class of investors in respect of whom the Respondent has consented to ICSID jurisdiction.

. . . .

81. Having considered and weighed the totality of the evidence adduced by Mr. Soufraki, the Tribunal, unanimously, comes to the conclusion that Claimant has failed to discharge his burden of proof. He has not demonstrated to the satisfaction of the Tribunal that he established and maintained his residence in Italy during the period from March 1993 until April 1994.

Having lost the case at the jurisdictional stage, Mr. Soufraki sought annulment of the decision against him,[38] alleging that the ICSID tribunal manifestly exceeded its powers when it failed to recognize his Italian certificate of nationality. However, the annulment panel rejected the claimant's assertions. It held that the arbitral tribunal was entitled to review the nationality certificate independently to determine Mr. Soufraki's nationality at the international level. It added that "it is a general principle that a state does not have the last word when a question is raised before an international tribunal concerning the interpretation of its national law, when it comes to a question on which the jurisdiction of the Tribunal depends."[39]

c. Status of Dual Nationals Under the Washington Convention and Other Arbitral Rules

It is a reality of modern life that individuals not infrequently possess two or more nationalities at the same time.[40] The situation is difficult when a person possesses two nationalities, one of which is that of the host state of the investment.

---

[38] *Soufraki v. United Arab Emirates*, ICSID Case No. ARB/02/7 (Decision of the Ad Hoc Committee on the Application for Annulment of Mr. Soufraki, June 5, 2007).

[39] *Id.* ¶ 59 (emphasis in the original).

[40] *See generally* Boll, *supra* note 25.

Article 25(2)(a)[41] of the Washington Convention includes a "negative" nationality requirement,[42] which does not allow such persons to bring a claim against the host state.[43] On this basis the tribunal in *Champion Trading v. Egypt* denied jurisdiction *ratione personae* with respect to three American claimants who also held Egyptian nationality. The tribunal confirmed its jurisdiction with respect to the other claimants, two American corporations. The individual claimants in that case were three members of the Wahba family, all of whom were born in the United States to an American mother, and enjoyed U.S. nationality by virtue of both jus soli and jus sanguinis. Their father was also a U.S. citizen and had been born in Egypt as an Egyptian citizen. The claimants were born and had spent most of their lives in the United States, and had only tenuous connections to Egypt; however, the tribunal found that by application of jus sanguinis, which was part of the Egyptian laws on nationality, they were Egyptian and therefore barred from bringing a claim against Egypt under the Convention.[44]

Schreuer suggests that a dual national might be able to circumvent the prohibition imposed by Article 25(2)(a) of the Washington Convention by renouncing the nationality of the host state just before initiating arbitration. He notes the following:

> Obviously, the benefits from such a step would have to be weighed against any costs arising from the surrender of the host State's nationality. Also, the investor would have to ensure that the renunciation of the nationality is valid under the host State's law. A written affirmation [by that state] to this effect is advisable.[45]

Also uncertain is the result where nationality has been involuntarily acquired or maintained. Thus, in *Champion Trading*, the arbitrators suggested that in certain circumstances dual nationals who hold host state nationality against their will would not be barred from ICSID arbitration:

> The Tribunal does not rule out that situations might arise where the exclusion of dual nationals could lead to a result which was manifestly absurd or unreasonable. . . . One

---

[41] See p. 296 *supra*.

[42] Schreuer, *supra* note 28, at 273.

[43] See id, at 273–76. On various aspects of the date of consent, see Chapter X *supra*. Washington Convention, art. 25(2)(a); Dolzer & Stevens, *supra* note 27, at 141. See also Report of the Executive Directors on the Convention on the Settlement of Disputes between States and Nationals of Other States (1965), ¶ 29, *reprinted in* ICSID, 2 *Documents Concerning the Origin and the Formulation of the Convention*, 1078–79 (1968): "It should be noted that under clause (a) of Article 25(2) a natural person who was a national of the State party to the dispute would not be eligible to be a party in proceedings under the auspices of the Centre, even if at the same time he had the nationality of another State. This ineligibility is absolute and cannot be cured even if the State party to the dispute had given its consent"; see also Brower & Brueschke, *supra* note 6, at 288.

[44] *Champion Trading*, *supra* note 37, at 4–8.

[45] Schreuer, *supra* note 28, at 272.

could envisage a situation where a country continues to apply the *jus sanguinis* over many generations. It might well for instance be questionable if the third or fourth foreign born generation, which has no ties whatsoever with the country of its forefathers, could still be considered to have, for the purposes of the Convention, the nationality of the State.[46]

These analyses may be contrasted with the dissenting opinion of Professor Orrego Vicuña in *Siag & Vecchi v. Egypt*,[47] where he opined that the nationality of natural persons for the purposes of the Washington Convention should be strictly evaluated in light of the purposes of the Washington Convention. Otherwise, he opined, there is the possibility for abuse of acquisition or loss of nationality on the part of claimants.[48] In *Siag & Vecchi v. Egypt*, the tribunal asserted jurisdiction *ratione personae* over the claims of Siag and Vecchi under the Egypt-Italy BIT. However, in his strong dissenting opinion Orrego Vicuña objected to Siag's standing.

Siag and Vecchi had relied on Italian nationality to submit their claims. Egypt objected to the jurisdiction of the tribunal on the basis that under the applicable Egyptian laws the claimants were also Egyptian nationals, and excluded from ICSID arbitration under Article 25(2)(a) of the Washington Convention. Both claimants countered that they had lost Egyptian nationality prior to filing the ICSID claim. The tribunal accepted claimants' argument, primarily on the basis of the expert testimony of Fuad Riad on the interpretation of applicable Egyptian law and its analysis.[49] In this context it considered Egypt's argument that the claimants' effective connections were to Egypt rather than to Italy. The majority of the *Siag* tribunal held that for the purposes of jurisdiction *ratione personae* under the Washington Convention, there is no need to determine the *effective* nationality of the claimants as might be the case under customary international law.[50] Indeed, the majority held that such a review would be irrelevant, because the Washington Convention is clear as to who may bring a claim:[51] So long as the claimant is not a dual national, there is no need to apply the *effective* nationality test.[52]

Orrego Vicuña found the interpretation of the majority, especially the latter part, to be inconsistent with the intentions of the Washington Convention's drafters. He noted that the countries that originally promulgated the Washington Convention, as it appears from the Report of the Executive Directors, were clearly concerned about being sued by their own nationals. Therefore, Orrego Vicuña rea-

---

[46] SN: *Champion Trading*, *supra* note 37, at 16–17. *See also* Farouk Yala, Champion Trading v. Egypt (*Observations*), 2004 Les Cahiers de l'Arbitrage/Gazette du Palais 19 (criticizing the tribunal's formalistic approach, particularly when faced with *authentic* foreign investment).

[47] *Siag*, *supra* note 32.

[48] *Id.* at 63.

[49] *Id.* at 40–41.

[50] Effective nationality was addressed at pp. 292–94 *supra*.

[51] *Siag*, *supra* note 32, ¶ 198.

[52] *Id.* ¶¶ 198–201.

soned, the negative nationality requirement of Article 25(2)(a), like a rule of *jus cogens*, must be interpreted as a mandatory requirement, which may not be derogated from even by consent. This would mean that in the circumstances of the case, the effective nationality of Siag should be considered.

> [The Washington] Convention goes beyond the strict technical situation of dual nationals and the dates used to this effect and covers additional situations that could contradict the prohibition in question, not to mention the fact that otherwise there could be uncontrollable abuse arising from acquisition or loss of nationalities.[53]

With respect to the date at which the negative nationality requirement must be satisfied,[54] Orrego Vicuña criticized the current tendency in the legal community to consider the acceptance date of the state's offer in an investment treaty as the date of consent, contending that such an approach was inadequate to protect state interests:[55]

> [C]ould it be held that the safeguard the State had under the Convention not to be taken to arbitration by those who were its own nationals at the time of expressing its consent, or at any rate at the time the investment was made, simply vanished? Could it be right that thereafter the process of eligibility would be controlled solely by the investor in the light of the situation prevailing at the time of its acceptance of consent, in disregard of the equivalent right of the State?[56]

Orrego Vicuña then suggested an alternative interpretation of the negative nationality requirement:

> In this context, an alternative reading of the Convention to the effect that the negative test applies not only at the date in which the investor consents but also at that in which the State consents, or at the date the investment was made as some treaties require, would be plausible and much in harmony with the meaning of the Convention in the light of its drafting history. In such a case, the interpretation given by the [ICSID] Institutional Rules would need to be supplemented or clarified.
>
> This would mean in fact that an investor applying for ICSID proceedings would be required not to be a national of the host State on both the date of expression of consent by the State, or the date of making the investment, and that of its own expression of consent, and then again at the time of registration. This would certainly prevent many kinds of abuse. . .[57]

Accordingly, he concluded that Mr. Siag was not a proper claimant under the Washington Convention, as his *effective nationality* was Egyptian.

The limitations imposed by dual nationality are not exclusive to the cases that are filed within the ICSID framework.[58] Such concerns may arise in cases filed under other arbitral rules as well. Most investment treaties are silent about the

---

[53] *Id.* at 63.

[54] See p. 296 *supra*.

[55] On the date of consent, see Chapter X *supra* and other authorities cited in note 43 *supra*.

[56] *Siag, supra* note 32, Partial Dissenting Opinion of Professor Francisco Orrego Vicuña, at 65.

[57] *Id.*

[58] The issue was extensively debated at Iran-U.S. Claims Tribunal where the tribunal eventually adopted the effective nationality rule as pronounced in *Nottebohm. See generally* Brower & Brueschke, *supra* note 6, at 288 *et seq.*

status of dual nationals.[59] But certain recent treaties have explicitly dealt with the issue. The Dominican Republic–Central American Free Trade Agreement, for example, provides:

> [I]nvestor of a Party means . . . a national . . . of a Party, that attempts to make, is making, or has made an investment in the territory of another Party; provided, however, that a natural person who is dual national shall be deemed to be exclusively a national of the State of his or her dominant and effective nationality.[60]

This provision appears to incorporate by reference the customary international law on dual nationality, as reflected in the *Nottebohm* decision. In the absence of such a treaty provision, a tribunal could nevertheless apply international law to fill any perceived lacuna, also permitting the application of the *effective nationality* test previously explained.[61]

2. Corporations and other Legal Persons

a. Treaty Provisions

Generally, investment treaties broadly define *investor* to encompass a variety of legal entities, including "legal person,"[62] "juridical person,"[63] "company,"[64] and so forth. Within these broad definitions, treaties usually provide an illustrative list of the entities that qualify such as "corporations, firms and associations,"[65] or "companies, association of companies, trading corporate entities and other organizations,"[66] or "any kind of corporation, company, association, partnership,

---

[59] United Nations Conference on Trade and Development (UNCTAD), *Scope and Definition*, 2 UNCTAD Series on Issues in International Investment Agreements, 36, U.N. Doc. UNCTAD/ITE/IIT/11 (1999).

[60] Dominican Republic–Central America Free Trade Agreement (2004), art. 10.28.

[61] In the context of NAFTA, Mexico in *Feldman v. Mexico* argued that Feldman, a U.S. citizen and permanent resident of Mexico, was effectively a dual-national under Article 1139, 201, and Annex 201.1. NAFTA Article 201 includes the following definition of *national*: "national means a natural person who is a citizen or permanent resident of a Party and any other natural person referred to in Annex 201.1." The tribunal, however, rejected Mexico's arguments and ruled that under general principles of international law, "in matters of standing in international adjudication or arbitration or other form of diplomatic protection, citizenship rather than residence is considered to deliver, subject to specific rules, the relevant connection [between a State and an individual]." *Feldman v. Mexico*, ICSID Case No. ARB(AF)/99/1 (Final Award, Dec. 16, 2002), ¶ 30.

[62] Ethiopia-Sudan BIT (2000), art. 1(b)(ii); Hungary-Yemen BIT (2004), art. 2.

[63] Belgium-Thailand BIT (2002), art. 1(1)(b); South Korea-Panama BIT (2001), art. 1(3).

[64] Belgium-Philippines BIT (1998), art. 1(b); Philippines-Thailand BIT (1995), art. 1.

[65] Benin-U.K. BIT (1987), art. 1(d); U.K.-Saint Lucia BIT (1983), art. 1(d).

[66] Belgium-Hong Kong BIT (1996), art. 1(2).

or other organization."[67] These definitions are wide enough to encompass both commercial and nonprofit entities. The following table offers a sample of some variations on the theme of who is an *investor*:

Definitions of Corporate Investors in Several Bilateral Investment Treaties

Greece-Republic of Korea (1995)	Finland-Algeria BIT (2005)	Argentina-Australia BIT (1995)	Republic of Korea-Panama BIT (2001)
Art. 3 "Investors" shall comprise, with regard to either Contracting Party: . . . . (b) legal persons constituted in accordance with the laws of that Contracting Party and having their principal place of business within its territory.	Art. 2. The term "investor" means, for either Contracting Party: . . . (b) Any legal entity such as company, corporation, firm, partnership, business association, institution or organisation, incorporated or constituted in accordance with the laws and regulations of the Contracting Party and having its registered office or central administration or principal place of business within the territory of	Art. 1(c) "investor" of a Contracting Party means: (i) in respect of Australia: . . . . (B) a company; and (ii) in respect of the Argentine Republic: . . . . (B) a legal person; 1(d) "company" means any corporation, association, partnership, trust or other legally recognised entity that is duly incorporated, constituted, set up, or otherwise duly organised: (i) under the law of Australia; or (ii) under the law of a third country and is owned or controlled, directly or indirectly, by an entity described in paragraph 1(d)(i) of this Article or by a natural	Art. 1(3) "investors" means any natural or juridical persons of one Contracting Party who invest in the territory of the other Contracting Party . . .

Continued

---

[67] U.S.-Ecuador BIT, art. 1(b). NAFTA uses the term "investor of a Party," defined as "a Party or state enterprise thereof, or a national or an enterprise of such Party, that seeks to make, is making or has made an investment." NAFTA, art. 1139. Article 201 defines "enterprise" as "any entity constituted or organized under applicable law, whether or not for profit, and whether privately-owned or governmentally-owned, including any corporation, trust, partnership, sole proprietorship, joint venture or other association." The Energy Charter Treaty, Art. 1(7)(ii), includes in the definition of "investor" "a company or other organization organized in accordance with the law applicable in that Contracting Party." *See also* other recent U.S. BITs, such as the U.S.-Argentina BIT (1992); UNCTAD, *supra* note 59, at 34 (discussion of nonprofit organizations and their engagement in education activities).

Greece-Republic of Korea (1995)	Finland-Algeria BIT (2005)	Argentina-Australia BIT (1995)	Republic of Korea-Panama BIT (2001)
	that Contracting Party.	person who is a citizen or permanent resident of Australia; regardless of whether or not the entity is organised for pecuniary gain, privately or otherwise owned, or organised with limited or unlimited liability; 1(e) "legal person" means any entity constituted according to the laws and regulations of the Argentine Republic or having its seat in the territory of the Argentine Republic . . .	

When it comes to the nationality of legal persons, investment protection instruments vary widely. Three points of contact between the investor and the state are normally considered to deal with nationality: (1) the place of incorporation or legal establishment, (2) the place of the seat (*siège sociale*) or central corporate administration, and (3) the nationality of the controlling shareholders. Each criterion presents its own complications.

According to the first concept, "a company is deemed to be attached to the legal order under which it was incorporated, irrespective of the place and seat of its economic activities."[68] An example of this approach may be found in Article 1(1)(b) of the Argentina-United States BIT.[69] Place of incorporation has the advantage of clarity and normally does not change over time.[70] However, such a criterion may not

---

[68] Dolzer & Stevens, *supra* note 27, at 35.

[69] Argentina-U.S. BIT, art. 1(b) (" 'company' of a Party means any kind of corporation, company, association, state enterprise, or other organization, legally constituted under the laws and regulations of a Party or a political subdivision thereof whether or not organized for pecuniary gain, and whether privately or governmentally owned . . ."); *see also* U.K.-Uruguay BIT (1991), art. 1(d): "[C]ompanies means: (i) in respect of the United Kingdom: corporations, firms, and associations incorporated or constituted under the law in force in any part of the United Kingdom or in any territory [to] which this Agreement is extended . . . (ii) in respect of the Oriental Republic of Uruguay: corporations, companies, firms and associations constituted or duly organized under its law in force."

[70] UNCTAD, *supra* note 59, at 37.

reflect the economic reality of the corporate entity's activities; many companies are founded in countries where they do no business at all, raising the question whether the home country would have intended to extend protection to such entities.[71]

The second defining concept "connotes the place where the effective management [of a company] takes place."[72] This approach is especially prevalent in German BIT practice. Article 1(4) of the German Model BIT of 1991, for example, provides:

> [T]he term "companies" means
>
> (a) in respect of the Federal Republic of Germany:
>
> > any juridical person as well as any commercial or other company or association with or without legal personality having its seat in the territory of the Federal Republic of Germany, irrespective of whether or not its activities are directed at profit . . . .[73]

The corporate seat reflects priorities opposite to those underlying the use of the place of incorporation as the determinant of corporate nationality: "The seat of a company may not be as easy to determine as the country of organization, but it does reflect a more significant economic relationship between the company and the country of nationality."[74]

The third concept looks to the nationality of the owners or controlling shareholders to determine the nationality of the corporation.[75] Although this approach may be difficult to apply in practice, it supports the recognition of genuine economic links between the corporation and the country of nationality.[76]

---

[71] *Id.* at 37–38; *see also* Dolzer & Stevens, *supra* note 27, at 36.

[72] UNCTAD, *supra* note 59, at 39.

[73] 1991 German Model Treaty on Encouragement and Reciprocal Protection of Investments, *reprinted in* 11 ICSID Rev.-F.I.L.J. 221 (1996); *see also* Bangladesh-Germany BIT (1981), art. 8(4)(a) (qualifying German company is as follows: "[A]ny juridical person as well as any commercial or other company or association with or without legal personality *having its seat in the German area of application* of the present Agreement and lawfully existing consistent with legal provisions, irrespective of whether the liability of its partners, associates or members is limited or unlimited and whether or not its activities are directed at profit" (emphasis added)).

[74] UNCTAD, *supra* note 59, at 39.

[75] *See, e.g.,* Philippines-Switzerland BIT (1997), art. 1(a)(ii) (qualifying Swiss companies include companies that are not incorporated under Swiss law but that are actually controlled by Swiss nationals); Switzerland-Nigeria BIT (2000), art. 1(a)(iii) (qualifying investors include "legal entities established in accordance with the legislation of an unspecified country, which are controlled, directly or indirectly, by nationals of a contracting Party"); Argentina-Australia BIT (1995), art. 1(c) (qualifying Australian companies include those incorporated "under the law of a third country and . . . owned or controlled, directly or indirectly, by an [Australian national]"). *See also* Argentina-Australia BIT (1995), art. 1(d) at p. 305 *supra.*

[76] UNCTAD, *supra* note 59, at 39.

Finally, some treaties combine these criteria, effectively narrowing the definition of a corporate investor by for example requiring both incorporation and seat,[77] or incorporation and control.[78] Conversely, some treaties specify either of these points of contact in the alternative, which make it easier to satisfy the corporate nationality requirements.[79]

b. Customary Law on Nationality of Corporations and Shareholder Standing

Customary international law displays (as do treaties) the same variety of approaches with respect to the criteria defining corporate nationality. Generally, under customary law a legal person is considered a national of the country where it was incorporated.[80] There was a reluctance to *pierce* the corporate form at customary international law. Thus, it was rare to consider a corporation a national of the country where its *siège sociale* or effective headquarters is located.[81] And: "The respect for the corporate form at international law is not normally affected by such

---

[77] Noah Rubins & N. Stephan Kinsella, *International Investment, Political Risk and Dispute Resolution* 281 (2005). *See also* Acconci, *supra* note 1, at 149–50; Russian Federation-Thailand BIT (2002), art. 1(a) (" 'investor' shall mean . . . legal persons, including companies . . . which are constituted or otherwise duly organized under the law of the Contracting Party and have their seat, together with real economic activities, in the territory of that same Contracting Party"); Switzerland-Zimbabwe BIT (1996), art. 1(1)(b) (qualifying companies include those incorporated under the laws of a Party which also have their seat in the territory of the same party).

[78] *See* Acconci, *supra* note 1, at 151 and material cited therein; *see also* Morocco-U.S. BIT (1985), art. 1(3) ("Company of a Party means: a company duly incorporated, constituted or otherwise duly organized under the applicable laws and regulations . . . in which [nationals] . . . have a substantial interest"); Senegal-U.S. BIT (1983), art. 1(b) (" 'Company of a Party' means a company duly incorporated . . . [in] a Party . . . in which [nationals] have a substantial interest as determined by such Party").

[79] *See, e.g.*, the Netherlands-Georgia BIT (1999), art. 1(b): "(ii) with . . . [regard] to either Contracting Party: legal persons constituted under the law of that Contracting Party; (iii) with regard to either Contracting Party: legal persons not constituted under the law of that Contracting Party but controlled, directly or indirectly, by natural persons as defined in (i) or by legal persons as defined in (ii)."

[80] *See* Schreuer, *supra* note 28, at 277; *see generally* Oppenheim's International Law, *supra* note 32, at 859–64; Yoram Dinstein, *Diplomatic Protection of Companies under International Law*, in *International Law: Theory and Practice* 505 (Karel Wellens ed., 1998); Christopher Staker, *Diplomatic Protection of Private Business Companies: Determining Corporate Personality for International Law Purposes*, 61 Brit. Y.B. Int'l L. 155 (1991).

[81] *See* Schreuer, *supra* note 28, at 278–79; Georges R. Delaume, *ICSID Arbitration and the Courts*, 77 AMJIL 784, 793–94 (1983); Larry C. Backer, *Comparative Corporate Law: United States, European Union, China and Japan* 467 (2002); Stanimir A. Alexandrov, *The "Baby Boom" of Treaty-Based Arbitrations and the Jurisdiction of ICSID Tribunals: Shareholders as "Investors" and Jurisdiction Ratione Temporis*, 4 L. & Prac. Int'l Cts. & Tribunals 19, 34 (2005); Dolzer & Stevens, *supra* note 27, at 35.

factors as the nationality of shareholders, and reflects the reluctance to "pierce the corporate veil."[82]

The ICJ's landmark decision in the *Barcelona Traction* case confirms this latter approach.[83] *Barcelona Traction*[84] arose out of the conduct of the government of Spain, which ultimately resulted in the bankruptcy of the Barcelona Traction company. The government of Belgium brought a claim against Spain on behalf of its nationals, who owned shares in the Canadian corporation Barcelona Traction. In the proceedings before the ICJ, one of Spain's preliminary objections to jurisdiction was that Belgium lacked standing, because Barcelona Traction was a Canadian corporation, and that Belgium consequently had no right to espouse shareholders' claims under international law. The ICJ joined its decision on this matter to the merits and in the end, 18 years later, agreed with Spain that only the state of incorporation of a company could sue on its behalf and dismissed the case.[85] It reasoned inter alia that most municipal laws of the world were based on the distinction between rights of a company and those of its shareholders.[86] The Court held that "an act directed against and infringing only the company's rights does not involve responsibility towards the shareholders, even if their interests are affected."[87] It added that "[t]he situation is different if the act complained of is aimed at the direct rights of the shareholder as such."[88] These rights include, for example, shareholder's voting rights, which were not breached.[89] Direct rights of shareholders are determined in accordance with the company laws of the country where it is incorporated.[90]

---

[82] Rubins & Kinsella, *supra* note 77, at 409; *see also*; Katherine E. Lyons, *Piercing the Corporate Veil in the International Arena*, 33 SYRJILC 523 (2006); Glenn Morris, *Piercing the Corporate Veil in Louisiana*, 52 La. L. Rev. 271 (1991); Carsten Alting, *Piercing the Corporate Veil in American and German Law—Liability of Individuals and Entities: A Comparative View*, Tulsa J. Comp. & Int'l L. 187 (1995); Omar Guerrero et al., *Piercing the Corporate Veil in Mexico*, Comp. L. Y.B. Int'l Bus. 375 (Dennis Campbell ed., 2004); Ignaz Seidl-Hohenveldern, *Corporations in and under International Law* (1987).

[83] *Barcelona Traction, Light and Power Co., Ltd. (Belgium v. Spain)* (Judgment, Feb. 5, 1970), ICJ Rep. 3 (1970).

[84] For a detailed account of the case and its implications for the modern investment treaty arbitration see Ian Laird, *A Community of Destiny—The* Barcelona Traction *Case and the Development of Shareholder Rights to Bring Investment Claims*, in *International Investment Law and Arbitration: Leading Cases from the ICSID, NAFTA, Bilateral Treaties and Customary International Law* 77 (Todd Weiler ed., Cameron May 2005).

[85] *Barcelona Traction*, *supra* note 83, at 46, ¶ 88.

[86] *Id*. at 33–40, ¶¶ 37–58.

[87] *Id*. at 36, ¶ 46.

[88] *Id*. at 36, ¶ 47; *see also* ILC Draft Articles on Diplomatic Protection, art. 12, U.N. Doc. A/61/10 (2006) ("To the extent that an internationally wrongful act of a State causes direct injury to the rights of shareholders as such, as distinct from those of the corporation itself, the State of nationality of any such shareholders is entitled to exercise diplomatic protection in respect of its nationals.").

[89] *Id*. at 37, ¶ 49.

[90] *Ahmadou Sadio Diallo (Guinea v. Democratic Republic of the Congo*, Preliminary Objections, Judgment, May 2007), ¶ 64.

Two decades later, the ICJ in the *Elettronica Sicula S.p.A. (ELSI)* case[91] seemingly abandoned the *Barcelona Traction* approach. In *ELSI*, the Court allowed the United States to espouse claims of two American companies that held controlling shares in ELSI, an Italian corporation—to be sure a corporation in the respondent state and not of a third country, as Canada in *Barcelona Traction*. The ICJ allowed the espousal without delving into the question of shareholder standing.[92]

In *Diallo*,[93] the ICJ found an opportunity to apply its dictum in *Barcelona Traction* with respect to the protection of direct rights of shareholders and seems to confirm *Barcelona Traction* on the general issue of shareholder standing to bring a claim. *Diallo* concerned Diallo, a Guinean national, who was the manager and a shareholder of two companies registered under the laws of the Democratic Republic of Congo (DRC). In 1995 the DRC detained and later deported Diallo on the ground that his "presence and conduct have breached public order in Zaire, especially in the economic, financial and monetary areas, and continue to do so."[94] Guinea espoused Diallo's claim and brought a case in the ICJ. The DRC acknowledged that Guinea could espouse Diallo's claim for his direct injuries but argued that Guinea lacked standing because the injury was suffered by the companies, not by Diallo; and the DRC had done nothing to interfere with the relationship between Diallo and the companies. However, the ICJ found the following:

> Guinea does indeed have standing in this case in so far as its action involves a person of its nationality, Mr. Diallo, and is directed against the allegedly unlawful acts of the DRC which are said to have infringed his rights, particularly his direct rights as *associé* [(shareholder)] of the two companies. . . .[95]

To the extent that it suggests *Barcelona Traction*'s rigid distinction between shareholders' and corporations' standing is still intact, the *Diallo* case came as a surprise and may be considered a step backward. Indeed, the ICJ's position in the *ELSI* case[96] seemed to be in line with the substantial progress made in the field of protection of shareholder rights in international law, whether in the form of

---

[91] *Case Concerning the Elettronica Sicula S.p.A. (ELSI)* (*U.S. v. Italy*, Judgment of July 20, 1989), ICJ Rep. 15 (1989).

[92] *See* Laird, *supra* note 84, at 85 and the material cited therein; *see also* Schreuer, *Shareholder Protection in International Investment Law*, 2(3) TDM 1, 4.

[93] *Diallo*, *supra* note 90.

[94] *Id.* ¶ 15.

[95] *Id.* ¶ 65.

[96] *See CMS Gas Transmission Co. v. Argentina*, ICSID Case No. ARB/01/08 (Decision on Objection to Jurisdiction of July 17, 2003), ¶ 44 (*ELSI* "evidences that the International Court of Justice itself accepted, some years [after *Barcelona Traction*], the protection of shareholders of a corporation by the State of their nationality in spite of the fact that the affected corporation had a corporate personality under the defendant State's legislation." *See also Azurix Corp. v. Argentina*, ICSID Case No. ARB/01/12 (Decision on Jurisdiction of Dec. 8, 2003), ¶ 71; *GAMI Inv., Inc. v. Mexico* (UNCITRAL arbitration, Final Award of Nov. 15, 2004), ¶ 30.

proliferation of investment treaties that provide for the direct right of shareholders to file claims against host governments,[97] or developments in municipal corporate laws taking a more favorable stance toward the control criterion—the latter of which may constitute a general principle of law under Article 38(1) of the ICJ Statute.[98]

Whether backward or not, the holdings of the ICJ in *Barcelona Traction* and subsequently in *Diallo* are likely to be cited and followed by some arbitral tribunals. But the better reading of these precedents is to limit their applicability to diplomatic protection cases.[99] A survey of the cases brought under various investment treaties suggests that the *Barcelona Traction* approach is not applied.[100]

The following excerpt from *CMS v. Argentina* summarizes the status of *Barcelona Traction* in the modern investment treaty arbitration.

CMS Gas Transmission Company v. Argentina

ICSID Case No. ARB/01/08 (Decision on Objection to Jurisdiction of July 17, 2003)

43. The parties have turned next to the discussion of the situation under international law, with particular reference to the meaning and extent of the Barcelona Traction decision. Counsel for the Republic of Argentina are right when arguing that that decision ruled out the protection of investors by the State of their nationality when that State is different from the State of incorporation of the corporate entity concerned, all of it in respect of damage suffered in a third State. However, Counsel for the Claimant are also right when affirming that this case was concerned only with the exercise of diplomatic protection in that particular triangular setting, and involved what the Court considered to be a relationship attached to municipal law, but it did not rule out the possibility of extending protection to shareholders in a corporation in different contexts. Specifically, the International Court of Justice was well aware of the new trends in respect of the protection of foreign investors under the 1965 Convention and the bilateral investment treaties related thereto.

44. Barcelona Traction is therefore not directly relevant to the present dispute. . . .

---

[97] See Laird, *supra* note 84, at 86.

[98] Statute of the International Court of Justice, June 26, 1945, *available at* http://www.icj-cij.org/. Recent commentators have noted the abandonment in a number of modern corporate laws of the rigid distinction between a corporation and its shareholders (i.e., the *Barcelona Traction* approach), defining a more prominent role for the *control* element. *See* Acconci, *supra* note 1, at 169–71.

[99] *GAMI*, *supra* note 96, ¶¶ 30–33.

[100] *See* Laird, *supra* note 84, at 89–90.

45. Diplomatic protection itself has been dwindling in current international law, as the State of nationality is no longer considered to be protecting its own interest in the claim but that of the individual affected.[101] To some extent, diplomatic protection is intervening as a residual mechanism to be resorted to in the absence of other arrangements recognizing the direct right of action by individuals. It is precisely this kind of arrangement that has come to prevail under international law, particularly in respect of foreign investments, the paramount example being that of the 1965 Convention.

46. The Republic of Argentina has advanced the argument that, when shareholders have been protected separately from the affected corporation, this occurred in cases where the shareholders were majority or controlling, not minority shareholders as in the instant case. This fact may be true, but it is equally true, as argued by the Claimant [. . . that the cases] were concerned with the possibility of protecting shareholders independently from the affected corporation, that is, solely with the issue of the corporate legal personality and its limits.

47. State practice further supports the meaning of this changing scenario. Besides accepting the protection of shareholders and other forms of participation in corporations and partnerships, the concept of limiting it to majority or controlling participations has given way to a lower threshold in this respect. Minority and non-controlling participations have thus been included in the protection granted or have been admitted to claim in their own right. Contemporary practice relating to lump-sum agreements,[102] the decisions of the Iran-United States Tribunal[103] and the rules and decisions of the United Nations Compensation Commission,[104] among other examples, evidence increasing flexibility in the handling of international claims.

48. The Tribunal therefore finds no bar in current international law to the concept of allowing claims by shareholders independently from those of the corporation concerned, not even if those shareholders are minority or non-controlling shareholders. Although it is true, as argued by the Republic of Argentina, that this is mostly the result of lex specialis and specific treaty arrangements that have so allowed, the fact is that lex specialis in this respect is so prevalent that it can now be considered the general rule, certainly in respect of foreign investments and increasingly in respect of other matters.[105] To the extent that customary international law or generally the traditional law of international claims might have followed a different approach, a proposition that is open to debate, then that approach can be considered the exception.

---

[101] SN: International Law Commission: Preliminary Report on Diplomatic Protection, by Mohammed Bennouna, Special Rapporteur, A/CN.4/484, Feb. 4 1998, at 5.

[102] SN: David J. Bederman, *Interim Report on Lump Sum Agreements and Diplomatic Protection*, in International Law Association, Committee on Diplomatic Protection of Persons and Property, *Report of the Seventieth Conference*, New Delhi (2002), 230, at 253–56.

[103] SN: For the jurisprudence of the U.S.-Iran Claims Tribunal *see generally* George H. Aldrich: *The Jurisprudence of the Iran-United States Claims Tribunal* (1996); Charles N. Brower & Jason D. Brueschke: *The Iran-United States Claims Tribunal* (1998).

[104] SN: United Nations Compensation Commission, Decision of the Governing Council on Business Losses of Individuals, S/AC.26/1191/4, 23 Oct. 1991, ¶ F & Decision 123 (2001).

[105] SN: International Law Association, Committee on Diplomatic Protection of Persons and Property, First Report, *Sixty-Ninth Conference*, London, 2000.

c. Washington Convention

The Washington Convention does not define the term *juridical person*. This omission was intentional so as to leave the ultimate decisions on this matter to arbitral tribunals.[106] The Convention in Article 25(2)(b) grants standing to such persons:

> 2) "National of another Contracting State" means:
>
> . . . .
>
> (b) any juridical person which had the nationality of a Contracting State other than the State party to the dispute on the date on which the parties consented to submit such dispute to conciliation or arbitration and any juridical person which had the nationality of the Contracting State party to the dispute on that date and which, because of foreign control, the parties have agreed should be treated as a national of another Contracting State for the purposes of this Convention.

Article 25(2)(b) thus has two parts. The first part, similar to Article 25(2)(a)[107] with respect to natural persons, provides that the legal person must have the nationality of a Contracting State to the Washington Convention and may not have the nationality of the host state.[108]

In the second part, however, the article provides a significant exception by granting standing to a legal person that is a national of the host state, provided it is controlled by non-nationals of the host state,[109] subject to the agreement of the parties in dispute.[110] The second part of Article 25(2)(b) was included by the drafters of the Convention to reflect the fact that laws of many jurisdictions require that foreign investment to be channeled through a locally incorporated company.[111] But for this exception, such companies would not have standing under the Washington Convention.[112]

---

[106] Schreuer, *supra* note 28, at 267.

[107] *See* note 41 *supra*.

[108] The concurrent possession of another third country (not the respondent) nationality does not bar jurisdiction. Al-Sharmani, *ICSID: Requirements Ratione Personae*, UNCTAD Course on Dispute Settlement-Module 2.4, 15, U.N. Doc. UNCTAD/EDM/Misc.232/Add.3 (2003). Arbitral tribunals under the Washington Convention have generally considered the criteria of place of incorporation or seat to determine nationality of a company. Schreuer, *supra* note 28, at 465–68

[109] Non-nationals in this context do not include nationals of states, which are not a member of the Washington Convention. *Id.* at 286.

[110] *See* Delaume, *supra* note 81, at 786–87. The Washington Convention does not require any specific form for an agreement of the disputing parties on nationality. It could be reached in an investment agreement, in a separate agreement, or it could be part of a government's offer to arbitrate in a treaty or legislation. Al-Sharmani, *supra* note 108, at 19–22. In the latter situation, the agreement is reached upon the acceptance of the offer. Schreuer, *supra* note 28, at 286.

[111] Amazu Asouzu, *A Review and Critique of Arbitral Awards on Article 25(2)(b) of the ICSID Convention*, 3 J. World Inv. 397, 398 (2002).

[112] Schreuer, *supra* note 28, at 290–91.

With respect to the second part of Article 25(2)(b), nationality must be objectively determined; an arbitral tribunal maintains its authority to examine the nationality of a company independently, even if there is an agreement on the issue of nationality.[113]

Determining who controls a company can be a complex matter. Normally, the test of *foreign* identity is *majority* control; if a local operating company is more than 50 percent owned by foreigners of qualifying nationality, the national of the host state is considered foreign for purposes of arbitral jurisdiction.[114] The additional criteria for determining control have been described by Schreuer as follows:

> On the basis of the Convention's preparatory works as well as the published cases, it can be said that the existence of foreign control is a complex question requiring the examination of several factors such as equity participation, voting rights and management. In order to obtain a reliable picture, all these aspects must be looked at in conjunction. There is no simple mathematical formula based on shareholding or votes alone.[115]

3. Shareholders Standing Under Investment Treaties and the Washington Convention

As noted in Chapter XI, under a number of investment treaties, shares in companies may qualify as an investment. The owners of the shares or shareholders, whether natural persons or corporations, may also qualify as investors in a target company or investment and have standing to bring a claim under a treaty, provided that they meet the nationality requirements of the applicable investment treaties and the Washington Convention, if applicable. Determining shareholder's standing is more complicated than merely determining the nationality of an individual or a corporation, however. A shareholder's standing may depend on whether it is a majority or minority shareholder, is a controlling or noncontrolling shareholder, and owns the shares directly or indirectly. Indirect ownership of shares could take place through various layers of companies, which could be incorporated in the claimant's state, the host state, or a third state. There are also consequences as to the quantum of damages: Can shareholders recover damages suffered by the company, or are they limited to the value of their individual shares? These issues are addressed in the following sections.

---

[113] See Schreuer, *supra* note 28, at 309; Al-Sharmani, *supra* note 108, at 14.
[114] See C. F. Amerasinghe, *Interpretation of Article 25(2)(b) of the ICSID Convention*, in *International Arbitration in the 21st Century: Towards "Judicialization" and Uniformity?* 241–42 (Richard B. Lillich & Charles N. Brower eds., 1993).
[115] Schreuer, *supra* note 28, at 321.

a. Minority and Noncontrolling Shareholders

i. Standing Under Investment Treaties

The starting point for examination of these issues is the text of the applicable treaty. Investment treaties generally grant standing to the majority shareholders who presumably control a corporation. The status of minority, noncontrolling shareholders is less clear, however. A number of treaties grant standing only to shareholders that have control over the company that is actually making the investment.[116] Such a provision could limit the standing of minority shareholders, unless they provide proof of control based upon the criteria discussed above.[117] "Similarly, some investment treaties only consider a company to be an 'investor' of a [home] contracting State if it carries on 'real economic activities' there."[118] Such provisions could limit the standing of shell companies. In the absence of clear language containing such a requirement, however, arbitral tribunals have refrained from denying standing. In *Saluka*, for example, the Czech Republic argued that Saluka was only a Dutch shell company, controlled by Japan's Nomura Group, and as such it lacked standing under the Netherlands-Czech Republic BIT. Although acknowledging that allowing shell companies to bring a claim increases the potential for treaty-shopping,[119] nonetheless the tribunal held that the Netherlands-Czech Republic BIT's definition of investor did not contain any additional requirement other than a company being constituted under the laws of the Contracting Parties to the BIT.[120]

ii. Standing Under the Washington Convention

As noted earlier the jurisdictional requirements of the Washington Convention are not necessarily the same as those of the investment treaty that provides the consent to arbitration; and if the case is filed under the Convention, arbitral tribunals must conduct a second level of inquiry to determine whether the Convention's requirement have been satisfied. Article 25 of the Washington Convention does not seem to limit standing of shareholders, however, even if they have minority status. A line of ICSID cases confirms this conclusion. In *CMS v. Argentina*, for example, the American company CMS owned 29 percent of the shares of TGN, an Argentine gas transmission company, which had entered into a concession agreement with Argentina. Argentina argued that CMS lacked standing under the BIT and the

---

[116] *See, e.g.*, U.S.-Canada Free Trade Agreement (1992), art. 1611.

[117] *See* p. 314 *supra*.

[118] Rubins & Kinsella, *supra* note 77, at 287 (citing North Korea-Thailand BIT (2002), art. 1(2)(b)). *See also* U.S.-Ecuador BIT, art. 2.

[119] *Saluka Inv. v. Czech Republic* (UNCITRAL arbitration, Partial Award on Liability, 2006), ¶ 240.

[120] *Id.* ¶ 241. *See also id.* ¶ 211, where the tribunal rejected the Czech Republic's argument that investment under the BIT must contribute to the local economy.

Washington Convention, because it was only a minority shareholder in TGN.[121] However, the tribunal found jurisdiction under both the BIT and the Washington Convention. The jurisdictional decision of the tribunal in *CMS v. Argentina* summarizes the relevant issues as well as the jurisprudence:[122]

> *CMS Gas Transmission Company v. Argentina*
>
> ICSID Case No. ARB/01/08 (Decision on Objection to Jurisdiction of July 17, 2003)
>
> 49. As mentioned above, the 1965 Convention is the paramount example of the approach now prevailing in international law in respect of claims arising from foreign investments. It is a well-known fact that Article 25(1) of that Convention did not attempt to define the term "investment," as no definition was generally acceptable. Against this background, all relevant bilateral investment treaties and other instruments embodying the consent of the parties to ICSID's jurisdiction have usually contained definition in this respect.[123]
>
> 50. A rather broad interpretation of "investment" has ensued from these expressions of consent. It should be recalled that the ownership of shares was one of the specific examples of investment given during the negotiations of the Convention as pertinent for parties to agree in the context of their expressions of consent to jurisdiction.[124] The definition of investment in the Argentina-United States BIT will be considered further below.
>
> 51. Precisely because the Convention does not define "investment," it does not purport to define the requirements that an investment should meet to qualify for ICSID jurisdiction. There is indeed no requirement that an investment, in order to qualify, must necessarily be made by shareholders controlling a company or owning the majority of its shares. It is well known incidentally that, depending on how shares are distributed, controlling shareholders can in fact own less than the majority of shares. The reference that Article 25(2)(b) makes to foreign control in terms of treating a company of the nationality of the Contracting State party as a national of another Contracting State is precisely meant to facilitate agreement between the parties, so as not to have the corporate personality interfering with the protection of the real interests associated with the investment. The same result can be achieved by means of the provisions of the BIT, where the consent may include non-controlling or minority shareholders.
>
> 52. Article 25(1) of the Convention is also relevant in another respect. In the *Fedax* case, Venezuela had objected to ICSID's jurisdiction on the ground that the dispute[d] transaction was not a "direct foreign investment." Although the transaction considered in that case was different from the one in the present case, the tribunal's holding is useful in the interpretation of the scope of that Article:
>
>> "However, the text of Article 25(1) establishes that the 'jurisdiction of the Centre shall extend to any legal dispute arising directly out of an investment.' It is apparent

---

[121] *CMS*, Decision on Jurisdiction, *supra* note 96, ¶ 36.

[122] Subsequent cases that confirm the *CMS* approach include: *Siemens v. Argentina*, ICSID Case No. ARB/02/8 (2007); *Enron & Ponderosa Assets v. Argentina*, ICSID Case No. ARB/01/3 (2004); *Champion Trading*, *supra* note 37.

[123] SN: *Fedax v. Venezuela* (Decision of the ICSID Tribunal on Objections to Jurisdiction, July 11, 1997, ¶¶ 21–26 with citations to the relevant cases and literature).

[124] SN: *Id.* ¶ 22.

that the term 'directly' relates in this Article to the 'dispute' and not the 'investment.' It follows that jurisdiction can exist even in respect of investments that are not direct, so long as the dispute arises directly from such transaction. This interpretation is also consistent with the broad reach that the term 'investment' must be given in light of the negotiating history of the Convention."[125]

53. With this background in mind, it is then possible for this Tribunal to examine the meaning of a number of decisions of ICSID tribunals that have dealt with the protection of shareholders. The parties have a different reading of these ICSID cases, with particular reference to AAPL v. Sri Lanka,[126] AMT v. Zaire,[127] Antoine Goetz et consorts v. Republique du Burundi,[128] Maffezini v. Spain,[129] Lanco v. Argentina,[130] Genin v. Estonia,[131] the Aguas or Vivendi Award[132] and Annulment[133] and CME v. Czech Republic.[134] For the Republic of Argentina, all these cases deal with shareholder rights, underlying arrangements and factual situations different from those given in the instant case, and hence do not support jurisdiction in this case. CMS, for its part, believes that, to the contrary, in all those cases the right of shareholders, including minority shareholders, to claim independently from the corporate entity affect has been upheld.

54. There can be no doubt that the factual setting of each case is different and that some may lend themselves more than others to illustrate points of relevance. In some cases, there has been majority shareholding or control by the investor, in others not; in some cases there has been expropriation affecting specifically the shares, in others not; in some cases, there has been no objection to jurisdiction, in others there has been.

55. However, there can be no doubt that most, if not all, such cases are immersed in the same trend discussed above in the context of international law and the meaning of the 1965 Convention. In the present case, the Claimant has convincingly explained that notwithstanding the variety of situations in ICSID's jurisprudence noted by the Republic of Argentina, the tribunals have in all such cases been concerned not with the question of [. . .] control but rather whether shareholders can claim independently from the corporate entity. In *Goetz* the tribunal reflected this prevailing trend in the following terms:

« . . . le Tribunal observe que la jurisprudence antérieure du CIRDI ne limite pas la qualité pour agir aux seules personnes morales directement visées par les mesures litigieuses mais l'étend aux actionnaires de ces personnes, qui sont les véritables investisseurs.»[135]

---

[125] SN: *Id.* ¶ 24.

[126] SN: *AAPL v. Sri Lanka* (ICSID Award of June 27, 1990).

[127] SN: *AMT v. Zaire* (ICSID Award of Feb. 21, 1997).

[128] SN: *Antoine Goetz v. République du Burundi* (Sentence du CIRDI du 10 Février 1999).

[129] SN: *Maffezini v. Spain,* ICSID Award of November 13, 2000, ¶ 64.

[130] SN: *Lanco v. Argentina* (Preliminary Decision of the ICSID Tribunal of Dec. 8, 1998).

[131] SN: *Genin v. Estonia* (ICSID Award of June 25, 2001).

[132] SN: *Compañía de Aguas del Aconquija v. Argentina* (ICSID Award of Nov. 21, 2000).

[133] SN: *Vivendi* (ICSID Annulment Decision of July 3, 2002).

[134] SN: *CME v. Czech Republic* (Partial Award of Sept. 13, 2001).

[135] SN: *Supra,* note [128], ¶ 89.

56. The Tribunal can therefore conclude that there is no bar to the exercise of jurisdiction in light of the 1965 Convention and its interpretation as reflected in its drafting history, the opinion of distinguished legal writers and the jurisprudence of ICSID tribunals.

iii. Damages Due Minority Shareholders

A difficult issue in investment treaty arbitration concerns the amount of damages that minority shareholders can recover—so-called derivative damages.[136] Investment treaties usually do not provide any guidance in this respect. NAFTA, the 2004 U.S. Model BIT, and U.S. treaties modeled after them are possible exceptions. In fact the NAFTA parties have argued that the extent of investor recovery under NAFTA article 1116 is different from that under article 1117.[136a] Under the former an investor may only claim damages for injuries suffered by it, whereas under the latter investors can claim damages suffered by the enterprise. In *GAMI v. Mexico*,[137] the United States tried to draw a fine line between the investors' rights under the two provisions by arguing that under Article 1116 the investor could only claim damages to its shareholding rights and could not claim damages to the enterprise. The tribunal, however, dismissed this argument stating the following:

> The fact that a host State does not explicitly interfere with share ownership is not decisive. The issue is rather whether a breach of NAFTA leads with sufficient directness to loss or damage in respect of a given investment. Whether [claimant] can establish such a prejudice is a matter to be examined on the merits. Uncertainty in this regard is not an obstacle to jurisdiction.[138]

Based on this Schreuer concludes "the distinction between direct rights of shareholders to ownership in the shares and their indirect rights in the assets of the company has not been sustained by practice."[138a] The *GAMI* tribunal ultimately did not find any breach of NAFTA; so the question of damages due to GAMI, a minority shareholder owning 14 percent of a Mexican company, remained moot. The tribunal's approach logically would have entitled the investor to recover damages caused to the enterprise in which it held shares, had it prevailed on the issue of liability.

---

[136] See generally Thomas Wälde & Borzu Sabahi, *Compensation, Damages and Valuation* in The Oxford Handbook of International Investment Law (Muchlinski, Ortino, & Schreuer eds., Oxford University Press 2008).

[136a] For the text of Article 1116 see p. 359 *infra*.

[137] *GAMI, supra* note 96.

[138] *Id.* ¶¶ 29–33.

[138a] Schreuer, *supra* note 92, at 19. *See also* Alexandrov, *supra* note 81, at 45.

Similarly, in *CMS v. Argentina* the Argentine government argued that CMS only had standing with respect to the damages caused to its 29 percent of the shares and not to the Argentine enterprise in which it held the shares (i.e., TGN). The tribunal dismissed that argument, however. Accordingly, the arbitral practice seems to suggest that the damages due to minority shareholders could be assessed based on the damage suffered by the enterprise in which they hold shares as well as any damage resulting from the diminution of their share value.[139] A number of related issues, however, need to be further clarified in the future, such as the potential for double-recovery or the distribution of the proceeds of the award among the shareholders and the company, in the event that the investor prevails.

b. Indirect Shareholders Controlling an Entity Incorporated in the Host State: Case Studies

In many instances the investment at issue is owned by a number of juridical entities incorporated in various jurisdictions.[140] In other cases the investment is owned by an entity that is itself owned by other entities or even a chain of entities, some or all of which may be incorporated in different countries, including the home state of the claimant. Confronted with such circumstances, a tribunal must determine whether claimant's ownership structure would affect its status as an investor for jurisdictional purposes.

In resolving these issues, international arbitration tribunals, whether under the Washington Convention or not, have been generally consistent: They pierce the corporate façade and go up the chain of ownership until they find an entity with standing to bring a treaty claim and stop at that point. A foreign investor directly or indirectly owning a local subsidiary in the host state is found to have standing if a foreign company in the chain of ownership is properly incorporated in a state that has a treaty with the host state where the investment is made. Once a juridical entity with standing is identified, tribunals accept that the formal requirements for jurisdiction have been satisfied. They usually do not pierce the veil any further to determine if the entity with standing is itself owned or controlled by investors that also have standing to bring a treaty claim.[141] Similarly, where a claimant foreign investor does not use a local subsidiary to own the investment in the host state, tribunals generally look only at the juridical status of the claimant investor to determine if it meets the treaty requirements. It is usually sufficient to sustain jurisdiction if the claimant is properly incorporated in a state that has a treaty with

---

[139] Wälde & Sabahi, *supra* note 136, at 1101 *et seq*. Meg N. Kinnear, Andrea K. Bjorklund, & John F. G. Hannaford, *Investment Disputes under NAFTA: An Annotated Guide to NAFTA Chapter 11, Article 1116*, 7 *et seq* (Kluwer 2006).

[140] *See, e.g.*, the cases discussed below.

[141] *See, e.g., Amco* and *Tokios* below.

the host state. However, there are two cases, *Aucoven* and *Loewen,* in which tribunals looked beyond the formal status of the claimant investor, either to determine the ownership of the claimant investor[142] or to determine if the claimant investor had independent economic substance.[143]

The following cases brought under the Washington Convention or other arbitral rules illustrate these issues.

i. Amco v. Indonesia

In *Amco v. Indonesia*,[144] the claimants requested ICSID arbitration of a dispute with the Indonesian government regarding the construction and management of a hotel in Jakarta. In 1964 an Indonesian company P. T. Blundas began building a hotel but ceased work in 1965 when it ran out of funds. The Indonesian government subsequently forced P. T. Blundas to reorganize under the name of P. T. Wisma (Wisma), and the government placed the new corporation under the control of a government cooperative. In 1968 Wisma concluded a Lease and Management Agreement with the American investor Amco Asia under which Amco Asia would finish the construction project and carry out management of the hotel for forty years.

Amco Asia itself was controlled by Pan American Development, Ltd., a Hong Kong corporation, which in turn was majority owned by a Mr. Tan, a citizen of the Netherlands. Pursuant to Indonesian investment law, Amco Asia obtained an investment license from Indonesia and formed a locally incorporated Indonesian company, P. T. Amco, to carry out the investment. The following shows the chain of ownership:

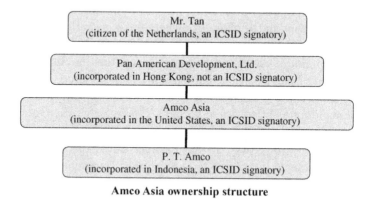

Amco Asia ownership structure

---

[142] *Loewen Group, Inc. & Loewen v. U.S.*, ICSID Case No. ARB (AF)/98/3 (2003), discussed below.

[143] *Autopista Concesionada de Venezuela, C.A. v. Bolivarian Republic of Venezuela*, ICSID Case No. ARB/00/5 (Decision on Jurisdiction of Sept. 27, 2001), 16 ICSID Rev.-F.I.L.J. 469 (2001) [hereinafter *Aucoven*], discussed below.

[144] *Amco Asia Corp. v. Republic of Indonesia*, ICSID Case No. ARB/81/1, 23 I.L.M. 351 (1984).

A dispute arose between P. T. Amco and Wisma after the construction was completed. In 1980 Wisma terminated Amco Asia's interest in the project by persuading the Indonesian government to engage in two allegedly expropriatory measures: It sent the Indonesian army to take the hotel by force, and it convinced the Indonesian Foreign Investment Board to revoke P. T. Amco's investment license. After the Indonesian courts sanctioned and affirmed these events, P. T. Amco, Amco Asia, and Pan American Development, Ltd., sought arbitration against Indonesia under the ICSID convention.[145] The asserted jurisdictional basis was that the U.S. company Amco Asia was entitled to bring a claim against Indonesia. In fact, the arbitration clause in the Lease and Management Agreement between Amco Asia and Wisma explicitly named the locally incorporated company, P. T. Amco, as a party to any future investor-state arbitration with Indonesia.

Indonesia objected to the tribunal's jurisdiction on the ground that "the *true* controller of P. T. Amco was not of American nationality, because, it alleg[ed], Amco Asia itself was controlled by Tan, a Dutch citizen residing in Hong Kong, through Pan American, a Hong Kong company of which Tan was the sole or main shareholder."[146] Indonesia thus asked the tribunal to pierce Amco Asia's corporate veil and go up the chain of ownership until it identified the *controlling* entity, and assess its jurisdiction on the basis of that investor's nationality.

The tribunal declined to enter the thicket into which Indonesia invited it:

> To take this argument into consideration, the Tribunal would have to admit first that for the purpose of article 25–2(b) of the [Washington] Convention, one should not take into account the legal nationality of the foreign juridical person which controls the local one, but the nationality of the juridical or natural persons who control the controlling juridical person itself: in other words, to take care of a control at the second, and possibly third, fourth, or xth degree.
>
> Such reasoning is, in law, not in accord with the Convention. Indeed, the concept of nationality there is a classical one, based on the law under which the juridical person has been incorporated, the place of incorporation, and the place of the social seat. An exception is brought to this concept in respect of juridical persons having the nationality, thus defined, of the Contracting state party to the dispute, where said juridical persons are under foreign control. But no exception to the classical concept is provided for when it comes to the nationality of the foreign controller, even supposing—which is not at all clearly stated in the Convention—that the fact that the controller is the national of one or another foreign state is to be taken into account. . . .[147]

The *Amco* tribunal refused to engage in an inquiry regarding the ultimate nationality of the foreign controlling party because such an investigation would open the door to an unending examination of the chain of control, and would be both exceedingly taxing on the arbitration process as well as undermine the objects and purposes of the ICSID Convention. Therefore, the tribunal saw no need to pierce

---

[145] *Id.*

[146] *Id.* at 362 (emphasis added).

[147] *Id.* at 362–63.

the corporate veil after it had identified an entity with standing—Amco Asia, the U.S. company. Amco Asia's objective status as an investor of a contracting state (the U.S.) sufficed to establish jurisdiction

ii. *Tokios v. Ukraine*[148]

Tokios v. Ukraine is the most compelling example of the tendency of tribunals to approach the nationality issue in a very formalistic manner. Claimant, Tokios Tokeles, was a Lithuanian company that asserted it was engaged in the business of advertising, publishing, and printing in Lithuania and outside its borders. In 1994 Tokios Tokeles created Taki spravy, a wholly owned subsidiary established under the laws of Ukraine for the purpose of conducting advertising, publishing, printing, and related activities in Ukraine and outside its borders. Tokios was thus formally a Lithuanian company that invested in Ukraine. However, Ukrainian nationals owned 99 percent of the outstanding shares of Tokios and comprised two-thirds of its management. The following shows the relationship between the investors and their investment as well as their nationalities:

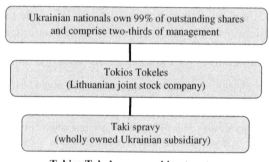

Tokios Tokeles ownership structure

After Tokios published a book that portrayed an opposition Ukrainian politician in a favorable light, Tokios alleged that the government of Ukraine engaged in a variety of retaliatory activities in violation of the bilateral investment treaty between Ukraine and Lithuania. These included numerous and invasive investigations under the guise of enforcing Ukrainian national tax laws; the pursuit of unsubstantiated legal actions in Ukrainian domestic courts, including actions to invalidate contracts entered into by Taki spravy; the administrative arrest of Taki spravy's assets; unreasonable seizure of financial and other documents; and falsely accusing Taki spravy of illegal activities. Although Tokios sought alternative means of resolving the dispute, it ultimately filed a Request for Arbitration with ICSID in 2002.

---

[148] *Tokios Tokeles v. Ukraine*, ICSID Case No. ARB/02/18 (Decision on Jurisdiction, Apr. 29, 2004).

Respondent Ukraine urged the tribunal to refuse jurisdiction on the grounds that Tokios was not a *genuine entity* of Lithuania because it was owned and controlled predominantly by Ukrainian nationals and because Tokios had no substantial business activities in Lithuania and maintained its administrative headquarters in Ukraine. The Respondent contended that Tokios was, in terms of economic substance, a Ukrainian investor situated for mere convenience in Lithuania, rather than a true Lithuanian investor.[149] Ukraine argued that extending jurisdiction in this case would, in essence, allow Ukrainian nationals to pursue international arbitration against their own government, which would be inconsistent with the object and purpose of the ICSID Convention. To avoid this result, Ukraine asked the tribunal to *pierce the corporate veil* (i.e., to take note of what Ukraine contended was the Claimant's lack of substantial business activity in Lithuania, to go up the chain of ownership to determine the nationality of its predominant shareholders, and to thus disregard both the formal situs in Lithuania of the claimant's place of incorporation and *siège social*).[150]

The tribunal rejected Ukraine's argument and found jurisdiction. It explained that, in the specific context of BITs, the Contracting Parties enjoy broad discretion to define corporate nationality: "Definitions of corporate nationality in national legislation or in treaties providing for ICSID's jurisdiction will be controlling for the determination of whether the nationality requirements of Article 25(2)(b) have been met."[151] Furthermore, "[a]ny reasonable determination of the nationality of juridical persons contained in national legislation or in a treaty should be accepted by an ICSID commission or tribunal."[152] Turning to the relevant treaty provisions, the tribunal noted that Article 1(2)(b) of the Ukraine-Lithuania BIT defines the term "investor," with respect to Lithuania, as "any entity established in the territory of the Republic of Lithuania in conformity with its laws and regulations."[153] The ordinary meaning of "entity" is "[a] thing that has a real existence."[154] The meaning of "establish" is to "[s]et up on a permanent or secure basis; bring into being, found (a ... business)."[155] Thus, according to the ordinary meaning of the terms of the Treaty, the Claimant was an *investor* of Lithuania if it had real legal existence in the territory of Lithuania in conformity with its laws and regulations.[156] The Treaty contains no additional requirements for an entity to qualify as an *investor* of Lithuania.[157]

---

[149] *Id.* ¶ 21.
[150] *Id.* ¶ 22.
[151] Schreuer, *supra* note 28, at 286.
[152] *Id.*
[153] *Tokios, supra* note 148, ¶ 28.
[154] *Id.* (citing *New Shorter Oxford English Dictionary* 830 (Thumb Index ed. 1993)).
[155] *Id.* (citing *id.* at 852).
[156] *Id.*
[157] *Id.*

The tribunal found that the object and purpose of the Treaty likewise confirm that piercing the veil was inappropriate as a means for restricting the scope of investors in Article 1(2)(b).[158] The tribunal noted that—unlike this case—several investment treaties allow a party to deny the benefits of the treaty to entities of the other party that are controlled by foreign nationals and that do not engage in substantial business activity in the territory of the other party.[159]

For example, the Ukraine-United States BIT states the following:

> Each Party reserves the right to deny to any company the advantages of this treaty if nationals of any third country control such company and, in the case of a company of the other Party, that company has no substantial business activities in the territory of the other Party....[160]

Similarly, the Energy Charter Treaty allows each party to deny the benefits of the agreement to "a legal entity if citizens or nationals of a third state own or control such entity and if that entity has no substantial business activities in the Area of the Contracting Party in which it is organized."[161] The tribunal found that these investment agreements confirm that state parties are capable of excluding from the scope of the agreement entities of the other party that are controlled by nationals of third countries or by nationals of the host country.[162]

> Under the terms of the Ukraine-Lithuania BIT, interpreted according to their ordinary meaning, in their context, and in light of the object and purpose of the Treaty, the *only relevant consideration is whether the Claimant is established under the laws of Lithuania*. We find that it is. Thus, the Claimant is an investor of Lithuania under Article 1(2)(b) of the BIT.[163]

Indeed, the tribunal noted that "ICSID tribunals have uniformly adopted the test of incorporation or seat rather than control when determining the nationality of a juridical person."[164] Moreover, "[t]he overwhelming weight of the authority . . . points

---

[158] *Id.* ¶ 31.

[159] *Id.* ¶ 33.

[160] Treaty between the United States of America and Ukraine Concerning the Encouragement and Reciprocal Protection of Investment, Mar. 4, 1994, at art. 1(2) (entered into force Nov. 16, 1996) (emphasis added).

[161] Energy Charter Treaty, art. 17(1).

[162] *Tokios, supra* note 148, ¶ 36.

[163] *Id.* ¶ 38 (emphasis added).

[164] *Id.* ¶ 42 citing Schreuer, *supra* note 28, at 279–80 (citing *Kaiser Bauxite Co. v. Jamaica*, ICSID Case No. ARB/74/3 (Decision on Jurisdiction of July 6, 1975)), 1 ICSID Rep. 296, 303 (1993); *SOABI v. Senegal*, ICSID Case No. ARB/82/1 (Decision on Jurisdiction of Aug. 1, 1984), 2 ICSID Rep. 175, 180–81; *Amco, supra* note 144, at 396; *see also Aucoven, supra* note 143, ¶ 108.

towards the traditional criteria of incorporation or seat for the determination of corporate nationality under Art. 25(2)(b)."[165] The *Tokios* majority refused to supplant the states' clear intent as expressed in the investment treaty.

In refusing to go up the ownership chain beyond the formal claimant, the tribunal found that the parties had established a clear definition of *investor* in the treaty; and because the definition was reasonable, there was no basis to consider anything except the evidence that the claimant met the objective test. The tribunal rejected the relevance of any "origin-of-capital" test on the question of jurisdiction, because such a test was "plainly absent from the text" of the governing treaty, and it would also be "inconsistent with the object and purpose of the treaty," in other words "to provide broad protection to investors and their investments in the territory of either party." The tribunal stated the following:

> The origin of the capital is not relevant to the existence of an investment . . . [T]he ICSID Convention does not require an 'investment' to be financed from capital of any particular origin . . . The origin of the capital used to acquire these assets is not relevant to the question of jurisdiction under the Convention.[166]

However, the *Tokios* award had a dissent by Prosper Weil. His dissenting opinion points out that the majority "[d]ecision rests on the assumption that the origin of the capital is not relevant," an assumption that the dissent alleges "[flies] in the face of the object and purpose of the ICSID Convention. . . ."[167] The dissent continues:

> The question boils down to determining whether Tokios Tokelės, even though undisputedly under Ukrainian control, is to be regarded as having "the nationality of a Contracting State other than the State party to the dispute," *i.e.*, the nationality of Lithuania, or whether, because undisputedly under Ukrainian control, it is to be regarded for the purposes of the Convention, as having the nationality of the Ukraine.[168]

iii. *CME* Cases

A group of two cases known as the *CME* Cases further illustrate the tendency of tribunals to end the jurisdictional analysis once they identify an entity with standing. The cases arose when the Czech Media Council, the media licensing authority in the Czech Republic, restructured a foreign investor's unusually successful television license, triggering a series of arbitrations brought by various parties against the Czech Republic on the grounds that the Czech Media Council engaged in expropriatory acts that violated the rights of the foreign

---

[165] *Id.* citing Schreuer, *supra* note 28, at 281.
[166] *Tokios, supra* note 148, ¶ 80.
[167] *Id.*, Dissenting Opinion, ¶ 6.
[168] *Id.* ¶ 15.

investors. Two investment treaty cases were brought by two formally different investors, each of which had standing under its respective treaties:

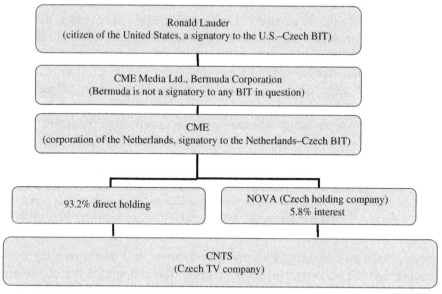

CME ownership structure

One claim was brought by Lauder, an American businessman who controlled the Bermuda corporation that in turn controlled CME. Lauder alleged that the Media Council's actions, which were attributed to the Czech government, violated his rights as an investor under the bilateral investment treaty to which the United States and the Czech Republic were party. The Respondent originally argued that jurisdiction was lacking because, inter alia, the Claimant failed to prove ownership or control of an investment within the Czech Republic and that the claim was not a dispute under the BIT. However, by the time of the closing submissions, the Respondent conceded that the United States-Czech Republic BIT was applicable to the dispute and that the Claimant controlled the investment, at least for purposes of jurisdiction over the dispute. Thus, the tribunal had jurisdiction because the parties agreed it would go up the ownership chain until there was a U.S. investor with standing under the United States-Czech Republic BIT.[169]

In *CME Czech Republic BV v. Czech Republic*, the claimant was CME, the Netherlands corporation that held an indirect 99 percent (93.2 plus 5.8) equity interest in Česká Nezávislá Televizní Společnos, spol s.r.o. (CNTS), the locally incorporated Czech television company. Relying on the BIT between the Netherlands and the Czech Republic (IPPA or the BIT), CME argued that its

---

[169] *Lauder v. Czech Republic* (UNCITRAL arbitration, Final Award of Sept. 3, 2001), ¶¶ 153–155.

ownership interest in CNTS qualified as a protected investment.[170] Prior to the arbitration, however, CME and the Czech Republic reached an agreement on the assignment of claims under the agreement, stating the following in a *common position*:

> Each investor which qualifies under the IPPA is entitled to protection of the IPPA from the time the investment is acquired by that investor. Investors are free to assign their investments protected by the IPPA. A claim which the first investor has under the IPPA may pass to a second qualifying investor if that claim has been transferred to the second investor either expressly or impliedly by operation of the law applicable to the transfer and the claim so transferred will be available to the first investor. If the first investor's claim does not so pass to the second investor, the first investor may still be able to make the claim.[171]

Thus, it appears that the parties took the *piercing* question out of the tribunal's hands by reaching a *common position* on the interpretation of the BIT *prior* to the actual arbitration, but after the events that gave rise to the claim. Thus, the tribunal went up the chain until it found a covered entity. The *CME* tribunal explained as follows:

> Only in exceptional cases, in particular in competition law, have tribunals or law courts accepted a concept of a "single economic entity" which allows discounting of the separate legal existences of the shareholder and the company, mostly, to allow the joining of a parent of a subsidiary to an arbitration. Also a "company group" theory is not generally accepted in international arbitration . . . and there are no precedents of which this Tribunal is aware for general acceptance. In this arbitration, the situation is even less compelling. Mr. Lauder, although apparently controlling CME Media Ltd., the Claimant's ultimate parent company, is not the majority shareholder of the company and the cause of action in each proceeding was based on different investment treaties.[172]

Taken together, these two cases are in line with the other cases discussed in this section: Once a tribunal identifies an entity with standing—here CME—it refuses to go up the chain of ownership to determine who controls it, which might have terminated this tribunal's treaty jurisdiction.

iv. Waste Management v. Mexico

This case concerned an agreement between the Mexican city of Acapulco and Acaverde, a Mexican company that provided waste disposal services. Acaverde was directly owned by AcaVerde Holdings, Ltd., a Cayman Islands company,

---

[170] *CME Czech Republic BV v. Czech Republic* (UNCITRAL arbitration, Final Award, Mar. 14, 2003).

[171] *Id.* ¶ 92.

[172] *Id.* ¶ 436 (citing *Barcelona Traction, supra* note 83, and *Holiday Inns v. Morocco*, ICSID Case No. ARB/72/1 (1977)).

which was acquired by a U.S. company; and this U.S. company later merged with yet another U.S. corporation (Waste Management).[173] Waste Management's control over Acaverde, the local Mexican investment, is as follows:

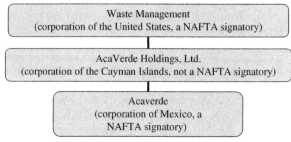

Waste Management ownership structure

When disputes arose over the level of service provided by Acaverde and the city's failure to pay invoices when due, Waste Management filed a claim against Mexico under NAFTA Chapter 11. Mexico argued that Waste Management did not have investor status for purposes of NAFTA Chapter 11 because Waste Management did not have a direct interest in the Mexican investment. Acaverde's direct shareholder, AcaVerde Holdings Ltd., was registered in the Cayman Islands, not a party to NAFTA.

The tribunal found that it had jurisdiction because NAFTA allows a foreign investor to hold its investment directly or indirectly:[174]

> If the NAFTA Parties had wished to limit their obligations of conduct to enterprises or investments having the nationality of one of the other Parties they could have done so. Similarly they could have restricted claims of loss or damage by reference to the nationality of the corporation which itself suffered direct injury. No such restrictions appear in the text. It is not disputed that at the time the actions said to amount to a breach of NAFTA occurred, *Acaverde was an enterprise owned or controlled indirectly by the Claimant*, an investor of the United States. The nationality of any intermediate holding companies is irrelevant to the present claim.[175]

This decision further confirms the principle that indirect control is sufficient to establish jurisdiction; that is to say, a tribunal went up the chain of ownership until it identified an entity with standing.

---

[173] *Waste Mgmt., Inc. v. United Mexican States*, ICSID Case No. ARB(AF)/00/3 (Final Award of Apr. 30, 2004), ¶ 77 [hereinafter *Waste Management*].

[174] *Id.* at 84, citing NAFTA, art. 1117, which provides in relevant part: "[a]n investor of a Party, on behalf of an enterprise of another Party that is a juridical person that the investor owns or controls directly or indirectly, may submit to arbitration under this Subchapter a claim that the other Party has breached: (a) a provision of Subchapter A. . . ."

[175] *Id.* at 85 (emphasis added).

v. Aguas del Tunari v. Bolivia

In *Aguas del Tunari* (AdT) *v. Bolivia*,[176] the claimant was a Bolivian corporation that entered into a forty-year water concession agreement with the Bolivian city of Cochabamba. The central question in the arbitration was whether AdT was "controlled directly or indirectly" by corporate nationals of the Netherlands, and therefore, under the Netherlands-Bolivia BIT.

In 1999 the government of Bolivia invited the private sector to participate in a tender for the development of a reliable supply of clean water to Cochabamba. International Water (IW) Ltd. (a Cayman corporation wholly owned by the U.S. Bechtel Enterprise Holding, Inc.) decided to pursue the tender by forming a Bolivian joint venture, AdT, in which it had a 55 percent investment. Its partners were Abengoa of Spain (25 percent) and four Bolivian companies (5 percent each), one of them ICE Agua y Energia, S.A., a major Bolivian contractor. The only bidder, AdT signed a concession agreement requiring the Founding Stockholder (i.e., Bechtel) to maintain more than 50 percent of the original equity percentage in voting shares of the Concessionaire for at least the first seven years of the concession. At the time of the concession, AdT's ownership was as follows:

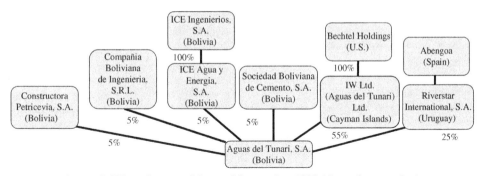

Aguas del Tunari, ownership as of September 1999 (time of concession)

Shortly after the concession was signed, Bechtel announced a joint venture with the Italian company Edison SpA, in which Edison and Bechtel would merge their water management projects—including AdT's parent company, IW Ltd.—into a single Dutch venture, International Water Holdings B.V. (IWH, B V). Because Edison would own a 50 percent stock interest in IW Ltd., Bechtel notified the Bolivian Waters Superintendency of the planned share transfer and requested permission to undertake this change in ownership, and the Bolivian Waters Superintendency granted its approval. However, instead of transferring its shares from IW Ltd. (Cayman) to a new Dutch corporation as originally planned, IW Ltd. opted first to *migrate* from the Cayman Islands to Luxembourg, where it became known as IW S.a.r.l., and which

---

[176] *Aguas del Tunari* (AdT) *v. Boliva*, ICSID Case No. ARB/02/3 (Jurisdictional Award, 2005).

was then acquired by the Dutch company International Water (Tunari), B.V. (IWT, B.V.), the joint venture in which Bechtel and Edison each held a 50 percent stake through IWH, B.V. The result was that as of December 1999, 55 percent of AdT's ownership was held in the following manner.

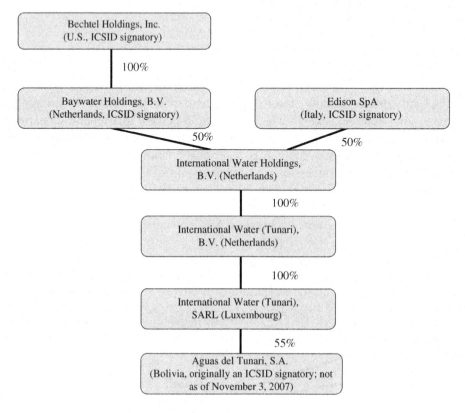

Aguas del Tunari, ownership as of December 1999 (following reorganization)

At approximately the same time the project commenced in late 1999, and contemporaneously with the changes in AdT's ownership, so did public protests and demonstrations against the water concession. In February 2000 the Bolivian government rolled back the higher water rates in the concession agreement; thereafter, the government cancelled the concession. After seventeen months of settlement negotiations, AdT filed a claim in ICSID for arbitration under the bilateral investment treaty between Bolivia and the Netherlands, where IWH, B.V., one of the intermediate holding companies, is registered.

Bolivia objected to the ICSID tribunal's jurisdiction, arguing that AdT was actually *controlled* by Bechtel and Edison, and not by a Dutch company, so that it should not be entitled to the protection of the Bolivia-Netherlands BIT. Although Bolivia conceded that 55 percent of AdT's chain of ownership passed through Netherlands companies, Bolivia disputed that these Netherlands companies (IWT, B.V. and IWH,

B.V.) had any economic substance. Instead, Bolivia claimed, these corporations were "mere shells" that lacked any real control over AdT. Bolivia thus asked the tribunal to go up the chain of ownership until it identified which entities had actual and ultimate control. AdT responded that there is no basis in international law for undertaking the sort of factual inquiry Bolivia requested of the tribunal. Indeed, in AdT's view, the element of Dutch *control* required by the BIT was satisfied by the fact that Dutch corporations held the requisite 55 percent stake in AdT.

In a two-to-one majority decision, the tribunal sided with AdT.[177] The tribunal held that *control* is a matter of ownership, and that international law does not recognize a "control test" that could determine reliably when a corporation is exercising "actual control" over a subsidiary. Moreover, relying on a control test as urged by Bolivia would undermine the purpose of BITs: "If an investor cannot ascertain whether their ownership of a locally-incorporated vehicle for the investment will qualify for protection, then the effort of the BIT to stimulate investment will be frustrated."[178] Although there was no definitive ruling on this point, the majority also indicated that routing an investment through a third-party nation to gain the protection of a BIT can be a legitimate corporate practice. Without endorsing the practice, the majority recognized that it is a matter of course that BITs "serve in many cases more broadly as portals" for investments originating in a number of countries and aimed at another state but which are routed through an intermediary state to gain the benefits of that BIT.[179]

vi. Aucoven v. Venezuela

An important case involving a change in nationality during the course of an investment is *Autopista Concesionada de Venezuela, C.A. v. Bolivarian Republic of Venezuela*,[180] which involved a Mexican investment in a highway project in Venezuela. The project was awarded to a consortium consisting of ICA, a Mexican engineering and construction firm, and Baninsa, a Venezuelan investment bank. Claimant Autopista Concesionada de Venezuela, C.A. (Aucoven) was an ICA subsidiary incorporated in Venezuela to serve as the concessionaire for the project.

At the time of Aucoven's incorporation, 99 percent of its shares were held by ICA; and Baninsa held one percent. ICA itself was a subsidiary of a very large Mexican conglomerate, ICA Holding. ICA Holding was also the parent company of an American subsidiary, Icatech Corporation. The United States is a signatory to the ICSID convention, Mexico is not.

---

[177] *Id.*, Jurisdictional Award of Oct. 21, 2005.

[178] *Id.* ¶ 247.

[179] *Id.* ¶ 332.

[180] *Aucoven, supra* note 143.

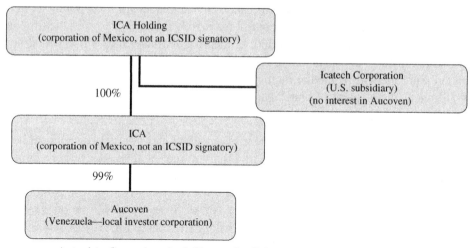

Autopista Concesionada de Venezuela, C.A. ownership at incorporation

As previously noted the ICSID Convention specifically provides a *foreign control* exception to the diversity requirement. Under the exception the parties can agree to consider the local (i.e., Venezuelan) juridical person a national of another Contracting State "because of foreign control."[181] In *Aucoven v. Venezuela*, the contracting parties explicitly agreed in the investment agreement that majority shareholding was the criterion to apply to determine foreign control.[182] Furthermore, the Venezuelan government confirmed the legality of the parties' agreement to use majority shareholding as the criterion for foreign control prior to the Claimant's demand for arbitration.[183]

During the Mexican peso crisis of the mid-1990s, ICA Holding decided to transfer to its U.S. subsidiary Icatech ownership of several international project companies to enhance its ability to obtain financing. Among the international project companies transferred to Icatech was Aucoven, the Venezuelan highway project concessionaire. In 1998, 15 months after Aucoven began the project, ICA Holding transferred 75 percent of its Aucoven shares to Icatech (with authorization from the Venezuelan Ministry of Infrastructure).[184] As a result, the American

---

[181] Washington Convention, art. 25(2)(b).

[182] Article 64 of the investment agreement provided that the parties agree to submit to ICSID any investment-related dispute if the shareholder or majority shareholders of the Concessionaire, i.e., *Aucoven*, came to be a national of a country in which the ICSID Convention is in force: ". . . Both the Republic of Venezuela . . . and the Concessionaire, agree to attribute to the Concessionaire, a legal person of Venezuela subject to foreign control for the date when this clause enters into force, the character of 'National of another Contracting State' for the purpose of applying this Clause and the provisions of the Convention." *Aucoven*, supra note 143, ¶ 79.

[183] *Id.* ¶ 30.

[184] *Id.* ¶¶ 25–26.

subsidiary Icatech became the majority shareholder of Aucoven. Both Aucoven's shareholders and the Ministry confirmed that the change in ownership rendered Aucoven subject to foreign control by Icatech for purposes of arbitration under ICSID.[185]

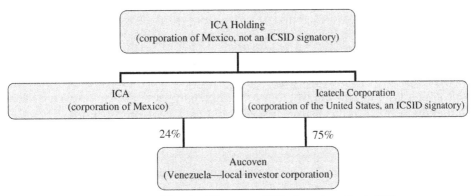

Aucoven ownership *after* 75 percent 1998 share transfer to ICA

Disputes arose between Aucoven and the Ministry, and Aucoven submitted a request for arbitration against Venezuela in June 2000, well over a year after the share transfer. Because Aucoven was by this point owned by Icatech, a U.S.-incorporated company, it asserted that there was ICSID jurisdiction. Venezuela argued that the tribunal lacked jurisdiction because although Aucoven was formally majority owned by a U.S. company, Aucoven was in reality controlled by a Mexican company; and because Mexico is not an ICSID contracting state, Aucoven could not bring an ICSID claim. Venezuela thus contended that the tribunal should go up the chain of ownership until it found *effective* control and that the nationality of the company in *effective* control should determine the jurisdictional question.

The tribunal found that jurisdiction existed. It noted that the "[c]onvention does not require any specific form for the agreement" set forth in the ICSID foreign control exception[186] and that the parties should have the autonomy to agree on an acceptable criterion regarding the meaning of nationality. In particular, the tribunal found that "an Arbitral Tribunal may not adopt a more restrictive definition of foreign control, unless the parties have exercised their discretion in a way inconsistent with the purposes of the Convention."[187] In analyzing Venezuela's argument

---

[185] *Id.* ¶¶ 28–30.
[186] *Id.* ¶ 105.
[187] *Id.* ¶ 114.

regarding the economic criteria to define the concept of foreign control, the tribunal noted the following:

> As a general matter . . . economic criteria often better reflect reality than legal ones. However, in the present case, such arguments of an economic matter are irrelevant. Indeed, exercising the discretion granted by the Convention, the parties have specifically identified *majority shareholding* as the criterion to be applied. They have not chosen to subordinate their consent to ICSID arbitration to other criteria.[188]

The tribunal found that the formal criteria of "majority shareholding" chosen by the parties was "reasonable." The tribunal then went on to find that there was no merit to Venezuela's argument that "Icatech would be a corporation of convenience exerting purely fictional control for jurisdiction purposes" or that "Aucoven's conduct in the context of the share transfer would have been misleading."

Aucoven v. Venezuela

ICSID Case No. ARB/00/5 (Decision on Jurisdiction of Sept. 27, 2001)

121. Direct shareholding confers voting right, and, therefore, the possibility to participate in the decision-making of the company. Hence, even if it does not constitute the sole criterion to define "foreign control," direct shareholding is certainly a reasonable test for control.

122. The actual circumstances prevailing in this case confirm this finding. Indeed, the Tribunal has found no indication supporting Venezuela's assertions that Icatech would be a corporation of convenience exerting a purely fictional control for jurisdiction purposes or that Aucoven's conduct in the context of the share transfer would have been misleading.

a) Icatech is not a Corporation of Convenience Exerting Merely Fictional Control over Aucoven

123. Icatech was incorporated in Florida on November 2, 1989, well before the conclusion of the Agreement, the share transfer and the emergence of the present dispute. Icatech, which has about 20 subsidiaries in different countries, is subject to economic, tax and social regulations in the United States, a country which is not considered a tax or regulatory haven.

124. As stated above (see para. 18), Aucoven requested Venezuela's approval of the share transfer at the very beginning of the project. As Aucoven alleged without being contradicted, it was difficult at that time for a Mexican company to finance projects because of the peso crisis. Since a connection to the United States enhanced the ability to obtain financing, again an assertion which remained unchallenged, ICA Holding

---

[188] *Id.* ¶ 119.

decided that Icatech would establish or acquire several international project companies including Aucoven. Such explanation which is being put forward by Aucoven in the context of the present proceedings (Hearing of June 28, 2001, transcript, p.175) is consistent with the one expressed in the request for approval of the share transfer: "On the other hand, I must indicate, Honorable Minister, that the purpose of the authorization requested herein is to create a new capital participation structure of the concessionaire company in charge of the project, construction, development, conservation and maintenance of the Caracas—La Guaira Expressway and Old Caracas—Highway and Related Services" (Letter from E. Perez Alfonso to Minister M. Orozco Graterol dated July 11, 1997, Ven. Ex. 25)

125. Further, in connection with corporate decision-making, the fact that Icatech exercises its voting rights (at least as far as major issues are concerned) in a way consistent with ICA Holding's strategy shows the group's coherence. It is certainly not sufficient to conclude that Icatech is a corporation of convenience.

126. On the basis of these facts, the Tribunal finds that Icatech cannot be regarded as a corporation of convenience. Hence, the assertion of ICSID jurisdiction based on the fact that Icatech holds 75% of Aucoven's shares does not constitute an abuse of the Convention purposes.

Thus, *Aucoven* suggests that when tribunals go up the ownership chain, it may be relevant to determine whether the entity with jurisdictional standing has independent economic substance.

vii. *Saluka v. Czech Republic*[189]

This dispute arose in the aftermath of the dissolution of the former Czechoslovak Republic in 1992 and creation of the new states of the Czech Republic and the Slovak Republic. This event occurred shortly after the end of the communist era (1990) when many banks in Central and Eastern Europe experienced solvency problems. As a result, a move toward privatization and reorganization of the banking sector began, which was intended to remedy those shortcomings. Investiční a Poštovní Banka a.s. (IPB), one of the four major Czech banks, was privatized and part of its shares were transferred to Saluka Investments, B.V. (Saluka) a Dutch holding company.

Saluka was a Dutch holding company, wholly owned by Nomura Group, a Japanese financial services consulting conglomerate with offices around the world. Nomura Group, through a complex series of transactions, using a U.K. subsidiary known as Nomura Europe plc., acquired a 46 percent minority but controlling interest in IPB, by purchasing the government's as well as private interests

---

[189] *Saluka, supra* note 119.

in IPB. In 1998 and 2000, Nomura Europe, plc., transferred these shares to Saluka. The ownership structure of Saluka at this time was as follows:

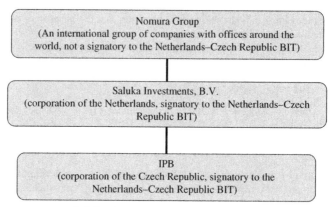

Saluka Ownership Structure

IPB, like other Czech banks, suffered from a *bad debt* problem; this later became the centerpiece of this dispute when the Czech Republic extended state aid to all the big banks to the exclusion of IPB. In 2001 Saluka commenced an arbitration under UNCITRAL rules against the Czech Republic pursuant to the BIT between the Netherlands and the Czech Republic. The Czech Republic raised several objections to the jurisdiction of the tribunal. It argued inter alia that the relationship between Saluka and Nomura was so close that they were in fact the same company; thus, the tribunal should pierce the corporate veil of Saluka and deny jurisdiction, because Nomura as the main interested party lacked standing under the Netherlands-Czech Republic BIT for want of requisite nationality.[190]

The tribunal, however, refused to pierce Saluka's veil; it however acknowledged that *piercing the corporate veil* could be a proper equitable remedy in other circumstances.[191]

Saluka Investments v. Czech Republic

UNCITRAL arbitration, Partial Award of Mar. 17, 2006

228. The Tribunal accepts—and the parties have made no attempt to conceal, either from the Tribunal or, in the Claimant's case, from the Czech authorities—the closeness of the relationship between Nomura and Saluka. In that respect, the companies concerned have simply acted in a manner which is commonplace in the world of commerce.

229. In dealing with the consequences of that way of acting, the Tribunal must always bear in mind the terms of the Treaty under which it operates. Those terms expressly give

---

[190] *Id.*, Partial Award of Mar. 17, 2006, ¶¶ 226–27.
[191] *Id.* ¶ 230.

> a legal person constituted under the laws of The Netherlands—such as, in this case, Saluka—the right to invoke the protection of the Treaty. To depart from that conclusion requires clear language in the Treaty, but there is none. The parties to the Treaty could have included in their agreed definition of "investor" some words which would have served, for example, to exclude wholly-owned subsidiaries of companies constituted under the laws of third States, but they did not do so. The parties having agreed that any legal person constituted under their laws is entitled to invoke the protection of the Treaty, and having so agreed without reference to any question of their relationship to some other third State corporation, it is beyond the powers of this Tribunal to import into the definition of "investor" some requirement relating to such a relationship having the effect of excluding from the Treaty's protection a company which the language agreed by the parties included within it.

Thus, the tribunal once again refused to go pierce the corporate veil to determine the ultimate beneficial owners of the investment.

viii. An Unusual Case: When a Tribunal Pierced the Veil but Denied Jurisdiction: *Loewen v. United States*

In one case a tribunal searched up the chain of ownership to identify the entity with effective control, and based its jurisdictional decision on the nationality of the entity with effective control. The *Loewen* case[192] began when an American funeral insurance company (O'Keefe) won a $500 million jury verdict in Mississippi against a Canadian competitor, The Loewen Group, Inc. (TLGI), and its American subsidiary, The Loewen Group International, Inc. (LGII) (collectively known as Loewen). Pursuant to Mississippi's rules, Loewen was faced with the choice of posting a 125 percent bond (US$625 million) to prevent O'Keefe from enforcing the judgment or executing on all Loewen's property in Mississippi and other states, while Loewen's appeal was pending. Because securing funds for the bond was nearly impossible and the alternative was loss of its property, Loewen thereafter decided to settle rather than continue with the appeal. Later, Loewen pursued its NAFTA claims, alleging, among other things, a denial of justice. Loewen claimed that the Mississippi court's actions and subsequent pressure were so improper as to constitute a violation of NAFTA's investment protections for which the United States should be held liable. The NAFTA tribunal agreed that the trial was a miscarriage of justice:

> By any standard of measurement, the trial involving O'Keefe and Loewen was a disgrace. By any standard of review, the tactics of O'Keefe's lawyers, particularly [its lead counsel], were impermissible. By any standard of evaluation, the trial judge failed to afford Loewen the process that was due.[193]

---

[192] *Loewen, supra* note 142.

[193] *Id.*, Final Award of June 26, 2003, ¶ 119.

Loewen filed its NAFTA arbitration in September 1999, and a hearing on the merits occurred in October 2001. However, after the hearing but before issuance of the tribunal's decision, Loewen filed for bankruptcy protection in the United States and Canada. As a result Loewen reorganized its businesses so that the ultimate parent became a U.S. corporation, instead of the previous arrangement in which the parent was the Canadian corporation TLGI. Of course under NAFTA, a U.S. corporation could not pursue a claim against the government of the United States; so in an attempt to preserve diversity in the NAFTA claim, Loewen assigned all its right, title, and interest in the NAFTA claim to a new Canadian corporation called NAFCANCO, whose only asset was the NAFTA claim, and whose sole business activity was pursuit of that claim.

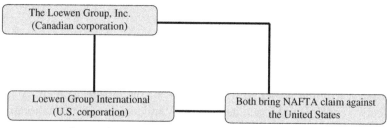

Loewen's corporate structure before reorganizing

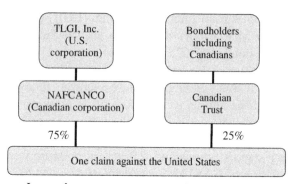

Loewen's corporate structure after reorganizing

The United States objected to the tribunal's jurisdiction, arguing, "A NAFTA claim cannot exist or cannot any longer exist, once the diversity of nationality has come to an end, so that the tribunal cannot continue with the resolution of the original dispute, there being no dispute left to resolve."[194] Loewen relied on

---

[194] *Id.* ¶ 232.

NAFTA Article 1109's provision for transfer of property by an investor to sustain its claim and the textual definition of investor: As a corporation properly incorporated in Canada, NAFCANCO was an *investor* of Canada under the definitions in the NAFTA text. NAFTA defines an *investor* quite broadly, and includes "an enterprise, *i.e.*, a company constituted or organized under the law of a Party or a branch located in the territory of a Party carrying out business activities there . . . ."[195]

The *Loewen* tribunal ruled against the claimant, disregarding the fact that NAFCANCO, the assignee owning the NAFTA claim, satisfied the formal requirements of NAFTA for jurisdictional standing. Instead, the tribunal went up the chain of ownership, identified the new U.S. holding company as the entity with effective control, and concluded it had no jurisdiction. The tribunal found the Claimant's assignment to NAFCANCO irrelevant:

> By the terms of the assignment, the only item being assigned was this NAFTA claim. All of the assets and business of [Loewen] have been reorganized under the mantle of an American corporation. All of the benefits of any award would clearly inure to the American corporation. Such a naked entity as NAFCANCO, even with its catchy name, cannot qualify as a continuing national for the purposes of this proceeding.[196]

The tribunal also noted, "[w]hatever the reasons for [Loewen's] decision to follow the bankruptcy route it chose, the consequences broke the chain of nationality that the Treaty requires."[197] Thus, the tribunal found that it lacked jurisdiction to determine the claims because NAFCANCO was "owned and controlled by a U.S. corporation."

Many commentators have expressed doubt about the basis for the *Loewen* decision, suggesting that the tribunal's reliance on a "continuous nationality requirement" was ultimately a pretext.[198] In petitioning the U.S. District Court for the District of Columbia to vacate the tribunal's award, Mr. Loewen indicated that the tribunal ignored the full extent of assignment of the NAFTA claims: NAFCANCO received 75 percent, but a Canadian trust also received 25 percent.[199] Thus, the tribunal found it legally relevant that the chain of conrol had changed during the course of the pursuit of the NAFTA claim, but failed to acknowledge that a "NAFTA disputing party" retained some interest in the claim.

---

[195] Counter-Memorial of Loewen Group Inc. on Matters of Jurisdiction and Competence, Mar. 29, 2002, ¶ 141, *available at* www.naftaclaims.com.

[196] *Loewen, supra* note 142, ¶ 237.

[197] *Id.* ¶ 234.

[198] *See* the discussion at p. 342 *infra*.

[199] Notice of Petition to Vacate, *Loewen v. U.S.*, No. Civ. A. 04–2151(RWR) 20 note 2 (D.D.C., Dec. 13, 2004), *available at* www.naftaclaims.com/.

C. Change of National Identity

A troubling issue for arbitral tribunals is how they should deal with cases in which the nationality of the claimant investor has changed during the course of the investment or during the course of the arbitral proceeding. The change of nationality can affect the tribunal's jurisdiction by moving the nationality to or from a state that has a different or no treaty relationship with the host state. The issue is examined in three contexts: first, under the customary international law where the continuous nationality rule applies; second, under various investment treaties; and third, under the Washington Convention.

1. Continuous Nationality Rule[200] Under Customary International Law

In the customary international law of diplomatic protection states may espouse claims of their nationals, subject to the application of the continuous nationality and other rules of international law such as the rule providing for the exhaustion of local remedies.[201] The continuous nationality rule requires that the injured person(s) have the nationality of the state that espouses their claim from the time of injury until the time when the claim is filed; furthermore, these person(s) must not have the nationality of the respondent state during this time period.[202] With respect to the time frame, two dates are critical: the date of the injury or *dies a quo* and the date when the claim is filed or *dies ad quem*.

There is in fact debate whether *dies ad quem*, or expiration date, should not be a later date.[203] After examining the jurisprudence of arbitral tribunals and state practice, Special Rapporteur of the United Nations International Law Commission on Diplomatic Protection John Dugard identified ten different dates ranging from the date of espousal of a claim until the date of payment or settlement of the case as possible alternatives for *dies ad quem* and concluded that the content of the rule is

---

[200] On continuous nationality *see* John Dugard, *First Report on Diplomatic Protection*, U.N. Doc. A/CN.4/506/Add.1 (2000); Maurice Mendelson, *Runaway Train: The Continuous Nationality Rule: From* the Panavezys-Saldutiskis Railway *Case to* Loewen, *in* Weiler, *supra* note 84, at 123; Jan Paulsson, *Continuous Nationality in* Loewen, 20 Arb. Int'l 213 (2004); Rubins & Kinsella, *supra* note 77, at 283–85; *cf. Oppenheim's International Law*, *supra* note 32, at 512.

[201] *See* Chapter XIII *infra* on exhaustion of local remedies.

[202] Mendelson, *supra* note 200, at 123; Brownlie, *supra* note 6, at 389; Amerasinghe, *supra* note 31, at 281.

[203] Oppenheim, for example, contains the most restrictive version of the rule, which requires the maintenance of nationality "[f]rom the time of the occurrence of the injury until the making of the award. . . ." *Oppenheim's International Law, supra* note 32, at 512. For additional sources see especially the following memorials of the parties in the *Loewen* case: *Loewen Group, Inc. v. U.S.*, ICSID Case No. RB(AF)/98/3 (Counter-Memorial of the Loewen Group on Matters of Jurisdiction and Competence, Mar. 29, 2002, at 19–26); *cf. Loewen v. U.S.* (Memorial of the U.S. on Matters of Jurisdiction Arising from the Restructuring of the Loewen Group, Inc., Mar. 1, 2002), at 13–17, *available at* www.naftaclaims.com.

uncertain.[204] Maurice Mendelson's recapitulation of the current status of the law on continuous nationality provides a balanced approach to the issue:

> [T]he current status of the continuous nationality rule in the context of diplomatic protection . . . seems to be as follows . . . [:] There is substantial support for a rule requiring the claimant State to have been the State of nationality at the time of the injury (though some would like to mitigate its harsher features). There is less, but still significant, support for a requirement that the victim should possess the same nationality up to the point of the formal presentation of the claim. It is, on the other hand, by no means settled that the victim needs to possess the claimant State's nationality at any later stage in the proceedings. The practice, the case-law and the opinions of the most highly qualified specialists are insufficiently consistent to require such an extension of the time period; and there are good reasons of theory and policy as to why it should not be extended. Finally, it is by no means clear that the same nationality has to be held continuously, rather than just at the key points, the *dies a quo* and the *dies ad quem*.[205]

2. Change of Nationality and the Jurisdiction of Arbitral Tribunals Under Investment Treaties

Usually, investment protection treaties do not expressly deal with change of nationality. However, possible guidance regarding the relevant dates may be found in the definitions of *investor* and *investment* as well as dispute resolution provisions of the treaties. Mendelson, for example, analyzes various issues that should be considered in approaching this issue in the context of the 2004 U.S. Model BIT as follows:

> Under the US [M]odel BIT, the substantive obligations of the host State are generally defined in relation to "covered investments" or "investors of the other party," with no temporal criteria in relation to nationality. Likewise, in the jurisdictional clauses, there are no express temporal criteria of the kind found in the context of the law of diplomatic protection. There may, however, be an implicit continuous nationality rule, to a limited extent. The substantive obligations are, as explained, owed to an "investor of a Party" or in respect of its "covered investments." This entails the investor being, in effect, a national of his or its State at the time of injury, since otherwise there will have been no breach of the BIT in respect of the investor. But when we come to the dispute settlement provisions, right of access to tribunals are give to a "disputing party" or "parties," and particularly to a "claimant," who is defined as "an investor of a Party." It could therefore be argued that he or it also has to be a national of the same State Party at the time of bringing the claim, the more so since, by definition, there are only two parties to BITs. But, in any event, there is nothing in the language to suggest that the same nationality has to be held *continuously* between two points, and still less that a change of nationality subsequent to the institution of proceedings will affect standing.[206]

. . .

---

[204] Dugard, First Report, *supra* note 200, at 10–11: "The following dates have been suggested and employed as the dies ad quem: the date on which the Government endorses the claim of its national, the date of the initiation of diplomatic negotiations on the claim, the date of filing of the claim, the date of the signature, ratification or entry into force of the treaty referring the dispute to arbitration, the date of presentation of the claim, the date of conclusion of the oral hearing, the date of judgement and the date of settlement." (Source notes omitted).

[205] Mendelson, *supra* note 200, at 123.

[206] *Id.* at 132–33 (emphasis in the original).

To summarise the position regarding IPTs [(investment protection treaties)], in some cases there is a continuous nationality rule, and in other cases not. But even where continuous nationality is required, in no case is there any basis in the treaty for holding that it needs to continue beyond the date of instituting proceedings.[207]

In *Loewen*, however, the tribunal departed from this analysis by importing the continuous nationality rule into NAFTA. The tribunal stated that the NAFTA Articles 1116 and 1117 only provided for *dies a quo*, which corresponded to the date of filing the claim, but they were silent on *dies ad quem*; this lacuna had to be filled pursuant to the rules of customary international law (i.e., the continuous nationality rule).[208] Then, following the United States' suggestion regarding the content of the continuous nationality rule, the tribunal stated that the claimants failed to maintain their Canadian nationality until the date of the award.[209] It did note that with investment treaties and a direct right of action for investors, "the need for a rigid rule of *dies ad quem* also was relaxed ... such relaxations came about specifically in the language of the treaties. There is no such language in the NAFTA document. . . ."[210]

The *Loewen* tribunal's ruling, including its application of the continuous nationality rule, has been widely criticized.[211] Similarly, the weight of customary authority seems to support the view that *dies ad quem* corresponds to the date of filing, not the date of rendering the award. Furthermore, it is doubtful whether the customary international rule of continuous nationality, which was developed in diplomatic protection context, should in any level be applicable in investment treaty arbitration.[212] The rationale underlying the diplomatic protection was a fiction rooted in the classic maxim uttered by de Vattel that the injury to the individual is that to the state[213] and the state protects its own right in espousing claims of its nationals. Given that investors now have direct right of action under treaties, this fiction contradicts the realities of the modern legal framework governing international investment. Insofar as the provisions of investment treaties explicitly or implicitly impose temporal requirements on maintaining nationality, these requirements are treaty provisions, which do not necessarily incorporate customary law.

---

[207] *Id.* at 134.

[208] *Loewen*, Award, *supra* note 142, ¶ 226.

[209] *Id.* ¶¶ 229–30

[210] *Id.* ¶ 230.

[211] *See, e.g.*, Mendelson, *supra* note 200; Paulsson, *supra* note 200; Don Wallace, *Fair and Equitable Treatment and Denial of Justice*: Loewen v. U.S. *and* Chattin v. Mexico, in *International Investment Law and Arbitrations: Leading Cases from the ICSID, NAFTA, Bilateral Treaties and Customary International Law* 696 (T. Weiler ed., Cameron May 2005); Noah Rubins, Loewen v. U.S.: *The Burial of an Investor-State Arbitration Claim*, 21 Arb. Int'l 1 (2005).

[212] Mendelson, *supra* note 200, at 124.

[213] E. de Vattel, *The Law of Nations* 161 (71 T & JW Johnson, Law Booksellers, 6th Am. ed.) (1844).

3. Change of Nationality and Jurisdiction of Arbitral Tribunals Under the Washington Convention

As to natural persons, it was noted earlier that Article 25(2)(a) of the Washington Convention requires them to possess the nationality of a Contracting Party other than the host state on two dates: on the date when the disputing parties consent to arbitration; and, on the date of the registration of a request for arbitration.[214] Change of nationality of a natural person to that of the host state after the registration date destroys the basis of jurisdiction *ratione personae*. A natural person, however, may change his nationality to that of another ICSID Contracting Party.[215]

As to juridical persons, the first part of Article 25(2)(b) of the Washington Convention requires that they possess the nationality of another ICSID Contracting Party and not possess the nationality of the host state. Unlike natural persons, the Convention requires these conditions to be satisfied only on one date: the date of consent. Subsequent to consent, a juridical person may lose the nationality of the original Contracting State and acquire nationality of another Contracting State but not that of the host state.[216]

The second part of Article 25(2)(b) also grants standing to a company incorporated in the host state, provided that: a) it is controlled by nationals of another ICSID Contracting Party; and b) the parties to a dispute have *agreed* to deem such a company as a foreign national. Here the issue involving change is perhaps slightly different as it does not revolve around the change of nationality of the juridical person per se; but rather, the consequences of change in who controls the juridical person. Maurice Mendelson explains various issues related to application of the second part of Article 25(2)(b) as follows:

---

[214] *See* p. 296 *supra*. As to date of consent under Article 25 of the ICSID Convention, when the disputing parties agree in an investment contract or in a *compromis* to submit their investment dispute to arbitration, date of consent is the date at which the parties execute these documents, which in the former case is before the dispute arises and in the latter, after it. When the government's offer to arbitrate is in an investment treaty or legislation, date of its consent is prior to a dispute. Date of consent under Article 25, however, is when the investor (whether a natural or a juridical person) accepts that offer. The investor could accept the government's offer before the dispute by, for example, sending a letter to that effect to the respective authorities. With very rare exceptions, however, investors accept such an offer after the dispute arises, by filing a claim with ICSID, in which case the date of consent will coincide with the date of filing.

[215] Schreuer, *supra* note 28, at 288. In an unlikely situation that an investor changes its nationality to that of host state between the date of consent and the registration date, jurisdiction may still exist, so long as the investor loses the host state nationality by the time the registration takes place. *Id.* at 274.

[216] *Cf. id.* at 289 (explaining that "[s]ubsequent to consent, a juridical person may lose the nationality of the original Contracting State and may acquire the nationality of a non-Contracting State or that of the host State without losing access to ICSID").

> Maurice Mendelson, *Runaway Train: The Continuous Nationality Rule: From the Panavezys-Saldutiskis Railway Case to Loewen,* in International Investment Law and Arbitration: Leading Cases from the ICSID, NAFTA, Bilateral Treaties and Customary International Law 128–9 (Todd Weiler ed., Cameron May 2005)
>
> [I]t is clear from the language [of Article 25(2)(b), second part] that the critical date for determining whether the [locally incorporated] entity is a national of the host State is that of consent to the jurisdiction of the Centre. What the terms of this provision do not cover expressly is what is the critical date for determining whether there is in fact *foreign control* (for this condition is not waivable by agreement). It must exist at the same date as the agreement to deem the company to have some other nationality, because of the words *"because of foreign control."* But what if foreign control disappears after the date of such agreement? Adherence simply to the date of consent, whilst warranted by the principle *expressio unius exclusio alterius,* might possibly be regarded as contrary to the intention of the drafters to restrict claims by national companies of the host State. The dispute settlement provisions of some BITs do in fact require foreign control immediately before the dispute arises also, which is permissible under the *ICSID Convention.* Schreuer, on the other hand, prefers the date of registration of the request.[217] What seems reasonably clear, in any event, though, is that a change of nationality is only relevant (if at all) under Article 25(2)(b), second part, if control falls into the hands of nationals of the host State, not if it simply changes into the control of nationals of some different Contracting State other than the host country. In other words, if control passes out of the hands of nationals of State A into that of nationals of State B, that should make no difference, provided at any rate that State B is not the host State. . . .

The early ICSID Case of *Klöckner v. Cameroon*[218] takes a more liberal approach to the interpretation of the Washington Convention. In *Klöckner v. Cameroon* the government of Cameroon signed two investment agreements with the German company Klöckner Group with respect to a fertilizer factory, which provided for ICSID arbitration of disputes. Both Cameroon and Germany were ICSID Contracting States. At the same time, the Cameroon government signed a third agreement, called the Establishment Agreement of 1973, with a Cameroonian company called SOCAME to run the fertilizer factory. The Establishment Agreement also contained an ICSID arbitration clause. When this agreement was signed, SOCAME was 51 percent owned by Klöckner and 49 percent by the government of Cameroon. Afterward, Klöckner failed to subscribe to a required capital increase and as a result lost its majority control over SOCAME. In 1978 after several months of unprofitable operation, the factory was shut down. Klöckner filed for arbitration in 1981, and Cameroon counterclaimed under the Establishment Agreement. Klöckner objected to the jurisdiction of the tribunal over the counterclaims, because, among other things, Klöckner had in 1978 lost its control over SOCAME; and the latter was then effectively under Cameroon's control. The tribunal ruled that it had jurisdiction over the counterclaim and disputes

---

[217] SN: Schreuer, *supra* note 32, at 324–32.

[218] *Klöckner Industrie-Anlagen GmbH v. United Republic of Cameroon and Société Camerounaise des Engrais,* ICSID Case No. ARB/81/2 (Award of Oct. 21, 1983), *reprinted at* 2 ICSID Rep. 9 (1993).

under the Establishment Agreement for the period ending in the change of control (1978), because until that date Klöckner had enjoyed the benefits of the Establishment Agreement.[219] Although the arbitrators focused more on questions of subject matter jurisdiction, they also summarized then-current thoughts about change of claimant identity and jurisdiction *ratione personae*:

> It is true that in 1978 a change occurred when the foreign interest lost majority control over [SOCAME].... Knowledgeable writers are divided on the issue of the effects on the ICSID arbitration clause of a subsequent change of nationality or control. On the one hand, Mr. Amerasinghe has maintained that this change affects neither the validity nor the effect of the forum clause because, in his view, the ICSID Convention implies that the relevant time for the fulfillment of the nationality requirement is that date when the consent to jurisdiction is effective for both parties. It also means that any change in the nationality of the juridical person after that date is immaterial for purposes of ICSID's jurisdiction.[220]
>
> This opinion finds support in a phrase contained in Article 25(2): "on the date on which the parties consented." On the other hand, Mr. Delaume[221] seems to be of a different view; in analyzing the hypothesis of an assignment to a third party of the investment agreement during its performance, he maintains that if the assignee is a "national of the State party to the agreement or of a non-contracting State," the Centre's jurisdiction would disappear.[222]

The tribunal, despite the fact that claimants did not have control over the locally incorporated company at the time of the registration, upheld its jurisdiction over the counterclaims.

---

[219] *Id.* at 16–17.

[220] SN: C. F. Amerasinghe, *The International Centre for the Settlement of Investment Disputes and Development through the Multinational Corporation*, 9 Vand. J. Transnat'l L. 793, 809–10 (1976).

[221] SN: G. Delaume, *Le Centre International pour le Règlement des Différends Relatifs aux Investissements (CIRDI)*, 109 J.D.I. 775, 797 (1982).

[222] *Klöckner, supra* note 218, at 16 (source notes altered).

XIII. Exhaustion of Local Remedies

A. Exhaustion of Local Remedies Under Customary International Law

The requirement of exhaustion of local remedies (or *local remedies rule*) is a longstanding rule of customary international law that was developed in the context of diplomatic protection.[1] Under this rule, where a state commits an act that injures a foreign person, the victim traditionally must *exhaust* all the *effective* domestic legal remedies before its home government can espouse its claim in the exercise of diplomatic protection. Exhaustion of local remedies in this sense is a precondition of the admissibility of international claims.[2] The exhaustion of local

---

[1] John Dugard, Special Rapporteur, International Law Commission, Second Report on Diplomatic Protection, U.N. Doc. A/CN.4/514 (Aug. 2001), at 10. On the exhaustion of local remedies, *see generally* John Dugard, Special Rapporteur, International Law Commission, Third Report on Diplomatic Protection, U.N. Doc. A/CN.4/523 (2002); Stephen M. Schwebel, *Arbitration and the Exhaustion of Local Remedies*, Just. Int'l L. 171 (Grotius 1994); Andrea Bjorklund, *Waiver and the Exhaustion of the Local Remedies Rule in NAFTA Jurisprudence*, NAFTA Inv. L. Arb. 253 (2004); P. Peters, *Exhaustion of Local Remedies: Ignored in Most Bilateral Investment Treaties*, 44(2) Neth. Int'l L. Rev. 233 (1997); A. A. Cancado Trindade, *The Application of the Rule of Exhaustion of Local Remedies in International Law: Its Rationale in the International Protection of Individual Rights* (Cambridge University Press 1983).

[2] Draft Articles on Responsibility of States for Internationally Wrongful Acts, Adopted by the U.N. International Law Commission in Its 53d Sess. (2001), art. 44 [hereinafter ILC Articles]. *See also* the excerpt from the *Interhandel* case at p. 354 *infra*. On the difference between admissibility and jurisdiction see I. Laird, *A Distinction without a Difference? An Examination of the Concepts of Admissibility and Jurisdiction in* Salini v. Jordan *and* Methanex v. U.S., *in International Investment Law and Arbitration: Leading Cases from the ICSID, NAFTA, Bilateral Treaties, and Customary International Law* 201 (Todd Weiler ed., Cameron May 2005). The local remedies rule does not apply when a claimant state has incurred a direct injury. I. Brownlie, *Principles of Public International Law* 477 (Oxford University Press, 6th ed., 2003).

remedies may also be required as a substantive element of some international wrongs, such as denial of justice.[3]

Borchard explained the rationale underlying the local remedies rule as follows:

> First, the citizen going abroad is presumed to take into account the means furnished by local law for the redress of wrongs; secondly, the right of sovereignty and independence warrants the local State in demanding for its courts freedom from interference, on the assumption that they are capable of doing justice; thirdly, the home Government of the complaining citizen must give the offending Government an opportunity of doing justice to the injured party in its own regular way, and thus avoid, if possible, all occasion for international discussions; fourthly, if the injury is committed by an individual or minor official, the exhaustion of local remedies is necessary to make certain that the wrongful act or denial of justice is the deliberate act of the State; and fifthly, if it is a deliberate act of the State, that the State is willing to leave the wrong unrighted. It is a logical principle that where there is a judicial remedy, it must be sought. Only if it is sought in vain and a denial of justice established, does diplomatic interposition become proper.[4]

The local remedies rule is subject to several exceptions that relieve foreign persons from pursuing them. The two main exceptions in investment treaty arbitration are waiver[5] by the state that has committed the wrongful act; and the futility[6] of the available local remedies.

---

[3] Denial of justice is one of the oldest international wrongs. Historically, it has played a prominent role in the development of the local remedies rule. John Dugard, Second Report, *supra* note 1, ¶ 10. Denial of justice and its relation to the local remedies rule are more fully discussed in Chapter XVII *infra*.

[4] E. Borchard, *The Diplomatic Protection of Citizens Abroad* 817–18 (Banks Law Publication 1915); *see also* K. Doehring, *Local Remedies, Exhaustion of*, in 3 *Encyclopedia of Public International Law* 238 (R. Bernhardt ed., Max Planck 1997); C. F. Amerasinghe, *Local Remedies in International Law* 43 et seq (Cambridge University Press, 2d ed., 2004); Mummery, *The Content of the Duty to Exhaust Local Remedies*, 58 Am. J. Int'l L. 389, 390 *et seq*. (1964).

[5] Dugard, Third Report, *supra* note 1, at 17–18. Waiver by a state, however, would arguably prevent a claim of denial of justice, which requires exhaustion as a substantive element, from crystallizing. *See* Section C.

[6] Dugard lists all the exceptions as follows: "Local remedies do not need to be exhausted where: (a) The local remedies are obviously futile (option 1); or they offer no reasonable prospect of success (option 2); or they provide no reasonable possibility of an effective remedy (option 3) [These options reflect the various terminology used to explain when local remedies are ineffective. Dugard later in this report prefers option 3, which in terms of strictness fills the middle ground between the three; i.e., it is less strict than option 1 and not as generous as option 2.]; (b) The respondent State has expressly or impliedly waived the requirement that local remedies be exhausted or is estopped from raising this requirement; (c) There is no voluntary link between the injured individual and the respondent State; (d) The internationally wrongful act upon which the international claim is based was not committed within the territorial jurisdiction of the respondent State; (e) The respondent State is responsible for undue delay in providing a local remedy; (f) The respondent State prevents the injured individual from gaining access to its institutions which provide local remedies." *Id.* at 5–6.

States can waive the exhaustion requirement in a variety of ways,[7] including in a treaty. This seems to be the case with most modern investment treaties, as is discussed in Section (b). There is some debate, however, over how explicit a waiver must be. In the *ELSI* case,[8] which involved requisition of a factory in Italy belonging to two American companies, the United States argued on behalf of the companies that Article XXVI of the Italy-U.S. FCN (Friendship, Commerce, and Navigation) Treaty (1948) made it unnecessary to exhaust local remedies. Article XXVI provided that "[a]ny dispute between the High Contracting Parties as to the interpretation or the application of this Treaty . . . shall be submitted to the International Court of Justice [(ICJ)]. . . ." The ICJ held the following:

> The Chamber has no doubt that the parties to a treaty can therein either agree that the local remedies rule shall not apply to claims based on alleged breaches of that treaty; or confirm that it shall apply. Yet the Chamber finds itself unable to accept that an important principle of customary international law should be held to have been *tacitly* dispensed with, in the absence of any words making clear an intention to do so. This part of the United States response to the Italian objection must therefore be rejected.[9]

This statement could be interpreted as ruling out implied waivers.[10] However, the modern view is that implied waivers are possible so long as the intention of the parties to that effect is clear.[11] Whether a waiver can be implied is in essence a treaty interpretation exercise, which should be undertaken on a case-by-case basis.

The so-called *futility* exception is the more important exception: An alien need not exhaust local remedies that are *obviously futile* or ineffective. What is futile or ineffective depends on the circumstances of the case.[12] The term *futility* was first used by Justice Bagge of the Swedish Supreme Court, sitting as arbitrator in the *Finnish Ships Arbitration*.[13] This case arose out of the taking of thirteen Finnish ships by the British government during World War I. The shipowners brought a claim against the Crown before the Admiralty Transport Arbitration Board of England, which dismissed it. The

---

[7] *See, e.g.*, J. Gillis Wetter & S. Schwebel, *Arbitration and the Exhaustion of Local Remedies*, 60 Am. J. Int'l L. 484, 499 (1966): "It may be presumed when a State and an alien agree to have recourse to arbitration, and do not reserve the right to have recourse to other remedies or require the prior exhaustion of other remedies, the intention of the parties is to have recourse to arbitration to the exclusion of any other remedy."

[8] *Case Concerning Elettronica Sicula S.p.A (ELSI) (U.S. v. Italy)*, 1989 I.C.J. Rep 15, 28 I.L.M. 1109 (1989).

[9] *Id.* ¶ 50 (emphasis added).

[10] Some commentators have even stated that there is a presumption against implied waiver. *See, e.g.*, G. Schwarzenberger, 1 *International Law: As Applied by International Courts and Tribunals*, 610–11 (Stevens, 3d ed. 1957). *See also* F. V. García Amador, *The Changing Law of International Claims* 467 (Oceana 1984).

[11] Dugard, Third Report, *supra* note 1, ¶¶ 53–55.

[12] Mummery, *supra* note 4, at 400–01.

[13] *Finnish Vessels in Great Britain During the War (Finland v. Great Britain)*, 7 ILR 231 (1934); 3 U.N.R.I.A.A. 1479 (1934).

claimants had a right of appeal to the ordinary courts on certain matters of law. Instead, they sought the diplomatic protection of their government, and the matter on the recommendation of the League of Nations was referred to arbitration. On behalf of the shipowners, the government of Finland argued that remedies *appearing* to be futile need not be exhausted. However, the British government contended that the threshold was higher and only *obviously futile* remedies need not be exhausted.[14] The sole arbitrator, Justice Bagge, agreeing with the latter view, held the following:

> As regards finally the third question, whether the local remedy shall be considered as not effective only where it is obviously futile on the merits of the case which are to be taken into account, to have recourse to the municipal remedy, or whether, as the Finnish Government suggest, [sic] it is sufficient that such a step only appears to be futile, a certain strictness in construing this rule appears justified by the opinion expressed by Borchard when mentioning the rule applied in prize cases. Borchard says (a.a. § 383): "In a few prize cases, it has been held that in face of a uniform course of decisions in the highest courts a reversal of the condemnation being hopeless, an appeal was excused; but this rule was most strictly construed, and if substantial right of appeal existed, failure to prosecute an appeal operated as a bar to relief."[15]

He then thoroughly examined the question of whether there was any appealable point of law that the claimants could have referred to the British courts; he concluded that there was none, and therefore the Finnish shipowners had exhausted local remedies.

Some cases have followed this test,[16] but it has been described as too strict.[17] One commentator has even noted that it "contributes very little to precision and objectivity of thought."[18] Based partly on such criticisms, in Dugard's third report on diplomatic protection,[19] he proposed using the following formulation: "provide no reasonable possibility of an effective remedy" (option 3),[20] instead of "obvious futility" (option 1), or "reasonable prospect of success" (option 2):

> John Dugard, Special Rapporteur, International Law Commission, *Third Report on Diplomatic Protection*, U.N. Doc. A/CN.4/523, 2002, at 12–13 (source notes omitted)
>
> 34. While the "obvious futility" test is too strict, that of "reasonable prospect of success" is probably too generous to the claimant. It seems wiser, therefore, to seek a formulation that invokes the concept of reasonableness but which does not too easily excuse the claimant from compliance with the local remedies rule. A possible solution is to be found in option 3, that there is an exemption from the local remedies rule where "there is no reasonable

---

[14] *Id.* at 1504.

[15] *Id.*

[16] *See, e.g., Ambatielos* claim, 12 U.N.R.I.A.A. 83, 119 (1956). Justice Bagge's approach was also in line with a prior decision of the Permanent Court of International Justice in the *Panevezys-Saldutiskis Railway case*, 76 P.C.I.J. Series A/B. 4, 19 (1939) (requiring the ineffectiveness of the remedies to be clearly shown).

[17] Dugard, Third Report, *supra* note 1, at 12.

[18] Mummery, *supra* note 4, at 401.

[19] See note 6 *supra*.

[20] *Cf.* Amerasinghe, *supra* note 4, at 206 *et seq.*

possibility of an effective remedy before courts of the respondent State." This formulation avoids the stringent language of "obvious futility" but nevertheless imposes a heavy burden on the claimant by requiring that he prove that in the circumstances of the case, and having regard to the legal system of the respondent State, there is no reasonable possibility of an effective remedy. This is a stricter test than that of "no reasonable prospect of success," the test employed in some legal systems for refusing leave to appeal to a higher court.

35. This test is adopted from the separate opinion of Sir Hersch Lauterpacht in the *Norwegian Loans* case, in which he stated, after considering the grounds on which it might be doubted that the Norwegian courts could afford any effective remedy:

> "However, these doubts do not seem strong enough to render inoperative the requirement of previous exhaustion of local remedies. The legal position on the subject cannot be regarded as so abundantly clear as to rule out as a matter of reasonable possibility an effective remedy before the Norwegian courts."

A number of writers have endorsed this view. Perhaps the best exposition of the test is given by Sir Gerald Fitzmaurice:

> "... Lauterpacht propounded the criterion of there being a 'reasonable possibility' that a remedy would be afforded, as being the test of effectiveness—or in other words he suggested that no means of recourse can be regarded as futile from the effectiveness standpoint unless there does not appear to be even a reasonable possibility that it will afford an effective remedy. This test is acceptable provided it is borne in mind that what there must be a reasonable possibility of is the *existence* of a possibly effective remedy, and that the mere fact that there is no reasonable possibility of the claimant obtaining that remedy, because his case is legally unmeritorious, does not constitute the type of absence of reasonable possibility which will displace the local remedies rule."

36. The text proposed arguably accords more with the reasoning of Arbitrator Bagge in the Finnish Ships Arbitration than that of "obvious futility"....

Terminological differences aside, the application of these tests poses difficulties insofar as in drawing a line beyond which the foreigner need not exhaust a local remedy. Several questions arise: What is an available or effective remedy? Does it include administrative or extra-legal remedies? Should the foreigner bring its international as well as domestic claims before local courts? There is no clear-cut answer to some of these questions, and various tribunals have taken divergent views. In the *Salem* case described in the following text, for example, the tribunal did not require Salem to exhaust an administrative remedy.[21] Subsequently, however, in the *Loewen* case the tribunal held that the claimant did have a remedy to exhaust.[22]

Ultimately, the determination of whether there are any remedies to exhaust turns on the circumstances of each case, keeping in mind that the local remedies rule "is

---

[21] *See* Section C *infra*.

[22] *Loewen Group, Inc. & Raymond L. Loewen v. U.S.*, ICSID Case No. ARB (AF)/98/3 (North American Free Trade Agreement [NAFTA], Award of June 26, 2003). *See* pp. 360 *et seq. infra* for the discussion of the case insofar as the exhaustion rule is concerned. *See also* Chapters XII and XVII for the discussion of continuous nationality issue and denial of justice aspects of this case, respectively.

a 'reasonable' rule, not a 'rigid' one, not a rule of infinite pursuit by platonically ideal parties with bottomless wallets to pay for legal fees, or professors wishing to create new legal theories. . . . "[23] Dugard has identified the following circumstances as those where local remedies need *not* be exhausted:[24]

- The local court has no jurisdiction over the dispute in question

- The national legislation justifying the acts of which the alien complains will not be reviewed by the courts

- The local courts are notoriously lacking in independence

- There is a consistent and well-established line of precedents adverse to the alien

- The courts of the respondent state do not have the competence to grant an appropriate and adequate remedy to the alien

- The respondent state does not have an adequate system of judicial protection

Following is an excerpt from the preliminary objections phase in the *Interhandel* case decided by the International Court of Justice (ICJ), where the question of exhaustion of local remedies was examined in detail. For ten years (1948–1957) the Swiss company Interhandel unsuccessfully pursued litigation in the U.S. courts to unblock its assets in the United States. Ultimately, its case was espoused by the Swiss government, which brought a claim before the ICJ on behalf of *Interhandel*. The ICJ dismissed the case because claimant had not exhausted local remedies.

Interhandel Case (Switzerland v. United States), Preliminary Objections, 1959 I.C.J. 6, 15–29, 26–29

By its decisions of February 16th and April 24th, 1942, based on the Trading with the Enemy Act of October 6th, 1917, as amended, the Government of the United States vested almost all of the shares of General Aniline and Film Corporation (briefly referred to as the GAF), a company incorporated in the United States, on the ground that these shares in reality belonged to the I.G. Farbenindustrie company of Frankfurt or that the GAF was in one way or another controlled by that enemy company.

It is not disputed that until 1940 I.G. Farben controlled the GAF through the Société internationale pour entreprises chimiques S.A. (I.G. Chemie), entered in the Commercial Register of the [Swiss] Canton of Bale-Ville in 1928. However, according to the contention of the Swiss Government, the links between the German company I.G. Farben and the

---

[23] Don Wallace, Jr., *Fair and Equitable Treatment and Denial of Justice: From* Chattin v. Mexico and Loewen v. U.S., *in International Investment Law and Arbitration: Leading Cases from the ICSID, NAFTA, Bilateral Treaties, and Customary International Law* 689 (Todd Weiler ed., Cameron May 2005).

[24] Dugard, Third Report, *supra* note 1, ¶¶ 38–44.

Swiss company I.G. Chemie were finally severed by the cancellation of the contract for an option and for the guarantee of dividends, a cancellation which was effected in June 1940, that is, well before the entry of the United States into the war. The Swiss company adopted the name of Société internationale pour participations industrielles et commerciales S.A. (briefly referred to as Interhandel). . . .

Towards the end of the war, under a provisional agreement between Switzerland, the United States of America, France and the United Kingdom, property in Switzerland belonging to Germans in Germany was blocked (Decree of the Federal Council of February 16th, 1945). The Swiss Compensation Office was entrusted with the task of uncovering property in Switzerland belonging to Germans or controlled by them. In the course of these investigations, the question of the character of Interhandel was raised, but as a result of investigations carried out in June and July, 1945, the Office, considering it to have been proved that Interhandel had severed its ties with the German company, did not regard it as necessary to undertake the blocking of its assets.

For its part, the Government of the United States, considering that Interhandel was still controlled by I.G. Farben, continued to seek evidence of such control. In these circumstances the Federal Department of Public Economy and the Federal Political Department ordered the Swiss Compensation Office provisionally to block the assets of Interhandel; this was done on October 30th, 1945. The Office then carried out a second investigation (November 1945–February 1946) which led it to the same conclusion as had the first.

On May 25th, 1946, an agreement was concluded between the three Allied Powers and Switzerland (the Washington Accord). Under one of the provisions of the Accord, Switzerland undertook to pursue its investigations and to liquidate German property in Switzerland. It was the Compensation Office which was "empowered to uncover, take into possession, and liquidate German property" (Accord, Annex, II, A), in collaboration with a Joint Commission "composed of representatives of each of the four Governments" (Annex, II, B). The Accord lays down the details of that collaboration (Annex, II, C, D, E, F) and provides that, in the event of disagreement between the Joint Commission and the Compensation Office or if the party in interest so desires, the matter may within a period of one month be submitted to a Swiss Authority of Review composed of three members and presided over by a Judge. "The decisions of the Compensation Office, or of the Authority of Review, should the matter be referred to it, shall be final" (Annex, III). In the event, however, of disagreement with the Swiss Authority of Review on certain given matters, "the three Allied Governments may, within one month, require the difference to be submitted to arbitration" (Annex, III).

The Washington Accord . . . provides:

> Article IV, paragraph 1.
>
> The Government of the United States will unblock Swiss assets in the United States. The necessary procedure will be determined without delay.
>
> Article VI.
>
> In case differences of opinion arise with regard to the application or interpretation of this Accord which cannot be settled in any other way, recourse shall be had to arbitration.

After the conclusion of the Washington Accord, discussions with regard to Interhandel between the Swiss Compensation Office and the Joint Commission as well as between representatives of Switzerland and the United States were continued without reaching any conclusion accepted by the two parties. The Office, while declaring itself ready to examine any evidence as to the German character of Interhandel which might be submitted to it, continued to accept the results of its two investigations; the Joint Commission challenged these results and continued its investigations. By its decision of January 5th, 1948, given on appeal by Interhandel, the Swiss Authority of Review annulled the blocking with retroactive effect. It had invited the Joint Commission to participate in the procedure, but the latter had declined the invitation. This question was not referred to the arbitration provided for in the Washington Accord.

In these circumstances, the Swiss Government considered itself entitled to regard the decision of the Swiss Authority of Review as a final one, having the force of res judicata vis-à-vis the Powers parties to the Washington Accord. Consequently, in a Note of May 4th, 1948, to the Department of State, the Swiss Legation at Washington invoked this decision and the Washington Accord to request the Government of the United States to restore to Interhandel the property which had been vested in the United States. On July 26th, 1948, the Department of State rejected this request, contending that the decision of the Swiss Authority of Review did not affect the assets vested in the United States and claimed by I.G. Chemie. On September 7th, 1948, in a Note to the Department of State, the Swiss Legation in Washington, still relying on its interpretation of the Washington Accord, maintained that the decision of the Swiss Authority of Review recognizing Interhandel as a Swiss company was legally binding upon the signatories of that Accord. It expressed the hope that the United States Government would accordingly release the assets of Interhandel in the United States, failing which the Swiss Government would have to submit the question to the arbitral procedure laid down in Article VI of the Washington Accord.

On October 12th, 1948, the Department of State replied to that communication, maintaining its previous view that the decision of the Swiss Authority of Review was inapplicable to property vested in the United States. It added that United States law in regard to the seizure and disposal of enemy property authorized non-enemy foreigners to demand the restitution of vested property and to apply for it to the courts. On October 21st, 1948, Interhandel, relying upon the provisions of the Trading with the Enemy Act, instituted proceedings in the United States District Court for the District of Columbia. . . .

Up to 1957 the proceedings in the United States courts had made little progress on the merits. Interhandel, though it had produced a considerable number of the documents called for, did not produce all of them; it contended that the production of certain documents was prohibited by the Swiss authorities as constituting an offence under Article 273 of the Swiss Criminal Code and as violating banking secrecy (Article 47 of the Federal Law of November 8th, 1934). The action brought by Interhandel was the subject of a number of appeals in the United States courts and in a Memorandum appended to the Note addressed by the Department of State to the Swiss Minister on January 11th, 1957, it was said that Interhandel had finally failed in its suit. It was then that the Swiss Government, on October 2nd, 1957, addressed to the Court the Application instituting the present proceedings. The assertion in the Note of January 11th, 1957, that Interhandel's claim was finally rejected proved, however, to be premature, as the Court will have occasion to point out in considering the Third Objection of the United States.

. . . .

Third Preliminary Objection

The Third Preliminary Objection [of the United States] seeks a finding that 'there is no jurisdiction in this Court to hear or determine the matters raised by the Swiss Application and Memorial, for the reason that Interhandel, whose case Switzerland is espousing, has not exhausted the local remedies available to it in the United States courts.'

Although framed as an objection to the jurisdiction of the Court, this Objection must be regarded as directed against the admissibility of the Application of the Swiss Government. Indeed, by its nature it is to be regarded as a plea which would become devoid of object if the requirement of the prior exhaustion of local remedies were fulfilled.

. . . .

The rule that local remedies must be exhausted before international proceedings may be instituted is a well-established rule of customary international law; the rule has been generally observed in cases in which a State has adopted the cause of its national whose rights are claimed to have been disregarded in another State in violation of international law. Before resort may be had to an international court in such a situation, it has been considered necessary that the State where the violation occurred should have an opportunity to redress it by its own means, within the framework of its own domestic legal system. A fortiori the rule must be observed when domestic proceedings are pending, as in the case of Interhandel, and when the two actions, that of the Swiss company in the United States courts and that of the Swiss Government in this Court, in its principal Submission, are designed to obtain the same result: the restitution of the assets of Interhandel vested in the United States.

The Swiss Government does not challenge the rule which requires that international judicial proceedings may only be instituted following the exhaustion of local remedies, but contends that the present case is one in which an exception to this rule is authorized by the rule itself.

The Court does not consider it necessary to dwell upon the assertion of the Swiss Government that "the United States itself has admitted that Interhandel had exhausted the remedies available in the United States courts." It is true that the representatives of the Government of the United States expressed this opinion on several occasions, in particular in the memorandum annexed to the Note of the Secretary of State of January 11th, 1957. This opinion was based upon a view which has proved unfounded. In fact, the proceedings which Interhandel had instituted before the courts of the United States were then in progress.

However, the Swiss Government has raised against the Third Objection other considerations which require examination.

In the first place, it is contended that the rule is not applicable for the reason that the measure taken against Interhandel and regarded as contrary to international law is a measure which was taken, not by a subordinate authority but by the Government of the United States. However, the Court must attach decisive importance to the fact that the laws of the United States make available to interested persons who consider that they have been deprived of their rights by measures taken in pursuance of the Trading with the Enemy Act, adequate remedies for the defence of their rights against the Executive.

It has also been contended on behalf of the Swiss Government that in the proceedings based upon the Trading with the Enemy Act, the United States courts are not in a position to adjudicate in accordance with the rules of international law and that the Supreme Court, in its decision of June 16th, 1958, made no reference to the many questions of international law which, in the opinion of the Swiss Government, constitute the subject of the present dispute. But the decisions of the United States courts bear witness to the fact that United States courts are competent to apply international law in their decisions when necessary. In the present case, when the dispute was brought to this Court, the proceedings in the United States courts had not reached the merits, in which considerations of international law could have been profitably relied upon.

The Parties have argued the question of the binding force before the courts of the United States of international instruments which, according to the practice of the United States, fall within the category of Executive Agreements; the Washington Accord is said to belong to that category. At the present stage of the proceedings it is not necessary for the Court to express an opinion on the matter. Neither is it practicable, before the final decision of the domestic courts, to anticipate what basis they may adopt for their judgment.

Finally, the Swiss Government laid special stress on the argument that the character of the principal Submission of Switzerland is that of a claim for the implementation of the decision given on January 5th, 1948, by the Swiss Authority of Review and based on the Washington Accord, a decision which the Swiss Government regards as an international judicial decision. 'When an international decision has not been executed, there are no local remedies to exhaust, for the injury has been caused directly to the injured State.' It has therefore contended that the failure by the United States to implement the decision constitutes a direct breach of international law, causing immediate injury to the rights of Switzerland as the Applicant State. The Court notes in the first place that to implement a decision is to apply its operative part. In the operative part of its decision, however, the Swiss Authority of Review 'Decrees: (1) that the Appeal is sustained and the decision subjecting the appellant to the blocking of German property in Switzerland is annulled . . .' The decision of the Swiss Authority of Review relates to the unblocking of the assets of Interhandel in Switzerland; the Swiss claim is designed to secure the restitution of the assets of Interhandel in the United States. Without prejudging the validity of any arguments which the Swiss Government seeks or may seek to base upon that decision, the Court would confine itself to observing that such arguments do not deprive the dispute which has been referred to it of the character of a dispute in which the Swiss Government appears as having adopted the cause of its national, Interhandel, for the purpose of securing the restitution to that company of assets vested by the Government of the United States. This is one of the very cases which give rise to the application of the rule of the exhaustion of local remedies.

For all these reasons, the Court upholds the Third Preliminary Objection so far as the principal Submission of Switzerland is concerned.

In its alternative claim, the Swiss Government asks the Court to declare its competence to decide whether the United States is under an obligation to submit the dispute to arbitration or conciliation. The Government of the United States contends that this claim, while not identical with the principal claim, is designed to secure the same object, namely, the restitution of the assets of Interhandel in the United States, and that for this reason the Third Objection applies equally to it. It maintains that the rule of the exhaustion of local remedies applies to each of the principal and alternative Submissions which seek 'a ruling by this Court to the effect that some other international tribunal now has jurisdiction to determine that very same issue, even though that issue is at the same time being actively litigated in the United States courts.'

The Court considers that one interest, and one alone, that of Interhandel, which has led the latter to institute and to resume proceedings before the United States courts, has induced the Swiss Government to institute international proceedings. This interest is the basis for the present claim and should determine the scope of the action brought before the Court by the Swiss Government in its alternative form as well as in its principal form. On the other hand, the grounds on which the rule of the exhaustion of local remedies is based are the same, whether in the case of an international court, arbitral tribunal, or conciliation commission. In these circumstances, the Court considers that any distinction so far as the rule of the exhaustion of local remedies is concerned between the various claims or between the various tribunals is unfounded.

It accordingly upholds the Third Preliminary Objection also as regards the alternative Submission of Switzerland.

Brownlie has commented on the case as follows:

> In the first place, particularly in respect of the alternative claim, it is very doubtful if the facts disclosed that the only interest of Switzerland was that of Interhandel and that no

direct injury to the applicant was involved. There was no remedy available to the latter in the United States courts for breach of treaty rights. Secondly, litigation lasting ten years and on which no term had been placed might not be regarded as "adequate" and "effective."[25]

B. Exhaustion of Local Remedies in Investment Treaty Arbitration

Whether exhaustion of local remedies is required in the context of an investment treaty dispute depends on the individual treaty text. Investment treaty tribunals rarely face the issue because most treaties expressly derogate from the exhaustion requirement under customary international law, by permitting the investor to resort to international arbitration for violation of an applicable treaty's substantive provisions without prior recourse to domestic courts or other remedies, as long as all other jurisdictional requirements are met.[26] Some bilateral investment treaties (BITs), such as the Czech Republic-Netherlands BIT, provide for waiting periods of six months or more before an investor can start arbitration.[27] Such waiting periods cannot be considered as an exhaustion requirement; they are merely "cooling off" periods.[28]

---

[25] Brownlie, *supra* note 2, at 480–81.

[26] *See, e.g*, Austria-United Arab Emirates BIT (2001), art. 10(5) ("If the investor chooses to file for arbitration, the host Contracting Party agrees not to request the exhaustion of local settlement procedures . . ."). "Most BITs do not even mention exhaustion of local remedies. A number of BITs concluded since 1995 explicitly include an obligation for the parties not to request the exhaustion of local remedies if the investor has opted to submit the dispute to international arbitration." United Nations Conference on Trade and Development (UNCTAD), *Bilateral Investment Treaties 1995–2006: Trends in Investment Rulemaking* 108 *et seq.* (2007). Schreuer notes that "the exhaustion of local remedies is generally not a requirement of modern investment arbitration." C. Schreuer, *The Co-Existence of Local and International Law Remedies*, British Institute of International and Comparative Law Third Investment Treaty Forum Conference Sept. 10, 2004, 2(4) TDM 1, 11 (2005).

[27] Article 8(2) of the Czech Republic-Netherlands BIT provides in relevant part that: "(2) Each Contracting Party hereby consents to submit a dispute referred to in paragraph (1) of this Article, to an arbitral tribunal, if the dispute has not been settled amicably within a period of six months from the date either party to the dispute requested amicable settlement."

[28] *See also* Chapter VII *supra*. Even longer periods, up to two years and beyond, may not be sufficient to exhaust all the domestic remedies in the modern legal systems of the world. The *Interhandel* case, discussed earlier, is a good example of possible delays in domestic litigation, ten years in that case, without reaching a final decision. Schreuer gives the example of Franco-Moroccan treaty of 1975, which provides for a two-year exhaustion period. He refers to it as "only remotely realistic time limit to achieve an exhaustion of local remedies. C. Schreuer, *The ICSID Convention: A Commentary* 393 (Cambridge University Press 2001). *Cf.* the discussion of the *Maffezini* case and its application of the most favored nation (MFN) clause of the Argentina-Spain BIT in Chapter XV *infra*.

It was noted earlier that sometimes it is not wholly clear whether a treaty waives the exhaustion requirement.[29] North American Free Trade Agreement (NAFTA) Chapter 11 is a good example of such a treaty, which may contain an implied waiver. In such situations one must interpret the relevant provisions of the treaty to ascertain whether the parties intended to waive the rule. The following excerpt by Andrea Bjorklund illustrates such an interpretation exercise:

> Andrea Bjorklund, *Waiver and the Exhaustion of the Local Remedies Rule in NAFTA Jurisprudence*, NAFTA Inves. L. & Arb. 260–62 (2004) (source notes omitted)
>
> C. NAFTA'S WAIVER (OR LACK THEREOF) OF THE LOCAL REMEDIES RULE
>
> The NAFTA, like other treaties, contains many interrelated provisions that cannot be understood in isolation. Examining the way in which the NAFTA appears to have waived the exhaustion of local remedies requires first an examination of some basic provisions outlining what classes of persons or entities may bring what kinds of claims, and the remedies to which claimants are entitled.
>
> Chapter 11 provides for two main types of claims. The first type comprises those claims brought under Article 1116 by an investor of one party, on its own behalf, for losses incurred because of a breach of a NAFTA obligation by another party. Such losses may include injury to its interest in an enterprise that is both a juridical person of that other party and controlled, directly or indirectly, by the investor. The second type of claim comprises those claims brought under Article 1117 by an investor of one party on behalf of an enterprise that is owned or controlled, directly or indirectly, by that investor and is also a juridical person of another party, when that other party has breached one of its NAFTA obligations. By allowing a claim (an "1117 claim") by an investor of one party on behalf of an enterprise of another party, Article 1117 circumvents the rule that an entity may not claim damages under international law against its own country. By specifying who may bring an international law claim on behalf of an enterprise—an investor who controls that enterprise, whether directly or indirectly—Article 1117 also avoids problems that might arise under the strict construction of corporate personality mandated by the International Court of Justice in Barcelona Traction.
>
> The primary difference between claims under Articles 1116 and 1117 is the award of damages; any damages or restitution payable under an 1117 claim go directly to the enterprise, rather than to the investor. In many cases a party's measure (NAFTA obligations extend to "measures"—laws, regulations, procedures, requirements, or practices—taken by the state parties) will have damaged both the investor's interest in the enterprise and the enterprise itself, giving rise to claims under both articles. The allocation of damages in such a case may be a challenge for the arbitrators, but does not implicate the exhaustion of local remedies rule. What is important with respect to exhaustion, however, is that in cases involving damage to an investor's interest in an enterprise, or in cases involving damage directly to an enterprise, that investor and that enterprise must also waive their rights to initiate or continue local remedies. Since the investor must control, directly or indirectly, the enterprise on whose behalf it is asserting a claim, it should be able to elicit such a waiver.
>
> The NAFTA countries did not explicitly waive exhaustion of local remedies in the text of the agreement. The operative provision, Article 1121, reads as follows:

---

[29] *See* p. 349 *supra*.

A disputing investor may submit a claim under Article 1116 to arbitration only if:

> (a) the investor consents to arbitration in accordance with the procedures set out in this Agreement; and
>
> (b) the investor and, where the claim is for loss or damage to an interest in an enterprise of another Party that is a juridical person that the investor owns or controls directly or indirectly, the enterprise, waive their right to initiate or continue before any administrative tribunal or court under the law of any Party, or other dispute settlement procedures, any proceedings with respect to the measure of the disputing Party that is alleged to be a breach referred to in Article 1116, except for proceedings for injunctive, declaratory or other extraordinary relief, not involving the payment of damages, before an administrative tribunal or court under the law of the disputing Party.

A similar provision exists for claims brought under Article 1117—in such cases both the investor and the enterprise must also "waive their right to initiate or continue before any administrative tribunal or court under the law of any Party, or any other dispute settlement procedures, any proceedings with respect to the measure of the disputing Party that is alleged to be a breach referred to in Article 1117," with the same exceptions for extraordinary relief noted above.

Though the language does not mention waiver of the local remedies rule, the requirement that the investor "waive its right to initiate or continue" actions in local tribunals can only with difficulty be interpreted as other than an implicit waiver. If an investor must not, after bringing a NAFTA claim initiate or continue to pursue its local remedy, it is likely that the state party is not requiring the investor to exhaust local remedies before bringing its NAFTA claim. The exceptions for injunctive, declaratory, and other extraordinary relief are also consistent with waiver of the exhaustion requirement; arbitral tribunals generally cannot order such relief, so permitting investors to preserve those rights complements, rather than replaces, arbitral proceedings. . . .

Exhaustion in cases brought under the International Centre for Settlement of Investment Disputes (ICSID) Convention is much more straightforward, because Article 26 of the ICSID Convention provides the following:

> Consent of the parties to arbitration under this Convention shall, unless otherwise stated, be deemed consent to such arbitration to the exclusion of any other remedy. A Contracting State may require the exhaustion of local administrative or judicial remedies as a condition of its consent to arbitration under this Convention.[30]

Schreuer comments that this provision "reverses the situation under traditional [i.e., customary,] international law in that the Contracting States waive the exhaustion of local remedies unless otherwise stated."[31] Pursuant to Article 26 of the ICSID Convention, if a state subjects its consent to exhaustion, then this requirement trumps the first sentence of Article 26.[32]

---

[30] Washington Convention, art. 26.
[31] Schreuer, *supra* note 28, at 388.
[32] *Id.* at 390–91.

C. Exhaustion of Local Remedies and the *Loewen* Case[33]

It was noted earlier that the local remedies rule may be required as a substantive element of an international wrong, rather than merely being a procedural prerequisite. In such situations, although the treaty may have waived the exhaustion requirement, as is the case with NAFTA,[34] the exhaustion may still be required to prove the international responsibility of the state. The NAFTA case of *Loewen v. United States*[35] is an example of the application of this requirement. In *Loewen*, the claimants were subject to arbitrary and discriminatory treatment during a lawsuit in the state courts of Mississippi. In their decision, the arbitrators reviewed an objection of the United States as both a matter of jurisdiction *and* liability, namely the extent to which claimants should have exhausted domestically available remedies before filing an international claim under NAFTA. In a previous jurisdictional decision, the tribunal had delayed resolution of the issue without clearly stating whether it would be treated as a matter of competence or substantive liability:

> [T]he rule of judicial finality is no different from the local remedies rule. Its purpose is to ensure that the State where the violation occurred should have an opportunity to redress it by its own means, within the framework of its own domestic legal system . . . Just as it was said that the function of the local remedies rule was to establish whether the point had been reached at which the home State may raise the issue on the international level . . . now it is the function of the rule to establish that State responsibility for a breach of an international obligation may be invoked.[36]

As addressed in the Final Award, the question of "finality" or "exhaustion of remedies" appeared to be primarily one of admissibility, that is, whether claimants had access to certain avenues of local relief that it "should have pursued before it could establish that the verdict and judgment at trial constituted a measure 'adopted or maintained' by [the United States] amounting to a violation of Art. 1105 [of NAFTA]."[37] The tribunal appears to have abandoned any question of

---

[33] *See also* the discussion of denial of justice in Chapter XVII.

[34] *See* p. 358 *supra*.

[35] *Loewen, supra* note 22. For the facts, see Chapters XII and XVII.

[36] *Id.*, Decision on Jurisdiction, ¶¶ 71–72. There was some confusion by the tribunal in its treatment of the relationship of exhaustion of local remedies and finality of judgments. *See* Wallace, *supra* note 23, at 691. The exhaustion rule in the context of judicial measures and international law standards of treatment is also based in part on the principle that states are free to organize their court systems and appeal mechanisms, as they see fit. Charles de Visscher, *Le déni de justice en droit international*, 52 R.C.A.D.I. 367, 397 (1935) ("L'organisation de ses tribunaux, la réglementation de sa procédure, sont en principe laissées à la discrétion de chaque État, le droit international restant indifférent au choix des moyens pour ne s'attacher qu'au résultat").

[37] *Loewen, supra* note 22, ¶ 207. For an explanation of the difference between substance, admissibility, and jurisdiction in the application of the local remedies rule under international law, *see* Christopher Greenwood, *State Responsibility for the Decisions of National Courts, Issues of State Responsibility before International Judicial Institutions* 55, 61–68 (2004); Brownlie, *supra* note 2, at 472–73.

exhaustion of remedies as an issue of jurisdiction, perhaps rightly deciding that NAFTA Article 1121 in any event amounted to a U.S. waiver of any jurisdictional objection on those grounds.[38]

The tribunal's basic premise, that the acts of a court of first instance do not normally rise to the level of an international wrong, is open to some debate[39] but solidly grounded in customary law. Normally, judicial systems in most countries are structured precisely to rectify court misconduct at the lower level; and therefore until available higher levels of domestic review have had the opportunity to correct a given miscarriage of justice, it cannot normally be said that there has been a state act capable of triggering international liability. As Rapporteur to the International Law Commission James Crawford explained, "an aberrant decision by an official lower in the hierarchy, which is capable of being reconsidered, does not of itself amount to an unlawful act."[40]

The United States suggested at least three such "domestic remedies":

> a. pursued an appeal in the Mississippi Supreme Court without posting a supersedeas bond. O'Keefe would have been free to execute on claimants' U.S. assets during the appeal, but the United States insisted that such a risk was acceptable, and any damage could have been reversed if claimants were successful in its court appeal.
>
> b. pursued protection under the bankruptcy laws of the United States (known as "Chapter 11," although the bankruptcy law has no connection whatever with NAFTA Chapter XI). Bankrupt status under U.S. federal law would have prevented O'Keefe from seizing claimants' assets pending court reorganization of the enterprise, freeing claimants to pursue an appeal in Mississippi Supreme Court without posting a bond.

---

[38] NAFTA, art. 1121 provides that a disputing investor may submit a NAFTA claim to arbitration only if "the investor ... waive[s its] right to initiate or continue before any administrative tribunal or court under the law of any Party, or other dispute settlement procedures, any proceedings with respect to the measure of the disputing Party that is alleged to be a breach ... before an administrative tribunal or court under the law of the disputing Party."

[39] See, e.g., A. O. Adede, *A Fresh Look at the Meaning of the Doctrine of Denial of Justice under International Law*, 14 Canadian Y.B. Int'l L. 72, 91 (1976) (contemplating possibility of denial of justice in case of an original judicial failure). Wallace believes that "the case where the original wrong is judicial is the very essence of the modern understanding of denial of justice—such is the *Loewen* case, a characterization that the *Loewen* Tribunal appears to have accepted." Wallace, *supra* note 23, at 679.

[40] James Crawford, Special Rapporteur, Second Report on State Responsibility, Int'l L. Commission, U.N. Doc. A/CN 4/498 (1999), ¶ 75. Or, as Alfred Rubin has noted, "Justice cannot be presumed to have been denied until it has been sought, and thus there must be an 'exhaustion of local remedies.'" Alfred Rubin, *Book Review—Application of the Rule of Exhaustion of Local Remedies in International Law*, 25 Harv. Int'l L. J. 517, 518 (1984).

c. sought discretionary review and stay of execution from the United States Supreme Court.[41]

The tribunal rejected the United States' contention that claimants should have pushed ahead with their appeal without posting the supersedeas bond. According to the arbitrators, such a route would have presented a real risk to claimants' economic survival. As a result, appeal to the Mississippi Supreme Court was not a "reasonably available remedy."[42] With regard to the other two possible *local remedies*, however, the tribunal was unconvinced that bankruptcy protection and appeal to the U.S. Supreme Court were not reasonably available alternatives to signing the settlement agreement with O'Keefe. "No doubt there are some situations," the arbitrators reasoned, "in which it would be reasonable to expect an impecunious claimant to file [for protection] under [U.S. bankruptcy law] in order to exercise an available right of appeal."[43]

Similarly, the tribunal claimed that it had insufficient information to decide whether appeal to the U.S. Supreme Court, and application for a stay of execution from that body, constituted a reasonably available remedy. This was despite the fact that the parties had submitted opinions from three of the most renowned constitutional law scholars in the United States: Lawrence Tribe, Charles Fried, and Drew Days. The arbitrators inexplicably considered themselves "not in a position to decide whether the opinion of Professor Days or that of Professor Tribe is to be preferred."[44] Holding that Loewen bore the burden of proving that it had exhausted available local remedies, the tribunal found its claim under Article 1105 inadmissible.

One troubling aspect of the tribunal's exhaustion decision is related to the nature of the determination whether local remedies were *reasonably available*. The term *reasonable* implies an objective, rather than subjective, standard of analysis, both under international law and domestic systems around the world.[45] In other words, the tribunal's task should have been to evaluate whether an average (or *reasonable*) person or company in claimants' position would have considered bankruptcy

---

[41] *Loewen*, supra note 22, ¶ 207. In fact, there was a fourth possible remedy, namely "collateral review" before a U.S. federal district court. Although this potential avenue of recourse was debated during the merits hearing, the tribunal did not appear concerned with claimants' failure to opt for it. This could be because of the U.S. Supreme Court's decision in *Pennzoil v. Texaco*, 481 U.S. 1 (1987), which would have made a collateral review petition potentially frivolous and sanctionable under U.S. civil procedure rules.

[42] *Loewen*, supra note 22, ¶ 208.

[43] *Id.* ¶ 209.

[44] *Id.* ¶ 211. The Tribunal evidently missed the opinion of Fried.

[45] *See generally* Mayo Moran, *Rethinking the Reasonable Person* (Oxford University Press 2003); *Military and Paramilitary Activities in and Against Nicaragua* (*Nicaragua v. U.S.*), 1986 I.C.J. 14, 141; Phanesh Koneru, *The International Interpretation of the U.N. Convention on the Sale of Goods: An Approach Based on General Principles*, 6 Minn. J. Global Trade 105, 151–52 (1997).

protection or U.S. Supreme Court appeal to be an available remedy under the circumstances, rather than speculating whether claimants in fact so believed.

Initially, the *Loewen* tribunal appeared to take an objective approach to the issue of available remedies. In response to the U.S. argument that Loewen's decision not to pursue local remedies was "voluntary" and the result of "business judgment," the arbitrators remarked, "The question is whether the remedies in question were reasonably available and adequate. If they were not, it is not to the point that Loewen entered into the settlement, even as a matter of business judgment."[46] In the very next paragraph, however, the tribunal appeared to reverse its position, finding that the availability of local remedies turned on claimants' *subjective* analysis at the time of the Mississippi court verdict regarding the various options available to the company.

> Here we encounter the central difficulty in Loewen's case. Loewen failed to present evidence disclosing its reasons for entering into the settlement agreement in preference to pursuing other options, in particular the Supreme Court option.[47] ... Although entry into the settlement agreement may well have been a reasonable course for Loewen to take, we are simply left to speculate on the reasons which led to the decision. ... Accordingly, our conclusion is that Loewen failed to pursue its domestic remedies, notably the Supreme Court option. ...[48]

Nothing in the Final Award indicates how the stated rule that availability of remedies is an objective inquiry can be reconciled with the tribunal's conclusion that Loewen should have submitted evidence on its subjective state of mind.

The tribunal's subjective approach merits particular attention. Assuming that the exhaustion or finality doctrine applies if local remedies are fully available and effective within the host state, the fact that a potential claimant in international proceedings erroneously believes that they are not should not make the claim admissible where otherwise it would not be. By the same token, if there are no reasonably available remedies within the host jurisdiction, it should make no difference to the admissibility of the international law complaint if the claimant in

---

[46] *Loewen, supra* note 22, ¶ 214. On Loewen's settlement of the dispute *see* Chapter XVII *infra* at p. 530.

[47] In fact: "The Tribunal was simply wrong. Claimants had submitted clear, uncontradicted, uncontested, comprehensive, and corroborated evidence why The Loewen Group, Inc. (TLGI) had settled the case. The Tribunal missed all of this evidence, a deeply embarrassing omission for so distinguished a panel. TLGI's reasons for settling were addressed in two declarations filed with the Tribunal in 2000, long before the 2003 Award. The first was the declaration of Wynne S. Carvill, the American attorney in charge of all post-verdict proceedings. It was supported by the equally clear declaration of a director of TLGI, John Napier Turner, the former Prime Minister of Canada. See Declaration of Wynne S. Carvill (May 24, 2000) (Exhibit C) and Declaration of Rt. Hon. John N. Turner, P.C., C.C., Q.C. (May 25, 2000) (Exhibit D). The United States never questioned, challenged, or cross-examined either of these declarations, nor did it put in counter-declarations rebutting this evidence." Petition to Vacate Arbitration Award, D.C. 13, 2004, U.S. District for the District of Columbia, Case No 1:04CV02151, at 15–16, *available at* http://ita.law.uvic.ca/documents/loewen-petitiontovacate.pdf.

[48] *Loewen, supra* note 22, ¶¶ 215–17.

fact believes that there are effective remedies but chooses not to take them for purely economic reasons. To create a different rule of law would subject international jurisprudence to the internal meditations of individual claimants—at best difficult to identify, and at worst simple to falsify.[49]

Naturally, there remains the question as to whether or not under an objective examination Loewen exhausted all reasonably available local remedies. As noted earlier, claimants and the United States each submitted opinions by eminent American jurists.[50] Tribe insisted that a writ of *certiorari*[51] from the U.S. Supreme Court was practically inconceivable in the *Loewen* case, to say nothing of a stay of enforcement pending resolution.[52] Days, meanwhile, opined that Loewen "could have sought and had a reasonable opportunity to obtain" U.S. Supreme Court review and a stay of execution.[53] The United States admitted that U.S. Supreme Court review is highly discretionary[54] and could not deny that statistically only a small number of cases each year are approved for appeal to the Court—less than two percent, in fact.[55] One wonders whether such a rare remedy could ever be deemed *reasonably available*, particularly under an objective standard. Indeed, international law authorities appear to agree that "[t]he remedies to be exhausted comprise all forms of recourse as of right . . . 'but not extra-legal remedies or remedies as of grace.' "[56] It is clear that a remedy available at the complete discretion of the court in question, and granted in only a small fraction of instances, cannot be considered recourse *as of right*. In specific instances international tribunals have readily made the distinction between remedies that must be exhausted and those that need not be. In the 1931 *George*

---

[49] On the foundations of the *reasonable man* standard and its policy underpinning in domestic jurisprudence, *see* Oliver Wendell Holmes, *The Common Law* 108 (1881); *Blyth v. Birmingham Waterworks Co.*, 156 Eng. Rep. 1047 (1856); *Vaughan v. Menlove*, 132 Eng. Rep. 490 (1837).

[50] In fact, as noted above, although the tribunal only mentioned one opinion on U.S. constitutional law from each side, it evidently misunderstood that claimants had submitted *two* opinions from leading Harvard Law School professors, Lawrence Tribe and Charles Fried.

[51] A "writ of *certiorari*" is a common law device whereby a superior court demands documents related to a particular case from the inferior court. *Black's Law Dictionary* 228 (6th ed. 1990). The U.S. Supreme Court, which under the Constitution is only required to accept jurisdiction over a very narrow category of disputes, uses a writ of *certiorari* to decide which cases it will review and which it will not. 28 U.S.C. § 1254.

[52] *Loewen*, *supra* note 22, Memorial of the Loewen Group, Inc. Concerning the Jurisdictional Objections of the United States of May 26, 2000 (*Jurisdictional Memorial*), ¶ 60 *et seq.*

[53] *Loewen*, *supra* note 22, Memorial of the United States of America on Matters of Competence and Jurisdiction of Feb. 18, 2000 at 59 *et seq.*

[54] *Id.*

[55] *Loewen*, *supra* note 22, Final Submission of the Loewen Group, Inc. Concerning the Jurisdictional Objections of the United States of July 27, 2000 at ¶ 71. Furthermore, the kinds of cases approved involve issues that are vastly different from the issue involved in the *Loewen* case.

[56] Brownlie, *supra* note 2, at 475; J. L. Brierly, *The Law of Nations* 281 (1963); *Finnish Ships Arbitration*, *supra* note 13.

Salem arbitration,⁵⁷ for example, an American sued the Egyptian government in a Cairo court for wrongful prosecution he had suffered in Egypt. The Cairo court dismissed his action, a decision affirmed by the court of appeals. The United States espoused Salem's claim, and the resulting arbitral tribunal examined Egypt's defense that Salem had not exhausted the remedy of *recours en requête civile*. The tribunal permitted the case to proceed, ruling that the local remedies rule is not absolute and—just as importantly—the *requête civile* was not a regular legal remedy such as an appeal as of right; it is only meant to re-open an already closed process.⁵⁸ For the local remedies rule to have practical application, tribunals should take a realistic view of domestic judicial systems, following the estimation of the ICJ that the foreign claimant's duty is not to exhaust every theoretical possibility of remedy.⁵⁹

Although obviously inspired by a treaty very different in purpose and wording from NAFTA, the approach of the European Court of Human Rights is illuminating. In applying the European Convention on Human Rights (ECHR), the Court has refused to allow the local remedies rule to become a formalistic or technical bar to relief for claimants otherwise harmed by treaty violations. In *Sovtransavto Holding v. Ukraine*,⁶⁰ a Russian company sought judicial redress in Ukraine against local minority shareholders in a joint venture, who had diluted the Russian shareholding to gain control of the enterprise. After losing in the court of first instance, Sovtransavto appealed to the Ukrainian Supreme Arbitrazh Tribunal. The appeal was dismissed without prejudice for late payment of court fees, but was time-barred by the time Sovtransavto redeposited the necessary amount and resubmitted its case. Although recognizing that the claimant had not necessarily exhausted all available local remedies, the ECHR found Ukraine had violated the Convention: "[T]he rule on the exhaustion of domestic remedies must be applied with some degree of flexibility and without excessive formalism and is neither absolute nor capable of being applied automatically."⁶¹ This flexible view of local remedies draws support from the fact that, unlike cases of diplomatic espousal, complaints before the ECHR (and NAFTA tribunals) are decided "in the context of machinery for the protection of . . . rights that the Contracting States have agreed to set up."⁶² Such a flexible, less formalistic approach is entirely consistent with the central purpose of investment treaties—protection of investor rights.

---

⁵⁷ *Salem Case*, 2 U.N.R.I.A.A. 1165 (1932).

⁵⁸ *Id.* at 1189.

⁵⁹ *ELSI, supra* note 8, at 42–48, 84 ILR 311, 348–54.

⁶⁰ *Sovtransavto Holding v. Ukraine*, 38 E.H.R.R. 44 (2004).

⁶¹ *Id.* ¶ 81.

⁶² *See Ilhan v. Turkey*, (2000) 34 ECHR 353, ¶ 59, where the Court's refusal to require exhaustion occurred despite an *express* provision in the Convention preserving the local remedies rule; European Convention on Human Rights, art. 26 ("The Commission may only deal with the matter after all domestic remedies have been exhausted, according to the generally recognized rules of international law"). By contrast, NAFTA makes no direct mention of local remedies, other than to say they must be *abandoned*. NAFTA, art. 1121. *See* p. 358 *supra*.

XIV. Election of Forum: National Courts and Contract Arbitrations

One of the most persistent problems in investor-state disputes is which forum will adjudicate the dispute. Although there are in theory many potential fora, three predominate: the national courts where the investment is made, an arbitral forum that the parties may have selected by contract, and an investment treaty tribunal. Chapter VI covered those situations where national courts may interfere with arbitrations by their insisting, through the use of antiarbitration injunctions, that only the national courts can resolve a particular dispute. But independent of a national court's position, the investor often has its own choice to make, because it may have the option—or the obligation—to choose one of the three predominant fora. The investor's exercise of its choice has resulted in numerous problems.

A. National Courts and Treaty Arbitration

Before the advent of modern investor-state arbitration, national courts and administrative tribunals in the host state played a central role in the resolution of disputes arising out of foreign investment. As explained elsewhere in this book, diplomatic espousal of claims is normally impermissible at customary international law unless the foreign investor has exhausted all effective local remedies within the host state's adjudicatory system.[1] For the most part, investment treaties have effectively done away with this "local remedies"

---

[1] *Finnish Shipowners Arbitration (Finland v. U.K.)* (Award of May 9, 1934), 3 R.I.A.A. 1479; *Panavesyz-Saldaiskis Railway Case (Estonia v. Lithuania)*, P.C.I.J. Rep. Ser. A/B, No. 76, at 18 (1939).

rule.[2] At the same time, however, many investment protection treaties include a clause requiring that the claimant elect once and for all which remedy it will pursue: national court adjudication or international arbitration. This kind of mandatory choice provision has become known as a "fork in the road" or waiver clause.[3]

1. *Fork in the Road* and Waiver: Treaty Texts

a. True *Fork in the Road* Provisions

The more common type of *fork in the road* provision, included in the bilateral investment protection treaties signed by many western European governments, requires that the investor-claimant choose a forum at the outset of the dispute resolution process. According to the terms of such a *true* fork in the road clause, a claimant irrevocably elects a remedy when it commences legal proceedings in either forum. Thus, a claimant's commencement of national court litigation precludes recourse to investment treaty arbitration at some later time (and, in theory, vice versa). Article 8(2) of the France-Argentina bilateral investment treaty (BIT), which requires an *irrevocable* election by the investor, provides an often-cited

---

[2] However, where the investor complains of measures in a host state's *judicial system*, remnants of the exhaustion of remedies rule appear to remain. In such cases the issue of local remedies may cease to be one of *jurisdiction*, and instead become one of *admissibility*. Loewen Group, Inc. & Loewen v. U.S., ICSID Case No. ARB(AF)/98/3 (Award of June 26, 2003), 42 I.L.M. 811 (2003), ¶ 207. For an explanation of the difference between substance, admissibility, and jurisdiction in the application of the local remedies rule under international law, see Christopher Greenwood, *State Responsibility for the Decisions of National Courts*, in *Issues of State Responsibility before International Judicial Institutions* 55, 61–68 (Malgosia Fitzmaurice & Dan Sarooshi eds., Oxford 2004); Ian Brownlie, *Principles of Public International Law* 472–73 (6th ed. Oxford 2003). Furthermore, a minority of investment treaties and national investment laws expressly maintain the requirement of exhaustion of local remedies. See, e.g., Netherlands-Malaysia BIT (1971), art. 12; Ghana-Romania BIT (1989), art. 4(3). Other investment treaties create an "exhaustion period" of litigation in local courts, during which the investor is required to pursue its claims in the domestic courts of the host state for a specified period. Thereafter it may commence international arbitration. See, e.g., Germany-Argentina BIT (1991), arts. 10(2), 10(3)(a); Netherlands-Jamaica BIT (1991), art. 9.

[3] On *fork in the road* clauses generally, see Michael Polkinghorne, *Investor-State Dispute Resolution under the Energy Charter Treaty: Which Fork? Which Road?*, Mealey's Int'l Arb. Rep., April 2004, at 13; Christoph Schreuer, *Travelling the BIT Route: Of Waiting Periods, Umbrella Clauses and Forks in the Road*, 5 J. World Inv. & Trade 231, 239–49 (2004); Lucy Reed, Jan Paulsson, & Nigel Blackaby, *Guide to ICSID Arbitration* 58–59 (Kluwer 2003); Noah Rubins & Stephan Kinsella, *International Investment, Political Risk and Dispute Resolution* 275 (Oceana 2005); *The Relationship between Local Courts and Investment Treaty Arbitration*, British Institute of International and Comparative Law Third Investment Treaty Forum Conference, Sept. 10, 2004, 2(4) Transnat'l Disp. Mgmt., 17–26 (A. Sheppard, J. Warner, & F. Ortino eds., Aug. 2005).

example of this type of fork in the road clause; it establishes that an investor's claim

> shall be submitted, at the request of the investor, either to the national courts of the contracting Party involved in the dispute, or to international arbitration. ... Once an investor has submitted the dispute either to the jurisdictions of the Contracting Party involved or to international arbitration, the choice of one or the other of these procedures shall be final.[4]

Most United States BITs concluded in the early 1990s incorporate a more complex formulation of the mandatory choice of dispute resolution method:

> 2. If [an investment] dispute cannot be settled amicably, the national or company concerned may choose to submit the dispute for resolution:
>
> (a) to the courts or administrative tribunals of the Party that is a party to the dispute; or
>
> (b) in accordance with any applicable, previously agreed dispute-settlement procedures; or
>
> (c) in accordance with the terms of paragraph 3(a).
>
> 3 (a). Provided that the national or company concerned has not submitted the dispute for resolution under paragraph 2 (a) or (b) and that six months have elapsed from the date on which the dispute arose, the national or company concerned may choose to consent in writing to the submission of the dispute for settlement by binding arbitration.[5]

The effect of both texts, however, is similar: An investor's treaty claims may be subject to the host state's jurisdictional objection that if the investor has already opted for national court adjudication of a dispute it has opted out of the arbitration procedure available pursuant to the treaty.[6]

b. Waiver Provisions

A growing number of investment protection treaties establish a different rule with respect to the choice of remedies, which has become known as the *waiver* approach: An investor must waive its rights to initiate or continue local litigation before it can file for treaty arbitration. Rather than establishing a true *fork in the road*, such waiver clauses prevent only a return to local courts once international arbitration has been selected. Thus, litigation within the host state's judicial or administrative law system prior to arbitration does not extinguish the investor's right to subsequently arbitrate the same dispute pursuant to the treaty.

---

[4] France-Argentina BIT (1991), art. 8(2).

[5] U.S.-Romania BIT (1992), art. VI(2)-(3). *See also* U.S.-Ecuador BIT (1993), art. VI.

[6] Reed et al., *supra* note 3, at 59. Such was the objection raised by Estonia and rejected by the tribunal in *Genin v. Republic of Estonia*, ICSID Case No. ARB/99/2 (Award of June 25, 2001), 17 ICSID Rev.-F.I.L.J. 395 (2002), ¶ 333.

At the same time, an investor that violates a definitive waiver requirement by continuing to pursue claims in litigation parallel to the arbitral procedure, or by reserving the right to do so, can fatally undermine its jurisdictional position in a treaty arbitration.[7]

One of the most important waiver clauses in investment treaties is the North American Treaty (NAFTA) Article 1121. This clause provides that a qualifying investor may submit a claim to NAFTA arbitration only if:

> the investor ... waive[s its] right to initiate or continue before any administrative tribunal or court under the law of any Party, or other dispute settlement procedures, any proceedings with respect to the measure of the disputing Party that is alleged to be a breach ... before an administrative tribunal or court under the law of the disputing Party.[8]

This waiver approach to forum selection has recently received broader application, because the United States has incorporated waiver provisions similar to NAFTA Article 1121 in its 2004 Model BIT as well as in the investment protection agreements recently concluded with Chile, Singapore, and Uruguay. Canada has also chosen the "waiver" approach over the "fork in the road" in its new model investment treaty.[9] Like NAFTA, these treaties allow investors to commence suit in a domestic court or administrative tribunal and then discontinue such proceedings in favor of international arbitration.[10]

2. The Policy Behind *Fork in the Road* and Waiver Provisions

Both waiver provisions and true *fork in the road* clauses are primarily designed to prevent duplicative dispute resolution activity, which is viewed as potentially abusive and unfair to the host state.[11] At the same time, an important difference in policy lies behind these two types of treaty text. The waiver approach encourages investors to investigate possible remedies within the host state's municipal law

---

[7] *Waste Mgmt., Inc. v. United Mexican States*, ICSID Case No. ARB(AF)/98/2 (Award of June 2, 2000), 40 I.L.M. 56 (2001) [hereinafter *Waste Mgmt. I*], ¶¶ 26–28 (dismissing claim on jurisdictional grounds where claimant had not effectively waived and ceased all local court proceedings prior to initiating claim). *See also* William S. Dodge, *Waste Mgmt., Inc. v. Mexico: Arbitral Award on Jurisdiction under NAFTA Where Requisite Waiver of Other Remedies Reserves, and Applicant Pursues, Municipal Law Claims in Other Fora*, 95 Am. J. Int'l L. 186 (2001).

[8] NAFTA, art. 1121.

[9] Canada Model Investment Promotion and Protection Agreement (2003), § C.

[10] *See* U.S. Model Bilateral Investment Treaty (2004); U.S.-Chile Free Trade Agreement (2003), art. 10.17; U.S.-Singapore Free Trade Agreement (2003), art. 15.17; U.S.-Uruguay BIT (2004), art. 26.

[11] *See, e.g., Waste Mgmt. I, supra* note 7, ¶ 27: "[I]t is possible to consider that proceedings instituted in a national forum may exist which do not relate to those measures alleged to be in violation of the NAFTA by a member state of the NAFTA, in which case it would be feasible that such proceedings could coexist simultaneously with an arbitration proceeding under the NAFTA. However, when both legal actions have a legal basis derived from the same measures, they can no longer continue simultaneously in light of the imminent risk that the Claimant may obtain the double benefit in its claim for damages."

system before turning to international arbitration. By contrast, a *fork in the road* provision discourages recourse to local courts and administrative tribunals whenever the investor is aware of and interested in preserving its rights to international arbitration under the investment protection treaty. Kantor explained an important advantage of the waiver approach in the context of local laws requiring that claims be asserted within twenty days after a dispute arises:

> Very few investors would like to make an irrevocable choice regarding what approach to take, what forum to follow, what litigation strategy to follow, indeed whether to litigate or not against a sovereign, in 20 days. Utilizing the waiver approach of course defers that decision to the time the investment arbitration claim is brought under [the applicable investment treaty]. At that time, the foreign investor must determine whether or not to waive the right to maintain or continue any pre-existing claim in an administrative tribunal or court with respect to the same measures, so the timing of when the decision has to be made is deferred under the waiver approach. That is very crucial if you are a foreign investor in deciding whether to pick a fight with the sovereign, and if so what approach to follow in that fight.[12]

In interpreting both types of forum choice provisions, the central question for international arbitration tribunals has been the extent to which a dispute being litigated in host state courts is so similar to that before the tribunal that it falls within the scope of an applicable forum election provision. In practice, it can be surprisingly complex to determine whether a particular court action related to an investment constitutes the investor's irrevocable *choice* of forum. In particular, arbitration tribunals have recognized that under local law investors may be required to defensively invoke local remedies of various kinds to avoid waiver or to otherwise comply with domestic legislation.[13]

3. Choice of Forum with Respect to *Disputes*

The determination of whether an investor must make (or be deemed to have made) a choice of forum depends in part on the wording of the applicable investment protection treaty. Most investment arbitration jurisprudence has dealt with *fork in the road* clauses rather than waiver provisions. Because most clauses refer to a choice of forum with respect to *disputes* rather than government *measures*, numerous tribunals have sought to determine whether domestic and international law disputes are sufficiently similar to trigger an applicable treaty's *fork in the road* provision. Schreuer explains, "The fork in the road provision and the consequent loss of access to international arbitration applies only if the same dispute between the same parties has been submitted to domestic courts or administrative tribunals of the host state before the resort to international arbitration."[14] As a result, many decisions have narrowed the preclusive effect of a *fork in the road*

---

[12] Mark Kantor, contribution to *The Relationship between Local Courts and Investment Treaty Arbitration*, 2(4) Transnat'l Dis. Mgmt. 23–24 (Aug. 2005).

[13] *CMS Gas Transmission Co. v. Republic of Argentina*, ICSID Case No. ARB/01/8 (Decision on Jurisdiction of July 17, 2003), 42 I.L.M. 788 (2003), ¶ 78; *Genin, supra* note 6, ¶ 333.

[14] Christoph Schreuer, *The ICSID Convention: A Commentary* 247–48 (2001).

clause to cases where the subject matter of the dispute in the local forum is the same as that submitted to arbitration,[15] and the parties in both domestic and international proceedings are identical.[16] In a similar formulation, drawn from both civil and common law precedent in the area of res judicata, investors may be barred from international treaty arbitration by a *fork in the road* clause where there is an identity of "parties, object, and cause of action" between domestic and international claims: the so-called triple-identity test.[17]

In *Alex Genin, Eastern Credit Limited, Inc. (ECL) and A.S. Baltoil v. Estonia*,[18] ECL, a U.S. corporation owned by Genin (also a U.S. citizen) acquired a controlling stake in the Estonian Innovation Bank (EIB). EIB then purchased from the Bank of Estonia a branch of the Estonian Social Bank, which was insolvent at the time. Shortly thereafter, EIB became aware of discrepancies in the branch's balance sheet. EIB sued the Estonian Social Bank in the local courts to recover its losses and won a substantial court judgment. However, because the Estonian Social Bank was unable to pay the full amount of the judgment, EIB was left with significant uncompensated losses. EIB then transferred its right to recover losses to ECL (the U.S. corporation), which initiated a lawsuit in a Texas court, seeking redress from the Bank of Estonia.[19] Thereafter, the Bank of Estonia adopted a regulation requiring that EIB's shareholders apply for permits to maintain their stake in EIB. EIB filed suit in Estonian court to challenge this requirement, and the Bank of Estonia then revoked EIB's banking license. EIB filed a second lawsuit in Estonia challenging the revocation. While these proceedings were pending, an Estonian court ordered the liquidation of EIB. EIB sought to stay the liquidation pending the outcome of the license revocation dispute, but this effort also failed. After EIB was liquidated, its second Estonian lawsuit challenging the revocation of its banking license was dismissed as moot.[20]

---

[15] *Lauder v. Czech Republic* (UNCITRAL arbitration, Award of Sept. 3, 2001), ¶ 162; *Middle East Cement Shipping & Handling Co. S.A. v. Arab Republic of Egypt*, ICSID Case No. ARB/99/6 (Award of Apr. 12, 2002), 18 ICSID Rev.-F.I.L.J. 602 (2003), ¶ 71; *Olguin v. Republic of Paraguay*, ICSID Case No. ARB/98/5 (Decision on Jurisdiction of Aug. 8, 2000), 6 ICSID Rep. 156 (2004), ¶ 30.

[16] *CMS, supra* note 13, ¶ 80; *Azurix Corp. v. Argentine Republic*, ICSID Case No. ARB/01/12 (Decision on Jurisdiction of Dec. 8, 2003), 43 I.L.M. 262 (2004), ¶ 88; *Genin, supra* note 6, ¶ 333.

[17] *Joy Mining Machinery Ltd. v. Egypt*, ICSID Case No. ARB/03/11 (Award on Jurisdiction of Aug. 6, 2004), ¶ 75; Mark W. Friedman, Jack J. Coe, William J. Park, Dietmar W. Prager, & Steven Smith, *Developments in International Commercial Dispute Resolution in 2003*, Int'l L. 265, 281 (2004) ("the ["fork in the road"] clause is triggered only where the parties and cause of action are identical"). In the absence of a BIT and in the more traditional contractual context, see *Benvenuti & Bonfant SRL v. People's Republic of the Congo*, 1 ICSID Rep. 340, ¶ 1.14 ("there could only be a case of *lis pendens* where there was identity of the parties, object and cause of action in the proceedings pending before both tribunals").

[18] *Genin, supra* note 6.

[19] *See id.* ¶¶ 43–51.

[20] *See id.* ¶¶ 53–61.

In 1999, Genin, ECL, and Baltoil, an Estonian subsidiary of ECL, initiated at the International Centre for Settlement of Investment Disputes (ICSID) an arbitration against Estonia under the United States-Estonia BIT.[21] One of Estonia's primary defenses was that the foreign investors' claims had been "previously litigated in Estonia and the U.S.," thus triggering the BIT's *fork in the road* provision and precluding recourse to international arbitration.[22] The *Genin* ICSID tribunal was thus faced with two questions: first, "to what extent were the issues litigated in Estonia and the United States identical to those raised by Claimants in this arbitration"; and second, "is it proper to consider EIB and Claimants as a 'group' and to view EIB's legal acts in Estonia as an 'election of remedy' for the group as a whole."[23]

The *Genin* tribunal concluded that the issues in the litigation and the international arbitration were distinct. It found that the object of EIB's second litigation in Estonia was "to contest the revocation of its license in Estonia," whereas the ICSID claimants sought compensation for the losses they suffered as a result of violations of the BIT and international law.[24] The *Genin* tribunal similarly distinguished the issues at stake in the U.S. litigation from the issues before the tribunal.[25] Furthermore, the *Genin* tribunal differentiated the parties in interest in the domestic and international dispute resolution processes. The tribunal held that EIB had engaged in litigation "on behalf of all the Bank's shareholders (including minority shareholders), as well as on behalf of its depositors, borrowers, and employees, all of whom were damaged by the cessation of EIB's activities."[26] By contrast, the ICSID claims were filed only for the benefit of the named claimants, not EIB.[27] More fundamentally, none of the parties to the ICSID dispute had ever been a party to the court litigation.[28] The *Genin* tribunal thus concluded that neither the parties nor the claims in the litigation and international arbitration were identical, and thus that the *fork in the road* provision of the United States-Estonia BIT did not prevent the claimants from pursuing arbitration under the treaty.

Like the *Genin* tribunal, two arbitral tribunals adjudicating claims arising out of the 2001 Argentine financial crisis applied a relatively strict test based on the *identity* of the parties, allowing claims based on the same governmental measure to be brought in both domestic litigation and international arbitration. In *CMS*

---

[21] See id. ¶ 1.
[22] Id. ¶ 321.
[23] Id. ¶ 330.
[24] Id. ¶¶ 332–33.
[25] See id. ¶ 334.
[26] Id. ¶¶ 333.
[27] See id. ¶¶ 332–33.
[28] In the second court litigation the parties were EIB and the Estonian Bank, whereas in the ICSID arbitration the parties were Genin, ECL, and Baltoil.

Gas Transmission v. Argentina,[29] CMS, a U.S. company, purchased a 29 percent equity stake in TGN, an Argentine gas company that held a license for the transportation of gas. Following the 2001 financial crisis, Argentina took several measures that had a serious negative effect on this investment. As a result, CMS filed a claim under the United States-Argentina BIT with ICSID.[30] Argentina argued that because TGN had previously challenged the disputed governmental measures in local courts, the *fork in the road* provision of the BIT precluded CMS from arbitrating claims related to the same measures.[31] CMS responded that TGN was a separate legal entity, and that TGN by its actions could not choose a forum for CMS.[32]

CMS Gas Transmission Co. v. Republic of Argentina

ICSID Case No. ARB/01/8 (Decision on Jurisdiction of July 17, 2003), *reprinted in* 30 I.L.M. 788, 800 (2003)

77. ....The Republic of Argentina argues that because TGN appealed a judicial decision to the Federal Supreme Court and other administrative remedies were sought, CMS cannot now submit the same dispute to arbitration under the Treaty.

78. The Claimant's view is different. First, there is no triggering of the "fork in the road" provision because TGN is a separate legal entity and is not the investor; only the investor can make the choice of taking a claim to the local courts or to arbitration, and CMS chose the ICSID arbitration option. Second, the court's decision appealed by TGN related to judicial proceedings initiated by the Argentine Ombudsman and in which TGN only intervened as a third party; moreover, both the Argentine Government and ENARGAS—the regulatory agency of the gas industry—also appealed that particular decision. It follows, the argument further elaborates, that the Licensee was only undertaking defensive and reactive actions in those proceedings. And third, CMS argues, not only are the parties to those proceedings and to the arbitration different but also the subject-matter of the dispute is not the same; TGN's claim concerns the contractual arrangements under the License while those of CMS concern the affected treaty rights.

79. The Claimant has also explained that TGN has been prevented from making a claim before the courts or through arbitration because of the provisions of Decree 1090/02 of June 26, 2002, and the Ministry of Economy Resolution 308/02 of August 20, 2002. These provisions direct the licensee to make its claims for breach of contract only in the context of the [license] renegotiation process under way and not before the court; if the latter action is followed, the licensee will be excluded from such renegotiation. This situation, it is further explained, evidences again that TGN could not bring a claim before the Argentine courts and has not done so. In any event, as mentioned above, such a claim would be entirely separate from that of CMS under the Treaty.

---

[29] *CMS, supra* note 13.
[30] *See id.* ¶¶ 1, 19–20.
[31] *See id.* ¶ 77.
[32] *See id.* ¶ 78.

80. Decisions of several ICSID tribunals have held that as contractual claims are different from treaty claims even if there had been or there currently was a recourse to the local courts for breach of contract, this would not have prevented submission of the treaty claims to arbitration. This Tribunal is persuaded that with even more reason this view applies to the instant dispute, since no submission has been made by CMS to local courts and since, even if TGN had done so—which is not the case—this would not result in triggering the "fork in the road" provision against CMS. Both the parties and the causes of action under separate instruments are different.

81. Had the Claimant renounced recourse to arbitration, for example by resorting to the courts of Argentina, this would have been a binding selection under the BIT. In that case, the Tribunal would agree with Counsel for the Republic of Argentina that although Carlos Calvo, a distinguished Argentine international jurist who fathered the Calvo Doctrine and Clause, will not become an honorary citizen of countries having entered into bilateral investment treaties, this would still be a binding decision. However, as no such renunciation took place, the Calvo Clause will not resuscitate in this context.

In *Azurix Corp. v. Argentina*,[33] the U.S. claimant established an Argentine subsidiary, ABA, to operate a privatized water and sewage utility under a concession contract with the Province of Buenos Aires.[34] During the 2001 Argentine financial crisis, the provincial authorities terminated the concession contract. Azurix later initiated ICSID arbitration against Argentina under the applicable United States-Argentina BIT. Argentina again argued that the *fork in the road* provision precluded Azurix from seeking arbitration under the BIT, because ABA had engaged in proceedings before administrative bodies and domestic courts in Argentina to contest the termination of the concession contract.[35] Azurix countered that "the parties and subject matter of the proceedings before the Argentine courts and the Tribunal are not the same," and in particular argued that the "causes of action before the Tribunal are independent of the Concession Agreement."[36]

The *Azurix* tribunal began by specifying that the triple identity test requires that both the plaintiffs *and* the defendants in domestic and international proceedings be the same before a *fork in the road* clause will be triggered. The tribunal emphasized that "[n]either of the parties [(i.e., Azurix and Argentina)] [was] a party to the proceedings before the local courts[, and e]ven if Azurix had joined ABA as a plaintiff in those courts, there [still] would not [have been] party identity since Argentina [was] not party to any of those proceedings."[37] The *Azurix* tribunal also found a lack of identity between the causes of action, based on the *CMS* tribunal's differentiation between contract and treaty claims. Because there was a lack of

---

[33] *Azurix, supra* note 16.
[34] *See id.* ¶¶ 19–22.
[35] *See id.* ¶ 37.
[36] *Id.* ¶ 38.
[37] *Id.* ¶ 90.

identity between parties and causes of action, the *Azurix* tribunal determined that the requirements of the triple identity test were not met.

Like the *CMS* and *Azurix* tribunals, the tribunal in *Occidental v. Ecuador* applied the *triple identity* test, holding that claims presented to the domestic courts did not preclude the investor from presenting international claims to the tribunal.[38] Occidental entered into a participation contract with an Ecuadorian state-owned entity, under which the companies agreed to jointly explore for and produce oil.[39] Until 2001 Ecuador reimbursed Occidental for the value-added tax (VAT) it paid on purchases required for its exploration and exploitation activities. Beginning in 2001 Ecuador refused to do so, arguing that the reimbursement was accounted for in the contractual participation formula. Ecuador issued a series of resolutions denying further VAT reimbursements to Occidental and other companies in the oil sector. These resolutions also required the return of previous VAT reimbursements.[40] Occidental filed four lawsuits in Ecuador to halt the enforcement of these measures. In addition, the company filed a claim under the United States-Ecuador BIT.[41]

Ecuador argued that Occidental was precluded by the BIT's *fork in the road* provision from resorting to international arbitration: "[T]he fact that [Occidental] has submitted four separate lawsuits to Ecuadorian courts constitutes an irrevocable choice to [resolve] . . . the present dispute [through] . . . the courts or administrative tribunals of [Ecuador]."[42] Ecuador emphasized that the domestic litigation involved the same governmental measures and denial of refunds. Because the dispute was the same, the *fork in the road* provision was triggered and should preclude Occidental from seeking duplicative relief at the international level.[43] Occidental responded that it had "not submitted an investment dispute to the courts of Ecuador and that it [had] not made any assertion or claim in such courts concerning its rights under the [BIT]."[44] Occidental argued that the causes of action were different because one arose under the BIT and the other under domestic law.[45]

The *Occidental* tribunal noted that the dispute "touch[ed] in part upon the Contract . . . as the [government measures] were based on the view that the VAT

---

[38] *Occidental v. Ecuador*, London Court of International Arbitration Administered Case No. U.N. 3467 (Final Award of July 1, 2004).
[39] *See id.* ¶ 1.
[40] *See id.* ¶¶ 2–3.
[41] *See id.* ¶¶ 4, 6.
[42] *Id.* ¶ 38.
[43] *See id.* ¶ 39.
[44] *Id.* ¶ 40.
[45] *See id.* ¶ 41.

was already reimbursed under the provisions of the Contract."[46] However, the tribunal emphasized that Occidental had "not submitted any Contract claims to the courts of Ecuador or for that matter to this Tribunal."[47] Because the claims were based on violations of the BIT (and not breaches of the contract), the *Occidental* tribunal refused to apply the forum selection clause: "To the extent that the nature of the dispute submitted to arbitration is principally, albeit not exclusively, treaty-based, the jurisdiction of the arbitral tribunal is correctly invoked."[48]

Unlike the panels that preceded it, however, the *Occidental* tribunal paid particular attention to the danger of a rigid approach to the *fork in the road* issue where local law establishes short deadlines for the exercise of rights and remedies:

> The "fork in the road" mechanism by its very definition assumes that the investor has made a choice between alternative avenues. This [in] turn requires that the choice be made entirely free and not under any form of duress .... [I]n the instant case the Ecuadorian Tax Law requires the taxpayer to apply to the courts within the brief period of twenty days following the issuance of any resolution that might affect it. If this is not done, ... the resolution becomes final and binding.
>
> The Tribunal is of the view that in this case the investor did not have a real choice. Even if it took the matter instantly to arbitration, which is not that easy to do, the protection of its right to object to the adverse decision of the [tax authority] would have been considered forfeited if the application to the local courts were not made within the period mandated by the Tax Code.[49]

4. Choice of Forum with Respect to *Measures*

As explained earlier, most *fork in the road* provisions apply to a given *dispute*, raising a range of questions about whether related claims are the same if they are based on different rules of law, brought by different entities, or initiated against different government agencies. However, a number of treaties that adopt the waiver approach, most notably NAFTA and its descendents, incorporate more specific language describing the type of court action that triggers the waiver requirement. As previously noted, NAFTA allows arbitral jurisdiction only where the claimant has irrevocably waived the right to pursue court relief "with respect to the *measure* of the disputing Party that is alleged to be a breach."[50] This type of waiver provision seems to be more restrictive than the provisions imposing a choice with respect to a *dispute* (discussed in the previous section). A tribunal interpreting such a provision probably does not need to apply the so-called triple identity test; it need only

---

[46] See id. ¶ 45.
[47] Id. ¶ 46.
[48] Id. ¶ 57.
[49] Id. ¶¶ 60–61.
[50] NAFTA, art. 1121 (emphasis added).

inquire whether the same measure underlies both international and domestic law claims. Once that is established, arbitral jurisdiction exists only if the investor has waived its right to local remedies. The investor must waive its right to commence or continue local proceedings even if its claims concerning the measure are based on breaches of different laws (i.e., breaches of local law as opposed to breaches of international law).

In the NAFTA arbitration *Waste Management Inc. v. Mexico*,[51] the city of Acapulco granted a municipal waste disposal concession to a U.S. corporation and its Mexican subsidiary, Acaverde. Pursuant to the terms of the concession agreement, the city, the state of Guerrero, and the Mexican state bank Banobras entered into a line of credit agreement that allowed Acaverde to demand payment in the event that the city was unable to make the necessary payments under the concession agreement. Thus, under the line of credit agreement, the bank guaranteed the city's obligation to pay. After a dispute arose over the terms of the concession and the line of credit agreement, Acaverde initiated two lawsuits in Mexico against the bank for the latter's failure to make payments on behalf of the city under the line of credit agreement. In addition, Acaverde commenced domestic arbitration against the city under the concession's dispute resolution clause. Waste Management also sought to initiate international arbitration against Mexico under NAFTA. With a view to satisfying the requirements of NAFTA Article 1121, Waste Management submitted a declaration to the NAFTA tribunal waiving the right "to initiate or continue . . . any proceedings [in all fora] with respect to the measures taken by [Mexico] that are alleged to be in breach of NAFTA Chapter Eleven and applicable rules of international law."[52] However, the waiver excluded "dispute settlement proceedings involving allegations that [Mexico] has violated duties imposed by sources of law other than Chapter Eleven of NAFTA, including the municipal law of Mexico."[53] In this way the claimant hoped that the Mexican courts would retain jurisdiction over issues of Mexican law, and the NAFTA tribunal would simultaneously adjudicate claims based on alleged treaty breaches.

Mexico argued that Waste Management's waiver was defective because the company continued to pursue domestic law remedies while prosecuting the NAFTA arbitration. Mexico added that the claims and relief sought in the Mexican proceedings were duplicative of those introduced in the international arbitration.[54] Waste Management countered that it had not alleged a breach of NAFTA or international law in the domestic litigation and arbitration, and therefore the parallel

---

[51] *Waste Mgmt. I, supra* note 7.
[52] *Id.* ¶¶ 4–5.
[53] *Id.*
[54] *See id.* ¶ 6.

proceedings "could [not] be held to have either caused prejudice to Mexico or forced it to defend duplicate allegations of NAFTA breaches simultaneously."[55]

The central inquiry for the *Waste Management* tribunal was whether the domestic Mexican law claims brought by its subsidiary were sufficiently connected to the international law claims brought by the parent company. Focusing on the text of Article 1121, the tribunal recognized that a single government *measure* could give rise to different claims in different fora, under distinct systems of law:

> It is clear that one and the same measure may give rise to different types of claims in different courts or tribunals. Therefore, something that under Mexican legislation would constitute a series of breaches of contract expressed as non-payment of certain invoices, violation of exclusivity clauses in a concession agreement, etc., could, under the NAFTA, be interpreted as a lack of fair and equitable treatment of a foreign investment by a government (Article 1105 of NAFTA) or as measures constituting "expropriation" under Article 1110 of the NAFTA.[56]

After analyzing Waste Management's claims before Mexican courts and in the local arbitration, the tribunal concluded that they were based upon the same government measure that lay at the root of the NAFTA arbitration.[57] Consequently, by continuing the domestic litigation and arbitration after it filed its NAFTA arbitration, Waste Management failed to satisfy the waiver requirement set forth in NAFTA Article 1121.[58] The *Waste Management* tribunal held that a full waiver of an investor's right to continue local proceedings was a condition precedent to the submission of an international claim to arbitration under NAFTA,[59] and that any such waiver "must be clear, explicit and categorical."[60] Because Waste Management submitted only a limited waiver, the tribunal dismissed its NAFTA claims for want of jurisdiction.[61]

The *Waste Management* decision might have been decided quite differently had Article 1121 referred to waiver of rights with respect to the *same dispute*, rather than the *same measure*. Applying different language, the tribunal might have taken into account a number of distinctions between Waste Management's claims

---

[55] *Id.*

[56] *Id.* ¶ 27.

[57] *See id.*

[58] *See id.* ¶¶ 27–30.

[59] *See id.* ¶¶ 13–14.

[60] *Id.* ¶ 18.

[61] *Id.* ¶ 18. After the *Waste Mgmt. I* decision, the claimant resubmitted the dispute to NAFTA arbitration. This time, Waste Mgmt. provided the tribunal with an effective waiver of its litigation rights in local courts (the domestic arbitration was also discontinued). Based on this new waiver document, the *Waste Mgmt. II* tribunal held that it had jurisdiction to decide Waste Mgmt.'s claims. *Waste Mgmt. Inc. v. Mexico*, Decision on Mexico's Preliminary Objection concerning the Previous Proceedings, ICSID Case No. ARB(AF)/00/3 (June 26, 2002), ¶¶ 3, 53 [hereinafter *Waste Mgmt. II*].

in domestic and international fora. It thus appears that a choice of forum clause focusing on a host state measure is more likely to reduce duplicative litigation and the risk of inconsistent decisions.

B. Investment Treaties and Contractual Forum Selection Clauses

Determining the appropriate forum for an investment dispute becomes even more problematic where the investor has agreed in its contract to a specific dispute resolution forum, either national courts or a nontreaty, perhaps local, arbitration. The central difficulty is that even when parties to an investment contract choose national courts or nontreaty arbitration as the exclusive forum for resolving their disputes, an applicable investment treaty can create an independent, parallel forum to which investors may bring disputes for adjudication.[62] Tribunals and expert commentary are divided on this issue. A few tribunals have found that contractually chosen national courts have exclusive jurisdiction, at least for *purely* contract claims, especially absent allegations of an independent breach of international law, such as denial of justice. Other tribunals have found that investment treaty jurisdiction exists in parallel with national court jurisdiction, with the national court competent to hear national law claims and the international tribunal competent to adjudicate international law claims, even when both sets of claims arise out of a single set of facts.

Part of the confusion in this area is caused by the failure of most investment treaties to expressly delineate the respective jurisdictions of national courts and international tribunals. Other instruments have been clearer. The declaration establishing the Iran-United States Claims Tribunal sought to preclude such confusion by creating an exception for contracts in which parties agreed to the sole jurisdiction of Iranian Courts.[63] Article II of the Declaration provided the following:

> An international arbitral tribunal (the Iran-United States Claims Tribunal) is hereby established for the purpose of deciding claims of nationals of the United States against Iran and claims of nationals of Iran against the United States ... whether or not filed with any court ... excluding claims arising under a binding contract between the parties

---

[62] *See Société Générale de Surveillance S.A. (SGS) v. Pakistan*, ICSID Case No. ARB/01/13 (Decision on Jurisdiction of Aug. 6, 2003) (where contractual remedy was local arbitration in Pakistan); *Compania de Aguas del Aconquija S.A. & Vivendi Universal (Formerly Compagnie Generale Des Eaux) v. Argentine Republic*, ICSID Case No. ARB/97/3 (Decision on Annulment of July 3, 2003), 41 I.L.M. 1135 (2002) [hereinafter *Vivendi*]; *Lanco Int'l, Inc. v. Argentine Republic*, ICSID Case No. ARB/97/6 (Preliminary Decision on Jurisdiction of Dec. 8, 1998), 40 I.L.M. 457 (2001); *Azinian v. United Mexican States*, ICSID Case No. ARB(AF)/97/2 (Award of Nov. 1, 1999), 39 I.L.M. 537 (2000); *see generally* Raul Emilio Vinuesa, *Bilateral Investment Treaties and the Settlement of Investment Disputes under ICSID: The Latin American Experience*, 8 NAFTA L. & Bus. Rev. Am. 501 (2002).

[63] *See generally* Ted L. Stein, *Jurisprudence and the Jurists' Prudence: The Iranian Forum Clause Decisions of the Iran-U.S. Claims Tribunal*, 78 Am. J. Int'l L. 1 (1984).

specifically providing that any disputes there under shall be within the sole jurisdiction of the competent Iranian courts.[64]

Honoring the forum clause exception of Article II, the Claims Tribunal in *Halliburton Co. v. Doreen/IMCO* determined that it lacked jurisdiction to arbitrate claims based on a purchase agreement that contained a provision stating, "All disputes arising in connection with this Purchase Agreement . . . shall be settled by submission to the Courts of Iran."[65]

One of the first investment arbitration decisions to examine the interaction of contractual and treaty-based dispute resolution procedures was *Azinian v. United Mexican States*. In this early NAFTA arbitration, the Mexican municipality city of Naucalpana was alleged to have breached a Concession Agreement with Desechos Solidos de Naucalpan S.A. de C.V. (DESONA), a Mexican corporate entity that was controlled by a group of American investors.[66] After the city nullified the contract, the American investors sought recovery under the contract in Mexican courts, where three levels of courts ruled in the municipality's favor. Thereafter, one investor argued that the actions of the municipality were attributable to the Mexican government under NAFTA, and he filed a NAFTA claim. In its decision on jurisdiction, the tribunal recognized the principle established in *Amco v. Indonesia*: "[A]n international tribunal is not bound to follow the result of a national court."[67] The arbitrators held that the investor's fundamental complaint was of contract breach, rather than of a treaty violation, and further held that because NAFTA does not allow investors to seek international arbitration for mere breaches of contract, the tribunal lacked jurisdiction to consider the merits of the investor's case.[68]

An important ICSID decision addressing the role of contractual forum selection clauses came in *Compañia de Aguas del Aconquija v. Argentina*. There, a contract between a French company and a province of Argentina required the parties to submit disputes to domestic courts, whereas a BIT between France and Argentina allowed parties to submit claims for ICSID arbitration.[69] Article 16.4 of the Concession Agreement expressly stated, "for purposes of interpretation and application of this Contract the parties submit themselves to the exclusive jurisdiction of the Contentious Administrative Tribunals of Tucumán."[70] However, Article 8 of the treaty between France and Argentina provided the following:

---

[64] The Declaration of the Government of the Democratic and Popular Republic of Algeria concerning the Settlement of Claims by the Government of the United States of America and the Government of the Islamic Republic of Iran, Jan. 19, 1981, 1 Iran-U.S. C.T.R. 9.

[65] *Halliburton Co., IMCO Services (U.K.) v. Doreen/Imco*, 1 Iran-U.S. Cl. Trib. Rep. 242 (1982).

[66] *Azinian, supra* note 62.

[67] *Amco v. Indonesia*, ICSID Case No. ARB/81/1 (Award of Nov. 20, 1984), 24 I.L.M. 1022, 1026 (1985).

[68] *Azinian, supra* note 62.

[69] *Vivendi, supra* note 62.

[70] *Id.*, Original Proceedings (Award of Nov. 21, 2000), 40 I.L.M. 426, 451.

> 1. Any dispute relating to investments made under this Agreement between one Contracting Party and an investor of the other Contracting Party shall, as far as possible, be settled amicably between the two parties concerned.
>
> 2. If any such dispute cannot be so settled within six months of the time when a claim is made by one of the parties to the dispute, the dispute shall, at the request of the investor, be submitted:
>
>> (i) Either to the domestic courts of the Contracting Party involved in the dispute;
>>
>> (ii) Or to international arbitration under the conditions described in paragraph 3 below.
>
> Once an investor has submitted the dispute to the courts of the Contracting Party concerned or to international arbitration, the choice of one or the other of these procedures is final.[71]

When the French company brought its claim to ICSID pursuant to Article 8(3) of the bilateral investment treaty, the initial ICSID tribunal held that it had jurisdiction to hear claims of violations of the bilateral investment treaty, despite the fact that those were similar to the claims made in Argentine courts under the Concession Agreement.[72] However, it went on to dismiss the claim on the merits based inter alia on the fact that "the Argentine Republic cannot be held liable unless and until Claimants have, as Article 16.4 of the Concession Contract required, asserted their rights in proceedings before the contentious administrative courts of Tucumán and have been denied their rights, either procedurally or substantively."[73] The claimant then started an ICSID annulment proceeding against this award; and the Annulment Committee, in a decision that has been followed by several tribunals,[74] held that the initial "Tribunal manifestly exceeded its powers by not examining the merits of the claims for acts of the Tucumán authorities under the BIT. . . ."[75] Most importantly, it articulated what has become known as the "principle of the independence of treaty and contract claims."[76] Excerpts of the Annulment Committee's decisions have been reproduced in the following text:

---

[71] France-Argentina BIT, *quoted in Vivendi, supra* note 62 (Award of Nov. 21, 2000), app. 1.

[72] *Vivendi, supra* note 62 (Award of Nov. 21, 2000), at 1138 (holding "neither the forum-selection provision of the Concession Contract nor the provisions of the ICSID Convention and the BIT on which the Argentine Republic relies preclude [the French company's] recourse to this Tribunal on the facts presented").

[73] *Id.* ¶ 78.

[74] *See, e.g., Jan de Nul N.V. & Dredging International N.V. v. Egypt*, ICSID Case No. ARB/04/13 (Decision on Jurisdiction of June 13, 2006), ¶ 80; *Bayindir Insaat Turizm Ticaret ve Sanyai A.S. v. Pakistan*, ICSID Case No. ARB/03/29 (Decision on Jurisdiction of Nov. 14, 2005), ¶ 148; *Eureko v. Poland*, ad hoc arbitration (Partial Award of Aug. 19, 2005), ¶ 101; *Sempra Energy v. Argentina*, ICSID Case No. ARB/02/16 (Decision on Jurisdiction of May 11, 2005), ¶¶ 95–99; *AES v. Argentina*, ICSID Case No. ARB/02/17 (Decision on Jurisdiction of April 26, 2005), ¶ 90 *et seq.; Siemens v. Argentina*, ICSID Case No. ARB/02/8 (Decision on Jurisdiction of Aug. 3, 2004), ¶ 180.

[75] *Vivendi, supra* note 62, ¶ 119.

[76] *See id.* ¶ 101; *see also Bayindir, supra* note 74, ¶ 166.

Compañia de Aguas del Aconquija S.A. & Vivendi Universal v. Argentine Republic

ICSID Case No. ARB/97/3 (Decision on Annulment of July 3, 2002), 41 I.L.M. 1135[77]

1. On 20 March 2001, Compañía de Aguas del Aconquija S.A. ("CAA") and Compagnie Générale des Eaux ("CGE;" CGE and CAA are referred to, collectively, as "Claimants") filed with the Secretary-General of the International Centre for Settlement of Investment Disputes ("ICSID") an application in writing (the "Application") requesting the partial annulment of an Award dated 21 November 2000 (the "Award") rendered by the Tribunal in the arbitration between Claimants and Respondent.

. . . .

B. The Tribunal's Award

9. The dispute underlying the arbitration arose out of certain alleged acts of the Argentine Republic and its constituent Province of Tucumán that, according to Claimants, caused the termination of a thirty-year concession contract (the "Concession Contract") entered into by Tucumán and CAA on 18 May 1995. In the arbitration, Claimants asserted that all of these acts were attributable to the Argentine Republic under international law and, as such, violated Argentina's obligations under the Agreement between the Government of the Argentine Republic and the Government of the Republic of France for Reciprocal Protection and Promotion of Investments of 3 July 1991 (the "BIT"). Relevant provisions of the BIT are set out later in this decision.

10. The Award that is the subject of the present annulment proceeding was rendered on 21 November 2000. In the Award, the Tribunal rejected the objections to its jurisdiction raised by the Argentine Republic. Having upheld its jurisdiction, the Tribunal nonetheless dismissed the claim.

. . . .

C. THE COMMITTEE'S ANALYSIS

. . . .

(b) Local Remedies and their Relation to Arbitration under the BIT

51. The role and effect, if any, of local remedies available to the investor under the France-Argentina BIT are addressed in Article 8 of the BIT, which is central to this case, and in certain articles of the ICSID Convention, especially Article 26.

52. In accordance with Article 26 of the Convention, consent to ICSID arbitration involves consent "to the exclusion of any other remedy." A Contracting State may qualify its consent by requiring, as a pre-condition to arbitration, "the exhaustion of local administrative or judicial remedies." Argentina did not impose such a pre-condition when it agreed to Article 8 of the BIT. Accordingly it is common ground (and the Tribunal so held) that the exhaustion of local remedies rule does not apply to claims under the BIT.

53. Article 8 of the BIT expressly gives investors a choice of forum. Article 8 provides in full as follows:

> 1. Any dispute relating to investments made under this Agreement between one Contracting Party and an investor of the other Contracting Party shall, as far as possible, be settled amicably between the two parties concerned.

---

[77] Some source notes have been omitted.

2. If any such dispute cannot be so settled within six months of the time when a claim is made by one of the parties to the dispute, the dispute shall, at the request of the investor, be submitted:

—Either to the domestic courts of the Contracting Party involved in the dispute;

—Or to international arbitration under the conditions described in paragraph 3 below.

Once an investor has submitted the dispute to the courts of the Contracting Party concerned or to international arbitration, the choice of one or the other of these procedures is final.

3. Where recourse is had to international arbitration, the investor may choose to bring the dispute before one of the following arbitration bodies:

—The International Centre for Settlement of Investment Disputes (ICSID), established by the Convention on the Settlement of Investment Disputes between States and Nationals of other States opened for signature in Washington on 18 March 1965, if both States Parties to this Agreement have already acceded to the Convention. Until such time as this requirement is met, the two Contracting Parties shall agree to submit the dispute to arbitration, in accordance with the rules of procedure of the Additional Facility of ICSID;

—An ad hoc arbitral tribunal established in accordance with the Arbitration Rules of the United Nations Commission on International Trade Law (UNCITRAL).

4. The ruling of the arbitral body shall be based on the provisions of this Agreement, the legislation of the Contracting Party which is a party to the dispute, including rules governing conflict of laws, the terms of any private agreements concluded on the subject of the investment, and the relevant principles of international law.

5. Arbitral decisions shall be final and binding on the parties to the dispute.

54. Two initial points may be made about these provisions. First, it is evident that the term "national jurisdictions" as used in Article 8(2) ("jurisdictions nationales"/"jurisdiciones nacionales" in the authentic French and Spanish texts; "domestic courts" in the UNTS English translation) refers to all the courts and tribunals of the Contracting Parties, and not just to those at the federal level. In a treaty between a unitary and a federal state, such as France and Argentina respectively, one would not expect any disparity in the application of a phrase such as "national jurisdictions:" all French courts and tribunals are national, as are, for the purposes of the BIT, all courts and tribunals of Argentina. The relevant distinction, as Article 8(2) makes clear, is between "national" and "international" tribunals, not between "national" and "provincial" courts. Thus, there is no disparity between the phrases "national jurisdictions [*i.e.*, courts]" and "jurisdictions [courts] of the Contracting Party" as used in the two paragraphs of Article 8(2). In consequence, the contentious administrative courts of Tucumán are to be considered as national courts falling within the scope of Article 8(2).

55. Secondly, Article 8 deals generally with disputes "relating to investments made under this Agreement between one Contracting Party and an investor of the other Contracting Party." It is those disputes which may be submitted, at the investor's option, either to national or international adjudication. Article 8 does not use a narrower formulation, requiring that the investor's claim allege a breach of the BIT itself. Read literally, the requirements for arbitral jurisdiction in Article 8 do not necessitate that the Claimant allege a breach of the BIT itself: it is sufficient that the dispute relate to an investment made under the BIT. This may be contrasted, for example, with Article 11 of the BIT, which refers to disputes "concerning the interpretation or application of this Agreement," or with Article 1116 of the NAFTA, which provides that an investor may submit to arbitration under Chapter 11 "a claim that another Party has breached an obligation under"

specified provisions of that Chapter. Consequently, if a claim brought before a national court concerns a "dispute relating to investments made under this Agreement" within the meaning of Article 8(1), then Article 8(2) will apply.[78] In the Committee's view, a claim by CAA against the Province of Tucumán for breach of the Concession Contract, brought before the contentious administrative courts of Tucumán, would *prima facie* fall within Article 8(2) and constitute a "final" choice of forum and jurisdiction, if that claim was coextensive with a dispute relating to investments made under the BIT.

(c) Scope and Application of Substantive Provisions of the BIT

56. Claimants' case before the Tribunal was based on Articles 3 and 5 of the BIT, which deal, respectively, with "fair and equitable treatment according to the principles of international law" and with "measures of expropriation . . . or any other equivalent measure."

. . . .

(ii) Manifest excess of powers: Article 52(1)(b)

86. It is settled, and neither party disputes, that an ICSID tribunal commits an excess of powers not only if it exercises a jurisdiction which it does not have under the relevant agreement or treaty and the ICSID Convention, read together, but also if it fails to exercise a jurisdiction which it possesses under those instruments.[79] One might qualify this by saying that it is only where the failure to exercise a jurisdiction is clearly capable of making a difference to the result that it can be considered a manifest excess of power. Subject to that qualification, however, the failure by a tribunal to exercise a jurisdiction given it by the ICSID Convention and a BIT, in circumstances where the outcome of the inquiry is affected as a result, amounts in the Committee's view to a manifest excess of powers within the meaning of Article 52(1)(b).

87. No doubt an ICSID tribunal is not required to address in its award every argument made by the parties, provided of course that the arguments which it actually does consider are themselves capable of leading to the conclusion reached by the tribunal and that all questions submitted to a tribunal are expressly or implicitly dealt with. In the present case, Claimants contend that, far from considering their claims concerning breach of the BIT prior to purportedly dismissing them, the Tribunal actually declined to decide Claimants' allegations since it considered that, in order to do so, it would have had to address issues which, according to the Concession Contract, fell within the exclusive jurisdiction of the Tucumán courts. Claimants argue that if the Tribunal was wrong as regards this approach—that is, if the Tribunal erred in finding that it could not consider the BIT claims, in the circumstances—it failed to exercise its treaty jurisdiction, a jurisdiction which it had itself upheld. On that assumption, its failure to do so could also be said to be manifest.

. . . .

The Tucumán claims

93. The . . . question . . . is whether the Tribunal, having validly held that it had jurisdiction over the Tucumán claims, was entitled nonetheless to dismiss them as it did. Claimants, for their part, submit that the Tribunal did not so much dismiss the Tucumán claims as decline to address them. They argue that the only reason those claims were dismissed was that they were held to be substantially identical with claims against Tucumán under the Concession Contract, which the Tribunal found it could not determine, and that the Tribunal's refusal to decide the Tucumán claims on this basis was a

---

[78] SN: Cf. *Waste Mgmt., Inc. v. Mexico (No. 1)*, 40 I.L.M. 56 (2001), at 68 ¶ 28.

[79] SN: Schreuer, *supra* note 14, at 937–38.

manifest excess of powers. The Respondent argues that, assuming the Tribunal had jurisdiction over these claims, it acted correctly in dismissing them on the basis of Article 16(4) of the Concession Contract, but that in any event this was not the only reason for dismissal since the Tribunal did consider the Tucumán claims on their merits.

94. In dealing with these issues, it is necessary first to consider the relationship between the responsibility of Argentina under the BIT and the rights and obligations of the parties to the Concession Contract (especially those arising from Article 16(4), the exclusive jurisdiction clause); and secondly, to consider precisely what the Tribunal decided with respect to the Tucumán claims.

95. As to the relation between breach of contract and breach of treaty in the present case, it must be stressed that Articles 3 and 5 of the BIT do not relate directly to breach of a municipal contract. Rather they set an independent standard. A state may breach a treaty without breaching a contract, and vice versa, and this is certainly true of these provisions of the BIT. The point is made clear in Article 3 of the ILC Articles, which is entitled "Characterization of an act of a State as internationally wrongful:"

> The characterization of an act of a State as internationally wrongful is governed by international law. Such characterization is not affected by the characterization of the same act as lawful by internal law.

96. In accordance with this general principle (which is undoubtedly declaratory of general international law), whether there has been a breach of the BIT and whether there has been a breach of contract are different questions. Each of these claims will be determined by reference to its own proper or applicable law—in the case of the BIT, by international law; in the case of the Concession Contract, by the proper law of the contract, in other words, the law of Tucumán. For example, in the case of a claim based on a treaty, international law rules of attribution apply, with the result that the state of Argentina is internationally responsible for the acts of its provincial authorities. By contrast, the state of Argentina is not liable for the performance of contracts entered into by Tucumán, which possesses separate legal personality under its own law and is responsible for the performance of its own contracts.

97. The distinction between the role of international and municipal law in matters of international responsibility is stressed in the commentary to Article 3 of the ILC Articles, which reads in relevant part as follows:

> (4) The International Court has often referred to and applied the principle. For example in the *Reparation for Injuries* case, it noted that "[a]s the claim is based on the breach of an international obligation on the part of the Member held responsible ... the Member cannot contend that this obligation is governed by municipal law." In the *ELSI* case, a Chamber of the Court emphasized this rule, stating that:

> 'Compliance with municipal law and compliance with the provisions of a treaty are different questions. What is a breach of treaty may be lawful in the municipal law and what is unlawful in the municipal law may be wholly innocent of violation of a treaty provision. Even had the Prefect held the requisition to be entirely justified in Italian law, this would not exclude the possibility that it was a violation of the FCN [Friendship, Commerce, and Navigation] Treaty.'

> Conversely, as the Chamber explained:

> '. . . the fact that an act of a public authority may have been unlawful in municipal law does not necessarily mean that that act was unlawful in international law, as a breach of treaty or otherwise. A finding of the local courts that an act was unlawful may well be relevant to an argument that it was also arbitrary; but by itself, and without more, unlawfulness cannot be said to amount to arbitrariness . . . Nor does it follow from a finding by a municipal court that an act was unjustified, or unreasonable, or

arbitrary, that that act is necessarily to be classed as arbitrary in international law, though the qualification given to the impugned act by a municipal authority may be a valuable indication.'

. . . .

(7) The rule that the characterization of conduct as unlawful in international law cannot be affected by the characterization of the same act as lawful in internal law makes no exception for cases where rules of international law require a State to conform to the provisions of its internal law, for instance by applying to aliens the same legal treatment as to nationals. It is true that in such a case, compliance with internal law is relevant to the question of international responsibility. But this is because the rule of international law makes it relevant, e.g. by incorporating the standard of compliance with internal law as the applicable international standard or as an aspect of it. Especially in the fields of injury to aliens and their property and of human rights, the content and application of internal law will often be relevant to the question of international responsibility. In every case it will be seen on analysis that either the provisions of internal law are relevant as facts in applying the applicable international standard, or else that they are actually incorporated in some form, conditionally or unconditionally, into that standard.

98. In a case where the essential basis of a claim brought before an international tribunal is a breach of contract, the tribunal will give effect to any valid choice of forum clause in the contract.[80] For example in the *Woodruff* case,[81] a decision of an American-Venezuelan Mixed Commission in 1903, a claim was brought for breach of a contract which contained the following clause:

> Doubts and controversies which at any time might occur in virtue of the present agreement shall be decided by the common laws and ordinary tribunals of Venezuela, and they shall never be, as well as neither the decision which shall be pronounced upon them, nor anything relating to the agreement, the subject of international reclamation.

99. The Commission in that case held that Woodruff was bound by this clause not to refer his contractual claim to any other tribunal. At the same time, the exclusive jurisdiction clause did not and could not preclude a claim by his government in the event that the treatment accorded him amounted to a breach of international law:

> [W]hereas certainly a contract between a sovereign and a citizen of a foreign country can never impede the right of the Government of that citizen to make international reclamation, wherever according to international law it has the right or even the duty to do so, as its rights and obligations can not be affected by any precedent agreement to which it is not a party;

> But whereas this does not interfere with the right of a citizen to pledge to any other party that he, the contractor, in disputes upon certain matters will never appeal to other judges than to those designated by the agreement, nor with his obligation to

---

[80] SN: That is, unless the treaty in question otherwise provides. *See, e.g.*, Article II (1) of the Claims Settlement Declaration of 19 Jan. 1981, 1 *Iran-U.S. Claims Tribunal Reports*, at 9, which overrode exclusive jurisdiction clauses concerning U.S. courts but not Iranian courts: see the cases cited by C. N. Brower & J. D. Brueschke, *The Iran-U.S. Claims Tribunal*, 60–72 (Martinus Nijhoff, 1998). The Committee does not need to consider whether the effect of Article 8 of the BIT is to override exclusive jurisdiction clauses in contracts underlying investments to which the BIT applies.

[81] SN: 9 *Reports of International Arbitral Awards*, 213.

keep this promise when pledged, leaving untouched the rights of his Government, to make his case an object of international claim whenever it thinks proper to do so and not impeaching his own right to look to his Government for protection of his rights in case of denial or unjust delay of justice by the contractually designated judges; ...

100. The Commission accordingly dismissed the claim "without prejudice on its merits, when presented to the proper judges," on the ground that "by the very agreement that is the fundamental basis of the claim, it was withdrawn from the jurisdiction of this Commission."

101. On the other hand, where "the fundamental basis of the claim" is a treaty laying down an independent standard by which the conduct of the parties is to be judged, the existence of an exclusive jurisdiction clause in a contract between the claimant and the respondent state or one of its subdivisions cannot operate as a bar to the application of the treaty standard.[82] At most, it might be relevant—as municipal law will often be relevant—in assessing whether there has been a breach of the treaty.

102. In the Committee's view, it is not open to an ICSID tribunal having jurisdiction under a BIT in respect of a claim based upon a substantive provision of that BIT, to dismiss the claim on the ground that it could or should have been dealt with by a national court. In such a case, the inquiry which the ICSID tribunal is required to undertake is one governed by the ICSID Convention, by the BIT and by applicable international law. Such an inquiry is neither in principle determined, nor precluded, by any issue of municipal law, including any municipal law agreement of the parties.

103. Moreover the Committee does not understand how, if there had been a breach of the BIT in the present case (a question of international law), the existence of Article 16(4) of the Concession Contract could have prevented its characterisation as such. A state cannot rely on an exclusive jurisdiction clause in a contract to avoid the characterisation of its conduct as internationally unlawful under a treaty.

104. The Respondent argues that, even if the Tribunal had jurisdiction, and even if it could not decline to exercise that jurisdiction by reference to the exclusive jurisdiction clause in the Concession Contract, this was not what the Tribunal did. According to the Respondent, it emerges clearly from the Award that the Claimants had no arguable case for a breach of Articles 3 or 5 of the BIT and that, at best, their claim was one for breach of contract: the issue of a treaty claim could only arise in the event that the contentious administrative tribunals of Tucumán denied Claimants justice, substantively or procedurally.

105. The question thus becomes how to characterize the Tribunal's decision. In considering that question, the Committee does not believe that it is material either that CGE was not a party to the Concession Contract or that the parties to the Concession Contract were CAA and the Province of Tucumán, as opposed to CAA and the federal

---

[82] SN: It is unnecessary for the Committee to pronounce on the content of the standard laid down in the BIT, in particular Article 3. It may be that *mere* breaches of contract, unaccompanied by bad faith or other aggravating circumstances, will rarely amount to a breach of the fair and equitable treatment standard set out in Article 3. The Tribunal did not, however, offer any interpretation of Article 3, nor seek to base itself on this consideration.

government. If the Tribunal was right in saying that it could not consider any allegation of breach of treaty which required it to interpret or apply the Concession Contract, then it is arguable that CGE could be in no better position than CAA. It is also arguable that this conclusion should apply even though CAA's contractual commitment was to a province, since the acts of that province form the nub of the claim. But it is one thing to exercise contractual jurisdiction (arguably exclusively vested in the administrative tribunals of Tucumán by virtue of the Concession Contract) and another to take into account the terms of a contract in determining whether there has been a breach of a distinct standard of international law, such as that reflected in Article 3 of the BIT.

106. Claimants made a series of allegations as to the conduct of Tucumán, much of which, they claim, involved measures taken in bad faith. Such action included alleged instances of: acts of the Ombudsman and other regulatory authorities; incitement of consumers, by legislators and others, not to pay their water bills; unauthorized tariff changes; the incorrect imposition of fines (never in fact collected) for allegedly deficient water quality; incorrect invoicing for municipal and provincial water taxes; conduct relating to the "black water" problem, which was blamed on CAA, but which CAA denied was its fault; unilateral changes by the provincial Governor to the second renegotiated agreement; and various post-termination conduct. This conduct, they contend, amounted on the whole to concerted action by the Tucumán authorities to frustrate the concession.

. . . .

108. [I]t is clear from the core discussion of the Tucumán claims, at paragraphs 77–81 of the Award, that the Tribunal declined to decide key aspects of the Claimants' BIT claims on the ground that they involved issues of contractual performance or non-performance. The Tribunal itself characterised these passages, in paragraph 81, as embodying its "decision" with respect to the Tucumán claims.

109. A key passage in this regard is found in paragraph 79, where the Tribunal said:

[G]iven the nature of the dispute between Claimants and the Province of Tucumán, it is not possible for this Tribunal to determine which actions of the Province were taken in exercise of its sovereign authority and which in the exercise of its rights as a party to the Concession Contract considering, in particular, that much of the evidence presented in this case has involved detailed issues of performance and rates under the Concession Contract.

110. This passage calls for two remarks. First, it is couched in terms not of decision but of the *impossibility* of decision, the impossibility being founded on the need to interpret and apply the Concession Contract.[83] Yet under Article 8(4) of the BIT the Tribunal had jurisdiction to base its decision upon the Concession Contract, at least so far as necessary in order to determine whether there had been a breach of the substantive standards of the BIT. Second, the passage appears to imply that conduct of Tucumán carried out in the purported exercise of its rights as a party to the Concession Contract could not, *a priori*, have breached the BIT. However, there is no basis for such an assumption: whether particular conduct involves a breach of a treaty

---

[83] SN: See also the Tribunal's summary where the Tribunal said it was "impossible . . . to distinguish or separate violations of the BIT from breaches of the Concession Contract without first interpreting and applying the detailed provisions of that agreement."

is not determined by asking whether the conduct purportedly involves an exercise of contractual rights.[84]

111. For these reasons, and despite certain passages of the Award in which the Tribunal seems to go further into the merits, the Committee can only conclude that the Tribunal, in dismissing the Tucumán claims as it did, actually failed to decide whether or not the conduct in question amounted to a breach of the BIT. In particular, the Tribunal repeatedly referred to allegations and issues which, it held, it could not decide given the terms of Article 16(4) of the Concession Contract, even though these were adduced by Claimants specifically in support of their BIT claim. Moreover, it offered no interpretation whatsoever either of Article 3 or of Article 5 of the BIT, something which was called for if the claims were to be dismissed on their merits.

. . . .

113. In the light of Article 8 of the BIT, the situation carried risks for Claimants. Having declined to challenge the various factual components of its treaty cause of action before the administrative courts of Tucumán, instead choosing to commence ICSID arbitration—and having thereby, in the Committee's view, taken the "fork in the road" under Article 8(4)—CAA took the risk of a tribunal holding that the acts complained of neither individually nor collectively rose to the level of a breach of the BIT. In that event, it would have lost both its treaty claim and its contract claim. But on the other hand it was entitled to take that risk, with its associated burden of proof. A treaty cause of action is not the same as a contractual cause of action; it requires a clear showing of conduct which is in the circumstances contrary to the relevant treaty standard. The availability of local courts ready and able to resolve specific issues independently may be a relevant circumstance in determining whether there has been a breach of international law (especially in relation to a standard such as that contained in Article 3). But it is not dispositive, and it does not preclude an international tribunal from considering the merits of the dispute.

114. It should be stressed that the conduct complained of here was not more or less peripheral to a continuing successful enterprise. The Tucumán conduct (in conjunction with the acts and decisions of Claimants) had the effect of putting an end to the investment. In the Committee's view, the BIT gave Claimants the right to assert that the Tucumán conduct failed to comply with the treaty standard for the protection of investments. Having availed itself of that option, Claimants should not have been deprived of a decision, one way or the other, merely on the strength of the observation that the local courts could conceivably have provided them with a remedy, in whole or in part. Under the BIT they had a choice of remedies.

115. For all of these reasons, the Committee concludes that the Tribunal exceeded its powers in the sense of Article 52(1)(b), in that the Tribunal, having jurisdiction over the Tucumán

---

[84] SN: See ILC Articles, commentary to art. 4, ¶ (6), commentary to art. 12, ¶¶ (9)–(10). See also C. Amerasinghe, *State Breaches of Contracts with Aliens and International Law*, 58 Am. J. Int'l L. 881, 910–12 (1964): "The general proposition that, where a state performs an act which is prohibited by a treaty to which it is a party, it will be responsible for a breach of international law to the other party or parties to the treaty requires no substantiation. In accordance with the same principle, an act which constitutes a breach of contract would be a breach of international law, if it is an act which that state is under an obligation not to commit by virtue of a treaty to which it and the national state of the alien are parties"; R. Jennings & A. Watts, *Oppenheim's International Law* 927 (Harlow, Longman, 9th ed., 1992): "It is doubtful whether a breach by a state of its contractual obligations with aliens constitutes *per se* a breach of an international obligation, unless there is some such additional element as denial of justice, or expropriation, or breach of treaty, in which case it is that additional element which will constitute the basis for the state's international responsibility."

claims, failed to decide those claims. Given the clear and serious implications of that decision for Claimants in terms of Article 8(2) of the BIT, and the surrounding circumstances, the Committee can only conclude that that excess of powers was manifest. It accordingly annuls the decision of the Tribunal so far as concerns the entirety of the Tucumán claims.

The *Vivendi* annulment decision highlights a number of significant issues.[85] First, *Vivendi* articulated a crucial distinction between contractual and treaty claims. Tribunals that have adopted this distinction include, among others: *SGS v. Pakistan, Siemens v. Argentina, Sempra Energy v. Argentina, AES v. Argentina, Eureko v. Poland, Bayindir v. Turkey*, and *Jan de Nul N.V. et al v. Egypt*.[86]

A second and related issue is the degree to which treaty claims and contract claims are truly distinct. The *Vivendi* annulment decision articulated the longstanding distinction between the two types of claims, but there are undoubtedly circumstances where no such distinction exists. In particular, as discussed in detail in Chapter XVIII, for those BITs that contain sweeping, mandatory umbrella clauses, a breach of a contract with a host state, and especially an investment contract, may ipso facto breach the BIT as well. Even without an umbrella clause, an investor may argue that a state's breach of contract may simultaneously constitute a breach of the fair and equitable treatment standard that most BITs contain.[87] Thus, the distinction, although theoretically sound, may in some circumstances prove illusory.

The third issue is whether an investor that has signed a contract containing an *exclusive* dispute resolution procedure may nonetheless ignore that procedure and instead commence a BIT arbitration to adjudicate its international law or treaty claims. The *Vivendi* Annulment Committee ruled that an investor can elect treaty adjudication notwithstanding the seemingly exclusive contractual dispute provision.[88] Other tribunals have reached the same conclusion, including *SGS v. Pakistan*,[89] *Lanco v. Argentina*,[90] *Salini v. Morocco*,[91] *Sempra Energy v.*

---

[85] For competing views of the *Vivendi* annulment decision, *see* Bernardo Cremades, *Litigating Annulment Proceedings—The Vivendi Matter: Contract and Treaty Claims*, in *Annulment of ICSID Awards* 87 (Gaillard & Banifatemi eds., 2004); Stanimir Alexandrov, *The Vivendi Annulment Decision and the Lessons for Future ICSID Arbitrations: The Applicants' Perspective*, in *id.* at 97; Carlos Ignacio Suarez Anzorena, Vivendi v. Argentina: *On the Admissibility of Requests for Partial Annulment and the Ground of a Manifest Excess of Powers*, in *id.* at 123.

[86] *See* note 74 *supra*.

[87] *See generally* Chapter XVII on fair and equitable treatment.

[88] *See Vivendi, supra* note 62, ¶ 101.

[89] *SGS v. Pakistan, supra* note 62, ¶ 155.

[90] *Lanco, supra* note 62, at 463.

[91] *Salini v. Morocco*, ICSID Case No. ARB/02/13 (Decision on Jurisdiction), 42 I.L.M. 609, 624 (2003).

Argentina,[92] *AES v. Argentina*,[93] *Eureko v. Poland*,[94] and *PSEG Global Inc. v. Turkey*.[95]

In another well-known decision, *SGS v. Philippines*,[96] the tribunal took a different approach, with a majority of the ICSID arbitrators ruling that the Switzerland-Philippines BIT was not "intended to *override* an exclusive jurisdiction clause in a contract, so far as contractual claims are involved."[97] In that case the Swiss company Société Générale de Surveillance S.A. (SGS) contracted with the Philippines to provide specialized import supervision services. When a dispute arose concerning money allegedly owed to SGS under the contract, SGS sought arbitration pursuant to the BIT. Article VIII(2) of the BIT provided, "the investor may submit the dispute either to the national jurisdiction of the Contracting Party in whose territory the investment has been made or to international arbitration."[98] Before considering the relevance of the contract's forum selection clause (see below), the tribunal, based on Article VIII(2) of the BIT alone, concluded, "in principle (and apart from the exclusive jurisdiction clause in the [contract]) it was open to SGS to refer the present dispute, as a contractual dispute, to ICSID arbitration."[99] However, the ICSID tribunal concluded that if it were to exercise jurisdiction over the contractual dispute as provided in Article VIII(2) of the BIT, it would nullify the forum selection clause of the contract, which stated, "All actions concerning disputes in connection with the obligations of either party to this Agreement shall be filed at the Regional Trial Courts of Makati or Manila."[100] Moreover, the tribunal believed that the Switzerland-Philippines BIT was a "framework treaty" designed to "support and supplement, not to override or replace, the actually negotiated investment arrangements made between the investor and the host State."[101] Based on those two findings, the tribunal concluded that the BIT was not intended to override the exclusive jurisdiction clause of the contract and thereby give SGS an alternative forum in which to resolve its contractual claims.[102] It reached this decision despite its holding that the *umbrella*

---

[92] *Sempra Energy, supra* note 74, ¶¶ 121–22.

[93] *AES, supra* note 74, ¶¶ 90 *et seq.*

[94] *Eureko, supra* note 74, ¶ 101.

[95] *PSEG Global Inc. & Konya Ilgin Elektrik Üretim ve Ticaret Ltd. Srketi v. Turkey*, ICSID Case No. ARB/02/5 (Award and Annex of Jan. 19, 2007), ¶ 158.

[96] *SGS v. Republic of Philippines*, ICSID Case No. Arb/02/06 (Decision of the tribunal on Objections to Jurisdiction of Jan. 29, 2004).

[97] *Id.* ¶ 143 (emphasis added).

[98] *Id.* ¶ 34, *quoting* Agreement of 1997 between the Swiss Confederation and the Republic of the Philippines on the Promotion and Reciprocal Protection of Investments.

[99] *Id.* ¶ 135.

[100] *Id.* ¶ 137.

[101] *Id.* ¶ 141.

[102] *Id.* ¶ 143.

clause of the BIT applied to all of the Philippines' contractual undertakings.[103] However, the tribunal also held that an arbitral tribunal could have jurisdiction when a contract refers disputes exclusively to another forum if there are "good reasons, such as *force majeure*, preventing the claimant from complying with its contract."[104] Furthermore, the tribunal affirmed that it could hear the contractual claims of SGS if proceedings in Philippines courts resulted in a miscarriage of justice, violating other terms of the BIT.[105] Because SGS could not demonstrate that local litigation would not provide adequate recourse, the tribunal stayed the ICSID arbitration pending a decision in the Philippines courts.[106]

In his dissenting opinion, Crivellaro offered an alternative interpretation of the Treaty and argued that the issue should not be whether the BIT was intended to "override" preexisting, freely negotiated contracts but whether the BIT was intended to "coexist" with such contracts.[107] According to Crivellaro's interpretation of Article VIII(2), when Switzerland and the Philippines signed the BIT, they intended to offer investors an unconditional right to an additional forum; and in the case of SGS, Article VIII(2) therefore permits an ex post facto forum choice.[108] As a policy matter, Crivellaro suggested that the majority's interpretation undermines the incentives that BITs provide for foreign investors, because those foreign investors lose their preferential privilege of a forum choice under BITs when provisions of an earlier contract are upheld.[109] Based on his interpretation of the contract and the practical implications of the majority's ruling, Crivellaro declared his opposition to the stay.[110]

A fourth issue is whether and where a claimant with a contractual dispute resolution clause can adjudicate its contractual claims, assuming they are distinct from its international law claims. The *Vivendi* Annulment Committee stated, "In a case where the essential basis of a claim brought before an international tribunal is a breach of contract, the tribunal will give effect to any valid choice of forum clause in the contract."[111] The tribunal in *SGS v. Pakistan* effectively adhered to this view

---

[103] This aspect of the case is discussed in detail in Chapter XVIII.

[104] *Id.* ¶ 154.

[105] The majority also found that the failure of the Philippines' courts to enforce an obligation to pay money owed to SGS on the contract would violate the BIT's "fair and equitable treatment" provision of art. IV. *Id.* ¶ 162. Additionally, a failure to observe obligations to pay SGS would violate art. X(2) of the BIT, which provides, "Each Contracting Party shall observe any obligation it has assumed with regard to specific investments in its territory by investors of the other Contracting Party." *Id.* ¶ 155.

[106] *Id.* ¶ 175.

[107] *Id.*, Declaration of Antonio Crivellaro of Jan. 29, 2004, ¶ 4.

[108] *Id.*

[109] *Id.* ¶ 5.

[110] *Id.* ¶ 15.

[111] *Vivendi, supra* note 62, ¶ 99.

by ruling that the claimant should pursue its contract claims in the contractual forum and its international claims in a treaty forum.[112] However, the BIT in that case, the Pakistan-Switzerland BIT, did not have a *fork in the road* or waiver clause. In the *Vivendi* annulment, the Argentina-France BIT did contain a *fork in the road* clause; and the tribunal consequently ruled that the claimant, by electing treaty arbitration, had forever relinquished its contract claims.[113] Later, the ICSID tribunal in *Joy Mining v. Egypt* followed the *Vivendi* Annulment Committee on this matter.[114] After finding that the sales contract between the parties did not constitute an investment under the BIT, and therefore that there could be no breach of the applicable investment treaty, the tribunal stated, "only the forum selection clause [in the contract] stands."[115] The contract clause gave the choice of UNCITRAL arbitration, but the claimant argued that clauses in agreements that created the right to "pursue other remedies" also allowed ICSID arbitration.[116] The tribunal disagreed, stating, "arbitration clauses, including ICSID clauses, need to be much more precise to be given the effect the Company attaches to those references."[117]

The tribunal in *Saluka Investments v. Czech Republic* was even more definitive in determining how contract claims could be brought. In this UNCITRAL arbitration, which was filed under the Netherlands-Czech Republic BIT, the Czech Republic brought a number of counterclaims against the investor, some of which alleged the investor had breached certain provisions of a share purchase agreement (SPA).[118] The tribunal noted that the SPA contained a forum selection clause, which provided that all disputes arising from the SPA were to be resolved through UNCITRAL arbitration in Zurich.[119] Then, relying on *Vivendi* Annulment Decision, it concluded that the essential basis of these counterclaims was breach of contract, and hence they had to be resolved in the forum specified in the SPA. In addition, the tribunal noted that Article 8(6) of the BIT required the parties to take into account "the provisions of special agreement relating to the investment"; it concluded that the arbitration clause in the SPA was just such an agreement and that it was required to give effect to it.[120]

---

[112] *SGS v. Pakistan*, supra note 62; *see also Joy Mining*, supra note 17, ¶¶ 90–91; *Saluka Inv. v. Czech Republic* (UNCITRAL arbitration, Decision on Jurisdiction over the Czech Republic's Counterclaim of May 7, 2004).

[113] *Vivendi*, supra note 62, ¶¶ 15, 113.

[114] *Joy Mining*, supra note 17, ¶¶ 90–91.

[115] *Id.* ¶ 89.

[116] *Id.* ¶ 94.

[117] *Id.*

[118] *Saluka Inv.*, supra note 112, ¶¶ 47–48.

[119] *Id.* ¶ 52.

[120] The claimant's claims were based on the BIT and not the purchase agreement and so were not subject to the clause.

Other tribunals have reached the opposite conclusion, finding that an investor can ignore a contractual dispute resolution clause and instead have its contractual claims adjudicated by a treaty tribunal. One such pre–*Vivendi* annulment case was *Lanco v. Argentina*. In *Lanco*, the government of Argentina awarded a concession agreement to a consortium of companies that included an American company, and that agreement provided that disputes should be submitted to the Federal Contentious Administrative Tribunals in the Argentine Republic.[121] When a contractual dispute arose, the American company invoked Article VII(3)(i) of the United States-Argentina BIT to request ICSID arbitration.[122] Article VII(3)(i) provides, "If the dispute cannot be settled amicably, the national or company concerned may choose to consent in writing to the submission of the dispute . . . to the International Centre for Settlement of Investment Disputes." In its decision on jurisdiction, the tribunal equated the alleged contractual breach with a breach of the investment treaty, and held that once the foreign investor had chosen ICSID arbitration pursuant to the BIT, Argentina was obligated to comply with ICSID arbitration proceedings despite the contrary forum selection clause included in the contract.[123]

Similarly, the BIT tribunal in *Eureko v. Poland* allowed the claimant to present its treaty claims to the tribunal. The tribunal first noted and followed the *Vivendi* annulment decision, finding that it had a duty to adjudicate any treaty claims.[124] In addition, like the *SGS v. Philippines* tribunal, it held that the umbrella clause in the BIT applied to Poland's contractual undertakings; so Poland's violation of a contractual commitment became a treaty violation as well.[125] However, unlike the *SGS v. Philippines* tribunal, the *Eureko* tribunal concluded that it had jurisdiction to hear Eureko's contract claims.[126]

Given the absence of textual clarity in many investment treaties, tribunals will undoubtedly continue to confront the problems of where a particular dispute will be heard and which claims an international tribunal may adjudicate.

---

[121] *Lanco, supra* note 62, at 460.
[122] *Id.* at 464.
[123] *Id.* at 473.
[124] *Eureko, supra* note 74, ¶ 112.
[125] *Id.* ¶¶ 57, 250.
[126] *Id.* ¶ 250.

XV. Discrimination

The principle of non-discrimination is one of the basic protections for foreign investors and investments in host nations.[1] Investment treaties provide guarantees against discrimination in three different ways. First, national treatment ensures that foreign investors will be treated no less favorably than similarly situated domestic investors. Second, most-favored-nation (MFN) treatment ensures that foreign investors will not be treated less favorably than investors from any third country.[2] Finally, some treaties contain a provision that prohibits arbitrary and discriminatory impairment of investments by the host state.[3] The following discussion analyzes the basic elements of these protections and the difficulties faced by tribunals adjudicating discrimination claims.

---

[1] Todd Weiler, *Prohibitions against Discrimination in NAFTA Chapter 11*, in *NAFTA Investment Law and Arbitration: Past Issues, Current Practice, Future Prospects* 27 (Weiler ed., Transnat'l Publishers, 2004).

[2] The non-discrimination principle may have roots in customary international law. According to some commentators, both national and MFN treatments emanated from more restricted customary rules. A. F. M. Maniruzzaman, *Expropriation of Alien Property and the Principle of Non-Discrimination in the International Law of Foreign Investment: An Overview*, 8 J. Transnat'l L. & Pol'y 57, 57 (1998); Ian Brownlie, *Principles of Public International Law* 546–47 (6th ed. Oxford 2003); *Restatement (Third) of the Foreign Relations of the United States* § 712 (1987) [hereinafter U.S. Restatement], Section 712(3) ("A state is responsible under international law for injury resulting from: . . . (3) other arbitrary or *discriminatory* acts or omissions by the state that impair property or other economic interests of a national of another state" (emphasis added)).

[3] *See also* the related discussion of arbitrary impairment clauses in Chapter XVII on fair and equitable treatment.

A. National Treatment

1. Introduction

The concept of national treatment is a key element of international trade and investment agreements.[4] On the one hand, capital-exporting nations seek basic assurances that their businesses will be able to compete on equal footing with investors in a host nation, including local enterprises.[5] Host nations, on the other hand, may be reluctant to extend national treatment protections wholesale to foreign investors, because of the competitive challenges that may result for their own investors.[6] This is especially true in former communist countries, where many domestic investors are state-owned or newly privatized enterprises. As a result, although the national treatment standard commonly appears in bilateral investment treaties (BITs),[7] where the host nation can analyze the advantages of national treatment for investors from a particular foreign nation, the standard is sometimes excluded from multilateral investment treaties.[8]

Host states do not always grant unlimited national treatment guarantees. Instead, many treaties incorporate exceptions for specified industries or economic sectors. In addition, most treaties grant to host states a wide margin of discretion in deciding whether and under what conditions to permit the entry of foreign investment.[9] The following excerpt from Rubins and Kinsella[10] explains some of the limitations that may circumscribe national treatment provisions:[11]

> Investment treaties vary as to whether they require national treatment to qualifying foreign investors only after an investment is established in the host state or in the pre-establishment

---

[4] See United Nations Conference on Trade and Development (UNCTAD), *National Treatment* 1 (1999) ("The national treatment standard is perhaps the single most important standard of treatment enshrined in international investment agreements").

[5] *Id.* at 8 ("[F]oreign and domestic investors should be subject to the same competitive conditions in the host country market, and therefore no government measure should unduly favour domestic investors").

[6] See Jian Zhou, *National Treatment in Foreign Investment Law: A Comparative Study from a Chinese Perspective*, 10 Touro Int'l L. Rev. 39, 89–90 (2000); *see also* Don Wallace, Jr & David B. Bailey, *The Inevitability of National Treatment of Foreign Direct Investment with Increasingly Few and Narrow Exceptions*, 31 Cornell Int'l L.J. 615 (1998).

[7] There are exceptions, however, and a few bilateral investment treaties (BITs) lack national treatment clauses. See, e.g., Sweden-China BIT (1982), art. 2; Norway-China BIT (1984), art. 4(3).

[8] Zhou, *supra* note 6, at 89–90.

[9] Cynthia Wallace, *Legal Control of the Multinational Enterprise* 84–85 (Martinus Nijhoff 1983). On entry, admission, and establishment of foreign investment, *see generally* United Nations Conference on Trade and Development (UNCTAD), *Admission and Establishment* (2002).

[10] Noah Rubins & N. Stephan Kinsella, *International Investment, Political Risk and Dispute Resolution* 227–28 (Oceana 2005).

[11] *See also* UNCTAD, *supra* note 4.

phase as well. The majority of BITs extend such protection only to established investments. The Energy Charter Treaty, for example, obliges each member State to provide national treatment to "investments in its Area" and primarily in the domains of "management, maintenance, use, enjoyment or disposal" of such investments.[12] Other treaties, particularly most of those concluded by the United States and Canada, ensure equal market access as well.[13] NAFTA, for example, grants national treatment to investors and investments with respect to "the *establishment, acquisition,* expansion, management, conduct, operation, and sale of other disposition of investments."[14] A number of investment protection instruments provide expressly for national treatment only as compared to local investors or investments that are in "like" or "similar" circumstances.[15] As noted below, some tribunals have applied the requirement of "like circumstances" as part of the national treatment obligation even where not expressly included in the relevant treaty text.

Many national treatment provisions in investment treaties are subject to certain specific limitations and exceptions. Such exclusions may relate to particular economic sectors, subject matters, or more general exceptions. The exceptions to national treatment in the U.S.-Argentina BIT, for example include:

> air transportation; ocean and costal shipping; banking; insurance; energy and power production; custom house brokers; ownership of real property; ownership of shares in the Communications Satellite Corporation; the provision on common carrier telephone and telegraph services; the provision of submarine cable services; use of land and natural resources.[16]

Other common subject-specific exceptions deal with taxation, intellectual property rights, financial incentives, and public procurement.[17] Express general exceptions may include measures aimed at protecting public health, order and morals, and national security.[18]

---

[12] SN: *See, e.g.,* Energy Charter Treaty (ECT), art. 10(7). *See also* Jamaica-U.K. BIT (1987), art. 3.

[13] SN: *See, e.g.,* U.S. Model BIT . . . art. 3 ("1. Each Party shall accord to investors of the other Party treatment no less favorable than that it accords, in like circumstances, to its own investors with respect to the establishment, acquisition, expansion, management, conduct, operation, and sale or other disposition of investments in its territory 2. Each Party shall accord to covered investments treatment no less favorable than that it accords, in like circumstances, to investments in its own territory of its own investors with respect to the establishment, acquisition, expansion, management, conduct, and sale or other disposition of investments.").

[14] SN: North American Free Trade Agreement (NAFTA), art. 1102(1).

[15] SN: *See, e.g.,* U.S. Model BIT, art. 3; NAFTA, art. 1102(1)-(2); Canada-Chile Free Trade Agreement (1997), art. G-02(1)-(2); U.K.-Belize BIT (1982), art. 3(1) ("Neither Contracting Party shall . . . subject investments or returns of nationals or companies of the other Contracting Party to treatment less favorable than that which it accords in the same circumstances to investments or returns of its own nationals").

[16] SN: Protocol to U.S.-Argentina BIT (1991). Pursuant to NAFTA's Annex II, each Contracting Party is permitted to make reservations with respect to industries in which restrictive measures are permissible. Existing exceptions include, *inter alia,* Mexico's primary energy sector and railroads, U.S. airlines and radio communications, and Canada's cultural industries.

[17] SN: *See, e.g.,* South Korea-Mongolia BIT (1991), art. 7 (b); U.S. Model BIT, *pass.*; U.K.-Jamaica BIT, art. 3; NAFTA, art. 1108(7)(a)-(b). *See also* Peter Muchlinski, *Multinational Enterprises and the Law,* 241, 269 (1995).

[18] SN: *See* Protocol to Germany-Pakistan BIT (1959) ("Measures taken for reasons of public security and order, public health or morality shall not be deemed as discrimination").

2. Application of the National Treatment Standard

In recent years, international tribunals have had numerous opportunities, especially under Article 1102 of the North American Free Trade Agreement (NAFTA), to examine and analyze the concept of national treatment.[19] The resulting decisions reveal a basic framework for adjudicating such claims centering on three fact-driven questions. First, what is the relative class of comparators (i.e., are the subjects in *like circumstances*)? What treatment did each comparator receive (i.e., was it more or less favorable; and was there a justification for less favorable treatment)?[20] Finally, what was the host state's intent and does it make any difference?

Despite deceptively simple treaty language, the application of the national treatment standard is quite complex.[21] For example, arbitral tribunals have questioned how broadly or narrowly *like circumstances* or similar language should be interpreted. They have also questioned the substantive content of *less favorable treatment*, whether such treatment can result from the strict observance of the host nation's law, and how the burden of proof should be allocated. It should be noted that the elements of the framework previously discussed are interrelated, and separating them into distinct categories may not fully reflect the complexity of the interrelationship. However, a rough categorization may help the observer to understand better the analytical approach that arbitrators have taken to date.

a. Relevant Class of Comparators: *Like Circumstances*

As a preliminary matter, it is important to recognize that the national treatment standard does not protect qualifying investors from each and every instance of differential treatment by a host government. The plain language of Article 1102 of NAFTA makes clear a limitation that most commentators agree is implicit in the concept of discrimination: National treatment only protects foreign investors or investments that are in *like circumstances* with a national investor or investment. In many cases the issue of *likeness* is relatively simple, because the claimant and a local business are in direct competition with one another (e.g., if they are bidding on the same contract, they would seem *prima facie* to be in *like circumstances*). Such

---

[19] The early NAFTA cases played a very important role in developing a methodology for applying the national treatment standard. *See S.D. Myers, Inc. v. Canada* (UNICTRAL Arbitration, First Partial Award of Nov. 13, 2000); *Pope & Talbot Inc. v. Canada* (UNCITRAL/NAFTA Arbitration, Final Merits Award, Apr. 10, 2001); *Feldman v. Mexico*, ICSID Case No. ARB(AF)/99/1 (Final Award of Dec. 16, 2002).

[20] *Pope & Talbot*, supra note 19 (Award of Apr. 10, 2001), ¶¶ 31–81; *see* Todd Weiler, *The Treatment of SPS Measures under NAFTA Chapter 11: Preliminary Answers to an Open-Ended Question*, 26 B.C. Int'l & Comp. L. Rev. 229, 240 (2003).

[21] *Feldman*, supra note 19, ¶ 166 ("Despite its deceptively simple language, the interpretive hurdles for Article 1102 [NAFTA's national treatment investment provision] are several").

was the case in *ADF v. United States*,[22] where the arbitration panel assumed, without discussion, that American-owned producers of steel were similarly situated with a Canadian-owned producer of steel.[23] Both businesses produced the same product and both were competing for the same contract. Thus, the treatment they had received could be compared for the purposes of the national treatment standard.

Determining the relevant class of comparators may not be as easy in every case, however. One of the first NAFTA investment disputes, *S.D. Myers, Inc. v. Canada*,[24] applied a "competitive relationship" test. In that case, a Michigan-based hazardous waste facility that contracted with Canadian companies to process their polychlorinated biphenyl (PCB) across the border challenged the Canadian government's decision to ban all exports of PCB. Relying on decisions of panels adjudicating trade disputes in the World Trade Organization/General Agreement on Tariffs and Trade (WTO/GATT) system, the tribunal stated that "like treatment" had to be considered in the overall legal context, which necessarily included an examination of the host nation's environmental and trade concerns, as well as any other "circumstances that would justify governmental regulation that treats [foreign investors] differently in order to protect the public interest."[25] The tribunal also relied on a 1993 declaration by the Organization for Economic Cooperation and Development (OECD), which stated that "likeness" effectively meant "same sector."[26] Based on this analysis, the tribunal concluded that the "word 'sector' has a wide connotation that includes the concepts of 'economic sector' and 'business sector.' "[27] The tribunal then found that the American waste facility was comparable to several Canadian businesses, because the companies "all were engaged in providing PCB waste remediation services."[28] The tribunal paid particular attention to the fact that the American company competed with the Canadian companies for prospective business, and that such competition could result in lost business opportunities for the Canadian companies.[29] Indeed, it was the American company's ability "to take business away from its Canadian competitors" that was a critical factor in establishing like circumstances under Article 1102 of NAFTA.[30]

---

[22] *ADF Group, Inc. v. U.S.*, ICSID Case No. ARB(AF)/00/1 (Final Award of Jan. 9, 2003).

[23] *Id.* ¶¶ 150–58.

[24] *S.D. Myers, supra* note 19.

[25] *Id.* ¶ 250; *see also id.* ¶¶ 244–47 (citing, in part, *Japan–Alcoholic Beverages*, WT/DS38/AB/R). World Trade Organization (WTO) jurisprudence interpreting the concept of *like product* with respect to national treatment for trade in goods has often been put to use by analogy in investment protection orbitration.

[26] *Id.* ¶ 248.

[27] *Id.* ¶ 250.

[28] *Id.*

[29] *Id.*

[30] *Id.*

Not all NAFTA cases have focused solely on the competitive relationship between companies when determining whether they are in like circumstances. In *Pope & Talbot Inc. v. Canada*,[31] an American lumber company argued that Canada had violated the national treatment standard by establishing quota limits through a regulation called Export Control Regime, which was designed to implement Canada's obligations under the Canada–United States Softwood Lumber Agreement (SLA). Under the SLA, Canada was required to charge a fee for exports of softwood lumber from the Canadian provinces of Alberta, British Columbia, Ontario, and Quebec whenever the exports of individual companies exceeded a certain volume. Exports from other provinces were not subject to these limitations. Among other things, Pope & Talbot argued that this regime granted more favorable treatment to investments that were located in the latter provinces. Canada replied that the limits set by the regime were the result of implementing the SLA, that they were thus legitimate policy measures adopted to reduce the threat of U.S. countervailing duty measures which at the time had only been imposed on the exports from the four designated provinces, and that the regime had been applied without regard to nationality to all lumber producers in Canada.

In analyzing the likeness of the comparators, the tribunal acknowledged the importance of the legal and factual context in determining likeness. This legal context included more than the language and history of NAFTA, and encompassed the SLA and Canada's obligations under that agreement.[32] As the tribunal noted, this latter context was important, because different "treatment will presumptively violate Article 1102(2), unless . . . [there] is a reasonable nexus to rational government policies that . . . do not distinguish, on their face or *de facto*, between foreign-owned and domestic companies."[33] Although the tribunal recognized that Canada's effective limitation on the export of softwood lumber adversely affected an American company more than some Canadian companies, the different treatment was based on the location within Canada of the American company, rather than its nationality. Further, the tribunal found Canada's explanation as to why the four provinces were singled out (i.e., the threat of the U.S. duties) to be a rational response to a legitimate policy concern.[34] It also emphasized that the policy was applied in equal measure to all lumber producers within a particular province. Given this legal and factual context, the tribunal held that the American company was not in like circumstances with any Canadian investor, and rejected its national treatment claim.[35] In effect, the tribunal found that Canada's obligations under the SLA took precedence over Canada's non-discrimination obligations under Article 1102 of NAFTA.

---

[31] *Pope & Talbot, supra* note 19.
[32] *Id.* ¶ 77.
[33] *Id.* ¶ 78.
[34] *Id.* ¶ 87.
[35] *Id.* ¶¶ 87–88.

The contextual analysis endorsed in *Pope & Talbot* was further supported by dicta in *Feldman v. Mexico*. In *Feldman*, the tribunal examined whether the Mexican government had violated Article 1102 of NAFTA by granting tax rebates to Mexican-owned resellers/exporters of cigarettes, but refusing the same rebates for an American-owned reseller/exporter. The Mexican government's denial of the rebates was because the U.S.-owned company could not produce itemized invoices specifically showing the amount of tax paid for the cigarettes, as required by Mexican law. The requirement was impossible to meet because the retail source of its purchases (i.e., Wal-Mart and Sam's Club) did not and could not provide such invoices. The claimant showed that similarly-situated Mexican companies, which purchased their cigarettes from the same retail sources (and, thus, could not have had itemized invoices), nonetheless received rebates during the relevant time. Finally, the U.S.-owned company offered evidence that the Mexican government had denied its export license and initiated an audit of the company, but not of the Mexican companies, after it challenged the Mexican government's denial of the rebates.[36]

The tribunal explained that "the concept of discrimination has been defined to imply *unreasonable* distinctions between foreign and domestic investors in like circumstances."[37] Although the US and Mexican companies appeared to be in substantially identical cirumstances—Mexico had, in fact, conceded the likeness of the American and Mexican companies—the tribunal nevertheless adopted a narrow interpretation of like circumstances. Then in dicta it dealt with whether Mexico's distinction in its laws between producers of cigarettes, on the one hand, and reseller/exporters of cigarettes, on the other, had any bearing on the determination of likeness. The tribunal noted that there may be "some rational basis for treating producers [of cigarettes] and re-sellers differently," and that such reasonable distinctions limited the "universe" of comparators in the case to resellers/exporters of cigarettes.[38] The tribunal then concluded that the U.S.-owned company and the Mexican exporters/resellers of cigarettes were in sufficiently similar circumstances.

The tribunal in *GAMI v. Mexico*[39] took a similar interpretative approach to the issue of likeness by giving weight to the government's policy choices. In *GAMI*, through

---

[36] *Feldman, supra* note 19, ¶¶ 155–56.

[37] *Id.* ¶ 170 (citing U.S. Restatement. Comment f) (emphasis in original).

[38] *Id.* ¶¶ 170–71. The tribunal stated that the following policy reasons could justify such a distinction: ". . . discouragement of smuggling (of cigarettes purportedly exported back into Mexico), which may deprive a government of substantial amounts of tax revenue, maintenance of high cigarette taxes to discourage smoking (as in Canada) and, as a Mexican government official has suggested, assisting producers in complying with trademark licensing obligations under private agreements. . . ." *Id.* ¶ 115.

[39] *GAMI Investments, Inc. v. Mexico* (NAFTA Arbitration under UNCITRAL Rules, Final Award of Nov. 15, 2004), 44 I.L.M. 545 (2005).

DISCRIMINATION

a nationalization program, the Mexican government had expropriated a number of sugar mills belonging to Grupo Azucarero México S.A. de C.V. (GAM), a Mexican company in which GAMI, a U.S. Delaware company, held a 14.1 percent stake. GAMI argued that Mexico's measures violated Article 1102 of NAFTA because its expropriated sugar mills were in like circumstances with other sugar mills that had not been expropriated. The tribunal rejected this argument, however, mainly because the government demonstrated a legitimate policy reason for the contested measure,[40] which was "neither applied in a discriminatory manner nor designed as a disguised barrier to equal opportunity."[41]

The question of likeness was also raised in *Methanex v. United States*.[42] In that case Methanex Corporation, a Canadian company and the largest producer of methanol in the world, claimed that certain measures adopted by the state of California that banned MTBE (methyl tertiary butyl ether), a gasoline additive and a methanol derivative, violated various articles of NAFTA, including Article 1102. Methanex asserted that the measures were intended to favor U.S. producers of ethanol, another gasoline additive, and that MTBE and methanol were *like* ethanol. The tribunal, however, stated that "it would be as perverse to ignore identical comparators if they were available and to use comparators that were less 'like,' as it would be perverse to refuse to find and to apply less 'like' comparators when no identical comparators existed."[43] Accordingly, it held that Methanex was more like domestic methanol producers than domestic ethanol producers. Because all producers of methanol (US and foreign) had been treated identically,[44] it dismissed Methanex's national treatment claim.

The "likeness" issue was also critical in *UPS v. Canada*.[45] In 2000, United Parcel Service of America (UPS), a U.S. company in the business of courier and package delivery, filed a claim against Canada for violating several NAFTA provisions, including Article 1102. UPS alleged that it was in like circumstances with the Canada Post Corporation, a Canadian company that had a legal monopoly over mail services, and also participated in the courier delivery sectors. The core of the UPS's likeness argument was that it "competed in the same market and for the same market share" and Canada Post non-monopoly products were generally substitutable with UPS courier products.[46]

---

[40] The government's goal was to ensure that the sugar industry was in the hands of solvent enterprises. *Id.* ¶ 114.

[41] *Id.*

[42] *Methanex v. U.S.* (NAFTA Arbitration under UNCITRAL rules, Award of Aug. 3, 2005).

[43] *Id.* Pt. IV, Ch. B ¶ 17.

[44] The *Methanex* tribunal also questioned whether the "like circumstances" analysis under the WTO and General Agreement on Tariffs and Trade (GATT) system was applicable in the context of investment treaty arbitration. *Id.* ¶ 30.

[45] *United Parcel Service v. Canada* (NAFTA Arbitration under UNCITRAL rules, Award of June 11, 2007).

[46] *Id.* ¶ 87.

Ultimately, the tribunal members could not reach a consensus on this issue. The majority held that the two entities were not alike, because Canada Post's mail service was different from UPS's courier service.[47] The majority noted that a number of states and international organizations, including the United States, the United Kingdom, and the World Customs Organization, recognized differences between courier and mailing services.[48] Furthermore, the difference was acknowledged in several international conventions.[49] Arbitrator Ronald Cass dissented, opining that UPS and Canada Post were "like service providers" and that their services were interchangeable.[50] In his view UPS had met its *prima facie* burden to demonstrate comparability, and Canada had failed to rebut the evidence.[51]

At least two non-NAFTA cases have also dealt with the issue of likeness: *Champion Trading v. Egypt*[52] and *Occidental v. Ecuador*.[53] In *Champion Trading*, the claimants, two American companies, alleged that Egypt had violated several provisions of the Egypt–U.S. BIT, including Article II(2)(a) on national treatment.[54] The claimants alleged that Egypt's design and implementation of a program to eliminate the government's debt to certain cotton producers who chose to sell their crop to the government rather than in the free market was *prima facie* discriminatory. They further argued that it was Egypt's burden to show that the

---

[47] *Id.* ¶¶ 98–99.

[48] *Id.* ¶ 103.

[49] *Id.* ¶ 115 (citing Annex F4 of the Kyoto Convention: "The Customs are necessarily involved in international postal traffic since, just as in the case of goods imported and exported by other means, they have to ensure that the appropriate duties and taxes are collected, enforce import and export prohibitions and restrictions, and in general ensure compliance with the laws and regulations which they are responsible for enforcing. Because of the special nature of postal traffic, however, the Customs formalities in respect of items carried by post are somewhat different from those applied to goods carried by other means. While individual postal items are restricted in size, their numbers are enormous and, to avoid creating unacceptable delays, special administrative arrangements are necessary to deal with them. These are made possible because in virtually all countries the postal services are furnished by public administrations or authorities, and the two public bodies involved in postal traffic, the Post and the Customs, cooperate very closely with one another").

[50] *Id.* ¶¶ 23, 63.

[51] *Id.* ¶ 39.

[52] *Champion Trading Co. & Ameritrade Int'l, Inc. v. Egypt*, ICSID Case No. ARB/02/9 (Award of October 27, 2006).

[53] *Occidental Exploration & Production Co. v. Ecuador*, LCIA Case No. UN3467 (Final Award of July 1, 2004).

[54] U.S.-Egypt BIT, art. II(2)(a) ("Each Party shall accord investments in its territory, and associated activities in connection with these investments of nationals or companies of the other Party, treatment no less favorable than that accorded in like situations to investments of its own nationals and companies or to investments of nationals and companies of any third country, whichever is most favorable").

program was based on reasonable, non-discriminatory policies that did not violate the national treatment principle. The tribunal at the outset noted that the non-discrimination provision of Article II(2)(a) prohibited discrimination based on nationality. As to whether the Egyptian recipients of settlement payments were in like situation as the claimants, the tribunal adopted the *Pope & Talbot* definition, and found that *in like situation* means operating within the same business or economic sector.[55] The tribunal eventually concluded that claimants and the Egyptian recipients were not sufficiently similar, mainly because claimants had not participated in the government's sale and purchase program at centers designated by the government. As a result, it dismissed the case.[56]

In *Occidental*, the tribunal interpreted likeness quite broadly,[57] comparing enterprises that belonged to different economic sectors, unlike the arbitrators in *Pope & Talbot* and *SD Myers*. The *Occidental* case arose out of a change in the official interpretation of Ecuador's value-added tax (VAT) reimbursement formula, which was included in a participation contract (the "Contract") entered into between Occidental Exploration and Production Co. (OEPC), a U.S. oil company, and Petroecuador, a state-owned corporation.[58] Under the Contract, OEPC regularly applied to the Ecuadorian Internal Revenue Service ("SRI") for the reimbursement of VAT paid by the company on certain expenses, and the SRI calculated the reimbursement based upon a particular formula.[59] In 2001, however, the government issued resolutions stopping the reimbursements to OEPC and other oil companies. It claimed that the VAT reimbursement amount was already reflected in the contract formula and the oil companies should not be further reimbursed for the VAT. It also demanded the return of the amounts previously paid.[60]

After unsuccessful recourse to local courts, OEPC commenced arbitration against Ecuador under the United States-Ecuador BIT.[61] The tribunal dismissed OEPC's expropriation claim, but found that Ecuador had breached its obligation to accord national treatment as well as other obligations.[62] The applicable national treatment clause, Article II(1) of the BIT, provides in relevant part:

---

[55] *Champion Trading Co.*, supra note 52, ¶ 130.
[56] *Id.* ¶¶ 155–56.
[57] Organization for Economic Cooperation and Development (OECD), *Declaration on International Investment and Multinational Enterprises, reprinted in* 15 I.L.M. 967 (1976).
[58] *Occidental*, supra note 53, ¶ 1.
[59] *Id.* ¶¶ 2, 27–28.
[60] *Id.* ¶¶ 3, 29.
[61] *Id.* ¶ 6.
[62] *Id.* ¶ 200.

> 1. Each Party shall permit and treat investment, and activities associated therewith, on a basis no less favorable than that accorded in like situations to investment or associated activities of its own nationals or companies, or of nationals or companies of any third country, whichever is the most favorable, subject to the right of each Party to make or maintain exceptions falling within one of the sectors or matters listed in the Protocol to this Treaty . . . .

OEPC argued that Ecuador had breached Article II(1) because a number of companies that exported other goods (e.g., flowers, mining, seafood products, lumber, and bananas) continued to receive the VAT refund. OEPC also argued that local companies in like situations not only included those involved in the same sector of activity as OEPC, such as oil producers, but also to companies engaged in exports, even in other economic sectors.[63] Finally, OEPC argued that Ecuador had failed to accord MFN treatment to OEPC because under the BITs between Ecuador and Spain and Argentina, the standard of treatment was not qualified by the reference to *in like situations*. OEPC was thus entitled to this less restrictive treatment under the MFN clause.[64]

Ecuador replied that in like situations could only refer to companies operating in the same sector, in this case oil producers. "The comparison . . . cannot be extended to other sectors because the whole purpose of the VAT refund policy is to ensure that the conditions of competition are not changed, a scrutiny that is relevant only in the same sector."[65] It further contended that it did not treat foreign-owned companies and national companies differently, because it had denied VAT refunds to Petroecuador as well, and there was nothing in that policy that intended to discriminate against foreign-owned companies.[66]

The tribunal agreed with OEPC: "In fact, in like situations cannot be interpreted in the narrow sense advanced by Ecuador, as the purpose of national treatment is to protect investors as compared to local producers, and this cannot be done by addressing exclusively the sector in which that particular activity is undertaken."[67] Discussions of *like products* in the WTO context (e.g., competitive relationship, etc.) were not specifically pertinent to the issues involved in the case.[68] Although the tribunal found that Ecuador had not intended to discriminate against foreign-owned companies, that was the

---

[63] *Id.* ¶ 168.
[64] *Id.* ¶ 170.
[65] *Id.* ¶ 171.
[66] *Id.* ¶ 172.
[67] *Id.* ¶ 173.
[68] "In fact, the purpose of national treatment in this dispute is the opposite of that under the GATT/WTO, namely it is to avoid exporters being placed at the disadvantage in foreign markets because of the indirect taxes paid in the country of origin, while in GATT/WTO the purpose is to avoid imported products being affected by a distortion of competition with similar domestic products because of taxes and other regulations in the country of destination." *Id.* ¶ 175.

consequence. "[T]he result of the policy enacted and the interpretation followed by the SRI in fact has been a less favorable treatment of OEPC."[69]

Given the different outcomes in *Feldman, Pope & Talbot, S.D. Myers,* and later cases such as *UPS* and *Champion Trading*, it may appear at first glance that an interpretative divide has developed regarding the definition and application of like circumstances. However, any conflict in the decisions may be more apparent than real. In each case, the tribunal employed a detailed examination of the factual and legal context to determine whether there were *like* circumstances. Each tribunal considered similarities between the investors and investments (the sector or competition tests). Furthermore, in the context of the NAFTA cases, arbitrators also considered the purpose of NAFTA and the government's right to impose reasonable, non-discriminatory policies.

The cases seem to suggest a two-pronged analysis for determining likeness: (1) an examination of the competitive relationship between the investors and investments, and (2) a determination whether there was a reasonable governmental basis for differential treatment. *Occidental v. Ecuador*, in so far as it suggests an extremely broad definition of likeness, has found only limited support in the arbitral awards[70] and scholarly writings.[71] Ultimately, whether investors and investments will be considered sufficiently comparable will hinge on a thorough analysis of the particular facts and circumstances.

b. Relevant Standard of Treatment: No Less Favorably

National treatment provisions apply to two types of governmental measures: (1) measures that are *de jure* discriminatory;[72] and (2) measures that are *de facto* discriminatory. The latter measures are not discriminatory on their face, but they *effectively* discriminate against foreign investors or investments that quality for BIT protection.

---

[69] *Id.* ¶ 177.

[70] The *Methanex* tribunal seemed to agree with *Occidental*'s statement regarding the differences between the international trade jurisprudence and international investment and the applicability of the concepts developed in the former field to the latter. *See Methanex, supra* note 42, at Pt. IV, Ch. B, ¶¶ 29, 37.

[71] *See, e.g.*, Susan Franck, *International Decision: Occidental Exploration & Production Co. v. Republic of Ecuador*, 99 Am. J. Int'l L. 675 (2005). *See also* Campbell McLachlan, Laurence Shore, & Matthew Weiniger, *International Investment Arbitration* 252 (Oxford University Press 2007) (characterizing the finding of the tribunal in this respect as "questionable"); Meg N. Kinnear, Andrea K. Bjorklund, & John F. G. Hannaford, *Investment Disputes under NAFTA: An Annotated Guide to NAFTA Chapter 11, Article 1102*, 1102-33, 34. (Kluwer 2006) ("Comparing foreign- and domestic-controlled enterprises that operate in different sectors may be reasonable in certain situations, but it also may hamper a government which has legitimate reasons to treat investors in certain economic sectors differently from those in other sectors").

[72] Such a measure could be a law promulgated by a government that explicitly grants benefits or subsidies only to local investors or investments.

The issue of whether treatment given to foreigners is less favorable than that enjoyed by locals, like the issue of like circumstances, depends primarily on the terms of the applicable treaty and the facts surrounding the alleged discriminatory treatment. Tribunals have considered the plain language of the national treatment provision of an agreement, the purpose of the provision in the context of the overall agreement, and the facts and legal regime surrounding the alleged discriminatory conduct to determine whether a foreign investor has been treated less favorably.

Again, the decision in *Pope & Talbot, Inc.* is instructive. The Canadian government challenged the discrimination claim by arguing that less favorable treatment required the investor to show that it had been treated worse than *all* other similarly situated Canadian investors. The tribunal rejected this argument based on the plain language of Article 1102 and the policy underlying NAFTA. The tribunal found that "no less favorable" treatment means "treatment equivalent to the 'best' treatment accorded to domestic investors or investments in like circumstances" to domestic investors.[73] Thus, the tribunal concluded that "no less favorable" had to mean "equivalent to, not better or worse than, the best treatment accorded to the comparator."[74]

Similarly, the tribunal rejected Canada's defense that *de facto* discrimination (*i.e.*, the discriminatory application of an otherwise neutral law) had to be established as a higher burden of proof—a *disproportionately disadvantaged* test. Under this test, the Canadian government argued, an American investor could not succeed on a claim of *de facto* discrimination unless it proved treatment worse than treatment received by *a majority* of similar Canadian investors.[75] The tribunal again turned to the plain language of Article 1102 and found that no such requirement appeared in NAFTA.[76] Nor could such an interpretation be squared with the policy objectives of NAFTA—that is, "to promote conditions of fair competition and to increase substantial investment opportunities."[77] On the contrary, the tribunal concluded:

> Simply to state this approach is to show how unwieldy it would be and how it would hamstring foreign owned investments seeking to vindicate their Article 1102 rights. Only in the simplest and most obvious cases of denial of national treatment could the complainant hope to make a case for recovery. The tribunal is unwilling to take a step that would so weaken the provisions and objectives of NAFTA and, for the reasons stated, rejects Canada's disproportionate disadvantage test.[78]

As for whether discrimination had in fact occurred, the tribunal seemed satisfied that the American company had demonstrated a *prima facie* case of less favorable

---

[73] *Pope & Talbot, Inc., supra* note 19, ¶ 42.
[74] *Id.*
[75] *Id.* ¶¶ 43–44 (footnotes omitted).
[76] *Id.* ¶ 44.
[77] *Id.* ¶ 70.
[78] *Id.* ¶ 72.

treatment. In fact, the parties agreed that the American company, as well as some Canadian companies, had been treated differently (and presumably less favorably) than other Canadian companies. The tribunal then turned its focus to whether "there is a reasonable nexus between the measure and a rational, non-discriminatory policy, whether those policies are embodied in statute, regulation or international agreement."[79] The tribunal concluded that there was in fact a sufficient basis for different treatment as between the companies in question, because Canada was required to implement the Softwood Lumber Agreement in this way.[80] On this basis, the tribunal held that there was no violation of the national treatment standard.

Feldman v. Mexico also addressed the meaning of less favorable treatment under Article 1102 of NAFTA. In that case, as previously noted, the tribunal examined a claim that the Mexican government had violated the national treatment standard by denying tax rebates to an American exporter while the rebates were available to similarly situated Mexican companies. Although the tribunal acknowledged that the record contained limited evidence of discrimination,[81] the majority concluded that the limited evidence was sufficient to establish "a presumption and *prima facie* case" of less favorable treatment.[82] The tribunal then determined that once the claimants had provided a sufficient showing of less favorable treatment, the burden shifted to the respondent government either to rebut that presumption or to provide a reasonable basis for the difference in treatment.[83]

Applying this standard, the majority of the tribunal found that the American company had met its initial burden by showing that no reseller/exporter of cigarettes in Mexico could qualify for rebates under Mexican law, the American reseller was denied such rebates, and yet at least one like Mexican company did receive the rebates for a period of time.[84] The Mexican government did not offer any evidence to rebut the resulting presumption that the American company had been treated less favorably than at least one Mexican company.[85] Accordingly, the tribunal determined that Mexico had violated the national treatment standard under Article 1102 of NAFTA by failing to provide the rebates to the American investor.

The result in *Pope & Talbot* and *Feldman* can usefully be compared to *ADF Group Inc.*[86] There, a Canadian-owned company challenged a United States highway

---

[79] *Id.* ¶ 81. For a discussion of the SLA see p. 402 *supra*.
[80] *Id.* ¶¶ 83–104.
[81] *Feldman*, *supra* note 19, ¶ 176.
[82] *Id.*
[83] *Id.* ¶¶ 176–77.
[84] *Id.* ¶ 176.
[85] *Id.*
[86] *ADF Group*, *supra* note 22.

construction program that had a "buy America" requirement for the steel used in bridge construction. Unlike the preceding cases, the tribunal failed to find a *prima facie* case of discrimination or less favorable treatment. The tribunal noted that under the bridge construction contract all companies were treated identically, whether foreign or domestic: they all had to use steel made in the United States.[87] In this regard, as the United States argued, the Canadian claimant could have used steel from its own facility located in the United States, purchased steel from another United States facility, or chosen not to bid on the contract.[88] Regardless of the option it chose, these were the same options that each prospective bidder faced. Thus, there was no less favorable treatment.

Moreover, although the Canadian company raised a claim of *de facto* discrimination, it submitted no proof that the implementation of the "buy America" policy resulted in less favorable treatment. To that end, as the tribunal noted, "specific evidence concerning the comparative economics of the situation would be relevant, including: whether the cost of fabrication [of steel] was significantly lower in Canada; whether fabrication capacity was unavailable at that time in the United States and whether transportation costs to Canada were sufficiently low to make up the differential."[89] Without such evidence, the tribunal concluded that the Canadian company had failed to establish that "the U.S. measures imposed (*de jure* or *de facto*) . . . less favorable treatment. . . ."[90]

c. Proof of Discriminatory Intent Based on Nationality[91]

Discriminatory intent has received considerable attention in recent national treatment cases. The issue is whether a government measure must be shown not only to accord less favorable treatment to qualified foreign investors, but also to have been designed by the government to achieve that effect. According to most arbitral tribunals, proof of discriminatory intent is not essential to establishing a breach of the national treatment standard. The *S.D. Myers* tribunal concluded that although intent may be important, "protectionist intent is not necessarily decisive on its own."[92] Rather, "protectionist intent" is one of many factors that should be considered in analyzing a national treatment claim.[93]

The tribunals in *Feldman* and *Pope & Talbot* reached the same conclusion from a slightly different angle. In these two cases, the respondents argued that Article 1102

---

[87] *Id.* ¶ 156.
[88] *Id.*
[89] *Id.* ¶ 157.
[90] *Id.*
[91] See generally Borzu Sabahi, *National Treatment—Is Discriminatory Intent Relevant?*, in *Investment Treaty Arbitration: A Debate and Discussion* (Weiler ed., Juris Publishing 2008); Sylvie Tabet, *National Treatment—Is Discriminatory Intent Relevant?*, in *id.*
[92] *Pope & Talbot, supra* note 19, ¶¶ 252–54.
[93] *Id.*

of NAFTA is only violated where the host country knew of the foreign investor's nationality and discriminated against it for that reason.[94] The tribunals in *Feldman* and *Pope & Talbot* rejected this requirement, because such a policy would be difficult or nearly impossible to prove and would effectively limit national treatment to *de jure* claims.[95] Instead, the tribunals determined that intentional discrimination is one factor to consider after a claimant establishes a *prima facie* case of discrimination. At this point the tribunal should consider, among other things, whether the policy was a result of intentional, discriminatory conduct or the policy "has a reasonable nexus to rational government policies."[96] Proof of discriminatory intent could also be difficult when there is little information available about the treatment or the existence of the comparable investors/investments.[97] In such situations the claimant "has to demonstrate that a certain measure was directed specifically against a certain investor by reason of his, her or its nationality. . . ."[98] Thus, when a claimant can show a differential treatment on a prima facie basis, the proof of intent could become irrelevant, because the burden of proof shifts to the government to prove that its measures had a reasonable connection to a rational policy.[99] This normally requires the government show that its motives or intentions were directed at something other than harming foreign investors/investments.

According to some commentators, proof of discriminatory intent could lead to an increase of the amount of damages that a foreign investor is entitled to receive.[100] In any event, clear proof of discriminatory intent can provide a tribunal with a measure of comfort in its decision that the government has indeed violated the national treatment obligation. Proof of discriminatory intent could be especially helpful when a measure is general in nature and ostensibly affects both domestic and foreign investors.

The issue of intent surfaced in *Methanex v. United States* in a perplexing way. The *Methanex* tribunal stated at the outset that, in principle, malign intent need not be proven to succeed in a national treatment claim.[101] The arbitrators nevertheless included intent as part of the test for violation of Article 1102 that the claimant was

---

[94] See *Feldman, supra* note 19, ¶ 181; *Pope & Talbot, supra* note 19, ¶ 79.

[95] See *Feldman, supra* note 19, ¶ 183 ("requiring a foreign investor to prove that discrimination is based on his nationality could be an insurmountable burden to the Claimant, as that information may only be available to the government"); *Pope & Talbot, supra* note 19, ¶ 79 (such an approach "would tend to excuse discrimination that is not facially directed at foreign owned investments").

[96] *Feldman, supra* note 19, ¶ 184; *see also, Pope & Talbot, supra* note 19, ¶ 79.

[97] See generally Sabahi, *supra* note 91.

[98] *Noble Ventures v. Romania*, ICSID Case No. ARB/01/11 (Award of Oct. 12, 2005), ¶ 180.

[99] See *Champion Trading, supra* note 52, ¶ 133.

[100] Brownlie, *supra* note 2, at 46.

[101] *Methanex, supra* note 42, at Pt. IV Ch. B ¶ 1.

expected to satisfy.[102] Despite the apparent contradiction, a close reading of the case reveals a unifying understanding of state intent in an earlier Partial Award rendered by the *Methanex* tribunal. The Partial Award dealt with the overarching jurisdictional issue of whether the government measures in question were "relating to" the claimant or its investments as required by NAFTA Article 1101(1).[103] In the earlier decision, the tribunal concluded that the Article 1101(1) requirement of "relating to" signified something more than a mere effect of the measure on the investor; it demanded proof of a "legally significant connection" between the measure and the affected investor/investment.[104] Upon the examination of the record, the tribunal ruled that Methanex's allegations did not meet this requirement, except the allegation that California had purposely targeted Methanex. With this ruling in the background, the analysis of the tribunal in the Final Award necessarily focused on whether the United States through California had intended to discriminate. Thus, the tribunal included intent as one of the requirements of the test for violation of Article 1102:

> [T]he better explanation for the *Methanex* tribunal's requirement of intent seems to be that it was case specific; the tribunal's decision was driven by the particular factual allegations of the claimant. These allegations narrowed the scope of the issues before the tribunal to those that were based on the intentional targeting of Methanex by the U.S.[105]

B. Most Favored Nation Treatment

1. Introduction

The MFN principle is one of the most venerable standards of treatment in international economic law.[106] The first examples of MFN clauses can be traced back to as early as the eleventh century.[107] The MFN clauses in modern investment treaties,

---

[102] *Id.*, Pt. IV, Ch. B, ¶ 12.

[103] *See* NAFTA, art. 1101(1) ("1. This Chapter applies to measures adopted or maintained by a Party relating to. . . ."); *see also* the parties' submissions regarding the requirements of intent under Article 1101 of NAFTA in jurisdictional filings of the *Methanex* case, *available at* http://naftaclaims.com/disputes_us_methanex.htm.

[104] *See Methanex*, *supra* note 42 (Partial Award of Aug. 7, 2002), ¶ 150.

[105] Sabahi, *supra* note 91.

[106] For a discussion of the historical background of MFN clauses see generally Endre Ustor, *First Report on the Most-Favoured Nation Clause*, II Y.B. Int'l L. Comm'n 157 *et seq.* (1969), U.N. Doc. A/CN.4/213; *see also* Scott Vesel, *Clearing a Path through a Tangled Jurisprudence: Most-Favored-Nation Clauses and Dispute Settlement Provisions in Bilateral Investment Treaties*, 32 Yale J. Int'l L. 125, 138–36 (2007).

[107] Ustor, *supra* note 106, at 159. For a discussion of the earlier forms of MFN clauses see Vesel, *supra* note 106, at 129–30.

however, are modeled primarily on similar clauses in the GATT and other international trade agreements.

MFN clauses, like national treatment clauses, are extremely common in modern investment treaties. A typical MFN clause of an investment treaty provides that each contracting state shall treat investors of the other contracting state no less favorably than it treats investors of a third country. Thus, the focus of an MFN clause is on discriminatory treatment as between foreign investors of different nationalities, as opposed to discrimination in favor of local investors, which is the focus of national treatment clauses.

MFN and national treatment clauses are often included in the same provision of an investment treaty.[108] Sometimes, however, the MFN clauses may appear as a separate provision.[109] A typical example of the former is Article 3(1) of the Albania-Croatia BIT: "Neither Contracting Party shall subject investments of the other Contracting Party to treatment less favorable than that which it accords to investments of its own investors or to investments of investors of any third State."[110] Similar to national treatment, some treaties provide MFN treatment only after the entry of investment into the host state (i.e., in the post-establishment stage),[111] others provide such protections in both pre- and post-entry period.[112] Finally, MFN treatment is often subject to exceptions, which may be included in the same clause[113] or in other parts of the treaty.[114]

---

[108] See, e.g., Bulgaria-Israel BIT (1993), art. 3; Egypt-Greece BIT (1993), art. 3 (1); Chile-Tunisia BIT (1998), art. 4 (2); U.K.-Kenya BIT (1999), art. 3 (1).

[109] See, e.g., New Zealand-Singapore BIT (2000), art 28; see also NAFTA, art. 1103.

[110] Albania-Croatia BIT (1993).

[111] E.g., Mongolia-Singapore BIT (1995); France-India BIT (1997); Chile-South Africa BIT (1998); Argentina-New Zealand BIT (1999).

[112] "Examples of BITs falling within this category are, among others, the agreements between Japan, on the one hand, and Vietnam (2003) and the Republic of Korea (2002) on the other hand. Other Japanese BITs, although in principle only apply to established investment, do provide MFN treatment at the entry stage. That is the case of the BITs between Japan and Bangladesh (1998), Hong Kong (China) (1997) and the Russian Federation (1998), respectively. Furthermore, most of the BITs of the United States and Canada—after the mid-1990s—fall within this category." UNCTAD, *Bilateral Investment Treaties 1995–2006: Trends in Investment Rulemaking* 38 n.53, U.N. Doc UNCTAD/ITE/IIT/2006/5 [hereinafter UNCTAD 2006]. For a detailed examination of various MFN clauses and legal implications of each clause see UNCTAD 2006 and UNCTAD, *Most-Favoured-Nation Treatment*, U.N. Doc UNCTAD/ITE/IIT/10 (1999) [hereinafter UNCTAD 1999].

[113] See, e.g., Philippines-Thailand BIT (1987), art. 4(1) ("Investments made by nationals of either Contracting Party in the territory of the other Contracting Party, as also the returns therefrom, shall be subject to a treatment no less favorable than that accorded to investments and returns made by its own nationals or companies or by the nationals or companies of any third State, whichever is more favorable to the nationals and companies, *in areas allowed by existing laws, rules and regulations*." (emphasis added))

[114] See, e.g., the complex MFN carve-outs in NAFTA, art. 2103 with respect to taxation measures.

MOST FAVORED NATION TREATMENT

A typical exception to MFN treatment denies the investors from a particular state covered by a BIT the more beneficial economic opportunities that are available in the host state through a customs union, free trade area, or similar regional institution to which the investor's state is not a member.[115]

2. Scope and Interpretation of Most Favored Nation Clauses

There is no formula for determining the scope of an MFN clause. Like other treaty provisions, the scope must be determined, through interpretation pursuant to Article 31 of the Vienna Convention on the Law of Treaties (VCLT),[116] first based on the ordinary meaning of the particular text. It is therefore essential to examine the precise language of each MFN clause and to identify what has been included in or excluded from it. Tribunals also commonly apply the interpretative principle of *ejusdem generis*, finding that the putative beneficiary of an MFN clause acquires only those rights that fall within the limits of the subject matter of the underlying treaty[117] or of the MFN clause more specifically, if it enumerates the subjects the clause is meant to cover.[118]

The following excerpt by Noah Rubins explains various interpretative approaches to the scope of the MFN provisions in investment treaties:

> Noah Rubins, *MFN Clauses, Procedural Rights, and a Return to the Treaty Text*, in *Investment Treaty Arbitration: A Debate and Discussion* (Weiler ed., Juris Publishing 2008)
>
> The debate over the scope of MFN clauses has taken on a general character, but this is misleading, in light of the textual focus of Article 31 of the Vienna Convention. MFN clauses are at once among the most ubiquitous provisions in investment protection

---

[115] *See, e.g.*, Botswana-China BIT (2000), art. 3(4); for a complete examination of the variations in exceptions see the UNCTAD studies cited in *supra* note 112.

[116] Vienna Convention on the Law of Treaties, May 23, 1969, art 31(1), U.N. Doc. A/CONF.39/27 [hereinafter VCLT].

[117] The *basic treaty* refers to the treaty with an MFN clause that is invoked to import better treatment accorded to foreign investors under other treaties.

[118] The principle has also been described as follows: "an MFN clause can only attract matters belonging to the same subject matter or the same category of subject as to which the clause relates." OECD, *International Investment Law* 142 (2005); *see also* International Law Commission (ILC), *Draft Articles on Most-Favored-Nation Clauses Art. 9*, U.N. Doc A/CN.4/SER.A/1978/Add.1, reprinted in 2 Y.B. Int'l L Commission (1978) (Article 9 provides that:

> 1. Under a most-favoured-nation clause the beneficiary State acquires, for itself or for the benefit of persons or things in a determined relationship with it, only those rights which fall within the limits of the subject matter of the clause.
>
> 2. The beneficiary State acquires the rights under paragraph 1 only in respect of persons or things which are specified in the clause or implied from its subject matter.)

On *ejusdem generis, see also* Pia Acconci, *Most-Favoured-Nation Treatment and the International Law on Foreign Investment*, in *Oxford Handbook of International Investment Law* (P. Muchlinski, F. Ortino, C. Schreuer, eds., Oxford University Press 2008).

treaties, and among the most varied. The most essential area of variation for present purposes is the list of matters to which the MFN clause is to apply.

The simplest form of MFN clauses provide no such list, and instead set forth only the obligation to provide "treatment no less favorable" than that offered to third-party investors and/or investments. Swiss bilateral investment treaties, for example, often provide for "treatment [not] less favourable than . . . that granted by each Contracting Party to the investments made within its territory by investors of the most favoured nation. . . ."[119] This basic language seems somewhat ambiguous, because it is unclear from the text whether the State's consent to arbitrate disputes, or the right to do so under particular conditions or according to specific rules, constitutes "treatment" for purposes of the MFN clause.

However, most investment treaties set forth what appears to be an exhaustive list of matters to which MFN treatment is meant to apply. This is the most common approach taken in United States investment protection treaties.[120] A typical MFN clause is also found in the New Zealand-Singapore BIT:

> *Except as otherwise provided for in this Agreement, each Party shall accord to investors and investments of the other Party, in relation to the establishment, acquisition, expansion, management, conduct, operation, liquidation, sale, transfer (or other disposition), protection and expropriation (including any compensation) of investments, treatment that is no less favourable than that it accords in like situations to investors and investments from any other State or separate customs territory which is not party to this Agreement.*[121]

Some German BITs codify this approach in a more concise manner, by limiting the scope of MFN treatment to investors' "activity in connection with investments" in the territory of the host State.[122] It seems relatively clear that these MFN clauses of limited scope are intended to cover the investment activities of the investor and/or its investment vehicle, *i.e.* matters related to making money, and not matters related to vindicating rights through international arbitration.

Finally, a number of investment treaties add to the general coverage of the MFN clause a qualification indicating that all matters covered by the treaty are subject to the MFN treatment obligation. The treaty between Spain and Argentina, for example, provides:

> *In all matters subject to this Agreement, this treatment shall not be less favourable than that extended by each Party to the investments made in its territory by investors of a third party.*[123]

This language would seem unambiguous. While consent to arbitration may not clearly fall within the category of "treatment" without further qualification, there can be little doubt that dispute resolution is one of the "matters covered" by the BIT.

Thus, there appear to be three textual approaches to the scope of MFN treatment in investment treaties. The limited MFN clause and the all-inclusive MFN clause yield an

---

[119] SN: Switzerland-Czechoslovakia BIT (1990), art. 4(2).

[120] SN: United States-Georgia BIT (1994), art. II(1).

[121] SN: New Zealand-Singapore BIT (2000), art. 2.

[122] SN: Germany-Syria BIT (1977), art. 3(2). Some BITs go still further, expressly limiting the MFN obligation to treatment accorded pursuant to the substantive provisions of the treaty (fair and equitable treatment, prohibition against arbitrary and discriminatory measures, etc. The Belgium/Luxembourg-Turkey BIT (1990), art. 3(3).

[123] SN: Spain-Argentina BIT (1991), art. 4(2).

"ordinary meaning" through a plain reading that is unambiguous. In the former clause type, the "ordinary meaning" would appear to exclude the application of the clause to procedural rights, while the latter type would appear on its face to permit the importation of procedural rights from third-party treaties. Only in the case of the most general formulation of MFN treatment, which appears in a minority of investment treaties, would there seem to be any ambiguity justifying reference to circumstances extraneous to the treaty itself. As explained below, however, many of the arbitral tribunals that have examined this issue have taken a different view.

3. Application of MFN Clauses to Substantive and Procedural Rights

The interpretation and application of MFN clauses can be challenging in practice. The focal point of current debate in this respect is the question of whether MFN clauses only apply to substantive rights, or to procedural rights as well. Arbitral tribunals have generally applied MFN clauses to substantive rights,[124] while the application of MFN to procedural rights, fueled by the decision of the tribunal in *Maffezini v. Spain*, has been subject to a tremendous amount of debate in the legal community.[125] The issue became more controversial when the tribunal in *Plama v. Bulgaria*[126] expressly disagreed with parts of the *Maffezini* tribunal's findings. Since then a number of other

---

[124] See, e.g., *MTD Equity Sdn. Bhd. & MTD Chile S.A. v. Chile*, ICSID Case No. ARB/01/7 (Award of May 25, 2004); *Tecnicas Medioambientales Tecmed S.A. v. Mexico*, ICSID Case No. ARB(AF)/00/2 (Award of May 29, 2003), 19 ICSID Rev.-F.I.L.J. 158 (2004); *ADF Group*, supra note 22, *Pope and Talbot*, supra note 19.

[125] See, e.g., Rubins & Kinsella, supra note 10, at 232–34; Walid Ben Hamida, *MFN Clause and Procedural Matters: Seeking Solutions from WTO Experiences*, in Investment Treaty Arbitration: A Debate and Discussion (T. Weiler ed., Juris Publishing 2008). For an overview of this debate over the scope of MFN clauses, see Ruth Teitelbaum, *Recent Developments in the Interpretation of Most Favored Nation Clauses*, 22(3) J. Int'l Arb. 225 (2005); Bruno Poulain, *Clauses de la Nation la Plus Favorisée et Clauses d'Arbitrage Investisseur-Etat: Est-ce la Fin de la Jurisprudence Maffezini?*, unpublished; Dana Freyer & David Herlihy, *Most Favored-Nation Treatment and Dispute Settlement in Investment Arbitration: Just How "Favored" Is "Most-Favored"?*, 20(1) ICSID Rev.-F.I.L.J. 58 (2005); Emmanuel Gaillard, *Establishing Jurisdiction through a Most-Favored Nation Clause*, N.Y.L.J. (June 2, 2005); Jurgen Kurtz, *The Delicate Extension of MFN Treatment to Foreign Investors*: Maffezini v. Kingdom of Spain, in International Investment Law and Arbitration: Leading Cases from ICSID, NAFTA, Bilateral Investment Treaties and Customary International Law 523 (T. Weiler ed., Cameron May 2005); Katja Scholz, *Having Your Pie and Eating It with One Chopstick–MFN Clauses and Procedural Rights*, 5 Pol'y Papers Transnat'l Econ. L. (2004); Enrique Fernández Masiá, *Atribución De Competencia A Traves De La Cláusula De La Nación Más Favorecida: Lecciones Extraidas De La Reciente Práctica Arbitral Internacional En Materia De Inversiones Extranjeras*, 13 Revista Electrónica De Estudios Internacionales (2007); Hsu Locknie, *MFN and Dispute Settlement: When the Twain Meet*, 7(1) J. W. Inv. & Trade 25 (2006).

[126] *Plama Consortium Ltd. v. Bulgaria*, ICSID Case No. ARB/03/24 (Decision on Jurisdiction of February 8, 2005), 20 ICSID Rev.-F.I.L.J. 262 (2005).

tribunals have followed one or the other of these awards, as was briefly discussed in Chapter VII.

a. Procedural Rights

Maffezini v. Spain provided the historical starting point for the debate surrounding the "upgrading" of procedural rights by application of MFN clauses. There, one of the jurisdictional issues was whether the Argentine claimant could bypass a requirement contained in the Argentina-Spain BIT[127] that investment disputes be litigated in local courts for eighteen months prior to any submission to arbitration. The claimant invoked the MFN clause of the Argentina-Spain BIT,[128] and sought to rely upon the dispute resolution clause of the Chile-Spain BIT, which contained no such exhaustion requirement. Spain replied that in accordance with the *ejusdem generis* principle, the MFN clause could cover only the subject matter of the underlying treaty, namely investment protection. In Spain's view, the MFN clause only applied to substantive matters, and not to procedure or arbitral jurisdiction.[129] The *Maffezini* tribunal rejected this argument, and ruled in favor of the claimant.[130]

Maffezini v. Spain, ICSID Case No. ARB/97/7 (Decision on Objection to Jurisdiction January 25, 2000)

43. The arguments outlined above are familiar to international lawyers and scholars. Indeed, many of the issues mentioned have been addressed in the *Anglo-Iranian Oil Company Case (Jurisdiction)*,[131] in the *Case concerning the rights of nationals of the United States of America in Morocco*[132] and in the *Ambatielos Case (merits: obligation to arbitrate)*,[133] as well as in the proceedings of the *Ambatielos case* before a Commission of Arbitration.[134]

---

[127] The dispute settlement clause of the BIT provided that "[t]he dispute may be submitted to international arbitration . . . if no decision has been rendered on the merits of the claim after the expiration of a period of eighteen months from the date on which the [local] proceedings . . . have been initiated." Argentina-Spain BIT (1991), art. X(3).

[128] The MFN clause of the BIT provided that "[i]n all matters subject to this Agreement, this treatment shall not be less favorable than that extended by each Party to the investments made in its territory by investors of a third country." *Id.* art. IV(2).

[129] *Maffezini v. Spain*, ICSID Case No. ARB/97/7 (Decision on Objection to Jurisdiction January 25, 2000), ¶ 41, 16 ICSID Rev.-F.I.L.J. 212 (2001).

[130] *Id.* ¶ 64.

[131] SN: I.C.J. Rep. 93 (1952); *See also* Sir Gerald Fitzmaurice: *The Law and Procedure of the International Court of Justice, 1951–1954: Points of Substantive Law. Part II*, at 84.

[132] SN: I.C.J. Rep. 176 (1952).

[133] SN: I.C.J. Rep. 10 (1953). See also generally, *International Law Reports* 547 (1953).

[134] SN: Award of the Commission of Arbitration established for the Ambatielos claim between Greece and the United Kingdom, dated March 6, 1956. United Nations, 12 *Reports of International Arbitral Awards* 91 (1963).

44. In addressing these issues, it must first be determined which is the basic treaty that governs the rights of the beneficiary of the most favored nation clause. This question was extensively discussed in the *Anglo-Iranian Oil Company Case,* where the International Court of Justice determined that the basic treaty upon which the Claimant could rely was that "containing the most-favored-nation clause."[135] The Court then held that:

> "It is this treaty which establishes the juridical link between the United Kingdom and a third-party treaty and confers upon that State the rights enjoyed by the third party. A third party treaty, independent of and isolated from the basic treaty, cannot produce any legal effect as between the United Kingdom and Iran: it is *res inter alios acta.*"[136]

45. This discussion has practical consequences for the application of the most favored nation clause. For if, as the tribunal believes, the right approach is to consider that the subject matter to which the clause applies is indeed established by the basic treaty, it follows that if these matters are more favorably treated in a third-party treaty then, by operation of the clause, that treatment is extended to the beneficiary under the basic treaty. If the third-party treaty refers to a matter not dealt with in the basic treaty, that matter is *res inter alios acta* in respect of the beneficiary of the clause.[137]

46. The second major issue concerns the question whether the provisions on dispute settlement contained in a third-party treaty can be considered to be reasonably related to the fair and equitable treatment to which the most favored nation clause applies under basic treaties on commerce, navigation or investments and, hence, whether they can be regarded as a subject matter covered by the clause. This is the issue directly related to the *ejusdem generis* rule.

47. The question was indirectly but not conclusively touched upon in the *Case concerning the rights of nationals of the United States of America in Morocco.* Here, the International Court of Justice was confronted with the question of whether the clause contained in a treaty of commerce could be understood to cover consular jurisdiction as expressed in a third-party treaty. However, the Court did not need to answer the question posed because its main finding was that the treaties from which the United States purported to derive such jurisdictional rights had ceased to operate between Morocco and the third states involved.[138]

48. The issue came into sharp focus in the *Ambatielos* case. Greece contended before the International Court of Justice that her subject—Ambatielos—had not been treated in the English courts according to the standards applied to British subjects and foreigners who enjoyed a most favored nation treatment under treaties in force. Such most favored nation treatment was relied upon as the basis of the claim and the request that the dispute be submitted to arbitration. The Court did not deal with the matter of the most favored nation clause, but this task would be undertaken by the Commission of Arbitration.

---

[135] SN: I.C.J. Rep., 109 (1952).

[136] SN: *Id.* at 109. For a discussion of this and other decisions relating to the most favored nation clause, the writings of authors and the work of the International Law Commission on the subject, see 2 *Yearbook of the International Law Commission* 199 (1970); 2 *Yearbook of the International Law Commission* 97 (1973); 2 *Yearbook of the International Law Commission* 1 Pt. 1 (1978); 2 *Yearbook of the International Law Commission* 7 Pt. 2 (1978).

[137] SN: It was on this basis that the International Court of Justice ruled against the extension of principles of international law envisaged in treaties between Iran and third parties to the United Kingdom, as these principles were unrelated to the basic treaty containing the clause, Judgment cit., *supra* note [135].

[138] SN: I.C.J. Rep. 191 (1952).

49. The Commission of Arbitration, to which the dispute was eventually submitted, subsequently confirmed the relevance of the *ejusdem generis* rule. It affirmed that "the most-favored-nation clause can only attract matters belonging to the same category of subject as that to which the clause itself relates."[139] However, the scope of the rule was defined in broad terms:

> "It is true that the 'administration of justice,' when viewed in isolation, is a subject-matter other than 'commerce and navigation,' but this is not necessarily so when it is viewed in connection with the protection of the rights of traders. Protection of the rights of traders naturally finds a place among the matters dealt with by treaties of commerce and navigation. Therefore it cannot be said that the administration of justice, in so far as it is concerned with the protection of these rights, must necessarily be excluded from the field of application of the most-favored-nation clause, when the latter includes 'all matters relating to commerce and navigation.' The question can only be determined in accordance with the intention of the Contracting Parties as deduced from a reasonable interpretation of the Treaty."[140]

50. The Commission accepted the extension of the clause to questions concerning the administration of justice and found it to be compatible with the *ejusdem generis* rule. It concluded that the protection of the rights of persons engaged in commerce and navigation by means of dispute settlement provisions embraces the overall treatment of traders covered by the clause. On the merits of the question, the Commission determined, however, that the third-party treaties relied upon by Greece did not provide for any "privileges, favours or immunities" more extensive than those resulting from the basic treaty and that "accordingly the most-favored nation clause contained in Article X has no bearing on the present dispute."[141]

. . . .

52. A number of bilateral investment treaties have provided expressly that the most favored nation treatment extends to the provisions on settlement of disputes. This is particularly the case of investment treaties concluded by the United Kingdom. Thus, Article 3(3) of the Agreement between the United Kingdom and Albania, stipulates: "For the avoidance of doubt it is confirmed that the treatment provided for in paragraphs (1) and (2) above shall apply to the provisions of Articles 1 to 11 of this Agreement."[142] Among the enumerated provisions are the clauses on dispute settlement and the consent to submit to conciliation or arbitration under ICSID. Here it is beyond doubt that the parties intended the most favored nation clause to include dispute settlement in its scope, thereby meeting the test proposed by the *Ambatielos* Commission of Arbitration. Furthermore, the parties included this model clause in the Agreement with the express purpose of "the avoidance of doubt."

53. In other treaties the most favored nation clause speaks of "all rights contained in the present Agreement"[143] or, as the basic Argentine-Spain BIT does, "all matters subject to

---

[139] SN: United Nations, *Reports of International Arbitral Awards* 107 (1963).

[140] SN: *Id.*

[141] SN: *Id.* at 109, 110.

[142] SN: Agreement between the United Kingdom and Albania, Mar. 30, 1994. Twelve other agreements made by the United Kingdom, which the tribunal has examined, contain the same model clause.

[143] SN: Agreement between Chile and the Belgian-Luxembourg Economic Union, July 15, 1992, art. 3(3).

this Agreement." These treaties do not provide expressly that dispute settlement as such is covered by the clause. Hence, like in the *Ambatielos* Commission of Arbitration it must be established whether the omission was intended by the parties or can reasonably be inferred from the practice followed by the parties in their treatment of foreign investors and their own investors.

54. Notwithstanding the fact that the basic treaty containing the clause does not refer expressly to dispute settlement as covered by the most favored nation clause, the tribunal considers that there are good reasons to conclude that today dispute settlement arrangements are inextricably related to the protection of foreign investors, as they are also related to the protection of rights of traders under treaties of commerce. Consular jurisdiction in the past, like other forms of extraterritorial jurisdiction, were considered essential for the protection of rights of traders and, hence, were regarded not merely as procedural devices but as arrangements designed to better protect the rights of such persons abroad.[144] It follows that such arrangements, even if not strictly a part of the material aspect of the trade and investment policy pursued by treaties of commerce and navigation, were essential for the adequate protection of the rights they sought to guarantee.

55. International arbitration and other dispute settlement arrangements have replaced these older and frequently abusive practices of the past. These modern developments are essential, however, to the protection of the rights envisaged under the pertinent treaties; they are also closely linked to the material aspects of the treatment accorded. Traders and investors, like their States of nationality, have traditionally felt that their rights and interests are better protected by recourse to international arbitration than by submission of disputes to domestic courts, while the host governments have traditionally felt that the protection of domestic courts is to be preferred. The drafting history of the ICSID Convention provides ample evidence of the conflicting views of those favoring arbitration and those supporting policies akin to different versions of the Calvo Clause.[145]

56. From the above considerations it can be concluded that if a third-party treaty contains provisions for the settlement of disputes that are more favorable to the protection of the investor's rights and interests than those in the basic treaty, such provisions may be extended to the beneficiary of the most favored nation clause as they are fully compatible with the *ejusdem generis* principle. Of course, the third-party treaty has to relate to the same subject matter as the basic treaty, be it the protection of foreign investments or the promotion of trade, since the dispute settlement provisions will operate in the context of these matters; otherwise there would be a contravention of that principle.

---

[144] SN: See, for example, *Magno Santovincenzo v. James F. Egan* (U.S. Supreme Court, Decision of Nov. 23, 1931), 284 U.S. Rep., 30, where it was held as follows: "[T]he provisions of Article V of the Treaty were of special importance, as they provided for extraterritorial jurisdiction of the United States in relation to the adjudication of disputes. It would thwart the major purpose of the Treaty to exclude from the important protection of these provisions citizens of the United States who might be domiciled in Persia." For this and other domestic decisions concerning the most favored nation clause see International Law Commission, Decisions of national courts relating to the MFN clause, Digest prepared by the Secretariat, Doc. A/CN.4/269, 2 *Yearbook of the International Law Commission*, 117 (1973).

[145] SN: *See generally* International Centre for Settlement of Investment Disputes (ICSID), *Analysis of Documents Concerning the Origin and the Formulation of the Convention* (1970).

Several tribunals have followed the *Maffezini* ruling, at least with respect to secondary procedural rights like pre-arbitration negotiation or litigation requirements.[146] The tribunal in *Gas Natural v. Argentina* was particularly adamant in its extension of MFN treatment to procedural rights:

> 57. This tribunal understands that the issue of applying a general most-favored-nation clause to the dispute resolution provisions of bilateral investment treaties is not free from doubt, and that different tribunals faced with different facts and negotiating background may reach different results. The tribunal is satisfied, however, that the terms of the BIT between Spain and Argentina show that dispute resolution was included within the scope of most-favored-nation treatment, and that our analysis set out in paragraphs 28–30 above is consistent with the current thinking as expressed in other recent arbitral awards. *We remain persuaded that assurance of independent international arbitration is an important—perhaps the most important—element in investor protection. Unless it appears clearly that the state parties to a BIT or the parties to a particular investment agreement settled on a different method for resolution of disputes that may arise, most-favored-nation provisions in BITs should be understood to be applicable to dispute settlement.*[147]

But *Maffezini* has frequently been challenged, particularly when the rights to be "imported" are more fundamentally related to the jurisdiction of the arbitral tribunal. In *Plama v. Bulgaria*,[148] a Cypriot company purchased the majority of the shares of a Bulgarian company, Nova Plama, which owned a refinery in Bulgaria. Later, the Bulgarian government took various measures that allegedly interfered with the operations of Nova Plama. Plama commenced ICSID arbitration against Bulgaria under both the Energy Charter Treaty (ECT) and the Cyprus-Bulgaria BIT. The BIT contained a limited investor-state arbitration clause common in investment treaties entered into by former Soviet-bloc countries, which only permitted investors to bring claims to arbitration related to the quantum of compensation for expropriation. Other issues were relegated to litigation in the host state's courts.[149] To avoid this limitation, Plama invoked the MFN clause of the Cyprus-Bulgaria BIT, seeking to import the dispute resolution clause in Bulgaria's treaty with Finland, which permitted investors to arbitrate all investment disputes. Plama argued that it was entitled to the better treatment that Bulgaria had granted to Finnish investors. The MFN clause in the Cyprus-Bulgaria BIT was generally worded: "Each Contracting Party shall apply to the investments in its territory by investors of the other Contracting Party a treatment which is not less favorable than that accorded to investments by investors of third states."[150] To determine the scope of the MFN clause, the *Plama* tribunal sought

---

[146] See, e.g., *Siemens v. Argentina*, ICSID Case No. ARB/02/8 (Decision on Jurisdiction August 3, 2004); *Gas Natural SDG S.A. v. Argentina*, ICSID Case No. ARB/03/10 (Award on Jurisdiction June 17, 2005); cf. *Salini Construtorri S.p.A. & Italstrade S.p.A. v. Jordan*, ICSID Case No. ARB/02/13 (Decision on Jurisdiction Nov. 9, 2004) (Tribunal refusing to extend a more narrowly worded MFN clause, which did not extend to "all rights" as did the clause in *Maffezini*).

[147] *Gas Natural*, supra note 146, ¶ 49 (emphasis added).

[148] *Plama*, supra note 126.

[149] Cyprus-Bulgaria BIT (1987), art. 4.

[150] *Id.* at art. 3(1).

guidance outside the text of the BIT, including the other treaties concluded by Bulgaria and the history of recent negotiations between Cyprus and Bulgaria.[151]

The arbitrators ultimately concluded that dispute resolution provisions did not fall within the scope of the MFN clause at issue. In light of the ambiguous treaty language, the arbitrators doubted that the contracting states intended to give investors the right to cherry pick procedural elements from various third-party treaties when initiating arbitration.[152]

In *dicta*, the *Plama* tribunal went further still. The arbitrators suggested that there should be a very strong presumption against importing procedural rights, even if an MFN clause is less ambiguous than the clause in the Cyprus-Bulgaria BIT. This view appears to be directly contrary[153] to the standard applied by *Maffezini* and adopted in *Gas Natural*. The *Plama* tribunal opined: "[A]n MFN provision in a basic treaty does not incorporate by reference dispute settlement provisions in whole or in part set forth in another treaty, unless the MFN provision in the basic treaty leaves no doubt that the Contracting Parties intended to incorporate them."[154] The *Plama* standard is difficult to reconcile with the VCLT, which requires interpretation in accordance with the "ordinary meaning" of the words—surely a less exacting standard than "[an interpretation that] leaves no doubt."[155] Moreover, in a surprising additional *dictum*, the arbitrators noted that "[t]he expression 'with respect to all matters' as appearing in MFN provisions in a number of other BITs (but not the Bulgaria-Cyprus BIT) does not alleviate the doubt [as to whether procedural rights are covered]."[156] In other words, the *Plama* tribunal opined that *even if* the Bulgaria-Cypress BIT had expressly extended to *all matters* covered therein (which it did not), the result would have been the same. The only authority cited for this conclusion is the decision in *Siemens v. Argentina*.[157] Oddly enough, the *Siemens* tribunal concluded that a *neutral* MFN clause, which did not include the phrase "with respect to all matters," was sufficiently clear to allow the importation of procedural rights.

---

[151] See *Plama*, *supra* note 126, ¶¶ 195–97.

[152] See *id*. ¶ 219. See also Kinnear et al., *supra* note 71, at 1103–23 (explaining that cherry picking undermines the *quid pro quo* underlying the adoption of various treaty provisions; it could be argued that investors who pick a favorable provision from a treaty should also be subject to the less favorable provisions of that treaty.

[153] See Stephen Fietta, *Most Favoured Nation Treatment and Dispute Resolution under Bilateral Investment Treaties: A Turning Point?*, 2(3) TDM 8 (2005).

[154] *Plama*, *supra* note 126, ¶ 223.

[155] *Id*.

[156] *Id*. ¶ 205.

[157] *Siemens*, *supra* note 146, ¶¶ 85–86.

b. MFN and Substantive Rights

As noted earlier, the application of MFN treatment to substantive treaty rights has not been as contentious as its application to procedural rights.[158] Two cases merit particular attention: *MTD v. Chile*[159] and *Tecmed v. Mexico*.[160]

In *MTD v. Chile*, the Malaysian claimant sought to invoke several provisions from Chile's BITs with Denmark and Croatia, to expand the scope of the fair and equitable treatment standard of the Malaysia BIT. These provisions included an observance of undertakings or an "umbrella" clause and the obligation to award permits, which the Chile-Malaysia BIT lacked. Article 3(1) of the Chile-Malaysia BIT provided that "[i]nvestments made by investors of either Contracting Party in the territory of the other Contracting Party shall receive treatment which is fair and equitable, and not less favourable than that accorded to investments made by investors of any third State."[161] The tribunal framed the question before it as whether the relevant provisions of the Denmark and Croatia treaties were part of the fair and equitable treatment standard. It answered this question in the affirmative, since "the fair and equitable standard of treatment has to be interpreted in the manner most conducive to fulfill the objective of the BIT to protect investments and create conditions favorable to investments."[162] The tribunal concluded that importing the relevant provisions of the Denmark and Croatia treaties would be consistent with this principle.[163] The arbitrators further bolstered this conclusion by noting that the imported provisions did not fall within any exceptions to MFN treatment enumerated in the Malaysia BIT.[164]

Later, in an application for annulment of the *MTD* award, Chile challenged the tribunal's MFN analysis, stating "the tribunal confused fair and equitable treatment with most-favoured-nation treatment under Article 3(1) of the BIT, rendering this aspect of the Award incomprehensible."[165] The annulment committee agreed with Chile, but refused to invalidate the award on that basis:

> [The tribunal's analysis of the MFN clause] appears to confuse the notion of fair and equitable treatment required by the first part of Article 3(1) of the Malaysia-Chile

---

[158] Cases in which the application of MFN to substantive rights has been at issue include *MTD v. Chile*, *Tecmed v. Mexico*, *Pope & Talbot v. Canada*, and *ADF v. Canada*.

[159] *MTD, supra* note 124.

[160] *Tecmed, supra* note 124.

[161] Chile-Malaysia BIT (1992).

[162] *MTD, supra* note 124, ¶ 104.

[163] *Id.*

[164] *Id.*

[165] *Id.*, Decision on Annulment of March 21, 2007, ¶ 63.

> BIT with the most-favoured-nation treatment, which is required by the second half. The most-favoured-nation clause in Article 3(1) is not limited to attracting more favourable levels of treatment accorded to investments from third States only where they can be considered to fall within the scope of the fair and equitable treatment standard. *Article 3(1) attracts any more favourable treatment extended to third State investments and does so unconditionally.* However, the uncertainty in the tribunal's handling of Article 3(1) was without incidence for its resolution of the case. As to Articles 3(1) of the Denmark BIT and 3(3) of the Croatia BIT, these are distinct from the notion of fair and equitable treatment but MTD's claims based on those provisions failed. . . .[166]

It is important to note that the *ad hoc* committee did not question that the MFN clause of the Chile-Malaysia BIT could import more favorable provisions from other BITs. In fact, the annulment committee's interpretation of the MFN clause was broader than that of the tribunal.[167] To interpret the Chile-Malaysia BIT's MFN clause in this way, the tribunal by necessity assumed that under the *ejusdem generis* principle the imported provisions belonged to the *same category* or *same subject matter* as those in the basic BIT. This is a liberal approach toward the application of the *ejusdem generis* and MFN, effectively allowing the importation of many substantive protections that do not exist in the basic treaty—here, for example, an umbrella clause. It remains to be seen whether future tribunals take a similar approach.

In *Tecmed v. Mexico*, the Spanish claimants sought to invoke the MFN clause of the Mexico-Spain BIT to extend its temporal limits by importing a more favorable provision in this regard from the Austria-Mexico BIT. The tribunal rejected the claimant's argument:

> The Arbitral tribunal is aware that the Claimant, relying on the decision in the case *Emilio Agustín Maffezini v. Kingdom of Spain*, refers in its closing statement to the most favored nation treatment provided for in Article 8(1) of the Agreement in order to enable retroactive application in view of the more favorable treatment in connection with that matter which would be afforded to an Austrian investor under the bilateral treaty on investment protection between the United Mexican States and Austria of June 29, 1998. The Arbitral tribunal will not examine the provisions of such Treaty in detail in light of such principle, because it deems that matters relating to the application over time of the Agreement, which involve more the time dimension of application of its substantive provisions rather than matters of procedure or jurisdiction, due to their significance and importance, go to the core of matters that must be deemed to be specifically negotiated by the Contracting Parties. These are determining factors for their acceptance of the Agreement, as they are directly linked to the identification of the substantive protection regime applicable to the foreign investor and, particularly, to the general (national or international) legal context within which such regime operates, as well as to the access of the foreign investor to the substantive provisions of such regime. Their application cannot therefore be impaired by the principle contained in the most favored nation clause.[168]

---

[166] *Id.* ¶ 64 (emphasis added).

[167] *See* quoted paragraph of the annulment committee's decision on pp. 424–25.

[168] *Tecmed, supra* note 124, ¶ 69.

C. Discriminatory Impairment

Provisions barring arbitrary and discriminatory impairment of investments first appeared in U.S. treaties of Friendship, Commerce, and Navigation. A typical clause of this sort provides that: "[n]either Party shall in any way impair by arbitrary[169] or discriminatory measures the management, operation, maintenance, use, enjoyment, acquisition, expansion, or disposal of investments...."[170] Variations of this clause separate "arbitrary" from "discriminatory" with the conjunctive "and."[171] These clauses, unlike national treatment or MFN clauses, specifically use the term *discrimination*. They do not, however, contain any reference to like circumstances/situations. The question therefore arises whether such clauses require such a comparison.[172]

As of 2007, arbitrary and discriminatory treatment clauses have been discussed in several cases,[173] but have not played a major role in determining liability in most. An exception is *Nykomb v. Latvia*.[174] In *Nykomb*, the dispute arose out of Latvia's refusal to pay a so-called "double tariff" under a contract with Nykomb's subsidiary for the supply of electricity. In 2001, Nykomb commenced arbitration against Latvia for breach of the ECT, arguing that non-payment of the double tariff violated Article 10(1) of the ECT, which prohibited "unreasonable or discriminatory measures."[175] Nykomb argued that Latvia violated this provision by paying the double tariff to two other companies, while denying it to Nykomb's subsidiary. Latvia countered that those other companies were different in nature, and that the different treatment was therefore justified. The tribunal accepted that the companies could in principle be different, but found that Latvia had not produced sufficient evidence of the criteria that it had used to set different tariffs for the other companies. Consequently, the tribunal

---

[169] In some treaties the word *arbitrary* has been replaced with *unreasonable*. See, e.g., Dutch-Czech BIT, art. 3(1).

[170] U.S.-Ecuador BIT (1993), art. II(3)(b).

[171] U.S.-Czech BIT (1991), art. 2(b). In the latter case, arguably an act only violates the treaty if it is both arbitrary *and* discriminatory. Such a strict interpretation would presumably impose a higher burden on the investor to prove a breach. Whether an act is considered arbitrary is discussed in Chapter XVII in the context of fair and equitable treatment.

[172] The issue was obliquely addressed by the tribunal in *Enron*, where the arbitrators found that there was no discrimination because the application of different solutions in different economic sectors was "not surprising." *Enron Corp. v. Argentine Republic*, ICSID Case No. ARB/01/3 (Final Award, May 22, 2007) ¶ 282.

[173] See, e.g., Case Concerning Elettronica Sicula, S.P.A. (*ELSI*) (*U.S. v. Italy*), 1989 I.C.J. Rep. 3; *Nykomb Synergistics Technology Holding AB v. Latvia* (SCC ECT Arbitration, Award of Dec. 16, 2003); *Noble Ventures v. Romania*, supra note 98; *Saluka Inves. v. Czech Republic* (UNCITRAL Arbitration, Partial Award, Mar. 17, 2006). For a discussion of these cases see Sabahi, *supra* note 91.

[174] *Nykomb*, *supra* note 173.

[175] ECT, art. 10(1).

deemed the companies to be comparable.[176] The *Nykomb* tribunal thus viewed like circumstances as a pre-requisite for liability under the arbitrary or discriminatory measures clause.

Arbitrary and discriminatory impairment clauses were also invoked by claimants in some of the cases filed against Argentina in the wake of the financial crisis.[177] In those cases the core arguments with respect to discrimination were largely similar. The claimants in these cases advocated a broad economic comparison,[178] arguing that Argentine had treated the energy sector differently (and less favorably) when compared to other (Argentine-dominated) economic sectors, in particular manufacturing. The *CMS* and *Enron* tribunals ultimately rejected the discrimination claim. However, in *LG&E,* the arbitrators found Argentina's conduct to have been discriminatory, implicitly approving the broad definition of likeness.[179] Despite different outcomes, all the tribunals considered the issue of similarity of circumstances, as did the tribunal in *Nykomb*.

In the end, it is unclear whether an arbitrary/discriminatory impairment clause adds anything to what is already available under the national treatment or the fair and equitable treatment standards.[180]

---

[176] *See id.* ¶ 34.

[177] *See, e.g., CMS Gas Transmission Co. v. Argentina*, ICSID Case No. ARB/01/8 (Final Award, May 12, 2005); *LG&E Energy Corp. v. Argentina*, ICSID Case No. ARB/02/1 (Partial Award on Liability Oct. 3, 2006); *Enron, supra* note 172.

[178] *Cf.* discussion of *Occidental* above.

[179] *CMS, supra* note 177, ¶ 290, *Enron, supra* note 177, ¶ 282; *cf. LG&E, supra* note 177, ¶ 146. *See also* the discussion of *Occidental's* approach to the likeness issue. For a discussion of *LG&E* see Sabahi, *supra* note 91.

[180] The *Saluka* tribunal found that the same discriminatory actions that violated the fair and equitable treatment standard also violated the discriminatory impairment clause of the Czech-Netherlands BIT. The methodology of the *Saluka* tribunal for determining a violation of the fair and equitable treatment clause was similar to the three-step national treatment test developed under NAFTA Chapter 11 jurisprudence. *See Saluka, supra* note 173, ¶¶ 294, 308. *See also* Sabahi, *supra* note 91 in this respect. *See also* Todd Weiler & Ian Laird, *Standards of Treatment in International Investment Law: The Move Towards Unification* in *Oxford History of International Investment Law* (P. Muchlinski, F. Ortino, C. Schreuer, eds., Oxford University Press 2008).

XVI. Expropriation

Expropriation is the taking by a government of privately owned property, also known in the common law as *eminent domain*. Such a taking is universally recognized as within the inherent power of a state over property located in its territory, and where the state expropriates only its own citizens' property, international law is not implicated.[1] Indeed, regardless of whether the property expropriated is in foreign hands, expropriation is not *per se* wrongful under customary international law or investment treaties unless certain other conditions are present.[2]

---

[1] *See* The Suez Canal Conference, Selected Documents, Egypt No. 1, Cmd. 9853, at 3 (1956) (France, the United States, and the United Kingdom "do not question the right of Egypt to enjoy and exercise all the powers of a fully sovereign and independent nation, including the generally recognized right, under appropriate conditions, to nationalize assets, not imposed with an international interest, which are subject to its political authority"); Riyaz Dattu, *A Journey from Havana to Paris: The Fifty-Year Quest for the Elusive Multilateral Agreement on Investment*, 24 Fordham Int'l L.J. 275, 278–79 (2000) ("in so far as measures of expropriation only affect the nationals of the state carrying them out, there are no interests of foreigners to be protected and, to date, international law has not limited a state's jurisdiction in this field"); *See also Chuidian v. Philippine Nat'l Bank*, 912 F.2d 1095, 1105 (9th Cir. 1990) ("Expropriation by a sovereign state of the property of its own nationals does not implicate settled principles of international law."); *de Sanchez v. Banco Central de Nicaragua*, 770 F.2d 1385, 1395–98 & notes 14 & 16 (5th Cir. 1985).

[2] *See* John A. Westberg & Bertrand P. Marchais, *General Principles Governing Foreign Investment as Articulated in Recent International Tribunal Awards and Writings of Publicists*, 7 ICSID Rev.-For. Inv. L.J. 453, 454 (1992) ("The general principle that a State may lawfully expropriate the property interests of a foreign non-State party located within its borders is universally recognized"). *See also* J. L. Brierly, *The Law of Nations* 224 (1955); E. De Vattel, *The Law of Nations* 139 (1916); S. Friedman, *Expropriation in International Law* 190 (1953); Gillian White, *Nationalization of Foreign Property* 146 (1961); John H. Herz, *Expropriation of Foreign Property*, 35 Am. J. Int'l L. 253 (1941); Lord McNair, *The Seizure of Property and Enterprises in Indonesia*, 6 Neth. Int'l L. Rev. 243 (1959).

The law of expropriation is concerned with the way states must treat foreign investment; expropriation is, in fact, a subset of the responsibility that a state has for injuries to nationals of another state. Like other elements of international investment protection law, the law of expropriation is *lex ferenda*—evolving over time. Issues of particular interest in recent years include the types of property protected from expropriation, either through the terms of a treaty or through customary international law,[3] the boundary between normal government regulation and impermissible *indirect* expropriation, and the valuation of property that has been expropriated.

A. Historical Overview of Expropriation[4]

1. Introduction

Before the era of modern investment treaties,[5] prohibition against expropriation under customary international law[6] or Friendship, Commerce, and Navigation

---

[3] *See, e.g.*, North American Treaty Agreement (NAFTA), art. 1139. The law of expropriation deals with the treatment of investments after they are made; under customary international law, a country is free to refuse entry to an investment. UNCTAD, Admission and Establishment, UNCTAD/ITE/IIT/10 (vol. II) (United Nations 1999) at 3.

[4] *See generally* A. Loewenfeld, *International Economic Law* 397–403(2002); J. E. S. Fawcett, *Some Foreign Effects of Nationalisation of Property*, 27 Brit. Y.B. Int'l L. 355 (1950); Isi Foighel, *Nationlization: A Study in the Protection of Alien Property in International Law* (Stevens 1957); Alexander P. Fachiri, *Expropriation in International Law*, 6 Brit. Y.B. Int'l L. 159 (1925); Frederick S. Dunn, The Protection of Nationals (1932); *See* Noah Rubins & N. Stephan Kinsella, *International Investment, Political Risk and Dispute Resolution*, 158 (2005); *cf.* John Fischer Williams, *International Law and the Property of Aliens*, 9 Brit. Y.B. Int'l L. 1 (1928).

[5] The first bilateral investment treaty was signed between Pakistan and Germany in 1959. Current investment treaties and investment chapters of free trade agreements, whether bilateral or multilateral, provide a variety of protections to foreign investors and their investments, such as fair and equitable treatment (e.g., NAFTA, art. 1105) and national treatment (NAFTA, art. 1102(1)). These protections have been discussed in detail in Chapters XV and XVII of this book.

[6] In 1961, Professors Louis Sohn and Richard Baxter published a draft Convention on the International Responsibility of States for Injuries to Aliens, which sought to define a compensable "taking of property" under customary international law: "... not only an outright taking of property but also any such unreasonable interference with the use, enjoyment, or disposal of property as to justify an inference that the owner thereof will not be able to use, enjoy, or dispose of the property within a reasonable period of time after the inception of such interference." Louis B. Sohn & R. R. Baxter, *Responsibility of States for Injuries to the Economic Interests of Aliens: II. Draft Convention on the International Responsibility of States for Injuries to Aliens*, 55 Am. J. Int'l L. 548, 553 (1961).

(FCN)[7] treaties was the principal protection for foreign investors.[8] Most arbitrations from the pre-investment treaty era sounded in expropriation.[9] So too, states espousing the claims of their nationals, in the exercise of diplomatic protection,

---

[7] FCN treaties provided that host states could not expropriate foreign investments without paying compensation. *See* U.S.-Italy Treaty of Friendship, Commerce and Navigation, 9 Bevans 261, art. V(2) (Feb. 2, 1948) ("The property of nationals, corporations and associations of either High Contracting Party shall not be taken [in Italian, "*espropriati*"] within the territories of the other High Contracting Party without due process of law and without the prompt payment of just and effective compensation."); U.S.-Iran Treaty of Amity, Economic Relations, and Consular Rights, 8 U.S.T. 899, art. IV(2) (Aug. 15, 1955) ("Such property shall not be taken except for a public purpose, nor shall it be taken without the prompt payment of just compensation.").

[8] Customary international law also provided some protection against "repudiation" of agreements. 1 *Restatement (Third) of Foreign Relations Law of the United States*, § 712(2) (American Law Institute 1987) [hereinafter *Restatement*] (expropriation involves "a repudiation or breach by the state of a contract with a national of another state"). The other common ground for international protection of investors was "denial of justice." For a comprehensive and historical treatment of this subject, *see* Alwyn V. Freemen, *International Responsibility of States for Denial of Justice* (Longman, Green & Co. Ltd. 1938). Denial of justice along other legal theories were the main legal bases for protection of foreign investor's property rights, particularly in the pre-twentieth century era. During the nineteenth century, for example, a number of cases, which by today's standards would involve expropriation, were "for the most part settled by the application of standards based on freedom of contract, the sanctity of private property, and the duty of the state to compensate the owners of property taken for the public use." Fawcett, *supra* note 4, at 356.

[9] *See, e.g., Aramco Arbitration*, 27 I.L.R. 117 (1958) (Saudi Arabian government granted Aramco exclusive rights to exploit and export oil and subsequently granted overlapping rights to transport the oil; tribunal held that government was in breach of the agreement with Aramco because it lacked the legal authority to void pre-existing contracts by creating subsequent, contradictory contracts); *Sapphire Int'l Petroleum Ltd. v. Nat'l Iranian Oil Co.*, 35 I.L.R. 136 (1963) (Sapphire provided financial guarantee to National Iranian Oil Company (NIOC), which NIOC could cash if Sapphire did not fulfill its obligations under a concession contract; NIOC subsequently announced that Sapphire had not fulfilled its obligations and cashed the guarantee; arbitral tribunal ruled (in default) that NIOC should refund the guarantee); *British Petroleum Exploration Co. (Libya) Ltd. v. Gov't of the Libyan Arab Republic*, 53 I.L.R. 297, 328 (1973) ("The BP Nationalization Law, and the actions taken thereunder by the Respondent, do constitute a fundamental breach of the BP Concession as they amount to a total repudiation of the agreement and the obligations of the Respondent thereunder, and, on the basis of rules of applicable systems of law too elementary and voluminous to require or permit citation, the Tribunal so holds. Further the taking by the Respondent of the property, rights and interests of the Claimant clearly violates public international law as it was made for purely extraneous political reasons and was arbitrary and discriminatory in character. Nearly two years have now passed since the nationalization, and the fact that no offer of compensation has been made indicates that the taking was also confiscatory."); *Texaco Overseas Petroleum Co./California Asiatic Oil Co.* [hereinafter *TOPCO*] *v. Gov't of the Libyan Arab Republic*, 17 I.L.M. 1, ¶ 68 (1978) (although the state has sovereignty to issue decrees "... a State cannot invoke its sovereignty to disregard commitments freely undertaken ... and cannot make null and void the rights of a contracting party which has performed its various obligations under the contract."); *Libyan American Oil Co.* [hereinafter *LIAMCO*] *v. Libyan Arab Republic*, 62 I.L.R. 140, 217 (1977) (Libya nationalized LIAMCO's concession rights; sole arbitrator held that "nationalization of concession rights ... if not discriminatory and not accompanied by a wrongful act or conduct, is not unlawful ... [here] there has been no conclusive evidence to prove sufficiently the discriminatory character of the nationalization measures complained of, and therefore, these measures do not constitute a wrongful act provided due compensation is paid to the concessionaire.").

typically alleged that the property of their nationals had been expropriated.[10] This was the case in those few claims adjudicated by the International Court of Justice and its predecessor, the Permanent Court of International Justice (PCIJ).[11] The focus of the expropriation debate at the time was more on the relevant standard of compensation than the liability issues.[12] On the liability side, the expropriation claims that arose during the greater part of the twentieth century generally involved nationalizations, socializations, confiscations, and other "direct expropriations"[13]—that is, where an investor's property was physically seized by or formally transferred to a foreign government.[14] Although as early as the 1960s scholars had examined complex issues involving indirect expropriations—that is,

---

[10] In 1938, U.S. Secretary of State Cordell Hull, in correspondence with the Mexican government, wrote "under every rule of law and equity, no government is entitled to expropriate private property, for whatever purpose, without provision for prompt, adequate and effective payment therefor." See G. Hackworth, *Digest of International Law* 657 (1943); *Banco Nacional de Cuba v. Sabbatino*, 376 U.S. 398 (1964); *West v. Multibanco Comermex, S.A.*, 807 F.2d 820, 832–33 (9th Cir. 1987) (describing the Hull Doctrine as follows: "The right to expropriate property is coupled with and conditioned on the obligation to make adequate, effective, and prompt compensation. The legality of an expropriation is in fact dependent upon the observance of this requirement" but observing that "there may be exceptions to this principle" and finding no taking); *Banco Nacional de Cuba v. Chase Manhattan Bank*, 658 F.2d 875, 888–93 (2d Cir. 1981) (describing history of Hull Doctrine). Likewise, when the U.S. Congress sought to pressure the State Department to exercise diplomatic protection, it referred to the prohibition against expropriation, which included repudiation of contracts. *See, e.g.*, Hickenlooper Amendment, 22 U.S.C. § 2370(e)(2) (West 2005).

[11] *Case Concerning the Factory at Chorzow*, 1925 P.C.I.J. (ser. A) No. 13 (determining compensation owed to Germany for the wrongful actions of Poland with respect to the factory at Chorzow, which in effect amounted to the taking of the property). *See also Mavrommatis Jerusalem Concessions*, (1925) P.C.I.J. (ser. A) No. 5 at 32–34 and 37–39 (Crown Agents for the Colonies on behalf of the British High Commissioner for Palestine conferred a concession on one individual to supply certain public utilities to the city of Jerusalem, but that concession overlapped with another concession previously granted to a different individual by the Ottoman empire. Under the terms of the second concession, the concessionaire could request the High Commissioner to terminate any infringing concession. The tribunal held that the request by the second concessionaire and its implementation would amount to expropriation, but the request was never made and the British government stated that it would not expropriate the concession); *Case Concerning Barcelona Traction, Light & Power Co.* (New Application: 1962) (*Belgium v. Spain*), 1970 I.C.J. 3 (Feb. 5) (Barcelona Traction, separate opinion of Judge Manfred Lachs ¶ 71) (stating with respect to the forced bankruptcy, seizure and sale of certain assets, "The same observations apply to the purported transfer of Ebro's Canadian share register, its Canadian registered offices, and its very seat itself (also Canadian), to the city of Barcelona . . . In short what really took place appears to have had the character of a disguised expropriation of the undertaking."); *Case Concerning Elettronica Sicula S.p.A. (ELSI) (U.S. v. Italy)*, 1989 I.C.J. 15 ¶¶ 115–19 (Jul. 20).

[12] The issue of standard of compensation and how it works in the modern practice is more fully discussed in Chapter XIX.

[13] *See* Ian Brownlie, *Principles of Public International Law* 509 (6th ed. 2003); Andreas Lowenfeld, *International Economic Law* 392 (Oxford University Press 2002).

[14] *See* Annex 10-B of the (2004) U.S. Model bilateral investment treaty (BIT) (defining "direct expropriation" as "where an investment is nationalized or otherwise directly expropriated through formal transfer of title or outright seizure").

effective transfer of property rights without physically seizing the property[15]—it was not until the 1980s and in the context of the Iran-U.S. Claims Tribunal that these more subtle aspects of the expropriation doctrine became the subject of a tremendous amount of advocacy and scholarly debate.

On the compensation side, the classic rule describing the applicable standard of compensation for expropriation, which is often stated by quoting the "Hull Formula," was drawn from a 1938 letter sent by U.S. Secretary of State Cordell Hull to the Mexican government concerning properties owned by U.S. nationals and nationalized by Mexico.[16] This letter stated:

> The Government of the United States merely adverts to a self-evident fact when it notes that the applicable precedents and recognized authorities on international law support its declaration that, under every rule of law and equity, no government is entitled to expropriate private property, for whatever purpose, without provision for prompt, adequate, and effective payment therefor.[17]

The Hull Formula of "prompt, adequate, and effective payment" seemed to define the law of international expropriation for the first half of the twentieth century.[18] No international tribunal sitting during this period held the appropriate remedy for expropriation of property was anything less than full compensation.[19]

2. Pre–World War II Period

One of the earliest international cases on expropriation was *Delagoa Bay and East African Railroad Co.*,[20] which addressed Portugal's cancellation of a concession contract owned by U.S. and British interests. As was then the practice, the interests

---

[15] See, e.g., Christie, *What Constitutes a Taking Under International Law?*, 33 Brit. Y. B. Int'l L. 307 (1962). *See also* Sohn & Baxter, *supra* note 6.

[16] See Hackworth, *supra* note 10, at 658.

[17] *Id.* at 658–59.

[18] See Patrick M. Norton, *A Law of the Future or a Law of the Past? Modern Tribunals and the International Law of Expropriation*, 85 A.M.J.I.L. 474 (1991); Andrew T. Guzman, *Why LDCs Sign Treaties That Hurt Them: Explaining the Popularity of Bilateral Investment Treaties*, Va. J. Int'l L. 639 (1998). *But see* Oscar Schachter, *Compensation for Expropriation*, 78 Am. J. Int'l L. 121 (1984) ("It is true that several 'traditional' decisions of international tribunals recognize an international obligation to pay compensation when alien property is taken by a state. However, contrary to what is often asserted, these decisions contain no reference to the 'prompt, adequate and effective' standard.").

[19] Norton, *supra* note 18, at 476–77. Cases in this period include *Norwegian Shipowners Claim (Nor. v. U.S.)*, 1 R. Int'l Arb. Awards 307 (1922); *British Claims in the Spanish Zone of Morocco*, 2 I.L.R. 157 (1925); *Goldenberg Case (Ger. v. Rom.)*, 2 R. Int'l Arb. Awards 901 (1928); *Smith v. Compañía Urbanizadora del Parque y Playa de Marianao*, 2 R. Int'l Arb. Awards 915 (1929); *Lena Goldfields, Ltd. v. Russia* (Judgment of Sept. 3, 1930), *reprinted in* 36 Cornell L. Rev. 42 (1950); *Shufeldt Claim*, 2 R. Int'l Arb. Awards 1079 (1930).

[20] *Delagoa Bay & E. Afr. RR. Co. (U.S. & Gr. Brit. v. Port.)* (1900), *in* Majorie Whiteman, 3 Damages Int'l L. 1694 (1943).

of the contract owners were espoused by their states, making *Delgoa Bay* a state-to-state arbitration despite the subject matter being a private interest. The tribunal held the cancellation amounted to an expropriation and that customary law, "universally accepted rules of law" in the language of the tribunal, required full compensation.[21] The tribunal nonetheless held that full compensation did not include compensation for future profits that were not "absolutely accurate but only comparatively likely."[22]

The seminal pre-World War II case was the 1928 PCIJ *Chorzow Factory Case*,[23] where Germany sought reparation from Poland on behalf of two German companies for the taking of properties owned by the companies in areas that were transferred to Poland under the treaties ending World War I.[24] The tribunal stated that in cases of expropriation:

> [R]eparation must, as far as possible, wipe out all consequences of the illegal act and reestablish the situation which would, in all probability, have existed if the act had not been committed."[25] It based this ruling both on the provisions of the relevant treaties between the States and on customary international law, stating full compensation was "a principle which seems to be established by international practice and in particular by the decisions of arbitral tribunals.[26]

Lena Goldfields Ltd. v. Russia was another early case involving expropriation, which was unusual at the time because it was commenced on the basis of an arbitration clause in a concession contract, allowing the concessionaire to represent itself directly rather than seeking state espousal of its claim.[27] The concession was to mine gold in Siberia, and the concessionaire claimed that official harassment by the Soviet Union, including criminal trials of its employees and nighttime raids of facilities, made it impossible to carry out the concession. Although the concessionaire did prevail in the arbitration, it was unable to enforce the award because the Soviet Union was not party to any arbitration award recognition treaties.[28]

---

[21] *Id.* at 1697.

[22] *Id.*

[23] *Chorzów, supra* note 11.

[24] *See Case Concerning the Factory at Chorzów* (Indemnity) 1927 P.C.I.J. (ser. B) No. 3, 9–15.

[25] *Chorzów, supra* note 11, at 47.

[26] *Id.* at 47–49.

[27] *Lena Goldfields, supra* note 19. For a history of *Lena Goldfields*, see V.V. Veeder, *The Lena Goldfields Arbitration: The Historical Roots of Three Ideas*, 47 Int'l & Comp. L.Q. 747 (1998).

[28] *See* Veeder, *supra* note 27, at 787–89. The U.K. (Lena Goldfields had U.K. nationality) was able to reach a diplomatic settlement with the U.S.S.R. 38 years after the arbitration, though the payment finally came from U.K. coffers.

In the *Norwegian Shipowners Claim*,[29] the tribunal held that contracts between Norwegian citizens and U.S. shipyards were property. When the U.S. government took control of shipyards following its entry into World War I and did not complete the contracts or return payments, the tribunal found that the U.S. measures amounted to expropriation.[30] It relied both on U.S. law and "international law, based on the respect for private property."[31] Other period cases include the *Spanish Zone of Morocco*,[32] *Goldenberg Case*,[33] *Walter Fletcher Smith Claim*,[34] and the *Shufeldt Claim*,[35] all reflecting some rule similar to the Hull Formula for full compensation for expropriation.

3. Post–World War II Period Until Present

By the 1950s a clear countermovement to the traditional rule stated in the Hull Formula emerged. Driven by social revolutions and decolonization, many young states began to argue for a right of economic self-determination, including the right to expropriate foreign-owned property without full compensation.[36] These arguments found expression in a series of the U.N. General Assembly resolutions beginning in 1962 with Resolution 1803.[37] This resolution, which marked the beginning of what came to be known as the New International Economic Order (NIEO), was followed by Resolutions 3171 (1973),[38] 3201 (1974),[39] and 3281 (1974),[40] which were discussed fully in Chapter II.

While the heated debate regarding these standards occupied the U.N. General Assembly, a handful of expropriation arbitrations during this period adhered more

---

[29] *Norwegian Shipowners Claim, supra* note 19.

[30] *Id.* at 334.

[31] *Id.*

[32] *Spanish Zone of Morocco, supra* note 19.

[33] *Goldenberg Case, supra* note 19.

[34] *Walter Fletcher Smith Claim (U.S. v. Cuba)*, 2 R. Int'l Arb. Awards 915 (1929).

[35] *Shufeldt Claim, supra* note 19.

[36] *See also* Chapter II on this issue.

[37] G.A. Res. 1803 (VIII), U.N. GAOR, 7th Sess., Agenda Item 39, U.N. Doc. A/RES/1803 (XVII) (1962); *see* "Political Barriers: The New International Economic Order" in Chapter II, *supra*.

[38] G. A. Res. 3171 (XXVIII), "Permanent Sovereignty over Natural Resources," U.N. GAOR, 28th Sess., U.N. Doc. A/9030 (XVIII) (1973).

[39] G.A. Res. 3201 (S-VI), "The Declaration on the Establishment of a New Economic Order," U.N. GAOR, 6th Special Sess., Agenda Item 7, U.N. doc. A/RES/3201 (S-VI) (1974).

[40] G.A. Res. 3281, "Charter of Economic Rights and Duties of States," 29 U.N. GAOR, 29th Sess., Supp. No.31, at 50, 51–55, U.N. Doc. A/9631 (1974).

closely to the traditional rule for compensation than to the new U.N. resolutions.[41] A number of these cases arose from the seizure by oil-exporting states of petroleum concessions previously granted to foreign companies. Many of these cases were decided with knowledge of both the early decisions requiring full compensation for expropriation as a matter of international law, as well as the newer U.N. resolutions proclaiming that expropriations and the level of compensation were firmly within the jurisdiction of the expropriator. Although tribunals differed slightly in how they balanced these competing authorities, they tended to affirm the traditional rule.[42] *British Petroleum Exploration Co. v. Libyan Arab Republic* was decided in the midst of the U.N. debate, but the arbitrator held that the taking was in "violat[ion of] public international law," especially as it was done without compensation.[43] The arbitrator in *TOPCO v. Libya* ruled that Libya was required to resume a concession contract it had nationalized. The arbitrator stated, in dicta, that full compensation remained the standard in international law, accepting Resolution 1803 as customary international law but rejecting the other resolutions because of the lack of consensus among states.[44] The arbitrator in *LIAMCO* accorded the later Resolutions somewhat more weight, stating they were not binding in international law, but did express "the recent dominant trend of international opinion,"[45] and that the Hull Formula was a "practical guide" but not the only standard in international law.[46] Ultimately, however, the arbitrator found that one of the "general principles" of international law was "equitable compensation," and that Libya was accordingly required to indemnify LIAMCO for the taking.[47] The tribunal in *Arbitration between Kuwait and American Independent Oil Co.*

---

[41] Cases include *Petroleum Dev. Ltd. v. Sheikh of Abu Dhabi*, 18 I.L.R. 144 (1951); *Ruler of Qatar v. Int'l Marine Oil Co.*, 20 I.L.R. 534 (1953); *Lighthouses Arbitration (Fr./Greece)*, 23 I.L.R. 299 (1956); *Aramco Arbitration, supra* note 9; *Sapphire, supra* note 9; *British Petroleum, supra* note 9; *TOPCO, supra* note 9; *LIAMCO, supra* note 9; *Arbitration between Kuwait and Am. Independent Oil Co. (AMINOIL)*, 21 I.L.M. 976 (1982).

[42] Some of the cases also address whether lump sum payments, which were negotiated between states to compensate nationals for expropriations rather than decided by judges or arbitrators, contributed to the development of international law. Some held that the political element in these settlements prevented them from establishing customary international law. *See, e.g., TOPCO, supra* note 9, at 24 ("lump sum payments are inspired basically by considerations of expediency and not of legality" and are therefore of no value). Others held that lump sums, as they are usually settled at only pennies on the dollar, undercut the traditional rule of full compensation for expropriation. *See, e.g., LIAMCO, supra* note 9, at 206.

[43] *British Petroleum, supra* note 9, at 329.

[44] *TOPCO, supra* note 9, at 30; *see also* Norton, *supra* note 18, at 480–81.

[45] *LIAMCO, supra* note 9, at 189.

[46] *Id.* at 218.

[47] *Id.* at 76, 86–87.

(*AMINOIL*) followed the holding in *TOPCO*, recognizing Resolution 1803 as a "codification" of customary international law of "appropriate compensation."[48] The tribunal further stated that the underlying purpose behind the rules governing expropriation was to maintain the future flow of investment.[49]

Beginning in the 1980s, another series of important expropriation decisions were issued by the Iran-U.S. Claims Tribunal.[50] The U.S.-Iran Treaty of Amity stated:

> [P]roperty shall not be taken except for a public purpose, nor shall it be taken without the prompt payment of just compensation. Such compensation shall be in an effectively realizable form and shall represent the full equivalent of the property taken; and adequate provision shall have been made at or prior to the time of taking for the determination and payment thereof.[51]

Many of the Iran-U.S. Claims Tribunal's decisions on expropriation additionally rested on the tribunal's articulation of international law on issues of liability as well as compensation. On the liability side, for example, the tribunal in *Starrett Housing*[52] crafted one of the most cited standards for indirect expropriation.[53] On the compensation side, in *American International Group v. The Islamic Republic of Iran*,[54] the tribunal stated "it is a general principle of public international law that even in a case of lawful nationalization the former owner of the nationalized property is normally entitled to compensation for the value of the property taken."[55] The tribunal in *Sola Tiles v. Iran* held the expropriation requirements of the treaty were the same standard required by general international law.[56]

The current state of the customary law of expropriation is arguably reflected in the 1987 Restatement (Third) of Foreign Relations Law:

> A state is responsible under international law for injury resulting from:
>
> (1) a taking by the state of the property of a national of another state that
>
> (a) is not for a public purpose, or

---

[48] *AMINOIL, supra* note 41, at 601.

[49] *See id.* at 603.

[50] *See generally* Charles N. Brower & Jason D. Brueschke, *Iran-United States Claims Tribunal* (1998).

[51] U.S.-Iran Treaty, *supra* note 7, art. IV, ¶ 2.

[52] *Starrett Housing Corp., Starrett Systems, Inc. Starrett Housing Int'l, Inc. v. Gov't of the Islamic Rep. of Iran, Bank Markazi Iran, Bank Omran, Bank Mellat*, Interlocutory Award No. ITL-32–24–1, Case No. 24 (Dec. 19, 1983) 4 Iran-U.S. Cl. Trib. Rep. 122, § IV(b) [hereinafter *Starrett Housing*].

[53] *See* p. 451 *infra*.

[54] *Am. Int'l Group v. Islamic Republic of Iran*, AWD 93–2–3, *reprinted at* 4 Iran-U.S. C.T.R. 96 (1983).

[55] *Id.*, AWD 93–2–3, slip op. at 14–15, 21.

[56] *Sola Tiles, Inc. v. Iran*, AWD 298–317–1, 14 IRAN-U.S. C.T.R. 223 (1987)

(b) is discriminatory, or

(c) is not accompanied by provision for just compensation;

> For compensation to be just under this Subsection, it must, in the absence of exceptional circumstances, be in an amount equivalent to the value of the property taken and be paid at the time of taking, or within a reasonable time thereafter with interest from the date of taking, and in a form economically usable by the foreign national.[57]

current CIL (§ 712 R.3d FR)

Accordingly, states may expropriate property of aliens provided that they do so in a nondiscriminatory way, for a public purpose, and most importantly on payment of full compensation.

The great majority of the modern investment treaties contain this expropriation standard as the following excerpt from a 2006 United Nations Conference on Trade and Development (UNCTAD) study confirms:

> Most agreements include the same four requirements for a lawful expropriation, namely public purpose, non-discrimination, due process and payment of compensation. Furthermore, most BITs [bilateral investment treaties] have similar provisions regarding the standard of compensation. Notwithstanding some variations in language, the overwhelming majority of BITs provide for prompt, adequate and effective compensation, based on the market or genuine value of the investment. However, BITs differ on the degree of specificity and sophistication concerning the calculation and payment of compensation. The normative convergence among the BITs regarding the conditions for expropriation reflects the important domestic reforms that most developing countries have undertaken during the last 20 years to improve their domestic investment climate.
>
> The above trend contrasts with the variety of means in BITs with respect to the newly emerging issue of indirect expropriations or regulatory takings. Recent investment disputes on this matter have caused some countries, in particular the United States and Canada, to redraft their model BITs. However, at least for the time being, most contracting parties to BITs continue to agree on broad and general clauses to delimit the scope of the expropriation provision—the kind of language that has led to controversy in the context of many investor-State disputes. On the other hand, countries may need more time to assess the impact of these awards on their BIT practice before arriving at any conclusions concerning the need to modify the expropriation clause.[58]

B. Investments and Property Protected Against Expropriation

A threshold determination as to whether an expropriation has occurred is to identify the foreign investor's investment or property rights in question. In 1982, Judge Rosalyn Higgins in her lecture in The Hague Academy of International Law said:

---

[57] *Restatement, supra* note 8, § 712.

[58] United Nations Conference on Trade and Development (UNCTAD), *Bilateral Investment Treaties 1995–2006: Trends in Investment Rulemaking* 52 (2007).

> I am very struck by the almost total absence of any analysis of conceptual aspects of property. So far as the concept of property itself is concerned, it is as if we international lawyers say: property has been defined for us by municipal legal systems; and in any event, we *know* property when we see it. But how can we know if an individual has lost *property* rights unless we really understand what property is?"(emphasis added)[59]

Investment treaties have to some degree remedied this problem because many include detailed provisions defining the types of investments protected from expropriation.[60] These treaty provisions tend to go beyond the scope of property protected by customary international law,[61] but there is still considerable debate whether such detailed treaty provisions have actually expanded the scope of customary international law itself.[62] Obviously, the starting point in determining whether a particular investment or property right is protected from expropriation is the text of the governing treaty, but where the treaty is silent, a tribunal will have to decide whether the property or property right at issue is within the evolving customary definition of protected property.

Contractual and quasi-contractual rights, as a subset of "property" protected by the law of expropriation, deserve special mention, particularly government-issued permits and contracts with government entities. Not all sources of customary international law treat these as a form of property capable of expropriation.[63] In *The Oscar Chinn Case*, the tribunal found that a shipowner had no "vested right" in continued profits contemplated in a contract, just because prices for shipped commodities were high when the owner started his business,[64] and in *McHarg, Roberts, Wallace, and Todd v. Islamic Republic of Iran*, the tribunal rejected a

---

[59] Rosalyn Higgins, *The Taking of Property by the State, Recent Developments in International Law* 176 Receuil des Cours 321, 268 (1982) (emphasis added).

[60] On the definitions of investment *see* Chapter XI *supra*; *see also* Noah Rubins, *Notion of "Investment" in International Investment Arbitration*, in *Arbitrating Foreign Investment Disputes: Substantive and Procedural Aspects* 283 (Horn ed., Kluwer Law Int'l 2004) (hereinafter Horn ed.).

[61] *Id.* at 323. *See also S.D. Myers v. Gov't of Canada* (UNCITRAL Partial Award, Nov. 12, 2000), 40 I.L.M. 1408 (2001) ¶¶ 281–82 [hereinafter *S.D. Myers*] ("[I]n legal theory, rights other than property rights may be 'expropriated' . . . Expropriations tend to involve the deprivation of ownership rights; regulations a lesser interference.").

[62] *See* Schachter, *supra* note 18, at 126 ("As a general rule, the repetition of common clauses in bilateral treaties does not create or support an inference that those clauses express customary law"); *but see* Brice M. Clagett, *Just Compensation in International Law: The Issues Before the Iran-United States Claims Tribunal*, in 4 *The Valuation of Nationalized Property in International Law*, 31, 76–77 (Richard B. Lillich ed., 1987) (in light of "the large number of treaties involved, the substantial uniformity of their provisions, and the indications in many of them or in their negotiating history that they were recognized to be declaratory of a legal rule, the better view is that they provide significant evidence of that rule" of law).

[63] *See* Higgins, *supra* note 59, at 271–73.

[64] 1934 P.C.I.J. (ser. A/B), No. 63, at 65, 88.

claim of expropriation of shares based only on evidence of a contract breach.[65] However, the arbitrator in the *LIAMCO* case dealt somewhat differently with the issue of "concessions rights as property":

> It is well-known that property in its general meaning is of two kinds: corporeal and incorporeal. The first, by unanimous opinion of jurists, covers all physical things, such as chattels, lands and various other things of material nature.
>
> On the other hand, incorporeal property comprises all interests and rights which, though incapable of immediate material composition, may produce corporeal things or may be evaluated in financial and economic terms. In other words, incorporeal property includes those rights that have a pecuniary or monetary value.
>
> Concession rights, as those of the present dispute, may be included under the class of incorporeal property. This assertion is recognized by international precedents, as was held for instance by the Permanent Court of Arbitration in its Award delivered on 13 October 1922 in the dispute between the United States of America and the Kingdom of Norway. This view is likewise in harmony with municipal law of most legal systems, and with the spirit of Islamic jurisprudence.[66]

More recently, in *CME v. Czech Republic*, the tribunal found that the investor's right to use a license to operate a television station constituted the "legal basis" of its investment.[67]

An investor's claim to vested property rights or reasonable expectations under a concession contract, licensing agreement, or other commercial contract with a governmental entity[68] may be enhanced by the presence of a *stabilization clause*, which will typically provide that the host government will not alter laws during the term of the agreement so as to prejudice the investor's rights.[69]

---

[65] 13 Iran-U.S. Cl. Trib. Rep. 286, 302 (1986) (no expropriation even though Iranian government's breach of service contract deprived claimant of its only source of income, thus rendering claimant's stock worthless). *See Restatement, supra* note 8, § 712 cmt. h. ("[N]ot every repudiation or breach by a state of a contract with a foreign national constitutes a violation of international law").

[66] *LIAMCO, supra* note 9, at 189. *See also AMINOIL, supra* note 41, at 1017 (Kuwait, after adjusting the original oil concession of 1948 several times, terminated Aminoil's concession and nationalized its assets; the nationalization was legal, but the government was required to compensate Aminoil.).

[67] *CME Czech Republic B.V. v. Czech Republic* (UNCITRAL, Partial Award of Sept. 3, 2001), ¶¶ 593, 599 [hereinafter *CME Partial Award*]; *see Norwegian Shipowners' Claims*, June 30, 1921, 1 Rep. Int'l Arb. Awards 309, 323 (1922) (where the U.S. government "took over the rights and duties of the shipbuilders towards the shipowners," the tribunal found a taking).

[68] Yet another permutation of contractual obligation involves sovereign debt, such as a bond of or loan to a government. This type of debt may or may not be a protected investment, depending in large part on the treaty definition. *See* p. 253 *supra*.

[69] *See EnCana Corp. v. Republic of Ecuador,* LCIA Case No. UN3481 (UNCITRAL, Final Award of Feb. 3, 2006), ¶ 67. *See also CMS Gas Transmission Co. v. Argentine Republic*, ICSID Case No. ARB/01/8 (May 12, 2005), ¶ 145; *AMINOIL, supra* note 41, at 977.

Investors have claimed that, even absent a stabilization clause, an investment agreement should benefit from the rule of *pacta sunt servanda*, much like a treaty.[70] When a host state's commitments are embodied not in a contract, but rather in a permit or decree, the issue becomes more complex; still, investors argue and arbitrators have held that the resulting *right* may amount to protected property under international law.[71]

How a particular right is treated under national law may further complicate the issue. Whether an investor possesses a vested property right or a legitimate expectation regarding a particular right (contractual or otherwise) may, at least in the first instance, turn on the legal status of that property under national law.[72] For example, concession contracts—which are invariably governed by the local law of the place where the concession was issued and is to be performed—may not provide the investor with a vested property right under a state's national law. In such cases, an investor claiming that its property rights have been expropriated will likely need to rely on treaty definitions and principles of customary international law,[73] or other legal theories such as "legitimate expectations"[74] or "reasonably to-be-expected economic benefit" to advance its cause.

---

[70] *Sapphire, supra* note 9, at 181 ("The rule *pacta sunt servanda* is the basis of every contractual relationship"); *TOPCO, supra* note 9 (commitments were undertaken pursuant to a stabilization clause in the contract, which were breached by Libya's nationalization decrees, thus incurring and liability for Libya). *See also* R. Y. Jennings, *State Contracts in International Law*, 37 Brit. Y.B. Int'l L. 156, 175 (1975). *See also* Chapter XVIII, *infra*, on umbrella clauses.

[71] *See Tecmed v. United Mexican States*, ICSID Case No. ARB (AF)/00/2 (May 29, 2003) 43 I.L.M. 133 (2004), ¶ 117 [hereinafter *Tecmed*] (Mexican government's refusal to renew a permit to operate a landfill that it purchased and the closure of landfill meant that "the economic or commercial value directly or indirectly associated with those operations and activities and with the assets earmarked for such operations and activities was irremediably destroyed"). *See* A. A. Fatouros, *State Guarantees to Aliens* (Columbia University Press 1962); *CME Partial Award, supra* note 67, ¶ 147 ("investment assets of CME in the Czech Republic also plainly include CNTS's tangible and intangible property—including its . . . intellectual property rights, such as its rights to air licensed programmes . . .").

[72] *See CMS, supra* note 69, ¶ 123. *See also Azurix Corp. v. Argentine Republic*, ICSID Case No. ARB/01/12 ¶ 47 (July 14, 2006); *Siemens A.G. v. Argentine Republic*, ICSID Case No. ARB/02/8 ¶¶ 69–80 & 267–69 (Feb. 6, 2007) (discussing potential application of local law with respect to property rights and interpretation of applicable treaties).

[73] *See generally, EnCana v. Ecuador, supra* note 69.

[74] *See* L. Yves Fortier & Stephen L. Drymer, *Indirect Expropriation in the Law of International Investment: I Know It When I See It, or Caveat Investor*, 19 ICSID Rev.-F.I.L.J. 293, 306–08 (2005). *Cf. Thunderbird v. Mexico* ¶ 208 (no expropriation where "the Tribunal has already found that the [claimant's subsidiaries] could not have operated based on a legitimate expectation in Mexico. Accordingly, as acknowledged by [the claimant], compensation is not owed for regulatory takings where it can be established that the investor or investment never enjoyed a vested right in the business activity that was subsequently prohibited.").

C. The Role of Investment Treaties

Although there is assuredly a body of customary international law concerning expropriation, in the context of investment treaty arbitration the starting point for any tribunal's analysis of an alleged expropriation is the language of the treaty itself. Some treaties include detailed provisions on expropriation, which may or may not alter customary international law.[75] Some treaties, such as the Argentina–United States BIT, are quite succinct:

> Investments shall not be expropriated or nationalized either directly or indirectly through measures tantamount to expropriation or nationalization (expropriation) except for a public purpose; in a nondiscriminatory manner; upon payment of prompt, adequate and effective compensation; and in accordance with due process of law and the general principles of treatment provided for in Article II (2). Compensation shall be equivalent to the fair market value of the expropriated investment immediately before the expropriatory action was taken or became known, whichever is earlier; be paid without delay; include interest at a commercially reasonable rate from the date of expropriation; be fully realizable; and be freely transferable at the prevailing market rate of exchange on the date of expropriation.[76]

Indeed, this paragraph concisely summarizes most of the fundamental principles concerning expropriation that investment treaties have generally adopted, and that customary international law also embraces. Other treaties contain a more detailed elaboration of the fundamental principles. For example, Article 1110 (Expropriation and Compensation) of the North American Free Trade Agreement (NAFTA) provides:

> Article 1110: Expropriation and Compensation
>
> 1. No Party may directly or indirectly nationalize or expropriate an investment of an investor of another Party in its territory or take a measure tantamount to nationalization or expropriation of such an investment ("expropriation"), except:
>
>   (a) for a public purpose;
>
>   (b) on a non-discriminatory basis;
>
>   (c) in accordance with due process of law and Article 1105(1); and
>
>   (d) on payment of compensation in accordance with paragraphs 2 through 6.
>
> 2. Compensation shall be equivalent to the fair market value of the expropriated investment immediately before the expropriation took place ("date of expropriation"), and shall not reflect any change in value occurring because the intended expropriation had become known earlier. Valuation criteria shall include going concern value, asset value including declared tax value of tangible property, and other criteria, as appropriate, to determine fair market value.

---

[75] Article 1121 of NAFTA, for instance, waives the requirement to exhaust local remedies, which is an established principle of customary international law. *See* William S. Dodge, *National Courts and International Arbitration: Exhaustion of Remedies and Res Judicata under Chapter Eleven of NAFTA*, 23 Hastings Int'l & Comp. L. Rev. 357 (1999–2000).

[76] Treaty between the United States of America and the Argentine Republic Concerning the Reciprocal Encouragement and Protection of Investment, Nov. 14, 1991, art. IV(1), 31 I.L.M. 124 (1992).

3. Compensation shall be paid without delay and be fully realizable.

4. If payment is made in a G7 currency, compensation shall include interest at a commercially reasonable rate for that currency from the date of expropriation until the date of actual payment.

5. If a Party elects to pay in a currency other than a G7 currency, the amount paid on the date of payment, if converted into a G7 currency at the market rate of exchange prevailing on that date, shall be no less than if the amount of compensation owed on the date of expropriation had been converted into that G7 currency at the market rate of exchange prevailing on that date, and interest had accrued at a commercially reasonable rate for that G7 currency from the date of expropriation until the date of payment.

6. On payment, compensation shall be freely transferable as provided in Article 1109.

7. This Article does not apply to the issuance of compulsory licenses granted in relation to intellectual property rights, or to the revocation, limitation or creation of intellectual property rights, to the extent that such issuance, revocation, limitation or creation is consistent with Chapter Seventeen (Intellectual Property).

8. For purposes of this Article and for greater certainty, a non-discriminatory measure of general application shall not be considered a measure tantamount to an expropriation of a debt security or loan covered by this Chapter solely on the ground that the measure imposes costs on the debtor that cause it to default on the debt.

The Energy Charter Treaty (in Article 13, Expropriation and Article 21, Taxation),[77] which was signed on December 17, 1994, and entered into force in April 1998,[78] both incorporates the basic principles concerning expropriation and applies them to tax measures:

Article 13 Expropriation

(1) Investments of Investors of a Contracting Party in the Area of any other Contracting Party shall not be nationalized, expropriated or subjected to a measure or measures having effect equivalent to nationalization or expropriation (hereinafter referred to as "Expropriation") except where such Expropriation is:

(a) for a purpose which is in the public interest;

(b) not discriminatory;

(c) carried out under due process of law; and

(d) accompanied by the payment of prompt, adequate and effective compensation.

Such compensation shall amount to the fair market value of the Investment expropriated at the time immediately before the Expropriation or impending Expropriation became known in such a way as to affect the value of the Investment (hereinafter referred to as the "Valuation Date").

---

[77] Energy Charter Treaty, art. 13 (Dec. 17, 1994), *available at* http://www.encharter.org/.
[78] As of March 1, 2007, there were forty-seven members of the Energy Charter (with an additional five countries with ratification pending) and nineteen observers to the Energy Charter.

Such fair market value shall at the request of the Investor be expressed in a Freely Convertible Currency on the basis of the market rate of exchange existing for that currency on the Valuation Date. Compensation shall also include interest at a commercial rate established on a market basis from the date of Expropriation until the date of payment.

(2) The Investor affected shall have a right to prompt review, under the law of the Contracting Party making the Expropriation, by a judicial or other competent and independent authority of that Contracting Party, of its case, of the valuation of its Investment, and of the payment of compensation, in accordance with the principles set out in paragraph (1).

(3) For the avoidance of doubt, Expropriation shall include situations where a Contracting Party expropriates the assets of a company or enterprise in its Area in which an Investor of any other Contracting Party has an Investment, including through the ownership of shares.

Article 21 Taxation

. . . .

(5) (a) Article 13 shall apply to taxes.

(b) Whenever an issue arises under Article 13, to the extent it pertains to whether a tax constitutes an expropriation or whether a tax alleged to constitute an expropriation is discriminatory, the following provisions shall apply:

(i) The Investor or the Contracting Party alleging expropriation shall refer the issue of whether the tax is an expropriation or whether the tax is discriminatory to the relevant Competent Tax Authority. Failing such referral by the Investor or the Contracting Party, bodies called upon to settle disputes pursuant to Article 26(2)(c) or 27(2) shall make a referral to the relevant Competent Tax Authorities;

(ii) The Competent Tax Authorities shall, within a period of six months of such referral, strive to resolve the issues so referred. Where non-discrimination issues are concerned, the Competent Tax Authorities shall apply the non-discrimination provisions of the relevant tax convention or, if there is no non-discrimination provision in the relevant tax convention applicable to the tax or no such tax convention is in force between the Contracting Parties concerned, they shall apply the non-discrimination principles under the Model Tax Convention on Income and Capital of the Organisation for Economic Cooperation and Development;

(iii) Bodies called upon to settle disputes pursuant to Article 26(2)(c) or 27(2) may take into account any conclusions arrived at by the Competent Tax Authorities regarding whether the tax is an expropriation. . . .

The recently-enacted U.S. Free Trade Agreement with Central America and the Dominican Republic[79] provides:

---

[79] U.S.-Costa Rica-Dom. Rep.-El Sal.-Guat-Hond.-Nicar. (Aug. 5, 2004), *available at* http://www.ustr.gov/Trade_Agreements/Bilateral/CAFTA/CAFTA-DR_Final_Texts/Section_Index.html.

Article 10.7: Expropriation and Compensation[80]

1. No Party may expropriate or nationalize a covered investment either directly or indirectly through measures equivalent to expropriation or nationalization ("expropriation"), except:

(a) for a public purpose;

(b) in a non-discriminatory manner;

(c) on payment of prompt, adequate, and effective compensation in accordance with paragraphs 2 through 4; and

(d) in accordance with due process of law and Article 10.5.

2. Compensation shall:

(a) be paid without delay;

(b) be equivalent to the fair market value of the expropriated investment immediately before the expropriation took place ("the date of expropriation");

(c) not reflect any change in value occurring because the intended expropriation had become known earlier; and

(d) be fully realizable and freely transferable.

3. If the fair market value is denominated in a freely usable currency, the compensation paid shall be no less than the fair market value on the date of expropriation, plus interest at a commercially reasonable rate for that currency, accrued from the date of expropriation until the date of payment.

4. If the fair market value is denominated in a currency that is not freely usable, the compensation paid—converted into the currency of payment at the market rate of exchange prevailing on the date of payment—shall be no less than:

(a) the fair market value on the date of expropriation, converted into a freely usable currency at the market rate of exchange prevailing on that date, plus

(b) interest, at a commercially reasonable rate for that freely usable currency, accrued from the date of expropriation until the date of payment.

5. This Article does not apply to the issuance of compulsory licenses granted in relation to intellectual property rights in accordance with the TRIPS Agreement [The Agreement on Trade Related Aspects of Intellectual Property Rights], or to the revocation, limitation, or creation of intellectual property rights, to the extent that such issuance, revocation, limitation, or creation is consistent with Chapter Fifteen (Intellectual Property Rights).[81]

---

[80] SN: Article 10.7 shall be interpreted in accordance with Annexes 10-B and 10-C.

[81] SN: For greater certainty, the reference to "the TRIPS Agreement" in paragraph 5 includes any waiver in force between the Parties of any provision of that Agreement granted by World Trade Organization (WTO) Members in accordance with the WTO Agreement.

The Free Trade Agreements that that United States has signed with Singapore,[82] Chile,[83] Australia,[84] Morocco,[85] Colombia,[86] and Peru[87] as well as the United States-Uruguay BIT[88] contain near identical provisions regarding expropriation.[89]

The case of *Goetz v. Burundi* illustrates the approach of a tribunal that hewed to the precise terms of a treaty, carefully applying the provisions to the facts before it:

> *Antoine Goetz v. République du Burundi*[90]
>
> ICSID Case No. ARB/95/3 (Decision of Feb. 10, 1999), 15 ICSID Rev.-F.I.L.J. 457, 513–16
>
> The proceedings were instituted on November 29, 1995 by Mr. Antoine Goetz and five other Belgian investors against Burundi. The dispute concerned AFFIMET, a company incorporated in Burundi involved in the production and marketing of precious metals, owned by the six Belgian investors. The company was granted a "certificate of free zone" by Burundi in 1993. The free zone regime conferred tax and customs exemptions. However, two years later Burundi withdrew the certificate on the grounds that the free zone regime no longer applied to companies involved in the extraction and sale of ore. As a result of the withdrawal of the certificate of free zone, the Belgian individuals incurred losses. They brought the case on a basis of consent to arbitration under the

---

[82] See Letter from United States Trade Representative Robert Zoellick to Singapore Minister for Trade and Industry George Yeo (May 6, 2003), *follow link for Exchange of Letters on Expropriation at* http://www.ustr.gov/Trade_Agreements/Bilateral/Singapore_FTA/Final_Texts/Section_Index.html.

[83] See U.S.-Chile Free Trade Agreement, art. 10.9 and Annexes 10-A and 10-D (Jun. 6, 2003), *available at* http://www.ustr.gov/Trade_Agreements/Bilateral/Chile_FTA/Final_Texts/Section_Index.html.

[84] See U.S.-Austl. Free Trade Agreement, art. 11.7 and Annexes 11-A and 11-B (Mar. 1, 2004), *available at http://www.ustr.gov/Trade_Agreements/Bilateral/Australia_FTA/Final_Text/Section_Index.html*

[85] See U.S.-Morocco Free Trade Agreement, art. 10.6 and Annexes 10-A and 10-B (Jun. 15, 2004), *available at* http://www.ustr.gov/Trade_Agreements/Bilateral/Morocco_FTA/Section_Index.html.

[86] See U.S.-Colom. Free Trade Agreement, art. 10.7 and Annex 10-B (Nov. 22, 2006), *available at* http://ustr.gov/assets/Trade_Agreements/Bilateral/Colombia_FTA/Final_Text/asset_upload_file630_10143.pdf

[87] See U.S.-Peru Free Trade Agreement, art. 10.7 and Annex 10-B (Apr. 12, 2006), a*vailable at* http://ustr.gov/assets/Trade_Agreements/Bilateral/Peru_TPA/Final_Texts/asset_upload_file483_9547.pdf

[88] See U.S.-Uruguay BIT, art. 6 and Annexes A and B (Nov. 5, 2005), a*vailable at* http://ustr.gov/assets/World_Regions/Americas/South_America/Uruguay_BIT/asset_upload_file582_6728.pdf

[89] Unlike NAFTA Chapter 11, these free trade agreements do not contain the "tantamount to nationalization or expropriation" language in the article regarding expropriation. They tend to use "equivalent to expropriation."

[90] Trans. by authors, 2000.

ICSID Convention contained in the 1989 bilateral investment treaty between the Belgium-Luxembourg Economic Union and Burundi (the "Investment Convention").

124. The international legality of the revocation of the free enterprise certificate must be viewed in light of Article 4 of the Investment Convention, entitled "Measures Expropriating or Restricting Property." There is no doubt that the disputed decision cannot itself be analyzed as a measure expropriating or restricting property, but the very terms of Article 4 state that the provision targets not only expropriatory and restrictive measures stricto sensu, but more broadly covers any measures "having similar effect." According to the terms of the first paragraph of this article, in effect the Republic of Burundi has undertaken not to "adopt any measure expropriating or restricting property, nor any other measure having a similar effect" with regard to investments located in its territory. Such measure can be adopted only where there is an exceptional need due to the interest of public utility, security, or national interest, in which case the following conditions must be satisfied:

a) the measures are adopted according to legal procedures;

b) they are neither discriminatory, nor contrary to any particular agreement;

c) they are accompanied by provisions for the payment of adequate and effective compensation.

This last condition is set forth in paragraph 2 of article 4, in the following terms:

> Compensation provided in paragraph 1(c) shall represent the commercial value of the given investment on the day before the measures were adopted, or, otherwise, on the day before the measures became publicly known. In either case, if an investment has no commercial value, or if the investor in question establishes that the commercial value of the expropriated investment is less than its real and objective value, then compensation shall be calculated on the basis of this [real and objective] value. Any compensation shall be paid in the currency of the investor's State or in another convertible currency. It shall be paid promptly, shall be capable of effective implementation, and shall include interest calculated from the date of the expropriation at a reasonable commercial rate. Compensation shall be freely transferable.

Since, according to the facts supplied to the Tribunal by the Claimants, the revocation of the free enterprise certificate forced them to cease all activities from August 13, 1996, the date of their last export, which deprived their investment of any utility and robbed the Claimant investors of the profit they could have obtained from their investments, the disputed measure can be regarded as a "measure having a similar effect" to measure expropriating or restricting property in the sense of Article 4 of the Investment Convention.

125. According to the terms of the first paragraph of Article 4 of the Investment Convention, a measure expropriating or restricting property or a measure having a similar result is internationally legal as long as certain conditions are met. It is only when one of these conditions is found to be lacking that the host State can be regarded as having breached its international obligations under the Investment Convention and, more specifically, as having transgressed the obligation set forth in Article 3 to ensure that investors of the other Party receive "constant protection and security."

126. First Condition: a measure such as the one applied to AFFIMET is only internationally legal if "imperatives of public utility, security, or national interest absolutely require it." It is perfectly clear from an overview of Burundi law that this condition must be taken into account. The facts of the case reveal that it was in the interest of the national economy that in 1992 the Burundi authorities instituted a free trade zone to promote investments. It was in this same interest that the authorities at first included gold in the activities whose national importance justified such a favorable regime, before excluding it from the regime some time

later. The change of regulations was preceded by in depth studies, one of which was carried out by an international consulting group. In the absence of an error of law or fact, a manifest error of judgment, or a usurpation of power, it is not for this Tribunal to substitute its own judgment for the discretionary analysis of the Government of Burundi of the "imperatives of public utility ... or national interest."[91] Therefore, the first condition for the international legality of the disputed measure is satisfied.

127. Second Condition: to be internationally legal, the measure must not only be validly motivated, but must also have been adopted "according to a legal procedure." It has been established above that this was indeed the case. The international legality of the measure, which depends in turn upon its legality under national law, is thus established in connection with this second condition.

128. Third Condition: in order to be internationally legal, the measure must be neither discriminatory nor contrary to a specific agreement between the investors and the host State. This condition poses no difficulty. As has been already noted, the Claimants do not assert that there was any discrimination with regard to similarly situated enterprises. Additionally, because the allocation of the free zone regime is not contractual in nature but instead constitutes a unilateral measure of the Burundi administration, there can be no question here of a measure "contrary to a specific agreement."

129. Now to the Last Condition: in order for the measure to be legal with regard to the Belgium-Burundi treaty, it must include provision for the payment of "adequate and effective compensation," with the compensation calculated according to the principles contained in paragraph 2 of Article 4, reproduced above. The Investment Convention thus embodies on the international level one of the guiding ideas of French administrative law—and, to some extent, Burundi law, namely that if the state imposes through its innate power a special and unusual burden on a private person in the public interest, this must result in monetary compensation. In the contractual sphere, this idea is found in the so-called "prince theory," which arbitral jurisprudence applies to state contracts,[92] according to which the administration can unilaterally modify certain definite contractual rights and obligations, or even terminate a contract, when the general interest so requires, but must in such cases indemnify the other contracting party. In the non-contractual sphere, this idea is the basis for the jurisprudence on State responsibility without fault as a result of its legislative or administrative acts—regulatory or individual—that impose a particular and unusual burden on a private party in the interest of the public at large.

130. In this case, the final condition set by Article 4 of the Investment Convention for the legality of a "measure having an effect similar" to an expropriation or property restriction is not currently satisfied, since the May 29, 1995 revocation of the free enterprise certificate was not accompanied by the adequate and effective compensation upon which the international legality of the revocation depended. However, the Tribunal does not consider this circumstance sufficient for international illegality to attach to the disputed measure. The Investment Convention requires adequate and effective compensation; unlike many national laws on expropriation, it does not require prior indemnification.

131. That is to say that the question of the international legality of the May 29, 1995 decision remains suspended. One of two outcomes applies. On the one hand, the Republic of Burundi can, within a reasonable time, satisfy the condition of adequate

---

[91] SN: *See* I.F. I. Shihata, "Recent Trends Relating to Entry of Foreign Direct Investment," 9 ICSID Rev.-F.I.L.J. 47, 58 (1994), which speaks of a "self-judging" analysis, measured, according to customary international law, by a standard of good faith.

[92] SN: *Southern Pacific Properties (Middle East) (SPP) v. Arab Republic of Egypt*, ARB/84/3 32 I.L.M., 970, ¶¶ 176–77 (1993); J. du Droit Int'l, 235 (1994).

and effective compensation by paying an amount according to the criteria and demands of Article 4(2) of the Investment Convention. In such a case, the international legality of the May 29, 1995 decision will be definitively established. Or, the Republic of Burundi may fail to satisfy this final condition for the measure's international legality within a reasonable time. In this case, Burundi will have violated the international obligation that it took on through the Belgium-Burundi Investment Convention, to which it acceded in the full and free exercise of its international sovereignty, to "not take any measure of expropriation or property restriction, nor any other measure having a similar effect with regard to investments located within its territory" except on certain conditions. The international responsibility of the government of Burundi would then be implicated at once for violating the obligation codified in Article 4 to refrain from taking any measure having an effect similar to an expropriation or property restriction and for violating the obligation codified in Article 3, to ensure Belgian investments within its territory "full protection and security."

132. It would be otherwise, however, if the Republic of Burundi decided to reestablish AFFIMET's status as a free enterprise. In such a case, the international legality of the Republic's action would no longer pose any problem. The reestablishment of AFFIMET as a free enterprise would naturally have only prospective effect, and the question of reparation for damages caused between the date the benefit was revoked and the date of its reestablishment could be raised. The tribunal considers nevertheless that since the revocation of the status was legal under national Burundi law and did not give rise to any liability of the Burundi government within the context of its internal law, there would be no cause for compensation of such damages, even assuming that they could be proven.

133. In other words, it behooves the Republic of Burundi, in order to establish the international legality of the disputed decision to revoke the agreement, to provide the claimants adequate and effective compensation as provided in Article 4 of the Belgium-Burundi Convention on Investment Protection, unless it wishes to effect restitution of the benefit of the free zone regime. The choice remains the sovereign prerogative of the Burundi government. Failing within a reasonable time to take one of these actions, the Republic of Burundi would be committing an internationally illegal act, which would lead this Tribunal to draw the appropriate conclusions.

This decision is unusual in giving Burundi a "second chance" to resolve the dispute in accordance with the terms of the treaty; most tribunals would have assessed the damages incurred by the investor.[93] The decision is also noteworthy for concluding without any analysis that the revocation of a "free enterprise license" was a measure having a "similar effect" to expropriation,[94] and thus violative of the treaty prohibition. The tribunal thus dealt in somewhat summary fashion with one of the central problems of modern investment law—at what point does a government act rise to the level of an indirect or regulatory expropriation.

---

[93] The case settled after this award.
[94] *Antoine Goetz v. Republic of Burundi*, ICSID Case No. ARB/95/3 (Introductory Note Feb. 10, 1999), ¶ 124, *available at* http://icsid.worldbank.org/.

D. The Problem of Indirect or Regulatory Expropriation

A particularly contentious issue in international investment law is defining precisely what types of government action constitute an expropriation. There is a variety of vocabulary in this area—seizure, confiscation, nationalization, sequestration, condemnation—and an even larger number of ways that property can be expropriated. Expropriation can be direct, indirect, regulatory, creeping, de facto, or a government act may be "tantamount to," "equivalent to," or "have similar effect as" expropriation.[95]

It should be said at the outset that any determination of whether there has been an indirect or regulatory expropriation is highly dependent on the particular facts of the dispute. Indeed, although there have been innumerable decisions and writings on this issue, the factual setting of a dispute is almost always more important than any particular doctrinal approach or formulation of the controlling legal principles. Leading commentators have long recognized that a case-by-case approach is imperative.[96]

Notwithstanding this fact-intensive approach, certain broad principles have evolved out of the decisions and the literature in the field. It is well-settled that the physical seizure of property without compensation by a government constitutes a direct expropriation. The history of international investment law is replete with outright physical seizure of mines, oil and gas fields, factories, businesses, and land. Although direct expropriations are not as prevalent now as in the past, especially with the demise of Marxist-Leninist regimes, they still occur.[97] Such physical seizures or the outright transfer of legal title of an investment cause few doctrinal

---

[95] *See* Don Wallace, Jr., *Case Study under NAFTA: Lessons for the Wise?*, Horn ed., *supra* note 60, at 255.

[96] *See* Christie, *supra* note 15; Fortier and Drymer, *supra* note 74, at 326–27 ("In most cases, the determination of when State conduct crosses the line between non-compensable regulation and compensable indirect expropriation tends to involve a balancing of several considerations. That many of these considerations are particular to a given case may be frustrating to those who seek not only clarity but definitiveness in international legal norms. Yet it is perhaps the only reasonable means of approaching an issue that touches both public and private interests and that can arise in such innumerable circumstances. Moreover, it is the reality of foreign investment (indeed, of any investment) in areas of genuine and legitimate public concern that both public and private interests are at play."); OECD, *International Investment Law* 22 (OECD Directorate for Financial and Enterprise Affairs, Working Papers on International Investment, Nov. 2004), [hereinafter OECD Paper on Expropriation] ("prudence requires [a recognition] that the list of criteria which can be identified today from state practice and existing jurisprudence is not necessarily exhaustive and may evolve. Indeed, new investment agreements are being concluded at a very fast pace and the number of cases going to arbitration is growing rapidly. Case-by-case consideration which may shed additional light will continue to be called for").

[97] *See, e.g.*, "Tin soldiers," *The Economist* (Feb. 15, 2007) ("It is becoming a familiar ritual. On February 9th Evo Morales, Bolivia's socialist president, flanked by troops, stood in front of the Vinto tin smelter and declared it nationalized. Last May he did the same to his country's natural-gas industry"). *See also* Guzman, *supra* note 18, at 647 (1998).

problems because both the character and consequence of such acts is readily apparent. Indeed, for purposes of legal classification, such direct expropriations are the easy cases.

Much more troublesome are those instances where there is no physical seizure or outright transfer of title, but instead where a government enacts a measure that interferes with property rights or diminishes the value of a property or property right. There is general agreement that government interference or other measures short of seizure can at some point constitute an expropriation. For example, in *Starrett Housing*, the tribunal observed:

> [T]he Government of Iran did not issue any law or decree according to which the [investment] expressly was nationalized or expropriated. However, it is recognized in international law that measures taken by a State can interfere with property rights to such an extent that these rights are rendered so useless that they must be deemed to have been expropriated, even though the State does not purport to have expropriated them and the legal title to the property formally remains with the original owner.[98]

More recently, in *Feldman v. Mexico* the tribunal declared:

> Recognizing direct expropriation is relatively easy: governmental authorities take over a mine or factory, depriving the investor of all meaningful benefits of ownership and control. However, it is much less clear when governmental action that interferes with broadly-defined property rights ... crosses the line from valid regulation to a compensable taking, and it is fair to say that no one has come up with a fully satisfactory means of drawing the line."[99]

Likewise, in *Tippetts* the tribunal stated, "A deprivation or taking of property may occur under international law through interference by a state in the use of that property or with the enjoyment of its benefits, even where legal title to the property is not affected,"[100] and in *Tecmed*, the tribunal concluded that "[u]nder international law, the owner is also deprived of property where the use or enjoyment of benefits related thereto is exacted or interfered with to a similar extent, even where legal ownership over the assets in question is not affected, and so long as the deprivation is not temporary."[101]

---

[98] *Starrett Housing, supra* note 52, § IV(b).

[99] *Marvin Feldman v. United Mexican States*, Case No. ARB. (AF)/99/1 (Dec. 16, 2002), 42 I.L.M. 625 (2003) ¶ 100 [hereinafter *Feldman*].

[100] *Tippetts, Abbett, McCarthy, Stratton v. TAMS-AFFA Consulting Engineers of Iran, the Gov't of the Islamic Rep. of Iran, Civil Aviation Organization, Plan and Budget Organization, Iranian Air Force, Ministry of Defence, Bank Melli, Bank Sakhteman, Mercantile Bank of Iran & Holland*, Award, Case No. 7, 6 Iran-U.S. Cl. Trib. Rep. 219 (June 22, 1984) [hereinafter *Tippetts*].

[101] *Tecmed, supra* note 71, ¶ 116; compare *Pope & Talbot, Inc. v. Gov't. of Canada* (Interim Award, Jun. 26, 2000), ¶ 96 [hereinafter *Pope & Talbot*] ("the Tribunal concludes that the Investment's access to the U.S. market is a property interest subject to protection under Article 1110. . . .").

The signal problem is defining with precision when an exercise of regulatory or police power[102] crosses the line and becomes compensable, and a vast literature makes clear that the line is neither bright nor clear. In international law, this difficulty is compounded by the fact that a police power justification for what would otherwise be an expropriation has, until recently, been little explored.[103] Although generally recognizing the primacy of the facts, international tribunals and commentators have nonetheless articulated many different formulations to determine when a government act is or is not expropriatory. For example:

> Indirect expropriation or nationalization is a measure that does not involve an overt taking, but that effectively neutralizes the enjoyment of the property.[104]

> Expropriation in international law connotes the deprivation of a person's use and enjoyment of his property, either as the result of a formal act having that consequence, or as the result of other actions which *de facto* have that effect. Expropriation involves the deprivation by State organs of a right of property either as such, or by permanent transfer of the power of management and control.[105]

> The nationalization, confiscation or expropriation of an investment, including "creeping" expropriation, due to unlawful government acts (or a series of acts) that deprive the investor of its fundamental rights in a project. The coverage excludes losses due to lawful regulation or taxation by host governments and actions provoked by the investor or foreign enterprise.[106]

---

[102] *Black's Law Dictionary* (8th ed., 2004), for example, defines "police power" as "1. The inherent and plenary power of a sovereign to make all laws necessary and proper to preserve the public security, order, health, morality, and justice. It is a fundamental power essential to government, and it cannot be surrendered by the legislature or irrevocably transferred away from government ... 2. A state's Tenth Amendment right [under the United States Constitution], subject to due-process and other limitations, to establish and enforce laws protecting the public's health, safety, and general welfare, or to delegate this right to local governments ... 3. Loosely, the power of the government to intervene in the use of privately owned property, as by subjecting it to eminent domain ..." See also "Indirect Expropriation" and "the Right to Regulate" in OECD Paper on Expropriation, *supra* note 96.

[103] See OECD Paper on Expropriation, *supra* note 96, at 18–19.

[104] *Lauder v. Czech Republic* (Final Award, Sept. 3, 2001) [hereinafter *Lauder*] ¶ 200. See also *CME Partial Award*, *supra* note 67, ¶ 604 ("effectively neutralize the benefit of the property").

[105] Ian Brownlie, *Principles of Public International Law* 508–09 (Oxford University Press, 6th ed., 2003).

[106] Overseas Private Investment Corporation Insurance Policy (on file with authors).

Measures taken by competent authorities ... in the legitimate, nondiscriminatory exercise of its police power, which reduce an investment value, do not constitute expropriation within the meaning of article III [of the Model BIT].[107]

[A]ny legislative action or administrative action or omission attributable to the host government which has the effect of depriving the holder of a guarantee of his ownership or control of, or a substantial benefit from, his investment, with the exception of non-discriminatory measures of general application which the governments normally take for the purpose of regulating economic activity in their territories.[108]

Expropriation under NAFTA includes not only open, deliberate and acknowledged takings of property, such as outright seizure or formal or obligatory transfer of title in favour of the host State, but also covert or incidental interference with the use of property which has the effect of depriving the owner, in whole or in significant part, of the use or reasonably-to-be-expected economic benefit of property even if not necessarily to the obvious benefit of the host State.[109]

A state is responsible under international law for injury resulting from:

> (1) a taking by the state of the property of a national of another state that (a) is not for a public purpose, or (b) is discriminatory, or (c) is not accompanied by provision for just compensation;
>
> ....
>
> (3) other arbitrary or discriminatory acts or omissions by the state that impair property or other economic interests of a national of another state.[110]
>
> ....
>
> A state is responsible as for an expropriation of property under [Subsection (1)] when it subjects alien property to taxation, regulation, or other action that is confiscatory, or that prevents, unreasonably interferes with, or unduly delays, effective enjoyment of an alien's property or its removal from the state's territory. Depriving an alien of control of his property, as by an order freezing his assets, might become a taking if it is long extended. A state is not responsible for loss of property or for other economic disadvantage resulting from bona fide general taxation, regulation, forfeiture for crime, or other action of the kind that is commonly accepted as within the police power of states, if it is not discriminatory ... and is not designed to cause the alien to abandon the property to the state or sell it at a distress price. As under

---

[107] Pamela B. Gann, *The U.S. Bilateral Investment Treaty Program*, 21 Stan. J. Int'l L. 373, 399 note 120 (1985).

[108] Convention Establishing the Multilateral Investment Guarantee Agency (MIGA), Oct. 11, 1985, art. 11(ii), 1508 U.N.T.S. 100.

[109] *Metalclad Corp. v. United Mexican States*, ICSID Case No. ARB (AF)/97/1 (Award of Aug. 30, 2000), ¶ 103.

[110] *Restatement, supra* note 8, § 712.

United States constitutional law, the line between "taking" and regulation is sometimes uncertain."[111]

In 2004, the United States government issued its updated Model Bilateral Investment Treaty (U.S. Model BIT). Article 6 of the U.S. Model BIT, in conjunction with its Annexes A and B, set forth the current U.S. view regarding customary international law on indirect expropriation.[112] Annex B to the U.S. Model BIT states:

> The Parties confirm their shared understanding that:
>
> 1. Article 6 [Expropriation and Compensation] (1) is intended to reflect customary international law concerning the obligation of States with respect to expropriation.
>
> 2. An action or a series of actions by a Party cannot constitute an expropriation unless it interferes with a tangible or intangible property right or property interest in an investment.
>
> 3. Article 6 [Expropriation and Compensation] (1) addresses two situations. The first is direct expropriation, where an investment is nationalized or otherwise directly expropriated through formal transfer of title or outright seizure.
>
> 4. The second situation addressed by Article 6 [Expropriation and Compensation] (1) is indirect expropriation, where an action or series of actions by a Party has an effect equivalent to direct expropriation without formal transfer of title or outright seizure.
>
>> (a) The determination of whether an action or series of actions by a Party, in a specific fact situation, constitutes an indirect expropriation, requires a case-by-case, fact-based inquiry that considers, among other factors:
>>
>>> (i) the economic impact of the government action, although the fact that an action or series of actions by a Party has an adverse effect on the economic value of an investment, standing alone, does not establish that an indirect expropriation has occurred;
>>>
>>> (ii) the extent to which the government action interferes with distinct, reasonable investment-backed expectations; and
>>>
>>> (iii) the character of the government action.

---

[111] *Id.* at cmt. g.

[112] *See* Annex A, U.S. Model BIT ("The Parties confirm their shared understanding that 'customary international law' generally and as specifically referenced in Article 5 [Minimum Standard of Treatment] and Annex B [Expropriation] results from a general and consistent practice of States that they follow from a sense of legal obligation").

> (b) Except in rare circumstances, non-discriminatory regulatory actions by a Party that are designed and applied to protect legitimate public welfare objectives, such as public health, safety, and the environment, do not constitute indirect expropriations.

As illustrated above and discussed below, although tribunal decisions and commentators have identified a number of factors that are relevant to adjudicating indirect expropriations, generally speaking, the most important factors are: (1) the effect of the government measures on an investment; (2) the intent, purpose, nature or character of the governmental act or measure, and (3) the degree of reliance on the government's representations. Other factors, such as (4) the duration of the effect of the governmental act or measure, (5) whether the investor has sought domestic remedies, (6) whether the government act has been validated by domestic courts, and (7) whether the government has transferred the investment to itself or to a third party, are considered by tribunals and commentators, albeit less frequently.

1. The Effect of the Government Measures

There is unanimous agreement that one of the most important factors in determining whether a government act is an indirect or regulatory expropriation is the effect or the consequences of the government act on the investor's property. In fact, in some arbitrations, the effect is the only factor the tribunal has considered.[113] In evaluating the effect or impact, tribunals have tended to focus on three factors: (1) whether the investor's fundamental rights have been affected, and in particular whether the investor remains in control of an ongoing business; (2) whether the entire value of the investment or business has been destroyed; or (3) (at least in theory) whether the value of the business has been significantly or substantially diminished.

---

[113] *See In the Matter of Revere Copper & Brass, Inc. v. Overseas Private Investment Corp.*, 56 I.L.R. 258 (1978) [hereinafter *Revere Copper*]; *CMS, supra* note 69, ¶ 262 ("The essential question is therefore to establish whether the enjoyment of the property has been effectively neutralized"); *Nykomb Synergetics Technology Holding, AB, Stockholder v. Republic of Latvia, Riga* (Award, Arb. Inst. of Stockholm Chamb. of Comm., Dec. 16, 2003) [hereinafter *Nykomb*] ¶ 4.3.1 ("The decisive factor for drawing the border line towards expropriation must primarily be the degree of possession . . . [taken] or control over the enterprise the disputed measures entail"). *But see* Rudolf Dolzer, "Indirect Expropriations: New Developments?, 11 N.Y.U. Envt'l L.J. 64 (2002); Fortier and Drymer, *supra* note 74 (distinguishing decisions that rely on the impact of the governmental action on the investor (the "sole effect doctrine") and those decisions that consider other factors).

First, one formulation, which has been adopted by certain tribunals[114] and by the U.S. Overseas Private Investment Corporation (OPIC),[115] requires that the deprivation pertain to the investor's "fundamental rights" in the investment.[116] Examples of "fundamental rights" include the right to control the day-to-day operations of the investment[117] and to be free from interference with management and shareholders' activities.[118] The NAFTA *Pope & Talbot* award is one of the principal decisions that has focused on the degree of control the investor was left with, as well as its ability to continue to operate an ongoing business.[119] There, the tribunal articulated a standard for "expropriation" that essentially required loss of control over the investment before the loss of value would be significant enough to constitute an expropriation:

> 100. . . . First of all, there is no allegation that the Investment has been nationalized or that the Regime is confiscatory. The Investor's (and the Investment's) Operations Controller testified at the hearing that the Investor remains in control of the Investment, it directs the day-to-day operations of the Investment, and no officers or employees of the Investment have been detained by virtue of the Regime. Canada does not supervise the work of the officers or employees of the Investment, does not take any of the proceeds of company sales (apart from taxation), does not interfere with management or shareholders' activities, does not prevent the Investment from paying dividends to its shareholders, does not interfere with the appointment of directors or management and does not take any other actions ousting the Investor from full ownership and control of the Investment.
>
> 101. The sole "taking" that the Investor has identified is interference with the Investment's ability to carry on its business of exporting softwood lumber to the U.S. While this interference has, according to the Investor, resulted in reduced profits for

---

[114] See *Thomas Earl Payne v. Gov't of the Islamic Rep. of Iran* (Award No. 245–335–2), 12 Iran-U.S. Cl. Trib. Rep. 3 (Aug. 8, 1986) [hereinafter *Payne*] ¶ 22, quoting *Tippetts, supra* note 100, ¶ 225; *Compañia del Desarrollo de Santa Elena v. Costa Rica* (Final Award), ICSID Case No. ARB/96/1 (Feb. 17, 2000) ¶¶ 77–78; *Feldman, supra* note 99, ¶¶ 118–19 (no "fundamental right of ownership" of investor to obtain a tax rebate for exportation of cigarettes).

[115] See 22 U.S.C. §§ 2191 *et seq.*

[116] See *supra* note 106; *Capital India Power Mauritius & Energy Enterprises (Mauritius) Co. v. Maharashtra Power Dev. Corp.*, ICC Arb. Case No. 12913/MS (Apr. 27, 2005) at 31, available at http://ita.law.uvic.ca/documents/Dabhol_award_050305.pdf (finding a "total expropriation of the Claimant's investment in the Project . . . result[ing] in depriving Claimant of its fundamental rights in the Project and the entire benefit of its investment therein"); *Bechtel Enterprises Int'l v. OPIC*, AAA Case No. 50 T195 0059 02 (Sep. 25, 2003) at 25, available at http://www.opic.gov/ (under the OPIC policy, governmental acts must "directly deprive the Investor of fundamental rights in the insured investment" and "rights are 'fundamental' if without them the Investor is substantially deprived of the benefits of the investment." The tribunal found that the closure of the policyholder's plant has "effectively destroyed the investment of Claimants").

[117] See Christie, *supra* note 15, at 337 ("the most fundamental right that an owner of property has is the right to participate in its control and management").

[118] *Pope & Talbot, supra* note 101, ¶ 100.

[119] See id.

the Investment, it continues to export substantial quantities of softwood lumber to the U.S. and to earn substantial profits on those sales.

102. Even accepting ... the allegations of the Investor concerning diminished profits, the Tribunal concludes that the degree of interference with the Investment's operations ... does not rise to an expropriation (creeping or otherwise) within the meaning of Article 1110. While it may sometimes be uncertain whether a particular interference with business activities amounts to an expropriation, the test is whether that interference is sufficiently restrictive to support a conclusion that the property has been "taken" from the owner. Thus, the *Harvard Draft* defines the standard as requiring interference that would "justify an inference that the owner will not be able to use, enjoy, or dispose of the property . . . " The *Restatement*, in addressing the question whether regulation may be considered expropriation, speaks of "action that is confiscatory, or that prevents, unreasonably interferes with, or unduly delays, effective enjoyment of an alien's property." Indeed, at the hearing, the Investor's Counsel conceded, correctly, that under international law, expropriation requires a "substantial deprivation." The Export Control Regime has not restricted the Investment in ways that meet these standards.

The reasoning in *Pope & Talbot* has been persuasive to other tribunals. For example, in *Feldman v. Mexico*, the tribunal declared:

Here, as in *Pope & Talbot*, the regulatory action (enforcement of longstanding provisions of Mexican law) has not deprived the Claimant of control of his company, [Corporación de Exportaciones Mexicanas, S.A. de C.V.] CEMSA, interfered directly in the internal operations of CEMSA or displaced the Claimant as the controlling shareholder. The Claimant is free to pursue other continuing lines of export trading, such as exporting alcoholic beverages, photographic supplies, or other products for which he can obtain from Mexico the invoices required under Article 4, although he is effectively precluded from exporting cigarettes. Thus, this Tribunal believes there has been no "taking" under this standard articulated in *Pope & Talbot*, in the present case.[120]

Similarly, in *CMS Gas v. Argentina*,[121] the tribunal stated:

Substantial deprivation was addressed in detail ... in the *Pope & Talbot* case. The Government of Argentina has convincingly argued that the list of issues to be taken into account for reaching a determination on substantial deprivation, as discussed in that case, is not present in the instant dispute. In fact, the Respondent has explained, the investor is

---

[120] *Feldman, supra* note 99, ¶ 152. See also *Methanex Corp. v. U.S.* (Final Award, Aug. 3, 2005) [hereinafter *Methanex*], Pt. IV, Ch. D, ¶¶ 15–17 (". . . the Tribunal concludes that the California ban was made for a public purpose, was non-discriminatory and was accomplished with due process . . . From the standpoint of international law, the California ban was a lawful regulation and not an expropriation. Nor has Methanex established that the California ban manifested any of the features associated with expropriation. In *Feldman v. Mexico*, the tribunal held that 'the regulatory action has not deprived the Claimant of control over his company ... interfered directly in the internal operations ... or displaced the Claimant as the controlling shareholder. The claimant is free to pursue other continuing lines of business activity ... this does not amount to Claimant's deprivation of control of his company' ... Methanex claims that it lost customer base, goodwill and market share ... [I]n a comprehensive taking, these items may figure in valuation. But it is difficult to see how they might stand alone, in a case like the one before the Tribunal.").

[121] *CMS, supra* note 69, ¶¶ 263–64.

in control of the investment; the Government does not manage the day-to-day operations of the company; and the investor has full ownership and control of the investment . . . The Tribunal is persuaded that this is indeed the case in this dispute and holds therefore that the Government of Argentina has not breached [the expropriation article of the United States-Argentina BIT].[122]

Thus, in circumstances where the investor retains full control of an ongoing business, many tribunals are likely to reject allegations of expropriation.

Second, many tribunals have analyzed whether the government measures have effectively destroyed the entire value of the investment, regardless of the degree of retained control. These tribunals have generally concluded that if the governmental measures deprive the owner of all of the benefits of its vested property rights, then an expropriation has occurred.[123] In *Tecmed*[124] the tribunal observed:

> To establish whether the Resolution is a measure equivalent to an expropriation . . . it must be first determined if the Claimant . . . was radically deprived of the economical use and enjoyment of its investments, as if the rights related thereto—such as the income or benefits

---

[122] See also *LG&E Energy Corp., LG&E Capital Corp., & LG&E Int'l Inc. v. Argentine Republic*, ICSID Case No. ARB/02/1 ¶¶ 199–200 (Oct. 3, 2006) ("Further, it cannot be said that Claimants lost control over their shares in the licensees, even though the value of the shares may have fluctuated during the economic crisis, or that they were unable to direct the day-to-day operations of the licensees in a manner different than before the measures were implemented. Thus, the effect of the Argentine State's actions has not been permanent on the value of the Claimants' shares, and Claimants' investment has not ceased to exist. Without a permanent, severe deprivation of LG&E's rights with regard to its investment, or almost complete deprivation of the value of LG&E's investment, the Tribunal concludes that these circumstances do not constitute expropriation."); *Enron Corp. & Ponderosa Assets, L.P. v. Argentine Republic*, Award (Ancillary Claim), ICSID Case No. ARB/01/3 ¶ 245 (May 22, 2007) [hereinafter *Enron & Ponderosa*] ("The list of measures considered in the *Pope & Talbot* case as tantamount to expropriation, which the Respondent has invoked among other authorities, is in the Tribunal's view representative of the legal standard required to make a finding of indirect expropriation. Substantial deprivation results in that light from depriving the investor of the control of the investment, managing the day-to-day operations of the company, arrest and detention of company officials or employees, supervision of the work of officials, interfering in the administration, impeding the distribution of dividends, interfering in the appointment of officials and managers, or depriving the company of its property or control in total or in part.") (citing *Pope & Talbot, supra* note 101, ¶ 100).

[123] See *CME Partial Award, supra* note 67, ¶ 604 ("measures that do not involve an overt taking but that effectively neutralize the benefit of the property of the foreign owner, are subject to expropriation claims. This is undisputed under international law."); *Phelps Dodge Corp. v. Islamic Repub. of Iran* (Award No. 217–99–2), 10 Iran-U.S. Cl. Trib. Rep. 121 (Mar. 19, 1986) ¶ 22 ("A deprivation or taking of property may occur under international law through interference by a state in the use of that property or with the enjoyment of its benefits, even where legal title to the property is not affected"); *Starrett Housing, supra* note 52, § IV(b) (appointment of Iranian manager demonstrated that "the government of Iran had interfered with the Claimant's property rights in the Project to an extent that rendered these rights so useless that they must be deemed to have been taken"); *Petrolane v. Gov't Islamic Republic of Iran*, 27 Iran-U.S. Cl. Trib. Rep. 64, 96 (1991) (prevention of exportation of excess equipment "deprived the Claimant of the effective use, benefit, and control of the equipment . . . in breach of contract, as well as constituting an expropriation"). *Cf.* Jan Paulsson & Zachary Douglas, *Indirect Expropriation in Investment Treaty Arbitration*, in Horn ed., *supra* note 60.

[124] *Tecmed, supra* note 71, ¶ 115.

related to the Landfill or to its exploitation—had ceased to exist. In other words, if due to the actions of the Respondent, the assets involved have lost their value or economic use for their holder and the extent of the loss. [citations omitted] This determination is important because it is one of the main elements to distinguish, from the point of view of an international tribunal, between a regulatory measure, which is an ordinary expression of the exercise of the state's police power that entails a decrease in assets or rights, and a de facto expropriation that deprives those assets and rights of any real substance.

Similarly, in *CME v. Czech Republic*, the tribunal found that the Czech Republic's alteration of the exclusive license to operate the television station "caused the destruction of CNTS [claimant's investment] operations, leaving CNTS as a company with assets but without business" and that there was "no immediate prospect at hand that CNTS can resume its broadcasting operations, as they were in 1996 before the legal protection of the use of the license was eliminated."[125] In *Middle East Cement v. Arab Republic of Egypt*, the tribunal evaluated the revocation of the investor's license to import cement, its main business, with four years remaining on the license. Because the revocation effectively terminated the investor's business, it constituted a measure tantamount to expropriation under the Egypt-Greece BIT.[126] The tribunal wrote, "[w]hen measures are taken by a State the effect of which is to deprive the investor of the use and benefit of his investment even though he may retain nominal ownership of the respective rights being the investment . . . the investor is deprived by such measures of parts of the value of his investment."[127] In *Biloune v. Ghana Investment Centre*, the tribunal found that "the conjunction of the stop work order, the demolition [of the investor's construction project], the summons [of the investor to governmental offices], the arrest [of the investor], the detention [of the investor] . . . and the deportation [of the investor] had the effect of causing the irreparable cessation of work on the project."[128]

A third approach concerns those circumstances in which an investor retains control, and where the investment still has some value, but that value has been significantly or substantially diminished by the government measures. In *Metalclad v. Mexico*, the tribunal stated that "A regulatory measure qualifies as expropriatory if it deprives the investor in whole *or in significant part*, of the use or reasonably-to-be-expected economic benefit of property."[129] Many other

---

[125] *CME Partial Award*, supra note 67, ¶¶ 591, 607.

[126] *Middle East Cement Shipping and Handling Co., S.A. v. Egypt*, ICSID Case No. ARB 99/6 (Apr. 12, 2002).

[127] *Id.* ¶ 107.

[128] Oct. 27, 1989, 95 I.L.R. 184, 209 (1990) [hereinafter *Biloune*].

[129] *Metalclad*, supra note 109, ¶ 103.

definitions of regulatory expropriation articulate a similar standard.[130] Although tribunals been unable to draw a sharp line between mere regulation and expropriation, the less residual value the investment in question retains, the more likely tribunals are to find state liability. For example, in one of the only cases expressly evaluating residual value of an ongoing enterprise, *CME v. Czech Republic*, the tribunal found liability where approximately 90.5 percent of the asset value was destroyed.[131]

Although the "substantial deprivation" standard exists at least as a matter of doctrinal theory, tribunals have in practice been reluctant to apply it. Thus, the *Metalclad* standard was specifically rejected in *Waste Management v. Mexico*,[132] where the tribunal noted that even though Mexico's breaches of the claimant's contract "had the effect of depriving [claimant] of the 'reasonably-to-be-expected economic benefit' of the project ... that will be true of any serious breach of contract: the loss of benefits or expectations is not a sufficient criterion for an expropriation, even if it is a necessary one."[133] The tribunal, after analyzing the cases, concluded "it is one thing to expropriate a right under a contract and another to fail to comply with the contract."[134] Although the *Waste Management* decision hinged more on the concept that mere breaches of contract cannot constitute an expropriation, other tribunals have refused to apply the "substantial deprivation" test where the investor retains control over the investment.

In particular, as set forth above, the series of decisions arising out of the Argentine government's promulgation of Argentina's Emergency Law of January 2002[135] have thus far[136] refused to apply the substantial deprivation test.[137] However, each of those tribunals has also held that although the Argentine Emergency Law of

---

[130] See, e.g., UNCTAD, *Series on Issues in International Investment Agreements, Taking of Property* 3–4 (2000) (indirect expropriation includes "official acts that effectuate ... a significant depreciation in the value of assets"); U.N. Conference on Trade and Development, *Bilateral Treaties in the Mid-1990s*, at 66 (1998) (expropriation may occur where conduct "*substantially* impairs" the property's value).

[131] See *CME Czech Republic B.V. v. Czech Republic* (UNCITRAL Final Award, Mar. 4, 2003) ¶ 620 [hereinafter *CME Final Award*].

[132] ICSID Case. No. ARB (AF)/00/3 (Apr. 30, 2004), 43 I.L.M. 967 (2004).

[133] *Id.* ¶ 159.

[134] *Id.* ¶ 175.

[135] Emergency Law No. 25.561.

[136] Through June 1, 2007.

[137] See *CMS*, supra note 69, ¶ 263; *LG&E*, supra note 122, ¶¶ 199–200; *Enron & Ponderosa*, supra note 122, ¶¶ 243–250.

2002 was not expropriatory,[138] it was nevertheless a violation of the fair and equitable standard, and each found liability on that basis.[139] It is thus possible that the "substantial deprivation" test will be wholly displaced by the fair and equitable treatment standard.

2. The Intent, Purpose, Nature, or Character of the Governmental Act or Measure

The degree to which a tribunal should consider the intent, purpose, nature, or character of the governmental act arguably now provokes more controversy than the question of the degree of deprivation itself. At one end of the spectrum are those sources that contend that these contextual factors should be given no weight in the calculus as to whether an indirect or regulatory expropriation has occurred; at the other end are those sources that contend that these contextual factors, which often reflect a sovereign state's legitimate exercise of the "police power," can be a broad and complete defense to any alleged expropriation. As the tribunal in *Azurix Corp. v. The Argentine Republic* observed, "[w]hether to consider only the effect of measures tantamount to expropriation or consider both the effect and purpose of the measures is a point on which not only the parties disagree but also arbitral tribunals."[140]

The government's intent or purpose for enacting a measure has generally been less important than the measure's consequences for the investment.[141] For example, in *Tecmed*, the tribunal noted that "[t]he government's intention is less important than the effects of the measures on the owner of the assets or on the benefits arising from

---

[138] In *Azurix, supra* note 72, ¶ 322, however, the tribunal found that "the impact on the investment attributable to the Province's actions was not to the extent required to find that, in the aggregate, these actions amounted to an expropriation; Azurix did not lose the attributes of ownership, at all times continued to control [its subsidiary] and its ownership of 90 percent of the shares was unaffected. No doubt the management of [its subsidiary] was affected by the Province's actions, but not sufficiently for the Tribunal to find that Azurix's investment was expropriated."

[139] See *CMS, supra* note 69, ¶¶ 266–84; *LG&E supra* note 122, ¶¶ 132–39; *Enron & Ponderosa, supra* note 122, ¶¶ 256–68. See also *Azurix, supra* note 72, ¶¶ 358–78.

[140] See *Azurix, supra* note 72, ¶ 309.

[141] See *CME Partial Award, supra* note 67, ¶ 608, quoting *Tippets* ("The intent of the government is less important than the effects of the measure on the owner, and the form of the measures of control or interference is less important than the reality of their impact"); *Biloune, supra* note 128, ¶ 26 ("The motivations for the actions and omissions of Ghanaian governmental authorities are not clear. But the Tribunal need not establish those motivations to come to a conclusion in this case. What is clear is that the conjunction of the [various governmental acts] had the effect of causing the irreparable cessation of work on the project"); *Metalclad, supra* note 109, ¶ 111; *S.D. Myers, supra* note 61, ¶¶ 281, 285 (noting in passing that a tribunal must examine the "purpose and effect" of governmental measures). *But see Methanex, supra* note 120, Pt. IV, Ch. D, ¶ 7.

such assets affected by the measures; and the form of the deprivation measure is less important than its actual effects."[142] Certain commentators have approved this approach on the grounds that determining the intention or purpose behind a governmental act or measure is difficult, if not impossible, to determine conclusively.[143]

A number of arbitral tribunals have failed or refused to consider the intent, purpose, character or nature of the government act.[144] Others have referred to the purpose of the governmental act or measure to support their conclusions. For example, in *Phillips Petroleum Co. Iran v. Iran*, in which the tribunal found that Iran's acts reflected an expropriatory purpose, the tribunal stated:

> [T]he Tribunal need not determine the intent of the Government of Iran; however, the effects of actions are consistent with a policy to nationalize a whole industry and to that end expropriate particular alien property interests, and are not merely the incidental consequences of an action or policy designed for an unrelated purpose, [and therefore] the conclusion that a taking has occurred is all the more evident.[145]

Still others have analyzed the government's purpose and have chosen to defer to the goals and methods adopted by a sovereign to regulate property within its borders rather than dismiss consideration of these concerns altogether.[146]

---

[142] *Tecmed*, supra note 71, ¶ 116.

[143] Burns H. Weston, *"Constructive Takings" under International Law: A Modest Foray into the Problem of "Creeping Expropriation,"* 16 Va. J. Int'l L. 103, 115–16 (1975) (questioning utility of trying to evaluate governmental motives or purposes of taking).

[144] *See Metalclad*, supra note 109, ¶ 111 ("The Tribunal need not decide or consider the motivation or intent of the adoption of the Ecological Decree") (excerpted more fully at p. 478 *infra*); *Phelps Dodge Corp. v. Islamic Repub. of Iran* (Award No. 217–99–2), 10 Iran-U.S. Cl. Trib. Rep. 121, 130 (Mar. 19, 1986) ("the Tribunal fully understands the financial, economic and social concerns that inspired the law pursuant to which it acted, but those reasons and concerns cannot relieve [Iran] of the obligation to compensate [claimant] for its loss"); *Compañia del Desarrollo de Santa Elena v. Costa Rica*, ICSID Case No. ARB/96/1 (Final Award, Feb. 17, 2000) ¶ 71 ("the purpose of protecting the environment for which the property was taken does not alter the legal character of the taking for which adequate compensation must be paid. The international source of the obligation to protect the environment makes no difference"); *Biloune*, supra note 128, ¶ 26 ("The motivations for the actions and omissions of the Ghanaian governmental authorities are not clear. But the Tribunal need not establish those motivations to come to a conclusion in the case.")

[145] *Phillips Petroleum Co. Iran v. Iran & Nat'l Iranian Oil Co.* (Award No. 425–39–2), 21 Iran-U.S. Cl. Trib. Rep. 79 (June 29, 1989) [hereinafter *Phillips Petroleum*] ¶ 97.

[146] *Siemens*, supra note 72, ¶ 273 ("On the other hand, the public purpose of the 2000 Emergency Law was to face the dire fiscal situation of the Government. This is a legitimate concern of Argentina and the Tribunal defers to Argentina in the determination of its public interest."); *James v. U.K.*, 98 Eur. Ct. H.R. (ser. A) 9, 32 (1986) (national authorities are "better placed than [an] international [court] to appreciate what is in the public interest"); Christie, supra note 15, at 332 (" 'Purpose,' however, is a much-abused word in international law. It is impossible to read many of the authors who have written widely on the subject of expropriation and nationalization without coming to suspect that, at least some of the time, they are not talking about the purpose which a State actually gives for its actions but rather about some "real" purpose, some subjective purpose, which motivates the State or, rather, the persons who have the supreme power in a State").

Regardless of a tribunal's doctrinal approach, it is clear that a tribunal will be far less likely to find that a government act is expropriatory if it is "a non-discriminatory regulation for a public purpose,"[147] and at least one early treaty expressly stated as much.[148] Professor Christie observed in 1962:

> The conclusion that a particular interference is an expropriation might also be avoided if the State . . . had a purpose in mind which is recognized in international law as justifying even severe, though by no means complete, restrictions on the use of property. Thus, the operations of a State's tax laws, changes in the value of a State's currency, actions in the interest of the public health and morality, will all serve to justify actions which because of their severity would not otherwise be justifiable [so long as the action is not discriminatory].[149]

If a tribunal is not convinced that a government act is an "ordinary measure of the State," then it is more likely to find that the act is expropriatory.[150] Likewise, if the tribunal finds that the reasons behind a governmental measure were unrelated to public policy concerns or that the measure was otherwise unjustified, the tribunal is more likely to find that an expropriation has occurred.[151] In respect of certain policy areas, a tribunal may, however, be willing to give a state more

---

[147] *See Methanex, supra* note 120, Pt. IV, Ch. D, ¶ 7; *Feldman, supra* note 99, ¶ 113; *Sea-Land Serv. v. Islamic Republic of Iran*, 6 Iran-U.S. Cl. Trib. Rep. 149, 166 (1984); *Restatement, supra* note 8, § 712, cmt. g (stating that a measure is not an indirect expropriation if it is "commonly accepted as within the police power of states, if it is not discriminatory . . . and it is not designed to cause the alien to abandon the property to the state or sell it at a distress price").

[148] *See* Protocol 1 to the European Convention for the Protection of Human Rights and Fundamental Freedoms, art. 1 (1952) (*entered into force* 1954): "Every natural or legal person is entitled to the peaceful enjoyment of its possessions. No one should be deprived of his possessions except in the public interest and subject to the conditions provided for by the law and by the general principles of international law. The preceding provisions shall not, however, in any way impair the right of a State to enforce such laws as it deems necessary to control the use of property in accordance with the general interest or to secure the payment of taxes or other contributions or penalties." *See* note 156 *infra* for full citation.

[149] Christie, *supra* note 15, at 331–32.

[150] *See CME Partial Award, supra* note 67, ¶ 603 ("The Council's actions and inactions, however, cannot be characterized as normal broadcasting regulator's regulations in compliance with and in execution of the law . . .").

[151] *See id., supra* note 67, ¶ 609 (emphasizing that the government agency's objective was to deprive the investor of the exclusive use of its license); *Siemens, supra* note 72, ¶ 273 ("Decree 669/01 became a convenient device to continue the process started more than a year earlier long before the onset of the fiscal crisis. From this perspective, while the public purpose of the 2000 Emergency Law is evident, its application through Decree 669/01 to the specific case of Siemens' investment and the public purpose of same are questionable."). *See also Metalclad, supra* note 109, ¶ 106 (noting that the investor's construction permit was denied "without any basis in the proposed physical construction or any defect in the site"); *Int'l Bank v. OPIC*, 11 I.L.M. 1216, 1224, 1227–28 (1972) (no expropriation by Dominican Republic when it denied permits for timber cutting, in light of the legitimate goals of the government and the nondiscriminatory nature of the regulations, as well as the limited period of interference with operations).

latitude to enact certain measures; for example, if it can be shown that they relate to a government's right to tax,[152] to control its currency,[153] or to regulate health, welfare, and the environment.[154] One tribunal has more recently made the observation that a tribunal must "balance two competing interests: the degree of the measure's interference with the right of ownership and the power of the State to adopt its policies."[155]

At least three arbitral tribunals—a NAFTA tribunal in a case against Mexico and two International Centre for Settlement of Investment Disputes (ICSID) tribunals in cases against Argentina—have expanded the scope of the "purpose" analysis to consider the proportionality of the measures.[156] In *Tecmed*, although the tribunal expressly gave more weight to effects than to purpose, it also considered "whether such actions or measures are proportional to the public interest presumably protected thereby and to the protection legally granted to the investments."[157] The tribunal concluded that "[t]he actions undertaken by the authorities to face these socio-political difficulties, where these difficulties do not have serious emergency or public hardship connotations, or wide-ranging and serious consequences, may not be considered from the standpoint of the [BIT] or international law to be sufficient to

---

[152] *See Restatement*, *supra* note 8, § 712 note 6 ("It is often necessary to determine, in the light of all the circumstances, whether an action by a state constitutes a taking or is a police power regulation or tax that does not give rise to an obligation to compensate even though a foreign national suffers loss as a consequence").

[153] The U.S. Foreign Claims Settlement Commission, for example, rejected a series of claims by Americans that losses due to foreign currency regulations enacted by Hungary, Romania, and Bulgaria in response to economic crises constituted a "nationalization, compulsory liquidation or other taking" in violation of international law. *Mascotte Claim*, Jan. 16, 1957, 26 I.L.R. 275 (1963) ("it is well established that a currency reform is an exercise of sovereign authority which does not give rise to a cause of action against the nation); *Endreny Claim* (Nov. 10, 1958), 26 I.L.R. 278 (1963); *Chobady Claim* (Feb. 5, 1958) 26 I.L.R. 292, 293 (plaintiff's grievance "is the consequence of severe currency devaluation . . . brought about by the general economic conditions rather than by any specific action of the Hungarian government which may be characterized as a [taking]"); *Evanoff Claim* (Aug. 13, 1958), 26 I.L.R. 301 (1963) (same regarding Bulgaria); *Muresan Claim*, *supra* note 153, at 295 (same regarding Romania).

[154] *See Methanex v. U.S.*, *supra* note 120, at Pt. IV, Ch. D, ¶¶ 7, 15.

[155] *LG&E Energy Corp.*, *supra* note 122, ¶ 189.

[156] The proportionality test also appears in European Court of Human Rights cases as a factor in determining whether a government's actions violate an individual's right to property under Protocol 1 to the European Convention for the Protection of Human Rights and Fundamental Freedoms. *See* Convention for the Protection of Human Rights and Fundamental Freedoms, 213 U.N.T.S. 222 (*entered into force* Sept. 3, 1953) *as amended by* Protocols Nos. 3, 5, 8, and 11 (*entered into force* Sept. 21, 1970; Dec. 20, 1971; Jan. 1, 1990, and Nov. 1, 1998 respectively); *Walker v. U.K.*, 2006 Eur. Ct. H.R. 37212/02 (2006). *See also Vasilyev v. Russia*, 2005 Eur. Ct. H.R. 66543/01 (2006).

[157] *Tecmed v. Mexico*, *supra* note 71, ¶ 122.

deprive the foreign investor of its investment with no compensation. . . ."[158] In *Azurix Corp. v. The Argentine Republic*, the tribunal wrote:

> The public purpose criterion as an additional criterion to the effect of the measures under consideration needs to be complemented . . . The European Court of Human Rights . . . [has] held that "a measure depriving a person of his property [must] pursue, on the facts as well as in principle, a legitimate aim 'in the public interest,'" and bear "a reasonable relationship of proportionality between the means employed and the aim sought to be realized." This proportionality will not be found if the person concerned bears "an individual and excessive burden." The Court considered that such "a measure must be both appropriate for achieving its aim and not disproportionate thereto." The Court found relevant that non-nationals "will generally have played no part in the election or designation of its [of the measure] authors nor have been consulted on its adoption," and observed that "there may well be legitimate reason for requiring nationals to bear a greater burden in the public interest than non-nationals."[159]

And in *LG&E Energy, et al. v. Argentina*, the tribunal observed, albeit in apparent dicta, that:

> With respect to the power of the State to adopt its policies, it can generally be said that the State has the right to adopt measures having a social or general welfare purpose. In such a case, the measure must be accepted without any imposition of liability, except in cases where the State's action is obviously disproportionate to the need being addressed.[160]

The critical and evolving test, then, is not whether the intent, purpose, nature, or character of the governmental act should be considered in the calculus of whether an indirect expropriation has occurred, but instead how the particular governmental act is to be characterized and how much the purpose, nature or character should weigh in the calculus. Two commentators have recently observed:

> [T]he advent of the so-called "purpose test," as expressed for example in the Draft U.S. Model BIT, is likely to have a far-reaching impact, designed as it is to shield *bona fide* regulatory measures whose purpose is to protect legitimate public welfare objectives from claims of indirect expropriation. Tribunals appear increasingly disinclined to adhere to extreme versions of the "sole effect" or "purpose" doctrines, and are wont in any case to consider both the character and the practical impact of governmental measures.[161]

3. Legitimate Reliance on Government Representations

A third critical factor is the extent of the investor's reliance on government representations. A tribunal is more likely to find that a government measure is an expropriation if the measure contradicts express or even implied representations that the government has made to the investor. The rationale underpinning this representations-and-reliance test was articulated in *AMINOIL*, where the

---

[158] *Id.* ¶ 147.

[159] *See Azurix, supra* note 72, ¶ 311 (internal citations omitted).

[160] *LG&E Energy Corp. supra* note 122, ¶ 195.

[161] Fortier & Drymer, *supra* note 74, at 326.

tribunal reasoned, "with reference to every long-term contract, especially such as involves an important investment, there must necessarily be economic calculations, and the weighing-up of right and obligation, of chances and risks, constituting the contractual equilibrium." Thus, in *Metalclad Corp. v. United Mexican States*, the claimant alleged that a variety of representations supported its claim for indirect expropriation, including assurances from federal officials that the claimant had done everything necessary to operate its investment and that a municipal permit would be granted as a matter of course.[162] The tribunal concluded that "[t]hese measures, taken together with the representations of the Mexican federal government, on which Metalclad relied . . . amount to an indirect expropriation."[163]

The existence of a representation by the government that supports a legitimate expectation is not, however, dispositive. For example, in *CMS Gas Transmission Company v. The Argentine Republic*, the tribunal concluded that although the government of Argentina "did not keep the commitments and obligations it had undertaken under its own legislation, regulations and the License to [the claimant],"[164] the Argentine government's failure to keep those commitments and obligations did not constitute an indirect expropriation.[165] Conversely, if a claimant cannot show that the government violated its representations and commitments, a claim of expropriation is far more difficult to support. The tribunal in *Methanex*, for example, noted that no special representations had been made to the investor in finding that the government measure at issue was not expropriatory,[166] and went on to specifically note that:

---

[162] *Metalclad, supra* note 109, ¶ 41.

[163] *Id.* ¶ 107. *See also Methanex, supra* note 120, Pt. IV, Ch. D, ¶ 7 ("[A] non-discriminatory regulation for a public purpose, which is enacted in accordance with due process and which affects, inter alios, a foreign investor or investment is not deemed expropriation and compensable *unless specific commitments had been given by the regulating government to the then putative foreign investor contemplating investment that the government would refrain from such regulation*") (emphasis added); *Revere Copper & Brass v. OPIC*, 56 I.L.R. 258, 17 I.L.M. 1321, 1331 ("We regard these principles as particularly applicable where the question is, as here, whether actions taken by a government contrary to and damaging to the economic interests of aliens are in conflict with undertakings and assurances given in good faith to such aliens as an inducement to their making investments affected by the action").

[164] *CMS, supra* note 69, ¶ 252.

[165] *Id.* ¶ 253–64.

[166] *Methanex, supra* note 120, Pt. IV, Ch. D, ¶ 10. *See also Opel Austria GmbH v. Council of the European Union*, T-115/94 ¶ 93 (1997) ("The principle of good faith is the corollary in public international law of the principle of protection of legitimate expectations which, according to the case-law, forms part of the Community legal order . . . Any economic operator to whom an institution has given justified hopes may rely on the principle of protection of legitimate expectations. . . .").

Methanex entered a political economy in which it was widely known, if not notorious, that governmental environmental and health protection institutions at the federal and state level ... continuously monitored the use and impact of chemical compounds and commonly prohibited or restricted the use of some of these compounds for environmental and/or health reasons.[167]

The case of *EnCana Corporation v. Republic of Ecuador* reflects the different approaches—and tensions—in the existing jurisprudence regarding the weight given to legitimate expectations of an investor. In *EnCana*, the claimant made two allegations that raised an indirect expropriation claim: (1) that Ecuador's enactment of certain regulations, ongoing denials of value-added tax (VAT) credits and refunds, and amendments to regulations wrongfully deprived EnCana's subsidiaries of certain tax refunds under Ecuadorian law, and (2) irrespective of the legality of those measures, Ecuador's actions had the effect equivalent to an indirect expropriation of the investment.[168] In resolving these claims, the tribunal stated that those claims faced a "double difficulty":

> 173. In the first place, foreign investments like other activities are subject to the taxes and charges imposed by the host State. In the absence of a specific commitment from the host State, the foreign investor has neither the right nor any legitimate expectation that the tax regime will not change, perhaps to its disadvantage, during the period of the investment. Of its nature all taxation reduces the economic benefits an enterprise would otherwise derive from the investment; it will only be in an extreme case that a tax which is general in its incidence could be judged as equivalent in its effect to an expropriation of the enterprise which is taxed.
>
> 174. In the second place, although the EnCana subsidiaries suffered financially from the denial of VAT and the recovery of VAT refunds wrongly made, they were nonetheless able to continue to function profitably and to engage in the normal range of activities, extracting and exporting oil (the price of which increased during the period under consideration).[169]

The *EnCana* tribunal went on to conclude that "only if a tax law is extraordinary, punitive in amount or arbitrary in its incidence would issues of indirect expropriation be raised. In the present case ... the denial of VAT refunds ... did not deny EnCana 'in whole or significant part' the benefits of its investment."[170] Under the *EnCana* approach, at least with respect to taxation issues,

---

[167] *Methanex*, supra note 120, Pt. IV, Ch. D, ¶ 9.
[168] *EnCana*, supra note 73, ¶ 171.
[169] *Id.* ¶¶ 173–74.
[170] *Id.* ¶ 177.

if an investor cannot show that it has been given a specific commitment by the host state, the investor must instead show that its investment has been rendered nearly valueless before an indirect expropriation will be deemed to have occurred.

4. Duration of Effect of Act or Measure

When multiple state actions are involved, determining whether there is an indirect expropriation "will depend on the duration of their cumulative effect. Unfortunately, there is no mathematical formula to reach a mechanical result. How much time is needed must be judged by the specific circumstances of each case."[171] Even if a government regulation results in the "substantial deprivation" of an investor's "fundamental rights" in its investment, there is no expropriation if the effects of the regulation are only temporary.[172] The investor must also show that the "deprivation is not merely ephemeral."[173] Thus, in *S.D. Myers v. Government of Canada*, the tribunal concluded that Canada's eighteen-month closure of the U.S. border to exports of chemicals was "[a]n opportunity [that] was delayed," but there was no expropriation in substantial part because the measure was temporary.[174] In contrast, in *Metalclad* the tribunal found that the government regulation was expropriatory where the "Decree had the effect of barring *forever* the operation of the landfill."[175] And in *LG&E Energy, et al.*, the tribunal wrote, "[g]enerally, the expropriation must be permanent, that is to say, it cannot have a temporary nature, unless the investment's successful development depends on the realization of certain activities at specific moments that may not endure variations."[176]

---

[171] *See Azurix, supra* note 72, ¶ 309.

[172] *See Tecmed, supra* note 71, ¶ 116. *See also Generation Ukraine v. Ukraine*, ICSID Case No. ARB/00/9 (Sep. 16, 2003) ¶¶ 20.32–21.33 [hereinafter *Generation Ukraine*], http://ita.law.uvic.ca/documents/GenerationUkraine_000.pdf, (failure of the city of Kiev to issue investor the documents necessary to proceed with the construction of commercial property was not an indirect expropriation under the U.S.-Ukraine BIT because although it might constitute administrative negligence, it "does not come close to creating a persistent or irreparable obstacle to the Claimant's use, enjoyment or disposal of its investment," particularly in light of the claimant's failure to challenge and correct the acts within the Ukrainian legal system).

[173] *Tippetts, supra* note 100, Pt. III. 1, ¶ 6.

[174] *S.D. Myers, supra* note 61, ¶¶ 283–84, 287 ("an expropriation usually amounts to a lasting removal of the ability of an owner to make use of its economic rights although it may be that, in some contexts and circumstances, it would be appropriate to view a deprivation as amounting to an expropriation, even if it were partial and temporary") *Id.* ¶ 283.

[175] *Metalclad Award, supra* note 109, ¶ 109 (emphasis added).

[176] *LG&E Energy, supra* note 122, ¶ 193.

5. Domestic Remedies Sought

Under many investment treaties, an investor is normally not required to exhaust domestic remedies before turning to an international investment tribunal for relief, but tribunals sometimes look favorably on those investors that have sought domestic remedies first. For example, in *Generation Ukraine*, in concluding that the government measure at issue was not expropriatory, the tribunal stated:

> an international tribunal may deem that the failure to seek redress from national authorities disqualifies the international claim, not because there is a requirement of *exhaustion* of local remedies but because the very reality of conduct tantamount to expropriation is doubtful in the absence of a *reasonable*—not necessarily exhaustive—effort by the investor to obtain correction.[177]

Similarly, in *Feldman*, the tribunal noted that "the Claimant could have availed himself early on of the procedures available under Mexican law to obtain a formal, binding ruling on the invoice issue from [the Ministry of Finance and Public Credit], but apparently chose not to do so."[178]

6. Transfer of the Investment to the Government or to Third Parties

The transfer of the investor's property to the government or a third party is typically a characteristic of direct expropriation rather than indirect expropriation.[179] Nonetheless, some tribunals have cited the fact that there has been no such transfer to support their findings that there has been no indirect expropriation. For example, in *Lauder*, the tribunal stated that "even assuming that the actions taken by the Media Council . . . had the effect of depriving the Claimant of his property rights, such actions would not amount to an appropriation—or the equivalent—by the State, since it did not benefit the Czech Republic or any person or entity related thereto . . ."[180] Likewise, in *S.D. Myers*, the panel defined expropriation as a taking "with a view to transferring ownership of that property to another person, usually the authority that exercised its de jure or de facto power to do the 'taking'" and then observed that "Canada realized no benefit from the measure. The evidence does not

---

[177] *Generation Ukraine, supra* note 172, ¶ 20.30 (emphasis in original).

[178] *Feldman, supra* note 120, ¶ 114 (internal citations omitted).

[179] *See, e.g., Enron & Ponderosa, supra* note 122, ¶ 243 ("In fact, the Tribunal does not believe there can be a direct form of expropriation if at least some essential component of property rights has not been transferred to a different beneficiary, in particular the State. In this case it can be argued that economic benefits might have been transferred to an extent from industry to consumer or from industry to another industrial sector, but this does not amount to affecting a legal element of the property held, such as the title to property.")

[180] *Lauder, supra* note 104, ¶ 203.

support a transfer of property or benefit directly to others."[181] In *Olguín v. Republic of Paraguay*,[182] the tribunal found that a Paraguayan finance company's failure to pay an investor the amount in local currency that he previously deposited in dollars because of a financial crisis that left the finance company bankrupt was not an expropriation under the Peru-Paraguay BIT.[183] The tribunal observed that even if the Paraguayan government's poor regulation caused the finance company's bankruptcy,

> For an expropriation to occur, there must be actions that can be considered reasonably appropriate for producing the effect of depriving the affected party of the property it owns, in such a way that whoever performs those actions will acquire, directly or indirectly, control, or at least [sic] the fruits of the expropriated property. Expropriation therefore requires a teleologically driven action for it to occur; omissions, however egregious they may be, are not sufficient for it to take place.[184]

As the delineation of an improper indirect expropriation continues to evolve, this factor's analytical importance is likely to wane, although recent practice suggests that tribunals are more likely to use this factor to support a finding of "no expropriation."

7. Other Factors

Other factors tribunals might consider in determining whether a government act or measure is expropriatory include whether the act has been validated by domestic courts,[185] whether the investor has suffered a denial of due process,[186] and whether the timing of the investor's complaint corresponds with the occurrence of the disputed government measures or follows it.[187] The following chart illustrates the factors considered in a number of leading cases.

---

[181] *S.D. Myers supra* note 61, ¶¶ 280, 287.

[182] *Eudoro A. Olguín v. Republic of Paraguay*, ICSID Case No. ARB/98/5 (July 26, 2001).

[183] The Peru-Paraguay BIT reads in relevant part: "None of the Contracting Parties will adopt, directly or indirectly, measures of expropriation, nationalization or whichever other methods with the same nature or effect, against investments owned by nationals of the other Contracting Party, except for purposes expressly established in the respective national Constitutions, and on the conditions that these measures are not discriminatory and that they are met with fair and reasonable payment." The BIT further requires that just compensation be provided immediately after the expropriation. *See* Convenio Entre la Republica Del Peru y la Republica Del Paragua Sobre Promocion y Proteccion Reciproca de Inversiones, art.VI (1994) (trans. by authors).

[184] *Id.* ¶ 84.

[185] *See Robert A. Azinian v. United Mexican States*, Award, Case No. ARB (AF)/97/2 (Nov. 1, 1999), ¶¶ 96–97 [hereinafter *Azinian*].

[186] *See Feldman, supra* note 99, ¶ 139. *See also Methanex, supra* note 120, Pt. IV, Ch. D, ¶ 7.

[187] *See Lauder, supra* note 104, ¶ 204.

Factors for Evaluating Whether a Government Measure Constitutes Expropriation

Case	Expropriation?	Loss of Control/Degree of Deprivation	Duration	Intent, Purpose, Nature	Proportionality	Exhaustion	Reliance on Government Reports	Benefit Transfer to Others	Ordinary State Measure	Denial of Due Process	Timing of Complaint
Revere Copper OPIC, 1978	Yes	x						x			
Starrett Housing Iran, 1983	Yes	x									
Tippets Iran, 1984	Yes	x	x					x			
Payne Iran, 1986	Yes	x	x					x			
Phelps Dodge Iran, 1986	Yes	x	x					x			
Phillips Petroleum Iran, 1989	Yes	x		x							
Biloune UNCITRAL Rules, 1990	Yes	x		x					x	x	
Azinian NAFTA, 1999	No			x		x			x		
Metalclad NAFTA, 2000	Yes	x	x	x			x		x	x	
Pope & Talbot NAFTA, 2000	No	x									

Case	Expro-priation ?	Loss of Control/ Degree of Deprivation	Duration	Intent, Purpose, Nature	Proportion-ality	Exhaustion	Reliance on Government Reports	Benefit Transfer to Others	Ordinary State Measure	Denial of Due Process	Timing of Complaint
S.D. Myers NAFTA, 2000	No	x	x	x				x			
CME UNCITRAL, 2001	Yes	x		x					x		
Lauder UNCITRAL, 2001	No	x						x	x		x
Olguín v. Paraguay ICSID, 2001	No	x		x				x			
Feldman NAFTA, 2002	No	x		x		x			x		x
CMS Gas ICSID, 2003	No	x					x				
Generation Ukraine ICSID, 2003	No	x				x	x		x		
Nykomb Stockholm, 2003	No	x	x			x					
Tecmed NAFTA, 2004	Yes	x	x	x	x				x		x

Case	Expropriation?	Loss of Control/ Degree of Deprivation	Duration	Intent, Purpose, Nature	Proportionality	Exhaustion	Reliance on Government Reports	Benefit Transfer to Others	Ordinary State Measure	Denial of Due Process	Timing of Complaint
Methanex NAFTA, 2005	No	x		x			x		x	x	
Azurix ICSID, 2006	No	x	x	x			x		x		x
EnCana LCIA, 2006	No	x		x	x		x		x		
LG & E ICSID, 2006	No	x	x	x	x			x	x		
Siemens ICSID, 2007	Yes	x		x		x	x		x		

LCIA, London Court of International Arbitration; OPIC, Overseas Private Investment Corporation; UNCITRAL, United Nations Commission on International Trade Law.

Many commentators have attempted to synthesize the various factors that may be considered in determining whether expropriation has occurred, such as in the following particularly insightful article:

> Jan Paulsson, Freshfields Bruckhaus Deringer, Paris. *Indirect Expropriation: Is the Right to Regulate at Risk?* From: Making the Most of International Investment Agreements: A Common Agenda. A symposium co-organized by ICSID, OECD, and UNCTAD. December 12, 2005, Paris
>
> Instead of embarking on a description of individual awards, I will rather propose the barebones of some conclusions emerging from this jurisprudence *in statu nascendi*.
>
> 1. The grounds on which a property owner adversely affected by regulation may be entitled to compensation are becoming much clearer. First among these is the notion of "reasonable investment-backed expectations"—not my favourite phrase but so often repeated that it cannot be ignored. Many will prefer the *Methanex* formulation: "specific commitments ... given by the regulating government to the then putative foreign investor contemplating investment that the government would refrain from such regulation."[188] Obvious examples of such expectation-creating commitments are contracts and licences. But there are other circumstances, presumably exceptional, where "policies in force earlier might have created legitimate expectations both of a procedural and substantive nature."[189]
>
> 2. To escape liability under international law, the relevant regulation must be legitimate and bona fide; it will fail that test if the stated objective is shown to be false, as in *S.D. Myers* when a Canadian restriction was revealed not to be motivated by environmental concerns, but rather a stratagem to protect national business interests.[190]
>
> 3. Regulatory acts must be consistent with due process. An inquiry into the public benefit would violate due process if it is perfunctory, one-sided, or otherwise skewed against the investor. More obviously, the forfeiture of a licence on the grounds of failure to respect the conditions of licence is unjustifiable if the licensee is given no opportunity to justify its conduct. And the cancellation of a license is not necessarily a regulatory act at all.
>
> 4. These restrictions on the power to regulate without giving compensation would be impotent if they could be swept aside by self-serving declarations. The state whose conduct is in question cannot "decide" that (i) there was no commitment to the investor, (ii) the regulation was bona fide, or (iii) due process was respected. As Professor Christie put it: "A State's declaration that a particular interference with an alien's enjoyment of his property is justified by the so called 'police power' does not preclude an international tribunal from making its own independent determination of this issue."
>
> 5. In many cases a claimant may seek recovery under several additional grounds, most commonly discrimination or a denial of fair and equitable treatment. When recovery is granted on such alternative grounds, the discussion of indirect expropriation may be obiter. If so, it is far preferable for arbitral tribunals to state that it is unnecessary to decide the expropriation claim, rather than seek to comfort losing respondents—"giving them something"—by declaring that there was no expropriation. Such obiter dicta may

---

[188] SN: At Pt. V, Chapter D, ¶ 7.

[189] SN: Francisco Orrego Vicuña, *Regulatory Authority and Legitimate Expectations: Balancing the Rights of the State and the Individual under International Law in a Global Society*, 5/3 Int'l L.F. 188 (2003).

[190] SN: *S.D. Myers Inc. v. Canada* (Partial Award, Nov. 13, 2000).

have an unintended and unfortunate effect on international jurisprudence, and create difficulties in entirely different contexts where the issues of discrimination and fair and equitable treatment do not arise, such as an investor's claims under an expropriation insurance policy governed by international law.

6. While it is tempting to import notions from the international law of human rights dealing with deprivations of property and violations of due process, there can be no assumptions about the perfect correspondence between instruments devised for quite different purposes. Human rights conventions deal with rights of individuals that are inalienable whether or not the concerned individuals have chosen to subject themselves to a given national system. Investment treaties contemplate the rights of *foreigners*, who as such have both advantages and disadvantages.

7. The magical formula for deciding claims of indirect expropriation is the international lawyer's equivalent of proving Fermat's Last Theorem.[191] The one who finds it would be justly famous—but unlike the case with respect to the proof of the Theorem, no one has done so yet. Most attempts founder quickly; they tend to degenerate into sterile or tautologous obsessions with nomenclature. For example, it may be tempting to suggest that a government which acts to procure public *benefits* should pay compensation for their acquisition, but when it acts to prevent a *harm* no compensation should be due. But as Professor Michelman wrote, almost as long ago as Professor Christie, outlawing billboards next to highways may be equally classified as the prevention of a harm (a nuisance) or as acquiring a benefit (increased safety).[192] Similar conceptual dead ends appear if one imagines that the solution lies in distinguishing between cases where the state acts as *purchaser* or as *policy-maker*, or whether or not there has been an *appropriation* by the State,[193] or whether the deprivation has met some standard of *comprehensiveness*.[194]

Justice Scalia of the US Supreme Court, I hope, discouraged more than one would-be author of the magical formula when he wrote that the ease of articulating regulatory purposes is so great that the use of such criteria "amounts to a test of whether the legislature has stupid staff."[195]

---

[191] SN: $10\, x^n + y^n = z^n$ has no non-zero integer solutions for x, y, and z when $n > 2$.

[192] SN: F. I. Michelman, *Property, Utility, and Fairness: Comments on the Ethical Foundations of "Just Compensation" Law*, 80 Harv. L. Rev. 1165 (1967).

[193] SN: This quickly leads to tortured reasoning, such as insisting that the cancellation of a permit is tantamount to its appropriation because the state has put itself in the position to grant it anew. In his brave bid to promote this approach, Professor Andrew Newcombe argues his way resolutely into a corner, and finds himself reduced to arguing that cases such as *Metalclad*, *CME v. Czech Republic*, and *Tecmed S.A.*, involving "state approval of investment activity in question and then subsequent state interference, . . . can be analogized to a form of indirect government appropriation of the investment in question," "The Boundaries of Regulatory Expropriation in International Law," 1 ICSID Rev., 16 (2005). Verily there is no end to what one might "analogize," and birds are like airplanes because both have wings, but reaching for such analogies is unlikely to contribute to solving problems relating to either avian flu or traffic congestion at Heathrow.

[194] SN: Why should farmer Jones be compensated for his lost hectare but not farmer Smith, just because farmer Smith had a bigger estate? Why should company A be compensated for the loss of its gambling business but not company B, just because company B also operated a bakery business?

[195] SN: *Lucas v. South Carolina Coastal Council*, 112 S. Ct. 2886, at 2898 (1992). The proposed dichotomy in that case was "harm/benefit."

8. It is unacceptable to ignore national law in the absence of an international norm. An international treaty may provide for the protection of contracts, property, or other private-law rights, but international law does not define such rights; one must look to national law. If an alleged *contract* has been annulled by national authorities competent to do so in accordance with due process of law, international law is powerless to find a contract to be expropriated;[196] if a national law does not consider a *lease* to be "property" but rather a contract, it is difficult to see how an investor invoking a treaty which calls vaguely for the protection of "property" (as opposed to "assets" explicitly defined as including "contractual rights") can enlist any international law definition in support of his cause.[197]

E. Case Study: *Metalclad v. Mexico*

One of the more important cases of indirect expropriation is *Metalclad v. Mexico*. In 1993 Metalclad, an American waste disposal company, acquired Confinamiento Tecnico de Residuos Industriales, S.A. de C.V. (COTERIN), a Mexican hazardous waste transfer company, to develop and operate a hazardous waste landfill in the Municipality of Guadalcazar (hereinafter Municipality of Guadalcazar) within the state of San Luis Potosí (SLP), Mexico. The governments of Mexico and SLP issued federal and state construction and operating permits for the landfill prior to Metalclad's purchase of COTERIN.[198]

In April 1994, Metalclad obtained an eighteen-month extension for the construction of the landfill from the relevant agency of the federal government, and it began and continued the construction of the landfill without interruption until October of that year. At that time, the Municipality ordered Metalclad to stop work because it had not obtained a municipal construction permit.[199] With the encouragement of the federal government officials, Metalclad applied for the permit and resumed its work.[200] During this time, Metalclad was subject to contradictory treatment; although federal officials supported its investment and even issued a second permit for the completion of its work, the governor of SLP and the Municipality did not do so. Metalclad continued its work openly and completed the construction in March 1995; because of local protest, however, it was unable to begin operating the landfill. In December 1995, thirteen months after Metalclad had applied for the municipal permit, the Municipality denied the permit. Metalclad did not receive any notification regarding the town council meeting where its application was considered;

---

[196] SN: Compare *Azinian* and *Wena*, two awards that seem irreconcilable.

[197] SN: See Zachary Douglas, *The Hybrid Foundations of Investment Treaty Arbitration*, 74 BYIL 151 (2004), an article which has quickly established itself as indispensable.

[198] *Id.* ¶¶ 28–36.

[199] *Id.* ¶ 40.

[200] *Id.* ¶¶ 41–42.

neither was it afforded any opportunity to appear in that meeting.²⁰¹ Finally, on September 20, 1997, the governor of SLP reentered the scene and issued an ecological decree that effectively and permanently prevented Metalclad's use of its investment by declaring the landfill area a protected zone for the protection of a rare cactus.²⁰² Thereafter, Metalclad filed a claim for arbitration, alleging breaches of seven articles of NAFTA Chapter 11, including Article 1110 on expropriation.

Metalclad Corporation v. United Mexican States (Award)

ICSID Case No. ARB(AF)/97/1 (Aug. 30, 2000)

102. NAFTA Article 1110 provides that "[n]o party shall directly or indirectly . . . expropriate an investment . . . or take a measure tantamount to, . . . expropriation . . . except (a) "for a public purpose; (b) on a non-discriminatory basis; (c) in accordance with due process of law and Article 1105(1); and (d) on payment of compensation. . . . ' "A measure" is defined in Article 102(1) as including "any law, regulation, procedure, requirement or practice.'

103. Thus, expropriation under NAFTA includes not only open, deliberate and acknowledged takings of property, such as outright seizure or formal or obligatory transfer of title in favour of the host State, but also covert or incidental interference with the use of property which has the effect of depriving the owner, in whole or in significant part, of the use of reasonably-to-be-expected economic benefit of property even if not necessarily to the obvious benefit of the host State.²⁰³ (emphasis added)

104. By permitting or tolerating the conduct of Guadalcazar in relation to Metalclad which the Tribunal has already held amounts to unfair and inequitable treatment breaching Article 1105 and by thus participating or acquiescing in the denial to Metalclad of the right to operate the landfill, notwithstanding the fact that the project was fully approved and endorsed by the federal government, Mexico must be held to have taken a measure tantamount to expropriation in violation of NAFTA Article 1110(1).

105. The Tribunal holds that the exclusive authority for siting and permitting a hazardous waste landfill resides with the Mexican federal government.

106. [T]he Municipality denied the local construction permit in part because of the Municipality's perception of the adverse environmental effects of the hazardous waste landfill and the geological unsuitability of the landfill site. In so doing, the Municipality acted outside its authority. [T]he Municipality's denial of the construction permit without

---

²⁰¹ *Id.* ¶ 54.

²⁰² *Id.* ¶ 59.

²⁰³ This paragraph of the award has been discussed by many scholars and in many reports, *see* Paulsson and Douglas, *supra* note 96; OECD Paper on Expropriation, *supra* note 96; Barry Appleton, *Regulatory Takings: The International Law Perspective, Colloquium Article*, 11 N.Y.U. Env. L.J. 35, 39 (2002). *See also* World Investment Report 2003, Ch. 4, *available at* http://www.unctad.org/.

any basis in the proposed physical construction or any defect in the site, and extended by its subsequent administrative and judicial actions ... effectively and unlawfully prevented the Claimant's operation of the landfill.

107. These measures, taken together with the representations of the Mexican federal government, on which Metalclad relied, and the absence of a timely, orderly or substantive basis for the denial by the Municipality of the local construction permit, amount to an indirect expropriation.

108. The present case resembles in a number of pertinent respects that of *Biloune, et al. v. Ghana Investment Centre, et al.*, 95 I.L.R.183, 207–10 (1993) (Judge Schwebel, President; Wallace and Leigh, Arbitrators). In that case, a private investor was renovating and expanding a resort restaurant in Ghana. As with Metalclad, the investor, basing itself on the representations of a government affiliated entity, began construction before applying for a building permit. As with Metalclad, a stop work order was issued after a substantial amount of work had been completed. The order was based on the absence of a building permit. An application was submitted, but although it was not expressly denied, a permit was never issued. The Tribunal found that an indirect expropriation had taken place because the totality of the circumstances had the effect of causing the irreparable cessation of work on the project. The Tribunal paid particular regard to the investor's justified reliance on the government's representations regarding the permit, the fact that government authorities knew of the construction for more than one year before issuing the stop work order, the fact that permits had not been required for other projects and the fact that no procedure was in place for dealing with building permit applications. Although the decision in *Biloune* does not bind this Tribunal, it is a persuasive authority and the Tribunal is in agreement with its analysis and its conclusion.

109. Although not strictly necessary for its conclusion, the Tribunal also identifies as a further ground for a finding of expropriation the Ecological Decree issued by the Governor of SLP on September 20, 1997. This Decree covers an area of 188,758 hectares within the "Real de Guadalcazar" that includes the landfill site, and created therein an ecological preserve. This Decree had the effect of barring forever the operation of the landfill.

110. The Tribunal is not persuaded by Mexico's representation to the contrary. The Ninth Article, for instance, forbids any work inconsistent with the Ecological Decree's management program. The management program is defined by the Fifth Article as one of diagnosing the ecological problems of the cacti reserve and of ensuring its ecological preservation. In addition, the Fourteenth Article of the Decree forbids any conduct that might involve the discharge of polluting agents on the reserve soil, subsoil, running water or water deposits and prohibits the undertaking of any potentially polluting activities. The Fifteenth Article of the Ecological Decree also forbids any activity requiring permits or licenses unless such activity is related to the exploration, extraction or utilization of natural resources.

111. The Tribunal need not decide or consider the motivation or intent of the adoption of the Ecological Decree. Indeed, a finding of expropriation on the basis of the Ecological Decree is not essential to the Tribunal's finding of a violation of NAFTA Article 1110. However, the Tribunal considers that the implementation of the Ecological Decree would, in and of itself, constitute an act tantamount to expropriation.

112. In conclusion, the Tribunal holds that Mexico has indirectly expropriated Metalclad's investment without providing compensation to Metalclad for the expropriation. Mexico has violated Article 1110 of the NAFTA.

Of particular interest is Paragraph 103 of the tribunal's decision, which articulated a now-famous definition of what constitutes an indirect expropriation. Dissatisfied with the NAFTA tribunal's decision, Mexico sought review in the courts of Canada, the situs of the arbitration. The Canadian court reached the following conclusions on NAFTA Article 1110:

> *United Mexican States v. Metalclad Corp. (Judicial Review)*
> British Columbia Superior Court (2001) BCSC 664, *available at* www.investmentclaims.com[204]
>
> Article 1110—Pre-Ecological Decree
>
> 77. Prior to its consideration of the Ecological Decree, the Tribunal concluded that the actions of Mexico constituted a measure tantamount to expropriation in violation of Article 1110. The Tribunal based this conclusion on its view that Mexico permitted or tolerated the conduct of the Municipality, which amounted to unfair and inequitable treatment breaching Article 1105, and that Mexico therefore participated or acquiesced in the denial to Metalclad of the right to operate the landfill. The Tribunal subsequently made reference to the representations by the Mexican federal authorities and the absence of a timely, orderly or substantive basis for the denial of the construction permit by the Municipality in concluding that there had been indirect expropriation. It is unclear whether the Tribunal equated a "measure tantamount to expropriation" with "indirect expropriation" or whether it made two separate findings of expropriation.
>
> 78. I agree with the submission of counsel for Mexico that the Tribunal's analysis of Article 1105 infected its analysis of Article 1110. I have held that the Tribunal decided a matter beyond the scope of the submission to arbitration when it concluded that Mexico had breached Article 1105. The Tribunal's statement that Mexico took a measure tantamount to expropriation was directly connected to its finding of a breach of Article 1105. The statement that Mexico permitted or tolerated the conduct of the Municipality is a clear reference to the Tribunal's view that Mexico failed to ensure a transparent and predictable framework for Metalclad's business planning and investment. Similarly, the Tribunal relied on the absence of a timely, orderly and substantive basis for the denial of the construction permit by the Municipality in making its statement that there had been indirect expropriation. This is also a reference to a lack of transparency.
>
> 79. The Tribunal based its conclusion that there had been a measure tantamount to expropriation/indirect expropriation, at least in part, on the concept of transparency. In finding a breach of Article 1105 on the basis of a lack of transparency, the Tribunal decided a matter beyond the scope of the submission to arbitration. In relying on the concept of

---

[204] Under the ICSID Convention, there is no possibility of appeal in domestic courts. *See* ICSID Convention, Article 54 (*entered into force* Oct. 14, 1966) *as amended and effective* Apr. 10, 2006. *Metalclad*, however, was decided under the Additional Facility Rules of the ICSID (as Mexico is not a member of the Washington Convention), and Article 3 of these rules provides that Additional Facility proceedings are outside the jurisdiction of the ICSID, so that none of the provisions of the Convention applies to them. Consequently, Mexico was able to challenge the award in the courts of British Columbia.

transparency, at least in part, to conclude that there had been an expropriation within the meaning of Article 1110, the Tribunal also decided a matter beyond the scope of the submission to arbitration.

80. In reaching this conclusion that there had been an expropriation within the meaning of Article 1110, the Tribunal made a comparison to the arbitration decision of *Biloune v. Ghana Investments Centre* (1990), 95 I.L.R. 183, which did not involve the concept of transparency. The Tribunal recognized that the *Biloune* decision was not binding on it but found the decision to be persuasive authority and agreed with it. In my view, the Tribunal did not independently rely on *Biloune* in concluding that there had been an expropriation prior to the issuance of the Ecological Decree. The Tribunal simply relied on *Biloune* as support for the conclusion it had already made that there had been an expropriation (which conclusion was based, at least in part, on the concept of transparency). There are substantial differences between the situation in the present case and the circumstances in *Biloune*. The main two distinctions are that in *Biloune* (i) the building was partially destroyed and then closed by government officials, and (ii) the investor was deported from the country and was not allowed to return. Apart from the Ecological Decree, the circumstances in the present case fall considerably short of those in *Biloune* and it would not logically follow that *Biloune* could be an independent basis for concluding that the actions in this case prior to the issuance of the Decree amounted to an expropriation.

Article 1110—Postecological Decree

81. Counsel for Mexico submits that the Tribunal improperly considered the Ecological Decree but that, in any event, it did not base its decision on the Decree. With respect, I cannot agree . . .

85. In view of my conclusion that the Tribunal did find that the Ecological Decree amounted to an expropriation of the Site, it is necessary to decide the following issues:

>   (a) was the Tribunal correct in its conclusion that it could consider the Ecological Decree?
>
>   (b) did the Tribunal decide a matter beyond the scope of the submission to arbitration when it concluded that the announcement of the Ecological Decree constituted an act tantamount to expropriation?
>
>   (c) if a patently unreasonable error is a basis under the *International CAA* for setting aside an arbitral award, was it patently unreasonable for the Tribunal to conclude that the announcement of the Ecological Decree constituted an act tantamount to expropriation?

(a) Consideration of the Ecological Decree

86. This issue can lead to a setting aside of the Award under s. 34(2)(a)(v) of the *International CAA* if the arbitral procedure was not in accordance with the agreement of the parties.

87. In considering the Ecological Decree, the Tribunal relied on Article 48 of the ICSID Additional Facility Rules, which are the arbitration rules selected by Metalclad pursuant to Article 1120 of the NAFTA. Article 48 reads as follows:

(1) Except as the parties otherwise agree, a party may present an incidental or additional claim or counter-claim, provided that such ancillary claim is within the scope of the arbitration agreement of the parties . . .

88. Counsel for Mexico submits that the claim based on the Ecological Decree was a separate claim and does not qualify as an ancillary claim. Although the term "ancillary claim" is used in both paragraphs of Article 48, the operative language is the phrase "incidental or additional claim." The use of the term "ancillary claim" was a shorthand method to refer back to the earlier-used phrase "incidental or additional claim." In my view, Metalclad's claim based on the Ecological Decree was an additional claim which, as required by Article 48, fell within the scope of the agreement to arbitrate (as contained in Section B of Chapter 11 of the NAFTA) . . .

91. I conclude that no error has been demonstrated in the arbitral procedure as a result of the Tribunal considering the claim based on the Ecological Decree.

(b) Beyond the Scope of the Submission

. . . .

94. In my opinion, the Tribunal's conclusion with respect to the Ecological Decree stands on its own and is not based on a lack of transparency or on the Tribunal's finding of a breach of Article 1105. The Tribunal considered the Decree in isolation of its other findings of breaches of the NAFTA. It specifically identified the issuance of the Decree as a further ground for a finding of expropriation . . .

(c) Patently Unreasonable Error

. . . .

99. The Tribunal gave an extremely broad definition of expropriation for the purposes of Article 1110. In addition to the more conventional notion of expropriation involving a taking of property, the Tribunal held that expropriation under the NAFTA includes covert or incidental interference with the use of property which has the effect of depriving the owner, in whole or in significant part, of the use or reasonably-to-be-expected economic benefit of property. This definition is sufficiently broad to include a legitimate rezoning of property by a municipality or other zoning authority. However, the definition of expropriation is a question of law with which this Court is not entitled to interfere under the *International CAA*.

100. The Tribunal reviewed the terms of the Ecological Decree and concluded that it had the effect of barring forever the operation of Metalclad's landfill and constituted an act tantamount to expropriation. It made reference to the Ninth Article of the Decree, which requires that all activities in the area are subject to guidelines established by the management plan for ensuring ecological preservation of the cacti reserve. The Tribunal also made reference to the Fourteenth Article of the Decree, which forbids the spillage or discharge of polluting agents on the soil, subsoil or water of the reserve area. In my view, the Tribunal's conclusion that the issuance of the Decree was an act tantamount to expropriation is not patently unreasonable.

Mexico settled the case shortly after this decision, leaving standing the tribunal's holding on indirect expropriation.

F. The Current U.S. Approach to Indirect or Regulatory Expropriation

The United States Constitution expressly prohibits the taking of private property "for public use ... without just compensation."[205] U.S. courts have developed an extensive body of case law applying this principle,[206] although despite the long history of this doctrine, they have been no more successful than international tribunals in identifying what is an impermissible regulatory taking for their own citizens.[207] Nevertheless, a careful evaluation of U.S. takings law is worthwhile because of the arguably more developed nature of U.S. takings law, the substantial impact of U.S. takings law on the international law of expropriation,[208] and the impact of international law on U.S. courts' interpretation of statutes[209] and common

---

[205] U.S. Constitution, Amendment V (1789) & Amendment XIV (1866). The government's authority to take private property is limited to public purposes. *See Brown v. Legal Foundation of Washington*, 538 U.S. 216, 231–32 (2003) ("While it confirms the State's authority to confiscate private property, the text of the Fifth Amendment imposes two conditions on the exercise of such authority: the taking must be for a 'public use' and 'just compensation' must be paid to the owner"); *Lingle v. Chevron*, 544 U.S. 528, 538 (2005) ("the Takings Clause presupposes that the government has acted in pursuit of a valid public purpose").

[206] This section analyzes how U.S. courts have treated takings under the U.S. Constitution. It does not analyze how U.S. courts have treated or defined expropriations under international law.

[207] *See, e.g., Lingle*, 544 U.S. at 538 ("Twenty-five years ago, the Court posited that a regulation of private property 'effects a taking if [it] does not substantially advance [a] legitimate state interes[t].' The lower courts in this case took that statement to its logical conclusion, and in so doing, revealed its imprecision. Today we correct course.") (citation omitted) (brackets in original).

[208] Discussed in this chapter in section (d).

[209] *See, e.g.,* OPIC Statute, 22 U.S.C. § 2198(b), ("As used in this subpart ... the term 'expropriation' includes, but is not limited to, any abrogation, repudiation, or impairment by a foreign government of its own contract with an investor with respect to a project, where such abrogation, repudiation, or impairment is not caused by the investor's own fault or misconduct, and materially adversely affects the continued operation of the project"); Foreign Sovereign Immunities Act (FSIA), 28 U.S.C. § 1605(a)(3) (denying immunity of foreign states in claims over "rights in property taken in violation of international law"); Second Hickenlooper Amendment, 22 U.S.C. § 2370(e)(2) (prohibiting federal courts from relying upon act of state ground to deny a determination if the merits concern "claim of title or other right to property ... based upon ... a confiscation or other taking ... in violation of the principles of international law"); First Hickenlooper Amendment, 22 U.S.C. § 2370(e)(1) (prohibiting foreign assistance to state that has "nationalized or expropriated or seized ownership or control of property" owned by U.S. nationals, without defining those terms; 26 U.S.C. § 1351(b) (defining "foreign expropriation loss" for tax purposes as "any loss sustained by reason of the expropriation, intervention, seizure, or similar taking of property by the government of any foreign country ... [including] a debt which becomes worthless"); International Claims Settlement Act of 1949, as amended, 22 U.S.C. § 1641b (authorizing Foreign Claims Settlement Commission to determine whether U.S. nationals' property had been subject to a "nationalization, compulsory liquidation, or other taking" by the governments of Bulgaria, Hungary, Romania in violation of international law).

law.[210] Consequently, according to several sources, "the line in international law is similar to that drawn in United States [takings] jurisprudence" in distinguishing between regulations deemed to be takings and other government regulations.[211]

In 1922, the U.S. Supreme Court first recognized that "government regulation of private property may, in some circumstances, be so onerous that its effect is tantamount to a direct appropriation."[212] At that time, Justice Holmes described, "[t]he general rule at least is that while property may be regulated to a certain extent, if regulation goes too far it will be recognized as a taking."[213] Since then, "[t]he rub, of course, has been—and remains—how to discern how far is 'too far.' "[214] In 2005, the United States Supreme Court broadly clarified the standard for regulatory takings under the U.S. Constitution:

> Our precedents stake out two categories of regulatory action that generally will be deemed *per se* takings for Fifth Amendment purposes. First, where government requires an owner to suffer a permanent physical invasion of her property—however minor—it must provide just compensation. A second categorical rule applies to regulations that completely deprive an owner of "*all* economically beneficial us[e]" of her property. We held in [the second case] that the government must pay just compensation for such "total regulatory takings," except to the extent that "background principles of nuisance and property law" independently restrict the owner's intended use of the property.
>
> Outside these two relatively narrow categories . . . , regulatory takings challenges are governed by the standards set forth in *Penn Central Transportation Co. v. New York City*. The Court in *Penn Central* acknowledged that it had hitherto been "unable to develop any 'set formula' " for evaluating regulatory takings claims, but identified "several factors that have particular significance." . . . The *Penn Central* factors—though each has given rise to vexing subsidiary questions—have served as the principal guidelines for resolving regulatory takings claims that do not fall within the physical takings or the ["total regulatory takings"] rule.[215]

---

[210] See *Banco Nacional de Cuba v. Sabbatino*, supra note 10; *Altmann v. Republic of Austria*, 317 F.3d 954, 968 (9th Cir. 2002), *aff'd* 541 U.S. 677 (2004) ("For guidance regarding the norms against takings in violation of international law, we may look to court decisions, United States law, the work of jurists, and the usage of nations"); *West v. Multibanco Comermex, S.A.*, 807 F.2d 829, 831 note 10 (9th Cir. 1987) ("in ascertaining the content of international [takings] law, we may look to various sources of law, including United States law"); *French v. Banco Nacional de Cuba*, 242 N.E.2d 704, 710 (N.Y. 1968) (citing to U.S. Fifth Amendment takings law in its expropriation analysis). See also *F. Hoffman-LaRoche v. Epigram S.A.*, 542 U.S. 155 (2004); and T.A. Aleinikoff, *International Law, Sovereignty, and American Constitutionalism: Reflections on the Customary International Law Debate*, 98 Am. J. Int'l L. 91 (2004).

[211] Restatement, supra note 8, § 712, rep. note 6; see Barry Appleton, *Regulatory Takings: The International Law Perspective*, 11 N.Y.U. Env. L.J. 35 (2002) ("international tribunals have come to essentially similar conclusions as U.S. domestic courts" that have addressed "cutting-edge issues of regulatory takings"); OECD Paper on Expropriation, supra note 96, at 22 ("However, a close examination of the relevant [international] jurisprudence reveals that, in broad terms, there are some criteria that tribunals have used to distinguish these concepts: i) the degree of interference with the property right, ii) the character of governmental measures, i.e. the purpose and the context of the governmental measure, and iii) the interference of the measure with reasonable and investment-backed expectations").

[212] *Lingle*, 544 U.S. at 538, citing *Pennsylvania Coal Co. v. Mahon*, 260 U.S. 393 (1922).

[213] *Mahon*, 260 U.S. at 415.

[214] *Lingle*, 544 U.S. at 537.

[215] See *id.* at 538.

Thus, when the government's action does not result in a *per se* taking under U.S. law, the Court's decision in *Penn Central Transportation Co. v. New York City*[216] provides the applicable factors for determining whether a regulation has taken property[217] in violation of the U.S. Constitution. Under the *Penn Central* test, a U.S. court examines three factors to determine whether a taking has occurred:

1. The degree to which the property right is impacted by the regulation

2. The investor's reasonable investment-backed expectations

3. The nature and character of the challenged government act.[218]

The purpose of the *Penn Central* test, like the constitutional guarantee itself, is "to bar Government from forcing some people alone to bear public burdens which, in all fairness and justice, should be borne by the public as a whole."[219] Consequently, these three factors are not exclusive,[220] and "careful examination and weighing of all the relevant circumstances"[221] is required.

Under the *Penn Central* test, a U.S. court must first consider the impact of the regulation on the property right.[222] When determining the magnitude of the economic impact, the value of the property that has been allegedly taken is generally compared to the value of the property as a whole that remains, rather than to discrete segments of that property.[223] Even a substantial decrease in property

---

[216] 438 U.S. 104 (1978).

[217] *See, e.g., Home Savings of America v. U.S.*, 51 Fed. Cl. 487, 495 (2002) (application of *Penn Central* test presupposes a property interest).

[218] *Penn Central*, 438 U.S. at 124. *See Kaiser Aetna v. U.S.*, 444 U.S. 164, 175 (1979) (replacing "distinct investment-backed expectations" set forth in *Penn Central* with "reasonable investment-backed expectations").

[219] *Penn Central*, 438 U.S. at 123–24 (quoting *Armstrong v. U.S.*, 364 U.S. 40, 49 (1960)).

[220] *See id.* at 24 (factors have "particular significance"); *Tahoe-Sierra Preservation Council v. Tahoe Regional Planning Agency*, 535 U.S. 302, 327 note 23 (2002) (*Penn Central* "does not supply mathematically precise variables, but instead provides important guideposts that lead to the ultimate determination whether just compensation is required") (quoting *Palazzolo v. Rhode Island*, 533 U.S. 606, 634 (2001) (J. O'Connor, concurring)).

[221] *Brown v. Legal Found. of Wash.*, 538 U.S. 216 (2003) (quoting *Palazzolo*, 533 U.S. at 636).

[222] *See Duquesne Light Co. v. Barach*, 488 U.S. 299, 310 (1989) ("it is not theory but the impact of the [regulation] which counts") (quoting *FPC v. Hope Natural Gas Co.*, 320 U.S. 591, 605 (1944)).

[223] *See Keystone Bituminous Coal Assoc. v. DeBenedictis*, 480 U.S. 470, 497 (1987); *Tahoe-Sierra*, 535 U.S. at 327 (focus is on "parcel as a whole"); *Andrus v. Allard*, 444 U.S. 51, 65–66 (1979) ("where an owner possesses a full 'bundle' of property rights, the destruction of one 'strand' of the bundle is not a taking, because the aggregate must be viewed in its entirety"). *Cf. Palazzolo* 533 U.S. at 631 ("Some of our cases indicate that the extent of deprivation effected by a regulatory action is measured against the value of the parcel as a whole, but we have at times expressed discomfort with the logic of this rule, a sentiment echoed by some commentators") (citations omitted).

value does not, in itself, establish a taking.[224] Rather, the alleged deprivation of property value must be "significant enough to satisfy the heavy burden placed upon one alleging a regulatory taking."[225] That "up-hill battle . . . is made especially steep" where there is no allegation or proof that the regulation "makes it commercially impracticable . . . to continue" to use the property as planned.[226]

The second *Penn Central* factor indicative of a taking is the deprivation of reasonable investment-backed expectations.[227] Although this factor gives rise to significant questions over the applicable legal and evidentiary standards, generally speaking, a party's reasonable investment-backed expectations derive primarily from the degree of the regulation, the investor's knowledge of the risks inherent in the industry, the reasonableness of the regulation, and the relationship of the property or contractual interest to the regulatory scheme at issue.[228] The range of investment-backed expectations that an owner of private property may reasonably hold is "greatly reduced in proportion to the amount of regulation. . . ."[229] Consequently, where the government can reasonably be expected to modify the contractual terms at issue, such modification may not constitute a taking.[230] In other words, what might otherwise be a taking may fail if the investors' expectations are low because the subject is regulated.

---

[224] See *Concrete Pipe & Prods. of Calif. v. Constr. Laborers Pension Trust*, 508 U.S. 602, 645 (1993) (no taking despite challenged act's effect of a 46 percent payout in shareholder equity); *Agins v. City of Tiburon*, 447 U.S. 255, 258, 262 (1980) (no taking despite alleged $2 million in damages where zoning ordinance still allowed up to five houses to be built); *Village of Euclid, Ohio v. Amber Realty Co.*, 272 U.S. 365, 384 (1926) (no taking despite 75 percent diminution in value of property); *Hadacheck v. Sebastian*, 239 U.S. 394, 405 (1915) (no taking despite 92.5 percent diminution).

[225] *Keystone*, 480 U.S. at 493.

[226] *Id.* at 495–96.

[227] See generally J. David Breemer & R. S. Radford, *The (Less?) Murky Doctrine of Investment-Backed Expectations after Palazzolo, and the Lower Courts' Disturbing Insistence on Wallowing on the Pre-Palazzolo Muck*, 34 Sw. U. L. Rev. 351 (2005).

[228] See *Ruckelshaus v. Monsanto*, 467, U.S. 986, 1008–1010 (1984); *Connolly v. Pension Benefit Guaranty Corp.*, 475 U.S. 211, 226–27 (1986); *Palazzolo*, 533 U.S. at 626–29; *Tahoe-Sierra*, 535 U.S. at 336–37.

[229] See *Bowen v. Public Agencies Opposed to Social Sec. Entrapment*, 477 U.S. 41, 52 (1986); *Energy Reserves Group, Inc.*, 459 U.S. at 413–414 (no taking when statute eliminated price escalation clauses where "supervision of the industry was extensive and intrusive" and regulatory conditions changed).

[230] See *Energy Reserves Group, Inc. v. Kansas Power & Light Co.*, 459 U.S. 400, 413 & 416 (1983); *City of El Paso v. Simmons*, 379 U.S. 497, 507–508 (1965); *Connolly*, 475 U.S. at 224 ("the fact that legislation disregards or destroys existing contractual rights does not always transform the legislation into an illegal taking") (citations omitted); *Norman v. Baltimore & Ohio R. Co.*, 294 U.S. 240, 307–308 (1935) ("[c]ontracts may create rights of property, but, when contracts deal with a subject matter which lies within the control of the Congress, they have a congenital infirmity").

The third *Penn Central* factor—the nature and character of the challenged law or regulation—evaluates whether the government's policy considerations outweigh what might otherwise be considered a regulatory taking. Such an examination and balancing is required because regulatory interference with property rights that "arises from a public program that adjusts the benefits and burdens of economic life to promote the common good" does not effectuate a taking.[231] As the U.S. Supreme Court declared in *Pennsylvania Coal Company v. Mahon*:

> Government hardly could go on if to some extent values incident to property could not be diminished without paying for every such change in the general law. As long recognized some values are enjoyed under an implied limitation and must yield to the police power.[232]

The case of *Miller v. Schoene*[233] illustrates this principle. In that case, the Commonwealth of Virginia, in response to an epidemic of cedar rust disease that threatened adjacent apple orchards, passed legislation that created a "comprehensive scheme" for the condemnation and destruction of infected cedar trees.[234] The Supreme Court rejected a takings challenge to the legislation, declaring:

> It would have been none the less a choice if, instead of enacting the present statute, the state, by doing nothing, had permitted serious injury to the apple orchards within its borders to go on unchecked. When forced to such a choice the state does not exceed its constitutional powers by deciding upon the destruction of one class of property in order to save another which, in the judgment of the legislature, is of greater value to the public.[235]

Thus, such an exercise of the "police powers" will not constitute an illegal taking under the U.S. Constitution, but rather meets the requirement that it is for "public use."

Because of the wide-ranging and often complicated nature of the lawmaking and regulatory process, determining the nature and character of the law or regulation likewise depends heavily on the particular facts of the case.[236] Consequently, this factor may include the examination of a number of considerations:

---

[231] See *Penn Central*, 438 U.S. at 124; *Connolly*, 475 U.S. at 225; *Lingle*, 544 U.S. at 538 ("the Takings Clause presupposes that the government has acted in pursuit of a valid public purpose").

[232] 260 U.S. 393, 413 (1922).

[233] 276 U.S. 272 (1928).

[234] See *id.* at 277–78.

[235] See *id.* at 279.

[236] See *Yee v. Escondido*, 503 U.S. 519, 523 (1992) (regulatory takings cases "necessarily entai[l] complex factual assessments of the purposes and economic effects of government actions").

1. The purpose and objective of the law or regulation in question[237]

2. Whether the law or regulation falls within the traditional authority of the legislative branch to legislate[238]

3. Whether the law or regulation is narrowly focused to promote the health and safety of the public[239]

4. Whether the law or regulation was necessitated by an emergency or averted a crisis[240]

5. Whether the law or regulation involves currency controls, particularly in response to an economic crisis[241]

---

[237] *See, e.g., Miller*, 276 U.S. 272; *Penn Central*, 438 U.S. at 127 ("[A] use restriction on real property may constitute a 'taking' if not reasonably necessary to the effectuation of a substantial public purpose, [citations omitted], or perhaps if it has an unduly harsh impact upon the owner's use of the property").

[238] *Kelo v. New London*, 540 U.S. 469, 483 (2005) ("legislatures [have] broad latitude in determining what public needs justify the use of the takings power"); *Norman v. Baltimore & Ohio R. Co.*, 294 U.S. 240, 307–308 (1935). ("Contracts, however express, cannot fetter the constitutional authority of the Congress. Contracts may create rights of property, but, when contracts deal with a subject-matter which lies within the control of the Congress, they have a congenital infirmity. Parties cannot remove their transactions from the reach of dominant constitutional power by making contracts about them."); *U.S. Trust Co. of N.Y. v. New Jersey*, 431 U.S. 1, 22–23 (1976) ("[A]s is customary in reviewing economic and social regulation, courts properly defer to legislative judgment as to the necessity and reasonableness of a particular measure").

[239] *See Penn Central*, 438 U.S. at 124–129 (citing examples of cases where courts found no takings because regulations advanced important public policies); *Exxon Corp. v. Eagerton*, 462 U.S. 176, 191–92 (1983) (legislative prohibition of pass-through tax, which nullified contractual obligations to reimburse appellants for any severance taxes, was a proper exercise of police power because it served a "'broad societal interest'" in "protecting consumers from excessive prices" (internal citations omitted)).

[240] *See Veix v. Sixth Ward Bldg. & Loan Ass'n*, 310 U.S. 32, 39 (1940) (an economic emergency "may furnish the occasion for the exercise of [the police] power"); *Home Bldg. & Loan Ass'n v. Blaisdell*, 290 U.S. 398, 437 (1934) ("The economic interests of the state may justify the exercise of its continuing and dominant protective power notwithstanding interference with contracts"); *Subway-Surface Supervisors Assoc. v. N.Y. City Transit Authority*, 375 N.E.2d 384, 390 (N.Y. 1978) (wage freeze of New York City employees, including the suspension of wage increases in a collective bargaining agreement, was "a necessary and appropriate step toward relieving the [city's] financial crisis and thereby continuing the performance of governmental services"); *Miller*, 276 U.S. at 279 (state may destroy one class of property in order to save another).

[241] *See Norman*, 294 U.S. at 292–93 (because the nature and value of U.S. currency falls within Congress' control, Congress acted within its powers when it de-pegged the U.S. dollar from the gold standard, notwithstanding the approximately 40 percent reduction in the value of the gold clause payment obligations.

U.S. jurisprudence on takings is becoming more relevant to international law because the U.S. government is now actively attempting to convert that body of national law into customary international law. In 2002, the U.S. Congress directed the executive branch to ensure that in future U.S. treaties, foreign investors in the United States were to have no greater rights in respect of regulatory expropriations than those enjoyed by U.S. investors under the U.S. Constitution.[242] In effect, foreign investments covered by the new treaties will be accorded nothing more than national treatment. It is indeed ironic that the United States—long the leading opponent of the Calvo Doctrine[243]—may now be considered its proponent, at least in regard to national treatment and indirect expropriation.

To implement the United States Congress' apparent adoption of the Calvo Doctrine, the United States has significantly modified the language and terms of recent U.S. treaties, as discussed in section D of this chapter. The United States' effort to inject U.S. takings jurisprudence into the body of customary international law raises at least three uncertainties. First, it is unclear what impact the new language of these recent treaties will have on previous U.S. investment treaties. The absence of such language in older treaties implies that the older treaties did not adopt the same standards. Second, the principles set out in the new treaties are not necessarily coterminous with existing customary international law.[244] It is not clear, for example, that the U.S. emphasis on the third factor—the purpose of the government act—will be adopted by future tribunals, especially in light of the many decisions that have rejected the need to examine the governmental purpose.[245] There may well be other inconsistencies.

---

[242] *See* 22 U.S.C.A. § 3802(b)(3)(D) ("Recognizing that United States law on the whole provides a high level of protection for investment, consistent with or greater than the level required by international law, the principal negotiating objectives of the United States regarding foreign investment are to reduce or eliminate artificial or trade-distorting barriers to foreign investment, while ensuring that foreign investors in the United States are not accorded greater substantive rights with respect to investment protections than United States investors in the United States, and to secure for investors important rights comparable to those that would be available under United States legal principles and practice, by . . . seeking to establish standards for expropriation and compensation for expropriation, consistent with United States legal principles and practice").

[243] *See* discussion in Chapter II *supra*.

[244] *See* Stephen M. Schwebel, *The Influence of Bilateral Investment Treaties on Customary International Law*, 98 Am. Soc'y Int'l L. Proc. 27 (2004).

[245] *See* awards discussed at pp. 461 *et seq., supra* note 141. *But see Methanex, supra* note 120, at Pt. IV, Ch. D, ¶ 7.

Third, the current U.S. approach fails to take into account the evolution and application of the fair and equitable standard.[246] For example, as the *CMS Gas v. Argentina* tribunal has concluded, there may be government measures that, although not expropriatory, still violate the fair and equitable standard.[247] Future international tribunals will undoubtedly confront and resolve such uncertainties.

---

[246] Because the "fair and equitable" standard in U.S. BITs and Free Trade Agreements is defined historically with respect to "international law"—and, more recently with respect to "customary international law"(*see, e.g.*, U.S. Model BIT, Annex A)—arbitral tribunals have broad latitude to discern the parameters of fair and equitable treatment. *See, e.g., Pope & Talbot, Inc. v. Govt. of Canada*, Award on the Merits of Phase Two (Apr. 10, 2001) ¶¶ 114–16 (interpreting the "fair and equitable" standard under NAFTA to permit the application of provisions contained in other BITs concluded by NAFTA Parties).

[247] *See CMS, supra* note 69, ¶¶ 252–84.

XVII. "Fair and Equitable Treatment" and "Full Protection and Security"

Among the most discussed standards of protection that investment treaties provide are "fair and equitable treatment" and "full protection and security." These concepts and their relation to the minimum standard of treatment of aliens under customary international law have inspired significant debate.[1] This discussion has mainly centered on whether these standards provide only as much protection as foreign investors receive in their capacity as aliens under the customary international law minimum standard of protection of aliens, or whether they offer a higher level of protection.[2] In a 2001 interpretive note, the Free Trade Commission of the North American Free Trade Agreement (NAFTA)[3] answered this question in the specific context of NAFTA, stating that fair and equitable treatment and full protection and security as codified in Article 1105 of that treaty provide no more protection than that available under customary international law.[4] The Free Trade Commission's articulation is binding only with respect to NAFTA, however, and the discussion has continued unabated in relation to other investment treaties.

Fair and equitable treatment and full protection and security are generally recognized as "absolute" or "objective" protections. This objectivity contrasts with national treatment and most-favored-nation treatment obligations, which are "relative,"

---

[1] "The international minimum standard of treatment of aliens affirms that there are certain rights created by international law states must grant to aliens regardless of their domestic legislation. The international minimum standard thus is in conflict with the principle of the Calvo doctrine, according to which aliens enjoy only those rights which are afforded to nationals, i.e. national treatment." Detlev Vagts, *Minimum Standard*, in 3 *Encyclopedia of Public International Law*, 215 (R. Bernhardt ed., 1992).

[2] *See* the discussion at pp. 493 *et seq. infra*.

[3] NAFTA Free Trade Commission (FTC) Notes of Interpretation (July 31, 2001), *available at* http://www.dfait-maeci.gc.ca/tna-nac/NAFTA-Interpr-en.asp.

[4] *Id.*

requiring a comparison of the treatment accorded to the claimant and to investors of other nationalities. In reviewing one NAFTA arbitration award, a Canadian court described the minimum standard of Article 1105 and its relation to the relative standards of treatment found in Articles 1102 and 1103 of the treaty:[5]

> [59] I now turn to a consideration of Article 1105. It is a companion provision to Articles 1102 and 1103. In simple terms, Article 1102 provides that a NAFTA Party must treat the investors of another NAFTA Party and their investments no worse than it treats its own investors and their investments. This is referred to as "national treatment." Article 1103 provides that a Party must treat the investors of another Party and their investments no worse than it treats the investors of any other Party or of a non-party and their investments. This is referred to as "most favored-nation treatment."
>
> [60] Articles 1102 and 1103 are both framed in relative terms by way of a comparison to the way in which the NAFTA Party treats other investors. On the other hand, Article 1105 is framed in absolute terms. In considering Article 1105, the way in which the Party treats other investors is not a relevant factor. Article 1105 is intended to establish a minimum standard so that a Party may not treat investments of an investor of another Party worse than this standard irrespective of the manner in which the Party treats other investors and their investments.
>
> [61] The rationale of Article 1105 was discussed in a partial arbitration award issued shortly after the Tribunal issued the Award in this case. In *S.D. Myers, Inc. v. Government of Canada* (13 November 2000), the Tribunal said the following about Article 1105:
>
>> The minimum standard of treatment provision of the NAFTA is similar to clauses contained in [bilateral investment treaties]. The inclusion of a "minimum standard" provision is necessary to avoid what might otherwise be a gap. A government might treat an investor in a harsh, injurious and unjust manner, but do so in a way that is no different than the treatment inflicted on its own nationals. The "minimum standard" is a floor below which treatment of foreign investors must not fall, even if a government were not acting in a discriminatory manner. (para. 259)[6]

---

[5] NAFTA, art. 1105(1) provides that "1. Each Party shall accord to investments of investors of another Party treatment in accordance with international law, including fair and equitable treatment and full protection and security."

[6] *United Mexican States v. Metalclad Corp.*, 2001 BCSC 664 (Supreme Court of British Columbia). *See also* Stephen Vasciannie, *The Fair and Equitable Treatment Standard in International Investment Law and Practice*, 1999 Brit Y.B. of Int'l Law 99, 105 (2000) ("The standard of fair and equitable treatment is one of the main noncontingent or absolute standards used in the field of protection of foreign investment. A noncontingent standard is one which applies to an entity in a given situation without reference to standards which are applicable to other entities. . . . [I]ts content does not vary according to how other entities are treated.").

The interpretative guidance with respect to the minimum standard that the Free Trade Commission provided for NAFTA has no application to other investment protection treaties. This leaves arbitral tribunals and litigating parties to ponder and debate the intent of contracting states as to the extent of protection required by "fair and equitable treatment" and "full protection and security" clauses. A review of the relatively extensive jurisprudence reveals several particularly important points of debate, including: (a) the relationship of fair and equitable treatment and full protection and security to customary international law; (b) the content of the "fair and equitable treatment" standard; and (c) the content of the "full protection and security" standard. These issues are discussed below.

A. The Relationship of "Fair and Equitable Treatment" and "Full Protection and Security" to Customary International Law

There has been ample debate among states and commentators as to whether fair and equitable treatment and full protection and security have become principles of customary international law. More than 2,500 bilateral and multilateral investment treaties have been concluded,[7] and the vast majority incorporate these standards using very similar language.[8] Because these treaty standards have become so widespread, some observers contend that they have by this ubiquity alone become part of customary international law:

> The process by which provisions of treaties binding only the parties to those treaties may seep into general international law and thus bind the international community as a whole is subtle and elusive. It is nevertheless a real process known to international law. As the UN International Law Commission put it:
>
>> An international convention admittedly establishes rules binding the contracting States only, and based on reciprocity; but it must be remembered that these rules become generalized through the conclusion of other similar conventions containing identical or similar provisions. (Report of the International Law Commission covering the work of its twelfth session, 2 *Yearbook of the International Law Commission* 145, U.N. DOC. A/4425 (1960).)

---

[7] A 2006 survey of the United Nations Conference on Trade and Development (UNCTAD) indicates that at the end of the 2005, out of almost 2,495 BITs, approximately 1,900 had entered into force. UNCTAD, *The Entry Into Force of Bilateral Investment Treaties (BITs)*, UNCTAD/WEB/ITE/IIA/2006/9, at 2, *available at* http://www.unctad.org/en/docs/webiteiia20069_en.pdf.

[8] *See, e.g.*, Albania-France BIT (1996), art. 3; Belarus-Switzerland BIT (1994), art. 3(2).

It is submitted that this is a process of which more than 2,000 BITs are the contemporary exemplar. The result is that, when BITs prescribe treating the foreign investor in accordance with customary international law, they should be understood to mean the standard of international law embodied in the terms of some two thousand concordant BITs. The minimum standard of international law is the contemporary standard.[9]

Other observers have maintained that this treaty practice has not created customary international law.[10] Among commentators who accept the evolutionary view of custom in this area, some suggest that the fair and equitable standard could be an independent rule of customary international law.[11] Others suggest that the standard is simply the modern expression of the minimum standard of treatment of aliens, which is in turn a recognized element of customary

---

[9] Stephen M. Schwebel, *The Influence of Bilateral Investment Treaties on Customary International Law*, 98 Am. Soc'y Int'l L. Proc. 27, 29 (2004). *See also* more generally on the effect of the BIT practice of states on creation of customary international law Charles Leben, *L'Évolution du droit international des investissements*, at http://www.dundee.ac.uk/cepmlp/journal/html/v017/article7–12.html (2000); Malcolm N. Shaw, *International Law* 748 (5th ed., Cambridge University Press 2003); Rudolf Dolzer, *New Foundations of the Law of Expropriation of Alien Property*, 75 Am. J. Int'l L. 553, 566–8 (1981); Steffen Hindelang, *Bilateral Investment Treaties, Custom and A Healthy Investment Climate: The Question of Whether BITs Influence Customary International Law Revisited*, 5 JWIT 789 (2004); *Mondev International Ltd. v. U.S.*, International Centre for Settlement of Investment Disputes (ICSID) Case No. ARB (AF)/99/2 (NAFTA) (Award, Oct. 11, 2002), ¶ 125.

[10] *ADF Group Inc. v. U.S.*, ICSID Case No. ARB(AF)/00/1 (NAFTA, Award of Jan. 9, 2003), ¶ 187 ("We are not convinced that the Investor has shown the existence, in current customary international law, of a general and autonomous requirement (autonomous, that is, from specific rules addressing particular, limited contexts) to accord fair and equitable treatment and full protection and security to foreign investments. The Investor for instance, has not shown that such a requirement has been brought into the corpus of present day customary law.").

[11] UNCTAD, for example, in its study of fair and equitable treatment, concluded that the concept could become part of customary international law as an independent standard of conduct, unrelated to the traditional minimum standard: "Nevertheless, it is also possible, as a matter of theory, that the standard of fair and equitable treatment has become a part of customary international law. This possibility arises from the fact that, in some instances, where a treaty provision is norm-creating in character, this provision may pass into customary law once certain criteria are satisfied. However, in the case of the fair and equitable standard, it is not likely that this has occurred in practice, essentially because States have not demonstrated any clear will to have the standard included in the body of customary international law." UNCTAD, *Fair and Equitable Treatment*, in 3 *UNCTAD Series on Issues in International Investment Agreements*, 17 (1999). *See also* F. A. Mann, *British Treaties for the Promotion and Protection of Investments*, in *Further Studies in International Law* 238 (Clarendon Press). *See also Pope & Talbot Inc. v. Canada* (UNCITRAL/NAFTA Arbitration, Award of Apr. 10, 2001), ¶¶ 110–13 (the tribunal stated that fair and equitable treatment under Article 1105 of NAFTA was additive to the requirement of international law; i.e., "investors . . . [were] entitled to the international law minimum, *plus* the fairness elements."); Schwebel, *supra* note 9.

international law.[12] The minimum standard, although difficult to define with precision, has been described as:

> a norm of customary international law which governs the treatment of aliens, by providing for a minimum set of principles which States, regardless of their domestic legislation and practices, must respect when dealing with foreign nationals and their property. While the principle of national treatment foresees that aliens can only expect equality of treatment with nationals, the international minimum standard sets a number of basic rights established by international law that States must grant to aliens, independent of the treatment accorded to their own citizens. Violation of this norm engenders the international responsibility of the host State and may open the way for international action on behalf of the injured alien provided that the alien has exhausted local remedies.[13]

The historic formulation of the minimum standard was articulated in the seminal 1926 *Neer* decision,[14] which resulted from a claim lodged by the United States with

---

[12] See, e.g., arguments advanced by the Czech Republic in *Saluka Inves. v. Czech Republic* (UNCITRAL, Partial Award of Mar. 17, 2006), ¶ 289. See also J. C. Thomas, *Reflections on Article 1105 of NAFTA: History, State Practice and the Influence of Commentators*, 17 ICSID Rev.-F.I.L.J. 21, 50 (2002) ("While the precise wording varied, it is evident that states propounding the negotiation of investment protection treaties saw a clear and intended link between constant (or full) protection and security, fair and equitable treatment, and the international minimum standard at general international law. The former were considered to be expression of the latter."). Most recently, Tudor suggests that the fair and equitable standard is a general principle of law. *See* Ioana Tudor, *The Fair and Equitable Treatment Standard in International Foreign Investment Law* (Oxford University Press, 2008).

[13] Organization for Economic Cooperation and Development (OECD), *Fair and Equitable Standard in International Investment Law*, 8 note 32 (Working Papers on International Investment, 2004/3, 2004). *See also* Andreas Hans Roth, *The Minimum Standard of International Law Applied to Aliens* 127 (1949) ("[T]he international standard is nothing else than a set of rules, correlated to each other and deriving from one particular norm of general international law, namely that the treatment of alien is regulated by the law of nations."); Antonio Cassese, *International Law* 120 (2d ed., 2005) ("[C]ustomary rules . . . have placed a major limitation upon state sovereignty. Although foreigners are under the territorial supremacy of the host State . . . , they also benefit from a host of rights laid down in international rules that confer international rights on their national State."); *Oppenheim's International Law* 931 (Sir Robert Jennings & Sir Arthur Watts eds., 1992) ("It has been repeatedly laid down that there exists in this matter a minimum international standard, and that a state which fails to measure up to that standard incurs international liability."); Alfred Verdross & Bruno Simma, *Universelles Völkerrecht: Theorie und Praxis* 801 (Duncker & Humblot 1984). Verdross and Simma refer to *Roberts v. United Mexican States*, where a mixed claims tribunal held that "such equality (with respect to nationals) is not the ultimate test of the propriety of the acts of the authorities in the light of international law. That test is, broadly speaking, whether aliens are treated in accordance with ordinary standards of civilization." Vagts, in accordance with other cited sources, suggests that the minimum standard, with respect to property, includes the right to enjoy such property unless it is taken for a public purpose and in exchange for fair compensation. *See also* Marjorie M. Whiteman, 8 *Digest of International Law*, 697–704 (1967); and *Restatement (Third) of Foreign Relations Law*, §§ 711–12 (1987). *Cf.* Ian Brownlie, *Principles of Public International Law* 527 (5th ed. Oxford University Press 1998) ("legal doctrine has opposed an 'international minimum standard,' 'a moral standard for civilized states,' to the principle of national treatment").

[14] L. F. H. Neer & Pauline E. Neer v. Mexico (Opinion rendered on Oct. 15, 1926), 21(3) Am. J. Int'l L. 555 (1927).

the Mexican-American Claims Commission on behalf of the family of Paul Neer, an American citizen who was killed in Mexico. The Mexican authorities had been unable to arrest the culprits.[15] The Commission stated that the host government's treatment of aliens would violate international law only if the treatment amounted "to an outrage, to bad faith, to willful neglect of duty, or to an insufficiency of governmental action so far short of international standards that every reasonable and impartial man would recognize its insufficiency."[16] Under the circumstances, and in light of the evidence provided by the Mexican authorities regarding various steps that had been taken to investigate the matter (including a prompt visit to the murder scene and investigating several people), the tribunal held that Mexico could not be held liable for failing to arrest those who had killed Mr. Neer.[17]

Some respondent states in contemporary investment disputes have argued that fair and equitable treatment and full protection and security require no better treatment than the minimum standard set out in *Neer*.[18] Arbitral tribunals have accepted that some treaty clauses limit the protection afforded to the historical minimum standard,[19] while other treaty texts should be interpreted to provide a higher level of protection.[20] In reaching these conclusions, tribunals have been guided by the applicable treaty's express terms as well as sources of supplementary guidance such as the NAFTA FTC Note and *travaux preparatoires*. Tribunals have noted that when the text of the clause links the standards of fair and equitable treatment and full protection and security to international law, the protection that such a clause provides may be limited to that available under customary law.[21] When these standards are described without express reference to international law, the dominant view is that they provide more protection than what is available under the customary minimum standard of treatment. In any event, there seems to be a consensus that the minimum standard of treatment of customary international law is evolving, and today prohibits conduct that would not have been considered egregious in 1926.[22] *Azurix v. Argentina* illustrates these interpretative approaches with respect to fair and equitable treatment as codified in the United States-Argentina BIT.

---

[15] *Id.*

[16] *Id.* at 556.

[17] *Id.* at 557.

[18] See, e.g., Canada in *ADF*, supra note 10, ¶ 121; Czech Republic in *Saluka*, supra note 12, ¶ 290.

[19] Such is the wording of NAFTA Art. 1105. See, e.g., *Mondev*, supra note 9, ¶ 125 (interpreting art. 1105 in light of FTC). *But see Pope & Talbot*, supra note 11, ¶ 110–13.

[20] See also the *Saluka* excerpt, pp. 499–500 *infra*, ¶ 294.

[21] *Azurix v. Argentina*, ICSID Case No. ARB/01/12 (U.S.-Argentina BIT, Final Award of July 14, 2006), ¶¶ 358 *et seq.*; *Saluka*, supra note 12, at 61 *et seq.*

[22] *Mondev*, supra note 9, ¶ 124.

Azurix v. Argentina

ICSID Case No. ARB/01/12 (U.S.-Argentina BIT Final Award of July 14, 2006) (source notes omitted)

In 1999, Azurix Corporation, a U.S. company, through two of its subsidiaries (AAS and OBA) participated in a bidding process to operate AGOSBA, a company owned by the Province of Buenos Aires, which was in charge of providing potable water and sewage service in the Province. Subsequently, Azurix subsidiaries incorporated Azurix Buenos Aires (ABA), which paid 438,555,554 Argentine pesos to the Province. Then, ABA, AGOSBA, and the Province signed an agreement, which granted ABA a 30-year concession for the distribution of potable water and the treatment and disposal of sewage in the Province. Soon after ABA took control of the operations, the parties' relationship began to deteriorate. One of the main reasons was the failure of the Province to complete certain algae removal works in a dam that was a major source of water for the city of Buenos Aires. As a result, the water became hazy and its odor became foul. This led to public protest, which the Province handled by advising the customers not to pay their water bills. In September 2001, Azurix filed a request for ICSID arbitration, alleging violation of the fair and equitable treatment and full protection and security standards of the United States-Argentina BIT.

---

358. The arguments exchanged by the parties raise the following issues:

1. Whether the standard of fair and equitable treatment is a standard which entails obligations for the parties to the BIT in the treatment of foreign investment which are additional to those required by the minimum standard of treatment of aliens under customary international law;

2. What conduct attributable to the State can be characterized as unfair and inequitable? In other words, what is the substantive content of the standard? . . .

359. In discussing the first issue, the Tribunal will start by considering the specific provision of the BIT on fair and equitable treatment and recall that the BIT is an international treaty that should be interpreted in accordance with the norms of interpretation established by the Vienna Convention. As already noted, the Vienna Convention is binding on the parties to the BIT. Article 31(1) of the Convention requires that a treaty be "interpreted in good faith in accordance with the ordinary meaning to be given to the terms of the treaty in their context and in the light of its object and purpose."

360. In their ordinary meaning, the terms "fair" and "equitable" used in Article 3(1) of the BIT mean "just," "even-handed," "unbiased," "legitimate." As regards the purpose and object of the BIT, in its Preamble, the parties state their desire to promote greater cooperation with respect to investment, recognize that "agreement upon the treatment to be accorded such investment will stimulate the flow of private capital and the economic development of the Parties," and agree that "fair and equitable treatment of investment is desirable in order to maintain a stable framework for investment and maximum effective

use of economic resources." It follows from the ordinary meaning of the terms fair and equitable and the purpose and object of the BIT that fair and equitable should be understood to be treatment in an even-handed and just manner, conducive to fostering the promotion of foreign investment. The text of the BIT reflects a positive attitude towards investment with words such as "promote" and "stimulate." Furthermore, the parties to the BIT recognize the role that fair and equitable treatment plays in maintaining "a stable framework for investment and maximum effective use of economic resources."

361. Turning now to Article II.2(a), this paragraph provides: "Investment shall at all times be accorded fair and equitable treatment, shall enjoy full protection and security and shall in no case be accorded treatment less than required by international law." The paragraph consists of three full statements, each listing in sequence a standard of treatment to be accorded to investments: fair and equitable, full protection and security, not less than required by international law. Fair and equitable treatment is listed separately. The last sentence ensures that, whichever content is attributed to the other two standards, the treatment accorded to investment will be no less than required by international law. The clause, as drafted, permits to interpret fair and equitable treatment and full protection and security as higher standards than required by international law. The purpose of the third sentence is to set a floor, not a ceiling, in order to avoid a possible interpretation of these standards below what is required by international law.

In recent years, certain states have sought to resolve conflicting interpretative approaches by including specific language in treaties describing the relationship between fair and equitable treatment, full protection and security, and customary international law. Canada, for example, in its recent model Foreign Investment Protection and Promotion Agreement,[23] expressly limited "fair and equitable treatment" to the standard of treatment required under customary international law:

Article 5

Minimum Standard of Treatment

1. Each Party shall accord to covered investments treatment in accordance with the customary international law minimum standard of treatment of aliens, including fair and equitable treatment and full protection and security.

2. The concepts of "fair and equitable treatment" and "full protection and security" in paragraph 1 do not require treatment in addition to or beyond that which is required by the customary international law minimum standard of treatment of aliens.

. . . .

---

[23] *See* Agreement between Canada and _____ for the Promotion and Protection of Investments, *at* http://www.international.gc.ca/tna-nac/documents/2004-FIPA-model-en.pdf [hereinafter 2004 Canadian Model FIPA]. *See also* NAFTA, art. 1105.

Commentary provided by the Canadian government with respect to this article explains:

> The Minimum Standard of Treatment ensures investments of investors fair and equitable treatment and full protection and security in accordance with the principles of customary international law. The minimum standard provides a "floor" to ensure that the treatment of an investment cannot fall below treatment considered as appropriate under generally accepted standards of customary international law.[24]

It is difficult to predict whether this debate will ever be resolved. Ultimately, for most investment tribunals, the outcome may be of marginal significance. Some recent decisions suggest that there is no practical difference between the fair and equitable treatment standard and the customary minimum standard when they are applied to most factual situations.

Saluka Investments B.V. v. Czech Republic

(UNCITRAL, Partial Award of Mar. 17, 2006), ¶¶ 291–94

291. Whatever the merits of this controversy between the parties may be, it appears that the difference between the Treaty standard [of fair and equitable treatment] laid down in Article 3.1 and the customary minimum standard, when applied to the specific facts of a case, may well be more apparent than real. To the extent that the case law reveals different formulations of the relevant thresholds, an in depth analysis may well demonstrate that they could be explained by the contextual and factual differences of the cases to which the standards have been applied.

292. Also, it should be kept in mind that the customary minimum standard is in any case binding upon a State and provides a minimum guarantee to foreign investors, even where the State follows a policy that is in principle opposed to foreign investment; in that context, the minimum standard of "fair and equitable treatment" may in fact provide no more than "minimal" protection. Consequently, in order to violate that standard, States' conduct may have to display a relatively higher degree of inappropriateness.

293. Bilateral investment treaties, however, are designed to promote foreign direct investment as between the Contracting Parties; in this context, investors' protection by the "fair and equitable treatment" standard is meant to be a guarantee providing a positive incentive for foreign investors. Consequently, in order to violate the standard, it may be sufficient that States' conduct displays a relatively lower degree of inappropriateness.

---

[24] Canada's Foreign Investment Protection and Promotion Agreements (FIPAs) Negotiating Programme, clarification on art. 5, *available at* http://www.dfait-maeci.gc.ca/. The Canadian model incorporates the clarification of the Minimum Standard of Treatment obligation included in the NAFTA FTC's Notes of Interpretation issued in July 2001. As noted above, the Notes and the FIPA clarification state that concepts such as fair and equitable treatment should be interpreted according to the customary international law minimum standard for the treatment of aliens. The FIPA also specifies that a tribunal's conclusion that a Party has breached another obligation of the treaty, such as national treatment, does not mean that the minimum standard of treatment had been violated.

294. Whichever the difference between the customary and the treaty standards may be, this Tribunal has to limit itself to the interpretation of the "fair and equitable treatment" standard as embodied in Article 3.1 of the Treaty. That Article omits any express reference to the customary minimum standard. The interpretation of Article 3.1 does not therefore share the difficulties that may arise under treaties (such as the NAFTA) which expressly tie the "fair and equitable treatment" standard to the customary minimum standard.[25] Avoidance of these difficulties may even be regarded as the very purpose of the lack of a reference to an international standard in the Treaty.[26] This clearly points to the autonomous character of a "fair and equitable treatment" standard such as the one laid down in Article 3.1 of the Treaty.[27]

The NAFTA Free Trade Commission Interpretation of July 2001

As already noted, the NAFTA Free Trade Commission added an additional element of complexity to the debate about fair and equitable treatment with its official interpretation of Article 1105, issued in July 2001 (the "FTC Interpretation").[28]

The NAFTA member states—and in particular the United States and Canada—appear to have been caught rather off guard by the first NAFTA arbitration cases, initiated in the late 1990s. In particular, many in governmental circles were surprised to find that international arbitral tribunals acting on the authority of the NAFTA text could apply the fair and equitable treatment standard to the administrative, regulatory, and judicial practices of "advanced" countries such as the United States and Canada. Canada received its first such surprise in the very first investor-state arbitration under NAFTA, *Ethyl v. Canada*,[29] which resulted in a settlement of C$20 million. Still more troublesome for the Canadian government

---

[25] SN: NAFTA, Art. 1105(1) [...] provides that:

Each Party shall accord to investments of investors of another Party treatment in accordance with international law, including fair and equitable treatment and full protection and security.

[26] SN: See G. Sacerdoti, *Bilateral Treaties and Multilateral Instruments on Investment Protection*, Receuil des Cours, Tome 269, at 341 (1997); R. Dolzer & M. Stevens, *Bilateral Investment Treaties* 60 (ICSID 1995); see also UNCTAD, *Fair and Equitable Treatment*, in Series on Issues in International Investment Agreements 40 (1999).

[27] Paragraph 294 of the *Saluka* award also provides guidance for interpreting and distinguishing various fair and equitable treatment clauses based on whether they are expressly linked to international law. The tribunal in *Azurix v. Argentina* took a similar approach. See *Azurix* (Final Award), *supra* note 21, ¶ 361.

[28] Pursuant to Article 2001(1) of the NAFTA, the FTC consists of cabinet-level representatives of the NAFTA Parties. Among other powers, it is authorized to render authoritative interpretations of the NAFTA text. Such interpretations, according to NAFTA, art. 1131(2), are binding on arbitral tribunals deciding NAFTA Chapter 11 cases.

[29] *Ethyl Corp. v. Canada* (UNCITRAL/NAFTA Arbitration, Decision on Jurisdiction, June 24, 1998).

was the *Pope & Talbot*[30] award, in which Canada was found to have breached the substantive protections of the treaty and also sought to intimidate a NAFTA claimant after its claim was filed. By 2001, the United States was also facing a number of serious arbitration claims, including *Loewen v. United States*,[31] in which the claimant challenged the fairness under international standards of U.S. judicial practices.

In part as a result of these concerns, the NAFTA member states convened the Free Trade Commission in 2001. The FTC Interpretation that emerged from this initiative was designed primarily to raise the threshold of international liability for conduct allegedly in breach of the "fair and equitable treatment" standard. In relevant part, the FTC Interpretation provides:

> 2. The concepts of "fair and equitable treatment" and "full protection and security" do not require treatment in addition to or beyond that which is required by the customary international law minimum standard of treatment of aliens.
>
> 3. A determination that there has been a breach of another provision of the NAFTA, or of a separate international agreement, does not establish that there has been a breach of Article 1105(1).[32]

The FTC Interpretation had a direct impact on some of the cases that were then pending before the NAFTA tribunals.[33] The NAFTA parties in those cases on the basis of the interpretation tried to constrain the meaning of fair and equitable treatment to the *Neer* standard referred to above.[34] In at least one arbitration,[35] the claimant argued that the FTC interpretation in fact constituted an amendment and therefore exceeded the scope of the FTC's authority under the treaty. It was also submitted that, in any event, the *Neer* standard was not directly applicable in the

---

[30] *Pope & Talbot v. Canada*, supra note 11.

[31] *Loewen Group, Inc. & Raymond L. Loewen v. U.S.*, ICSID Case No. ARB (AF)/98/3 (NAFTA, Award of June 26, 2003).

[32] Paragraph 3 of the FTC Interpretation seems to have been inspired by the *S.D. Myers* arbitration, in which the tribunal held that a violation of national treatment (art. 1102) can constitute in itself a contravention of the requirement to provide fair and equitable treatment (art. 1105). The tribunal added that in some cases, the breach of a rule of international law by a host state may not be decisive in determining that a foreign investor has been denied fair and equitable treatment, but the fact that a host state has breached a rule of international law that is specifically designed to protect investors will tend to weigh heavily in favor of finding a breach of the fair and equitable treatment. *S. D. Myers, Inc. v. Canada* (UNCITRAL/NAFTA Arbitration, First Partial Award, Nov. 2000), ¶ 264.

[33] See, e.g., *Pope & Talbot v. Canada*, supra note 11, ¶ 114; *Mondev*, supra note 9, ¶ 125.

[34] See pp. 495–96 supra.

[35] *Methanex Corp. v. U.S.* (UNCITRAL/NAFTA Arbitration, Award of Aug. 3, 2005).

NAFTA context, because it dealt only with the physical security of aliens, and had nothing to say about the protection of their investment.[36] Insofar as the content of the minimum standard is concerned, NAFTA tribunals have given relatively little effect to the FTC interpretation.[37] NAFTA arbitrators have tended to apply the terms of Article 1105 according to the plain meaning of the text.[38] In doing so, they have acted no differently than their brethren who apply the terms of BITs.[39]

B. The Meaning of Fair and Equitable Treatment

The "fair and equitable" standard has become one of the most actively debated concepts in investment protection law. Investors generally seek to apply the legal terms literally and broadly, while respondent states try to narrow the scope of protection as much as possible. In recent years, fair and equitable treatment has become the protective principle that investors most frequently invoke:

> Without exaggeration, Article 1105 [the NAFTA fair and equitable provision] has become the alpha and omega of investor-state arbitration under Chapter 11 of NAFTA. Every pending claim alleges a violation of Article 1105. Likewise, every award rendered against a NAFTA party rests at least in part on the denial of 'fair and equitable treatment.' These disputes have placed over $2 billion in controversy; their outcome will influence both future deployments of capital and the regulatory practices of host states.[40]

---

[36] See The Meaning of Article 1105(1) of the NAFTA Agreement: Second Opinion of Professor Sir Robert Jennings, Q.C., *Methanex v. U.S.* (Sept. 6, 2001).

[37] *Pope & Talbot v. Canada*, supra note 11, ¶ 118 (interpreting Article 1105 to require that covered investors and investments receive the benefits of fair and equitable treatment and full protection and security under ordinary standards applied in the NAFTA countries, without any threshold limitation that state conduct be "egregious," "outrageous," "shocking," or otherwise extraordinary); *Mondev v. U.S.*, supra note 9, ¶ 116.

[38] See, e.g., *Waste Mgmt. v. United Mexican States*, ICSID Case No. ARB(AF)/00/3 (Final Award of Apr. 30, 2004), ¶¶ 86–99; *GAMI Inves. Inc. v. Mexico* (NAFTA/UNCITRAL Arbitration, Final Award of November 15, 2004), ¶¶ 83–110. See also, Ian Laird, *Betrayal, Shock and Outrage: Recent Developments in NAFTA Article 1105*, in NAFTA Investment Law and Arbitration: Past Issues, Current Practice, Future Prospects, 73–74 ("Although the NAFTA parties have persistently argued their position that the fair and equitable treatment standard should be equated to the historical international minimum standard of treatment found in cases such as *Neer*, none of the NAFTA Chapter 11 tribunals ruling on the fair and equitable treatment standard accepted those arguments").

[39] See *Saluka*, supra note 12, ¶ 291.

[40] Charles H. Brower, *Fair and Equitable Treatment under NAFTA's Investment Chapter*, 96 Am. Soc'y Int'l L. Proc. 9 (2002). See also in general the comments by J. Christopher Thomas, Jack J. Coe, & Murray J. Belman, in id. See also non-NAFTA cases such as *Azurix*, supra note 21; *Saluka*, supra note 12; *CMS Gas Transmission Co. v. Argentina*, ICSID Case No. ARB/01/8 (Award of May 12, 2005); *Occidental Exploration & Production Company v. Ecuador*, LCIA Case No. UN3467 (Final Award of July 1, 2004).

1. History of the "Fair and Equitable Treatment" Standard

The concept of fair and equitable treatment pre-dates the advent of modern investment protection treaties. One early reference to what would become the fair and equitable treatment standard can be found in the Havana Charter of 1948,[41] a multilateral instrument intended to establish the International Trade Organization (ITO). Article 11(2) of the Charter required that foreign investments be provided "just and equitable treatment." The standard was articulated in somewhat different terms in several proposed plurilateral agreements throughout the 1950s and 1960s, including the Bogotá agreement of 1948,[42] the Abs-Shawcross Draft Convention on Investments Abroad,[43] and the OECD draft convention on the protection of foreign investment.[44] At about the same time, the United States began to include similar clauses in Friendship, Commerce and Navigation (FCN) treaties. Thus, a number of post–World War II treaties included clauses requiring that qualifying foreign enterprises receive "equitable treatment" or "fair and equitable treatment."[45]

---

[41] "[A]n important starting point concerning the fair and equitable treatment was the Havana Charter, a multilateral text prepared as the basis for establishment of an International Trade Organization." Vasciannie, *supra* note 6, at 107. "Though the Havana Charter did not enter into force, its use of the term 'just and equitable' has served as a precedent for subsequent efforts to reach multilateral agreement on treatment standards for foreign investments in international law." *Id.*, at 100. *See also*, OECD, *supra* note 13, at 3. However, the provision in the Havana Charter did not apply directly. Rather, the ITO was to require that its members include the standard in subsequent agreements.

[42] Article 22 of the Bogotá agreement provided that foreign capital should receive equitable treatment and that states shall not take "unjustified, unreasonable or discriminatory measures that would impair the legally acquired rights or interests of nationals of other countries. . . ." *See* Vasciannie, *supra* note 6, at 109. Hence, "though the Bogotá agreement was not implemented, its provision for the non-contingent standard of equitable treatment helped to give currency to the term in multilateral deliberations on foreign investments."

[43] The Draft Convention on Investment Abroad was proposed in 1959 under the leadership of Hermann Abs and Lord Shawcross. H. Abs & H. Shawcross, *The Proposed Convention to Protect Private Foreign Investment*, 9 J. Public L. 115 (1960).

[44] The Draft Convention on the Protection of Foreign Property was adopted by the OECD Council in 1967. According to the OECD working paper, "[T]he draft Convention although never opened for signature, represented the collective view and dominant trend of OECD countries on investment issues and influenced the pattern of deliberations of foreign investment in that period." *See* OECD, *supra* note 13, at 4.

[45] One commentator suggests that the term "fair and equitable treatment" as used by the United States is the equivalent of the "equitable treatment" set out in various FCN treaties. *See* Kenneth J. Vandevelde, *The Bilateral Treaty Program of the United States*, 21 Cornell Int'l L. J. 201 (1988). The author refers to FCN treaties with, *e.g.*, Ireland (1950), Greece (1954), Israel (1954), France (1960), Pakistan (1961), Belgium (1963), and Luxembourg (1963), and the Federal Republic of Germany, Ethiopia, and the Netherlands.

The adoption of the fair and equitable treatment standard accelerated in the late 1960s and in the 1970s, when it was widely incorporated in bilateral investment treaties.[46] Today it is nearly a universal feature of investment protection instruments.[47]

2. The Definition of "Fair and Equitable" Treatment

Claimants in treaty disputes have often advocated a "plain meaning" or "ordinary meaning" interpretation of the term *fair and equitable treatment*.[48] According to this view, where a foreign investor benefits from such protection, a tribunal should assess whether the host state acted with respect to the investor and its investment in a manner that comports with the normal business understanding of fairness.[49]

Vienna Convention on the Law of the Treaties. General Rule of Interpretation, art. 31(1)

A treaty shall be interpreted in good faith in accordance with the ordinary meaning to be given to the terms of the treaty in their context and in light of its object and purpose.

Applying the "plain or ordinary meaning" approach to fair and equitable treatment can be more difficult than it first appears. Government officials, arbitrators, and scholars have given different meanings to the fair and equitable

---

[46] Vasciannie, *supra* note 6, at 108–11; *see also* OECD, *supra* note 13, at 3–4.

[47] *See* Brower, *supra* note 40, at 9 ("similar language appears in hundreds of bilateral investment treaties (BITs)"). Ibrahim Shihata, *Legal Treatment of Foreign Investments: The World Bank Guidelines* 233–37 (1993) (a study of 335 BITs negotiated by most of the Western industrialized countries demonstrated that 92 percent of these treaties contained a "fair and equitable treatment" provision). *See also* Kenneth J. Vandevelde, *United States Investment Treaties: Policy and Practice* 76–78 (1992) (absolute standards of the BIT require the host state to provide covered investment with fair and equitable treatment); Dolzer & Stevens, *supra* note 26, at 58 ("Nearly all recent BITs require that investments and investors covered under the treaty receive 'fair and equitable treatment,' in spite of the fact that there is no general agreement on the precise meaning of this phrase").

[48] OECD, *supra* note 13, at 25.

[49] *See* Vasciannie, *supra* note 6, at 103.

treatment standard in different factual contexts and at different times.[50] Some commentators have observed that the broad terms with which the standard has been formulated may be a virtue, as they "promote flexibility in the investment process."[51] A more prevalent concern is that the breadth and imprecision of the term may allow arbitrators excessive latitude in deciding a case, and might ultimately create the risk that fair and equitable claims will be decided on the basis of the arbitrators' own subjective conception of justice and fairness.[52] In this regard, the United States has argued in defending NAFTA claims brought against it that "fair and equitable treatment" is too subjective to have any effective legal content.[53] At the same time, a number of U.S. statutes contain similar phrases. For example, the Federal Gas Act requires that natural gas rates be "fair and equitable."[54] Indeed, the U.S. Supreme Court has also had occasion to define "fair and equitable."[55]

Fears that arbitrators would decide cases on the basis of purely subjective conceptions of "fairness" have not materialized in the cases decided to date. Instead, faced with an express but broad treaty provision, investment arbitration tribunals have begun to develop objective and concrete meaning. In so doing, the tribunals have generally agreed on two general points. First, violation of the fair and

---

[50] *See id*; Courtney C. Kirkman, *Fair and Equitable Treatment*: Methanex v. United States *and the Narrowing Scope of NAFTA Article 1105*, 34 Law & Pol'y Int'l Bus. 343 (2002); Stefan Matiation, *Arbitration with Two Twists*: Loewen v. United States *and Free Trade Commission Intervention in NAFTA Chapter 11 Disputes*, 24 U. Pa. J. Int'l Econ. L. 451 (2003); David A. Gantz, *Pope and Talbot v. Canada*, 97 Am. J. Int'l L. 937 (2003); R. Dolzer, *Fair and Equitable Treatment: A Key Standard in Investment Treaties*, 39 Int'l L. 87 (2005); and C. Schreuer, *Fair and Equitable Treatment in Arbitral Practice*, 6(3) JWIT 357 (2005).

[51] Vasciannie, *supra* note 6, at 104.

[52] The OECD, for example, points out that "a number of governments seem to be concerned that, the less guidance is provided for arbitrators, the more discretion is involved and the closer the process resembles decisions *ex aequo et bono, i.e.* based on the arbitrators' notions of 'fairness' and 'equity.'" OECD, *supra* note 13, at 3. Similarly, "virtually any governmental action can be called unfair or inequitable. But if unfairness or inequity is determined by reference not to international law but to subjective considerations of fairness or equity, the standards of conduct to which states are to be held can become divorced from law." J. C. Thomas, ASIL Proc., *supra* note 40, at 16.

[53] *See, e.g., Mondev, supra* note 9, 5 Transcript of the Hearing, 968–69 (May 24, 2002), *available at* www.state.gov. *Cf.* S. Schwebel, *The United States 2004 Model Bilateral Investment Treaty: An Exercise in the Regressive Development of International Law*, in *Global Reflections on International Law, Commerce and Dispute Resolution Liber Amicorum in Honour of Robert Briner* 819–20 (ICC Publishing, Pub. No. 693, 2005) (stating that the new U.S. Model BIT of 2004, which expressly limits the definition of fair and equitable treatment, embodies regressive changes).

[54] 15 U.S.C. § 3371(a)(2)(B)(i). *See also* U.S. Bankruptcy Code, 11 U.S. § 1129(b).

[55] *Bank of America S.A. v. 203 North LaSalle St. Partnership*, 526 U.S. 434, text accompanying note 13 *et seq.* (1999) (interpreting "fair and equitable" requirement in bankruptcy code).

equitable standard does not necessarily involve bad faith on the part of the state.[56] Otherwise, the fair and equitable treatment standard would lose its objective nature.[57] However, proof of bad faith conduct on the part of the respondent state could serve as a strong indicator that violation has occurred.[58] Second, arbitrators tend to agree that the application of the fair and equitable standard depends on the facts presented in a particular case:

> When a tribunal is faced with the claim by a foreign investor that the investment has been unfairly or inequitably treated or not accorded full protection and security, it is bound to pass upon that claim on the facts and by application of any governing treaty provisions. A judgment of what is fair and equitable cannot be reached in the abstract; it must depend on the facts of the particular case. It is part of the essential business of courts and tribunals to make judgments such as these. In doing so, the general principles referred to in Article 1105(1) and similar provisions must inevitably be interpreted and applied to the particular facts.[59]

Many commentators have taken a similar approach, urging that "a tribunal must 'decide whether in all circumstances the conduct in issue is fair and equitable or unfair and inequitable.'"[60]

But even when a tribunal is guided principally by the specific facts of a case, there remains a need to attribute more specific content to this broad legal term. As examined in the remainder of this section, tribunals have frequently identified and

---

[56] See, e.g., *Azurix* (Final Award), *supra* note 21, ¶ 372 (stating that arbitral tribunals have concluded that bad faith or malicious intentions on the part of the host state are not part of the fair and equitable standard, although they could aggravate the situation. Citing *CMS, supra* note 40, ¶ 280).

[57] See, e.g., *CMS, supra* note 40, ¶ 280 ("[fair and equitable treatment] is an objective requirement unrelated to whether the Respondent has had any deliberate intention or bad faith in adopting the measures in question.").

[58] *CME Czech Republic B.V. (The Netherlands) v. Czech Republic* (UNCITRAL, Netherlands-Czech Republic BIT, Partial Award of Sept. 13, 2001), ¶ 526 (relying on an article by Detlev Vagts to conclude that the fair and equitable treatment standard would be violated by: "Regulatory Action *without bona fide* governmental purpose (or without bona fide timing) *designed* to make the investor's business unprofitable"). *See also* Detlev F. Vagts, *Coercion and Foreign Investment Re-Arrangements*, 72(1) Am. J. Int'l L. 17 (1978); *Genin, Eastern Credit Limited, Inc. & A.S. Baltoil v. Estonia*, ICSID Case No. ARB/99/2 (Award of June 25, 2001), ¶ 367 ("While the exact content of [the fair and equitable treatment] standard is not clear, the Tribunal understands it to require an "international minimum standard" that is separate from domestic law, but that is, indeed, a minimum standard. Acts that would violate this minimum standard would include acts showing a willful neglect of duty, an insufficiency of action falling far below international standards, or even subjective bad faith"). The *Genin* tribunal may have been quoting without attribution the *Neer* decision. *Neer, supra* note 14. At the same time, the *Genin* tribunal did not mention the *Neer* requirement that "every reasonable and impartial man would readily recognize" the inadequacy of the treatment received, perhaps ignoring the objective element of the customary law test.

[59] *Mondev, supra* note 9, ¶ 118; *see also* OECD, *supra* note 13, at 25 ("Where the fair and equitable standard is invoked the central issue remains simply whether the actions in questions are in all circumstances fair and equitable or unfair and inequitable").

[60] F. A. Mann, *British Treaties for the Promotion and Protection of Investments*, 52 Brit. Y.B. Int'l L. 241, 244 (1981).

incorporated specific legal principles and concepts into the fair and equitable treatment standard. This approach seems to be consistent with commentators' expectations that the fair and equitable standard will be developed by the "praetorian" work of investment treaty tribunals.[61]

a. Arbitrary Treatment

One recurring theme in the literature on fair and equitable treatment is that the standard is closely related to the concept of arbitrariness. A United Nations Commission on Trade and Development (UNCTAD) study concluded:

> Still with reference to plain meaning, however, if there is discrimination on arbitrary grounds, or if the investment has been subject to arbitrary or capricious treatment by the host State, the fair and equitable standard has been violated.[62]

Certain tribunals, such as those in *Waste Management*[63] and *Genin*,[64] have concluded that arbitrary conduct is also unfair and inequitable. It is unclear, however, whether the concept of arbitrariness actually clarifies the fair and equitable treatment standard. In the International Court of Justice (ICJ) case *ELSI v. Italy*,[65] an applicable treaty provision prohibited "arbitrary and discriminatory measures."[66] In arguing that Italy had breached this provision, the United States urged that the treaty be interpreted by reference to its literal terms:

> The prohibition of "arbitrary" measures conveys above all the commitment of the respective Governments not to injure the investments and related interests of foreign investors by the unreasonable or unfair exercise of governmental authority. Following standard dictionary definitions, an "arbitrary" act may be one which is characterized by absolute power or an abuse

---

[61] OECD, *supra* note 13, at 25–26, *citing* Patrick Juillard, *L'évolution des sources du droit des investissements*, in 250 Receuil des Cours 83 (1994). Although concepts such as arbitrariness and legitimate expectations have found a prominent place within the fair and equitable treatment standard, some arbitral awards are based instead on the cumulative impact of a number of less significant irregularities by the government. In *PSEG v. Turkey*, the arbitral tribunal listed a number of irregularities, including Turkey's failure to engage in negotiation of a build-operate-transfer contract with the investors. *PSEG Global v. Turkey*, ICSID Case No. ARB/02/5 (Award of Jan. 19, 2007), ¶¶ 246–256.

[62] UNCTAD, *supra* note 11, at 37.

[63] *Waste Mgmt*, *supra* note 38, ¶ 98. *See also S. D. Myers*, *supra* note 32, ¶ 263 ("The Tribunal considers that a breach of Article 1105 occurs only when it is shown that an investor has been treated in such an unjust or arbitrary manner that the treatment rises to the level that is unacceptable from the international perspective. . .").

[64] *Genin*, *supra* note 58, ¶ 367. Although it did not expressly link arbitrary conduct with the breach of the fair and equitable treatment standard, the *Genin* tribunal found that the same state action violated both the fair and equitable treatment standard and a separate prohibition on arbitrary impairment contained in the applicable U.S.-Estonia BIT.

[65] *Case Concerning Elettronica Sicula S.p.A (ELSI) (U.S. v. Italy)*, 1989 I.C.J. Rep. 15, 28 I.L.M. 1109 (1989).

[66] *See Case Concerning Elettronica Sicula, S.p.A. (ELSI) (U.S. v. Italy)*, 1 *I.C.J. Pleadings, Oral Arguments*, 75 (Mem. of the U.S.) (emphasis omitted).

of discretion. "Arbitrary actions" include those which are not based on fair and adequate reasons (including sufficient legal justification), but rather arise from the unreasonable or capricious exercise of authority. The terms "oppressive" and "unreasonable" are thus synonyms of "arbitrary." As used in Italian and United States legal practice with reference to governmental action, "arbitrary" actions include those which are unreasonable, in the sense that they are not based on sufficient or legitimate reasons, or are unduly unjust or oppressive.[67]

In *Metalclad*, Mexico took a similar approach to defining the fair and equitable standard. Mexico argued that:

> [t]he concept of fair and equitable treatment is not precisely defined. It offers a general point of departure in formulating an argument that the foreign investor has not been well treated by reason of discriminatory or other unfair measures being taken against its interests. . . . At most it can be said that the concept connotes the principle of non-discrimination and proportionality in treatment of foreign investors.[68]

Naturally, tribunals must still decide how these concepts interrelate, and whether "arbitrary" is equivalent to "unfair and inequitable." While the United States argued in *ELSI* that "arbitrary" and "unfair" are roughly synonymous, at least one prominent commentator has contended that they are not:

> [W]hile it may be suggested that arbitrary, discriminatory or abusive treatment is contrary to customary international law, unfair and inequitable treatment is a much wider conception which may readily include such administrative measures . . . as are not plainly illegal in the accepted sense of international law.[69]

Tribunals working with the diverse texts of investment treaties, including varied articulations of the fair and equitable treatment standard, will undoubtedly find it difficult to establish any agreed-upon typology of government measures, separating "arbitrary" from "unfair," "inequitable," "unreasonable" or "oppressive." In addition, separate clauses in certain BITs prohibiting "arbitrary impairment" further complicate the interpretative task.[70] A typical arbitrary impairment clause provides:

> (b) Neither Party shall in any way impair by arbitrary or discriminatory measures the management, operation, maintenance, use, enjoyment, acquisition, expansion, or

---

[67] *Id.* at 76–77 (source notes omitted).

[68] *Mexico v. Metalclad Corp.* (Mexico's Outline of Argument) ¶ 526 (citing P. Muchlinski, *Multinational Enterprises and the Law* (1995)).

[69] *See* F. A. Mann, *supra* note 60. Mann appears later to have moderated this expansive statement: "In some cases, it is true, treaties merely repeat, perhaps in slightly different language, what in essence is a duty imposed by customary international law; the foremost example is the familiar provision whereby states undertake to accord fair and equitable treatment to each other's nationals and which in law is unlikely to amount to more than a confirmation of the obligation to act in good faith, or to refrain from abuse or arbitrariness." F. A. Mann, *The Legal Aspects of Money* 510 (1982).

[70] *See, e.g.*, U.S.-Argentina BIT (1991), art. II(2)(b). For another variation, *see* Netherlands-Czech BIT (1991), art. 3(1), where the word "arbitrary" has been replaced by the word "unreasonable"; or U.K.-Albania BIT (1994), art. 2(2). *The Restatement (Third) of the Foreign Relations Law of the United States* (1987) defines "an arbitrary act" as "an act that is unfair and unreasonable, and inflicts serious injury to established rights of foreign nations." *The Restatement (Third) of the Foreign Relations Law of the United States*, § 712, cmt 11 (1987).

disposal of investments. For purposes of dispute resolution under Articles VI and VII, a measure may be arbitrary or discriminatory notwithstanding the fact that a Party has had or has exercised the opportunity to review such measure in the courts or administrative tribunals of a Party.[71]

The question arises whether a fair and equitable treatment provision should be interpreted to prohibit conduct that is already sanctioned by an express prohibition against arbitrary treatment. The principle of effectiveness, codified in Article 31 of the Vienna Convention, would require that each clause be interpreted in such a way as not to make it redundant.[72] If arbitrary impairment is no more than a form of unfair and inequitable treatment, arbitrary impairment clauses would appear unnecessary. The tribunal in *LG&E v. Argentina*, however, found that the respondent state had not violated the applicable arbitrary impairment clause but that its conduct nevertheless constituted a breach of the requirement to provide fair and equitable treatment.[73] This suggests that arbitrary impairment is not co-extensive with unfair and inequitable treatment, but that there is some overlap between the two.

On the other hand, the tribunal in *Saluka*, interpreting a variation of the same type of clause ("unreasonable impairment"), stated that:

> [i]nsofar as the standard of conduct is concerned, a violation of the non-impairment requirement does not therefore differ substantially from a violation of the "fair and equitable treatment" standard. The non-impairment requirement merely identifies more specific effects of any such violation, namely with regard to the operation, management, maintenance, use, enjoyment or disposal of the investment by the investor.[74]

The BIT practice of the United States could also be seen to suggest that the arbitrary impairment standard is subsumed within the obligation to provide fair and equitable

---

[71] U.S.-Kazakhstan BIT (1992), art. II(2)(b).

[72] *Corfu Channel Case* (1949) 24 I.C.J. Rep.; *see also* 1 *Oppenheim's International Law* 1280–81 (9th ed., R. Jennings & A. Watts, eds., 1992).

[73] *LG&E v. Argentina*, ICSID Case No. ARB/02/1 (Decision on Liability, Oct. 3, 2006), ¶¶ 161–3. *Cf. Lauder v. Czech Republic*, where the tribunal found that there had been a breach of the arbitrary impairment standard under the U.S.-Czech Republic BIT, but found that the fair and equitable treatment standard had not been violated. *Lauder v. Czech Republic* (UNCITRAL Arbitration, Decision of Sept. 3, 2001), ¶¶ 260 & 293. The *Lauder* tribunal's analysis however leaves no doubt that there is substantial overlap between the two standards ("most of the arguments denying the existence of any arbitrary and discriminatory measure from the Czech Republic as from 1996 also apply to the Respondent's compliance with the obligation to provide fair and equitable treatment"). *Id.* ¶ 294. *See also CMS, supra* note 40, ¶¶ 290 & 292 ("The standard of protection against arbitrariness and discrimination is related to that of fair and equitable treatment. Any measure that might involve arbitrariness or discrimination is in itself contrary to fair and equitable treatment. The standard is next related to impairment: the management ... must be impaired by measures adopted. ... This Tribunal is not persuaded by the Claimant's view about arbitrariness because there has been no impairment, for example, in respect of the management and operation of the investment").

[74] *Saluka, supra* note 12, ¶ 461. *See also Occidental, supra* note 40, ¶ 159–66.

treatment. The disappearance of the "arbitrary impairment" clause from the 2004 U.S. Model BIT suggests that the drafters might have viewed such provisions as unnecessary in light of the current interpretation of other treaty clauses.

There remains substantial doubt concerning the extent to which the fair and equitable treatment standard overlaps with the prohibition on arbitrary impairment. The more central question will be whether future tribunals are able to identify concrete legal formulations to apply the fair and equitable treatment standard in a predictable way. In the words of the *ADF v. United States* tribunal, "any general requirement to accord 'fair and equitable treatment' and 'full protection and security' must be disciplined by being based on State practice and judicial or arbitral case law or other sources of customary or general international law."[75]

b. Legitimate or Reasonable Expectations and Stability

A number of tribunals have used the concept of "reasonable" or "legitimate" expectations in assessing state conduct to determine whether the "fair and equitable treatment" standard has been violated. The test generally applied in these cases is whether the state or its agencies made representations, gave assurances, or otherwise took actions upon which the foreign investor relied in the exercise of reasonable business judgment, and then changed its position in a way that frustrated the investor's resulting expectations.[76]

One of the most often cited cases applying the legitimate expectations test is *Tecmed v. Mexico*.[77] *Tecmed* concerned the refusal by Mexican authorities to renew a Spanish investor's license to operate a hazardous waste landfill in the municipality of Hermosillo, in the state of Sonora, Mexico. The operating license of the landfill at the time of the investment was valid indefinitely. Later, the

---

[75] *ADF, supra* note 10, ¶ 184.

[76] For a detailed examination of the origins of legitimate expectations doctrine, *see* Separate Opinion of Prof. Thomas Wälde in *Thunderbird Gaming v. United Mexican States* (UNCITRAL/NAFTA, Jan. 26, 2006). Professor Wälde believes that the principle of legitimate expectations is a manifestation of the good faith principle, which is a general principle of law (on good faith as a general principle of law, *see* Bin Cheng, *General Principles of Law as Applied by International Courts and Tribunals* 105 *et seq.* (Cambridge University Press 2006)). Wälde also notes that in common law the principle is referred to as estoppel (or *venire contra factum proprium*). The principle is well established in the jurisprudence of the European Court of Justice and developed systems of administrative law and the World Trade Organization (WTO) panel jurisprudence (with respect to the conditions of competition). *See id.* ¶¶ 25–30 and sources cited therein.

[77] *Tecnicas Medioambientales Tecmed S.A. v. United Mexican States*, ICSID Case No. ARB(AF)/00/2 (Award of May 29, 2003). The case was initiated pursuant to the Mexico-Spain BIT (1996).

Instituto Nacionale de Ecologia (INE),[78] an environmental agency of the Mexican government, changed the license terms to require renewal on an annual basis. In July 1997, a new mayor took office in the municipality. This, coupled with the widespread public protests against the landfill operation in its location, led to an understanding between the investor and INE pursuant to which investor would continue operating the landfill until a new location was found for its operation. In November 1998, when the investor applied for the renewal of its license, however, INE rejected its application, and later ordered the landfill to be shut down,[79] giving rise to arbitration.

In its final award, the tribunal outlined the expectations protected by the fair and equitable treatment standard:[80]

> The Arbitral Tribunal considers that this provision of the Agreement [requiring fair and equitable treatment], in light of the good faith principle established by international law, requires that Contracting Parties provide to international investments treatment that does not affect the basic expectations that were taken into account by the foreign investor to make the investment. The foreign investor expects the host State to act in a consistent manner, free from ambiguity and totally transparently in its relations with the foreign investor, so that it may know beforehand any and all rules and regulations that will govern its investments, as well as the goals of the relevant policies and administrative practices or directives, to be able to plan its investment and comply with such regulations. . . . The foreign investor also expects the host State to act consistently, i.e. without arbitrarily revoking any preexisting decisions or permits issued by the State that were relied upon by the investor to assume its commitments as well as to plan and launch its commercial and business activities.[81]

Applying this test, the *Tecmed* tribunal concluded that the investor reasonably understood that the license would continue in full force and effect until the

---

[78] The Hazardous Materials, Waste, and Activities Division of the National Ecology Institute of Mexico, an agency of the Federal Government of the United Mexican States within the Ministry of the Environment, Natural Resources and Fisheries (SEMARNAP). INE directs Mexico's national policy on ecology and environmental protection and is also the regulatory body overseeing environmental issues. *Id.* ¶ 36.

[79] *Id.* ¶¶ 38–39.

[80] A number of other tribunals have relied on a similar test in cases involving other fact patterns. *See, e.g., Parkerings Compagniet AS v. Lithuania*, ICSID Case No. ARB/05/8 (Award of Sept. 11, 2007), ¶ 330; *Siemens v. Argentina*, ICSID Case No. ARB/02/8 (Award of Feb. 6, 2007), ¶ 298; *LG&E, supra* note 73, ¶ 127; *Azurix, supra* note 21, ¶ 371; *Saluka, supra* note 12, ¶ 302; *Eureko B.V. v. Poland* (ad hoc arbitration, Partial Award on Liability, Aug. 19, 2005), ¶ 235; *CMS, supra* note 40, ¶ 268; *Occidental, supra* note 40, ¶ 185; *MTD Equity Sdn. Bhd. & MTD Chile S.A. v. Republic of Chile*, ICSID Case No. ARB/01/7 (Award of May 25, 2004), ¶¶ 114–15.

[81] *Tecmed, supra* note 77, ¶ 154 (emphasis added). For a criticism of *Tecmed*, see Zachary Douglas, *Nothing if Not Critical for Investment Treaty Arbitration: Occidental Eureko and Methanex*, 22 Arb. Int'l 27, 28 (2006) ("The *Tecmed* 'standard' is actually not a standard at all; it is rather a description of perfect public regulation in a perfect world, to which all states should aspire but very few (if any) will ever attain").

effective relocation date.[82] According to the *Tecmed* tribunal, the conduct of INE was in conflict with what a reasonable and unbiased market participant would consider fair and equitable, and this resulted in a violation of the BIT provision on fair and equitable treatment.[83]

The tribunal in *Thunderbird v. Mexico*[84] was one of the first to define expressly the concept of legitimate expectations in the context of international investment protection law.[85] The issue of legitimate expectations in *Thunderbird* arose in the context of an inquiry by the investor and answer to that inquiry by the Ministry of the Interior of Mexico (SEGOB) regarding the legality of the investor's proposed operations in Mexico, which involved gambling machines. On the basis of the investor's description of the machines, SEGOB stated that if the machines operated as described, and were not mere slot machines but involved some skill, then they would not be prohibited under the Mexican law. However, slot machines in which the principal factor of operation is luck were prohibited under the Federal Law of Games and Sweepstakes of Mexico.[86] On the basis of SEGOB's answer, Thunderbird began expanding its activities in Mexico. Later, SEGOB started closing down Thunderbird's gaming facilities, maintaining the equipment used there was no more than slot machines. Thunderbird resorted to proceedings in the Mexican courts to challenge SEGOB's measures, but to no avail. In the NAFTA arbitration that ensued, Thunderbird argued that according to SEGOB's answer to its inquiry, it legitimately expected to continue its operations, had detrimentally relied on the government's representations in making its investments in Mexico, and had suffered damages as a result of the frustration of its expectations. The tribunal defined the legitimate expectations test as follows:

> Having considered recent investment case law and the good faith principle of international customary law, the concept of "legitimate expectations" relates, within the context of the NAFTA framework, to a situation where a Contracting Party's conduct creates reasonable and justifiable expectations on the part of an investor (or investment) to act in reliance on said conduct, such that a failure by the NAFTA Party to honour those expectations could cause the investor (or investment) to suffer damages.
>
> The threshold for legitimate expectations may vary depending on the nature of the violation alleged under the NAFTA and the circumstances of the case.[87]

The tribunal, ultimately, rejected Thunderbird's allegations, finding that SEGOB's answer to Thunderbird's inquiry had not created any legitimate expectations,

---

[82] *Id.*

[83] *Id.* ¶ 166.

[84] *Thunderbird, supra* note 76.

[85] *Metalclad* was the first case involving the direct application of such a "reasonable expectations" test. For a discussion of the case *see* p. 521 *infra*.

[86] *Thunderbird, supra* note 76, ¶ 55.

[87] *Id.* ¶¶ 147–48.

because the claimant had not described the nature of the gaming machines correctly in the initial request for an opinion, and the machines were in fact gambling machines under Mexican law.[88]

According to *Tecmed*, investors expect host states to act consistently, transparently, and in predictable and rational manner. In addition, the *Tecmed* standard (as noted above, criticized by some commentators as unrealistically stringent) requires stability of the legal framework, at least to the extent that "the conditions existing at the time of [investment] remain unchanged."[89] The *Saluka* tribunal added to that list a host state's obligation to treat investors in non-discriminatory manner.[90] A few tribunals, such as *Saluka* and *LG & E*, have also suggested that investors must share part of the risk of adverse change in business conditions in this context. In *LG & E*, for example, the tribunal stated, "the investor's fair expectations cannot fail to consider parameters such as business risk or industry's regular patterns."[91]

The legitimate expectations of the investor as formulated by *Tecmed* and further described by other tribunals encompass a wide array of governmental conduct and/or measures. The breadth of these expectations could imply that the test is being used as a catch-all phrase to refer to the majority of the fact situations subsumed under fair and equitable treatment. Some of the relevant concepts, such as arbitrariness[92] and transparency,[93] have been discussed separately in this chapter. The obligation of the state to treat investors in a non-discriminatory manner was discussed in Chapter XV, above.

Two approaches seem to emerge from arbitral practice in regard to creation of reasonable expectations: first, a narrow approach, requiring specific assurances from the government to the investor regarding a particular business relationship; and second, a broad approach, according to which expectations could be created based on assurances provided in generally applicable laws of a country, and more generally, upon the existing legal framework at the time of the investment. The legitimate expectation test in the latter sense seems to be equivalent to or overlap with the concept of stability of the legal framework. Some tribunals have treated the stability of the legal framework as a subcategory of legitimate expectations,[94] while others view

---

[88] *Id.* ¶¶ 150–53.

[89] *Parkerings*, supra note 80, ¶ 330.

[90] *Saluka*, supra note 12, ¶ 309. For a commentary on this issue see Borzu Sabahi, *National Treatment—Is Discriminatory Intent Relevant?*, in *Investment Treaty Arbitration: A Debate and Discussion* (T. Weiler ed., Juris Publishing 2008).

[91] *LG&E*, supra note 73, ¶130. See also *Saluka*, supra note 12, ¶ 305 ("No investor may reasonably expect that the circumstances prevailing at the time the investment is made remain totally unchanged. To determine whether frustration of the foreign investor's expectations was justified and reasonable, the host State's legitimate right subsequently to regulate domestic matters in the public interest must be taken into consideration as well . . .").

[92] See p. 507 *supra*.

[93] See p. 519 *infra*.

[94] See, e.g., *Parkerings*, supra note 80, ¶¶ 326 et seq.

the protection of expectations as a separate subcategory of fair and equitable treatment.[95] The latter categorization implies that even in the absence of legitimate expectations, governments are bound to provide a stable legal framework. This conclusion, however, seems to obviate the need to include stabilization clauses in investment contracts. The continued prevalence of such clauses suggests that investors do not enjoy any unconditional right to legal or contractual stability absent a stabilization clause, or a similar government undertaking that could be the source of an expectation of stability.

Arbitral tribunals have applied the legitimate expectations test in a variety of fact patterns, including the revocation of a license to operate,[96] inconsistent actions of different branches of a government,[97] and change of the regulatory framework governing the investment.[98]

The first group of cases applying this standard involves government interference with the investors' license to operate a business. In *Tecmed* (as explained briefly above), the Mexican government changed its position with respect to to renewal of Tecmed's permit to operate a hazardous waste landfill, contrary to assurances it had made. The tribunal found Mexico had breached the fair and equitable treatment standard under the Spain-Mexico BIT.[99] Similarly, in *Metalclad*, the tribunal found that Mexico had assured the U.S. investor that local permits for a landfill were not needed, and that the investor reasonably relied on those representations when it made its investment:

> 87. Relying on the representations of the federal government, Metalclad started constructing the landfill, and did this openly and continuously, and with the full knowledge of the federal, state, and municipal governments, until the municipal "Stop Work Order" on October 26, 1994. The basis of this order was said to have been Metalclad's failure to obtain a municipal construction permit.
>
> . . .
>
> 89. Metalclad was entitled to rely on the representations of federal officials and to believe that it was entitled to continue its construction of the landfill. In following the advice of these officials, and filing the municipal permit application on November 15, 1994, Metalclad was merely acting prudently and in the full expectation that the permit would be granted.[100]

---

[95] See, e.g., PSEG, supra note 61, ¶¶ 241 et seq. See also C. Schreuer, *Fair and Equitable Treatment in Arbitral Practice*, Standard, 6(3) JWIT 357 (2005).

[96] See, e.g., *Metalclad Corp. v. United Mexican States*, ICSID Case No. ARB(AF)/97/1 (NAFTA, Aug. 30, 2000); and *Tecmed*, supra note 77.

[97] MTD, supra note 80.

[98] CMS, supra note 40; Occidental, supra note 40. See also *Sempra Energy v. Argentina*, ICSID Case No. ARB/02/16 (Award of Sept. 28, 2007), ¶¶ 303 & 113–14.

[99] Tecmed, supra note 77, ¶¶ 166 & 174.

[100] Metalclad, supra note 96.

Because the project was ultimately scuttled as a result of the local authorities' demand that the investor apply for a permit, the Tribunal found Mexico liable to the U.S. investor for violation of the fair and equitable treatment standard.[101]

MTD v. Chile,[102] an ICSID arbitration proceeding initiated pursuant to the Malaysia-Chile BIT, involved a fair and equitable treatment claim based upon inconsistent government actions. There, the investors intended to build a housing complex in a location close to the capital of Chile, Santiago. They obtained necessary approvals from Chile's investment promotion agency. Later, however, the municipality where the land was located refused to issue the necessary permits, because pursuant to certain land use regulations the housing complex could not be built at the desired location. The claimants alleged that Chile had acted unfairly and inequitably[103] when it "created and encouraged strong expectations that the Project, which was the object of the investment, could be built in the specific proposed location and entered into a contract confirming that location but then disapproved that location as a matter of policy after MTD irrevocably committed its investment to build the Project in that location."[104] The tribunal found that Chile was obliged to act coherently and to apply policies consistently, and it held that Chile's rejection of MTD's investment after an initial approval violated this obligation.[105]

---

[101]   *Id.* ¶¶ 97–101. *See also CME* (Partial Award), *supra* note 58. CME initiated arbitration pursuant to the Netherlands-Czech Republic BIT. CME had established a company in the Czech Republic, CNTS, which operated a very successful television channel, TV Nova. A Czech subsidiary, CET 21, held the broadcast license for TV Nova. CME's investment in CNTS was governed by a "Memorandum of Association" that memorialized this structure. This contract had been negotiated and approved by a Czech quasi-governmental agency during the license approval process. A few years later, the Czech agency took steps that effectively ousted CME from TV Nova. "The Media Council [the relevant Czech government entity] violated the Treaty when dismantling the legal basis of the foreign investor's investments by forcing the foreign investor's joint venture company CNTS to give up substantial accrued legal rights . . . . The Media Council jointly with CEDC [, (a German company under the same ultimate control as CME, which sold a 66 percent stake to CME)] developed the investment scheme by creating the 1993 split structure which was thereafter also used by other broadcasters. CME and its predecessor as foreign investor could reasonably rely on this structure which was developed in close conjunction with and approved by the Media Council." On this basis, the tribunal held that the "Media Council breached its obligation of fair and equitable treatment by evisceration of the arrangements in reliance upon which the foreign investor was induced to invest." *Id.* ¶ 611.

[102]   *MTD, supra* note 80.

[103]   The applicable fair and equitable clause in this case was imported from the Chile-Croatia BIT by application of the MFN clause of the Chile-Malaysia BIT. *See* Chapter XV, *supra*.

[104]   *See MTD, supra* note 80, ¶ 116.

[105]   *Id.* ¶¶ 163–67. Chile brought an ICSID annulment proceeding against award in this case. The annulment committee upheld the decision. *See MTD v. Chile*, ICSID Case No. ARB/01/7 (Decision on Annulment, Mar. 21, 2007).

The third common fact pattern involves a change of regulatory framework and the failure to provide a stable legal regime for investment. This fact pattern raises particularly difficult questions balancing the government's right to regulate with the investor's legitimate expectations that the framework will remain unchanged.[106] Three cases, *CMS*,[107] *Occidental*,[108] and *Parkerings*,[109] highlight the wide spectrum of solutions that the arbitral tribunals have adopted.

The *CMS* case arose out of the Argentinean financial crisis of the late 1990s.[110] In the early 1990s, Argentina created a new regulatory framework for the gas transportation and distribution sector, including various guarantees designed to attract foreign investment: currency convertibility was introduced in 1991, operating companies were to receive a tariff sufficient to ensure a reasonable rate of return in real terms, and so forth. CMS, a U.S. corporation, acquired 29 percent of the Argentine gas transportation company TGN. CMS's decision to invest was based in part on the terms of the new regulatory regime. Starting in 1998, the Argentine economy began to deteriorate, and in 2001 Argentina suffered a serious financial crisis. In its efforts to control the crisis, Argentina eventually nullified several of the central elements of the regulatory regime to which TGN was subject. Finally, in January 2002, the government passed the Emergency Law, which abrogated the one-to-one peg between the Argentine peso and U.S. dollar and forcibly converted dollar-denominated contracts into pesos at the newly-devalued exchange rate. CMS brought an ICSID arbitration under the Argentina-United States BIT, alleging violation of several standards including fair and equitable treatment. In particular, CMS alleged a violation of fair and equitable treatment "insofar as [Argentina had] profoundly altered the stability and predictability of the investment environment, an assurance that was key to its decision to invest."[111]

The tribunal, citing cases such as *CME* and *Tecmed*, considered the stability and predictability of the legal and regulatory environment to be an important part of fair and equitable treatment:

> 274. The Treaty Preamble makes it clear, however, that one principal objective of the protection envisaged is that fair and equitable treatment is desirable "to maintain a stable

---

[106] *Saluka, supra* note 12, ¶ 306 ("The determination of a breach of [fair and equitable treatment] . . . requires a weighing of the Claimant's legitimate and reasonable expectations on the one hand and the Respondent's legitimate regulatory interests on the other").

[107] *CMS, supra* note 40.

[108] *Occidental, supra* note 40.

[109] *Parkerings, supra* note 80.

[110] *See generally CMS, supra* note 40, ¶¶ 59–67.

[111] *Id.* ¶ 267.

framework for investments and maximum effective use of economic resources." *There can be no doubt, therefore, that a stable legal and business environment is an essential element of fair and equitable treatment.*

> 275. The measures that are complained of did in fact entirely transform and alter the legal and business environment under which the investment was decided and made. The discussion above, about the tariff regime and its relationship with a dollar standard and adjustment mechanisms unequivocally shows that these elements are no longer present in the regime governing the business operations of the Claimant. *It has also been established that the guarantees given in this connection under the legal framework and its various components were crucial for the investment decision.*[112]

Not every alteration of the existing regulatory framework is as obvious as it was in *CMS v. Argentina*. Such changes do not necessarily involve the enactment of new legislation or the abolition of existing regulations. A similar effect is sometimes achieved by transforming the interpretation of existing laws. This was the case in *Occidental Exploration and Production Company* (OEPC) *v. Ecuador*.[113] There, OEPC entered into a hydrocarbon production contract with Petroecuador, an Ecuadorian state-owned corporation. The contract included a participation formula, called "Factor X," based on which the parties calculated the share of oil production that OEPC could keep. In addition, OEPC was entitled to reimbursement of the value-added tax (VAT) paid on domestic purchases made to conduct its operations. OEPC regularly applied to the Ecuadorian Internal Revenue Services (SRI) and received VAT reimbursements pursuant to this entitlement. Later, however, the government disqualified OEPC from VAT reimbursements, insisting the VAT already was built into Factor X and therefore was part of OEPC's oil take. In addition, Ecuador demanded that OEPC return all VAT already received. The tribunal, relying on *Tecmed,* concluded that "the framework under which the investment was made and operates has been changed [by reinterpreting it] in an important manner by the actions adopted by the SRI."[114] Ecuador was therefore found to have violated the fair and equitable treatment standard.

Not all changes in a regulatory framework have been found to violate the fair and equitable standard. In *Parkerings v. Lithuania*, for example, the tribunal held that the government had the right to change its legal regime, and that the claimants could not expect that applicable legislation would not change.[115] A consortium of investors won a bid to create, operate, and enforce a public parking system in the city of Vilnius. The consortium entered into a contractual agreement with the city of Vilnius to this effect. Shortly thereafter, the Lithuanian central government contended that certain provisions of the agreement, particularly the proposed method of calculating

---

[112] *Id.* ¶¶ 274–75 (emphasis added). Argentina brought proceedings to annul the *CMS* award. The arbitrators' decision was roundly criticised on a number of points by the annulment committee, but ultimately was left unchanged. *CMS Gas Transmission Co. v. Argentina* ICSID Case No. ARB/01/8 (Decision on Application for Annulment). *See also LG&E, supra* note 73, ¶ 130.

[113] *Occidental, supra* note 40.

[114] *Id.* ¶¶ 184.

[115] *Parkerings, supra* note 80, ¶¶ 331–33.

and collecting parking fees, were in conflict with existing Lithuanian laws. Subsequently, the Lithuanian parliament enacted new legislation depriving the parking venture of some of the anticipated fees. Meanwhile, other government agencies raised concerns about the impact of planned parking lots on the historical part of Vilnius. After several failed attempts to amend the agreement to harmonize it with Lithuanian law, the municipality terminated the agreement.

The foreign lead partner of the parking consortium initiated ICSID arbitration pursuant to the 1992 Norway-Lithuania BIT, alleging violation of several articles of the BIT, including a provision requiring "equitable and reasonable treatment." The claimant argued that its legitimate expectations had been frustrated by the changes that took place after it entered into the agreement with the city authorities.[116] The tribunal noted that the government had not given any explicit or implicit assurance that the legal regime would not change.[117] Another pertinent consideration was that Lithuania was at the time a country in transition, and any businessman should have expected that change in the law could occur.[118] The foreign investor could have secured stability by inserting a stabilization clause in the concession contract. Instead, the agreement made explicit reference to the applicability of Lithuanian law. Therefore, the tribunal concluded that the claimant's legitimate expectations had not been frustrated; the claimant could not have had any such expectations as to legal stability in the first place.[119]

The *Parkerings* decision suggests a closely circumscribed conception of legitimate expectations, limited to understandings about future state conduct created by specific assurances from the government. Unlike in *CMS*, the tribunal in *Parkerings* did not accept that the legal framework itself, as it existed at the time when the agreement was signed, could be the source of any protected expectations. This difference in approach could be partly due to differences in the legal regimes governing foreign investments in the two countries. The Argentine legal regime at issue in

---

[116] *Id.* ¶¶ 320 *et seq.*

[117] *Id.* ¶ 334.

[118] *Id.* ¶ 335.

[119] *Id.* ¶¶ 320 *et seq.* The claimant also argued that the municipality was aware of the existence of the proposals to amend the relevant Lithuanian laws, and acted contrary to the claimant's legitimate expectations by withholding this information during the negotiation of the agreement. The tribunal dismissed this claim, holding that "the Tribunal considers that the Claimant's expectations are, in substance, of a contractual nature. The acts and omissions of the Municipality of Vilnius, in particular any failure to advise or warn the claimant of likely or possible changes to Lithuanian law, may be breaches of the Agreement but that does not mean they are inconsistent with . . . the Treaty." *Id.* ¶ 345.

CMS contained specific guarantees addressed to foreign investors, which were explicitly recognized by the tribunal, whereas the Lithuanian legal regime appears to have been devoid of provisions aimed at attracting foreign investment.[120] Furthermore, in *Parkerings*, the claimant's proffered evidence failed to demonstrate that it had engaged in reasonable due diligence with respect to the nature and extent of pending legal evolution in Lithuania.

c. Transparency

An emerging additional element of fair and equitable treatment is the requirement that host states ensure a reasonable level of administrative transparency. A number of investment treaty arbitration tribunals have held that this principle is encompassed by the fair and equitable treatment standard.[121] The same conclusion has been proposed by international organizations such as UNCTAD.[122] Some investment treaties, particularly those concluded in the past decade, contain separate provisions dealing with transparency.[123] These novel treaty provisions often require the publication of laws and regulations constituting the investment framework, as well as the exchange of related information between the state parties to the treaty.[124] Such provisions do not normally establish any direct right for foreign investors. However, a few recent investment treaties have expanded the scope of

---

[120] *CMS, supra* note 40, ¶ 275. *Cf. Parkerings, supra* note 80, ¶¶ 334–38.

[121] *See* cases mentioned at p. 522 *infra*.

[122] UNCTAD, *supra* note 11, at 51 ("The concept of transparency overlaps with fair and equitable treatment in at least two significant ways. First, transparency may be required, as a matter of course, by the concept of fair and equitable treatment. If laws, administrative decisions and other binding decisions are to be imposed on a foreign investor by a host State, then fairness requires that the investor is informed about such decisions before they are imposed. This interpretation suggests that where an investment treaty does not expressly provide for transparency, but does for fair and equitable treatment, then transparency is implicitly included in the treaty"). Other international institutions have also embraced the principle of transparency. For example, the concept of transparency and the procedural requirements for ensuring it are clearly embodied in the General Agreement on Tariffs and Trade (GATT), art. X. Similarly, a WTO working group has concluded that "fair and equitable treatment" can be interpreted as "requiring parties to adhere to basic norms of transparency." WTO, Working Group on the Relationship between Trade and Investment, *Transparency*, Note by the Secretariat, WT/WGTI/W/109 (Mar. 27, 2002). *See also LG & E, supra* note 73, ¶ 131 ("Thus, this Tribunal, having considered, as previously stated, the sources of international law, understands that the fair and equitable standard consists of the host State's consistent and transparent behavior, free of ambiguity that involves the obligation to grant and maintain a stable and predictable legal framework necessary to fulfill the justified expectations of the foreign investor").

[123] *See, e.g.*, Energy Charter Treaty, art. 20. *See also* 2004 Canadian Model FIPA, *supra* note 23, art. 19; and U.S. Model BIT 2004, art. 11.

[124] *See* UNCTAD, *Bilateral Investment Treaties 1995–2006: Trends in Investment Rulemaking* 76 *et seq.* (2007).

transparency obligations by requiring governments to provide an opportunity for private parties to play a role in the rule-making process.[125]

Arbitral tribunals that have examined the transparency concept in the context of fair and equitable treatment appear generally to have focused upon the exchange of information between the government and the investor in the context of an ongoing investment project. In some instances, these tribunals have viewed the host state's openness obligation to extend beyond the publication of laws. As explained below, a few awards have imposed a duty proactively to clarify possible ambiguities in the legal framework or in the relationship between the parties to the project.

---

[125] Article II of the U.S. Model BIT (2004) provides:

Article 11: Transparency

1. Contact Points

(a) Each Party shall designate a contact point or points to facilitate communications between the Parties on any matter covered by this Treaty.

(b) On the request of the other Party, the contact point(s) shall identify the office or official responsible for the matter and assist, as necessary, in facilitating communication with the requesting Party.

2. Publication

To the extent possible, each Party shall:

(a) publish in advance any measure referred to in Article 10(1)(a) that it proposes to adopt; and

(b) provide interested persons and the other Party a reasonable opportunity to comment on such proposed measures.

3. Provision of Information

(a) On request of the other Party, a Party shall promptly provide information and respond to questions pertaining to any actual or proposed measure that the requesting Party considers might materially affect the operation of this Treaty or otherwise substantially affect its interests under this Treaty.

(b) Any request or information under this paragraph shall be provided to the other Party through the relevant contact points.

(c) Any information provided under this paragraph shall be without prejudice as to whether the measure is consistent with this Treaty.

4. Administrative Proceedings

With a view to administering in a consistent, impartial, and reasonable manner all measures referred to in Article 10(1)(a), each Party shall ensure that in its administrative proceedings applying such measures to particular covered investments or investors of the other Party in specific cases:

(a) wherever possible, covered investments or investors of the other Party that are directly affected by a proceeding are provided reasonable notice, in accordance with domestic procedures, when a proceeding is initiated, including a description of the nature of the proceeding, a statement of the legal authority under which the proceeding is initiated, and a general description of any issues in controversy;

(b) such persons are afforded a reasonable opportunity to present facts and arguments in support of their positions prior to any final administrative action, when time, the nature of the proceeding, and the public interest permit; and

(c) its procedures are in accordance with domestic law.

One of the first investment treaty decisions to resolve a claim based upon a state's alleged failure to act transparently came in *Metalclad v. Mexico*.[126] Metalclad acquired a hazardous waste landfill in San Luis Potosí, Mexico. The Mexican federal and state authorities issued construction and operating permits for the landfill prior to this purchase.[127] At the same time, Metalclad inquired whether it would need additional municipal construction permits. Federal officials replied with assurances that no other permits would be required, and extended the federal construction permit for an additional eighteen months.[128] Later, local authorities demanded that Metalclad obtain a municipal permit and eventually refused to issue one. The resulting NAFTA tribunal considered whether Mexico had treated Metalclad fairly and equitably. In making this determination, the tribunal was guided by the legal principles codified in NAFTA itself, particularly Article 102(1) on transparency.[129] The tribunal defined transparency in this context as follows:

> Prominent in the statement of principles and rules that introduces the Agreement is the reference to "transparency" (NAFTA Article 102(1)). The Tribunal understands this to include the idea that all relevant legal requirements for the purpose of initiating, completing and successfully operating investments made, or intended to be made, under the Agreement should be capable of being readily known to all affected investors of another Party. There should be no room for doubt or uncertainty on such matters. Once the authorities of the central government of any Party (whose international responsibility in such matters has been identified in the preceding section) become aware of any scope for misunderstanding or confusion in this connection, it is their duty to ensure that the correct position is promptly determined and clearly stated so that investors can proceed with all appropriate expedition in the confident belief that they are acting in accordance with all relevant laws.[130]

The *Metalclad v. Mexico* tribunal expressly based its ruling with respect to fair and equitable treatment on the Mexican government's failure to maintain the appropriate level of transparency in dealing with the foreign investor.[131] The tribunal particularly noted that the investor had been led to believe that it did not need a local permit; furthermore, there was no procedure for handling local construction permit applications. In addition the arbitrators took account of the fact that the decision to deny the permit was made *in absentia*. The investor never learned that a decision was being made, and was afforded no opportunity to participate in the process.[132] On this basis,

---

[126] For a more extensive discussion of *Metalclad*'s facts and its significance for the doctrine of indirect expropriation, see Chapter XVI *supra* at pp. 476 *et seq.*

[127] *Id.* ¶¶ 77–78.

[128] *Id.* ¶ 80.

[129] See id. ¶ 76 *et seq.* NAFTA, art. 102(1), which sets out the objectives of NAFTA, provides in the relevant part that: "The objectives of this Agreement, as elaborated more specifically through its principles and rules, including national treatment, most-favored-nation treatment and transparency, are to . . . c) increase substantially investment opportunities in the territories of the Parties. . . ."

[130] *Id.* ¶ 76.

[131] *Metalclad, supra* note 96, ¶¶ 88, 99.

[132] *Id.* ¶ 88.

the tribunal concluded that the authorities' actions, together with deficiencies in the permit process, had violated the treaty:[133]

> Mexico failed to ensure a transparent and predictable framework for Metalclad's business planning and investment. The totality of these circumstances demonstrates a lack of orderly process and timely disposition in relation to an investor of a Party acting in the expectation that it would be treated fairly and justly in accordance with the NAFTA.[134]

Mexico sought to annul the *Metalclad* award in British Columbia, which was the place of the arbitration.[135] Judge Tysoe set aside the tribunal's decision with respect to fair and equitable treatment (although he left other dispositive conclusions against Mexico untouched), on grounds that transparency had not become part of customary international law,[136] and that there were "no transparency obligations contained in (NAFTA) Chapter 11."[137] However, the court did not grapple with what could have been a central question: does fair and equitable treatment encompass the principle of transparency? Judge Tysoe's decision has been characterized by a number of commentators as "questionable."[138] The case was settled (with nearly full payment by Mexico) before the judgment could be reviewed by a court of appeals.

Subsequent tribunals, some relying on the *Metalclad* reasoning, have held that fair and equitable treatment requires a government to act transparently, despite the absence of any reference to the concept in most bilateral investment treaties. In *Tecmed v. Mexico*,[139] for example, the tribunal found that the fair and equitable standard requires that a host government act "totally transparently" when dealing with a foreign investor.[140] In *Maffezini v. Spain*,[141] the tribunal held that "the lack of transparency . . . is incompatible with [the host state's] commitment to ensure the investor a fair and equitable treatment."[142] In *Waste Management v. Mexico*, the tribunal undertook a survey of jurisprudence applying and interpreting fair and

---

[133] *Id.* ¶ 97.

[134] *Id.* ¶ 99.

[135] See *Metalclad v. Mexico* (Judicial Review Proceedings), *supra* note 6.

[136] *Id.* ¶ 68.

[137] *Id.* ¶ 72.

[138] See *Pope & Talbot*, *supra* note 11. H. C. Alvarez, *Setting Aside Additional Facility Awards: The Metalclad Case*, in Annulment of ICSID Awards 267 (E. Gaillard & Y. Banifatemi eds., Juris Publishing & Internat'l Arb. Inst. 2004); H. Olasolo, *Have Public Interests Been Forgotten in NAFTA Chapter 11 Foreign Investor/Host State Arbitration? Some Conclusions from the Judgment of the Supreme Court of British Columbia on the Case of Mexico v. Metalclad*, 189–210 NAFTA: L. & Bus. Rev. Am. (2002); T. Weiler, *Good Faith and Regulatory Transparency: The Story of Metalclad v. Mexico*, in International Investment Law and Arbitration: Leading Cases from the ICSID, NAFTA, Bilateral Treaties and Customary International Law 701 (T. Weiler ed., Cameron May 2005).

[139] Facts of *Tecmed* were discussed in pp. 510–12 *supra*.

[140] *Tecmed, supra* note 77, ¶ 154.

[141] *Maffezini v. Spain*, ICSID Case No. ARB/97/7 (Argentina-Spain BIT, Award of Nov. 13, 2000).

[142] *Id.* ¶ 83.

equitable treatment, and then concluded that the standard will not permit a "lack of transparency and candour in an administrative process."[143]

In sum, some arbitral decisions suggest that the host state's failure to act transparently is sufficient to breach fair and equitable treatment, while other arbitrators and commentators appear to favor the view that opacity in government administration will only provide a valid basis for a claim of unfair and inequitable treatment if accompanied by other irregularities.

d. Coercion of Foreign Investors

Once an investment has been made, foreign investors can be vulnerable to government pressure or harassment. Particularly in capital-intensive sectors, long-term projects are in some sense hostage to the host state.[144] As one might expect, this type of government conduct is precisely one of the areas targeted by investment protection treaties. It is therefore unsurprising that investment arbitration tribunals have found unjustified government pressure or coercion to violate the fair and equitable treatment standard. In *CME v. Czech Republic*,[145] for instance, the tribunal sanctioned the Czech government's improper pressure on the investor through administrative proceedings designed to dissuade the investor from pursuing certain investment plans:

> *CME Czech Republic B.V. v. Czech Republic*
>
> (UNCITRAL Arbitration, Partial Award on Liability, Sept. 13, 2001)
>
> 480. The events in 1996 as documented by the exhibits to the parties' submissions are decisive in sustaining the conclusion that the Media Council in 1996 forced ÈNTS and CME to agree to undermine the legal protection of CME's investment. Considering the interpretation of the documents and the witness statements, the Tribunal is of the view that the Council, in order to re-establish its control over the broadcasting operations of CET 21/ÈNTS (which operations were disconnected from the licence-holder by the 1993 split structure), "made a very intensive effort" . . . to force CET 21/ÈNTS and its shareholders to surrender the 1993 split structure. . . .

---

[143] *Waste Mgmt., supra* note 38, ¶ 98. The *Waste Management* tribunal ultimately rejected the claims based upon the fair and equitable treatment standard. *See also PSEG, supra* note 61, ¶ 174 ("There is thus a cumulative lack of transparency that, short of bad faith, comes at the very least close to negligence, compounded by the fact that various witnesses admitted not having read key documents or taken appropriate action on them for long periods").

[144] N. Rubins & S. Kinsella, *International Investment, Political Risk, and Dispute Resolution* 5 (Oceana Publications 2005 ("At the outset of a project, foreign investors tend to demand additional concessions or higher returns as a result of the perceived risk of entry and the intensive exposure of the start-up phase. Once the investment is underway, however, the host government is less prepared to maintain the start-up conditions, since the risk often will have declined, along with the cost of financing. Where a project is long-term with heavy capital investment (sunk costs) at the start, and uses assets that are not easily sold or converted to other purposes, the government has a great deal of leverage over the foreign investor, who cannot . . . abandon his investment plans if conditions deteriorate. This imbalance creates an almost irresistible temptation for local officials to extract short-term political advantage by shifting foreign investment profits to constituents either within the government or the public at large").

[145] *CME, supra* note 58.

"FAIR AND EQUITABLE TREATMENT" AND "FULL PROTECTION AND SECURITY"

> 484. The Council put the issue of CET 21's legal structure on the agenda of the Council Meeting on June 28 and June 29, 1996 and decided at that meeting in respect of ÈNTS that a warning of illegality of broadcasting shall be sent to ÈNTS, which shall include a time-period for remedy, ending on August 27, 1996. Further, the Council decided to postpone a decision on a cancellation of Condition No. 17 of the Licence, "because of the preliminary question of proceedings before a court and proceedings at the State Prosecutor's Office." . . .
>
> 490. The purpose of initiating administrative proceedings against ÈNTS was solely to put pressure on CET 21 and ÈNTS, with the aim of elimination of the 1993 split structure. . . .
>
> 507. The witness stated that only because of the exercise of coercion was the legal basis for the investment changed. Only the amendment of the MOA to be redrafted along the lines that would satisfy the Media Council could have solved the situation which otherwise would have been destructive for CME's investment.
>
> 508. Also, the witness Ms. Landová, who, in the years 1993 to 1997 worked as a senior member of the staff of the office of the Council, supported this position. She clearly stated that the Council initiated administrative proceedings for unauthorized broadcasting against ÈNTS in order to put pressure on ÈNTS to change the MOA and to make the other changes requested by the Council. . . .
>
> 511. According to the statement of Mr. Josefík, who later became the Chairman of the Media Council, the administrative proceedings must have been seen in the eyes of ÈNTS as a real threat. . . .
>
> 513. This threat was fundamental because a withdrawal of the Licence in the same way as interference with ÈNTS' broadcasting operations would have destroyed the Claimant's investment in the Czech Republic.
>
> 514. CME, at this point of time, could not take the risk of entering into longlasting legal battles, civil law and/or administrative law proceedings, as such proceedings would carry the danger that, if the lawsuits were to be lost, CME's investment would have been irreversibly destroyed.
>
> 515. The Claimant decided to give in, which is a normal commercial consequence in any situation of unlawful pressure, when the affected victim of such pressure has to make a careful assessment.
>
> 516. Such a decision for a compromise, however, does not make the Council's unlawful acts legal and cannot be deemed as a waiver of CME's rights under the Treaty. This is the considered conclusion of the Arbitral Tribunal. . . .
>
> 521. A threat does not become legal upon the victim's surrender to the threat and the surrender cannot be deemed as a waiver of its legal rights. The possibility that the threatening State Authority would not exercise its powers or that law courts would grant sufficient relief do not qualify the victim's surrender as voluntary.

Occasionally, harassment or coercion occurs *after* arbitration has began. In *Pope & Talbot*, for example, the tribunal concluded that Canada's threats after the claimant investor had initiated NAFTA arbitration violated the fair and equitable treatment standard:

> 67. Applying Canada's view of the customary international law standard embodied in the Interpretation, the Tribunal must determine whether the conduct giving rise to the April 10, 2001 Award under Article 1105 was, to use Canada's term, egregious. The Tribunal finds that it was.

68. A lengthy statement of facts, as found by the Tribunal, is set out in paragraphs 156–181 of that Award. Briefly, the Tribunal found that when the Investor instituted the claim in these proceedings, Canada's Softwood Lumber Division (SLD) changed its previous relationship with the Investors and the Investment from one of cooperation in running the Softwood Lumber Regime to one of threats and misrepresentation. Figuring in this new attitude were assertions of non-existent policy reasons for forcing them to comply with very burdensome demands for documents, refusals to provide them with promised information, threats of reductions and even termination of the Investment's export quotas, serious misrepresentations of fact in memoranda to the Minister concerning the Investor's and the Investment's actions and even suggestions of criminal investigation of the Investment's conduct. The Tribunal also concluded that these actions were not caused by any behaviour of the Investor or the Investment, which remained cooperative until the overraching of the SLD became too burdensome and confrontational. One would hope that these actions by the SLD would shock and outrage every reasonable citizen of Canada, *they did shock and outrage the Tribunal.*

69. For these reasons, the Tribunal concludes that the conduct of the SLD in the Verification Review Episode violated the fair and equitable treatment requirement under Article 1105, even using Canada's strict formulation of that requirement.[146]

e. Denial of Justice

The concept of "denial of justice," one of the most venerable of international wrongs,[147] appears to occupy the very core of the fair and equitable treatment standard.[148] The Annexes to the U.S. Model BIT of 2004 and new U.S. FTAs expressly link the access to meaningful justice with fair and equitable treatment.[149]

---

[146] *Pope & Talbot, supra* note 11, ¶¶ 67–69.

[147] Alwyn Freeman traces the origins of denial of justice to the institution of private reprisals, which existed before the emergence of the modern state. Alwyn V. Freeman, *The International Responsibility of States for Denial of Justice* 309 (Kraus Reprint Co. 1938). *See also* Hans W. Spiegel, *Origin and Development of Denial of Justice*, 32 Am. J. Int'l L. 63 (1938). For more recent commentaries see Don Wallace, Jr., *Fair and Equitable Treatment and Denial of Justice: From Chattin v. Mexico and Loewen v. USA*, in *International Investment Law and Arbitration: Leading Cases From the ICSID, NAFTA, Bilateral Treaties, and Customary International Law* 669–700 (Todd Weiler ed., Cameron May 2005); and Jan Paulsson, *Denial of Justice in International Law* 82 (Cambridge University Press 2005).

[148] *See, e.g., Vivendi v. Argentina (II)*, ICSID Case No. ARB/97/3 (Award of Aug. 20, 2007), ¶ 7.4.11. *See also Loewen, supra* note 148, (First Memorial of Loewen Group Inc., Oct. 18, 1999), ¶ 176, *available at* www.naftaclaims.com.

[149] U.S. Model BIT 2004, art. 5(2)(a) ("'fair and equitable treatment' includes the obligation not to deny justice in criminal, civil, or administrative adjudicatory proceedings in accordance with the principle of due process embodied in the principal legal systems of the world"); U.S.-Chile Free Trade Agreement (FTA), art. 10.4(2)(a) (same).

The exact definition of denial of justice has long been subject to debate. According to the OECD:[150]

> The principle of "denial of justice" has been considered as being part of customary international law and is used in three senses.[151] In the broadest sense, it "seems to embrace the whole field of State responsibility, and has been applied to all types of wrongful conduct on the part of the State towards aliens"[;[152]] it includes therefore acts or omissions of the authorities of any of the three branches of government, *i.e.*, executive, legislative or judiciary.[153] In the narrowest sense, it is "limited to refusal of a State to grant an alien access to its courts or a failure of a court to pronounce a judgment."[154] There is also an intermediary sense, in which it is "employed in connection with the improper administration of civil and criminal justice as regards an alien, including denial of access to courts, inadequate procedures, and unjust decisions."[155] The majority of the cases examined approach fair and equitable treatment in the intermediate sense.

The irregularities that fall within the denial of justice in the intermediate sense have also been referred to as denial of procedural and substantive justice.[156] Such a violation could be committed by any of the three branches of government.[157] Some time ago, a leading commentator defined procedural denial of justice broadly: "fair courts, really open to aliens, administering justice honestly [and]

---

[150] OECD, *supra* note 13, at 28 (some of the source notes have been omitted).

[151] SN: F. V. Garcia-Amador et al., *Recent Codification of the Law of State Responsibility for Injuries to Aliens* 180 (1974).

[152] SN: *idem*.

[153] The broadest meaning of "denial of justice" has been criticized, because it expands the concept to an extent equal to any breach of international law, depriving the words of any specific meaning. Freeman, *supra* note 147, at 105; Clyde Eagleton, *Denial of Justice in International Law*, 22 Am. J. Int'l L. 538, 558 (1928); *see also B. E. Chattin (U.S.) v. United Mexican States*, 4 RIAA 282, at 286 (1927). For further references, see Paulsson, *supra* note 147, at 46.

[154] A typical example of such an approach may be found in Guerrero, *Report of the Subcommittee of Experts*, League of Nations Doc. C.196.M.70.1927 V, at 90. The narrow approach was also reflective of Latin American countries' resentment toward the development of the concept of the minimum standard, and pressures exerted on them by the United States, sentiments which led to the emergence of the Calvo Doctrine. Wallace, *supra* note 147, at 677.

[155] SN: *Id.* note 22. [*See also* the *Harvard Research Draft on International Law* definition of denial of justice: "[D]enial of justice exists where there is a denial, unwarranted delay or obstruction of access to courts, gross deficiency in the administration of judicial or remedial process, failure to provide those guarantees which are generally considered indispensable to the proper administration of justice or a manifestly unjust judgement. An error of a national court which does not produce manifest injustice is not a denial of justice."]

[156] *See, e.g.*, Freeman, *supra* note 147. *Cf.* Paulsson, *supra* note 147, at 82. Commentators and arbitral tribunals have distinguished between situations where a wrong is committed by the courts, and where the wrong is committed by another branch of the government, but local courts fail to redress the injustice. The former category has been referred to as *déni de justice* and the latter *défi de justice*. Spiegel, *supra* note 147, at 73. "Of course this is just a verbal distinction. Such terminological distinctions have been abundant. Preoccupation with them has often confounded the consideration and understanding of this subject." Wallace, *supra* note 147.

[157] Freeman, *supra* note 147, at 28.

impartially, without bias or political control, seem [to be] essential elements of a fair trial and objective justice required of all systems."[158] Denial of substantive justice refers to "gross defects in the substance of the [court] judgment itself, [including misapplication of national law]."[159]

The denial of justice may take a variety of forms. Jan Paulsson, on the basis of a survey of cases, identifies a range of specific manifestations of justice denied, including denial of access to justice, targeted legislation, repudiation by a state of an agreement to arbitrate, governmental interference, manipulation of the composition of the courts, executive public pressure, failure to execute judgments, inadequate measures against perpetrators of crimes against foreigners, and more.[160]

One question with respect to these categories is the role of the exhaustion of local remedies in assessing whether denial of justice has occurred.[161] There seems to be some consensus that when denial of justice is committed by the judiciary or an authority whose actions are susceptible to judicial review, local remedies (an appeal to higher courts) must be exhausted before a valid denial of justice claim can arise.[162] Exhaustion of local remedies is not required when there is no reasonable possibility of obtaining an effective remedy or pursuing local remedies would be "obviously futile."[163] This exception could be particularly relevant when actions are committed by nonjudicial branches of the government.[164] However, it remains unclear to what extent available remedies must be exhausted before responsibility for denial of justice is established. The following excerpt by Professor Wallace explains some of the questions that may arise in this context:

> A different question was addressed in the *Finnish Ships* case. Finnish Ships examined what exhaustion of local remedies consists of if the local remedies rule did apply. Would

---

[158] Edwin Borchard, *The "Minimum Standard" of the Treatment of Aliens*, 38 Mich. L. Rev. 445–1 (1939–1940).

[159] Freeman, *supra* note 147, at 309. Jan Paulsson, in a recent study, suggests that substantive denial of justice is no longer a cause of action. He maintains that "[i]f a judgment is *grossly* unjust, it is because the victim has not been afforded fair treatment. That is the basis for responsibility, not the misapplication of national law in itself." Paulsson, *supra* note 147, at 82 (emphasis in the original).

[160] For a list of the categories see Paulsson, *supra* note 147, at vi and 131–207.

[161] On exhaustion of local remedies see generally Chapter XIII.

[162] *See, e.g.*, Paulsson, *supra* note 147, at 107–12 & 130.

[163] John Dugard, Special Rapporteur, International Law Commission, *Third Report on Diplomatic Protection*, UN Doc. A/CN.4/523, 2002, at 6, ¶ 19. Justice Bagge in Finnish Ships Arbitration referred to such remedies as "obviously futile." *Finnish Ships Arbitration (Great Britian v. Finland)*, 3 UNRIAA 1479 (1934). *Cf.* Paulsson, *supra* note 147, at 118 (preferring "reasonable possibility of an effective remedy" in Dugard's third report over the "obviously futile" formulation of Justice Bagge).

[164] Paulsson, *supra* note 147, at 109. The local remedies rule and its application in this context have engendered substantial debate in the legal community. The issue became the focal point in *Loewen v. U.S. See* pp. 529 *et seq. infra*.

> only ordinary remedies have to be pursued, or extraordinary ones? Non-judicial ones? In court, would every conceivable argument have to be made before remedies were deemed exhausted? Not all these questions are answered with respect to every fact situation. Justice Bagge sitting by designation in *Finnish Ships* did however, after thoroughly examining the facts of the matter, authoritatively rule what the "exhaust" standard means. Yes, one had to do much and more; but the remedies to be pursued had to be adequate and effective; this is a "reasonable" rule, not a "rigid" one, not a rule of infinite pursuit by platonically ideal parties with bottomless wallets to pay for legal fees, or professors wishing to create new legal theories; the reasoned calculations of experienced counsel of whether redress was likely was relevant, possibly controlling. The received wisdom that remedies must be "non-existent," or "futile" because of judicial bias is not the only reason to stop. Another reason to stop, and not continue to butt your head against a wall, is "the existence of a uniform body of jurisprudence in the upper court which renders any modification of the lower court's decision altogether improbable" – it is objectively knowable by learned and competent counsel and bench that further pursuit would not succeed.
>
> One can conclude that the historical deposit of international law is not sufficiently worked out: that denial of justice through original judicial failure (or for that matter, at the stage of redress) and the local remedies rule have not been knitted together either conceptually or temporally; nor is it clear how many different judicial stages may be involved in the combination of the two.[165]

In some cases, claimants have specifically alleged that the host state has committed denial of justice.[166] In other cases, however, the claimant has made no specific reference to denial of justice; but the facts of the case lead the tribunal to find nevertheless that a denial of justice has occurred. The latter category includes the state's refusal to honor arbitration agreements.[167] Once a state agrees to arbitrate a particular category of disputes, it is bound by that agreement. Its subsequent repudiation of such an agreement has been categorized by influential observers as a denial of justice or a transgression against customary law, which arguably would violate the fair and equitable treatment standard.[168] However characterized, a state will normally be held responsible for the consequences of such a breach. In *Salini v. Jordan*,[169] an ICSID tribunal accepted jurisdiction over the claim that Jordan had agreed to arbitrate the resolution of the underlying dispute but refused to participate in arbitration when a dispute later arose. The tribunal concluded that it had the

---

[165] Wallace, *supra* note 147, at 683–84 (source notes omitted).

[166] See, e.g., Loewen, *supra* note 31; *Feldman v. Mexico*, ICSID Case No. ARB (AF)/99/1 (Award of Dec. 16, 2002).

[167] See, e.g., the *Himpurna California Energy Ltd. v. Indonesia* (UNCITRAL Arbitration, Interim Award of Sept. 26, 1999), 25 Y.B. Comm. Arb. 109, ¶ 184 ("The present Arbitral Tribunal considers that it is a denial of justice for the courts of a State to prevent a foreign party from pursuing its remedies before a forum to the authority of which the state consented, and on the availability of which the foreigner relied in making investments explicitly envisaged by that state...").

[168] See Stephen M. Schwebel, *International Arbitration: Three Salient Problems* 61–143 (1987), and the sources there cited; Paulsson, *supra* note 147, at 149 *et seq.*; I. Brownlie, *System of the Law of Nations* 80 (Clarendon Press 2001).

[169] *Salini Construtorri S.p.A & Italstrade S.p.A. v. Jordan*, ICSID Case No. ARB/02/13 (Italy-Jordan BIT, Award of Jan. 31, 2006), ¶ 179.

power to determine whether those facts, if proven, violated the "just and equitable treatment" standard in the Italy-Jordan BIT, as well as the BIT's umbrella clause.[170]

In *Amco v. Indonesia*,[171] the claimant specifically alleged a denial of justice. A tribunal presided by Judge Rosalyn Higgins held that the procedural irregularities surrounding the revocation of the claimant's investment license by the Indonesian Foreign Investment Board constituted a denial of justice, although the board decision had been substantively correct under Indonesian law.[172] The tribunal noted that although the board was an administrative body, there was no "provision of international law that makes impossible a denial of justice by an administrative body."[173]

The *Loewen* case is perhaps the most discussed modern arbitral award where denial of justice was at the center of the dispute.[174] Loewen owned a number of funeral homes and associated insurance companies in Canada and the United States, and was the second largest operator of such enterprises in North America. Loewen's local competitor in Mississippi, Jerry O'Keefe, brought suit in Mississippi court based upon failed negotiation for the purchase of certain funeral homes in Jackson, Mississippi. The net amount of the transaction had the deal gone through was approximately US$1 million. Mr. O'Keefe retained Willy Gary, a flamboyant trial lawyer. Gary engaged in a range of suspect litigation tactics, particularly seeking to provoke the jury's baser instincts in his client's favor. The jury returned a verdict of US$500 million: approximately US$26 million compensatory damages, US$74 million pain and suffering/emotional distress,

---

[170] *Id.* ¶¶ 165–66. Other authorities view a breach of an arbitration agreement as a breach of customary international law but not necessarily of the fair and equitable treatment standard. *See, e.g.*, Overseas Private Investment Corporation (OPIC), Memorandum of Determinations: Expropriation Claim of MidAmerican Energy Holdings Company (formerly CalEnergy Co., Inc.), Contracts of Insurance Nos. E374, E453, E527, & E759 (Nov. 10, 1999). *See also* OPIC Memorandum of Determinations, Expropriation Claim of Bank of America as Trustee: India-Contract of Insurance No. F401, at 20 (Sept. 30, 2003); *Restatement (Third) of Foreign Relations Law of the United States* § 712, Comm. *h* (Am. L. Inst., 1987) ("[A] state may be responsible ... if, having committed itself to a special forum dispute settlement, such as arbitration, it fails to honor such commitment; or if it fails to carry out a judgment or award rendered by such ... special forum"). This has long been the position in certain international conventions as well. *See, e.g.*, Article 18, 1899 Hague Convention on the Pacific Settlement of International Disputes ("The Arbitration Convention implies the engagement to submit loyally to the Award"); Article 37, 1907 Hague Convention on the Pacific Settlement of International Disputes ("Recourse to arbitration implies an engagement to submit in good faith to the award").

[171] *Amco Asia Corp. v. Republic of Indonesia*, ICSID Case No. ARB/81/1 (Resubmitted Case, Award of June 5, 1990). The facts of the case were extensively discussed in Chapter XII, at pp. 320 *et seq. supra*.

[172] *Id.* ¶ 139; *cf.* Paulsson's criticism of the tribunal's finding. Paulsson, *supra* note 147, at 125–26.

[173] *Amco*, *supra* note 171, ¶ 137.

[174] Facts of *Loewen* as far as the issues of nationality of the investors are concerned were detailed in Chapter XII, and are also set forth in Noah Rubins, *Loewen v. United States: The Burial of an Investor-State Claim*, 20(1) Arb. Int'l 1 (2005). Three of the authors of this book, Christopher F. Dugan, Professor Don Wallace, Jr., and Noah Rubins, represented the claimant in the *Loewen* case.

and US$400 million punitive damages. The verdict had a catastrophic impact. Loewen's market capitalization was instantaneously cut by half a billion dollars. Meanwhile, the company's assets were subject to imminent seizure, unless it posted a bond in the amount of US$625 million (125 percent of the judgment amount) in accordance with local law. Under these circumstances, Loewen agreed to pay O'Keefe a settlement of US$175 million.

A number of irregularities tainted the trial. For example, during the jury selection process, O'Keefe's lawyer asked jurors whether they could be impartial in a case between a "Canadian foreigner and Jerry O'Keefe who had fought the Japs [sic] at Pearl Harbor."[175] On a number of other occasions, the trial judge did not prevent O'Keefe's lawyer from employing xenophobic rhetoric and playing upon the jurors' racial and economic preconceptions. Finally, the judge gave erroneous instructions to the jury about the nature of compensatory as opposed to punitive damages.

In determining whether these problems constituted a denial of justice, the *Loewen* tribunal cited the following formulation from the award in *Mondev v. United States*:

> The test is not whether a particular result is surprising, but whether the shock or surprise occasioned to an impartial tribunal leads, on reflection, to justified concerns as to the judicial propriety of the outcome, bearing in mind on the one hand that international tribunals are not courts of appeal, and on the other hand that Chapter 11 of NAFTA (like other treaties for the protection of investments) is intended to provide a real measure of protection. In the end the question is whether, at an international level and having regard to generally accepted standards of the administration of justice, a tribunal can conclude in the light of all the available facts that the impugned decision was clearly improper and discreditable, with the result that the investment has been subjected to unfair and inequitable treatment. This is admittedly a somewhat open-ended standard, but it may be that in practice no more precise formula can be offered to cover the range of possibilities.[176]

The *Loewen* tribunal concluded that "[b]y any standard of measurement, the trial involving O'Keefe and Loewen was a disgrace. By any standard of review, the tactics of O'Keefe's lawyers, particularly [O'Keefe's lawyer] Mr. Gary, were impermissible. By any standard of evaluation, the trial judge failed to afford Loewen the process that was due."[177] Nevertheless, in a much-criticized decision,[178] the arbitrators dismissed

---

[175] Before jury selection began, O'Keefe's legal team erected a billboard in downtown Jackson, portraying Mr. O'Keefe surrounded by the flags of the United States and Mississippi. The flags of Canada and Japan were also depicted, in a position suggesting that O'Keefe represented local interests against foreigners.

[176] *Mondev, supra* note 9, ¶ 127 *cited in Loewen, supra* note 31, ¶ 133.

[177] *Loewen, supra* note 31, ¶ 119. *See also id.* ¶ 137.

[178] *See, e.g.*, Rubins, *supra* note 174; and Maurice Mendelson, Runaway Train: The Continuous Nationality Rule from the *Panevezys-Saldustiskis Case* to *Loewen*, in T. Weiler ed. 2005, *supra* note 138, at 1230. Professor Thomas Wälde's straw poll of the votes of arbitration practitioners revealed that 90 percent of those responding considered the *Loewen* award to be erroneous. E-mail dated Oct. 28, 2003, to OGEMID listserv, available at TDM archives, available at www.transnational-dispute-management.com. *See also* Jacques Werner, *Making Investment Arbitration More Certain—A Modest Proposal*, 4(5) JWIT 767 (2003); Wallace, *supra* note 147.

Loewen's claims, including the claim based upon the fair and equitable treatment clause, because they concluded that Loewen had failed to exhaust local remedies as required under international law.[179] The tribunal found that Loewen could have filed a petition for permission to appeal to the U.S. Supreme Court, or could have filed for bankruptcy under the U.S. bankruptcy code.[180]

The *Loewen* decision highlights that the exhaustion of local remedies may be a substantive element of denial of justice claims. As noted above, this is not overly controversial. However, the Loewen tribunal's assessment of whether the claimant in fact had any meaningful domestic remedy at its disposal is one of several aspects of the case that has given rise to heated debate.[181]

With a few notable exceptions,[182] relatively few investment arbitration tribunals have had occasion to consider the term *denial of justice* specifically. Rather, they tend to discuss the broader standard of fair and equitable treatment. This could be the result of the debates surrounding the notion of denial of justice, its relation to the local remedies rule, or the sufficiency of fair and equitable treatment to analyze various fact patterns.

C. Full Protection and Security

Most investment treaties require that host states provide foreign investors and their investments "full protection and security,"[183] "the most constant protection and security,"[184] or some similarly-formulated level of protection. As with "fair and equitable treatment," the content of the obligation to ensure full protection and security has been subject to wide-ranging debate. As an initial matter, some commentators have suggested that full protection and security should be interpreted in the same spirit

---

[179] *See generally* Chapter XIII *supra*.

[180] *Loewen, supra.* note 31, ¶¶ 207–17.

[181] *Cf.* discussion of the *Salem* case, in Chapter XIII *supra*. Later, in response to the situation that arose in *Loewen*, the Mississippi Supreme Court changed its requirement that parties post bond to obtain a stay of enforcement pending appeal. *Loewen, supra* note 31, ¶ 187.

[182] *Azinian v. Mexico*, ICSID Case No. ARB(AF)/97/2 (NAFTA, Award of Nov. 1, 1999); and *Feldman, supra* note 166.

[183] *See, e.g.*, NAFTA, art. 1105 (1). Argentina–U.S. BIT (1994), art. II(2)(a); China-Germany BIT (2003), art. 4(1).

[184] *See, e.g.*, Energy Charter Treaty (1994), art. 10(1).

as fair and equitable treatment.[185] As discussed in more detail below, both standards of protection have been found to prohibit a similar type of treatment. It has been suggested that the primary distinction is that fair and equitable treatment targets affirmative action by the state, while full protection and security relates primarily to the state's failure to take certain action.[186]

1. Historical Development of the Obligation to Ensure Protection and Security

Although far more attention in recent years has been given to other standards of treatment, such as compensation for expropriation, national treatment, and fair and equitable treatment, "full protection and security" is one of the more venerable international obligations contained in treaties relating to the treatment of foreigners and their property. The precise terms, as noted above, have varied, and the scope of coverage has gradually evolved over the decades from aliens, to their property, and finally to qualifying investors and investments.

In the nineteenth and early twentieth centuries, the United States and other capital-exporting countries developed and negotiated treaties of Friendship, Commerce and Navigation. Many FCN treaties specifically provided for the protection of foreigners and their property.

Treaty of Friendship, Commerce and Navigation Between Argentina and the United States Signed July 27, 1853[187]

Article VIII

All merchants, commanders of ships and others, citizens of the United States, shall have full liberty, in all the territories of the Argentine Confederation, to manage their own affairs themselves, or to commit them to the management of whomsoever they please, as broker, factor, agent or interpreter. The citizens of the two contracting parties shall reciprocally receive and enjoy full and perfect protection for their persons and property.

---

[185] Thomas, *supra* note 12, at 22–39. *See also Asian Agric. Prod. Ltd. v. Sri Lanka*, ICSID Case No. ARB/87/3 (Award of June 21, 1990, Separate Opinion of Samuel Asante), 30 I.L.M. 577, 634 (1991).

[186] James Crawford, *International Law Commission's Articles on States Responsibility* 82 (Cambridge University Press 2002) ("Conduct attributable to the State can consist of actions or omissions. Cases in which the international responsibility of a State has been invoked on the basis of an omission are at least as numerous as those based on positive acts, and no difference in principle exists between the two").

[187] Treaty of Friendship, Commerce and Navigation between Argentina and the United States (1853), art. VIII, *available at* http://www.yale.edu/lawweb/avalon/diplomacy/argentina/argen02.htm.

Protection and security clauses like the one reproduced above were initially less prominent in FCN treaties than provisions governing tariffs and other trade barriers. Nevertheless, by the mid–twentieth century, FCN treaties almost invariably contained a protection and security clause. The treaty between the United States and Germany of December 8, 1923, for example, obligated each signatory to accord to nationals of the other party "the most constant protection for their persons and property," and protection in any case no less than that required by international law.[188]

While the concept of protection and security was taking root in international commercial treaties, customary international law was developing in the area of state responsibility for the protection of aliens and their property.[189] Both treaties and customary law appear to have focused on the physical security of foreigners and their property. This emphasis arose out of an apprehension of the risk of xenophobic violence and the inadequacy of local police forces in host states after World War I.[190] A typical example of such a case was *Neer*, described above, which involved the murder of an American citizen in Mexico. Another notable case (which took place before World War I) involved the lynching of eleven Italian citizens by a New Orleans mob. The U.S. government observed that although the injury "'was not inflicted directly by the United States, the President nevertheless feels that it is the solemn duty . . . of the National Government to pay a satisfactory indemnity.'"[191] The protection standard that developed in this context imposed on states a duty of "due diligence."[192] This duty, at the time, required states to provide aliens and their property with a reasonable level of police protection, against harm done by non-state actors.[193]

After World War II, the number of the FCN treaties increased. By that time, foreign direct investment had come to be viewed as a valuable tool for promoting economic

---

[188] See Thomas, *supra* note 12, at 39. An almost identical provision was included in the U.S.-Italy FCN treaty of 1949, followed by language emphasizing legal due process: "To these ends, persons accused of crime shall be brought to trial promptly, and shall enjoy all the rights and privileges which are or may hereafter be accorded by applicable law and regulations; . . . while in the custody . . . shall receive reasonable and humane treatment."

[189] Robert R. Wilson, *The International Law Standard in Treaties of the United States* 103–104 (Harvard University Press 1953)

[190] Rubins & Kinsella, *supra* note 144, at 218.

[191] See J. B. Moore, 6 *A Digest of International Law*, 837–41 (G.P.O., 1906).

[192] Brownlie, *System of the Law of Nations, supra* note 168, at 161.

[193] Brownlie reproduces a letter dated 1887 from the United States regarding the claim of D. G. Negrete addressed to the government of Spain as the statement of the law even today. The letter provides in relevant part that "[t]he measure of diligence to be exercised by a government in the repression of disorder is not that of an insurer but such as prudent governments are, under the circumstances of the case, accustomed to exercise." *Id*. at 168. *See also Responsibility of States for Damage Done in Their Territory to the Person or Property of Foreigners*, 23 Am. J. Int'l L. Spec. Supp. 131, 187 *et seq*. (1929).

and social development and postwar reconstruction. It was understood that one prerequisite to such investment was basic physical security for investors and their property. In the Havana Charter, signed in 1948 as part of the failed attempt to establish an international trade organization, member states recognized that "the international flow of capital will be stimulated to the extent that Members afford Nationals of other countries opportunities for investment and security for existing and future investments."[194] Consistent with this principle, many postwar FCN treaties provided for "full protection and security" and the mandatory submission of disputes arising in relation to the implementation of treaty obligations to state-to-state adjudication at the International Court of Justice. The OECD's 1967 Draft Convention on the Protection of Foreign Property, the first major attempt to create a multilateral instrument in the area of investment protection, continued the tradition of provisions already found in most FCN treaties, guaranteeing "the most constant protection and security" to alien-owned property, as well as banning all impairment of the management, maintenance, use, enjoyment, or disposal by unreasonable or discriminatory measures.[195]

2. Modern Investment Treaties and the Meaning of Protection and Security

Most modern investment treaties incorporate provisions requiring full protection and security of investments.[196] Investment protection treaties rarely offer any further guidance to decision makers in relation to the meaning of "full protection and security." The tribunal in *Saluka v. Czech Republic* succinctly summarized the existing arbitral decisions in this regard:

> The host State is . . . obliged to exercise due diligence.[197] As the tribunal in *Wena*, quoting from *American Manufacturing and Trading*,[198] stated,
>
>> The obligation incumbent on the [host state] is an obligation of vigilance, in the sense that the [host state] shall take all measures necessary to ensure the full enjoyment of protection and security of its investments and should not be permitted to invoke its own legislation to detract from any such obligation.[199]
>
> Accordingly, the standard obliges the host State to adopt all reasonable[200] measures to protect assets and property from threats or attacks which may target particularly foreigners or certain

---

[194] Havana Charter, art. 12.

[195] OECD, *Draft Convention on the Protection of Foreign Property* (1967), art. 1(a), *reprinted at* 7 I.L.M. 117 (1968). *Cf.* the discussion of arbitrary impairment at p. 507 *supra*.

[196] *See, e.g.*, UNCTAD, *supra* note 124, at 28.

[197] SN: Dolzer & Stevens, *supra* note 26, at 61.

[198] SN: *AMT*, ICSID Case No. ARB/93/1, ¶ 28.

[199] SN: *Wena*, ICSID Case No. ARB/98/4, ¶ 84.

[200] For an extended analysis of actions that could be considered "reasonable" in this context, *see generally* Helge E. Zeitler, *The Guarantee of "Full Protection and Security" in Investment Treaties Regarding Harm Caused by Private Actors*, 3 Stockholm Int'l Arb. Rev. 1 (2005).

groups of foreigners.[201] The practice of arbitral tribunals seems to indicate, however, that the "full security and protection" clause is not meant to cover just any kind of impairment of an investor's investment, but to protect more specifically the *physical integrity* of an investment against interference by use of force.[202]

As the *Saluka* panel observed, a number of tribunal decisions suggest that states are obliged to ensure only the physical security of investments, but not their legal or economic security.[203] Moreover, there seems to be general consensus that the obligation to protect does not imply the imposition upon host states of strict liability. [204]

As already noted, the full protection and security standard not only protects foreign investors against destructive actions by a government or its instrumentalities; but it may also impose state liability for harm caused by third parties.[205] Because other treaty provisions cover most instances of arbitrary, affirmative state acts, protection and security clauses are now most frequently invoked in relation to state omissions.[206] In *Wena v. Egypt*,[207] the Egyptian Hotels Company (EHC), a public company affiliated with the Egyptian tourism authority, and Wena Hotels, a British company, entered into leasehold arrangements to develop and operate two hotels, one in Luxor and the other in Cairo. Soon after the lease contracts were signed, the parties disagreed as to their respective obligations under the contracts. These disagreements culminated to the seizure of the hotels by the EHC. The tribunal held Egypt liable for its failure to prevent the EHC from taking the hotels although it was aware of EHC's plans, and for its subsequent failure to restore the hotels to Wena.[208]

In *Asian Agricultural Products Ltd. v. Sri Lanka*, AAPL, a Hong Kong corporation, entered into a joint venture, Serendib Seafoods Ltd., which was to

---

[201] SN: *See* OECD Working Papers, *supra* note 13, at 26–28 ("obligation of vigilance and protection").

[202] *Saluka, supra* note 12, ¶ 484 (emphasis added).

[203] *See also Noble Ventures v. Romania*, ICSID Case No. ARB/01/11 (Award, Oct. 12, 2005), ¶ 164 ("it seems doubtful whether that provision can be understood as being wider in scope than the general duty to provide for protection and security of foreign nationals found in the customary international law of aliens"). *But see CME, supra* note 58.

[204] *See, e.g., Asian Agric. Prod. Ltd. v. Sri Lanka*, ICSID Case No. ARB/87/3, 30 I.L.M. 577, 599–601 (1991).

[205] *Id.*

[206] *AMT, supra* note 198; and *CME, supra* note 58.

[207] *Wena Hotels Ltd. v. Arab Republic of Egypt*, ICSID Case no. ARB/98/4 (Award of Dec. 8, 2000), 41 ILM 896 (2002).

[208] *Id.* ¶¶ 84–95. *See also* note 209 *infra*.

cultivate and export shrimp to Japan. Shortly after Serendib started operations, the area where the farm was located came under the control of Tamil rebels. Despite Serendib's cooperation with Sri Lankan officials in identifying members of farm's staff who were aiding the rebels, government forces attacked and destroyed the farm. As a result, AAPL initiated ICSID arbitration under the Sri Lanka-United Kingdom BIT. It claimed a violation of Article 2(2) of the BIT requiring full protection and security. In this regard, AAPL insisted that this provision imposed strict liability upon the state for all harm that had befallen the company, whatever its cause. While the tribunal rejected this extreme interpretation, it nevertheless found that Sri Lanka had failed to provide the requisite level of protection.[209]

Asian Agricultural Products Ltd. v. Sri Lanka

ICSID Case No. ARB/87/3, 30 I.L.M. 577, 599–601 (1991)

45. The Claimant's primary submission—as previously explained (supra, § 26)—is based on the assumption that the "full protection and security" provision of Article 2(2) created a "strict liability" which renders the Sri Lankan Government liable for any destruction of the investment even if caused by persons whose acts are not attributable to the Government and under circumstances beyond the State's control.

For sustaining said construction introducing a new type of objective absolute responsibility called "without fault," the Claimant's main argument relies on the existence in the text of the Treaty of two terms: "enjoy" and "full," a combination which sustains, according to the Claimant, that the Parties intended to provide the investor with a "guarantee" against all losses suffered due to the destruction of the investment for whatever reason and without any need to establish who was the person that caused said damage. In other words, the Parties substituted the "due diligence" standard of general international law by a new obligation creating an obligation to achieve a result ("obligation de resultat") providing the foreign investor with a sort of "insurance" against the risk of having his investment destroyed under whatever circumstances.

46. The Tribunal is of the opinion that the Claimant's construction of Article 2(2) as explained hereinabove cannot be justified under any of the canons of interpretation previously stated (supra, § 40).

47. . . . [T]he words "shall enjoy full protection and security" have to be construed according to the "common use which custom has affixed" to them, their "usus loquendi," "natural and obvious sense," and "fair meaning." In fact, similar expressions, or even stronger wordings like the "most constant protection," were utilized since last century in a number of bilateral treaties concluded to encourage the flow of international economic exchanges and to provide the citizens and national companies established on the territory of the other Contracting Party with adequate treatment for them as well as to their property ("Traite

---

[209] *AAPL, supra* note 185, ¶ 50.

d'Amitie, de Commerce et Navigation," concluded between France and Mexico on November 27, 1886—cf. A Ch. KISS, Repertoire de la Pratique Francaise . . . , op. cit., Tome III, 1965, § 1002, p. 637; the Treaty concluded in 1861 between Italy and Venezuela, the interpretation of which became the central issue in the *Sambiaggio* case adjudicated in 1903 by the Italy/Venezuela Mixed Claims Commission–U.N. Reports of International Arbitral Awards, vol. X, p. 512ss.).

48. The Arbitral Tribunal is not aware of any case in which the obligation assumed by the host State to provide the nationals of the other Contracting State with "full protection and security" was construed as absolute obligation which guarantees that no damages will be suffered, in the sense that any violation thereof creates automatically a "strict liability" on behalf of the host State.

[The] *Sambiaggio* case seems to be the only reported case in which such argument was voiced, but without success. The Italian Commissioner AGNOLI, referred in his Report to: "The protection and security . . . which the Venezuelan Government explicitly guarantees by Article 4 of the Treaty of 1861 to Italians residing in Venezuela" (U.N. Reports, op. cit., p. 502). The Venezuelan Commissioner ZULOAGA responded by indicating that: "Governments are constituted to afford protection, not to guarantee it" (Ibid., p. 511). The Umpire RALSTON put an end to the Italian allegation by emphasizing that:

> "If it had been the contract between Italy and Venezuela, understood and consented by both, that the latter should be held liable for the acts of revolutionists—something in derogation of the general principles of international law—this agreement would naturally have found direct expression in the protocol itself and would not have been left to doubtful interpretation" (Ibid. p. 521).

49. In the recent case concerning *Elettronica Sicula S.P.A. (ELSI)* between the U.S.A and Italy adjudicated by a Chamber of the International Court of Justice, the U.S.A. Government invoked Article V(1) of the Bilateral Treaty which established an obligation to provide "the most constant protection and security," but without claiming that this obligation constitutes a "guarantee" involving the emergence of a "strict liability" (Section 2—Chapter V of the U.S.A. Memorial dated May 15, 1987, where reference is made, on the contrary at page 135 to the: "One well-established aspect of the international standard of treatment . . . that States must use "due diligence" to prevent wrongful injuries to the person or property of aliens within their territory").

In its Judgment of July 20, 1989, the ICJ Chamber clearly stated that:

"The reference in Article V to the provision of "constant protection and security" cannot be construed as the giving of a warranty that property shall never in any circumstances be occupied or disturbed" (C.I.J. Recueil, 1989, § 108, p. 65).

Consequently, both the oldest reported arbitral precedent and the latest I.C.J ruling confirms that the language imposing on the host State an obligation to provide "protection and security" or "full protection and security required by international law" (the other expression included in the same Article V) could not be construed according to the natural and ordinary sense of the words as creating a "strict liability." The rule remains that:

> "The State into which an alien has entered . . . is not an insurer or a guarantor of his security. . . . It does not, and could hardly be asked to, accept an absolute responsibility for all injuries to foreigners" (Alwyn V. Freeman, Responsibility of States for Unlawful Acts of Their Armed Forces, Sijthoff, Leiden, 1957, p. 14).

This conclusion, arrived at more than three decades ago, still reflects—in the Tribunal's opinion—the present status of International Law Investment Standards as reflected in "the worldwide BIT network" (cf. K.S. GUDGEON, "Valuation of Nationalized Property Under United States and other Bilateral Investment Treaties." Chapter III, in the

Valuation of Nationalized Property in International Law, Ed. by Richard B. Lillich, vol. IV, (1987), p.120).

50. In the opinion of the present Arbitral Tribunal, the addition of words like "constant" or "full" to strengthen the required standard of "protection and security" could justifiably indicate the Parties' intention to require within their treaty relationship a standard of "due diligence" higher than the "minimum standard" of general international law. But, the nature of both the obligation and ensuing responsibility remain unchanged, since the added words "constant" or "full" are by themselves not sufficient to establish that the Parties intended to transform their mutual obligation into a "strict liability."

More recently, some tribunals have interpreted full protection and security clauses more broadly, concluding that the government's duty to protect foreign investors extends beyond physical security.[210] In doing so, some arbitrators have relied expressly upon the relationship between fair and equitable treatment and full protection and security. The following excerpt from *Azurix* provides an example of this approach.

Azurix Corp. v. The Argentine Republic

ICSID CASE No. ARB/01/12 (Final Award of July 14, 2006)

[The facts in *Azurix* were described at p. 497 *supra*]

The facts in 406. While the cases of *AAPL* and *AMT* refer to physical security, there are other cases in which tribunals have found that full protection and security has been breached because the investment was subject to unfair and inequitable treatment—*Occidental v. Ecuador*—or, conversely, they have held that the obligation of fair and equitable treatment was breached because there was a failure to provide full protection

---

[210] *See, e.g., Occidental, supra* note 40, ¶ 187; *CME, supra* note 58, ¶ 613 ("The host State is obligated to ensure that neither by amendment of its laws nor by actions of its administrative bodies is the agreed and approved security and protection of the foreign investor's investment withdrawn or devalued. . ."); *Enron Corp. & Ponderosa Assets, L.P. v. Argentine Republic*, ICSID Case No. ARB/01/3 (Award of May 22, 2007), ¶ 286 ("There is no doubt that historically this particular standard has been developed in the context of physical protection and security of the company's officials, employees, or facilities. The Tribunal cannot exclude as a matter of principle that there might be cases where a broader interpretation could be justified, but then it becomes difficult to distinguish such situation from one resulting in the breach of fair and equitable treatment, and even from some form of expropriation"). *See particularly Azurix, supra* note 21, ¶¶ 406–08 (see excerpts below); and *Siemens, supra* note 80, ¶ 303 ("As a general matter and based on the definition of investment, which includes tangible and intangible assets, the Tribunal considers that the obligation to provide full protection and security is wider than "physical" protection and security. It is difficult to understand how the physical security of an intangible asset would be achieved").

and security—*Wena Hotels v. Egypt*. The inter-relationship of the two standards indicates that full protection and security may be breached even if no physical violence or damage occurs as it was the case in *Occidental v. Ecuador*.

407. In some bilateral investment treaties, fair and equitable treatment and full protection and security appear as a single standard, in others as separate protections. The BIT falls in the last category; the two phrases describing the protection of investments appear sequentially as different obligations in Article II.2(a): "Investment shall at all times be accorded fair and equitable treatment, shall enjoy full protection and security and...." The tribunal in Occidental based its decision on a clause worded exactly like in the BIT, and nonetheless considered that, after it had found that the fair and equitable standard had been breached, "the question of whether in addition there has been a breach of full protection and security under this Article becomes moot as a treatment that is not fair and equitable automatically entails an absence of full protection and security."[211]

408. The Tribunal is persuaded of the inter-relationship of fair and equitable treatment and the obligation to afford the investor full protection and security. The cases referred to above show that full protection and security was understood to go beyond protection and security ensured by the police. It is not only a matter of physical security; the stability afforded by a secure investment environment is as important from an investor's point of view. The Tribunal is aware that in recent free trade agreements signed by the United States, for instance, with Uruguay, full protection and security is understood to be limited to the level of police protection required under customary international law. However, when the terms "protection and security" are qualified by "full" and no other adjective or explanation, they extend, in their ordinary meaning, the content of this standard beyond physical security. To conclude, the Tribunal, having held that the Respondent failed to provide fair and equitable treatment to the investment, finds that the Respondent also breached the standard of full protection and security under the BIT.

The *Azurix* tribunal based its conclusion in part on the specific language of the Argentina-United States BIT, which does not expressly link the state's obligation to provide full protection and security to customary international law.[212] Subsequent tribunals have taken a cautious approach to this broader view of full protection and security. The tribunal in *LG&E*, for example, noted that only in exceptional circumstances should such a broad interpretation of the standard be adopted.[213] The question remains whether any additional substantive protection would result from the *Azurix* approach. In nearly every case where state action unrelated to physical security was found to violate the full protection and security standard, the same conduct (or omission) was also found to constitute a breach of fair and equitable treatment.[214]

---

[211] SN: *Occidental, supra* note 40, ¶ 187.
[212] See the discussion of the interpretive principles at pp. 496–97 *supra*. Cf. NAFTA, art. 1105 at note 5 *supra*.
[213] *LG&E, supra* note 73, ¶ 258.
[214] See note 210 *supra*.

XVIII. Umbrella Clauses

A. Introduction

Most bilateral and multilateral investment treaties provide investors with a relatively standard set of protections, including the rights to national treatment, most-favored-nation treatment, fair and equitable treatment, and compensation for expropriation.[1] Some treaties arguably provide investors with an additional layer of protection by specifically requiring host states to observe the obligations and honor the commitments they have undertaken vis-à-vis foreign investments. Known as "umbrella clauses,"[2] these provisions appear to provide a route through which investors can seek to transform their contractual claims into treaty claims, although their interpretation and application has thus far been uncertain.

These clauses were necessitated because there is considerable authority that a breach of a contract by a state does not necessarily amount to a breach of

---

[1] Calvin A. Hamilton & Paula I. Rochwerger, *Trade and Investment: Foreign Direct Investment through Bilateral and Multilateral Treaties*, 18 N.Y. Int'l L. Rev. 1, 14–16 (2005).

[2] These clauses are variously referred to as "mirror effect," *pacta sunt servanda*, observance of undertakings, sanctity of contract, and respect clauses. On umbrella clauses in general, *see* Thomas W. Wälde, *The "Umbrella" Clause in Investment Arbitration: A Comment on Original Intentions and Recent Cases*, 6(2) J. World Inv. & Trade 184, 192 (2005); C. Schreuer, *Travelling the BIT Route: Of Waiting Periods, Umbrella Clauses and Forks in the Road*, 5(2) J. World Inv. & Trade 231 (2004); Anthony Sinclair, *The Origins of the Umbrella Clause in the International Law of Investment Protection*, 20 Arb. Int'l 411 (2004); Katia Yanaca-Small, *Interpretation of the Umbrella Clause in Investment Agreements* (OECD, Working Papers on International Investment 2006/3, 2006).

international law.[3] In fact, half a century ago, when foreign investment mainly took place through concession contracts involving oil and gas as well as minerals, investors had little non-contractual protection against a state's failure to honor those contracts.[4] Umbrella clauses were an answer to this shortcoming; they effectively created a cause of action under international law for breach of contract, thus providing additional remedies and protections to foreign investors. One of the main rationales for this extension was to make clear that the concept of *pacta sunt servanda*, which applies to state-to-state relationships, also applies to relationships between investors and states.[5]

B. Historical Background and Various Formulations of Umbrella Clauses

The history of the emergence of these clauses in investment protection instruments was succinctly explained in *Eureko v. Poland*.

Eureko B.V. v. Republic of Poland

Partial Award and Dissenting Opinion, ad hoc UNCITRAL Arbitration, IIC 98, Aug. 19, 2005

251. The provenance of "umbrella clauses" has been traced to proposals of Elihu Lauterpacht in connection with legal advice he gave in 1954 in respect of the Iranian Consortium Agreement, described in detail in an article in Arbitration International by Anthony Sinclair.[6] It found expression in Article 11 of a draft Convention on Investments Abroad ("the Abs-Shawcross Draft") of 1959, which provided: "Each Party shall at all

---

[3] *Oppenheim's International Law* 927 (Sir Robert Jennings & Sir Arthur Watts eds., 1992); Stephen Schwebel, *On Whether the Breach by a State of a Contract with an Alien Is a Breach of International Law*, in *International Law at the Time of Its Codification* 401 (1987); *see also* International Law Commission articles on state responsibility, art. 3, which provides in the relevant part that "[t]he characterization of an act of a State as internationally wrongful is governed by international law. Such characterization is not affected by the characterization of the same act as lawful by internal law." James Crawford, *The International Law Commission's Articles on State Responsibility* 86 (Cambridge University Press 2002).

[4] *See generally* Chapter II *supra*.

[5] Wälde, *supra* note 2, at 192; *see also* G.A. Res. 1803, ¶ 8 (1962) (this resolution, which some believe reflected the status of customary law at the time, provided in relevant part that "Foreign investment agreements freely entered into by or between sovereign States shall be observed in good faith. . . .").

[6] SN: "The Origin of Umbrella Clause in International Law of Investment Protection," 20 *Arbitration International* 411, 414–18.

times ensure the observance of any undertakings which it may have given in relation to investments made by nationals of any other Party."[7] It was officially espoused in Article 2 of the OECD Draft Convention on the Protection of Foreign Property of 1967, in whose preparation, Lauterpacht, as a representative of the United Kingdom, played a part. It provided that: "Each Party shall at all times ensure the observance of undertakings given by it in relation to property of nationals of any other Party."[8] The commentary to the draft Convention stated that, "Article 2 represents an application of the general principle of pacta sunt servanda—the maintenance of the pledged word—which also applies to agreements between States and foreign national."[9] Commenting on this article in his Hague Academy lectures in 1969, Professor Prosper Weil concluded that: "The intervention of the umbrella treaty transforms contractual obligations into international obligations . . ." ("Problèmes relatifs aux contrats passés entre un état et un particulier.").[10] The late Dr. F. A. Mann described the umbrella clause as "a provision of particular importance in that it protects the investor against any interference with his contractual rights, whether it results from a mere breach of contract or a legislative or administrative act, and independently of the question whether or not such interference amounts to expropriation. . . ."[11] The leading work on bilateral investment treaties states that: "These provisions seek to ensure that each Party to the treaty will respect specific undertakings towards nationals of the other Party. The provision is of particular importance because it protects the investor's contractual rights against any interference which might be caused by either a simple breach of contract or by administrative or legislative acts. . . ."[12] The United Nations Centre on Transnational Corporations, in a 1988 study on BITS, found that an umbrella clause "makes the respect of such contracts [between the host State and the investor] . . . an obligation under the treaty."[13] These and other relevant sources are authoritatively surveyed in Christoph Schreuer, "Travelling the BIT Route: Of Waiting Periods, Umbrella Clauses and Forks in the Road,"[14] as well in as Stanimir A. Alexandrov, "Breaches of Contract and Breaches of Treaty."[15]

Umbrella clauses have been drafted in a variety of forms. Article II(2)(c) of the Argentina–United States BIT is a typical example of an umbrella clause (and perhaps the most argued over), which provides that "(2)(c) Each Party shall observe any obligation it may have entered into with regard to investments."[16] Article 2 of the

---

[7] SN: *Ibid.*, p. 421.

[8] SN: *Ibid.*, pp. 427–433.

[9] SN: *Ibid.*, p. 123, note 1(a).

[10] SN: *Receuil des Cours* III (1969), p. 130.

[11] SN: "British Treaties for Protection and Promotion of Investments," 52 *British Yearbook of International Law* 241, at 246 (1941).

[12] SN: R. Dolzer and M. Stevens, Bilateral Investment Treaties (1995), at 81–2.

[13] SN: United Nations Centre on Transnational Corporations, *Bilateral Investment Treaties* 39 (1988).

[14] SN: 5 The Journal of World Investments & Trade, 249–255 (2004).

[15] SN: 5 J. World Inves. & Trade, 564–72 (2004).

[16] Argentina-U.S. BIT (1994), art. II(2)(c).

U.K. Model BIT provides in relevant part that "(2) Each Contracting Party shall observe any obligation it may have entered into with regard to investments of nationals or companies of the other Contracting Party."[17] Article 10(1) of Energy Charter Treaty contains a broadly drafted umbrella clause: "Each Contracting Party shall observe any obligations it has entered into with an Investor or an Investment of an Investor of any other Contracting Party."[18] This treaty also has an opt-out provision in Article 26(3)(C), whereby contracting states may limit their consent to submit disputes to arbitration with respect to the umbrella clause. Not all investment treaties have umbrella clauses, however. NAFTA Chapter 11, for instance, does not have an umbrella clause.[19] The U.S. Model BIT of 2004, unlike the U.S. Model BIT of 1992, does not have such a broadly drafted clause. Instead, Article 24(1) limits the protection for contracts to claims arising out of a breach of an "investment agreement."[20]

C. Arbitral Decisions Involving Umbrella Clauses

As a consequence of these clauses, and instead of relying on specific contractual agreements and remedies, investors have sought to bring their contractual claims within the ambit of bilateral and multilateral investment treaties. The response of arbitral tribunals to such claims has been remarkably mixed thus far; indeed, the proper interpretation of umbrella clauses is one of the most contentious issues in international investment law. Two camps have emerged. The first views such clauses restrictively, limiting their application to, perhaps, sovereign acts, and refusing to extend treaty protection to "mere" contractual breaches. The second camp insists that umbrella clauses "mean what they say," elevating contractual breaches into treaty breaches.

---

[17] U.K. Model BIT, art. 2 *cited in* Yanaca-Small, *supra* note 2, at 25.

[18] For a commentary see T. Wälde, *Contract Claims under the Energy Charter Treaty's Umbrella Clause: Original Intentions versus Emerging Jurisprudence*, in *Investment Arbitration and the Energy Charter Treaty*, Ch. 4, Pt. 1 (C. Ribeiro ed., Juris Publishing 2006).

[19] See also Unified Agreement for the Investment of Arab Capital in the Arab States (1980).

[20] "Investment agreement" under the model BIT is defined as follows: "investment agreement" means a written agreement between a national authority of a Party and a covered investment or an investor of the other Party, on which the covered investment or the investor relies in establishing or acquiring a covered investment other than the written agreement itself, that grants rights to the covered investment or investor: (a) with respect to natural resources that a national authority controls, such as for their exploration, extraction, refining, transportation, distribution, or sale; (b) to supply services to the public on behalf of the Party, such as power generation or distribution, water treatment or distribution, or telecommunications; or (c) to undertake infrastructure projects, such as the construction of roads, bridges, canals, dams, or pipelines, that are not for the exclusive or predominant use and benefit of the government. 2004 U.S. Model BIT, art. 1 (source notes omitted).

Sgs Société Générale de Surveillance S.A. [hereinafter SGS] v. *Islamic Republic of Pakistan*

ICSID Case No. ARB/01/13 (Decision on Objections to Jurisdiction Nov. 2003) (some of the footnotes omitted)

[In 1994, SGS, a Swiss corporation, entered into an agreement with the Islamic Republic of Pakistan to provide Pre-Shipment Inspection (PSI) services for goods exported from certain countries to Pakistan. Later, the parties questioned each other's performance under the agreement. In 2000, Pakistan initiated domestic arbitration pursuant to the arbitration clause of the agreement. In 2001, SGS commenced an arbitration before ICSID against Pakistan alleging that Pakistan through various measures had breached its obligations under Pakistan-Switzerland BIT. Pakistan replied that the tribunal lacked jurisdiction to consider breaches of the PSI agreement because they were before the domestic arbitration tribunal. The tribunal agreed with Pakistan, but went on to consider whether the existence of an umbrella clause—Article 11—in the Pakistan-Swiss BIT would change that conclusion.]

5. Does Article 11 of the [Pakistan-Switzerland] BIT transform purely contractual claims into BIT claims?

163. Article 11 of the BIT states:

> Either Contracting Party shall constantly guarantee the observance of the commitments it has entered into with respect to the investments of the investors of the other Contracting Party.

As noted earlier, during the hearing on the Respondent's Objections to Jurisdiction, counsel for the Claimant characterized this clause as an "elevator" or "mirror effect" clause that takes breaches of contract under municipal law and elevates them immediately to the level of a breach of an international treaty. Counsel for the Claimant freely acknowledged that this interpretation was "far-reaching," but asserted that nevertheless this is what the article means and that the Claimant's view of its meaning was supported by the commentary on articles of this type found in other bilateral investment treaties.

164. It appears that this is the first international arbitral tribunal that has had to examine the legal effect of a clause such as Article 11 of the BIT. We have not been directed to the award of any ICSID or other tribunal in this regard, and so it appears we have here a case of first impression. We begin, as we commonly do, by examining the words actually used in Article 11 of the BIT, ascribing to them their ordinary meaning in their context and in the light of the object and purpose of Article 11 of the Swiss-Pakistan Treaty and of that Treaty as a whole.

165. A treaty interpreter must of course seek to give effect to the object and purpose projected by that Article and by the BIT as a whole. That object and purpose must be ascertained, in the first instance, from the text itself of Article 11 and the rest of the BIT.[21] Applying these familiar norms of customary international law on treaty interpretation, we do not find a convincing basis for accepting the Claimant's contention that Article 11 of the BIT has had the effect of entitling a Contracting Party's investor, like SGS, in the face of a valid forum selection contract clause, to "elevate" its claims grounded solely in a contract with another Contracting Party, like the PSI Agreement, to

---

[21] SN: *ADF Group Inc. v. U.S.*, [hereinafter *ADF*] ICSID Case No. ARB(AF)/00/1 (Final Award), *available at* www.state.gov/documents/organization/16586.pdf.

claims grounded on the BIT, and accordingly to bring such contract claims to this Tribunal for resolution and decision.

166. Firstly, textually, Article 11 falls considerably short of saying what the Claimant asserts it means. The "commitments" the observance of which a Contracting Party is to "constantly guarantee" are not limited to contractual commitments.[22] The commitments referred to may be embedded in, e.g., the municipal legislative or administrative or other unilateral measures of a Contracting Party. The phrase "constantly [to] guarantee the observance" of some statutory, administrative or contractual commitment simply does not to our mind, necessarily signal the creation and acceptance of a new international law obligation on the part of the Contracting Party, where clearly there was none before. Further, the "commitments" subject matter of Article 11 may, without imposing excessive violence on the text itself, be commitments of the State itself as a legal person, or of any office, entity or subdivision (local government units) or legal representative thereof whose acts are, under the law on state responsibility, attributable to the State itself. As a matter of textuality therefore, the scope of Article 11 of the BIT, while consisting in its entirety of only one sentence, appears susceptible of almost indefinite expansion. The text itself of Article 11 does not purport to state that breaches of contract alleged by an investor in relation to a contract it has concluded with a State (widely considered to be a matter of municipal rather than international law) are automatically "elevated" to the level of breaches of international treaty law. Thus, it appears to us that while the Claimant has sought to spell out the consequences or inferences it would draw from Article 11, the Article itself does not set forth those consequences.

167. Considering the widely accepted principle with which we started, namely, that under general international law, a violation of a contract entered into by a State with an investor of another State, is not, by itself, a violation of international law, and considering further that the legal consequences that the Claimant would have us attribute to Article 11 of the BIT are so far-reaching in scope, and so automatic and unqualified and sweeping in their operation, so burdensome in their potential impact upon a Contracting Party, we believe that clear and convincing evidence must be adduced by the Claimant.[23] Clear and convincing evidence of what? Clear and convincing evidence that such was indeed the shared intent of the Contracting Parties to the Swiss-Pakistan Investment Protection Treaty in incorporating Article 11 in the BIT. We do not find such evidence in the text itself of Article 11. We have not been pointed to any other evidence of the putative common intent of the Contracting Parties by the Claimant.

168. The consequences of accepting the Claimant's reading of Article 11 of the BIT should be spelled out in some detail. Firstly, Article 11 would amount to incorporating by reference an unlimited number of State contracts, as well as other municipal law

---

[22] SN: The Claimant has, for instance, not tried to distinguish between (a) a contract between a Contracting Party and an investor of the other Contracting Party, the applicable law of which is the national law of the Contracting Party and (b) a State contract with a private investor the applicable law of which is specified as "international law" or "general principles of law." The seminal lectures of Prosper Weil, *Problèmes relatifs aux contrats passés éntre un état et un particulier*, 3 *Hague Recueil des Cours*, Tome 128, at 157–88 (1969), explored the theoretical consequences of "internationalization" of contracts the lex contractus of which is determined to be international law or general principles of law, such as the natural resources concessions granted, in an earlier day, by, e.g., Iran, Abu Dhabi, and Qatar. The Claimant's reading of Article 11 of the BIT apparently extends to every contract, or other commitment, that a Contracting Party has entered into or assumed, or may in the future enter into or undertake with respect to an investor of the other Contracting Party.

[23] The Swiss government itself later disputed this tribunal interpretation. *See also Eureko v. Poland*, ¶ 254, at p. 548 *infra*.

instruments setting out State commitments including unilateral commitments to an investor of the other Contracting Party. Any alleged violation of those contracts and other instruments would be treated as a breach of the BIT. Secondly, the Claimant's view of Article 11 tends to make Articles 3 to 7 of the BIT substantially superfluous. There would be no real need to demonstrate a violation of those substantive treaty standards if a simple breach of contract, or of municipal statute or regulation, by itself, would suffice to constitute a treaty violation on the part of a Contracting Party and engage the international responsibility of the Party. A third consequence would be that an investor may, at will, nullify any freely negotiated dispute settlement clause in a State contract. On the reading of Article 11 urged by the Claimant, the benefits of the dispute settlement provisions of a contract with a State also a party to a BIT, would flow only to the investor. For that investor could always defeat the State's invocation of the contractually specified forum, and render any mutually agreed procedure of dispute settlement, other than BIT-specified ICSID arbitration, a dead-letter, at the investor's choice. The investor would remain free to go to arbitration either under the contract or under the BIT. But the State party to the contract would be effectively precluded from proceeding to the arbitral forum specified in the contract unless the investor was minded to agree. The Tribunal considers that Article 11 of the BIT should be read in such a way as to enhance mutuality and balance of benefits in the inter-relation of different agreements located in differing legal orders.

. . . .

171. We believe, for the foregoing considerations, that Article 11 of the BIT would have to be considerably more specifically worded before it can reasonably be read in the extraordinarily expansive manner submitted by the Claimant. The appropriate interpretive approach is the prudential one summed up in the literature as *in dubio pars mitior est sequenda*, or more tersely, *in dubio mitius*.[24]

172. The Claimant vigorously submits that any view of Article 11 of the BIT other than the one urged by it, would render Article 11 inutile, a result abhorrent to the principle of effectiveness in treaty interpretation. We are not persuaded that rejecting SGS's reading of Article 11 would necessarily reduce that Article to "pure exhortation," that is, to a non-normative statement. At least two points may be usefully made in this connection. Firstly, we do not consider that confirmation in a treaty that a Contracting Party is bound under and pursuant to a contract, or a statute or other municipal law issuance is devoid of appreciable normative value, either in the municipal or in the international legal sphere. That confirmation could, for instance, signal an implied affirmative commitment to enact implementing rules and regulations necessary or appropriate to give effect to a contractual or statutory undertaking in favor of investors of another Contracting Party that would otherwise be a dead letter. Secondly, we do not preclude the possibility that under exceptional circumstances, a violation of certain provisions of a State contract with an investor of another State might constitute violation of a treaty provision (like Article 11 of the BIT) enjoining a Contracting Party constantly to guarantee the observance of contracts with investors of another Contracting Party. For instance, if a Contracting Party were to take action that materially impedes the ability of an investor to prosecute its claims before an international arbitration tribunal (having previously agreed to such arbitration in a contract with the investor), or were to refuse to go to such arbitration at all and leave the investor only the option of going before the ordinary courts of the Contracting Party (which actions need not amount to "denial of justice"), that Contracting Party may arguably be regarded

---

[24] SN: See in this connection, e.g., Appellate Body Report, EC Measures Concerning Meat and Meat Products (Hormones), WT/DS26/AB/R; WT/DS48/AB/R (adopted Jan. 16, 1998), ¶¶ 163–65. Footnote 154 in this Appellate Body Report sets out a representative collection of the pertinent literature on this interpretative principle. . . .

as having failed "constantly [to] guarantee the observance of [its] commitments" within the meaning of Article 11 of the Swiss-Pakistan BIT. The modes by which a Contracting Party may "constantly guarantee the observance of" its contractual or statutory or administrative municipal law commitments with respect to investments are not necessarily exhausted by the instant transubstantiation of contract claims into BIT claims posited by the Claimant.

173. The Tribunal is not saying that States may not agree with each other in a BIT that henceforth, all breaches of each State's contracts with investors of the other State are forthwith converted into and to be treated as breaches of the BIT. What the Tribunal is stressing is that in this case, there is no clear and persuasive evidence that such was in fact the intention of both Switzerland and Pakistan in adopting Article 11 of the BIT. Pakistan for its part in effect denies that, in concluding the BIT, it had any such intention. SGS, of course, does not speak for Switzerland. But it has not submitted evidence of the necessary level of specificity and explicitness of text. We believe and so hold that, in the circumstances of this case, SGS's claim about Article 11 of the BIT must be rejected.

The tribunal in *SGS v. Pakistan* was the first to adopt the restrictive interpretation. As the reasoning of the decision makes clear, the tribunal was extremely reluctant to expand a single sentence, which it considered imprecisely worded, into a wide-ranging guarantee of contractual commitments. The *SGS* tribunal identified the salient issues: textual interpretation; extraneous evidence, such as the negotiating history of the contracting states' intent; the practical consequences of a broad interpretation; the impact of a broadly interpreted umbrella clause on other substantive treaty protections; and the consequences for any contractually selected dispute resolution procedure. The *SGS* panel left no doubt where it stood.

But the *SGS v. Pakistan* decision was by no means the last word; indeed, other tribunals, such as that in *Eureko v. Poland*, have sharply disagreed.

Eureko B.V. v. Republic of Poland

Partial Award and Dissenting Opinion, ad hoc UNCITRAL Arbitration, IIC 98, Aug. 19, 2005

(4) Art. 3.5 – The Umbrella Clause

244. Article 3.5 of the Treaty provides that each Contracting Party "shall observe any obligations it may have entered into with regard to investments of investors of the other Contracting Party." (A clause of such substance is often called "the umbrella clause.") Thus, insofar as the Government of Poland has entered into obligations vis-a-vis Eureko with regard to the latter's investments, and insofar as the Tribunal has found that the Respondent has acted in breach of those obligations, it stands, prima facie, in violation of Article 3.5 of the Treaty.

245. The Tribunal has found that Respondent bound itself, by the combined effect of the terms of the [Share Purchase Agreement (SPA)] and its First Addendum [, which were entered into between Eureko B.V., a Dutch company, and Big Bank Gdanski S.A., on one hand, and Polish Treasury, on the other], to conduct an IPO that would

afford Eureko the facility of gaining control of PZU, [a Polish company] and that it deliberately violated that obligation. It has found that obligation pertains to an investment of Eureko. The question accordingly arises, quite apart from the Government of Poland being in breach of Articles 3.1 and 5 of the Treaty on the grounds stated above, is it in further breach of Article 3.5? In the view of the Tribunal, the answer to that question must be in the affirmative, for the reasons that follow.

246. The plain meaning—the "ordinary meaning"—of a provision prescribing that a State "shall observe any obligations it may have entered into" with regard to certain foreign investments is not obscure. The phrase, "shall observe" is imperative and categorical. "Any" obligations is capacious; it means not only obligations of a certain type, but "any"—that is to say, all—obligations entered into with regard to investments of investors of the other Contracting Party.

247. This Tribunal is interpreting and applying a Treaty, a bilateral investment treaty, one of more than two thousand such treaties. In so doing, as stated earlier in this Award, it applies public international law. The authoritative codification of the law of treaties is the Vienna Convention on the Law of Treaties, a treaty in force among the very great majority of the States of the world community. Article 31, paragraph 1, of that Convention provides that: "A treaty shall be interpreted in good faith in accordance with the ordinary meaning to be given to the terms of the treaty in their context and in the light of its object and purpose."

248. The ordinary meaning of Article 3.5 has been set out in paragraph 244 above. The context of Article 3.5 is a Treaty whose object and purpose is "the encouragement and reciprocal protection of investment," a treaty which contains specific provisions designed to accomplish that end, of which Article 3.5 is one. It is a cardinal rule of the interpretation of treaties that each and every operative clause of a treaty is to be interpreted as meaningful rather than meaningless. It is equally well established in the jurisprudence of international law, particularly that of the Permanent Court of International Justice and the International Court of Justice, that treaties, and hence their clauses, are to be interpreted so as to render them effective rather than ineffective.

249. It follows that the effect of Article 3.5 in this proceeding cannot be overlooked, or [folded into] the Treaty's provisions for fair and equitable treatment, national treatment, most-favored-nation treatment, deprivation of investments, and full protection and security. On the contrary, Article 3.5 must be interpreted to mean something in itself.

250. The immediate, operative effects of Article 3.5 are two. The first is that Eureko's contractual arrangements with the Government of Poland are subject to the jurisdiction of the Tribunal, a conclusion that reinforces the jurisdictional conclusions earlier reached in this Award. The second is that breaches by Poland of its obligations under the SPA and its First Addendum, as read together, that are not breaches of Articles 3.1 and 5 of the Treaty nevertheless may be breaches of Article 3.5 of the Treaty, since they transgress Poland's Treaty commitment to "observe any obligations it may have entered into" with regard to Eureko's investments.

. . . .

252. There have been only a few cases that treat the umbrella clause. The earliest appears to be *Fedax v. The Republic of Venezuela*.[25] The Respondent had failed to honor promissory notes issued by the Government of Venezuela. The bilateral investment treaty—the Agreement between the Netherlands and Venezuela provided . . . that: "Each Contracting Party shall observe any obligation it may have entered into with regard to the

---

[25] SN: 37 *International Legal Material* 1391 (1998).

treatment of investments of nationals of the other Contracting Party." The Tribunal found that the non-payment of the contractual obligation to pay amounted to a violation of the BIT. The Tribunal held: ". . . the Republic of Venezuela is under the obligation to honor precisely the terms and conditions governing such investment, laid down mainly in Article 3 of the Agreement, as well as to honor the specific payments established in the promissory notes issued, and the Tribunal so finds. . . ."

253. In *SGS Société Générale de Surveillance S.A. vs. Islamic Republic of Pakistan*,[26] the Tribunal passed upon the meaning of an umbrella clause that provided, in Article 11 of the BIT: "Either Contracting Party shall constantly guarantee the observance of commitments it has entered into with respect to the investments of investors of the other Contracting Party." The Claimant maintained that that clause "had the effect of elevating a simple breach of contract claim to a treaty claim under international law." (Para. 98.) The Tribunal held to the contrary, principally on the following grounds: (a) the text of Article 11 is not limited to contractual commitments. If the Claimant's position were to be accepted, the meaning of Article 11 "appears susceptible of almost indefinite expansion" (Para. 166). (b) The legal consequences that the Claimant attributes to Article 11 "are so far-reaching in scope, and so automatic and unqualified and sweeping in their operation, so burdensome in their potential impact upon a Contracting Party," that clear and convincing evidence must be adduced by the Claimant that such was the shared intent of the Contracting Parties to the BIT (Para. 167). No such evidence had been introduced. (c) Acceptance of the Claimant's reading would amount to incorporating by reference an unlimited number of State contracts, as well as other municipal law instruments setting out State commitments (Para. 168). (d) It would also tend to make the substantive protections of the BIT "substantially superfluous" (ibid). There would be no real need to demonstrate a violation of those substantive treaty standards if a simple breach of contract would suffice to constitute a treaty violation. (e) Such acceptance would also enable an investor at will to nullify any freely negotiated dispute settlement clause in a State contract (ibid.) (f) Article 11 was located not among the substantive obligations of the BIT ("fair and equitable treatment" etc.) but at the end of the Treaty, before its final provisions. (g) In respect of the expansive interpretation of the Claimant of the obligations of the State, the approach rather should prudentially be in dubio mitius (Para. 171). The Tribunal acknowledged that Switzerland and Pakistan could have agreed that breaches of each State's contracts with investors of the other State shall be treated as breaches of the BIT, but it concluded that evidence of such agreement—which Pakistan denied—had not been submitted (Para. 173).

254. In a letter to ICSID of October 1, 2003, the Swiss Government stated that it was "alarmed about the very narrow interpretation given to the meaning of [the umbrella clause] by the Tribunal, which not only runs counter to the intention of Switzerland when concluding the Treaty but is quite evidently neither supported by the meaning of similar articles in BITS concluded by other countries nor by academic comments on such provisions."

255. In *SGS Société Générale de Surveillance S.A. vs. Republic of the Philippines*, a subsequent Tribunal took a decidedly different approach. It interpreted a BIT provision, Article X(2), reading: "Each Contracting Party shall observe any obligation it has assumed with regard to specific investments in its territory by investors of the other Contracting Party." It observed that that provision "uses the mandatory term 'shall' in the same way as substantive" articles of the treaty. It held that the term "any obligation" is capable of applying to obligations arising under national law, e.g., those arising from a contract. "Interpreting the actual text of Article X(2), it would appear to say, and to

---

[26] SN: ICSID Case No. ARB/01/13.

say clearly, that each Contracting Party shall observe any legal obligation that it has assumed, or will in the future assume, with regard to specific investments covered by the BIT." It added that that article was adopted within the framework of the BIT, "and has to be construed as intended to be effective within that framework." It continued: "The object and purpose of the BIT supports an effective interpretation of Article X(2). The BIT is a treaty for the promotion and reciprocal protection of investments . . . It is legitimate to resolve uncertainties in its interpretation so as to favour the protection of covered investments." It added, ". . . if commitments made by the State towards specific investments do involve binding obligations or commitments under the applicable law, it seems entirely consistent with the object and purpose of the BIT to hold that they are incorporated and brought within the framework of the BIT by Article X(2)."[27] (Paras. 115–118.)

256. This [*SGS v. Phillippines*] Tribunal's conclusion that "Article X(2) means what it says," the Tribunal acknowledged, "is however contradicted by the decision of the Tribunal in *SGS v. Pakistan*." The Tribunal proceeded to consider, and trenchantly criticize, the essential reasoning of that latter Award. It held that this umbrella clause was not susceptible of almost indefinite expansion, because to be applicable the State must have assumed a legal obligation vis-a-vis the specific investment. "This is very far from elevating to the international level all the municipal legislative or administrative or other unilateral measures of a Contracting Party." It further held that the question is not determined by a presumption against a broad interpretation of an umbrella clause. An umbrella clause need not be interpreted to override dispute settlement clauses of particular contracts. The Tribunal gave some weight to the location of the umbrella clause apart from the substantive articles of the BIT but that was not decisive. "Not only are the reasons given by the Tribunal in *SGS v. Pakistan* unconvincing: the Tribunal failed to give any clear meaning to the 'umbrella clause.'" It went on to hold that the Tribunal in *SGS v. Pakistan* found that a broad interpretation of the umbrella clause would convert investment contracts into treaties, but that that is not what the clause says. "It does not convert questions of contract law into questions of treaty law." It "addresses not the scope of the commitments entered into with regard to specific investments but the performance of these obligations, once they are ascertained." ". . . Article X(2) makes it a breach of the BIT for the host State to fail to observe binding commitments, including contractual commitments, which it has assumed with regard to specific investments. But it does not convert the issue of the extent or content of such obligations into an issue of international law." (Paras. 121–128.)

257. This Tribunal finds the foregoing analysis of the Tribunal in *SGS v. the Republic of the Philippines*, a Tribunal which had among its distinguished members Professor Crawford, cogent and convincing. While having the greatest respect for the distinguished members of the Tribunal in *SGS v. the Islamic Republic of Pakistan*, it is constrained to say that it finds its analysis of the umbrella clause less convincing.

258. The Tribunal adds to the considerations advanced in the Philippines Award its conclusion that to give effect to the plain meaning of an umbrella clause by no means renders the other substantive protections of a BIT superfluous. As Professor Schreuer points out in his cited article, "The BIT's substantive provisions deal with non-discrimination, fair and equitable treatment, national treatment, MFN treatment, free transfer of payments and protection from expropriation. These issues are not normally covered in contracts." (At p. 253.) This Tribunal feels bound to add that reliance by the Tribunal in *SGS v. Pakistan* on the maxim *in dubio mitius* so as effectively to presume that sovereign rights override the rights of a foreign investor could be seen as a reversion to a doctrine that has

---

[27] SN: 19 Mealey's Int'l Arb. Rep. Feb. 2004, at E-1.

been displaced by contemporary customary international law, particularly as that law has been reshaped by the conclusion of more than 2000 essentially concordant bilateral investment treaties.

259. Moreover, insofar as the placement of the umbrella clause in the BIT—among the substantive obligations or with the final clauses—is of any significance (in this Tribunal's view, little), it should be noted that Article 3.5 of the BIT between the Netherlands and Poland places its umbrella clause amidst the rendering of the Parties' substantive obligations.

260. In view of the foregoing analysis, the Tribunal concludes that the actions and inactions of the Government of Poland that are in breach of Poland's obligations under the Treaty—those that have been held to be unfair and inequitable and expropriatory in effect—also are in breach of its commitment under Article 3.5 of the Treaty to "observe any obligations it may have entered into with regards to investments of investors" of the Netherlands.

The differing approaches that the *Eureko* and *SGS (Pakistan)* adopted have framed the debate. A recent tribunal, *El Paso v. Argentina*, aligned itself with the restrictive camp, and usefully summarized some of the cases on both sides.

El Paso Energy International Company v. Argentina

ICSID Case No. ARB/03/05 (Decision on Jurisdiction, Apr. 26, 2006)[28]

67. Considering that the Claimant's case comprises some claims which concern breaches of purported contractual relationships between the foreign investor and the Respondent—whose existence will be determined at the merits level—the question for the Tribunal is whether Article II(2)(c) of the U.S.–Argentina BIT is an umbrella clause whose effect would be, according to the Claimants, to transform all contractual undertakings into international law obligations and, accordingly, to turn breaches of the slightest such obligations by the Respondent into breaches of the BIT.

. . . .

70. This Tribunal considers that a balanced interpretation is needed, taking into account both State sovereignty and the State's responsibility to create an adapted and evolutionary framework for the development of economic activities, and the necessity to protect foreign investment and its continuing flow. It is bearing this in mind that the Tribunal will deal with the controversial question of the so-called "umbrella clause," which is still not moot: as stated recently by Emmanuel Gaillard, "[t]his question has divided practitioners and legal commentators and remains unsettled in the international arbitral case law," (New York Law Journal, Thursday, 6 October 2005). The question is whether, through an "umbrella clause," sometimes also called an "observance-of-undertakings clause," in a BIT, contractual claims of an investor

---

[28] *See also BP Am. Prod. Co. v. Argentina*, ICSID Case No. ARB/04/8 (Decision on Jurisdiction, July 26, 2006). This decision was rendered three months after *El Paso*.

having a contract either with the State or with an autonomous entity are automatically and ipso jure "transformed" into treaty claims benefiting from the dispute settlement mechanism provided for in the BIT. There is an ongoing debate on that question, as divergent positions have been adopted by different ICSID tribunals. Umbrella clauses are not always drafted in the same manner, and some decisions insist on the variations in the drafting to explain different analyses. This Tribunal is not convinced that the clauses analysed so far really should receive different interpretations. The broadest clauses read like that contained in the relevant clause of Article II(2)(c) in the U.S. Argentina BIT, which provides that:

> "Each Party shall observe any obligation it may have entered into with regard to investments."

71. The first tribunal to be faced with the interpretation of such clause on the availability of international arbitration based on a BIT for purely contractual claims was the Tribunal, presided by Judge Feliciano, in *SGS v. Pakistan*.... The Tribunal did not consider, as is well known, that this clause "elevates" all contract claims stemming from a contract with the State to the level of claims for a breach of the Treaty, in other words that it transforms any contract claim into a treaty claim. The arguments put forward by the Tribunal are, in the view of this Tribunal, more than conclusive. These arguments can be summarised in the following manner.

72. Firstly, Article 11 refers to commitments in general, not only to contractual commitments. Therefore, if one considers that it elevates contract claims to the status of treaty claims, it should result as an unavoidable consequence that all claims based on any commitment in legislative or administrative or other unilateral acts of the State or one of its entities or subdivisions are to be considered as treaty claims . . .

73. Secondly, and consequently, if any violation of any commitment of the State is a violation of the Treaty, this renders useless all substantive standards of protection of the Treaty . . .

74. A last point to be made, however, which brings some nuances to its findings in the *SGS v. Pakistan* case, is that the Tribunal does not exclude the possibility that States decide to consider, in a BIT, that the slightest violation of a contract between a State and a foreign investor amounts to a violation of the Treaty, but then this has to be stated clearly and unambiguously. . . . This general reasoning is quite convincing, keeping in mind that the words "contract" or "contractual obligations" do not even appear in the so-called umbrella clause.

75. As is also well known, this analysis was strongly criticised by another ICSID Tribunal, presided by Dr. El-Kosheri, in a similar case, *SGS v. Philippines*, in its 2004 Decision on Jurisdiction (above, § 69), in which it had to deal with an "umbrella clause" embodied in Article X(2) of the BIT:

> "Each Contracting Party shall observe any obligation it has assumed with regard to specific investments in its territory by investors of the other Contracting Party."

Here too, it seems useful to this Tribunal to summarise the main steps of the reasoning followed. First, the Tribunal in *SGS v. Philippines* indeed considered that this general provision transformed any contractual obligation of the State into a treaty obligation:

> "It uses the mandatory term 'shall' in the same way as substantive Articles III-VI. The term 'any obligation' is capable of applying to obligations arising under national law, e.g., those arising from a contract . . . Interpreting the actual text of Article X(2), it would appear to say, and to say clearly, that each Contracting Party shall observe any legal obligation it has assumed, or will in the future assume, with regard to specific investments covered by the BIT (Decision, § 115, emphasis by this Tribunal)."

Second, after having underscored the difference in the language of the umbrella clauses in *SGS v. Pakistan* and *SGS v. Philippines*, the Tribunal criticised the reasoning of its predecessor and mainly emphasised that if it does not elevate the contract claims, into treaty claims the umbrella clause has no real far-reaching meaning.

76. This Tribunal should like to stress, on the contrary, that the interpretation given in *SGS v. Philippines* does not only deprive one single provision of far-reaching consequences but renders the whole Treaty completely useless: indeed, if this interpretation were to be followed—the violation of any legal obligation of a State, and not only of any contractual obligation with respect to investment, is a violation of the BIT, whatever the source of the obligation and whatever the seriousness of the breach—it would be sufficient to include a so-called "umbrella clause" and a dispute settlement mechanism, and no other articles setting standards for the protection of foreign investments in any BIT. If any violation of any legal obligation of a State is ipso facto a violation of the treaty, then that violation need not amount to a violation of the high standards of the treaty of "fair and equitable treatment" or "full protection and security." Apart from this general and very important remark, the Tribunal also wishes to point to the fact that quite contradictory conclusions have been drawn by the Tribunal in *SGS v. Philippines*: among other things, the Tribunal stated that, although the umbrella clause transforms the contract claims into treaty claims, first "it does not convert the issue of the extent or content of such obligations into an issue of international law" (Decision, § 128, original emphasis), which means that the "contract claims/treaty claims" should be assessed according to the national law of the contract and not the treaty standards, and, second, that the umbrella clause does not "override specific and exclusive dispute settlement arrangements made in the investment contract itself" (Decision, § 134), which explains that the Tribunal has suspended its proceedings until the "contract claims/treaty claims would be decided by the national courts in accordance with the dispute settlement provisions of the contract," stating that "the Tribunal should not exercise its jurisdiction over a contractual claim when the parties have already agreed on how such a claim is to be resolved, and have done so exclusively"(Decision, § 155). In other words, the Tribunal asserts that a treaty claim should not be analysed according to treaty standards, which seems quite strange, and that it has jurisdiction over the contract claims/treaty claims, but at the same time that it does not really have such jurisdiction—until the contract claims are decided. This controversy has been going on ever since these two contradictory decisions.

77. Some have adopted the *SGS v. Philippines* position but not drawn the same consequences from it. [I]n *Eureko B. V. v. Poland* (Partial Award of 19 August, 2005), [for example,] the Tribunal, presided by Mr. Yves Fortier, accepted the idea that, as a result of the umbrella clause in the BIT—Article 3(5) of the BIT provided that "[e]ach Contracting Party shall observe any obligation it may have entered into with regard to investors of the other Contracting Party"—the smallest obligation of a State with regard to investments was protected by the BIT and could give rise to an ICSID obligation. This decision was, however, accompanied by a strong dissent of the arbitrator Rajski, who emphasised the systemic consequences a broad interpretation of so-called "umbrella clauses." ...

In *Noble Ventures Inc. v. Romania* (above, § 69), the Tribunal, presided by Professor Bockstiegel, followed the same line of reasoning [as Eureko], stating quite generally that "[a]n umbrella clause is usually seen as transforming municipal law obligations into obligations directly cognizable in international law" (Award, § 53). The Tribunal, while it considered the umbrella clause as an exception to the "well established rule of general international law that in normal circumstances per se a breach of a contract by the State does not give rise to direct international responsibility on the part of the State," certainly did not interpret that exception restrictively, as exceptions should be interpreted, although it mentioned the necessity theoretically to adopt such an interpretation when it stated: "as with any other exception to established general rules of law the identification of a provision as an umbrella clause can as a consequence proceed only from a strict, if not indeed restrictive, interpretation of its terms" (Decision, § 55). In the words used by the Tribunal in *Noble Ventures Inc. v. Romania*, the breach of a contract being assimilated by the umbrella clause to a breach of the BIT, is thus "internationalized" (Decision, § 54). Again, the problem faced by such reasoning, according to this Tribunal, is that, by necessary implication, all municipal law commitments must necessarily be as well "internationalised," as the so-called umbrella clause does not differentiate among obligations; it refers to any obligation and not specifically to contractual obligations, the consequence being that the division between the national legal order and the international legal order is completely blurred. One of the arguments presented by the ICSID Tribunal in Noble Ventures was that the "elevation" theory was prompted by the object and purpose of the BIT, and that "[a]n interpretation to the contrary would deprive the investor of any internationally secured legal remedy in respect of investment contracts that it has entered into with the host State" (Decision, § 52). In this Tribunal's opinion, this is not a good reason, and it can explain why. Either the foreign investor has a commercial contract with an autonomous State entity or it has an investment agreement with the State, in which some "clauses exorbitantes du droit commun"[29] are inserted. In both cases, it is more than likely that the foreign investor will have managed to insert a dispute settlement mechanism into the contract; usually, in a purely commercial contract, that mechanism will be commercial arbitration or the national courts, while in an investment agreement it will generally be an international arbitration mechanism such as that of ICSID. In other words, in the so-called State contracts, there is usually an "internationally secured legal remedy," while in the mere commercial contracts governed by national law, there is no reason why such a mechanism should be available, as stated by Judge Schwebel, when he said that "it is generally accepted that, so long as it affords remedies in its Courts, a State is only directly responsible, on the international plane, for acts involving breaches of contract, where the breach is not a simple breach . . . but involves an obviously arbitrary or tortuous element. . . ." (International Arbitration: Three Salient Problems, Cambridge, Cambridge University Press, 1987, p. 111).

78. Some have adopted the *SGS v. Pakistan* position, either by insisting on certain specificities of the case, or by presenting a general approach. In *Salini v. Jordan*, decided in 2004 (*Salini Costruttori S.p.A. & Italstrade S.p.A. v. Hashemite Kingdom of Jordan*, Decision on Jurisdiction, 29 November 2004, ICSID case No. ARB/02/13, http://www.worldbank.orm/icsid/cases/salini-decision.pdf), the Tribunal, presided by Judge Gilbert Guillaume, answered in the negative the question of the "elevation" of contract claims into treaty claims, insisting on the generality of the language used in the so-called umbrella clause in Article 2(4), which stated that "[e]ach Contracting Party shall create and maintain in its territory a legal framework apt to guarantee the investors the continuity of legal treatment, including the compliance, in good faith, of all undertakings assumed with regard to each specific investor." In *Joy Machinery Limited v. Arab Republic of Egypt*, (Award of 6 August 2004, ICSID case No. ARB/02/11, http://www.worldbank.ora/icsid/cases/ioy-mining-award.pdf), the Tribunal, presided by Professor Orrego Vicuna, noted that a discussion of the "umbrella clause" was not necessary for the outcome of the case but, in order to "make certain clarifications," took a firm position against the transformation of all contractual claims into treaty claims in the specific case. . . .

---

[29] In French administrative law, the phrase *clauses exorbitantes du droit commun* refers to certain terms that are not usually found in private civil contracts. The inclusion of such terms in a contract implies that the contract is administrative and hence subject to administrative law including to special powers of the government to unilaterally modify or alter it.

79. In this Tribunal's view, it is necessary to distinguish the State as a merchant from the State as a sovereign. This is not new: in the above case of *Joy Machinery Limited v. Arab Republic of Egypt*, the ICSID Tribunal stated: "A basic general distinction can be made between commercial aspects of a dispute and other aspects involving the existence of some forms of State interference with the operation of the contract involved" (Decision, § 72). The same approach was taken by the ad hoc Committee on annulment presided by Mr. Yves Fortier in the Vivendi II case, where the distinction between contract claims and treaty claims was clearly stated ... (*Compania de Aguas del Aconquija, S.A. et Compagnie Générale des Eaux (Vivendi Universal) v. Argentine Republic*, Decision on Annulment of 3 July 2002, ILM, Vol. 41, 2002, p. 1135 § 96).[30]

80. The view that it is essentially from the State as a sovereign that the foreign investors have to be protected through the availability of international arbitration is confirmed, in the Tribunal's opinion, by the language in the new 2004 US Model BIT, which clearly elevates only the contract claims stemming from an investment agreement stricto sensu, that, is an agreement in which the State appears as a sovereign, and not all contracts

---

[30] The *El Paso* tribunal emphasized that the State acting as a merchant must be distinguished from State acting as a sovereign, which reflects the classic distinction between actions *jure gestionis* and *jure imperii* in international law. A State's actions in the former capacity do not violate international law, whereas those in the latter capacity do. Distinguishing between these two categories of State actions is, however, easier said than done. In fact, tribunals have so far refrained from suggesting any criteria for this purpose. Instead, they have provided examples of each category. For instance, *Fedax v. Venezuela* applied the umbrella clause to a promissory note (arguably a commercial contract). *Joy Machinery*, however, characterized a bank guarantee as a commercial contract and refused to apply the umbrella clause. *El Paso* characterized a contract containing a stabilization clause as an investment contract, which presumably a government would enter into as a sovereign. Regardless of whether an umbrella clause's coverage should be limited to government's actions in its capacity as a sovereign or not, development of criteria for distinguishing the two categories would make the application of the law more predictable and hence is desirable. The United Nations Convention on Jurisdictional Immunities of States, which was adopted by U.N. General Assembly in December 2004 (*see* G.A. Res. 59/38, U.N. Doc. A/RES/59/38 (Dec. 16, 2004)) could provide some initial guidance for this purpose. The convention in Article 2(1) and (2) provides in relevant part that:

> (c) "commercial transaction" means:
>
> (i) any commercial contract or transaction for the sale of goods or supply of services;
>
> (ii) any contract for a loan or other transaction of a financial nature, including any obligation of guarantee or of indemnity in respect of any such loan or transaction;
>
> (iii) any other contract or transaction of a commercial, industrial, trading or professional nature, but not including a contract of employment of persons.
>
> 2. In determining whether a contract or transaction is a "commercial transaction" under paragraph 1 (c), reference should be made primarily to the nature of the contract or transaction, but its purpose should also be taken into account if the parties to the contract or transaction have so agreed, or if, in the practice of the State of the forum, that purpose is relevant to determining the non-commercial character of the contract or transaction.

See also Section 1605(a)(2) of the United States Foreign Sovereign Immunities Act, which limits a foreign sovereign's immunity to its "commercial activity." Section 1603(d) provides in the relevant part that "[t]he commercial character of an activity shall be determined by reference to the nature of the course of conduct or particular transaction or act, rather than by reference to its purpose."

signed with the State or one of its entities to the level of treaty claims, as results from its Article 24(1)(a).[31]

81. In view of the necessity to distinguish the State as a merchant, especially when it acts through instrumentalities, from the State as a sovereign, the Tribunal considers that the "umbrella clause" in the Argentine-US BIT, which prescribes that "[e]ach Party shall observe any obligation it may have entered into with regard to investments," can be interpreted in the light of Article VII (1),[32] which clearly includes among the investment disputes under the Treaty all disputes resulting from a violation of a commitment given by the State as a sovereign State, either through an agreement, an authorisation, or the BIT. . . . Interpreted in this way, the umbrella clause in Article II of the BIT, read in conjunction with Article VII, will not extend the Treaty protection to breaches of an ordinary commercial contract entered into by the State or a State-owned entity, but will cover additional investment protections contractually agreed by the State as a sovereign—such as a stabilization clause—inserted in an investment agreement.

82. In conclusion, in this Tribunal's view, following the important precedents set by Tribunals presided over by Judge Feliciano, Judge Guillaume and Professor Orrego Vicuna, an umbrella clause cannot transform any contract claim into a treaty claim, as this would necessarily imply that any commitments of the State in respect to investments, even the most minor ones, would be transformed into treaty claims. These far-reaching consequences of a broad interpretation of the so-called umbrella clauses, quite destructive of the distinction between national legal orders and the international legal order, have been well understood and clearly explained by the first Tribunal which dealt with the issue of the so-called "umbrella clause" in the *SGS v. Pakistan* case and which insisted on the theoretical problems faced. It would be strange indeed if the acceptance of a BIT entailed an international liability of the State going far beyond the obligation to respect the standards of protection of foreign investments embodied in the Treaty and rendered it liable for any violation of any commitment in national or international law "with regard to investments." A well known specialist of ICSID, Christoph Schreuer, has strikingly described what some of the practical consequences of a broad interpretation of the umbrella clauses could be . . . ("Travelling the BIT Route. Of Waiting Periods, Umbrella Clauses and Forks in the Road," Journal of World Investment & Trade, Vol. 5, 2004, p. 255). It is the firm conviction of this Tribunal that the investors will not use appropriate restraint—and why should they?—if the ICSID tribunals offer them

---

[31] Article 24(1)(a) of the 2004 U.S. Model BIT provides that:

1. In the event that a disputing party considers that an investment dispute cannot be settled by consultation and negotiation: (a) the claimant, on its own behalf, may submit to arbitration under this Section a claim

(i) that the respondent has breached

(A) an obligation under Articles 3 through 10,

(B) an investment authorization, or

(C) an investment agreement; and

(ii) that the claimant has incurred loss or damage by reason of, or arising out of, that breach. . . ."

[32] Article VII(1) of Argentine-U.S. BIT provides that: "For purposes of this Article, an investment dispute is a dispute between a Party and a national or company of the other Party arising out of or relating to (a) an investment agreement between that Party and such national or company; (b) an investment authorization granted by that Party's foreign investment authority (if any such authorization exists) to such national or company; or (c) an alleged breach of any right conferred or created by this Treaty with respect to an investment."

unexpected remedies. The responsibility for showing appropriate restraint rests rather in the hands of the ICSID tribunals.

. . . .

84. In the Tribunal's view, this umbrella clause does not extend its jurisdiction over any contract claims that the Claimants might present as stemming solely from the breach of a contract between the investor and the Argentine State or an Argentine autonomous State entity. Moreover, in the Tribunal's view, it is especially clear that the umbrella clause does not extend to any contract claims when such claims do not rely on a violation of the standards of protection of the BIT, namely, national treatment, MFN clause, fair and equitable treatment, full protection and security, protection against arbitrary and discriminatory measures, protection against expropriation or nationalisation either directly or indirectly, unless some requirements are respected. However, there is no doubt that if the State interferes with contractual rights by a unilateral act, whether these rights stem from a contract entered into by a foreign investor with a private party, a State autonomous entity or the State itself, in such a way that the State's action can be analysed as a violation of the standards of protection embodied in a BIT, the treaty-based arbitration tribunal has jurisdiction over all the claims of the foreign investor, including the claims arising from a violation of its contractual rights. Moreover, Article II, read in conjunction with Article VII(I), also considers as treaty claims the breaches of an investment agreement between Argentina and a national or company of the United States.

85. In other words, the Tribunal, endorsing the interpretation first given to the so-called "umbrella clause" in the Decision *SGS v. Pakistan*, confirms what it mentioned above (§ 65), namely, that it has jurisdiction over treaty claims and cannot entertain purely contractual claims, which do not amount to a violation of the standards of protection of the BIT. It adds that, in view of Article VII(1) of the US-Argentina BIT, a violation of an investment agreement entered into by the State as a sovereign and a national or company of the United States is deemed to be also a violation of the Treaty and can thus give rise to a treaty claim.

86. The answer to the question raised above (§ 66), that is, whether the existence of a so-called umbrella clause changes the Tribunals intermediary conclusion to the effect that it has no jurisdiction over purely contractual claims, and that it can only entertain treaty claims, is clearly in the negative. Indeed, the Tribunal has jurisdiction only over the treaty claims, the latter including, pursuant to the wording of Article VII(1), the claims based on the violation of an investment agreement entered into by the foreign investor with the State as a sovereign.

D. Conclusion

This debate covers a number of important issues. First and most obvious is how are tribunals to interpret the actual words of the umbrella clauses? Leaving aside clauses that do not incorporate mandatory language, such as those clauses at issue in *Joy Machinery*[33] and *Salini v. Jordan*,[34] the typical umbrella clause seems

---

[33] *Joy Mining*, p. 555 *supra*.

[34] *Salini v. Jordan*, p. 555 *supra*.

to be definitive in its meaning: words such as *shall* and *any* would not appear to allow tribunals to refuse enforcement because they find the consequences of an ordinary-meaning interpretation to be too severe and far reaching. The *SGS v. Pakistan* tribunal, however, cited the maxim *in dubio pars mitior est sequenda* (in doubt, the gentler course is to be followed) in adopting what it considered a prudently restrictive interpretation. But gentler to whom? To the state in respect of its sovereignty, or to the investor, whose rights investment treaties explicitly seek to protect? Because the acknowledged purpose of most treaties is that very protection, a mandatory umbrella clause should at a minimum create a strong presumption that any specific host state undertaking to an investor that can reasonably be construed as within the scope of the particular treaty term (*commitment, obligation*) is indeed a treaty obligation.

Second, the tribunals that have adopted restrictive interpretations often note that a state's breach of contract is ordinarily not an international wrong, and find no reason "absent clear and convincing evidence" to alter what they consider an established and longstanding rule. Although the observation that contract breaches are not international wrongs is undoubtedly the majority rule, there is some support for the proposition to the contrary.[35] Moreover, so restrictive an approach ignores the norm-creating potential of treaties. As is the case with the fair and equitable treatment standard, an argument can be made that the progressive adoption of clearly expressed mandatory umbrella clauses moves the international legal regime closer to extending the venerable concept of *pacta sunt servanda* to all investment (but not commercial) contracts. Indeed, the historic precedents to umbrella clauses that the *Eureko* tribunal identified are concrete evidence of this evolution: that history suggests that the original drafters of umbrella clause language consciously and expressly intended to extend international protection to investment contract commitments and obligations.

Third, tribunals that adhere to the restrictive approach object that interpreting umbrella clauses broadly will "blur" the distinction between the national and international legal orders by elevating "mere" contractual disputes to the plane of international law. That is surely true, but so do investment treaties as a whole. That, indeed, is the very purpose of these legal instruments—to create for a foreign investor the juridical standing to bring an international claim on its own behalf, when in the past such standing was limited to espousal by states. Elevating "mere" contractual disputes involving foreign investors to the international level is fully consistent with a central goal of both the international commercial arbitration system and the investment treaty regime: to create a neutral, impartial forum for the

---

[35] *See, e.g.*, Jennings, *State Contracts with Aliens*, 37 Brit. Y.B. Int'l L. 178, 182 (1961); S. Schwebel, *International Protection of Contractual Arrangement*, 53 Am. Soc'y Int'l L. Proc. 266 (1959); *see also* the following cases: *Illinois Central Railrod Co. Claim*, 4 U.N.R.I.A.A. 134 *et seq.*; *El Trinfu*, 4 U.N.R.I.A.A. 661; Feller, *The Mexican Claims Commission, 1923–1934*, ch. 9 (Macmillan 1935); *cf.* I. Brownlie, *The Principles of Public International Law* 522 *et seq.* (6th ed., Oxford University Press 2003); *Restatement (Third) of Foreign Relations Law of the United States* (West 1987), Comm. *h*.

resolution of transnational disputes. Similarly, a broad interpretation is consistent with the goal of depoliticizing investment disputes. There is no apparent reason—and certainly none in the language of most umbrella clauses—why this expanded standing should exclude investment contract commitments that are covered prima facie by a mandatory umbrella clause.

Fourth, as the decisions above note, the interpretive rule of effectiveness must be dealt with. It is an undisputed maxim of law, both internationally and nationally, that all the words and clauses of a legal instrument should be given effect. If, for example, the word *commitments* does not cover specific investment contract commitments made by a state to investors, then what does it cover? Both the *SGS v. Pakistan* and the *El Paso* tribunals suggest that tribunals should read the word *sovereign* into umbrella clauses, limiting their reach to sovereign or noncommercial or tortious acts. The restrictive tribunals often justify their rejection of a broad interpretation by conceding that certain state actions relating to a contract—such as a refusal to comply with a contractual arbitration procedure—would indeed breach an umbrella clause. But limiting umbrella clause protection to these types of acts would not give full effect to such a clause, because such acts would in all likelihood violate other treaty protections.[36]

In fact, any state act that invokes the state's sovereign power to block or frustrate or repudiate a specific investment commitment will probably violate some other substantive treaty protection. For example, in *Metalclad v. Mexico*, the tribunal found that the Mexican government made a commitment to Metalclad concerning permits required for the construction of the landfill. Mexico's failure to fulfill that commitment frustrated Metalclad's legitimate expectations, and thus violated the fair and equitable treatment standard of NAFTA.[37] It can accordingly be argued that a state's breach of its sovereign commitments—made through legislative or executive branches—breaches substantive norms regardless of whether an umbrella claim is present.[38] Thus, in *CMS v. Argentina*, the tribunal held that Argentina's repudiation of the legislative and executive commitments it had made to foreign investors violated the fair and equitable standard.[39]

---

[36] See Chapter XVII at p. 528 *supra*, discussing how refusal to arbitrate breaches the fair and equitable standard.

[37] *Metalclad v. Mexico*, ICSID Case No. ARB(AF)/97/1 (Final Award, Aug. 30, 2000), ¶¶ 97–101.

[38] *Cf.* note 30, *supra*.

[39] *CMS v. Argentina*, ICSID Case No. ARB/01/08 (Award, May 12, 2005), ¶¶ 275–81. The *CMS* tribunal also held that Argentina breached the umbrella clause of the Argentina-U.S. BIT "to the extent that legal and contractual obligations pertinent to the investment have been breached and have resulted in the violation of the standards of protection under the Treaty." *Id.* ¶ 303. Argentina later challenged this finding in an annulment proceeding. The basis of the challenge, however, was that the government commitments at issue were made to TGN, the CMS's subsidiary, rather than the CMS itself. The annulment committee agreed with Argentina. *CMS* (Annulment Decision, Sept. 23, 2007), ¶¶ 89–100. The annulment committee dismissed Argentina's challenge to the tribunal's finding of the breach of fair and equitable treatment. *Id.* ¶¶ 81–85.

CONCLUSION

The only type of host state commitment whose breach is not clearly covered by existing international law is a "mere" contractual commitment. Thus, limiting an umbrella clause to only those sovereign state acts that likely violate other treaty protections would render the umbrella clause itself superfluous and, consequently, ineffective. It may thus be doubted whether tribunals have the power to limit breaches to "sovereign" acts where no such limitation appears in the text of the investment. Indeed, it can be argued that the *SGS v. Pakistan* tribunal reversed the proper burden: in view of the relative clarity and mandatory nature of the treaty provision, what was required was clear and convincing evidence that the clause did *not* apply to state contractual commitments that clearly relate to investors.

Fifth, the restrictive approach tribunals have properly identified a serious problem with any broad interpretation of umbrella clauses: how to reconcile contractual dispute resolution procedures with treaty dispute resolution procedures. Even if one accepts that the state parties to an umbrella clause intended that the clause apply to investment contract promises (such as Switzerland's position, *see Eureko v. Poland*, para. 254), those states neither anticipated nor prescribed a method of reconciling the two disparate dispute resolution procedures. As the restrictive approach tribunals note, creating a treaty remedy for an investment contract dispute may create a dispute resolution procedure never contemplated by the contract parties, and displace the procedure that was expressly contemplated and bargained for. It is at least surprising that a treaty would allow a private investor the option of abandoning a freely selected contractual dispute resolution procedure.[40]

Finally, the restrictive approach tribunals may be overstating the impact of broadly interpreted umbrella clauses in finding that such clauses would render other treaty protections redundant or nugatory. One can easily imagine situations in which a state has neither signed an investment contract nor made any specific commitments with respect to a particular investment. For example, a foreign investor could build a pharmaceutical factory, as to which there were no specific state commitments. Any decision by the state to nationalize the factory without adequate compensation, or to nationalize the factory because it was owned by an investor from a disfavored country, would likely violate antiexpropriation and antidiscrimination treaty protections, but not an umbrella clause. Many similar scenarios can be readily articulated. Thus, the fear that umbrella clauses could displace the whole of international investment protection appears to be illusory.

---

[40] However, the problem of competing dispute resolution procedures is an intrinsic part of the investment treaty legal landscape. *See generally* Chapter XIV *supra*.

XIX. Damages, Compensation,[1] and Non-Pecuniary Remedies

A. Introduction

The subject of damages and compensation is one of the most complex areas of investment arbitration practice. This is because of some confusion over terminology, the lack of sufficiently developed rules on the subject, and the multidisciplinary nature of compensation analysis, which in addition to law may require knowledge of accounting and finance.

---

[1] Both the terms *damages* and *compensation* denote a monetary payment due as a result of harm caused by an action contrary to obligations arising under law or contract. *See* Eibe H. Riedel, *Damages*, in 1 *Encyclopedia of Public International Law* [hereinafter EPIL] 929–30 (R. Bernhardt ed., 1992) ("The question of damages arises when a subject of international law is in breach of an international obligation, thereby incurring responsibility and, as a legal consequence, must render reparation for internationally wrongful acts or omissions ... Although the terminology used in the literature and case-law concerning reparations is far from uniform (sometimes "reparation," "restitution" or "indemnity" are used synonymously as generic terms covering all types of reparations, while "damages" or "compensation" specially denote payment for actual loss sustained or injury inflicted upon persons or property), the basic idea behind all types of legal consequences for breaches of international obligations is to make good the injury caused to persons or property by a State or other subject of international law"). *See also* Ian Brownlie, *Principles of Public International Law* 442 (2003) ("[T]he terminology of the subject is in disorder. . . . ['damages' refers to] a loss, *damnum,* whether it is a financial quantification of physical injury or damage, or of other consequences of a breach of duty. 'Reparation . . . to refer to all measures which a plaintiff may expect to be taken by a defendant state: payment of compensation (or restitution) . . . [and] 'Compensation' . . . to describe reparation in the narrow sense of the payment of money as a 'valuation' of the wrong done"). The terms *compensation* and *damages* have been used interchangeably in this chapter.

Until recently, the concept of damages has defied attempts at simplification or codification. The 1930 Hague Codification Conference was one of the earliest attempts to codify certain principles governing this subject at a global level.[2] Its failure to some extent may be attributed to the lack of consensus among the participants with respect to the appropriate measure of damages.[3] Seventy years later, in 2001, the U.N. International Law Commission adopted the Draft Articles on Responsibility of States for Internationally Wrongful Acts.[4] These articles are

---

[2] *See* Edwin M. Borchard, *Responsibility of States, at the Hague Codification Conference,* 24 Am. J. Int'l L. 517, 518 (1930). For earlier attempts to codify the rules on damages *see* Draft Convention on the Responsibility of States for Damage Done in Their Territory to the Person or Property of Foreigners, Apr. 1, 1929, by reporter Edwin M. Borchard, Harvard Law School. On suggestion of the secretary of the International Law Commission, this 1929 draft was revised in 1961, *see* the 1961 Draft Convention *in* Louis B. Sohn & R. R. Baxter, *Responsibility of States for Injuries to the Economic Interests of Aliens,* 55 Am. J Int'l L. 545, 548 *et seq.* (1961), in particular arts. 6–10, 12, 27, 30–32, 34. Another attempt to codify the international law of damages was made in 1967 by the OECD in the *Draft Convention on the Protection of Foreign Property,* 71 I.L.M. 117 (1968). For one of the earliest treatises on the subject, *see* Marjorie M. Whiteman, *Damages in International Law* (Government Printing Office 1937–1943).

[3] Borchard, *supra* note 2, at 524.

[4] The International Law Commission's Articles on the Responsibility of States for Internationally Wrongful Acts [hereinafter ILC Articles] were adopted by the ILC on May 31, 2001. *See* Report of the ILC, 53d Sess., *available at* http://www.un.org/law/ilc. In December 2001, the U.N. General Assembly took note of the ILC Articles, and since then they remain on the agenda of the General Assembly for adoption or other future appropriate actions. *See* G.A. Res. 56/83, U.N. Doc. A/RES/56/83 (Jan. 28, 2002); and G.A. Res. 59/35, U.N. Doc. A/RES/59/35 (Dec. 16, 2004)). For the text of the articles and a commentary, *see* James Crawford, *The International Law Commission's Articles on State Responsibility* (Cambridge University Press 2002). With respect to the authority of the ILC Articles as a source of law, scholars have taken different positions. Some believe that the ILC Articles are not a formal source of law, but only a subsidiary means of ascertaining rules of law. Clive Parry, *The Sources and Evidences of International Law* 23–24, 114 (Oceana 1965). Others have argued that these articles form part of international law, since they were drawn up by an organ of the United Nations. *See* the exchange of e-mails between Giorgio Sacerdoti and Maurice Mendelson on this topic, *available at* Transnational Dispute Management (TDM), OGEMID Archives, Aug. 26, 2006.

INTRODUCTION

considered by many to constitute a codification of customary international law.[5] Although primarily meant to regulate the treatment of damages in state-to-state relationships, the ILC Articles may also be applicable to investor-state relationships and thus constitute a useful starting point for the present discussion of damages.[6]

Article 31(1) of the ILC Articles, entitled "Reparation," provides: "The responsible state is under an obligation to make full reparation for the injury caused by the internationally wrongful act."[7] "Reparation" is a broad term that covers a wide spectrum of pecuniary and non-pecuniary remedies available to the injured party under international law.[8] These remedies include "restitution, compensation and satisfaction, either singly or in combination."[9] *Satisfaction* will not be discussed here, as it concerns reparation in state-to-state disputes

---

[5] *Noble Ventures v. Romania*, ICSID Case No. ARB/01/11 (Award of Oct. 12, 2005), ¶ 69.

[6] Some commentators have advised caution when applying the ILC Articles in mixed private-public relationships such as investor-state arbitration. *See Int'l Thunderbird Gaming v. Mexico* (United Nations Commission on International Trade Law [UNCITRAL] Arbitration under Chapter 11 of NAFTA, Separate Opinion of Thomas W. Wälde (Dissent in Part), Jan. 26, 2006), ¶ 13 ("[I]nvestment treaties such as the NAFTA deal with a significantly different context from the one envisaged by traditional public international law: At its heart lies the right of a private actor to engage in an arbitral litigation against a (foreign) government over governmental conduct affecting the investor. That is fundamentally different from traditional international public law, which is based on solving disputes between sovereign states and where private parties have no standing. Analogies from such inter-state international law have therefore to be treated with caution . . ."). *See also* Zachary Douglas, *The Hybrid Foundations of Investment Treaty Arbitration*, *in* 74 Brit. Y.B. Int'l L. 151, 189 (2003) ("In summary, investment treaties create a sub-system of international law to regulate the relationship between states and private investors that arises upon a breach of the treaty, without prejudice to the general law of state responsibility that governs the relationship between the contracting states. The ILC's Articles on State Responsibility do not detract from this conclusion; to the contrary they provide the necessary conceptual framework to distinguish between the general system of state responsibility and sub-systems of responsibility. The sub-system created by investment treaties is by definition *sui generis*. An uncritical transplantation of secondary rules that govern, *inter alia*, the consequences of a diplomatic protection claim between two state parties is inappropriate").

[7] ILC Articles, *supra* note 4, art. 31(1).

[8] *Id.*, and accompanying commentary.

[9] *See id.*, art. 34.

specifically.[10] *Restitution* is often referred to as the primary remedy, but for practical purposes does not occupy a prominent place in the menu of remedies sought and awarded in investment arbitrations.[11] *Compensation* is therefore the most common remedy awarded by international tribunals, and is the principal focus of this chapter.

Section B examines the function of reparation by analyzing the dictum of the Permanent Court of International Justice in the *Chorzów Factory* case.[12] Section C covers non-pecuniary remedies, including restitution and specific performance. Section D examines standards of compensation for expropriation and other treaty breaches. Section E explains a variety of valuation methods that have been used by international tribunals. Section F discusses the specific problem of valuing projects that have not become profitable. Section G examines compensation for breach of contract. Section H examines factors limiting the amount of compensation, such as absence of causation, contributory fault, and the obligation to mitigate damages. Section I examines the role of equity in awarding damages. Finally, sections J and K provide an overview of interest, costs, and attorneys' fees.

---

[10] *See, e.g., CMS Gas Transmission Co. v. Argentina*, ICSID Case No. ARB/01/8 (Final Award of May 12, 2005), ¶ 399 ("As this is not a case of satisfaction due to an injured State, satisfaction can be ruled out at the outset"). *See also* Commentary on the ILC Articles, *available at* http://untreaty.un.org/ilc/texts/instruments/english/commentaries/9_6_2001.pdf, Commentary on Article 37, ¶¶ 3–4; ("'Satisfaction,' on the other hand, is the remedy for those injuries, not financially assessable, which amount to an affront to the State. These injuries are frequently of a symbolic character, arising from the very fact of the breach of the obligation, irrespective of its material consequences for the State concerned. The availability of the remedy of satisfaction for injury of this kind, sometimes described as non-material injury is well-established in international law. The point was made, for example, by the Tribunal in the *Rainbow Warrior* arbitration: There is a long established practice of States and international Courts and Tribunals of using satisfaction as a remedy or form of reparation (in the wide sense) for the breach of an international obligation. This practice relates particularly to the case of moral or legal damage done directly to the State, especially as opposed to the case of damage to persons involving international responsibility"), *Rainbow Warrior* (New Zealand/France), 20 U.N.R.I.A.A. 217, at 272–73, ¶ 122 (1990). *See also* Eibe H. Riedel, *Satisfaction*, in 4 *Encyclopedia of Public International Law* 320–21 (R. Bernhardt ed., 1992); Ian Brownlie, *Principles of Public International Law* 444 (2003) ("Satisfaction is an aspect of reparation in the broad sense. However, it is not easy to distinguish between pecuniary satisfaction and compensation in the case of breaches of duty not resulting in ... damage or loss of property. Claims of this sort are commonly expressed as a claim for an 'indemnity.' If there is a distinction, it would seem to be in the intention behind the demand. If it is predominantly that of seeking a token of regret and acknowledgement of wrongdoing then it is a matter of satisfaction").

[11] *But see* Christine Gray, *The Choice Between Restitution and Compensation*, 10 Eur. J. Int'l L. 413 (noting that the International Court of Justice in *Paraguay v. U.S. (Provisional Measures)*, 37 I.L.M. 810 (1998), "left the availability of restitution open; it made no ringing re-endorsements of the famous dictum in the *Chorzow Factory* case as to the primacy of this remedy").

[12] *Case Concerning the Factory at Chorzów*, Merits, P.C.I.J. (ser. A) No. 17, at 47 (1928).

B. The Function of Reparation: To Eliminate the Consequences of an Illegal Act

As noted earlier, Article 31 of the ILC Articles[13] requires that a state make full reparation for the injury caused by its wrongful conduct. Injury "includes any damage, whether material or moral, caused by the intentionally wrongful act of a State."[14] The Permanent Court of International Justice (PCIJ) in the *Case Concerning the Factory at Chorzów* described the function of damages:

> The essential principle contained in the actual notion of an illegal act—a principle which seems to be established by international practice and in particular by the decisions of arbitral tribunals—is that *reparation must, so far as possible, wipe out all the consequences of the illegal act and re-establish the situation which would, in all probability, have existed if that act had not been committed.* Restitution in kind, or, if this is not possible, payment of a sum corresponding to the value which a restitution in kind would bear; the award, if need be, of damages for loss sustained which would not be covered by restitution in kind or payment in place of it—such are the principles which should serve to determine the amount of compensation due for an act contrary to international law.[15]

This passage has become one of the most cited in the area of reparation.[16] Although the *Chorzów Factory* formulation was originally articulated in the context of expropriation, it has been also relied on in cases involving other breaches of international law.[17] The statement is actually quite complex, which makes its application challenging.[18] The central direction to re-establish a counterfactual

---

[13] See p. 565 *supra.*

[14] ILC Articles, *supra* note 4, art. 31(2).

[15] *Factory at Chorzów, supra* note 12, at 47. See also *Lusitania Case,* 7 R.I.A.A., Vol. 32, at 39 (1923), emphasis in original, *cited in CMS, supra* note 10, ¶ 401 ("the fundamental concept of 'damages' is ... reparation for a loss suffered; a judicially ascertained compensation for wrong. The remedy should be commensurate with the loss, so that the injured party may be made whole.").

[16] The P.C.I.J.'s statement was arguably *obiter dictum* and not a *ratio decidendi*, as restitution in kind as a remedy had been ruled out by the agreement of the parties. *Texaco Overseas Petroleum Co./California Asiatic Oil Co. & Gov't of the Libyan Arab Republic,* Award of January 19, 1977, 17 I.L.M. 1, ¶ 98 (1978) [hereinafter *TOPCO*].

[17] *See, e.g., CMS, supra* note 10, ¶ 400; see also *Case Concerning the Gabcíkovo-Nagymaros Project,* 1997 I.C.J. 92 (Decision of Sept. 25, 1997), ¶ 149.

[18] *Amoco Int'l Fin. Corp. v. Iran,* Partial Award No. 310-56-3, 15 Iran-U.S. Cl. Trib. Rep. 189, ¶ 191 ("In spite of the fact that it is nearly sixty years old, this judgment [*Chorzow Factory* case] is widely regarded as the most authoritative exposition of the principles applicable in this field, and is still valid today. It must be recognized, however, that its treatment of compensation is fairly complex and must be carefully analyzed").

situation may require constructing hypothetical scenarios to imagine how the affected investment would have performed had the wrongful act not occurred.[19]

The *Chorzów Factory* formula also specifies the two main forms that reparation can take: first, "restitution," and then "compensation." Restitution has been defined as "re-establishing the situation that would have existed had the wrongful act not occurred."[20] Compensation, however, is designed to cover "any financially assessable damage including loss of profits insofar as it is established."[21]

Despite the PCIJ's expressed preference for restitution, in practice such a remedy is rarely granted. In her Hague Academy lecture of 1982, Judge Higgins summarized some of the reasons underlying this phenomenon in the context of the expropriation of property:

> In many cases, of course, *restitutio* is not sought.... There can be a variety of reasons for this. It can be because restitution is indeed impossible—for example, if the nationalized assets have already passed into the hands of *bona fide* third party purchaser ... ; the nationalized property may no longer exist in the same form; ... damages [may] represent a compensation that is satisfactory in all the circumstances ... Problems of effectiveness in relation to restitution are of course closely related to the difficulty of

---

[19] In *Chorzow Factory,* the PCIJ appointed financial experts to determine the value of expropriated property. It directed the experts to answer two questions, the first of which required valuing the factory at the time of taking; and the second at the time of the calculation, *supra* note 12, at 51. The Court explained the rationale underlying each question as follows:

> The purpose of question I is to determine the monetary value, both of the object which should have been restored in kind and of the additional damages, on the basis of the estimated value of the undertaking including stocks at the moment of taking possession by the Polish Government, together with any probable profit that would have accrued to the undertaking between the date of taking possession and that of the expert opinion.
>
> On the hand, question II is directed to the ascertainment of the present value on the basis of the situation at the moment of the expert enquiry and leaving aside the situation presumed to exist in 1922.
>
> This question contemplates the present value of the undertaking from two points of view: firstly, it is supposed that the factory had remained essentially in the state in which it was on July 3rd 1922, and secondly, the factory is to be considered in the state in which it would (hypothetically but probably) have been in the hands of ... [the owners], if, instead of being taken in 1922 by Poland, it had been able to continue its supposedly normal development from that time onwards. The hypothetical nature of this question is considerably diminished by the possibility of comparison with other undertakings of the same nature directed by ... [one of the owners], and, in particular, with the Piesteritz factory, the analogy of which with Chorzow, as well as certain differences between the two, have been many times pointed out during the present proceedings." *Id.* at 52.

[20] See ILC Articles, *supra* note 4, art. 35 and Commentary ("Restitution involves the re-establishment as far as possible of the situation which existed prior to the commission of the internationally wrongful act, to the extent that any changes that have occurred in that situation may be traced to that act"); *see also CME Czech Republic B.V. v. Czech Republic* (Final Award of Mar. 14, 2003), ¶ 400.

[21] See ILC Articles, *supra* note 4, art. 36.

ordering specific performance against a state. Arbitration Tribunals feel that ... they cannot order specific performance. ...²²

Consequently, compensation has become the most common remedy that international tribunals consider and award in investor-state disputes.²³

C. Non-Pecuniary Remedies: Specific Performance and Other Injunctive Relief

Although compensation is the most prevalent form of reparation, two other remedies—specific performance and injunctive relief—merit some discussion.²⁴ Two basic questions arise: first, whether tribunals have the power to award such remedies;²⁵ and second, assuming that the answer to the first question is affirmative, whether there are any practical or legal bars to enforcement of such awards. The answer to both questions depends in part upon the provisions of applicable investment treaties and arbitration rules, which constitute part of the law applicable to an arbitration proceeding.

Investment treaties (and in particular BITs) do not generally limit the power of arbitral tribunals to grant non-pecuniary remedies. Exceptions include the recent

---

22 Rosalyn Higgins, *The Taking of Property by the State*, 176 Recueil des Cours 259, 315–17 (1982). *See also CME v. Czech Republic* (Partial Award of Sept. 31, 2001), ¶ 618 ("The Respondent is obligated to 'wipe out all the consequences' of the Media Council's unlawful acts and omissions, which caused the destruction of the Claimant's investment. Restitution in kind is not requested by the Claimant (as restitution in kind is obviously not possible, ENTS' broadcasting operations having been shut down for two years). Therefore, the Respondent is obligated to compensate the Claimant by payment of a sum corresponding to the value which a restitution in kind would bear"). *But see* the Libyan oil concession cases of 1970s (*BP Exploration Co. (Libya) Ltd. v. Libya*, 53 I.L.R. 297 (1973), *TOPCO, supra* note 16, *Libyan Arab Am. Oil Co. v. Libya* [hereinafter *LIAMCO*], 62 I.L.R. 140 (1977)). *See also* Gray, *supra* note 11, at 416 ("The idea that restitution is the primary remedy for all the breaches of international law has caused controversy in the past. One of the problems in establishing the primacy of restitution lies in the large gap *between* practice and theory").

23 *See also* Charles N. Brower & Jason D. Brueschke, *The Iran-United States Claims Tribunal* 473 (Martinus Nijhoff Publishers 1998). *But see* Thomas Wälde & Borzu Sabahi, *Compensation, Damages and Valuation in International Investment Law*, in *Oxford Handbook of International Investment Law* 1058 et seq. (P. Muchlinski, F. Ortino, & C. Schreuer eds., Oxford University Press 2008) (suggesting that in the modern practice of investment arbitration, restitution as a remedy should receive more attention).

24 A notable example of specific performance in state contract disputes is *TOPCO, supra* note 16, at 1 ("For the first time in the history of international arbitration relating to economic development contracts, an arbitral tribunal held that the injured parties were entitled to *restitutio in integrum* and that the sovereign state was obliged to perform specifically its contractual obligations with private foreign investor").

25 On this issue, *see* Martin Endicott, *Remedies in Investor-State Arbitration: Restitution, Specific Performance and Declaratory Awards,* in *New Aspects of International Investment Law* 520 et seq. (Kahn & Wälde eds., Martinus Nijhoff Publishers 2007).

model BITs of the United States and Canada, which expressly limit the remedies that a tribunal may award.[26] Similarly, pursuant to Article 1135 of NAFTA, claimants may receive only monetary damages (including interest) or restitution of property, or a combination thereof.[27]

Most arbitral rules do not restrain the power of tribunals in this respect. However, Article 54(1) of the ICSID Convention, which obliges the state parties to recognize as binding awards rendered under the Convention, limits this obligation to the enforcement of *"pecuniary* obligations."[28] During the negotiation of the ICSID Convention, some delegates favored an additional restriction on the power of ICSID tribunals to award non-pecuniary remedies, mainly because of doubts concerning enforceability.[29] The Chairman of the drafting committee, Aron Broches, stated that the provision adopted would not curtail the power of the tribunals to award non-monetary remedies, but that enforcement would be limited to monetary obligations.[30]

The power of an ICSID tribunal to award injunctive relief was raised in *Enron & Ponderosa v. Argentina*.[31] Having considered Argentina's objection that the tribunal did not have such authority, the arbitrators concluded:

> 79. An examination of the powers of international courts and tribunals to order measures concerning performance or injunction and of the ample practice that is available in this respect, leaves this Tribunal in no doubt about the fact that these powers are indeed available. The Claimants have convincingly invoked the authority of the Rainbow Warrior, where it was held:
>
>> "The authority to issue an order for the cessation or discontinuance of a wrongful act or omission results from the inherent powers of a competent tribunal which is confronted with the continuous breach of an international obligation which is in force and continues to be in force. The delivery of such an order requires, therefore, two essential conditions intimately linked, namely that the wrongful act has a continuing

---

[26] *See* 2004 U.S. Model BIT, art. 34; 2004 Canada Model BIT, art. 44. *See also* U.S.-Chile Free Trade Agreement (FTA), art. 10.25; Energy Charter Treaty (ECT), art. 26(8); North American Free Trade Agreement (NAFTA), art. 1135.

[27] NAFTA, art. 1135 ("Where a Tribunal makes a final award against a Party, the Tribunal may award, separately or in combination, only: (a) monetary damages and any applicable interest; (b) restitution of property, in which case the award shall provide that the disputing Party may pay monetary damages and any applicable interest in lieu of restitution . . .").

[28] Washington Convention, art. 54(1) (emphasis added).

[29] *See* Christoph Schreuer, *Non-Pecuniary Remedies in ICSID Arbitration*, 20(4) Arb. Int'l 325, 325 (2004).

[30] *Id. citing* Aaron Broches, 2 *History of the Convention*, 990 (1968).

[31] *Enron Corp. & Ponderosa Assets, L.P. v. Argentina*, ICSID Case No. ARB/01/3 (Award on Jurisdiction, Jan. 14, 2004).

character and that the violated rule is still in force at the time in which the order is issued."[32]

80. The same holds true under the ICSID Convention. In *Goetz v. Burundi* such a power was indeed resorted to by the Tribunal, and the fact that it was based on a settlement agreement between the parties does not deprive the decision of the Tribunal of its own legal force and standing. A scholarly opinion invoked by the Claimants is also relevant in this context, having an author concluding that it is

"... entirely possible that future cases will involve disputes arising from ongoing relationships in which awards providing for specific performance or injunctions become relevant."[33]

Apart from the limitations to enforcement that may result from applicable arbitral rules or investment treaties,[34] claimants seeking to enforce non-pecuniary awards may encounter, in the formulation of the ILC Articles, "material or legal impossibility."[35] Martin Endicott explains this problem:

Martin Endicott, *Remedies in Investor-State Arbitration: Restitution, Specific Performance and Declaratory Awards*, in New Aspects of International Investment Law 540–41 (Kahn & Wälde eds., Martinus Nijhoff Publishers 2007)

(i) *Impossibility*

Restitution will be materially impossible in situations such as where the subject-matter of the dispute has been destroyed, has irremediably deteriorated (for example, when a confiscated ship has been sunk), has perished and where it has passed into the hands of a bona fide third party. In the *Rhodope Forests* case, Bulgaria had unlawfully confiscated forests belonging to Greek nationals. Restitution was denied on the ground that the condition of the forests had changed and third parties had acquired rights over them.[36]

Whether the position of a third party will preclude restitution will depend on circumstances such as whether the third party acted in good faith at the time of acquiring the disputed rights.[37]

Legal impossibility, such as where a respondent State's constitution prevents it from annulling or amending non-federal legislation, as a limit to the claim for restitution has been recognized in several treaties on the pacific settlement of disputes.[38] Treaty

---

[32] SN: *Rainbow Warrior*, R.I.A.A., Vol. 20, 1990, 217, at 270, ¶ 114, as cited in James Crawford, *The International Law Commission's Articles on State Responsibility* (2002), at 196, note 457 and associated text . . .

[33] SN: Christoph H. Schreuer, *The ICSID Convention: A Commentary* 1126 (2001), ¶ 73 . . .

[34] *See* discussion of the Washington Convention, art. 54(1) and NAFTA, art. 1135.

[35] *See* ILC Articles, *supra* note 4, art. 35 and the commentary on restitution.

[36] SN: *Forests of Central Rhodope, in* 3 *R.I.A.A.,* 1405, 1432 (1933).

[37] SN: Crawford, *Commentary,* [*supra* note 4,] 216 [10].

[38] SN: General Act for the Pacific Settlement of Disputes (Sept. 26, 1928 & Apr. 28, 1949); German-Swiss Treaty on Arbitration and Conciliation (1921) 12 L.N.T.S., 280.

practice has been to provide for reparation in another form in such circumstances.[39] It is not recognised by the [ILC Articles] however. Under Article 32, the respondent State is not entitled to invoke the political or administrative obstacles resulting from its internal law as justification for the failure to provide full reparation....[40]

(ii) *Disproportionate burden*

Restitution is also barred where there is a grave disproportionality between the burden and the benefit, although it has been suggested that this may only be the case "if the delinquency can also be atoned by a pecuniary indemnification."[41] This bar to restitution is based on considerations of equity and reasonableness. The [ILC Articles] indicate a preference for the wishes of the injured State in any case where the balancing exercise does not clearly favour compensation over restitution. The balance will also favour the injured State in any case where the failure to provide restitution would jeopardize its political independence or economic stability.[42]

The issue of legal impossibility was raised in *LG&E v. Argentina*.[43] In that case, the claimant asked the tribunal during the damages phase of the arbitration to invite Argentina to provide an assurance that the gas regulatory framework that had been in place before the dispute arose would be restored. The tribunal rejected that proposal, on grounds that such an order would be equivalent to restitution:

> The judicial restitution required in this case would imply modification of the current legal situation by annulling or enacting legislative and administrative measures that make over the effect of the legislation in breach. The Tribunal cannot compel Argentina to do so without a sentiment of undue interference with its sovereignty. Consequently, the Tribunal arrives at the same conclusion: the need to order and quantify compensation.[44]

The tribunal also noted that Argentina had an opportunity to restore the regulatory framework after the award on liability was rendered, but had chosen not to do so. Therefore, there would be no purpose in issuing such an order.[45]

---

[39] SN: *Gray Judicial Remedies in International Law* 15, e.g., ECT, art. 26(8) ECT, European Convention on Human Rights, art. 50 (1950) provides that, if the internal law of the State involved allows only partial reparation, an injured party may claim "just satisfaction" before the European Court of Human Rights (ECHR).

[40] SN: Crawford, *Commentary*, [*supra* note 4,] 216 [8].

[41] SN: J. H. W. Verzijl, *International Law in Historical Perspective*, Pt. VI, 744 (Leyden Sijthoff 1973).

[42] SN: Crawford, *Commentary*, [*supra* note 4,] 217 [11].

[43] *LG&E v. Argentina*, ICSID Case No. ARB/02/1 (Damages Award, July 25, 2007). *LG&E* was among the cases brought against Argentina in the wake of the Argentine's financial crisis. The events that gave rise to this claim were described in Chapter XVII, p. 516 *supra* in the context of the description of *CMS v. Argentina*. *See also* pp. 157–58 *supra*.

[44] *Id.* ¶ 87.

[45] *Id.* ¶ 86.

D. Standard of Compensation

1. Standard of Compensation for Expropriation

The proper standard of compensation for expropriation is a central issue in the calculation of damages. The choice of the proper standard of compensation is crucial in assessing the amount of damages, as it "invariably affects the method for calculating the compensation that will be awarded."[46] The appropriate level of compensation for expropriation has been one of the most debated issues in international law.[47] Until the recent proliferation of BITs, developed and developing countries took opposing positions on this issue. The former advocated the Hull formula of "prompt, adequate and effective compensation," whereas the latter championed "appropriate" compensation, which for some suggested less than full or adequate compensation. The details of this debate were discussed in Chapter XVI. For purposes of this chapter, this debate has minor practical significance. In modern treaty-based investment arbitration, the governing law includes the text of the applicable treaty,[48] the majority of which contain provisions specifying the standard of compensation due to an investor whose property has been expropriated. The United States-Ecuador BIT, for example, provides:

> 1. Investments shall not be expropriated or nationalized either directly or indirectly through measures tantamount to expropriation or nationalization ("expropriation") except: for a public purpose; in a nondiscriminatory manner; *upon payment of prompt, adequate and effective compensation;* and in accordance with due process of law and the general principles of treatment provided for in Article II (3).[49]

The treaty then further defines "prompt, adequate and effective":

> Compensation shall be equivalent to the fair market value of the expropriated investment immediately before the expropriatory action was taken or became known, whichever is earlier; be calculated in a freely usable currency on the basis of the prevailing market rate of exchange at that time; be paid without delay; include interest

---

[46] Brower & Brueschke, *supra* note 23, at 473.

[47] *Id.* at 472; *Amoco Int'l Fin. Corp. v. Iran* ("[t]he rules of customary international law relating to the determination of the nature and amount of the compensation to be paid, as well as the conditions of its payment, are less well settled"). *See also* Markham Ball, *Assessing Damages in Claims by Investors Against States,* 32 ICSID Rev.-F.I.L.J. 408, 413 *et seq.* (2001).

[48] *See* Chapter IX, *supra.*

[49] *See* U.S.-Ecuador BIT, art.III(1) (1993) (emphasis added).

at a commercially reasonable rate from the date of expropriation; be fully realizable and be freely transferable.[50]

Many other investment treaties contain similar provisions.[51]

An important issue in determining the amount of compensation for expropriated property is setting the date on which valuation is to be made. Most BITs provide for the payment of the fair market value of the property before the taking became known.[52] This requires a tribunal, among other things, to fix a date for the taking, which is normally also the date for valuing the expropriated property. "The significance of identifying the date of taking lies in its bearing on the factors that may properly be taken into account in assessing the 'fair market value' of the Property. . . ."[53] Normally, events that occured after the date of taking are not considered in determining the fair market value of the property. For example, in the *Santa Elena* case the tribunal determined the date of the taking to be the date of a governmental decree issued on May 5, 1978, by which the Costa Rican government had effectively expropriated claimant's property. The tribunal then stated that:

> [i]f the relevant date were the date of this Award [i.e., 2000], then the Tribunal would have to pay regard to the factors that would today be present to the mind of a potential purchaser . . . If, on the other hand, the relevant date is 5 May 1978, factors that arose thereafter—though not necessarily subsequent statements regarding facts that existed as of that date—must be disregarded.[54]

Determination of the date of the taking is particularly difficult in indirect expropriation cases.[55] In such situations, because a combination of several actions often leads to an effective taking, the choice of the date can become somewhat arbitrary, as no single act deprives the investor of its property. Various possibilities are conceivable. At one extreme, the date of the taking may be the date of the first act in the series of acts

---

[50] *Id.*

[51] *See, e.g.,* Germany-Bangladesh BIT (1981), art. 3(2); U.K.-United Arab Emirates BIT (1992), art. 6(1); Switzerland-India BIT (1997), art. 5(1); France-Hong Kong BIT (1995), art. 5(1); Netherlands-South Africa BIT (1995), art. 6(c); NAFTA, art. 1110; ECT, art. 13. *See also* Rudolf Dolzer & Margrete Stevens, *Bilateral Investment Treaties* 109 (Martinus Nijhoff Publishers 1995).

[52] *See id.* The latter criterion (*i.e.,* valuing the property at a time before the taking becomes known) reduces the negative impact on the value of the expropriated property, such as a drop in share price once an expropriation becomes known.

[53] *Compania de Desarollo de Santa Elena, S.A. v. Costa Rica,* ICSID Case No. ARB/96/1 (Final Award of Feb. 17, 2000), ¶ 84. The date of the taking becomes especially important when there is a significant lapse of time between the taking and the date of the award, because during this time interest will accrue. Therefore, the earlier the date of the taking, the larger the amount of the award.

[54] *Id.*

[55] *See, e.g., Lauder v. Czech Republic* (UNCITRAL Arbitration under Chapter 11 of NAFTA, Final Award, Sept. 2, 2001), ¶ 200, *cited in CMS, supra* note 10, ¶ 261.

that led to expropriation.⁵⁶ Another appropriate date may be "the day when the interference has ripened into a more or less irreversible deprivation of the property rather than on the beginning date of the events."⁵⁷ Arbitral tribunals, despite the difficulty, usually identify the date of a particular state action as the valuation date.⁵⁸ Exceptions are sometimes made when the expropriatory measures are ongoing and changing over time, or where value of the expropriated property has appreciated substantially since the expropriation. This was the situtation in *ADC v. Hungary*,⁵⁹ where the tribunal observed:

> 496. The present case is almost unique among decided cases concerning the expropriation by States of foreign owned property, since the value of the investment after the date of expropriation (1 January 2002) has risen very considerably while other arbitrations that apply the *Chorzów Factory* standard all invariably involve scenarios where there has been a decline in the value of the investment after regulatory interference. It is for this reason that application of the restitution standard by various arbitration tribunals has led to use of the date of the expropriation as the date for the valuation of damages.
>
> 497. However, in the present, *sui generis*, type of case the application of the *Chorzów Factory* standard requires that the date of valuation should be the date of the Award and not the date of expropriation, since this is what is necessary to put the Claimants in the same position as if the expropriation had not been committed.⁶⁰

On this basis, the tribunal awarded the claimants compensation calculated as of the date of the award.⁶¹

The legality or illegality of the expropriation may also have an impact on the amount of compensation to be awarded. In *Chorzów Factory*, the PCIJ opined that where the state act is legal, compensation is limited to the value of the property at the moment of taking, excluding lost profits; if the state act is illegal, then lost profits may also be recoverable.⁶² The Iran-U.S. Claims Tribunal considered these issues in *Amoco v.*

---

56   W. Michael Reisman & Robert D. Sloane, *Indirect Expropriation and its Valuation in the BIT Generation*, 74 Brit. Y.B. Int'l L. 140 (2003) ("At one extreme, a tribunal could elect to set the moment of expropriation at the date of the first governmental act or omission in the series of deleterious measures that, in the aggregate, constitute the expropriation").

57   *Id.* at 140. *See also id. at* note 120, citing *Malek v. Iran*, 28 Iran-U.S. Cl. Trib. Rep. 246, ¶ 114 (citing *Int'l Technical Products Corp. v. Iran*, 9 Iran-U.S. Cl. Trib. Rep. 206, 241 *and Foremost Teheran Inc. v. Iran*, 10 Iran-U.S. Cl. Trib. Rep. 228, 249).

58   Reisman and Sloane have argued that in indirect expropriation cases, the date of the valuation need not correspond to the time of the taking. Reisman et al., *supra* note 56, at 147.

59   *ADC Affiliate Ltd. & ADC & ADMC Mgmt. Ltd. v. Republic of Hungary*, ICSID Case No. ARB/03/16 (Award of Oct. 2, 2006).

60   *Id.* ¶¶ 496–97.

61   *Id.* ¶ 499.

62   *Chorzow Factory*, *supra* note 12.

Iran,[63] which is excerpted below. In particular, Judge Brower raised the issue of whether lost profits should always constitute part of compensation for expropriated property.[64]

Amoco International Finance Co. v. Islamic Republic of Iran

Award No. 310–56–3 (July 14, 1987), 15 Iran-U.S. C.T.R. 189–289

2. The Effects of Lawfulness or Unlawfulness of Expropriation on the Standard of Compensation

189. Both Parties consider that this issue must be decided by reference to customary international law. The Tribunal agrees. Article IV, paragraph 2 of the Treaty determines the conditions that an expropriation should meet in order to be in conformity with its terms and therefore defines the standard of compensation only in case of a lawful expropriation. A nationalization in breach of the Treaty, on the other hand, would render applicable the rules relating to State responsibility, which are to be found not in the Treaty but in customary law.

190. The Claimant asserts that in case of unlawful expropriation compensation would be more than the "full equivalent" standard which applies to lawful expropriation. The Respondents argue that in case of lawful expropriation the measure of compensation must be substantially less than for a wrongful expropriation and assert that in such a case compensation is limited to the unjustified enrichment realized by the nationalizing State, with no compensation for lost profit.

191. By and large, both Parties refer to the same authorities in the discussion of their respective theses, but give them opposite interpretations. They agree that the leading case in this context is Case Concerning the Factory at Chorzów (*Germany v. Poland*), 1928 P.C.I.J., Ser. A. No. 17 (Judgment of 13 September 1928) ("*Chorzów Factory*"), decided by the Permanent Court of International Justice in 1928. The Tribunal shares this view.

---

[63] *Amoco Int'l Fin. Corp. v. Iran, supra* note 18, ¶ 196.

[64] *Id.* Concurring Opinion of Judge Brower, ¶¶ 17–18 ("In my view *Chorzów Factory* presents a simple scheme: If an expropriation is lawful, the deprived party is to be awarded damages equal to "the value of the undertaking" which it has lost, including any potential future profits, as of the date of taking; in the case of an unlawful taking, however, either the injured party is to be actually restored to enjoyment of his property, or, should this be impossible or impractical, he is to be awarded damages equal to the greater of (i) the value of the undertaking at the date of loss (again including lost profits), judged on the basis of information available as of that date, and (ii) its value (likewise including lost profits) as shown by its probable performance subsequent to the date of loss and prior to the date of the award, [*footnote omitted*], based on actual post-taking experience, plus (in either alternative) any consequential damages. Apart from the fact that this is what *Chorzów Factory* says, it is the only set of principles that will guarantee just compensation to all expropriated parties"). *See also* Brower & Brueschke, *supra* note 23, at 517 ("The Tribunal's precedents thus confirm that expected future profitability must be included in the calculation of compensation under the Treaty for a going concern"). *See also Thomas Earl Payne v. Iran*, 12 Iran-U.S. Cl. Trib. Rep. 3, *Phelps Dodge Corp.*, 19 Iran-U.S. Cl. Trib. Rep. 121.

STANDARD OF COMPENSATION

In spite of the fact that it is nearly sixty years old, this judgment is widely regarded as the most authoritative exposition of the principles applicable in this field, and is still valid today. It must be recognized, however, that its treatment of compensation is fairly complex and must be carefully analyzed.

192. Undoubtedly, the first principle established by the Court is that a clear distinction must be made between lawful and unlawful expropriations, since the rules applicable to the compensation to be paid by the expropriating State differ according to the legal characterization of the taking. Id. at 46–47. Such a principle has been recently and expressly confirmed by the celebrated AMINOIL case, also invoked by both Parties. AMINOIL, *supra*, para. 138, 21 Int'l Legal Mat'ls at 1031.

193. According to the Court in *Chorzów Factory*, an obligation of reparation of all the damages sustained by the owner of expropriated property arises from an unlawful expropriation. The rules of international law relating to international responsibility of States apply in such a case. They provide for restitutio in integrum: restitution in kind or, if impossible, its monetary equivalent. If need be, "damages for loss sustained which would not be covered by restitution" should also be awarded. See *Chorzów Factory*, *supra*, at 47. On the other hand, a lawful expropriation must give rise to "the payment of fair compensation," id. at 46, or of "the just price of what was expropriated." *Id.* at 47. Such an obligation is imposed by a specific rule of the international law of expropriation.

194. The difficulty, obviously, is in determining the practical consequences of the distinction between reparation of the damage caused by a wrongful expropriation and payment of compensation in case of lawful expropriation. The legal bases of the two concepts are totally different and, logically, the practical methods to be used in order to derive the amount due should also differ. On this question, the principles enunciated by the *Chorzów Factory* case are equally important and have not lost their validity.

195. In *Chorzów Factory* the Court dealt with the question of reparation of the damages resulting from an unlawful expropriation. The analysis of the Court was so thorough, however, and its comparisons with the reverse hypothesis so systematic, that the judgment is also illuminating in analyzing the lawful expropriation before us.

196. Restitutio is well defined by the Court. It means the restitution in kind or, if that is impossible, the payment of the monetary equivalent. In both cases the principle on which it lies is the same: "that reparation must, as far as possible, wipe out all the consequences of the illegal act and reestablish the situation which would, in all probability, have existed if this act had not been committed." *Id.* at 47. One essential consequence of this principle is that the compensation "is not necessarily limited to the value of the undertaking at the moment of dispossession" (plus interest to the day of payment). According to the Court, "this limitation would be admissible only if the Polish Government [the expropriating State] has had the right to expropriate, and if its wrongful act consisted merely in not having paid . . . the just price of what was expropriated." *Id.* This last statement is of paramount importance: It means that the compensation to be paid in case of a lawful expropriation (or of a taking which lacks only the payment of a fair compensation to be lawful) is limited to the value of the undertaking at the moment of the dispossession, i.e., "the just price of what was expropriated."

197. Obviously the value of an expropriated enterprise does not vary according to the lawfulness or the unlawfulness of the taking. This value can not depend on the legal characterization of a fact totally foreign to the economic constituents of the undertaking, namely the conduct of the expropriating State. In the traditional language of international law it equates the damnum emergens, which must be compensated in any case. Such a conclusion was already accepted by this Tribunal in Sedco Inc. and National Iranian Oil Company, Award No. ITL 59–129–3, pp. 11–12 (27 March 1986), reprinted in 25 Int'l Legal Mat'ls 629. The difference is that if the taking is lawful the value of the

undertaking at the time of the dispossession is the measure and the limit of the compensation, while if it is unlawful, this value is, or may be, only a part of the reparation to be paid. In any event, even in case of unlawful expropriation the damage actually sustained is the measure of the reparation, and there is no indication that "punitive damages" could be considered.

. . . .

3. The Standard of Compensation in Case of Lawful Expropriation

207. The standard of "just compensation" for a lawful expropriation referred to in Article IV, paragraph 2, of the Treaty is more precisely defined in the last sentence of the paragraph, which provides that "such compensation shall be in an effectively realizable form and shall represent the full equivalent of the property taken."

208. As previously noted, by the phrase "just compensation" the parties to the Treaty chose one of the various ways of describing the compensation due in case of nationalization. It is therefore apparent that the wording chosen in Article IV, paragraph 2, has as a first purpose and effect to exclude consideration of factors foreign to the value of the expropriated assets, such as excessive past profits or the rate of return on the initial investment, which have been invoked in a few cases of nationalization in order to reduce the compensation due to an amount less than the full value of these assets. Although counsel for the Respondents made some references to the rate of return on Amoco's initial investment, the Respondents do not appear to suggest that this factor should enter into the calculation of the compensation due, and no other factor of this kind was invoked.

209. "Just compensation" has generally been understood as a compensation equal to the full value of the expropriated assets. This is confirmed in the wording of Article IV, paragraph 2, which refers to "the full equivalent of the property taken." The Tribunal does not see any material difference between this phrase and the usual term of "just compensation." The Tribunal has expressed this point in the Sedco case, where it held that full compensation was the standard to be applied. See *Sedco, Inc. & Nat'l Iranian Oil Co.*, *supra*, Award No. ITL 59–129–3 at 11–13. Such a finding, however, leaves without a precise answer the difficult question of the proper method to be used in order to determine what the "full value" or "full equivalent" of the property taken means in figures. This question of method goes beyond the issue of the standard of compensation, because several methods are available and the choice between them depends on the particular circumstances of each case. This will be dealt with in the following section. . . .

2. The Standard of Compensation for Breach of Investment Treaty Obligations Other than Expropriation

While most investment treaties expressly define the level of compensation that must be paid to a qualifying foreign investor whose property is expropriated,[65] there is no equivalent treaty provision defining the proper standard of compensation due to investors harmed as a result of the breach of other treaty protections,

---

[65] See e.g., U.S.-Ecuador BIT (1993), art. III. *See also* the relevant provisions of the investment treaties cited in note 51 *supra*.

such as fair and equitable treatment or national treatment.[66] This lacuna has not prevented arbitral tribunals from devising practical and coherent approaches to the calculation of damages,[67] but they have faced a number of recurring issues. Where tribunals have found the respondent state liable for multiple breaches of a treaty, including expropriation, some have applied the standard of compensation dictated by the treaty for expropriation, on the theory that this measure provides the highest level of compensation, which makes it unnecessary to assess damages for other breaches that would yield lower levels of compensation.[68] When tribunals have found only breaches of investment treaty provisions other than expropriation, they have adopted at least two different approaches. Some have applied the standard of compensation for expropriation. This approach seems to have been used where the effect of the breach of the respective nonexpropriation standard of protection has been total or near-total deprivation of property rights, similar to that of an expropriation.[69] In *CMS v. Argentina,* for example, the tribunal found that no expropriation had occurred, but held Argentina to be in breach of other obligations under the United States-Argentina BIT, including fair and equitable treatment. With respect to the standard of fair market value compensation, the tribunal held that "[as] this standard figures prominently in respect of expropriation, it is not excluded that it might also be appropriate for breaches different from expropriation if their effect results in important long-term losses."[70]

However, a breach of the fair and equitable treatment standard or denial of national treatment may not result in a total deprivation of property rights or even in significant losses, but may lead to some diminution in the value of the investment.[71]

---

[66] See, e.g., *LG&E v. Argentina,* supra note 43, ¶ 30; *CMS v. Argentina,* supra note 10, ¶ 409; *S.D. Myers Inc. v. Canada* (UNCITRAL Arbitration, Second Partial Award, Oct. 2002), ¶ 94 [hereinafter *Myers*] ("By not identifying any particular methodology for the assessment of compensation in cases not involving expropriation, the Tribunal considers that the drafters of the NAFTA intended to leave it open to tribunals to determine a measure of compensation appropriate to the specific circumstances of the case . . ."); *MTD Equity Sdn. Bhd. & MTD Chile S.A. v. Chile,* ICSID Case No. ARB/01/7 (May 25, 2004), ¶ 238.

[67] *Myers,* supra note 66, ¶¶ 97–100.

[68] See, e.g., *Metalclad Corp. v. Mexico,* ICSID Case No. ARB(AF)/97/1 (Award of Aug. 30, 2000); *Tecnicas Medioambientales Tecmed S.A. v. The United Mexican States (Spain v. Mexico),* ICSID Case No. ARB(AF)/00/2 (2003).

[69] *Compania de Aguas del Aconquija & Vivendi v. Argentina* (Vivendi II), Award, ICSID Case No. ARB/97/3 (Award of Aug. 20, 2007), ¶¶ 8.2.8 (breaches of fair and equitable treatment and expropriation clauses "caused more or less equivalent harm").

[70] See *CMS,* supra note 10, ¶ 410. See also *Myers,* supra note 66, ¶¶ 303–19; *Pope & Talbot v. Canada* (Damages Award), ¶¶ 81–90; *Azurix v. Argentina,* ICSID Case No. ARB/03/30 (Final Award of July 14, 2006), ¶ 420 (citing *CMS v. Argentina,* ¶ 410 on the same point); and *Vivendi II,* supra note 69, ¶¶ 8.2.9–8.2.11; *LG&E,* supra note 43, ¶ 31.

[71] In *Feldman v. Mexico,* the tribunal found that the standard of fair market value was inappropriate to measure a loss accruing as a result of the breach of the national treatment standard. *Marvin Roy Feldman Karpa v. United Mexican States,* ICSID Case No. ARB(AF)/99/1 (Award), ¶ 194.

Arbitral tribunals have adopted a variety of approaches in such cases, developing case-specific methodologies, and sometimes taking into account the particular characteristics of affected rights. The starting point for this analysis has consistently been the PCIJ's decision in the *Chorzów Factory* case.[72]

Occidental v. Ecuador is a good example of such a case-specific approach. There, the tribunal found breaches of several standards of protection, including national treatment, fair and equitable treatment, and the prohibition against arbitrary impairment of investments. The claimant's request for relief, seeking reimbursement of certain value-added taxes paid on various costs, was central to the tribunal's reasoning. The tribunal did not enunciate any conceptual standard, but awarded the claimant what it sought.[73] Under the circumstances, this was deemed to be reasonable, because the requested relief was the return of precise sums of money, the amount of which was not in dispute.

In *MTD v. Chile,* the claimant invested in a housing project near Chile's capital, Santiago, after the investment promotion agency of Chile had issued a development license. Later, it was discovered that the project did not comply with local zoning regulations, and the local authorities refused to rezone the area and allow the project to continue. The investor filed an ICSID claim, and the tribunal ruled that Chile had breached its obligation to provide fair and equitable treatment. In assessing the amount of damages, the tribunal applied the *Chorzów Factory* standard, without clarifying whether it would take any particular form in a case involving breach of fair and equitable treatment:[74]

> The Tribunal first notes that the BIT provides for the standard of compensation applicable to expropriation, "prompt, adequate and effective" (Article 4(c)). It does not provide what this standard should be in the case of compensation for breaches of the BIT on other grounds. The Claimants have proposed the classic standard enounced by the Permanent Court of Justice in the *Factory at Chorzów*: compensation should "wipe out all the consequences of the illegal act and re-establish the situation which would, in all probability, have existed if that had not been committed." The Respondent has not objected to the application of this standard and no differentiation has been made about the standard of compensation in relation to the grounds on which it is justified. Therefore, the Tribunal will apply the standard of compensation proposed by the Claimants to the extent of the damages awarded.[75]

---

[72] See, e.g., *CMS, supra* note 10, ¶ 400; *Occidental Exploration & Prod. Co. v. Ecuador,* London Court of International Arbitration (LCIA) Case No. UN3467 (U.S.-Ecuador BIT), (Final Award of July 1, 2004), ¶ 210; *Myers, supra* note 66 (First Partial Award of Nov. 13, 2000), ¶ 311; *MTD, supra* note 66, ¶ 238; *Vivendi II, supra* note 69, ¶ 8.2.4; *LG&E, supra* note 43, ¶ 31. Note that in all of these awards the tribunals did not find that expropriation had taken place, but held that the respondent state had violated the standard of fair and equitable treatment or national treatment.

[73] Borzu Sabahi, *The Calculation of Damages in International Investment Law,* in *New Aspects of International Investment Law* 587–88 (Kahn & Wälde eds., Martinus Nijhoff Publishers 2007).

[74] See *MTD, supra* note 66, ¶ 238.

[75] *Id.* (Source notes omitted.)

The *MTD* tribunal then calculated the claimant's actual investment in the project, minus amounts that had been invested prior to governmental approval and those invested after the project had been blocked by the zoning regulation.[76] The tribunal also deducted the "residual value of the investment and the damages that can be attributed to business risk . . ."[77] from the aggregate amount.

In *LG&E v. Argentina*,[78] the tribunal held that Argentina had breached the fair and equitable treatment requirement of the Argentina-United States BIT, but had not expropriated the claimant's investment. Distinguishing the earlier cases of *CMS* and *Azurix,* it ruled that full compensation, which was the applicable standard of expropriation cases, was not appropriate in the case before it. The arbitrators instead based compensation on the dividends that the claimants would have received had it not been for the Argentine government's alteration of the legal regime governing the gas transportation industry. Further, because the tribunal accepted Argentina's defense that a state of necessity existed (at least for a limited period of time) as a result of the financial crisis, it did not award damages while the economic crisis was at its worst.

LG&E v. Argentina

ICSID Case No. ARB/02/1 (Damages Award, July 25, 2007) (source notes omitted)

33. At the heart of the Claimants' argument lies the valuation of their loss by reference to the fair market value [(FMV)] of that loss. Respondent do[es] not oppose the use of the FMV, but rather, the method for its estimation.

34. To determine the FMV of their loss, the Claimants establish the value of the gas distribution companies (and of LG&E's investment using the percentage of shares owned) based on stock price and large share purchase values. The only difference in the valuation for the expropriation claim and the other claims is in the subtraction of the residual value in the later case. Argentina proposes DCF as the method to calculate such value but does not conduct a calculation.

35. In the Tribunal's view, this type of valuation is appropriate in cases of expropriation in which the claimants have lost the title to their investment or when interference with property rights has led to a loss equivalent to the total loss of investment. However, this is not the case. The Tribunal rejected the claim for indirect expropriation put forward by the Claimants on the basis that Argentina's measures:

---

[76] *Id.* ¶ 239–40.
[77] *Id.* ¶ 241.
[78] *LG&E, supra* note 43. The facts underlying the case were explained in Chapters VII and XV *supra,* at pp. 157–58 and 516, respectively.

> "did not deprive the investors of the right to enjoy their investment [...] the true interests at stake here are the investments' asset base, the value of which has rebounded since the economic crisis of December 2001 and 2002 [...] the effect of the Argentine State's actions has not been permanent on the value of the Claimants' shares, and Claimants' investment has not ceased to exist."
>
> 36. For the Tribunal, compensation in this case cannot be determined by the impact on the asset value; it does not reflect the actual damage incurred by Claimants. The measure of compensation has to be different.

The *LG&E* tribunal rejected both parties' suggested methods for calculating damages, and adopted a third method, which after taking into account the parties' comments, was encapsulated in the following formula:

> The Tribunal's method to quantify compensation calculates the dividends that Claimants would have received but for Argentina's breaches and subtracts from such dividends those that were actually received by Claimants. Losses during the State of Necessity period are subsequently subtracted. The method was adjusted to account for the Claimants' comments on the methodological shortcomings and the verification of the dividend figures and the [Producer Price Index (PPI)] data. Compound interest at the rate of six-month U.S. Treasury bills will be added.[79]

The concept of legitimate expectations may also play a role in determining the standard of compensation. Thomas Wälde, in a dissenting opinion in *Thunderbird v. Mexico*,[80] discussed this issue in detail. In *Thunderbird v. Mexico,* the investor alleged that it had detrimentally relied on a letter issued by Mexican authorities in response to the investor's inquiry as to the legality of its proposed gaming activities in Mexico, and as a result, its legitimate expectations had been frustrated. The majority of the tribunal dismissed the case in its entirety, mainly because the investor in its inquiry to the Mexican authorities had not correctly disclosed the character of the gaming machines that it intended to operate there. Professor Wälde, however, disagreed with the majority regarding the application of the standard of legitimate expectations to the facts. In examining the issue of compensation for the frustration of the investor's legitimate expectations, he opined that "a 'legitimate expectation' can only ... lead to compensation if there was 'detrimental reliance,' i.e., a link between the expectation and investment made—a principle which in American takings law has led to the notion of 'investment-backed expectations.'"[81] Professor Wälde then went on to compare damages due in case of the frustration of an investor's legitimate expectations with the compensation that should be paid in case of the cancellation of a concession contract:

> But a legitimate expectation under Art. 1105 of the NAFTA [which guarantees fair and equitable treatment] is a much weaker legal position than a long-term concession

---

[79] *Id.* ¶ 106.

[80] *Thunderbird, supra* note 6.

[81] *Id.* ¶ 119.

contract. As all precedents show, governments retain flexibility to reverse a legitimate expectation in a reasonable way with transitional measures. A comfort letter may create a legally protected legitimate expectation even if it is not crystal-clear; but it is by far not the equal of a proper long-term concession contract. Even if we had a long-term, legally valid concession contract, one would have to take into account that the initial high profitability stemming from a successful start-up operation of a newcomer in a hitherto largely closed market is likely to give way as other competitors move in and thus, in the normal process of economic logic, depress the profitability. In cases of legitimate expectation (detrimental reliance), at most the government owes the investor the "negative interest," i.e., the expenditure the investor has undertaken with confidence in the reliability of the government position communicated. But it does not give a claim to the "positive interest," i.e., to be placed into a situation as if the government had committed in the form of a valid long-term concession contract.[82]

It should be noted that a few arbitration awards have provided guidance regarding the award of damages in national treatment cases.[83] No uniform methodology for calculating compensation has emerged, however.[84]

E. Valuation of Assets

The proper valuation of assets is crucial in determining the quantum of damages in investment arbitration. Indeed, the choice of valuation methodology may ultimately be more significant than the applicable legal standard. The protagonists at this stage of arbitration proceedings may not so much be lawyers as accountants and financial experts.[85] They proffer their theories about what method should be used to value the assets, and the tribunal then determines whether to accept those methods or not. A ribunal's acceptance of a method does not, however, guarantee that it will be applied in the way that a

---

[82] See *Thunderbird* (Separate Opinion), *supra* note 6, ¶ 121. For a detailed analysis of legitimate expectations in the context of compensation for breach of a long-term contract, *see Aminoil v. Kuwait*, 21 I.L.M. 976 (1982). There, the tribunal was to determine the compensation due to Aminoil for the cancellation of its oil concession. The tribunal opined that "Both Parties to the present litigation have invoked the notion of 'legitimate expectations' for deciding on compensation. That formula is well-advised, and justifiably brings to mind the fact that, with reference to every long-term contract, especially such as involve an important investment, there must necessarily be economic calculations, and the weighing-up of rights and obligations, of chances and risks, constituting the contractual equilibrium cannot be neglected—neither when it is a question of proceeding to necessary adaptations during the course of the contract, nor when it is a question of awarding compensation. It is in this fundamental equilibrium that the very essence of the contract consists." *Id.* ¶ 148. The tribunal went on to calculate damages based on the claimant's reasonable rate of return on its investment. *Id.* ¶ 160.

[83] See, e.g., *S.D. Myers, Inc. v. Canada* (First Partial Award, Nov. 13, 2000), ¶ 309; and *Feldman v. Mexico, supra* note 71.

[84] See Wälde & Sabahi, *supra* note 23, at 1084.

[85] Ball, *supra* note 47, at 417–18.

party has suggested. Tribunals often adjust the amounts that a method yields to satisfy the rules of law or equity that they deem applicable.[86]

There are a number of general approaches to determining the value of an asset. One of the most frequently cited is based on the fair market value of the enterprise affected.[87] Fair market value has been defined as "the price that a willing buyer would have paid a willing seller for the asset on the date of the taking in circumstances in which each had good information, each desired to maximize his financial gain, and neither was under duress or threat."[88] Tribunals may consider any of a number of factors in assessing fair market value.[89] One is the enterprise's share price on the stock market before the illicit actions led to the depreciation of the shares' value.[90] If the enterprise's shares are not traded on a public stock market, or if the given exchange is too illiquid to provide accurate indicators of asset value, a tribunal may try to identify a private sale of a comparable enterprise within the same business sector and estimate the price by analogy.[91] If there was any recent offer to acquire a stake in the injured enterprise, the tribunal may use that price as the starting point for its determination of value. In *CME v. Czech Republic,* for instance, the tribunal relied on just such an offer as the starting point of its analysis.[92]

---

[86] *See, e.g., CMS, supra* note 10, ¶ 456. *See also Sedco Inc. v. Iran,* 21 Iran-.U.S. Cl. Trib. Rep. 31, ¶¶ 59–63; *Himpurna California Energy Ltd. v. Pt. Perusahaan Listruik Negara* (UNCITRAL Arbitration), 14(12) Mealey's Int'l Arb. Rep. 12/99 A-1 (1999), ¶¶ 519–20 [hereinafter *Himpurna*].

[87] The fair market value of an enterprise may differ depending on whether it is a going concern—i.e., it has reached profitability and has the power to generate cash—or it is a new company with an uncertain prospect of profitability. *See* pp. 587–88 *infra*. On fair market value see most recently I. Marboe, *Compensation and Damages in International Law: Limits of Fair Market Value,* 7(5) J.W.I.T. 723 (2007).

[88] P. Friedland & E. Wong, *Measuring Damages for the Deprivation of Income-Producing Assets: ICSID Case Studies,* 6 ICSID Rev.-F.I.L.J. 400, 404 (1991).

[89] Business valuators usually compare and reconcile the result of valuations based on these indicators. *IVSC General Valuation Concepts and Principles,* ¶ 9.2.1 (International Valuation Standards, 7th ed., 2005) cited in Mark Kantor, *Valuation for Arbitrators: Uses and Limits of Income-Based Valuation Methods,* 4(6) TDM 2 (2007).

[90] *Id.*

[91] *See, e.g., Sedco Inc. v. Iran,* 15 Iran-U.S. Cl. Trib. 23, 27–8 *cited in* Brower & Brueschke, *supra* note 23, at 596–97 (the tribunal considered the evidence of the price paid for the sale of comparable oil rigs, with the caveat that the evidence produced related to a "comparable" sale, meaning that substantial justification was required to prove its relevance). *See also* Ball, *supra* note 47, at 418; W. C. Lieblich, *Determining the Economic Value of Expropriated Income-Producing Property in International Arbitrations,* 8 J. Int'l Arb. 59, 62 (1991).

[92] *CME, supra* note 20, ¶ 564 ("... the SBS transaction entered into between CME Media Ltd and SBS gives an objective view of the FMV[(fair market value)] of CNTS [(the expropriated company)] in Feb./Mar. 1999 by a third party purchase on the basis of arms-length negotiations"). *See also Sola Tiles, Inc. v. Iran,* 14 Iran-U.S. Cl. Trib. Rep. 223 (where the tribunal took into account the estimations by two potential buyers of the company as the start point of analysis).

Where no such benchmarks are available, such as where the enterprise to be valued is unique,[93] assessment based on comparables is obviously impossible. In any event, very often tribunals look to other accounting and financial methods of valuation to assess the value of an enterprise or property rights. The following excerpt provides a summary of some of the leading methodological approaches.

Paul D. Friedland & Eleanor Wong, *Measuring Damages for the Deprivation of Income-Producing Assets: ICSID Case Studies*, 6 ICSID Rev.-F.I.L.J. 400, 405–08 (1991)

1. Book Value Methods

As used in the context of valuing assets, book value means the difference between a company's assets and liabilities as recorded on its financial statements, or the amount at which the expropriated tangible asset appears on the balance sheet in accordance with generally accepted accounting principles. Book value has been viewed as a means of returning to the former owner of expropriated property his investment in the property. It is the amount that remains after deducting the liabilities from the assets of a company in the amounts that such items appear on the company's book of accounts and is usually referred to in accounting terms as owner's equity.

The Book Value Method has usually been advanced as an appropriate method of valuing an asset when the asset is an enterprise or tangible asset of such enterprise. Where the asset "taken" is a contract right, such as when the state revokes or repudiates an agreement or license, the Book Value Method is less obviously applicable and is generally not used.

Commentators have criticized the use of the Book Value Method to value expropriated enterprises. Balance sheets do not measure the ability of a firm's assets to generate cash. They therefore do not measure the assets' economic value. More particularly, the Book Value Method, based on balance sheet figures, fails to reflect the economic value of the firm or assets for the following reasons. First, assets are recorded on the balance sheet at their historical cost, which may diverge considerably from their current cost. The longer the lapse between the time the asset was purchased and the date of the balance sheet, the less realistic is the historical cost of the asset as a measure of such asset's current value. Furthermore, identical assets may have entirely different book values because they were purchased at different prices. Second, assets may be depreciated for accounting purposes at rates which may bear little relationship to the reduction in their economic productivity, and their book value is their depreciated historical cost. Third, the balance sheet fails to reflect certain intangible assets and other important elements of an enterprise, such as contractual rights, management skills, technical expertise, and relationships with customers and suppliers, sometimes called "goodwill," which may contribute importantly to its success. Fourth, assets and other elements of enterprise economically productive principally when used as part of an integrated whole. It is often inappropriate to attempt to determine a business's value by deriving a value for each asset or element separately, and then adding them together. The whole may be of greater value than the sum of its parts.[94]

---

[93] Lieblich, *supra* note 91, at 62.

[94] SN: For examples of the application of this method *see Oil Fields of Texas v. Iran*, 12 Iran-U.S. C. Trib. Rep. 308 *cited in* Brower & Brueschke, *supra* note 23, at 601.

2. Replacement Value Method

The Replacement Value Method measures the value of an expropriated going concern enterprise, based on the amount of cash that would be required to purchase the individual assets that have been expropriated as of the date of expropriation. The method therefore implicitly assumes that the asset taken is replaceable in its entirety. To the extent that the investor is able to purchase an asset identical to the one taken and, by re-employing the new asset, use it to generate the cash flows which he would have received from the asset taken, the Replacement Value Method would yield a figure which accurately values that asset taken. However, if the assumption of replaceability is false, use of the Replacement Value Method would fail to return to an investor the value of his asset. In the context of the taking of long-term contracts or investments in local enterprises, the assumption of replaceability breaks down into several respects. First, there may be unique features to the investor's asset which cannot be reproduced. Thus, for example, even if the investor received a sum of money sufficient to re-establish a mining operation of which he was deprived, that money may not fully reflect the value of his loss if there are no comparable mining opportunities in which the investor could re-invest the money received. Second, it will seldom be the case that individual discrete assets are taken by the State. Thus although the Replacement Value Method avoids some of the problems raised by the use of historical cost figures in the Book Value Method, it does not reflect the greater value which the individual assets may have together in an enterprise.[95]

3. Liquidation Value Method

As its name implies, the Liquidation Value Method is most appropriately applied when the enterprise to be valued demonstrates lack of profitability. The Liquidation Value Method values such an enterprise as the sum of the amounts at which the individual assets comprising the enterprise could be sold less any liabilities which the enterprise might have to meet. In fact, the Liquidation Value Method may be viewed as a specific application of the DCF Method. If an owner of an unprofitable enterprise could realize a greater sum from the sale of the individual assets comprising the enterprise than its continued operation, assuming rational economic behavior, such owner would liquidate rather than continue to operate the enterprise. The cash flow which such an enterprise could be expected to generate would therefore simply be the price of each asset comprising the enterprise when sold off. No discount rate would need to be applied to the cash flow since one would assume that the sale of assets would take place in the immediate future. The significant difference between the Liquidation Value Method and the Book Value Method is that the former uses the sales price of individual assets at the date of the taking while the latter uses historical acquisition cost figures.

4. DCF Method (Discounted Cash Flow Method)

The DCF method values an income-producing asset by estimating the cash flow which the asset would be expected to generate over the course of its life, and then discounting that cash flow by a factor which reflects the time value of money and the risk associated with such cash flow. It involves first calculating the cash receipts expected in each future

---

[95] SN: *See, e.g.,* Brower & Brueschke, *supra* note [23], at 565, citing *Thomas Earl Payne v. Iran*, 12 Iran-U.S. Cl. Trib. Rep. 3.

year, then subtracting that year's expected cash expenditure. The result is the net cash flow for the year. Because cash to be received in the future is worth less than the same amount of cash received today, the net cash flow for each future year is discounted to determine its value on the valuation date, which is usually referred to as its "present value" as of that date. This discounting is accomplished through the application of a discount rate which reflects the time value of money, expected inflation and any risk attached to the cash flows. The discount rate is usually measured by examining the rate of return available in the market on alternative investments having risk comparable to that of the asset or enterprise being valued. The sum of the present values of the net cash flows for each of the future years is the value of the asset or enterprise as determined by the DCF method.

In the business and academic communities, the DCF Method is frequently regarded as the most appropriate method of valuing an income-producing asset because it recognizes that the economic value of the asset to its owner is a function of the cash which such asset can be expected to produce in the future.

The DCF Method is also a useful and flexible tool. It can be adapted to value different kinds of income producing assets with different abilities to generate cash at different times and different lives. Through the risk factor in the discount rate, the DCF Method also explicitly recognizes the uncertainty which is inherent in valuing an income-producing asset. While opponents of the DCF Method have charted that it is speculative, the DCF Method in fact has the advantage of forcing the parties to articulate the various factors which enter into their calculations and, where some individual items are too speculative to properly constitute damages, they may be excluded on an item by item basis. The DCF Method is merely a valuation took. The final determination of damages obtained by its use it will naturally depend on the figures which are plugged into the DCF formula.[96]

F. Valuation of Enterprises or Projects That Have Not Become Profitable

In valuing enterprises or projects, tribunals have frequently limited the amount of damages to the actual value of investment-related expenditures, excluding any consideration of future profitability as an element of value.[97] In modern economics, the value of an enterprise that has an established history of profitability, that is, a going-concern, is determined on the basis of its ability to generate cash flows to equity holders. A start-up enterprise with no track record of

---

[96] *See, e.g., Himpurna, supra* note 86. *See also Starret Housing Corp. v. Iran,* 16 Iran-U.S. Cl. Trib. Rep. 112 (1987).

[97] *See, e.g., PSEG Global Inc. & Konya Ilgin Elektrik Üretim ve Ticaret Ltd. Srketi v. Turkey,* ICSID Case No. ARB/01/10 (Award of Jan. 19, 2007), ¶¶ 310–15; *Autopista Concesionada de Venezuela, C.A. v. Venezuela,* ICSID Case No. ARB/00/5 (Award of Sept. 23, 2003), ¶ 351 [hereinafter *Aucoven*]; *Metalclad, supra* note 68; *Asian Agric. Prod. v. Sri Lanka* (Award of June 27, 1990), *in* 4 ICSID Rep., at 245, 292–293; *Am. Mfg. & Trading v. Republic of Zaire,* ICSID Case No. ARB/93/1 (Award of Feb. 21, 1997), ¶ 7.14; United Nations Compensation Commission (U.N.C.C.) Governing Council (G.C.) Decision 9, U.N.C.C. G.C., Resumed 4th Sess., U.N. Doc. S/AC.26/1992/9 (1992).

profitability may not always be subject to valuation on the basis of the same criterion. A new enterprise's profitability prospects may be so uncertain that factoring them into the value of the enterprise would be speculative and inappropriate. The award of the tribunal in the damages phase of the *Metalclad* case is illustrative in this regard. The tribunal awarded only the value of the investment expenditures, because it considered that Metalclad had insufficient history of operations and profits to quantify them with any precision.[98]

Metalclad Corp. v. United Mexican States (Final Award)

Metalclad Corp. v. Mexico

ICSID Case No. ARB(AF)/97/1 (Award of Aug. 30, 2000)

119. Normally, the fair market value of a going concern which has a history of profitable operation may be based on an estimate of future profits subject to a discounted cash flow analysis. *Benvenuti and Bonfant v. The Government of the People's Republic of Congo*, 1 ICSID Reports 330; 21 I.L.M. 758; *AGIP SpA v. the Government of the People's Republic of Congo*, 3 ICSID Reports 306; 21 I.L.M. 737.

120. However, where the enterprise has not operated for a sufficiently long time to establish a performance record or where it has failed to make a profit, future profits cannot be used to determine going concern or fair market value. In *Sola Tiles, Inc. v. Iran* (1987) (14 Iran-U.S.C.T.R. 224, 240–42; 83 I.LR 460, 480–81, the Iran-U.S. Claims Tribunal pointed to the importance in relation to a company's value of "its business reputation and the relationship it has established with its suppliers and customers." Similarly, in *Asian Agricultural Products v. Sri Lanka* (4 ICSID Reports 246 (1990) at 292), another ICSID Tribunal observed, in dealing with the comparable problem of the assessment of the value of good will, that its ascertainment "requires the prior presence on the market for at least two or three years, which is the minimum period needed in order to establish continuing business connections."

121. The Tribunal agrees with Mexico that a discounted cash flow analysis is inappropriate in the present case because the landfill was never operative and any award based on future profits would be wholly speculative.

122. Rather, the Tribunal agrees with the parties that fair market value is best arrived at in this case by reference to Metalclad's actual investment in the project. Thus, in *Phelps Dodge Corp. v. Iran* (10 Iran-U.S.C.T.R. 121 (1986)), the Iran-US. Claims Tribunal concluded that the value of the expropriated property was the value of claimant's investment in that property. In reaching this conclusion, the Tribunal considered that the property's future profits were so dependent on as yet unobtained preferential treatment from the government that any prediction would be purely speculative, (*Id.* at 132–33). Similarly, in the Biloune case (see above), the Tribunal concluded that the value of the expropriated property was the value of the claimant's investment in that property. While the Tribunal recognized the validity of the

---

[98] See also *PSEG, supra* note 97.

principle that lost profits should be considered in the valuation of expropriated property, the Tribunal did not award lost profits because the claimants could not provide any realistic estimate of them. In that case, as in the present one, the expropriation occurred when the project was not yet in operation and had yet to generate revenue. (95 I.L.R, at 228–229). The award to Metalclad of the cost of its investment in the landfill is consistent with the principles set forth in *Chorzów Factory* (Claim for Indemnity (Merits)), *Germany v. Poland*, P.C.I.J., Series A., No. V (1928) at p. 47, namely, that where the state has acted contrary to its obligations, any award to the claimant should as far as is possible, wipe out all the consequences of the illegal act and reestablish the situation which would in all probability have existed if that act had not been committed (the status quo ante).

123. Metalclad asserts that it invested $20,474,528.00 in the landfill project, basing its value on its United States Federal Income Tax Returns and Auditors' Workpapers of Capitalized Costs for the Landfill reflected in a table marked Schedule A and produced by Metalclad . . . in the course of document discovery. The calculations include landfill costs Metalclad claims to have incurred from 1991 through 1996 for expenses categorized as the COTERIN acquisition, personnel, insurance, travel and living, telephone, accounting and legal, consulting, interest, office, property, plant and equipment, including $328,167.00 for "other."

124. Mexico challenges the correctness of these calculations on several grounds, of which one is the lack of supporting documentation for each expense item claimed. However, the Tribunal finds that the tax filings of Metalclad, together with the independent audit documents supporting those tax filings, are to be accorded substantial evidential weight and that difficulties in verifying expense items due to incomplete files do not necessarily render the expenses claimed fundamentally erroneous, See Biloune, 35 I.L.R. at 223–24.

125. The Tribunal agrees, however, with Mexico's position that costs incurred prior to the year in which Metalclad purchased COTERIN are too far removed from the investment for which damages are claimed. The Tribunal will reduce the Award by the amount of the costs claimed for 1991 and 1992.

In some breach of contract cases, as discussed below, arbitral tribunals have calculated damages taking future cash flows into account, even where the project in question had no established record of profits.[99]

G. Awarding Lost Profits for Breach of Contract

According to most commentators, breach of a contract generally implicates an obligation of the breaching party to compensate the innocent party for both the amount expended in performance of the contract and for the profits that the innocent party would have earned during the life of the contract.[100] This formulation has

---

[99] *See, e.g., Karaha Bodas Co. v. Pertamina*, 16(3) Mealey's Int'l Arb. Rep., at 3/01 (2001); and *Himpurna, supra* note 86. In both cases the tribunals awarded lost profits for unfinished projects. The difference between their approach, however, could be attributed to the existence of "take or pay" clauses in the underlying contracts, which shifted the risk of failure of the project in each case to the government. *See* Sabahi, *supra* note 73, at 570.

[100] *See generally* G. H. Treitel, *Remedies for Breach of Contract: A Comparative Account* 84 *et seq.* (Oxford University Press 1988).

its roots in Roman law: The first element of damages is traditionally referred to as *damnum emergens;* the second is called *lucrum cessans.*[101] Calculation of the amount of *damnum emergens* is not usually controversial, as it does not involve contemplation of any counter-factual scenario.[102] Calculation of the amount of the *lucrum cessans,* however, often becomes the epicenter of the parties' and their damages experts' battle, especially when the business in question is relatively new, without a substantial history of profitability, but there is a long-term contract[103] that requires calculating profits over a long period of time. The general principle in awarding lost profits is that they must be reasonably certain and not speculative.[104]

Below are excerpts from the *Himpurna* case, a summary of the discussion of damages in the *Karaha Bodas* case, and an excerpt of a critique of the *Karaha Bodas* award by Prof. Louis Wells. These texts shed light on various aspects of awarding lost profits. Himpurna and Karaha Bodas were both independent power producers in Indonesia, both of which had entered into long-term "take or pay" contracts to generate and supply electricity. Both companies commenced arbitration against the government and its respective agencies as a result of the measures taken by the Indonesian government during the Asian financial crisis of the late 1990s.[105]

The Himpurna claim was brought to arbitration under an Energy Sales Contract (ESC) signed between the parties on December 2, 1994. Under the ESC, PLN (the Indonesian power utility) was to buy electricity on a "delivered or made available" basis from a geothermal project developed by the claimant in Java. PLN had to pay the price in U.S. dollars. But when the claimant issued its first invoice on March 1, 1998, PLN refused to fulfill its obligation because of the Asian financial crisis of 1997–1998. Indeed, a Presidential Decree issued on January 1998 had postponed

---

[101] Wälde and Sabahi have questioned the appropriateness of this formula for measuring losses suffered as a result of the breach of an investment contract: "The damnum emergens/lucrum cessans combination needs to be seen as arising in a time when valuation was mainly backwards/historic and based on the accounting value of individual items of property. That did not represent market value properly as the combination of all items—the package value—and the ability to make profits was not taken into account. The lucrum cessans add-on was therefore meant, at least until payment of a judgement, to compensate for the short-comings of a purely historic and cost-based focus on individual property items. Insofar, it made perfect sense and was legitimate. It seems that (without further analysis into the history of the concept) it envisaged actions like damage to a workshop; compensation had then to enable the owner to repair and replace the workshop, but also pay the profits he or she would have made until the workshop was operating again." Wälde & Sabahi, *supra* note 23, at 20.

[102] There may, however, be difficulties of proof if records were lost or are in the possession of a hostile host state. *See, e.g., Biloune & Marine Drive Complex v. Ghana* (Award of June 30, 1990), *reprinted in* 19 Y.B. Comm. Arb. 11 (1994).

[103] *See also* discussion regarding the calculation of the value of an enterprise or project that has not become profitable at pp. 587 *et seq. supra.*

[104] *See also* authorities cited in *supra* note 97.

[105] Although not treaty arbitrations, both cases involved compensation-related questions similar to those that tribunals typically confront in such arbitrations.

the project indefinitely. The impasse remained unresolved and the claimant initiated arbitration proceedings on August 14, 1998. The tribunal ultimately ruled that PLN had breached its obligations under the contract, and the excerpt below demonstrates the tribunal's approach to calculation of damages for breach of the ESC.

Himpurna California Energy Ltd. (Bermuda) v. Pt. (Persero) Perusahan Listruik Negara (Indonesia)

14(12) Mealey's Int'l Arb. Rep. 12/99, A1 (1999)

438. In addition to asking for an award in the amount of unpaid invoices, the Claimant proceeds conventionally to quantify its damages under two headings, reflecting wasted costs and lost profits, respectively. The former, traditionally referred to as *damnum emergens,* represents the aggregate of what the claimant lists as "capital invested and expended;" to this amount, the Claimant seeks to add interest. The latter, traditionally spoken of as *lucrum cessans,* assigns a present value to the expected future revenue stream; the nominal amounts are thus decreased by applying two discount rates: one reflecting the time value of money (i.e., the notion that a dollar to be received in the future is worth less than a dollar received today), the other a risk premium.

. . . .

441. In this case as in so many others, it is impossible to establish damages as a matter of scientific certainty. This does not, however, impede the course of justice. "It is well settled that the fact that damages cannot be settled with certainty is no reason not to award damages when a loss has been incurred."[106] Approximations are inevitable. Moreover, considerations of fairness enter into the picture, to be assessed—inevitably— by reference to particular circumstances. The fact that the Arbitral Tribunal is influenced in this respect by equitable factors does not mean that it shirks the discipline of deciding on the basis of legal obligations. The *Sapphire* award was based on "general principles of law" but nevertheless decided *ex aequo et bono* when assessing damages. And as the *Aminoil* award held: "It is well known that any estimate in purely monetary terms of amounts intended to express the value of an asset, of an undertaking, of a contract, or of services rendered, must take equitable principles into account."

442. The *Sapphire* and *Aminoil* awards were on the firm footing of significant international precedents. The International Court of Justice [ICJ] in 1956 upheld a complaint against the judgment of an administrative tribunal which had awarded damages *ex aequo et bono,* finding no intent "to depart from principles of law" but rather the consequence of the fact that "the precise determination of the actual amount to be awarded could not be based on any specific rule of law." The ICJ made the point even more limpidly in its judgment in the *North Sea Continental Shelf* case in 1969: ". . . in short, it is not a question of applying equity simply as a matter of abstract justice, but of applying a rule of law which itself requires the application of equitable principles."

443. With respect to the evaluation of financial data, some introductory observations of a general nature may serve to clarify the Arbitral Tribunal's approach.

---

[106] *SPP v. Arab Republic of Egypt* (ICSID Award of May 20, 1992), 19 I.C.C.A. Y.B. 84 (1994).

444. When a DCF method for evaluating damages in the context of a contractual breach is followed, any comparisons with precedents involving the evaluation of expropriated business ventures must be made with great care. In the latter situation, there is generally no basis to apply the *contractual* reliance damages (damnum emergens), but only the expectancy damages (lucrum cessans). An undertaking has been expropriated; the prejudice suffered by its former owner is simply the worth of the venture as a going concern. That worth is crystallised in an analysis which discounts the future revenue stream of the enterprise to establish its present value. Leaving aside special considerations justifying higher recovery in the case of *wrongful* expropriation, there is no separate evaluation of sunk costs, whether or not represented by physical assets. That the claimant has been dispossessed of the walls and machinery of a factory does not lead to a separate recovery on that account. Had there been no expropriation, past investments would have been recovered through subsequent revenues. Since those revenues are fully accounted for in the DCF going-concern evaluation, an award of lost investment as well would be an unacceptable double recovery.

445. In contractual cases such as this, it is usual that claimants seek recoupment of their entire investment as a discrete element of compensation. Claimants are on solid grounds when they ask to be reimbursed monies they have actually spent in reliance on the contract; recovery of lost future profits is less certain. The value of the asset taken in an expropriation case may be higher or lower than the amounts the claimant expended in developing the asset. (Positive subsequent developments such as improved market conditions, or successful exploration campaigns, may have resulted in a higher value; negative developments such as failed exploration campaigns, or a fall in price, may have had the opposite effect.) In the case of a breach of contract, the wasted cost is what the claimant has spent in reliance on the agreement, without reference to how judicious or providential those expenditures turned out to be. . . .

446. On this footing, however, the quantification of lost profits must result in a lower amount to avoid double counting. This is so because future net cash flow generally includes all the amortization of revenue stream when also claiming recoupment of all investments is wanting to have your cake and eat it too. If the DCF method is applied in a contractual scenario to measure nothing but net cash flows (thus excluding the accrual accounting notion of "income" which may cover non-cash items such as depreciation), there is no room for recovery of wasted costs. In other words, when the victim of a breach of contract seeks recovery of sunken costs, confident that it is entitled to its damnum, it may go on to seek lost profits only with the proviso that its computations reduce future net cash flows by allowing a proper measure of amortization. . . .

In *Karaha Bodas,* after finding that Pertamina, the Indonesian national oil company, breached its contract with Karaha Bodas, a Cayman Islands company, a tribunal awarded Karaha Bodas US$111.1 million in lost expenditures and US$150 million in lost profits.[106a] Under the contract at issue, Karaha Bodas was to develop geothermal energy in the project area and to build generating facilities.[107] After the Government of Indonesia suspended the project during the Asian financial crisis of

---

[106a] *Karaha Bodas Co. v. Pertamina, supra* note 99.

[107] *Id.* ¶ 3.

1997–1998, Karaha Bodas filed for arbitration, claiming that Pertamina had assumed the risk of such decrees under the contract, and that such decrees were thus not an excuse for Pertamina's nonperformance.[108] The tribunal decided that Pertamina could not rely on the decrees as an excuse for nonperformance and was therefore liable to Karaha Bodas for damages.[109]

To compensate for its lost expenditures, Karaha Bodas sought damages based on its capital investment (US$94.6 million) plus a rate of return of between 15 percent and 16 percent.[110] In response, Pertamina argued that Karaha Bodas had assumed the risk that it would not be able to recoup its expenses when it entered into the contract, and that the investments it had made were wasteful.[111] The tribunal ultimately agreed with Karaha Bodas that as the non-breaching party, it was entitled to recover the value of its initial investment.[112] However, the tribunal decided that the appropriate rate of return to award on that investment was a "risk-free rate" that represented "the least non-speculative yield that a prudent person could have earned by placing the amount in question at a secured type of investment."[113] Using a "risk-free rate" of 5.8 percent, the tribunal ordered Pertamina to pay Karaha Bodas US$111.1 million as damages for *damnum emergens*.[114]

Karaha Bodas also requested compensation for lost profits of US$512.5 million, relying on projected cash flows over the thirty-year period of the project.[115] In response, Pertamina maintained that Karaha Bodas could not have obtained financing to complete the project, and therefore the company could not prove that it was ready, willing, and able to perform the contract.[116] Furthermore, Pertamina argued that Karaha Bodas' calculation of lost profits was based on a suspect estimate of geothermal reserves, and that the project could not have generated the volume of electricity that Karaha Bodas projected.[117] The tribunal found that lost profits were a proper component of damages, but that:

> as in other legal systems, recovery is limited to damages that were foreseeable when the contract was made and that are the immediate and direct result of the breach. To limit the

---

[108] *Id.* ¶ 41.
[109] *Id.* ¶¶ 55, 78.
[110] *Id.* ¶ 80.
[111] *Id.* ¶¶ 84–90.
[112] *Id.* ¶¶ 91–99.
[113] *Id.* ¶ 107.
[114] *Id.* ¶¶ 107–08.
[115] *Id.* ¶ 113.
[116] *Id.* ¶ 115.
[117] *Id.* ¶ 117.

recovery of the victim of a breach to its actual expenditures is to transform it into a lender, which is commercially intolerable when the party was at full risk for the amount of investments made an the strength of the contract.[118]

After considering Karaha Bodas' foreseeable damages "subject to the vagaries of a number of risks typical of this kind of project in a country such as Indonesia,"[119] the tribunal fixed lost profits at US$150 million.[120]

Louis T. Wells, *Double-Dipping in Arbitration Awards? An Economist Questions Damages Awarded to Karaha Bodas Company in Indonesia*, 19 Arb Int'l 471, 473–77 (2003)

This case [(Karaha Bodas)] raises many issues, such as the role of Indonesian and foreign courts, procedural questions, whether IMF pressure on Indonesia constitutes something beyond an act of government, the appropriate venue for challenging the validity of a contract that purportedly did not conform to the decree authorising the investments, and so on. But, the basis and method used by the arbitrators to calculate the damages award is one of the most important.

The claimants argued for, and the arbitrators awarded, two categories of damages: *damnum emergens* (expenses incurred) and *lucrum cessans* (lost profits). In so doing, the claimants and the arbitrators equated *damnum emergens* with investment that had been made by the claimants.

If this event had involved a normal trade transaction, say the cancellation of a contract to purchase an aeroplane, the two-part award might well be appropriate. *Damnum emergens* would include the costs incurred for manufacturing the aeroplane before the cancellation and, likely, sales costs associated with the deal. *Lucrum cessans* would account for the foregone profit on that sale. The Indonesian generating facility was, however, not a normal trade transaction; rather, it had the characteristics of foreign direct investment. Like many recent foreign direct investments, this one had special contractual elements, but it was not a short-term sales contract. The errors from treating the project as a sales transaction began with the arbitrators' interpretation of *damnum emergens* as being equivalent to investment and with the decision to aggregate both investment and future profits in determining the amount of the award. Although the award document makes it frustratingly difficult to determine exactly how the arbitrators calculated the profits part of the award, from an economist's point of view, the total amount awarded was likely excessive.

In most involuntary or efficient takings of investments, the goal of compensation ought to be to leave the investor in the same position it would have been in had the property not been taken. The principal guideline for calculating compensation is fair market value (FMV) of the property. Such a standard will usually lead to Pareto optimal results: the party initiating the breach will be better off (the Indonesians will not have to pay for unneeded electricity) and the other party (Karaha Bodas Co.) will not be worse off than if the event had not occurred.

In calculating the FMV of commercial property, or an ongoing business, analysts are likely to begin with the net present value (NPV) of the expected future stream of cash

---

[118] *Id.* ¶ 121–22.

[119] *Id.* ¶ 124.

[120] *Id.* ¶ 136.

flow from the project as a measure. They would not add to the resulting figure the amount of investment. Rather, if the investment had a residual value to the investor at the end of the calculation period, that residual would be discounted and included in the NPV. In the case of KBC, there was no residual value; the project, including all assets and improvements, reverted free of cost to Pertamina at the end of 30 years. Projecting the stream of earnings for 30 years requires some heroic assumptions, especially for a project that has not yet been completed and thus has no track record; in some cases, such projections are essential, as uncertain as they might be; but there are advantages in seeking another approach when another is feasible.

When the investment is very recent, or still in the process of being made, there is an obvious and often easier alternative to using NPV of future cash flow to determine FMV. If the project was expected to generate "normal" rates of return for the business, then the amount of investment itself provides a reasonable starting point for determining FMV. In most cases, the FMV of recently acquired assets is unlikely to be substantially different from the cost of those assets. Cost of investment will approximate what a buyer might pay; moreover, the investor who receives his investment back can invest the sum in another project, earn normal returns, and be equally well off. For most unfinished projects, this should end the calculations.

If one starts with investment as a measure of FMV, however, one must be willing to ask whether there are reasons why the market value might differ substantially from the amount spent, and make appropriate adjustments. There are indeed reasons that might justify modifications. First, if some of the investment was wasteful, or represented over-invoiced transactions with affiliates, the market value would be less than the amount invested. Indonesians claimed that this was the case in KBC[.] [W]ithout deciding whether any portion of the investment was wasteful or over invoiced, the arbitrators determined that even wasteful investment should be reimbursed in full, a position sharply at odds with FMV as the standard. Secondly, if the investor brought some kind of technology or other intangible asset to the project that added to its future cash flow but was not reflected in the investment figures, the project might have an FMV greater than the reported investment. That does not seem to support a case for greatly increasing the valuation of the KBC project over the amount invested; the geothermal projects are not at the forefront of technology, or at least no argument was reported in the arbitral decision that investors brought important proprietary technology or other intangible assets to the project. Thirdly, adjustments might be required for an investment that was in "exploratory" or "research"-type activities; that is, if the investor undertook a significant gamble. If the exploration yielded negative results by the time of the taking, the project would have an FMV less than the investment, perhaps even zero, and the award should be reduced accordingly. If the gamble turned out positive, the FMV would be higher than the investment. KBC does seem to have faced some risk in terms of the geothermal resources; it is not clear, however, whether KBC had resolved questions about the amount of steam available by the time of the postponement of the project. Although the NPV approach might be an easier measure of FMV in a "gambling" project, the arbitrators did not use that argument to explain the award to KBC. Fourthly, the FMV might be different from the amount of investment if the deal reflected corruption, lack of competitive "bidding," or ignorance on the part of the other party. Under this argument, the tribunal would have to assess the ability of an investor to continue to collect the resulting abnormally high return; the FMV might be more, or possibly even less, than the investment. In fact, the defendant alleged that at least one of the latter conditions was present in the KBC project, an allegation that KBC denied. However, even if a party in KBC's position advanced such an argument (and KBC did not), it is not clear that the tribunal ought to make an award based on adjustments to reflect extra value accruing from these factors. Finally, a tribunal might subtract the value of those future earnings that result from an inappropriate monopoly position.

In sum, one could estimate FMV by starting with *either* the investment *or* the NPV of expected cash flows, but they should not be added together. It appears from the award document that the arbitrators in the case double counted in determining the amounts owed by Pertamina and PLN by awarding the amount of the investment (with no adjustment of the kinds indicated above) *plus* the NPV of expected cash flows.[121]

H. Factors Potentially Limiting the Amount of Compensation

Several factors may justify a reduction of the compensation to which the victim of an internationally wrongful act otherwise would be entitled. Some of these factors were already discussed in the earlier parts of this chapter.[122] For instance, it has been noted that an award of lost profits can be problematic when based on speculative forecasts regarding the future profitability of a new enterprise,[123] and that compensation for such an enterprise may therefore be limited to investment outlays, excluding future profits.[124] It should also be apparent that "double recovery" is not permitted, meaning that the injured party cannot

---

[121] *See also* D. W. Bowett, *Claims Between States and Private Entities: The Twilight Zone of International Law,* 35 Cath. U. L. Rev. 929, 941 (1986) ("[W]hen the private claimant receives, by way of an award, compensation representing the value of his assets, plus any loss of profits in the interim period between the act of nationalization, breach of contract or expropriation and the date of the award, at that date he receives back the value of his business. His 'capital' is returned to him. He is presumed to invest that capital elsewhere so that it will earn him profits in some other business, in some other country. Why, therefore, should the private claimant expect the tribunal to award him loss of profits under the terminated contract for the same period during which the same capital is earning a second set of profits elsewhere? On the assumption that he has put his returned capital to good use, the claimant, in effect, is claiming a double recovery for loss of profits. Such a claim seems both illogical and unethical"). *Cf.* Brower's dissent in *Amoco, supra* note 18.

[122] For example, an injury may be caused by something other than a wrongful act, in which case there will be no legal remedy. "There are many forms of harm of which the law takes no account. Damage so done and suffered is called *damnum sine injuria*, and the reasons for its permission by the law are various and not capable of exhaustive statement. For example, the harm done may be caused by some person who is merely exercising his own rights, as in the case of the loss inflicted on individual traders by competition in trade, or where the damage is done by a man acting under necessity to prevent a greater evil." R. F. V. Heuston, *Salmond on the Law of Torts* 13 (17th ed. 1977). *Cited in Black's Law Dictionary* (8th ed. 2004), *damnum sine injuria.*

[123] *See* pp. 587 *et seq. supra.*

[124] *See id.*

recover twice for the same injury.[125] In this subsection, three additional concepts will be discussed: (1) causation; (2) contributory fault; and (3) the obligation to mitigate damages.

1. Causation

Article 31 of the ILC Articles requires reparation only for injury caused by an internationally wrongful act. This provision embodies the general principle of law that there must be a close link between the wrongful act and the injury.[126] Thus, damages are available to the extent that the injured party can prove that its injuries resulted from the illegal acts.[127] The main question that arises here is the extent to which this cause-and-effect analysis can be followed to its logical conclusion. The dissenting opinion of Justice Andrews in the classic New York court case of *Palsgraf* in the field of tort law frames the issue:

> [A]s we have said, we cannot trace the effect of an act to the end, if end there is. Again, however, we may trace it part of the way. A murder at Sarajevo may be the necessary antecedent to an assassination in London twenty years hence. An overturned lantern may burn all Chicago. We may follow the fire from the shed to the last building. We rightly say the fire started by the lantern caused its destruction. A cause, but not the proximate cause. What we do mean by the word "proximate" is that, because of convenience, of public policy, of a rough sense of justice, the law arbitrarily declines to trace a series of events beyond a certain point. This is not logic. It is practical politics.[128]

Thus, for practical reasons most legal systems impose limits on the length of the causal chain that can be followed from state action to compensable injury. Similarly, arbitral tribunals and claims settlement commissions have employed a variety of qualifying terms—proximate, foreseeable, direct causation, and so forth—to

---

[125] Double recovery could occur in a variety of ways. For example, a potential for double recovery may exist in parallel proceedings involving the same dispute, which may take place on the international level. For example, in the *CME* and *Lauder* arbitrations against the Czech Republic, two BIT arbitrations were commenced in relation to the same investment and state measures, under the Netherlands-Czech BIT and the Czech Republic-U.S. BIT. Ultimately, one of the claimants prevailed, and one lost. If claimants had won in both cases, there could have been potential for double recovery. Alternatively, parallel proceedings may take place at the international level and at the local court level. This issue was also raised in *CME v. Czech Republic*, where the claimant had resorted to local courts. The tribunal noted that the claimant had not recovered anything from the local proceedings, and hence there was no danger of double recovery. With respect to the other issues pending before the local courts, the tribunal stated that the Czech courts would decide whether to consider the arbitral award in the *CME* case in their future decisions. See *CME*, supra note 20, ¶ 489.

[126] Bin Cheng, *General Principles of Law as Applied by International Courts and Tribunals* 253 (Stevens & Sons Ltd. 1953) (". . . the principle of integral reparation in responsibility has to be understood in conjunction with that of proximate or effective causality which is valid both in municipal and international law"); *see also* ILC Articles, supra note 4, Commentary to art. 31, ¶ 9.

[127] *Id.*

[128] *Palsgraf v. Long Island Railroad Co.*, 162 N.E. 99 (N.Y. 1928).

describe the extent to which the cause-and-effect relationship should be curtailed. The following excerpt from the ILC Commentary 10 on Article 31 discusses this issue:[129]

> The allocation of injury or loss to a wrongful act is, in principle, a legal and not only a historical or causal process. Various terms are used to describe the link which must exist between the wrongful act and the injury in order for the obligation of reparation to arise. For example, reference may be made to losses "attributable [to the wrongful act] as a proximate cause,"[130] or to damage which is "too indirect, remote, and uncertain to be appraised,"[131] or to "any direct loss, damage, including environmental damage and the depletion of natural resources, or injury to foreign Governments, nationals and corporations as a result of" the wrongful act.[132] Thus causality in fact is a necessary but not a sufficient condition for reparation. There is a further element, associated with the exclusion of injury that is too "remote" or "consequential" to be the subject of reparation. In some cases, the criterion of "directness" may be used,[133] in others "foreseeability,"[134] or "proximity."[135] But other factors may also be relevant: for example, whether State organs deliberately caused the harm in question, or whether the harm caused was within the ambit of the rule which was breached, having regard to the purpose of that rule.[136] In other words, the requirement of a causal link is not necessarily the same in relation to every breach of an international obligation. In international as in national law, the question of remoteness of damage "is not a part of the law which can be satisfactorily solved by search for a

---

[129] ILC Articles, Commentary, *supra* note 4.

[130] SN: *See* U.S.-Germany Mixed Claims Commission, Administrative Decision No. II, 7 U.N.R.I.A.A., 23, 30 (1923). *See also* Dix, *ibid*, vol. 9, at 121 (1902), and the Canadian statement of claim following the disintegration of the Cosmos 954 Soviet nuclear-powered satellite over its territory in 1978: 18 I.L.M. 907, ¶ 23 (1979).

[131] SN: *See* the *Trail Smelter* arbitration, 3 U.N.R.I.A.A., 1905, 1931 (1938, 1941). *See also* A. Hauriou, *Les dommages indirects dans les arbitrages internationaux*, 31 R.G.D.I.P. 209 (1924), citing the Alabama arbitration as the most striking application of the rule excluding indirect damages.

[132] SN: Security Council Resolution 687 (1991), ¶ 16. This was a chapter VII resolution, but it is expressed to reflect Iraq's liability under international law as a result of its unlawful invasion and occupation of Kuwait. The United Nations Compensation Commission and the Governing Council have provided some guidance on the interpretation of the requirements of directness and causation under ¶ 16. *See, e.g., Claims Against Iraq (Category B. Claims)*, Report of Apr. 14, 1994 (S/AC.26/1994/1), reproduced in 109 I.L.R., at 127; approved by Governing Council Decision 20, May 26, 1994 (S/AC.26/Dec.20), reproduced in 109 I.L.R., at 622; *Well Blowout Control Claim*, Report of Nov. 15, 1996 (S/AC.26/1996/5), reproduced in 109 I.L.R., 480, at 506–511, ¶¶ 66–86; approved by Governing Council Decision 40, Dec. 17, 1996 (S/AC.26/Dec.40), reproduced in 109 I.L.R., at 669.

[133] SN: As in Security Council resolution 687 (1991), ¶ 16.

[134] SN: *See, e.g.*, the *Naulilaa* case (responsibility of Germany for damage caused in the Portuguese colonies in the south of Africa) (*Portugal v. Germany*), 2 U.N.R.I.A.A., 1011, 1031 (1928).

[135] SN: For comparative reviews of issues of causation and remoteness *see, e.g.*, H. L. A. Hart & A. M. Honoré, *Causation in the Law* (Clarendon Press 2nd ed. 1985); A. M. Honoré, *Causation and Remoteness of Damage*, in 9 *International Encyclopedia of Comparative Law*, Pt. 1, Ch. VII, at 156 (A. Tunc, ed.); K. Zwiegert & H. Kötz, *Introduction to Comparative Law* 601–27 (esp. 609ff.) (trans. J. A. Weir, Clarendon Press 3d ed. 1998); B. S. Markesinis, *The German Law of Obligations, Volume II. The Law of Torts: A Comparative Introduction* 95–108 (Clarendon Press 3d ed. 1997), with many references to the literature.

[136] SN: *See, e.g.*, the decision of the Iran-U.S. Claims Tribunal in *Islamic Republic of Iran v. U.S.*, Cases Nos. A15(IV) & A24, Award No. 590-A15 (IV)/A24-FT (Dec. 28, 1998).

single verbal formula."[137] The notion of a sufficient causal link which is not too remote is embodied in the general requirement in article 31 that the injury should be in consequence of the wrongful act, but without the addition of any particular qualifying phrase.

The following excerpt from *S.D. Myers* demonstrates the application of this principle in an investment arbitration case.

S.D. Myers, Inc. (SDMI) v. Canada

In a NAFTA Arbitration under UNCITRAL Rules, Second Partial Award, Oct. 21, 2002

140. In its First Partial Award the Tribunal determined that damages may only be awarded to the extent that there is a sufficient causal link between the breach of a specific NAFTA provision and the loss sustained by the investor. Other ways of expressing the same concept might be that the harm must not be too remote, or that the breach of the specific NAFTA provision must be the *proximate* cause of the harm.

141. The assessment of damages is not always a precise science. This case illustrates the point. Although the expert accountants for both sides stated that SDMI's loss of profit or contribution margin was capable of assessment, their respective quantifications were subjective and based on the exercise of their judgement.

142. The Tribunal reviews the legal framework for assessing damages and the many factors that the Parties, not always in agreement, stated should be taken into account. This leads to an award of damages, which is the Tribunal's judgement of what is appropriate in this case. In some circumstances, in the calculations, a fixed percentage or dollar amount is expressed. In others it is not. In all circumstances, the result is based on the Tribunal's appreciation of the evidence and its interpretation of the applicable law.

143. Article 1116 is relevant to the scope of recovery. It states that an investor can claim for:

> ... *loss or damage by reason of, or arising out of* ... a breach of Section A of Chapter 11. Article 1117, which is not in issue in this arbitration, provides the same remedy when an investor claims on behalf of its investment.

144. SDMI relies on authorities that include decisions of the Iran-United States Claims Tribunal, but they concern the measure of damages in an expropriation. While some assistance can be obtained from a consideration of these authorities, the NAFTA deals explicitly with the measure of damages for an expropriation and those provisions are not controlling in this case.

145. SDMI says that it is entitled to ... lost profits and consequential damages (such as the loss of competitive advantage and market share). ... It states that this Tribunal has established that there is a ... need for a direct causal link between Canada's unlawful international conduct and the occurrence of damages. Several authorities are referred to in support of this proposition.

---

[137] SN: P. S. Atiyah, *An Introduction to the Law of Contract* 466 (Clarendon Press 5th ed. 1995).

146. CANADA characterises any loss of profits by SDMI as consequential and not recoverable.

147. The concept of foreseeability of damages is referred to by both parties. SDMI says that the damages . . . *must have been reasonably anticipated by the disputing parties at the time of the breach.* SDMI also asserts that a special intention to harm an investor . . . *permits the Tribunal to award damages even in they would otherwise by considered to be too remote.*

148. In summary, SDMI seeks to recover the present value of the net income stream it says was lost by reason of the interim orders closing the Canadian border, plus a loss of opportunity it says it would have had to invest or use the money derived from that income stream and actual out-of-pocket losses suffered by it. Loss of opportunity is also characterised as *consequential.*

149. SDMI contends that in response to egregious conduct the Tribunal can and should award damages that otherwise would not be recoverable as too remote. Even if it were possible legally to award damages that were otherwise too remote on the basis of the misconduct of a respondent, and the Tribunal has made no such finding in this case, such damages would be clearly punitive, and thus prohibited by Article 1135(4).

150. Characterising SDMI's loss of profit claim as a claim for consequential damages is neither helpful nor consonant with the authorities. Insofar as it arises out of the provision of a cross-border service, there is an argument that the claim is not recoverable in proceedings under Chapter 11 of the NAFTA, but that does not make it a claim for consequential damages other than in a non-legal, descriptive, sense.

151. Professor Whiteman states appropriately:

> Damages are disallowed when they are "not a natural consequence" of the wrongful act for which the respondent government is liable under international law. At times such losses are referred to as "consequential" and are disallowed on that account.

152. The authorities are clear that claims for loss of profits are recoverable. The issue is remoteness. The tribunal in *Shufeldt* said that a respondent's obligation is:

> . . . to recoup or compensate . . . for damages . . . which result directly or indirectly . . . and . . . such compensation includes both damages suffered and profits lost. . . . The Shufeldt tribunal continued to note that the profits . . . lost . . . must be the direct fruit of the contract and not too remote or speculative.

153. SDMI calls in aid the concept of foreseeability to support its claim for damages. CANADA responds stating that while it knew that SDMI was contemplating entering the market, at the time the interim measure was enacted, it did not know the extent to which SDMI had made preparation and did not know that MYERS Canada existed.

154. Foreseeability is a concept found in the law of contract. The authorities referred to by the Disputing Parties confirm that this is so. Using contractual measures of damage in the context of this case is not helpful. It led SDMI to contend that the question is whether the damages claimed were foreseeable by both parties *at the time of the breach*, which is misconceived in a contractual context. This in turn provoked CANADA's rejoinder concerning its lack of knowledge at the time of the breach.

155. In its Memorial, SDMI quotes the Tribunal in Shufeldt, which held that damages should be direct and . . . reasonably supposed to have been in the contemplation of both parties as the probable result of the breach. SDMI then states that . . . [t]o be foreseeable, the damages claimed must have been reasonably anticipated by the disputing parties at the time of the breach.

156. The phrase *reasonably anticipated* does not refer to the concept of foreseeability as it is used in the law of contract. It is used in the context of speculation. Claimed profits must not be merely speculative. They must have been anticipated reasonably; in that sense, reasonably foreseeable at the time of the breach.

157. After referring to submissions concerning directness and foreseeability, the Amoco Asia Tribunal quoted French law stating:

> [t]he debtor can only be liable for the damages which were foreseen or foreseeable at the time the contract was entered into . . .

158. Insofar as the word *foreseeability* is used in the context of what was anticipated, what was realistic, it is appropriate. In this context it is a descriptive word, not a legal term of art.

159. The inquiry in this case is more akin to ascertaining damages for a tort or delict. The damages recoverable are those that will put the innocent party into the position it would have been in had the interim measure not been passed. The focus is on causation, not foreseeability in the sense used in the law of contract. In contract law, foreseeability may limit the range of recoverability. That is not the case in the law of tort or delict. Remoteness is the key.

160. Similarly, a debate as to whether damages are direct or indirect is not appropriate. If they were caused by the event, engage Chapter 11 and are not too remote, there is nothing in the language of Article 1139 that limits their recoverability.[138]

A separate but related question is how to measure the extent to which a particular wrongful act contributed to an injury. This issue becomes especially relevant where two or more events have played a role in bringing about damage to a claimant. In such situations, there is some authority for the proposition that, unless the respondent can prove that "some part of the injury can

---

[138] See also *Lauder*, supra note 55. *Lauder* involved the same facts as *CME, see* pp. 325 *et seq. supra,* except that the arbitration was commenced by the ultimate owner of TV Nova, Ronald Lauder, under the U.S.-Czech Republic BIT. Unlike *CME,* however, the claimant did not recover any damages. The tribunal dismissed all of Mr. Lauder's claims, except for arbitrary impairment. Ultimately, the tribunal did not award any damages, because causation had not been proven. *See id.* ¶ 235.

be shown to be severable in causal terms from that attributed to the responsible State,"[139] it will be held responsible for all of the consequences.[140]

2. Contributory Fault

Article 39 of the ILC Articles provides that "[i]n the determination of reparation, account shall be taken of the contribution to the injury by wilful or negligent action or omission of the injured State or any person or entity in relation to whom reparation is sought."[141] Commentary 2 elaborates on this issue by stating that:

> Article 39 recognizes that the conduct of the injured State, or of any person or entity in relation to whom reparation is sought, should be taken into account in assessing the form and extent of reparation. This is consonant with the principle that full reparation

---

[139] See ILC Articles, *supra* note 4, Commentary to art. 31, ¶ 13.

[140] *Id.* See also U.N.C.C. Decision 9, *supra* note 97. U.N.C.C. Decision 15 interpreting Decision 9 further illustrates the role of contributory negligence under international law. Decision 15 deals with the compensation for losses that resulted from Iraq's invasion of Kuwait but also partly from the United Nations' Trade Embargo imposed on Iraq by U.N. Security Council Resolution 661 (1990). Decision 15 provides in relevant part:

> 9. The first four sentences of paragraph 6 of Decision 9 are now considered in turn. The object is to provide further guidance for Commissioners when they assess claims in respect of business losses of individuals, corporations and other entities. The guidance is also intended to help claimants in presenting their claims. It will be for Commissioners to draw on the principles in this guidance when making their judgements on actual cases which will stand or fall according to their specific factual and legal situations.
>
> I. "The trade embargo and related measures, and the economic situation caused thereby, will not be accepted as the basis for compensation."
>
> (i) The practical effect of this statement is that any loss, damage, or injury resulting solely from the trade embargo and related measures, and the economic situation caused thereby, is not eligible for compensation.
>
> . . . .
>
> II. "Compensation will be provided to the extent that Iraq's unlawful invasion and occupation of Kuwait constituted a cause of direct loss, damage, or injury which is separate and distinct from the trade embargo and related measures."
>
> (i) The practical effect of this statement is that compensation will be provided, if and to the extent that loss, damage, or injury resulting directly from Iraq's unlawful invasion and occupation of Kuwait was actually suffered and would have been suffered irrespective of whether the trade embargo and related measures had been in force.
>
> (ii) Particularly in the case of larger and more complex claims, the Commissioners may decide that some losses listed in a claim are a direct result of Iraq's unlawful invasion and occupation of Kuwait and should be compensated and that other losses listed in the same claim resulted solely from the embargo and related measures and are therefore ineligible for compensation. In this situation partial compensation would in principle be payable.

Compensation for Business Losses Resulting from Iraq's Unlawful Invasion and Occupation of Kuwait Where the Trade Embargo and Related Measures Were Also a Cause, Decision 15, U.N.C.C. G.C., 8th Sess., U.N. Doc. S/AC.26/1992/15_*/ (1992), ¶ 9 (Commentary on ¶ 6 of Decision 9).

[141] See ILC Articles, *supra* note 4, Commentary to art. 39.

is due for the injury—but nothing more—arising in consequence of the internationally wrongful act. It is also consistent with fairness as between the responsible State and the victim of the breach.[142]

Detailed examination of contributory negligence appears to be relatively rare in investment treaty arbitration. In *MTD v. Chile*,[143] the tribunal substantially reduced the amount of damages awarded because the claimant had failed to undertake reasonable due diligence before investing substantial sums in the project.[144] Arbitral tribunals in *Bogdanov*[145] and *Azurix*[146] have applied similar principles, but without using the term "contributory negligence."

3. Obligation to Mitigate Losses

This general principle of law,[147] which normally requires that the injured party take reasonable steps to mitigate its losses,[148] has also been invoked in arbitral practice. In the *CME* case,[149] for instance, Czech Republic argued that CME had failed to mitigate its losses. The tribunal, although acknowledging that this principle is "one of the established legal principles in arbitral case law," rejected this contention, having found that the investors, under the circumstances, had done their utmost to overcome the consequences of the government's acts.[150]

I. Role of Equity

> Thomas W. Wälde & Borzu Sabahi, *Compensation, Damages and Valuation in International Investment Law*, in Oxford Handbook of International Investment Law (P. Muchlinski, F. Ortino, & C. Schreuer eds., Oxford University Press 2008)
>
> In conventional international law, in particular in ICJ jurisprudence, equitable circumstances play a role not only, for example, in boundary determinations, but also in other

---

[142] *Id.*

[143] See *MTD*, *supra* note 66. This case is currently subject to an annulment proceeding.

[144] *Id.* ¶¶ 242-46. Contributory fault, i.e., business risk not to be attributed to breach of fair and equitable treatment, was estimated at 50 percent.

[145] *Bogdanov (Russia) v. Moldova* (Stockholm Chamber of Commerce [SCC] Arbitral Award of Sept. 22, 2005), at 19.

[146] *Azurix*, *supra* note 70, ¶ 426.

[147] *See, e.g., Middle East Cement Shipping & Handling Co. S.A. v. Egypt*, ICSID Case No. ARB/99/6 (Award of Apr. 12, 2002), ¶ 167.

[148] See ILC Articles, *supra* note 4, Commentary to art. 31, ¶ 11.

[149] See *CME*, *supra* note 20, ¶ 303.

[150] *Id.* ¶ 482. See also *Middle East Cement v. Egypt*, *supra* note 147, ¶¶ 166-71.

areas.[151] Equity ... on the other hand, plays a minor role in international commercial arbitration. It is largely recognised that the parties have to explicitly agree for a tribunal to apply an "ex aequo et bono" approach.[152] Tribunals relying on equity ... as a concept beyond the legal rules applicable risk their awards set aside.[153] ... Equitable circumstances should therefore—very much in the international law tradition[154]—be seen as a "legal"—not "ex aequo et bono"—criterion that allows correction of outcomes achieved by application of normal standards, but not consistent with the overall purpose and policy of the investment treaty.

Some investment arbitration awards and treaties have considered equitable circumstances in assessing damages.[155] Others—where the compensation award had little relation to the reasoning—have stated that it is "considered just and reasonable to take some measure of account of all elements of an undertaking."[156] What arises from this less than conclusive evidence is that tribunals cannot replace a proper application of the existing law on compensation exclusively by equitable considerations; equitable circumstances, however, can be relied upon in order to determine the exact point of compensation on a range that has been suggested by the competing valuations of the parties. The principle therefore corrects the results that appear excessive; in essence, it can serve as an emergency brake for tribunals when faced with exorbitant values produced by an application of the ... DCF method when the tribunal has difficulties in controlling the speculations inherent in this method otherwise. The *Himpurna v Indonesia* (a long-term contract dispute) tribunal felt

---

[151] SN: *See, e.g., Corfu Channel Case (U.K. v. Albania)* Assessment of the Amount of Compensation Due from the People's Republic of Albania to United Kingdom, I.C.J. Rep. at 244 & 248 (1949). [On equity in international law see M. Akehurst, *Equity and General Principles of Law*, 25 Int'l & Comp. L. Q. 801 (1976); *see also* S. Rosenne, *Equitable Principles and the Compulsory Jurisdiction of International Tribunals*, in Festschrift Bindschedler (Bern, 1980)].

[152] SN: *See generally* Gary Born, *International Commercial Arbitration* (Transnat'l Publishers & Kluwer 2d ed. 2001) at 556–57.

[153] SN: Seidl-Hohenveldern, ["L'évaluation des dommages dans les arbitrages transnationaux" 33 Annuaire français de droit international 7 (1987)], at 27.

[154] SN: *Cf. e.g.*, in particular the *North Sea Continental Shelf* (1969) case where the ICJ used equitable circumstances to correct a practically and politically problematic solution indicated by the more formal criteria of boundary delimitation. *Ibid.*, ¶¶ 90–91.

[155] SN: In *Santa Elena v. Costa Rica*, for instance, the tribunal relied on the jurisprudence of *Iran-USCT* in Philips Petroleum where the latter tribunal, itself relying on *Starrett Housing*, opined that in determining the fair market value of a company the tribunal should consider all the circumstances including the equitable circumstances. See *Santa Elena*, *supra* note [53], ¶ 92 and references therein. *Cf.* E. Lauterpacht, *International Law and Private Foreign Investment* 4 J. Global Legal Stud. 259 (1997) at 269; *LIAMCO*, *supra* note 22, at 150–52 & 160 ("reasonable equitable indemnification").

[156] SN: *Aminoil*, *supra* note [82], ¶ 164; J. F. Lalive in a personal discussion (with Michael Schneider present) explained to Thomas Wälde that the parties had agreed on a specific compensatory amount and that the tribunal was asked, without further explanation, to simply endorse it. This would explain the missing link between the amount and the reasoning. That has been disputed by Hunter and Sinclair, [*Changed Circumstances: Aminoil Revisited* in *International Investment Law and Arbitration: Leading Cases from the ICSID, Nafta, Bilateral Treaties and Customary International Law* (T. Weiler ed., Cameron May 2005)].

it necessary to apply, under a different name, the principle of equitable circumstances (labelled: abuse of right).[157]

Tribunals ultimately when choosing between competing and equally plausible and legitimate valuation methods, and in weighing the significant assumptions (in particular discount rate and risk factors) underlying such models cannot avoid exercising discretion. This is where they will be influenced by equitable considerations.[158]

J. Interest

1. Overview

Given the size of claims brought under investment protection treaties, it is hardly surprising that the interest to accrue on any final award is of significant concern to the parties. Indeed, pre-award interest alone may total millions of dollars,[159] where the award is rendered long after the breach occurs. In the *American Independent Oil Company* case, the tribunal awarded US$96 million in interest on damages totalling US$83 million.[160] The claimant in *Santa Elena* received interest nearly three times the damage award, as the expropriation in question had taken place twenty-two years before the close of the arbitration proceedings.[161]

Arbitral tribunals faced with a request to award interest have to answer a number of questions. First, should interest be awarded at all? Second, at what rate should interest be awarded? Third, from which date should interest begin to

---

[157] SN: *Himpurna v. Indonesia, supra* note [86]. In this case Indonesia had entered into a take or pay contract with Himpurna. Later as a result of the financial crisis of 1997, it became unable to fulfill its obligations under the contract. The tribunal reasoned that the strict application of the NPV/DCF method to value Himpurna's investment would amount to abuse of rights. It could have reached the same results, however, more easily by applying a higher discount rate (e.g., at or more than 25 percent), given the high-risk nature of a one-sided contract in a developing country, and, secondly, by rather applying the equitable circumstances corrective function.

[158] SN: Aldrich, [*The Jurisprudence of the Iran-United States Tribunal* (Clarendon Press 1996)], at 241 ("I believe that when they are making a complex judgment such as one regarding the amount of compensation due for expropriation or rights to lift and sell petroleum products, equitable considerations will inevitably be taking into account, whether acknowledged or not").

[159] *See generally* John Y. Gotanda, *Awarding Interest in International Arbitration,* 90 Am. J. Int'l L. 40 (1996).

[160] *Aminoil, supra* note 82, ¶ 178.

[161] *Santa Elena, supra* note 53, ¶¶ 95, 107.

accrue? Fourth, should the award include pre- and/or post-award interest? And fifth, should the interest rate be compounded, and if so, how frequently?[162]

Most systems of municipal law have their own answers to these questions. Indeed, many jurisdictions (including many states within the United States) establish a statutory rate of interest, to be applied to all money judgments. In contrast, some Islamic countries that apply Sharia law prohibit awarding any interest.[163] Although in the international commercial arbitration context the parties' choice of substantive law would often establish the rules governing the question,[164] claimants under BITs or regional investment treaties must normally rely on the discretion of the tribunal and principles of customary international law.[165]

The following excerpt by Wälde and Sabahi provides some possible answers to the first four questions presented above. The last question, on compounding of interest, is discussed separately in the next section.

Thomas W. Wälde & Borzu Sabahi, *Compensation, Damages and Valuation in International Investment Law*, in Oxford Handbook of International Investment Law (P. Muchlinski, F. Ortino, & C. Schreuer eds., Oxford University Press 2008)

(c) Rate of Interest

The rates vary between six-month U.S. certificates of deposit (reflecting a prudent, risk-free standard corporate re-investment practice), prime borrowing rates (reflecting high-class corporate borrowers), rates derived from the contractual relationship[166] or rates that have to be specifically proved by claimants for their particular case.[167] There

---

[162] *See generally* Martin Hunter & Volker Triebel, *Awarding Interest in International Arbitration*, 6 J. Int'l Arb. 1 (1990); Mauro Rubino-Sammartano, *International Arbitration Law and Practice* 815–17 (Kluwer 2000).

[163] It should be noted that in some Islamic jurisdictions awarding interest is considered illegal. Arbitrators in such situations may consider incorporating pre-award interest into the principal amount to be awarded. Otherwise, the award could be subject to challenge under the laws of any relevant Islamic country. *See generally* Gotanda, *supra* note 159; Wälde & Sabahi, *supra* note 23.

[164] In most legal systems, the award of interest is normally considered a substantive, not a procedural, matter. *But see* Gotanda, *supra* note 159, at 50–53.

[165] *Pope & Talbot v. Canada* (UNCITRAL Arbitration (NAFTA), Award in Respect of Damages, May 31, 2002), ¶¶ 88–90 (holding that "the NAFTA provisions are an independent basis for determining interest recovery; otherwise domestic law could prevent the award of any interest. Of course, applicable rules of international law, which are expressly made part of these proceedings by virtue of Article 1131(1), also call for the award of appropriate interest, including compounding, as one of the elements of compensation").

[166] SN: Brower & Brueschke, *supra* note [23], at 624–25; *see especially Anaconda v. Iran*, 13 Iran-US Cl. Trib. Rep. 199 (1988) with a discussion of usury (rates over 12 percent).

[167] SN: Gotanda, [*Awarding Compound Interest in International Disputes*, Oxford University Comparative Law Forum 2004, available at http://papers.ssrn.com/s013/papers.cfm?abstract_id = 561263.], text accompanying notes 276–77.

are many candidates for the right interest rate as confirmed by precedents.[168] Absolute figures—such as the interest rates quoted—are of no relevance at all since they will reflect rates of interests prevailing at the time. Interest rates can be either generic (i.e., generally prevailing at the time for first-class companies) or individualised (e.g., the specific rates payable by the particular claimant-investor or companies in its class). The proper approach seems to be to apply generic rates[169] except if the claimant proves satisfactorily that, with prudent management, it would have achieved or had to pay a higher rate.[170]

Another significant difference is if the interest rate is derived from either an investment or a debt perspective. Debt-based interest rates are logically higher as they include profit, risk, and cost elements for the lender. The proper approach again seems to be to choose a rate that a prudent investor managing another individual's money would have chosen with minimal risk-taking.[171] Only if the claimant-investor can prove that it had to increase its debt level rather than invest this type of money should the higher debt-related interest rate be used.

(d) Date from which the Interest Should Accrue

Article 38(2) of the ILC Articles provides that the interest obligation start "from the date when the principal sum should have been paid until the date the obligation is fulfilled." That presumably translates in takings cases into the date of the taking (when compensation under international law—"prompt"—is payable). In quasi-expropriatory breach of contract cases, the relevant starting date is when the contract was no longer fulfilling a

---

[168] SN: *Aminoil, supra* note [82], ¶ 178 ("In order to establish what is due in 1982, account must be taken both of a reasonable rate of interest, which could be put at 7.5 percent, and of a level of inflation which the Tribunal fixes at an overall rate of 10 percent—that is to say at a total annual increase of 17.5 percent in the amount due, over the amount due for the preceding year."); [*Sylvania v. Iran*, 8 Iran-U.S.Cl. Trib. 298 (1985)] (12.2 percent; these rates reflected then prevailing high interest rates in an inflationary environment); *Santa Elena, supra* note [53] (a rate that was either 13.13 percent simple interest or 6.40 percent compound interest—supposedly 30 percent lower than "generally prevailing rates," C. N. Brower & J. Wong, [*General Principles of Valuation: The Case of* Santa Elena in Weiler ed. 2005, *supra* note 156,] at 773–74); rates were subsequently derived from a relevant benchmark—here six-month U.S. certificate of deposit rates. Sometimes, rates prevailing in the host state were applied. Presumably, the rate in the investor's home state is in most cases the pertinent one. Brower & Brueschke, *supra* note [23], at 621–23; *Metalclad, supra* note [68], ¶ 128 (6 percent compounded annually, before and after the judgment).

[169] SN: See the *S. S. Wimbledon* case, PCIJ Series A, No. 1, p. 23 (1923) (where the PCIJ determined a rate of 6 percent on the basis of the "present financial situation of the world" and the conditions prevailing for "public loans"—that is the equivalent, today, of the U.S. government bonds (with the issue open if a long-term rate, somewhat higher, or a short-term rate (e.g., six months certificate of deposit rates) is to be chosen. *PSEG v Turkey, supra* note [97] (six-month LIBOR plus 2).

[170] SN: Gotanda, *supra* note [167], text following n.299 (suggests that claimant should show it would have invested the money owed or (after n.188) that it had to pay the cost of additional financing charges because of the breach and the resultant outstanding claim against respondent).

[171] SN: That is essentially something akin to the six-month rate on risk-free U.S. dollars or Euro certificates of deposit or bank rates, depending on whether the investor operates mainly in a U.S. dollars or Euro financial environment. *Siemens v. Argentina*, [ICSID Case No. ARB/02/8 (Award of Feb. 6, 2007)] ¶ 126: 2.66 percent: U.S. six-month Certificates of Deposit.

useful economic function. Should one use investment arbitration to adjudicate on all contract issues (e.g., under the umbrella clause), it would be the date from which damages are due under the law applicable . . . It is not enough, however, to refer to "circumstances of each case" and arbitral "discretion" to define the starting date.[172]

[A] possible date is when the breach becomes effective as against the investor;[173] but states may often not be aware of difficulties of this nature, in particular in cases of general regulation where the anti-foreigner discrimination emerges only subsequently when its implementation is anticipated or when it is actually applied. In such a scenario, however, the investor in principle shall not profit from fixing a too early date, when for instance the investor had continued its operations unharmed because the new rule was not yet applied; nor should the state profit by setting a later date (e.g., substantially after the harm was done because the state claims ignorance of both breach and harm).

It is essential that the starting date for interest to be aligned with the ending date of the calculation of the principal of the compensation/damage.[174]

(e) Pre-award and Post-award Interest

National laws often distinguish between pre-judgment and post-judgment interest [rates].[175] There is no particular reason to distinguish between these concepts in investment arbitration.[176] . . . In general, the pre-award interest rate should therefore be the [same as the] post-award interest rate. The only question is if they should be expressed in nominal terms (x-percent) or in reference to a benchmark (e.g., US$ prime borrowing rate as published each July 1 in the *Wall Street Journal*). Since the past is known to the tribunal, it might be better to express the interest rate for the past in nominal, absolute terms, and leave at least the possibility of a substantial change of interest rates open by expressing the post-award interest rate as an absolute figure (on the day of the judgment), but open it up for automatic adaptation if the underlying benchmark quotation should change.

---

[172] SN: Crawford, *supra* note [4], at 238, 239, n.652.

[173] SN: The practice of Iran-U.S. Claims Tribunal was "from the date that compensable damages arose due to the taking or from the date that a debt or other obligation became due." See Brower & Brueschke, *supra* note [23], at 629, with the references in n.2990.

[174] SN: This approach is possibly already implicit in the Wimbledon case, *supra* note [169]; interest was payable only from the "moment when the amount of the sum due has been fixed and the obligation to pay has been established."

[175] SN: Gotanda, *supra* note [167]; *Metalclad, supra* note [68], ¶ 120.

[176] Indeed, arbitral tribunals in investment treaty cases seem to have been more concerned with whether to award interest in the absence of a timely request by claimants. In *Sempra Energy*, e.g., the tribunal refused to award interest in the post-award stage because claimants had not asked for it in a timely fashion. *Sempra Energy v. Argentina,* ICSID Case No. ARB/02/16 (Award of Sept. 28, 2007), ¶¶ 484–6 (Sempra relied on *Enron v. Argentina* in this respect. *See Enron & Ponderosa Assets v. Argentina,* ICSID Case No. ARB/01/3 (Award of May 22, 2007), ¶¶ 451–52).

2. Compound or Simple Interest?[177]

Until relatively recently, commentators noted a certain tendency of international arbitral tribunals to award simple rather than compound interest.[178] However, even a century ago the economic realism of compound interest was understood in many quarters[179] and today there is general recognition that compound interest is usually necessary to make an injured party truly whole. Professor Gaetano Arangio-Ruiz, the Special Rapporteur of the United Nations International Law Commission on State Responsibility, reviewed the authorities in depth, and concluded that "compound interest should be awarded whenever it is proved that it is indispensable in order to ensure full compensation for the damage suffered by the injured State."[180] The underlying policy supporting compound interest was cogently articulated by the tribunal in *Santa Elena v. Costa Rica:*

> In particular, where an owner of property has at some earlier time lost the value of his asset but has not received the monetary equivalent that then became due to him, the amount of compensation should reflect, at least in part, the additional sum that his money would have earned, had it, and the income generated by it, been reinvested each year at generally prevailing rates of interest. It is not the purpose of compound interest to attribute blame to, or to punish, anybody for the delay in the payment made to the expropriated owner; it is a mechanism to ensure that the compensation awarded the Claimant is appropriate in the circumstances.[181]

Nevertheless, according to some observers there remains insufficient uniformity of state practice to establish either simple or compound interest as a clear rule of international law.[182] Some arbitrators in investment-related cases continue to reject compounding of interest in certain circumstances. This is particularly true where the host country (whose legal system will often inform

---

[177] See generally F. A. Mann, *Compound Interest as an Item of Damage in International Law*, in *Further Studies in International Law* 377 (Clarendon Press 1990); Gotanda, *supra* note 167. See also Natasha Affolder, *Awarding Compound Interest in International Arbitration*, 12 Am. Rev. Int'l Arb. 45 (2001).

[178] *See, e.g.,* Yves Derains, Études Pierre Bellet 113 (1991) ("the analysis of jurisprudence reveals that arbiters have the greatest reluctance in granting compound interest"); *Santa Elena, supra* note 53, ¶ 97 ("there is a tendency in international jurisprudence to award only simple interest").

[179] *Fabiani's Case*, Moore's Dig. Int'l L. 4878–915 (1905) (awarding compound interest); *Affaire des Chemins de Fer Zeltweg-Wolfsberg*, 3 U.N.R.I.A.A. 1795, 1808 (1934) (same); *Kuwait v. Aminoil*, 66 Int'l L. Rep. 518, 613 (1982) (same); *Santa Elena, supra* note 53, ¶ 106 (same); *Flexi-Van v. Iran*, 9 Iran-US CTR 206; *Wena Hotels Ltd. v. Arab Republic of Egypt*, ICSID Case No. ARB/98/4, 41 I.L.M. 896 (2002) (same). See also *Norwegian Shipowners' Claims*, 1 U.N.R.I.A.A. 307, 341 (1922) (recognizing possibility of compound interest); *Great Britain v. Spain* (Spanish Zone of Morocco), 2 U.N.R.I.A.A. 615, 650 (1924) (same).

[180] Gaetano Arangio-Ruiz, *Second Report on State Responsibility*, 2 Y.B. I.L.C. 1, 30 (1989). See also Mann, *supra* note 177, at 380.

[181] *Santa Elena, supra* note 53, ¶ 104.

[182] Mann, *supra* note 177, at 378; International Law Commission, Report on Draft Articles on Responsibility of States for Internationally Wrongful Acts, *found in* Crawford, *supra* note 4, at 236 & 271; *McKesson HBOC, Inc. v. Islamic Republic of Iran*, 211 F.3d 1101, 1111–12 (2001).

the decision on interest) is a civil law jurisdiction, which tends to recognize compound interest only in limited situations.[183] Furthermore, where the operation of law calls for the application of a relatively high statutory interest rate,[184] some arbitrators fear over-compensating the claimant for losses when international law calls only for "full" restitution. In *CME v. Czech Republic,* for instance, both these considerations influenced the decision on compounding. The tribunal applied the Czech statutory rate of 12 percent, but declined to award compound interest:

> *CME Czech Republic B.V. v. Czech Republic*
>
> (UNCITRAL, Final Award of Mar. 13, 2003)
>
> 642. The Tribunal does not grant compound interest in this case. Civil Law Countries, such as the Czech Republic, only provide for simple interest by specifying the rate to be applied by statute . . . . Czech law only grants compound interest on the basis of an agreement by the parties (Art. 369 Commercial Code). Such an agreement does not exist.
>
> 643. Moreover, in accord with international law principles and international arbitration practice, the Tribunal does not award compound interest since the purpose of compensation—to "fully" compensate the damage sustained—in this case does not require the awarding of compound interest, having regard to the generous interest provision of the Czech Statute.
>
> 644. In respect of international law, arbitral tribunals in the past awarded compound interest infrequently. The Iran-US Claim Tribunal has rejected claims for compound interest, even in cases where the claimant was entitled to compound interest under the relevant contract, in order to insure that the compensation was not out of the proportion [sic] to the possible loss that was incurred (see *Anaconda-Iran Inc. v. Iran* (1986) 13 Iran-US CTR 199; *R.J. Reynolds Tobacco Co. v. Iran* (1984) 7 Iran-US CTR 181; *Sylvania Technical Systems v. Iran* (1984) 5 Iran-US CTR 141). At the same time, that Tribunal has recognized that "no uniform rule relating to interest has emerged from the practice in transnational arbitration." (*McCullough & Company v. The Ministry of Post, Telegraph and Telephone, The National Iranian Oil Company, and Bank Markazi* (1986), 11 Iran-US CTR 3, 28.)
>
> 645. However, in recent years international arbitral tribunals, particularly those acting under bilateral investment treaties, have increasingly have awarded compound interest essentially in recognition of the prevalent contemporary commercial reality that companies that borrow pay compound interest. . . . Among the circumstances which justify the award of compound interest are back-to-back financing obligations of the investor (F.A. Mann, I.c., p. 384).
>
> 646. The Claimant did not demonstrate that it borrowed money from banks and paid compound interest . . . .

---

[183] In *Aucoven v. Venezuela,* for example, the tribunal noted that Venezuelan law allowed compound interest only when the parties had expressly agreed thereto. It also noted that international law did not include a rule requiring compound interest. *Aucoven, supra* note 97, ¶¶ 389–97. See also *Occidental, supra* note 72 (4 percent simple interest awarded).

[184] *See id.* ¶ 391.

> 647. The Tribunal does not find particular circumstances in this case justifying the award of compound interest. The calculation of the compensation itself . . . fully compensates Claimant for the damage suffered. Awarding simple interest compensates the loss of use of the principal amount of the award in the period of delay.

Arbitrators in both the commercial and investment treaty context will normally be more comfortable awarding compound interest where there is a provision for such a remedy in the parties' contract,[185] or in cases where the claimant has been required as a result of the respondent's default to obtain supplementary financing that itself involves compound interest.[186] The choice of compound or simple interest is generally made on a case-by-case basis, as is the frequency of the compounding.[187]

K. Arbitration Costs and Attorneys' Fees[188]

1. Introduction

Article 39 of the United Nations Commission on International Trade Law (UNCITRAL) Arbitration Rules enumerates various expenses that may be incurred and recovered as part of an award in an ad hoc arbitration:

(a) The fees of the arbitral tribunal . . .

(b) The travel and other expenses incurred by the arbitrators;

---

[185] On contractually-agreed compound interest, *see* Affolder, *supra* note 177, at 54 *et seq.*

[186] ICC Case No. 5514 (1990), 1992 J. de Droit Int'l 1022. In other cases, arbitrators awarded compound interest because the respondent did not object, *see, e.g.,* ICC Case No. 5684, or because the parties' relations led to the establishment of a cash account, *see* ICC Case No. 6075.

[187] *See, e.g., Metalclad, supra* note 68, ¶ 131 (annually compounded); *Maffezini v. Spain,* ICSID Case No. ARB/97/7 (2000), ¶ 96 (LIBOR for Spanish peseta compounded annually), *Santa Elena, supra* note 53, ¶¶ 96 *et seq.* (compounded semi-annually); *Wena, supra* note 179, 41 ILM 896, 919 (compounded quarterly at 9 percent; Don Wallace, Jr. (arbitrator) questioning the choice of quarterly compounding); *Aminoil, supra* note 82, ¶ 178 (compounded annually at 17 percent); *MTD, supra* note 66 (annual LIBOR rate as of Nov. 5th (the day after breach) of each year, compounded annually); and *Azurix, supra* note 70, ¶ 440 (rate set at U.S. 6-month certificates of deposit, compounded semi-annually); *PSEG, supra* note 97, ¶ 348 (LIBOR plus 2 percent compounded semi-annually); *Siemens, supra* note 171, ¶¶ 399–401 (interest compounded annually); *Sempra, supra* note 176, ¶ 486("successive 6-month LIBOR rates, plus a 2 percent annualized premium or portion thereof. Interest shall be compounded semi-annually"); *Enron, supra* note 176, ¶ 452 (6-month average LIBOR rate plus 2 percent for each year, or proportion thereof, compounded annually).

[188] *See generally* Mauro Rubino-Sammartano, *International Arbitration Law and Practice* 811–15 (Kluwer 2000); John Gotanda, *Chapter 3, Attorney's Fees and Costs* in *Damages in Private International Law,* at 6 (manuscript on file with the authors); Noah Rubins, *The Allocation of Costs and Attorney's Fees in Investor-State Arbitration,* 18 ICSID Rev.-F.I.L.J. 109 (2003). For a survey of the cost decisions in investment arbitration awards, *see* separate opinion of Thomas Wälde in *Thunderbird, supra* note 6.

(c) The costs of expert advice and of other assistance required by the arbitral tribunal;

(d) The travel and other expenses of witnesses to the extent such expenses are approved by the arbitral tribunal;

(e) The costs for legal representation and assistance of the successful party . . .

(f) Any fees and expenses of the appointing authority.

In arbitration administered by ICSID, the LCIA, the Stockholm Chamber of Commerce (SCC), or other arbitral institutions, similar expenses are bound to be incurred. In addition, the administering body charges certain fees, some of which are fixed and others determined on a case-by-case basis as the arbitration progresses.[189] The main question is who should bear the costs. The issue is central, because the costs incurred may be quite substantial.[190] International arbitral tribunals (as well as courts) may adopt one of two contrary approaches to the allocation of costs: (1) "costs follow the event" and (2) the so-called American rule.[191]

"Costs follow the event" is a rule that requires the losing party to bear the expenses of the winning party, at least in proportion to the degree to which the other side has prevailed.[192] In many jurisdictions, courts allocate costs and legal fees according to the "costs follow the event" principle, requiring the losing party to pay both court costs and attorneys' fees unless the judge finds that the circumstances justify a different allocation.[193]

---

[189] As of May 2008, ICSID required payment of a US$25,000 filing fee. *See* ICSID Schedule of Fees, *available at* http://icsid.worldbank.org/.

[190] In *CSOB v. Slovakia,* for instance, each party was represented by a major international law firm, and each in its cost submission requested in excess of US$14 million.

[191] For the purpose of costs allocation, the expenses enumerated above may be split into two categories: first, "arbitration costs," encompassing all the enumerated items as well as costs of the administering body, except item (e), the costs of legal representation; and second, "costs of legal representation," which are alternatively referred to as "legal fees," "legal costs," and "attorneys' fees." Tribunals sometimes adopt this distinction by ordering the loser to bear the arbitration costs, whereas each party bears its own legal costs.

[192] Accordingly, the tribunal or the court in jurisdictions where this principle is followed will have the power to "allocate" the costs of the proceedings to the loser. This phenomenon is also referred to as *cost-shifting.*

[193] This is the case in France, Brazil, Germany, Sweden, and Mexico. *See Access to Civil Procedure Abroad,* § 9.9.3 (H. J. Snijders ed., 1996) (stating "the general rule [in England] is that costs follow the event: the losing party will be ordered to pay the winning party's costs"); S. O'Malley & A. Layton, *European Civil Practice,* § 56.57 (1989) ("The awarding of costs as between parties to litigation is in the discretion of the court, although normally the successful party will obtain an order for costs against the unsuccessful party"); *Doing Business in Ireland* § 16.01[4] (P. Ussher & B. J. O'Connor eds., 1996) (noting that in Ireland a successful litigant is "usually awarded costs against the unsuccessful party, but this is at the court's discretion"); O'Malley & Layton, *supra,* § 52.57 (noting that the practice in Northern Ireland concerning costs and fees is substantially the same as in England and the Republic of Ireland)."

Allocating costs pursuant to the "costs follow the event" principle appears to be prevalent in international commercial arbitration. Most national arbitration laws and international arbitration rules grant arbitrators broad authority to allocate arbitration and legal costs between the parties as they see fit.[194] Although it is difficult to formulate any generally applicable rule or pattern to describe their decisions,[195] international arbitrators often render decisions in accordance with the "costs follow the event principle." Indeed, Professor Gotanda opines that "the principle that costs follow the event is . . . so well-accepted that it may be viewed

---

[194] John Y. Gotanda, *Supplemental Damages in Private International Law* 142 (1998). *See also* ICC Rules of Arbitration, art. 31; *Prudential-Bache Trade Corp. (U.S.) v. Kyocera Corp. (Japan)*, Case No. 6070/BGD (Aug. 25, 1994), *reported in* Mealey's Int'l Arb. Rep., May 1995, at 7 (US$14.5 million award, including attorneys' fees and costs); *Ministry of Defense & Support for Armed Forces of Iran v. Harsco/Bowen-McLaughlin-York Co.*, Case No. 7263/CK (Sept. 18, 1996) (costs award of US$1.7 million). *See also* LCIA Rules of Arbitration, art. 28; AAA International Arbitration Rules, art. 31(d). *See also* the chart below:

Arbitral Rule	Allocation of Costs
ICSID & Additional Facility Rules	ICSID Convention, art. 61(2): "In the case of arbitration proceedings the Tribunal shall, except as the parties otherwise agree, assess the expenses incurred by the parties in connection with the proceedings, and shall decide how and by whom those expenses, the fees and expenses of the members of the Tribunal and the charges for the use of the facilities of the Centre shall be paid. . . ."
	Additional Facility, Rule 59(1): "Unless the parties otherwise agree, the Tribunal shall decide how and by whom the fees and expenses of the members of the Tribunal, the expenses and charges of the Secretariat and the expenses incurred by the parties in connection with the proceeding shall be borne. . . ."
LCIA	Article 28.3: "The Arbitral Tribunal shall also have the power to order in its award that all or part of the legal or other costs incurred by a party be paid by another party, unless the parties agree otherwise in writing. . . ."
SCC Institute	Article 40(2): "The Arbitral Tribunal decides on the apportionment of the arbitration costs as between the parties with regard to the outcome of the case and other circumstances."
	Article 41: "Unless the parties have agreed otherwise, the Arbitral Tribunal may . . . order the losing party to compensate the other party for legal representation and other expenses for presenting its case.
UNCITRAL Rules	Article 40(1): "Except as provided in paragraph 2, the costs of arbitration shall in principle be borne by the unsuccessful party. However, the arbitral tribunal may apportion each of such costs between the parties if it determines that apportionment is reasonable, taking into account the circumstances of the case."
	Article 40(2): "With respect to the costs of legal representation and assistance referred to in article 38, paragraph (e), the arbitral tribunal, taking into account the circumstances of the case, shall be free to determine which party shall bear such costs or may apportion such costs between the parties if it determines that apportionment is reasonable."

[195] John Gotanda, *Awarding Costs and Attorney's Fees in International Commercial Arbitrations*, 21 Mich. J. Int'l L. 1 25 (1999) ("there is no consensus" as to the proper allocation of costs in investment arbitration); A. Redfern & M. Hunter, *Law and Practice of International Commercial Arbitration* 407 (2d ed. 1991) ("It is impossible to identify any general practice as to the treatment of costs in international commercial arbitration").

as a general principle of international law."[196] In 1991, however, the Secretariat of the International Chamber of Commerce's (ICC) Court of Arbitration released a study on cost-shifting in commercial arbitration awards rendered between March 1989 and September 1991 in ICC proceedings.[197] The study revealed that in 81 percent of cases where the claimant prevailed, the arbitrators ordered the respondent to bear all or most of the arbitrators' fees and administrative costs. In 50 percent of these same cases, the tribunal ordered the respondent to pay some portion of the claimant's reasonable legal fees. In cases where the claimant was partially or completely unsuccessful, tribunals awarded administrative costs to the respondent 33 percent of the time, and in 20 percent of cases the respondent received some or all of its legal fees as part of the final award. In the commercial arbitration context, the decision whether to shift costs is sometimes influenced by the provisions of procedural or substantive law applicable to the proceedings.[198]

The American rule, in contrast with the widespread (and perhaps spreading) practice described above, requires that each party bear its own costs, particularly the costs of legal representation.[199] This approach has been followed in a number of investment arbitration decisions, apparently not out of any sense of obligation to follow the American rule, but because of the circumstances of the case and equitable considerations. Indeed, in investment arbitration it is difficult to formulate any generally applicable rule or pattern to describe tribunals' decisions with respect to the allocation of costs.[200] Earlier awards tended to follow the American rule by splitting the arbitration costs and ordering the parties to bear their own legal costs.[201] However, more recently tribunals appear to have started to allocate costs more frequently on the basis of the costs-follow-the-event rule. In so doing, however, they tend more readily to shift arbitration costs than legal fees to the losing side.[202] Some arbitral rules also make a distinction between these categories of expenses.[203]

---

[196] Gotanda, *id.* at 34 & notes 159–60.

[197] Yves Derains & Eric Schwartz, *A Guide to the New ICC Rules of Arbitration* 341–44 (1998).

[198] *See, e.g., Triumph Tankers Ltd. v. Kerr McGee Refining Corp.* (SMA Award No. 2642 of Mar. 28, 1990), *reprinted in* 18 Y.B. Comm. Arb. 112, 120 (1993); ICC Case No. 6962, *reprinted in* 19 Y.B. Comm. Arb. 185, 192 (1994); ICC Case No. 5946, *reprinted in* 16 Y.B. Comm. Arb. 97, 118 (1991).

[199] This is known as the American Rule, first articulated by the U.S. Supreme Court in *Arcambel v. Wiseman*, 3. U.S. 306 (1796).

[200] *Compañia de Aguas del Aconquija, S.A. v. Argentine Republic,* ICSID Case No. ARB/97/3 (Award of Nov. 21, 2000), ¶ 94 ("ICSID tribunals, and international arbitration tribunals generally, have not followed a uniform practice with respect to the award of costs and fees"); Gotanda, *supra* note 195, at 25 ("there is no consensus" as to the proper allocation of costs in investment arbitration). One of the reasons underlying this diverse practice is the wide discretion granted to arbitrators under applicable arbitral rules, providing ample room for interpretation and flexibility.

[201] *See* survey of awards, below.

[202] *Id.*

[203] *See, e.g.,* UNCITRAL Rules, art. 40.

Investment arbitration tribunals take into account several factors in deciding whether to allocate costs against the defeated party, and on what basis to allocate those costs. First, costs are frequently *not* awarded against an unsuccessful claimant where the *bona fides* of the claims are clear.[204] Second, arbitrators appear reluctant to award attorneys' fees where the issues of law are novel, or when the substantive law applicable to the merits of the case is unclear.[205] Finally, the behavior of both parties is a recurring consideration. Where the losing party has conducted itself properly, or the prevailing party is guilty of misconduct, either in relation to the subject of the dispute or during the arbitration proceedings, arbitrators are less likely to shift the costs against the losing party.[206]

The following sections of this chapter examine costs awards rendered in investment arbitration conducted under the UNCITRAL, ICSID, and ICSID Additional Facility rules.

2. Survey of Some Investment Arbitration Awards Rendered under the United Nations Commission on International Trade Law Rules[207]

Article 38 of the UNCITRAL Rules enumerates the expenses that are covered by the term "costs." Article 40 sets forth the rules applicable to the allocation of costs:

> 1. Except as provided in paragraph 2, the costs of arbitration shall in principle be borne by the unsuccessful party. However, the arbitral tribunal may apportion each of such costs between the parties if it determines that apportionment is reasonable, taking into account the circumstances of the case.
>
> 2. With respect to the costs of legal representation and assistance referred to in article 38, paragraph (e), the arbitral tribunal, taking into account the circumstances of the case, shall be free to determine which party shall bear such costs or may apportion such costs between the parties if it determines that apportionment is reasonable.

In contrast to the arbitration rules of ICSID, ICC, LCIA, and the SCC, which accord arbitrators complete discretion in allocating costs,[208] the UNCITRAL Rules create a

---

[204] *See, e.g., Tradex Hellas, S.A. v. Greece,* ICSID Case No. ARB/94/2 (Award of Apr. 29, 1999), ¶¶ 206–207 (no costs awarded where claimant succeeded at jurisdictional phase, but lost on merits, and where "by no means [can the] claim . . . be considered as frivolous"). *See also* N. Rubins, *supra* note 188, at 204–206.

[205] *See, e.g., Maffizini v. Kingdom of Spain,* ICSID Case No. ARB/97/7 (Award of Nov. 13, 2000), ¶ 99 (no costs awarded to successful claimant where "each party has been successful on the key points of their respective positions").

[206] *See, e.g., Olguín v. Paraguay,* ICSID Case No. ARB/98/5 (Award of July 26, 2001), ¶ 85 (no costs awarded to respondent where conduct of Paraguay towards claimant was "less than exemplary" and Paraguay had delayed proceedings by violating ICSID procedures). Tribunals like the one in *Southern Pacific Prop. Ltd. v. Egypt,* however, have rendered very large costs awards without any explanation or indication that such factors were absent.

[207] UNCITRAL has four articles (arts. 38–41) on costs. For a commentary on these articles *see* David D. Caron, Matti Pellonpää, & Lee M. Caplan, *The UNCITRAL Arbitration Rules: A Commentary* 927 *et seq.* (Oxford University Press 2006).

[208] *See* ICSID Arbitration Rules, Rule 28; ICC Arbitration Rules, art. 31; and LCIA Arbitration Rules, art. 28.

presumption that the losing party in arbitration will, "in principle," cover both sides' administrative costs.[209] Article 40(2), however, expressly excludes the prevailing party's legal fees from the cost-shifting presumption, granting to the arbitrators freedom to allocate such expenses as they see fit.[210] As with other rules, however, the UNCITRAL Rules permit an award of legal costs (attorneys' fees) only if they were "claimed during the arbitral proceedings, and only to the extent that the arbitral tribunal determines that the amount of such costs is reasonable."[211] It is unclear at what stage of the arbitral proceedings the prevailing party would need to present its claim for legal fees, or whether a tribunal sould *sua sponte* offer the parties an opportunity to make submissions on the issue of costs.[212] In some investment arbitrations, arbitrators have ordered a separate exchange of submissions on the allocation of fees and expenses, after rendering a decision on the merits.[213]

A survey of published decisions of arbitral tribunals operating under the UNCITRAL Arbitration Rules suggests that there is no clear pattern of cost allocation.[214] Some arbitral awards, however, do underline certain factors that will be important in an UNCITRAL tribunal's deliberation on this issue. In the NAFTA arbitration *Ethyl Corporation v. Canada,* the tribunal rejected several of Canada's challenges to the tribunal's jurisdiction, and joined several others to the merits.[215] The tribunal held that Ethyl's claims suffered from several defects, but that the weaknesses were procedural and did not affect jurisdiction.[216] However, the tribunal found that if Ethyl had complied with certain procedural requirements of NAFTA, delay and expense

---

[209] UNCITRAL Rules, art. 40(1).

[210] For a discussion of drafting history of this article *see* Caron et al., *supra* note 207, at 948–49.

[211] UNCITRAL Rules, art. 38(e).

[212] This issue, to some extent, depends on the arrangements made at the beginning of the arbitral process as to whether the issues of jurisdiction, liability, and damages should be briefed together or in separate stages. In some cases, it may not be economically sound to bifurcate a case, or the parties may prefer not to do so. In such cases the parties' arguments in this respect should in theory be presented in the final round of briefings, which would also include all arguments regarding jurisdiction, liability, and damages. *Cf.* ICSID Arbitration Rule 28, which allows submissions on costs after the closure of the proceedings.

[213] *Pope & Talbot v. Canada* (UNCITRAL, Award in Respect Of Damages, May 31, 2002), ¶ 92 (tribunal requested the parties "provide to the Tribunal . . . their proposals in writing for dealing with costs"); *Waste Mgmt. v. United Mexican States II,* ICSID Case No. ARB(AF)/00/3 (Decision on Mexico's Preliminary Objection Concerning the Previous Proceedings), ¶¶ 52–53 (June 26, 2002) (reserving "to a later stage questions relating to the costs and expenses of the present phase of the proceedings").

[214] *See* separate opinion of Thomas Wälde in *Thunderbird, supra* note 6.

[215] *See Ethyl Corp. v. Canada* (Award on Jurisdiction, June 28, 1998), ¶ 96. The case was settled prior to any award on the merits, after a Canadian court found that Canada's statute banning shipments of the gasoline additive MMT was illegal under Canadian law. *See* http://www.dfait-maeci.gc.ca/tna-nac/ethyl-en.asp.

[216] *Id.* ¶ 87.

could have been avoided.[217] As a result, the tribunal ordered Ethyl to bear Canada's administrative and legal costs associated with these specific aspects of the jurisdictional proceedings.[218]

In *Lauder v. Czech Republic*, the tribunal recognized that under the UNCITRAL Rules, "the costs of arbitration shall in principle be borne by the unsuccessful party."[219] Although it rejected the claimant's complaint and found in favor of the respondent, the tribunal exercised its discretion to depart from the general rule, requiring each party to bear its own legal and administrative costs.[220] The tribunal's decision to split costs equally was influenced by its finding that the Czech Republic had engaged in some improper behavior, both substantively toward the claimant and during the proceedings with respect to document production.[221] The closely related dispute in *CME v. Czech Republic* resulted in the opposite outcome, an award for the claimant. In that case, the tribunal ordered the Czech Republic to pay CME US$750,000 in legal costs and related expenditures, as well as two-thirds of the administrative costs.[222]

In *Himpurna California Energy Ltd. v. PT. PLN (Persero)*, Himpurna, which was awarded more than US$391 million in damages, sought US$2.2 million in legal costs and US$723,000 to cover the tribunal's administrative expenses. The tribunal, which was constituted under the UNCITRAL rules, ordered the state-owned respondent to reimburse the claimant a significant portion of the administrative expenses but refused the claimant's request for attorneys' fees. The arbitrators followed the Rule 40 presumption with regard to arbitration costs, but ordered each side to cover its own costs of legal representation, citing three independent reasons. First, the legal system of Indonesia, the arbitral situs, did

---

[217] *Id.* ¶¶ 88, 92.

[218] *See id.* ¶¶ 89, 92, 96(3).

[219] *Lauder, supra* note 55, ¶ 317.

[220] *Id.* ¶ 319.

[221] *See id.* ¶ 318. *See also GAMI Inv. v. Mexico* (UNCITRAL Arbitration under Chapter 11 of NAFTA, Final Award, Nov. 15, 2004). In that case, the tribunal dismissed GAMI's allegations, but decided that each party should bear its own legal costs and half of the arbitration costs. In reaching this conclusion, the tribunal implied that Mexico would have been eligible to recover its legal and arbitration costs had it not insisted on a separate jurisdictional hearing, which led to substantial additional expense. *Id.* ¶¶ 134–36.

[222] *See CME v. Czech Republic* (Partial Award of Sept. 13, 2001), ¶ 264.

not allow the recovery of most legal fees. Indeed, the tribunal noted that "both parties come from countries [the United States and Indonesia] where litigants broadly bear their own costs." Second, the claimant recovered only a fraction of its monetary claim (Himpurna had sought compensation totalling US$2.3 billion). Finally, the tribunal held that PLN's breach of contract "was not the fruit of self-interested calculations, but of its powerlessness in the face of macroeconomic and political developments [i.e., the 1998 Asian financial crisis]."[223]

In *Methanex v. United States* and *Thunderbird v. Mexico*,[224] which were brought under Chapter 11 of NAFTA and the UNCITRAL rules, the arbitral tribunals awarded both arbitration and legal costs to the victorious respondent states. In *Methanex*, the tribunal noted that the United States had emerged as the prevailing party on issues of both jurisdiction and merits. As a result, Methanex was the unsuccessful party within the meaning of Article 40(1) of UNCITRAL Rules and had to bear the costs of arbitration (US$1.5 million). Similarly, and based on Article 38(e) of the UNCITRAL Rules,[225] the tribunal ordered Methanex to pay US$2,989,423 to the United States for the latter's reasonable legal fees. The tribunal saw no reason to apportion these amounts between the parties, given that the only issues that the United States had lost during the process were of minor significance.[226]

In *Thunderbird*, the tribunal noted that Mexico had generally prevailed, except on issues of jurisdiction and admissibility. With respect to the recovery of legal fees, the tribunal applied the criteria set out in *Azinian v. Mexico*:[227]

> Mexico may in principle recover an appropriate portion of the costs of its legal representation and assistance. In this regard, the amount of US$1,502,065.84 claimed by Mexico appears to be reasonable in light of the scope and length of the present arbitral proceedings. Mexico did not however prevail on all issues. In consideration of this fact, the Tribunal shall exercise its discretion and allocate the costs on a [three-quarters to one-quarter] basis. Accordingly, the Tribunal hereby determines that Thunderbird shall reimburse Mexico in the amount of US$1,126,549.38 in respect of the costs of legal representation for this arbitration.

---

[223] *Himpurna California Energy Ltd. v. PT. PLN (Persero)* (Award of May 4, 1999), *reprinted in* 25 Y.B. Comm. Arb. 13, 106–107 (2000). Another UNCITRAL award ordering a respondent to pay a successful claimant for administrative costs (approximately US$65,000) but not legal fees was rendered in *Biloune, supra* note 102, at 30–31.

[224] *Methanex Corp. v. U.S.* (UNCITRAL Arbitration under Chapter 11 of NAFTA, Pt. V, Final Award of Aug. 3, 2005).

[225] See p. 614 *supra*.

[226] *Methanex* (Final Award), *supra* note 224, Pt. V, ¶¶ 9–12.

[227] *Robert Azinian v. United Mexican States*, ICSID Case No. ARB(AF)/97/2 (Arbitral Award of Nov. 1, 1999), cited in *Thunderbird, supra* note 6, ¶ 217.

Applying the same rationale and proportions, it ordered the claimant to reimburse Mexico for its share of the advance on costs, amounting to US$126,313.02.[228]

In *EnCana v. Ecuador*,[229] the tribunal ordered Ecuador to reimburse EnCana for the arbitration costs, and each party to bear its own legal fees and related expenses, notwithstanding the fact that Ecuador was the prevailing party within the meaning of Article 40(1) of the UNCITRAL Rules. It noted that "this is not an inflexible rule and the Tribunal has a discretion to order otherwise."[230] It also considered that under the circumstances it would be inequitable for EnCana to bear the costs.

The cases of the Iran-U.S. Claims Tribunal, which were conducted under a modified version of the UNCITRAL Rules,[231] illustrate the lack of consensus surrounding costs awards. Although cost-shifting was not uncommon, panels at the Claims Tribunal tended to award less in costs than the prevailing party requested. There is some speculation that this was due to the influence of Iranian arbitrators, and concern for the customs of Iranian parties, unaccustomed to the magnitude of legal fees often encountered in American litigation. One panel succinctly summarized the pre-1985 practice:

> [T]hus far the Tribunal has not awarded costs in all cases, and even when it has, the amounts have generally been less than claimed. Chamber Two has never awarded any

---

[228] *Id.* ¶ 221. *Cf. id.* Separate Opinion of Thomas Wälde, ¶¶ 124 *et seq.* (opining that although cost-shifting may be common in civil law litigation, it is not so in North American litigation and arbitration and should be reserved for cases involving misconduct on the part of the parties); *see also Link Trading v. Moldova* (UNCITRAL Arbitration, Award, Apr. 18, 2002). In *Link Trading*, the tribunal dismissed all the claimant's allegations and ordered it to bear the arbitration costs as well as part of Moldova's legal costs. However, the tribunal ultimately awarded only US$22,200 of the US$144,422 claimed by Moldova. In doing so, the arbitrators took into account that there had been no hearing, that the respondent's counsel had appeared fairly late in the proceedings and prepared only a limited number of submissions, and that the rest of the amount put forward by Moldova was unsubstantiated. *Id.* ¶¶ 93–6.

[229] *EnCana Corp. v. Republic of Ecuador* (Canada-Ecuador BIT), LCIA Case UN3481 (Arbitration under the UNCITRAL Rules, Award of Feb. 3, 2006). Facts of *EnCana* were discussed at p. 467 *supra*.

[230] *Id.* ¶ 201. In *Occidental v. Ecuador*, which was brought under the U.S.-Ecuador BIT and conducted under the UNCITRAL Rules administered by the LCIA, the tribunal noted that both parties had prevailed in respect of important aspects of the dispute. Therefore, it ordered Ecuador, which had breached the BIT and was liable for damages in excess of US$70 million, to bear 55 percent of the arbitration costs and each party to bear its own legal costs. *Occidental, supra* note 72, ¶ 216.

[231] The modified version of the UNCITRAL rules applied by the Iran-U.S. Claims Tribunal can be found at http://www.iusct.org/index-english.html.

costs, Chamber One has awarded relatively small amounts of costs in only a few cases, and Chamber Three has in general awarded costs to the successful party in an amount well below the one claimed, using a range between $5,000 and $25,000 with costs of $70,000 awarded in one case. No distinction has been made between costs for legal representation and assistance and other costs, where costs were awarded.[232]

According to one commentator's view of Claims Tribunal practice, "[i]n most cases, only 'reasonable' costs are granted to the winning side without any attempt to justify the amount awarded, or to itemize."[233]

3. Awards Rendered under the International Centre for Settlement of Investment Disputes Rules

The ICSID Arbitration Rules and Additional Facility Rules provide that, absent contrary agreement between the parties, the award of costs and legal expenses is left to the discretion of the tribunal.[234] Article 61(2) of the ICSID Convention provides that:

> In the case of arbitration proceedings the Tribunal shall, except as the parties otherwise agree, assess the expenses incurred by the parties in connection with the proceedings, and shall decide how and by whom those expenses, the fees and expenses of the members of the Tribunal and the charges for the use of the facilities of the Centre shall be paid. Such decision shall form part of the award.

This provision effectively allows a tribunal to decide how to allocate both legal fees and related costs ("expenses incurred by the parties in connection with the proceedings") and arbitration costs, unless the parties agree otherwise.[235] Article 58 of the ICSID Additional Facility Rules grants tribunals under those rules comparable authority.

Article 28 of the ICSID Arbitration Rules deals with the procedure for allocating the costs of arbitration proceedings:

> (1) Without prejudice to the final decision on the payment of the cost of the proceeding, the Tribunal may, unless otherwise agreed by the parties, decide:
>
> (a) at any stage of the proceeding, the portion which each party shall pay, pursuant to Administrative and Financial Regulation 14, of the fees and expenses of the Tribunal and the charges for the use of the facilities of the Centre;
>
> (b) with respect to any part of the proceeding, that the related costs (as determined by the Secretary-General) shall be borne entirely or in a particular share by one of the parties.

---

[232] SN: *Sylvania Technical Systems, Inc. v. Gov't of the Islamic Republic of Iran*, 8 Iran-U.S. C. Trib. Rep. 298, 324 (1985).

[233] Stephen J. Toope, *Mixed International Arbitration* 380 (1990).

[234] ICSID Convention, art. 61(2) and Additional Facility, Rule 59(1).

[235] *See also* Schreuer, Commentary, *supra* note 33, at 1223–24.

(2) Promptly after the closure of the proceeding, each party shall submit to the Tribunal a statement of costs reasonably incurred or borne by it in the proceeding and the Secretary-General shall submit to the Tribunal an account of all amounts paid by each party to the Centre and of all costs incurred by the Centre for the proceeding. The Tribunal may, before the award has been rendered, request the parties and the Secretary-General to provide additional information concerning the cost of the proceeding.

This article, unlike Article 40 of the UNCITRAL Rules, contemplates a procedural timetable during which the parties should provide the necessary information to substantiate their claims regarding the costs of the proceedings, and allowing the tribunal to inquire about these costs. As with UNCITRAL Arbitration Rules, however, no uniform pattern emerges from an overview of resulting awards.

One of the most striking costs awards was rendered in 1992 in *Southern Pacific Properties Ltd. v. Egypt*, where an ICSID tribunal awarded the prevailing party US$5 million in administrative costs and attorneys' fees as part of a damages award of US$27.7 million. The arbitral tribunal provided little reasoning, but did underscore the importance of costs awards in making a successful investor whole:[236]

> [T]here is little doubt that the legal costs incurred in obtaining the indemnification must be considered part and parcel of the compensation, in order to make whole the party who suffered the loss and had to litigate to obtain compensation. . . . In light of these considerations, the Tribunal concludes that the total costs to be reimbursed to the Claimants for legal and accounting work which has been relevant or useful to the present ICSID proceedings amounts to US$5,092,000. Undoubtedly, this is a high figure, but it is justified by the extraordinary length and complication of the proceedings in this case.[237]

In the NAFTA case of *Azinian v. United Mexican States*, which was decided under the Additional Facility Rules, the tribunal did not award any costs against the unsuccessful claimant, although it recognized that the ordinary practice in such circumstances is to make the losing claimant "bear the costs of the arbitration, as well as to contribute to the prevailing respondent's reasonable costs of representation."[238] Rather, the tribunal allocated costs equally between the parties, citing several factors as justification: that NAFTA was a new system, and

---

[236] *Southern Pac. Prop. Ltd. v. Egypt* (Award of May 20, 1992), *reprinted in* 19 Y.B. Comm. Arb. 51, 82–83 (1994).

[237] *Id.*, 3 ICSID Rep. 45, 238–39 (1992).

[238] *Azinian v. United Mexican States*, ICSID Case No. ARB(AF)/97/2 (Award of Nov. 1, 1999), ¶¶ 125–27.

therefore the claimant could not be expected to understand fully the extent of his rights; that the claimant had presented his case in an "efficient and professional manner"; that Mexico's actions, while ultimately lawful, tended to invite litigation; and that an award of costs against the claimants would ultimately be borne by innocent parties.[239]

Similarly, the award in *Vacuum Salt Products Ltd. v. Republic of Ghana* included no allocation of arbitration or legal costs, although the claimant was wholly unsuccessful, and the case was dismissed for lack of jurisdiction. The parties were ordered to bear their own legal costs and to share the arbitration costs equally.[240]

The award in *Genin v. Estonia* again underlines the potential importance of party conduct in the allocation of costs. There, the claimant concealed important facts from the tribunal until very late in the proceedings. On the other hand, the respondent government had revoked the claimant's license in an "awkward manner" and without notice or the opportunity to challenge the action. The tribunal noted that "either of these factors, alone, might have impelled an award of costs against the offending party." However, in dismissing Genin's claim, the tribunal found that the conduct on both sides had a balancing effect, leading to an order that each side bear its own legal expenses and half of the administrative costs.[241] The NAFTA tribunal in *Metalclad v. United Mexican States* likewise declined to award costs to the successful party, in this case the claimant. Without explaining the specific factors that led to its conclusion, the tribunal found that "it is equitable in this matter for each party to bear its own costs and fees, as well as half the advance payments made to ICSID."[242] In *World Duty Free v. Kenya*,[243] the tribunal stated that ordinarily it would have followed the rule of costs follow the event, but that under the circumstances of the case, none of the parties had emerged as the winner in the traditional sense. Consequently, it ordered each party to bear its own legal costs and to share equally the arbitration costs.[244]

---

[239] See id. ¶ 126.

[240] *Vacuum Salt Prods. Ltd. v. Republic of Ghana*, ICSID Case No. ARB/92/1 (Award of Feb. 1, 1994), *reprinted in* 20 Y.B. Comm. Arb. 11, 33 (1995). *See also L.E.S.I. DIPENTA v. Algeria*, ICSID Case No. ARB/03/08 (Decision on Jurisdiction, Jan. 10, 2005), ¶ 43 (tribunal ordered each party bear its own legal costs and equally share the arbitration costs); *Noble Ventures Inc. v. Romania*, ICSID Case No. ARB/01/11 (Final Award, Oct. 12, 2005), ¶¶ 230–36 (the tribunal considered that although Noble Ventures lost on all its claims, it had prevailed with respect to certain legal issues. Therefore, the tribunal found it fair and reasonable that each party bear its own legal costs and share the arbitration costs equally); *Joy Mining Machinery Ltd. v. Egypt*, ICSID Case No. ARB/03/11 (Award on Jurisdiction, July 30, 2004).

[241] *Genin v. Estonia*, ICSID Case No. ARB/99/2 (Award of June 25, 2001), ¶¶ 380–83.

[242] *Metalclad, supra* note 68, ¶ 130.

[243] *World Duty Free Co. Ltd. v. Republic of Kenya*, ICSID Case No. ARB/00/7 (Oct. 4, 2006).

[244] *Id.* ¶¶ 190–91.

The tribunal in *Agip v. Congo,* which awarded the claimant more than US$3 million in damages, ordered the host state to bear all of the administrative costs and expenses, but ordered each party to cover its own attorneys' fees.[245] In *Azurix v. Argentina,* the tribunal took a similar approach. It first considered the success and failure of the parties in the arguments that they had presented to the tribunal during the proceedings. For instance, it noted that the claimant had prevailed on the merits, but had failed in a request for provisional measures, and that Argentina had failed in its objections to the jurisdiction and its challenge to the president of the tribunal. The tribunal also considered the fact that the claimant had not complied with a request for the production of certain documents. On this basis, it ordered that each party pay its own legal costs, and that arbitration costs be borne by Argentina, except for US$34,496, which was to be borne by the claimant.[246]

The tribunal in *Telenor v. Hungary*[247] applied the "costs follow the event" rule, and awarded arbitration and legal costs to Hungary as the prevailing party.[248] The Norwegian claimant was ordered to pay Hungary's legal fees, which were approximately US$1.25 million. In addition, Telenor had to reimburse Hungary for its share of the ICSID administrative costs. In ordering Telenor to pay these sums, the tribunal considered *inter alia* that Telenor's conduct during the proceedings had made it difficult both for the tribunal and for Hungary to litigate the case, adding to the costs of the proceedings.[249] In *ADC v. Hungary,*[250] the tribunal similarly shifted costs, ordering Hungary to pay more than US$7.5 million to ADC for arbitration costs and legal fees. The tribunal quoted Judge Holtzman of the Iran-U.S. Claims Tribunal,[251] who suggested that in assessing requests for reimbursement of costs, a reasonableness test should be applied. In applying that test, the tribunal rejected Hungary's argument that ADC's costs

---

[245] *Agip S.p.A. v. People's Republic of Congo,* ICSID Case No. ARB/77/1 (Award of Nov. 30, 1979), *reprinted in* 1 ICSID Rep. 306, 329 (1993). *See also Inceysa Vallisoletana S.L. v. Republic of El Salvador,* ICSID Case No. ARB/03/26 (Aug. 2, 2006), ¶ 338.

[246] *Azurix, supra* note 70, ¶ 441.

[247] *Telenor Mobile Commc'ns A.S. v. Republic of Hungary,* ICSID Case No. ARB/04/15 (Sept. 15, 2006).

[248] *See also CSOB v. Slovak Republic,* where the tribunal ordered the losing party, Slovakia, to contribute US$10,000,000 to CSOB's costs and to bear its own costs and expenses. CSOB had to bear the rest of its costs, almost US$6 million. *CSOB v. Slovak Republic,* ICSID Case No. ARB/97/4 (Final Award, 2004), ¶ 372.

[249] *Id.* ¶ 107.

[250] *ADC, supra* note 59.

[251] *Id.* ¶ 534 citing separate opinion of Judge Holtzman at 7; reported in Iranian Assets Litig. Rep. 10, 860, 10, 863; 8 Iran-US C.T.R. 329, 332–33.

were unreasonable because they were 75 percent more than Hungary's, dismissing the idea that "the reasonableness of the quantum of the Claimants' claim for costs should be judged by the amount expended by the Respondent."[252] It also noted that Hungary's decision to change counsel and experts during the proceedings, engaging a relatively younger legal team, could have explained the discrepancy between the parties' costs.

4. Calculation of Government Legal Fees

Until recently, there was only one published investment arbitration decision in which a respondent government received an award of attorneys' fees against an unsuccessful private claimant (*Ethyl v. Canada*).[253] It was therefore very difficult to predict how an arbitral tribunal would determine the rate at which a government should be compensated for the work of its staff attorneys. Arbitrators might take any of three approaches. First, they could award the respondent government attorneys' fees as if its lawyers were engaged in comparable private practice. Second, the government could receive an amount based on the attorneys' actual salary, for time spent on the case. Finally, the arbitrators could simply award a "reasonable" fee, as the UNCITRAL Rules suggest, perhaps between the amounts that would follow from the first two valuation methods.

There now have been at least three additional cases (*Methanex, Thunderbird,* and *Telenor*) in which respondent states have been reimbursed for legal fees. In *Thunderbird,* the Mexican government asked for its own in-house lawyers' costs as well as the fees paid to outside counsel. Outside counsel submitted affidavits as to their costs, and the tribunal simply stated that "the amount of US$1,502,065.84 claimed by Mexico appears to be reasonable in light of the scope and length of the present arbitral proceedings."[254] In *Methanex,* the U.S. government's cost submission

---

[252] *Id.* ¶ 535. Most recently, the tribunal in *Vivendi v. Argentina* awarded attorney's fees and arbitration costs to the claimant for the jurisdictional phase of the case (approximately US$ 702,000) because the respondent had reasserted several jurisdictional objections, which had been dismissed in the earlier phases of the case by the original tribunal as well as by the annulment committee. Furthermore, some of these arguments had also been raised and rejected in other arbitral proceedings pending against Argentina. Such objections were held unnecessarily to magnify the cost of the proceedings, without any reasonable chance of success. With respect to the parties' expenses during the merits phase, the tribunal ordered each to bear its own attorney's fees and pay half of the arbitration costs. *Vivendi II, supra* note 69, ¶¶ 10.2.1–10.2.6.

[253] See pp. 616–17 *supra.*

[254] *Thunderbird, supra* note 6, ¶ 220.

included more extensive explanation as to why these costs were reasonable. Ultimately, the tribunal found these arguments convincing.

> *Methanex Co. v. United States of the America*
>
> Submission on Costs of Respondent United States of America, July 19, 2004, *available at* www.naftaclaims.com
>
> Costs for legal representation and assistance as referenced in Article 38(e) are discussed in the attached witness statements of Barton Legum, Mary Reddy, and John Rinaldi. The Tribunal should award the full amount of these costs, which is $942,455.25. (Rinaldi Statement at Tab 3).
>
> The amount of these costs is not only reasonable, it is quite conservative. Unlike attorneys in the private sector, attorneys for the United States Department of State have only one client and do not bill for their time by matter. Therefore, the United States has made a reasonable estimate of the cost of attorney time devoted to the Methanex case in the following manner. Mr. Legum, who supervised the attorneys assigned to the Methanex case, estimated the percentage of their time that was devoted to working on the case during each year of these proceedings. (See Witness Statement of Barton Legum ("Legum Statement") ¶ 10.) The costs of these attorneys' salaries and benefits in each of those years were obtained from the Executive Director's Office in the Legal Adviser's Office at the Department of State. (See Witness Statement of Mary Reddy ("Reddy Statement") ¶ 4.) Multiplying the appropriate percentage by the cost of salary and benefits for each attorney and then adding the results yields the total estimated cost of legal representation by the United States in this case, $942,455.25. (See Rinaldi Statement at Tab 3.)
>
> This estimate is conservative in many respects, as discussed in Mr. Legum's Witness Statement. First, the State Department could have retained outside counsel and paid prevailing market rates for attorneys' time, rather than the salaries and benefits of its employees. Using the hourly billable rate for attorneys in the market with the experience of the attorneys in the NAFTA Arbitration Division would yield a much higher estimate of the costs of legal representation in this case. (See Legum Statement ¶ 11; Reddy Statement ¶ 2.)
>
> Second, some attorneys who devoted significant time to this case are excluded from this calculus, including, for example, Deputy Legal Adviser Ronald Bettauer, and Assistant Legal Adviser for International Claims and Investment Disputes, Mark Clodfelter, as well as attorneys in other agencies of the federal and California state governments. These attorneys—at federal agencies including the Department of Commerce, the Department of Justice, the Department of the Treasury, the Environmental Protection Agency, and the U.S. Trade Representative's Office, and California agencies including the Attorney General's Office, the State Water Resources Control Board, and the Air Resources Board—spent many hours reviewing and commenting on the United States' submissions in this case.
>
> Third, the value of administrative support services has not been included in this calculation, although many hours of secretarial and paralegal time were devoted to this case. Similarly, the value of intern and student law clerk time is not included here. Accordingly, the Tribunal should award the United States the full amount of its costs for attorney time, in the amount of $942,455.25.

XX. Annulment and Set Aside

Many consider the finality of awards to be one of the primary advantages of arbitration.[1] Hyperbolically describing the immunity of arbitration awards from judicial review on the merits, one nineteenth-century Scottish judge remarked that an arbitrator "may believe what nobody else believes, and he may disbelieve what all the world believes. He may overlook or flagrantly misapply the most ordinary principles of law, and there is no appeal for those who have chosen to submit themselves to his despotic power."[2] In contrast, the loser in a national court case may well be able to persuade an appellate court to disregard the legal or factual findings of the lower court.

The modern system of international arbitration—including some types of investment arbitration—is indeed intended to avoid the multitiered appeals mechanisms of national court systems. Judicial review at the situs of the arbitration is usually limited, and international treaties prevent the relitigation in non-situs courts of issues already resolved by arbitration tribunals. However, there is still a very real role for national courts and other bodies to assess the correctness of awards. Where a defeated host state is dissatisfied with the arbitrators' decision,[3] it

---

[1] Samuel A. Haubold, *Opting out of the U.S. Legal System: The Case for International Arbitration,* 10 Int'l L. Practicum 43, 44 (1997) ("Most parties who elect to arbitrate rather than litigate do so because they want finality"). *But compare* William H. Knull, III & Noah D. Rubins, *Betting the Farm on International Arbitration: Is it Time to Offer an Appeal Option?,* 11 Am. Rev. Int'l Arb. 531 (2000) (many parties to international arbitration consider neutrality and predictability to be the primary advantages of arbitration, and would prefer *ex ante* some level of appeal on the merits).

[2] *Mitchell v. Cable* [1848] 10 D. 1297.

[3] A claimant that has lost its case can also seek to set aside the award. However, losing investors are less likely to seek to overturn awards, as success in such an effort would simply put the claimant back at square one, obliged to restart the arbitration from the beginning with a new tribunal.

normally has at least one opportunity to challenge the arbitral award, known as annulment or set aside. The scope of this review is determined by the situs of the arbitration: The International Centre for Settlement of Investment Disputes (ICSID) annulment procedure controls ICSID awards, and the national arbitration law of the situs controls non-ICSID arbitrations.

In ICSID proceedings, the losing party can only request annulment under Article 52 of the Washington Convention.[4] Article 52 calls for the establishment of an "ad hoc Committee" of arbitrators that is empowered to examine the procedural propriety of the award, and if it finds one of the enumerated defects, to partially or completely annul it.[5] In theory, once the annulment process is complete, the host state is obligated to honor any final award as if it were a judgment of that state's own courts, subject only to possible sovereign immunity defenses under the laws of the place of execution.[6]

However, many investment arbitration cases take place outside the self-contained Washington Convention system, and are instead conducted pursuant to the ICSID Additional Facility Rules, United Nations Commission on International Trade Law (UNCITRAL) arbitration rules, or under the auspices of one of the prominent commercial arbitration institutions. Most commonly, an investment dispute is arbitrated outside of ICSID because at least one of the states involved in the dispute (the host state or the investor's home state) is not a party to the Washington Convention. A claimant might also choose non-ICSID arbitration because the transaction generating the dispute may not qualify as an "investment" for purposes of Article 25 of the Washington Convention but might still fall within the broader scope of an investment treaty or other document evidencing

---

[4] Convention on the Settlement of Investment Disputes Between States and Nationals of Other States of March 18, 1965, 4 I.L.M. 524 (1966).

[5] *See generally* M. Feldman, *The Annulment Proceedings and the Finality of ICSID Arbitral Awards*, 2 ICSID Rev.-F.I.L.J. 85 (1987); D. Caron, *Reputation and Reality in the ICSID Annulment Process: Understanding the Distinction Between Annulment and Appeal*, 7 ICSID Rev.-F.I.L.J. 92 (1993); A. Giardina, *ICSID: A Self-Contained, Non-National Review System*, in *International Arbitration in the 21st Century* (Lillich & Brower eds., Transnat'l Publishers 1994).

[6] *See* Washington Convention, art. 55. Argentina, however, has indicated it may not enforce or recognize International Centre for Settlement of Investment Disputes (ICSID) awards against it arising out of the 2000–2001 financial crisis. U.S. State Department, 2005 Investment Climate Statement: Argentina, http://www.state.gov/e/eeb/ifd/2005/41948.htm ("Several government of Argentina officials have hinted that Argentina will not pay any ICSID awards resulting from the pesification of contracts").

consent to arbitration.[7] Finally, the claimant may have a range of options open to it, and could decide that the International Chamber of Commerce, Stockholm Chamber of Commerce, or ad hoc arbitration under UNCITRAL Rules better suited the dispute at hand and the investor's strategic interests.

If the award is from a non-ICSID tribunal, the challenge is normally governed by the law of the situs of the arbitration. Thus, the bases on which a losing party can seek to annul an award will vary from state to state. Some states may have relatively broad grounds for challenging an award, although others, especially those that have adopted the UNCITRAL Model Law[8] or some variant of it, are more restrictive.

The most important characteristic of almost all annulment procedures is that it is generally much narrower than an appeal of a national court judgment. Although, as noted, there is considerable variation among the available procedures, most reviewing courts (and ICSID annulment committees) are precluded from substituting their analysis of the facts or the law for that of the tribunal. Instead, annulment actions tend to focus on asserted procedural deficiencies of the award, although reviewing bodies sometimes use a procedural basis as a pretext for a more substantive review. This generally narrow scope of review reflects the goal of treating an arbitration award as final.

A. International Centre for Settlement of Investment Disputes Annulment

The ICSID annulment process is in theory a narrow one. The only permissible grounds for annulment under Article 52 of the Washington Convention are: (a) the tribunal was not properly constituted; (b) the tribunal manifestly exceeded its

---

[7] *See generally* Chapter XI on definition of investment. Some contracts for the sale of goods, for example, may fall within the definition of "investment" for purposes of a bilateral investment treaty (BIT). *See, e.g.*, Agreement among the Government of Brunei Darussalam, Republic of Indonesia, Malaysia, Republic of the Philippines, Republic of Singapore, and the Kingdom of Thailand for the Promotion and Protection of Investments, signed Dec. 15, 1987 (the Association of South East Asian Nations [ASEAN] Investment Agreement), Art. I(3) ("every kind of asset" qualifies as investment, arguably including contract rights). Such contracts, however, usually do not satisfy the definition of investment under Article 25(1) of the Washington Convention. *Asian Express v. Greater Colombo Economic Comm'n, described in* Ibrahim Shihata & Antonio Parra, *The Experience of the International Centre for Settlement of Investment Disputes*, 14 ICSID Rev.-F.I.L.J. 299, 308 (1999); ICSID, *Annual Report* 6 (1985) (investment arbitration refused registration by the ICSID Secretariat on grounds that the claim arose out of a contract for the sale of goods and therefore did not arise out of an investment within the scope of the Washington Convention).

[8] United Nations Commission on International Trade Law (UNCITRAL), Model Law on International Commercial Arbitration (1985, amended in 2006), *available at* www.uncitral.org/uncitral/en/uncitral_texts/arbitration/1985Model_arbitration.html.

powers; (c) there was corruption of a tribunal member; (d) there was a serious departure from a fundamental rule of procedure; or (e) the award did not state the reasons on which it is based. The annulment process begins when a party requests the establishment of a new ICSID panel, referred to as the *ad hoc committee*. The ad hoc committee determines whether one of the preceding five grounds exists, and if it does, the committee can annul the decision in whole or in part. Annulment voids the decision, rather than modifying it, as is possible with an appeal. It is also possible for a party seeking annulment of an award to request at that time a stay of enforcement for the duration of the proceeding, perhaps on the posting of a bond for the total amount of the award.[9]

A great deal has been written about the process and jurisprudence of ad hoc annulment committees under the Washington Convention.[10] From the inception of ICSID to 2007, at least eighteen annulment requests have been filed,[11] out of 248 total ICSID disputes.[12] Of the sixteen annulment proceedings concluded as of 2007, five attempts have been successful (three in the 1980s,[13] and two more

---

[9] Martina Polasek, *Introductory Note to Three Decisions on the Stay of Enforcement of an ICSID Award*, 20(2) ICSID Rev.–F.I.L.J. 581 (2005).

[10] *See, e.g.*, Caron, *supra* note 5, at 21; David R. Sedlak, Comment, *ICSID's Resurgence in International Investment Arbitration: Can the Momentum Hold?*, 23 Penn. St. Int'l L. Rev. 147, 162–71 (2004); Daniel Q. Posin, *Recent Developments in ICSID Annulment Procedures*, 13 World Arb. & Mediation Rep. 170, 171 (2002); Monroe Leigh, *Arbitration—Annulment of Arbitral Award for Failure to Apply law Applicable Under ICSID Convention and Failure to State Sufficiently Pertinent Reasons*, 81 Am. J. Int'l L. 222, 224 (1987); *Annulment of ICSID Awards* (Gaillard & Banifatemi eds., Juris Publishing 2002).

[11] In each of the two cases of *Amco v. Indonesia* and *Klöckner v. Cameroon*, two annulment applications were filed. They have been counted as one in calculating the number of the filed annulment cases, however.

[12] Data obtained in September 2007 from the list of ICSID cases, *available at* http://icsid.worldbank.org.

[13] *Klöckner Industrie-Anlagen GmbH v. United Republic of Cameroon & Société Camerounaise des Engrais*, ICSID Case No. ARB/81/2 (Ad hoc Committee Decision on Annulment of May 3, 1985), 114 J. du Droit Int'l 163 (1987); *Amco Asia Corp. v. Republic of Indonesia*, ICSID Case No. ARB/81/1 (Ad hoc Committee Decision on the Application for Annulment of May 16, 1986), 25 I.L.M. 1439 (1986); *Maritime International Nominees Establishment v. Republic of Guinea*, ICSID Case No. ARB/84/4 (Ad hoc Committee Decision on Annulment of Dec. 22, 1989) (partially annulled, then resubmitted and settled).

recently[14]), and eleven either unsuccessful, discontinued, or remain unpublished.[15] Two annulment petitions are pending.[16] After initial concern that the first two ad hoc committees (i.e., those in *Amco* and *Klöckner* cases) were interpreting the procedural grounds for annulment too broadly, the next committees followed a more stringent approach, rejecting most annulment requests. However, the recent decisions of *Aguas de Aconquija & Vivendi v. Argentina* and later *Patrick Mitchell* may indicate the emergence of a somewhat more activist approach to the interpretation of grounds for annulment under the Washington Convention.

Article 52 lay dormant for the first nineteen years of the ICSID Convention. The first annulment petition was *Klöckner v. Cameroon*, in 1985, in response to which the ad hoc committee concluded that the tribunal manifestly exceeded its powers.[17] In *Klöckner*, the ad hoc committee found that merely postulating a legal principle without demonstrating its existence was an inadequate application of the governing law, as required by the Convention. The legal principle at issue was a French law that permitted a party to refuse performance of its contractual obligations when

---

[14] *Compañia de Aguas del Aconquija S.A. & Vivendi Universal v. Argentine Republic*, ICSID Case No. ARB/97/3 (Decision on Annulment of July 3, 2002), [English original] 19 ICSID Rev.-F.I.L.J. 89 (2004) [hereinafter *Vivendi Annulment Decision*]; and *Patrick Mitchell v. Democratic Republic of the Congo*, ICSID Case No. ARB/99/7 (Decision on Annulment of Nov. 1, 2006) (annulling the award).

[15] *CMS Gas Transmission Co. v. Argentine Republic*, ICSID Case No. ARB/01/8 (Decision on Annulment of Sept. 25, 2007) (the award was approved on all major points including the damages analysis, with the exception of the umbrella clause analysis, which was annulled); *Industria Nacional de Alimentos & Indalsa Perú v. Perú* (previously *Empresas Lucchetti, S.A. & Lucchetti Peru, S.A. v. Republic of Peru*), ICSID Case No. ARB/03/4 (Decision on Annulment, Sept. 5, 2007) (annulment denied); *Hussein Nuaman Soufraki v. United Arab Emirates*, ICSID Case No. ARB/02/7 (Decision of the Ad Hoc Committee on the Application for Annulment of Mr. Soufraki, June 5, 2007) (annulment denied); *Wena Hotels Ltd. v. Arab Republic of Egypt*, ICSID Case No. ARB/98/4 (Decision on Application for Annulment of Feb. 5, 2002), 41 I.L.M. 933 (2002) (annulment denied); *Repsol YPF Ecuador S.A. v. Empresa Estatal Petroleos del Ecuador* (Petroecuador), ICSID Case No. ARB/01/10 (Decision on Application for Annulment), Jan. 8, 2007 (annulment denied); *Southern Pacific Properties (Middle East) Ltd. v. Arab Republic of Egypt*, ICSID Case No. ARB/84/3 (settled before annulment decision was made); *Philippe Gruslin v. Malaysia*, ICSID Case No. ARB/99/3 (discontinued for lack of payment); *Consortium R.F.C.C. v. Kingdom of Morocco*, ICSID Case No. ARB/00/6 (Decision on Application for Annulment, Jan. 18, 2006); *MTD Equity Sdn. Bhd. & MTD Chile S.A. v. Republic of Chile*, ICSID Case No. ARB/01/7 (Decision on the Application for Annulment, Mar. 21, 2007); *CDC Group PLC v. Republic of Seychelles*, ICSID Case No. ARB/02/14 (Decision on the Application for Annulment, June 29, 2006); *Joy Mining Machinery Ltd. v. Arab Republic of Egypt*, ICSID Case No. ARB/03/11 (settled before annulment issued).

[16] *Azurix Corp. v. Argentine Republic*, ICSID Case No. ARB/01/12 (annulment proceeding registered Dec. 11, 2006); *Siemens A.G. v. Argentine Republic*, ICSID Case No. ARB/02/8 (annulment proceeding registered July 16, 2007).

[17] *Klöckner Industrie-Anlagen GmbH v. United Republic of Cameroon & Société Camerounaise des Engrais*, ICSID Case No. ARB/81/2 (May 3, 1985) (decision annulling award of Oct. 21, 1983).

confronted with a material failure to perform by the other party.[18] Although the tribunal technically did provide reasons for its decision, relying on such a "basic principle" of the law chosen by the parties was deemed by the ad hoc committee too cursory a basis for the tribunal's decision.[19]

The next annulment, *Amco v. Indonesia*,[20] involved two annulment proceedings. The first annulment committee found both a serious departure from a fundamental rule of procedure and that the tribunal manifestly exceeded its powers because it failed to apply the proper Indonesian law in calculating the amount of the investment in the project at issue. This miscalculation resulted in a gross overstatement of the investment, and thereby altered the outcome of the arbitration.[21]

Together, the decisions in *Klöckner* and *Amco* sparked concerns that the ad hoc panels were actually reviewing the merits of the case and ignoring the fundamental arbitral principle of finality. The Secretary General of ICSID himself warned the ICSID Administrative Council of the "danger" that "both investors and contracting states might be deterred from making use of ICSID arbitration" if the practice of annulment called into question the effectiveness and finality of the ICSID process.[22] One of the grounds for annulment—that the tribunal manifestly exceeded its powers—is especially susceptible to criticism because it often requires a more intensive examination of the merits than the other grounds.[23] The time and expense involved in annulment proceedings are also a cause of concern for critics. The entire arbitration process including the annulment in *Klöckner* took more than nine years, and more than eleven years in *Amco*.[24] The risk of ICSID awards becoming as vulnerable to appeal as disputes in litigation, compounded by the time and expense of seeking annulment, generated widespread criticism of the ICSID annulment process in the 1980s and 1990s.[25]

A counterargument to these concerns was that neither annulment altered the initial award or actually determined that the losing party should win. Rather, in *Klöckner,*

---

[18] *Id.*

[19] *Id.* After the first annulment proceedings, the case was resubmitted to a new tribunal, which issued a new award on Jan. 26, 1988. Thereafter, a second annulment committee rejected the second annulment application.

[20] *Amco v. Indonesia, supra* note 13.

[21] *Id.* The case was resubmitted to a new tribunal, which rendered its award on June 5, 1990. A second annulment committee rejected the annulment application on all major points.

[22] Report of the Secretary General to the Administrative Council at its Twentieth Annual Meeting 2 (Oct. 2, 1986), reprinted in Int'l Arb. Rep., at 128 (Feb. 1987).

[23] Thomas W. Wälde, *ICSID "Annulment Committee,"* 1(2) Oil, Gas & Energy Law Intelligence (Mar. 2003), *available at* http://www.gasandoil.com/ogel/samples/freearticles/article_75.htm.

[24] *See, e.g.,* Leigh, *supra* note 10, at 225.

[25] *Id.*

the committee sent the case back to a second arbitral tribunal to decide the case on the merits after determining the appropriate legal standard. This is different from an appeals process because the ad hoc committee did not look at the merits of the case.[26] The committee in *Amco* did not consider itself competent to recalculate the amount of damages but instead annulled the entire decision.[27] The second tribunal in *Amco* supported the view that an ad hoc committee's role is strictly limited, and rejected the argument that an annulment committee's reasoning is binding on the new tribunal's decision.[28]

Perhaps in response to the earlier criticism, the committees in the next few annulment proceedings refused to set aside the awards. For example, in *Wena Hotels Limited v. Arab Republic of Egypt,* the original ICSID tribunal had found that Egypt failed to afford Wena fair and equitable treatment as well as full protection and security for its investments in Egypt. In response, Egypt sought annulment on three grounds: (1) that the tribunal manifestly exceeded its powers, (2) that it engaged in a serious departure from a fundamental rule of procedure, and (3) that it failed to state the reasons for the award.[29] The ad hoc committee systematically rejected each of the three grounds. Specifically, it rejected the claim that the tribunal manifestly exceeded its powers by not applying the proper law because the parties had never agreed on a governing law, so the tribunal's choice-of-law analysis was within its powers.[30] It rejected the serious departure claim because Egypt had an opportunity to present its case regardless of the tribunal's alleged procedural inadequacies. Finally, the committee rejected the claim that the tribunal failed to state its reasons because the tribunal had, in fact, provided reasons, although sometimes implicitly, and because the annulment claim as framed by Egypt would have required an improper review of the appropriateness of the stated reasons.[31]

In contrast, the recent decision of the ad hoc committee in *Aguas de Aconquija and Vivendi* may indicate a renewal of the broad approach toward the interpretation of the grounds for annulment. The claimants in *Aguas de Aconquija and Vivendi*[32] sought annulment on the same three grounds as the respondents in *Wena Hotels.*

---

[26] Posin, *supra* note 10, at 171.

[27] Leigh, *supra* note 10, at 224.

[28] Peter D. Trooboff & Christopher T. Curtis, *International Investment Disputes–Res Judicata Effect of Partially Annulled ICSID Award,* 83 Am. J. Int'l L. 106, 109 (1998).

[29] *Wena Hotels, supra* note 15; *see also* Posin, *supra* note 10, at 171.

[30] *Id.*

[31] *Id.*

[32] *Vivendi Annulment Decision, supra* note 14. *See* Chapter XIV *supra* for excerpts of this decision.

The ad hoc committee granted a partial annulment, finding that the tribunal had acted improperly by upholding its jurisdiction to hear the claimants' claims under the relevant treaty, but then declining to decide a significant portion of those claims.[33] The committee concluded that the tribunal had exceeded its powers by refusing to exercise them,[34] a curious textual interpretation of Article 52. When the Argentinean government requested a supplementary decision and rectification of the committee's decision, this request was denied.[35]

The ad hoc committee in *Patrick Mitchell v. Congo*[36] also took a somewhat broader approach to interpreting the grounds for annulment. In *Patrick Mitchelle,* Congo commenced an annulment proceeding based on grounds of manifest excess of powers and failure to state reasons. With respect to the "manifest excess of powers" ground the committee stated that it had two aspects: positive and negative. The former refers to situations where an arbitral tribunal does something that is not supposed to do; and the latter refers to situations where an arbitral tribunal fails to do something that it was obligated to do.[37] The ad hoc committee ultimately accepted Congo's arguments and annulled the award, because among other things the arbitral tribunal had improperly assumed jurisdiction where there was no investment within the meaning of the Washington Convention. Having reached this conclusion, the ad hoc committee did not have any reason to examine Congo's challenges to the merits of the award; nevertheless, it examined them, and concluded that the award, assuming that the tribunal had jurisdiction, could not be annulled.

To summarize, of the thirteen decisions rendered thus far, six have resulted in at least a partial annulment. That seems to be a surprisingly high percentage for a review process intended to be very narrow. The two pending requests will likely further clarify the permissible scope of review and will determine whether the newer cases actually mark the expansion of this process.

---

[33] *Id. See also* Claudia Frutos-Peterson, *Introductory Note to* Aguas de Aconquija & Vivendi v. Argentine Republic, 17(2) ICSID Rev.-F.I.L.J. 87 (2002), *available at* http://icsid.worldbank.org/.

[34] *Vivendi Annulment Decision, surpa* note 14, ¶ 119 ("The Tribunal manifestly exceeded its powers by not examining the merits of the claims for acts of the Tucumán authorities under the BIT and its decision with regard to those claims is annulled").

[35] Frutos-Peterson, *supra* note 33.

[36] For an extended discussion of the facts and parts of the legal reasoning of the case, see Chapter XI.

[37] *Patrick Mitchell, supra* note 14, ¶ 20.

B. Challenge to Non-ICSID Investment Arbitration Awards

Where an investment arbitration is conducted outside the self-contained ICSID system, the losing party can challenge the award under the normal arbitration framework established by national law, as modified, perhaps, by a relevant treaty.[38] Thus, the losing party in a non-ICSID investment arbitration can initiate an action in the appropriate court of the place of arbitration, requesting set aside on the basis of the situs' national arbitration law. Although most countries have implemented legislation that tightly limits the proper grounds on which such relief will be given, the opportunity remains in some cases to reopen the merits of the case, either by application of a broad arbitration statute or broad interpretation of a narrow one.[39] Particularly in investment arbitration, where public policy concerns and popular pressure can sometimes loom large, there is a real possibility that national courts will overturn the arbitrators' substantive decision.

A number of recent cases have demonstrated that, in any case, a final award does not necessarily mean speedy payment for the investor. Increasingly, governments ordered to pay substantial sums for violation of investment protection treaties or investment agreements will use all avenues available to them to challenge international investment arbitration awards, pushing investor-state disputes into national courts. It is possible that this trend will strengthen in North American Free Trade Agreement (NAFTA) arbitrations, the most active investment arbitration system where industrialized, capital-exporting countries (Canada and the United States) also become respondents as a general matter.[40] Although some developing countries that sign investment treaties, such as Mexico and NAFTA, view the occasional defeat in arbitration as part of the cost of increased foreign direct investment, neither Canada nor the United States appears to have been prepared to be hauled

---

[38] For example, the North American Free Trade Agreement (NAFTA) expressly recognizes the possibility of actions in national courts to "revise, set aside or annul" awards, requiring the victorious party to refrain from enforcement until the losing side has had the opportunity to pursue such relief. NAFTA, art. 1136(3)(b).

[39] Professor Brower has argued that the NAFTA Parties' agreement to "final" and "binding" arbitration precludes judicial review of the merits of NAFTA awards, even if local law at the place of arbitration allows a full appeal. Charles H. Brower, II, *Structure, Legitimacy, and NAFTA's Investment Chapter,* 36 Vanderbilt J. Transnat'l L. 37, 83 (2003); Charles H. Brower, II, *Beware the Jabberwock: A Reply to Mr. Thomas,* 40 Colum. J. Transnat'l L. 465, 479–84 (2002). This is, however, a minority view.

[40] The Energy Charter Treaty (ECT), like NAFTA, binds capital-exporting states to one another and contains investor-state dispute resolution provisions similar to those found in NAFTA and bilateral investment treaties. *See* Chapter III. Its subject matter, however, is limited to the energy sector, and to date the dispute resolution provisions have been used in only seven cases.

before international tribunals under NAFTA.[41] The realization that international law is a two-way street has engendered sharp political pressure in Canada and the United States to scale back the power of NAFTA tribunals—a campaign that may lead to additional challenges of NAFTA awards.[42]

1. The Standard of Judicial Review

As noted, for non-ICSID awards the national courts and law of the legal situs of arbitration control a losing party's attempt to set aside the award. There are no international treaties restricting a state's legal approach to the review of arbitration awards rendered in its own territory.[43] There is considerable variation in national legislation on arbitration around the world, although harmonization is growing. Most modern national arbitration statutes provide a very short list of grounds for annulling international arbitration awards, analogous to the exceptions to recognition and enforcement of awards contained in Article V of the New York Convention.

The UNCITRAL Model Law on International Commercial Arbitration,[44] although adopted verbatim in only a few countries,[45] has served as an authoritative guide for many jurisdictions seeking to modernize and harmonize legislation on arbitration. The UNCITRAL Model Law establishes six bases for setting aside awards at the arbitral situs: (1) invalidity of the agreement to arbitrate; (2) lack of notice to a party or other inability to present the case; (3) inclusion in the award of matters outside the scope of submission; (4) irregularity in the composition of the tribunal or the arbitral procedure; (5) nonarbitrability of the subject matter; and (6) violation of domestic public policy.[46]

Of these, the first defect is practically impossible to establish in investment arbitration initiated under investment treaties, as the agreement to arbitrate consists, on the one hand, of an international agreement between sovereign states or comparable national legislation, and on the other, of the claimant's request for arbitration. Few of the bases for invalidity common in the commercial arbitration

---

[41] Guillermo A. Alvarez & William W. Park, *The New Face of Investment Arbitration: NAFTA Chapter 11,* 28 Yale J. Int'l L. 365, 367 (2003) ("when the shoe is on the other foot perceptions of fairness may be quite different, and the industrialized countries may not be enthusiastic about playing by the same rules").

[42] *See* discussion above at p. 500 regarding NAFTA Free Trade Commission's interpretation of July 2001.

[43] W. Craig, *Uses and Abuses of Appeal from Awards,* 4 Arb. Int'l 174 (1988); Hamid Gharavi, *The International Effectiveness of the Annulment of an Arbitration Award* 29 (2002).

[44] *Available at* http://www.uncitral.org/.

[45] The UNCITRAL Web site, at http://www.uncitral.org/english/status/status-e.htm, provides a list of "enactments" of the Model Law, but this list is somewhat misleading. Many of the countries and jurisdictions noted there introduced legislation based on the Model Law, but sometimes with substantial modifications.

[46] UNCITRAL Model Law, art. 34(2).

context, such as coercion, fraud, lack of identity of the parties, and so forth, apply to investment arbitration. Nonarbitrability of the subject matter and procedural irregularity are grounds for challenge that have yet to appear prominently in cases related to investment arbitration awards, but which could find increasing currency should challenges become more common.[47] In practice, the most common of the Model Law grounds, on which losing parties base their challenges to investment arbitration awards, are that the arbitrators decided issues outside the scope of their authority or that the award violates public policy.

2. Grounds for Setting Aside Relevant to Investment Arbitration

a. Excess of Authority

It has often been said that the consent of the parties is the cornerstone of arbitration. Commercial arbitrators' power to adjudicate disputes normally emerges not from operation of law but directly out of the contractual delegation of authority from the parties.[48] The particular contours of this delegation are found in the parties' agreement to arbitrate. As a result, nearly all national arbitration laws recognize[49] that tribunals only have jurisdiction to decide issues that the parties have agreed to submit to them and according to the parameters the parties specify (most commonly in advance). Where arbitrators go beyond the scope of this "mandate," their awards may be set aside by national courts at the place of arbitration as an "excess of authority."[50]

The range of issues that losing parties may assert under the "excess of powers" rubric is extremely broad and therefore difficult to characterize generally. The subjects complained about fall most commonly into one of two categories. First, the defeated party may assert that the arbitrators' departure from the agreed-on rules of procedure is so serious that the parties' agreement to arbitrate has been subverted. One frequently cited defect of this kind is consolidation, where disputes between a single party on one side and multiple parties on the other are merged into one proceeding. In *Oxford Shipping Co. Ltd. v. Nippon Yusen Kaisha*,[51] an English court ruled that arbitrators could not consolidate disputes without the consent of the parties involved. Many commentators agree that consolidation can amount to a rewriting of the arbitration agreement because the parties agreed to arbitrate disputes between

---

[47] For a general overview of national arbitration laws and their position on annulment, see Georges Delaume, *The Finality of Arbitration Involving States*, 5 Arb. Int'l 21 (1989).

[48] This is in contrast to the common institution of "statutory arbitration," as in labor disputes in the United States, removed by operation of law from the purview of courts and into the competence of arbitrators.

[49] See, e.g., UNCITRAL Model Law, art. 34(2)(iii); Bulgarian Law on International Commercial Arbitration, art. 47(5); Estonian Arbitration Act, art. 7(4); Mexico Civil Code, art. 1457(1)(c).

[50] A. Redfern & M. Hunter, *Law and Practice of International Commercial Arbitration* 3–8 (3d ed. 1999); *Waste Mgmt., Inc. v. United Mexican States*, ICSID Case No. ARB(AF)/98/2 (Award of June 2, 2000), ¶ 16.

[51] [1984] 2 Lloyd's Rep. 374.

themselves, not with other parties.[52] Nevertheless, courts have refused to annul on this ground where the complaining party could be deemed to have accepted the procedure. In the *Organisation pour les investissements et les aides economiques et techniques de l'Iran (OIAETI) v. Société Eurodif et Sofidif et Commissariat à l'energie atomique (SOFIDIF)* case, the French Court of Cassation reversed a Paris court's decision annulling an award against several Iranian public companies where the arbitrators had consolidated various disputes.[53]

Likewise, in the case of *Karaha Bodas Company* (KBC) *v. Pertamina*,[54] an UNCITRAL tribunal that was sited in Switzerland consolidated claims KBC had brought against Pertamina and PLN, two Indonesian state-owned entities, under closely related project contracts. Pertamina strenuously opposed enforcement of the award, in part on grounds that this consolidation was in excess of the arbitrators' mandate. An enforcing court in the United States rejected Pertamina's challenge, finding that the two respondent parties were closely related and suffered no detriment from the consolidation.[55] The issue of consolidation is less likely to be troublesome for NAFTA and Central America Free Trade Agreement (CAFTA) tribunals because those treaties provide a detailed procedure for merging related claims. But with multiple treaty claims now arising more and more frequently out of a single government measure, as in the Argentina financial crisis,[56] and decisions to consolidate cases perhaps more likely, challenges based on procedural excess of powers may also become more common.

The second class of "excess of mandate" challenges are those dealing with the substantive issues the arbitral tribunal has decided, and whether they fall within the scope of the agreement to arbitrate. In the investment context, this type of challenge could be mounted where the tribunal has accepted jurisdiction over issues beyond the scope of consent, such as tort claims or purely commercial disputes unrelated to an "investment" as required by most investment treaties. In addition, losing states frequently try to open the merits of the dispute to judicial review by asserting that the arbitrators were mistaken in their choice of law or incorrectly applied the law to the facts at hand. Under most legal systems, arbitrators must decide according to the

---

[52] T. Carbonneau, *Cases and Materials on the Law and Practice of Arbitration* 27 (2000).

[53] *OIAETI v. SOFIDIF*, Court of Cassation, Decision of Mar. 8, 1988, *reprinted at* 1987 Revue de l'Arbitrage 339.

[54] Unpublished, 2000.

[55] *Karaha Bodas Co. L.L.C. v. Pertamina*, 190 F. Supp.2d 936 (S.D. Tex. 2001) *aff'd*, 335 F.3d 357 (5th Cir.), *cert. denied*, 125 S.Ct. 59 (2004).

[56] Numerous ICSID cases have been filed against Argentina, pursuant to investment treaties of Argentina with a number of countries, especially the United States, as a result of Argentine's "emergency measures," in 2001–2002. As these treaties do not contain any procedure for consolidation of related claims, the practical solution adopted in some of the Argentine cases has been the choice of the same arbitrators to decide the related cases. For a discussion of these issues *see generally* Chapter VIII.

law chosen by the parties. Also, unless the parties expressly agree otherwise, the arbitrators exceed their powers when they rule as amiable compositeurs, according to general principles of justice and equity.[57]

In *Bridas S.A.P.I.C. et al. v. Turkmenistan et al.*, the claimant was awarded compensation for lost profits for breach of contract, with damages determined by a discounted cash flow method at a discount rate of approximately 10 percent.[58] Turkmenistan moved to set aside the award in the U.S. court (the situs of the arbitration was Texas), contending that neither party had argued for that particular rate, and that the arbitrators had in fact "split the baby," setting the discount rate between the parties' estimates without any basis in law. The court rejected this challenge, finding that the arbitrators had provided sufficient reasoning to conclude that they applied the law in their deliberations. "It is not th[e] Court's role," it concluded, "to sit as the panel did and reexamine the evidence under the guise of determining whether the arbitrators exceeded their powers."[59]

b. Nonarbitrability

Countries differ widely as to what kinds of disputes may be submitted to arbitration. In many jurisdictions, certain areas of law are considered too laden with public welfare concerns to permit private adjudication.[60] Even in the United States, which espouses a strong pro-arbitration policy, antitrust and securities disputes were not arbitrable until relatively recently. Today, courts in most developed countries tend to rule in favor of arbitrability when in doubt, as did the Second Circuit in *Kerr-McGee Refining Corp. v. M/T Triumph,* revising the annulment of an award based on the Racketeer Influenced and Corrupt Organizations (RICO) racketeering statute.[61] Nevertheless, in some countries certain fields of law—such as antitrust disputes,[62]

---

[57] *Inter-Arab Inves. Guarantee Corp. v. Banque Arabe d'Investissements,* Paris Cour d'Appel, decision of Oct. 23, 1997 ("the arbitrators had to decide in law and to give reasons for their decision"). In other jurisdictions, *amiable composition* is permitted as long as the parties do not prohibit it. This is the case in the United States, where arbitrators in some commercial contexts need not even provide written reasons for their award unless the parties expressly require it. See G. Born, *International Commercial Arbitration* 557 (Transnat'l Publishers & Kluwer Law Int'l 2d ed. 2001).

[58] *Bridas S.A.P.I.C., Bridas Energy Int'l, Intercontinental Oil & Gas Ventures, & Bridas Corp. v. Turkmenistan, Balkannebitgazsenagat & Turkmenneft,* Civil Action No. H 99 2171 (S.D. Tex. Oct. 1, 2001).

[59] *Id.* at 27 (citing *National Oil Corp. v. Libyan Sun Oil Co.,* 733 F. Supp. 800, 819 (D. Del.).

[60] See, e.g., the problems raised by limitations on the French government's authority to consent to ICSID arbitration in connection with the construction and operation of Euro Disneyland. Jacques Ribs, *Ombres et incertitudes de l'arbitrage pour les personnes morales de droit publique français,* 64 Juris-Classeur Périodique I.3465 (1990).

[61] 924 F.2d 467 (2d Cir. 1991).

[62] Ludwig von Zumbusch, *Arbitrability of Antitrust Claims under U.S., German, and E.E.C. Law: The International Transaction Criterion and Public Policy,* 22 Tex. Int'l L. J. 291, 304–12 (1987).

securities transactions,[63] and intellectual property[64]—are, for policy reasons, still within the exclusive jurisdiction of local courts.[65]

It is somewhat surprising that no investment arbitration award has yet been challenged on the basis of nonarbitrability. This may be because of an accident of fate, that to date the situs of most challenged awards has been in countries with broad local rules on arbitrability (for example, Canada and Sweden). The proliferation of arbitration proceedings in Latin America, however, may eventually alter this trend, and several European countries, notably France, also maintain tight limits on the arbitration of government-related disputes.

c. Public Policy

In most jurisdictions, awards that violate public policy are subject to annulment. *Public policy* is a term that evades precise definition.[66] An oft-cited definition of public policy was offered by the U.S. Court of Appeals for the Second Circuit in *Parsons*,[67] which characterized public policy as "the forum State's most basic notions of morality and justice."[68] The term public policy can refer to domestic, international, or transnational public policy (i.e., public policy common among states). There is, however, a consensus that the domestic public policy is broader than the international public policy,[69] and the latter broader than the transnational public policy.[70]

Some arbitration statutes note that annulment is possible where international public policy is offended,[71] although others make domestic public policy the relevant norm.[72] Still other national statutes are unclear whether local or international public

---

[63] Hans van Houtte, *Arbitration Involving Securities Transactions*, 12 Arb. Int'l 405 (1996).

[64] Marc Blessing, *The Arbitrability of Intellectual Property Disputes*, 12 Arb. Int'l 191 (1996).

[65] Karl-Heinz Böckstiegel, *Public Policy and Arbitrability*, ICCA Congress Series 177, 181–82 (1986).

[66] International Law Association (ILA), *Interim Report on Public Policy as a Bar to Enforcement of International Arbitral Awards* (2000), at 4, *available at* www.ila-hq.org [hereinafter ILA 2000 Report].

[67] *Parsons & Whittemore Overseas Co. v. Société Générale de l'Industrie du Papier*, 508 F. 2d 969 (2d Cir. 1974).

[68] *Id.* at 974.

[69] ILA 2000 Report, *supra* note 66, at 6.

[70] *Id.*

[71] French Civil Code, art. 1504.

[72] UNCITRAL Model Law, art. 36(1). No such statutory ground (public policy) exists under the U.S. Federal Arbitration Act, but courts there accept the ground as a "specific application of the more general doctrine, rooted in the common law, that a court may refuse to enforce contracts that violate law or public policy." *United Paperworkers Int'l Union v. Misco, Inc.*, 484 U.S. 29, 42 (1987).

policy or both should serve as the basis for challenge, leading to a great deal of confusion and debate.[73] In the international commercial arbitration context, courts in developed countries around the world have been hesitant to set aside awards on the basis of public policy, given the vagueness of the standard and the potential for its abuse.[74] In the words of England's Court of Appeal, public policy

> is never argued at all but when other points fail. It has to be shown that there is some element of illegality or that the enforcement of the award would be clearly injurious to the public good or, possibly, that enforcement would be wholly offensive to the ordinarily reasonable and fully informed member of the public.[75]

Most frequently cited as likely violations of public policy are contracts or concessions obtained by bribery,[76] and illegal or immoral agreements, or denial of due process in the conduct of arbitration. In some cases, an award can be subject to public policy challenge if the award or underlying transaction creates a monopoly or overly dominant market position for the winning party.[77] According to the law in most jurisdictions, the mere violation of local law by the arbitrators[78] or minor defects in the arbitral process[79] will not be enough to set aside the resulting award. Instead, it must be fundamentally unconscionable for the national court to give effect to the arbitration award—a test that is rarely, if ever, met.

An illustrative case is *Parsons and Whittemore Overseas Co. v. Société Générale de l'Industrie du Papier*,[80] where a U.S. engineering firm sought relief on public policy grounds from an award rendered against it for failing to complete a project in Egypt as a result of U.S. government's actions against Egypt during the Six Day War. The Second Circuit found that although U.S. policy supported the U.S. company's position, this was not enough to annul the award. Public policy could only be invoked "where enforcement would violate the forum state's most basic notions of morality and justice," as the exception was "not meant to enshrine the vagaries of international

---

[73] *See, e.g.,* Swiss Law on Private International Law, art. 190(2). The same problem exists with respect to the New York Convention, art. V(2)(b) and several other conventions, as well as domestic statutes. It has been suggested that the public policy ground in these contexts should be interpreted narrowly and correspond to international public policy. *See* ILA, *Final Report on Public Policy as a Bar to Enforcement of International Arbitral Awards* (2002), at 2–3, available at www.ila-hq.org.

[74] Pro-arbitration bias of the courts is another reason for this outcome. *Id.* at 4.

[75] *Deutsche Schachtbau- und Tiefbohrgesellschaft GmbH v. Ras Al Khaimah Nat'l Oil Co.*, [1987] 2 All E.R. 769, 779 (Ct. App. 1987).

[76] *European Gas Turbines SA-v- Westman Int'l Ltd* (Sept. 30, 1993), 1994 Rev. Arb. 359.

[77] *See, e.g., DO Zdravilisce Radenska v. Kajo-Erzeugnisse Essenzen GmbH* (Supreme Court of Slovenia, decision of Oct. 20, 1993), *reprinted at* 24 Y.B. Comm. Arb. 920 (1999) (annulling arbitration award rendered in Yugoslavia on grounds that the contract in dispute violated competition law and therefore Slovenian public policy).

[78] *General Electric Co. v. Renusagar Power Co. Ltd.*, [1994] 81 Company Cases 171 (India S.C.).

[79] *See, e.g.,* Moscow City Court, Decision of Nov. 10, 1994, Model Arb. Law Case No. 146.

[80] 508 F. 2d 969 (2d Cir. 1974).

politics."[81] European courts have been similarly circumspect about public policy challenges, stating that nonrecognition or set aside of international arbitration awards is appropriate only when "the arbitral procedure suffered from a serious deficiency affecting the bases of civil and economic life."[82]

Nevertheless, in developing countries that as yet have a less favorable attitude toward arbitration in general, broader concepts of public policy find application. In particular, the subject matter of "investment arbitration" may lend itself to a finding by courts of the host state that an award violates international public policy or national public policy. Often governments of both developing and developed countries are forced to compensate for harm caused to private investors by regulations dealing with the environment, safety, subsidies, or the exploitation of natural resources. It is therefore not difficult to imagine a court finding that the harm to the general public in the respondent state is sufficient to support a challenge on the basis of public policy. No investment treaty arbitration award has yet been challenged in this way, although in the arbitration case of *Karaha Bodas Company v. Pertamina*, the Indonesian government-owned oil company made and lost public policy arguments similar to those that could be raised in investment arbitrations.[83]

Like "excess of powers," the public policy challenge is frequently used by losing respondents, particularly states, to draw courts into the merits of the dispute. By arguing that the arbitrators have made a substantive decision that leads to an unjust or morally unconscionable result, respondents hope national courts at the place of arbitration will be reluctant to place their imprimatur on the resulting award and will effectively act as a court of appeal on the merits. Most courts in developed countries, however, have refused to take the bait. In one such action to set aside an award, the Swiss Supreme Court rebuffed the respondent, stating it refused to "decide as an appellate instance; the merits of an award cannot be reviewed under the cover of public policy."[84]

d. Procedural Irregularity

Perhaps the most multifaceted ground for challenge of international arbitration awards under nearly all national arbitration statutes is related to the proper conduct of the proceedings. Courts in most countries will set aside an award if the arbitration was carried out in a fundamentally arbitrary or unfair way. This principle can be related to public policy concerns, and claims of procedural irregularity are frequently combined

---

[81] *Id.* at 974.

[82] German Bundesgerichtshof Judgment of May 15, 1986, *published in* N.J.W. (Nov. 26, 1986), at 3027.

[83] *Karaha Bodas Co., LLC v. Pertamina*, 364 F.3d 274, 300–08 (5th Cir.), *cert. denied*, 125 S.Ct. 59 (2004).

[84] Swiss Federal Tribunal, Judgment of Jan. 8, 1995, *reprinted at* 22 Y.B. Comm. Arb. 789 (1997).

with a public policy challenge. A wide range of questionable practices could subject an award to set aside at the place of arbitration, including ex parte communications, manifestly unequal treatment of the parties, unauthorized consolidation of proceedings as indicated above, bias or corruption of one or more arbitrators, or denial of basic due process.

Generally speaking, however, courts do not hold arbitrators to the same procedural formalities as would bind judges in national litigation. In particular, arbitrators enjoy broad powers to arrange hearings as they see fit, including the examination of witnesses, submission of briefs, and timing of oral hearings. This is especially true in the international context, where a fusion of civil-law and common-law elements has engendered flexible practices that sometimes bear little resemblance to pure court procedures in either civil- or common-law countries. Furthermore, in many jurisdictions it is not enough that there has been a fundamental defect of procedure; the moving party must also show that, but for the irregularity, the arbitrators' decision would have been different.

In the U.S. case of *Generica v. Pharmaceutical Basics,* for example, the losing side claimed that the arbitrators had denied it the opportunity to cross-examine a particularly damaging witness.[85] Insisting that this denial violated fundamental due process, the losing party sought to block enforcement of the award in federal district court. The court dismissed the motion on three grounds, each illustrative of the limits of the procedural defect ground for annulment. First, it confirmed the arbitral tribunal's broad freedom to organize and conduct the arbitration. The arbitrators' mode of evidence gathering was "not such a fundamental procedural defect that it violated our due process jurisprudence." Second, the court found that if it were to itself closely examine the testimony of the damaging witness, or the arbitrators' decision not to allow cross-examination, that would "amount to an impermissible request that this Court review the arbitrator's factfinding." Finally, the Court determined that in any case the outcome of the arbitration was unlikely to have been affected by the limitation on cross-examination.

Investment arbitration tribunals have rarely provided ammunition to losing states that seek set aside on grounds of procedural defect. The arbitrators involved in these often massive cases are among the most experienced and qualified in the world. Acutely aware of the criticisms leveled against NAFTA and other investment arbitration regimes as "anti-democratic" and arbitrary, these tribunals have proven themselves as a general rule meticulous in their observance of procedural rules, proper techniques of communication with the parties, and thorough evidence collection. In addition, because the stakes in these cases are usually high, witness statements are usually voluminous and evidentiary hearings lengthy, further undermining any attack on the procedural inadequacy or unfairness of the arbitration.

---

[85] 1996 U.S. Dist. LEXIS 13716 (E.D. Ill. Sept. 18, 1996).

e. "Manifest Disregard of the Law" and Other "Substantive" Grounds

National arbitration statues may contain grounds for annulment that go beyond the grounds recognized in international treaties or the UNCITRAL Model Law. For example, under the U.S. Federal Arbitration Act (FAA),[86] if an international arbitration's situs is within the United States, both the domestic and international sections of the FAA apply, including extrastatutory grounds for set aside such as "manifest disregard of the law."[87] This standard was drawn from *Wilko v. Swan*, where the U.S. Supreme Court remarked, in dicta, that under normal circumstances "the interpretations of the law by the arbitrators in contrast to manifest disregard are not subject, in the federal courts, to judicial review for error in interpretation."[88] Although the Supreme Court gave little or no guidance as to the contours of "manifest disregard" or when such behavior by arbitrators would justify annulling an award, the federal appeal courts have incorporated the idea into arbitration jurisprudence. Domestic arbitration awards in the United States are rarely vacated under the manifest disregard standard, and even less frequently in the international context. Even so, courts have occasionally set awards aside on the merits, particularly where they found "no rational basis" for the arbitrators' decision.[89]

The issue of manifest disregard arose in the NAFTA case of *Loewen v. United States*, where the losing claimant asked the federal court to set aside the award on that ground:

> In the Matter of Arbitration between Raymond L. Loewen, Petitioner, and the United States of America, Respondent, Notice of Petition to Vacate, United States District Court for the District of Columbia, Case 1:04-cv-02151-RWR, Filed 12/13/2004, at 5 & 13–14, available at www.naftaclaims.com [Facts of the *Loewen* case were explained in Chapter XII]
>
> B. Grounds for Vacating the Award
>
> Section 10 of the FAA, 9 U.S.C. § 10, sets out the statutory grounds for vacating an arbitration award. At a minimum, the following grounds of the FAA are relevant here:
>
> (3) Where the arbitrators were guilty of misconduct in refusing to postpone the hearing, upon sufficient cause shown, or in refusing to hear evidence pertinent and material to the controversy; or of any other misbehavior by which the rights of any party have been prejudiced; or

---

[86] 9 U.S.C. § 201, *et seq.*

[87] Yusuf Ahmed Alghanim & Sons, W.L.L. v. Toys "R" Us, Inc., 126 F.3d 15, 24–25 (2d Cir. 1997); Indus. Risk Insurers v. M.A.N. Guttehoffnungshutte GmbH, 141 F.3d 1434, 1441 (11th Cir. 1998); Spector v. Torenberg, 852 F. Supp. 201, 205–206 (S.D.N.Y. 1994).

[88] 363 U.S. 427, 436–437 (1953) overruled on other grounds by *Rodriguez de Quijas v. Shearson/American Express, Inc,* 490 U.S. 477 (1989).

[89] *Ainsworth v. Kurnick,* 960 F.2d 939 (11th Cir. 1992); *Shearson Lehman Bros., Inc. v. Hedrich,* 639 N.E.2d 228 (Ill. App. 1994).

(4) Where the arbitrators exceeded their powers, or so imperfectly executed them that a mutual, final, and definite award upon the subject matter submitted was not made.

FAA caselaw also recognizes that an award may be vacated if the arbitrators act in "manifest disregard of the law." The "manifest disregard of the law" concept, while not set forth in the FAA, is widely accepted as a ground for vacating arbitration awards. *See, e.g., Brabham v. A.G. Edwards & Sons Inc.*, 376 F.3d 377, 381 (5th Cir. 2004) ("[M]anifest disregard is an accepted nonstatutory ground for vacatur."); *Montes v. Shearson Lehman Bros., Inc.*, 128 F.3d 1456, 1460 (11th Cir. 1997) ("[E]very other circuit . . . has expressly recognized that 'manifest disregard of the law' is an appropriate reason to review and vacate an arbitration panel's decision.").

. . . .

B. The Tribunal's Manifest Disregard of the Objective Standard for "Reasonably Available" Local Remedies

In its 2003 Award, the Tribunal concluded that TLGI [(Loewen Group Inc.)] was required to exhaust local remedies before obtaining international relief, so long as such remedies were "reasonably available." First, the Tribunal stated the legal standard it would apply:

> 169. Availability is not a standard to be determined or applied in the abstract. It means reasonably available to the complainant in the light of its situation, including its financial and economic circumstances as a foreign investor, as they are affected by any conditions relating to the exercise of any local remedy.
>
> . . . .
>
> 214. Respondent argues that, because entry into the settlement agreement was a matter of business judgment, Loewen voluntarily decided not to pursue its local remedies. That submission does not dispose of the point. The question is whether the remedies in question were reasonably available and adequate. If they were not, it is not to the point that Loewen entered into the settlement, even as a matter of business judgment. It may be that the business judgment was inevitable or the natural outcome of adverse consequences generated by the impugned court decision.

Thus, the Tribunal recognized and concluded that the controlling law concerning exhaustion was a standard of "reasonable availability." Any standard based on reasonable availability is normally an objective standard.[90] However, the Tribunal then disregarded that legal standard, refusing to consider the extensive expert testimony provided by Professor Laurence Tribe and Professor Charles Fried, former Solicitor General of the United States, that TLGI did not have a reasonably available alternative to settlement. *See* Expert Witness Statements of Laurence Tribe and Charles Fried. Instead, the Tribunal disposed of the exhaustion issue on a different legal principle: whether TLGI subjectively believed it had any reasonable alternative to settlement. Furthermore, as discussed below, it improperly applied that standard by overlooking all the evidence of TLGI's state of mind. But more importantly, it manifestly disregarded the law that it had deemed controlling: whether there was, objectively, a reasonably available alternative.

As a result of its failure to apply the proper legal standard, the Tribunal engaged in misbehavior by which the rights of the Petitioner have been prejudiced. In failing to carry out

---

[90] SN: *See, e.g., Dep't Justice v. Federal Labor Relations Auth.*, 991 F.2d 285, 291 (5th Cir. 1993) (describing reasonable availability as an objective standard); *Brehm v. Eisner*, 746 A.2d 244, 260 (Del. 2000) (referring to the "objective test of reasonable availability").

its duties and apply the proper legal standard, the Tribunal acted in manifest disregard of the law and exceeded its powers, or so imperfectly executed them, that a mutual, final, and definite award upon the subject matter submitted was not made. *See Montes v. Shearson Lehman Bros., Inc.*, 128 F.3d 1456, 1460 (11th Cir.1997) ("To manifestly disregard the law, one must be conscious of the law and deliberately ignore it."); *Jeffrey M. Brown Assocs., Inc. v. Allstar Drywall & Acoustics, Inc.*, 195 F. Supp. 2d 681, 84–685 (E.D. Pa. 2002) ("'Manifest disregard of the law' encompasses situations in which it is evident from the record that the arbitrator recognized the applicable law, yet chose to ignore it.").

In most countries other than the United States, the merits of an arbitral tribunal's reasoning and decision are generally beyond challenge, unless they can be fit within one of the permissible "procedural" defect categories described above, such as excess of powers or public policy. In some jurisdictions, however, local courts are given limited authority to act as appeals court over arbitration proceedings that take place within their territory. The English Arbitration Act 1996, for example, allows losing parties a full appeal as to points of law but not issues of fact as long as certain prerequisites are met.[91] However, English courts are given a great deal of discretion in dismissing challenges to arbitration awards, and presumably often do so where the respondent seeks to set aside an international award on the merits. The Argentine civil code permits appeal of both law and facts, providing that "the same appeal may be instituted against an arbitral award as may be instituted against court judgments, as long as such appeal has not been waived in the agreement to arbitrate."[92] Other statutes take a middle position, similar to "manifest disregard" in the United States, allowing vacatur[93] where the arbitrators have failed to apply the law chosen by the parties to govern their dispute.[94]

The adoption and adaptation of the UNCITRAL Model Law has sharply reduced the number of countries where judicial appeal of arbitration awards on the merits is expressly permitted by local law. In particular, most of the new states of the former Soviet Union have excluded judicial review of law and fact, and many countries in Latin America have amended their legislation as traditional hostility to international arbitration has faded. This leaves losing states in investment arbitration with decidedly fewer options, particularly where the parties have carefully chosen the place of arbitration with regard to the vacatur provisions of national arbitration law.

---

[91] English Arbitration Act 1996, art. 69.
[92] Argentine Civil Code, art. 758. *See also* Iraqi Civil Code, art. 273–74.
[93] Vacatur is an order to set aside or annul an award. *Black's Law Dictionary* (8th ed. 2004).
[94] Oman Arbitration Act, art. 53(4), *at* http://www.gccarbitration.com/english/rules/oman-2.htm.

C. Waiver of Objections

Under the law of many jurisdictions, certain otherwise permissible grounds for setting aside international arbitration awards may be unavailable to the challenging party because it failed to object to the alleged defect during the arbitration itself. This rule is particularly applicable in connection with jurisdictional objections, based on the principle that "a party may not submit a claim to arbitration and then challenge the authority of the arbitrator to act after receiving an unfavorable result."[95]

Some arbitration statutes are explicit in this regard. The Swedish Arbitration Act, for example, separates grounds for set aside into two separate categories, the waivable and the unwaivable. Under the Act, an award can be declared void regardless of the losing party's behavior only where the award is not in writing, violates Swedish public policy, or deals with inarbitrable subject matter.[96] As for all other grounds for vacatur, the Act states,

> A party shall not be entitled to rely upon a circumstance which, through participation in the proceedings without objection, or in any other manner, he may be deemed to have waived.[97]

From the prevailing party's perspective, the rule that grounds for vacatur may be waived is particularly useful in blocking challenges based on alleged procedural defects. From the losing party's point of view, the rule serves as a warning to bring all possible objections during the arbitration, despite the possibility that this kind of aggressive stance could alienate the arbitral tribunal.

D. Agreements to Narrow the Grounds for Annulment

It is generally accepted that the parties to an arbitration clause may to some extent narrow the grounds on which an arbitral award may be set aside by national courts.[98] Although in some jurisdictions parties may not be able to waive their right to some form of judicial review of arbitration awards,[99] the choice of certain arbitration rules

---

[95] *Fortune, Alsweet & Eldridge, Inc. v. Daniel,* 724 F.2d 1355 (9th Cir. 1983).

[96] Swedish Arbitration Act, art. 33, *available at* http://www.chamber.se/arbitration/english/laws/skiljedomslagen_eng.html.

[97] Swedish Arbitration Act, art. 34.

[98] Robert Fischer & Roger Haydock, *International Commercial Disputes: Drafting an Enforceable Arbitration Agreement,* 21 Wm. Mitchell L. Rev. 941, 973 (1996).

[99] Professor Park suggests that at least in three areas, judicial review should be impossible to waive, in the interests of fairness and integrity of the arbitral system: (1) arbitrability; (2) the right to be heard; and (3) international public policy. William Park, *Safeguarding Procedural Integrity in International Arbitration,* 63 Tul. L. Rev. 647, 707 (1989). In New York, for instance, the right to cross-examination has been deemed a fundamental element of due process, and therefore probably unwaivable. S. J. Stein & D. R. Wotman, *International Commercial Arbitration in New York* 87–96 (1986).

may effect such a waiver. In particular, the London Court of International Arbitration Rules (rarely used in investment arbitration) provide that in choosing arbitration under that system "the parties also waive irrevocably their right to any form of appeal, review or recourse to any state court or other judicial authority, insofar as such waiver may be validly made."[100] Neither the ICSID Additional Facility nor the UNCITRAL Rules contain such a provision. However, even where arbitral rules are silent, many legal systems recognize the validity of "exclusion agreements," by which the parties voluntarily restrict judicial review or eliminate it altogether.[101] Furthermore, as noted above, failure to object to procedural irregularities during the arbitration may effect an implied waiver of recourse under some legal systems.

Although some jurisdictions, such as Switzerland, allow a waiver of the right to set aside arbitral awards at the place of arbitration, it is doubtful that most legal systems would allow the parties to waive the right to object to confirmation of the award at the place of enforcement.[102] The significance of the Swiss and former Belgian legislation is that it effectively shifts the locus of control from the arbitral situs, which often has little connection with the parties or their transaction, to the place of enforcement, which is likely to be where one of the parties has substantial assets. Public policy, as codified in the New York Convention, demands that states be able to refuse enforcement that would contravene their fundamental interests or societal goals.

For most modern investment arbitrations, where there is rarely, if ever, a contractual agreement to arbitrate (because they are mainly commenced based on the consent of the governments in investment treaties), the issue of contractually narrowed judicial review is purely academic. Many other investment arbitration cases, however, arise out of concession agreements, which could theoretically contain such a clause. If more UNCITRAL and ICSID Additional Facility investment arbitration awards come to be challenged in national courts, private concessionaires may begin to consider pushing their government counterparts for language restricting the scope of judicial review to an absolute minimum.

---

[100] LCIA Rules (1998), art. 26.9.

[101] *See, e.g.,* Swiss federal law on arbitration, the Loi Fédéral de Droit International Privé (LDIP), art. 192, which allows express waiver of all judicial review where all parties are non-Swiss. The most extreme expression in a law of limited judicial review was under the Belgian arbitration law in force until 2000, which *as a default rule* allowed no action for annulment of arbitral awards rendered in Belgium in disputes between foreign parties. Law of Mar. 27, 1985 (Belg.) enacting Code Judiciaire, art. 1717.

[102] *Karaha Bodas,* 190 F. Supp.2d at 943–45 (holding that party had right to oppose confirmation of award despite contractual provision expressly renouncing any right to appeal).

E. The Effect of Annulled Investment Arbitration Awards

Where a respondent in investment arbitration successfully annuls an award at the place of arbitration, the effectiveness of this victory is unclear. A set aside in one country may not be honored by judges in other jurisdictions.[103] Although the New York Convention clearly designates the arbitral situs as the most appropriate venue for judicial challenge to international arbitration awards, an annulment from a national court does not firmly close the book on enforcement outside that jurisdiction.

The New York Convention exception to enforcement based on annulment or vacatur at the place of arbitration is worded permissively: "recognition and enforcement of the award **may** be refused ... if ... the award ... has been set aside or suspended by a competent authority of the country in which ... the award was made."[103'] Because of this permissive language, in *Hilmarton Limited v. Omnium de Traitement et de Valorisation*,[104] the French Cour de Cassation upheld a lower court's decree confirming a foreign arbitral award despite the fact that the award had been set aside by a court in Switzerland, the arbitral situs. The court held that although the Swiss court had applied Swiss arbitration law in deciding to deprive the award of legal force in Switzerland, the award "remains in existence even if set aside, and its recognition in France is not contrary to international public policy." This is not the first time that French courts have held that courts at the place of arbitration and the place of enforcement are equally competent to assess the validity of international arbitration awards.[105]

Similarly, in *In re Chromalloy Aeroservices Inc. v. Arab Republic of Egypt*,[106] the U.S. District Court for the District of Columbia granted the plaintiff's motion to confirm an arbitration award rendered in Egypt against the Egyptian Air Force, although Egypt had successfully moved to set aside the award in the Egyptian courts. The federal district court relied largely on the parties' explicit waiver of judicial review in their agreement to arbitrate, as well as the possible lack of independence of the Egyptian courts, both somewhat unusual and important considerations. However, the court also stated in more general terms that in the United States, because foreign court judgments are not a ground for set aside under

---

[103] A comprehensive and thoughtfully written commentary on the problem of enforcing annulled arbitration awards can be found in Gharavi, *supra* note 43.

[103'] New York Convention, art. V(1)(e).

[104] *Société Hilmarton v. OTV*, Decision No. 484, French Cour de Cassation, First Civil Chamber (1994) Rev. Arb. 327–28. *See also Award Upheld in France Despite Annulment by Swiss Court*, Mealey's Int'l Arb. Rep., May 1994.

[105] *See, e.g., Pabalk Ticaret Sirkeri v. Norsolor*, French Cour de Cassation (Decision of Oct. 9, 1984), *reprinted in* 1985 Rev. Arb. 430 (1985).

[106] 939 F. Supp. 907 (D.D.C. 1996).

the domestic provisions of the Federal Arbitration Act, Article VII of the New York Convention allows U.S. courts to ignore such foreign decisions and enforce awards.

Except in France,[107] the status of annulled awards remains undetermined in most jurisdictions; in many countries the issue has yet to be confronted.[108] Many commentators have supported *Hilmarton, Chromalloy,* and similar court decisions as evidence of a growing trend around the world bolstering the enforceability of international arbitration awards.[109] To be sure, such cases tend to improve the currency of international awards and ensure against biased courts at the arbitral situs, especially where the situs court is in the host country. However, within the context of investment arbitration, as opposed to the commercial variety, an annulled award may be more effective, mainly because of the presence of a sovereign as defendant. Where the award is against a sovereign state, widely accepted rules of sovereign immunity make enforcement extremely difficult: In most jurisdictions, the judgment creditor may only execute on the government's commercial assets, a rule that normally excludes the vast majority of property that states hold outside their own territory.[110] Taking an enforcement campaign to the local courts of the defendant state is even less likely to succeed, given the lack of judicial independence and extensive immunity conferred by national law in most capital-importing countries. Collection of investment arbitration awards therefore rests largely on voluntary compliance, both inside and outside the Washington Convention system. Although voluntary compliance has not been perfect, breaking down in cases such as *LETCO v. Liberia*[111] and *SOABI v. Senegal,*[112] losing states have generally paid awards against them.

---

[107] See discussion of *Hilmarton* below. See also *Direction Générale de l'aviation civile de l'Emirat de Dubai v. Société Internationale Bechtel,* Paris Court of Appeal, Chamber 1C (Sept. 27, 2005).

[108] See P. Ramaswamy, *Enforcement of Annulled Awards: An Indian Perspective,* 19 J. Int'l Arb. 461, 472 (2002) ("an Indian court is unlikely to enforce an award annulled abroad because of the 'territorial' view that the Indian courts have taken").

[109] Emmanuel Gaillard & Jenny Edelstein, Baker Marine *and* Spier *Strike a Blow to the Enforceability in the United States of Awards Set Aside at the Seat,"* 3 Int. Arb. L. Rev. 37 (2000). *But compare* Gharavi, *supra* note 43 (suggesting that enforcement of annulled arbitration awards is contrary to the goals of predictability and harmonization of arbitration law).

[110] Indeed, most industrialized countries own very little commercial property at all, particularly after the massive privatizations of the 1990s. It is difficult to imagine, for example, how an investor who wins an award against Canada or the United States under NAFTA would ever be able to force compliance by execution on assets.

[111] *Liberian Eastern Timber Co. v. Republic of Liberia,* 650 F. Supp. 73 (S.D.N.Y. 1987) (enforcement of ICSID award blocked by Liberia's claims of sovereign immunity).

[112] *Société Ouest Africaine de Bétons Industriels v. Sénégal* (French Cour de Cassation, decision of June 11, 1991), 2 ICSID Rep. 337 (The exequatur granted to enforce and recognize the ICSID award against Senegal was valid; Senegal could not challenge this outcome on the basis of sovereign immunity; the latter defense could be raised later in the execution stage).

F. Case Studies of Non-ICSID Challenge Proceedings

The preceding analysis of the most commonly recognized bases for annulling international arbitration awards indicates that courts have greatly narrowed the available grounds. In many countries the review of international arbitral awards is one of the narrowest known to the law, and it is presumed that an exceedingly narrow approach to judicial review is in keeping with the expectations of the parties, which—at least in the commercial context—have expressly chosen to remove their dispute from the jurisdiction of national courts. But no matter how long the odds, motions to set aside awards are by no means uncommon. The more a state stands to lose by paying the award, the more likely it is to seek annulment, even if the chances of success are small. Not only are investment arbitration awards frequently large, even by international arbitration standards, but they are also colored by issues of sovereignty and political ideology. These concerns may create domestic political pressure on losing states that compel them to challenge the awards against them, if only to prove to constituents at home that all possible avenues have been explored. In part as a result of these considerations, three well-known investment arbitration awards have been challenged by respondent governments in recent years. In one case, the government's petition was partially granted, and in the other two cases it was dismissed.

1. *Metalclad v. United Mexican States*

The *Metalclad* case[113] arose out of the American claimant company's purchase of a site in San Luis Potosí, Mexico, to operate as a hazardous waste landfill. The Mexican federal authorities repeatedly approved the project, and assured Metalclad that no further permits were required. However, local opposition to building the waste disposal facility grew, along with intense pressure on state and local authorities to prevent the landfill from beginning operations. Meanwhile, Metalclad invested several million dollars in completing the site for use, obtaining additional assurances from officials in Mexico City that operations would be in compliance with all regulatory requirements. Nevertheless, the local municipality obtained a court order preventing the opening of the facility. Although the court order was eventually vacated, the governor of San Luis Potosí also issued an Ecological Decree designating the landfill site a natural preserve for the protection of rare cactus. Metalclad requested arbitration against Mexico under NAFTA, to be conducted pursuant to the ICSID Additional Facility arbitration rules. The situs of arbitration was Vancouver, British Columbia, although most of the proceedings actually took place in Washington, D.C.

---

[113] *Metalclad Corp. v. United Mexican States,* ICSID Case No. ARB(AF)/97/1 (Award of Aug. 30, 2000), *published in* 40 I.L.M. 36 (2001); *see* pp. 476 *et seq. supra* for a fuller description of facts.

In its August 2000 award, the tribunal awarded Metalclad US$16,685,000, finding that Mexico had violated Metalclad's rights under NAFTA. Most importantly, the arbitrators held that Mexico's federal authorities had led Metalclad to believe that it had obtained all permits necessary to begin construction of the landfill. The tribunal found that Mexico had therefore breached its obligation under Article 1105 of NAFTA to provide American investors "fair and equitable treatment" by failing "to ensure a transparent and predictable framework for Metalclad's business planning and investment." Furthermore, the arbitrators determined that the local authorities' deprivation of the economic benefit of its investment constituted expropriation, requiring prompt, adequate, and effective compensation under NAFTA Article 1110.

Soon after the award was rendered, Mexico filed an action in the Supreme Court of British Columbia (the court of appropriate jurisdiction under British Columbian law), asking the Canadian court to vacate the award. After extensive briefing and oral argument the court rendered an opinion on May 2, 2001.[114]

An important threshold issue that the court faced was which of two local arbitration statutes applied. The British Columbia International Commercial Arbitration Act (ICAA) applies to all arbitrations considered both international and commercial. The ICAA, based largely on the UNCITRAL Model Law, establishes a relatively narrow scope of judicial review, limiting annulment to cases of serious procedural defects. However, the British Columbia Commercial Arbitration Act (CAA), which applies in all other cases, allows courts to reexamine the merits of the dispute and set aside an award for misapplication of law. Mexico contended that the CAA was the governing legislation because investment arbitration deals with government regulations and therefore cannot be considered "commercial."[115]

The court disagreed. Investment, it held, is an inherently commercial activity, and therefore falls within the ambit of the ICAA. As the UNCITRAL Model Law drafters advised in a footnote to the definitions section of the Law, "[t]he term 'commercial' should be given a wide interpretation so as to cover matters arising from all relationships of a commercial nature."[116] As a result, the international rather than domestic statute governed Mexico's challenge, excluding mistakes of law as an acceptable basis for vacatur. As quickly became clear, however, this ruling did not prevent the court from delving deeply—probably too deeply—into the merits of the Metalclad dispute.

---

[114] *United Mexican States v. Metalclad Corp.*, 2001 B.C.S.C. 664 (2001). *See also* Yelena Faynblyum, *The Metalclad Appeal: A Pyrrhic Victory?*, available at http://www.cba.org/cba/newsletters/Environmental-06–2001/ec03.asp.

[115] *United Mexican States v. Metalclad, supra* note 114, ¶¶ 44–45.

[116] UNCITRAL Model Law, article 1(1), note 1.

CASE STUDIES OF NON-ICSID CHALLENGE PROCEEDINGS

The United Mexican States v. Metalclad Corporation

2001 BCSC 664 (B.C. Supreme Ct. 2001)(Tysoe, J.)

STANDARD OF REVIEW

[50] The extent to which this Court may interfere with an international commercial arbitral award is limited by the provisions of International CAA. Section 5 of the Act reads as follows:

In matters governed by this Act,

> (a) a court must not intervene unless so provided in this Act, and
>
> (b) an arbitral proceeding of an arbitral tribunal or an order, ruling or arbitral award made by an arbitral tribunal must not be questioned, reviewed or restrained by a proceeding under the Judicial Review Procedure Act or otherwise except to the extent provided in this Act.

Subsection 34(1) of the Act states that recourse to a court against an arbitral award may only be made in accordance with subsections (2) and (3). Subsection (3) contains a limitation period which is not relevant to this matter. The pertinent portions of subsection (2) read as follows:

An arbitral award may be set aside by the Supreme Court only if

> (a) the party making the application furnishes proof that

. . .

>> (iv) the arbitral award deals with a dispute not contemplated by or not falling within the terms of the submission to arbitration, or it contains decisions on matters beyond the scope of the submission to arbitration . . . , or
>>
>> (v) the composition of the arbitral tribunal or the arbitral procedure was not in accordance with the agreement of the parties . . . , or
>
> (b) the court finds that

. . .

>> (ii) the arbitral award is in conflict with the public policy in British Columbia.

[51] The leading British Columbia authority on s. 34 is *Quintette Coal Limited v. Nippon Steel Corporation*, [1991] 1 W.W.R. 219 (B.C.C.A.), a decision which has been followed by several other courts in Canada. In that case, the B.C. Court of Appeal refused to interfere with an arbitration award setting prices to be paid for the supply of coal. After referring to numerous authorities, Gibbs J.A., on behalf of the majority of the Court, commented on the standard of review in the following terms:

> It is important to parties to future such arbitrations and to the integrity of the process itself that the court express its views on the degree of deference to be accorded the decision of the arbitrators. The reasons advanced in the cases discussed above for restraint in the exercise of judicial review are highly persuasive. The "concerns of international comity, respect for the capacities of foreign and transnational tribunals, and sensitivity to the need of the international commercial system for predictability in the resolution of disputes" spoken of by Blackmun J. [in *Mitsubishi Motors Corp. v. Soler Chrysler-Plymouth Inc.*, 473 U.S. 614 (1985)] are as compelling in this jurisdiction as they are in the United States or elsewhere. It is meet therefore, as a matter of policy, to adopt a standard which seeks to preserve the autonomy of the forum selected

by the parties and to minimize judicial intervention when reviewing international commercial arbitral awards in British Columbia. (p. 229)

Gibbs J.A. also stated that unless the arbitral award contained decisions beyond the scope of the submission to arbitration, the court has no jurisdiction to set the award aside under s. 34(2)(a)(iv) even if it could be shown that the arbitration tribunal had erred in interpreting the contract.

[55] During the course of their submissions, counsel made reference in general terms to the issue of whether the Tribunal exceeded its jurisdiction. The concept of "excess of jurisdiction" is the standard which was previously applied to decisions of administrative tribunals and arbitral bodies. The International CAA does not utilize the term "excess of jurisdiction" or the like but, instead, sets out with particularity the grounds on which the court may set aside an arbitral award. Rather than making reference to terms like "excess of jurisdiction" and jurisdictional errors," I prefer to utilize the wording contained in the International CAA (although I will use such terms when reciting submissions of counsel).

. . . .

ARTICLE 1105 – MINIMUM STANDARD

[62] . . . What the Myers tribunal correctly pointed out is that in order to qualify as a breach of Article 1105, the treatment in question must fail to accord to international law. Two potential examples are "fair and equitable treatment" and "full protection and security," but those phrases do not stand on their own. For instance, treatment may be perceived to be unfair or inequitable but it will not constitute a breach of Article 1105 unless it is treatment which is not in accordance with international law. In using the words "international law," Article 1105 is referring to customary international law which is developed by common practices of countries. It is to be distinguished from conventional international law which is comprised in treaties entered into by countries (including provisions contained in the NAFTA other than Article 1105 and other provisions of Chapter 11).

. . . .

[64] After these Reasons for Judgment had been prepared in draft, counsel for Metalclad provided a copy of the arbitral award in *Pope & Talbot Inc. v. Canada* (April 10, 2001), in which the tribunal declined to follow the interpretation of Article 1105 given by the Myers tribunal. The Pope & Talbot tribunal concluded that "investors under NAFTA are entitled to the international law minimum, plus the fairness elements." The tribunal based its interpretation on the wording of the corresponding provision in the Model Bilateral Investment Treaty of 1987, which has been adopted by numerous countries. The provision states that investment shall be accorded fair and equitable treatment, shall enjoy full protection and security and shall in no case be accorded treatment less than that required by international law. The tribunal rejected the submission of the United States (as intervenor) that the language of Article 1105 demonstrated that the NAFTA Parties did not intend to diverge from the customary international law concept of fair and equitable treatment. The tribunal reasoned that the United States relied solely on the language of Article 1105 and did not offer any other evidence that the NAFTA Parties intended to reject the "additive" character of bilateral investment treaties.

[65] With respect, I am unable to agree with the reasoning of the Pope & Talbot tribunal. It has interpreted the word "including" in Article 1105 to mean "plus," which has a virtually opposite meaning. Its interpretation is contrary to Article 31(1) of the Vienna Convention, which requires that terms of treaties be given their ordinary meaning. The evidence that the NAFTA Parties intended to reject the "additive" character of bilateral investment treaties is found in the fact that they chose not to adopt the language used in such treaties and I find it surprising that the tribunal considered that other evidence was required. The NAFTA Parties chose to use different language in Article 1105 and the

natural inference is that the NAFTA Parties did not want Article 1105 to be given the same interpretation as the wording of the provision in the Model Bilateral Investment Treaty of 1987.

[68] On my reading of the Award, the Tribunal did not simply interpret Article 1105 to include a minimum standard of transparency. No authority was cited or evidence introduced to establish that transparency has become part of customary international law. In the Myers award, one of the arbitrators wrote a separate opinion and surmised an argument that the principle of transparency and regulatory fairness was intended to have been incorporated into Article 1105. The arbitrator crafted the argument by assuming that the words "international law" in Article 1105 were not intended to have their routine meaning and should be interpreted in an expansive manner to include norms that have not yet technically passed into customary international law. However, the arbitrator did not decide the point because it had not been fully argued in the arbitration and he was not aware of the argument having been made in any earlier case law or academic literature. In my view, such an argument should fail because there is no proper basis to give the term "international law" in Article 1105 a meaning other than its usual and ordinary meaning.

[69] Although I do not agree with the argument posed by the arbitrator in the Myers award, it may be argued that the court would have no ability to set the award aside under the International CAA if the arbitrator had based the award on that argument. While the interpretation of Article 1105 would have been flawed, it may be that the arbitrator would not have decided a matter outside the scope of the submission to arbitration.

[70] In the present case, however, the Tribunal did not simply interpret the wording of Article 1105. Rather, it misstated the applicable law to include transparency obligations and it then made its decision on the basis of the concept of transparency.

[71] In addition to specifically quoting from Article 1802 in the section of the Award outlining the applicable law, the Tribunal incorrectly stated that transparency was one of the objectives of the NAFTA. In that regard, the Tribunal was referring to Article 102(1), which sets out the objectives of the NAFTA in clauses (a) through (f). Transparency is mentioned in Article 102(1) but it is listed as one of the principles and rules contained in the NAFTA through which the objectives are elaborated. The other two principles and rules mentioned in Article 102, national treatment and most-favored nation treatment, are contained in Chapter 11. The principle of transparency is implemented through the provisions of Chapter 18, not Chapter 11. Article 102(2) provides that the NAFTA is to be interpreted and applied in light of the objectives set out in Article 102(1), but it does not require that all of the provisions of the NAFTA are to be interpreted in light of the principles and rules mentioned in Article 102(1).

[72] In its reasoning, the Tribunal discussed the concept of transparency after quoting Article 1105 and making reference to Article 102. It set out its understanding of transparency and it then reviewed the relevant facts. After discussing the facts and concluding that the Municipality's denial of the construction permit was improper, the Tribunal stated its conclusion which formed the basis of its finding of a breach of Article 1105; namely, Mexico had failed to ensure a transparent and predictable framework for Metalclad's business planning and investment. Hence, the Tribunal made its decision on the basis of transparency. This was a matter beyond the scope of the submission to arbitration because there are no transparency obligations contained in Chapter 11.

[73] The Tribunal went on to state that the acts of the State of SLP and the Municipality, for which Mexico was responsible, also failed to comply with the requirements of Article 1105 but it did not state any reasons for this conclusion. Based on the preceding discussion, the Tribunal must have been referring to the acts of the State of SLP and the Municipality which contributed to the perceived failure to provide a transparent and predictable framework for Metalclad's business planning and investment.

[74] I should add that I would have reached the same conclusion even if I had agreed with the analysis of Article 1105 by the Pope & Talbot tribunal. Even with the broader interpretation of Article 1105, the Tribunal still made a decision on a matter outside the scope of the submission to arbitration by basing its finding of a breach on the concept of transparency.

. . . .

CONCLUSION

[133] In order to have this Court set aside the Award in its entirety, Mexico was required to successfully establish that all three of the Tribunal's findings of breaches of Articles 1105 and 1110 of the NAFTA involved decisions beyond the scope of the submission to arbitration or that the Award should be set aside in view of Metalclad's allegedly improper acts or the Tribunal's alleged failure to answer all questions submitted to it. Although Mexico succeeded in challenging the first two of the Tribunal's findings of breaches of Articles 1105 and 1110, it was not successful on the remaining points. Accordingly, the Award should not be set aside in its entirety.

[136] Although I have concluded that the Tribunal made decisions on matters outside the scope of the submission to arbitration when it found the first two breaches of Articles 1105 and 1110, I should not be taken as holding that there was no breach of Article 1105 and no breach of Article 1110 until the issuance of the Ecological Decree. The function of this Court is limited to setting aside arbitral awards if the criteria set out in s. 34 of the International CAA are shown to exist. I express no opinion on whether there was a breach of Article 1105 or a breach of Article 1110 prior to the issuance of the Decree on grounds other than those relied upon by the Tribunal. If Metalclad wishes to pursue the portion of the interest contained in the Award which I have set aside, by establishing a breach of Article 1105 or Article 1110 prior to the issuance of the Decree without regard to the concept of transparency, the matter is remitted to the Tribunal.

This decision engendered considerable controversy.[117] To be sure, the transparency obligation that the arbitral tribunal relied on is contained in Article 102 of NAFTA, not in Chapter 11's substantive standards of treatment, and therefore might have been rejected as an independent ground for state liability under the treaty. But as at least one Mexican commentator has recognized, the *Metalclad* tribunal made no mention of a "breach" of NAFTA Article 102 as a basis for its award against Mexico.[118] The *Metalclad* tribunal's task, as it saw it, was simply to give content to the elusive notion of "fair and equitable treatment" contained in Article 1105. The tribunal viewed the lack of regulatory transparency as a clearly unfair circumstance, and its reference to the term in Article 102 was simply to underline that the NAFTA parties appeared to share this view. It seems logical and preferable for the arbitrators to have sought principles for defining unfairness from the text of

---

[117] *See, e.g.,* Ian A. Laird, *The Weakening of the International Rule of Law in the NAFTA Zone,* presentation prepared for May 3, 2002, CD Howe/Munk Centre Conference on NAFTA Chapter 11, at 12–14.

[118] Francisco González de Cossío, *Mexican Experience with Investment Arbitration,* 3 J.W.I. 473, 481 (2002).

NAFTA itself, which the state parties agreed to, rather than drawing on general principles of law or their own subjective sense of justice. Mexico's breach, as the tribunal clearly stated in its award, was of Article 1105, because its failure to adhere to standards of transparency was unfair and inequitable.

Because the British Columbia court upheld the *Metalclad* award on most points, and in particular declined to overturn the tribunal's finding that Mexico had expropriated the claimant's property, the modification of the damages award against Mexico was relatively insignificant. The partial set aside was criticized nonetheless, and there was widespread confidence that Metalclad's appeal to the Canadian Supreme Court would be successful and lead to the reinstatement of the entire award. Shortly after the appeal was filed, the parties agreed to a settlement, whereby Mexico paid US$16 million to Metalclad, which abandoned all further litigation.[119] The British Columbia's court's decision, however, continues to reverberate. Although many believe that the court's approach intruded too far into the merits of the case, respondent states may be emboldened to seek to set aside awards against them, hoping local judges at the place of arbitration will, like the British Columbian Supreme Court, give less deference in such cases than in the commercial arbitration context.

C. Tollefson, Metalclad v. United Mexican States Revisited: Judicial Oversight of NAFTA's Chapter Eleven Investor-State Claim Process, 11 Minn. J. Global Trade 183 (2002)

II. Judicial Review of Jurisdiction With Respect to Awards Under Chapter Eleven

. . . .

B. Private Commercial Arbitration v. Chapter 11 Arbitration: Implications for Judicial Review

Mexico argued forcefully that private commercial arbitrations and arbitrations under Chapter Eleven differ significantly in a variety of key respects and that therefore it would be a mistake to employ the same approach to judicial review in both contexts.[120] A compelling argument in its favor is that the investor-state claim procedure is sui generis, possessing many characteristics that would tend to justify a greater degree of judicial supervision than would otherwise be appropriate in the review of awards in private commercial arbitrations.[121] Unlike private commercial arbitrations, a claimant

---

[119] *Metalclad to Receive $16 Million NAFTA: Mexico Pays the Newport Beach Company to End 5-Year Dispute Over Dump Site*, L.A. Times, Oct. 27, 2001, at C8.

[120] SN: *See* Petitioner's Outline of Argument 178–85, at 53–56, Metalclad (No. L002904); see also Outline of Argument of Intervenor Attorney General of Canada 30, at 12, *United Mexican States v. Metalclad Corp.*, [2001] 89 B.C.L.R.3d 359 (Can.) (No. L002904).

[121] SN: Petitioner's Outline of Argument 179, at 54; 184, at 55–56, Metalclad (No. L002904); see also Outline of Argument of Intervenor Attorney General of Canada 5 & 7, at 3–4, Metalclad (No. L002904).

under Chapter Eleven is not seeking to enforce an agreement to which it is a party.[122] Its right to seek arbitration is entirely derivative of NAFTA, an international treaty.[123] The fact that an investor can seek such relief represents a significant departure from the general international law principle that only sovereign States are entitled to enforce international treaty obligations.[124] It also represents a departure from the private law principle that strangers to an agreement cannot invoke its arbitration process because it is only the parties to the agreement who have consented to resolve their disputes in this manner.[125]

Thus, while in private commercial arbitrations, the parties to the arbitration agreement are the same parties that ultimately appear in court on an application for review, this is not the case with arbitrations under Chapter Eleven.[126] In the latter circumstance, the need to review the award so as to respect the autonomy of the "parties" to resolve their dispute in a preferred arbitral forum is greatly diminished.[127]

There are a variety of other factors that tend to support the position adopted by Mexico that Chapter Eleven awards should be subjected to an enhanced level of judicial scrutiny. Perhaps most compelling among these is that while private commercial arbitrations deal with matters primarily of concern to the immediate private disputants, Chapter Eleven claims have a strong public character. Frequently, as in the present case and many other pending and decided Chapter Eleven disputes, the issues to be decided have broad implications for public policy affecting the ability of governments to promote sustainable development and take measures that protect public health and the environment.[128] The desirability of ensuring that trade and investment liberalization do not undermine these goals is expressly recognized throughout NAFTA.[129] Indeed, it is in recognition of the need to harmonize trade and environmental objectives, and to encourage public discussion and debate regarding these issues, that the procedural rules and practices governing Chapter Eleven arbitrations are increasingly departing from those that have traditionally governed private commercial arbitrations.[130] Thus, in recent Chapter Eleven decisions, tribunals have held that the strict principle of confidentiality that has tended to hold sway in arbitrations between private parties does not apply with

---

[122] SN: Petitioner's Outline of Argument 8, at 4, Metalclad (No. L002904); see also Outline of Argument of Intervenor Attorney General of Canada, 8 at 4, Metalclad (No. L002904).

[123] SN: Petitioner's Outline of Argument 58, at 15, Metalclad (No. L002904).

[124] SN: *See id.* 72, at 19.

[125] SN: Metalclad, 89 B.C.L.R.3d 57, at 376–77; see also Andrea K. Bjorklund, *Contract Without Privity: Sovereign Offer and Investor Acceptance*, 2 Chi. J. Int'l L. 183 (2001) (discussing lack of privity theme in private commercial law).

[126] SN: Outline of Argument of Intervenor Attorney General of Canada 8–10, at 4–5, Metalclad (No. L002904).

[127] SN: *See* discussion supra Pt. III.B.

[128] SN: *See* Lucien J. Dhooge, *The North American Free Trade Agreement and the Environment: The Lessons of* Metalclad Corp. v. United Mexican States, 10 Minn. J. Global Trade 209, 273–82 (2001) (for a discussion of the public policy implications).

[129] SN: *See* Metalclad, 89 B.C.L.R.3d 54 at 375.

[130] SN: In particular, note the reference to sustainable development and environmental protection contained in the NAFTA preamble, art. 1114 and the North American Agreement on Environmental Cooperation as discussed in Dhooge, *supra* note [128], at 274–75.

the same force when a sovereign state is a party to the arbitration.[131] For similar reasons, Chapter Eleven tribunals have allowed non-parties to participate in arbitral proceedings through the filing of amicus briefs.[132] Finally, once again unlike private commercial arbitrations, NAFTA specifically allows parties other than the disputants to take part in Chapter Eleven proceedings.[133]

C. A "Pragmatic and Fundamental" Approach?

Mexico therefore submitted that Justice Tysoe was not constrained by the deferential standard of review traditionally employed in the review of private commercial arbitral awards.[134] Rather, it urged him to employ a more flexible test that Canadian courts have employed to determine the appropriate standard of review when petitioned to review decisions of domestic tribunals and agencies.[135] This so-called "pragmatic and functional" approach calls upon the court to consider a variety of case-specific factors before determining the appropriate standard of review.[136] According to Mexico, applying this approach would vest the court with a broader discretionary and more context-specific basis on which to review the Tribunal's decision.[137]

Justice Tysoe was not prepared to adopt the pragmatic and functional test approach. Echoing submissions made by Metalclad,[138] he voiced concern about importing into the realm of arbitral review a test "developed as a branch of statutory interpretation in respect of domestic tribunals created by statute."[139] In his view, the standard of review to be employed under the ICAA was inherent in the language of the Act. It was unnecessary and unhelpful, he intimated, to bring extraneous legal concepts or tests to bear on this task.

Other courts will likely be tempted to follow Justice Tysoe's lead in concluding that applications to set aside Chapter Eleven awards should be approached solely with reference to the express statutory language contained in the applicable domestic review statute. The only source of potential uncertainty is reviews conducted in the United States where, as

---

[131] SN: The sui generis nature of the Chapter 11 process is also implicitly recognized in the recent decision of the Parties to issue an interpretive statement on this issue. See Interpretive Statement, *supra* note 24; Jeff Sallot & Heather Scoffield, *Agreement Means More Open NAFTA*, Globe & Mail, Aug. 1, 2001, at B1–2; Jan Cienski, *NAFTA Chapter 11 Facing Closer Public Scrutiny*, Nat'l Post, Aug. 1, 2001, at C5.

[132] SN: Charles H. Brower II, *Investor-State Disputes Under NAFTA: The Empire Strikes Back*, 40 Colum. J. Transnat'l L. 43, 47–8 (2001).

[133] SN: NAFTA, art. 1127–1129, 32 I.L.M. at 645.

[134] SN: Petitioner's Outline of Argument 202, at 62, Metalclad (No. L002904).

[135] SN: *Id.*

[136] SN: Relevant factors include: "1) the presence or absence of a privative clause; 2) the relative expertise of the tribunal, as compared to the Court; 3) the nature of the decision being made (i.e., whether it is a question of law or fact), 4) whether the decision to be made is 'polycentric' (i.e., necessarily involves a consideration of often-conflicting and multi-facetted issues); and 5) the purpose of the provision." *Id.* 203, at 62.

[137] SN: *See id.* 204, at 63.

[138] SN: *See* Respondent's Outline of Argument 169, at 57, Metalclad (No. L002904): "the question of the appropriate standard of review does not arise under the International Commercial Arbitration Act. The provisions of that legislation set out a complete code governing the Court's authority to set aside an arbitral award including the bases for review, and implicitly, the standard of review to be applied. There is no need to look beyond the language of the statute to determine the appropriate standard of review." *Id.*

[139] SN: *See Metalclad*, 89 B.C.L.R.3d ¶ 54 at 375.

has been noted, Chapter Eleven awards will fall to review under the Federal Arbitration Act.[140] As with laws based on the UNCITRAL model, the FAA expressly provides that an award may be vacated on the basis that the tribunal exceeded its authority.[141] However, American courts have interpreted the FAA as leaving open an additional common law ground for setting aside an award known as the "manifest disregard" standard.[142] This non-statutory standard emerges from dicta in the 1953 U.S. Supreme Court case of *Wilko v. Swan*.[143] Many courts have since relied on the comments in Wilko as an additional ground for arbitral review, although this manifest disregard standard has also been the subject of judicial criticism.[144] The standard has been characterized as "something beyond and different from a mere error of law or failure on the part of the arbitrators to understand or apply the law,"[145] that arises where the arbitrator "understood and correctly stated the law but proceeded to ignore it."[146] Of late, the vitality of this standard has been cast into serious doubt[147] but the U.S. Supreme Court has not yet pronounced its fate.

2. CME v. Czech Republic

The *CME* case arose out of investments in the broadcasting sector by American businessman Ronald S. Lauder (son of Estée Lauder). In 1994, Czech Republic B.V. (CME), a Dutch Antilles company controlled by Lauder, acquired Česká Nezávislá Televizní Společnost, spol. s.r.o. (CNTS), a Czech company that ran the first independent television station in the Czech Republic, TV Nova. Innovative and sometimes controversial programming (including a famous naked weather girl) made TV Nova very successful. After a falling out with Lauder, CME's local director, Dr. Zelezny, used his connections with the state media regulatory body, the Media Council, to deprive the company of its exclusive licensing arrangement. As a result, CME's business was seriously harmed. Lauder first initiated arbitration in London in his capacity as an individual investor under the United States-Czech Republic BIT, and six months later CME filed a claim against the government under the Netherlands-Czech Republic BIT, which resulted in the formation of a tribunal in Stockholm.

In September 2001, the Stockholm arbitral tribunal rendered an award on liability, finding for CME and holding that the Czech Republic had violated a range of

---

[140] SN: 9 U.S.C. 1–16 (1994).

[141] SN: 9 U.S.C. 10(a)(4).

[142] SN: 346 U.S. 427, 436 (1953).

[143] SN: *Id.*

[144] SN: This is especially true in Eleventh and Seventh Circuit decisions. *See, e.g., Raiford v. Merrill Lynch*, 903 F.2d 1410, 1412 (11th Cir. 1990); *Bavarati v. Josephthal, Lyon & Ross, Inc.*, 28 F.3d 704, 706 (7th Cir. 1994). *See also Gelander*, supra note 138, at 636–37.

[145] SN: *Siegal v. Titan Indus. Corp.*, 779 F.2d 891, 892 (2d Cir. 1985), quoted in *Gelander*, supra note 137, at 636.

[146] SN: *Id.*

[147] SN: *Baker Marine (Nig.) Ltd. v. Chevron (Nig.) Ltd.*, 191 F.3d 194 (2d Cir. 1999).

obligations under the Netherlands-Czech Republic BIT.[148] In preparation for a future phase of the arbitration to determine the amount of damages due to CME, the tribunal ruled that the breaches in question gave rise to an obligation on the Czech Republic to compensate CME for the "full market value" of its investment.[149] Shortly after the liability award was rendered, the Czech Republic applied to the Svea Court of Appeal in Stockholm to set aside the award. As part of the filing of that action, the Czech government posted a bond for the full amount of the award, such that CME would promptly receive payment on its claim should the Czech challenge fail.[150] The Swedish Arbitration Act, which governed the annulment action, roughly tracks the UNCITRAL Model Law in this area, with a few important modifications. Most significantly, the Swedish statute specifically bars challenges on several of the permissible grounds if the moving party waived the objection by not raising it in the course of the arbitration proceedings.[151]

On May 15, 2003, the Swedish Court rendered its opinion, rejecting the Czech Republic's motion to set aside the award.[152] The Czech Republic first put forward the argument that the Stockholm arbitration was procedurally defective, because Jaroslav Hándl, the arbitrator it appointed, had been excluded from many of the deliberations that led to the drafting of the award. After Hándl had expressed his disagreement with the other two arbitrators (Wofgang Kühn and Stephen Schwebel) at the first post-hearing deliberation session, he was allegedly marginalized in the subsequent process, did not receive all drafts of the award in a timely fashion, and did not have enough time to review and comment on those drafts before the next draft was prepared. Ultimately, Hándl refused to sign the award, submitted a separate opinion, and then resigned from the tribunal.[153]

---

[148] *CME Czech Rep. B.V. v. Czech Republic* (Partial Award of Sept. 13, 2001).

[149] In the final phase of the arbitration on the quantification of damages, which proceeded simultaneously with the Czech Republic's challenge of the Partial Award, the tribunal awarded CME $269 million plus 10 percent interest per annum. *CME Czech Rep. B.V. v. Czech Republic* (Final Award of Mar. 13, 2003).

[150] *Czech Republic Will Pay Immediately If Stockholm Court Upholds Award*, PRNewsWire-FirstCall, Mar. 31, 2003, *available at* http://www.finanznachrichten.de/nachrichten/artikel-1931445.asp. It is somewhat puzzling why the Czech Republic chose to post the bond and challenge the award in Sweden. Had it not done so, CME would likely have been required to enforce the award in the Czech Republic, as that was probably the only jurisdiction with identifiable and seizable assets of the Republic. The Republic's courts might well have been more receptive to the Republic's objections.

[151] See p. 647 *supra*.

[152] *Czech Republic v. CME Czech Republic B.V.* (Svea Court of Appeal, Case No. T 8735–01, decision of May 15, 2003) [hereinafter Stockholm Court Decision].

[153] Hándl was replaced by Ian Brownlie during the final damages phase. Brownlie also ended up in the minority, issuing a lengthy separate opinion but also signing the final award.

After hearing extensive testimony from the arbitrators themselves, the Swedish court rejected this argument.[154] The Court explained that the parties and Swedish law delegate a great deal of authority to the arbitrators, within the framework of applicable rules, to organize their deliberations as they see fit. The lack of restrictions under Swedish law and the UNCITRAL arbitration rules was designed precisely to secure the flexibility necessary to defeat any attempts by a dissenting arbitrator to stall the process and block the issuance of an award adverse to the party that appointed him or her. Furthermore, the Court concluded from the evidence presented that arbitrator Hándl had not in fact been excluded from deliberations in any significant way, and suggested that if he was marginalized at all, this was the natural consequence of his minority opinion.

> [The Chairman] appears the whole time to have treated Hándl correctly and Hándl appears to have been afforded an opportunity to submit his comments to the extent which reasonably may be dictated by considerations of courtesy between colleagues. Hándl's feeling of having been excluded is probably, in all essential regards, connected to the fact that he did not meet with support for his opinion in the case.[155]

The Court added that Hándl had received ample time to review drafts, and in fact the schedules he proposed for reviewing the award were unjustifiably slow.[156]

The Czech Republic also advanced several reasons why the Stockholm tribunal exceeded its mandate in rendering the award on liability. Perhaps the central argument presented was that the tribunal had ignored the terms of the submission to arbitration by ignoring the proper system of applicable law. The choice-of-law clause of the Netherlands-Czech BIT called for application of the terms of the BIT, Czech law, and international law, with no indication which body of law, if any, should take precedence. The Czech Republic asserted that the arbitrators had completely disregarded Czech law and had invoked rules not part of international law. Therefore, it argued, the entire award was the result of an impermissible decision on the basis of general equity (*ex aequo et bono* or amiable composition) and should be annulled. The Swedish Court disagreed, noting that the arbitrators had spent a great deal of time discussing whether the BIT required them to apply Czech law and had ultimately decided that the clause provided a "menu" of options from which they had full discretion to choose. Under the Swedish Arbitration Act, it stated, "an excess of mandate may be involved only where the arbitrators' interpretation of the choice of law clause proves to be baseless such that their assessment may be equated with . . . having ignored a provision regarding applicable law."[157] The tribunal's decision to apply primarily international law, the Court concluded, was perfectly reasonable in light of the BIT language. The

---

[154] Stockholm Court Decision, *supra* note 152, at 85–90.
[155] *Id.* at 89.
[156] *Id.* at 90.
[157] *Id.* at 91.

Court refused to delve into various sections of the Stockholm award to see which sources of law the tribunal applied in each instance, since "it is sufficient to clarify whether the arbitral tribunal applied any of the [applicable] sources of law. . . . The fact that each legal statement in the award is not directly derived citing a rule of law cannot be deemed to mean that the tribunal conducted a general assessment of reasonableness."[158]

The Czech Republic next argued that the Stockholm tribunal had exceeded its mandate because principles of *res judicata* and *lis pendens* barred the proceedings in light of the pendency of Ronald Lauder's parallel arbitration in London. The Stockholm court rejected this challenge as well, for two reasons. First, there was no identity of parties, since the claimants were different in the two arbitrations, and therefore the doctrines had no effect on the Stockholm tribunal. Second, the Czech Republic waived any possible challenge on this ground at the annulment stage by refraining from making the same argument before the arbitral tribunal. Excess of mandate, the Court underlined, like all other challenges not based on public policy, is subject to the rule that "a party is not entitled to invoke a circumstance which, through participating in the arbitration proceedings without objection or otherwise, he may be deemed to have waived."[159] During the arbitration, the Czech Republic "expressly waived raising an objection of lis pendens or res judicata," and therefore could not interpose that argument during the annulment case in court.[160]

The other "excess of mandate" argument was that the tribunal had erroneously invoked a theory of "joint tortfeasors" to find that the Republic was liable for injury to CME despite the intervening actions of a private party, Dr. Zelezny. "Without the conclusion that there existed joint tortfeasors, the Republic could not have been held liable for the injury incurred by CME's investment and the outcome of the case would have been different."[161] This argument, more perhaps than any of the others, clearly attacked the tribunal's reasoning and factual findings on the merits, rather than the scope of the parties' agreement to arbitrate. Nevertheless, the Stockholm Court dismissed the challenge on its own terms, finding that the arbitrators' decision in fact did not depend on any "joint tortfeasors" concept, and that this notion was introduced only in passing as a response to objections the Czech Republic itself had raised.[162]

---

[158] *Id.* at 94.

[159] *Id.* at 96.

[160] On the same grounds of waiver, the Court dismissed two additional Czech "excess of mandate" arguments, namely that the tribunal had impermissibly included preliminary decisions on damages in an award that was expressly limited to liability and that the arbitrators had found the Republic liable for treaty violations that occurred before CME acquired its investment. *Id.* at 101–104.

[161] *Id.* at 41.

[162] *Id.* at 100–101.

As a last resort, the Czech Republic also argued that the CME award violated Swedish public policy, or, in the words of the Swedish arbitration statute, that the Stockholm award and the manner in which in came about were "manifestly incompatible with the principles on which the legal system of Sweden is based."[163] The Czech Republic's position was that the same defects, particularly the exclusion of the Czech arbitrator from deliberations and the tribunal's assumption of jurisdiction despite the pendency of parallel proceedings in London, when taken together also constituted a public policy breach sufficient to annul the award. The Court rejected this submission with minimal discussion, simply stating that the Czech Republic had "no shown ample reason for why the arbitration award or the manner in which it came about should be in violation of order public and thereby invalid based on the grounds asserted."[164] It is surprising that the Czech Republic offered no additional grounds for public policy violation. Once the Swedish court had found that the defects complained of were too insignificant to justify setting aside the award under the "excess of powers" rubric, it was seemingly a foregone conclusion that the identical facts would not support the public policy ground, either. The Czech Republic might have tried to assert that the overwhelming size of the award, more than $300 million with interest, would have a crippling effect on the functioning of the Czech government and a devastating effect on public welfare in the country. Given that the Swedish statute concentrated on national, rather than international public policy, it is unlikely that this argument would have won the day, either. But given widespread grassroots outcry concerning the negative effects of large investment arbitration awards on development, the heavy burden of large investment arbitration awards on the host state's populace could play a major role in future public policy challenges.[165]

3. S.D. Myers v. Canada

An export regulation was the source of the dispute in *S.D. Myers v. Canada*.[166] S.D. Myers (SDMI) was a U.S. corporation engaged in the treatment and disposal of toxic waste materials called polychlorinated biphenyls (PCBs). It established a Canadian subsidiary to contract for the export of PCBs to SDMI's U.S.-based facilities for treatment. In order to promote a homegrown Canadian PCB handling industry, the Canadian government implemented a ban on the export of the PCB wastes from Canada.[167] SDMI claimed that this export ban violated several

---

[163] *Id.* at 105.

[164] *Id.*

[165] Gus van Harten, *Private Authority and Transnational Governance: The Contours of the International System of Investor Protection*, 12(4) Rev. Int'l Pol. Econ. 600, 601 (2005); Elizabeth Blackwood & Stephen McBride, *Investment Arbitration as the Achilles Heel of Globalization?: The Ongoing Conflict between the Rights of Capital and the Rights of States*, 25(3) Pol. & Soc'y 43 (2006).

[166] *S.D. Myers, Inc. v. Gov't of Canada* (Partial Award of Nov. 13, 2000) [hereinafter Myers Partial Award].

[167] *Id.* ¶¶ 122–23.

substantive provisions of NAFTA, including national treatment, fair and equitable treatment, the prohibition on performance requirements, and expropriation without compensation.[168]

The tribunal ruled that although the goal of maintaining a domestic PCB-processing capacity was a legitimate goal, it was achieved in a way that unnecessarily compromised Canada's NAFTA obligation to treat American investors no less favorably than Canadian investors, and therefore violated Article 1102. A majority of the arbitrators also found that Canada's actions in blocking the export of PCBs, largely because of the arbitrary and unjust manner in which the measures discriminated against SDMI, also violated the fair and equitable treatment standard of Article 1105. Arbitrator Chiasson dissented on this point, insisting that violation of the antidiscrimination clause of Article 1102 could not, standing alone, also be deemed a breach of Article 1105. The tribunal denied SDMI's expropriation claim, however, noting that

> [E]xpropriations tend to involve the deprivation of ownership rights; regulations [are] a lesser interference. The distinction between expropriation and regulation screens out most potential cases of complaints concerning economic intervention by a state and reduces the risk that governments will be subject to claims as they go about their business of managing public affairs.[169]

Apparently emboldened by the *Metalclad* court decision, on February 8, 2001, Canada applied to the Federal Court of Canada in Ottawa, pursuant to the federal Commercial Arbitration Code,[170] seeking to annul the tribunal's decision. Canada contended that the tribunal purported to resolve disputes not properly before it, thereby acting beyond the scope of its jurisdiction. Canada also argued that the tribunal misinterpreted NAFTA's jurisdictional provisions by extending the benefits of Chapter 11 to a company that was not an investor with respect to the relevant investment, and that it had misapplied NAFTA's substantive provisions, Articles 1102 and 1105.

At the outset, Canada argued for a very liberal standard of review for NAFTA awards, relying on the British Columbia court's *Metalclad* decision and a line of Canadian case law on the vacatur of domestic arbitration awards. Canada's position took direct aim at the legitimacy of the NAFTA system in general, arguing essentially that the issues in dispute were too important to the Canadian public to allow arbitrators full discretion.

---

[168] *Id.* ¶¶ 130–44.

[169] *Id.* ¶ 184.

[170] The *Myers* arbitration was sited in Toronto, Canada, in the province of Ontario, as is Ottawa. According to one commentator, this forum was chosen because under Canadian law, the annulment of arbitration awards rendered in Canada against foreign states, as in *Metalclad*, are governed by provincial statute, whereas challenges to awards against Canada itself must be brought under federal law. Patricia Isela Hansen, *Judicialization and Globalization in the North American Free Trade Agreement*, 38 Tex. Int'l L. J.489, 498 (2003).

> NAFTA Chapter Eleven arbitrations differ substantially from a private commercial arbitration in terms of the extent to which their decisions might affect interests beyond those of the immediate parties to the dispute. Claims under NAFTA Chapter Eleven are not contractual disputes but challenges to government "measures," [defined as] "any law, regulation, procedure, requirement or practice." ... The decisions of NAFTA Chapter Eleven Tribunals have important public policy implications that impact upon, and are of interest to Canadians generally.[171]

Canada further suggested that NAFTA arbitration tribunals are not necessarily qualified to properly decide the momentous issues they face, as they "are not standing tribunals with established or recognized expertise in trade matters."[172] As a result, Canada argued that NAFTA awards "do not attract extensive judicial deference where the issue is whether the award under review falls within the terms of the submission to arbitration, or contains decisions on matters beyond the scope of the submission to arbitration."[173] The standard of review in such matters, according to Canada, should be "correctness," that is, a complete *de novo* review of the tribunal's decisions and replacement of the arbitrators' discretion with the court's. Canada insisted that the "patently unreasonable" standard of review, the most commonly applied level of deference in international commercial arbitration under Canadian law,[174] should be discarded in NAFTA cases.

The thrust of Canada's attack on the *S.D. Myers* award was that the tribunal had acted outside the scope of its mandate in several ways. Most of these grounds for vacatur were based on the tribunal's allegedly erroneous finding that it had jurisdiction to decide the dispute before it. For example, Canada argued during the arbitration that the claimant was not an "investor" as defined in NAFTA, and therefore the Chapter 11 dispute resolution provisions could not apply to its claim against Canada. The annulment brief described in great detail the corporate structure of the American claimant and its related Canadian enterprise, arguing that the two were not directly affiliated, and therefore not linked closely enough to make Myers an "investor."[175] This line of argumentation appeared designed to appeal to the court's perceived willingness to reopen the factual as well as legal findings of the arbitrators.

Other arguments in the Canadian papers were even more thinly disguised attempts to reopen the merits of the dispute. Clearly taking inspiration from the Czech Republic's

---

[171] *Attorney Gen. of Canada v. S.D. Myers, Inc.*, Court File No. T-81-03, Memorandum of Fact and Law of the Applicant Attorney General of Canada [hereinafter Myers Motion to Set Aside], ¶¶ 137–38, *available* at www.naftaclaims.com.

[172] *Id.* ¶ 136.

[173] *Id.* ¶ 134.

[174] Under this standard, a court will interfere only if a careful review of the factual and legislative record demonstrates that the decision under review violates the most basic notions of justice, is clearly irrational, or is unsustainable on the evidence. *Nat'l Corn Growers Ass'n v. Canada (Import Tribunal)*, [1990] 2 S.C.R. 1324, 1370.

[175] Myers Motion to Set Aside, *supra* note 171, ¶¶ 147–175.

positions in *CME*, Canada argued that the arbitrators exceeded their authority by awarding damages for injuries for actions or harm falling outside the treaty's scope. Because SDMI was not a real "investor," Canada's actions had little to do with any harm that SDMI sustained, which was largely felt in the company's main U.S. facilities. "By awarding damages to a person other than the investor or the investment and for damages beyond those related to the investment, the Tribunal's awards deal with a dispute not falling within the terms of the submission to arbitration."[176]

Despite Canada's schooled excision of the word, this argument was nothing more than a disagreement over the arbitrators' "causation" decision—a key element of the tribunal's liability holding. Just as the Czech Republic argued in *CME* that the tribunal exceeded its jurisdiction by ignoring the intervening actions of a private party, Mr. Zelezny, Canada sought to recast substance as procedure, liability as jurisdiction. Canada used the same approach later in its brief, framing a challenge to the tribunal's discrimination finding as an allegation of excess of powers. The tribunal had found that Canada breached NAFTA Article 1102 by treating SDMI differently than it treated Canadian operators in the same industry. Canada claimed that the discrimination holding resulted from an excess of powers because Article 1102 applies only where better treatment is accorded to local companies in "like circumstances," and because the comparators used by the tribunal were not actually comparable. At its core, this was an argument about the substantive legal criteria for finding that Article 1102 was violated, and not about the scope of submission to arbitration at all. As Myers argued in its response to Canada's court submission,

> Canada's approach would transform [the "excess of mandate" provision of the Arbitration Act] from a narrow jurisdictional ground for setting aside an award into a broad right of appeal, that would effectively transfer to the courts in the place of arbitration the jurisdiction intended to be vested in the arbitrators.[177]

Although Canada next argued that the Myers award should be set aside on public policy grounds, it offered no independent basis for this assertion. Instead, it simply contended that the defects it had characterized as an "excess of powers" also contravened Canadian public policy and should therefore lead to vacatur on that ground as well.[178] The connection between the two grounds for vacatur arose from the assertion that "the 'fundamental principles of law and justice' inherent in the use of the term 'public policy' in the [UNCITRAL] Model Law include[s] the principle that a tribunal could not exceed its jurisdiction in the course of the inquiry."[179]

---

[176] *Id.* ¶ 179.

[177] *Attorney Gen. of Canada v. S.D. Myers* (Respondent's Memorandum of Fact and Law, June 16, 2003), at 26.

[178] Myers Motion to Set Aside, *supra* note 171, ¶¶ 171, 232, 236.

[179] *Id.* ¶ 146.

The federal court rejected each of Canada's claims and dismissed its petition.

THE ATTORNEY GENERAL OF CANADA

Applicant

-and-

S.D. MYERS, INC.

Respondent

-and-

THE UNITED MEXICAN STATES ("MEXICO")

Intervener

REASONS FOR ORDER

Kelen J:

[1] This is an application pursuant Article 34 of the *Commercial Arbitration Code*, a schedule to the *Commercial Arbitration Act*, R.S.C. 1985, c. 17 (2nd Supp.), to set aside decisions dated November 13, 2000 ("liability award"), October 21, 2002 ("damages award") and December 30, 2003 ("costs award") made by an Arbitral Tribunal established pursuant to the *North American Free Trade Agreement* ("NAFTA").

The arbitration proceedings

[15] On July 28, 1998 SDMI delivered a Notice of Intent to submit a claim to arbitration under NAFTA Chapter 11. Three months later, it delivered its Notice of Arbitration and Statement of Claim alleging that the Canadian ban on exports of PCBs breached NAFTA articles 1102, 1105 and two other Articles which were not upheld by the Tribunal.

The Tribunal's Decision

[18] Based on the evidence the Tribunal found that the interim and final orders favoured Canadian nationals over non-nationals, and that the effect of the orders was to prevent SDMI and its investment from carrying out the Canadian business that they planned to undertake. It further found that "there was no legitimate environmental reason for introducing the ban."

. . . .

THE ISSUES

[25] The issues in this application are:

whether the arbitral awards exceeded the scope of the arbitration agreement in Part B of the NAFTA Chapter 11 by dealing with a dispute or disputes not contemplated by Chapter 11 of the NAFTA; and,

whether the awards contravene the public policy of Canada.

[26] With respect to the first issue Canada, and Mexico, which intervened in support of Canada, raise the following sub-issues:

whether the Tribunal erred in concluding that for the purposes of NAFTA Chapter 11, SDMI was an "investor" and Myers Canada was its "investment";

whether the Tribunal misconstrued the obligation of National Treatment in NAFTA Article 1102 as permitting a comparison between the treatment accorded SDMI and Myers Canada with Canadian companies, and wrongly concluded that SDMI and Myers Canada were "in like circumstances" with Canadian companies for the purposes of Article 1102;

whether the Tribunal erred in concluding that under international law, a breach of an obligation related to investment protection supports a finding that a State Party breached NAFTA Article 1105 and that in the circumstances of this case, a breach of Article 1102 essentially establishes a breach of Article 1105; and,

whether the Tribunal exceeded the scope of the submission to arbitration by applying Chapter 11 obligations to "cross-border trade in services" which are governed by Chapter 12;

ANALYSIS

The objectives and interpretation of NAFTA

[27] The relevant objectives of NAFTA are set out in Article 102, and can be paraphrased as follows:

to eliminate trade barriers in the free trade zone of Canada, United States and Mexico;

to promote conditions of fair competition in the free trade area;

to substantially increase investment opportunities in the free trade area;

and to create effective procedure for the application of NAFTA and for the resolution of disputes under NAFTA.

[28] The objectives also provide that the parties "shall interpret and apply" NAFTA in light of its objectives and in accordance with "applicable rules of international law."

[29] Under Chapter 11, NAFTA has created an obligation on Canada to treat a U.S. company which chooses to invest and compete in Canada in a fair and non-discriminatory manner, and that the provisions of NAFTA shall be interpreted and applied in a manner which fulfills this objective.

[30] Article 1114 of NAFTA allows Canada to adopt a legitimate environmental measure without regard to Chapter 11. However, the Tribunal found that the Canadian law banning exports of PCBs was not a measure for a legitimate environmental purpose, but was for the purpose of protecting Canadian industry from U.S. competition. Therefore, Article 1114 is not in issue.

The meaning of the pertinent Chapter 11 NAFTA provisions

[31] In Article 1102 of NAFTA, Canada, the United States of America and the United States of Mexico, have agreed that each country will accord investors from the other two countries no less favourable treatment than it accords its own investor with respect "to the establishment, acquisition, expansion, management, conduct, operation, and sale or other disposition of investments."

[32] Moreover, NAFTA provides, unlike its predecessor, the Canada-U.S. Free Trade Agreement, a mechanism which allows individual investors to settle disputes with respect to alleged discriminatory treatment. This creates a powerful and significant new cause of action to protect investors against state protection. It also creates an impartial, efficient and timely arbitration process to settle such disputes. This arbitration process

only applies to disputes with respect to Chapter 11 claims by "investors" with respect to "investments of investors."

Limited jurisdiction of the Federal Court for judicial review

[33] Canada and Mexico assert that the appropriate standard of review in this case is "correctness" because this international arbitration involves a State, and the State has only consented to arbitration to the extent provided in NAFTA. They state that this is a different situation from where private parties have agreed that the international arbitration will decide the whole matter in issue between the private parties.

[34] Canada submits at paragraph 87 of its Memorandum:

> A corner stone of the law of arbitration is the requirement that parties consent to the arbitration. That consent must comprehend not only the fact of arbitration but also the specific issues to be resolved by arbitration and may stipulate the governing law. An arbitration tribunal only has jurisdiction over those specific issues that the parties have agreed to submit and any award that goes beyond those issues exceeds the scope of the submission to arbitration.

Canada's authority is Alan Redfern & Martin Hunter, *Law and Practice of International Commercial Arbitration*, 3d ed. (London: Sweet & Maxwell, 1999). (The co-author, Professor Martin Hunter, a world expert on the subject, was chose by the parties to be the chairman of the Arbitration Tribunal in this case.)

[35] The limited extent of the Court's jurisdiction to review is under Article 34 of the *Commercial Arbitration Code*. The Canadian jurisprudence that examines the limited jurisdiction for judicial review of a NAFTA Chapter 11 arbitration tribunal is:

. . . .

[37] In *Feldman, supra*, Chilcott J. at paragraph 77 states:

> In my view, a high level of deference should be accorded to the Tribunal especially incases where the Applicant Mexico is in reality challenging a finding of fact. The panel who has heard the evidence is best able to determine issues of credibility, reliability and onus of proof.

And at paragraph 97 he concludes:

> I accept the proposition that judicial deference should be accorded to arbitral awards generally and to international commercial arbitration in particular.

[42] It is noteworthy, that Article 34 of the Code does not allow for judicial review if the decision is based on an error of law or an erroneous finding of fact if the decision is within the jurisdiction of the Tribunal. The principle of non-judicial intervention in an arbitral award within the jurisdiction of the Tribunal has been often repeated.

[44] In analyzing the Court's jurisdiction under this subparagraph, the arbitral awards may only be set aside if the applicant, in this case the Attorney General of Canada, furnishes proof on one of two grounds:

the awards deal with a dispute not contemplated by or not falling within their terms of the submission to arbitration; or,

the awards contain decisions on matters beyond the scope of the submission to arbitration.

[45] With respect to the first ground, I am not satisfied that the award deals with a dispute not contemplated by or not falling within the terms of the submission to arbitration, namely whether Canada breached Articles 1102 and 1105 of NAFTA in relation to the respondent. In fact, this is the dispute submitted by the respondent to arbitration.

[46] The second ground is more difficult. The Attorney General submits that the arbitral decision that SDMI falls within the definition of an "investor" or that Myers Canada is "an investment of the investor" in accordance with the definitions in Article 1139 of NAFTA are matters beyond the scope of the submission to arbitration by applying Chapter 11 obligations to "cross-border trade in services" which are governed by Chapter 12, and Chapter 12 is beyond the scope of arbitration.

Matters beyond the scope of arbitration go to jurisdiction

[47] Article 21 of *UNCITRAL Arbitration Rules* give the Arbitration Tribunal the power to rule on objections regarding its jurisdiction. Article 21(3) requires that any plea that the Tribunal does not have jurisdiction be raised not later than the Statement of Defence. Article 21(4) requires that "in general" the Tribunal should rule on its jurisdiction as a preliminary question, however, the Tribunal may proceed with the arbitration and rule on its jurisdiction as part of its final award. In this case, SDMI submits that Canada did not object to the jurisdiction of the Tribunal as required in Article 21 of the *UNCITRAL Arbitration Rules,* and is now barred from seeking judicial review on this basis.

[48] The Court has considered the Notice of Arbitration and the Statement of Claim submitted by the respondent and Canada's Statement of Defence. Canada submits that it challenged the jurisdiction of the Arbitration Tribunal in paragraph 4 of its Statement of Defence under the heading "The Facts":

> ¶ 4. Except as expressly submitted below, Canada denies the facts alleged in paragraphs 2, 4–12 and 16–57 of the Claim and puts Myers to the strict proof of every fact alleged in those paragraphs.

Canada submits that this plea satisfies the requirements of Article 21(3) of the Arbitral Rules because paragraphs 6 to 12 of the Statement of Claim are under the heading "Jurisdiction of this Tribunal," and alleged that the claim is within the jurisdiction of the Tribunal.

[49] Article 21 requires that a party make a clear objection to the jurisdiction of the Arbitration Tribunal as soon as possible, and not later than the Statement of Defence. In reviewing paragraph 4 of Canada's Statement of Defence, the Court concludes that Canada did not make a clear objection to the Tribunal's jurisdiction. The plain and ordinary meaning of the Rules are that a party must make a specific, express objections to jurisdiction, and must ask the Tribunal to rule on its jurisdiction as a preliminary question. At that stage, parties can seek judicial review before the arbitration proceeds in, what was in this case, a lengthy and expensive arbitration. I find paragraph 4 of Canada's Statement of Defence obtuse with respect to jurisdiction.

[53] Jurisdiction is a term of art and a legal objection must be raised clearly at the outset of the arbitration. Canada failed to do so in this case, and cannot now argue that the Tribunal did not have jurisdiction to render the three decisions which are the subject of these applications for judicial review. To find otherwise would undermine the clear and express procedures incorporated in NAFTA for the resolution of disputes.

Judicial Review under Article 34(2)(b)(ii)–Public Policy

[55] Article 34(2)(b)(ii) of the Code provides that a Court may judicially review and set aside an award where "it is in conflict with the public policy of Canada." "Public policy" does not refer to the political position or an international position of Canada but refers to "fundamental notions and principles of justice." Such a principle includes that a tribunal not exceed its jurisdiction in the course of an inquiry, and that such a "jurisdictional error" can be a decision which is "patently unreasonable," such as a complete disregard of the law so that the decision constitutes an abuse of authority amounting to a flagrant injustice.

[56] In the case at bar, the Tribunal's findings with respect to the two jurisdictional questions, and with respect to Article 1102, are not "patently unreasonable," "clearly irrational," "totally lacking in reality" or "a flagrant denial of justice." Accordingly, the Court concludes that there is no aspect of the Tribunal decisions under review which "conflicts with the public policy of Canada."

Standard of review on legal meaning of definitions in NAFTA and the application of NAFTA Chapter 12

[57] I will undertake this review in the alternative that I am wrong in my conclusion above that Canada did not properly plead jurisdiction before the Tribunal so that Canada is now barred from seeking judicial review on this basis.

[58] On the two issues raised by Canada and Mexico that go the jurisdiction or the "scope of the submission to arbitration," the standard of review on a pure questions of law is correctness, and on a mixed question of law and fact is reasonableness.

[60] For these reasons, I will review the arbitral award with respect to the legal meaning of the word "investor" and "investment of an investor" in NAFTA on the standard of correctness. With respect to the application of the facts to the definitions, I will review the award on the standard of reasonableness.

[61] With respect to the second issue related to jurisdiction, namely whether Chapter 11 applies to cross-border trade in services under Chapter 12, the same two standards will be applied.

[65] The Court concludes that the broad nature of the definition of "investment of an investor of a Party," in particular the use of the words "controlled directly or indirectly," together with the objective of NAFTA that it shall be interpreted and applied to meet the objectives of NAFTA, support the finding of the Tribunal at paragraph 231:

> On the evidence and on the basis of its interpretation of NAFTA, the Tribunal concludes that SDMI was an "investor" for the purposes of Chapter 11 of NAFTA and that Myers Canada was an "investment."

[66] Since the language of NAFTA permits this finding, the Court also concludes that this finding was not *ex aequo et bono,* as submitted by Canada. The Tribunal did not exercise any equitable or chancery court power. It only exercised its power to properly interpret and apply the definition in Article 1139 of "investment of an investor of a Party" to the facts.

[67] The Attorney General states that the domestic law of Canada is applicable to determine whether Myers Canada is controlled by SDMI. (See paragraph 160 of the Memorandum of Fact of Law of the Attorney General of Canada. NAFTA is to be interpreted according to the provisions of NAFTA and the principles of international law.)

[68] Therefore, the references to the *Canadian Business Corporations Act* relied upon by the Attorney General are not relevant for determining whether SDMI, as a question of fact, controlled, indirectly or directly, Myers Canada in the ordinary meaning of the word "controlled."

[69] The position of the Attorney General is a narrow, legalistic, restrictive interpretation contrary to the objectives of NAFTA and contrary to the purposive interpretation which NAFTA Article 2.01 and Article 31 of the Vienna Convention stipulate.

Chapter 12—Cross-border trade in services

[71] Canada and Mexico argue that the respondent's activities in Canada are properly characterized as cross-border trade in services and are therefore governed by Chapter 12 of NAFTA. The Court is off the view that the different chapters of NAFTA overlap, and

that NAFTA rights are cumulative, unless there is a direct conflict. Since SDMI did have an investment in Canada with respect to waste remediation services, SDMI is entitled to the protection under Chapter 11 toward its investment, as well as the rights and protection afforded by Chapter 12 with respect to its trade in services. The rights and obligations under Chapter 12 are not mutually exclusive or inconsistent with the rights and obligations under Chapter 11. Accordingly, the Tribunal correctly applied Chapter 11 rights and obligations to SDMI.

Judicial review of the issue: did the export ban of PCBs breach Canada's obligations under Article 1102 (National Treatment)

[72] In the event that I am wrong about the Court not having the power to judicially review this issue under Article 34 of the Code, I will briefly do so. Article 1102 requires Canada accord to investors and investments of a national of another party, the U.S. in this case, treatment no less favourable than it accords, "in like circumstances," to its own investors, with respect to "the establishment, acquisition, expansion, management, conduct, operation and sale or other disposition of investments."

[73] There is no dispute that the Canadian ban on PCB exports sought to protect Canadian companies from U.S. competition, and was not for a legitimate environmental purpose. The applicant, with the support of Mexico, submits that the phrase "in like circumstances" means that the Tribunal must compare U.S. investors in like circumstances with Canadian investors and U.S. investments in Canada with Canadian investments in like circumstances. The Tribunal found at paragraph 251:

From the business perspective, it is clear that SDMI and Myers Canada were in "like circumstances" with Canadian operators such as Chem-Security and Cintex. They all were engaged in providing PCB waste remediation services. SDMI was in a position to attract customers that might otherwise have gone to the Canadian operators because it could offer more favourable prices and because it had extensive experience and credibility. It was precisely because SDMI was in a position to take business away from its Canadian competitors that Chem-Security and Cintex lobbied the Minister of Environment to ban exports when the U.S. authorities opened the border.

[74] This is a question of mixed fact and law. The Court concludes that the Tribunal's decision was reasonably open to it. The authorities show that the comparison of "in like circumstances" is a flexible benchmark, which can be expanded and contracted like an accordion to suit the particular facts of each case. In this case the Tribunal used a broad comparator, which was reasonably open to the Tribunal. Accordingly, the Court would not set aside this decision under Article 1102 if this was within the Court's jurisdiction.

These three case studies generally illustrate the deference that most courts will likely give to the investment arbitration process, similar to the deference given to the commercial arbitration process.

XXI. Enforcement of Awards

Enforcement of an arbitration award is a broad and sometimes ambiguous term that is often used to refer to any postaward attempt by a claimant to obtain the fruits of its victory. It can include (1) confirmation or exequatur proceedings at the situs of the arbitration; (2) proceedings to have the award enforced as a judgment in jurisdictions other than the situs; and (3) proceedings to execute upon an award by seizing the respondent's assets, either at the situs or in other jurisdictions where assets can be found. A different law governs each of the three types of proceedings: confirmation is governed by the *lex arbitri* of the situs; enforcement in nonsitus jurisdictions is usually governed by international treaty, as adopted or modified by national law; and execution is governed almost exclusively by the national law of the particular forum where the assets are located. As used in this chapter, *enforcement* refers to any affirmative attempt by a victorious party to confirm or collect an award.

Enforcement is discussed less frequently than other arbitration topics because it is usually not necessary to compel compliance with an arbitration award. In the vast majority of cases, the rendering of an arbitral award is promptly followed either by payment or by a negotiation process between winner and loser to define the mode of payment (i.e., in installments, through asset transfers, or other mutually beneficial mechanisms).[1] One practitioner has estimated that up to 95 percent of arbitration awards (commercial and otherwise) are satisfied

---

[1] Jane L. Volz & Roger S. Haydock, *Foreign Arbitral Awards: Enforcing the Award against the Recalcitrant Loser,* 21 Wm. Mitchell L. Rev. 867, 870 (1996) ("The majority of arbitral awards are honored, without resistance, by the losing party. The vast number of arbitrations, and the lack of data exhibiting enforcement difficulties, illustrate the positive results of international arbitrations. . . . The lack of adverse data is a reasonable confirmation of its phenomenal success"); Pierre Lalive, *Enforcing Awards,* in *Sixty Years of ICC Arbitration* 317, 319 (ICC Publishing 1984) (voluntary compliance with ICC awards exceeds 90 percent). *See also* Alan Redfern, Martin Hunter, N. Blackaby, & C. Partasides, *Law and Practice of International Commercial Arbitration* § 10–01 (Sweet & Maxwell, 4th ed. 2004).

without recourse to any formal enforcement mechanism.[2] Most courts are supportive of attempts to enforce awards, consistent with their support of international arbitration in general. For example, U.S. courts have began signaling that they will not tolerate extensive litigation to resist awards, even where a party's attempt to resist consists solely of resisting a confirmation or exercising its limited right to annul. In *B.L. Harbert International v. Hercules Steel*,[3] the court criticized parties that are "poor losers" in arbitration, noting that "[i]f we permit parties who lose in arbitration to freely relitigate their cases in court, arbitration will do nothing to reduce congestion in the judicial system; dispute resolution will be slower instead of faster; and reaching a final decision will cost more instead of less."[4] The court further suggested that sanctions are "an idea worth considering" where a party "assumes a never say die attitude and drags the dispute through the court system without an objectively reasonable belief that it will prevail."[5] In so holding, the court reasoned that "[a] realistic threat of sanctions may discourage baseless litigation over arbitration awards and help fulfill the purposes of the pro-arbitration policy contained in the [U.S. Federal Arbitration Act]."[6]

This widespread compliance is a saving grace for international arbitration. The arbitral system, although generally efficient in adjudicating transnational disputes, lacks any direct compulsory power. After all, arbitration, even investment treaty arbitrations, is merely a creature of some form of contract, and contracting parties cannot give a tribunal more authority than they have themselves. Arbitrator-sanctioned seizure of assets, therefore, would in most countries amount to vigilante justice, as governments jealously retain their general police powers. Although some national

---

[2] Leslie Nelson, *International Joint Ventures*, 2-SPG I.N.L.E.G.P. 75, 78 (1990) ("In any case, it is estimated that approximately 95 percent of international arbitration and conciliation awards are complied with voluntarily."); D. Wang, *International Center for the Settlement of Investment Disputes*, United Nations Conference on Trade and Development (UNCTAD) Course on Dispute Settlement, Module 2.9, UNCTAD/EDM/Misc.232/Add.8, at 2 (2003) ("voluntary compliance [with ICSID awards] is the norm").

[3] *B.L. Harbert Int'l, LLC v. Hercules Steel Co.*, 441 F.3d 905 (11th Cir. 2006).

[4] *Id.* at 907.

[5] *Id.* at 913.

[6] *Id.* at 914; *see also, Sparan Masonry, LLC v. Hoar Constr., LLC*, 2007 WL 951773, 3 (S.D. Fla. Mar. 28, 2007) (noting that an "attempt to gain a 'second bite at the apple' is frowned upon and sanctionable," and cautioning counsel "to refrain from filing such frivolous challenges in the future"); *SII Inves. v. Jenks*, 2006 WL 2092639, 5–6 (M.D. Fla. July 27, 2006) (sanctioning plaintiff who "ignored the Eleventh Circuit's stern notice to those who pursue unwarranted judicial review" by filing a "baseless lawsuit," and noting that the *Hercules Steel* court had "forcefully warned any arbitration loser to stop and think carefully before seeking to overturn an arbitration award"); *Reuter v. Merrill, Lynch, Pierce, Fenner & Smith, Inc.*, 440 F. Supp. 2d 1256, 1266–67 (N.D. Ala. 2006) (sanctioning brokerage customers for bringing a motion to vacate an arbitral decision, where the motion was "both frivolous and ha[d] no real legal basis").

arbitration laws grant limited direct enforcement capabilities to duly appointed arbitrators, in the vast majority of cases involving recalcitrant losers, judicial enforcement is essential to compel payment.[7]

A. Confirmation

A useful definition of confirmation (or exequatur) is the procedure by which the winning party in an arbitration seeks, at the situs of the arbitration, to transform the award into a binding court judgment that is capable of enforcement and execution against the losing party, either in the situs or in other jurisdictions. This section deals with confirmation at the situs of the arbitration; the next section covers enforcement (including "confirmation") in other jurisdictions pursuant to international treaty.

Confirmation at the situs is governed by national arbitration law. In recent years, many countries have adopted, usually with modifications, the United Nations Commission on International Trade Law (UNCITRAL) Model Law on International Commercial Arbitration.[8] In Canada, for example, the Model Law covers certain types of international arbitration, whereas national law applies to local arbitrations and possibly some international arbitrations.[9] Other jurisdictions, such as England and the great majority of the U.S. states, continue to apply their own laws to the confirmation of international arbitration awards.[10]

The UNCITRAL Model Law sets out a basic confirmation procedure in Article 35, Recognition and Enforcement:

> (1) An arbitral award, irrespective of the country in which it was made, shall be recognized as binding and, upon application in writing to the competent court, shall be enforced subject to the provisions of this article and of article 36.[11]

---

[7] Volz & Haydock, *supra* note 1, at 871 & note 12.

[8] According to the United Nations Commission on International Trade Law (UNCITRAL) Web site as of 2007 more than fifty jurisdictions had adopted the UNCITRAL Model Law with some modifications. *See* http://www.uncitral.org/uncitral/en/uncitral_texts/arbitration.html.

[9] *See United Mexican States* (Petitioner) *v. Metalclad Corp.* (Respondent), 2001 BCSC 664, at 9–11.

[10] *See* English Arbitration Act 1996, § 66 (enforcement of the award) & § 99 *et seq.* (recognition and enforcement of certain foreign awards); United States Federal Arbitration Act, 9 U.S.C. § 207. The following states in the U.S., however, have adopted the UNCITRAL Model Law: California, Connecticut, Illinois, Louisiana, Oregon, and Texas.

[11] Article 36 deals with grounds for refusing enforcement and recognition. *See generally* Chapter XX.

(2) The party relying on an award or applying for its enforcement shall supply the original award or a copy thereof. If the award is not made in an official language of this State, the court may request the party to supply a translation thereof into such.[12]

The Model Law illustrates well the modern trend to very limited judicial review of arbitration awards. Of course, the precise scope of judicial review in the confirmation process is determined by the national arbitration laws of the situs, which as discussed in the preceding chapter,[13] are often wider than the review contemplated by the Model Law.

In contrast to the normal confirmation process, awards issued by ICSID under the Washington Convention are, in theory, self-confirming. Article 54 of the ICSID Convention provides:

(1) Each Contracting State shall recognize an award rendered pursuant to this Convention as binding and enforce the pecuniary obligations imposed by that award within its territories as if it were a final judgment of a court in that State. A Contracting State with a federal constitution may enforce such an award in or through its federal courts and may provide that such courts shall treat the award as if it were a final judgment of the courts of a constituent state.

(2) A party seeking recognition or enforcement in the territories of a Contracting State shall furnish to a competent court or other authority which such State shall have designated for this purpose a copy of the award certified by the Secretary-General. Each Contracting State shall notify the Secretary-General of the designation of the competent court or other authority for this purpose and of any subsequent change in such designation.

(3) Execution of the award shall be governed by the laws concerning the execution of judgments in force in the State in whose territories such execution is sought.

Thus, ICSID awards in some ways have the juridical character of a national court judgment, and a victorious claimant can bypass the confirmation process and attempt to enforce the award directly in any state that is a signatory to the Washington Convention.[14] The obligation to enforce, however, is limited to pecuniary obligations.[15]

---

[12] Article 35(2) was amended by the Commission at its thirty-ninth session, in 2006. "The Model Law does not lay down procedural details of recognition and enforcement, which are left to national procedural laws and practices. The Model Law merely sets certain conditions for obtaining enforcement under article 35(2). It was amended in 2006 to liberalize formal requirements and reflect the amendment made to article 7 on the form of the arbitration agreement. Presentation of a copy of the arbitration agreement is no longer required under article 35(2)." UNCITRAL, Explanatory Note by the UNCITRAL Secretariat on the 1985 Model Law on International Commercial Arbitration as amended in 2006, *available at* http://www.uncitral.org/uncitral/en/uncitral_texts/arbitration/1985Model_arbitration.html.

[13] *See* Chapter XX, at p. 651 *supra*.

[14] *See generally* C. Schreuer, *The ICSID Convention: A Commentary* 1100 *et seq.* (Cambridge University Press 2001). *See also* E. Baldwin, M. Kantor, M. Nolan, *Limits to Enforcement of ICSID Awards*, 23(1) J. Int'l Arb. 1 (2006).

[15] On the obligation of ICSID Contracting Parties to enforce pecuniary obligations *see* Chapter XIX on damages, at 570.

B. Enforcement of Awards Under the New York Convention

With regard to international commercial arbitration between private parties, widespread compliance with arbitration awards is largely the result of the nearly universal application of the Convention on the Recognition and Enforcement of Foreign Arbitral Awards (hereinafter the New York Convention).[16] This treaty allows the beneficiary of a valid arbitral award to execute on the loser's assets in most countries around the world, because after a recognition proceeding is complete, the award is transformed into local court judgment at the place of enforcement. The New York Convention is one of the most widely ratified international agreements in the world,[17] and its successful implementation and application over the last fifty years is one of the principal reasons for the rapid expansion of international arbitration.

A recent and leading example of enforcement under the New York Convention was *Karaha Bodas Co. v. Pertamina*. That dispute involved an aborted investment by Karaha Bodas Company, a Cayman Islands company owned by a group of U.S., Japanese, and Indonesian investors that began to develop a geothermal power facility in the West Java region of Indonesia. The dispute began when the Indonesian government forced Karaha Bodas to abandon the project in 1998 in the wake of the Asian financial crisis. Following Indonesia's termination of the project, Karaha Bodas filed a claim before a Geneva-based arbitral panel convened under the UNCITRAL Rules. In 2000, the tribunal ruled in Karaha Bodas's favor, awarding it approximately US$261 million in damages. Thereafter, as the Swiss and Indonesian courts denied Pertamina's vacatur petitions, Karaha Bodas began enforcement proceedings in the courts of Canada, Hong Kong, Singapore, and the United States. Although the dispute did not arise out of an investment treaty, it is in many ways similar. The resulting procedures are a very useful example of the enforceability of international arbitration awards, including non-ICSID treaty awards, as the reviewing courts engaged in an unusually painstaking analysis of the New York Convention and the factors that govern a reviewing court's discretion to refuse to enforce an arbitration award.

---

[16] Other treaties, such as the Inter-American Convention, may also be relevant to enforcement. Inter-American Convention on International Commercial Arbitration (also known as the *Panama Convention*), adopted in Panama (1975), 14 I.L.M. 336 (1975).

[17] The New York Convention presently has at least 142 signatories. *See* UNCITRAL status report at www.uncitral.org/uncitral/en/uncitral_texts/arbitration/NYConvention_status.html.

ENFORCEMENT OF AWARDS

Karaha Bodas Co., L.L.C. v. Perusahaan et al.

364 F.3d 274 (5th Cir.), *cert. denied* 125 S. Ct. 59 (2004)

ROSENTHAL, District Judge [sitting by designation]:

. . . .

This appeal arises from an arbitral award (the "Award") made in Geneva, Switzerland, involving contracts negotiated and allegedly breached in Indonesia. The Award imposed liability and damages against Perusahaan Pertambangan Minyak Dan Gas Bumi Negara ("Pertamina"), which is owned by the government of Indonesia, in favor of Karaha Bodas Company, L.L.C. ("KBC"), a Cayman Islands company. KBC filed this suit in the federal district court in Texas to enforce the Award under the United National Convention on the Recognition and Enforcement of Foreign Arbitral Awards (the "New York Convention"), and filed enforcement actions in Hong Kong and Canada as well. While those enforcement proceedings were pending, Pertamina appealed the Award in the Swiss courts, seeking annulment. When that effort failed, and after the Texas district court granted summary judgment enforcing the Award, Pertamina obtained an order from an Indonesian court annulling the Award.

Pertamina appealed to this court. During the appeal, Pertamina filed in the district court a motion to set aside the judgment under Federal Rule of Civil Procedure 60(b)(2), based on newly-discovered evidence Pertamina contended should have been disclosed during the arbitration, and under Rule 60(b)(5), based on the Indonesian court's decision annulling the arbitration Award. . . .

Pertamina urges this court to reverse the district court's decision enforcing the Award on several grounds under the New York Convention. We conclude that the record forecloses Pertamina's arguments that procedural violations and other errors during the arbitration preclude enforcement. We reject Pertamina's argument that the Indonesian court's order annulling the Award bars its enforcement under the New York Convention; this argument is inconsistent with the arbitration agreements Pertamina signed and with its earlier position that Switzerland, the neutral forum the parties selected, had exclusive jurisdiction over an annulment proceeding. We reject Pertamina's efforts to delay or avoid enforcement of the Award as evidencing a disregard for the international commercial arbitration procedures it agreed to follow. In short, we affirm the district court's judgment enforcing the Award, for the reasons set out in detail below.

I. Background

A. Procedural and Factual History

KBC explores and develops geothermal energy sources and builds electric generating stations using geothermal sources. Pertamina is an oil, gas, and geothermal energy company owned by the Republic of Indonesia. In November 1994, KBC signed two contracts to produce electricity from geothermal sources in Indonesia. Under the Joint Operation Contract ("JOC"), KBC had the right to develop geothermal energy sources in the Karaha area of Indonesia; Pertamina was to manage the project and receive the electricity generated. Under the Energy Sales Contract ("ESC"), PLN agreed to purchase from Pertamina the energy generated by KBC's facilities. Both contracts contained almost identical broad arbitration clauses, requiring the parties to arbitrate any disputes in Geneva, Switzerland under the Arbitration Rules of the United Nations Commission on International Trade Law ("UNCITRAL").

On September 20, 1997, the government of Indonesia temporarily suspended the project because of the country's financial crisis. The government of Indonesia indefinitely suspended the project on January 10, 1998. On February 10, 1998, KBC notified Pertamina and PLN that the government's indefinite suspension constituted an event of "force majeure" under the contracts. KBC initiated arbitration proceedings on April 30, 1998. In its notice of arbitration, KBC appointed Professor Piero Bernardini, vice-chair of the International Chamber of Commerce's ("ICC") International Court of Arbitration and member of the London Court of International Arbitration, to serve as an arbitrator. Pertamina, however, did not designate an arbitrator in the contractually allotted thirty days. The JOC and ESC both provided that if a party failed to appoint an arbitrator within thirty days, the Secretary-General of the International Center for Settlement of Investment Disputes ("ICSID") was to make the appointment. After notifying Pertamina, PLN, and the government of Indonesia, the ICSID appointed Dr. Ahmed El-Kosheri, another vice-chair of the ICC, as the second arbitrator. As specified in the JOC and ESC, the two appointed arbitrators then selected the chairman of the arbitration panel, Yves Derains, the former Secretary-General of the ICC.

Pertamina raised threshold challenges to the Tribunal's consolidation of the claims KBC raised under the JOC and the ESC into one arbitration proceeding and to the selection of the panel. In October 1999, the Tribunal issued a Preliminary Award, rejecting Pertamina's threshold challenges and ruling that the government of Indonesia was not a party to the contracts or to the arbitration proceeding.

KBC filed its Revised Statement of Claim in November 1999. Pertamina received a number of extensions before it filed its reply to the Revised Statement of Claim in April 2000. KBC filed a rebuttal to that reply in May 2000. In response to KBC's rebuttal, Pertamina sought additional discovery and a continuance of the proceedings, claiming that KBC had raised assertions and added elements to its case-in-chief not contained in the Revised Statement of Claim.

. . . .

In the Final Award, the Tribunal found that under the JOC and the ESC, Pertamina and PLN had accepted the risk of loss arising from a "Government Related Event." The Tribunal interpreted the contracts as "putting the consequences of a Governmental decision which prevents the performance of the contract at Pertamina's . . . sole risk." The Tribunal awarded KBC $111.1 million, the amount KBC had expended on the project, and $150 million in lost profits.

In February 2001, Pertamina appealed the Award to the Supreme Court of Switzerland. While that appeal was pending, KBC initiated this suit in the federal district court to enforce the Award.

B. The District Court Decisions

Pertamina challenged enforcement of the Award in the federal district court on four grounds under Article V of the New York Convention: (1) the procedure for selecting the arbitrators was not in accordance with the agreement of the parties; (2) the Tribunal improperly consolidated the claims into one arbitration; (3) Pertamina was "unable to present its case" to the Tribunal; and (4) enforcement of the damages Award would violate the public policy of the United States. As to the first two grounds, Pertamina contended that the decision to consolidate the claims under the two contracts was procedurally improper and that KBC's unilateral appointment of an arbitrator violated the ESC arbitration provision. As to the third ground, Pertamina argued that the Tribunal improperly reversed its finding in the Preliminary Award that Pertamina did not breach the contracts by holding Pertamina liable for nonperformance in the Final Award; that the Tribunal's denial of Pertamina's request for discovery of FPL's records prevented Pertamina from fully presenting its case; and that the Tribunal's denial of a continuance after KBC filed its rebuttal to the reply to the Revised Statement of Claim prevented Pertamina from fully preparing to meet KBC's contentions. As to the fourth ground, Pertamina argued that the Award violated the international abuse of rights doctrine and punished Pertamina for obeying the Indonesian government's decree....

Pertamina continued its appeal seeking annulment of the Award to the Supreme Court of Switzerland while the enforcement action was pending in the district court in Texas. The Texas district court slowed the proceedings in deference to Pertamina's request that the Swiss court first be allowed to decide whether to annul the Award. In April 2001, the Swiss Supreme Court dismissed Pertamina's claim because of untimely payment of costs. Pertamina moved for reconsideration; the Swiss court denied that motion in August 2001. In December 2001, the district court enforced the Award, rejecting each of Pertamina's grounds for refusal.... Having failed in its effort to annul the Award in the Swiss courts, Pertamina filed suit in Indonesia seeking annulment. In August 2002, an Indonesian court annulled the Award. KBC continued with enforcement suits in Hong Kong and Canada. In October 2002, while this appeal was pending, Pertamina discovered in the Canadian proceeding that FPL and one other KBC investor, Caithness, had held a political risk insurance policy covering the KBC project through Lloyd's of London. Pertamina also learned that Lloyd's had paid $75 million under that insurance policy to FPL and Caithness for the losses resulting from the Indonesian government's suspension of the project.

. . . .

The district court also rejected Pertamina's claim that Indonesia had primary jurisdiction to decide to annul the Award and declined to give effect to the Indonesian court's annulment order as a defense to enforcement. The district court imposed judicial estoppel to preclude Pertamina from asserting that Indonesian procedural law had governed the arbitration and that Indonesian courts had primary jurisdiction to review the Award. Finally, the district court rejected Pertamina's argument that the amount of the Award should be offset by the $75 million insurance payment.
This appeal followed....

II. Analysis

A. The New York Convention

The New York Convention provides a carefully structured framework for the review and enforcement of international arbitral awards. Only a court in a country with primary jurisdiction over an arbitral award may annul that award. Courts in other countries have secondary jurisdiction; a court in a country with secondary jurisdiction is limited to deciding whether the award may be enforced in that country. The Convention "mandates very different regimes for the review of arbitral awards (1) in the [countries] in which, or under the law of which, the award was made, and (2) in other [countries] where recognition and enforcement are sought." Under the Convention, "the country in which, or under the [arbitration] law of which, [an] award was made" is said to have primary jurisdiction over the arbitration award. All other signatory states are secondary jurisdictions, in which parties can only contest whether that state should enforce the arbitral award. It is clear that the district court had secondary jurisdiction and considered only whether to enforce the Award in the United States.

Article V enumerates specific grounds on which a court with secondary jurisdiction may refuse enforcement. In contrast to the limited authority of secondary-jurisdiction courts to review an arbitral award, courts of primary jurisdiction, usually the courts of the country of the arbitral situs, have much broader discretion to set aside an award.

While courts of a primary jurisdiction country may apply their own domestic law in evaluating a request to annul or set aside an arbitral award, courts in countries of secondary jurisdiction may refuse enforcement only on the grounds specified in Article V. The New York Convention and the implementing legislation, Chapter 2 of the Federal Arbitration Act ("FAA"), provide that a secondary jurisdiction court must enforce an arbitration award unless it finds one of the grounds for refusal or deferral of recognition or enforcement specified in the Convention. The court may not refuse to enforce an arbitral award solely on the ground that the arbitrator may have made a mistake of law or fact. "Absent extraordinary circumstances, a confirming court is not to reconsider an arbitrator's findings." The party defending against enforcement of the arbitral award bears the burden of proof. Defenses to enforcement under the New York Convention are construed narrowly, "to encourage the recognition and enforcement of commercial arbitration agreements in international contracts. . . ."

E. The Public Policy Challenge to the Arbitral Award

Pertamina asserts that the Award violated public policy because it violated the international law doctrine of abuse of rights. Pertamina contends that the Award imposes punishment for obeying a government decree. Pertamina also asserts that KBC's failure to disclose the political risk insurance policy during the arbitration makes enforcement of the Award a violation of public policy.

Under Article V(2)(b) of the New York Convention, a court may refuse to recognize or enforce an arbitral award if it "would be contrary to the public policy of that country." The public policy defense is to be "construed narrowly to be applied only where enforcement would violate the forum state's most basic notions of morality and justice." "The general pro-enforcement bias informing the convention . . . points to a narrow reading of the public policy defense." Erroneous legal reasoning or misapplication of law is generally not a violation of public policy within the meaning of the New York Convention.

An action violates the abuse of rights doctrine if one of the following three factors is present: (1) the predominant motive for the action is to cause harm; (2) the action is totally unreasonable given the lack of any legitimate interest in the exercise of the right and its exercise harms another; and (3) the right is exercised for a purpose other than that for which it exists. The abuse of rights doctrine is not established in American law and KBC's actions do not meet the factors required to trigger its application. The evidence in the record is that KBC pursued the arbitration to recover its costs, expenses, and lost profits from the nonperformance of the JOC and ESC. The record does not support Pertamina's argument that enforcing the Award penalizes obedience to a governmental decree. The Tribunal explained in the Final Award that the JOC and ESC shifted the risk of loss resulting from a government-ordered suspension onto Pertamina and PLN. Pertamina is challenging the substance of the Tribunal's interpretation of the JOC and ESC. An arbitration tribunal's contract interpretation does not violate public policy unless it "violates the most basic notions of morality and justice." The Tribunal's interpretation of the JOC and ESC does not approach this steep threshold.

Despite the Fifth Circuit's affirmance of the District Court's enforcement decision (and its entry of judgment thereon), Pertamina continued its long campaign to nullify or avoid the award. It refused to pay voluntarily, resisted the parallel enforcement actions in Canada, Hong Kong, and Singapore, and started a new action against Karaha Bodas in the Cayman Islands. Because of Pertamina's refusal to pay, Karaha Bodas was forced to execute against Pertamina's assets in Hong Kong and New York. During the execution process in New York, the government of Indonesia intervened, arguing that almost all of Pertamina's revenues belonged to the government, not Pertamina. Ultimately, after numerous hearings and appeals, Karaha Bodas in 2006 collected the entire award, plus post-judgment interest, totaling almost $320 million.[18] Although this dispute provides an extreme example, it nonetheless demonstrates that the international arbitration enforcement process can be effective, even against a recalcitrant state and its instrumentalities.

C. Execution in Investment Arbitrations

Investment arbitration presents execution problems that are not present in commercial arbitrations, particularly when the losing party is a state or one of its instrumentalities. First, any substantial assets that foreign governments maintain outside their own territory are frequently held not by the state itself, but by state-owned corporations (national airlines, for example). Most courts hesitate to "pierce the corporate veil" to allow enforcement against such assets, because respect for the corporate form is considered an essential component for the efficient operation of international commerce.[19] Even more important is the issue of sovereign immunity. When the claimant in an investment arbitration manages to locate assets held in the losing state's name, most countries' legal systems provide a strong shield to protect those assets from judicial attachment or execution, in the interest of international comity and diplomatic relations. In many jurisdictions sovereign immunity has weakened in recent decades, but the issue remains central to any execution attempt against a government, and raises a range of complex legal questions that are frequently litigated.

---

[18] The dispute generated multiple parallel court decisions. *See Karaha Boda Co., L.L.C. v. Perusahaan Pertambangan Minyak Dan Gas Bumi Negara,* 2004 ABQB 918, [2004] A.J. No. 1440, 2004 AB.C. LEXIS 1460 (Dec. 9, 2004) (denying Pertamina's application to set aside judgment enforcing arbitral award); *Karaha Bodas Co., LLC. V. Persusahaan Pertambangan Minydak Dan Gas Bumi Negara,* [2003] 2 HKLRD 381 CFI, 2003 WL 17616 (Dec. 2002) (granting Karaha Bodas's application for recognition and enforcement of the arbitral award); Notification on the Content of the Decision of the Supreme Court of the Republic of Indonesia, number: 01/Banding/Wasit.int/2002, Jo. No. 86/PDT.G/2002/PN.JKT.PST, Concerning the Decision dated Mar. 8, 2004, *Karaha Bodas Co. L.L.C. v. Perusahaan Pertamina, Cs* (annulling Central Jakarta District Court decision and endorsing Karaha Bodas's position).

[19] *See Letelier v. Chile,* 748 F.2d 790 (2d Cir. 1984).

August Reinisch,[20] European Court Practice Concerning State Immunity From Enforcement Measures, 17(4) Eur. J. Int'l L. 803 (Sept., 2006)

Immunity from execution or immunity from enforcement measures is distinct from jurisdictional immunity. Immunity from jurisdiction refers to a limitation of the adjudicatory power of national courts,[21] whereas immunity from execution restricts the enforcement powers of national courts or other organs.

In the course of the twentieth century many European states have changed from an absolute to a restrictive jurisdictional immunity concept. With regard to limiting a broad immunity from enforcement measures, however, a more hesitant approach prevailed in the case law of most European countries. Traditionally, it seemed that, unlike "restrictive" or "relative" adjudicatory immunity concepts, immunity from execution was considered to be absolute. This may have led to its characterization as "the last bastion of State immunity."[22]

The main reason for this difference between absolute and relative immunity is usually seen in the more intrusive character of enforcement measures compared with merely adjudicatory powers.[23] However, also in the field of enforcement measures immunity is no longer generally considered to be the unequivocal rule. A number of national courts have clearly expressed their opinion that enforcement immunity is also no longer absolute. They do, however, wrestle with the precise conditions and criteria under and by which such enforcement immunity should be granted or denied. Equally, scholarly conceptualizations concerning the correct delimitation between permissible and impermissible enforcement actions frequently encounter difficulties.[24]

In addition to the possibility of waiving enforcement immunity, the most important general trend points towards opening up certain types of state property, not serving public purposes, to measures of execution. However, contrary to the requirements of immunity from jurisdiction, the distinctive criterion is not the nature of the act in issue but rather the purpose of the property to be subjected to enforcement measures. This implies that limitations on enforcement immunity are less intrusive than in the field of immunity from jurisdiction. Thus, a more cautious view is also reflected in various national and international codification attempts.

---

[20] SN: Professor of International and European Law at the University of Vienna and Professorial Lecturer at the Bologna Center of SAIS/Johns Hopkins University. E-mail: Aug..reinisch @univie.ac.at.

[21] SN: See H. Fox, *The Law of State Immunity* (2002); H. Lauterpacht, *The Problem of Jurisdictional Immunities of Foreign States*, 28 British Y.B. Int'l L. (1951) 220; I. Pingel-Lenuzza, *Les immunités des états en droit international* (1997); C. Schreuer, *State Immunity: Some Recent Developments* (1988); I. Sinclair, *Law of Sovereign Immunity—Recent Developments*, 167 RdC (1980) 113; P. Trooboff, *Foreign State Immunity: Emerging Consensus on Principles*, 200 RdC (1986) 200 and the contributions to 10 *Netherlands Y.B. Int'l L.* [hereinafter *NYIL*] (1979).

[22] SN: *ILC Report on Jurisdictional Immunities of States and their Property* in: [1991] Y.B. Int'l L. Commission [hereinafter *YBILC*], ii. Pt. Two, 1, at 56.

[23] SN: Cf. Schreuer, *supra* note [21], at 126; Sinclair, *supra* note [21], at 218.

[24] SN: See L. J. Bouchez, *The Nature and Scope of State Immunity from Jurisdiction and Execution*, 10 NYIL (1979) 3, at 17ff.

National immunity legislation regularly prohibits enforcement measures against foreign states in principle. One of the few pieces of such genuine European statutory law, the 1978 UK State Immunity Act (SIA)[25] is an example of this approach.[26] It permits enforcement measures only "in respect of property which is for the time being in use or intended for use for commercial purposes."[27]

A rather peculiar approach is pursued by the 1972 European Convention on State Immunity,[28] which prohibits enforcement measures in general, subject only to the possibility of an express waiver.[29] As a substitute for generally non-available enforcement measures, the Convention stipulates that the Contracting States shall give effect to judgments delivered against them in accordance with the provisions of the Convention.[30] As between states which have made an optional declaration in accordance with Article 24 of the Convention and with respect to judgments concerning industrial or commercial activities, enforcement measures remain possible against property "used exclusively in connection with such an activity."[31] The solution offered by the European Convention clearly does not, and does not purport to, codify existing customary law on the subject. Rather, it represents a compromise between states adhering to a rule of absolute immunity from enforcement measures and those permitting such measures under certain conditions, "in that it combines an obligation of States to give effect to judgments with a rule permitting no execution."[32]

. . . .

B *The Major Distinction in the Application of the Concept of Restrictive Immunity*

While in the field of jurisdictional immunity the nature of an act as *iure imperii* or *iure gestionis* is decisive, concerning immunity from execution it is prevailingly the purpose of the property against which enforcement measures are sought that determines whether or not immunity will be granted.[33]

In one of the best-known enforcement immunity cases, the *Philippine Embassy Bank Account Case*, the German Constitutional Court stated that

---

[25] SN: State Immunity Act 1978, c. 33 (U.K.), 17 I.L.M. (1978) 1123.

[26] SN: S. 13(2) U.K. SIA, *supra* note [25], provides: "subject to sub-sections 3 and 4 below b) the property of a State shall not be subject to any process for the enforcement of a judgment or arbitration award or, in an action in rem, for its arrest, detention or sale." Similarly, s. 1609 of the U.S. Foreign Sovereign Immunities Act of 1976 (FSIA), 15 I.L.M. (1976) 1388, provides: "subject to existing international agreements to which the United States is a party at the time of enactment of this act the property in the United States of a foreign State shall be immune from attachment arrest and execution except as provided in sections 1610 and 1611 of this chapter."

[27] SN: S. 13(4) U.K. SIA, *supra* note [25].

[28] SN: European Convention on State Immunity 1972 (European Convention), May 16, 1972, in force since June 11, 1976, ETS No. 74, 11 I.L.M. (1972) 470.

[29] SN: *Ibid.*, art. 23.

[30] SN: *Ibid.*, art. 20(1).

[31] SN: *Ibid.*, art. 26.

[32] SN: Council of Europe, Explanatory Report on the European Convention on State Immunity (1972), *available at* http:// conventions.coe.int/Treaty/EN/Reports/HTML/074.htm, ¶ 92.

[33] SN: Bouchez, *supra* note [24], at 25; Fox, *supra* note [21], at 399.

[t]here is a general rule of international law that execution by the State having jurisdiction on the basis of a judicial writ of execution against a foreign State, issued in relation to non-sovereign action (*acta iure gestionis*) of that State upon that State's things located or occupied within the national territory of the State having jurisdiction, is inadmissible without assent by the foreign State, insofar as those things serve sovereign purposes of the foreign State at the time of commencement of the enforcement measure.[34]

This view, confirming a basic distinction between property serving sovereign, on the one hand, and non-sovereign purposes, on the other hand, is reflected in many other court decisions in European countries. A Dutch court qualified it as a "rule of international law ... that public service assets are exempt from measures of execution in another country."[35] More recently the rule was upheld in a Belgian judgment in which the court "*confirme, dans le cadre de l'immunité d'exécution, la distinction entre les biens affectés à des fins souveraines (iure imperii) et les biens affectés aux fins de gestion (iure gestionis).*"[36] Similarly, according to the Italian Constitutional Court, in order "[t]o deny immunity from execution ... it is also necessary that the property to which the request for attachment or the process of execution refers is not destined to accomplish public functions (*jure imperii*) of the foreign State."[37] Similarly, the Italian Court of Cassation found that "the idea that immunity from execution in the forum State is limited to the assets of the State ... used in the exercise of sovereign functions or devoted to public purposes is now accepted as a rule in the international community."[38] Even Swiss courts, which have been very liberal in denying immunity from enforcement measures to foreign states, respect the immunity of assets allocated for the performance of acts of sovereignty.[39]

As will be shown below, it is the exact determination of whether or not this requirement of a public purpose is fulfilled which forms the core issue of the majority of enforcement immunity decisions.

. . . .

3 The Main Types of Exceptions to Immunity from Execution

---

[34] SN: *Philippine Embassy Case, supra* note 22, at 164 (I.L.R.), confirmed in the *NIOC Revenues Case,* Bundesverfassungsgericht, 12 Apr. 1983, BVerfGE 64, 1, 65 I.L.R. 215, at 242. *See also Spanish Consular Bank Accounts Case,* Landgericht, Stuttgart, Sept. 21, 1971, 65 I.L.R. 114, at 117, where the court had held that "there is a rule of customary international law under which execution against the property of a foreign State which is devoted to sovereign purposes is not admissible."

[35] SN: *Cabolent v. NIOC,* The Hague Court of Appeal, Nov. 28, 1968, 1 *NYIL* (1970) 225; 47 I.L.R. 138, at 148.

[36] SN: *Leica AG v. Central Bank of Iraq et Etat Irakien,* Cour d'Appel, Brussels, 15 Feb. 2000 [2001] JT 6 "confirms, in the context of immunity from execution, the distinction between goods destined for sovereign purposes (*iure imperii*) and goods destined for non-sovereign purposes (*iure gestionis*)."

[37] SN: *Condor & Filvem v. Ministry of Justice,* Case No. 329, July 15, 1992; 101 I.L.R. 394, at 402.

[38] SN: *Libya v. Rossbeton SRL,* Case No. 2502, May 25, 1989, 87 I.L.R. 63, at 66.

[39] SN: "A foreign State which in a particular case does not enjoy jurisdictional immunity is not entitled to immunity from execution either, unless the measures of execution concern assets allocated for the performance of acts of sovereignty": *République Arabe d'Egypte v. Cinetel,* Tribunal fédéral suisse, July 20, 1979, 65 I.L.R. 425, at 430.

A Waiver of Immunity from Execution

As with immunity from jurisdiction, it is generally accepted that immunity from enforcement measures may be waived by a state. This is clearly reflected in Articles 18 and 19 of the UN Convention which permit enforcement measures if expressly consented to by states,[40] and it is also found in the ECHR,[41] the ILA Draft Convention,[42] and national immunity legislation. This exception to enforcement immunity is even recognized in countries adhering to an absolute immunity standard.

. . . .

The general rule is that a separate waiver is required for purposes of enforcement measures and that a waiver of immunity from jurisdiction does not normally also imply a waiver of immunity from enforcement.[43] The requirement of a separate waiver is also clearly expressed in the UN Convention,[44] the ILC Draft Articles,[45] and national legislation.[46]

When national courts have to interpret waivers of immunity from enforcement measures they tend to limit the scope of such waivers in order to avoid a possible conflict with immunities derived from consular or diplomatic law.

. . . .

The most difficult issues with respect to waivers concern the question whether a waiver of immunity has to be express or whether it can also be implied and, if the possibility of an implied waiver is recognized, which acts constitute such waiver. Both the UN

---

[40] SN: See [U.N. GAOR, 59th Sess., Supp. No. 22 (A/59/22), Dec. 16, 2004, Annex I. The Convention was opened for signature on Jan. 17, 2005. See Stewart, *The U.N. Convention on Jurisdictional Immunities of States and Their Property*, 99 A.J.I.L. (2005) 194.].

[41] SN: Art. 23 ECHR, *supra* note [28], provides: "[n]o measures of execution or preventive measures against the property of a Contracting State may be taken in the territory of another Contracting State except where and to the extent that the State has expressly consented thereto in writing in any particular case."

[42] SN: Art. VIII A of the ILA Draft Convention [(International Law Association, Montreal Draft Articles for a Convention on State Immunity 1982, 22 I.L.M. (1983) 287)], at 291, provides: "[a] foreign State's property in the forum State, shall not be immune from any measure for the enforcement of a judgment or an arbitral award if: 1. The foreign State has waived its immunity either expressly or by implication from such measures. A waiver may not be withdrawn except in accordance with its terms."

[43] SN: See Bouchez, *supra* note [24], at 23.

[44] SN: Art. 20 U.N. Convention provides: "[w]here consent to the measures of constraint is required under articles 18 and 19, consent to the exercise of jurisdiction under article 7 shall not imply consent to the taking of measures of constraint."

[45] SN: Art. 18(2) ILC Draft Articles [(Draft Articles on Jurisdictional Immunities of States and Their Property [1991] YBILC, ii, Pt. Two, 13)].

[46] SN: S. 13(3) U.K. SIA, *supra* note [25], dealing with enforcement immunity, states that "a provision merely submitting to the jurisdiction of the courts is not to be interpreted as a consent for the purposes of this subsection."

Convention[47] and the ECHR[48] seem to require express consent. The ILA Draft Convention, however, clearly contemplated the possibility of an implied waiver of immunity from execution.[49]

In this context particular problems have arisen when courts have been requested to interpret the meaning of arbitration clauses accepted by states. The restrictive language of the UN Convention, the ILC Draft Articles, and the ECHR indicates that a mere arbitration clause does not imply a waiver of enforcement immunity but rather requires an additional, express consent to such enforcement measures. This approach has been traditionally adhered to by courts in Europe.[50] Nevertheless, some national courts have been ready to interpret arbitration agreements more broadly.

By this broad interpretation French courts have changed their interpretation of language found in the ICC Arbitration Rules which provided: "[b]y submitting the dispute to arbitration by the International Chamber of Commerce, the parties shall be deemed to have undertaken to carry out the resulting award without delay and to have waived their right to any form of appeal insofar as such waiver can validly be made."[51] Initially this provision was interpreted by French courts not to imply a waiver from execution measures.[52] However, in the *Creighton* decision the Cour de Cassation changed its approach and held:

> L'engagement pris par un Etat signataire de la clause d'arbitrage d'exécuter la sentence dans les termes de l'article 24 du règlement d'arbitrage de la chambre de commerce international implique renonciation de cet Etat à l'immunité d'exécution.[53]

. . . .

Most immunity instruments and the case law of European courts provide for an exception from immunity for property serving non-governmental purposes. For instance, the UN

---

[47] SN: Both arts. 18(a) and 19(a) U.N. Convention, *supra* note 16, require that a "State has expressly consented."

[48] SN: Art. 23 ECHR, *supra* note [28], requires that a "State has expressly consented" to enforcement measures "in writing in any particular case."

[49] SN: Art. VIII A 1 of the ILA Draft Convention, *supra* note [42], provides for an exception to immunity if "[t]he foreign State has waived its immunity either expressly or by implication from such measures."

[50] SN: See *Duff Dev. v. Kelantan Gov't* [1923] 1 Ch 385 (CA), 2 I.L.R. 124, [1924] AC 797 (HL).

[51] SN: Art. 24(2) ICC Rules of Conciliation and Arbitration, in force from Jan. 1, 1988 until Dec. 31, 1997.

[52] SN: In *Eurodif et Sofidif*, *supra* note 101, 65 I.L.R. 93, at 98, the French Cour d'Appel, Paris held with regard to Art. 24 ICC Rules of Conciliation and Arbitration that "this stipulation constitutes merely an undertaking to submit voluntarily the award and to recognise its binding force but does not contain any allusion to the immunity from execution from which a party might be entitled to benefit. It cannot therefore be interpreted as implying the waiver of a right with which it is not intended to deal."

[53] SN : *Société Creighton v. Ministre des Finances de l'Etat du Qatar et autre,* Cour de cassation (1st Civil Chamber), 6 July 2000, Bulletin civil I, no 207, [2001] *Revue de l'arbitrage* 114. The same result had already been reached by a lower French court with regard to ad hoc arbitration in *Société Bec Frères v. Office des Céréales de Tunisie,* Cour d'Appel, Rouen, 20 June 20, 1996 [1997] *Revue de l'arbitrage* 263, 113 I.L.R. 485. "The acceptance by a State signing an arbitral clause to enforce an award according to Article 24 of the Arbitration Rules of the International Chamber of Commerce implies a renunciation of the immunity from enforcement of that State."

Convention exempts from immunity property "specifically in use or intended for use by the State for other than government non-commercial purposes";[54] similarly the ILA Draft Convention speaks of enforcement measures against property "in use for the purposes of commercial activity."[55] The UK SIA provides for enforcement measures against property which "is for the time being in use or intended for use for commercial purposes."[56]

. . . .

One of the more controversial issues with regard to enforcement immunity remains the question whether the denial of such immunity requires some connection or nexus between the property against which enforcement measures are sought and the underlying claim or the entity involved. In fact, there are a number of different types of nexus requirements in international instruments, national legislation, and court practice that may lead to different results in specific situations.

One nexus requirement—which is clearly expressed in the US FSIA[57]—demands a connection between the property and the underlying claim. Similarly, the ILA Draft Convention requires that "[t]he property is in use for the purposes of commercial activity or was in use for the commercial activity upon which the claim is based."[58]

. . . .

Another related type of nexus prerequisite can be seen in a required connection between the property and the defendant state entity. The ILC Draft Articles stipulated that one of the two main types of links is present, requiring that the property "has a connection with the claim which is the object of the proceeding or with the agency or instrumentality against which the proceeding was directed."[59] This nexus requirement was severely criticized by some states. In fact, the wording of the nexus requirement in the ILC Draft Articles remained controversial until the end of the ILC's deliberations on this subject.[60] In the new UN Convention it has been modified in so far as the link between the property and the underlying claim has been discarded, leaving a "connection with the entity against which the proceeding was directed" as the only nexus requirement.[61]

. . . .

---

[54] SN : Art. 19(c) U.N. Convention, *supra* note [40].

[55] SN: Art. VIII A 2 of the ILA Draft Convention, *supra* note [42].

[56] SN: S. 13(4) U.K. SIA, *supra* note [25].

[57] SN: S. 1610(a)(2) U.S. FSIA, *supra* note [26], permits execution measures if "the property is or was used for the commercial activity upon which the claim is based."

[58] SN: Art. VIII A 2 ILA Draft Convention, *supra* note [42].

[59] SN: Art. 18(1)(c) ILC Draft Articles, *supra* note [45], provided: '[N]o measures of constraint, such as attachment, arrest and execution, against property of a State may be taken in connection with a proceeding before a court of another State unless and except to the extent that ... the property is specifically in use or intended for use by the State for other than government non-commercial purposes and is in the territory of the State of the forum and has a connection with the claim which is the object of the proceeding or with the agency or instrumentality against which the proceeding was directed.'

[60] SN: See Hess, *The International Law Commission's Draft Convention on the Jurisdictional Immunities of States and their Property*, 4 *EJIL* 269, at 277f (1993).

[61] SN: Art. 19(c) U.N. Convention. . . .

The availability for enforcement measures of property used for *iure gestionis* or non-public purposes, or, as it is somewhat awkwardly put in the UN Convention, for "other than government non-commercial purposes,"[62] is recognized in many states.[63] The true difficulty lies in defining and identifying the scope of property not used for sovereign purposes and thus subject to enforcement jurisdiction.[64] In the case law reviewed one can clearly recognize that the broad categories, identifying types of property generally considered to serve sovereign or non-commercial purposes as they are found in the UN Convention and other immunity instruments, have been followed and refined.

. . . .

Diplomatic and consular premises as well as related property serving diplomatic or consular functions are the paradigmatic examples of property serving non-commercial purposes and thus being immune from execution.

. . . .

Warships and other military equipment are generally regarded as not available for enforcement measures.[65] This is clearly reflected in the UN Convention which expressly characterizes "property of a military character or used or intended for use in the performance of military functions" as government non-commercial property.[66]

. . . .

That central bank funds, as typically non-commercial property, are immune from enforcement measures is reflected in the UN Convention which exempts "property of the central bank or other monetary authority of the state" from the types of property possibly subject to execution measures.[67] A similar, though more limited, exemption can be found in the ILA Draft Convention[68] and in the [Institut de Droit International (IDI)] Resolution.[69] The UK SIA provides that "[p]roperty of a State's central bank or other monetary authority shall not be regarded . . . as in use or intended for use for commercial purposes."[70]

. . . .

---

[62] SN: Art. 19(c) U.N. Convention, *supra* note [40], based on Art. 18(1)(c) ILC Draft Articles.

[63] SN: See *supra* text at note [34].

[64] SN: *See Société de droit irakien Rafidain Bank et crts v. Consarc Corp., société de droit américain et crts.* Cour d'Appel, Brussels, Mar. 10, 1993 [1994] JT 787, where the court reasoned that "*l'immunité d'exécution a pour but de soustraire certains biens de l'Etat étranger aux mesures d'exécution de ses créanciers*," ("immunity from execution aims at removing certain assets of a foreign State from measures of execution of its creditors"), but did not make it clear which assets might be available for execution.

[65] SN: See Fox, *supra* note [21], at 391.

[66] SN: Art. 21(1)(b) U.N. Convention, *supra* note [40].

[67] SN: Art. 21(1)(c) U.N. Convention, *supra* note [40].

[68] SN: Art. VII(C)3 of the ILA Draft Convention, supra note [42], prohibits attachment or execution if "[t]he property is that of a State central bank held by it for central banking purposes."

[69] SN: Art. 4(2)(c) IDI Resolution, *supra* note 15, accords immunity from measures of constraint to "property of the central bank or monetary authority of the State in use or set aside for use for the purposes of the central bank or monetary authority."

[70] SN: S. 14(4) U.K. SIA, *supra* note [25].

Embassy and consular[71] accounts, at least as far as they are used for running a diplomatic or consular mission, are normally considered to serve non-commercial (public) purposes and are thus protected by immunity from execution measures, in particular immunity from attachment. This exemption is also expressly provided for in the UN Convention, which clarifies that the immunity is not limited to embassy accounts, but extends to "property, including any bank account, which is used or intended for use for the purposes of the diplomatic mission of the State or its consular posts, special missions, missions to international organizations, or delegations to organs of international organizations or to international conferences."[72] The underlying idea of protecting the functioning of state missions (*ne impediatur legatio*) is generally accepted by national courts. However, questions have arisen with regard to issues such as mixed accounts, burden of proof, past, present, or future use of accounts, and related problems.[73]

. . . .

While embassy or consular accounts serve as the basis for most of the litigation concerning execution against foreign state property, other tangible or intangible assets may also become the object of attempted enforcement measures. In such cases, it is the purpose of the assets which usually serves as the distinguishing criterion in order to determine whether or not it should be protected by immunity. For instance, in the course of French litigation aimed at enforcing an arbitration award made against Yugoslavia, debts owed by the French national airline to the Yugoslav state were held not to be subject to attachment because they were intended to cover overflight charges which directly related to the "exercise of that State of its prerogative powers linked to its national and international sovereignty as that sovereignty applies to its territory and airspace."[74]

. . . .

Apart from measures of constraint aimed at enforcing judgments already delivered against a state, the need may arise for provisional measures before final judgment to be imposed. The most important provisional measures are pre-judgment attachments of property in order to secure assets for the eventual enforcement of a subsequent judgment, followed by pre-judgment attachments for the purpose of establishing jurisdiction. This applies mostly to the attachment of bank accounts[75] and seizure of commercial ships.[76] The question arises whether the rules concerning enforcement immunity also apply to provisional measures or whether distinct rules are called for. It

---

[71] SN: With regard to immunity from execution, national courts generally do not distinguish between diplomatic and consular accounts. See *Spanish Consular Bank Accounts Case,* Landgericht, Stuttgart, Sept. 21, 1971, 65 I.L.R. 114.

[72] SN: Art. 21(1)(a) U.N. Convention, *supra* note [40].

[73] SN: Fox, *supra* note [21], at 380ff, 404ff.

[74] SN: *Socialist Federal Republic of Yugoslavia v. Société Européenne d'Etudes et d'Entreprises, Crédit Lyonnais, Air France and Others,* Tribunal de grande instance, Paris, July 3, 1985, 82 I.L.R. 58, at 73.

[75] SN: For instance, *Neustein v. Republic of Indonesia,* [Oberster Gerichtshof, Aug. 6, 1958, 65 I.L.R. 3].

[76] SN: For instance, *Russia v. Pied-Rich BV,* [Hooge Raad der Nederlanden (Netherlands Supreme Court), May 28, 1993 [1994] NYIL 512].

seems that the established practice of most European courts disregards such differentiation and uses the same test with regard to the permissibility of pre- and post-judgment measures.[77] For instance, the Italian Court of Cassation held:

> According to an international customary law principle, the assets of a foreign State are exempt from provisional and executive measures, provided that the assets are used in the exercise of sovereign functions or to attain public goals. Hence, also in case of conservatory or enforcement acts, immunity from jurisdiction can be applied to activities carried out in the exercise of the powers of a public authority, whereas it is excluded in case of private activities.[78] The German decisions in the *Central Bank of Nigeria*[79] and the *NIOC* cases[80] also concerned pre-judgment attachments, and both used the purpose test that would also have been used in regular enforcement proceedings.

. . . .

The US FSIA, however, introduced an important distinction by prohibiting pre-judgment attachments in order to establish the jurisdiction of US courts and by generally requiring an explicit waiver for any pre-judgment attachment.[81] Similarly, the UK SIA requires "written consent" for the "giving of any relief,"[82] such as a *Mareva* injunction[83] prohibiting a defendant from removing funds from the forum state.

. . . .

The ILA Draft Convention specifically addresses pre-judgment measures, which it permits in order to avoid a situation in which a defendant state tries to frustrate the execution of an eventual judgment.[84]

The position of United States courts, summarized in the *Connecticut Bank of Commerce* case, is not markedly different from the law of other jurisdictions.[85]

---

[77] SN: Schreuer, *supra* note [21], at 162.

[78] SN: *Libia v. Condor Srl*, Corte di Cassazione, Aug. 23, 1990 [1991] *Rivista di diritto internazionale* 679.

[79] SN: *Central Bank of Nigeria Case*, [Landgericht, Frankfurt, Dec. 2, 1975 [1976] Neue Juristische Wochenschrift 1044, 65 I.L.R. 131, at 137].

[80] SN: *NIOC Revenues Case, supra* note [34].

[81] SN: S. 1610(d) U.S. FSIA, *supra* note [26].

[82] SN: S.13(2) and (3) U.K. SIA, *supra* note [25].

[83] SN: *Mareva Compania Naviera SA v. Int'l Bulk Carriers Ltd.* [1975] 2 Lloyd's Rep. 509.

[84] SN: Art. VIII D of the ILA Draft Convention, *supra* note [42], provides: "[i]n exceptional circumstances, a tribunal of the forum State may order interim measures against the property of a foreign State, available under this Convention for attachment, arrest, or execution, including prejudgment attachment of assets and injunctive relief, if a party presents a prima facie case that such assets within the territorial limits of the forum State may be removed, dissipated or otherwise dealt with by the foreign State before the tribunal renders judgment and there is a reasonable probability that such action will frustrate execution of any such judgment."

[85] Nancy Turck, *French and U.S. Courts Define Limits of Sovereign Immunity in Execution and Enforcement of Arbitral Awards,* 17 Arb. Int'l 327 (2001).

Connecticut Bank of Commerce v. Republic of Congo

309 F.3d 240, 251–54 (5th Cir. 2002)

Until 1952, the United States generally afforded foreign sovereigns absolute immunity from the jurisdiction of the courts, including complete immunity from execution. Verlinden B.V. v. Central Bank of Nigeria, 461 U.S. 480, 486, 76 L. Ed. 2d 81, 103 S. Ct. 1962 (1983). Unlike state or federal sovereign immunity, foreign sovereign immunity does not derive from the constitution. *Id.* Foreign sovereign immunity instead derives from concerns of grace and comity between nations. As a result, the Supreme Court regularly deferred to the Executive Branch in determining whether to take jurisdiction over a case concerning a foreign sovereign. *Id.* The Executive was in a better position to anticipate the foreign relations consequences of subjecting a foreign state to suit in a U.S. court. Under the theory of absolute sovereign immunity, the Executive would regularly recommend that courts decline to take jurisdiction over any case against a foreign sovereign.

In 1952, the State Department issued the "Tate Letter," which announced the Department's adoption of the "restrictive" theory of foreign sovereign immunity. *Id.* at 486–87. Under the restrictive theory, which many other nations had already adopted, the State Department would continue to recommend immunity in suits concerning a foreign state's sovereign, public acts. The Department, however, would recommend denying immunity in suits based on a foreign sovereign's strictly commercial activities. The Tate Letter did nothing to modify the complete immunity enjoyed by foreign sovereigns from execution against their property. If a plaintiff successfully obtained a final judgment against a foreign sovereign, he still had to rely on the foreign state to pay the judgment voluntarily. H.R. REP. NO. 94–1487, at 8, 27 ("The traditional view in the United States concerning execution has been that the property of foreign states is absolutely immune from execution. . . . Even after the "Tate Letter" of 1952, this continued to be the position of the Department of State and of the courts."); RESTATEMENT (THIRD) OF THE FOREIGN RELATIONS LAW OF THE UNITED STATES § 460 cmt. a (1987) (hereinafter "RESTATEMENT").

The FSIA shifted the responsibility to make determinations about foreign sovereign immunity from the State Department to the courts. Verlinden, 461 U.S. at 488. For the most part, the FSIA codifies the restrictive theory of sovereign immunity as described in the Tate Letter. Id. But the FSIA also modified the rule barring execution against a foreign state's property by "partially lowering the barrier of immunity from execution, so as to make this immunity conform more closely with the provisions on jurisdictional immunity in the bill." H.R. REP. NO. 94–1487, at 27 (emphasis added). For both immunity from jurisdiction and immunity from attachment, "commercial activity" generally constitutes the touchstone of the immunity determination. But immunity from execution is nevertheless narrower than jurisdictional immunity. De Letelier v. Republic of Chile, 748 F.2d 790, 798–99 (2d Cir. 1984). In De Letelier, the Second Circuit surveyed both the history of immunity from execution and the international law context at the time Congress passed the FSIA. The court concluded that Congress intended to lift immunity from execution only "in part," that it did not intend to reverse completely the historical and international antipathy to executing against a foreign state's property even in cases where a judgment could be had on the merits. *Id.* It attributed the differences in phrasing between the jurisdictional (§ 1605) and execution (§ 1610) immunity sections in the FSIA to a deliberate choice to narrow the scope of immunity from execution.

Two subsections of the FSIA spell out the exceptions to immunity from execution. 28 U.S.C. § 1610(a) governs the immunity from execution of property belonging to foreign states. 28 U.S.C. § 1610(b) governs the immunity from execution of property belonging to an "agency or instrumentality" of a foreign state engaged in commercial activity in the United States. Subsection (a), regarding property belonging directly to a foreign state, permits execution only narrowly, when the property is "in the United States" and "used for a commercial purpose in the United States." Subsection (b) is broader; it permits execution of "any property in the United States" belonging to the agency or instrumentality, regardless of how the agency or instrumentality uses the property. Subsection (a) is generally thought to be more restrictive than subsection (b). De Letelier, 784 F.2d at 799 (explaining that Congress "was more cautious when lifting immunity from execution against property owned by the State itself").

Because subsection (a) is intended to be narrower than subsection (b), we pay close attention to the differences in phrasing between the sections. Subsection (a) allows courts to execute only when the property is "used for a commercial activity," whereas subsection (b) permits execution of "any property," regardless of its use. The focus in subsection (a) is plainly on the "use" to which the property is put. As the Restatement explains, "For purposes of post-judgment attachment and execution, the Foreign Sovereign Immunities Act draws a sharp distinction between the property of states and the property of state instrumentalities. . . . The property of states may be attached only if it is or was used in commercial activity; the property of state instrumentalities may be attached without any such limitation, so long as the instrumentality itself is engaged in commercial activity in the United States." RESTATEMENT § 460 cmt. b.

Restricting execution against property belonging to foreign states depending on the "use" of that property, rather than its source, helps accomplish the purpose of limiting execution against property directly belonging to a foreign state more severely than execution against property belonging to an instrumentality. The premise is that agencies or instrumentalities engaged in commercial activity are akin to any other player in the market, and that their functions are primarily commercial. *Id.* On the other hand, the "primary function of states is government." *Id.* One of the chief motifs of the FSIA is to limit as much as possible disrupting the "public acts" or "jure imperii" of sovereigns, while restricting their purely commercial activity. H.R. REP. 94–1487, at 7. Confiscating funds that are being put immediately to some sovereign use interrupts a sovereign's public acts regardless of what kind of activity generated the funds, commercial or noncommercial.

An example helps clarify the point. Consider an airplane owned by a foreign government and used solely to shuttle a foreign head-of-state back and forth for official visits. If the plane lands in the United States, it would not be subject to attachment or execution. The plane is not "used for" any commercial activity, in the U.S. or elsewhere. It plainly would not matter how the foreign government bought the plane, raised the purchase price, or otherwise came into ownership. Even if the government received the plane as payment from a U.S. company in an obviously commercial transaction, that would not somehow transform the "use" of the plane into a commercial use. Regardless of how the government came to own the plane, a U.S. court could never under the terms of the FSIA confiscate a plane used solely to transport a foreign head-of-state on official business. Attaching the plane and selling it in execution of a judgment would go too far in interrupting the public acts of a foreign state.[86]

---

[86] SN: The Third Circuit relied on similar reasoning in *City of Englewood v. Socialist People's Libyan Arab Jamahiriya*, 773 F.2d 31 (3d Cir. 1985), in rejecting an attempt to attach real property used as a residence for Libya's Head of Mission to the United Nations. The city of Englewood argued that the property was subject to attachment because it was "acquired by Libya in a commercial transaction between a seller and a buyer." *Id.* at 36. The court rejected this argument, reasoning that if "acquisition of property in a particular commercial transaction or act indelibly stamped the property as used for commercial activity, even foreign embassies and chancelleries would be subject to execution. Plainly Congress did not intend a result so inconsistent with recognized principles of international law." *Id.* at 36–37. The determinative issue, according to the Englewood court, was not whether the property was acquired in a commercial transaction but instead whether Libya's present use of the property was commercial. *Id.* at 37.

> The phrase "used for" in § 1610(a) is not a mere syntactical infelicity that permits courts to look beyond the "use" of property, and instead try to find any kind of nexus or connection to a commercial activity in the United States. The statute means what it says: property of a foreign sovereign, unlike property belonging to a mere agency or instrumentality, may be executed against only if it is "used for" a commercial activity. That the property is revenue from or otherwise generated by commercial activity in the United States does not thereby render the property amenable to execution.

After remand to the lower court, a subsequent appeal clarified the above analysis:[87]

> [W]e agree that determining the commercial (or non-commercial) status of a property's use requires a more holistic approach. Specifically, we think that an analysis applied to such a question should examine the totality of the circumstances surrounding the property. This analysis should include an examination of the uses of the property in the past[88] as well as all facts related to its present use, with an eye toward determining whether the commercial use of the property, if any, is so exceptional that it is "an out of character" use for that particular property.[89]
>
> This holistic approach is also consistent with the reasoning in our earlier decision in this case. There, Af-Cap's predecessor argued that courts should look at the source as opposed to the use of the property to determine its commercial nature. In rejecting this contention, we utilized [an airplane] analogy.
>
> . . . .
>
> Tweaking this analogy a bit, consider that the airplane had been used on rare occasions for commercial activities—for example, it was temporarily used to fill in for a disabled plane in the foreign country's commercial fleet. It would strain reason to conclude that these limited, emergency usages rendered the plane subject to garnishment now and forever irrespective of the fact that its use was otherwise almost exclusively non-commercial. Indeed, permitting the attachment and selling of such a plane in execution of a judgment would also "go too far in interrupting the public acts of a foreign state." Thus, we conclude that under the FSIA, foreign property retains its immunity protection where its commercial uses, considered holistically and in context, are bona fide exceptions to its otherwise non-commercial use.[90]

---

[87] *Af-Cap Inc. v. Republic of Congo*, 383 F.3d 361, 369 (5th Cir. 2004).

[88] SN: We disagree with the district court's alternative holding that evidence of past commercial use cannot be considered for purposes of establishing the commercial or noncommercial nature of property under the FSIA. According to the court, § 1610(a) only applies to "present and impending uses." Instead, we think that the consideration of evidence of past use is an indispensable part of a court's FSIA inquiry. A court forbidden to consider how property has been used in the past would be hard-pressed to accurately determine whether the predominant use of that property is commercial or sovereign.

[89] SN: In this analysis, we also think it would be appropriate for a court to consider whether the use of the property in question was being manipulated by a sovereign nation to avoid being subject to garnishment under the FSIA.

[90] *Af-Cap*, *supra* note 87, at 370–71.

Parties attempting to collect investment arbitration awards may also confront problems concerning the enforcing court's jurisdiction over the foreign state, above and beyond the problem of locating that state's assets. This problem is particularly acute in the United States. Although the U.S. Foreign Sovereign Immunities Act (FSIA), on its face, provides automatic personal jurisdiction as long as there is subject matter jurisdiction and proper service of process, 28 U.S.C. § 1330(b), many U.S. courts have found that they must nonetheless engage in what is known as a "minimum contacts" analysis to determine whether there is personal jurisdiction over a sovereign defendant.[91] Specifically, many courts have found that because the U.S. Supreme Court has held that personal jurisdiction is a constitutional limitation on judicial authority (having its roots in the Fifth Amendment's Due Process Clause), the FSIA's statutory grant of personal jurisdiction may only be exercised where minimum contacts exist between the defendant and the United States.[92]

Recent cases have begun to retreat from this position. Thus, the D.C. Circuit has held that there is no constitutional element to section 1330(b)'s grant of personal jurisdiction because foreign sovereigns and their instrumentalities (which, by necessity, are the only parties against whom § 1330(b) jurisdiction may be asserted) are not "persons" entitled to due process protections. These cases grow out of the Supreme Court's 1992 decision in *Republic of Argentina v. Weltover*.[93] In *Weltover*, a breach of contract case against the Republic of Argentina and its central bank, the Supreme Court raised, but did not answer, the question of whether foreign states and their instrumentalities are "persons" to whom due process protection is owed.[94] In raising the issue, the Court cited its prior decision in *South Carolina v. Katzenbach*,[95] specifically noting its holding that the states of the United States are not "persons" within the meaning of the Fifth Amendment and that they are therefore not entitled to due process protection.[96] As a result of the Supreme Court's holding in *Weltover*, an emerging trend in U.S. courts is that foreign sovereigns and their instrumentalities are not "persons" within the meaning of the Fifth Amendment and that personal jurisdiction under Section 1330(b) may be asserted

---

[91] See *Int'l Shoe Co. v. Washington*, 326 U.S. 310, 316 (1945) (holding that "due process requires only that in order to subject a defendant to a judgment *in personam*, if he be not present within the territory of the forum, he have certain minimum contacts with it such that the maintenance of the suit does not offend 'traditional notions of fair play and substantial justice'") quoting *Milliken v. Meyer*, 311 U.S. 457 (1941).

[92] *See, e.g., Texas Trading & Milling Corp. v. Federal Republic of Nigeria*, 647 F.2d 300, 308 (2d Cir. 1981) (noting that Section 1330 "cannot create personal jurisdiction where the Constitution forbids it").

[93] 504 U.S. 607 (1992).

[94] *Id.* at 609.

[95] 383 U.S. 301, 323–24 (1966).

[96] *Id.*

against such parties without regard to due process considerations.[97] Even where Circuits have not expressly held that foreign sovereigns are not "persons" entitled to due process, lower courts have increasingly begun to question earlier decisions holding otherwise,[98] and many courts have left the question open by assuming without deciding that foreign sovereigns are "persons" for the purposes of the Fifth

---

[97] See *I.T. Consultants, Inc. v. Islamic Republic of Pakistan*, 351 F.3d 1184, 1191 (D.C. Cir. 2003) (declining to conduct minimum contacts analysis because foreign states are not "persons" protected by the Fifth Amendment); *Price v. Socialist People's Libyan Arab Jamarihiriya*, 294 F.3d 82, 96 (D.C. Cir. 2002) (holding that "foreign states are not "persons" protected by the Fifth Amendment"); *Cassirer v. Kingdom of Spain*, 461 F. Supp. 2d 1157, 1168 (C.D. Cal. 2006) ("Nothing in the [FSIA] suggests that a minimum contacts analysis must be conducted or that foreign sovereigns should be viewed as 'persons' for purposes of due process analysis"); *Altmann v. Republic of Austria*, 142 F. Supp. 2d 1187, 1208 (C.D. Cal. 2001) ("this Court holds that a foreign state is not a "person" under the Due Process Clause of the United States Constitution"), *aff'd on other grounds*, 317 F.3d 954 (9th Cir. 2002), *aff'd on other grounds*, 124 S. Ct. 2240 (2004); *Cruz v. U.S.*, 387 F. Supp. 2d 1057, 1067 (N.D. Cal. 2005) ("the reasoning of *Price*, which this Court finds sound, counsels against affording the Mexican banks in this case the status of 'persons' within the scope of that term as used in the Due Process Clause"); *Nikbin v. Islamic Republic of Iran*, 471 F. Supp. 2d 53, note 3 (D.D.C. 2007) (The Constitution's Due Process Clause imposes no limitation on a court's exercise of personal jurisdiction over a foreign state because a foreign state is not a 'person' within the meaning of the Fifth Amendment"); *Gilmore v. Palestinian Interim Self-Government Authority*, 422 F. Supp. 2d 96, 103–04 (D.D.C. 2006) ("foreign states are not 'persons' protected by the Fifth Amendment"); *Abur v. Republic of Sudan*, 437 F. Supp. 2d 166, note 11 (D.D.C. 2006) ("The Constitution's Due Process Clause imposes no limitation on a court's exercise of personal jurisdiction over a foreign state because a foreign state is not a 'person' within the meaning of the Fifth Amendment"); *Sisso v. Islamic Republic of Iran*, 448 F. Supp. 2d 76, note 7 (D.D.C. 2006) ("The Constitution's due process clause imposes no limitation on a court's exercise of personal jurisdiction over a foreign state because a foreign state is not a 'person' within the meaning of the Fifth Amendment"); *Rux v. Republic of Sudan*, No. 04 Civ. 428, 2005 WL 2086202, **13, 18–19 (E.D. Va. 2005) ("the Due Process Clause does not apply to foreign states"), *affirmed in part, appeal dismissed in part*, *Rux v. Republic of Sudan*, 461 F.3d 461 (4th Cir. 2006), *cert. denied*, 127 S. Ct. 1325 (2007). *But see Frontera Resources Azerbaijan Corp. v. State Oil Co. of Azerbaijan*, 479 F. Supp. 2d 376, 384 (S.D.N.Y. 2007) (where "although the Court largely agree[d] with the D.C. Circuit's analysis" the court nonetheless declined to follow the D.C. Circuit based on insufficient information to determine whether SOCAR was an "agent of the state," and based on the fact that "the holding of *Texas Trading* remains good law within the Second Circuit, and any expressions of uncertainty in *Weltover* and *Hanil Bank* are insufficient to justify a ruling to the contrary").

[98] For example, the Second Circuit has expressly noted that, in the wake of *Weltover*, it is unsettled whether foreign states and their instrumentalities are entitled to due process protection. The issue first came before the Second Circuit in *Hanil Bank v. PT Bank Negara Indonesia*, 148 F.3d 127 (2d Cir. 1998). In *Hanil Bank*, the Second Circuit questioned the continued validity of its earlier holding that foreign states were entitled to due process protection, although the court refused to rule on the question of whether a foreign sovereign was a person for due process purposes, having found that the defendant's extensive contacts with the forum rendered it unnecessary to address the question. *Id.* at 134 ("we need not resolve the exact status of a foreign sovereign for due process analysis because we believe, in any event, that the due process requirements have been met here"). *See also Weininger v. Castro*, 462 F. Supp.2d 457, note 29 (S.D.N.Y. 2006) (noting that although the Supreme Court has not decided the issue, it has signaled that the approach established by the Second Circuit may be incorrect, as foreign states may not be persons under the Due Process clause).

Amendment's due process analysis.[99] Earlier cases such as *Creighton*, which declined to find that foreign sovereigns and their instrumentalities are not "persons" within the meaning of the Fifth Amendment, have also been criticized as undermining the international arbitration regime and perhaps violating the United States' commitments under the New York Convention.[100]

D. Sovereign Immunity and the Washington Convention

It was noted earlier that pursuant to Article 54 of the Washington Convention, ICSID awards are intended to be the equivalent of a final judgment of the court of a Contracting Party. This is certainly an advantage and a "distinct feature"[101] of ICSID awards when compared to New York Convention and other awards. Article 55 of the Washington Convention, however, somewhat diminishes that advantage by providing an important exception to Article 54 as follows: "Nothing in Article 54 shall be construed as derogating from the law in force in any Contracting State relating to immunity of that State or of any foreign State from execution." This short clause leaves intact the whole panoply of sovereign immunity defenses that a state could assert in the courts of the place of enforcement during the execution stage.

---

[99] See *Boeing Co. v. Egyptair*, 2007 WL 1315716, *2 (2d Cir. May 7, 2007) (assuming that the minimum contacts requirement of the Due Process Clause applies to foreign instrumentalities, while noting that it is an open question whether foreign sovereigns are subject to due process analysis); *Altmann v. Republic of Austria*, 317 F.3d 954, 970 (9th Cir. 2002) ("[a]ssuming that a foreign state is a 'person' for purposes of the Due Process Clause," court found that defendant had sufficient contacts with jurisdiction to exercise personal jurisdiction); *S & S Davis Int'l, Inc. v. Republic of Yemen*, 218 F.3d 1292, 1303–04 (11th Cir. 2000) ("We do not need to determine the precise constitutional status of a foreign sovereign because we find that due process requirements have been met in this case") (citing *Hanil Bank*, 148 F.3d at 134).; *TMR Energy Ltd. v. State Property Fund of Ukraine*, 411 F.3d 296, 299–302 (D.C. Cir. 2005) (refusing to resolve issue of whether foreign instrumentality is "person" under Fifth Amendment and resolving personal jurisdiction challenge instead by finding that the defendant was an alter-ego of Ukraine, and therefore not an instrumentality of the state). Similarly, other courts have refused to directly engage in a minimum contacts analysis, finding personal jurisdiction over sovereigns based on the text of the FSIA. *See, e.g., S & S Davis Int'l, Inc. v. Yemen*, 218 F.3d 1292, 1303 (11th Cir. 2000) (where service was proper, "[t]he parties agreed to arbitration, a final award was determined, and the defendants have failed to satisfy that award. Therefore, under the FSIA, personal jurisdiction exists"). *See also* Joseph W. Dellapenna, *Refining the Foreign Sovereign Immunities Act*, 9 Willamette J. Int'l L. & Disp. Res. 57, 69 (2001) (suggesting that no contacts analysis is necessary to find personal jurisdiction under the FSIA, since any of the subject matter jurisdiction requirements are themselves dependent on sufficient contacts).

[100] *See, e.g.,* Karen Halverson, *Is a Foreign State a "Person"? Does it Matter?: Personal Jurisdiction, Due Process and the Foreign Sovereign Immunities Act*, 34 N.Y.U. J. Int'l L. & Pol'y 115, 183–84 (2001).

[101] Schreuer, *supra* note 14, at 1100.

In *AIG v. Kazakhstan*,[102] for example, AIG tried to execute an ICSID award in British High Court against certain cash and securities belonging to the Central Bank of Kazakhstan, which were held by third parties in London. The Kazakh government, based on the U.K. Sovereign Immunity Act of 1978, argued among other things that the identified assets were immune, because under that Act only those state assets that are intended for commercial use are subject to execution,[103] and Central Bank assets are explicitly exempt from execution under the Act.[104] The British High Court sided with the Kazakh government and dismissed the case.

In at least three other enforcement proceedings involving Washington Convention awards, two in France[105] and one in the United States,[106] losing states have successfully avoided execution based on the sovereign immunity defenses available to them under the laws of the place of execution. In sum, these cases highlight the potential challenges that investors may face when they wish to enforce a Washington Convention award.

E. Conclusion

As the preceding sections demonstrate, enforcing an investment treaty arbitration award against a recalcitrant state may be the most difficult, lengthy, and expensive phase of an investor-state arbitration. In recent years, some nations have sought to restrict or rescind their participation in the investor-state treaty regime.[107] Such attempts would make the enforcement process even more problematic.

---

[102] *AIG Capital Partners, Inc. & CJSC Tema Real Estate Co. v. Kazakhstan*, ICSID Case No. ARB/01/6 (Oct. 7, 2003) (unpublished); *AIG Capital Partners, Inc. v. Republic of Kazakhstan*, [2005] EWHC 2239 (Comm) (Oct. 20, 2005) (enforcement decision in High Court of Justice, Queen's Bench Division, England), *available at* www.investmentclaims.com.

[103] U.K. Sovereign Immunity Act of 1978, § 13(2)(b) ("the property of a State shall not be subject to any process for the enforcement of a judgment or arbitration award, or in an action in rem, for its arrest, detention or sale").

[104] *Id.*, § 14(4) ("Property of a State's central bank or monetary authority shall not be regarded for the purposes of subsection (4) of section 13 above as in use or intended for use for commercial purposes . . .").

[105] *Benvenuti & Bonfant v. Congo*, ICSID Case No. ARB/77/2 (Award, Aug. 8, 1980). *See also* the decisions of the French courts on the enforcement of this award in 1 ICSID Rep. 366–75. The second award that the claimants sought to enforce in France was *Société Ouest Africaine des Bétons Industriels (SOABI) v. Senegal*, ICSID Case No. ARB/82/1 (Award, Feb. 25, 1988), 2 ICSID Rep. 114 (1994). The decisions of the French courts on the enforcement of this award may be accessed at 2 ICSID Rep. 337–42.

[106] *Liberian Eastern Timber Corp.* [hereinafter *LETCO*] *v. Republic of Liberia*, ICSID Case No. ARB/83/2, (Award, Mar. 31, 1986), 2 ICSID Rep. 346. The decisions of the U.S. courts in the enforcement proceedings in this case may be accessed at 2 ICSID Rep. 384–96.

[107] For example, Bolivia has formally withdrawn from the Washington Convention (*Bolivia Withdraws from ICSID*, Latin Lawyer, May 22, 2007).

XXII. The Future of International Investment Arbitration

The world is ever more committed to economic development, and foreign direct investment and other capital flows have become a vital component of that development. The protection of these investment flows is of growing importance and customary international law is evolving to deal with disputes that arise. The newly emerged international arbitration system, the subject of this book, has become the primary form of such protection. It is our view that this system, or something like it, is here to stay.

For many years international investment arbitration occupied a quiet niche in international law. However, with the recent explosion of activity in the area—the conclusion of investment treaties and the resulting proliferation of disputes—investment arbitration faces a host of challenges. The number, size, and scope of recent arbitrations have attracted attention from civil society groups, socially minded non-governmental organizations (NGOs), legal scholars, and governments themselves. Several groups have been increasingly vocal in decrying the shortcomings of investment arbitrations in meeting various needs.[1] Some have been upset with investment arbitration's impact on sensitive issues, from environmental to social.[2] Concern has been expressed over perceived inconsistencies in investment arbitration awards.[3] Additionally, various states and other governmental organizations have responded negatively when faced with the difficulties

---

[1] *See, e.g.,* Guillermo Alvarez & William Park, *The New Face of Investment Arbitration: NAFTA Chapter 11,* 28 Yale J. Int'l L. 365, 383–86 (2003) (discussing various complaints about NAFTA arbitrations).

[2] *See, e.g.,* Howard Mann & Konrad von Moltke, *NAFTA's Chapter 11 and the Environment: Addressing the Impacts of the Investor-State Process on the Environment,* Int'l Inst. for Sustainable Dev. Working Paper (1999).

[3] *See, e.g.,* Susan D. Franck, *The Legitimacy Crisis in Investment Treaty Arbitration: Privatizing Public International Law through Inconsistent Decisions,* 73 Fordham L. Rev. 1521 (2005).

that can come from investment arbitration.[4] How investment arbitration institutions and others involved in arbitrations respond to these concerns will shape how international investment arbitration moves forward. Various suggestions have been made on how to reshape investment arbitration to better fit the needs of both investors and states; some of the more frequently repeated suggestions include improving transparency in the process, allowing greater amicus participation, and developing an appeal process. This chapter examines some trends in both the conclusion and the development of the content of investment treaties; it also examines some of the issues and challenges that may significantly influence international investment arbitration well into the future.

A. Trends in the Conclusion and Amendment of Investment Treaties[5]

The 1990s witnessed an unprecedented proliferation of investment treaties. Today, we have more than 2,500 bilateral investment treaties and a number of other multilateral treaties that contain investment chapters, including the North American Free Trade Agreement (NAFTA), the Energy Charter Treaty (ECT), the Dominican Republic–Central America Free Trade Agreement (DR-CAFTA), and the Association of South East Asian Nations (ASEAN) Investment Agreement. The statistics suggest that although the treaty conclusion pace has slowed, governments continue to agree to such treaties.[6] The question for many is whether the investment treaty system will thrive or lose its appeal, and a variety of factors may play a role in this context. On the investor side, developments such as investors' success—or failure—in recovering

---

[4] *See, e.g.*, Bipartisan Trade Promotion Authority Act 2002, Pub. L. No. 107–210, § 2102(b)(3), 19 U.S.C.A. § 3802, *available at* http://www.sice.oas.org/Trade/tradeact/act7.asp (in response to several arbitrations brought against the United States, the United States under its own laws provides "a high level" of foreign investment protection, which it believes sufficient, and sets limits on what rights the United States will offer to foreign investors under treaties). *See also* pp. 703–704 *infra*, explaining reactions of Ecuador, Bolivia, and Venezuela.

[5] *See generally* United Nations Conference on Trade and Development (UNCTAD), *Bilateral Investment Treaties 1995–2006: Trends in Investment Rulemaking*, U.N. Doc. UNCTAD/ITE/IIT/2006/5 (2007).

[6] *Id.* at 1 (the number of bilateral investment treaties [BITs] signed each year has decreased from a high in 2001, although the number of free trade agreements [FTAs] and other agreements on economic cooperation containing investment provisions began to increase).

awards against Argentina in the aftermath of the 1999 to 2002 Argentinean financial crisis will certainly have an effect.[7]

States could act at a fundamental level by terminating their investment treaties. In 2005, for example, the Czech cabinet proposed to parliament that it terminate the Czech Republic BITs with the European Union (EU) member countries.[8] These treaties, particularly the Czech Republic-Netherlands BIT, have been the source of several investment treaty cases against the republic.[9] The supposed rationale underlying the Czech cabinet's proposal was that the treaties were incompatible with the Czech Republic's obligations under Article 307[10] of the European Communities Treaty (EC Treaty).[11] Similarly, in 2007, Ecuador signaled that it might not renew its BIT with the United States, which has been the source of many investment

---

[7] As of November 2007, six awards resulting from the financial crisis had been rendered against Argentina, amounting to approximately US$800 million. Argentina has commenced at least four annulment proceedings against them. The Argentine government has protested and has continued to litigate the cases. *See* Wailin Wong, *Argentina Treasury Attorney: World Bank Claims Could Reach $80 Billion,* Dow Jones Newswire, Jan. 21, 2005 (Argentine Attorney of the Treasury criticizing ICSID as "more extraordinarily unfavorable" than any other justice system in the world). In what has become known as the *Rosatti Doctrine,* Argentina's Minister of Justice Horacio Rosatti stated that any award that "confers a higher status on a foreign investor than on an Argentinean investor" would violate the Argentinean Constitution and be nonenforceable. Aníbal Sabater, *The Weaknesses of the "Rosatti Doctrine,"* 15 Am. Rev. Int'l Arb. 465 (2004). Now that it has lost in a number of cases, Argentina seems to be seeking a global solution for the thirty odd cases still pending.

[8] Luke Peterson, *Czech Republic Pursues Shake-Up of Its Bilateral Investment Treaties,* Inves. Treaty News (ITN) (Nov. 21, 2005).

[9] *See, e.g., CME Czech Republic B.V. v. Czech Republic* (UNCITRAL Arbitration, Final Award of Mar. 14, 2003) (US$270 million award against the Czech Republic); *Saluka Inves. v. Czech Republic* (UNCITRAL Arbitration, Partial Award of Mar. 17, 2006) (government liable on the merits; compensation to be determined).

[10] Article 307 states:

> The rights and obligations arising from agreements concluded before 1 January 1958 or, for acceding States, before the date of their accession, between one or more Member States on the one hand, and one or more third countries on the other, shall not be affected by the provisions of this Treaty.
>
> To the extent that such agreements are not compatible with this Treaty, the Member State or States concerned shall take all appropriate steps to eliminate the incompatibilities established. Member States shall, where necessary, assist each other to this end and shall, where appropriate, adopt a common attitude.
>
> . . . .
>
> Consolidated Version of the Treaty Establishing the European Community, Dec. 24, 2002 [hereinafter EC Treaty].

[11] Peterson, *Czech Republic, supra* note 8.

disputes.[12] Speculation about the viability of the system as a whole began when Bolivia, in 2007, became the first country to withdraw from the International Centre for Settlement of Investment Disputes (ICSID) Convention.[13] Venezuela has sent similar signals.[14] Beyond these examples, however, it is unlikely that the investment treaty regime will unravel. The sheer number of the BITs and other relevant treaties would make it extremely difficult to do so.

Although efforts to withdraw from investment treaties have not been numerous, several European countries have started to amend their BITs. The driving force behind these amendments is the European Commission, the executive branch of the EU. In recent years, the European Commission has identified potential incompatibilities between the bilateral investment treaties of states acceding to the EU, as well as of some existing members, and the EC Treaty.[15] In 2003 the European Commission initially focused its investigation on the BITs of eight of the recently acceding members from Central and Eastern Europe[16] with the United States.[17] The core argument of the European Commission was that the respective BITs undermine obligations of these joining members under Article 307 of the EC Treaty. In 2003 the European Commission, the United States, and the eight acceding members signed a memorandum of understanding whereby they agreed to amend these BITs by including exceptions to national and most-favored-nation provisions with respect to several sectors, such as agriculture, audio-visual services, and hydrocarbons.[18]

---

[12] Luke Peterson, *Ecuador Announces That It Wants Out of US Investment Treaty*, Int'l L. Rep., May 9, 2007, at 5. Ecuador has thus far not terminated its BIT with the United States; however, on October 29, 2007 it notified the International Centre for Settlement of Investment Disputes (ICSID) that under the Washington Convention, art. 25(4) it will not submit to the jurisdiction of the Centre and disputes related to the management of its non-renewable natural resources, including mining and hydrocarbon resources. For a text of the letter in Spanish, *see* Hernán Pérez Loose, OGEMID e-mail dated Nov. 15, 2007, *available at* OGEMID archives, at www.transnational-dispute-management.com.

[13] News Release, ICSID, Bolivia Submits a Notice under Article 71 of the ICSID Convention (May 16, 2007).

[14] Saul Hudson, *Venezuela to Quit IMF, World Bank*, Reuters, Apr. 30, 2007.

[15] Specifically with European Commission Treaty, art. 307, *supra* note 10.

[16] Bulgaria, Estonia, Latvia, Lithuania, Poland, Romania, and the Czech and Slovak Republics.

[17] The EC at the outset pushed for the termination of these treaties. Later, however, it retreated from this position, because of the willingness of the U.S. officials to resolve the issue through negotiation.

[18] Understanding Concerning Certain U.S. Bilateral Investment Treaties signed by the United States, the European Commission, and acceding and candidate countries for accession to the European Union, Sept. 22, 2003, *available at* http://www.state.gov/s/1 /2003/44366.htm. The interpretation of these exceptions seems to lie at the heart of a dispute between Cargill, the U.S. agricultural company, and Poland. *Cargill, Inc. v. Poland* (UNCITRAL Arbitration) (the case was originally filed under the ICSID Additional Facility rules as ICSID Case No. ARB(AF)/04/2. In 2005, however, the parties discontinued those proceedings and with the tribunal's consent agreed to pursue the matter under the UNCITRAL Arbitration Rules). *See* the list of concluded cases at the ICSID Web site, http://icsid.worldbank.org.

Later the European Commission expanded its investigation to some of the older members of the EU, such as Austria, Finland, Sweden, and Denmark, and requested that they bring some of their preaccession BITs with non-EU members into compliance with the EC Treaty.[19] However, these countries have refused to take action, maintaining that a mere potential for conflict between their obligations under their BITs with those under the EC Treaty is not sufficient to render the BITs ineffective; rather, they insist that the European Commission must demonstrate that they have actually violated a provision of the EC treaty.[20] As a result, the EC filed claims against three out of the four countries (Austria, Sweden, and Finland) before the European Court of Justice (ECJ).[21] As of November 2007, the ECJ had not rendered its decision on this issue.[22]

All in all these developments suggest that the global investment treaty regime, even if it requires a burdensome, expensive, and difficult process of renegotiation and amendment, will remain in place.

B. Trends in the Development of Substantive and Procedural Provisions of Investment Treaties

The core provisions of investment treaties have remained largely unchanged, but more recent investment agreements of some countries are much more detailed. Governments of the NAFTA countries (particularly the United States and Canada)

---

[19] Press release, Internal Market, Infringement cases against the U.K., Portugal, Denmark, Austria, Sweden, and Finland (IP/05/352, Mar. 22, 2005), *available at* http://europa.eu/rapid/pressReleasesAction.do?reference=IP/05/352&format=HTML&aged=1&language=EN&guiLanguage=fr.

[20] Damon Vis-Dunbar, *European Governments Defend BITs in Lawsuit Brought by EU Executive Branch*, ITN (Mar. 16, 2007).

[21] *See* Action brought on June 2, 2006—*Comm'n of the European Communities v. Kingdom of Sweden*, Case C-249/06, O.J. C178/27 (2006); Action brought on May 5, 2006—*Comm'n of the European Communities v. Republic of Austria*, Case C-205/06, O.J. C165/30 (2006); Action brought on Feb. 27, 2007—*Comm'n of the European Communities v. Republic of Finland*, Case C-118/07.

[22] The issue of the incompatibility between the EC Treaty and the obligations of the European Union (EU) members under their BITs was the centerpiece of a recent arbitral award, *Eastern Sugar v. Czech Republic*. In that case, the Czech Republic argued that the Czech-Netherlands BIT, which was the basis of the claim, was implicitly terminated after the accession of the Czech Republic to the EU on May 1, 2004, insofar as it was in conflict with the EC Treaty. It relied *inter alia* on a letter by the European Commission addressed to the Czech government and a European Commission internal note. According to these documents, in the post-accession period, BITs between EU member states are not applicable to matters that fall within the competence of the community and should be terminated. The arbitral tribunal ultimately rejected the Czech Republic's arguments in this regard. *See Eastern Sugar v. Czech Republic*, SCC Case No. 088/2004 (Mar. 27, 2007), ¶¶ 118–29. In December 2007, the EU members signed the Treaty of Lisbon, amending the Treaty on European Union and the Treaty establishing the European Community, 2007 O.J. (C 306). If this treaty, as planned, comes into force in 2009, it will grant exclusive competence to the European Commission with respect to foreign direct investment. It remains to be seen how this development impacts the existing and future investment treaties of the EU members.

have insisted on more detailed investment treaties,[23] a consequence of their experience as parties to several investment arbitrations under Chapter 11 of NAFTA. Although perhaps not taking matters as far as the NAFTA signatories, other governments certainly have made changes in their general attitude to investment agreements. For example, China has adopted a more liberal approach in its recent BITs: A comparison between China's older BIT with New Zealand and more recent Chinese BITs with Germany and the Netherlands demonstrates that the latter BITs permit direct investor-state arbitration for violation of all substantive protection of the BITs.[24] In contrast, the older Chinese BITs limited investor-state arbitration to determination of the compensation for expropriation.[25]

One area where more detailed treaties have attracted particular attention is the issue of transparency in investment arbitration proceedings, including confidentiality and third-party participation. Other innovative new features of investment treaties include tightening up the language of some of the substantive standards of protection in certain BITs,[26] as well as adding new provisions such as those precluding frivolous claims.[27]

1. Confidentiality in Investor-State Arbitration

Because many investor-related disputes arise from the application of government regulations in areas of public concern, such as energy, natural resources, the environment, and public health, some entities (particularly NGOs) have been quick to criticize the importation of commercial arbitration's confidentiality provisions. The following excerpt is typical of the NGO position on confidentiality:

> While such confidentiality may be attractive for investors seeking to exercise their rights away from the glare of public scrutiny, it ought to be deeply worrying to the sustainable development community. As far as can be ascertained, emerging disputes under bilateral investment treaties appear to be targeting government regulations in key areas of public policy such as water, energy, environment and health. Despite this, the resolution of such disputes is left in the hands of secretive tribunals that take no account of the wider public interests at stake, nor of the various safeguards available under domestic legal systems. Clearly, this system, which may have been well-suited for purely commercial arbitration,

---

[23] The U.S. Model BIT of 2004, for example, contains thirty-seven articles compared to pre-NAFTA models, which contained sixteen articles. Treaty between the Government of the United States of America and the Government of [Country] Concerning the Encouragement and Reciprocal Protection of Investment (Model BIT 2004), *available at* http://www.ustr.gov/assets/ Trade_Sectors/Investment/Model_BIT/asset_upload_file847_6897.pdf [hereinafter U.S. Model BIT].

[24] *See, e.g.,* China-Germany BIT (2003), art. 8.

[25] *See, e.g.,* China-New Zealand BIT (1988), art. 13(3).

[26] *See, e.g.,* the U.S. approach in its new Model BIT to define fair and equitable treatment or indirect expropriation. On these, *see* respectively Chapters XVII and XVI.

[27] For example, the 2004 U.S. Model BIT includes provisions for special state-to-state arbitration early in the process to preclude frivolous claims. U.S. Model BIT, *supra* note 23, at art. 37. *See also* Won-Mog Choi, *The Present and Future of the Investor-State Dispute Settlement Paradigm,* 10 J. Int'l Econ. L. 725 (2007).

is deeply unsatisfactory in an era when investment agreements are starting to be wielded as trump cards against sensitive public policies.[28]

There has been a great deal of discussion about the openness of investment arbitration proceedings, and it should be said that both private investors and governments have important reasons to oppose unfettered public access. Investors may fear the disclosure of confidential business information, trade secrets, investment strategies, and other sensitive information that could harm their future business. Meanwhile, governments are often reluctant to expose to public view the extent to which narrow interest groups have captured administrative and regulatory structures, fearful of gaining an exaggerated reputation as a poor host for foreign investment.

However, these and other arguments appear to be gradually losing ground, replaced by a realization that the vitality of the investor-state arbitration process, and its continued utility as a catalyst for investment flows, to some degree depends on solid legitimacy in the court of public opinion. As a result, some elements of the arbitral proceedings have been made publicly accessible. And in 2002, for example, United Parcel Service (UPS) requested that the entire NAFTA arbitration it initiated against Canada be made fully open to the public. Canada agreed, making *UPS v. Canada* one of the first investor-state arbitrations to be conducted in a truly open fashion.[29]

2. Amicus Curiae Briefs in Investor-State Arbitration

Some commentators have suggested amicus curiae submissions as a method to allow some public participation in investment arbitration on matters of public concern and to alleviate widespread frustration and hostility against the new international investment arbitration regime, particularly among environmental organizations.[30] *Amicus curiae* is a Latin phrase, literally translated as "friend of the court."[31] In American court practice, nonparties to an action with a strong interest in the subject matter often petition the court for permission to make a submission.

---

[28] Luke Peterson, *Changing Investment Litigation, Bit by BIT*, 5(4) Bridges Between Trade & Sustainable Dev. (May 2001) at 5, 8.

[29] UPS Press Release, UPS Proposal to Open NAFTA Arbitration Hearing to Public Accepted (July 23, 2002), *available at* http://biz.yahoo.com/cnw/020723/ups_nafta_hearing_1.html.

[30] Dan Price, Testimony before the Subcommittee on Trade of the House Committee on Ways and Means, Hearing on the Summit of the Americas and Prospects for Free Trade in the Hemisphere (May 8, 2001), *available at* http://waysandmeans.house.gov/trade/107cong/5-8-01/5-8pric.htm.

[31] *Black's Law Dictionary* 82 (6th ed. 1990); *see also Aguas Provinciales de Santa Fe S.A., Suez, Sociedad General de Aguas de Barcelona S.A. & Inter Aguas Servicios Integrales del Agua S.A. v. Argentina*, ICSID Case No. ARB/03/17 (Order in Response to a Petition for Participation as an Amicus Curiae, Mar., 17 2006), ¶ 13.

As discussed extensively in Chapter VII, some civil society groups have obtained the right to submit amicus curiae briefs in several instances, including, prominently, *Methanex* and *UPS*.[32] ICSID tribunals also have given permission for amici in several cases involving water rights.[33] As a result of these pressures, NAFTA parties issued an interpretive note officially granting NAFTA tribunals the right to accept such submissions, and[34] ICSID followed suit by promulgating a new amended rule 37.[35] Similar movements are underway in an United Nations Commission on International Trade Law (UNCITRAL) Working Group on the subject.[36] The civil society groups are looking for more, though, seeking the right to participate in the cases as a party.[37] At least one arbitral tribunal has held that

---

[32] *E.g., Methanex Corp. v. U.S.* (Decision of the Tribunal on Petitions from Third Persons to Intervene as Amici Curiae, Jan. 15, 2001); *United Parcel Service (UPS) v. Canada* (Decision on Jurisdiction, Nov. 22, 2003); *see also Aguas Argentinas, S.A., Suez, Sociedad General de Aguas de Barcelona, S.A. & Vivendi Universal, S.A. v. Argentina*, ICSID Case No. ARB/03/19 (Order in Response to Petition for Transparency and Participation as *Amicus Curiae*, May 19, 2005); *Biwater Gauf Ltd. vs. United Republic of Tanzania*, ICSID Case No. ARB/05/22 (Procedural Order No. 5 (Amicus Curiae), Feb. 2, 2007). Both *Methanex* and *UPS* were arbitrated under UNCITRAL rules.

[33] In one water rights case, *Aguas del Tunari S.A. v. Republic Bolivia*, ICSID Case No. ARB/02/3, some three hundred petitioners sought *amicus* status. See Jack Coe, *Transparency in the Resolution of Investor-State Disputes—Adoption, Adaptation, and NAFTA Leadership*, 54 U. Kan. L. Rev. 1339 (2006).

[34] Free Trade Comm'n, Statement on Non-Disputing Party Participation (2004), *available at* http://www.state.gov/documents/organization/38791.pdf ("No provision of the North American Free Trade Agreement . . . limits a Tribunal's discretion to accept written submissions from a person or entity that is not a disputing party. . . .").

[35] ICSID Rules, art. 37 (allowing *amicus* submissions if the "non-disputing party submission does not disrupt the proceeding or unduly burden or unfairly prejudice either party").

[36] *See* Jan Paulsson & Georgios Petrochilos, *Revision of the UNCITRAL Arbitration Rules*, report to the UNCITRAL Secretariat 71–72 (2006), *available at* www.uncitral.org/pdf/english/news/arbrules_report.pdf. These revisions may deal with a number of issues peculiar to investment arbitration.

[37] *See, e.g., UPS*, *supra* note 32, Amicus Petitions by the Canadian Union of Postal Workers and the Council of Canadians, Nov. 8, 2000, *available at* http://naftaclaims.com/Disputes/Canada/UPS/UPSAmicusPetitionCUPW.pdf.

NAFTA does not allow such participation.[38] It remains to be seen how future tribunals deal with this issue.

C. Future Jurisprudence of Investment Protection: Possible Problems and Solutions

The jurisprudence of investment protection is evolving rapidly. The reasons for this are varied, and the development is welcomed by some and criticized by others. The evolution can be seen in previous discussions in this book of fair and equitable treatment,[39] full protection and security,[40] expropriation,[41] most favored nation treatment,[42] and national treatment.[43] The norms in these areas are both elaborate and expanding, and the multiplicity of proceedings and awards[44] may begin to confuse the picture for some. New theories about the contours of this area of law and the practice of borrowing from other legal disciplines such as administrative law add to the complexity of these issues.[45]

---

[38] *Id.,* Decision on Petitions for Intervention and Participation as Amici Curiae, Oct. 17, 2001, ¶¶ 35–43, *available at* http://naftaclaims.com/Disputes/Canada/UPS/UPSDecisionRe ParticipationAmiciCuriae.pdf.

[39] *See* Chapter XVII.

[40] *Id.*

[41] *See* Chapter XVI.

[42] *See* Chapter XV.

[43] *Id.*

[44] As of November 23, 2007, awards (jurisdiction, merits, damages, annulment) were rendered in various ad hoc and institutional arbitrations. *See* www.investmentclaims.com. ICSID Secretariat reported that as of July 2007, it had registered a total of 236 cases. 24(1) ICSID News, 2.

[45] For example, some scholars have suggested that investment treaty arbitration is more similar to administrative review of governmental action than to commercial arbitration. *See* Thomas W. Wälde, *The Specific Nature of Investment Arbitration—Report of the Director of Studies of the English-Speaking Section of the Center*, in New Aspects of International Investment Law (Kahn & Wälde eds., Martinus Nijhoff Publishers 2007); *see also* Gus van Harten, *Investment Treaty Arbitration and Public Law* (Oxford University Press 2007); This potentially opens the door for arbitral tribunals to resort to analogy to administrative law to fill the gaps in the international investment law. Similar analogies have been made to international human rights law and potential applicability of its norms in the investment field. On the concept of indirect expropriation, for example, *Tecmed v. Mexico* first imported such norms from the European Court of Human Rights jurisprudence into investment treaty arbitration. *See* Chapter XVI.

The amounts involved in investment arbitrations are often large, and some actions challenge national environmental and other regulations, previously yet erroneously thought by some to be immune from international scrutiny. Thus many NGOs question the very legitimacy of privately initiated international arbitration[46]; and some states, notably the United States, long a principal advocate of investment dispute resolution, when confronted with the possibility of losing a case,[47] appeared to be getting cold feet.[48] As a consequence of these developments, there is a clamor for solutions for these problems, particularly the *problem* of *incoherence* in the emerging jurisprudence.[49] There are a number of suggested solutions to this situation.

One, inertia, may carry the day, and we will simply muddle along as we are doing currently. That is to say, as we have more experience with cases, what now appears to be a collection of disparate results will become a more solid body. Unlike in the past, awards are increasingly published,[50] and the many lawyers working on these cases as counsel and arbitrators, a veritable college of lawyers[51] as well as interested

---

[46] *See, e.g.,* Synthesis of Major Concerns expressed by the Center for International Environmental Law (CIEL) and the International Institute for Sustainable Development (IISD) in Investment Tent at the Americas Trade and Sustainable Development Forum in Miami, Nov. 2003, *available at* http://www.ciel.org/Tae/FTAA_Synthesis_24Nov03.html ("The fact that investment disputes are decided not by a standing and impartial court, but by practicing commercial lawyers whose independence is not guaranteed, undermines the legitimacy of the proceedings and decisions"). *See also* Charles H. Brower II, *Structure, Legitimacy and NAFTA's Investment Chapter*, 36 Vand. J. Int'l L. 37 (2003); and Franck, *supra* note 3.

[47] The United States long thought of itself as a capital exporter; it is also the largest importer of capital, specifically foreign direct investment (FDI). Incidentally, it has yet to lose a case.

[48] Daniel Price, *NAFTA Chapter 11: Investor-State Dispute Settlement: Frankenstein or Safety Valve?*, 26 Can.-U.S. L.J. 107 (2001) (". . . countries that have traditionally been claimants are now defendants. Remember, most BITs were concluded with developing countries that have very little investment either in the United States or Canada. These rules and mechanisms were thus perfectly acceptable to the U.S. when invoked against the laws and actions of developing countries. Now NAFTA has come along and said to the United States and Canada, 'you too can be a defendant.' And now these very same rules and procedures are seen as threats to sovereignty and democracy. The shoe is on the other foot, and it is not as comfortable.")

[49] *See, e.g.,* Franck, *supra* note 3.

[50] Apart from hard copies of the awards published in International Legal Materials, Mealey's or other publications, several Web sites make the awards available to the public. *See, e.g.,* www.investmentclaims.com; www.worldbank.org/icsid; www.naftaclaims.com; www.law.uvic.ca/newcombe.

[51] *Cf.* Oscar Schachter, *The Invisible College of International Lawyers*, 72 NW. U. L. Rev. 217 (1977).

scholars, will begin to sort all this out.⁵² This is especially likely because of the lively and full commentaries now available on Web sites such as those of Ian Laird and Todd Weiler⁵³ and Listservs such as that of Thomas Wälde.⁵⁴ In 2007 several

---

52   Although it is too early to be very specific, is it possible that paragraph 154 from *Tecnicas Medioambientales Tecmed S.A. v. The United Mexican States*, ICSID Case No. ARB (AF)/00/2 (2003) [hereinafter *Tecmed*], is the kind of language that may become the standard in a particular area, cited by subsequent arbitrators?

> The Arbitral Tribunal considers that this provision of the Agreement, in light of the good faith principle established by international law, requires the Contracting Parties to provide to international investments treatment that does not affect the basic expectations that were taken into account by the foreign investor to make the investment. The foreign investor expects the host State to act in a consistent manner, free from ambiguity and totally transparently in its relations with the foreign investor, so that it may know beforehand any and all rules and regulations that will govern its investments, as well as the goals of the relevant policies and administrative practices or directives, to be able to plan its investment and comply with such regulations. Any and all State actions conforming to such criteria should relate not only to the guidelines, directives or requirements issued, or the resolutions approved thereunder, but also to the goals underlying such regulations. The foreign investor also expects the host State to act consistently, i.e. without arbitrarily revoking any preexisting decisions or permits issued by the state that were relied upon by the investor to assume its commitments as well as to plan and launch its commercial and business activities. The investor also expects the state to use the legal instruments that govern the actions of the investor or the investment in conformity with the function usually assigned to such instruments, and not to deprive the investor of its investment without the required compensation.
> . . .

A number of other tribunals since then have quoted the above standard. *See, e.g., Parkerings-Compagniet AS v. Lithuania*, ICSID Case No. ARB/05/8 (Award of Sept. 11, 2007), ¶ 330; *Siemens v. Argentina*, ICSID Case No. ARB/02/8 (Award of Feb. 6, 2007), ¶ 298; *LG&E v. Argentina*, ICSID Case No. ARB/02/1 (Decision on Liability Oct. 3, 2006), ¶ 127; *Azurix Corp. v. Argentina*, ICSID Case No. ARB/01/12 (Final Award July 14, 2006), ¶ 371; *Saluka*, supra note 9, ¶ 302; *Eureko B.V. v. Poland*, ad hoc arbitration (Partial Award on Liability Aug. 19, 2005), ¶ 235; *CMS Gas Transmission Co. v. Argentina*, ICSID Case No. ARB/01/08 (Final Award May 12, 2005), ¶ 268; *Occidental Exploration & Prod. Co. v. Republic of Ecuador*, LCIA Case No. UN3467 (Final Award July 1, 2004), ¶ 185 [hereinafter *Occidental*]; *MTD Equity Sdn. Bhd. & MTD Chile S.A. v. Republic of Chile*, ICSID Case No. ARB/01/7 (Award of May 25, 2004), ¶¶ 114–5 [hereinafter *MTD*]. Note that this development takes place notwithstanding the absence of formal *stare decisis* in international arbitration or international courts. *See, e.g.,* in the context of NAFTA Chapter 11, J. C. Thomas, *A Reply to Professor Brower*, 40 Col. J. Transnat'l L. 433, 462 ("The NAFTA Parties recognized that although an award is binding only on the parties to the dispute, practically speaking, NAFTA tribunals would be interested in the awards of other tribunals and that although *stare decisis* does not apply, a body of jurisprudence would emerge over time").

53   Ian Laird and Todd Weiler, for instance, manage www.investmentclaims.com. Todd Weiler also manages www.naftaclaims.com. *See also* Prof. Andrew Newcombe's Web site at www.law.uvic.ca/newcombe.

54   Thomas W. Wälde is moderator of an online Listserv called OGEMID. This electronic discussion list has been set up under the auspices of the Centre for Energy, Petroleum & Mineral Law & Policy (CEPMLP) "to provide professionals with a special interest in oil-gas-energy-mining and infrastructure investment, legislative reform, contracting, arbitration and other forms of dispute management with a forum for peer discussion." *See* http://www.dundee.ac.uk/cepmlp/journal/html/ogemidannounce.html.

conferences and publications were dedicated to the function of precedent in investment arbitration.[55]

However, there is a question whether the current system will be allowed to muddle through. Some, especially those entities that lose in arbitration, may be unwilling to wait for the development of this area of law to run its course. For those in this situation, current options are limited. In the case of ICSID arbitrations, a losing party can seek annulment[56] (this is not an appeal on the merits, but, even if unsuccessful, can introduce delay in enforcement). In the case of the ICSID Additional Facility (used in NAFTA cases because Mexico is not an ICSID party and Canada has only recently become one) arbitrations under the UNCITRAL rules, or any other ad hoc or institutional arbitration, national courts provide only limited recourse.[57]

Confronted with these perceived problems, suggestions have been made to improve the system. These include a permanent trial court[58] or, less radically, a permanent roster of arbitrators.[59] Presumably, it is thought that either suggestion

---

[55] British Institute of International and Comparative Law (BIICL), The Emerging Jurisprudence of International Investment Law, BIICL 9th Investment Treaty Forum (Sept. 14, 2007); International Arbitration Institute (IAI), The Precedent in International Arbitration Seminar (Dec. 14, 2007); see also Matthew Weiniger ed., Precedent in Investment Arbitration, TDM Special Issue (2008); Christoph Schreuer & Matthew Weiniger, *Conversations Across Cases–Is There a Doctrine of Precedent in Investment Arbitration?*, in *The Oxford Handbook of International Investment Law* (Muchlinski, Ortino, & Schreuer eds., Oxford University Press 2008). The questions raised in the BIICL conference highlight some of the issues that the legal community is now facing: "Is there 'jurisprudence' in international law? Is there one emerging in international investment law? If there is an emerging jurisprudence, how is it created? Is there, as we have seen in the development of the common law, a *de facto* system of precedent in international law, generally, and in investment law, particularly? What is the evidence of the emergence of this system? Does this system, if it exists, operate satisfactorily? If not, why not, and how should it operate?" Ian Laird, *Forum Introductory Remarks*, The Emerging Jurisprudence of International Investment Law, BIICL 9th Investment Treaty Forum, Sept. 14, 2007, London.

[56] *See* Chapter XX.

[57] United Nations Convention for the Recognition and Enforcement of Foreign Arbitral Awards, New York, June 10, 1958, *available at* http://www.jus.uio.no/lm/un.arbitration.recognition.and.enforcement.convention.new.york.1958/.

[58] Barton Legum, *Trends and Challenges in Investor-State Arbitration,* 19 Arb. Int'l 1143, 1147 (2003) ("if the result of the next few years is a collection of disparate decisions with widely varying and case-specific approaches to the issues presented, states may be tempted to consider replacing the system of ad hoc tribunals with a standing one that is perhaps capable of producing more consistent and coherent results").

[59] *See, e.g.,* Gus van Harten & Martin Loughlin, *Investment Treaty Arbitration as a Species of Global Administrative Law,* E.J.I.L. 17 121, 147–48 (2006) (discussing criticisms of appointing non-permanent arbitrators).

would lead to greater consistency in awards and their rationales.[60] The most prominent set of suggestions calls for the creation of some type of appellate body.[61] Thus the United States Trade Promotion Act calls for[62] "(iv) . . . an appellate body or similar mechanism to provide coherence to the interpretations of investment provisions in trade agreements . . . ." Presumably pursuant to this call, the new U.S. Model BIT provides the following:

> If a separate, multilateral agreement enters into force between the Parties that establishes an appellate body for purposes of reviewing awards rendered by tribunals constituted pursuant to international trade or investment arrangements to hear investment disputes, the Parties shall strive to reach an agreement that would have such appellate body review awards rendered under Article 34 in arbitrations commenced after the multilateral agreement enters into force between the Parties.[63]

The U.S. Model BIT also provides that

> [W]ithin three years after the date of entry into force of this Treaty, the Parties shall consider whether to establish a bilateral appellate body or similar mechanism to review awards rendered under Article 34 in arbitrations commenced after they establish the appellate body or similar mechanism.[64]

The investment chapters of recent U.S. FTAs and draft FTAs have similar provisions.[65] On October 22, 2004, ICSID released a discussion paper on possible improvements in its arbitration system, including a discussion of a possible appellate

---

[60] Again, we should make clear that we do not necessarily accept the charge that there is that much inconsistency, greater, for example, than that in domestic litigation. *Cf.* Jonathan Charney, *Is International Law Threatened by Multiple International Law Tribunals?* 271 Recueil des Cours 101, 347 (1998) ("in several core areas of international law the different international tribunals of the late twentieth century do share a coherent understanding of that law").

[61] The notion appears to derive from the World Trade Organization (WTO) Appellate Body; of course, the latter is different in that it deals with state-to-state disputes and an integrated set of agreements and norms. *See* Developments on Discussions for the Improvement of the Framework for ICSID Arbitration and the Participation of Developing Countries, South Center Analytical Note, SC/TADP/AN/INV/1, ¶¶ 53-54. Meanwhile, the functioning of ICSID will continue to be an important element in the future of investment treaty arbitration. *Cf.* note 45 above.

[62] Bipartisan Trade Promotion Authority Act, *supra* note 4, at (b)(3)(G)(iv).

[63] U.S. Model BIT, *supra* note 23, *at* art. 28(10); *cf.* US-Uruguay BIT (2004), art. 28(10).

[64] U.S. Model BIT, *supra* note 23, Annex D; *cf.* US-Uruguay BIT, *supra* note 63, at Annex E.

[65] *See e.g.*, Dominican Republic-Central America-U.S. Free Trade Agreement (2004), art. 10.20(10); U.S.-Morocco Free Trade Agreement (2004), art. 10.19(10); U.S.-Chile Free Trade Agreement (2003), art. 10.19(10); Singapore- U.S. Free Trade Agreement (2003), art. 15.19(10). All of the treaties are available at the U.S. Trade Representative's Web site, http://www.ustr.gov/Trade_Agreements/Bilateral/Section_Index.html.

body.[66] In a follow-up paper, which was issued on May 12, 2005, discussion on the subject was not included.[67]

Is the idea of an appellate body a good one? Is it feasible? Surely, there would be many issues to be resolved. Would there be one or more such bodies?[68] How would it be *attached* to the more than 2,500 existing BITs and other relevant agreements? Presumably, both government and private parties would have to give timely consents.[69]

In the coming years, the system of international investment arbitration will undoubtedly evolve, and the various reform proposals may be adopted in greater or lesser degree. Regardless of the changes that are adopted, we are confident the system itself will survive.

---

[66] ICSID Secretariat, *Possible Improvements of the Framework for ICSID Arbitration*, Discussion Paper (Oct. 22, 2004), ¶ 6, *available at* http://www.worldbank.org/icsid/improve-arb.pdf ("A further, potentially most important, issue that has been raised is whether an appellate mechanism is desirable to ensure coherence and consistency in case law generated in ICSID and other investor-to-State arbitrations initiated under investment treaties").

[67] The Secretariat stated that ". . . it would be premature to attempt to establish such an ICSID mechanism at this stage, particularly in view of the difficult technical and policy issues raised in the Discussion Paper." ICSID, *Suggested Changes to the ICSID Rules and Regulations*, Working Paper of the ICSID Secretariat (May 12, 2005), ¶ 4, *available at* http://www.worldbank.org/icsid/052405-sgmanual.pdf.

[68] Presumably having one such body (possibly added to ICSID), as opposed to more, would assure more consistency.

[69] One suggestion (possibly for existing investments and/or disputes) is to seek a *compromis* from the disputing parties after the dispute has arisen, but before any arbitration has begun, agreeing to appellate jurisdiction in the new ICSID appellate body (assuming there is one). Would this work? Would it be available in non-ICSID disputes? One can think of many other questions of this sort.

Select Bibliography

Chapter 1

Akinsanya, Adeoye, *International Protection of Direct Foreign Investments in the Third World*, 36 Int'l Comp. L. Q. 58 (1987).

American Law Institute, *Restatement (Third) of the Foreign Relations Law of the United States* (American Law Institute 1987).

Barsh, Russel L., *A Special Session of the U.N. General Assembly Rethinks the Economic Rights and Duties of States*, 85 Am. J. Int'l. L. 192 (1991).

Brownlie, Ian, *Principles of Public International Law* (Oxford Univ. Press 6th ed. 2003).

Cable, James, *Gunboat Diplomacy: Political Applications of Limited Naval Force* (Praeger 1981).

Cobb, Matthew B., *The Development of Arbitration in Foreign Investment*, 16(4) Mealey's Int'l Arb. Rep. 12 (April 2001).

Cremades, Bernardo M., *Promoting and Protecting International Investments*, 2000 Int'l Arb. L. Rev. 53.

Egger, Peter and Michael Pfaffermayr, *The Impact of Bilateral Investment Treaties on Foreign Direct Investment*, 32 J. Comp. Econ. 788 (2004).

Freeman, Alwyn V., *The International Responsibility of States for Denial of Justice* (Kraus Reprint Co. 1938).

Geiger, Rainer, *Towards a Multilateral Agreement on Investment*, 31 Cornell Int'l L.J. 467 (1998).

IMF, *Balance of Payments Manual* (4th ed. 1977).

International Bank for Reconstruction and Development, *Report of the Executive Directors on the Convention on the Settlement of Investment Disputes Between States and Nationals of Other States*, 4 I.L.M. 524 (1965).

Jolly, Curtis M., Mary Knapp, and Tridoyo Kusumastanto, *U.S. Competitive Position and Capital Investment Flows in the Economic Citizen Market: Constraints and Opportunities of the U.S. Investor Program*, 57(2) Am. J. Econ. and Sociology 155 (1998).

Nathan, K. V. S. K., *The ICSID Convention: The Law of the International Centre for Settlement of Investment Disputes* (Juris Publishing 2000).

OECD, *Code of Liberalization of Capital Movements* (OECD 2003).

———, *Code of Liberalization of Current Invisible Operations* (OECD 1997).

Peterson, Luke E., *Bilateral Investment Treaties and Development Policy-Making* (IISD 2004).

Pritchard, Robert, ed., *Economic Development, Foreign Investment and the Law* (Kluwer Law Int'l/International Bar Association 1996).

Ruddy, Frank, *Book Review: Foreign Investment in the Present and a New International Economic Order*, 84 Am. J. Int'l. L. 961 (1990).
Salacuse, Jeswald W. and Nicholas P. Sullivan, *Do BITs Really Work?: An Evaluation of Bilateral Investment Treaties and Their Grand Bargain*, 46 Harv. Int'l L.J. 67 (2005).
Shihata, Ibrahim, *Legal Treatment of Foreign Investment: The World Bank Guidelines* (Martinus Nijhoff 1993).
Sornarajah, M., *The International Law on Foreign Investment* (Cambridge Univ. Press 1994).
———, *Power and Justice in Foreign Investment Arbitration*, 14(3) J. Int'l Arb. 103 (1997).
Toope, Stephen J., *Mixed International Arbitration: Studies in Arbitration Between States and Private Persons* (Grotius 1990).
Tumman, John Peter and Craig F. Emmert, *The Political Economy of U.S. Foreign Direct Investment in Latin America: A Reappraisal*, 39-3 Latin American Research Review 9 (2004).
UNCTAD, *Bilateral Treaties in the Mid-1990s*, UNCTAD/ITE/IIA/2006/5 (United Nations 1998).
———, *World Investment Report 2006: FDI from Developing and Transition Economies: Implications for Development*, UNCTAD/WIR/2006 (United Nations 2006).
Weiler, Todd and Thomas W. Wälde, *Investment Arbitration under the Energy Charter Treaty in the Light of New NAFTA Precedents: Towards a Global Code of Conduct for Economic Regulation*, 1(2) Oil, Gas & Energy Law Intelligence 2 (2003).
Wilkins, Mira, *The History of Foreign Investment in the United States to 1914* (Harvard Univ. Press 1989).

Chapter 2

Aldrich, George H., *The Jurisprudence of the Iran-United States Claims Tribunal* (1996).
Al-Nauimi, Najeeb and Richard Meese, eds., *International Legal Issues Arising under the United Nations Decade of International Law* (Martinus Nijhoff 1995).
Amerasinghe, C. F., *Issue of Compensation for the Taking of Alien Property in the Light of Recent Cases and Practice*, 41 Int'l & Comp. L. Q. 22 (1992).
———, *Local Remedies in International Law* (Cambridge Univ. Press 2004).
American Law Institute, *Restatement (Third) of the Foreign Relations Law of the United States* (American Law Institute 1987).
Avramovich, Michael, *The Protection of International Investment at the Start of the Twenty-First Century: Will Anachronistic Notions of Business Render Irrelevant the OECD's Multilateral Agreement on Investment?* 31 J. Marshall L. Rev. 1201 (1998).
Blumenwitz, Dieter, "Treaties of Friendship, Commerce and Navigation" in *Encyclopedia of Public International Law* (Rudolf Bernhardt, ed., 1997).
Borchard, Edwin M., *Decisions of the Claims Commissions, United States and Mexico*, 20(3) Am. J. Int'l Law 536 (1926).
———, *The Diplomatic Protection of Citizens Abroad* (Banks Law Publication 1915).
———, *Government Liability in Tort*, 34 Yale L.J. 1 (1924).
Briggs, Herbert W., *The Settlement of the Mexican Claims Act of 1942*, 37 Am. J. Int'l L. 222 (1943).
Brower, Charles N. and Jason Brueschke, *The Iran-United States Claims Tribunal* (Martinus Nijhoff Publishers 1998).
Brownlie, Ian, *Principles of Public International Law* (Oxford Univ. Press 6th ed. 2003).

Cable, James, *Gunboat Diplomacy: Political Applications of Limited Naval Force* (Praeger 1981).

Clagett, Brice M., *The Expropriation Issue Before the Iran-United States Claims Tribunal: Is "Just Compensation" Required by International Law or Not?*, 16 L. & Pol'y in Int'l Bus. 813 (1984).

Clodfelter, Mark, *U.S. State Department Participation in International Economic Dispute Resolution*, 42 S. Texas L. R. 1273 (2001).

Cobb, Matthew B., *The Development of Arbitration in Foreign Investment*, 16(4) Mealey's Int'l Arb. Rep. 12 (April 2001).

Colomé, M. A. Ruíz, *Lump Sum Agreements in Spanish Practice*, 6 Spanish Y.B. Int'l L. 1 (2002).

Cornell, Peter and Arwen Handley, *Himpurna and Hub: International Arbitration in Developing Countries*, 15(9) Mealey's Int'l Arb. Rep. 39 (Sept. 2000).

Dalrymple, Christopher K., *Politics and Foreign Investment: The Multilateral Investment Guarantee and the Calvo Clause*, 29 Cornell Int'l L.J. 161 (1996).

Dodge, William S., *National Courts and International Arbitration: Exhaustion of Remedies and Res Judicata under Chapter Eleven of NAFTA*, 23 Hastings Int'l & Comp. L. Rev. 357 (2000).

Fales, Haliburton, *A Comparison of Compensation for Nationalization of Alien Property with Standards of Compensation under United States Domestic Law*, 5 Nw. J. Int'l L. & Bus. 871 (1983).

Fatouros, Arghyrios A., *Government Guarantees to Foreign Investors* (Columbia Univ. Press 1962).

Feller, Abraham Howard, *The Mexican Claims Commissions, 1923–1934, A Study in the Law and Procedure of International Tribunals* (Macmillan 1935).

Gaffney, John P., *Due Process in the World Trade Organization*, 14 Am. U. Int'l L. Rev. 1173 (1999).

Gianturco, Delio E., *Export Credit Agencies: The Unsung Giants of International Trade and Finance* (Quorum Books 2001).

Henkin, Louis et al., *International Law* (3d ed. 1993).

Higgins, Rosalyn, *Problems and Process: International Law and How We Use It* (Kluwer Law Int'l 1994).

Hobbes, Thomas, *Leviathan* (1660).

Hyde, Charles, *International Law* (1945).

Jennings, Sir Robert and Sir Arthur Watts, eds., *Oppenheim's International Law* (1992).

Jones, David Lloyd, *Act of Foreign State in English Law: The Ghost Goes East*, 22 Va. J. Int'l L. 433 (1982).

Lee, Donna, *Discrepancy Between Theory and Reality: Hong Kong's Court of Final Appeal and the Acts of State Doctrine*, 35 Colum. J. Transnat'l L. 175 (1997).

Legum, Barton, *The Innovation of Investor-State Arbitration Under NAFTA*, 43 Harv. Int'l L.J. 531 (2002).

Lillich, Richard B., *The Protection of Foreign Investment* (Syracuse Univ. Press 1965).

Lillich, Richard B. and Burns H. Weston, *Lumps Sum Agreements: Their Continuing Contribution to the Law of International Claims*, 82 Am. J. Int'l L. 69 (1988).

Link, Troland S., "Foreign Sovereign Immunity, Expropriation, Act of State, and Community" in *Commercial Law and Practice, Handbook Series Number 703* (Practicing Law Institute 1994).

Mann, F. A., *British Treaties for the Promotion and Protection of Investments*, 52 Brit. Y.B. Int'l L. 241 (1981).

Mehren, Robert von and P. Nicholas Kourides, *International Arbitration Between States and Foreign Private Parties: The Libyan Nationalization Cases*, 75 Am. J. Int'l. L. 476 (1981).

Mendelson, Maurice, "Runaway Train: Continuous Nationality Rule from Panavezys-Saldutiskis Railway Case to Loewen" in *International Investment Law and Arbitration: Leading Cases from the ICSID, NAFTA, Bilateral Treaties and Customary International Law* (Todd Weiler, ed., Cameron May 2005).

Orrego Vicuña, Fransisco, "Changing Approaches to the Nationality of Claims in the Context of Diplomatic Protection and International Dispute Settlement" in *Liber Amicorum Ibrahim Shihata: International Finance & Development Law* (Sabine Schlemmer-Schulte & Ko-Yung Tung, eds., 2001).

Percival, Sir John H., *International Arbitral Tribunals and the Mexican Claims Commissions*, 19(3) J. Comp. Legis. & Int'l L 98 (1937).

Phillips, G. Godfrey, *The Anglo-Mexican Special Claims Commission*, 49 L. Q. Rev. 226 (1933).

Robin, Patricia McKinstry, *The BIT Won't Bite: The American Bilateral Investment Treaty Program*, 33 Am. U.L. Rev. 931 (1984).

Rubins, Noah and N. Stephan Kinsella, *International Investment, Political Risk, and Dispute Resolution* (Oceana 2005).

Shaw, Malcolm N., *International Law* (Cambridge Univ. Press 5th ed. 2003).

Shea, Donald, *The Calvo Clause* (Univ. of Minnesota Press 1955).

Shihata, Ibrahim, *MIGA and Foreign Investment* (Martinus Nijhoff 1988).

―――, *Towards a Greater Depoliticization of Investment Disputes: The Roles of ICSID and MIGA* (ICSID 1992).

Sinclair, Ian, *Nationality of Claims: British Practice*, 27 Brit. Y.B. Int'l L. 125 (1950).

Singer, Michael, *The Act of State Doctrine of the United Kingdom: An Analysis, with Comparison to United States Practice*, 75 Am. J. Int'l L. 283 (1981).

Sornarajah, M., *The International Law on Foreign Investment* (Cambridge Univ. Press 1994).

―――, *Power and Justice in Foreign Investment Arbitration*, 14(3) J. Int'l Arb. 103 (1997).

Summers, Lionel, *La Clause Calvo: Tendences Nouvelles,* 12 Rev. de Droit Int'l 229 (1933).

Syrett, Harold C., ed., *The Papers of Alexander Hamilton* (1974).

Von Hennigs, Reinhard, *25th Anniversary of the Foreign Sovereign Immunities Act: European Convention on State Immunity and Other International Aspects of Sovereign Immunity*, 9 Willamette J. Int'l L. & Disp. Res. 185 (2001).

Weiler, Todd, "Saving Oscar Chin: Non-Discrimination in International Investment Law" in *Arbitrating Foreign Investment Disputes: Procedural and Substantive Aspects* (Norbert Horn, ed., Kluwer 2004).

Weston, Burns H. et al., *International Claims: Their Settlement by Lump Sum Agreements* (Transnational Publishers 1999).

Yergin, Daniel, *The Prize: The Epic Quest for Oil, Money & Power* (1992).

Chapter 3

Amissah, Austin, *The ACP/EEC Conciliation and Arbitration Rules*, 8 Arb. Int'l 167 (1992).

Arieti, Samuel A., *The Role of Mercosur as a Vehicle for Latin American Integration*, 6 Chi. J. Int'l L. 761 (2006).

Broches, Aron, *The Convention of the Settlement of Investment Disputes: Some Observations on Jurisdiction*, 5 Colum. J. Transnat'l L. 263 (1966).

―――, *Development of International Law by the International Bank for Reconstruction and Development*, 1965 ASIL Proc. 33.

Bruner, Christopher M., *Hemispheric Integration and the Politics of Regionalism: The Free Trade Area of the Americas (FTAA)*, 33 U. Miami Inter-Am. L. R. 1 (2002).

SELECT BIBLIOGRAPHY

Brusco, Gianluca, "Eurocentrism and Political Conditionality: The Case of the Lomé Convention" in *Europe, Diplomacy and Development* (Carol Cosgrove-Sacks, ed., 2001).

Cremades, Bernardo M., *Promoting and Protecting International Investments*, 2000 Int'l Arb. L. Rev. 53.

Denza, Eileen and Shelagh Brooks, *Investment Protection Treaties: United Kingdom Experience*, 36 Int'l & Comp. L. Q. 908 (1987).

Geiger, Rainer, *Towards a Multilateral Agreement on Investment*, 31 Cornell Int'l L.J. 467 (1998).

Goldhaber, Michael D., *A "Completely Appalling" Decision*, American Lawyer/Focus Europe, Summer 2004.

Grigera Naón, Horacio, *Foreign Investment Arbitration in Latin America: The New Environment*, ABA Sec. Int'l L. & Pract. (Winter 1995).

———, *The Settlement of Investment Disputes Between States and Private Parties*, 1 J. World Inv. 59 (2000).

Happ, Richard, *Dispute Resolution under Energy Charter Treaty*, 45 German Y.B. Int'l L. 331 (2003).

Hopkins, Lauren A., *Protecting Costa Rica's Osa Peninsula: CAFTA's Citizen Submission Process and Beyond*, 31 Vt. L. Rev. 381 (2007).

Hudson, David M. and Daniel C. Turner, *International and Interstate Approaches to Taxing Business Income*, 6 Nw. J. Int'l L. & Bus. 562 (1984).

International Chamber of Commerce, *Bilateral Treaties for International Investment* (1977).

Jackson, John H., William J. Davey, and Alan O. Sykes, *Legal Problems of International Economic Relations* (West Group 4th ed. 2002).

Kelley, G., *Multilateral Investment Treaties: A Balanced Approach to Multinational Corporations*, 39 Colum. J. Transnat'l L. 483 (2001).

Malanczuk, Peter, *State-State and Investor-State Dispute Settlement in the OECD Draft Multilateral Investment Agreement*, 3 J. Econ. L. 417 (2000).

OECD, *Draft Convention on the Protection of Foreign Property*, 7 I.L.M. 117 (1967).

Paulsson, Jan, *Arbitration Without Privity*, 10 ICSID Rev.—F.I.L.J. 232 (1995).

Ramsaran, Ramesh F., *Negotiating the Lomé IV Convention* (1990).

Reisman, W. Michael, *Unratified Treaties and Other Unperfected Acts in International Law: Constitutional Functions*, 35(3) Vand. J. Int'l L. 729 (2003).

Robert, Maryse et al., "Negotiating Investment Rules" in *An Integrated Approach to the European Union-Mercosur Association* (Paolo Giordano, ed., 2002).

Rosenbloom, H. David and Stanley I. Langbein, *United States Tax Treaty Policy: An Overview*, 19 Colum. J. Transnat'l L. 359 (1981).

Rubins, Noah, *Loewen v. United States: The Burial of an Investor-State Arbitration Claim*, 21(1) Arb. Int'l 1 (2005).

Salacuse, Jeswald W., "The Energy Charter Treaty and Bilateral Investment Treaty Regimes" in *The Energy Charter Treaty* (Thomas Wälde, ed., 1996).

Schwarzenberger, Georg, *Foreign Investments and International Law* (Fredrick A. Praeger 1969).

Schwebel, Stephen M., "The United States 2004 Model Bilateral Investment Treaty: An Exercise in the Regressive Development of International Law" in *Global Reflections on International Law, Commerce and Dispute Resolution, Liber Amicorum in Honour of Robert Briner* (ICC Publishing 2005).

Sholz, Wesley, *International Regulation of Foreign Direct Investment*, 31 Cornell Int'l L.J. 485 (1998).

Sornarajah, M., *The International Law on Foreign Investment* (Cambridge Univ. Press 1994).

Turner, Gillian, *Investment Protection through Arbitration: The Dispute Resolution Provisions of the Energy Charter Treaty*, 1 Int'l Arb. L. Rev. 166 (1998).

Vandevelde, Kenneth J., *United States Investment Treaties: Policy and Practice* (Kluwer 1992).
Vizentini, Paulo and Marianne Wiesebron, eds., *Free Trade for the Americas?: The United States' Push for the FTAA Agreement* (Zed Books 2004).
Wälde, Thomas, *Investment Arbitration under the Energy Charter Treaty: From Dispute Settlement to Treaty Implementation*, 12 Arb. Int'l 429 (2004).
Weiler, Todd, ed., *International Investment Law & Arbitration: Leading Cases from the ICSID, NAFTA, Bilateral Treaties and Customary International Law* (Cameron May 2005).
———, *NAFTA Investment Law and Arbitration: Past Issues, Current Practice, Future Prospects* (Transnational Publishers 2004).

Chapter 4

Alley, Edwin R., *International Arbitration: The Alternative of the Stockholm Chamber of Commerce*, 22 Int'l Law. 837 (1988).
Barron, William M., *Court-Ordered Consolidation of Arbitration Proceedings in the United States*, 4(1) J. Int'l Arb. 81 (1987).
Born, Gary B., *International Commercial Arbitration in the United States: Commentary and Materials* (Kluwer Law Int'l 2003).
Caron, David D., Lee M. Caplan, and Matti Pellonpää, *The UNCITRAL Arbitration Rules: A Commentary* (Oxford Univ. Press 2006).
Chao, Cedric and James Schurz, *International Arbitration: Selecting the Proper Forum*, 17(2) Mealey's Int'l Arb. Rep. 41 (2002).
Chiu, Julie, *Consolidation of Arbitral Proceeding and International Arbitration*, 7(2) J. Int'l Arb. 53 (1990).
Craig, Lawrence, William W. Park and Jan Paulsson, *International Chamber of Commerce Arbitration* (Oceana 3d ed. 2000).
Doak Bishop, R. and William Russell, *Survey of Arbitration Awards under Chapter 11 of the North American Free Trade Agreement*, 19 J. Int'l Arb. 505 (2002).
Dore, Isaak, *The UNCITRAL Framework for Arbitration in Contemporary Perspective* (Graham & Trotman/Martinus Nijhoff 1993).
Feldman, Mark, *The Annulment Proceedings and the Finality of ICSID Arbitral Awards*, 2 ICSID Rev.—F.I.L.J. 85 (1987).
Gaillard, Emmanuel, *L'affaire Sofidif ou les difficultés de l'arbitrage multipartite*, 3 Revue de l'Arbitrage 275 (1987).
Gaillard, Emmanuel and Yas Banifatemi, *The Meaning of "And" in Article 42(1), Second Sentence, of the Washington Convention: The Role of International Law in the ICSID Choice of Law Process*, 18 ICSID Rev.—F.I.L.J. 375 (2003).
Gaillard, Emmanuel and Yas Banifatemi, eds., *Annulment of ICSID Awards* (Juris Publishing 2004).
Gotanda, John Y., *Awarding Costs and Attorney's Fees in International Commercial Arbitrations*, 21 Mich. J. Int'l L. 1 (1999).
Hascher, Dominique T., *Consolidation of Arbitration by American Courts: Fostering or Hampering International Commercial Arbitration*, 1(2) J. Int'l Arb. 127 (1984).
Karrer, Pierre, *Arbitration Costs: Poker and Hide-and-Seek*, 3(1) J. Int'l Arb. 35 (1986).
Larsen, Clifford, *International Commercial Arbitration*, ASIL Insights (April 1997).
Park, William W., *The Lex Loci Arbitri and International Commercial Arbitration*, 32 Int'l Comp. L.Q. 21 (1983).

Redfern, Alan, Martin Hunter, Nigel Blackaby, and Constantine Partasides, *The Law and Practice of International Commercial Arbitration* (Sweet & Maxwell 4th ed. 2004).
Reisman, W. Michael, *The Breakdown of the Control Mechanism in ICSID Arbitration*, 4 Duke L.J. 739 (1989).
Rubins, Noah, *The Arbitral Seat is No Fiction*, 16(1) Mealey's Int'l Arb. Rep. 12 (2001).
Smutny, Abbey Cohen, *Arbitration before International Center for the Settlement of Investment Disputes*, 1(2) Oil, Gas, and Energy Law Intelligence (March 2003).
Van den Berg, Albert J., *Consolidated Arbitrations and the 1958 New York Arbitration Convention*, 2(4) Arb. Int'l 367 (1986).
Van Hof, J.J., *Commentary on the UNCITRAL Arbitration Rules: The Application by the Iran-U.S. Claims Tribunal* (Kluwer 1991).
Veeder, V. V., *Consolidation: More News from the Front Line*, 3(3) Arb. Int'l 262 (1987).
———, *Multi-party Disputes: Consolidation under English Law*, 2(4) Arb. Int'l 310 (1986).
Von Haersolte-van Hof, Jacomijn, *Consolidation under the English Arbitration Act 1996*, 13(4) Arb. Int'l 427 (1997).
Wetterfors, Jonas, *The First Investor-State Arbitration Award under The 1994 Energy Charter Treaty, Nykomb Synergetics Technology Holding AB, Sweden ("Nykomb") v. The Republic of Latvia: A Case Comment*, 2(1) T.D.M. (January 2005).

Chapter 5

Born, Gary B., *International Commercial Arbitration in the United States: Commentary and Materials* (Kluwer Law Int'l 2003).
Read, Pippa, *Delocalization of International Commercial Arbitration: Its Relevance in the New Millennium*, 10 Am. Rev. Int'l Arb. 177 (1999).
Schreuer, Christoph, *The ICSID Convention: A Commentary* (Cambridge Univ. Press 2000).

Chapter 6

Barrington, Louise, *Hubco v. WAPDA: Pakistan Top Court Rejects Modern Arbitration*, 11 Am. Rev. Int'l Arb. 385 (2000).
Cornell, Peter and Arwen Handley, *Himpurna and Hub: International Arbitration in Developing Countries*, 15(9) Mealey's Int'l Arb. Rep. 39 (Sept. 2000).
Gaillard, Emmanuel, ed., *Anti-Suit Injunctions in International Arbitration* (Juris Publishing & Staempfli Publishers 2005).
Kantor, Mark, *International Project Finance and Arbitration with Public Sector Entities: When Arbitrability Is a Fiction?* 24 Fordham Int'l L.J. 1122 (2001).
Lau, Martin, *Note on Société Générale de Surveillance SA v. Pakistan*, 19 Arb. Int'l 179 (2003).
Lew, Julian D. M., "Anti-Suit Injunctions Issued by National Courts to Prevent Arbitration Proceedings" in *Anti-Suit Injunctions in International Arbitration* (Emmanuel Gaillard, ed., 2005).
Majeed, Nudrat, *Commentary on the Hubco Judgment*, 16 Arb. Int'l 431 (2000).
Park, William W., *The Lex Loci Arbitri and International Commercial Arbitration*, 32 Int'l Comp. L.Q. 21 (1983).
Sarkar, Rumu, *Transnational Business Law, A Development Perspective* (Kluwer Law Int'l 2003).
Scherer, Matthias and Teresa Giovannini, *Anti-Arbitration and Anti-Suit Injunctions in International Arbitration: Some Remarks Following a Recent Judgment of the Geneva Court*, 2005(3) Stock. Int'l Arb. Rev. 201.

Chapter 7

Alexandrov, Stanimir, *Non-Appearance before the International Court of Justice*, 33 Colum. J. Transnat'l L. 41 (1995).

Amerasinghe, C. F., *Evidence in International Litigation* (Martinus Nijhoff 2005).

———, *Local Remedies in International Law* (Cambridge Univ. Press 2004).

Atik, Jeffery, "Legitimacy, Transparency and NGO Participation in the NAFTA Chapter 11 Process" in *NAFTA Investment Law and Arbitration: Past Issues, Current Practice, Future Prospects* (Todd Weiler, ed., Transnational Publishers 2004).

Bornstein, Brian E. and Julie M. Levitt, *Much Ado About 1782: A Look at the Recent Problems with Discovery in the United States for Use in Foreign Litigation under Section 1782*, 20 U. Miami Inter-Am. L. Rev. 429 (1989).

Broches, Aron, "The Convention on the Settlement of Investment Disputes Between States and Nationals of Other States: Applicable Law and Default Procedure" in *International Arbitration: Liber Amicorum for Martin Domke* (Pieter Sanders, ed., 1967).

Brower, Charles N. and Ronald E.M. Goodman, *Provisional Measures and the Protection of ICSID Jurisdictional Exclusivity Against Municipal Proceedings*, 6 ICSID Rev.—F.I.L.J. 431 (1991).

Caron, David D., Lee M. Caplan, and Matti Pellonpää, *The UNCITRAL Arbitration Rules: A Commentary* (Oxford Univ. Press 2006).

Crawford, James, *The International Law Commission's Articles on State Responsibility: Introduction, Text, and Commentaries* (Cambridge Univ. Press 2002).

De Fina, Antonio A., *Different Strokes for Different Folks: Institutional Appointment of Arbitrators*, Arb. and Disp. Res. L.J. 31 (March 2000).

Doak Bishop, R. and Lucy Reed, *Practical Guidelines for Interviewing, Selecting, and Challenging Party-Appointed Arbitrators in International Commercial Arbitration*, 14 Arb. Int'l 395 (1998).

Fitzmaurice, Sir Gerald, *The Problem of the Non-Appearing Defendant Government*, 51 Brit. Y.B. Int'l L. 89 (1980).

Fouchard, Philippe, *Fouchard Gaillard Goldman on International Commercial Arbitration* (Kluwer Law Int'l 1999).

Goldstein, Marc J., *Interpreting the New York Convention: When Should an Interlocutory Arbitral "Order" Be Treated as an "Award"?*, 2000 Swiss Arb. Assn. Bull. 830.

Green, J. C., *Are International Institutions Doing Their Job?*, 90 ASIL Proc. 62 (1996).

Griffith, Gavan, *Constitution of Arbitral Tribunals: The Duty of Impartiality in Tribunals or Choose Your Arbitrator Wisely*, 16 The Arbitrator: Journal of the Institute of Arbitrators Australia 229 (1998).

Hascher, Dominique T., *ICC Practice in Relation to the Appointment, Confirmation, Challenge and Replacement of Arbitrators*, 6(2) ICC Int'l Ct. Arb. Bull. 4 (1995).

Hellbeck, Eckhard R. and Carolyn B. Lamm, *Publicis Communication v. True North Communications, Inc.: Recognition and Enforcement of an Arbitral Tribunal's "Order,"* 3 Int'l Arb. L. Rev. N-45 (2000).

Helsing, Siegfried and John M. Townsend, *Bridging the Common Law-Civil Law Divide in International Arbitration*, 18(1) Arb. Int'l 59 (2002).

Highet, Keith, *Nonappearance and Disappearance before the ICJ*, 81 Am. J. Int'l L. 237 (1987).

Hirsch, Moshe, *The Arbitration Mechanism of the International Centre for the Settlement of Investment Disputes* (Martinus Nijhoff 1993).

Hunter, Martin and Jan Paulsson, *A Code of Ethics for Arbitrators in International Commercial Arbitration*, 13 Int'l Bus. Law. 153 (1985).

Lalive, Pierre, *The First World Bank Arbitration (Holiday Inns v. Morocco)—Some Legal Problems*, 50 Brit. Y.B. Int'l L. 123 (1980).

Lowenfeld, Andreas, *The Party-Appointed Arbitrator in International Controversies*, 30 Tex. Int'l L.J. 59 (1995).

Mackenzie, Ruth, "The Amicus Curiae in International Courts: Towards Common Procedural Approaches?" in *Civil Society, International Courts and Compliance Bodies* (Tullio Treves et al., eds., T.M.C. Asser Press 2005).

Marchac, Grégoire, *Interim Measures in International Commercial Arbitration under the ICC, AAA, LCIA and UNCITRAL Rules*, 10 Am. Rev. Int'l Arb. 123 (1999).

Masood, Arshad, *Default Procedure in Arbitration under the World Bank Convention*, 22 L. Rev. (India) 1 (1970).

———, *Provisional Measures of Protection in Arbitration under the World Bank Convention*, 1 Delhi L. R. 138 (1972).

McLaren, Douglas E., *Party-Appointed vs. List-Appointed Arbitrators*, 20 J. Int'l Arb. 233 (2003).

Miles, Wendy, *Practical Issues for Appointment of Arbitrators*, 20 J. Int'l Arb. 219 (2003).

Mistelis, Loukas, "Confidentiality and Third Party Participation" in *International Investment Law and Arbitration: Leading Cases from the ICSID, NAFTA, Bilateral Treaties and Customary International Law* (Todd Weiler, ed., Cameron May 2005).

Muller, Eva, *How Do International Institutions Select Arbitrators?*, 17 J. Int'l Arb. 157 (2000).

Northcote, William, *Default, Ex parte and Want of Prosecution Proceedings in International Commercial Arbitration*, 14 Advocate's Q. 319 (1992).

Parra, Antonio, "The Practices and Experience of ICSID" in *Conservatory and Provisional Measures in International Arbitration* (International Chamber of Commerce 1993).

———, *The Screening Power of the ICSID Secretary*, 2(1) News from ICSID 10 (1985).

Pietrowski, Robert, *Evidence in International Arbitration*, 22(3) Arb. Int'l 373 (2006).

Redfern, Alan, *Dangerous Dissents*, 71(3) J. Chartered Inst. Arb. 200 (2005).

———, *The 2003 Freshfields Lecture: Dissenting Opinions in International Commercial Arbitration; The Good, the Bad and the Ugly*, 20(3) Arb. Int'l 223 (2004).

———, *The Standards and Burden of Proof in International Arbitration*, 10(3) Arb. Int'l 317 (1994).

Redfern, Alan, Martin Hunter, Nigel Blackaby, and Constantine Partasides, *The Law and Practice of International Commercial Arbitration* (Sweet & Maxwell 4th ed. 2004).

Rubins, Noah, *The Arbitral Seat is No Fiction*, 16(1) Mealey's Int'l Arb. Rep. 12 (2001).

———, *In God We Trust, All Others Pay Cash: Security for Costs in International Commercial Arbitration*, 11 Am. Rev. Int'l Arb. 307 (2000).

———, *Swembalt v. Latvia: An Overview and the Dilemma of Default*, 2004(2) Stock. Arb. Rep. 119.

Rubins, Noah and N. Stephan Kinsella, *International Investment, Political Risk, and Dispute Resolution* (Oceana 2005).

Salomon, Claudia T., *Selecting an International Arbitrator: Five Factors to Consider*, 17(10) Mealey's Int'l Arb. Rep. 25 (2002).

Sandifer, Durward, *Evidence Before International Tribunals* (Univ. Press of Virginia 1975).

Schlosser, Peter F., *Coordinated Transnational Interaction in Civil Litigation and Arbitration*, 12 Mich. J. Int'l L. 150 (1990).

Schreuer, Christoph, *The ICSID Convention: A Commentary* (Cambridge Univ. Press 2000).

Schwartz, Johnson, *Court-Assisted Discovery in Aid of International Commercial Arbitrations: Two Recent U.S. Cases Regarding the Applicability of 28 U.S.C. § 1782*, 15(9) J. Int'l Arb. 53 (1998).

Schwebel, Stephen M. and J. Gillis Wetter, "Arbitration and the Exhaustion of Local Remedies" in *Justice in International Law* (Grotius 1994).

Smit, Hans, *American Assistance to Litigation in Foreign and International Tribunals: Section 1782 of Title 28 of the U.S.C. Revisited*, 25 Syracuse J. Int'l L. & Com. 1 (1998).

———, *International Litigation Under the United States Code*, 65 Colum. L. Rev. 1015 (1965).

Steger, Debra P., "Amicus curiae: Participant or Friend?" in *European Integration and International Co-ordination: Studies in Transnational Economic Law in Honour of Claus-Dieter Ehlermann* (Armin von Bogdandy et al., eds., Kluwer Law Int'l 2002).

Tallerico, Thomas J., *Bifurcation and Direct Testimony Witness Statements in International Commercial Arbitration*, 20(3) J. Int'l Arb. 295 (2003).

Tupman, W. Michael, *Challenge and Disqualification of Arbitrators in International Commercial Arbitration*, 38 Int'l & Comp. L. Q. 26 (1989).

Verbist, Herman, *The Practice of the ICC International Court of Arbitration with Regard to the Fixing of the Place of Arbitration*, 12(3) Arb. Int'l 347 (1996).

Von Mehren, George M., *Submitting Evidence in International Arbitration: A Common Lawyer's Guide*, 20 J. Int'l Arb. 285 (2003).

Voser, Nathalie and Neomi Rao, *Background Information on the IBA Guidelines on Conflicts of Interest in International Arbitration*, 5 Bus. L. Int'l 433 (2004).

Weiler, Todd, *Restrictions on Submissions of Amicus Briefs to NAFTA Investment Arbitral Tribunals*, 1(2) Oil, Gas, and Energy Law Intelligence (2003).

Yu, Hong-Lin and Laurence Shore, *Independence, Impartiality and Immunity of Arbitrators—US and English Persepctives*, 52 Int'l Comp. L. Q. 935 (2003).

Chapter 8

Alvarez, Henri, *Arbitration under North American Free Trade Agreement*, 16(4) Arb. Int'l 393 (2000).

Brower, Charles N., *A Crisis of Legitimacy*, 26 Nat'l L.J. B9 (Oct. 7, 2002).

———, *The Coming Crisis in the Global Adjudication System*, 13 World Arb. & Med. Rep. 270 (2002).

Carbonneau, Thomas E., *Cases and Materials on the Law and Practice of Arbitration* (Juris Publishing 2000).

Crivellaro, Antonio, *Consolidation of Arbitral and Court Proceedings in Investment Disputes*, 4(3) L. & Pract. of Int'l Ct. & Trib. 371 (2005).

De Rosa, Paolo, *The Recent Wave of Arbitration against Argentina under Bilateral Investment Treaties: Background and Principal Legal Issues*, 36 U. Miami Inter-Am. L. Rev. 41 (2004).

Frick, Joachim G., *Arbitration and Complex International Contracts* (Kluwer 2001).

Gaillard, Emanuel, *Consolidation of Arbitral Proceedings and Court Proceedings, in Complex Arbitrations: Perspectives on their Procedural Implications, Special Supplement*, ICC Int'l Ct. Arb. Bull. (December 2003).

Hanotiau, Bernard, *Complex Arbitrations: Multiparty, Multicontract, Multi-Issue and Class Actions* (Kluwer Law Int'l 2006).

Hascher, Dominique T., *Consolidation of Arbitration by American Courts: Fostering or Hampering International Commercial Arbitration*, 1(2) J. Int'l Arb. 127 (1984).

Jarvin, Sigvard, *Consolidated Arbitrations, the New York Convention, and the Dutch Arbitration Act 1986*, 3 Arb. Int'l 254 (1987).

Kodama, Yoshi, *Dispute Settlement under the Multilateral Agreement on Investment: The Quest for an Effective Investment Dispute Settlement Mechanism and its Failure*, 16(3) J. Int'l Arb. 45 (1999).

Chapter 9

Broches, Aron, *Observations on the Finality of ICSID Awards*, 6 ICSID Rev.—F.I.L.J. 321 (1991).

———, *The Convention on the Settlement of Investment Disputes Between States and Nationals of Other States*, 136 Recueil des Cours de L'Academie de Droit International 331 (1972).

Cheng, Bin, *General Principles of Law as Applied by International Courts and Tribunals* (Grotius 1987).

Gaillard, Emmanuel and Yas Banifatemi, *The Meaning of "And" in Article 42(1), Second Sentence, of the Washington Convention: The Role of International Law in the ICSID Choice of Law Process*, 18 ICSID Rev.—F.I.L.J. 375 (2003).

Reisman, W. Michael, *The Regime for Lacunae in the ICSID Choice of Law Provision and the Question of Its Threshold*, 15 ICSID Rev.—F.I.L.J. 362 (2000).

Rubins, Noah, *The Arbitral Innovations of Recent U.S. Free Trade Agreements: Two Steps Forward, One Step Back*, 2003 Int'l Bus. L.J. 865.

Schreuer, Christoph, *Diversity and Harmonization of Treaty Interpretation in Investment Arbitration*, 3(2) T.D.M. (2006).

———, *The ICSID Convention: A Commentary* (Cambridge Univ. Press 2000).

Sornarajah, M., *Settlement of International Investment Disputes* (Kluwer 2000).

Chapter 10

Amerasinghe, C. F., *Jurisdiction of International Tribunals* (Kluwer Law Int'l 2003).

Asouzu, Amazu A., *International Commercial Arbitration and African States: Practice, Participation and International Development* (Cambridge Univ. Press 2001).

Ben Hamida, Walid, *L'arbitrage Etat-investisseur étranger: Regards sur les Traités et Projets Récents*, 131 Journal du Droit International 419 (2004).

Berhnhardt, Rudolf, ed., *Encyclopedia of Public International Law* (1992).

Born, Gary B., *International Commercial Arbitration in the United States: Commentary and Materials* (Kluwer Law Int'l 2003).

Broches, Aron, "Bilateral Investment Protection Treaties and Arbitration of Investment Disputes" in *The Art of Arbitration: Essays on International Arbitration: Liber Amicorum Pieter Sanders* (Jan C. Schultsz and Albert Jan van den Berg, eds., 1982).

Carter, Barry E., Philip R. Trimble, and Curtis A. Bradley, *International Law* (Aspen 4th ed. 2003).

Delaume, Georges R., "Consent to ICSID Arbitration" in *The Changing World of International Law in the Twenty-First Century* (Joseph J. Norton et al., eds., Kluwer 1998).

Dolzer, Rudolf and Margrete Stevens, *Bilateral Investment Treaties* (Martinus Nijhoff 1995).

Fischer, Peter and Thomas Wälde, eds., *Collection of International Concessions and Related Instruments, Contemporary Series* (1976).

Friedland, Paul, *U.S. Courts' Misapplication of the "Agreement in Writing" Requirement for Enforcement of an Arbitration Award Agreement Under the N.Y. Convention*, 13(5) Mealey's Int'l Arb. Rep. 15 (1998).

Grigera Naón, Horacio, *The Settlement of Investment Disputes Between States and Private Parties: An Overview from the Perspective of the ICC*, 1 J. World Inv. & Trade, 59 (2000).

———, *Arbitration in Latin America*, 5 Int'l Arb. 137 (1989).

Hill, Richard, *The Writing Requirement of the New York Convention Revisited: Are There Black Holes in International Arbitration?*, 13(11) Mealey's Int'l Arb. Rep. 11 (1998).

Hirsch, Moshe, *The Arbitration Mechanism of the International Centre for the Settlement of Investment Disputes* (Martinus Nijhoff 1993).

Kelsen, Hans, *The Principle of Sovereign Equality of State As A Basis for International Organization*, 53(2) Yale L.J. 207 (1944).

Lemenez de Kerdelleau, Guillaume, *State Consent to ICSID Arbitration: Article 22 of the Venezuelan Investment Law*, 4(3) T.D.M. (June 2007).

Lillich, Richard B., *The Protection of Foreign Investment* (Syracuse Univ. Press 1965).

Mann, F. A., *An Agreement 'In Writing' to Arbitrate*, 3(2) Arb. Int'l 171 (1987).

Oceana Publications, *Investment Laws of the World* (Oceana 1972),

Parra, Antonio, *Principles Governing Foreign Investment, as Reflected in National Investment Codes*, 7 ICSID Rev.—F.I.L.J. 428 (1992).

———, *Role of ICSID in Settlement of Investment Disputes*, 16(1) ICSID News (1999).

Paulsson, Jan, *Arbitration Without Privity*, 10 ICSID Rev.—F.I.L.J. 232 (1995).

Redfern, Alan, Martin Hunter, Nigel Blackaby, and Constantine Partasides, *The Law and Practice of International Commercial Arbitration* (Sweet & Maxwell 4th ed. 2004).

Rubins, Noah, *Investment Arbitration in Brazil*, 4(6) J. World Inv. & Trade, 1071 (2003).

Saleh, Samir, *Commercial Arbitration in the Arab Middle East* (Graham & Trotman 1984).

Schreuer, Christoph, *Consent to Arbitration*, 2(5) T.D.M. (2005).

———, *The ICSID Convention: A Commentary* (Cambridge Univ. Press 2000).

Sornarajah, M., *Settlement of International Investment Disputes* (Kluwer 2000).

Chapter 11

Adeoye Akinsanya, *International Protection of Direct Foreign Investments in the Third World*, 36 Int'l Comp. L. Q. 58 (1987).

Ben Hamida, Walid, "The *Mihaly v. Sri Lanka* Case: Some Thoughts Relating to the Status of Pre-Investment Expenditures" in *International Investment Law and Arbitration: Leading Cases from ICSID, NAFTA, Bilateral Treaties and Customary International Law* (Todd Weiler, ed., Cameron May 2005).

———, *Two Nebulous ICSID Features: The Notion of Investment and the Scope of Annulment Control: Ad Hoc Committee's Decision in Patrick Mitchell v. Democratic Republic of Congo*, 24 J. Int'l Arb. 287 (2007).

Bliesener, D. H., *La Compétence du CIRDI dans la Pratique Arbitrale*, 68 Revue de Droit International et Comparé 95 (1991).

Broches, Aron, "Bilateral Investment Protection Treaties and Arbitration of Investment Disputes" in *Selected Essays: World Bank, ICSID, and Other Subjects of Public and Private International Law* (Martinus Nijhoff 1995).

———, *The Convention of the Settlement of Investment Disputes: Some Observations on Jurisdiction*, 5 Colum. J. Transnat'l L. 263 (1966).

Delaume, Georges R., *Convention on the Settlement of Investment Disputes Between States and Nationals of Other States*, 1 Int'l Law. 64 (1966).

Dolzer, Rudolf and Margrete Stevens, *Bilateral Investment Treaties* (Martinus Nijhoff 1995).

Endicott, Martin, "The Definition of Investment in ICSID Arbitration: Development Lessons for the WTO?" in *Sustainable Development in World Trade Law* (Markus Gehring & Marie-Claire Cordonier Segger, eds., 2005).

Graham, Edward and Paul Krugman, *Foreign Direct Investment in the United States* (Institute for International Economics 1991).

Hirsch, Moshe, *The Arbitration Mechanism of the International Centre for the Settlement of Investment Disputes* (Martinus Nijhoff 1993).

Hornick, Robert, *The Mihaly Arbitration: Pre-Investment Expenditure as a Basis for ICSID Jurisdiction*, 20 J. Int'l Arb. 189 (2003).

ICSID, *Convention on the Settlement of Investment Disputes Between States and Nationals of Other States* (ICSID 1970).

IMF, *Balance of Payments Manual* (4th ed. 1977).

Kurtz, Jürgen, *A General Investment Agreement in the WTO? Lessons from Chapter 11 of NAFTA and the OECD Multilateral Agreement on Investment*, 23 U. Pa. J. Int'l Econ. L. 713 (2002).

Lamm, Carolyn, *The Jurisdiction of the International Centre for Settlement of Investment Disputes*, 6 ICSID Rev.—F.I.L.J. (1991).

Lamm, Carolyn and Abby Cohen Smutny, *The International Centre for Settlement of Investment Disputes: Responses to Problems and Changing Requirements*, 12(11) Mealey's Int'l Arb. Rep. 11 (1997).

Mohtashami, Reza, *Patrick Mitchell Annulment Decision (Observations)*, 2006(3) Stock. Int'l Arb. Rev. 203.

Moore, Michael M., *International Arbitration Between States and Foreign Investors: The World Bank Organization*, 18 Stan. L. Rev. 1369 (1966).

Nathan, K. V. S. K., *The ICSID Convention: The Law of the International Centre for Settlement of Investment Disputes* (Juris Publishing 2000).

———, *Submissions to the International Centre for Settlement of Investment Disputes in Breach of the Convention*, 12 J. Int'l Arb. 27 (1995).

Parra, Antonio, *Principles Governing Foreign Investment, as Reflected in National Investment Codes*, 7 ICSID Rev.—F.I.L.J. 428 (1992).

———, *Provisions on the Settlement of Investment Disputes in Modern Investment Laws, BITs, and Multilateral Instruments on Investment*, 12 ICSID Rev.—F.I.L.J. 287 (1997).

———, "The Scope of New Investment Laws and International Instruments" in *Economic Development, Foreign Investment and the Law* (Robert Pritchard, ed., 1996).

Riesenfeld, Stefan A., "Foreign Investments" in *Encyclopedia of Public International Law* (Rudolf Bernhardt, ed., 1992).

Robin, Patricia McKinstry, *The BIT Won't Bite: The American Bilateral Investment Treaty Program*, 33 Am. U.L. Rev. 931 (1984).

Rubins, Noah and N. Stephan Kinsella, *International Investment, Political Risk, and Dispute Resolution* (Oceana 2005).

Schmidt, John T., *Arbitration under the Auspices of the International Centre for Settlement of Investment Disputes: Implications of the Decision on Jurisdiction in Alcoa Minerals of Jamaica, Inc. v. Government of Jamaica*, 17 Harv. Int'l L.J. 90 (1976).

Schreuer, Christoph, *Commentary on the ICSID Convention*, 11 ICSID Rev.—F.I.L.J. 318 (1996).

———, *The ICSID Convention: A Commentary* (Cambridge Univ. Press 2000).

Shihata, Ibrahim and Antonio Parra, *The Experience of the International Centre for Settlement of Investment Disputes*, 14 ICSID Rev.—F.I.L.J. 299 (1999).

Sirefman, Josef P., *The World Bank Plan for Investment Dispute Arbitration*, 20 Arb. J. 168 (1965).

Sornarajah, M., *The International Law on Foreign Investment* (Cambridge Univ. Press 1994).

Tupman, W. Michael, *Case Studies in the Jurisdiction of the International Centre for Investment Disputes*, 35 Int'l & Comp. L. Q. 813 (1986).

UNCTAD, *International Investment Agreements: Flexibility for Development*, UNCTAD/ITE/IIT/18 (United Nations 2000).

———, *Trends in International Investment Agreements*, UNCTAD/ITE/IIT/13 (United Nations 1999).

Chapter 12

Acconci, Pia, *Determining the Internationally Relevant Link Between a State and a Corporate Investor*, 5 J. World Inv. & Trade 139 (2004).

Alexandrov, Stanimir, *The "Baby Boom" of Treaty-Based Arbitrations and the Jurisdiction of ICSID Tribunals: Shareholders as "Investors" and Jurisdiction Ratione Temporis*, 4 L. & Pract. of Int'l Ct. & Trib. 19 (2005).

Alting, Carsten, *Piercing the Corporate Veil in American and German Law: Liability of Individuals and Entities: A Comparative View*, Tulsa J. Comp. & Int'l L. 187 (1995).

Amerasinghe, C. F., *Interpretation of Article 25(2)(b) of the ICSID Convention*, in International Arbitration in the 21st Century: Towards "Judicialization" and Uniformity? (Richard B. Lillich & Charles N. Brower, eds., 1993).

———, *Jurisdiction of International Tribunals* (Kluwer Law Int'l 2003).

Asouzu, Amazu A., *A Review and Critique of Arbitral Awards on Article 25(2)(b) of the ICSID Convention*, 3 J. World Inv. 397 (2002).

Backer, Larry C., *Comparative Corporate Law: United States, European Union, China and Japan* (Carolina Academic Press 2002).

Boll, Alfred M., *Multiple Nationality and International Law* (Martinus Nijhoff 2007).

Borchard, Edwin M., *The Protection of Citizens Abroad*, 43 Yale L.J. 359 (1934).

Brower, Charles N. and Jason Brueschke, *The Iran-United States Claims Tribunal* (Martinus Nijhoff Publishers 1998).

Brownlie, Ian, *Principles of Public International Law* (Oxford Univ. Press 6th ed. 2003).

Delaume, Georges R., *ICSID Arbitration and the Courts*, 77 Am. J. Int'l L. 784 (1983).

Dinstein, Yoram, "Diplomatic Protection of Companies under International Law" in *International Law: Theory and Practice* (Karel Wellens, ed., 1998).

Dolzer, Rudolf and Margrete Stevens, *Bilateral Investment Treaties* (Martinus Nijhoff 1995).

Guerrero, Omar et al., *Piercing the Corporate Veil in Mexico*, Comp. L. Y.B. Int'l Bus. 375 (2004).

Happ, Richard and Noah Rubins, *Awards and Decisions of ICSID Tribunals in 2004*, 47 German Y.B. Int'l L. 878 (2004).

Jennings, Sir Robert and Sir Arthur Watts, eds., *Oppenheim's International Law* (1992).

Kinnear, Meg N., Andrea K. Bjorklund and John F.G. Hannaford, *Investment Disputes under NAFTA: An Annotated Guide to NAFTA* Chapter 11, Article 1116 (Kluwer 2006).

Laird, Ian, "A Community of Destiny: The Barcelona Traction Case and the Development of Shareholder Rights to Bring Investment Claims" in *International Investment Law and Arbitration: Leading Cases from the ICSID, NAFTA, Bilateral Treaties and Customary International Law* (Todd Weiler, ed., Cameron May 2005).

Lyons, Katherine E., *Piercing the Corporate Veil in the International Arena*, 33 Syracuse J. Int'l L. & Com. 523 (2006).

Mendelson, Maurice, "Runaway Train: Continuous Nationality Rule from Panavezys-Saldutiskis Railway Case to Loewen" in *International Investment Law and Arbitration: Leading Cases from the ICSID, NAFTA, Bilateral Treaties and Customary International Law* (Todd Weiler, ed., Cameron May 2005).

Morris, Glenn, *Piercing the Corporate Veil in Louisiana*, 52 La. L.R. 271 (1991).

Orrego Vicuña, Fransisco, "Changing Approaches to the Nationality of Claims in the Context of Diplomatic Protection and International Dispute Settlement" in *Liber Amicorum Ibrahim Shihata: International Finance & Development Law* (Sabine Schlemmer-Schulte & Ko-Yung Tung, eds., 2001).

Paulsson, Jan, *Continuous Nationality in Loewen*, 20 Arb. Int'l 213 (2004).

Randelzhofer, Albrecht, "Nationality" in *Encyclopedia of Public International Law* (Rudolf Bernhardt, ed., 1997).

Rubins, Noah, *Loewen v. United States: The Burial of an Investor-State Arbitration Claim*, 21(1) Arb. Int'l 1 (2005).

Rubins, Noah and N. Stephan Kinsella, *International Investment, Political Risk, and Dispute Resolution* (Oceana 2005).

Schreuer, Christoph, *The ICSID Convention: A Commentary* (Cambridge Univ. Press 2000).

———, *Shareholder Protection in International Investment Law*, 2(3) T.D.M. 4 (2005).

Seidl-Hohenveldern, Ignaz, *Corporations in and under International Law* (Grotius 1987).

Sinclair, Anthony, *Nationality of Individual Investors in ICSID Arbitration: Hussein Nuaman Soufraki v. United Arab Emirates*, 2004 Int'l Arb. L. Rev. 191.

Staker, Christopher, *Diplomatic Protection of Private Business Companies: Determining Corporate Personality for International Law Purposes*, 61 Brit. Y.B. Int'l L. 155 (1991).

Vattel, Emmerich de, *The Law of Nations* (6th American ed. 1844).

Wälde, Thomas and Borzu Sabahi, "Compensation, Damages and Valuation in International Investment Law" in *The Oxford Handbook of International Investment Law* (Peter Muchlinski et al., eds., Oxford Univ. Press 2008).

Wallace, Jr., Don, "Fair and Equitable Treatment and Denial of Justice: *Loewen v. US* and *Chattin v. Mexico*" in *International Investment Law and Arbitrations: Leading Cases from the ICSID, NAFTA, Bilateral Treaties and Customary International Law* (Todd Weiler, ed., Cameron May 2005).

Weis, Paul, *Nationality and Statelessness in International Law* (Hyperion Press 1979).

Wisner, Robert and Nick Gallus, *Nationality Requirements in Investor-State Arbitration*, 5 J. World Inv. & Trade 927 (2004).

Yala, Farouk, *Soufraki v. United Arab Emirates (Observations)*, 2004 Les Cahiers de l'Arbitrage/Gazette du Palais 22.

Chapter 13

Adede, A. O., *A Fresh Look at the Meaning of the Doctrine of Denial of Justice under International Law*, 14 Can. Y. B. Int'l L. 72 (1976).

Black's Law Dictionary (6th ed. 1990).

Borchard, Edwin M., *The Diplomatic Protection of Citizens Abroad* (Banks Law Publication 1915).

Brierly, James Leslie, *The Law of Nations* (Clarendon Press 1963).

Brownlie, Ian, *Principles of Public International Law* (Oxford Univ. Press 6th ed. 2003).

Doehring, Karl, "Local Remedies, Exhaustion of" in *Encyclopedia of Public International Law* (Rudolf Bernhardt, ed., 1997).

García-Amador, F. V., *The Changing Law of International Claims* (Oceana 1984).

Greenwood, Christopher, "State Responsibility for the Decisions of National Courts" in *Issues of State Responsibility before International Judicial Institutions* (Malgosia Fitzmaurice & Dan Sarooshi, eds., 2004).

Holmes, Oliver Wendell, *The Common Law* (1881).

Koneru, Phanesh, *The International Interpretation of the U.N. Convention on the Sale of Goods: An Approach Based on General Principles*, 6 Minn. J. Global Trade 105 (1997).

Laird, Ian, "A Distinction Without a Difference? An Examination of the Concepts of Admissibility and Jurisdiction in *Salini v. Jordan* and *Methanex v. USA*" in *International Investment Law and Arbitration: Leading Cases from the ICSID, NAFTA, Bilateral Treaties, and Customary International Law* (Todd Weiler, ed., Cameron May 2005).

Moran, Mayo, *Rethinking the Reasonable Person* (Oxford Univ. Press 2003).

Mummery, David R., *The Content of the Duty to Exhaust Local Remedies*, 58 Am. J. Int'l L. 389 (1964).

Peters, P., *Exhaustion of Local Remedies: Ignored in Most Bilateral Investment Treaties*, 44(2) Neth. Int'l L. Rev. 233 (1997).

Rubin, Alfred, *Book Review: Application of the Rule of Exhaustion of Local Remedies in Int'l Law*, 25 Harv. Int'l L. J. 517 (1984).

Schreuer, Christoph, *The ICSID Convention: A Commentary* (Cambridge Univ. Press 2000).

Schwarzenberger, Georg, *International Law: As Applied by International Courts and Tribunals* (Stevens 3d ed. 1957).

Schwebel, Stephen M., and J. Gillis Wetter, *Arbitration and the Exhaustion of Local Remedies*, 60 Am. J. Int'l L. 484 (1966).

———, "Arbitration and the Exhaustion of Local Remedies" in *Justice in International Law* (Grotius 1994).

Trindade, A. A. Cancado, *The Application of the Rule of Exhaustion of Local Remedies in International Law: Its Rationale in the International Protection of Individual Rights* (Cambridge Univ. Press 1983).

UNCTAD, *Bilateral Investment Treaties 1995–2006: Trends in Investment Rulemaking*, UNCTAD/ITE/IIA/2006/5 (United Nations 2007).

Visscher, Charles de, *Le Déni de Justice en Droit International*, 52 Recueil des Cours de L'Academie de Droit International 367 (1935).

Wallace, Jr., Don, "Fair and Equitable Treatment and Denial of Justice: *Loewen v. US* and *Chattin v. Mexico*" in *International Investment Law and Arbitrations: Leading Cases from the ICSID, NAFTA, Bilateral Treaties and Customary International Law* (Todd Weiler, ed., Cameron May 2005).

Chapter 14

Alexandrov, Stanimir, "The Vivendi Annulment Decision and the Lessons for Future ICSID Arbitrations: The Applicants' Perspective" in *Annulment of ICSID Awards* (Emmanuel Gaillard & Yas Banifatemi, eds., 2004).

Anzorena, Carlos Ignacio Suarez, "*Vivendi v. Argentina*: On the Admissibility of Requests for Partial Annulment and the Ground of a Manifest Excess of Powers" in *Annulment of ICSID Awards* (Emmanuel Gaillard & Yas Banifatemi, eds., 2004).

British Institute of International and Comparative Law Third Investment Treaty Forum Conference, *The Relationship Between Local Courts and Investment Treaty Arbitration*, 10 Sept. 2004, 2(4) T.D.M. (2005).

Brownlie, Ian, *Principles of Public International Law* (Oxford Univ. Press 6th ed. 2003).

Cremades, Bernardo M., "Litigating Annulment Proceedings—The Vivendi Matter: Contract and Treaty Claims" in *Annulment of ICSID Awards* (Emmanuel Gaillard & Yas Banifatemi, eds., 2004).

Dodge, William S., *Waste Management, Inc. v. Mexico: Arbitral Award on Jurisdiction Under NAFTA Where Requisite Waiver of Other Remedies Reserves, and Applicant Pursues, Municipal Law Claims in Other Fora*, 95 Am. J. Int'l L. 186 (2001).

Friedman, Mark W. et al., *Developments in International Commercial Dispute Resolution in 2003*, 2004 Int'l Law. 265.

Greenwood, Christopher, "State Responsibility for the Decisions of National Courts" in *Issues of State Responsibility before International Judicial Institutions* (Malgosia Fitzmaurice & Dan Sarooshi, eds., 2004).

Jennings, Sir Robert and Sir Arthur Watts, eds., *Oppenheim's International Law* (1992).

Kantor, Mark, *The Relationship Between Local Courts and Investment Treaty Arbitration*, 2(4) T.D.M. (2005).

Polkinghorne, Michael, *Investor-State Dispute Resolution under the Energy Charter Treaty: Which Fork? Which Road?*, 19(4) Mealey's Int'l Arb. Rep. 13 (2004).

Reed, Lucy, Jan Paulsson and Nigel Blackaby, *Guide to ICSID Arbitration* (Kluwer 2003).

Rubins, Noah and N. Stephan Kinsella, *International Investment, Political Risk, and Dispute Resolution* (Oceana 2005).

Schreuer, Christoph, *The ICSID Convention: A Commentary* (Cambridge Univ. Press 2000).

———, *Travelling the BIT Route: Of Waiting Periods, Umbrella Clauses and Forks in the Road*, 5 J. World Inv. & Trade 231 (2004).

Stein, Ted L., *Jurisprudence and the Jurists' Prudence: The Iranian Forum Clause Decisions of the Iran-U.S. Claims Tribunal*, 78 Am. J. Int'l L. 1 (1984).

Vinuesa, Raul Emilio, *Bilateral Investment Treaties and the Settlement of Investment Disputes under ICSID: The Latin American Experience*, 8 NAFTA L. & Bus. Rev. Am. 501 (2002).

Chapter 15

Acconci, Pia, "Most-Favoured-Nation Treatment and the International Law on Foreign Investment" in *The Oxford Handbook of International Investment Law* (Peter Muchlinski et al., eds., Oxford Univ. Press 2008).

American Law Institute, *Restatement (Third) of the Foreign Relations Law of the United States* (American Law Institute 1987).

Ben Hamida, Walid, "MFN Clause and Procedural Matters: Seeking Solutions from WTO Experiences" in *Investment Treaty Arbitration: A Debate and Discussion* (Todd Weiler, ed., Juris Publishing 2008).

Brownlie, Ian, *Principles of Public International Law* (Oxford Univ. Press 6th ed. 2003).

Fietta, Stephen, *Most Favoured Nation Treatment and Dispute Resolution under Bilateral Investment Treaties: A Turning Point?*, 2(3) T.D.M. 8 (2005).

Franck, Susan D., *International Decision: Occidental Exploration & Production Co. v. Republic of Ecuador*, 99 Am. J. Int'l L. 675 (2005).

SELECT BIBLIOGRAPHY

Freyer, Dana and David Herlihy, *Most Favored-Nation Treatment And Dispute Settlement In Investment Arbitration: Just How "Favored" Is "Most-Favored"?*, 20(1) ICSID Rev.—F.I.L.J. 58 (2005).

Gaillard, Emmanuel, *Establishing Jurisdiction Through a Most-Favored Nation Clause*, N.Y.L.J., June 2, 2005.

ILC, *Draft Articles on Most-Favored-Nations Clauses Art. 9*, 2 Y.B. Int'l L. Comm'n (1978).

Kinnear, Meg N., Andrea K. Bjorklund and John F.G. Hannaford, *Investment Disputes under NAFTA: An Annotated Guide to NAFTA Chapter 11, Article 1116* (Kluwer 2006).

Kurtz, Jürgen, "The Delicate Extension of MFN Treatment to Foreign Investors: *Maffezini v Kingdom of Spain*" in *International Investment Law and Arbitration: Leading Cases from ICSID, NAFTA, Bilateral Investment Treaties and Customary International Law* (Todd Weiler, ed., Cameron May 2005).

Locknie, Hsu, *MFN and Dispute Settlement: When the Twain Meet*, 7(1) J.W. Inv. & Trade 25 (2006).

Maniruzzaman, A.F.M., *Expropriation of Alien Property and the Principle of Non-Discrimination in the International Law of Foreign Investment: An Overview*, 8 J. Transnat'l L. & Pol'y 57 (1998).

Masiá, Enrique Fernández, *Atribución De Competencia A Traves De La Cláusula De La Nación Más Favorecida: Lecciones Extraidas De La Reciente Práctica Arbitral Internacional En Materia De Inversiones Extranjeras*, 13 Revista Electrónica De Estudios Internacionales (2007).

McLachlan, Campbell, Laurence Shore and Matthew Weiniger, *International Investment Arbitration* (Oxford Univ. Press 2007).

OECD, *International Investment Law* (OCED 2005).

Rubins, Noah and N. Stephan Kinsella, *International Investment, Political Risk, and Dispute Resolution* (Oceana 2005).

Sabahi, Borzu, "National Treatment—Is Discriminatory Intent Relevant?" in *Investment Treaty Arbitration: A Debate and Discussion* (Todd Weiler, ed., Juris Publishing 2008).

Scholz, Katja, *Having Your Pie and Eating it with One Chopstick—MFN Clauses and Procedural Rights*, 5 Pol'y Papers Transn'l Econ. L. (2004).

Tabet, Sylvie, "National Treatment—Is Discriminatory Intent Relevant?" in *Investment Treaty Arbitration: A Debate and Discussion* (Todd Weiler, ed., Juris Publishing 2008).

Teitelbaum, Ruth, *Recent Developments in the Interpretation of Most Favored Nation Clauses*, 22(3) J. Int'l Arb. 225 (2005).

UNCTAD, *Bilateral Investment Treaties 1995–2006: Trends in Investment Rulemaking*, UNCTAD/ITE/IIA/2006/5 (United Nations 2007).

———, *Most-Favoured-Nation Treatment*, UNCTAD/ITE/IIT/10 (United Nations 1999).

———, *National Treatment*, UNCTAD/ITE/IIT/11 (United Nations 1999).

Ustor, Endre, *First Report on the Most-Favoured Nation Clause*, II Y.B. Int'l L. Comm'n 157 (1969).

Vesel, Scott, *Clearing a Path through a Tangled Jurisprudence: Most-Favored-Nation Clauses and Dispute Settlement Provisions in Bilateral Investment Treaties*, 32 Yale J. Int'l L. 125 (2007).

Wallace, Cynthia, *Legal Control of the Multinational Enterprise* (Martinus Nijhoff 1983).

Wallace, Jr., Don, and David B. Bailey, *The Inevitability of National Treatment of Foreign Direct Investment with Increasingly Few and Narrow Exceptions*, 31 Cornell Int'l L.J. 615 (1998).

Weiler, Todd, "Prohibitions against Discrimination in NAFTA Chapter 11" in *NAFTA Investment Law and Arbitration: Past Issues, Current Practice, Future Prospects* (Todd Weiler, ed., 2004).

Weiler, Todd and Ian Laird, "Standards of Treatment in International Investment Law: The Move towards Unification" in *The Oxford Handbook of International Investment Law* (Peter Muchlinski et al., eds., Oxford Univ. Press 2008).

Zhou, Jian, *National Treatment in Foreign Investment Law: A Comparative Study from a Chinese Perspective*, 10 Touro Int'l L. Rev. 39 (2000).

Chapter 16

Appleton, Barry, *Regulatory Takings: The International Law Perspective, Colloquium Article*, 11 N.Y.U. Env. L. J. 35 (2002).

American Law Institute, *Restatement (Third) of the Foreign Relations Law of the United States* (American Law Institute 1987).

Black's Law Dictionary (6th ed. 1990).

Breemer, J. David and R.S. Radford, *The (Less?) Murky Doctrine of Investment-Backed Expectations after Palazzolo, and the Lower Courts' Disturbing Insistence on Wallowing on the Pre-Palazzolo Muck*, 34 Sw. U. L. Rev. 351 (2005).

Brierly, James Leslie, *The Law of Nations* (Clarendon Press 1963).

Brower, Charles N. and Jason Brueschke, *The Iran-United States Claims Tribunal* (Martinus Nijhoff Publishers 1998).

Brownlie, Ian, *Principles of Public International Law* (Oxford Univ. Press 6th ed. 2003).

Christie, G., *What Constitutes a Taking Under International Law?*, 33 Brit. Y.B. Int'l L. 307 (1962).

Clagett, Brice M., "Just Compensation in International Law: The Issues Before the Iran-United States Claims Tribunal" in *The Valuation of Nationalized Property in International Law* (Richard B. Lillich, ed., 1987).

Dattu, Riyaz, *A Journey from Havana to Paris: The Fifty-Year Quest for the Elusive Multilateral Agreement on Investment*, 24 Fordham Int'l L.J. 275 (2000).

Dodge, William S., *National Courts and International Arbitration: Exhaustion of Remedies and Res Judicata under Chapter Eleven of NAFTA*, 23 Hastings Int'l & Comp. L. Rev. 357 (2000).

Dolzer, Rudolf, *Indirect Expropriations: New Developments?*, 11 N.Y.U. Envt'l L.J. 64 (2002).

Dunn, Frederick S., *The Protection of Nationals* (Johns Hopkins Press 1932).

Fachiri, Alexander P., *Expropriation in International Law*, 6 Brit. Y.B. Int'l L. 159 (1925).

Fatouros, Arghyrios A., *Government Guarantees to Foreign Investors* (Columbia Univ. Press 1962).

Fawcett, J. E. S., *Some Foreign Effects of Nationalisation of Property*, 27 Brit. Y.B. Int'l L. 355 (1950).

Foighel, Isi, *Nationalization: A Study in the Protection of Alien Property in International Law* (Stevens 1957).

Fortier, L. Yves and Stephen L. Drymer, *Indirect Expropriation in the Law of International Investment: I Know It When I See It, or Caveat Investor*, 19 ICSID Rev.—F.I.L.J. 293 (2005).

Freeman, Alwyn V., *The International Responsibility of States for Denial of Justice* (Kraus Reprint Co. 1938).

Friedman, S., *Expropriation in International Law* (Ivor Carlyon Jackson trans., 1953).

Gann, Pamela B., *The U.S. Bilateral Investment Treaty Program*, 21 Stan. J. Int'l L. 373 (1985).

Guzman, Andrew T., *Why LDCS Sign Treaties that Hurt Them: Explaining the Popularity of Bilateral Investment Treaties*, 38 Va. J. Int'l L. 639 (1998).

Hackworth, Green H., *Digest of International Law* (U.S. G.P.O. 1943).

Herz, John H., *Expropriation of Foreign Property*, 35 Am. J. Int'l L. 253 (1941).

Higgins, Rosalyn, *The Taking of Property by the State, Recent Developments in International Law* 176 Receuil des Cours 259 (1982).

Jennings, Robert Y., *State Contracts in International Law*, 37 Brit. Y.B. Int'l L. 156 (1975).

Lowenfeld, Andreas, *International Economic Law* (Oxford Univ. Press 2002).

McNair, Lord, *The Seizure of Property and Enterprises in Indonesia*, 6 Neth. Int'l L. Rev. 243 (1959).

Norton, Patrick M., *A Law of the Future or a Law of the Past? Modern Tribunals and the International Law of Expropriation*, 85 Am. J. Int'l. L. 474 (1991).

Paulsson, Jan and Zachary Douglas, "Indirect Expropriation in Investment Treaty Arbitration" in *Arbitrating Foreign Investment Disputes: Substantive and Procedural Aspects* (Norbert Horn, ed., Kluwer Law Int'l 2004).

Rubins, Noah, "Notion of 'Investment' in International Investment Arbitration" in *Arbitrating Foreign Investment Disputes: Substantive and Procedural Aspects* (Norbert Horn ed,. Kluwer Law Int'l 2004).

Rubins, Noah and N. Stephan Kinsella, *International Investment, Political Risk, and Dispute Resolution* (Oceana 2005).

Schachter, Oscar, *Compensation for Expropriation*, 78 Am. J. Int'l L. 121 (1984).

Schwebel, Stephen M., *The Influence of Bilateral Investment Treaties on Customary International Law*, 98 ASIL Proc. 27 (2004).

Sohn Louis B., and R. R. Baxter, *Responsibility of States for Injuries to the Economic Interests of Aliens: II. Draft Convention on the International Responsibility of States for Injuries to Aliens*, 55 Am. J. Int'l L. 548 (1961).

UNCTAD, *Bilateral Treaties in the Mid-1990s,* UNCTAD/ITE/IIA/2006/5 (United Nations 1998).

———, *Series on Issues in International Investment Agreements, Taking of Property*, UNCTAD/ITE/IIT/15 (United Nations 2000).

Vattel, Emmerich de, *The Law of Nations* (Charles Fenwick trans., 1916).

Veeder, V. V., *The Lena Goldfields Arbitration: The Historical Roots of Three Ideas*, 47 Int'l & Comp. L.Q. 747 (1998).

Westberg, John A. and Bertrand P. Marchais, *General Principles Governing Foreign Investment as Articulated in Recent International Tribunal Awards and Writings of Publicists*, 7 ICSID Rev.—F.I.L.J. 453, 454 (1992).

Weston, Burns H., *"Constructive Takings" under International Law: A Modest Foray into the Problem of "Creeping Expropriation"* 16 Va. J. Int'l L. 103 (1975).

White, Gillian, *Nationalization of Foreign Property* (Praeger 1961).

Whiteman, Marjorie, *Damages in International Law* (U.S. G.P.O. 1943).

Williams, John Fischer, *International Law and the Property of Aliens*, 9 Brit. Y.B. Int'l L. 1 (1928).

Chapter 17

Abs, Hermann, and Lord Shawcross, *The Proposed Convention to Protect Private Foreign Investment*, 9 J. Public L. 115 (1960).

Alvarez, Henri, "Setting Aside Additional Facility Awards: The Metalclad Case" in *Annulment of ICSID Awards* (Emmanuel Gaillard & Yas Banifatemi, eds., Juris Publishing 2004).

SELECT BIBLIOGRAPHY

American Law Institute, *Restatement (Third) of the Foreign Relations Law of the United States* (American Law Institute 1987).
Borchard, Edwin M., *The 'Minimum Standard' of the Treatment of Aliens*, 38 Mich. L. Rev. 445 (1939–1940).
Brower II, Charles H., *Fair and Equitable Treatment Under NAFTA's Investment Chapter*, 96 ASIL Proc. 9 (2002).
Brownlie, Ian, *Principles of Public International Law* (Oxford Univ. Press 6th ed. 2003).
———, *System of the Law of Nations* (Clarendon Press 1983).
Cassese, Antonio, *International Law* (Oxford Univ. Press 2d ed. 2005).
Cheng, Bin, *General Principles of Law As Applied by International Courts and Tribunals* (Grotius 1987).
Crawford, James, *The International Law Commission's Articles on State Responsibility: Introduction, Text, and Commentaries* (Cambridge Univ. Press 2002).
Dolzer, Rudolf, *Fair and Equitable Treatment: A Key Standard in Investment Treaties*, 39 Int'l Law. 87 (2005).
———, *New Foundations of the Law of Expropriation of Alien Property*, 75 Am. J. Int'l L. 553 (1981).
Douglas, Zachary, *Nothing if Not Critical for Investment Treaty Arbitration: Occidental, Eureko and Methanex*, 22 Arb. Int'l 27 (2006).
Dugard, John, *Third Report on Diplomatic Protection*, UN Doc. A/CN.4/523 (ILC 2002).
Eagleton, Clyde, *Denial of Justice in International Law*, 22 Am. J. Int'l L. 538 (1928).
Freeman, Alwyn V., *The International Responsibility of States for Denial of Justice* (Kraus Reprint Co. 1938).
Gantz, David A., *Pope and Talbot v. Canada*, 97 Am. J. Int'l L. 937 (2003).
Hindelang, Steffen, *Bilateral Investment Treaties, Custom and A Healthy Investment Climate: The Question of Whether BITs Influence Customary International Law Revisited*, 5 J. World Inv. & Trade 789 (2004).
Jennings, Sir Robert and Sir Arthur Watts, eds., *Oppenheim's International Law* (1992).
Juillard, Patrick, *L'évolution des Sources du Droit des Investissements*, 250 Receuil des Cours 83 (1994).
Kirkman, Courtney C., *Fair and Equitable Treatment: Methanex v. United States and the Narrowing Scope of NAFTA Article 1105*, 34 L. & Pol'y in Int'l Bus. 343 (2002).
Laird, Ian, *Betrayal, Shock and Outrage: Recent Developments in NAFTA Article 1105*, in NAFTA Investment Law and Arbitration: Past Issues, Current Practice, Future Prospects (Todd Weiler, ed., 2004).
Mann, F. A., *British Treaties for the Promotion and Protection of Investments*, 52 Brit. Y.B. Int'l L. 241 (1981).
———, "British Treaties for the Promotion and Protection of Investments" in *Further Studies in International Law* (Clarendon Press 1990).
———, *The Legal Aspects of Money* (Clarendon Press 1982).
Matiation, Stefan, *Arbitration with Two Twists: Loewen v. United States and Free Trade Commission Intervention in NAFTA Chapter 11 Disputes*, 24 U. Pa. J. Int'l Econ. L. 451 (2003).
Moore, John Bassett, *A Digest of International Law* (U.S. G.P.O. 1906).
OECD, *Draft Convention on the Protection of Foreign Property*, 7 I.L.M. 117 (1967).
Olasolo, Hector, *Have Public Interests Been Forgotten in NAFTA Chapter 11 Foreign Investor/Host State Arbitration? Some Conclusions from the Judgment of the Supreme Court of British Columbia on the Case of Mexico v. Metalclad*, 8(1/2) NAFTA L. & Bus. Rev. Am. 189 (2002).
Paulsson, Jan, *Denial of Justice in International Law* (Cambridge Univ. Press 2005).

Responsibility of States for Damage Done in Their Territory to the Person or Property of Foreigners, 23 Am. J. Int'l L. Spec. Supp. 131 (1929).

Roth, Andreas Hans, *The Minimum Standard of International Law Applied to Aliens* (A. W. Sijthoff 1949).

Rubins, Noah and N. Stephan Kinsella, *International Investment, Political Risk, and Dispute Resolution* (Oceana 2005).

Sabahi, Borzu, "National Treatment—Is Discriminatory Intent Relevant?" in *Investment Treaty Arbitration: A Debate and Discussion* (Todd Weiler, ed., Juris Publishing 2008).

Schreuer, Christoph, *Fair and Equitable Treatment in Arbitral Practice*, 6(3) J. World Inv. & Trade 357 (2005).

Schwebel, Stephen M., *The Influence of Bilateral Investment Treaties on Customary International Law*, 98 ASIL Proc. 27 (2004).

———, *International Arbitration: Three Salient Problems* (Grotius 1987).

———, "The United States 2004 Model Bilateral Investment Treaty: An Exercise in the Regressive Development of International Law" in *Global Reflections on International Law, Commerce and Dispute Resolution, Liber Amicorum in Honour of Robert Briner* (ICC Publishing 2005).

Shaw, Malcolm N., *International Law* (Cambridge Univ. Press 5th ed. 2003).

Shihata, Ibrahim, *Legal Treatment of Foreign Investment: The World Bank Guidelines* (Martinus Nijhoff 1993).

Spiegel, Hans W., *Origin and Development of Denial of Justice*, 32 Am. J. Int'l L. 63 (1938).

Thomas, J. Christopher, *Reflections on Article 1105 of NAFTA: History, State Practice and the Influence of Commentators*, 17 ICSID Rev.—F.I.L.J. 21 (2002).

Tudor, Ioana, *The Fair and Equitable Treatment Standard in International Foreign Investment Law* (Oxford Univ. Press 2008).

UNCTAD, *Bilateral Investment Treaties 1995–2006: Trends in Investment Rulemaking*, UNCTAD/ITE/IIA/2006/5 (United Nations 2007).

———, *The Entry Into Force of Bilateral Investment Treaties (BITs)*, UNCTAD/WEB/ITE/IIA/2006/9 (United Nations 2006).

———, *Series on Issues in International Investment Agreements, Fair and Equitable Treatment*, UNCTAD/ITE/IIT/11 (United Nations 1999).

Vagts, Detlev F., *Coercion and Foreign Investment Re-Arrangements*, 72(1) Am. J. Int'l L. 17 (1978).

———, "Minimum Standard" in *Encyclopedia of Public International Law* (Rudolf Bernhardt, ed., 1997).

Vandevelde, Kenneth J., *The Bilateral Treaty Program of the United States*, 21 Cornell Int'l L.J. 201 (1988).

Vasciannie, Stephen, *The Fair and Equitable Treatment Standard in International Investment Law and Practice*, 70 Brit. Y.B. Int'l L. 99 (2000).

Verdross, Alfred and Bruno Simma, *Universelles Völkerrecht: Theorie und Praxis* (Duncker & Humblot 1984).

Wallace, Jr., Don, "Fair and Equitable Treatment and Denial of Justice: *Loewen v. US* and *Chattin v. Mexico*" in *International Investment Law and Arbitrations: Leading Cases from the ICSID, NAFTA, Bilateral Treaties and Customary International Law* (Todd Weiler, ed., Cameron May 2005).

Weiler, Todd, "Good Faith and Regulatory Transparency: The Story of *Metalclad v. Mexico*" in *International Investment Law and Arbitration: Leading Cases from the ICSID, NAFTA, Bilateral Treaties and Customary International Law* (Todd Weiler, ed., Cameron May 2005).

Werner, Jacques, *Making Investment Arbitration More Certain—A Modest Proposal*, 4(5) J. World Inv. & Trade 767 (2003).

Whiteman, Marjorie, *Damages in International Law* (U.S. G.P.O. 1943).

Wilson, Robert R., *The International Law Standard in Treaties of the United States* (Harvard Univ. Press 1953).

Zeitler, Helge E., *The Guarantee of "Full Protection and Security" in Investment Treaties Regarding Harm Caused by Private Actors*, 2005(3) Stock. INT'L ARB. Rev. 1.

Chapter 18

American Law Institute, *Restatement (Third) of the Foreign Relations Law of the United States* (American Law Institute 1987).

Brownlie, Ian, *Principles of Public International Law* (Oxford Univ. Press 6th ed. 2003).

Crawford, James, *The International Law Commission's Articles on State Responsibility: Introduction, Text, and Commentaries* (Cambridge Univ. Press 2002).

Hamilton, Calvin A. and Paula I. Rochwerger, *Trade and Investment: Foreign Direct Investment through Bilateral and Multilateral Treaties*, 18 N.Y. Int'l L. Rev. 1 (2005).

Jennings, Robert Y., *State Contracts in International Law*, 37 Brit. Y.B. Int'l L. 156 (1975).

Jennings, Sir Robert and Sir Arthur Watts, eds., *Oppenheim's International Law* (1992).

Schreuer, Christoph, *Travelling the BIT Route: Of Waiting Periods, Umbrella Clauses and Forks in the Road*, 5 J. World Inv. & Trade 231 (2004).

Schwebel, Stephen M., *International Protection of Contractual Arrangement*, 53 ASIL Proc. 266 (1959).

———, "On Whether the Breach by a State of a Contract with an Alien is a Breach of International Law" in *International Law at the Time of Its Codification: Essays in Honour of Roberto Ago* (A. Giuffrè 1987).

Sinclair, Anthony, *The Origins of the Umbrella Clause in the International Law of Investment Protection*, 20 Arb. Int'l 411 (2004).

Wälde, Thomas, "Contract Claims under the Energy Charter Treaty's Umbrella Clause: Original Intentions versus Emerging Jurisprudence" in *Investment Arbitration and The Energy Charter Treaty* (Clarisse Ribeiro, ed., Juris. Publishing 2006).

———, *The "Umbrella" Clause in Investment Arbitration: A comment on Original Intentions and Recent Cases*, 6(2) J. World Inv. & Trade 184 (2005).

Chapter 19

Affolder, Natasha, *Awarding Compound Interest In International Arbitration*, 12 Am. Rev. Int'l Arb. 45 (2001).

Akehurst, Michael, *Equity and General Principles of Law*, 25 Int'l Comp. L. Q. 801 (1976).

Arangio-Ruiz, Gaetano, *Second Report on State Responsibility*, 2 Y.B. Int'l L. Comm'n 1 (1989).

Atiyah, P. S., *An Introduction to the Law of Contract* (Clarendon Press 5th ed. 1995).

Ball, Markham, *Assessing Damages in Claims by Investors Against States*, 32 ICSID Rev.—F.I.L.J. 408 (2001).

Borchard, Edwin M., *Responsibility of States, At The Hague Codification Conference*, 24 Am. J. Int'l L. 517 (1930).

SELECT BIBLIOGRAPHY

Bowett, D. W., *Claims Between States and Private Entities: The Twilight Zone of International Law*, 35 Cath. U. L. Rev. 929 (1986).

Broches, Aron, *History of the Convention* (ICSID 1968).

Brower, Charles N. and Jason Brueschke, *The Iran-United States Claims Tribunal* (Martinus Nijhoff Publishers 1998).

Brownlie, Ian, *Principles of Public International Law* (Oxford Univ. Press 6th ed. 2003).

Cheng, Bin, *General Principles of Law As Applied by International Courts and Tribunals* (Grotius 1987).

Crawford, James, *The International Law Commission's Articles on State Responsibility: Introduction, Text, and Commentaries* (Cambridge Univ. Press 2002).

Derains, Yves and Eric Schwartz, *A Guide to the New ICC Rules of Arbitration* (Kluwer Law Int'l 1998).

Derains, Yves, *Études Pierre Bellet* (Litec 1991).

Dolzer, Rudolf and Margrete Stevens, *Bilateral Investment Treaties* (Martinus Nijhoff 1995).

Douglas, Zachary, *The Hybrid Foundations of Investment Treaty Arbitration*, 74 Brit. Y.B. Int'l L. 189 (2003).

Friedland, Paul and Eleanor Wong, *Measuring Damages for the Deprivation of Income-Producing Assets: ICSID Case Studies*, 6 ICSID Rev.—F.I.L.J. 400 (1991).

Gotanda, John Y., *Awarding Costs and Attorney's Fees in International Commercial Arbitrations*, 21 Mich. J. Int'l L. 1 (1999).

———, *Awarding Interest in International Arbitration*, 90 Am. J. Int'l L. 40 (1996).

———, *Damages in Private International Law* (Hague Academy of Int'l Law 2007).

———, *Supplemental Damages in Private International Law* (Kluwer Law Int'l 1998).

Gray, Christine, *The Choice Between Restitution and Compensation*, 10 Eur. J. Int'l L. 413 (1999).

Hart, H.L.A. and Tony Honoré, *Causation in the Law* (Clarendon Press 2d ed. 1985).

Heuston, R. F. V., *Salmond on the Law of Torts* (Sweet & Maxwell 17th ed. 1977).

Higgins, Rosalyn, *The Taking of Property by the State, Recent Developments in International Law*, 176 Receuil des Cours 259 (1982).

Honoré, Tony, "Causation and Remoteness of Damage" in *International Encyclopedia of Comparative Law* (J.C.B. Mohr 1971).

Hunter, Martin and Volker Triebel, *Awarding Interest in International Arbitration*, 6 J. Int'l Arb. 1 (1990).

Lieblich, William C., *Determining the Economic Value of Expropriated Income-Producing Property in International Arbitrations*, 8 J. Int'l Arb. 59 (1991).

Mann, F. A., "Compound Interest as an Item of Damage in International Law" in *Further Studies in International Law* (Clarendon Press 1990).

Markesinis, Sir Basil, *The German Law of Obligations, Vol. II, The Law of Torts: A Comparative Introduction* (Clarendon Press 3d ed. 1997).

OECD, *Draft Convention on the Protection of Foreign Property*, 7 I.L.M. 117 (1967).

O'Malley, Stephen and Alexander Layton, *European Civil Practice* (Sweet & Maxwell 1989).

Paulsson, Jan, *Denial of Justice in International Law* (Cambridge Univ. Press 2005).

Parry, Clive, *The Sources and Evidences of International Law* (Oceana 1965).

Redfern, Alan and Martin Hunter, *Law and Practice of International Commercial Arbitration* (Sweet & Maxwell 2d ed. 1991).

Reisman, W. Michael and Robert D. Sloane, *Indirect Expropriation and Its Valuation in the BIT Generation*, 74 Brit. Y.B. Int'l L. 140 (2003).

Riedel, Eibe H., "Damages" in *Encyclopedia of Public International Law* (Rudolf Bernhardt, ed., 1992).

———, "Satisfaction" in *Encyclopedia of Public International Law* (Rudolf Bernhardt, ed., 1992).

Rubino-Sammartano, Mauro, *International Arbitration Law and Practice* (Kluwer 2000).

Rubins, Noah, *The Allocation of Costs and Attorney's Fees in Investor-State Arbitration*, 18 ICSID Rev.—F.I.L.J. 109 (2003).

Snijders, Henk J, ed., *Access to Civil Procedure Abroad* (Kluwer Law Int'l 1996).

Sohn Louis B., and R. R. Baxter, *Responsibility of States for Injuries to the Economic Interests of Aliens: II. Draft Convention on the International Responsibility of States for Injuries to Aliens*, 55 Am. J. Int'l L. 548 (1961).

Toope, Stephen J., *Mixed International Arbitration: Studies in Arbitration Between States and Private Persons* (Grotius 1990).

Ussher, Patrick and Brian O'Connor, eds., *Doing Business in Ireland* (Matthew Bender 1996).

Wälde, Thomas and Borzu Sabahi, "Compensation, Damages and Valuation in International Investment Law" in *The Oxford Handbook of International Investment Law* (Peter Muchlinski et al., eds., Oxford Univ. Press 2008).

Whiteman, Marjorie, *Damages in International Law* (U.S. G.P.O. 1943).

Zwiegert, Konrad and Hein Kötz, *Introduction to Comparative Law* (J.A. Weir, trans., Clarendon Press 3d ed. 1998).

Chapter 20

Alvarez, Guillermo A. and William W. Park, *The New Face of Investment Arbitration: NAFTA Chapter 11*, 28 Yale J. Int'l L. 365 (2003).

Black's Law Dictionary (6th ed. 1990).

Blackwood, Elizabeth and Stephen McBride, *Investment as the Achilles Heel of Globalization?: The Ongoing Conflict Between the Rights of Capital and the Rights of States*, 25(3) Pol'y & Society 43 (2006).

Blessing, Marc, *The Arbitrability of Intellectual Property Disputes*, 12 Arb. Int'l 191 (1996).

Böckstiegel, Karl-Heinz, "Public Policy and Arbitrability" in *ICCA Congress Series* (Pieter Sanders, ed., Kluwer 1986).

Born, Gary B., *International Commercial Arbitration in the United States: Commentary and Materials* (Kluwer Law Int'l 2003).

Brower II, Charles H., *Beware the Jabberwock: A Reply to Mr. Thomas*, 40 Colum. J. Transnat'l L. 465 (2002).

———, *Structure, Legitimacy, and NAFTA's Investment Chapter*, 36 Vand. J. Transnat'l L. 37, 83 (2003).

Carbonneau, Thomas E., *Cases and Materials on the Law and Practice of Arbitration* (Juris Publishing 2000).

Caron, David D., *Reputation and Reality in the ICSID Annulment Process: Understanding the Distinction Between Annulment and Appeal*, 7 ICSID Rev.—F.I.L.J. 1 (1992).

Cossio, Francisco González de, *Mexican Experience with Investment Arbitration*, 3 J. World Inv. 473 (2002).

Craig, Laurence, *Uses and Abuses of Appeal from Awards*, 4 Arb. Int'l 174 (1988).

Delaume, Georges R., *The Finality of Arbitration Involving States*, 5 Arb. Int'l 21 (1989).

Feldman, Mark, *The Annulment Proceedings and the Finality of ICSID Arbitral Awards*, 2 ICSID Rev.—F.I.L.J. 85 (1987).

Fischer, Robert and Roger Haydock, *International Commercial Disputes: Drafting an Enforceable Arbitration Agreement*, 21 Wm. Mitchell L. Rev. 941 (1996).

Gaillard, Emmanuel and Yas Banifatemi, eds., *Annulment of ICSID Awards* (Juris Publishing 2004).

Gaillard, Emmanuel and Jenny Edelstein, *Baker Marine and Spier Strike a Blow to the Enforceability in the United States of Awards Set Aside at the Seat*, 3 Int'l Arb. L. Rev. 37 (2000).

Gharavi, Hamid, *The International Effectiveness of the Annulment of an Arbitration Award* (2002).

Giardina, Andrea, "ICSID: A Self-Contained, Non-National Review System" in *International Arbitration in the 21st Century* (Richard B. Lillich & Charles N. Brower, eds., Transnational Publishers 1994).

Hansen, Patricia Isela, *Judicialization and Globalization in the North American Free Trade Agreement*, 38 Tex. Int'l L. J. 489 (2003).

Harten, Gus van, *Private Authority and Transnational Governance: The Contours of the International System of Investor Protection*, 12(4) Rev. Int'l Political Econ. 600 (2005).

Haubold, Samuel A., *Opting out of the U.S. Legal System: The Case for International Arbitration*, 10 Int'l L. Practicum 43 (1997).

Houtte, Hans van, *Arbitration Involving Securities Transactions*, 12 Arb. Int'l 405 (1996).

ICSID, *Annual Report* (ICSID 1985).

Knull III, William H. and Noah Rubins, *Betting the Farm on International Arbitration: Is it Time to Offer an Appeal Option?* 11 Am. Rev. Int'l Arb. 531 (2000).

Leigh, Monroe, *Arbitration-Annulment of Arbitral Award for Failure to Apply Law Applicable Under ICSID Convention and Failure to State Sufficiently Pertinent Reasons*, 81 Am. J. Int'l L. 222 (1987).

McClendon, J. Stewart and Rosabel E. Everard Goodman, *International Commercial Arbitration in New York* (World Arbitration Institute 1986).

Park, William W., *Safeguarding Procedural Integrity in International Arbitration*, 63 Tul. L. Rev. 647 (1989).

Polasek, Martina, *Introductory Note to Three Decisions on the Stay of Enforcement of an ICSID Award*, 20(2) ICSID Rev.—F.I.L.J. 581 (2005).

Posin, Daniel Q., *Recent Developments in ICSID Annulment Procedures*, 13 World Arb. & Med. Rep. 170 (2002).

Ramaswamy, P., *Enforcement of Annulled Awards: An Indian Perspective*, 19 J. Int'l Arb. 461 (2002).

Redfern, Alan and Martin Hunter, *Law and Practice of International Commercial Arbitration* (Sweet & Maxwell 2d ed. 1991).

Ribs, Jacques, *Ombres et Incertitudes de L'arbitrage pour les Personnes Morales de Droit Publique Français*, 64 Juris-Classeur Périodique I.3465 (1990).

Sedlak, David R., *Comment: ICSID's Resurgence in International Investment Arbitration: Can the Momentum Hold?* 23 Penn. St. Int'l L. Rev. 147 (2004).

Shihata, Ibrahim and Antonio Parra, *The Experience of the International Centre for Settlement of Investment Disputes*, 14 ICSID Rev.—F.I.L.J. 299 (1999).

Trooboff, Peter D. and Christopher T. Curtis, *International Investment Disputes—Res Judicata Effect of Partially Annulled ICSID Award*, 83 Am. J. Int'l L. 106 (1998).

von Zumbusch, Ludwig, *Arbitrability of Antitrust Claims under U.S., German, and E.E.C. Law: the International Transaction Criterion and Public Policy*, 22 Tex. Int'l L. J. 291 (1987).

Wälde, Thomas, *ICSID 'Annulment Committee'*, 1(2) Oil, Gas & Energy Law Intelligence (March 2003).

Chapter 21

Baldwin, Edward et al., *Limits to Enforcement of ICSID Awards*, 23(1) J. Int'l Arb. 1 (2006).
Dellapenna, Joseph W., *Refining the Foreign Sovereign Immunities Act*, 9 Willamette J. Int'l L. & Disp. Res. 57 (2001).
Halverson, Karen, *Is a Foreign State a "Person"? Does it Matter?: Personal Jurisdiction, Due Process and the Foreign Sovereign Immunities Act*, 34 N.Y.U. J. Int'l L. & Politics 115 (2001).
Lalive, Pierre, "Enforcing Awards" in *Sixty Years of ICC Arbitration* (ICC Publishing 1984).
Nelson, Leslie, *International Joint Ventures*, 2 Int'l L. Prosp. 75 (1990).
Redfern, Alan, Martin Hunter, Nigel Blackaby and Constantine Partasides, *The Law and Practice of International Commercial Arbitration* (Sweet & Maxwell 4th ed. 2004).
Reinisch, August, *European Court Practice Concerning State Immunity from Enforcement Measures*, 17(4) Eur. J. Int'l L. 803 (2006).
Schreuer, Christoph, *The ICSID Convention: A Commentary* (Cambridge Univ. Press 2000).
Turck, Nancy, *French and U.S. Courts Define Limits of Sovereign Immunity in Execution and Enforcement of Arbitral Awards*, 17 Arb. Int'l 327 (2001).
UNCTAD, *Course on Dispute Settlement—Module 2.9. ICSID: Binding Force and Enforcement*, UNCTAD/EDM/Misc.232/Add.8 (United Nations 2003).
Volz, Jane L. and Roger S. Haydock, *Foreign Arbitral Awards: Enforcing the Award against the Recalcitrant Loser*, 21 Wm. Mitchell L. Rev. 867 (1996).

Chapter 22

Alvarez, Guillermo A. and William W. Park, *The New Face of Investment Arbitration: NAFTA Chapter 11*, 28 Yale J. Int'l L. 365 (2003).
Black's Law Dictionary (6th ed. 1990).
Brower II, Charles H., *Structure, Legitimacy, and NAFTA's Investment Chapter*, 36 Vand. J. Transnat'l L. 37, 83 (2003).
Charney, Jonathan, *Is International Law Threatened by Multiple International Law Tribunals?* 271 Recueil des Cours 101 (1998).
Choi, Won-Mog, *The Present and Future of the Investor-State Dispute Settlement Paradigm*, 10 J. Int'l Econ. L. 725 (2007).
Coe, Jack, *Transparency in the Resolution of Investor-State Disputes-Adoption, Adaptation, and NAFTA Leadership*, 54 Kan. L. Rev. 1339 (2006).
Franck, Susan D., *The Legitimacy Crisis in Investment Treaty Arbitration: Privatizing Public International Law through Inconsistent Decisions*, 73 Fordham L. Rev. 1521 (2005).
Harten, Gus van, *Investment Treaty Arbitration and Public Law* (Oxford Univ. Press 2007).
Harten, Gus van and Martin Loughlin, *Investment Treaty Arbitration as a Species of Global Administrative Law*, 17(1) Eur. J. Int'l L. 121 (2006).
Legum, Barton, *Trends and Challenges in Investor-State Arbitration*, 19 Arb. Int'l 1143 (2003).
Peterson, Luke E., *Changing Investment Litigation, Bit by BIT*, 5(4) Bridges Between Trade and Sustainable Development 5 (May 2001).
Price, Daniel, *NAFTA Chapter 11: Investor-State Dispute Settlement: Frankenstein or Safety Valve?* 26 Can.-U.S. L.J. 107 (2001).
Sabater, Aníbal, *The Weaknesses of the "Rosatti Doctrine,"* 15 Am. Rev. Int'l Arb. 465 (2004).
Schachter, Oscar, *The Invisible College of International Lawyers*, 72 Nw. U.L. Rev. 217 (1977).

SELECT BIBLIOGRAPHY

Schreuer, Christoph and Matthew Weiniger, "Conversations Across Cases—Is There a Doctrine of Precedent in Investment Arbitration? " in *The Oxford Handbook of International Investment Law* (Peter Muchlinski et al., eds., Oxford Univ. Press 2008).

Thomas, J. Christopher, *A Reply to Professor Brower*, 40 Colum. J. Transnat'l L. 433 (2002).

UNCTAD, *Bilateral Investment Treaties 1995–2006: Trends in Investment Rulemaking*, UNCTAD/ITE/IIA/2006/5 (United Nations 2007).

Wälde, Thomas, "The Specific Nature of Investment Arbitration-Report of the Director of Studies of the English-Speaking Section of the Center" in *New Aspects of International Investment Law* (Philippe Kahn and Thomas Wälde, eds., Martinus Nijhoff 2007).

Index

A

AAA (American Arbitration Association), 78, 111–112, 144
Abs-Shawcross Draft Convention on Investments Abroad (1959), 48, 503
Act of state doctrine, 20–23
Additional Facility Rules. See International Centre for the Settlement of Investment Disputes
Ad hoc arbitration, 35–36, 236
African, Caribbean, and Pacific (ACP) Group of States, 55
Albania
    Albania-Croatia BIT, 414
    Law on Foreign Investment (1993), 230–231
Algiers Accords (1981), 41–42
American Arbitration Association (AAA). See AAA
American rule on costs. See Costs of Arbitration
Amicus curiae submissions, 167–177
    future trends, 707–709
    NGO participation, 173–177
Annulment and set aside, 199, 627–673
    agreements to narrow grounds for, 647–648
    effect of annulled awards, 649–650
    ICSID
        Ad hoc Committee, 628
        ICSID awards, 629–634, 712
    non-ICSID awards, 635–646
        case studies, 644–646, 651–673
        excess of authority, 637–639, 642, 663
        grounds for setting aside, 637–646
            "manifest disregard for the law," 644–646
            nonarbitrability, 639–640
            procedural irregularity, 642–643
            public policy challenge, 640–642
            substantive grounds, 644–646
        judicial review, standard of, 636–637
        national law of situs controlling, 628, 635, 636
    vacatur, 646, 649
    waiver of objections, 647
Anti-arbitration injunctions, 105–116
Anti-dumping claims, consolidation of, 194–195
Appellate body, proposal for, 713
Appointment of tribunal, 84
Arbitration. See also Arbitration awards; specific treaties and regional agreements
    ad hoc arbitration, 35–36
    amicus curiae, 167–177, 707–709
    annulment and set aside, 627–673. See also Annulment and set aside
    arbitrators. See Arbitrators
    briefing, 153
    choice of procedural law, 92–93
    confidentiality, 706–707
    consolidation of claims, 185–199. See also Consolidation of claims

INDEX

Arbitration (*continued*)
   costs and attorneys' fees, 611–625
   counterclaims, 153–156
   default, 126–128
   defenses, 156–158
   description of course of, 117–183
   dismissals, 119
   document production, 161–163
   effect of annulled awards, 649–650
   evidence, 158–163. *See also* Evidence
   exhaustion of local remedies, 119–120.
       See also Exhaustion of remedies
   filing, premature, 119
   forum elections. *See* Forum elections
   forum rules, 133
   future of, 2–3, 701–714
   hearings, 177–179
   ICSID. *See* International Centre for
       Settlement of Investment Disputes
   initial session, 134–137
   interim relief, 137–147
   jurisdiction. *See* Jurisdictional issues
   language of, 83, 130, 133–134
   letters of intent, 120
   merits phase of, 153–177
   MFN. *See* Most-favored nation treatment
   modern system of, 45–75
   multilateral investment treaties, 54–75.
       See also Multilateral investment
       treaties
   national investment legislation, 75
   nonarbitrability, 639–640
   origins of, 45–50
   procedural law, 91–99
   registration or approval of requests for,
       125–126
   remedies. *See* Remedies for foreign
       investors
   request for, 118, 122–125
   role of, 2–3
   sanctions, 119
   settlement, 116–117, 118
   situs of, 132–133
   submission to, binding and irrevocable
       nature of, 126
   U.S. procedures, 163–167
   waiting periods, 117–119, 121
   witness statements, 158–163

Arbitration awards, 179–182
   annulment. *See* Annulment and
       set aside
   challenge of, 182–183
   drafting of, 180–182
   enforcement of, 182–183, 198–199,
       675–700. *See also* Enforcement
       of awards
   time limit for issuance, 179–180
Arbitrators
   appointment of, 128–131
   disqualification of, 129
   qualifications of, 130–131
   tribunal chairman, selection of,
       128–129
   tribunal composition, 128–134
Argentina
   Argentina-Australia BIT, 305
   Argentina-Spain BIT, 119–120, 418
   choice of arbitrators and consolidation
       of suits against, 188–189
   Colonia Protocol, 67
   costs and attorneys' fees, 623
   discriminatory impairment, 427
   Emergency Law of January 2002,
       460–461
   expropriation, 457–458, 466
   fair and equitable treatment, 516–517,
       560, 579, 581–583
   forum election cases, 374–376,
       381–391
   France-Argentina BIT on governing law,
       84, 368–369, 381–391, 394
   investment treaty arbitration against,
       89–90
   legal impossibility, 572
   Mercosur, 64
   Netherlands-Argentina BIT, 203
   U.S.-Argentina BIT, 157–158, 221, 306,
       375, 395, 442
       fair and equitable treatment, 496–497
       full protection and security, 539
       umbrella clauses, 543
Armenia, 254
Association of South East Asian Nations
   (ASEAN), 67–68, 241, 702
Assumption of risk, 269–270
Attorneys' fees, 611–625

INDEX

Australia
  Argentina-Australia BIT, 305
  Australia-Czech Republic BIT, 238
  U.S.-Australia Free Trade Agreement, 446
Austria
  Austria-Croatia BIT, 297
  Austria-Mexico BIT, 425
  EC claims against (2007), 705
  lump sum agreement with German Democratic Republic, 38–39
Awards. *See* Arbitration awards
Azerbaijan
  U.S.-Azerbaijan BIT, 236

B

Bad faith, 388, 389, 496, 506
Barriers to recovery by foreign investors, 13–26
  act of state doctrine, 20–23
  Calvo Doctrine, 16–19, 488
  choice of law, 23
  in foreign investor's home courts, 19–23
  in host country courts, 13–19
  inefficient local courts, 15–16
  jurisdictional issues, 19–20
  local bias, 13
  political barriers, 23–26
  state immunity, 14–15
Belgium
  Canadian electric company with Belgian shareholders, Spain's refusal to pay, 33
Bifurcation, 147
Bilateral investment treaties (BITs), *See also specific countries and regions;* and Index of Treaties
  arbitration under Washington Convention, 52
  consent to arbitration, 220
  consolidation of claims, 195–196
  corporate investors, definition of, 305
  effect of, 7
  exhaustion of local remedies, 120
  international dispute resolution, 234
  interpretation of, 205–209
  investor-state arbitration, 46, 69
  models. *See specific names*
  national treatment standards, 398–399
  non-pecuniary remedies, 569
  role of, 51–54
  termination of, 703
  waiting periods, 117
Binational claims commissions, 36–37
BITs. *See* Bilateral investment treaties
Bjorklund, Andrea, 358–359
Bogotá agreement, 503
Bolivia
  Mercosur, 64
  Mexico-Bolivia Free Trade Agreement, 196
  Netherlands-Bolivia BIT, 329–331
  withdrawal from ICSID, 704
Borchard, E., 348
Brazil
  expropriation of property by, 243
  Mercosur, 64
Breach of contract
  lost profits, 589–596
Bribery, 641
Briefing, 153
  amicus curiae, 167–177, 707–709
  posthearing, 179
Broches, Aron, 42–43, 211–212, 237, 257, 258
Brower, Charles N., 57–58
Brownlie, I., 356–357
Buenos Aires Protocol, 66–67
Bulgaria, 145–146, 417, 422–423
  Cyprus-Bulgaria BIT, 422–423
Burundi and expropriation case, 446–449
Byrd Amendment (2000), 194–195

C

CAFTA (Central America Free Trade Agreement), 702. *See also* Dominican Republic–Central American–United States Free Trade Agreement
Calvo, Carlos, 16
Calvo Doctrine, 16–19, 69, 488
Cameroon, 210, 344–345, 631–633

INDEX

Canada
  Canada–U.S. Softwood Lumber Agreement, 402
  compensation, limitation of, 599–601
  consolidation of anti-dumping related claims, 194–195
  costs and attorneys' fees, 618
  courier services, 404–405
  espousal of claims by, 29–30
  expropriation, 468, 469–470
  fair and equitable treatment, 501, 524–525, 529–531
    customary international law and, 498–499
  forum selection and waiver, 370
  government legal fees, 624–625
  jurisdictional issues, 148–149
    amicus curiae, 168–171
    preliminary vs. merits issues, 149–153
  manifest disregard for law, 644–646
  methanol and claims against California, 404
  Model BIT. *See* Canada Model BIT
  NAFTA, 56–61, 635. *See also* North American Free Trade Agreement
  non-ICSID case studies, 664–673
Canada-Chile Free Trade Agreement (CCFTA), 252
  consolidation of claims, 196
Canada Model BIT
  consolidation of claims, 196
  non-pecuniary remedies, 570
Cárdenas, Lázaro, 11
Cayman Islands, 327–328, 329
CCFTA. *See* Canada-Chile Free Trade Agreement
Central America Free Trade Agreement (CAFTA), 702. *See also* Dominican Republic–Central American–United States Free Trade Agreement
Ceylon, suspension of U.S. aid to, 244
Charter of Economic Rights and Duties of States (CERDS), 25, 27
Chile
  CCFTA. *See* Canada-Chile Free Trade Agreement

Chile-Croatia BIT, 424
Chile-Denmark BIT, 424
Chile-Malaysia BIT, 424–425, 515
Chile-Spain BIT, 120, 418
forum selection and waiver, 370
Mercosur, 64
national investment laws, 254
U.S.-Chile Free Trade Agreement, 196
China, 706
Choice of forum. *See* Forum elections
Choice of law, 23
  clauses in treaties, 204
  procedural law, 92–93
Choice of situs, 83
Civil law systems, approach of, 14–15, 158
Civil society groups, amicus submissions by, 171, 173–177
Clauses exorbitantes du droit commun, 555
Colonia Protocol, 66, 67
Columbia
  Mercosur, 64
  U.S.-Colombia Free Trade Agreement, 446
Common-law systems, approach of, 14, 158, 482–483
Communist regimes, 23–24, 25. *See also* Soviet Union
Compensation. *See* Damages
Compromis, 220, 221, 242–246, 258–259
Confidentiality issues, 142, 706–707
Confirmation, 677–678
Consent to arbitral jurisdiction, 208–209, 219–246
  arbitration clauses in investment contracts, 225–230
  irrevocability of consent, 222
  limitations on consent clauses, 223–225
  methods of state consent, 220–221
Consolidation of claims, 89–90, 185–199
  by courts, 197–198
  by French Court of Cassation, 197–198
  ICC rules, 196–199
  ICSID and, 186–189
  NAFTA Article 1126, 190–195
  other bilateral and multilateral investment treaties, 195–196
  UNCITRAL Rules, 189–190

Continued Dumping and Subsidy Offset Act
of 2000 (Byrd Amendment),
194–195
Continuous nationality rule, 340–341, 342
Contract claims relinquished by electing
treaty arbitration, 394–395
Contractual and quasi-contractual rights,
439–440
Contributory fault, 602–603
Convention on the Settlement of Investment
Disputes between States and
Nationals of other States. *See*
Washington Convention
Cooling off periods, 117–119
Corporations and other legal entities,
304–314
Costa Rica, 245–246, 574–575, 605, 609
Costs of arbitration, 85–86, 611–625
   American rule, 612, 614
   financial guarantees to cover, 142
   follow the event principle, 612–614
Counterclaims, 153–156
Croatia
   Albania-Croatia BIT, 414
   Austria-Croatia BIT, 297
   Chile-Denmark BIT, 424
Custom, role of, 214
Customary international law
   continuous nationality rule, 340–341
   diplomatic espousal claims, 32–33
   Draft Articles on Responsibility of States
for Internationally Wrongful Acts,
564–565
   espousal claims, 32–33
   exhaustion of local remedies,
347–357
   expropriation, 430, 441, 488
   governing law, 208, 213
   limitations of, 42
   minimum standards, 495–496
   piercing corporate veil, 308
   siège sociale, 308
Cyprus-Bulgaria BIT, 422–423
Czech Republic
   Australia-Czech Republic BIT, 238
   BITs with EU member countries, 703
   coercion of foreign investors,
523–524
   costs and attorneys' fees, 617
   definition of investment in, 281–282
   fair and equitable treatment, 499–500,
509, 513
   full protection and security, 534–535
   interest, 610–611
   Netherlands-Czech Republic BIT,
154–156, 204, 236–237, 281, 315,
336–337, 357, 394
   non-ICSID case studies, 660–664
   obligation to mitigate losses, 603
   UK-Czech Republic BIT, 283

D

Damages
   compensation standards, 566, 568,
573–583
      breach of investment treaty obligations,
578–583
      expropriation, 573–578
   costs and attorneys' fees, 611–625
      American rule, 612, 614
      awards under ICSID rules, 620–624
      awards under UNCITRAL rules,
615–620
      government legal fees, calculation
of, 624–625
      reasonableness, 624
   "costs follow the event" principle,
612–614
   damnum emergens, 590, 593
   derivative, 318–319
   double recovery, 596–597
   equity, 603–605
   fair market value, 584
   injunctive relief, 569–572
   interest, 605–611
      compound or simple, 609–611
      pre-/post-award, 606
   legal impossibility, 571-2
   limitation of compensation, 596–603
      causation, 597–602
      contributory fault, 602–603
      mitigation obligations, 603
   lost profits for breach of contract,
589–596

Damages (*continued*)
  lucrum cessans, 590
  material or legal impossibility, 571–572
  minority shareholders, 318–319
  non-pecuniary damages and, 563–625
  reparation, 565, 567–569
  restitution, 566, 568
  specific performance, 569–572
  valuation of assets, 583–587
  valuation of unprofitable enterprises or projects, 587–589
Damnum emergens, 590, 593
Days, Drew, 362
De facto discrimination, 408–409, 411
De facto expropriation, 450, 469
Default of party, 126–128
Defenses
  absence of consent, 156
  countermeasures, 156
  distress, 156
  force majeure, 156
  forum election cases, 374–375
  host state defenses, 156–158
  necessity, 156, 157–158
  self-defense, 156
de Fina, A. A., 130
De jure discrimination, 408, 411, 412
Delaume, G.R., 257
Deliberation and drafting of awards, 180–182
Denmark
  Chile-Denmark BIT, 424
Developing countries
  FDI's effect on, 4–5, 8
  hostile environment in, 23–24
  investment protection and, 8–9
  less developed countries (LDCs), 2, 5, 6
  public policy and arbitration in, 642
Dies ad quem, 342
Dies a quo, 342
Diplomatic espousal, 27–33, 42
Discrimination, 397–427
  burden of proof, 412
  competitive relationship test, 401
  de *facto*, 408–409, 411
  de jure, 408, 411, 412
  discriminatory impairment, 426–427

  disproportionately disadvantaged test, 409
  intent as part of test for violation, 412–413
  like circumstances, 400–408
  likeness, 404–405, 407, 408
  MFN clauses, 397, 413–425
    scope and interpretation of, 415–417
    substantive and procedural rights, 417–425
  national treatment standard, 398–443
    application of, 400–413
    relevant class of comparators, 400–408
    relevant standard of no less favorably, 408–411
  proof of discriminatory intent based on nationality, 411–413
  tax rebates as, 403
  unreasonable distinctions, 403
Discriminatory impairment, 426–427
Dismissals in arbitration, 119
Distress, 156
Diversity jurisdiction, 13
Document production, 161–163
Dominican Republic–Central American–United States Free Trade Agreement (DR-CAFTA), 71–74
  annulment and set aside, 638
  Article 1.2, 71–72
  Article 10.7, 444–445
  consent to arbitration, 241, 242
  consolidation of claims, 196
  expropriation and compensation, 444–445
  governing law, 208
  nationality of investors, 304
Draft Articles on Responsibility of States for Internationally Wrongful Acts, 564–565
Draft Convention on the Protection of Foreign Property, 48
DR-CAFTA. *See* Dominican Republic–Central American–United States Free Trade Agreement
Dual nationals, status of, 300–304
Due process, 470, 641, 697
Dugard, John, 350–352

E

ECHR. *See* European Convention on Human Rights
Economic development of host states, 272–276
ECT. *See* Energy Charter Treaty
Ecuador
   Ecuador-UK BIT, 250
   forum election cases, 376–377
   likeness and discrimination claims, 405–408
   Mercosur, 64
   U.S.-Ecuador BIT, 296, 376–377, 406–407, 573–574, 703
   value-added tax on oil companies, 406–407
EDF (European Development Fund)
Effective control, 333
Effective nationality principle, 292–294, 303–304
Egypt
   Egypt-Greece BIT, 459
   exhaustion of remedies, 364–365
   Investment Law of 1989, 234
   Law No. 43 of 1974 Concerning the Investment of Arab and Foreign Funds and the Free Zone, 233–234
   likeness and discrimination claims, 405–406
   nationality of investor, 301–303
   set aside of award, 649
Ejusdem generis principle, 418, 425
Embargo of Mexican petroleum, 11
Eminent domain, 429
Energy Charter Treaty (ECT)
   Article 13, 443–444
   Article 21, 444
   consent to arbitration, 241
   expropriation, 443–444
   investor-state arbitration, 61–64
   MFN treatment, 422
   nationality of investors, 324
   preinvestment protection, 285
   taxation, 444
   umbrella clauses, 544
Energy Efficiency and Related Environmental Aspects, 62

Enforcement of awards, 182–183, 198–199, 675–700
   confirmation, 677–678
   execution problems, 684–699
   New York Convention, 679–684
   sovereign immunity and Washington Convention, 699–700
English Arbitration Act (1950), 197
English Arbitration Act (1996), 646
Equal market access, 63
Equity
   damages, 603–605
   remedies, 336
Espousal
   diplomatic espousal, 27–33, 42, 225, 298
Estonia
   forum election cases, 372–373
   U.S.-Estonia BIT, 373
Ethiopia, suspension of U.S. aid to, 244
European Commission on incompatibilities between the bilateral investment treaties of states acceding to EU, 704–705
European Convention on Human Rights (ECHR), 365
European Court of Human Rights, 365
European Development Fund (EDF), 55
European Union, 54–55, 704–705. *See also individual countries*
Evidence
   compulsory production, 165–167
   document production, 161–163
   FAA, 163–165
   hybrid system, 159
   IBA Rules, 159–160
   marshalling of, 158–163
   request for preservation of, 141–142
   Section 1782 to compel testimony or production of document, 165–167
   third-party evidence, 163–167
   witness statements, 159–160
Exclusive contractual dispute provision, 391–394
Execution of awards, 684–699
Exequatur, 677–678
Exhaustion of remedies
   BITs, 120
   customary international law, 347–357

Exhaustion of remedies (*continued*)
　futility of, 348, 349–352, 527
　ICSID, 359
　investment treaty arbitration, 357–359
　local remedies, 30–32, 119–120,
　　347–365
　NAFTA, 360–361
　Netherlands-Czech Republic BIT, 357
　reasonably available, 362–363
　recours en requête civile, 365
　waiting periods, 357
　waivers, 348–349
Expropriation, 429–489
　compensation standards, 573–578
　contractual and quasi-contractual rights,
　　439–440
　creeping, 450
　customary international law,
　　430, 441
　de facto, 450, 469
　de jure taking power, 469
　direct, 450
　domestic remedies sought, 469
　DR-CAFTA, 444–445
　due process, 470
　ECT, 62, 443–444
　fundamental rights, 468
　government measures, 455–461
　　duration of effect of, 468
　　intent, nature, or character of,
　　　461–465
　　reliance on, 465–468
　historical overview, 430–438
　　post-World War II period until present,
　　　435–438
　　pre-World War II period, 433–435
　Hull formula. *See* Hull formula
　indirect or regulatory, 430, 450–476
　lex ferenda, 430
　NAFTA, 442–443
　other factors, 470–476
　pacta sunt servanda, 441
　Penn Central test, 484–486
　per se taking, 484
　protection of investments and property
　　against, 438–441
　public use, 486
　purpose analysis, 464–465
　reasonable investment-backed
　　expectations, 485
　stabilization clauses, 440–441
　substantial deprivation test, 460–461, 468
　transfer of investment of government or
　　third parties, 469–470
　U.S. approach to, 482–489
　U.S. model BIT, 454–455
　U.S. takings law and customary
　　international law, 488

F

FAA. *See* Federal Arbitration Act
Fair and equitable treatment, 427, 491–539
　arbitrary impairment clause example,
　　508–509
　arbitrary treatment, 507–510
　bad faith, 506
　coercion of foreign investors, 523–525
　compensation, standard of, 579
　definition of, 214, 504–531
　denial of justice, 525–531
　denial of justice, definition of, 526–527
　ECT, 62
　expropriation and U.S. takings law, 489
　history of, 503–504
　legitimate or reasonable expectations and
　　stability, 510–519
　minimum standards, 495–496
　NAFTA, 500–502
　national treatment standard vs., 491–492
　plain or ordinary meaning, 504–505
　public international law, 214
　relationship to customary international
　　law, 493–502
　transparency, 519–523
Fair market value, 584
FCN treaties. *See* Friendship, Commerce,
　　and Navigation (FCN) treaties
FDI. *See* Foreign direct investment
Federal Arbitration Act (FAA), 163–165,
　　644, 650, 676
Fees of arbitrators, 85–86
Fifth Amendment, 697
Financial guarantees to cover costs and
　　eventual award, 142

INDEX

Finland
  EC claims against (2007), 705
  Finland-Algeria BIT, 305
Force majeure, 156, 393
Foreign assistance, withholding as retribution for expropriation of U.S. property, 243–246
Foreign Assistance Act of 1961, 243–244
Foreign direct investment (FDI)
  control and management of, 248
  defined, 1
  distinguished from portfolio investment, 248–249
  effects of, 4–5
  LDCs and, 2
Foreign Sovereign Immunities Act (FSIA, 1976), 20, 112, 697
Fork in the road treaty provisions and waiver, 368–377
Former Soviet countries, 398, 646
Forum elections, 367–395
  disputes, 371–377
  fork in the road treaty provisions, 368–371
  investment treaties and contractual forum selection clauses, 380–395
  irrevocable, 371
  mandatory procedural law, 93–95, 133
  measures, 377–380
  national courts and treaties, 367–380
  policy behind *fork in the road* treaty provisions, 370–371
  triple identity test, 372
France
  Court of Cassation
    judicial consolidation and, 197–198, 638, 649
    set aside of award and, 649
  France-Argentina BIT on governing law, 84, 368–369, 381–391, 394
  invasion and puppet government in Mexico, 27
  trends in arbitration in, 640
Free Trade Agreements (FTAs). *See also specific countries and regions*
  appellate body, proposal for, 713

DR-CAFTA. *See* Dominican Republic-Central American-United States Free Trade Agreement
FTAA. *See* Free Trade Area of the Americas
Mexico-Bolivia, 196
NAFTA. *See* North American Free Trade Agreement
Southern Cone free trade zone. *See* Mercosur or Mercosul
U.S.-Australia, 446
U.S.-Chile, 196, 446
U.S.-Colombia, 446
U.S.-Morocco, 241–242, 446
U.S.-Peru, 446
U.S.-Singapore, 252–253
Free Trade Area of the Americas (FTAA), 68–71
  consent to arbitration, 242
Free Trade Commission. *See* NAFTA Free Trade Commission (FTC)
Friedland, Paul D., 585–587
Friendship, Commerce, and Navigation (FCN) treaties, 37, 426, 430–431, 503, 532–534
FSIA. *See* Foreign Sovereign Immunities Act
FTAA. *See* Free Trade Area of the Americas
FTC. *See* NAFTA Free Trade Commission
Full protection and security, 491–539
  historical development, 532–534
  MFN vs., 491–492
  minimum standards, 495–496
  modern investment treaties and meaning of protection and security, 534–539
  national treatment standard vs., 491–492
  relationship to customary international law, 493–502
Futility of available local remedies, 349–352
Future jurisprudence of investment protection, 709–714

G

General Claims Convention (1923), 36
Germany
  Germany-Russia BIT, 283

Germany (*continued*)
   lump sum agreement of German Democratic Republic with Austria, 38–39
   Model BIT of 1991 on definition of company, 307
   reparation from Poland at end of WWI, 434
Ghana, 141–142
   contract arbitration clauses and, 227–230
Globalization, 10
Good Neighbor Policy (FDR administration), 11
Gotanda, John Y., 613–614
Governing law, 84–85, 201–217
   host state law, 209–213
   NAFTA, 202–203
   rules chosen by parties, 202–204
Greece
   banishment and confiscation of property of U.S. citizen by, 28–29
   Egypt-Greece BIT, 459
   Greece-Republic of Korea BIT, 305
Guinea, Republic of, 111–112, 144
Gunboat diplomacy, 9, 26–27

H

Hague Codification Conference (1930), 564
Havana Charter of 1948, 48, 503, 534
Hearings, 177–179
Helms Amendment, 244–246
Hickenlooper Amendment, 243–244
Higgins, R., 20, 438–439
High-fructose corn syrup (HFCS) producers' suit against Mexico, 192–194
History of investment dispute resolution, 11–43
  barriers to recovery by foreign investors, 13–26
  diplomatic espousal, 27–33
  early investment protection regimes, 34–42
  gunboat diplomacy, 26–27
  harms suffered by foreign investors, 11–13
  limitations of historic dispute settlement processes, 42–43
  traditional remedies for foreign investors, 26–33
Hobbes, Thomas, 14
Hong Kong and consolidation of claims, 198
Hopkins, Lauren A., 72–75
Host state law, 209–213
Hull formula, 26, 433, 435, 436

I

IBA. *See* International Bar Association
ICC. *See* International Chamber of Commerce
ICJ. *See* International Court of Justice
ICSID and ICSID Convention (or Washington Convention), 49–51, 77
  Additional Facility Rules, 147, 185, 280, 620, 628, 648, 651, 712
  annulment, 628
  anti-arbitration injunctions (Art. 26), 110–116
  appointment of tribunal, 128–129
  arbitration awards, enforcement of and sovereign immunity, 699–700
  Arbitration Rules. *See* Rules of Procedure for Arbitration Proceedings
  amicus curiae, 172, 708
  ancillary claims including counterclaims, 153
  annulment procedure, 628, 629–634, 712
  appellate body, proposal for, 713–714
  appointment of tribunal, 84, 128–129
  arbitration procedure, 91
  Article 25, 233, 236, 256–259, 301–303, 315
    annulment and set-aside, 628
    change of nationality, 343–345
    investment characteristics, 265–276
  Article 25(1), 154, 222
  Article 26, 138, 359
  Article 36, 126
  Article 38, 187
  Article 39, 141, 146–147

Article 42, 202, 203–204, 209–213
Article 44, 95–97, 173
Article 45, 127
Article 47, 142
Article 52, 97, 199, 628, 629–630
Article 54, 570, 678, 699
Article 55, 699
Article 61, 620
award and enforcement, 87–89, 182–183
BITs provision for arbitration under, 52
characteristics of investment, 248
confirmation, 678
civil society groups, 171
consent clauses, 224
consolidation of claims, 89–90, 186–189
contracting parties, 343
cost and speed, 85–86
costs and attorneys' fees, award of, 620–624
counterclaims, 154
creation and role of, 50–51
default judgments, 127
defenses, 157–158
definitions of investment and jurisdiction, 256–276
development of, 49–50
document production, 161
dual jurisdictional requirements, 259–260
dual nationals, 300–304
exhaustion of remedies, 359
entered into force (1966), 50
foreign control exception, 333
forum election cases, 374–375, 381–392
governing law, 84–85
host state law, 209
ICSID, creation of, 50–51
ICSDI Institutional Rules, 82, 221, 303
initial session of tribunal, 134
interim measures, 86–87, 137–138
  effect of recommendation, 140
  enforcement of, 138, 140
  enjoining parallel domestic proceedings, 143–146
  expedited procedure, 147
  obtaining evidence, 141
  power to provide, 138–140
  preventing excessive disclosure of information, 141
  requests for, 140–141
  securing financial guarantees, 141
Investment. See Investment, concept of
Investor. See Nationality of investor
jurisdictional requirements of ICSID Convention, 82, 122, 125, 202, 259
jurisdictional issues, 259, 260–265, 343–345
language of arbitration, 83, 133
minority and noncontrolling standing, 315–318
national investment legislation, 75, 235–236
nationality of investor, 291–292, 313–314, 343–345
natural persons, provisions regarding, 295–296
place of arbitration, 83
qualified investors, 294–339
Request for Arbitration, 122–126
Rules of Procedure for Arbitration Proceedings, 78, 95, 97
  Article 28, 620–621
  comparison with UNCITRAL Rules, 81–90
  Rule 1, 123
  Rule 2, 123–124
service of process, 122–125
shareholder standing, 314–339
situs of arbitration, 132
subject matter jurisdiction, 256–257, 697
travaux preparatoire, 161, 256–259
unity of investment, 276–280
withdrawal from, 704
World Bank Report of Executive Directors on, 97–98
World Bank role, 50–51
ILC. See International Law Commission
Illegal agreements, 641
IMF (International Monetary Fund), 1
Immigration and Nationality Act (U.S.), 297
Immunity. See also Sovereign immunity
  restrictive immunity from execution, concept of, 686–693
  state immunity, 14–15, 20
Impossibility, 571–572

India, Union Carbide gas plant tragedy (1984), 15
Indirect investment, 248, 319–339
Indonesia
  annulment and set aside, 632–633, 642
  effect of legal system on investment in, 12–13
  fair and equitable treatment, 529
  forum election cases, 381
  national court intervention in UNCITRAL case, 102–104
In dubio pars mitior est sequenda, 559
Inefficiency of local courts, 15–16
Injunctions, 569–572
  anti-arbitration, 105–110
Institutions that administer arbitrations, 77–78
Interest, 605–611
  compound or simple, 609–611
  pre-/post-award, 606
Interim relief, 137–147
  case law review, 140–146
  confidentiality, 142
  in contexts other than investment arbitration, 146
  enforcement of, 138
  expedited procedure, 147
  financial guarantees, 142
  ICSID recommendation, effect of, 140
  legal framework for, 138–140
  to obtain evidence, 141–142
  requests for, 140–141
  stay of parallel domestic proceedings, 143–146
  timing, 146–147
International Bank for Reconstruction and Development (IRBD), 7
International Bar Association on taking of evidence, 159–160, 162–163
International Centre for Settlement of Investment Disputes. *See* entry for ICSID and ICSID Convention
International Chamber of Commerce (ICC)
  Article 6, 127–128
  choice of option to arbitrate under, 629
  consolidation of claims, 196–197
  default judgments, 127–128
  dispute referral, 55
  injunction against arbitration by, 107–110
  International Court of Arbitration, 79, 126
  jurisdiction, 259, 280
  registration of requests for arbitration, 126
  rules, 79–80
  situs of arbitration, 132
International Court of Justice (ICJ)
  on content of international law, 213–214
  default judgments, 127
  expropriation, 432
  interim measures, 146
  on lump sum agreements, 39–40
International law. *See also* Customary international law
  defined, 213–214
  sources of, 214–216
International Law Commission
  Articles on Responsibility of States for Internationally Wrongful Acts, 157, 564–565, 567, 598–599, 602–603
International Monetary Fund (IMF), 1
International Trade Organization (ITO), 48
Intervention
  diplomatic espousal, 27–33, 42
  local court intervention, 104–105
Investment, concept of, 247–289
  assumption of risk, 269–270
  characteristics of under the ICSID Convention, 265–276
    assumption of risk, 269–270
    assumption of risk, 269–270
    contribution to economic development of host state, 272–276
    duration of activity, 266–269
  definitions
    historical perspective, 247–249
    in investment treaties, 250–253
    jurisdiction of arbitral tribunals and, 256–276
    Washington (ICSID) Convention and, 256–276
  definitions of in investment protection instruments, 250–256
  definitions of in national investment law, 254–256

INDEX

foreign direct investment, 248
indirect investment, 248
jurisdictional issues. *See*
Jurisdictional issues
portfolio investment, 248, 249
preinvestment protection, 285–289
regularity of profit and
return, 269
substantial commitment, 271
unity of investment under the ICSID
Convention, 276–280
Washington (ICSID) Convention
Article 25 on, 265–276
decisions based on type of
investment, 260–265
Investment contracts, arbitration
clauses in, 225–230
Investment guarantee programs, 40–41
Investment protection
future jurisprudence of, 709–714
purpose of, 5–10
Investment treaties. *See* Bilateral investment
treaties (BITs); Multilateral
investment treaties; Treaties
Investor. *See* Nationality of investor
Iran-U.S. Claims Tribunal, 190, 294,
380–381, 433, 575
costs and attorneys' fees, 619–620
expropriation decisions, 437
Iran-U.S. relations, 41–42, 146
Italy
Italy-Jordan BIT, 529
Italy-Morocco BIT, 187–188
Italy-United Arab Emirates
BIT, 298–300
Italy-U.S. FCN (Friendship, Commerce,
and Navigation) Treaty, 349
nationality, determination of, 298–300
national's store looted by Venezuelan
soldiers, 36

J

Jay Treaty (1794), 34–35
Jecker claim against Mexico (1860), 27
Jordan
Italy-Jordan BIT, 529

Judicial review of non-ICSID awards,
636–637
Jurisdictional issues, 147–153, 219–220
amicus curiae, 168–171
arbitral rules other than Washington
Convention, 280–285
bifurcation, 147
Calvo Doctrine, 16–19, 488
change of national identity and
investment treaties, 341–342
change of national identity and
Washington Convention, 343–345
civil society groups and amicus
submissions, 171–172
compromis, 220, 221, 242–246, 258–259
consent to arbitral jurisdiction, 208–209,
219–246
contract arbitration clauses, 225–230
contribution to economic development
of host state, 272–276
counterclaims, 154
definitions of investment, 256–276,
280–285
in foreign investor's home courts, 19–20
ICSID requirements, 82, 202
decisions based on type of investment,
260–265
Qualified investor. *See* Nationality of
investor
investment protection treaties as consent
to arbitration, 236–242
methods of accepting government's offer
to arbitrate, 221–222
national investment legislation, 230–236
pacta sunt servanda, 222
personal jurisdiction, 697
preliminary vs. merits issues, 149–153
ratione personae, 343, 345
subject matter jurisdiction, 256–257
submitting case under Washington
Convention and investment treaty
or law, 259
substantial investment
commitment, 271
travaux preparatoire, 256–259
Jus cogens, 303
Jus sanguinis, 296–297
Jus soli, 297

K

King, Jonas, 28–29
Kinsella, N. Stephan, 398–399
Korea, Republic of
    Foreign Investment Promotion Act, 255
    Greece-Republic of Korea BIT, 305
    Republic of Korea-Panama BIT, 305

L

Laird, Ian, 711
Language of arbitration, 83, 130, 133–134
Latin America. *See also individual countries*
    Calvo Doctrine in, 16–19, 69, 488
    Dominican Republic–Central American–United States Free Trade Agreement (DR-CAFTA), 71–74
    environmental politics in, 69–71
    Free Trade Area of the Americas (FTAA), 68–71
    gunboat diplomacy in, 26–27
    trends in arbitration in, 640
Latvia, double tariff case, 426–427
Less developed countries (LDCs), 2, 5, 6
Lex arbitri, 91, 133, 675
Libya and nationalization of concession contract, 436–437
License as legal basis of investment, 440
Liechtenstein and nationality issues, 292–294, 304
Lis pendens, 663
Lithuania
    Norway-Lithuania BIT, 518
    Ukraine-Lithuania BIT, 322–324
Local remedies rule, 347–365, 527 *See also* Exhaustion of remedies
Lomé Conventions, 54–56, 241
London Court of International Arbitration Rules, 648
Lost profits for breach of contract, 589–596
Lucrum cessans, 590
Lump sum agreements, 38–40

M

MAI. *See* Multilateral Agreement on Investment
Malaysia
    Chile-Malaysia BIT, 424–425, 515
Manifest disregard for law, 644
Mauritania Investment Code, 231
Maximilian, Emperor, 27
Mendelson, Maurice, 341, 343–344
Mercosur or Mercosul (Mercado Común del Sur), 64–67, 241
Merits phase of arbitration, 153–177
Methanol and claims against California, 404
Mexican-American Claims Commission, 496
Mexican Constitution, 297
Mexico
    Austria-Mexico BIT, 425
    Calvo Doctrine, opposition to, 16
    Constitution, 297
    damages, 588–589
    expropriation, 433, 469
    fair and equitable treatment, 510–515, 521–522
    forum election cases, 378–380, 381
    Free Trade Agreement between Mexico and Bolivia, 196
    Jecker claim against (1860), 27
    Mexico-Bolivia Free Trade Agreement, 196
    NAFTA, 56–61, 635. *See also* North American Free Trade Agreement
    nationalization of petroleum industry, 11
    peso crisis, 332
    Spain-Mexico BIT, 425, 514
    sugar mills expropriated by, 403–404
    tax on soft drinks, 192–194
    tax rebates to Mexican resellers/exporters of cigarettes, 403
    umbrella clauses, 560
    U.S.-Mexico General Claims Commission, 36
MFN. *See* Most-favored nation treatment
MIGA (Multilateral Investment Guarantee Agency), 41
Mitigation, 603

Model treaties
    BITs. *See* Canada Model BIT; U.K. Model
        BIT; U.S. Model BIT of 2004
    differences between U.S. and European, 54
    Morocco, 143–144
    dual jurisdictional requirements and,
        259–260
    Italy-Morocco BIT, 187–188
    U.S.-Morocco Free Trade Agreement,
        241–242, 446
Most-favored nation treatment
    (MFN), 62, 63, 66
    Albania-Croatia BIT, 414
    discrimination, 397, 407, 413–425
    exhaustion of local remedies, 120
    fair and equitable treatment and full
        protection and security vs.,
        491–492
    scope and interpretation of clauses,
        415–417
    substantive and procedural rights,
        417–425
    waiting periods and, 119
Multilateral Agreement on Investment
    (MAI), 54, 74–75
    consolidation of claims, 195–196
Multilateral Investment Guarantee Agency
    (MIGA), 41
Multilateral investment treaties, 54–75
    consent to arbitration, 241
    consolidation of claims, 195–196
    Lomé Conventions, 54–56, 241

N

NAFTA. *See* North American Free
    Trade Agreement
NAFTA Free Trade Commission (FTC),
    56–57
    amicus curiae, 170–171, 172
    fair and equitable treatment and full
        protection and security, 491, 493
    FTC Interpretation of July 2001,
        500–502
National court intervention, 367–380
    in ICSID arbitration, 112–116
    in UNCITRAL case, 102–104

National investment legislation,
    75, 230–236
    definition of investment in, 254–256
Nationality of investor, 142–143, 291–345
    applicable law, 296–300
    change of national identity, 340–345
    continuous nationality rule,
        340–341, 342
    corporations and other legal entities,
        304–314
        customary law on nationality of,
            308–312
        indirect shareholder control of entity
            incorporated in host state,
            319–339
        minority and noncontrolling
            shareholders, 315–319
    diplomatic espousal claims, 32–33
    DR-CAFTA, 304
    ECT, 324
    effective nationality principle, 292–294,
        303–304
    forum election cases, 381
    investment treaty and Washington
        Convention provisions, 304–308
    jurisdiction
        arbitral tribunals under investment
            treaties and change of national
            identity, 341–342
        change of national identity and
            Washington Convention, 343–345
    jus cogens, 303
    jus sanguinis, 296–297
    jus soli, 297
    natural persons, 292–294, 295–304
        applicable law, 296–300
        dual nationals, status of, 300–304
        investment treaty and Washington
            Convention provisions, 295–296
    proof of discriminatory intent based on
        nationality, 411–413
    qualified investors under investment
        treaties and Washington
        Convention, 294–339
    standing of shareholders, 314–339
        under investment treaties, 315
        under Washington Convention,
            315–318

Nationalization of industries.
    See Expropriation
National treatment standard, 62, 66,
        398–399, 427
    compensation, standard of, 579
    disproportionately disadvantaged test, 409
    fair and equitable treatment and, 491–492
    protectionist intent, 411
Natural persons. *See* Nationality of investor
Netherlands
    consolidation of claims, 198
    Czech Republic-Netherlands BIT, 154–156
    Netherlands-Argentina BIT, 203
    Netherlands-Bolivia BIT, 329–331
    Netherlands-Czech Republic BIT,
        204, 236–237, 281, 315, 336–337,
        357, 394
        non-ICSID challenge proceedings case
            studies, 662
    Netherlands-Poland BIT, 282
    non-ICSID case studies, 661
New International Economic Order (NIEO),
        5, 23–26, 52, 62–63, 435
New York Convention on the Recognition
        and Enforcement of Foreign
        Arbitral Awards, 87–88, 101, 139,
        182
    set aside, 648, 649
    enforcement of awards, 679–684
    national court intervention not allowed, 105
New Zealand, 706
NGOs. *See* Non-governmental organizations
NIEO. *See* New International
        Economic Order
Nonarbitrability and non-ICSID awards,
        639–640
Non-discrimination, 397–427. *See also*
        Discrimination
Non-governmental organizations (NGOs), 5
    amicus submissions by, 173–177
    confidentiality issues for, 706–707
Nonparty public interest groups, 167–177
Non-pecuniary remedies. *See* Damages
North American Free Trade Agreement
        (NAFTA), 56–61, 412–413, 702
    amicus curiae, 168–171
    Annex 201.1, 297
    Annex 1137.2, 121

Article 102, 521, 656
Article 201, 297
Article 1101, 149–153, 413
Article 1102, 400–404, 409–413, 492,
        665, 667
Article 1103, 492
Article 1105, 361–362, 491, 500–502,
        656–657, 665
Article 1110, 442–443, 477, 479–481, 652
Article 1116, 342
Article 1117, 342
Article 1118, 99
Article 1119, 121
Article 1120, 192
Article 1121, 361, 370, 378–379
Article 1126, 185, 190–196
Article 1128, 168–169
Article 1135, 570
Article 1139, 251–252, 253, 284–285
Chapter 11, 54, 56–61, 328, 358, 477
competitive relationship test, 401
confidentiality issues, 707
consent to arbitration, 241
consolidation of claims, 90, 185, 190–195
costs and attorneys' fees, 618
courier services, 404–405
definition of investment, 251–252, 284
delivery of documents, 121
derivative damages, 318
dies ad quem, 342
dies a quo, 342
discrimination cases, 404–405
ECT Article 26, 62
exhaustion of local remedies, 360–361
expropriation and compensation,
        442–443, 453
fair and equitable treatment, 500–502,
        524–525
forum election cases, 378–380
FTC Interpretation of July 2001, 500–502
government legal fees, 624–625
investment, definition of, 251–252
jurisdictional issues, 148–149
    amicus curiae, 168–171
    preliminary vs. merits issues, 149–153
minority shareholders, 318
nationality, determination of, 297
national treatment standard, 400–413

non-ICSID awards case studies, 651–660
notice of claim, 121
waivers, 361, 370
Norway
Norway-Lithuania BIT, 518
Notice of arbitration claims, 121

O

Organization for Economic Cooperation and Development (OECD)
  denial of justice, 526
  discrimination test, 401
  draft convention on protection of foreign investment, 503, 534
  investment protection role of, 7, 48–49, 196, 250, 285
  Multilateral Agreement on Investment (MIA), 54, 74–75
  protection of foreign property, 53–54

P

Pacta sunt servanda, 222, 441, 542, 559
Pakistan
  anti-arbitration injunctions and, 107–110, 112–116
  fair and equitable treatment, 545–548, 560, 561
  Pakistan–Switzerland BIT, 112–116, 394
Panama
  Republic of Korea-Panama BIT, 305
Paraguay
  Buenos Aires Protocol, 67
  Mercosur, 64
  Peru-Paraguay BIT, 470
Paulsson, Jan, 474, 527
Permanent Court of International Justice (PCIJ), 432
Personal jurisdiction, 19, 697–698
Peru
  electricity company owned privately, 276–280
  Mercosur, 64
  Peru-Paraguay BIT, 470
  U.S.-Peru Free Trade Agreement, 446

Philippines
  Switzerland-Philippines BIT, 392–393
Piercing corporate veil, 684
  customary international law, 308
  indirect shareholders, 319
  siège sociale, 323
Place of arbitration, 83
Plain or ordinary meaning, 504–505
Poland
  Netherlands-Poland BIT, 282
  reparation to Germany at end of WWI, 434
Political barriers to recovery by foreign investors, 23–26
Political risk insurance, 41
Polluter pays principle, 62
Portfolio investment, 248–249
Portugal, 433–434
Posthearing briefs, 179
Preinvestment protection, 285–289
Private capital, 45, 48
Priyatna Abdurrasyid, 102–104
Procedural rules, 77–90
  ICSID Rules of Procedure for Arbitration Proceedings, 78
  International Chamber of Commerce Rules, 79–80
  Stockholm Chamber of Commerce Rules, 79
  UNCITRAL Arbitration Rules, 80–81
Profit and return, 269
Protectionist intent, 411
Public international law, 213–217
  equitable principles, 216
  ICJ, 213–214
Public policy challenge to award, 640–642, 667, 683

Q

Qualified investors, 294–339
  applicable law, 296–300
  corporations and other legal entities, 304–314
  juridical person, definition of, 313
  natural persons, 295–304
  standing in host state, 319

R

Racketeer Influenced and Corrupt Organizations (RICO) Act, 639
Ratione personae, 343, 345
Read, Pippa, 92–95, 104–105
Recours en requête civile, 365
Reinish, August, 685–693
Remedies for foreign investors. *See also* Damages
 diplomatic espousal, 27–33, 42
 election of, 368
 equitable, 336
 exhaustion of local remedies, 119–120, 347–365. *See also* Exhaustion of remedies
 gunboat diplomacy, 9, 26–27
 history of, 26–33
 limitations of historic remedies, 42
 piercing corporate veil, 336
 reasonably available, 362–363
Reparation, 565, 567–569
Request for Arbitration, 122–125
 registration or screening of, 125–126
Res judicata, 663
Restatement (Third) of Foreign Relations Law, 437–438
Restitution. *See* Damages
Roosevelt, Franklin D., 11
Rubins, Noah, 398–399, 415–417
Russian Federation
 Germany-Russia BIT, 283
Ryan, Patti, 59

S

Sabahi, Borzu, 603–605, 606–608
Sanctions in arbitration, 119
Satisfaction as remedy, 566
Schreuer, C.H., 95–96, 97, 186–187, 238–241, 248, 260, 265–266, 272, 359, 371–372
Schreuer, Christoph, 110–111
Self-defense, 156
Service of process, 121, 122, 697
Set aside of award. *See* Annulment and set aside
Settlement, 116–117, 118
Shareholders
 indirect control of entity incorporated in host state, 319–339
 minority and noncontrolling derivative damages, 318–319
 standing under investment treaties, 315
 standing under Washington Convention, 315–318
 standing, generally, 314–339
Siège sociale, 308, 323
Singapore
 forum selection and waiver, 370
 U.S.-Singapore Free Trade Agreement, 252–253
Slovak Republic, 144–145
Somalia Investment Act, 232
Southern Cone free trade zone. *See* Mercosur or Mercosul (Mercado Común del Sur)
Sovereign immunity
 compromis, 242–246
 enforcement of awards and Washington Convention, 699–700
 in foreign investor's courts, 20
 in host country, 14–15
Soviet Union, 434, 646
Spain
 Argentina-Spain BIT, 119–120, 418
 Barcelona street car company seized by government, 11–12
 Canadian electric company with Belgian shareholders, Spain's refusal to pay, 33
 Chile-Spain BIT, 120, 418
 fair and equitable treatment, 510–512, 513, 514, 522
 financial guarantees to cover costs, 142
 Spain-Mexico BIT, 425, 514
Specific performance, 569–572
Speed of arbitration, 85–86
Sri Lanka
 Sri Lanka-UK BIT, 536
 U.S.-Sri Lanka BIT, 286–289
Standing, 314–339
State immunity, 14–15, 20. *See also* Sovereign immunity

Stay of parallel domestic proceedings, 143–146
Steven, Lee A., 57–58
Stockholm Chamber of Commerce, 79, 283, 629
Substantial deprivation test, 460–461, 468
Sweden
  Arbitration Act, 647, 662
  EC claims against (2007), 705
Switzerland
  anti-arbitration injunctions in, 111–112
  exhaustion of local remedies in, 352–357
  Pakistan–Switzerland BIT, 112–116, 394
  Switzerland-Philippines BIT, 392–393
  waiver of right to set aside awards, 648

T

Takings. *See* Expropriation
Tanzania national investment laws, 255
Taxation, 444
Third-party evidence, 163–167
Timing
  appointment of tribunal, 129
  arbitration awards, time limit for issuance, 179–180
  arbitration waiting periods, 117–119, 121
  duration of investment activity, 266–269
  indirect or regulatory expropriation government measures, duration of effect of, 468
  initial session of tribunal under ICSID Rules of Procedure, 134
  interim relief, 146–147
  waiting periods and exhaustion of remedies, 357
Tollefson, C., 657–660
Transparency, 519–523
Travaux preparatoires, 161, 256–259, 496
Treaties. *See also* Bilateral investment treaties (BITs); *specific types and by name; see also* Index of Treaties
  change of nationality, 341–342
  choice-of-law clauses, 204
  compensation standards for breach of obligations, 578–583
  as consent to arbitration, 236–242
  consolidation of related claims, 185–199
  contractual forum selection clauses and, 380–395
  definitions of investment in, 250–253
  election of remedies, 368
  exhaustion of local remedies, 357–359
  fork in the road provisions and waiver, 368–371
  forum election and national courts, 367–380
  full protection and security, 534–539
  interpretation of, 204–209
  jurisdictional requirements for submitting case under both Washington Convention and investment treaty or law, 259
  jurisdiction and change of national identity, 341–342
  minority and noncontrolling shareholder standing, 315
  model treaties, 53–54
  multilateral investment treaties, 54–75
  natural persons, provisions regarding, 295–296
  provisions regarding corporations and other legal persons, 304–308
  qualified investors under, 294–339
  roles of in expropriation, 442–449
  shareholder standing, 314–339
  substantive and procedural provisions, trends in development of, 705–709
  trends in, 702–705
Tribe, Laurence, 362
Turkmenistan, 639

U

UK Model BIT, 53–54, 543–544
Ukraine
  definition of investment in, 254
  Ukraine-Lithuania BIT, 322–324
  Ukraine-U.S. BIT, 324
Umbrella clauses, 541–561
  arbitral decisions, 392–393, 544–558
  in dubio pars mitior est sequenda, 559
  historical background, 542–544
  restrictive approach, 561

INDEX

UNCITRAL. *See* United Nations Commission on International Trade Law
UNCITRAL Model Law on International Commercial Arbitration, 636–637, 644, 646, 652, 661, 667, 677–678
UNCTAD. *See* United Nations Conference on Trade & Development
Union Carbide gas plant tragedy (1984), 15
United Kingdom
  Ecuador-UK BIT, 250
  interim measures, 146
  Jay Treaty (1794), 34–35
  Model BIT. *See* UK Model BIT
  Sovereign Immunity Act, 700
  Sri Lanka-UK BIT, 536
  United Kingdom-Czech Republic BIT, 283
United Nations
  Charter on use of force, 9
  Compensation Commission, 294
  Economic and Social Council (ECOSOC), 48
  General Assembly resolutions. *See* United Nations General Assembly (UNGA)
  International Law Commission, 564
  Secretary General questionnaire on foreign investment (1961), 46–48
United Nations Commission on International Trade Law (UNCITRAL)
  ad hoc arbitration, 236
  amicus curiae, 168–171
  appointment of tribunal, 84, 128–129
  Arbitration Rules, 80–81
    Article 2, 121
    Article 15(1), 169–170
    Article 19.3, 155
    Article 21(4), 152–153
    Article 25(4), 169
    Article 38, 615–616
    Article 39, 611–612
  award and enforcement, 87–89
  choice of option to arbitrate under, 629
  comparison with ICSID Rules, 81–90
  consolidation of related claims, 89–90, 185, 189–190
  contract arbitration clauses, 227–230
  cost and speed, 85–86
  costs and attorneys' fees, 615–620, 618
  definition of investment, 284
  disqualification of arbitrators, 129
  document production, 161
  governing law, 84–85
  government legal fees, 624–625
  hearings, 177–179
  interim measures, 86–87
  jurisdiction, 259, 280–282
  jurisdictional issues, 148–149, 149–153
  language of arbitration, 83, 133–134
  Mercosur, 66
  model law, 629
  monetary awards, 139
  notices of claim, 121
  place of arbitration, 83, 132–133
  Request for Arbitration, 122–125
  service of process, 122–125
  Working Group, 171
United Nations Conference on Trade & Development (UNCTAD), 5, 438, 507
United Nations Convention on the Recognition and Enforcement of Foreign Arbitral Awards. *See* New York Convention on the Recognition and Enforcement of Foreign Arbitral Awards
United Nations General Assembly (UNGA)
  Charter of Economic Rights and Duties of States (CERDS), 25
  Resolution 824, 45
  Resolution 1803, 24, 435, 437
  Resolution 3171, 435
  Resolution 3201, 435
  Resolution 3281, 435
  resolutions sponsored by NIEO movement, 23–24
United States. *See also specific acts, treaties, conventions, etc.*
  anti-dumping related claims, consolidation of, 194–195
  BITs with other countries. *See individual countries*
  Canada–U.S. Softwood Lumber Agreement, 402

consolidation of claims, 198
Constitution. *See* U.S. Constitution
costs and attorneys' fees, 618
expropriation of U.S. property, 243–246
fair and equitable treatment, 529–531
government legal fees, 624–625
Immigration and Nationality Act, 297
indirect or regulatory expropriation, 482–489
jurisdictional issues, 148–149
   amicus curiae, 168–171
   preliminary vs. merits issues, 149–153
model BIT. *See* U.S. Model BIT of 2004
NAFTA, 56–61. *See also* North American Free Trade Agreement
nationality of investor, 301–302
Section 1782 to compel testimony or production of document, 165–167
third-party evidence taking in, 163–167
Unity of investment, 276–280
Uruguay
   forum selection and waiver, 370
   Mercosur, 64
U.S. Constitution
   on diversity jurisdiction, 13
   personal jurisdiction, 697
   on regulatory takings, 483
U.S.-Iran Treaty of Amity, 437
U.S. Model BIT of 2004, 53–54, 72, 318
   appellate body, proposal for, 713
   change of nationality, 341
   consent to arbitration, 242
   consolidation of claims, 90, 185, 196
   definition of investment, 252
   expropriation, 454–455
   fair and equitable treatment, 510, 525
   forum selection and waiver, 370
   non-pecuniary remedies, 570
   umbrella clauses, 544

V

Vacatur, 646, 649. *See also* Annulment and set aside
van den Berg, Albert, 102–104

VCLT. *See* Vienna Convention on the Law of Treaties
Venezuela
   investment law, 232–233
   Italian national's store looted by soldiers of, 36
   Mercosur, 64
   withdrawal from ICSID, 704
Venue and Union Carbide gas plant tragedy (1984), 14–15
Vienna Convention on the Law of Treaties (VCLT), 415, 423, 504, 509

W

Waiting periods, 117
Waivers, 348–349
   fork in the road treaty provisions, 368–370
   NAFTA, 370
   of objections, 647
Wälde, Thomas W., 603–605, 606–608, 711
Wallace, Don, Jr., 60, 527–528
Washington Convention. *See* ICSID and ICSID Convention
Weiler, Todd, 57, 711
Wells, Louis T., 594–596
Wiltse, Jessica S., 69–71, 74
Witnesses, 158–163, 643
Wong, Eleanor, 585–587
World Bank
   consent to arbitrate, 220
   ICSID role of, 50–51, 97–98
   investment protection role of, 7, 49–50
   on investor-state arbitration, 8–9
   MIGA (Multilateral Investment Guarantee Agency), 41
   political risk insurance, 41
   situs of arbitration, 132
World War I and expropriation, 434–435
World War II and expropriation, 435–438

Table of Cases

A

AAPL v. Sri Lanka. *See* Asian Agricultural Prods. v. Sri Lanka

Abu Dhabi Gas Liquefaction Co. v. Eastern Bechtel Corp. (London Ct. Appeal, June 23, 1982), 197, 197n.42

Abur v. Republic of Sudan (D.D.C. 2006), 698n.97

Adams v. Mexico (Notice of Claim, Feb. 16, 2001), 123n.25

ADC Affiliate Ltd. & ADC & ADMC Mgmt. Ltd. v. Republic of Hungary (Award, Oct. 2, 2006), 575, 575nn.59–61, 623, 623nn.250–251

ADF Group, Inc. v. U.S.
- Final Award, Jan. 9, 2003, 401, 401n.22, 410, 410n.86, 417n.124, 424n.158, 494n.10, 496n.18, 510, 510n.75, 545n.21
- Minutes of First Session of Tribunal, Feb. 3, 2001, 134, 147n.103

AES v. Argentina (Decision on Jurisdiction, Apr. 26, 2005), 382n.74, 391–392, 392n.93

Af-Cap Inc. v. Republic of Congo (5th Cir. 2004), 696n.87

Affaire des Chemins de Fer Zeltweg-Wolfberg (1934), 609n.179

Agins v. City of Tiburon (1980), 485n.224

AGIP S.p.A. v. People's Republic of the Congo (Award, Nov. 30, 1979), 140n.73, 141, 141n.76, 588, 623, 623n.245

Aguas Argentinas S.A., Suez, Sociedad General de Aguas de Barcelona, S.A. & Vivendi Universal, S.A. v. Argentina
- Decision of Jan. 23, 2005, 168n.178, 189n.15, 708n.32
- Order in Response to a Petition for Transparency and Participation as Amicus Curiae, May 19, 2005, 96n.18, 172nn.203 & 205

Aguas del Tunari (AdT) v. Republic of Bolivia (Aug. 29, 2002), 168n.178, 329–331, 708n.33

Aguas Provinciales de Santa Fe S.A., Suez, Sociedad General de Aguas de Barcelona S.A. & Inter Aguas Servicios Integrales de Agua S.A. v. Argentina (2005), 173–176, 189n.15
- Order in Response to a Petition for Participation as Amicus Curiae, Mar. 17, 2006, 172n.205, 707n.31
- Order in Response to a Petition by Five Nongovernmental Organizations for Permission to Make an Amicus Curiae Submission, Feb. 12, 2007, 173n.206

TABLE OF CASES

Ahmadou Sadio Diallo (Guinea v. Democratic Republic of the Congo) (Preliminary Objections, Judgment, May 2007), 309n.90, 310, 310n.93

AIG Capital Partners, Inc., & CJSC Tema Real Estate Co. v. Kazakhstan (Oct. 7, 2003)
- (unpublished), 700, 700n.102
- enforcement decision in High Court of Justice, Queen's Bench Division, England, Oct. 20, 2005, 700n.102

Ainsworth v. Kurnich (11th Cir. 1992), 644n.89

Air (PTY) Ltd. v. Int'l Air Transport Assoc. (IATA) & CSA in liquidation, Republic and Canton of Geneva Judiciary (Court of First Instance, May 2, 2005), 106n.13

Alcoa Minerals of Jamaica, Inc. v. Jamaica (Decision on Jurisdiction and Competence, July 6, 1975), 187n.8, 259, 259n.63

Alex Genin, Eastern Credit Limited, Inc. (ECL) and A.S. Baltoil v. Estonia. *See* Genin v. Estonia

Altmann v. Republic of Austria (9th Cir. 2002), 483n.210, 698n.97, 699n.99

Ambatielos Case (1953), 418–419

Ambatielos Case before a Commission of Arbitration (1956), 418, 420–421

Amco Asia Corp. v. Republic of Indonesia, 320–322
- Award on Jurisdiction, Sept. 25, 1983, 7n.25, 320n.144, 324n.164
- Decision on Request for Provisional Measures, Dec. 9, 1983, 140n.73, 142, 143n.82
- Award, Nov. 20, 1984, 319n.141, 381, 381n.67
- Decision on the Application for Annulment, May 16, 1986, 88n.60, 211, 211n.34, 217n.54, 630n.11, 630n.13, 631–633, 632, 632nn.20–21
- Resubmitted Case, Decision on Jurisdiction, May 10, 1988, 154n.113
- Resubmitted Case, Award, June 5, 1990, 529, 529n.171, 529n.173

American Bell Int'l v. Gov't of the Islamic Republic of Iran (Award, June 11, 1984), 154n.112

American Independent Oil Co. Case. *See* Arbitration between Kuwait and American Independent Oil Co. (AMINOIL)

American Int'l Group v. The Islamic Republic of Iran (1983), 437, 437n.54

American Mfg. & Trading v. Republic of Zaire (Award, Feb. 21, 1997), 249n.14, 317, 317n.127, 534n.198, 535n.206, 587n.97

Amgen, Inc. v. Kidney Ctr. Del. County, Ltd., 165nn.161 & 163

AMINOIL. *See* Arbitration between Kuwait and American Independent Oil Co.

Amoco Int'l Fin. Corp. v. Islamic Republic of Iran (Award, July 14, 1987), 567n.18, 573n.47, 575–578, 576n.63, 596n.121

AMT v. Zaire. *See* American Mfg. & Trading v. Republic of Zaire

Anaconda v. Iran (1988), 606n.166, 610

Andrus v. Allard (1979), 484n.223

Anglo-Iranian Oil Co. Case (U.K. v. Iran)
- Judgment, July 22, 1952, 42n.90, 146n.100
- Jurisdiction, 418, 419

Application of Oxus Gold plc for Assistance Before a Foreign Tribunal, In the Matter of, 167, 167nn.172 & 174

Aramco Arbitration (1958), 431n.9, 436n.41

Arbitration between Kuwait and American Independent Oil Co. (AMINOIL) (1982), 436–437, 436n.41, 440n.66, 465, 577, 583n.82, 591, 604n.156, 605, 605n.160, 607n.168, 609n.179, 611n.187

TABLE OF CASES

Arcambel v. Wiseman (1796), 614n.199
Archer Daniels Midland Co. & Tate & Lyle Ingredients Americas, Inc. v. United Mexican States (Order of the Consolidation Tribunal, May 20, 2005), 186n.4, 192n.20, 193nn.22–23
Argentina, Republic of v. Weltover (Supreme Court, 1992), 697, 698
Armstrong v. U.S. (1960), 484n.219
Asian Agricultural Prods. v. Sri Lanka (Award, June 27, 1990), 205, 317, 317n.126, 532n.185, 535–538, 535nn.204–205, 536n.209, 587n.97, 588
Asian Agricultural Prods. v. Sri Lanka (Award, June 27, 1990), 205, 317, 317n.126, 532n.185, 535–538, 535nn.204–205, 536n.209, 587n.97, 588
Asian Express v. Greater Colombo Economic Comm'n (1999), 629n.7
Atlantic Triton v. Guinea, 140n.73, 144n.89
Attorney Gen. of Canada v. S.D. Myers, Inc. *See* S.D. Myers, Inc. v. Canada
Aucoven v. Venezuela
- Decision on Jurisdiction, Sept. 27, 2001, 224, 224n.24, 225n.28, 320, 320n.143, 324n.164, 331–335, 331n.180, 332n.182
- Award, Sept. 23, 2003, 262, 587n.97, 610n.183

Autopista Concesionada de Venezuela, C.A. v. Bolivarian Republic of Venezuela. *See* Aucoven v. Venezuela
Azinian v. United Mexican States (Award, Nov. 1, 1999), 380n.62, 381, 381n.66, 470n.185, 471, 476n.196, 531n.182, 618–618, 618n.227, 621, 621n.238
Azurix Corp. v. Argentina
- Decision on Jurisdiction, Dec. 8, 2003, 208n.27, 266n.87, 310n.96, 372n.16, 375–376, 461nn.138–140, 465, 465n.159, 468n.171
- Final Award, July 14, 2006, 441n.72, 461, 473, 496–498, 496n.21, 497, 500n.27, 502n.40, 506n.56, 511n.80, 538–539, 538n.210, 579n.70, 581, 603n.146, 611n.187, 623, 623n.246, 711n.52
- Annulment proceeding registered Dec. 11, 2006, 631n.16

B

Baker Marine (Nig.) Ltd v. Chevron (Nig.) Ltd. (2d Cir. 1999), 660n.147
Banco Nacional de Cuba v. Chase Manhattan Bank (1981), 432n.10
Banco Nacional de Cuba v. Sabbatino (1964), 21–22, 244n.95, 432n.10, 483n.210
Bank of Am. S.A. v. 203 North LaSalle St. Partnership (1999), 505n.55
Bank of the U.S. v. Devaux (1809), 13n.5
Barcelona Traction, Light and Power Co., Case Concerning (Belgium v. Spain) (Judgment, Feb. 5, 1970), 11n.2, 33, 33n.63, 40n.82, 309, 309nn.83–85, 311, 311n.98, 327n.172, 358, 432n.11
Bavarati v. Josephthal, Lyon & Ross, Inc. (7th Cir. 1994), 660n.144
Bayindir Insaat Turizm Ticaret Ve Sanyai A. (Scedil) v. Pakistan (Decision on Jurisdiction, Nov 14, 2005), 98n.22, 260n.73, 265n.81, 267, 267n.95, 270n.123, 271, 271n.131, 382n.74
B. E. Chattin (U.S.) v. United Mexican States (1927). *See* Chattin v. Mexico
Bechtel Enters. Int'l v. OPIC (Sept. 25, 2003), 456n.116
Benvenuti & Bonfant SRL v. People's Republic of the Congo (Award, Aug. 8, 1980), 372n.17, 588, 700n.105
Betteroads Asphalt Corp. v. U.S., 244nn.98–99

Biloune v. Ghana Inves. Ctr.
- Award, Oct. 27, 1989, 118–119, 227–230
- Award, June 30, 1990, 118–119, 141n.74, 459, 459n.128, 461n.141, 462n.144, 471, 478, 480, 588, 589, 590n.102, 618n.223

Biwater Gauff Ltd. v. United Republic of Tanzania (Procedural Order No. 3, Sept. 29, 2006), 140n.73, 143, 143n.84, 172n.202, 173, 175–176, 708n.32

Blad v. Bamfield (1674), 22

B.L. Harbert Int'l v. Hercules Steel (11th Cir. 2006), 676, 676nn.3–6

Blyth v. Birmingham Waterworks Co. (1856), 364n.49

Boeing Co. v. Egyptair (2d Cir. May 7, 2007), 699n.99

Bogdanov (Russia) v. Moldova (Award, Sept. 22, 2005), 603, 603n.145

Bowen v. Public Agencies Opposed to Social Sec. Entrapment (1986), 485n.229

BP Am. Prod. Co. v. Argentina (Decision on Jurisdiction, July 26, 2006), 552n.28

BP Exploration Co. (Libya) Ltd. v. Gov't Libyan Arab Republic (1973), 225n.28, 569n.22

Brabham v. A.G. Edwards & Sons Inc. (5th Cir. 2004), 645

Brehm v. Eisner (Del. 2000), 645n.90

Bridas S.A.P.I.C., Bridas Energy Int'l, Intercontinental Oil & Gas Ventures, & Bridas Corp. v. Turkmenistan, Balkannebitgazsenagat & Turkmenneft (S.D. Tex. Oct. 1, 2001), 639, 639nn.58–59

British Claims in the Spanish Zone of Morocco (1925), 433n.19, 435, 435n.32

British Petroleum Exploration Co. (Libya) Ltd. v. Gov't of the Libyan Arab Republic (1973), 431n.9, 436, 436n.41

Brown v. Legal Found. of Washington (2003), 482n.205, 484n.221

Burton v. Bush (1980), 164, 164n.155

C

Cable and Wireless Plc. v. IBM U.K. Ltd. (2002), 106n.14

Cabolent v. NIOC (1970), 687n.35

Camuzzi Int'l A.A. v. Argentina (Decision on Objection to Jurisdiction, May 11, 2005), 90n.66, 90, 188, 188n.14

Canfor Corp., Tembec Inc., Tembec Inves. Inc., Tembec Indus. Inc., Terminal Forests Prod. Ltd. v. U.S.
- Order of the Consolidation Tribunal, Sept. 7, 2005, 186n.4, 194–195, 194n.32
- Decision on Jurisdiction in the Consolidated Arbitration, June 6, 2006, 195n.33

Capital India Power Mauritius & Energy Enters. (Mauritius) Co. v. Maharashtra Power Dev. Corp. (Apr. 27, 2005), 456n.116

Cargill, Inc. v. Poland (UNCITRAL Arbitration, 2005), 704n.18

Casado and Allende Found. v. Chile (Decision on Conservatory Measures, Sept. 25, 2001), 140n.70, 145, 145n.94, 146, 146n.102

Case concerning the rights of nationals of the United States of America in Morocco (1952), 418

Cassirer v. Kingdom of Spain (C.D. Cal. 2006), 698n.97

CCL v. Kazakhstan (2001), 222n.14, 227n.32, 232n.40

CDC Group PLC v. Republic of Seychelles (Decision on the Application for Annulment, June 29, 2006), 631n.15

Central Bank of Nigeria Case Landgericht, Frankfurt (Dec. 2, 1975 [1976]), 693, 693n.79

Ceskoslovenska Obchodni Banka v. Slovakia (Decision on Objection to Jurisdiction of May 24, 1999), 263, 273n.141, 279n.173

TABLE OF CASES

Ceylon Case, 244n.96

Champion Trading Co. v. Egypt
- Decision on Jurisdiction, Oct. 21, 2003, 299n.37, 301, 301n.44, 302n.46, 316n.122
- Award, Oct. 27, 2006, 405, 405n.52, 408, 412n.99

Chattin v. Mexico (1927), 59n.67, 342n.211, 352n.23, 526n.153

Chobady Claim (1958), 464n.153

Chorzów Factory Case (Germany v. Poland) (1928), 216, 216n.49, 432n.11, 434, 434nn.23–25, 566–569, 566nn.11–12, 567nn.15 & 18, 568n.19, 575–577, 576n.64, 580, 589

Chromalloy Aeroservices Inc.v. Arab Republic of Egypt, In re (D.D.C. 1996), 649–650

Chuidian v. Philippine Nat'l Bank (1990), 429n.1

CME Czech Republic B.V. (The Netherlands) v. Czech Republic
- Partial Award on Liability, Sept. 13, 2001, 159n.139, 177n.209, 182n.212, 237n.59, 317, 17n.134, 440, 440n.67, 452n.104, 458n.123, 459, 459n.125, 461n.141, 463nn.150–151, 472, 506n.58, 515n.101, 516, 523–525, 523n.145, 535n.206, 569n.22, 617n.222, 661n.148
- Final Award, Mar. 14, 2003, 10n.34, 177n.209, 180–182, 185n.2, 188, 204n.16, 269, 269n.111, 325–327, 327n.170, 460, 460n.131, 568n.20, 584, 584n.92, 597n.125, 601n.138, 603, 603n.140, 603n.149, 610–611, 617, 660–664, 661n.149, 667, 703nn.9 & 11
- Svea Court of Appeal Decision, May 15, 2003, 661n.152, 662nn.154–157, 663nn.158–162, 664nn.163–164

CMS Gas Transmission Co. v. Argentina
- Decision on Objection to Jurisdiction, July 17, 2003, 99n.25, 158, 209, 209n.28, 266n.87, 310n.96, 311–312, 315–318, 319, 371n.13, 372n.16, 374–375, 460n.137, 461n.141, 466, 466nn.164–165, 472, 489, 489n.247, 560
- Final Award, May 12, 2005, 157, 157n.126, 427, 427n.177, 440n.69, 457, 502n.40, 506nn.56–57, 509n.73, 511n.80, 514n.98, 516–519, 516n.107, 517n.112, 519n.120, 560n.39, 566n.10, 567nn.15 & 17, 572n.43, 574n.55, 579, 579n.66, 579n.70, 581, 584n.82, 711n.52
- Decision on Annulment of Sept. 25, 2007, 560n.39, 631n.15

Comm'n of the European Communities v. Kingdom of Sweden (2006), 705n.21

Comm'n of the European Communities v. Republic of Austria (2006), 705n.21

Comm'n of the European Communities v. Republic of Finland (2007), 705n.21

Compañia de Aguas del Aconquija, S.A. & Vivendi Universal v. Argentine Republic
- Award, Nov. 21, 2000, 317, 317nn.132–133, 381, 381n.69, 382n.71, 382n.75, 383–391, 391n.85, 393, 394n.113, 395, 614n.200
- Decision on Annulment, July 3, 2002, 239, 239n.69, 380n.62, 556, 631, 631n.14, 633, 633n.32, 634n.34
- Vivendi II (Award, Aug. 20, 2007), 525n.148, 579nn.69–70, 580n.72, 624n.252

Compañia del Desarrollo de Santa Elena S.A. v. Republic of Costa Rica (Final Award, Feb. 17, 2000), 96n.18, 237n.62, 245, 245n.100, 456n.114, 462n.144, 574, 574nn.53–54, 604n.155, 605, 605n.161, 607n.168, 609, 609n.178, 609n.179, 609n.181, 611n.187

Compania Espanola de Petroleos, S.A. v. Nereus Shipping, S.A., 198n.48

Compania Minera Condesa SA and Compania de Minas Buenaventura SA v. BRGM-Pérou S.A.S. (Dec. 19, 1997), 106n.13

Concrete Pipe & Prods. of Calif. v. Constr. Laborers Pension Trust (1993), 485n.224

Condor & Filvem v. Ministry of Justice (July 15, 1992), 687n.37

Connecticut Bank of Commerce v. Republic of Congo (5th Cir. 2002), 693–696

Connolly v. Pension Benefit Guaranty Corp. (1986), 485n.228, 485n.230, 486n.231

Consortium R.F.C.C. v. Morocco
- Decision on Jurisdiction, July 16, 2001, 265n.81
- Award of 2003, 188, 188n.10, 267, 267n.93, 270n.122, 272n.138, 273n.142
- Decision on Application for Annulment, Jan. 18, 2006, 631n.15

Consorzio Groupement L.E.S.I.-DIPENTA v. Algeria (Award, Jan. 10, 2005), 98n.24

Corfu Channel Case (U.K. v. Albania)
- Assessment of the Amount of Compensation Due, 1949, 604n.151
- Merits, 1949, 216, 216n.50, 509n.72

Corn Prod. Int'l Inc. v. United Mexican States
- Decision of the Consolidation Tribunal, May 20, 2005, 186n.4, 192nn.20–21, 193n.23
- Decision on Jurisdiction in the Consolidated Arbitration, June 6, 2006, 195

Cruz v. U.S. (N.D. Cal. 2005), 698n.97

CSOB v. Slovakia
  Decision on Jurisdiction, May 24, 1999, 145n.92, 208n.27, 278–279
  Final Award, 2004, 140n.73, 144, 623nn.248–249, 612n.190

D

David v. Goliath (Nov. 2002), 59
Delagoa Bay & E. Afr. RR. Co. (U.S. & Gt. Brit. v. Port.) (1943), 433–434, 433n.20
Department of Justice v. Federal Labor Relations Auth. (5th Cir. 1993), 645n.90
de Sanchez v. Banco Central de Nicaragua (1985), 429n.2
Deutsche Schachtbau- und Tiefbohrgesellschaft GmbH v. Ras Al Khaimah Nat'l Oil Co. (Ct. App. 1987), 641n.75
Diallo Case. *See* Ahmadou Sadio Diallo
Direction Générale de l'aviation civile de l'Emirat de Dubai v. Société Internationale Bechtel (2005), 650n.107
Diversion of Water from the Meuse Case (Netherlands v. Belgium) (1937), 216, 216n.48
DO Zdravilisce Radenska v. Kajo-Erzeugnisse Essenzan GmbH (Supreme Court of Slovenia, decision of Oct. 20, 1993), 641n.77
Duff Dev. v. Kelantan Gov't (1923), 689n.50
Duke Energy Int'l Peru Invs. No. 1, Ltd. v. Peru, 259n.62, 276, 276n.167, 277–280
Duquesne Light Co. v. Barach (1989), 484n.222

E

Eastern Sugar v. Czech Republic (Mar. 27, 2007), 705n.22
Electricidad Argentina S.A. & EDF Int'l S.A. v. Argentine Republic (2004), 189n.15
Elettronica Sicula S.p.A. (ELSI) (U.S. v. Italy), Case Concerning
- Judgment of July 20, 1989, 32, 310, 310n.91, 349, 349n.8, 365n.59, 426n.173, 432n.11, 507–508, 507n.65
- Mem. of the U.S. 1989, 507n.66

El Paso, City of v. Simmons (1965), 485n.230
El Paso Energy Int'l Co. v. Argentine Republic (Decision on Jurisdiction, Apr. 26, 2006), 222n.15, 552–558, 556n.30
ELSI case. *See* Elettronica Sicula S.p.A.

El Triunfu (4 U.N.R.I.A.A.), 559n.35
Emilio Augustín Maffezini v. Kingdom of Spain. *See* Maffezini v. Kingdom of Spain
Empresas Lucchetti, S.A. & Lucchetti Peru, S.A. v. Republic of Peru (2007). *See* Industria Nacional de Alimentos & Indalsa Perú v. Perú
EnCana v. Ecuador
- Jurisdictional Award, Feb. 27, 2004, 222n.14, 237n.59
- UNCITRAL, Final Award of Feb. 3, 2006, 440n.69, 441n.73, 467, 467nn.168–170, 473, 619, 619n.229

Endreny Claim (1963), 464n.153
Energy Reserves Group, Inc. v. Kansas Power & Light Co. (1983), 485nn.229–230
Englewood, City of v. Socialist People's Libyan Arab Jamarihiriya (3d Cir. 1985), 695n.86
Enron Corp. & Ponderosa Asset v. Argentina
- Award on Jurisdiction, Jan. 14, 2004, 157, 158, 208n.27, 217n.54, 316n.122, 570, 570n.31, 608n.176, 611n.187
- Ancillary Claim, May 22, 2007, 458n.122, 460n.137, 461n.139, 469n.179
- Final Award, May 22, 2007, 157n.128, 426n.172, 538n.210

Erie R.R. Co. v. Tompkins (1938), 13n.5
Ethiopia Case, 244n.96
Ethyl Corp. v. Canada
- Award on Place of Arbitration, Nov. 1997, 83n.28, 99, 119, 616, 624
- Decision on Jurisdiction, June 24, 1998, 99n.25, 500, 500n.29
- Award on Jurisdiction, June 28, 1998, 616nn.215–216, 617nn.217–218

Euclid, Ohio, Village of v. Amber Realty Co. (1926), 485n.224
Eureko B.V. v. Poland (Partial Award, ad hoc UNCITRAL Arbitration, Aug. 19, 2005), 282, 282n.187, 283n.191, 382n.74, 391, 392, 392n.94, 395, 395n.124, 511n.80, 542–543, 546n.23, 548–552, 554, 559, 561, 711n.52
Eurodif et Sofidif, 689n.52
European Gas Turbines SA v. Westman Int'l Ltd. (Sept. 30, 1993), 641n.76
Evanoff Claim (1963), 464n.153
Exxon Corp. v. Eagerton (1983), 487n.239

F

Fabiani's Case (1905), 609n.179
Fedax N.V. v. Venezuela (Award, July 11, 1997), 259n.65, 264, 270n.118, 316n.123, 549, 556n.30
Feldman v. Mexico (Final Award, Dec. 16, 2002), 304n.61, 400n.19, 400n.21, 403, 403n.36, 408, 410–411, 410n.81, 412n.96, 451n.99, 456n.114, 457, 457n.120, 463n.147, 469, 469n.178, 470n.186, 472, 528n.166, 531n.182, 579n.71, 583n.83, 670
F. Hoffman-LaRoche v. Epigram S.A. (2004), 483n.210
Finnish Ships Arbitration (Finland v. U.K.) (Award, May 9, 1934), 31, 31n.55, 119n.8, 349, 349n.13, 367n.1, 527–528, 527n.163
Fireman's Fund Ins. Co. v. Mexico (Decision on the Preliminary Question of Jurisdiction, July 17, 2003), 262, 284, 284n.207, 285n.210
Flexi-Van v. Iran, 609n.179
Fomento v. CCT (May 14, 2001), 106n.13
Foremost Teheran Inc. v. Iran, 575n.57
Forests of Central Rhodope (1933), 571, 571n.36

Fortune, Alsweet & Eldridge, Inc. v. Daniel (9th Cir. 1983), 647n.95
FPC v. Hope Natural Gas Co. (1944), 484n.222
Francisco v. M/T Stolt Achievement (2001), 106n.14
French v. Banco National de Cuba (N.Y. 1968), 483n.210
Frontera Resources Azerbaijan Corp. v. State Oil Co. of Azerbaijan (S.D.N.Y. 2007), 698n.97

G

Gabcikovo-Nagymaros Project, Case Concerning (Decision, Sept. 25, 1997), 156n.123, 157n.129, 567n.17
GAMI Inv., Inc. v. Mexico (Final Award, Nov. 15, 2004), 310n.96, 311n.99, 318, 318n.137, 403–404, 403n.39, 502n.38, 617n.221
Gas Natural SDG, S.A. v. Argentine Republic (Award on Jurisdiction, June 17, 2005), 120n.11, 217n.54, 422–423, 422nn.146–147, 423
General Elec. Co. v. Renusagar Power Co. (India S.C. 1994), 641n.78
Generation Ukraine v. Ukraine (Award, Sept. 16, 2003), 222n.14, 468n.172, 469, 469n.177, 472
Generica v. Pharmaceutical Basics (E.D. Ill. Sept. 18, 1996), 643
Genin, Eastern Credit Ltd. & A.S. Baltoil v. Estonia (Award, June 25, 2001), 317, 317n.131, 369n.6, 371n.13, 373, 506n.58, 507n.64, 622, 622n.241
Gentini (Italy v. Venezuela) (1903), 36, 36n.71, 215n.46
Germany v. Poland. *See* Chorzów Factory Case (1928)
Gilmore v. Palestinian Interim Self-Government Auth. (D.D.C. 2006), 698n.97
Goetz v. République du Burundi (Sentence du CIRDI du 10 Février 1999), 317, 317n.128, 446–449, 449n.94, 571
Goldenberg Case (Ger. v. Rom.) (1928), 433n.19, 435, 435n.33
Gotaverken Arendal AB [v.] Libyan General National Maritime Transport Co., 94n.9
Great Britain v. Spain (1924), 609n.179
Gruslin v. Malaysia (Award, Nov. 27, 2000), 96n.17, 128n.40, 224n.25, 631n.15
Guinea v. Maritime Int'l Nominees Establishment. *See* Maritime Int'l Nominees Establishment (MINE) v. Republic of Guinea

H

Hadacheck v. Sebastian (1915), 485n.224
Halliburton Co., IMCO Servs. (U.K.) v. Doreen/Imco (1982), 381, 381n.65
Hanil Bank v. PT Bank Negara Indonesia (2d Cir. 1998), 698nn.97–98, 699n.99
Helnan Int'l Hotels A/S/ v. Egypt (2006), 262
Hilmarton Ltd. v. OTV. *See* Société Hilmarton Ltd. v. Omnium de Traitement et de Valorisation
Himpurna Calif. Energy Ltd. (Bermuda) v. Republic of Indonesia
  • Interim Award, Sept. 26, 1999, 102, 102n.3, 528n.167, 584n.86, 587n.96, 589n.99, 590–592, 604–605, 605n.157
  • Final Award, Oct. 16, 1999, 102, 102n.3, 104, 104n.5, 105, 617–618, 618n.223
Hitachi Ltd. v. Rupali Polyester (June 10, 1998), 92n.3
Holiday Inns S.A. v. Morocco, 88n.60, 140n.73, 143, 144n.89, 277, 327n.172
Home Bldg & Loan Ass'n v. Blaisdell (1934), 487n.240

Home Sav. of Am. v. U.S. (2002), 484n.217
Hubco v. WAPDA (2000), 107–110, 107n.16, 108–110
Hub Power Co. v. Pakistan WAPDA. *See* Hubco v. WAPDA
Hudson v. Guestier, 22

I

Ilhan v. Turkey (2000), 365n.62
Illinois Central R.R. Co. Claim (4 U.N.R.I.A.A.), 559n.35
Impreglio v. Pakistan (Decision on Jurisdiction, Apr. 22, 2005), 222n.14
Inceysa Vallisoletana S.L. v. Republic of El Salvador (Award, Aug. 2, 2006), 223–224, 253n.37, 623n.245
Indus. Risk Insurers v. M.A.N. Guttehoffnungshutte GmbH (11th Cir. 1998), 644n.87
Industria Nacional de Alimentos & Indalsa Perú v. Perú (Decision on Annulment, Sept. 5, 2007), 631n.15
In re. *See name of party*
Integrity Ins. Co. v. Am. Centennial Ins. Co. (1995), 165nn.160 & 162
Intel Corp. v. Advanced Micro Devices, Inc (2004), 166–167
Inter-Arab Inves. Guarantee Corp. v. Banque Arabe d'Investissements (Decision, Oct. 23, 1997), 639n.57
Interhandel Case (Switzerland v. U.S.), 30n.52, 31, 352–356, 357n.28
International Bank v. OPIC (1972), 463n.151
International Shoe Co. v. Washington (1945), 20n.19, 697n.91
International Technical Prods. Corp. v. Iran, 575n.57
International Thunderbird Gaming v. Mexico (2006). *See* Thunderbird Gaming v. Mexico
Iran v. U.S., 190, 294n.9
Islamic Republic of Iran v. U.S. (Award, Dec. 28, 1998), 598n.136
I.T. Consultants, Inc. v. Islamic Republic of Pakistan (D.C. Cir. 2003), 698n.97

J

James v. U.K. (1986), 462n.146
James Miller Ltd. v. Whitworth Street Estates (1970), 92, 92n.4
Jan de Nul N.V. & Dredging Int'l v. Egypt (Decision on Jurisdiction, June 13, 2006), 260n.74, 382n.74, 391
Jeffrey M. Brown Assocs., Inc. v. Allstar Drywall & Acoustics, Inc. (E.D. Pa. 2002), 646
Joy Mining Machinery v. Egypt (Award on Jurisdiction, Aug. 6, 2004), 260n.77, 264, 265n.81, 266n.83, 268, 268n.103, 269, 269n.113, 270n.117, 271, 271n.132, 272n.138, 372n.17, 394n.112, 555–556, 556n.30, 558n.33, 622n.240, 631n.15

K

Kaiser Aetna v. U.S. (1979), 484n.218
Kaiser Bauxite Co. v. Jamaica (Decision on Jurisdiction of July 6, 1975), 187n.8, 324n.164

Karaha Bodas Co. LLC v. Perusahan Pertambangan Minyak Dan Gas Numi Negara (Indonesia)
- Award of 1999, 189, 189n.16, 190n.19, 198, 198n.51, 589n.99, 590, 592–596, 593nn.108–117, 594nn.118–120, 638, 638n.54
- S.D. Tex. 2001, 638, 638n.55, 648n.102, 679
- 5th Cir. 2004, 642, 642n.83, 680–684, 684n.18

Kardassopoulos v. Georgia (Decision on Jurisdiction, July 6, 2007), 260n.72, 263

Kazakhstan, Republic of v. Biedermann Int'l (1999), 166n.166, 167

Kelo v. New London (2005), 487n.238

Kerr-McGee Refining Corp. v. M/T Triumph (2d Cir. 1991), 639

Keystone Bituminous Coal Assoc. v. DeBenedictis (1987), 484n.223, 485nn.225–226

Klöckner Industrie-Anlagen GmbH v. United Republic of Cameroon and Société Camerounaise des Engrais (Ad hoc Committee Decision on Annulment, May 3, 1985), 88n.60, 210, 210n.33, 211, 344, 345n.222, 630n.11, 630n.13, 631–632, 631n.17, 632nn.18–19

L

Lanco v. Argentina (Preliminary Decision of the ICSID Tribunal of Dec. 8, 1998), 317, 317n.130, 380n.62, 391, 391n.90, 395, 395n.121

Lauder v. Czech Republic (Final Award, 2001), 98, 98n.24, 123n.25, 159n.137, 185n.2, 188, 326n.169, 372n.15, 452n.104, 469, 469n.180, 470n.187, 472, 509n.73, 574n.55, 597n.125, 601n.138, 617, 617nn.219–220

Leica AG v. Central Bank of Iraq et Etat Irakien (Cour d'Appel, Brussels, Feb. 15, 2000), 687n.36

Lena Goldfields, Ltd. v. Russia (1930), 433n.19, 434, 434n.27

Léon Participaciones Argentinas S.A. v. Argentine Republic (2004), 189n.15

L.E.S.I. Dipenta v. Algeria (Decision on Jurisdiction, Jan. 10, 2005), 265n.81, 272n.140, 622n.240

L.E.S.I., S.p.A. & Astaldi, S.p.A. v. Algeria (Decision of July 12, 2006), 265n.81, 268n.109

LETCO v. Liberia
- Decision on Jurisdiction of Oct. 24, 1984, 271n.130
- Award, Mar. 31, 1986, 217n.54, 650, 700n.106
- S.D.N.Y. 1987, 650n.111

Letelier v. Chile (2d Cir. 1984), 684n.19, 694

L.F.H. Neer & Pauline E. Neer v. Mexico (1927), 495–496, 495nn.14 & 15–17, 506n.58, 533

LG&E Capital Corp. and LGE Int'l Inc. v. Argentina
- Decision on Liability, Oct. 3, 2006, 157, 157nn.127 & 130, 158, 158n.132, 177n.209, 263, 427, 427n.177, 458n.122, 460n.137, 464n.155, 465, 465n.160, 468, 468n.176, 473, 509, 509n.73, 511n.80, 513, 513n.91, 517n.112, 519n.122, 539, 539n.213, 711n.52
- Damages Award, July 25, 2007, 572, 572n.43, 579n.66, 580n.72, 581–583, 581n.78

LIAMCO. *See* Libyan Arab Am. Oil Co.

Liberian Eastern Timber Co. v. Republic of Liberia. *See* LETCO v. Liberia

Libia v. Condor Srl Corte di Cassazione (Aug. 23, 1990), 693n.78

Libya v. Rossbeton SRL (Case No. 2502, May 25, 1989), 687n.38

Libyan Arab Am. Oil Co. (LIAMCO) v. Libyan Arab Republic (1977), 46n.8, 431n.9, 436nn.41–42, 440n.66, 569n.22, 604n.155

The Libyan Nationalization Cases (1981), 25n.37, 46n.8
Lighthouses Arbitration (Fr./Greece) (1956), 436n.41
Lingle v. Chevron (2005), 482nn.205 & 207, 483nn.212 & 214–215, 486n.231
Link Trading v. Moldova (2002), 619n.228
Loewen Group, Inc. & Raymond L. Loewen v. U.S., 337–339
- Notice of Claim, 124n.26
- Counter-Memorial of the Loewen Group on Matters of Jurisdiction and Competence, Mar. 29, 2002, 340n.203
- Interim Relief, 140n.73
- Award, June 26, 2003, 59n.67, 274n.150, 320, 320n.142, 340n.200, 342, 342nn.208 & 211, 342n.211, 351n.22, 352n.23, 360–365, 360n.37, 361n.40, 362nn.41–42, 363n.46, 364nn.52–55, 368n.2, 501, 501n.31, 505n.50, 527n.164, 528n.166, 529–531, 529n.174, 530nn.176–177, 531n.180
- Notice of Petition to Vacate, Dec. 13, 2004, 339n.199, 644–646

Lucas v. South Carolina Coastal Council (1992), 475n.195
Lusitania Case (1923), 567n.14

M

Maffezini v. Kingdom of Spain
- Decision on Request for Provisional Measures, Oct. 28, 1999, 87n.50, 140n.73, 142, 142n.79
- Decision on Objections to Jurisdiction, Jan. 25, 2000, 119, 119n.5, 120, 120n.11, 417–418, 417n.125, 418n.129
- Award, Nov. 13, 2000, 317, 317n.129, 422–423, 425, 522, 522nn.141–142, 611n.187, 615n.205

Magno Santovincenzo v. Egan (1931), 421n.144
Malaysian Historical Salvors Sdn, Bhd v. Malaysia (Award, May 28, 2007), 260n.76, 264, 266n.83, 268, 268nn.105 & 110, 269, 269n.114, 270, 270n.126, 271, 271n.133, 273–274, 275nn.152 & 157
Malek v. Iran, 575n.57
Mareva Compania Naviera SA v. Int'l Bulk Carriers Ltd. (1975), 693n.83
Maritime Int'l Nominees Establishment (MINE) v. Republic of Guinea
- DC Cir. Decision of 1982, 111n.24, 112n.26
- Decision on Annulment, 1984, 97–98, 98n.21, 111–112, 144
- Guinea v. Maritime Int'l Nominees Establishment (Geneva Court Decision, Oct. 7, 1986), 111n.23
- Award (in the resubmitted case), Jan. 6, 1988, 86n.49, 140nn.72–73, 144nn.90–91
- Ad hoc Committee Decision on Annulment of Dec. 22, 1989, 630n.13

Mascotte Claim (1963), 464n.153
Mavrommatis Jerusalem Concessions (1925), 432n.11
Maxum Founds., Inc. v. Salus Corp., 198n.48
McCullough & Co. v. The Ministry of Post, Tel. & Tel., The Nat'l Iranian Oil Co., and Bank Markazi (1986), 610
McHarg, Roberts, Wallace, and Todd v. Islamic Republic of Iran (1986), 439–440, 440n.65
McKesson Corp. v. Islamic Rep. of Iran (1900), 217n.51, 609n.182
Meadows Indem. Co. v. Nutmeg Ins. Co. (1994), 165n.160

TABLE OF CASES

Metalclad Corp. v. United Mexican States
- Final Award, Aug. 30, 2000, 140n.73, 168, 269n.112, 453n.109, 459, 459n.129, 460, 461n.141, 462n.144, 463n.151, 466, 466n.162, 468, 468n.175, 471, 476–481, 512n.85, 514, 514n.96, 514n.100, 521–522, 521nn.126–132, 522nn.133–134, 560, 560n.37, 579n.68, 587n.97, 588–589, 607n.168, 608n.175, 611n.187, 622, 622n.242, 651–652, 651n.113, 657–660, 658n.128, 659nn.134 & 138, 665, 665n.170. *See also* United Mexican States v. Metalclad Corp.
- United Mexican States v. Metalclad Corp. (Judicial Review Proceedings in B.C. Supreme Ct. 2001). See Metalclad Corp. v. United Mexican States , 479–481, 479n.204, 492n.6, 508, 508n.68, 522, 522nn.135–137, 652nn.114–115, 653–657, 657n.120, 668–673, 677n.9

Methanex v. United States
- Submission on Costs of Respondent, July 19, 2000, 624, 625
- Decision of the Tribunal on Petitions from Third Persons to Intervene as Amici Curiae, Jan. 15, 2001, 168nn.178–179, 708
- Preliminary Award on Jurisdiction and Admissibility, Aug. 7, 2002, 149–153, 161n.141, 168, 170–171, 347n.2, 404, 408n.70, 412–413, 412n.101, 413n.104, 708n.32
- Final Award, Aug. 3, 2005, 284n.206, 404n.42, 457n.120, 461n.141, 463n.147, 464n.154, 466, 466n.166, 467n.167, 470n.186, 473, 488n.245, 501n.35, 502n.36, 618, 618nn.224–226

MHS v. Malaysia. *See* Malaysian Historical Salvors Sdn, Bhd v. Malaysia

Middle East Cement Shipping & Handling Co. v. Arab Republic of Egypt (Award, Apr. 12, 2002), 86n.45, 263, 281n.182, 372n.15, 459, 459nn.126–127, 603nn.147 & 150

Mihaly Int'l Corp. v. Socialist Democratic Republic of Sri Lanka (Award, Mar. 15, 2002), 271n.130, 286–289, 286nn.214–216, 288n.218, 291n.1

Military and Paramilitary Activities in and Against Nicaragua (Nicaragua v. U.S.) (Judgment on Jurisdiction and Admissibility, 1984), 98n.23

Miller v. Schoene (1928), 486, 487n.237, 487n.240

Milliken v. Meyer (1941), 697n.91

MINE v. Guinea. *See* Maritime Int'l Nominees Establishment (MINE) v. Republic of Guinea

Ministry of Defense & Support for Armed Forces of Iran v. Harsco/Bowen-McLaughlin-York Co. (Costs award, Sept. 18, 1996), 613n.194

Misima Mines Pty., Ltd. v. Papua New Guinea, 128n.40

Mitchell v. Cable (1848), 627n.2

Mitsubishi Motors Corp. v. Soler Chrysler-Plymouth Inc. (1985), 653

Mondev Int'l Ltd. v. U.S. (Final Award, Oct. 11, 2002), 214n.40, 217n.55, 494n.9, 496nn.19 & 22, 496n.22, 501n.33, 502n.37, 505n.53, 506n.59, 530, 530n.176

Montes v. Shearson Lehman Bros., Inc. (11th Cir. 1997), 645–646

MTD Equity Sdn. Bhd. & MTD Chile S.A. v. Chile
- Award, May 25, 2004, 52, 86n.44, 260n.70, 264, 291n.2, 417n.124, 424, 424n.158, 511n.80, 514n.97, 515, 515nn.102 & 104–105, 579n.66, 580, 580n.72, 580nn.74–75, 581, 603, 603nn.143–144, 611n.187, 711n.52
- Decision on Annulment, Mar. 21, 2007, 515n.105, 631n.15

Muresan Claim, 464n.153

Myers. *See* S.D. Myers, Inc. v. Canada

N

Nagel v. Czech Republic (Award, Sept. 9, 2003), 283, 283n.194, 289n.222
National Corn Growers Ass'n v. Canada (Import Tribunal) (1990), 666n.174

National Oil Corp v. Libyan Sun Oil Co. (D. Del.), 639n.59
Naulilaa Case (Portugal v. Germany) (1928), 598n.134
NBC v. Bear Stearns (1999), 164n.158, 165n.160, 166nn.166–167, 167
Neer. *See* L.F.H. Neer & Pauline E. Neer v. Mexico
Neustein v. Republic of Indonesia (Oberster Gerichtshof, Aug. 6, 1958), 692n75
Nikbin v. Islamic Republic of Iran (D.D.C. 2007), 698n.97
NIOC Revenues Case, Bundesverfassungsgericht (Apr. 12, 1983), 687n.34, 693, 693n.80
Noble Ventures v. Romania (Final Award, Oct. 12, 2005), 412n.98, 426n.173, 535n.203, 554–555, 565n.5, 622n.240
Norman v. Baltimore & Ohio R. Co. (1935), 485n.230, 487n.238, 487n.241
North American Dredging Co. of Tex. (U.S.A.) v. United Mexican States (1926), 17–19
North Sea Continental Shelf Case (1969), 216, 591, 604n.154
Norwegian Loans, Case of Certain (France v. Norway) (1957), 31n.57, 351
Norwegian Shipowners Claim (Norway v. U.S.) (1922), 433n.19, 435, 435n.29, 440n.67, 609n.179
Nottebohm (Liechtenstein v. Guatemala), 292n.4, 292nn.6–7, 293–294, 298, 298n.33, 303n.58, 304
Nykomb Synergistics Technology Holding, AB, Stockholder v. Republic of Latvia, Riga (Award, Arb. Inst. of Stockholm Chamb. of Comm., Dec. 16, 2003), 426–427, 426n.173, 455n.113, 472

O

Occidental Exploration & Prod. Co. v. Ecuador (Final Award, July 1, 2004), 376–377, 376n.38, 405–406, 405n.53, 406n.58, 408, 408nn.70–71, 427nn.178–179, 502n.40, 509n.74, 511n.80, 516–517, 516n.108, 517, 517n.113, 538n.210, 539n.211, 580, 580n.72, 610n.183, 619n.230, 711n.52
OIAETI v. SOFIDIF. *See* Organisation pour les investissements et les aides economiques et techniques de l'Iran (OIAETI) v. Société Eurodif et Solidif et Commissariat à l'energie atomique (SOFIDIF)
Oil Fields of Texas v. Iran, 585n.94
Oil Platforms, Case Concerning (Islamic Republic of Iran v. U.S.) (1996), 148, 150, 150n.106
Olguin v. Republic of Paraguay
 • Decision on Jurisdiction of Aug. 8, 2000, 372n.15
 • Award, July 26, 2001, 470, 470n.182, 472, 615n.206
Opel Austria GmbH v. Council of the European Union (1997), 466n.166
Organisation pour les investissements et les aides economiques et techniques de l'Iran (OIAETI) v. Société Eurodif et Solidif et Commissariat à l'energie atomique (SOFIDIF) (Decision, Mar. 8, 1988), 638, 638n.53
Oscar Chin Case (U.K. v. Belgium) (Dec. 12, 1934), 42n.91, 439
Owens-Corning Fiberglass Corp. v. Gov't of Iran (Award, May 13, 1983), 154n.112
Oxford Shipping Co. v. Nippon Yusen Kaisha (1984), 197n.43, 637

P

Pabalk Ticaret Sirkeri v. Norsolor (Decision, Oct. 9, 1984), 649n.105
Palazzolo v. Rhode Island (2001), 484nn.220–221 & 223, 485n.228
Palsgraf v. Long Island Railroad Co. (N.Y. 1928), 597, 597n.128
Panavezys-Saldutiskis Railway Case (Estonia v. Lithuania), 33n.65, 340n.200, 344, 350n.16, 367n.1

Paraguay v. U.S. (Provisional Measures) (1998), 566n.11
Parkerings-Compagniet AS v. Lithuania (Award, Sept. 11, 2007), 511n.80, 513n.89, 513n.94, 516–519, 516n.109, 517–519, 517n.115, 518nn.116–119, 519n.120, 711n.52
Parsons & Whittemore Overseas Co. v. Société Générale de l'Industrie du Papier (2d Cir. 1974), 640–641, 640nn.67–68, 641n.80, 642n.81
Party-Appointed v. List-Appointed Arbitrators (2003), 128n.39
Patrick Mitchell v. Democratic Republic of the Congo (Annulment Decision, Nov. 1, 2006), 260n.75, 263, 265n.81, 266n.82, 266n.84, 271n.129, 272n.135, 272n.139, 273, 273n.142, 273n.144, 273n.146, 631, 631n.14, 634n.37
Payne v. Iran (Award, 1986), 456n.114, 471, 576n.64, 586n.95
Penn Central Transp. Co. v. New York City (1978), 483–487, 483n.215, 484nn.216 & 218–220, 486n.231, 487n.237, 487n.239
Pennsylvania Coal Co. v. Mahon (1922), 483nn.212–213, 486
Pennzoil v. Texaco (1987), 362n.41
Petrobart v. Kyrgyz Republic (2005), 230n.33
Petrolane v. Gov't Islamic Republic of Iran (1991), 458n.123
Petroleum Dev. Ltd. v. Sheikh of Abu Dhabi (1951), 436n.41
Phelps Dodge Corp. v. Islamic Repub. of Iran (Award, 1986), 458n.123, 462n.144, 471, 576n.64, 588
Philippe Gruslin v. Malaysia (2000). *See* Gruslin v. Malaysia
Philippine Embassy Bank Account Case (Apr. 12, 1983), 686–687, 687n.34
Phillips Petroleum Co. Iran v. Iran & Nat'l Iranian Oil Co. (Award, June 29, 1989), 462, 462n.145, 471
Plama Consortium Ltd. v. Republic of Bulgaria
- Decision on Jurisdiction, Feb. 8, 2005, 64, 64n.87, 119n.6, 120n.11, 140n.73, 145, 417, 417n.126, 422–423, 422n.148, 423nn.151 & 157
- Order, Sept. 6, 2005, 145nn.96–97
Pope & Talbot Inc. v. Canada
- Interim Award, June 26, 2000, 177n.209, 261, 284, 284n.204, 402–403, 402n.31, 406, 408–412, 409n.73, 411n.92, 412nn.94–96, 417n.124, 424n.158, 451n.101, 456, 456n.118, 457, 458n.122, 471, 489n.246, 522n.138, 654, 656
- Final Merits Award, Apr. 10, 2001, 400nn.19–20, 494n.11, 496n.19, 501, 501n.30, 501n.33, 502n.37, 524, 525n.146
- Award in Respect of Damages, May 31, 2002, 579n.70, 606n.165, 616n.213
Price v. Socialist People's Libyan Arab Jamarihiriya (D.C. Cir. 2002), 698n.97
Prosecutor v. Erdemovic (1997), 214–215
Prudential-Bache Trade Corp. (U.S.) v. Kyocera Corp. (Japan) (Award including attorneys' fees and costs, Aug. 25, 1994), 613n.194
PSEG Global Inc. v. Konya Ilgin Elektrik Üretim ve Ticaret Ltd. Srketi v. Turkey (Award, Jan. 19, 2007), 392, 392n.95, 507n.61, 514n.95, 523n.143, 587n.97, 607n.169, 611n.187
Publicis Commc'n v. True North Commc'ns (2000), 139n.68
Pyramids Case. See Southern Pac. Props. (Middle East) Ltd. v. Arab Republic of Egypt

Q

Quintette Coal Limited v. Nippon Steel Corporation (1991), 653

TABLE OF CASES

R

Raiford V. Merrill Lynch (11th Cir. 1990), 660n.144
Rainbow Warrior (New Zealand/France) (1990), 566n.10, 571n.32
Repsol YPF Ecuador S.A. v. Empresa Estatal Petroleos del Ecuador (Decision on Application for Annulment, Jan. 8, 2007), 631n.15
Republic of. *See name of republic*
République Arabe d'Egypte v. Cinetel (Tribunal fédéral suisse, July 20, 1979), 687n.39
Reuter v. Merrill, Lynch, Pierce, Fenner & Smith, Inc. (N.D. Ala., 2006), 676n.6
Revere Copper & Brass Inc. v. Overseas Private Inv. Corp. (1978), 220n.4, 455n.113, 466n.163, 471
Reynolds Jamaica Mines Ltd. v. Jamaica (1977), 187n.8
R.J. Reynolds Tobacco Co. v. Iran (1984), 610
Robert A. Azinian v. United Mexican States (1999). *See* Azinian v. United Mexican States
Roberts v. United Mexican States, 495n.13
Rodriguez de Quijas v. Shearson/American Express (1989), 644n.88
Roz Trading, Ltd., In the Matter of, 167, 167n.173, 168, 168n.175
Ruckelshaus v. Monsanto (1984), 485n.228
Rudolf v. Venezuela, 13n.6
Ruler of Qatar v. Int'l Marine Oil Co. (1953), 436n.41
Russia v. Pied-Rich BV (Netherlands Supreme Court, May 28, 1993), 692n76
Rux v. Republic of Sudan (E.D. Va. 2005), 698n.97

S

Sabbatino Case. *See* Banco Nacional de Cuba v. Sabbatino
St. Mary's Mead Med. Ctr. of Evansville, Inc. v. Disco Aluminum Prods. Co. (1992), 164n.155
Saipem S.p.A. v. Bangladesh (Decision on Jurisdiction and Recommendation on Provisional Measures, Mar. 21, 2007), 265n.81, 267, 267n.99, 270n.124
Salem Case (1932), 364–365, 365n.57, 531n.181
Salini Costruttori S.p.A. & Italstrade S.p.A. v. Hashemite Kingdom of Jordan
  • Decision on Jurisdiction, Nov. 29, 2004, 120n.11, 347n.2, 422n.146, 555, 558
  • Award, Jan. 31, 2006, 528, 528n.169
Salini Costruttori S.p.A. & Italstrade S.p.A. v. Kingdom of Morocco (Decision on Jurisdiction, July 23, 2001), 98n.22, 187–188, 188n.9, 224, 224n.23, 239, 239n.66, 259–260, 259n.65, 260n.73, 262, 265n.81, 266n.82, 267, 267n.91, 268, 270n.119, 272n.139, 275, 391, 391n.91
Saluka Inves. B.V. v. Czech Republic
  • Decision on Jurisdiction over the Czech Republic's Counterclaim, May 7, 2004, 154–155, 154nn.114–115, 155n.118, 156, 177n.209, 237n.59, 265, 281–282, 335–337, 394, 394n.112
  • Partial Award, Mar. 17, 2006, 281n.184, 315n.119, 426n.173, 427n.180, 495n.12, 496n.18, 496n.20, 499–500, 500n.27, 502nn.39–40, 509, 509n.74, 511n.80, 513, 513nn.90–91, 516n.106, 535, 535n.202, 703n.9, 711n.52
S & S Davis Int'l, Inc. v. Republic of Yemen (11th Cir. 2000), 699n.99
Santa Elena v. Costa Rica. *See* Compañia del Desarrollo de Santa Elena S.A. v. Republic of Costa Rica
Sapphire Int'l Petroleum Ltd. v. Nat'l Iranian Oil Co. (1963), 431n.9, 436n.41, 441n.70, 591

Schooner Exchange v. McFadden (1812), 20n.23, 22
S.D. Myers, Inc. v. Canada
- First Partial Award, Nov. 13, 2000, 177n.209, 284, 284n.205, 400n.19, 401, 401n.24, 406, 408, 439n.61, 461n.141, 468, 468n.174, 469, 470n.181, 472, 474, 474n.190, 492, 501n.32, 507n.63, 580n.72, 583n.83, 664–667, 664nn.166–167, 665nn.168–170, 665n.170, 668–673
- Attorney Gen. of Canada v. S.D. Myers, Inc. (Motion to Set Aside, 2000), 666nn.171–175, 667nn.176 & 178–179, 668–673
- Second Partial Award, Oct. 21, 2002, 579nn.66–67, 599–601
- Attorney Gen. of Canada v. S.D. Myers (Respondent's Memorandum of Fact and Law, June 16, 2003), 667n.177

Sea-Land Serv. v. Islamic Republic of Iran (1984), 463n.147
Security Life Ins. Co. of Am. & Duncanson & Holt, Inc., Arbitration Between, 165n.161
Sedco, Inc. & Nat'l Iranian Oil Co. (Award, Mar. 27, 1986), 577, 578, 584n.91
Sedco, Inc. v. Petroleos Mexicanos Mexican Nat. Oil Co. (Pemex) (1985), 106n.14
Sedelmayer v. Russian Fed'n (Final Award, 1998), 241n.77. 283, 283n.201
Sempra Energy Int'l v. Argentina
- Decision on Objection to Jurisdiction, May 11, 2005, 90, 90n.66, 188, 188n.14, 382n.74, 391–392, 392n.92, 608n.176, 611n.187
- Award, Sept. 28, 2007, 514n.98

SGS Société Générale de Surveillance S.A. v. Islamic Republic of Pakistan
- Decision on Jurisdiction, Aug. 6, 2003, 106n.14, 112–113, 112nn.30–31, 140n.73, 240, 240n.71, 380n.62, 391, 391n.89, 393, 394n.112, 545–548, 550–551, 552, 553–561
- Decision of the Supreme Court of Pakistan, July 3, 2002, 113–116

SGS Société Générale de Surveillance S.A. v. Republic of the Philippines (Decision on Jurisdiction, Jan. 29, 2004), 222n.14, 240, 240n.75, 392, 392n.96, 395, 550–551, 553–554
Shearson Lehman Bros., Inc. v. Hedrich (Ill. App. 1994), 644n.89
Shufeldt Claim (1930), 433n.19, 435, 435n.35, 600
Siag & Vecchi v. Egypt (Decision on Jurisdiction and Partial Dissenting Opinion, April 11, 2007), 260n.71, 265, 266n.86, 298n.32, 299n.37, 302
Siegal v. Titan Indus. Corp. (2d Cir. 1985), 660n.145
Siemens A.G. v. Argentine Republic
- Decision on Jurisdiction, Aug. 3, 2004, 120n.11, 382n.74, 422n.146, 423, 423n.157, 441n.72, 462n.146, 463n.151
- Award, Feb. 6, 2007, 208n.27, 316n.122, 391, 473, 511n.80, 538n.210, 607n.171, 611n.187, 711n.52
- Annulment proceeding registered, July 16, 2007, 631n.16

SII Inves. v. Jenks (M.D. Fla., July 27, 2006), 676n.6
Sisso v. Islamic Republic of Iran (D.D.C. 2006), 698n.97
Smith v. Compañia Urbanizadora del Parque y Playa de Marianao (1929), 433n.19
SOABI v. Senegal
- Decision on Jurisdiction, Aug. 1, 1984, 279, 324n.164, 650
- Award, Feb. 25, 1988, 279n.175, 700n.105
- French Cour de Cassation, decision, June 11, 1991, 650n.112

Socialist Federal Republic of Yugoslavia v. Société Européenne d'Etudes et d'Entreprises, Crédit Lyonnais, Air France and Others (Tribunal de grande instance, Paris, July 3, 1985), 692n74
Société Bec Frères v. Office des Céréales de Tunisie (Cour d'Appel, Rouen, June 20, 1996), 689n.53

Société Creighton v. Ministre des Finances de l'Etat du Qatar et autre Cour de cassation (1st Civil Chamber, July 6, 2000), 689n.53

Société de droit irakien Rafidain Bank et crts v. Consarc Corp., société de droit américain et crts Cour d'Appel, Brussels (Mar. 10, 1993), 691n.64

Société Européenne d'Etudes et d'Entreprise v. People's Federal Republic of Yugoslavia (SEEE) (Trib. Canton. Vaud. Feb. 12, 1957), 94

Société Hilmarton Ltd. v. Omnium de Traitement et de Valorisation (French Cour de Cassation, First Civil Chamber 1994), 649–650, 649n.104

Société Ouest-Africaine des Bétons Industriels (SOABI) v. The Republic of Senegal. *See* SOABI v. Senegal

Sola Tiles, Inc. v. Iran (1987), 437, 437n.56, 584n.92, 588

Soufraki v. United Arab Emirates (Decision of the Ad Hoc Committee on the Application for Annulment, June 5, 2007), 300n.38, 631n.15

Soufraki v. United Arab Emirates (Award, July 7, 2007), 298–300, 298n.35, 299n.37

South Carolina v. Katzenbach (1966), 697

Southern Pac. Props. (Middle East) Ltd. v. Arab Republic of Egypt
- Decision on Jurisdiction, Nov. 27, 1985, 86n.45, 222n.15, 233–234
- Award, May 20, 1992, 75n.144, 86n.45, 203n.10, 233n.44, 233n.45, 448n.92, 591n.106, 615n.206, 621, 621n.236
- Request for Annulment, (settled before annulment decision was made, 1993), 631n.15

South-West Africa Case (1950), 216, 216n.47

Sovtransavto Holding v. Ukraine (2004), 365, 365n.60

Spanish Consular Bank Accounts Case (Landgericht, Stuttgart, Sept. 21, 1971), 687n.34, 692n.71

Sparan Masonry, LLC v. Hoar Constr., LLC (S.D. Fla., Mar. 28, 2007), 676n.6

Spector v. Torenberg (S.D.N.Y. 1994), 644n.87

SPP v. Egypt. *See* Southern Pac. Props. (Middle East) Ltd. v. Arab Republic of Egypt

S.S. Wimbledon Case (1923), 607n.169, 608n.174

Stanton v. Paine Webber Jackson & Curtis, Inc., 165n.160, 165n.163

Starrett Housing Corp., Starrett Systems, Inc., Starrett Housing Int'l, Inc. v. Gov't of the Islamic Rep. of Iran, Bank Markazi Iran, Bank Omran, Bank Mellat (1983), 437, 437n.52, 451, 451n.98, 458n.123, 471, 587n.96

Subway-Surface Supervisors Assoc. v. N.Y. City Transit Auth. (1978), 487n.240

Suez, Sociedad General de Aguas de Barcelona, S.A. & Vivendi Universal, S.A. v. Argentine Republic (Order in Response to Petition for Transparency and Participation as Amicus Curiae, May 19, 2006), 171n.202, 172n.203, 174n.206, 177n.207, 261, 266n.87

Sui On Construction Co. & Moon Yik Co., In re (Decision, Sept. 12, 1986), 198n.47

Sweden (Nykomb) v. The Republic of Latvia (2005), 79n.12

Swembalt v. Latvia, 127n.37

Sylvania Technical Sys., Inc. v. Gov't of the Islamic Republic of Iran (1985), 607n.168, 620n.232

T

Tahoe-Sierra Preservation Council v. Tahoe Reg'l Planning Agency (2002), 484nn.220 & 223, 485n.228

Talenti v. Clinton (D.C. Cir. 1996), 244n.98

TABLE OF CASES

Taunton-Collins v. Cromie & Others (1964), 197n.44

Tecmed v. Mexico. *See* Tecnicas Medioambientales Tecmed S.A. v. Mexico

Tecnicas Medioambientales Tecmed S.A. v. Mexico (Spain v. Mexico) (Award, May 29, 2003), 417n.124, 424–425, 424n.158, 425n.168, 441n.71, 451, 451n.101, 456, 458n.124, 462n.142, 464, 464n.157, 468n.172, 472, 510–514, 510n.77, 511n.81, 514nn.96 & 99, 522, 522nn.139–140, 579n.68, 709n.45, 711n.52

Telenor v. Hungary (Award, June 16, 2006), 120n.11, 261, 623, 623n.247, 624

Tembec v. U.S. (Order of the Consolidation Tribunal, Sept. 7, 2005), 194n.32 *See also* Canfor Corp., Tembec Inc., Tembec Inves. Inc., Tembec Indus. Inc., Terminal Forests Prod. Ltd. v. U.S.

Terminal Forest Prod. Ltd. v. U.S. (Order of the Consolidation Tribunal, Sept. 7, 2005), 194n.32. *See also* Canfor Corp., Tembec Inc., Tembec Inves. Inc., Tembec Indus. Inc., Terminal Forests Prod. Ltd. v. U.S.

Texaco Overseas Petroleum Co. & Calif. Asiatic Oil Co. (TOPCO) v. Gov't of the Libyan Arab Republic
- Preliminary Award, Nov. 27, 1975), 225–226
- Award, January 19, 1977, 24–25, 25n.33, 46n.8, 219n.3, 431n.9, 436–437, 436n.42, 441n.70, 567n.16, 569n.22, 569n.24

Texas Trading & Milling Corp. v. Federal Republic of Nigeria (2d Cir. 1981), 697n.92, 698n.97

Thunderbird Gaming v. Mexico (Jan. 26, 2006), 263, 441n.74, 510n.76, 512, 512nn.84 & 86–87, 513n.88, 565n.6, 582, 582nn.80–81, 583n.82, 611n.188, 616n.214, 618, 618n.227, 624, 624n.254

Tippetts, Abbett, McCarthy, Stratton v. TAMS-AFFA Consulting Eng'rs of Iran, the Gov't of the Islamic Rep. of Iran, Civil Aviation Org., Plan and Budget Org., Iranian Air Force, Ministry of Defence, Bank Melli, Bank Sakhteman, Mercantile Bank of Iran & Holland (1984), 451, 451n.100, 456n.114, 471

TMR Energy Ltd. v. State Property Fund of Ukraine (D.C. Cir. 2005), 699n.99

Tokios Tokeles v. Ukraine (Decision on Jurisdiction, Apr. 29, 2004), 182n.212, 207n.20, 223, 223n.22, 240n.74, 319n.141, 322–325, 322n.148

TOPCO. *See* Texaco Overseas Petroleum Co./California Asiatic Oil Co. v. Gov't of the Libyan Arab Republic

Tradex Hellas, S.A. (Greece) v. Albania
- Decision on Jurisdiction, Dec. 24, 1996, 122n.22, 221n.10, 222, 222n.14, 231n.37, 234–235, 235n.51, 256n.49, 266n.88
- Award, Apr. 29, 1999, 615n.204

Trail Smelter (1938, 1941), 598n.131

Triumph Tankers Ltd. v. Kerr McGee Refining Corp. (SMA Award, Mar. 28, 1990), 614n.198

U

U.K. v. Boeing Co. (2d Cir. 1993), 198n.48

Union Carbide Corp. Gas Plant Disaster at Bhopal, India, In re (1986), 15n.12

United Mexican States v. Metalclad Corp. (B.C. Supreme Ct. 2001). *See* Metalclad Corp. v. United Mexican States

United Paperworkers In'l Union v. Misco, Inc. (1987), 640n.72

United Parcel Serv. of Am., Inc. v. Canada
- Decision of the Tribunal on Amicus Curiae, Oct. 17, 2001, 170–171, 190n.19, 707–708
- Award on Jurisdiction, Nov. 22, 2002, 148–149, 149n.105, 170nn.195–196, 708n.32
- Final Award, May 24, 2007, 284, 284n.202, 404, 404n.45, 408

UPS v. Canada. *See* United Parcel Serv. of Am., Inc. v. Canada

U.S. Diplomatic and Consular Staff in Teheran, Case Concerning (1980), 146n.101

U.S. Trust Co. of N.Y. v. New Jersey (1976), 487n.238

V

Vacuum Salt Prods. Ltd. v. Ghana (Award, Feb. 16, 1994), 122n.20, 140n.73, 141–142, 142n.77, 622, 622n.240

Vasilyev v. Russia (2006), 464n.156

Vaughan v. Menlove (1837), 364n.49

Veix v. Sixth Ward Bldg & Loan Ass'n (1940), 487n.240

Verlinden B.V. v. Central Bank of Nigeria 103 S. Ct. 1962 (1983). (1983), 694

Victor Pey Casado v. Chile (Decision on Interim Measures, Sept. 25, 2001), 87n.50

Vivendi II. *See* Compañia de Aguas del Aconquija, S.A. & Vivendi Universal v. Argentina

Vladikavkazksy Ry. Co. v. N.Y. Trust Co. (1934), 23n.28

W

Walker v. U.K. (2006), 464n.156

Walter Fletcher Smith Claim (U.S. v. Cuba), 435, 435n.34

Ware v. Hylton, 22

Waste Mgmt., Inc. v. United Mexican States
- Award, June 2, 2000, 370n.7, 637n.50
- Decision on Mexico's Preliminary Objection concerning the Previous Proceedings, June 26, 2002, 379n.61, 616n.213
- Final Award, Apr. 30, 2004, 327–328, 328n.173, 370n.11, 378–379, 378n.51, 385n.78, 460, 502n.38, 507, 507n.63, 522, 523n.143

Weininger v. Castro (S.D.N.Y. 2006), 698n.98

Well Blowout Control Claim (1996), 598n.132

Wena Hotels Ltd. v. Arab Republic of Egypt
- Decision on Jurisdiction, May 25, 1999, 99n.25
- Award, Dec. 8, 2000, 89n.62, 212n.36, 262, 476n.196, 534–535, 534n.199, 535nn.207–208, 539, 609n.179, 611n.187
- Decision on Application for Annulment, Feb. 5, 2002, 212–213, 213n.37, 631n.15, 633, 633nn.29–31

West v. Multibanco Comermex, S.A. (9th Cir. 1987), 432n.10, 483n.210

The Western Maid (1922), 14n.9

Westland (1989), 189n.17

Weyerhauser Co. v. Western Seas Shipping Co. (9th Cir. 1984), 198n.48

Wilko v. Swan (1953), 88n.54, 644, 660
W.L.L. v. Toys "R" Us, Inc. (2d Cir. 1997), 644n.87
World Duty Free Co. v. Kenya (Oct. 4, 2006), 227n.32, 622, 622nn.243–244

Y

Yaung Chi Oo v. Myanmar (dismissed on jurisdictional grounds), 68
Yee v. Escondido (1992), 486n.236

Index of Treaties, Conventions, and International Agreements

A

Abs-Shawcross Draft Convention on Investments Abroad, 48–49, 53n.37
Accord Entre le Gouvernement de la Republique Francaise et le Gouvernement de la Republique Argentine sûr L'Encouragement et la Protection Reciproques des Investissements, 84n.38
Agreement Among the Government of Brunei Darussalam, Republic of Indonesia, Malaysia, Republic of the Philippines, Republic of Singapore, and the Kingdom of Thailand for the Promotion and Protection of Investments. See ASEAN Investment Agreement
Agreement Between Chile and the Belgian–Luxembourg Economic Union, 420n.143
Agreement Between Japan and the Islamic Republic of Pakistan Concerning the Promotion and Protection of Investment, 238n.64
Agreement Between the Government of Australia and the Government of the People's Republic of China on the Reciprocal Encouragement and Protection of Investments, 237n.60
Agreement Between the Government of Canada and the Government of Republic of Ecuador for the Promotion and Reciprocal Protection of Investments, 203n.7
Agreement Between the Government of Panama and Foreign Investors for the Development of the Cerro Colorado Copper Deposits, 226n.29
Agreement Between the Government of Sweden and the Government of Malaysia Concerning the Mutual Protection of Investments, 237n.60
Agreement Between the Government of the United Kingdom of Great Britain and Northern Ireland and the Government of Republic of Albania for Promotion and Protection of Investments, 236n.57, 420n.142
Agreement Between the Government of the United Kingdom of Great Britain and Northern Ireland and the Government of Republic of Bolivia, 80n.15
Agreement Between the Kingdom of Netherlands and Republic of Poland on Encouragement and Reciprocal Protection of Investments, 202n.6
Agreement Between the Portuguese Republic and the United Mexican States on the Reciprocal Promotion and Protection of Investments, 237n.59
Agreement Between the Republic of Austria and the German Democratic Republic on the Settlement of Unresolved Questions Relating to Property Rights, 38–39

INDEX OF TREATIES, CONVENTIONS, AND INTERNATIONAL AGREEMENTS

Agreement Between the Republic of Turkey and the Arab Republic of Egypt Concerning the Reciprocal Promotion and Protection of Investment, 80n.15
Agreement Between the Swiss Confederation and the Islamic Republic of Pakistan on the Promotion and Reciprocal Protection of Investments, 113n.33
Agreement for Reciprocal Promotion and Protection of Investments between the Kingdom of Spain and the Republic of El Salvador ("Spain–El Salvador BIT"), 223n.21
Agreement on Encouragement and Reciprocal Protection of Investments between the Kingdom of the Netherlands and the Argentine Republic, 203n.8
Agreement on Encouragement and Reciprocal Protection of Investments Between the Kingdom of the Netherlands and the Czech and Slovak Republic, 237n.58
Agreement on Trade Related Aspects of Intellectual Property Rights. *See* TRIPS Agreement
Albania–Croatia BIT, 414, 414n.110
Albania–France BIT, 236n.57, 493n.8
Albania–Greece BIT, 235
Algiers Accords of 1981, 41–42, 82n.24
Argentina–Australia BIT, 305–306, 307n.75
Argentina–France BIT, 261, 394
Argentina–New Zealand BIT, 414n.111
Argentina–Spain BIT, 120, 261, 357n.28, 418, 418n.127, 420, 522n.141
Argentina–United Kingdom BIT, 261
Argentina–U.S. BIT, 248n.8, 263, 306, 306n.69, 316, 442, 516, 531n.183, 539, 543, 543n.16, 557–558, 557n.32, 560n.39, 581
ASEAN Investment Agreement, 67–68, 67n.108, 68n.115, 241, 241n.80, 250n.16, 253n.38, 271n.129, 285n.211, 294n.14, 629n.7, 702
Australia–Czech Republic BIT, 238
Australia–India BIT, 117n.3
Austria–Croatia BIT, 297, 297n.29

Austria–Mexico BIT, 425
Austria–United Arab Emirates BIT, 357n.26

B

Bangladesh–Germany BIT, 307n.73
Belarus–Switzerland BIT, 493n.8
Belgium & Luxemburg–Burundi BIT (or Investment Convention), 447–449
Belgium & Luxemburg–Rwanda BIT, 253n.37
Belgium–Burundi Investment Convention, 449
Belgium–Hong Kong BIT, 304n.66
Belgium/Luxembourg–Turkey BIT, 416n.122
Belgium–Philippines BIT, 304n.64
Belgium–Thailand BIT, 304n.63
Benin–U.K. BIT, 304n.65
Bolivia–Mexico Free Trade Agreement, 196
Bolivia–Netherlands BIT, 330
Botswana–China BIT, 415n.115
Buenos Aires Protocol, 66–67, 66n.101, 67n.104
Bulgaria–Cyprus BIT, 423
Bulgaria–Israel BIT, 414n.108

C

CAFTA. *See* Central America Free Trade Agreement
Calvo Doctrine, 69
Canada Model Agreement for Promotion and Protection of Investment, 196, 196n.36, 251n.20, 370n.9, 498, 570n.26
Canada–Chile Free Trade Agreement (CCFTA), 196, 196n.38, 252, 252n.27, 253n.36, 399n.15
Canada–Costa Rica BIT, 285n.211
Canada–Czech BIT, 247n.2
Canada–Ecuador BIT, 237n.59
Canada–Panama BIT, 202n.6
Canada–South Africa BIT, 294n.11

Canada–U.S. Free Trade Agreement (CUSTFA), 70
Canada–U.S. Softwood Lumber Agreement (SLA), 402
Canadian Model FIPA, 498, 519n.123
Cartagena Free Trade Agreement, 51
CCFTA. *See* Canada-Chile Free Trade Agreement
Central America Free Trade Agreement (CAFTA), 638, 702
Chile–Croatia BIT, 424–425, 515n.103
Chile–Denmark BIT, 424–425
Chile–Malaysia BIT, 424–425, 424n.161, 515n.103
Chile–New Zealand FTA, 253n.37
Chile–South Africa BIT, 414n.111
Chile–Spain BIT, 120, 418
Chile–Tunisia BIT, 414n.108
China Model BIT, 285n.211
China–Germany BIT, 531n.183, 706, 706n.24
China–Hungary BIT, 241
China–Netherlands BIT, 706
China–New Zealand BIT, 706, 706n.25
Colonia Investment Protocol of Mercosur, 51, 64n.90, 65–67, 65nn.91–98, 66nn.99–101, 67n.104, 241n.83
Concession Agreement with Desechos Solidos de Naucalpan S.A. de C.V. (DESONA), 381
Convention for the Protection of Human Rights and Fundamental Freedoms, 464n.156
Convention for the Settlement of Investment Disputes, 245
Convention on the International Responsibility of States for Injuries to Aliens, 430n.6
Convention on the Settlement of Investment Disputes between States and Nationals of other States. *See* Washington Convention
Convention Respecting Claims between the United States and Mexico, 37n.76
Croatia–India BIT, 117n.3
Cyprus–Bulgaria BIT, 422, 422n.149
Czech Republic–Netherlands BIT, 154–155, 155n.116, 281, 281n.185, 357, 357n.27, 427n.180, 703
Czech Republic–U.S. BIT, 597n.125

D

Declaration of the Government of the Democratic and Popular Republic of Algeria Concerning the Settlement of Claims by the Government of the United States of America and the Government of the Islamic Republic of Iran. *See* Algiers Accords of 1981
Denmark–Lithuania BIT, 253n.38
Dominican Republic–Central America–U.S. Free Trade Agreement (DR–CAFTA), 71–74, 196, 196n.37, 208n.25, 241, 241n.81, 242, 304, 304n.60, 444, 444n.79, 713n.65
Draft Convention on Investment Abroad, 503n.43
Draft Convention on the Protection of Foreign Property, 48–49, 49n.14, 503n.44, 534, 534n.195
Draft Convention on the Responsibility of States for Damage Done in Their Territory to the Person or Property of Foreigners, 564n.2
Draft U.S. Model BIT, 465
DR–CAFTA. *See* Dominican Republic-Central American-United States Free Trade Agreement
Dutch–Czech BIT, 426n.170

E

EC Treaty, 55n.45, 703–705, 704n.15
ECA (Environmental Cooperation Agreement), 73
ECT. *See* Energy Charter Treaty
Ecuador–United Kingdom BIT, 250
Egypt–Denmark BIT, 262
Egypt–Greece BIT, 414n.108, 459
Egypt–Italy BIT, 299n.37, 302

INDEX OF TREATIES, CONVENTIONS, AND INTERNATIONAL AGREEMENTS

El Salvador–Spain BIT, 253n.37
Energy Charter Treaty (ECT), 51, 61–64, 61n.74, 77n.2, 79, 241, 241nn.79 & 83, 285, 295n.19, 305n.67, 324, 324n.161, 399, 399n.12, 422, 426, 443–444, 443n.77, 519n.123, 544, 570n.26, 635n.40, 702
Environmental Cooperation Agreement (ECA), 73
Ethiopia–Sudan BIT, 304n.62
European Communities Treaty. *See* EC Treaty
European Convention on Human Rights (ECHR), 365, 365n.62, 572n.39
European Convention on State Immunity (European Convention), 686n.28
Exploration and Production Sharing Agreement Between Government of Qatar and Wintershall Aktiengesellschaft and Others, 226n.29

F

Federal Republic of Germany–U.S.S.R. Agreement Concerning the Promotion and Reciprocal Protection of Investments, 283n.200
Finland–Algeria BIT, 305–306
France–Argentina BIT, 84–85, 239, 368, 369, 381, 382nn.71–72, 383–391
France–Chile BIT, 117n.1
France–Hong Kong BIT, 574n.51
France–India BIT, 414n.111
Franco–Moroccan treaty of 1975, 357n.28
Free Trade Agreement between Mexico and Bolivia, 196
Free Trade Area of the Americas (FTAA), 242
Friendship, Commerce, and Navigation (FCN) treaties, 32, 37, 53n.37, 532–534, 532n.187

G

General Agreement on Tariffs and Trade (GATT), 401, 407n.68, 519n.122
General Claims Convention, 36

German Model BIT, 307, 307n.73
German–Swiss Treaty on Arbitration and Conciliation, 571n.38
Germany–Argentina BIT, 368n.2
Germany–Bangladesh BIT, 574n.51
Germany–Pakistan BIT, 46n.6, 51n.29, 399n.18, 430n.5
Germany–Russia BIT, 283
Germany–Somalia BIT, 294n.12
Germany–Syria BIT, 416n.122
Ghana–Romania BIT, 120n.10, 368n.2
Greece–Egypt BIT, 263
Greece–Georgia BIT, 263
Greece–Republic of Korea BIT, 305–306

H

Hague Conventions for the Pacific Settlement of International Disputes, 47
Havana Charter on Trade and Employment, 48, 503, 503n.41, 534, 534n.194
Hungary–Yemen BIT, 304n.62

I

ICSID Convention (or Washington Convention), 45n.2, 49–50, 49n.19, 52, 80n.17, 82, 82n.25, 83, 83n.27, 83n.30, 84, 84n.36, 85n.39, 86n.47, 87–88, 88nn.55–59, 91, 95, 95n.11, 96n.18, 101n.2, 110n.22, 112, 113, 115, 116, 122n.17, 125–128, 125n.29, 126n.34, 128n.42, 132, 132n.54, 138–141, 138n.63, 147n.104, 154, 163, 171, 172n.203, 183n.216, 186–188, 199, 201nn.1–2, 202, 202n.4, 203–204, 209–210, 211–213, 217n.52, 220–222, 221n.12, 222n.17, 224n.25, 232, 233, 234, 236, 236n.54, 239n.65, 256–289, 256n.51, 257n.57, 292, 295–297, 295n.18, 296n.21, 297n.28, 300–302, 313–315, 321, 323, 332, 343, 344, 345, 359, 359n.30, 382n.72, 383, 384, 570n.28, 571n.34, 613n.194, 620–621, 628–635, 628nn.4 & 6, 699–700, 704

Inter–American Convention on International Commercial Arbitration, 679
International Centre for Settlement of Investment Disputes Convention. *See* ICSID Convention
Investment Convention. *See* Belgium & Luxemburg-Burundi BIT
Iran–U.S. Claims Tribunal, 437
Italy–Egypt BIT, 265
Italy–Jordan BIT, 529
Italy–Morocco BIT, 239n.67, 262
Italy–Philippines BIT, 253n.37
Italy–U.A.E. BIT, 298, 299
Italy–U.S. FCN (Friendship, Commerce, and Navigation) Treaty, 349

J

Jamaica–U.K. BIT, 399n.12
Jay Treaty of Amity, Commerce, and Navigation, 34–35, 34nn.66–67

K

Kyoto Convention, 405n.49

L

Lomé Conventions, 54–55, 54n.44, 55nn.46–49, 56n.53, 241
Lomé III, 55, 55nn.46 & 48–51
Lomé IV, 55, 55n.47, 241n.83

M

Malaysia–Chile BIT, 264, 424–425, 515
Malaysia–Netherlands BIT, 120n.10
Malaysia–U.K. BIT, 275n.156
Mercado Común de Sur (Mercosur or Mersocul), 64–67, 241
Mexico–Bolivia Free Trade Agreement, 196
MIGA Convention, 232
Model Bilateral Investment Treaty of 1987, 654–655

Model Tax Convention, 444
Mongolia–Singapore BIT, 414n.111
Morocco–U.S. BIT, 308n.78
Multilateral Agreement on Investment (MAI), 54, 74–75

N

NAFTA. *See* North American Free Trade Agreement
Netherlands–Argentina BIT, 203
Netherlands–Bolivia BIT, 329
Netherlands–Czech Republic BIT, 204, 236, 265, 315, 326, 336, 394, 506n.58, 515n.101, 597, 660–662
Netherlands–Georgia BIT, 308n.79
Netherlands–Jamaica BIT, 368n.2
Netherlands–Malaysia BIT, 368n.2
Netherlands–Poland BIT, 262, 282, 282n.189, 552
Netherlands–South Africa BIT, 574n.51
Netherlands–Venezuela BIT, 264
New York Convention on the Recognition and Enforcement of Foreign Arbitral Awards, 47, 87–88, 87n.53, 92, 101, 105n.12, 133n.58, 139, 183n.215, 221n.11, 641n.73, 649, 679, 682–683, 691n.62, 691nn.66–67, 699
New Zealand–Singapore BIT, 414n.109, 416, 416n.121
North American Agreement on Environmental Cooperation (NAAEC), 73–74, 658n.130
North American Free Trade Agreement (NAFTA), 51, 56–61, 56nn.55 & 57–60, 58n.66, 80n.17, 90n.67, 121, 185, 202, 203, 203n.7, 207n.21, 240, 241, 241nn.78 & 83, 251n.21, 261–263, 281, 281n.208, 297, 297n.26, 318, 339, 358–359, 361n.38, 370, 378–379, 399n.14, 400, 442–443, 491–493, 500–502, 570n.26, 571n.34, 574n.51, 635–636, 635n.38, 638, 702
North Korea–Thailand BIT, 315n.118
Norway–China BIT, 398n.7

INDEX OF TREATIES, CONVENTIONS, AND INTERNATIONAL AGREEMENTS

Norway–Hungary BIT, 261
Norway–Lithuania BIT, 518

O

OECD Draft Convention on the Protection of Foreign Property, 249n.14
OECD Draft Multilateral Investment Agreement, 66n.101, 251n.24

P

Pakistan–Switzerland BIT, 112–116, 240, 545
Panama Convention, 679
Peru–Paraguay BIT, 470, 470n.183
Philippines–Sweden BIT, 294n.14
Philippines–Switzerland BIT, 307n.75
Philippines–Thailand BIT, 304n.64 414n.113

R

Republic of Korea–Panama BIT, 305–306
Russian Federation–Germany BIT, 241n.77, 295, 296n.20
Russian Federation–Thailand BIT, 308n.77

S

Senegal–U.S. BIT, 308n.78
Singapore–U.S. Free Trade Agreement, 713n.65
Singapore–Vietnam BIT, 294n.14
SLA. *See* Canada-United States Softwood Lumber Agreement
Slovakia–Czech Republic BIT, 263
South Korea–Mongolia BIT, 399n.17
South Korea–Panama BIT, 304n.63
South Korea–U.K. BIT, 294n.11
Spain–Argentina BIT, 416n.123
Spain–El Salvador BIT, 223n.21
Spain–Mexico BIT, 514
Sri Lanka–U.K. BIT, 207, 536

Sweden–China BIT, 398n.7
Sweden–India BIT, 117n.3
Sweden–Malaysia BIT, 237
Swiss–Pakistan BIT, 548
Swiss–Pakistan Investment Protection Treaty, 545–546
Switzerland–Czechoslovakia BIT, 416n.119
Switzerland–India BIT, 574n.51
Switzerland–Nigeria BIT, 307n.75
Switzerland–Zimbabwe BIT, 308n.77

T

Trade Related Aspects of Investment Measures (TRIMS) Agreement, 74
Treaty of Asuncion, 64n.90, 65nn.91–92
Treaty of Lisbon, 705n.22
Treaty of Rome. *See* EC Treaty
TRIPS Agreement, 445, 445n.81
Tunisia–U.K. BIT, 294n.14
Turkey–Pakistan BIT, 261

U

U.K.–Belize BIT, 399n.15
U.K.–Chile BIT, 247n.2
U.K.–Czech Republic BIT, 283, 283n.195
U.K.–Egypt BIT, 264
U.K.–Egypt IPPA, 262
U.K.–Jamaica BIT, 399n.17
U.K.–Kenya BIT, 414n.108
U.K.–Kyrgyz BIT, 167
U.K.–Malaysia BIT, 264
U.K. Model BIT, 544, 544n.17
U.K.–Oman BIT, 253n.37
U.K.–Saint Lucia BIT, 304n.65
U.K.–Slovenia BIT, 285n.16
U.K.–Tonga BIT, 294n.12
U.K.–U.A.E. BIT, 294n.13, 296n.23, 574n.51
U.K.–Uruguay BIT, 306n.69
U.K.–Yemen BIT, 285n.17
Ukraine–Lithuania BIT, 207, 223, 323
Ukraine–U.S. BIT, 324, 324n.160, 468n.172
Unified Agreement for the Investment of Arab Capital in the Arab States, 544n.19

United Nations Convention on the Recognition and Enforcement of Foreign Arbitral Awards of 1958. *See* New York Convention on the Recognition and Enforcement of Foreign Arbitral Awards

U.S.–Argentina BIT, 117n.2, 157–158, 157n.130, 158n.131, 207, 221, 240, 251n.19, 305n.67, 374, 375, 395, 399n.16, 442n.76, 458, 497, 502n.40, 552–553, 558, 579

U.S.–Australia Free Trade Agreement, 446n.84

U.S.–Azerbaijan BIT, 117n.2, 236, 236n.56

U.S.–Canada Free Trade Agreement, 315n.116

U.S.–Chile Free Trade Agreement, 90n.68, 121n.13, 196, 196n.39, 242n.87, 446n.83, 525n.149, 570n.26, 713n.65

U.S.–Colombia Free Trade Agreement, 446n.86

U.S.–Czech BIT, 326, 426n.171, 509n.73, 601n.138, 660

U.S.–Democratic Republic of the Congo BIT, 247n.2, 263, 273

U.S.–Ecuador BIT, 285n.16, 296, 296n.23, 305n.67, 315n.118, 369n.5, 406, 426n.170, 502n.40, 573, 573n.49, 578n.65, 580n.72

U.S.–Egypt BIT, 405, 405n.54

U.S.–Estonia BIT, 373, 506n.58, 507n.64

U.S.–Georgia BIT, 416n.120

U.S.–Haiti BIT, 77n.2, 80n.15

U.S.–Iran Treaty of Amity, Economic Relations, and Consular Rights, 431n.7, 437

U.S.–Italy Treaty of Friendship, Commerce and Navigation, 431n.7, 533n.188

U.S.–Kazakhstan BIT, 509n.71

U.S. Model Bilateral Investment Treaty, 54n.41, 69, 72, 90, 90n.68, 121n.13, 185, 196, 196n.35, 221n.12, 242, 242n.87, 250n.17, 252, 252n.29, 253, 253n.34, 318, 341, 370, 370n.10, 399nn.13 & 17, 454, 454n.112, 489n.246, 505n.53, 510, 519n.123, 520n.125, 525, 525n.149, 544, 544n.20, 556, 557n.32, 706nn.23 & 27, 713, 713nn.63–64

U.S.–Morocco Free Trade Agreement, 90n.68, 241–242, 242n.85, 446n.85, 713n.65

U.S.–Peru Free Trade Agreement, 446n.87

U.S.–Romania BIT, 369n.5

U.S.–Singapore Free Trade Agreement (USSFTA), 252–253, 252n.29, 370n.10

U.S.–Sri Lanka BIT, 286, 288

U.S.–Trinidad and Tobago BIT, 250n.17

U.S.–Ukraine BIT, 324n.160, 468n.172

U.S.–Uruguay BIT, 252, 252n.29, 370n.10, 446n.88, 713nn.63–64

V

Vienna Convention on The Law of Treaties (VCLT), 204n.18, 205, 415, 415n.116, 497, 509, 549, 654

Viet Nam–Finland BIT, 247n.2

W

Washington Accord, 353–356

Washington Convention. *See* ISCID Convention

WTO Agreement, 445n.81

CPSIA information can be obtained at www.ICGtesting.com
Printed in the USA
BVOW09s0051291115

428541BV00011B/23/P